Book 5

The Bedford Anthology of
World Literature
The Nineteenth Century, 1800–1900

EDITED BY

Paul Davis
Gary Harrison
David M. Johnson
Patricia Clark Smith
John F. Crawford

THE UNIVERSITY OF NEW MEXICO

BEDFORD / ST. MARTIN'S   Boston ♦ New York

For Bedford/St. Martin's

Executive Editor: Alanya Harter
Associate Developmental Editor: Joshua Levy
Production Editor: Stasia Zomkowski
Senior Production Supervisor: Nancy Myers
Marketing Manager: Jenna Bookin Barry
Editorial Assistant: Jeffrey Voccola
Production Assistant: Kerri Cardone
Copyeditor: Melissa Cook
Map Coordinator: Tina Samaha
Text and Cover Design: Anna George
Cover Art: Rickshaws, 1875 by Hiroshige III Utagawa. © Asian Art & Archaeology, Inc. /
    CORBIS
Composition: Stratford Publishing Services, Inc.
Printing and Binding: R. R. Donnelley & Sons Company

President: Joan E. Feinberg
Editorial Director: Denise B. Wydra
Editor in Chief: Karen S. Henry
Director of Marketing: Karen Melton
Director of Editing, Design, and Production: Marcia Cohen
Managing Editor: Elizabeth M. Schaaf

Library of Congress Control Number: 2002112262

7   6   5   4   3   2
f   e   d   c   b   a

For information, write: Bedford/St. Martin's, 75 Arlington Street, Boston, MA 02116
(617-399-4000)

ISBN: 0–312–40264-3

Acknowledgments

Machado de Assis, "Adam and Eve" from *The Devil's Church and Other Stories,* translated by Jack Schmitt and Lorie Ishimatsu. Translation copyright © 1977 by the University of Texas Press. Reprinted with the permission of the publisher.

Bakin Takizawa, "Shino and Hamaji," translated by Donald Keene, from *Anthology of Japanese Literature,* edited by Donald Keene. Copyright © 1955 by Grove Press, Inc. Reprinted with the permission of Grove/ Atlantic, Inc.

(Acknowledgments and copyrights are continued at the back of the book on pages 1142–1144, which constitute an extension of the copyright page. It is a violation of the law to reproduce these selections by any means whatsoever without the written permission of the copyright holder.)

PREFACE

❧ *The Bedford Anthology of World Literature* has a story behind it. In 1985, a group of us received a grant from the National Endowment for the Humanities. Our task: to develop and team teach a new kind of literature course—one that drew from the rich literary traditions of Asia, India, the Middle East, and the Americas as well as from the masterpieces of the Western world. We learned so much from that experience—from our students and from each other—that we applied those lessons to an anthology published in 1995, *Western Literature in a World Context*.

In that first edition of our anthology, our goal was to add works that truly represented *world* literature to the list of Western classics and to place great literary works in their historical and cultural contexts. We've kept that focus in the newly titled *Bedford Anthology*—but we've also drastically reshaped, redesigned, and reimagined it to make it the book you hold today. We talked to hundreds of instructors and students in an effort to identify and confirm what they considered challenging about the world literature course. The design and content of these pages represent our attempt to meet these challenges.

The study and teaching of world literature have changed significantly in the past twenty to thirty years. Formerly, most world literature courses consisted of masterpieces of Western literature, while the literary traditions of Asia, Africa, and Latin America were virtually ignored. The movement to broaden the canon to more accurately represent our world—and to better represent oral and marginalized traditions in the West—has greatly increased the number of texts taught in world literature courses today. Although the specifics remain controversial, nearly all teachers of literature are committed to the ongoing revaluation and expansion of the canon.

The last few decades have also seen instructors reconsidering the traditional methods of teaching world literature. In the past, most world literature courses were designed along formalistic or generic principles. But the expanded canon has complicated both of these approaches. There are no developed criteria for defining masterworks in such formerly ignored genres as letters and diaries or for unfamiliar forms from non-Western cultures, and we are frequently reminded that traditional approaches sometimes impose inappropriate Eurocentric perspectives on such works. As content and methodology for the course have been evolving, recent critical theory has reawakened interest in literature's historical and cultural contexts. All of these factors have both complicated and enriched the study of world literature. With this multivolume literature anthology, we don't claim to be presenting the definitive new canon of world literature or the last word on how to teach it. We have, however, tried to open new perspectives and possibilities for both students and teachers.

One anthology — six individual books. *The Bedford Anthology of World Literature* is now split into six separate books that correspond to the six time periods most commonly taught. These books are available in two packages: Books 1–3 and Books 4–6. Our motivation for changing the packaging is twofold and grows out of the extensive market research we did before shaping the development plan for the book. In our research, instructors from around the country confirmed that students just don't want to cart around a 2,500-page book — who would? Many also said that they focus on ancient literatures in the first semester of the course and on the twentieth century in the second semester. In addition, many instructors teach an introduction

The Bedford Anthology of World Literature has been dynamically reimagined, redesigned, and restructured. We've added a second color, four hundred images, three hundred pronunciation guides, forty maps, six comparative time lines — and much more.

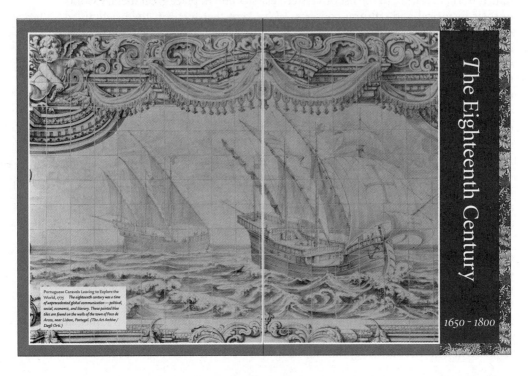

Portuguese Caravels Leaving to Explore the World, 1775   *The eighteenth century was a time of unprecedented global communication — political, social, economic, and literary. These painted blue tiles are found on the walls of the town of Paço de Arcos, near Lisbon, Portugal. (The Art Archive / Dagli Orti.)*

The Eighteenth Century

1650 - 1800

to world literature that is tailored specifically to the needs of their students and their institution and thus want a text that can be adapted to *many* courses.

We believe that the extensive changes we've made to *The Bedford Anthology of World Literature*—breaking the anthology into six books rather than only two, creating a new two-color design, increasing the trim size, and adding maps, illustrations, numerous pedagogical features, an expanded instructor's manual, and a new companion Web site—will make the formidable task of teaching and taking a world literature course both manageable and pleasurable.

An expanded canon for the twenty-first century. In each of the six books of *The Bedford Anthology,* you'll find a superb collection of complete longer works, plays, prose, and poems—the best literature available in English or English translation. Five of the books are organized geographically and then by author in order of birth date. The exception to this rule is Book 6, which, reflecting our increasingly global identities, is organized by author without larger geographical groupings.

Aphra Behn's Oroonoko *is one of the texts we include in its entirety—highlighting important issues of race, gender, and slavery in the eighteenth century.*

❧ APHRA BEHN
1640–1689

Aphra Behn.
Engraving from
*Histories and
Novels,* 1696

*This is the earliest
surviving image
of Behn. (The
Huntington Library,
San Marino, CA)*

Poet, playwright, and novelist Aphra Behn was one of the most prolific writers of her time. During a period in England when women were strongly discouraged from seeking literary recognition, she not only managed to earn a living as a professional writer but also directly engaged such traditionally "masculine" themes as political corruption, sexual politics, and social reform. In *Oroonoko* (1688), she openly addresses the complexities of rulership, sexual desire, and social injustice. Though her talent as a writer earned her much popularity and praise, the supposed presumptuousness and boldness of her work resulted in vicious attacks on her moral integrity. Associating her entrance into the public sphere of print and stage with prostitution, the satirist Robert Gould labeled her a vile "Punk[1] and Poetesse." Largely because of this stigma of indecency, publishers and scholars ignored Behn's work for years after her death. Only recently has she returned to center stage as a great literary talent, a major contributor to the development of the early English NOVEL, and a revolutionary figure in the tradition of women's writing in English.

Mystery, Travel, and Espionage. It is difficult to pin down the facts of Behn's early life. According to many sources, she was born near Canterbury to Bartholomew Johnson, a barber, and Elizabeth Denham. Her surprisingly advanced education and language skills (she was learned in Latin and French), which would have been unusual for a barber's daughter, might be attributed to a close association with the well-to-do family of Colonel Colepeper and to frequent exposure to Huguenot[2] and Dutch immigrants in Canterbury. Some recent scholarship, however, claims she was born in Kent and the daughter of John and Amy Amis or Amies. This would make her a possible relation, through her father, of Francis, Lord Willoughby of Parham, who at one time held a position for the British government in the West Indies. We know that in 1663 Behn traveled to the West Indies with her family after her father was named lieutenant-general of the colony of Surinam.[3] Though the stay in Surinam only lasted two months (her father died on the voyage), this experience influenced the writing of her most famous narrative work, *Oroonoko.*

The circumstances surrounding the adoption of Aphra Behn's last name are even more cloudy than those of her birth. Though there is no extant marriage record, scholars speculate that after the trip to Surinam, Behn wed a London merchant or seaman of Dutch or German descent. If

[1] **punk:** Prostitute.

[2] **Huguenots:** French Protestants who were members of the Reformed Church established in France by John Calvin circa 1555. Because of religious persecution, they fled to other countries in the sixteenth and seventeenth centuries.

[3] **Surinam:** A British sugar colony on the South American coast below Venezuela.

she married, she and her husband were together for only a short time before either he died or the two parted ways to live separate lives. More interesting is the suggestion that Behn imagined a spouse for herself so that she could gain the respectable title of widow. Several critics comment that, assuming Behn's maiden name was Johnson, taking the last name Behn creates an intriguing allusion to the famous seventeenth-century playwright Ben (Behn) Jonson.

The creation of a fictional husband may well seem like a bold act for a woman of the seventeenth century, but Behn was not one to shy away from taking chances or embarking on daring adventures. In 1666, for example, she served as a spy for Charles II (r. 1660–85) in the Anglo-Dutch War.[4] Recruited by her associate Thomas Killigrew, she was charged with convincing one William Scot to be a double agent, reporting on expatriots, and providing information on Dutch military plans. Her foray into espionage was largely ignored, and she was never repaid for her expenses. Deep in debt and forced to borrow money for the cost of her return to England, it is likely that she spent some time in debtor's prison in 1688.

Writing Politics and the Politics of Writing. Aphra Behn lived through a period of monumental political unrest and social change. In 1642, two years after her birth, England became embroiled in a bloody civil war over religious authority, class privileges, and economic practices, among other issues. Charles I (r. 1625–49) was brought to trial and executed in 1649. Despite the promise of a new kind of governance, the ensuing rule of Oliver Cromwell[5]—under whom Britain was called the "Commonwealth," then the "Protectorate"—proved only that a citizen given the power to govern may be more ineffective and tyrannical than a monarch. The period known as the Restoration, beginning in 1660 with the restoration of Charles II as king of England, saw a newfound celebration of, and freedom in, the arts but did not provide long-term political stability. Charles's successor, James II (r. 1685–88), was quickly ousted and sent into exile, primarily because he was a professed Roman Catholic. In what is called the "Glorious Revolution" of 1688,[6] the Dutch Protestant William of Orange and his wife Mary came to power.

As shown by her service as a spy for Charles II, Behn was dedicated to the preservation of the monarchy and to the system of aristocratic rule. Much of her work is informed by this sociopolitical agenda. In texts

WWW For links to more information about Behn and a quiz on *Oroonoko,* see *World Literature Online* at bedfordstmartins.com/worldlit.

[4] **Anglo-Dutch War:** Battles between the British and the Dutch for control of the seas and trade routes (1652–84).

[5] **Oliver Cromwell** (1599–1658): A soldier, politician, and staunch Puritan who attacked the bishops of the Church of England and advocated widespread political and religious reform. He came to power as "Lord Protector" of England (1653–58) shortly after the execution of Charles I.

[6] **Glorious Revolution:** The birth of a son to the Catholic James II led prominent statesmen in England to invite Dutchman William of Orange and his wife, Mary, to assume the throne. William arrived in 1688, promised to protect the Protestant faith and the liberties of the English, and took the throne without opposition. James II, denounced by Parliament, fled to France.

We've tried to assemble a broad selection of the world's literatures. We've updated our selection of European texts; we have also included American writers who have had significant contact with world culture and who have influenced or defined who we are as Americans. And of course we have added many works from non-Western traditions, both frequently anthologized pieces and works unique to this anthology, including texts from Mesopotamia, Egypt, Israel, India, Persia, China, Japan, Arab countries of the Middle East, Africa, native America, Latin America, and the Caribbean.

Over thirty-five complete, longer works. These include Homer's *Odyssey* and *The Epic of Gilgamesh* in Book 1, Dante's *Inferno* and Kalidasa's *Shakuntala* in Book 2, Marlowe's *Doctor Faustus* and Shakespeare's *The Tempest* in Book 3, Bashō's *Narrow Road through the Backcountry* in Book 4, Dostoevsky's *Notes from Underground* in Book 5, and Achebe's *Things Fall Apart* in Book 6.

When a work is too long to be produced in its entirety, we've presented carefully edited selections from it; examples include the Rig Veda, *Ramayana, Mahabharata,* Qur'an, *The Song of Roland,* Ibn Hazm's *The Dove's Necklace, The Book of Margery Kempe,* Attar's *Conference of the Birds,* Cervantes's *Don Quixote,* Swift's *Gulliver's Travels,* Equiano's *Interesting Narrative,* Benjamin Franklin's *Autobiography,* Chikamatsu's *The Love Suicides at Amijima,* and Cao Xueqin's *The Story of the Stone.* In most cases the excerpts are not fragments but substantial selections wherein the structure and themes of the whole work are evident. The anthology also contains a generous selection of prose writing—short stories, letters, and essays.

Several hundred lyric poems. *The Bedford Anthology* includes the work of such fine poets as Sappho, Bhartrhari, Nezahualcoyotl, Petrarch, Kakinomoto Hitomaro, Rumi, Li Bai, Heine, Mirabai, Ramprasad, Baudelaire, Dickinson, Ghalib, Akhmatova, Neruda, Rich, and Walcott. Unique *In the Tradition* clusters collect poems that share a tradition or theme: poetry about love in Books 1, 2, and 3, Tang dynasty poetry in Book 2, Indian devotional poetry in Book 3, and poetry on war in Book 6.

Literature in context. In addition to individual authors presented in chronological order, *The Bedford Anthology* features two types of cross-cultural literary groupings. In the more than thirty ***In the World*** clusters, five to six in each book, writings around a single theme — such as the history of religions, science, love, human rights, women's rights, colonialism, the meeting of East and West, imperialism, and existentialism — and from different countries and cultural traditions are presented side by side, helping students understand that people of every culture have had their public gods, heroes, and revolutions, their private loves, lives, and losses. Titles include "Changing Gods: From Religion to Philosophy," in Book 1; "Muslim and Christian at War," in Book 2; "Humanism, Learning, and Education" in Book 3; "Love, Marriage, and the Education of Women," in Book 4; "Emancipation," in Book 5; and "Imagining Africa," in Book 6. The second type of grouping, ***In the Tradition,*** presents poetry on love in Books 1, 2, and 3 and literature on war and American multiculturalism in Book 6. These clusters gather together such widely disparate writers as Hammurabi, Heraclitus, Marcus Aurelius, Ibn Battuta, Marco Polo, Sei Shonagon, Galileo, Bartolomé de las Casas, Mary Wollstonecraft, Mary Astell, Shen Fu, Karl Marx, Elizabeth Cady Stanton, Swami Vivekananda, Aimé Césaire, and Bharati Mukherjee.

In the World clusters bring together texts from different literary traditions and help students make thematic connections and comparisons.

IN THE WORLD

The Spirit of Inquiry

Voltaire's *Candide,* a relentless attack on human illusions, rigid dogma, and institutional cruelty of all kinds, is a reflection of the late-seventeenth- and eighteenth-century spirit of inquiry in Europe that encouraged people to question their cultural assumptions and their accepted place in the world. Confident in their ability to discern the laws of nature and perhaps in turn those of human society, ENLIGHTENMENT thinkers — called the *philosophes* in France — were determined to shrug off conventional ways of thinking in order not only to see the world anew but also to dismantle old institutions and design new ones along better models. In contrast to Voltaire's Pangloss, who believes that this is the best of all possible worlds, the *philosophes* felt that society was ready for a major overhaul, and by using reason, empirical investigation, and mechanical ingenuity, they hoped to overcome superstition, prejudice, and the abuses of religion and politics. Faith in the power of reason to effect change brought with it a strong sense of hope that — through education, reflection, and the application of new ideas and inventions — human beings might progress to a state of near perfection.

DARING TO KNOW

In "What Is the Enlightenment?" (1784), the great German philosopher Immanuel Kant (1724–1804) defines enlightenment as "man's release from his self-incurred tutelage. Tutelage is man's inability to make use of his understanding without direction from another." In the Horatian motto *sapere aude* — "dare to know" — Kant found the principle upon which Western philosophy hinged in the eighteenth century: Dare to reason independently and question authority, even

339

Helping students and teachers navigate the wide world of literature. The hundreds of instructors we talked to before embarking on *The Bedford Anthology* shared with us their concerns about teaching an introduction to world literature course, no matter what their individual agendas were. One concern was the sheer difficulty for students of reading literature that not only spans the period from the beginning of recorded literatures to the present but also hails from vastly different cultures and historical moments. Another was the fact that no one instructor is an expert in *all* of world literature. We've put together *The Bedford Anthology of World Literature* with these factors in mind and hope that the help we offer both around and with the selected texts goes a long way toward bringing clarity to the abundance and variety of world writings.

Helping students understand the where and when of the literature in the anthology. Each book of *The Bedford Anthology* opens with an extended overview of its time period as well as with a **comparative time line** that lists what happened, where, and when in three overarching categories: history and politics; literature; and science, culture, and technology. An interactive version of each time line serves as the portal to the online support offered on our Book Companion Site. In addition,

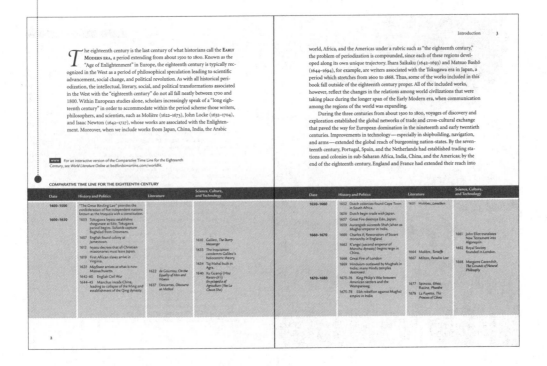

"Time and Place" boxes in the introductions to the different geographical groupings of writers further orient students in the era and culture connected with the literature they're reading by spotlighting something interesting and specific about a certain place and time.

Maps included throughout the anthology show students where in the world various literatures came from. Besides the maps that open each geographical section and show countries in relation to the larger world at a given time in history, we've supplied maps that illustrate the shifting of national boundaries; industrial growth; the effects of conquest, conquerors, and colonialism; and the travels of Odysseus, Ibn Battuta, and Bashō.

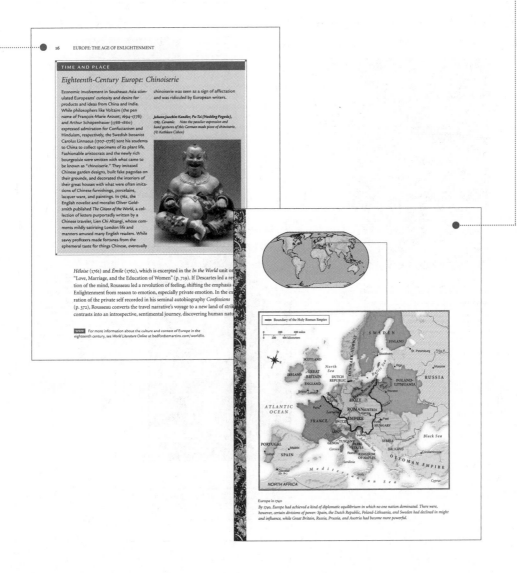

16   EUROPE: THE AGE OF ENLIGHTENMENT

TIME AND PLACE

Eighteenth-Century Europe: Chinoiserie

Economic involvement in Southeast Asia stimulated Europeans' curiosity and desire for products and ideas from China and India. While philosophers like Voltaire (the pen name of François-Marie Arouet; 1694–1778) and Arthur Schopenhauer (1788–1860) expressed admiration for Confucianism and Hinduism, respectively, the Swedish botanist Carolus Linnaeus (1707–1778) sent his students to China to collect specimens of its plant life. Fashionable aristocrats and the newly rich bourgeoisie were smitten with what came to be known as "chinoiserie." They imitated Chinese garden designs, built fake pagodas on their grounds, and decorated the interiors of their great houses with what were often imitations of Chinese furnishings, porcelains, lacquer ware, and paintings. In 1762, the English novelist and moralist Oliver Goldsmith published *The Citizen of the World*, a collection of letters purportedly written by a Chinese traveler, Lien Chi Altangi, whose comments mildly satirizing London life and manners amused many English readers. While savvy profiteers made fortunes from the ephemeral taste for things Chinese, eventually

chinoiserie was seen as a sign of affectation and was ridiculed by European writers.

Johann Joachim Kandler, Pu-Tai (Nodding Pagoda), 1765. Ceramic. Note the peculiar expression and hand gestures of this German-made piece of chinoiserie. (© Kathleen Cohen)

Héloïse (1761) and *Émile* (1762), which is excerpted in the *In the World* unit on "Love, Marriage, and the Education of Women" (p. 719). If Descartes led a revolution of the mind, Rousseau led a revolution of feeling, shifting the emphasis of Enlightenment from reason to emotion, especially private emotion. In the exploration of the private self recorded in his seminal autobiography *Confessions* (p. 372), Rousseau converts the travel narrative's voyage to a new land of striking contrasts into an introspective, sentimental journey, discovering human nature

www   For more information about the culture and context of Europe in the eighteenth century, see *World Literature Online* at bedfordstmartins.com/worldlit.

— Boundary of the Holy Roman Empire

Europe in 1740
By 1740, Europe had achieved a kind of diplomatic equilibrium in which no one nation dominated. There were, however, certain divisions of power: Spain, the Dutch Republic, Poland-Lithuania, and Sweden had declined in might and influence, while Great Britain, Russia, Prussia, and Austria had become more powerful.

The anthology's many illustrations—art, photographs, frontispieces, cartoons, and cultural artifacts—are meant to bring immediacy to literature that might otherwise feel spatially and temporally remote. A few examples are a photo of the Acropolis today juxtaposed with an artist's rendering of what it looked like newly built, a sketch of the first seven circles of Dante's hell, a scene from Hogarth's *Marriage à la Mode,* the ad Harriet Jacobs's owner ran for her capture and return, an editorial cartoon mocking Darwin's evolutionary theories, and a woodcut depicting Japanese boats setting out to greet Commodore Perry's warship in their harbor.

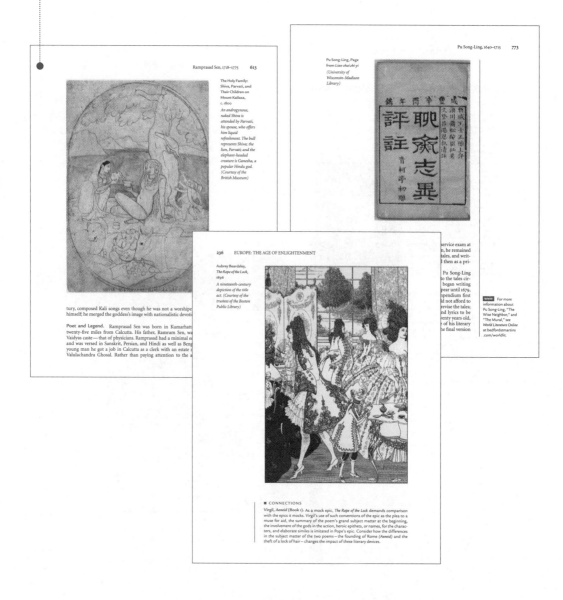

Ramprasad Sen, 1718–1775   613

The Holy Family: Shiva, Parvati, and Their Children on Mount Kailasa, c. 1800
An androgynous, naked Shiva is attended by Parvati, his spouse, who offers him liquid refreshment. The bull represents Shiva; the lion, Parvati; and the elephant-headed creature is Ganesha, a popular Hindu god. (Courtesy of the British Museum)

tury, composed Kali songs even though he was not a worshipe[...]
himself; he merged the goddess's image with nationalistic devoti[...]

Poet and Legend.   Ramprasad Sen was born in Kumarhatt[...]
twenty-five miles from Calcutta. His father, Ramram Sen, w[...]
Vaidyas caste—that of physicians. Ramprasad had a minimal e[...]
and was versed in Sanskrit, Persian, and Hindi as well as Beng[...]
young man he got a job in Calcutta as a clerk with an estate [...]
Valulachandra Ghosal. Rather than paying attention to the a[...]

Pu Song-Ling, 1640–1715   773

Pu Song-Ling, Page from *Liao-zhai zhi-yi* (University of Wisconsin-Madison Library)

service exam at [...]
n, he remained [...]
tales, and writ-[...]
then as a pri-[...]

Pu Song-Ling [...]
to the tales cir-[...]
began writing [...]
pear until 1679, [...]
pendium first [...]
d not afford to [...]
revise the tales; [...]
nd lyrics to be [...]
enty years old, [...]
of his literary [...]
he final version [...]

www For more information about Pu Song-Ling, "The Wise Neighbor," and "The Mural," see *World Literature Online* at bedfordstmartins .com/worldlit.

236   EUROPE: THE AGE OF ENLIGHTENMENT

Aubrey Beardsley, *The Rape of the Lock,* 1896
A nineteenth-century depiction of the title act. (Courtesy of the trustees of the Boston Public Library)

■ CONNECTIONS
Virgil, *Aeneid* (Book 1). As a mock epic, *The Rape of the Lock* demands comparison with the epics it mocks. Virgil's use of such conventions of the epic as the plea to a muse for aid, the summary of the poem's grand subject matter at the beginning, the involvement of the gods in the action, heroic epithets, or names, for the characters, and elaborate similes is imitated in Pope's epic. Consider how the differences in the subject matter of the two poems—the founding of Rome (*Aeneid*) and the theft of a lock of hair—changes the impact of these literary devices.

Practical and accessible editorial apparatus helps students understand what they read. Each author in the anthology is introduced by an informative and accessible literary and biographical discussion. The selections themselves are complemented with generous footnotes, marginal notes, cross-references, and critical quotations. Phonetic pronunciation guides are supplied in the margins of introductory material and before the selections for unfamiliar character and place names. Providing help with literary and historical vocabulary, bold-faced key terms throughout the text refer students to the comprehensive glossary at the end of each book.

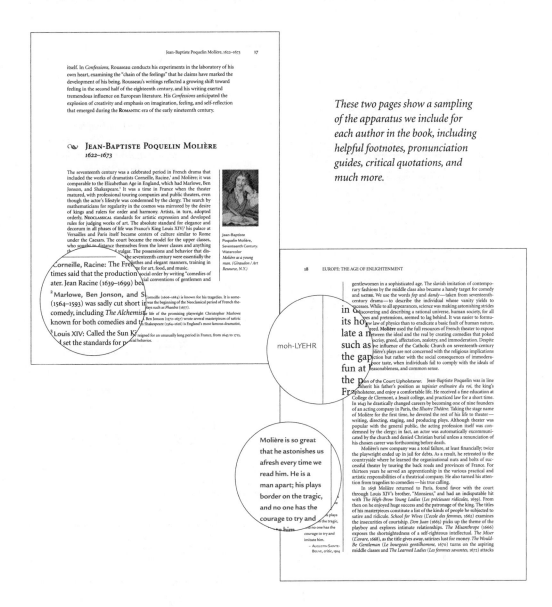

These two pages show a sampling of the apparatus we include for each author in the book, including helpful footnotes, pronunciation guides, critical quotations, and much more.

These terms cover the generic conventions of fiction, poetry, and drama; historical forms such as epic, epigram, and myth; and relevant historical periods such as the European Enlightenment or the Edo period in Japan.

Making connections among works from different times and places. At the end of each author introduction are two catalysts for further thought and discussion. **Questions** in the Connections apparatus tie together Western and world texts, both those within a single book and selections from other centuries, making the six books more of a unit and aiding in their interplay. **Further Research bibliographies**

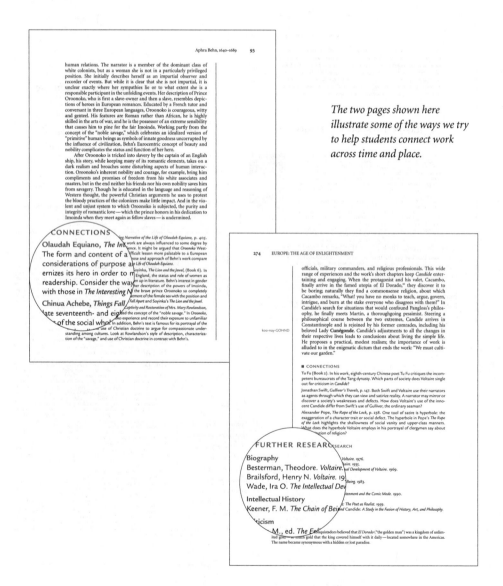

The two pages shown here illustrate some of the ways we try to help students connect work across time and place.

provide sources for students who want to read more critical, biographical, or historical information about an author or a work.

Print and online ancillaries further support the anthology's material. Two instructor's manuals, *Resources for Teaching THE BEDFORD ANTHOLOGY OF WORLD LITERATURE,* accompany Books 1–3 and Books 4–6 (one for each package), providing additional information about the anthology's texts and the authors, suggestions for discussion and writing prompts in the classroom and beyond, and additional connections among texts in the six books.

We are especially enthusiastic about our integrated Book Companion Site, *World Literature Online,* which provides a wealth of content and information that only the interactive medium of the Web can offer. **Web links** throughout the anthology direct

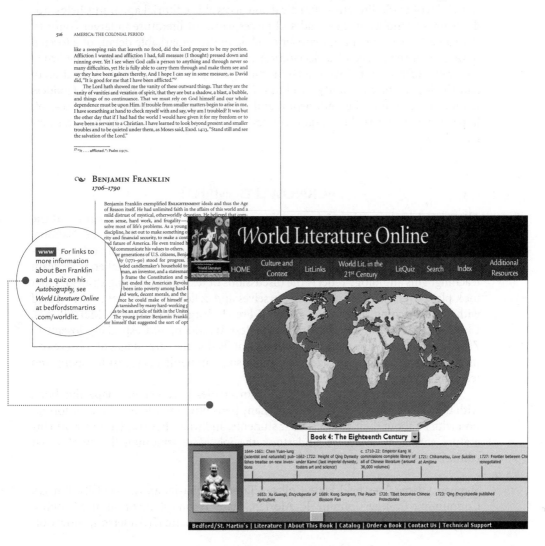

students to additional content on the Web site, where interactive illustrated time lines and maps serve as portals to more information about countries, texts, and authors. Culture and Context overviews offer additional historical background and annotated research links that students can follow to learn more on their own. Illustrated World Literature in the Twenty-First Century discussions trace the enduring presence in contemporary culture of the most frequently taught texts in world literature courses. Maps from the book are available online. Quizzes in LitQuiz offer an easy way for instructors to assess students' reading and comprehension. And LitLinks—annotated research links—provide a way for students to learn more about individual authors.

This wide variety of supplementary materials, as well as the broad spectrum of literary texts, offers teachers choices for navigating the familiar and the unfamiliar territories of world literature. Practical and accessible editorial apparatus helps students understand what they read and places works of literature in larger contexts. For some, the excitement of discovery will lie in the remarkable details of a foreign setting or in the music of a declaration of love. Others will delight in the broad panorama of history by making connections between an early cosmological myth and the loss of that certainty in Eliot's *The Waste Land* or between the Goddess Inanna's descent into the underworld and Adrienne Rich's descent into the sea. We hope all who navigate these pages will find something that thrills them in this new anthology.

ACKNOWLEDGMENTS

This anthology began in a team-taught, multicultural "great books" course at the University of New Mexico, initially developed with a grant from the National Endowment for the Humanities. The grant gave us ample time to generate the curriculum for the course, and it also supported the luxury and challenge of team teaching. This anthology reflects the discussions of texts and teaching strategies that took place over many years among ourselves and colleagues who have participated with us in teaching the course—Cheryl Fresch, Virginia Hampton, Mary Rooks, Claire Waters, Richard K. Waters, Mary Bess Whidden, and especially Joseph B. Zavadil, who began this anthology with us but died in the early stages of its development. Joe's spirit—his courage, wit, scholarship, humanity, and zest for living and teaching—endures in this book.

Reviewers from many colleges and universities have helped shape this book with their advice and suggestions. And many perceptive instructors shared information with us about their courses, their students, and what they wanted in a world literature anthology when we undertook the job of refashioning this book's first edition. We thank them all:

Stephen Adams, Westfield State College; Tamara Agha-Jaffar, Kansas City, Kansas, Community College; Johnnie R. Aldrich, State Technical Institute at Memphis; Allison Alison, Southeastern Community College; Jannette H. Anderson, Snow College; Kit Andrews, Western Oregon University; Joan Angelis, Woodbury University; Shirley Ariker, Empire State College; Sister Elena F. Arminio, College of Saint Elizabeth; Rose Lee Bancroft, Alice Lloyd College; John Bartle, Hamilton College; Amy M. Bawcom, University of Mary Hardin-Baylor; M. Susan Beck, University of Wisconsin-River Falls; Frank Beesley, Dalton State College; Peter Benson, Farleigh Dickinson University; Michael Bielmeier, Silver Lake College; Dale B. Billingsley, University of Louisville; Mark Bingham, Union University; Stephen Black, Dyersburg State Community College; Neil Blackadder, Knox College; Tyler Blake, MidAmerica Nazarene University; Gene Blanton, Jacksonville State University; James Boswell Jr., Harrisburg Area Community College; Lisa S. Bovelli, Itasca Community College; Lois Bragg, Gallaudet University; Kristin Ruth Brate, Arizona Western College; Marie Brenner, Bethel College; Linda Brown, Coastal Georgia Community College; Keith Callis, Crichton College; Charles P. Campbell, New Mexico Tech.; Zuoya Cao, Lincoln University; William Carpenter, College of ME Atlantic; May Charles, Wheeling Jesuit College; R. J. Clougherty, Tennessee Technical College; Helen Connell, Barry University; Lynn Conroy, Seton Hill College; Sue Coody, Weatherford College; Thomas A. Copeland, Youngstown State University; Peter Cortland, Quinnipiac College; R. Costomiris, Georgia Southern University; H. J. Coughlin, Eastern Connecticut State University; Marc D. Cyr, Georgia Southern University; Sarah Dangelantonio, Franklin Pierce College; James Davis, Troy State University; Barbara Dicey, Wallace College; Wilfred O. Dietrich, Blinn College; Michael Dinielli, Chaffey College; Matt Djos, Mesa State College; Marjorie Dobbin, Brewton-Parker College; Brian L. Dose, Martin Luther College; Dawn Duncan, Concordia College; Bernie Earley, Tompkins-Cortland Community College; Sarah M. Eichelman, Walters State Community College; Robert H. Ellison, East Texas Baptist University; Joshua D. Esty, Harvard University; Robert J. Ewald, University of Findlay; Shirley Felt, Southern California College; Lois Ferrer, CSU Dominguez Hills; Patricia Fite, University of the Incarnate Word; Sr. Agnes Fleck, St. Scholastica College; Robert Fliessner, Central State University; M. L. Flynn, South Dakota State University; Keith Foster, Arkansas State University; John C. Freeman, El Paso Community College; Doris Gardenshire, Trinity Valley Community College; Susan Gardner, University of North Carolina-Charlotte; Jerry D. Gibbens, Williams Baptist College; Susan Gilbert, Meredith College; Diana Glyer, Azusa Pacific University; Irene Gnarra, Kean University; R. C. Goetter, Glouster Community College; Nancy Goldfarb, Western Kentucky University; Martha Goodman, Central Virginia Community College; Lyman Grant, Austin Community College; Hazel Greenberg, San Jacinto College South; Janet Grose, Union University; Sharon Growney-Seals, Ouachita Technical College; Rachel Hadas, Rutgers University; Laura Hammons, East Central Community College; Carmen Hardin, University of Louisville; Darren Harris-Fain, Shawnee State University; Patricia B. Heaman, Wilkes University; Charles Heglan, University of South Florida; Dennis E. Hensley, Taylor University; Kathleen M. Herndon, Weber State University; Betty Higdon, Reedley College; David Hoegberg, Indiana University; Diane Long Hoeveler, Marquette University; Tyler Hoffman, Rutgers University; Lynn Hoggard, Midwestern State University; Greg Horn, Southwest VA Community College; Roger Horn, Charles County Community

College; Malinda Jay-Bartels, Gulf Coast Community College; Mell Johnson, Wallace State Community College; Kathryn Joyce, Santa Barbara City College; Steven Joyce, Ohio State University-Mansfield; Ronald A. T. Judy, University of Pittsburgh; Alan Kaufman, Bergen Community College; Tim Kelley, Northwest-Shoals Community College; Shoshanna Knapp, Virginia Technical College; Jim Knox, Roane State Community College; Mary Kraus, Bob Jones University; F. Kuzman, Bethel College; Kate Kysa, Anoka-Ramsey Community College; Linda L. Labin, Husson College; Barbara Laman, Dickinson State University; R. Scott Lamascus, GA-Southwestern State University; Sandi S. Landis, St. Johns River Community College; Ben Larson, York College; Craig Larson, Trinidad State Junior College; Linda M. Lawrence, Georgia Military College; Simon Lewis, C. of Charleston; Gary L. Litt, Moorhead State University; H. W. Lutrin, Borough of Manhattan Community College; Dennis Lynch, Elgin Community College; Donald H. Mager, Johnson C. Smith University; Barbara Manrique, California State University; W. E. Mason, Mid-Continent College; Judith Matsunobu, Atlantic Community College; Noel Mawer, Edward Waters College; Patrick McDarby, St. John's University; Judy B. McInnis, University of Delaware; Becky McLaughlin, University of Southern Alabama; Edward E. Mehok, Notre Dame College of Ohio; Patricia Menhart, Broward Community College; Arthur McA. Miller, New College of Florida; Mark James Morreale, Marist College; Toni Morris, University of Indianapolis; Philip Mosley, Penn State–Worthington; George Mower, Community College of Alleghany County; L. Carl Nadeau, University of St. Francis; Walter Nelson, Red Rocks Community College; Steven Neuwirth, Western Connecticut State University; Carol H. Oliver, St. Louis College of Pharmacy; Richard Orr, York Technical College; Geoffrey Orth, Longwood College; Ramenga M. Osotsi, James Madison University; Bonnie Pavlis, Riverside Community College; Craig Payne, Indian Hills College; Leialoha Perkins, University of Hawaii; Ralph Perrico, Mercyhurst College; Charles W. Pollard, Calvin College; Michael Popkin, Touro College; Victoria Poulakis, Northern Virginia Community College; Alan Powers, Bristol Community College; Andrew B. Preslar, Lamar University; Evan Radcliffe, Villanova University; Belle Randall, Cornish College of the Arts; Elaine Razzano, Lyndon State College; Lucia N. Robinson, Okaloosa-Walton Community College; John Rooks, Morris College; William T. Ross, University of South Florida; Andrew Rubenfeld, Stevens Institute of Technology; Elizabeth S. Ruleman, Tennessee Wesleyan College; Olena H. Saciuk, Inter-American University; Mary Lynn Saul, Worcester State College; MaryJane Schenck, University of Tampa; Kevin Schilbrack, Wesleyan College; Deborah Schlacks, University of Wisconsin; Michael Schroeder, Savannah State University; Helen Scott, Wilkes University; Asha Sen, University of Wisconsin; Mary Sheldon, Washburn University; Lisa Shoemaker, State Technical Community College; Jack Shreve, Allegany College of Maryland; Meg Simonton, Albertson College; Susan Sink, Joliet Junior College; Henry Sloss, Anne Arundel Community College; T. Sluberski, Concordia University; Betty Smith, The Criswell College; Jane Bouman Smith, Winthrop University; John Somerville, Hillsdale College; Claudia Stanger, Fullerton College; Patrick Sullivan, Manchester Community-Technical College; Joan S. Swartz, Baptist

Bible College of PA; Leah Swartz, Maryville University; Sister Renita Tadych, Silver Lake College; Janet Tarbuck, Kennebee Valley Technical College; Gina Teel, Southeast Arkansas College; Daniel Thurber, Concordia University; John Paul Vincent, Asbury College; Paul Vita, Morningside College; Tim Walsh, Otera Junior College; Julia Watson, Ohio State University; Patricia J. Webb, Maysville Community College; Lynne Weller, John Wood Community College; Roger West, Trident Technical College; Katherine Wikoff, Milwaukee School of Engineering; Evelyn M. Wilson, Tarrant County College; Carmen Wong, John Lyle Community College; Paul D. Wood, Paducah Community College; Fay Wright, North Idaho College; and finally, Pamela G. Xanthopoulos, Jackson State Community College.

We also want to thank a special group of reviewers who looked in depth at the manuscript for each book, offering us targeted advice about its strengths and weaknesses:

Cora Agatucci, Central Oregon Community College; Michael Austin, Shepherd College; Maryam Barrie, Washtenaw Community College; John Bartle, Hamilton College; Jeffry Berry, Adrian College; Lois Bragg, Gallaudet University; Ron Carter, Rappahannock Community College; Robin Clouser, Ursinus College; Eugene R. Cunnar, New Mexico State University; Karen Dahr, Ellsworth Community College; Kristine Daines, Arizona State University; Sarah Dangelantonio, Franklin Pierce College; Jim Doan, Nova SE University; Melora Giardetti, Simpson College; Audley Hall, North West Arkansas Community College; Dean Hall, Kansas State University; Wail Hassan, Illinois State University; Joris Heise, Sinclair Community College; Diane Long Hoeveler, Marquette University; Glenn Hopp, Howard Payne University; Mickey Jackson, Golden West College; Feroza Jussawalla, University of New Mexico; Linda Karch, Norwich University; David Karnos, Montana State University; William Laskowski, Jamestown College; Pat Lonchar, University of the Incarnate Word; Donald Mager, The Mott University; Judy B. McInnis, University of Delaware; Becky McLaughlin, University of South Alabama; Tony J. Morris, University of Indianapolis; Deborah Schlacks, University of Wisconsin; James Snowden, Cedarville University; David T. Stout, Luzerne County Community College; Arline Thorn, West Virginia State College; Ann Volin, University of Kansas; Mary Wack, Washington State University; Jayne A. Widmayer, Boise State University; and William Woods, Wichita State University.

No anthology of this size comes into being without critical and supportive friends and advisors. Our thanks go to the Department of English at the University of New Mexico (UNM); its chair, Scott Sanders, who encouraged and supported our work; and Margaret Shinn and the office staff, who provided administrative and technical assistance. Among our colleagues at UNM, we particularly want to thank Gail Baker, Helen Damico, Reed Dasenbrock, Patrick Gallacher, Feroza Jussawalla, Michelle LeBeau, Richard Melzer, Mary Power, Diana Robin, and Hugh Witemeyer. Several graduate students also helped with this project: Jana Giles contributed the final section on American multicultural literature; Mary Rooks wrote the sections on Aphra Behn and Wole Soyinka and served heroically as our assistant, record keeper, all-purpose editor, and consultant.

We have benefited from the knowledge and suggestions of those who have corrected our misunderstandings, illuminated topics and cultures with which we were unfamiliar, critiqued our work, and suggested ways to enrich the anthology: Paula Gunn Allen, Reynold Bean, Richard Bodner, Machiko Bomberger, Robert Dankoff, Kate Davis, Robert Hanning, Arthur Johnson, Dennis Jones, James Mischke, Harlan Nelson, Barrett Price, Clayton Rich, Julia Stein, Manjeet Tangri, William Witherup, Diane Wolkstein, and William Woods.

Resources for Teaching THE BEDFORD ANTHOLOGY OF WORLD LITERATURE was expertly developed, edited, and assembled by Mary Rooks, assisted by Julia Berrisford. Along with Mary, Shari Evans, Gabriel Gryffyn, and Rick Mott each wrote a section of the manual. The manual itself was a large and challenging endeavor; we are grateful to its authors for their enthusiasm and hard work.

A six-volume anthology is an undertaking that calls for a courageous, imaginative, and supportive publisher. Chuck Christensen, Joan Feinberg, Karen Henry, and Steve Scipione at Bedford/St. Martin's possess these qualities; we especially appreciate their confidence in our ability to carry out this task. Our editor, Alanya Harter, and her associate, Joshua Levy, have guided the project throughout, keeping us on track with a vision of the whole when we were discouraged and keeping the day-to-day work moving forward. In particular, they helped us to reconceptualize the anthology's format and content. Without their suggestions, unacknowledged contributions, and guidance, this anthology would not be what it is today. They were assisted by many others who undertook particular tasks: The brilliant design was conceived by Anna George; Genevieve Hamilton helped to manage the art program, and together with Julia Berrisford she managed the final stages of development. Martha Friedman served as photo researcher, and Tina Samaha developed the maps. Jeff Voccola acted as editorial assistant, taking on many tasks, including the onerous ones of pasting up and numbering the manuscript. Ben Fortson expertly and efficiently supplied the pronunciation guides. Harriet Wald tirelessly and imaginatively oversaw the content and production of the Web site, an enormous task; she was helped along the way by Coleen O'Hanley, Chad Crume, and Dave Batty. Jenna Bookin Barry enthusiastically developed and coordinated the marketing plan, especially challenging when six books publish over a span of six months.

We were blessed with a superb production team who took the book from manuscript to final pages. For Books 4 and 6, we owe special thanks to Senior Production Editor Karen Baart, whose dedication and eye for detail made the project better in every way. Stasia Zomkowski efficiently served as production editor for Book 5 and Ara Salibian for Book 1; they were ably assisted by Courtney Jossart and Kerri Cardone. Melissa Cook's careful and thoughtful copyediting helped to give consistency and clarity to the different voices that contributed to the manuscript. Managing Editor Elizabeth Schaaf oversaw the whole process and Senior Production Supervisor Catherine Hetmansky realized our final vision of design and content in beautifully bound and printed books.

Most of all, we thank our families, especially Mary Davis, Marlys Harrison, and Mona Johnson, for their advice, stamina, and patience during the past three years while this book has occupied so much of our time and theirs.

Paul Davis
Gary Harrison
David M. Johnson
Patricia Clark Smith
John F. Crawford

A NOTE ON TRANSLATION

Some translators of literary works into English tended to sacrifice form for literal meaning, while others subordinated literal meaning to the artistry of the original work. With the increasing number of translations of world literature available by a range of translators, it has become possible to select versions that are clear and accessible as well as literally and aesthetically faithful to the original. Thus our choice of Robert Fagle's *Iliad* and *Odyssey,* Horace Gregory's poems by Catullus, Mary Barnard's poems by Sappho, Theodore Morrison's *Canterbury Tales,* Edward Seidensticker's *Tale of Genji,* and Willa and Edwin Muir's *The Metamorphosis,* among others.

There are those who question whether poetry can ever be adequately translated from one language and culture into another; our concern, however, is not with what might be lost in a translation but with what is gained. The best translations do not merely duplicate a work but re-create it in a new idiom. Coleman Barks's poems of Rumi, Stephen Mitchell's poems of Rilke, Miguel León-Portilla's translations of Nahuatl poetry, and David Hinton's poems of the Tang dynasty are in a way outstanding English poems in their own right. And William Kelly Simpson's love poems of ancient Egypt, Robert and Jean Hollander's *Inferno,* Richard Wilbur's *Tartuffe,* W. S. Merwin's poems of Ghalib, Judith Hemschemeyer's poems of Anna Akhmatova, and Robert Bly's poems of Pablo Neruda are examples of translations done by major poets whose renderings are now an important part of their own body of work.

Barbara Stoler Miller's translation of the Bhagavad Gita and Donald Keene's translation of Chikamatsu's *Love Suicides at Amijima* communicate the complexity of a literary work. Richard Bodner's contemporary translation of Bashō's *Narrow Road through the Backcountry,* especially commissioned, does justice to both the prose and the resonant haiku in that work. David Luke's excellent translation of *Death in Venice* pays tribute to Thomas Mann's original German and is at the same time very readable.

More is said about the translations in this book in the notes for individual works.

About the Editors

Paul Davis (Ph.D., University of Wisconsin), professor emeritus of English at the University of New Mexico, has been the recipient of several teaching awards and academic honors, including that of Master Teacher. He has taught courses since 1962 in composition, rhetoric, and nineteenth-century literature and has written and edited many scholarly books, including *The Penguin Dickens Companion* (1999), *Dickens A to Z* (1998), and *The Life and Times of Ebeneezer Scrooge* (1990). He has also written numerous scholarly and popular articles on solar energy and Victorian book illustration.

Gary Harrison (Ph.D., Stanford University), professor and director of undergraduate studies at the University of New Mexico, has won numerous fellowships and awards for scholarship and teaching. He has taught courses in world literature, British Romanticism, and literary theory at the University of New Mexico since 1987. Harrison's publications include a critical study on William Wordsworth, *Wordsworth's Vagrant Muse: Poetry, Poverty and Power* (1994); and many articles on the literature and culture of the early nineteenth century.

David M. Johnson (Ph.D., University of Connecticut), professor emeritus of English at the University of New Mexico, has taught courses in world literature, mythology, the Bible as literature, philosophy and literature, and creative writing since 1965. He has written, edited, and contributed to numerous scholarly books and collections of poetry, including *Fire in the Fields* (1996) and *Lord of the Dawn: The Legend of Quetzalcoatl* (1987). He has also published scholarly articles, poetry, and translations of Nahuatl myths.

Patricia Clark Smith (Ph.D., Yale University), professor emerita of English at the University of New Mexico, has taught courses in world literature, creative writing, American literature, and Native American literature since 1971. Her many publications include a collection of poetry, *Changing Your Story* (1991); the biography *As Long as the Rivers Flow* (1996); and *On the Trail of Elder Brother* (2000).

John F. Crawford (Ph.D., Columbia University), associate professor of English at the University of New Mexico–Valencia, has taught medieval, world, and other literature courses since 1965 at a number of institutions, including California Institute of Technology, Herbert Lehmann College of CUNY, and, most recently, the University of New Mexico. The publisher of West End Press, Crawford has also edited *This Is About Vision: Interviews with Southwestern Writers* (1990) and written articles on multicultural women poets of the Southwest.

Pronunciation Key

This key applies to the pronunciation guides that appear in the margins and before most selections in *The Bedford Anthology of World Literature*. The syllable receiving the main stress is CAPITALIZED.

a	mat, alabaster, laugh	MAT, AL-uh-bas-tur, LAF
ah	mama, Americana, Congo	MAH-mah, uh-meh-rih-KAH-nuh, KAHNG-goh
ar	cartoon, Harvard	kar-TOON, HAR-vurd
aw	saw, raucous	SAW, RAW-kus
ay (or a)	may, Abraham, shake	MAY, AY-bruh-ham, SHAKE
b	bet	BET
ch	church, matchstick	CHURCH, MACH-stik
d	desk	DESK
e	Edward, melted	ED-wurd, MEL-tid
ee	meet, ream, petite	MEET, REEM, puh-TEET
eh	cherub, derriere	CHEH-rub, DEH-ree-ehr
f	final	FIGH-nul
g	got, giddy	GAHT, GIH-dee
h	happenstance	HAP-un-stans
i	mit, Ipswich, impression	MIT, IP-swich, im-PRESH-un
igh (or i)	eyesore, right, Anglophile	IGH-sore, RITE, ANG-gloh-file
ih	Philippines	FIH-luh-peenz
j	judgment	JUJ-mint
k	kitten	KIT-tun
l	light, allocate	LITE, AL-oh-kate
m	ramrod	RAM-rahd
n	ran	RAN
ng	rang, thinker	RANG, THING-ker
oh (or o)	open, owned, lonesome	OH-pun, OHND, LONE-sum
ong	wrong, bonkers	RONG, BONG-kurz
oo	moot, mute, super	MOOT, MYOOT, SOO-pur
ow	loud, dowager, how	LOWD, DOW-uh-jur, HOW
oy	boy, boil, oiler	BOY, BOYL, OY-lur
p	pet	PET
r	right, wretched	RITE, RECH-id
s	see, citizen	SEE, SIH-tuh-zun
sh	shingle	SHING-gul
t	test	TEST
th	thin	THIN
th	this, whether	*TH*IS, WEH-*th*ur
u	until, sumptuous, lovely	un-TIL, SUMP-choo-us, LUV-lee
uh	about, vacation, suddenly	uh-BOWT, vuh-KAY-shun, SUH-dun-lee
ur	fur, bird, term, beggar	FUR, BURD, TURM, BEG-ur
v	vacuum	VAK-yoo-um
w	western	WES-turn
y	yesterday	YES-tur-day
z	zero, loser	ZEE-roh, LOO-zur
zh	treasure	TREH-zhur

Where a name is given two pronunciations, usually the first is the most familiar pronunciation in English and the second is a more exact rendering of the native pronunciation.

In the pronunciations of French names, nasalized vowels are indicated by adding "ng" after the vowel.

Japanese words have no strong stress accent, so the syllables marked as stressed are so given only for the convenience of English speakers.

CONTENTS

◆ India: Jewel in the Colonial Crown   955

∾ Japan: From Isolation to Nationalism   *1071*

The Bedford Anthology of
World Literature
The Nineteenth Century, 1800–1900

Rue Auber, Paris, 1878 (photograph). *By the end of the nineteenth century, the United States, Japan, and almost all of Europe had become industrialized and urbanized. The Industrial Revolution had sparked an increase in production and trade, and many people had moved from rural communities to cities in order to meet the ever-increasing demand for factory workers and to realize their own dreams of prosperity. Because of explosive population growth, nineteenth-century cities saw dramatic poverty — but also an explosion of the arts, culture, and international trade. (Art Resource)*

The Nineteenth Century

1800 - 1900

*I*n Europe and in the Western hemisphere as a whole, the nineteenth century symbolically began with the American (1776) and French (1789) Revolutions, uprisings inspired by Enlightenment rationalism that would in turn inspire liberal movements to free trade and make government more representational and later anticolonial movements worldwide for the next two centuries. At the same time, the Industrial Revolution, which began in the last third of the eighteenth century, transformed material conditions and increased the opportunities for trade, emigration, and colonization, so that by the end of the nineteenth century industrial Europe controlled much of the world, and Westernization both threatened and attracted the nations of Asia and Africa.

REVOLUTIONARY LIBERALISM

Nineteenth-century Europe inherited revolutionary LIBERALISM, an ideology that rejects authoritarian government and defends freedom of speech, association, and

www For an interactive version of the Comparative Time Line for the Nineteenth Century, see *World Literature Online* at bedfordstmartins.com/worldlit.

COMPARATIVE TIME LINE FOR THE NINETEENTH CENTURY

Date	History and Politics	Literature	Science, Culture, and Technology
1770–1780	1776 American Revolution	1774 Goethe, *The Sorrows of Young Werther*	
1780–1790	1789 French Revolution		
1790–1800	1791 U.S. Bill of Rights ratified.		1791 Paine, *Rights of Man*
	1791 Slave revolt begins in Haiti, led by Toussaint-Louverture. Haitian independence declared in 1804.	1792 Wollstonecraft, *Vindication of the Rights of Woman*	1793 David, *The Murder of Marat*
			1795 Haydn completes the twelve London symphonies.
	1793 Reign of Terror begins in France; Louis XVI beheaded.		
	1794 Slavery abolished in French colonies.	1794 Blake, *Songs of Innocence and Experience*	1796 Jenner develops vaccine against smallpox.
	1795 British capture the Cape Colony from the Dutch in South Africa.		
	1796 Edict of Peking forbids the importation of opium into China.	1798 Wordsworth and Coleridge, *Lyrical Ballads*	1798 Malthus, *Essay on the Principle of Population*
			1799 Rosetta Stone found near Rosetta, Egypt.
1800–1810	1798–1801 Napoleon invades Egypt.		
	1802 British gain control over central India.		
	1803 Louisiana Purchase	1803 *The Travels of Mirza Abu Taleb Khan*	
	1804 Napoleon becomes emperor of France.		1807 Fulton's *Clermont* navigates in the Hudson River.
	1808 Slave trade abolished throughout British empire.	1808 Goethe, *Faust*, Part I	
			1808 Beethoven, *Symphony No. 5*

religion, and the right to own property. Eighteenth-century reformers had sought to overthrow monarchies and landed aristocracies and to establish constitutional governments in their place. These new governments would broaden the base of power and recognize the increasing role of industry and trade around the world throughout the nineteenth century. Great Britain saw an expansion in the number of registered voters, voters who curtailed the power of wealthy landowners by staging an ongoing "bloodless revolution" consisting of a series of Reform Bills. In most other European countries the same process was less peaceful. France repeated Napoleon's transformation of a "republic" into an "empire" several times, initiating each new republic with fighting in the streets. In 1848, the great year of revolution throughout Europe, there were armed revolts in France, Germany, Italy, Austria, and areas of eastern Europe that were part of the Ottoman empire.

In Asia, the traditional societies of China and Japan attempted to resist liberalization by isolating themselves from outside influences. China fought against British influence in a series of "opium wars" at the middle of the century, while at the same time suppressing a thirteen-year effort by Taiping rebels to overthrow the

Date	History and Politics		Literature		Science, Culture, and Technology	
1800–1810 (cont.)	1808	United States prohibits importation of slaves from Africa.	1809	Shen Fu, *Six Records from a Floating Life*	1809	Lamarck, *Principles of Zoology*
1810–1820	1809	Ecuador gains independence from Spain.			1810	Goya, *The Disasters of War*
	1810	Height of Napoleon's power	1812	The Brothers Grimm, *Fairy Tales*	1811	Stephenson, first locomotive
	1811	Luddites destroy factory machines in northern England.	1812	Byron, *Childe Harold's Pilgrimage*, Part I		
	1813	Simón Bolívar becomes dictator in Venezuela.				
	1814	Lord Hastings, governor of India, declares war on Gurkhas in Nepal.	1814	Bakin, *Hakkenden*, Part I	1816	Rossini, *The Barber of Seville*
	1815	Battle of Waterloo	1818	Mary Shelley, *Frankenstein*		
	1818	France abolishes slave trade.	1818	de Stael, *French Revolution*		
	1818	British defeat the Maratha Confederacy in India.	1819	Keats, *Odes*		
			1819	Hoffmann, "The Mines of Falun"		
			1819	Goethe, *Divan of West and East*	1819	Gericault, *The Raft of Medusa*
1820–1830					1820	Ampère discovers electrical current.
	1821	Greek war of independence begins.			1821	First fossilized skeleton of a dinosaur discovered.
	1822	Brazil becomes independent of Portugal.				
	1823	Mexico becomes a republic.			1822	Schubert, *Unfinished Symphony*
	1823	Monroe Doctrine				

tired Qing dynasty. Its victories would prove short-lived. The Qing survived only until 1911, when it was finally defeated by the republican forces of Sun Yat-sen. In Japan, which had vigorously resisted Western intrusions until the 1850s, Meiji reformers, while paying lip service to conservative, traditional ideology, instituted constitutional reform and encouraged industrialization.

EMANCIPATION

The liberation movements inspired by the Enlightenment philosophy that made *liberté, fraternité,* and *egalité* (liberty, fraternity, and equality) the bywords of the French Revolution also prompted a worldwide movement to abolish slavery. Toussaint-Louverture led a slave revolt that ended slavery in Haiti in 1801 and emboldened the abolition movement. The British brought the slave trade to a close in 1807 and outlawed slavery in their colonies in 1833. Although the United States abolished the slave trade in 1808, it took the Civil War (1861–65) to abolish slavery in the South. Simón Bolívar's revolutions in the first quarter of the century constitutionally eliminated slavery in many Latin American countries; once slavery was abolished in Brazil in 1888 it had been purged from the Western Hemisphere

Date	History and Politics	Literature	Science, Culture, and Technology
1820–1830 (cont.)	1824 Slavery abolished in Central America.	1827 Heine, *Book of Songs* (tr. 1846)	1825 Erie Canal finished.
		1828 Nerval, translation of Goethe's *Faust*	
	1829 Slavery abolished in Mexico.		
1830–1840	1830 Revolution in Paris; Louis Phillipe becomes king of France.	1830 Balzac begins *The Human Comedy*	1830 Delacroix, *Liberty Guiding the People*
	1830 Indian Removal Act; Native Americans relocated to west of the Mississippi.	1830 Stendhal, *The Red and the Black*	1832 Horoshige, *Fifty Three Stages of the Tohaido*
	1830 Belgium gains independence.	1831 Prince, *The History of Mary Prince*	1833 Lyell, *Principles of Geology*
	1833 Abolition of slavery in British colonies.	1832 Goethe, *Faust,* Part II	1833 Hokusai, *Thirty-six Views of Mt. Fuji*
		1832 Rai Sanyo dies.	1834 Babbage invents principle of the computer.
	1836 The Alamo	1837 Pushkin, *The Bronze Horseman*	
	1837 Victoria becomes queen of Great Britain.		1838 Daguerre develops the daguerreotype photographic process.
	1839 Independent Republic of Natal founded by Boers.	1839 Poe, "The Fall of the House of Usher"	
			1839 Goodyear vulcanizes rubber.
1840–1850	1840–1848 First Opium War between British and China, Chinese ports opened to British traders.		1840 de Tocqueville, *Democracy in America*
	1841 Britain proclaims sovereignty over Hong Kong.		

entirely. In 1861, Tzar Alexander II in Russia freed the serfs. In India, Ram Mohun Roy (1772–1833) and other reformers began a movement to reform the caste system, a rigidly enforced class hierarchy. The Meiji government in Japan ended the feudal class system there in 1871 and granted legal equality to the *etu*, the traditional slave class. The Berlin Conference in 1885 committed the most important Muslim leaders to act against slavery in the Middle East. Though slavery persisted in some parts of Africa and the Islamic world at the end of the nineteenth century, the abolition movement had achieved major victories nearly everywhere else.

NATIONALISM

As revolutionaries and reformers sought to expand the role and power of the growing middle classes, the merchants and factory owners of these new classes wanted to eliminate trade barriers. By consolidating smaller states into larger nations, they hoped to enlarge their markets and their spheres of economic influence. Sometimes national unity was led by liberal republicans, as in the *Risorgimento* in Italy; sometimes it was led by conservative politicians such as the Meiji reformers in Japan, who made the restoration of the emperor their central goal,

Date	History and Politics	Literature	Science, Culture, and Technology
1840–1850 (cont.)		1843 Hirata Atsutane dies.	1843 Prescott, *History of the Conquest of Mexico*
	1844 Daniel O'Connell found guilty of conspiracy against British rule in Ireland.		1844 Turner, *Rain, Steam, and Speed*
	1844 Dominican Republic becomes independent of Haiti.	1845 Douglass, *Narrative of the Life of Frederick Douglass, an American Slave*	
	1846 First Sikh War ends; Treaty of Lahore		1846 Smithsonian Institution founded.
	1846 Polish revolt	1846 Whittier, *Songs of Freedom*	1846 Howe invents sewing machine.
	1848 Revolt in Paris; Louis Napoleon elected president.	1847 C. Brontë, *Jane Eyre*	1846 Berlioz, *Damnation of Faust*
	1848 Revolution in Vienna; Metternich resigns.	1847 E. Brontë, *Wuthering Heights*	
	1848 Revolutions in Venice, Berlin, Milan, Parma, and Rome.	1848 Marx and Engels, *The Communist Manifesto*	
	1848 Czech Revolt in Prague	1848 Stanton and Mott, *Declaration of Sentiments and Resolutions*	
	1848 Treaty of Guadalupe Hildago ends Mexican-U.S. War.		
	1849 Mazzini proclaims Rome a republic.		
	1849 Revolts in Dresden and Baden.	1849 Kierkegaard, *The Sickness unto Death*	1849 California Gold Rush
	1849 British defeat Sikhs at Chillianwalla.		
	1849 Britain annexes the Punjab.		

or Prussia's Otto von Bismarck (1815–1898), who unified Germany into a military power. Whether liberal or conservative at heart, such unifications inspired nationalistic fervor. Artists and writers expressed their love of nation by collecting folk stories and ballads, writing in the language of the common people, and resurrecting or creating a mythic history of their nation. Among the "national epics" of the period are the Waverly novels of Sir Walter Scott (1771–1832), which developed a romantic history of Scotland; the historical romances of Takizawa Bakin (p. 1076) (1767–1848), which narrated a mythic history of medieval Japan; and the epic of Polish nationhood, Adam Mickiewicz's (1798–1855) *Pan Tafdeusz* (1834). The ideals of freedom, liberty, and nationhood inspired writers not only to poetry but also to military action: The English poet Lord Byron (p. 189) (1788–1824) died while fighting for Greek independence.

SCIENCE AND INDUSTRY

The Enlightenment faith in the power of science was edified by the important discoveries of scientists such as French biologist Louis Pasteur (1822–1895), who developed the germ theory of disease; Russian chemist Dmitri Mendeleyev

Date	History and Politics	Literature	Science, Culture, and Technology
1850–1860	1850 Outbreak of Anglo-Kaffir War	1850 Tennyson, *In Memoriam*	
	1850–1864 Taiping Rebellion in China	1851 Melville, *Moby-Dick*	
	1852 South African Republic (Transvaal) established.	1852 Stowe, *Uncle Tom's Cabin*	
	1854 Commodore Perry negotiates first Japanese-American treaty.		
	1854 Republican Party formed in United States.		
	1855 Crimean War	1855 Whitman, *Song of Myself*	
	1856 Britain annexes Oudh, India, and Natal.	1856 Melville, "Bartleby the Scrivener"	
	1857 Peace of Paris ends Anglo-Persian War.	1857 Baudelaire, *Les fleurs du mal*	
	1857 Sepoy Rebellion against British rule		
	1857 Irish Republican Brotherhood (Fenians) founded.		
	1858 Treaty of Tientsin ends Anglo-Chinese War.		
	1858–1863 Mexican civil war; Maximillian named emperor.		1859 Gounod, *Faust*
	1859 Franco-Austrian War	1859 Darwin, *The Origin of Species*	1859 First oil well drilled at Titusville, Pa.
		1859 Mill, *On Liberty*	

(1834–1907), who formulated the periodic table of the elements; and British physicist Michael Faraday (1791–1867), who discovered the theoretical foundations of electricity. In the nineteenth century, the scientific method was extended to areas of study that are now considered the province of the social sciences: economics, politics, anthropology, and sociology. With each new application of scientific study, the conviction grew that nature was an orderly system of laws and that mankind, by discovering those laws, could control the natural world. But for many, this faith was shaken by Charles Darwin (p. 349) (1809–1882), whose *Origin of Species* (1859) seemed to describe a world that operated by chance. Instead of a harmonious and orderly creation, Darwin had discovered, in British poet Alfred, Lord Tennyson's (p. 389) (1809–1892) words, a "Nature red in tooth and claw."

The power of science became visible in the achievements of the Industrial Revolution, which started in the last third of the eighteenth century. Industrialization gradually changed the process of manufacturing, modes of transportation, and much of the physical world. The steam engine facilitated railways and factory towns. By the end of the nineteenth century, the United States, Japan, and all of the European nations except Russia had become industrialized.

Date	History and Politics	Literature	Science, Culture, and Technology
1860–1870	1860 Garibaldi proclaims Victor Emmanuel II king of Italy.		1861 Pasturization introduced following Pasteur's work on microorganisms.
	1860 Abraham Lincoln elected president.		
	1861 Emancipation of the serfs in Russia.	1861 Jacobs, *Incidents in the Life of a Slave Girl*	1863 Joseph Lister introduces antiseptic surgery.
	1861 U.S. Civil War begins.		
	1862 Bismarck becomes Prussian prime minister.		1863 Manet, *Olympia*
		1864 Dostoyevsky, *Notes from Underground*	
	1863 Emancipation Proclamation		1865 Mendel develops laws of genetic inheritance.
	1865 End of U.S. Civil War; Lincoln assassinated.	1865 Dickens, *Our Mutual Friend*	
	1866 Austro-Italian War		
	1867 Tokugawa shogunate ends in Japan, replaced by Meiji emperor.	1867 Zola, *Thérèse Raquin*	1867 Nobel manufactures dynamite.
	1868 Russia sells Alaska to United States.		1868 Brahams, *German Requiem*
	1868 Revolution in Spain	1869 Ghalib dies.	
	1869 Opening of Suez Canal	1869 Rimbaud, *Poems*	
1870–1880	1870 Franco-Prussian War		
	1870 Revolt in Paris; Third Republic established.	1871 Eliot, *Middlemarch*	1871 Stanley meets Livingstone.
	1871 Paris Commune		1872 Whistler, *The Artist's Mother*
	1871 Germany unified under Prussian emperor.		1873 Japan adopts European calendar.

COLONIALISM

Agricultural nations were affected by industrialization in their own way. As Western nations sought to expand their markets and secure sources of raw materials, they established colonies throughout the world, especially in Asia and Africa. Gradually, they set themselves up as the colonial owners or managers of much of the rest of the globe; by 1900 the imperial nations controlled more than four-fifths of the world's land surface. Western-made maps of Asia and Africa were colored to identify their absentee owners. Britain, the most successful of the colonial powers, circled the globe in British red with an empire on which the sun never set.

While imperial powers exploited the economic and human resources of colonized countries and undermined those societies' traditional cultures, they also bestowed the mixed blessings of new Western institutions, ideas, and material goods on their colonies. In India, the urban middle class benefited from the inexpensive textiles imported from British factories, but these manufactured fabrics put many Indian hand-loom weavers out of work. The middle class also gained access to Western education. In Bengal and other Indian provinces, young writers

Date	History and Politics	Literature	Science, Culture, and Technology
	1873 Republic proclaimed in Spain.		
	1873 Famine in Bengal		
	1874 End of Ashanti War	1874 Flaubert, "A Simple Heart"	1874 First impressionist exhibition, Paris
			1875 Bizet, *Carmen*
			1875 Schliemann, *Troy and Its Remains*
		1876 Mallarmé, "L'Après-midi d'un faune"	1876 Wagner's *Ring Cycle* first performed.
	1877 Satsuma Revolt in Japan suppressed.	1876 Rassundari Devi, *Amar Jiban*	1876 Bell invents telephone.
	1878 Russia defeats the Ottoman empire.		
	1879 British-Zulu War		1879 Edison develops incandescent lamp.
1880–1890	1880 Boer Republic under Kruger	1880 Dostoevsky, *The Brothers Karamazov*	1880 Rodin, *The Thinker*
		1881 Machado de Assis, *Epitaph of a Small Winner* (tr. 1952)	
			1885 Benz develops prototype of automobile.
	1885 Congo becomes personal possession of Leopold II of Belgium.	1883 Nietzsche, *Thus Spoke Zarathustra*	
	1885 French establish a protectorate in Indochina.	1884 Twain, *Huckleberry Finn*	1885 Van Gogh, *The Potato Eaters*
	1886 First Indian National Congress	1886 Tolstoy, *The Death of Ivan Ilych*	1886 Statue of Liberty dedicated.

inspired by the English Romantic poets they had studied in British colonial schools created a new Indian poetry written in Bengali and other vernacular languages. As the British colonial administration brought together the disparate Indian states, these new vernacular literatures contributed to a growing nationalism. Ironically, the liberal political ideas of British philosophers that were part of the standard colonial curriculum helped inspire the Indian independence movement that began late in the nineteenth century.

ROMANTICISM AND REALISM IN LITERATURE

Although Western ideas were assimilated to some degree in many non-Western countries, there was nonetheless a deep distrust of Western thought and in particular of scientific materialism. Confronting the onslaught of Western culture, many Japanese and Indian writers looked for ways to adopt the material benefits of technology without giving up their spiritual and cultural traditions. Indian writer Rabindranath Tagore (p. 973) (1861–1941) suggested that an appropriate cultural exchange between equals would be for the West to trade science to the East in

Date	History and Politics	Literature	Science, Culture, and Technology
1880–1890 (cont.)		1889 Kipling, "Ballad of East and West"	1888 Eastman develops hand camera.
	1889 Political parties founded in Japan.		1889 Eiffel Tower
1890–1900	1890 First general election in Japan	1890 Dickinson, *Poems* (published posthumously)	1890 Frazer, *The Golden Bough*
	1890 Battle at Wounded Knee		1890 W. James, *The Principles of Psychology*
		1890 Ogai, "The Dancing Girl"	
	1891 Famine in Russia	1891 Doyle, *The Adventures of Sherlock Holmes*	
		1892 Gilman, "The Yellow Wallpaper"	
		1892 Chopin, "Desiree's Baby"	1892 Diesel patents heavy oil engine.
			1892 Monet paints Rouen Cathedral.
		1893 Pardo Bazan, "The Oldest Story"	1893 Dvorak, *New World Symphony*
	1894–1895 Sino-Japanese War ends in defeat of Chinese.	1894 Chopin, "The Story of an Hour"	1894 Debussy, *L'Après-midi d'un faune*
	1895 Rhodesia founded.	1895 Tagore, "The Hungry Stones"	1895 Röntgen discovers X-rays.
		1895 Pardo Bazan, "The Revolver"	1895 First motion picture
		1895 Freud and Breuer, *Studies in Hysteria*	

return for Eastern spiritual knowledge. In the colonial relationship, however, the exchange was unequal. Along with Western material goods, the East also took in Western missionaries, teachers, and literary models. By the end of the century the dominant Western literary movements, Romanticism and Realism, were also influential in such Eastern nations as India and Japan.

Like Eastern writers, European **ROMANTICS** dominant in the first half of the century rejected scientific rationalism. They turned inward and explored consciousness and personal experience, areas ignored by scientists. They invoked the spirit world, elevated feeling over thought, and celebrated the spontaneous and unpredictable. The English Romantic poet William Wordsworth (1770–1850) lamented the power of science to destroy the beauty of nature: "Our meddling intellect," he wrote, "misshapes the beauteous forms of things:—We murder to dissect." Wordsworth and others' emphasis on the inner life of the individual, use of expressive poetic forms, and celebration of the myths of nationhood were elements of Romanticism that influenced writers in many other parts of the world.

Realists who tended to write prose rather than poetry appeared later in the century. Looking at a world blackened by industry where human beings seemed

Date	History and Politics	Literature	Science, Culture, and Technology
1890–1900 (cont.)		1895 Stanton, *The Woman's Bible*	
		1895 Ichiyo, "The Thirteenth Night"	1896 Nobel endows Nobel Prizes.
	1897 Greeks defeated in war with Ottomans.	1898 Syed Ahmed Khan dies.	
	1899 Boer War	1899 Nitobé, *Bushido: The Soul of Japan*	
	1899 Dreyfus pardoned.		
	1899 Boxer Rebellion in China.		
1900–1910			1900 Planck develops quantum theory.
	1901 Death of Queen Victoria	1902 Conrad, *Heart of Darkness*	1900 Freud, *Interpretation of Dreams*
	1901 Commonwealth of Australia formed.	1902 Gorky, *Lower Depths*	1902 Gauguin, *Riders to the Sea*
	1902 Anglo-Japanese Treaty recognizes independence of Korea and China.	1904 Chekhov, *The Cherry Orchard*	1903 Wright brothers' first flight.
	1902 End of Boer War		1904 Weber, *The Protestant Ethic and the Spirit of Capitalism*
	1903 British complete conquest of Nigeria.		
	1905 Sinn Fein Party founded in Dublin.		1904 Puccini, *Madame Butterfly*
	1905 Russo-Japanese War ends with Japanese victory.		1905 Einstein, Special Theory of Relativity
	1905 Revolution in Russia; tsar establishes a national assembly.		

transformed into machines, realists attempted to describe everyday life in everyday language. They sometimes described their point of view as "scientific," for scientists such as Darwin had taught them to look at human society objectively, as part of the physical world. Their panoramic novels, crowded with characters and surveying complex networks of social relationships, became the dominant literary form in nineteenth-century Europe. The great nineteenth-century realist novelists — Charles Dickens (1812–1870) and George Eliot (1819–1880) in Britain, Honoré de Balzac (1799–1850) and Gustave Flaubert (p. 435) (1821–1880) in France, Fyodor Dostoevsky (p. 462) (1821–1881) and Leo Tolstoy (p. 617) (1828–1910) in Russia, Henry James (1843–1916) and Mark Twain (1835–1910) in America — inspired the novels that became the dominant literary genre of the twentieth century in Europe and in many other parts of the world. In the Bengali Renaissance of the late nineteenth century, B. C. Chatterjee (1838–1894) and Rabindranath Tagore (1861–1941) pioneered the realist novel in India. By the end of the century, realist fiction like that of Higuchi Ichiyo (p. 1103) (1872–1896) and Mori Ōgai (p. 1083) (1862–1922) had become the dominant literary genre in Japan.

Date	History and Politics	Literature	Science, Culture, and Technology
1900–1910 (cont.)	1905 Norway separates from Sweden.		1905 Artist group Les Fauves founded.
	1905 Sun Yat-sen organizes a union to expel Manchus from China.		1909 Peary reaches North Pole.
1910–1920	1910 Union of South Africa established.		1910 Stravinsky, *The Firebird*
	1910 Japan annexes Korea.		1911 Mahler, *Das Lied von der Erde*
	1910 Revolution in Portugal		1911 Matisse, *Red Studio*
	1910 China abolishes slavery.		1912 Titanic disaster
	1911 Mexican civil war		1913 Russell and Whitehead, *Principia Mathematica*
	1912 Sun Yat-sen founds Kuomintang (Chinese National Party).		
	1913 Balkan War		1913 Bohr develops theory of atomic structure.
	1914 World War I begins.	1915 Iqbal, *Asrar-e-Khudi* (*The Secrets of the Self*)	1913 Armory Show introduces cubism and postimpressionism in United States.
		1917 Hu Shih, a leader in the May Fourth movement	1914 Ford pioneers the assembly line.
1920–1930			
		1924 Forster, *A Passage to India*	
		1924 Guenon, *East and West*	

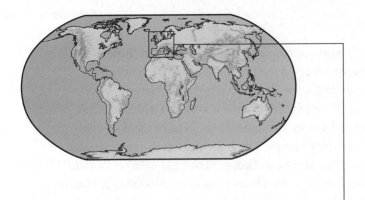

European Industry and Railways 1870

By the second half of the eighteenth century, the Industrial Revolution had transformed material conditions and increased opportunities for trade and travel. By 1870, coal mining, ironworking, and textile production had become major European industries. Train lines were constructed to allow easy travel throughout the whole of Europe—a concept unheard of a century before. Trade between nations flourished. A profound economic and social disparity opened between the affluent owner of production—the bourgeoisie—and the low-paid worker in the mills and mines—the proletariat—setting the stage for a century of violent upheaval.

EUROPE
Industry and Nationalism

∿ Symbolically, the nineteenth century in Europe began on July 14, 1789, the decisive day when French revolutionaries took over the Bastille, a French prison. Thomas Jefferson had summed up the political ideals of the Enlightenment in the Declaration of Independence; the French Jacobins turned those ideals into the revolutionary slogan, "liberté, fraternité, egalité"° and took to the streets. Even though they espoused the democratic, antimonarchical ideals of the Enlightenment, Jacobins broke with their predecessors' commitment to reasoned and evolutionary change. The superstition and oppression of the past, they believed, could be overthrown only by arms, not by argument. Their violent successes were examples emulated around the world by those who similarly wanted to throw off feudal oppression, outdated monarchy, or colonial exploitation.

REVOLUTION AND LIBERATION

In the century that followed the storming of the Bastille, revolutionary movements arose throughout Europe. The year 1848 became the "year of revolution," in which virtually simultaneous armed insurrections occurred, beginning in Paris and spreading to nearly every other European country. Appropriately, 1848 was also the year in which Karl Marx (1818–1883) and Friedrich Engels (1820–1895) (p. 680) published *The Communist Manifesto,* which characterized history as an ongoing series of class struggles. Revolutionary victories for democratic reforms were often countered by reactionary retreats reasserting the privileges of the ruling classes, but the struggles continued throughout the century. In some cases, as in Britain democratic gains were achieved with relatively little violence. In other places, however, the struggle to overthrow the old regimes of aristocrats and kings left the streets

liberty, fraternity, equality

Paris, February 1848. Engraving

The year 1848 was the "year of revolution" in Europe, in which armed uprisings occurred in nearly every European country. The first of these insurrections occurred in Paris, in February, when, angered by widespread unemployment and food shortages, students, workers, and the unemployed took to the streets. During the height of the demonstrations, forty to fifty people were killed when panicked police opened fire on a crowd. King Louis Philippe eventually abdicated the throne and fled to England, and a republic was soon established in France. (The Bridgeman Art Library)

flowing with blood. The French Revolution is remembered most vividly in images of the guillotine and the Reign of Terror.

These liberation movements were inspired by ENLIGHTENMENT philosophers whose most significant nineteenth-century successors were the English UTILITARI-ANS Jeremy Bentham (1748–1832) and John Stuart Mill (1806–1873). Bentham and Mill argued that the purpose of government was to enable "the greatest happiness of the greatest number," and they proposed measures to rationalize and centralize governmental institutions. Mill's classic essay *On Liberty* (1859) not only declared it a human right to be free of tyrants but, more important, addressed the issue of how, under a constitutional government, the rights of the minority could be protected from the tyranny of the majority. These ideas reached far beyond Britain; in

India, for example, the works of Bentham and Mill were standard texts in the British colonial schools; they soon became instrumental in the emancipation and women's rights movements worldwide.

Many revolutionary movements were more nationalistic than democratic. In Germany and Italy, nationalism weakened loyalties to local princes and enabled reformers to unify smaller states into nations. Throughout Europe, loyalty to national identities aroused more passionate allegiance than the Enlightenment's ideal of rational universalism. The "new" nations of Europe, made powerful by consolidation and aggressive by nationalism, pushed against their boundaries. Bismarck, the German chancellor, fought Denmark for the duchies of Schleswig and Holstein in 1864, fought Austria for control of several northern German states in 1866, and fought France in 1870 and 1871 for the provinces of Alsace and Lorraine. When such expansionist struggles quieted in Europe, the act of acquisition was often transported overseas, particularly to Africa and Asia, where European nations fought to annex nations there and make them into colonial possessions.

No figure of the nineteenth century better embodies its contradictory impulses than Napoleon Bonaparte (1769–1821). Son of a Corsican attorney, Napoleon was a commoner who rose to power as a military strategist in the aftermath of the French Revolution. He began as an officer in the revolutionary army of the people, but he became the emperor of most of Europe, a dictator who replaced the ruling monarchs with members of his own family. If he personified the ideals of the Revolution, he also represented their betrayal. As the charismatic "unifier" of Europe, he abolished the power of hereditary princes only to become the tyrant that German philosopher Friedrich Nietzsche (p. 198) (1844–1900) would later describe as "the synthesis of brute and Superman."

The century produced a pantheon of heroes, many of whom pursued the contradictory goals of liberation and imperial conquest. While they fought for freedom and independence from the monarchs and feudal lords who had inherited power, they also inspired nationalistic fervor as they consolidated smaller states into nations or pursued dreams of empires abroad. The impulse to liberation was embodied in such figures as Giuseppe Mazzini (1805–1872) and Giuseppe Garabaldi (1807–1882) in Italy, Thaddeus Kosciusko (1746–1817) in Poland, and Simón Bolívar (1783–1830) in Latin America. Leaders like Germany's dictatorial chancellor Otto von Bismarck (1815–1898) and Britain's Cecil Rhodes (1853–1902), who consolidated British colonial power in southern Africa, carried out some of the century's nationalistic and imperial excesses.

www For more information about the culture and context of Europe for the Nineteenth Century, see *World Literature Online* at bedfordstmartins.com/worldlit.

THE INDUSTRIAL REVOLUTION

As a series of inventions that mechanized textile manufacture sprung up in Britain, the INDUSTRIAL REVOLUTION was underway in the mid eighteenth century, transforming manufacturing, transportation, and agriculture. The new machines enabled the creation of factories and, with the use of steam power to run the machines, factories could be clustered in cities. Although some of these machines were developed in the eighteenth century, the complementary demographics of industrial cities was largely a nineteenth-century phenomenon, and industry and

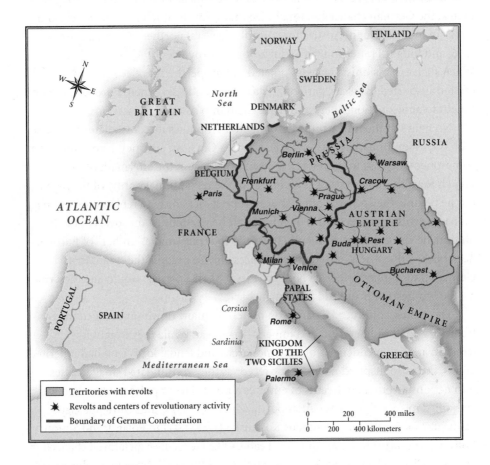

Centers of Revolution, 1848

By 1848, food shortages, overpopulation, and unemployment among the working classes of Europe helped turn ideological turmoil into revolution. One such revolt staged by the French in 1848 inspired others throughout the continent to do the same. Citizens rose up in one capital after another across central and eastern Europe. Although these revolutions ultimately failed to oust established governments, rulers were forced to reconsider their policies.

urbanization came together best in Britain. By the end of the century, the United States, Japan, and all European nations except Russia followed suit in becoming industrialized and urbanized, and even in Russia, as Anton Chekhov's (p. 703) (1860–1904) *The Cherry Orchard* (1904) makes clear, the old feudal society was a thing of the past. The effects of industrialization were felt worldwide through trade and colonization.

The Industrial Revolution was a manifestation of the scientific materialism of the Renaissance and the Enlightenment. After breaking down the processes of production into their component parts and analyzing how those parts worked together, the factory system rationalized manufacture by dividing labor among many workers. This "specialization of labor" was a central concept in Adam Smith's (1723–1790) eighteenth-century treatise, *Wealth of Nations* (1776). Smith believed that a rational economy would be accompanied by a harmonious society brought into being by the guiding "invisible hand" of the competitive marketplace. However, his economic theory did not predict the visible horrors of industrial cities and the class struggles that became increasingly hostile as the nineteenth century wore on.

Workers were lured from the countryside to join the growing urban proletariat, the working class, in quickly built boomtowns with few public services, poor sanitation, and crowded housing. Disease was rampant in these new cities. Industrial workers, whose wages were set by the forces of competition, had no protection against unemployment or brutal working conditions. Men, women, and children worked long hours—sometimes as many as fourteen a day, six days a week. With few safety measures to protect workers from the machines, industrial accidents were common. Removed from nature at work, crammed into crowded tenements at home, and reduced to cogs in the industrial machine, these human beings seemed to be creatures from a new age, mere animals caught in a daily struggle for survival.

ROMANTICISM

Like the political revolutions in America, France, the Caribbean, Poland, and Spanish America, a revolution in philosophy and the arts sought to liberate its practitioners from the rules and conventions of earlier generations. The works of French writer Jean-Jacques Rousseau (1712–1778) represent this societal transformation in its broadest sense. His *Discourse on Inequality* (1754) and *On Social Contract* (1762) provided a conceptual framework for and increased interest in the individualism and political equality espoused by revolutionary politics, and his *New Heloise* (1761), *Émile* (1762), and *Confessions* (1781, 1788) inspired a turn from reason and to feeling and imagination. Whereas the Enlightenment had heralded reason and empirical experimentation as the primary means to discover truth and as the key agents of change, ROMANTICS celebrated instead imagination and feeling as ways to truly connect with the world and oneself. Furthermore, for the Romantics, imagination and feeling were modes of truth that could free the mind from the imperial hold of the external world, the human heart from the restraints of social decorum, the citizen from the chains of political tyranny, and the artist from rules and convention.

Rousseau's injunction to follow feeling, not reason, in Book Seven of *Confessions* may serve as a kind of manifesto for the Romantic hero seeking universal truth in private self-reflection: "I have only one faithful guide upon which I can depend; the chain of the feelings which have marked the development of my being. . . ." Following that chain of feeling, individuals could trace what the Romantics considered a fall from "innocence"—the essential goodness and simplicity innate to all human beings—into "experience"—the alienating effects of culture and society. Nowhere was innocence more visible than in the child or peasant, whose sensibilities and habits had not been tainted by the corrupt influences of civil society. As English poet William Wordsworth's (p. 236) (1770–1850) "Ode: Intimations of Immortality" (1807) suggests, society distracts children from their innate powers of innocence; conforming to social convention, the child learns to "fit his tongue / To dialogues of business, love, or strife" and so becomes alienated from his or her true self. That inner self, however, survives as a spiritual trace that can be tapped by feeling and imagination. Many Romantic poems, like Wordsworth's "Ode," reflect the poet's recognition of and attempt to recuperate from this fall from innocence into experience. Although they believe that one's original state of innocence can never be recovered, Romantic poets value the creative endeavor of searching out some compensatory state of mind or being—what Wordsworth calls "abundant recompense" in "Lines Composed a Few Miles above Tintern Abbey."

Though Romanticism took many forms and rose up in different eras in different places, Romantic poetry as a whole is characterized by its reaction against the conventions and rules of NEOCLASSICAL poetry and by its emphasis on the innate, the subjective, the emotional, and the ideal. Neoclassical poets of the eighteenth century held up a mirror to nature; Romantic poets illuminated nature with the light of the imagination. Nature serves not as a palette for the Romantic poet's paintbrush but as a companion spirit that guides the poet in the act of creation. The Romantic poet looks, as English poet William Blake (p. 208) (1757–1827) says, not with the eye but through the eye, in order to see nature not so much as a source of external impressions as a creative power that helps to free unconscious resources and break down the boundaries between the self and the other, the inner and the outer.

As in Wordsworth's "Ode," these meditations are often also longings for the infinite, an elusive ideal, or an unattainable other. Thus, many Romantic poems involve quests, similar to those of the medieval knight in search of the Holy Grail and Dante's journey toward Beatrice. Indeed, in the late eighteenth century the word *romantic* was associated with the medieval and the Gothic. Unlike the medieval knight, however, the hero of the Romantic quest enacts a self-conscious meditation on his failure to attain the object of his desire. English poet John Keats's (p. 281) (1795–1821) "Ode to a Nightingale" (1820), for example, celebrates the possibility for and the near achievement of a fusion between the "I" of the poem and the Nightingale, the spirit of song; on the wings of "poesy" the narrator transcends his everyday, separate existence and for a moment loses his identity in the object. And yet, as the poem's final lines recognize, that fulfillment must of necessity be partial and cut short, for absolute identity with the object of desire can only be achieved with death. Romantic poetry pairs desire and despair, and a celebration of the imagination with disappointment because, in Keats's words, "the fancy cannot cheat so well / As she is fam'd to do."

Despite their tendencies toward solitude and private reverie, Romantic poets, perhaps paradoxically, were deeply engaged with social issues and politics, particularly with the French Revolution. When the young Wordsworth visited France in the first year of the Revolution, he found "The land all swarmed with passion" and the people "risen up/Fresh as the morning star." Romantic writers hoped that their poetry and philosophy would effect a similar transformation of society and its misguided values by transforming the consciousness of the individual. Thus, the most private reverie resonates with social and historical aspiration. As English poet Percy Bysshe Shelley (1792–1822) writes in "Ode to the West Wind" (composed in 1821), the poet's words are the "The trumpet of prophecy" for a world organized by the principles of human sympathy and love rather than self-interest and greed.

REALISM

The Romantics were often disheartened by the world around them. Wordsworth suggested that materialism, a preoccupation with "getting and spending," had devastated the spiritual awareness of his time, and Blake, observing the effects of the Industrial Revolution, lamented England's "green and pleasant land" now blighted and blackened by factories and their waste. Their disillusionment was magnified in the eyes of many writers later in the century, who found little reason for optimism or hope in the world produced by industrialization. These writers, now often called realists, focused on the "unnatural" life in the cities where repetitive work had reduced laborers to machines and where money defined relationships between people. Writers and artists saw the urban middle classes, with their self-serving materialism and vulgar display of wealth, as soulless, much like the dehumanized workers. Vacuous and narcissistic, they suffered from *ennui*—boredom with the emptiness of their lives. Danish theologian Søren Kierkegaard (p. 675) (1813–1855) diagnosed this condition as despair in *The Sickness unto Death.* To find a deeper spiritual meaning to life, he posits, one must first despair and realize that one is "sick." Russian novelist Leo Tolstoy (p. 617) (1828–1910) dramatized this kind of awakening in *The Death of Ivan Ilych* (1886); Ivan's illness and suffering leads to a painful enlightenment.

The proletariat as a literary character lacked the appealing persona and the folk wisdom of the peasants who had been celebrated by the Romantics. As for the bourgeoisie, they were "Philistines," uncultured and ignorant of art and intellectual thought, said Matthew Arnold (1822–1888); Gustave Flaubert (1821–1880), speaking for many writers, asserted, "Hatred of the Bourgeois is the beginning of wisdom." Lacking subjects for idealization, realists attempted instead to describe as accurately as they could the life around them. Novelists Charles Dickens (p. 670) (1812–1870) in England, Emilia Pardo Bazan (p. 670) (1852–1921) in Spain, and Émile Zola (p. 398) (1840–1902) in France visited factories and slums and exposed the social problems created by industrialization in *Hard Times, The Women Orator,* and *Germinal,* respectively. The Romantics had idealized human beings as creatures defined by their desire for freedom. Like Fyodor Dostoevsky's (p. 462) (1821–1881) cynical Grand Inquisitor, realists were convinced that the great mass of humanity would trade freedom for bread.

Science seemed to have material explanations for everything, and when Charles Darwin's (p. 349) (1809–1882) evolutionary theory, first published in 1859 in *The Origin of Species,* reduced humans to animals and explained creation as a random process, many were ready to accept Nietzsche's assertion that "God is dead." Lacking belief in an orderly universe, the realists simply tried to describe ordinary people and everyday things objectively, without suggesting that they were part of a larger design or had any deep spiritual meaning. Flaubert, in "A Simple Heart," seems to be mocking the search for such significance when he makes Felicité's holy spirit a bedraggled parrot. The NATURALISTS, writers such as Émile Zola in France and Theodore Dreiser (1871–1945) in America, went one Darwinian step further than the realists: Life is not simply ordinary and trivial, they suggested, it is physically determined; and human beings, like the rest of the animal creation, are driven by biological needs and instinctual desires.

In spite of their cynicism and apparent objectivity, realists often affirmed, sometimes inadvertently, the importance of feeling and the power of imagination. The realist in Flaubert looked on such provincial characters as Felicité and Madame Bovary with ironic disdain, but in a Romantic gesture, he was so drawn to identify with the latter that he exclaimed, "I am Madame Bovary." For all his shallowness and petty materialism, when faced with death Tolstoy's Ivan Ilych accepts his common humanity; as he does, he elicits our sympathy. An awareness of loss and the presence of death had tempered the idealism of the Romantics; the cold objectivity of the realists was softened by their recognition of the universality of the human condition.

LITERATURE ABOUT WOMEN

The Industrial Revolution changed the literary marketplace. The steam printing press, invented in 1810, made it possible to produce large quantities of inexpensive magazines and books, which were sold to a growing reading public. Besides books of instruction and religious tracts—two of the most popular genres at the time—novels were being published by the many new publishing houses and read by a growing number of literate readers. This new audience included large numbers of women, who were particularly interested in reading works by and about women. Among the major European novelists of the period were Jane Austen (1775–1817), the Brontë sisters—Charlotte (1816–1855) and Emily (1818–1848)—and George Eliot (1819–1880) in England; Madame de Staël (1766–1817) and George Sand (1804–1876) in France; and Emilia Pardo Bazan (1852–1921) in Spain. Many of the period's most important novels, even those written by men, have female protagonists, among them Flaubert's *Madame Bovary* (1857), Tolstoy's *Anna Karenina* (1877), and Eliot's *Middlemarch* (1872). Women's lives especially interested realist novelists, because most avenues for heroic public action were closed to women; women were confined to the sphere of the commonplace and the everyday. In the selections that follow, this realist literature about women is represented by Flaubert's "A Simple Heart" (1877), the biography of a servant woman; and Emilia Pardo Bazan's "The Revolver" (1895), a story about a husband's psychological oppression of his wife.

Henrik Ibsen (p. 556) (1828–1906), the Norwegian father of realist drama, devoted so many of his plays to exploring women's issues that he was honored by a feminist organization. *Hedda Gabler* (1890), one of the last of his social dramas, shocked its Victorian audiences with its manipulative and nihilistic heroine, who destroys those around her and ultimately herself.

Nineteenth-Century Europe: The Death of Lord Byron

In 1821, Greeks set out to free themselves from four hundred years of Turkish rule. Their struggle rallied liberals throughout Europe, who were happy to see the cause of liberty spreading to the country that had invented the idea of democracy. Committees were formed to support Greece and idealistic young men journeyed south to join the battle. Lord Byron, who had come to love Greece during his travels there in 1809–10, was placed on the London Greek Committee, even though scandal over his sexual escapades had driven him from England into self-imposed exile in Italy.

In 1823 Byron took an active part in the battle. He mustered a small force, outfitted them in elaborately plumed "Homeric helmets," and in July set sail for Greece. Besides soldiers, he also had money from the London committee as well as several thousand pounds of his own in tow. He stopped for a few months in the Ionian Isles deliberating how best to support the cause of Greek independence without just joining one of the bickering factions. In December Byron made it past the Turkish naval blockade and landed at Missolonghi, a town on the south central coast of Greece.

His role in Missolonghi, however, was more banker and diplomat than general. The troops he mustered fell into disarray, and Byron never had a chance to lead them in battle. His time was taken up responding to requests for money, administering support from abroad, and fighting off illness. The climate at Missolonghi was unhealthful. Swamps encircled the town and the winter weather was damp and rainy. In mid February, Byron suffered an attack of fever. His doctors counseled him to leave, but he insisted "it is proper that I should remain in Greece; and it were better to die doing something than nothing." In mid April, after a chilling ride in a rain storm, Byron fell into a fever and, weakened by the treatment of his doctors who bled him with leeches, died within a week.

Although he did not die in battle, he nevertheless became a hero, a symbol of the Romantic spirit of liberty and independence. A member of the London Greek Committee told him, "Your present endeavor is certainly the most glorious ever undertaken by man." His death was commemorated by memorial services in nearly every town in Greece and Byron's statue dominates the Garden of Heroes at Missolonghi. Scandal had denied him a place of burial in the Poet's Corner in Westminster Abbey. He was buried in his family's vault at the parish church in Nottinghamshire.

Lodovico Liparini, **Lord Byron Swearing Oath on Tomb of Marcos Batzaris.** *Batzaris was the leader of the Greek war of independence. He had corresponded with Byron, who took over his army. (The Art Archive/Civiche Raccolte Museo L. Bailo Treviso/Dagli Orti)*

∾ Johann Wolfgang von Goethe
1749–1832

YOH-hahn
VOHLF-gahng
fon GAY-tuh

Goethe's lifetime, from 1749 to 1832, may encompass the greatest shift in consciousness of any period in Western thought. It bridges the Enlightenment, with its belief in reason, objectivity, and rational control, and the Romantic age, which celebrated feeling, subjectivity, and imagination. At the heart of the period and at just about the midpoint of Goethe's life was the French Revolution, the event that, more than any other, came to symbolize the violent transition from rational order to passionate subjectivity that was taking place.

More than any other single figure, Goethe was the man of this age. Poet, playwright, autobiographer, novelist, critic, and journalist, Goethe seemed to try his hand at nearly every literary form. And he was a painter, theater manager, statesman, bureaucrat, educational theorist, and scientist as well—a "Renaissance man."[1] Goethe's masterwork, the long dramatic poem *Faust,* the story of another Renaissance man, is the defining work of German literature in the nineteenth century. Heinrich Heine, in *The Romantic School,* remarked that "the German people is itself that learned Doctor Faust. It is itself that spiritualist who finally through his intellect has grasped the inadequacy of the intellect and demands material pleasures and restores to the flesh its rights."

Sturm und Drang.   Born in Frankfurt into an affluent bourgeois family, Goethe had a happy childhood before going off to the University of Leipzig when he was sixteen. There he published his first volumes of poetry, but he left for health reasons before completing his degree. In 1770 he went to the University of Strasbourg to study law, where he met J. G. Herder,[2] the critic and philosopher who was the formative influence on the **Sturm und Drang** (storm and stress) movement, a German literary movement of the 1770s that sought to overthrow the cult of rationalism by emphasizing feeling, imagination, and natural simplicity. The Sturm und Drang, led by Herder, Friedrich Schiller,[3] and Goethe, was the first onslaught of German Romanticism. Influenced by Herder, Goethe wrote *Götz von Berlichingen* (1773), the first major literary work of the movement, and *The Sorrows of Young Werther* (*Die Leiden des Jungen Werther*) (1774), its major work. The story of a sensitive young man driven to suicide by his alienation from the conventional world, his emotional

SHTOORM oont
DRAHNG

---

[1] **Renaissance man:** A term used to describe a person who is accomplished in many disciplines, especially in both the sciences and the arts, like such multidimensional persons from the European Renaissance as Leonardo Da Vinci.

[2] **J. G. Herder:** (1744–1803) German folklorist, critic, and translator; a primitivist who believed that nature was best comprehended through the senses and feelings rather than through reason.

[3] **Friedrich Schiller:** (1759–1805) German dramatist whose idealistic dramas promoting freedom were the most popular plays on the nineteenth-century German stage. The best known of his nine plays are *The Robbers* (1781); *Mary Stuart* (1801), about Mary of Scotland; and *The Maid of Orleans* (1802), about Joan of Arc.

Johann Heinrich
Wilhelm Tischbein,
*Goethe in the
Campagna,* 1787
*This portrait of
Goethe as a young
man, with his coat
draped dramatically
around his body,
evokes his Romantic
sensibilities. (Art
Resource)*

absolutism, and his frustrated passion for a country girl, *Werther* was an immediate sensation. Werther's blue coat and yellow waistcoat became the fashion, and a rash of suicides occurred in the wake of the novel's popularity, similar to those that followed Chikamatsu's *shinju* plays in Japan.[4] The Scottish writer Thomas Carlyle (1795–1881) said that Goethe's book caught the spirit of the age and gave expression to "the nameless unrest and longing discontent which was then agitating every bosom."

VIGH-mar   **Return to Classical Ideals.**   In 1775 Goethe moved to **Weimar,** where he spent most of the rest of his life working as Minister of State for the reigning duke, Charles Augustus, while continuing to write and carry out scientific investigations. The poems of his early years in Weimar modify the extreme emotionalism of his Sturm und Drang works to reveal a growing objectivity. Nature becomes less a projection of the author's moods than something existing in its own right. This more classical bent in Goethe's work was encouraged by his visit to Italy in 1786–87. The works from this Italian period, especially *Iphigenie in Tauris* (1787) and *Roman Elegies* (1788–89), celebrate classical ideals and humanity's power to free itself from the delusions of its own consciousness.

In the 1790s Goethe, like nearly all Europeans of the time, was caught up in the French Revolution and its aftermath. He accompanied Augustus on a disastrous military campaign in France in 1792. Out of these experiences, Goethe wrote several books: the war dramas *Hermann and Dorothea* (1797) and *The Natural Daughter* (1804), and his most important work during this period, *Wilhelm Meister's Apprenticeship* (*Wilhelm Meister's Lehrjahr*) (1796), a Bildungsroman — a novel devoted to describing the learning process, or the "apprenticeship," of a young person learning about life. Goethe had worked on the novel for several years, and

---

[4] **Chikamatsu's . . . Japan:** Chikamatsu Monzaemon's (1653–1724) play *The Love Suicides at Amijima* (1721) was such a popular work that the Japanese government took steps to curb the number of suicides in its wake. (Book 4)

it might be said to describe his own learning process during his first two decades in Weimar.

Collaboration with Schiller.   Among Goethe's most productive years were those at the turn of the century when he collaborated with Friedrich Schiller. From 1794 until Schiller's death in 1805, the two writers formed a friendship and literary collaboration similar to that of Wordsworth and Coleridge[5] in England. Schiller's classicism reinforced the classical direction in Goethe's work, and the two men worked together on several literary magazines and other writing projects. Schiller especially encouraged Goethe's work on *Faust.*

Late Works.   After Schiller's death, Goethe's writing took a more Romantic direction in the psychological novel *Elective Affinities* (*Die Wahlverwandschaften*) (1809), which explores the night side of human relationships. Goethe also continued his scientific work, publishing in 1805–10 his most important scientific papers, *Theory of Color*. In the later years of his life, Goethe became interested in non-Western literature, developing an ideal of a **Weltliteratur** (world literature)[6] that transcended national differences to advance a universal civilization. His own poems in *Divan of West and East* (*West-Östlichen Diwan*) (1819) were inspired by Persian poetry and attempt to marry East and West.[7] By the last decade of his life, Goethe had become a reigning sage, and Weimar a place of pilgrimage for writers, artists, and intellectuals from all over Europe.

VELT-li-tuh-rah-toor

Faust, **an Autobiographical Work.**   Goethe worked on *Faust* throughout his life. *Urfaust,* an early version of the poem that was not published during Goethe's lifetime, was probably written in the early 1780s. The first published version, *Faust, a Fragment,* appeared in 1790 and the completed *Faust, Part I* in 1808. *Faust, Part II,* which Goethe worked on in the last years of his life, was published after his death in 1832. In the play's final verses, he challenges his readers to make sense of it: "Our play is rather like the whole life of man / We make a start, we make an end — / But make a whole of it? Well, do so if you can."

Goethe's challenge defines one of the central critical issues presented by *Faust:* whether or not it can be read as a unified and coherent work of art. Because it was written at different periods throughout Goethe's life, many commentators have read it as an autobiographical poem telling of Goethe's intellectual and creative growth. Like Goethe, Faust is a RENAIS-SANCE man. Restless and dissatisfied with the limitations of his human

---

[5] **Wordsworth and Coleridge:** *Lyrical Ballads* (1798), a collaborative volume including poems by both of these poets, ushered in the Romantic movement in England. See pp. 236, 255.

[6] *Weltliteratur:* Works that transcend local and national concerns to treat universal human themes.

[7] *Divan of West and East:* Some lyrics from *Divan of West and East* can be found in *In the World:* East and West, on p. 1045.

Henry Moses, *Faust and Mephistopheles in the Witches Cave, 1820*

This English engraving depicts the "Witch's Kitchen" section of Faust, Part I. *Note how the engraver includes imagery from the text: the monkeys playing with the globe, the hearth, the forms in the steam, and the "bizarre paraphernalia of witchcraft." (Courtesy of the Trustees of the Boston Public Library)*

situation, he seeks greater knowledge and experience. The two warring souls within him may characterize two competing aspects of Goethe's character, his **ENLIGHTENMENT**, scientific side, and his intuitive, poetic side. The two aspects of human nature represented by **Mephistopheles** and Faust, worldly cynicism and optimistic striving, may also reveal crucial contradictions in Goethe's own character.

meh-fis-TAH-fuh-leez

Faust as Everyman.   But Faust is also a representative of the time, a kind of Everyman transitioning from the Enlightenment into the Romantic age and embodying in his own mind and experience the contradictions of the period. The original folk stories of the Faust legend emerged in the late Middle Ages as a way of articulating the change from the church-dominated hierarchical consciousness of the Middle Ages to the humanism of the Renaissance. The struggle between these competing points of view can be seen in Christopher Marlowe's version of the story, *The Tragical History of Doctor Faustus* (c. 1592).[8] Goethe's *Faust* reflects a similar transition, from the Enlightenment's ideal of objective utopi-

---

[8] *The Tragical History of Doctor Faustus:* Christopher Marlowe's play appears in Book 3 of this anthology.

anism to the subjectivity of Romanticism. At the core of Goethe's verse play are the contradictory wagers between God and Satan and Mephistopheles and Faust: God challenges Satan to make Faust discontented; Faust bets Mephistopheles that he cannot make him contented. Many of the play's ambiguities and the questions that it leaves unanswered at its end derive from this contradiction: Is Faust saved or damned? Is he ever satisfied with his lot? Is the work tragic or comic?

By basing his drama on a folk story, Goethe exemplifies the Romantic interest in the primitive, for in the simple stories of the people the Romantics thought they could get beneath the veneer of civilization and get at the true nature of things. But Goethe significantly transformed the original folk story. *Faust* is no longer the story of the contest between good and evil or between the power of the church and the individual. Goethe's *Faust* explores instead alternative worldviews, different aspects of Faust's consciousness. When he rejects *word* and *mind* as adequate translations for the beginning of the Gospel of St. John and substitutes instead, "In the beginning was the Deed," Faust bespeaks the division within himself and the choice that Mephistopheles will offer him. Rejecting *mind,* Faust turns his back on his past, on his role as an Enlightenment scholar. Affirming the *Deed,* he chooses experience and action, to become a man of the world, of the body rather than the mind, of the parts of himself that he has previously ignored. From this perspective, Mephistopheles is not so much a separate character or a representation of evil as he is a projection of Faust's consciousness, a representative of one of the "two souls" that reside within Faust's breast. The poem pits Mephistopheles' cynicism and despair against Faust's optimism; it explores the interplay between the physical and spiritual, the human and divine.

Mephistopheles does not offer Faust a chance to break rules or to challenge authority but rather a chance to explore another reality. Rather than mind, he offers body; rather than idea, he offers experience. But the immersion in experience is dangerous; acting in the moment, from emotional spontaneity rather than rational consideration, can have tragic consequences. Valentine's death, for example, is an unforeseen result of Faust's affair with Margaret. Unthinking action inevitably leads to errors. And Faust's search for the fullest expression of his nature leads to tragic errors that result in the destruction of Margaret, her family, and Baucis and Philemon. If Mephistopheles is not a representative of evil in Goethe's poem, Faust is not an unqualified representative of good. In both aspects of his character, the divided Faust is caught in ambiguities and paradoxes.

Nineteenth-century readers tended to see *Faust* as a drama of a man redeemed by striving, for in spite of his mistakes Faust never ceases searching for the good. He is never satisfied with the limitations of the experiences that Mephistopheles offers him. These early critics often pointed to the last act in Part II, where Faust drains a marsh to develop a construction project, as an indication that he has transcended his selfishness and redeemed his earlier errors by engaging in altruistic service to humankind. Modern readers, less enamored of grand development projects and less willing to affirm action for its own sake, have not been

---

Voilá un homme!

(There is a man!)

—Napoleon on Goethe

---

www   For more information about Goethe and *Faust* and information about the Twenty-First-Century relevance of *Faust,* see *World Literature Online* at bedfordstmartins .com/worldlit.

so easily convinced that Faust has grown. After all, they point out, Baucis and Philemon are sacrificed so that Faust's project can proceed. The ending of the play, then, is problematic. Is it tragic or comic? Is Faust redeemed, or is the end a cosmic mockery? Stuart Atkins suggests these paradoxical ambiguities when he describes *Faust* as "the drama of a man destroyed by the larger force than himself which is life and yet enjoying triumph in inevitable defeat."

■ CONNECTIONS

In the World, "Heroes and Heroines," p. 179. As an intellectual who has mastered nearly all of the important academic disciplines, Faust is a hero of the intellect, larger than life as Napoleon was as a military and political leader. Is Faust's deal with Mephistopheles heroic? Are the qualities that ultimately redeem Faust from damnation heroic?

Marlowe, *Doctor Faustus* (Book 3). Marlowe and Goethe draw on the same legend for their Faust stories. Taking Marlowe's version as closer to the traditional legend, how does Goethe alter his source, such as the change in the ending, in which Faust is saved from damnation? How might Goethe's changes be seen as representative of the time in which he wrote?

Dostoevsky, *The Grand Inquisitor,* p. 541; Kalidasa, *Shakuntala* (Book 2). Faust can be seen as a man tormented by Western dualism — the division between mind and body that characterizes Western thought from the time of Plato on. Faust recognizes his self-division by speaking of the "two souls" within him. Dostoevsky dramatizes the split between mind and body in his work in the debate between Jesus, who offers mankind spiritual freedom, and the Grand Inquisitor, who offers bread for the body. In what ways is Faust's self-division related to the choice presented by Dostoevsky? Compare *Faust* and *The Grand Inquisitor* with Kalidasa's *Shakuntala,* a work Goethe greatly admired in which eroticism and the spiritual are aspects of a single worldview. Can Goethe's Faust be said to espouse a similar "monism" by the end of the play?

Conrad, *Heart of Darkness* (Book 6). Conrad's Kurtz, an extraordinary and accomplished man like Faust, and also like Faust a believer in enlightenment and progress, is a more cynically treated version of the intellectual hero. Is Kurtz's succumbing to "the horror" comparable to Faust's deal with Mephistopheles? What differences between Goethe's worldview and Conrad's may account for Faust's redemption and Kurtz's death?

■ FURTHER RESEARCH

Biography
Fairley, Barker. *A Study of Goethe.* 1947.
Hatfield, Henry. *Goethe: A Critical Introduction.* 1963.
Lucacs, Georgy. *Goethe and His Age.* Tr. Robert Anchor. 1969.
Reed, Terence. *Goethe.* 1984.

Criticism
Arndt, W. and Cyrus Hamlin, eds. *Faust.* 2000. A critical edition that includes
    background materials and critical essays on the play.
Atkins, Stuart. *Goethe's Faust: A Literary Analysis.* 1964.
Brown, Jane K. Faust: *Theater of the World.* 1992.
———. *Goethe's Faust: The German Tragedy.* 1986.

Mason, Eudo C. *Goethe's* Faust: *Its Genesis and Purport.* 1967.

Other Versions of the Faust Story
Mann, Thomas. *Doktor Faustus.* 1947. A satire of Hitler's Third Reich.
Marlowe, Christopher. *Doctor Faustus.* 1592–93. (Book 3)

■ PRONUNCIATION

Johann Wolfgang Von Goethe: YOH-hahn VOHLF-gahng fon GAY-tuh
Altmayer: AHLT-mire
Auerbach: OW-ur-bahk
Euphorion: yoo-FORE-ee-on
Mephistopheles: meh-fis-TAH-fuh-leez
Proktophantasmist: prahk-toh-fan-TAZ-mist
Sturm und Drang: SHTOORM oont DRAHNG
Wagner: VAHG-nur
Walpurgisnacht: vahl-POOR-gis-nahkt
Weimar: VIGH-mar
Weltliteratur: VELT-li-tuh-rah-toor

FROM

 Faust

Translated by Charles E. Passage

CHARACTERS IN THE PROLOGUE IN HEAVEN

THE LORD	MICHAEL
RAPHAEL	MEPHISTOPHELES
GABRIEL	

CHARACTERS IN THE TRAGEDY

FAUST	A STUDENT
MEPHISTOPHELES	ELIZABETH, *an acquaintance of* MARGARET
WAGNER, *a student*	WITCHES, *old and young;*
LIESCHEN	WIZARDS; WILL-O'-THE-WISP;
MARGARET *(also* GRETCHEN*)*	PROKTOPHANTASMIST; THE BEAUTY;
MARTHA, MARGARET'*s neighbor*	SERVIBILIS; MONKEYS; SPIRITS; ANIMALS;
VALENTINE, MARGARET'*s brother*	APPRENTICES; COUNTRY-FOLK; CITIZENS;
OLD PEASANT	BEGGAR; STUDENTS; *etc.*

CHARACTERS IN PART II

FAUST	LEMURS
MEPHISTOPHELES *in various guises*	*The* FOUR GRAY WOMEN: WANT, GUILT,
ARIEL	CARE, DISTRESS
BAUCIS	A PENITENT
PHILEMON	DOCTOR MARIANUS
A TRAVELER	CHORUS OF ANGELS *and* PENITENTS *and*
THE THREE MIGHTY MEN	*various Heavenly characters*
LYNCEUS	

And he is half aware that he is mad;
From heaven he demands the fairest star,
From earth all peaks of pleasure to be had,
And nothing near and nothing far
Will calm his troubled heart or make it glad.

THE LORD:

Though now he serves me but confusedly,
I soon shall guide him on toward what is clear.
310   The gardener knows, when green comes to the tree,
That flowers and fruit will deck the coming year.

MEPHISTOPHELES:

What will you bet you lose him if you give
Me your permission now to steer
Him gently down my path instead?

THE LORD:

As long as he on earth may live,
To you such shall not be gainsaid.
Man errs as long as he can strive.

MEPHISTOPHELES:

Thank you for that; for with the dead
I never hankered much to be.
320   It is the plump, fresh cheeks that mean the most to me.
I'm out to corpses calling at my house;
I play the way the cat does with the mouse.

THE LORD:

Good, then! The matter is agreed!
Divert this spirit from his primal source,
And if you can ensnare him, lead
Him with you on your downward course;
And stand abashed when you have to confess:
A good man harried in his dark distraction
Can still perceive the ways of righteousness.

MEPHISTOPHELES:

330   All right! It won't be any long transaction.
I have no fears at all for my bet's sake.
And once I've won, let it be understood
You will admit my triumph as you should.
Dust shall he eat, and call it good,
Just like my aunt,² the celebrated snake.

THE LORD:

There too feel wholly free to try;
Toward your kind I have borne no hate.
Of all the spirits that deny,

---

² **aunt:** Usually translated "cousin," an allusion to Satan.

340
The scoffer burdens me with slightest weight.
Man's activeness can all too easily go slack,
He loves to be in ease unqualified;
Hence I set a companion at his side
To goad him like a devil from the back.
　　　But you, true sons of gods, may you
Rejoice in beauty that is full and true!
May that which is evolving and alive
Encompass you in bonds that Love has wrought;
And what exists in wavering semblance, strive
To fix in final permanence of thought.

[*The heavens close, the* ARCHANGELS *disperse.*]

MEPHISTOPHELES:

350
From time to time I like to see the Boss,
And with him like to keep things on the level.
It's really nice in one of such high class
To be so decent with the very Devil.

THE FIRST PART OF THE TRAGEDY

Night

FAUST *restless in his chair at his desk in a narrow and high-vaulted Gothic room.*

FAUST:
I've read, alas! through philosophy,
Medicine and jurisprudence too,
And, to my grief, theology
With ardent labor studied through.
And here I stand with all my lore,
Poor fool, no wiser than before!

360
I'm Master, I'm Doctor, and with my reading
These ten years now I have been leading
My scholars on wild-goose hunts, out
And in, cross-lots, and round about—
To find that nothing can be known!
This burns my very marrow and bone.
I'm shrewder, it's true, than all the tribes
Of Doctors and Masters and priests and scribes;
Neither doubts nor scruples now can daunt me,
Neither hell nor devils now can haunt me—

370
But by the same token I lose all delight.
I don't pretend to know anything aright,
I don't pretend to have in mind
Things I could teach to improve mankind.
Nor have I lands nor treasure hoards,

Nor honors and splendors the world affords;
No dog would want to live this way!
And so I've yielded to magic's sway,
To see if spirits' force and speech
Might not bring many a mystery in reach;

380   So I no longer need to go
On saying things that I don't know;
So I may learn the things that hold
The world together at its core,
So I may potencies and seeds behold,
And trade in empty words no more.

O if, full moon, you did but shine
Your last upon this pain of mine,
Whom I have watched ascending bright
Here at my desk in mid of night;

390   Then over books and papers here,
Sad friend, you would come into view.
Ah, could I on some mountain height
Rove beneath your mellow light,
Drift on with spirits round mountain caves,
Waft over meadows your dim light laves,
And, clear of learning's fumes, renew
Myself in baths of healing dew!

Am I still in this prison stall?
Accursed, musty hole-in-the-wall,

400   Where the very light of heaven strains
But dully through the painted panes!
By these enormous book-piles bounded
Which dust bedecks and worms devour,
Which are by sooty charts surrounded
Up to the vaultings where they tower;
With jars shelved round me, and retorts,
With instruments packed in and jammed,
Ancestral junk together crammed—
Such is your world! A world of sorts!

410   Do you still wonder why your heart
Is choked with fear within your breast?
Why nameless pain checks every start
Toward life and leaves you so oppressed?
Instead of Nature's living sphere
Wherein God placed mankind of old,
Brute skeletons surround you here
And dead men's bones and smoke and mold.

Flee! Up! And out into the land!
Does not this mystic book indeed,

420   From Nostradamus'[3] very hand,
       Give all the guidance that you need?
       Then you will recognize the courses
       Of stars; within you will unfold,
       At Nature's prompting, your soul's forces
       As spirits speech with spirits hold.
       In vain this arid brooding here
       The sacred signs to clarify—
       You spirits who are hovering near,
       If you can hear me, give reply!

[He opens the book and glimpses the sign of the macrocosm.]

430   Ha! Suddenly what rapture at this view
       Goes rushing through my senses once again!
       I feel a youthful joy of life course new
       And ardent through my every nerve and vein.
       Was it a god who wrote these signs whereby
       My inward tempest-rage is stilled
       And my poor heart with joy is filled
       And with a mystic impulse high
       The powers of Nature all around me are revealed?
       Am I a god? I feel so light!
440   In these pure signs I see the whole
       Of operative Nature spread before my soul.
       Now what the wise man says I understand aright:
       "The spirit world is not locked off from thee;
       Thy heart is dead, thy mind's bolt drawn!
       Up, scholar, and bathe cheerfully
       Thy earthly breast in rosy dawn!"

[He contemplates the sign.]

       How all things interweave to form the Whole,
       Each in another finds its life and goal!
       How each of heaven's powers soars and descends
450   And each to each the golden buckets lends;
       On fragrant-blessed wings
       From heaven piercing to earth's core
       Till all the cosmos sweetly rings!
          O what a sight!—A sight, but nothing more!
       Where can I grasp you, Nature without end?
       You breasts, where? Source of all our lives,[4]
       On which both heaven and earth depend,

---

[3] **Nostradamus:** French astrologer and physician Michel de Notredame (1503–1566).

[4] **You . . . lives:** The image is that of a mother-earth goddess, perhaps like the ancient Diana of Ephesus, who was represented with innumerable breasts that gave suck to all creatures.

Toward you my withered heart so strives—
You flow, you swell, and must I thirst in vain?

[*Impatiently he turns pages of the book and glimpses the sign of the Earth Spirit.*]

460   How differently I am affected by this sign!
You, Spirit of the Earth, are nearer me,
I feel more potent energy,
I feel aglow as with new wine.
I feel the strength to brave the world, to go
And shoulder earthly weal and earthly woe,
To wrestle with the tempests there,
In shipwreck's grinding crash not to despair.
Clouds gather over me—
The moon conceals its light—
470   The lamp has vanished!
Mists rise!—Red lightnings dart and flash
About my head—Down from
The vaulted roof cold horror blows
And seizes me!
Spirit implored, I feel you hovering near.
Reveal yourself!
O how my heart is rent with fear!
With new emotion
My senses riot in wild commotion!
480   My heart surrenders to you utterly!
You must! You must! though it cost life to me!

[*He seizes the book and mystically pronounces the sign of the Spirit.
A reddish flame flashes. The* SPIRIT *appears in the flame.*]

SPIRIT:
    Who calls me?
FAUST [*cowering*]:
                    Ghastly shape!
SPIRIT:
                                    With might
You have compelled me to appear,
You have long sucked about my sphere,
Now—
FAUST:
            No! I cannot bear the sight!
SPIRIT:
    You begged so breathlessly to bring me near
To hear my voice and see my face as well;
I bow before your strong compulsive spell,
And here I am!—What childish fear
490   Besets you, superman! Where is the soul that cried?

Where is the heart that made and bore a world inside
Itself and sought amid its gleeful pride
To be with spirits equal and allied?
Where are you, Faust, whose voice called out to me,
Who forced yourself on me so urgently?
Are you the one who, having felt my breath,
Now tremble to your being's depth,
A terrified and cringing worm?

FAUST:

Shall I give way before you, thing of flame?

500   I am your equal. Faust is my name!

SPIRIT:

In tides of life, in action's storm
I surge as a wave,
Swaying ceaselessly;
Birth and the grave,
An endless sea,
A changeful flowing,
A life all glowing:
I work in the hum of the loom of time
Weaving the living raiment of godhead sublime.

FAUST:

510   O you who roam the world from end to end,
Restless Spirit, I feel so close to you!

SPIRIT:

You are like the spirit you comprehend,
Not me!

[*Disappears.*]

FAUST [*overwhelmed*]:

Not you?
Whom then?
I, image of the godhead!
Not even rank with you!

[*A knock.*]

God's death! I know who's there — my famulus[5] —
This puts an end to my great joy!

520   To think that dry-bones should destroy
The fullness of these visions thus!

[*Enter* WAGNER *in a dressing gown and nightcap, a lamp in his hand.* FAUST *turns around impatiently.*]

WAGNER:

Excuse me! I heard you declaiming;

---

[5] **famulus:** A graduate assistant to a professor.

It surely was a Grecian tragedy?
There I would like some more proficiency,
Today it gets so much acclaiming.
I've sometimes heard it said a preacher
Could profit with an actor for a teacher.

FAUST:

Yes, if the preacher is an actor too,
As may on some occasions be the case.

WAGNER:

530   Oh, cooped up in one's museum all year through
And hardly seeing folks except on holidays,
Hardly by telescope, how can one find
Persuasive skills wherewith to guide mankind?

FAUST:

Unless you feel it you will not succeed;
Unless up from your soul it wells
And all your listeners' hearts compels
By utmost satisfaction of a need,
You'll always fail. With paste and glue,
By grinding others' feasts for hash,
540   By blowing your small flame up too
Above your paltry pile of ash,
High praise you'll get in apes' and children's sight,
If that's what suits your hankering—
But heart with heart you never will unite
If from your heart it does not spring.

WAGNER:

Delivery makes the speaker's real success,
And that's just where I feel my backwardness.

FAUST:

Try for an honest win! Why rail
Like any bell-loud fool there is?
550   Good sense and reason will prevail
Without a lot of artifice.
If you have serious things to say,
Why hunt for words out of your way?
Your flashy speeches on which you have pinned
The frilly cutouts of men's artistry
Are unrefreshing as the misty wind
That sighs through withered leaves autumnally!

WAGNER:

Oh Lord! How long is art,
How short our life! And ever
560   Amid my work and critical endeavor
Despair besets my head and heart.

How difficult the means are to come by
That get one back up to the source,
And then before one finishes mid-course,
Poor devil, one must up and die.

FAUST:

Is that the sacred font, a parchment roll,
From which a drink will sate your thirst forever?
Refreshment will delight you never
Unless it surges up from your own soul.

WAGNER:

570　But what delight there is in pages
That lead us to the spirit of the ages!
In seeing how before us wise men thought
And how far glorious progress has been brought.

FAUST:

O yes, up to the furthest star!
My friend, the eras and past ages are
For us a book with seven seals.[6]
What you the spirit of the ages call
Is only those men's spirits after all
Held as a mirror that reveals
580　The times. They're often just a source of gloom!
You take one look at them and run away.
A trash can and a littered storage room,
At best a plot for some heroic play
With excellent pragmatic saws
That come resoundingly from puppets' jaws.

WAGNER:

But then the world! The mind and heart of man!
To learn about those things is our whole aim.

FAUST:

Yes, call it learning if you can!
But who dares call a child by its right name?
590　The few who such things ever learned,
Who foolishly their brimming hearts unsealed
And to the mob their feelings and their thoughts revealed,
Were in all ages crucified or burned.
But it is late into the night, my friend,
We must break off now for the present.

WAGNER:

I would have liked to stay awake and spend
The time in talk so learned and so pleasant.
But since tomorrow will be Easter Day,

---

[6]**book . . . seals:** See Revelation 5:1.

I'll ask some further questions if I may.
600   I have industriously pursued my studying;
I know a lot, but would like to know everything.

[Exit.]

FAUST [*alone*]:
Why hope does not abandon all such brains
That cling forever to such shallow stuff!
They dig for treasure and are glad enough
To turn up angleworms for all their pains!
     May such a human voice presume to speak
Where spirits closed around me in full ranks?
And yet for this one time I give you thanks,
Of all earth's sons the poorest and most weak.
610   You pulled me back from the despair and panic
That threatened to destroy my very mind.
That vision loomed so vast and so titanic
That I felt dwarfed and of the dwarfish kind.
     I, image of the godhead, who supposed
Myself so near eternal verity,
Who reveled in celestial clarity,
My earthly substance quite deposed,
I, more than cherub, whose free strength presumed
To flow through Nature's veins, myself creating,
620   Thereby in godlike life participating,
How I must pay for my expostulating!
There by a word of thunder I was consumed!
     Your equal I dare not pretend to be;
If I had power to make you come to me,
I did not have the power to make you stay.
In that brief moment's ecstasy
I felt so small and yet so great;
You thrust me backwards cruelly
To my uncertain human fate.
630   Who will instruct me? What must I not do?
Should I give every impulse play?
Alas, our very actions, like our sorrows too,
Build obstacles in our life's way.
     On the most glorious things mind can conceive
Things strange and ever stranger force intrusion;
Once we the good things of this world achieve,
We term the better things cheat and delusion.
The noble feelings that conferred our life
Are paralyzed amid our earthly strife.
640   If Fantasy once soared through endless space
And hopefully aspired to the sublime,

She is content now with a little place
When joys have foundered in the gulf of time.
Deep down within the heart Care builds her nest
And causing hidden pain she broods,
And brooding restlessly she troubles joy and rest;
Assuming ever different masks and moods,
She may appear as house and home, as child, as wife,
As poison, dagger, flood, or fire;
650 You dread what never does transpire,
And what you never lose you grieve for all your life.

      I am not like the gods! Too sharp I feel that thrust!
I am more like the worm that burrows in the dust,
That living there and finding sustenance
Is crushed beneath a passing foot by chance.

      Is all of this not dust that these walls hold
Upon their hundred shelves oppressing me?
The rubbish which with nonsense thousandfold
Confines me in this world of moths distressfully?
660 Should I find *here* the things I need?
When in perhaps a thousand books I read
That men have been tormented everywhere,
Though one may have been happy here and there? —
What is your grinning message, hollow skull,
But that your brain, like mine, once sought the day
In all its lightness, but amid the twilight dull,
Lusting for truth, went miserably astray?
And all you instruments make fun of me
With wheel and cog and drum and block:
670 I stood before the door, you should have been the key;
Your wards are intricate but do not turn the lock.
Mysterious in broad daylight,
Nature's veil can not be filched by you,
And what she keeps back from your prying spirit's sight
You will not wrest from her by lever or by screw.
You old contrivances unused by me,
You served my father's needs, hence here you stay.
You, ancient scroll, have blackened steadily
As long as dull lamps on this desk have smoked away.
680 Better if I had squandered my small estate
Than sweat and by that little be oppressed!
Whatever you inherit from your late
Forebears, see that it is possessed.
Things unused are a burden of great weight;
The hour can use what it alone creates, at best.

      But why does my gaze fix on that spot over there?

Is that small bottle then a magnet to my eyes?
Why is all suddenly so bright and fair
As when in a dark wood clear moonlight round us lies?
690   Rare phial, I salute you as I draw
You down with reverence and with awe.
In you I honor human skill and art.
You essence of all lovely slumber-flowers,
You extract of all subtle deadly powers,
Unto your master now your grace impart!
I see you, and my suffering is eased,
I clasp you, and my strugglings have ceased,
The flood tide of my spirit ebbs away.
To open seas I am shown forth by signs,
700   Before my feet the mirror-water shines,
And I am lured to new shores by new day.

        A fiery chariot comes on airy pinions
Down toward me! I feel ready now and free
To rise by new paths unto aether's wide dominions,
To newer spheres of pure activity.
This higher life! This godlike ecstasy!
And you, but now a worm, have you acquired such worth?
Yes, only turn your back decisively
Upon the lovely sun of earth!
710   By your presumptuous will, fling wide the portals
Past which each man would rather slink away.
Now is the time to prove by deeds that mortals
Yield not to gods in dignity's array:
To shrink not back from that dark cavern where
Imagination sees itself to torment damned,
To press on toward that thoroughfare
Around whose narrow mouth all hell is spanned:
To take that step with cheer, to force egress —
Though at the risk of passing into nothingness.

720   Come down, you glass of crystal purity,
Come forth out of your ancient case to me
Who have not thought of you these many years.
You used to gleam amid my father's feasts
And used to gladden earnest guests
As you were passed from hand to hand with cheers.
Your gorgeous braid of pictures deftly twined,
The drinker's pledge to tell of them in rhyme
And drain your hollow rondure at one time,
These bring back many youthful nights to mind;
730   I shall not this time pass you to a neighbor,
To prove my wit upon your art I shall not labor;

Here is a juice that makes one drunk with no delay.
Its brownish liquid streams and fills your hollow.
This final drink which now shall follow,
Which I prepared and which I choose to swallow,
Be it a festive high salute to coming day!

[*He lifts the glass to his lips.*]
[*A peal of bells and choral song.*]
CHORUS OF ANGELS:
    Christ is arisen!
    Joy to the mortal
    Whom the pernicious
740   Lingering, inherited
    Dearths encompassed.
FAUST:
    What bright clear tone, what whirring drone profound
    Makes me put this glass from my lips away?
    Do you deep bells already sound
    The solemn first hour of the Easter Day?
    Do you choirs sing the song that once such comfort gave
    When angels sang it by the darkness of a grave
    Assuring a new covenant that day?
CHORUS OF WOMEN:
    With spices enbalmed
750   Here we had carried Him,
    We, His devoted,
    Here we had buried Him;
    With winding cloths
    Cleanly we wrapped Him;
    But, alas, we find
    Christ is not here.
CHORUS OF ANGELS:
    Christ is arisen!
    Blessed the loving
    Who stood the troubling,
760   Stood the healing,
    Chastening test.
FAUST:
    Why seek here in the dust for me,
    You heavenly tones so mighty and so mild?
    Ring out around where gentle souls may be.
    I hear your tidings but I lack for faith,
    And Miracle is Faith's most favored child.
    As high as to those spheres I dare not soar
    Whence sound these tidings of great joy;

Yet by these sounds, familiar since I was a boy,
770 I now am summoned back to life once more.
Once there would downward rush to me the kiss
Of heavenly love in solemn Sabbath hour;
Then plenitude of bell tones rang with mystic power
And prayer had the intensity of bliss;
Past comprehension sweet, a yearning
Drove me to wander field and forest where
Amid a thousand hot tears burning
I felt a world arise which was most fair.
The merry games of youth are summoned by that song,
780 And free delight of springtime festival;
And by that memory with childlike feeling strong
I am kept from this final step of all.
Sing on, sweet songs, in that celestial strain!
A teardrop falls, the earth has me again!

CHORUS OF DISCIPLES:

If from the dead
He has ascended,
Living, sublime,
Glorious on high,
If He in His growth
790 Nears creative joy,
We, alas, are still here
On the bosom of earth.
He has left His own
Behind here to languish,
Master, we mourn
Thy happiness.

CHORUS OF ANGELS:

Christ is arisen
From the womb of decay;
Bonds that imprison
800 You, rend gladsome away!
For you as you praise Him,
Proving your love,
Fraternally sharing,
Preaching and faring,
Rapture proclaiming,
For you the Master is near,
For you He is here.

Outside the City Gate

All sorts of people coming out for a walk.

SEVERAL APPRENTICES:
>But why go up the hill?

OTHERS:
>We're going to the Hunting Lodge up there.

THE FIRST ONES:
810
>We'd rather walk out to the Mill.

ONE APPRENTICE:
>I'd suggest you go to the Reservoir.

THE SECOND:
>It's not a pleasant walk, you know.

OTHERS:
>How about you?

A THIRD:
>   I'll go where the others go.

A FOURTH:
>Come on to Burgdorf! There you're sure to find good cheer,
>The prettiest girls and also first-rate beer,
>And the best fights you'll ever face.

A FIFTH:
>You glutton, do you itch to go
>For your third drubbing in a row?
>I have a horror of that place.

SERVING GIRL:
820
>No, no! I'm going back now, if you please.

ANOTHER:
>We'll surely find him standing by those poplar trees.

THE FIRST GIRL:
>For me that's no great lucky chance;
>He'll walk at your side and he'll dance
>With none but you upon the lea.
>What good will your fun be to me?

THE OTHER GIRL:
>He won't be there alone today; he said
>He'd bring along the curlyhead.

SCHOLAR:
>Damn! How those lusty wenches hit their stride!
>Brother, come on! We'll walk it at their side.
830
>Strong beer, tobacco with a bite,
>A girl decked in her best, just suit my appetite.

GIRL OF THE MIDDLE CLASS:
>Just see those handsome boys! It certainly
>Is just a shame and a disgrace;
>They could enjoy the very best society,
>And after serving girls they chase.

SECOND SCHOLAR [*to the* FIRST]:
>   Don't go so fast! Behind us are two more,
>   Both very nicely dressed;
>   One is my neighbor from next door
>   In whom I take an interest.
840 They walk demurely, but you'll see
>   How they will overtake us finally.

THE FIRST:
>   No, Brother, I don't like things in my way.
>   Quick! Let's not lose these wildfowl on our chase.
>   The hand that wields the broom on Saturday
>   On Sunday will provide the best embrace.

CITIZEN:
>   No, this new burgomaster, I don't care for him,
>   And now he's in, he daily gets more grim.
>   And for the city, what's he done?
>   Don't things get worse from day to day?
850 More rules than ever to obey,
>   And taxes worse than any yet, bar none.

BEGGAR [*sings*]:
>   Kind gentlemen and ladies fair,
>   So rosy-cheeked and gay of dress,
>   Be good enough to hear my prayer,
>   Relieve my want and my distress.
>   Let me not vainly tune my lay.
>   Glad is the giver and only he.
>   Now that all men keep holiday,
>   Be there a harvest day for me.

ANOTHER CITIZEN:
860 There's nothing better for Sunday or a holiday
>   Than talk about war and war's alarms,
>   When off in Turkey people up in arms
>   Are battling in a far-off fray.
>   You sip your glass, stand by the window side,
>   And down the river watch the painted vessels glide,
>   Then come home in the evening all at ease,
>   Blessing peace and the times of peace.

THIRD CITIZEN:
>   Yes, neighbor, that's the way I like it too:
>   Let them beat out each other's brains,
870 Turn everything up wrong-end-to,
>   So long as here at home our good old way remains.

OLD WOMAN [*to the* MIDDLE-CLASS GIRLS]:
>   Heyday! How smart! My young and pretty crew!
>   Now who could help but fall for you? —

But don't act quite so proud. You'll do!
And what you're after, I could help you to.

MIDDLE-CLASS GIRL:

Come, Agatha! I don't want to be seen
In public with such witches. It's quite true
My future lover last Saint Andrew's E'en
In flesh and blood she let me view[7] —

THE OTHER GIRL:

880   She showed me mine too in her crystal glass,
A soldier type, with dashing friends behind him;
I look for him in every one I pass
And yet I just don't seem to find him.

SOLDIERS:

Castles and towers,
Ramparts so high,
Girls of disdainful
Scorn-casting eye,
I'd like to win!
Keen is the contest,
890   Grand is the pay!
     We'll let the trumpets
Sound out the call,
Whether to joy
Or to downfall.
There's an assault!
That is the life!
Maidens and castles
Surrender in strife.
Keen is the contest,
900   Grand is the pay!
And then the soldiers
Go marching away.

[*Enter* FAUST *and* WAGNER.]

FAUST:

From ice are released the streams and brooks
At springtime's lovely, life-giving gaze;
Now hope smiles green down valley ways;
Old Winter feebly flees to nooks
Of rugged hills, and as he hies
Casts backward from him in his flight
Impotent showers of gritty ice

---

[7] My . . . view: On November 30 Saint Andrew, the patron saint of the unmarried, offers visions of future lovers and spouses.

910   In streaks over meadows newly green.
        But the sun permits of nothing white,
        Everything is growth and striving,
        All things are in colors reviving,
        And lack of flowers in the countryside
        By gay-clad humans is supplied.
        Turn and from these heights look down
        And backwards yonder toward the town.
        From the hollow, gloomy gate
        Streams a throng in motley array.
920   All want to sun themselves today.
        The Lord's resurrection they celebrate
        For they are themselves new risen from tombs:
        From squalid houses' dingy rooms,
        From tradesman's and apprentice' chains,
        From crushing streets and choking lanes,
        From roof's and gable's oppressive mass,
        From their churches' everlasting night,
        They are all brought forth into the light.
        See now, just see how swiftly they pass
930   And scatter to fields' and gardens' grass
        And how so many merry boats
        The river's length and breadth there floats,
        How almost sinking with its load
        That last barque pushes from the quay.
        From even the hillside's distant road
        Bright costumes glimmer colorfully.
        Sounds of village mirth arise,
        Here is the people's true paradise.
        Both great and small send up a cheer:
940   "Here I am human, I can *be* human here!"

WAGNER:
        Doctor, to take a walk with you
        Is an honor and a gain, of course,
        But come here alone, that I'd never do,
        Because I am a foe of all things coarse.
        This fiddling, shouting, bowling, I detest
        And all that with it goes along;
        They rage as if by fiends possessed
        And call it pleasure, call it song!

        [*Peasants under the linden tree. Dance and song.*]
        The shepherd for the dance got dressed
950   In wreath and bows and fancy vest,
        And bravely did he show.

Beneath the linden lass and lad
Were dancing round and round like mad.
Juchhe! Juchhe!
Juchheisa! Heisa! He!
So went the fiddlebow.
    In through the crowd he pushed in haste
And jostled one girl in the waist
All with his sharp elbow.
960   The buxom lass, she turned her head,
"Well, that was stupid, now!" she said.
Juchhe! Juchhe!
Juchheisa! Heisa! He!
"Don't be so rude, fine fellow!"
    The ring spun round with all its might,
They danced to left, they danced to right,
And see the coattails go!
And they got red, and they got warm,
And breathless waited arm in arm,
970   Juchhe! Juchhe!
Juchheisa! Heisa! He!
A hip against an elbow.
    "Don't be so free! How many a maid
Has been betrothed and been betrayed
By carrying on just so!"
And yet he coaxed her to one side,
And from the linden far and wide
Juchhe! Juchhe!
Juchheisa! Heisa! He!
980   Rang shout and fiddlebow.

OLD PEASANT:

Doctor, it's really nice of you
Not to shun our mirth today,
And such a learnèd master too,
To mingle with the folk this way.
Therefore accept our finest stein
Filled with cool drink and let me first
Present it with this wish of mine:
May it not only quench your thirst—
May all its count of drops be added to
990   The sum of days that are allotted you.

FAUST:

I take the cooling drink you offer me
And wish you thanks and all prosperity.

[*The people gather around in a circle.*]

OLD PEASANT:

Indeed it was most kind of you
On this glad day to come here thus,
For in the evil days gone by
You proved a friend to all of us.
Many a man is here alive
Because your father in the past
Saved him from raging fever's fury
1000   When he had stemmed the plague at last.
And as a young man you went too
Among the houses of the pest;
Many a corpse they carried out
But you came healthy from the test.
You bore up under trials severe;
The Helper yonder helped the helper here.

ALL:

Good health attend the proven man,
Long may he help, as help he can!

FAUST:

Bow to Him yonder who provides
1010   His help and teaches help besides.

[*He walks on with* WAGNER.]

WAGNER:

What feelings must be yours, O noble man,
Before the veneration of this crowd!
O fortunate indeed is one who can
So profit from the gifts with which he is endowed!
The fathers show you to their sons,
Each asks and pushes in and runs,
The fiddle stops, the dancer waits,
They stand in rows where you pass by,
And all their caps go flying high:
1020   A little more and they would bend the knee
As if there passed the Venerabile.

FAUST:

Only a few steps more now up to yonder stone
And we shall rest from our long walk. Up there
I often used to sit and brood alone
And rack myself with fasting and with prayer.
Then rich in hope, in faith secure,
By wringing of hands, by tears and sighs,
I sought the plague's end to assure
By forcing the Lord of the skies.
1030   Praise sounds like mockery on the people's part.
If you could only read within my heart

How little father and son
Were worthy of the fame they won!
My father was a man of honor but obscure
Who over Nature and her holy spheres would brood
In his own way and with capricious mood,
Though wholly upright, to be sure.
With other adepts of the art he locked
Himself in his black kitchen and from lists
1040 Of endless recipes sought to concoct
A blend of the antagonists.[8]
There a Red Lion — a wooer to aspire —
Was in a warm bath with the Lily wed,
And both were then tormented over open fire
From one into the other bridal bed.
If the Young Queen was then espied
In rainbow hues within the flask,
There was our medicine; the patients died,
And "Who got well?" none thought to ask.
1050 Thus we with hellish tonics wrought more ills
Among these valleys and these hills,
And raged more fiercely, than the pest.
I gave the poison out to thousands with my hand;
They withered, and I have to stand
And hear the ruthless killers blessed.

WAGNER:

How can such things make you downcast?
Has not a good man done sufficient
In being conscientious and proficient
At skills transmitted from the past?
1060 If you respect your father in your youth,
You will receive his fund of knowledge whole;
If as a man you swell the store of truth,
Your son can then achieve a higher goal.

FAUST:

O happy he who still can hope
To rise out of the sea of errors here!
What one most needs to know exceeds his scope,
And what one knows is useless and unclear.
But let us not spoil hours that are so fair
With these dark melancholy thoughts of mine!
1070 See how beneath the sunset air
The green-girt cottages all shine.

---

[8]Using actual sixteenth-century terms, Goethe describes the manufacture of "the Philosopher's Stone" in an alchemist's laboratory ("black kitchen").

The sun moves on, the day has spent its force,
Yonder it speeds, new day eliciting.
O that I am swept upward on no wing
To follow it forever in its course!
Then I would see by deathless evening rays
The silent world beneath my feet,
All valleys calmed, all mountaintops ablaze,
And silver brooks with golden rivers meet.
1080 No mountains then would block my godlike flight
For all the chasms gashed across their ways;
And soon the sea with its warmed bays
Would open to my wondering sight.
But now the goddess seems to sink down finally;
But a new impulse wakes in me,
I hasten forth to drink her everlasting light,
With day in front of me and at my back the night,
With waves down under me and over me the sky.
A glorious dream, dreamed while the day declined.
1090 Alas, that to the pinions of the mind
No wing corporeal is joined as their ally.
And yet inborn in all our race
Is impulse upward, forward, and along,
When overhead and lost in azure space
The lark pours forth its trilling song,
When over jagged pine tree heights
The full-spread eagle wheels its flights,
And when across the seas and plains
Onward press the homing cranes.

WAGNER:

1100 I have had moody hours of my own,
But such an impulse I have never known.
The spectacle of woods and fields soon cloys,
I'll never envy birds their pinionage;
But how we *are* borne on by mental joys
From book to book, from page to page!
How sweet and fair the winter nights become,
A blessed life glows warm in every limb,
And oh! if one unrolls a noble parchment tome,
The whole of heaven then comes down to him.

FAUST:

1110 By one impulse alone are you possessed,
O may you never know the other!
Two souls abide, alas, within my breast,
And each one seeks for riddance from the other.
The one clings with a dogged love and lust

With clutching parts unto this present world,
The other surges fiercely from the dust
Unto sublime ancestral fields.
If there are spirits in the air
Between the earth and heaven holding sway,
1120   Descend out of your golden fragrance there
And to new life of many hues sweep me away!
Yes, if a magic mantle were but mine,
And if to far-off lands it bore me,
Not for all costly raiment placed before me
Would I exchange it; kings' cloaks I would decline!

WAGNER:

Do not invoke that well-known troop
That stream above us in the murky air,
Who from all quarters down on mankind swoop
And bring the thousand perils they prepare.
1130   With whetted spirit fangs down from the north
They pitch upon you with their arrowy tongues;
Out of the morning's east they issue forth
To prey with parching breath upon your lungs;
And if the south up from the desert drives
Those which heap fire on fire upon your brain,
The west brings on the swarm that first revives
Then drowns you as it drowns the field and plain.
They listen eagerly, on mischief bent,
And to deceive us, willingly comply,
1140   They often pose as being heaven sent
And lisp like angels when they lie.
But let us go. The world has all turned grey,
The air is chill, mist closes out the day.
With nightfall one enjoys a room. —
Why do you stand and stare with wondering gaze?
What so arrests you out there in the gloom?

FAUST:

Do you see that black dog that through the stubble strays?

WAGNER:

He looks quite unremarkable to me.

FAUST:

Look close! What do you take the beast to be?

WAGNER:

1150   A poodle, searching with his natural bent
And snuffing for his master's scent.

FAUST:

Do you see how he spirals round us, snail-
shell-wise, and ever closer on our trail?

And if I'm not mistaken, he lays welts
Of fire behind him in his wake.

WAGNER:

I see a plain black poodle, nothing else;
Your eyes must be the cause of some mistake.

FAUST:

I seem to see deft snares of magic laid
For future bondage round our feet somehow.

WAGNER:

1160   I see him run about uncertain and afraid
Because he sees two strangers, not his master now.

FAUST:

The circle narrows, he is near!

WAGNER:

You see! It's just a dog, no phantom here.
He growls, he doubts, lies belly-flat and all,
And wags his tail. All doggish protocol.

FAUST:

Come here! Come join our company!

WAGNER:

He's just a foolish pup. You see?
You stop, and he will wait for you,
You speak to him, and he'll jump up on you,
1170   Lose something, and he'll fetch it quick,
Or go in water for a stick.

FAUST:

You must be right, I see there's not a trace
Of spirits. It's his training he displays.

WAGNER:

A sage himself will often find
He likes a dog that's trained to mind.
Yes, he deserves your favor totally,
A model scholar of the students, he.

[*They go in through the city gate.*]

Study Room

FAUST *entering with the poodle.*

FAUST:

From field and meadow I withdraw
Which deepest darkness now bedecks,
1180   With holy and foreboding awe
The better soul within us wakes.
Asleep now are my wild desires,
My vehement activity;
The love of mankind now aspires,

The love of God aspires in me.
>Be quiet, poodle! Why should you romp and rove?
What are you snuffing there at the sill?
Go and lie down behind the stove,
I'll give you my best pillow if you're still.
1190 Out there on the hill-road back to town
You amused us by running and frisking your best;
Now accept your keep from me; lie down
And be a welcome and quiet guest.
>Ah, when in our close cell by night
The lamp burns with a friendly cheer,
Then deep within us all grows bright
And hearts that know themselves grow clear.
Reason begins once more to speak
And hope begins to bloom again,
1200 The brooks of life we yearn to seek
And to life's source, ah! to attain.
>Stop growling, poodle! With the sacred tones that rise
And now my total soul embrace,
Your animal noise is out of place.
We are accustomed to having men despise
What they do not understand;
The good and the beautiful they misprize,
Finding it cumbersome, they scowl and growl;
Must a dog, like men, set up a howl?
1210 But alas! with the best of will I feel no more
Contentment welling up from my heart's core.
Why must the stream so soon run dry
And we again here thirsting lie?
These things experiences familiarize.
But this lack can find compensation,
The supernatural we learn to prize,
And then we long for revelation,
Which nowhere burns more nobly or more bright
Than here in the New Testament. Tonight
1220 An impulse urges me to reach
Out for this basic text and with sincere
Emotion make its holy meaning clear
Within my own beloved German speech.

[*He opens a volume and sets about it.*]
It says: "In the beginning was the *Word*."[9]
Already I am stuck! And who will help afford?

---

[9] "In . . . *Word*.": John 1:1.

Mere word I cannot possibly so prize,
I must translate it otherwise.
Now if the Spirit lends me proper light,
"In the beginning was the *Mind*" would be more nearly right.
1230   Consider that first line with care,
The pen must not be overhasty there!
Can it be mind that makes and shapes all things?
It should read: "In the beginning was the *Power*."
But even as I write down this word too,
Something warns me that it will not do.
Now suddenly the Spirit prompts me in my need,
I confidently write: "In the beginning was the *Deed!*"
       If I'm to share this room with you,
Poodle, that howling must be curbed.
1240   And stop that barking too!
I cannot be disturbed
By one who raises such a din.
One of us must give in
And leave this cell we're in.
I hate to drive you out of here,
But the door is open, the way is clear.
But what is this I see?
Can such things happen naturally?
Is this reality or fraud?
1250   My poodle grows both long and broad!
He rises up with might;
No dog's shape this! This can't be right!
What phantom have I harbored thus?
He's like a hippopotamus
With fiery eyes and ghastly teeth.
O, I see what's beneath!
For such a mongrel of hell
The Key of Solomon works well.[10]

SPIRITS [*in the corridor*]:
     Captive inside there is one of us,
1260   Stay out here, follow him none of us.
Like a fox in an iron snare
A lynx of hell is cornered in there.
But take heed!
Hover to, hover fro,
Above, below,
And pretty soon he'll be freed.

---

[10] **Key of Solomon:** *Solomon's Key*, or the *Clavicula Salomonis*, was a standard book used by magicians in the Middle Ages. It gave the rules for controlling spirits.

If you can help him in aught
Don't leave him caught.
Many a turn he has done
1270 Helping us every one.

FAUST:

To deal with the beast before
Me, I'll use the spell of the four:[11]
    Salamander shall kindle,
Undine shall coil,
Sylph shall dwindle;
Kobold shall toil.
    Lacking the lore
Of the elements four,
Not knowing aright
1280 Their use and might,
None shall be lord
Of the spirit horde.
    Vanish in flame,
Salamander!
Together rush and stream,
Undine!
In meteor glory gleam,
Sylph!
Bring help to the house,
1290 Incubus! Incubus!
Step forth and make an ending! Thus!
    None of the four
Lurks in the beast.
He lies and grins at me as before,
I have not harmed him in the least.
You'll hear me tell
A stronger spell.
    Do you, fellow, live
As hell's fugitive?
1300 See this sign[12] now
To which they bow,
The black hordes of hell!
    With hair abristle he starts to swell.
    Forfeiter of bliss,
Can you read this?

---

[11] **the spell of the four:** The spirits of the four elements: Fire, Water, Air, and Earth.

[12] **this sign:** The sign INRI or JNRJ, abbreviation for "Jesus the Nazarene, King of the Jews" (*Jesus Nazarenus Rex Judaeorum*), which Pilate had inscribed on the cross that held the body of Jesus at the crucifixion (John 19:19). Faust apparently holds a crucifix over the shape-shifting spirit-beast.

The never-created
Of name unstated,
Diffused through all heavens' expanse,
Transpierced by the infamous lance?

1310   Back of the stove he flees from my spells,
There like an elephant he swells,
He fills the room entire,
He melts like a mist of sleet.
Rise ceilingwards no higher!
Fall down at your master's feet.
You see that mine is no idle threat.
With sacred flame I will scorch you yet.
Await not the might
Of the triply burning light![13]

1320   Await not the sight
Of my arts in their fullest measure!

[*As the mist falls away,* MEPHISTOPHELES *steps forth from behind the stove, dressed as a traveling scholar.*]

MEPHISTOPHELES:
Why all the fuss? What is the gentleman's pleasure?

FAUST:
So this was what was in the cur!
A traveling scholar? That's the best joke I've heard yet.

MEPHISTOPHELES:
I salute you, learned Sir.
You had me in a mighty sweat.

FAUST:
What is your name?

MEPHISTOPHELES:
For one so disesteeming
The word, the question seems so small to me,
And for a man disdainful of all seeming,

1330   Who searches only for reality.

FAUST:
With gentlemen like you, their nature is deduced
Quite often from the name that's used,
As all too patently applies
When you are named Corrupter, Liar, God of Flies.[14]
All right, who are you then?

---

[13] triply . . . light: The "sign" of the Trinity.

[14] Corrupter . . . Flies: The "Baal-Zebub the god of Ekron" of II Kings 1:2, usually etymologized as "the god of flies" or "the fly-god."

MEPHISTOPHELES:
        Part of that Force which would
 Do evil ever yet forever works the good.

FAUST:
 What sense is there beneath that riddling guise?

MEPHISTOPHELES:
 I am the Spirit that constantly denies!
 And rightly so; for everything that's ever brought
1340 To life deserves to come to naught.
 Better if nothing ever came to be.
 Thus all that you call sin, you see,
 And havoc — evil, in short — is meant
 To be my proper element.

FAUST:
 You call yourself a part, yet stand quite whole before me there?

MEPHISTOPHELES:
 It is the modest truth that I declare.
 Now folly's little microcosm, man,
 Boasts *him*self whole as often as he can. . . .
 I am part of the part which once was absolute,
1350 Part of the Darkness which gave birth to Light,
 The haughty Light, which now seeks to dispute
 The ancient rank and range of Mother Night,
 But unsuccessfully, because, try as it will,
 It is stuck fast to bodies still.
 It streams from bodies, bodies it makes fair,
 A body hinders its progression; thus I hope
 It won't be long before its scope
 Will in the bodies' ruination share.

FAUST:
 I see your fine objectives now!
1360 Wholesale annihilation fails somehow,
 So you go at it one by one.

MEPHISTOPHELES:
 I don't get far, when all is said and done.
 The thing opposed to Nothingness,
 This stupid earth, this Somethingness,
 For all that I have undertaken
 Against it, still remains unshaken;
 In spite of tempest, earthquake, flood, and flame
 The earth and ocean calmly stay the same.
 And as for that damned stuff, the brood of beasts and man,
1370 With them there's nothing I can do.
 To think how many I have buried too!
 Fresh blood runs in their veins just as it always ran.

And so it goes. Sometimes I could despair!
In earth, in water, and in air
A thousand growing things unfold,
In dryness, wetness, warmth, and cold!
Had I not specially reserved the flame,
I wouldn't have a thing in my own name.

FAUST:

So you shake your cold devil's fist
1380   Clenched in futile rage malign,
So you the endless Power resist,
The creative, living, and benign!
Some other goal had best be sought,
Chaos' own fantastic son!

MEPHISTOPHELES:

We really shall give this some thought
And talk about it more anon.
Right now, however, might I go?

FAUST:

Why you should ask, I don't quite see.
Now that we've made acquaintance, though,
1390   Come any time to visit me.
Here is the window, there the doors,
The chimney too is practical.

MEPHISTOPHELES:

Must I confess? To leave this room of yours
There is a trifling obstacle.
The witch's foot[15] there on the sill —

FAUST:

The pentagram distresses you?
But tell me now, O son of hell,
If that prevents you, how did you get through?
Could such a spirit be so blind?

MEPHISTOPHELES:

1400   Observe it carefully. It's ill designed.
One point there, facing outward as it were,
Is just a bit disjoined, you see.

FAUST:

Now what a lucky chance for me!
And so you are my prisoner?
And all by merest accident!

MEPHISTOPHELES:

The poodle did not notice when in he went.

---

[15] **witch's foot:** Another term for the pentagram, a symbol made up of interlocking triangles to form a five-pointed star used to ward off evil spirits.

Things now take on a different shape:
The Devil's caught and can't escape.

FAUST:

But why not use the window to withdraw?

MEPHISTOPHELES:

1410   With devils and with spirits it's a law:
Where they slipped in, they must go out.
The first is up to us, the second leaves no doubt:
There we are slaves.

FAUST:

                So hell has its own law?
I find that good, because a pact could then
Perhaps be worked out with you gentlemen?

MEPHISTOPHELES:

What once is promised, you will revel in,
No skimping and no spreading thin.
But such things can't be done so fast,
We'll speak of that when next we meet.

1420   And now I beg you first and last
To let me make my fair retreat.

FAUST:

Just for a single moment yet remain
And tell me of some pleasant news.

MEPHISTOPHELES:

No, let me go now! I'll come back again,
Then you can ask me all you choose.

FAUST:

I never had a plan so bold
As capturing you. You walked into the snare.
Whoever holds the Devil, let him hold!
A second time he will not have him there.

MEPHISTOPHELES:

1430   I am quite ready, if you choose,
To keep you company and stay,
But on condition that I use
My worthy skills to while the time away.

FAUST:

I'd like to see them, so feel free,
Just so the skills work pleasantly.

MEPHISTOPHELES:

Your senses will, my friend, gain more
In this hour than you've known before
In one whole year's monotony.
And what my dainty spirits sing you,

1440   The lovely images they bring you

Will be no empty magic play.
Your sense of smell shall be delighted,
Your sense of taste shall be excited,
And feelings will sweep you away.
No preparation shall we need;
We are assembled, so proceed!

SPIRITS:
Vanish, you gloomy
Vaultings above!
Lovelier hue
1450   Of aether's blue
Be shed in here!
O might the darkling
Clouds melt for once!
Stars begin sparkling;
Mellower suns
Shine now in here.
Sons of the air,
Of beauty rare,
Hover thronging,
1460   Wafting in light.
Ardent longing
Follows their flight.
Raiment in strands
Shed as streamer bands
Cover the lands,
Cover the groves
Where lovers vow,
Lost in reverie,
Lifelong loves.
1470   Arbors on arbors!
Lush greenery!
Masses of grapes
Tumble from vines
Into presses and vats,
Gush now as brooks
Of foaming wines,
Trickle as rills
Through gorges that wind,
Leaving the hills
1480   Far behind,
Widening to lakes
Around the abundance
Of verdant heights.
And then the birds

Drink delight,
Fly to the sun,
Fly to the bright
Islands that gleam
Drifting and glittering
1490　Upon the stream;
There we hear choirs
Of jubilant throngs,
See them on meadows,
At dances and songs,
Disporting free
In festivity;
Climbing, some,
Over the peaks,
Skimming, some,
1500　Over the lakes,
Still others fly;
All toward the high
Joy of existence,
All toward the distance
Of loving stars.

MEPHISTOPHELES:

He is asleep. Well done, my dainty, airy youngsters!
You lulled him loyally, my songsters!
I am much in your debt for such a concert.
You are not yet the man to hold the Devil fast!
1510　Around him your sweet dream illusions cast
And steep him in a sea of fancy;
But now I need a rat's tooth to divest
This threshold of its necromancy.
No lengthy incantation will be needed,
Here comes one rustling up, and my word will be heeded.
The Master of the rats and mice,
Of bedbugs, flies, and frogs and lice,
Commands you boldly to appear
And gnaw this carven threshold clear
1520　Where he has daubed a jot of oil—
Ah, there you scamper up to toil!
Get right to work! I'm hemmed in by the wedge
That's right there on the outer edge.
Just one more bite and then it's done.—
Now, till we meet again, Faustus, dream on!

FAUST [*waking*]:

Have I been once again betrayed?
The spirit throng has fled so utterly

> That I but dreamed the Devil came and stayed
> And that a poodle got away from me?

Study Room (II)

FAUST:
1530   A knock? Come in! Who now comes bothering me?

MEPHISTOPHELES:
    It's I.

FAUST:
        Come in!

MEPHISTOPHELES:
            A third call there must be.

FAUST:
    Come in, then!

MEPHISTOPHELES:
             That's the way I like to hear you.
    We shall, I trust, get on quite well,
    For I have come here to dispel
    Your moods, and as a noble squire be near you,
    Clad all in scarlet and gold braid,
    With my short cape of stiff silk made,
    A rooster feather on my hat,
    A long sharp rapier at my side,
1540   And I advise you to provide
    Yourself a costume just like that,
    So you, untrammeled and set free,
    Can find out just what life can be.

FAUST:
    No matter what might be my own attire,
    I would feel life cramped anyway.
    I am too old merely to play,
    Too young to be without desire.
    What can the world give me? Renounce,
    Renounce shalt thou, thou shalt renounce!
1550   That is the everlasting song
    Dinned in our ears throughout the course
    Of all our lives, which all life long
    Each hour sings until it's hoarse.
    Mornings I wake with horror and could weep
    Hot tears at seeing the new sun
    Which will not grant me in its sweep
    Fulfillment of a single wish, not one,
    Which mars anticipated joys
    Themselves with willful captiousness
1560   And with a thousand petty frets destroys

My eager heart's creativeness.
At nightfall I must lie down ill at ease
Upon my couch of misery where
There will be neither rest nor peace,
Wild dreams will terrify me even there.
The god that in my heart abides
Can stir my soul's profoundest springs;
He over all my energies presides
But cannot alter outward things.
1570   Existence is a weight by which I am oppressed,
With death desired, life something to detest.

MEPHISTOPHELES:
And yet Death never is a wholly welcome guest.

FAUST:
O happy he around whose brow Death winds
The blood-stained wreath in victory's radiance,
Or he whom in a girl's embrace Death finds
After the hectic whirling of the dance!
O, had I in my exultation sunk
Down dead before the lofty Spirit's power!

MEPHISTOPHELES:
And yet a brownish potion was not drunk
1580   By someone on a certain midnight hour.

FAUST:
Spying, it seems, amuses you.

MEPHISTOPHELES:
                        I dare
Not claim omniscience, but of much I am aware.

FAUST:
If from that harrowing confusion
A sweet familiar tone drew me away,
Belied me with a child's profusion
Of memories from a former day,
I now curse everything that holds the soul
Enchanted by the lures of sorcery
And charms it in this dreary hole
1590   By sweet illusion and duplicity!
Cursed be the lofty self-opinion
With which the mind itself deludes!
Cursed be phenomena's dominion
Which on our senses so intrudes!
Cursed be the cheating dream obsessions
With name and fame that have us so beguiled!
Cursed be what we have deemed possessions:
Servant and plow, and wife and child!

Cursed be old Mammon when with treasure
1600 He lures to deeds adventurous
Or when for idleness and pleasure
He spreads the pillows soft for us!
Cursed be the nectar of the grape!
Cursed be love at its happiest!
And cursed be hope! And cursed be faith!
And cursed be patience more than all the rest!

CHORUS OF SPIRITS [*invisible*]:
Woe! Woe!
You have destroyed
The beauteous world
1610 With mighty fist;
It crumbles, it collapses!
A demigod has shattered it!
We carry
The fragments to the void,
We grieve
For beauty so destroyed.
More mightily,
Son of earth,
More splendidly
1620 Bring it to birth,
Rebuild it in the heart of you!
Begin a new
Life course
With senses clear,
And may new songs
Hail it with cheer!

MEPHISTOPHELES:
These are the minions
From my dominions.
Precociously wise,
1630 Deeds and desires they now advise.
Out of solitude
Where senses and saps are glued,
To the wide world's view
They lure and summon you.
    Cease toying with your sorrow then,
Which tears your life as vulture-talons tear;
The worst of company makes you aware
You are a man with other men.
This does not indicate
1640 That you're to run with the pack;
I am not one of the great,

But if you want a track
Through life together with me,
I'll adapt myself quite willingly
To be yours right here and now.
I am your fellow,
If it suits you, to the grave,
I am your servant and your slave.

FAUST:

And what am I supposed to do for you?

MEPHISTOPHELES:

1650   There's lots of time before that's due.

FAUST:

No, no! The Devil is an egoist
And does not willingly assist
Another just for God's sake. I insist
You make all your conditions clear;
Such a slave is one to fear.

MEPHISTOPHELES:

I'll bind myself to be your servant *here*
And at your beck and call wait tirelessly,
If when there in the *yonder* we appear
You will perform the same for me.

FAUST:

1660   The yonder is of small concern.
Once you have smashed this world to pieces,
The other one may come to be in turn.
It is out of this earth that my joy springs
And this sun shines upon my sufferings;
Once free of them, this trouble ceases;
Then come what may and as time brings.
About all that I do not wish to hear,
Whether in future there is hate and love
And whether in that yonder sphere
1670   There is a new beneath and new above.

MEPHISTOPHELES:

In this mood you dare venture it. Just make
The compact, and I then will undertake
To turn my skills to joy. I'll give you more
Than any man has ever seen before.

FAUST:

Poor, sorry Devil, what could you deliver?
Was human mind in lofty aspiration ever
Comprehended by the likes of you?
Do you have food that does not satisfy? Or do
You have red gold that will run through

1680   The hand like quicksilver and away?
A game that none may win who play?
A girl who in my very arms
Will pledge love to my neighbor with her eyes?
Or honor with its godlike charms
Which like a shooting star flashes and dies?
Show me the fruit that rots right on the tree,
And trees that every day leaf out anew!

MEPHISTOPHELES:

Such a demand does not daunt me,
Such treasures I can furnish you.
1690   But still the time will come around, good friend,
When we shall want to relish things in peace.

FAUST:

If ever I lie down upon a bed of ease,
Then let that be my final end!
If you can cozen me with lies
Into a self-complacency,
Or can beguile with pleasures you devise,
Let that day be the last for me!
This bet I offer!

MEPHISTOPHELES:

          Done!

FAUST:

          And I agree:
If I to any moment say:
1700   Linger on! You are so fair!
Put me in fetters straightaway,
Then I can die for all I care!
Then toll bells for my funeral,
Then of your service you are free,
The clock may stop, the clock hand fall,
And time be past and done for me!

MEPHISTOPHELES:

Consider well, we shall remember this.

FAUST:

And that would be quite right of you.
I have committed no presumptuousness.
1710   I am a slave no matter what I do,
Yours or another's, we may dismiss.

MEPHISTOPHELES:

I will begin right with your doctoral feast
And be your slave this very day.
For life and death's sake, though, just one thing, if I may:
Just write a line or two at least.

FAUST:

> You ask for written forms, you pedant? Can
> You never have known man, or known the word of man?
> Is it not enough that by the word I gave
> The die of all my days is finally cast?
1720
> Does not the world down all its rivers rave,
> And should a promise hold me fast?
> But this illusion in our hearts is set
> And who has ever wanted to uproot it yet?
> Happy the man whose heart is true and pure,
> No sacrifice he makes will he regret!
> A parchment, though, with seal and signature,
> *That* is a ghost at which all people shy.
> The word is dead before the ink is dry
> And wax and leather hold the mastery.
1730
> What, evil spirit, do you want from me?
> Bronze, marble, parchment, paper? And then
> Am I to write with stylus, chisel, or a pen?
> The choice is yours and wholly free.

MEPHISTOPHELES:

> Why carry on so heatedly
> And force your eloquence so high?
> Just any little scrap will do;
> You sign it with a drop of blood.

FAUST:

> If that is satisfactory to you,
> We'll let it stand at that absurdity.

MEPHISTOPHELES:

1740
> Blood is a juice of very special kind.

FAUST:

> I'll honor this pact, you need not be afraid!
> The aim of all my strength and mind
> Will be to keep this promise I have made.
> I puffed myself up far too grand;
> In your class I deserve to be.
> The mighty Spirit spurned me and
> Nature locks herself from me.
> The thread of thought is snapped off short,
> Knowledge I loathe of every sort.
1750
> Let us now sate our ardent passion
> In depths of sensuality!
> Let miracles of every fashion
> Be brought in veils of mystery!
> Let us plunge in the flood of time and chance,
> Into the tide of circumstance!

Let grief and gratification,
Success and frustration
Spell one another as they can;
Restless doing is the only way for man.

MEPHISTOPHELES:

1760   There is no goal or limit set.
Snatch tidbits as impulse prompts you to,
Take on the wing whatever you can get!
And may you digest what pleases you.
Just help yourself and don't be coy.

FAUST:

But I tell you there is no talk of joy.
I vow myself to frenzy, agonies of gratification,
Enamored hatred, quickening frustration.
Cured of the will to knowledge now, my mind
And heart shall be closed to no sorrow any more

1770   And all that is the lot of human kind
I want to feel down to my senses' core,
Grasp with my mind their worst things and their best,
Heap all their joys and troubles on my breast,
And thus my self to their selves' limits to extend,
And like them perish foundering at the end.

MEPHISTOPHELES:

Believe me, many a thousand year
I've chewed this rugged food, and I well know
That from the cradle to the bier
No man digests this ancient sourdough.

1780   This whole, believe the likes of us,
For deity alone was made.
He dwells in timeless radiance glorious,
Us he has relegated to the shade,
You, day and night alone can aid.

FAUST:

But I am set on it.

MEPHISTOPHELES:

Easy said!
There's just one thing that could go wrong:
Time is short and art is long;
You could, I think, be taught and led.
Choose a poet for your associate,

1790   Let the gentleman's thoughts have their free bent
To heap upon your reverend pate
All noble qualities he can invent:
The lion's nobility,
The fleetness of the hind,

The fiery blood of Italy,
The Northman's steadfast mind.
Have him for you the secret find
Of magnanimity and guile combined,
Then make you fall in love by plan
1800   While youthful passions are in flame.
I'd like myself to meet just such a man,
I'd give him "Sir Microcosm" for a name.

FAUST:

What am I then, if seeking to attain
That toward which all my senses strain,
The crown of mankind, is in vain?

MEPHISTOPHELES:

You're after all—just what you are.
Wear wigs of a million ringlets as you will,
Put ell-thick soles beneath your feet, and still
You will remain just what you are.

FAUST:

1810   I feel that I have fruitlessly amassed
All treasures of the human mind,
And now when I sit down at last
No fresh strength wells within my heart, I find;
I'm not one hair's breadth taller nor one whit
Closer to the infinite.

MEPHISTOPHELES:

These matters, my good Sir, you see
Much in the ordinary light;
We must proceed more cleverly
Before life's joys have taken flight.
1820   What the Devil! You've got hands and feet,
You've got a head, you've got a prat;
Are all the things that I find sweet
Less mine for all of that?
If I can buy six stallions, can
I not call their strength also mine?
I race along and am a proper man
As if their four-and-twenty legs were mine.
Come on, then! Let this brooding be!
And off into the world with me!
1830   I tell you, any speculative fellow
Is like a beast led round and round
By demons on a heath all dry and yellow
When on all sides lies good green pasture ground.

FAUST:

But how do we begin?

MEPHISTOPHELES:
                              First we will get away.
　　What kind of dungeon is this anyway?
　　What kind of life do you lead if
　　You bore yourself and bore the youngsters stiff?
　　Leave that to Neighbor Sleek-and-Slow.
　　Why go on threshing straw? There is no doubt
1840　　The best things that you know
　　You dare not tell the boys about.
　　I hear one now out in the hall.
FAUST:
　　I simply cannot see him now.
MEPHISTOPHELES:
　　The poor lad has been waiting, after all,
　　And must not go uncomforted somehow.
　　Come, lend your cap and gown to me;
　　The mask will suit me admirably.

[*He changes clothes.*]
　　Just trust my wits and I'll succeed.
　　A quarter of an hour is all I need.
1850　　Meanwhile get ready for your travels with all speed.

                                                        [*Exit* FAUST.]

MEPHISTOPHELES [*in* FAUST's *long gown*]:
　　Scorn reason and the lore of mind,
　　Supremest powers of mankind,
　　Just let the Prince of Lies endow
　　Your strength with his illusions now
　　And I will have you unconditionally—
　　Fate has conferred on him a mind
　　That urges ever onward with incontinency,
　　Whose eager striving is of such a kind
　　That early joys are overleaped and left behind.
1860　　I'll drag him through wild life at last,
　　Through shallow insipidity,
　　I'll make him wriggle, stultify, stick fast,
　　And in his insatiety
　　His greedy lips will find that food and drink float past.
　　He will vainly beg refreshment on the way.
　　Had his lot not been with the Devil cast,
　　He would go to the Devil anyway.

[*Enter a* STUDENT.]
STUDENT:
　　I've been here just a short time, Sir,
　　And come to you with deference

1870 To meet a man, and see and hear,
Of whom all speak with reverence.
MEPHISTOPHELES:
I must approve your courtesy.
A man like other men you see.
Have you inquired around elsewhere?
STUDENT:
Take me, I entreat you, in your care.
I come with fresh blood, spirits high,
And money in tolerable supply.
My mother was loath to have me go,
But I would like to learn and know.
MEPHISTOPHELES:
1880 Then this is just the place to come.
STUDENT:
Frankly, I'd rather be back home.
I feel confined within these walls,
I'm ill at ease amid these halls,
The space is cramped, you never see
Green country or a single tree.
And in these rooms with benches lined
I lose my hearing, sight, and mind.
MEPHISTOPHELES:
It all depends on habit. Right at first
The infant will not take its mother's breast,
1890 But then it finds relief from thirst
And soon it feeds away with zest.
So you to Wisdom's breast will turn
And every day more strongly yearn.
STUDENT:
I'll hang upon her neck with all affection
If you will set me in the right direction.
MEPHISTOPHELES:
First tell me, before we go on,
What course have you decided on?
STUDENT:
I want to be quite erudite;
I'd like to comprehend aright
1900 What all there is on earth, in heaven as well,
In science and in nature too.
MEPHISTOPHELES:
You're on the right track, I can tell;
Just see that nothing distracts you.
STUDENT:
With body and soul it shall be done.

But to be frank, I would like in some ways
A little freedom and some fun
On pleasant summer holidays.

MEPHISTOPHELES:

Make good use of your time, so fast it flies.
You'll gain time if you just will organize.

1910   And so, dear friend, I would advise
First off *collegium logicum*.   a course in logic
There you will get your mind well braced
In Spanish boots[16] so tightly laced
That it will henceforth toe the taut
And cautiously marked line of thought
And not go will-o'-the-wisping out
And in, across, and round about.
They will spend days on teaching you
About how things you used to do—

1920   Like eating, drinking—just like that,
Need One! Two! Three! for getting at.
For with thought-manufacturies
It's like a weaver's masterpiece:
A thousand threads one treadle plies,
The shuttles dart back to and fro,
Unseen the threads together flow,
A thousand knots one movement ties;
Then comes the philosopher to have his say
And proves things have to be this way:

1930   The first being so, the second so,
The third and fourth are so-and-so;
If first and second were absent, neither
Would third and fourth be present either.
All scholars find this very clever,
None have turned weavers yet, however.
Whoever wants to know and write about
A living thing, first drives the spirit out;
He has the parts then in his grasp,
But gone is the spirit's holding-clasp.

1940   *Encheiresin naturae*[17] chemists call it now,
Mocking themselves, they know not how.

STUDENT:

I don't just get all you imply.

---

[16] Spanish boots: An instrument of torture consisting of metal boots that were screwed tighter and tighter.

[17] *Encheiresin naturae:* "Nature's hand-hold," the term of J. R. Spielmann, an eighteenth-century chemist, for the power that holds biological components together in a living organism.

MEPHISTOPHELES:
>   It will go better by and by,
>   Once you have all these things principified
>   And properly classified.

STUDENT:
>   I feel as dazed by all you've said
>   As if a mill wheel spun inside my head.

MEPHISTOPHELES:
>   Above all else you next must turn
>   To metaphysics. See that you learn
1950 >   Profoundly and with might and main
>   What does not fit the human brain.
>   For what fits in — or misfits — grand
>   Resounding phrases are on hand.
>   But this semester most of all
>   Keep schedule, be punctual.
>   You'll have five classes every day;
>   Be in there on the stroke of the bell.
>   See that you are prepared as well,
>   With paragraphs worked up in such a way
1960 >   That you can see with just a look
>   There's nothing said but what is in the book;
>   And take your notes with dedication
>   As if the Holy Ghost gave the dictation!

STUDENT:
>   No second time need I be told,
>   I see its usefulness all right;
>   What one gets down in black and white
>   One can take home and feel consoled.

MEPHISTOPHELES:
>   But name your field of concentration!

STUDENT:
>   I don't feel law is just the thing for me.

MEPHISTOPHELES:
1970 >   I cannot blame you there especially,
>   Well do I know the law school situation.
>   Laws are perpetrated like disease
>   Hereditary in some families;
>   From generation to generation they are bred
>   And furtively from place to place they spread.
>   Sense turns to nonsense, wise works to a mire.
>   Woe that you are a grandson and born late!
>   About the legal right that is innate
>   In man, they do not so much as inquire.

STUDENT:

1980   You make my own aversion still more great.
He whom you teach is fortunate.
I'd almost take theology, in a way.

MEPHISTOPHELES:

I wouldn't want to lead you astray.
That branch of learning, once you do begin it,
It's so hard to avoid the path of sin,
There's so much hidden poison lurking in it
And you can hardly tell this from the medicine.
Again it's best to follow only one man there
And by that master's statements swear.
1990   Cling hard and fast to words, in sum;
Then through sure portals you will come
To Certainty's own templed home.

STUDENT:

But words must have ideas too behind them.

MEPHISTOPHELES:

Quite so! But just don't fret too much to no avail,
Because just when ideas fail
Words will crop up, and timely you will find them.
With words you can most excellently dispute,
Words can a system constitute,
In words you can put faith and not be shaken,
2000   And from a word not one iota can be taken.

STUDENT:

Forgive me for so importuning you,
But I must trouble you again.
Would you say just a telling word or two
About the course in medicine?
Three years is a short time, and O my God!
The field itself is far too broad.
With just a little hint alone
One feels it would not seem so great.

MEPHISTOPHELES [*aside*]:

I've had enough of this dry tone,
2010   I've got to play the Devil straight.

[*aloud*]

The gist of medicine is grasped with ease;
You study through the great world and the small
To let it go on after all
As God may please.
In vain you'll go a-roving scientifically,
There each learns only what he can;
But one who grasps the moment, he

Is truly the right man.
You've got a good build on the whole,
2020   And you won't lack for impudence;
If you just have self-confidence
You'll have the trust of many a soul.
And learn to manage women, of that make sure;
For all their endless Ah!'s and Oh!'s
And thousand woes
Depend on one point only for their cure,
And if you're halfway decent about that,
You'll have them all under your hat.
First, by a title win their confidence
2030   That your skills many skills transcend,
Then you can finger every little thing and be
Welcome where others wait for years on end.
Know how to take her little pulse, and grasp her
With slyly passionate glances while you clasp her
Around her trim and slender waist
To see how tightly she is laced.

STUDENT:
Now that's more like it! The where and how I see!

MEPHISTOPHELES:
Grey, my dear friend, is all of theory,
And verdant is life's golden tree.

STUDENT:
2040   I swear it's all just like a dream to me.
Might I come back another time to sound
Your wisdom to its depths profound?

MEPHISTOPHELES:
I'll gladly do anything I may.

STUDENT:
It's just impossible to go away
Unless you take my album here and sign.
Would you do me the honor of a line?

MEPHISTOPHELES:
With pleasure.

[*He writes and gives the album back.*]

STUDENT [*reads*]:
Eritis sicut Deus, scientes bonum et malum.[18]

[*He respectfully closes the book and takes his leave.*]

---

[18] *Eritis . . . malum:* "Ye shall be as gods, knowing good and evil" (Genesis 3:5); Satan's temptation to Eve in the Garden of Eden.

MEPHISTOPHELES:
>   Just follow that old saying and my cousin, the snake,
2050   And you will surely tremble for your God's-likeness' sake!

[*Reenter* FAUST.]
FAUST:
>   And where do we go now?
MEPHISTOPHELES:
>   The choice is up to you.
>   We'll see the small world first, and then the great one too.
>   What joy, what profit will be yours
>   As you sail glibly through this course!
FAUST:
>   But with this long beard on my face
>   I lack for easy social grace.
>   This bold attempt will never work with me,
>   I never could get on in company,
>   In front of others I feel small and harassed,
2060   I'll be continually embarrassed.
MEPHISTOPHELES:
>   Good friend, all that is needed, time will give.
>   Once you have confidence, you will know how to live.
FAUST:
>   How do we travel, though, and get about?
>   Do you have servants, coach and pair?
MEPHISTOPHELES:
>   All we need do is spread this mantle out
>   And it will take us through the air.
>   But see that on this daring flight
>   Beginning now you travel light.
>   A little fire gas I will now prepare
2070   Will lift us to the upper air,
>   And if we're light, we'll go up fast from here.
>   Congratulations on your new career!
>   . . .

WITCH'S KITCHEN[19]

A large cauldron stands over the fire on a low hearth. Amid the steam rising from it various forms are seen. A MONKEY *sits by the kettle skimming it and watching that it does not boil over. The* HE-MONKEY *sits nearby with the young ones, warming himself. Walls and ceiling are hung with the most bizarre paraphernalia of witchcraft.*

---

[19]Scene V, "Auerbach's Cellar in Leipzig," in which Mephistopheles astounds some drunken students by drawing wine from a table, has been omitted.

FAUST:

>I am revolted by this crazy witchery;
>I shall be cured, you guarantee,
>In this stark raving rookery?

2340
>Must I seek counsel from an aged crone?
>And will her filthy cookery
>Take thirty years off from my flesh and bone?
>Alas for me if you can nothing better find!
>Already hope has vanished, I despair.
>Has neither Nature nor a wholesome mind
>Devised a balm to cure me anywhere?

MEPHISTOPHELES:

>Ah, now, my friend, you're talking sense once more.
>There is a natural way to make you young again,
>But that is in another book, and on that score

2350
>It forms a curious chapter even then.

FAUST:

>I want to hear it.

MEPHISTOPHELES:

>   Good! A way without recourse
>To money, medicine, or sorcery:
>Straight to the fields direct your course
>And start to dig immediately;
>There keep yourself and keep your mind
>Within a circle close confined,
>Eat only unadulterated food,
>Live with the beasts as beast, and count it good
>To strew the harvest field with your own dung;

2360
>There is no better way, believe me,
>Up to age eighty to stay young.

FAUST:

>I am not used to that, nor could I ever stand
>To take a shovel in my hand.
>For me that narrow life would never do.

MEPHISTOPHELES:

>Well, then it's to the witch for you.

FAUST:

>But why just this old hag? What makes
>You say that *you* can't brew the cup?

MEPHISTOPHELES:

>A pretty pastime that! I could put up
>A thousand bridges in the time it takes.

2370
>This work needs skill and knowledge, it is true,
>But it requires some patience too.
>A quiet mind may work for years on end

But time alone achieves the potent blend.
And as for what there may be to it,
There's many an odd ingredient.
The Devil taught her how to brew it,
But by himself the Devil cannot do it.

[*catching sight of the* ANIMALS]
  Ah, see the cute breed by the fire!
  That is the maid, that is the squire.

[*to the* ANIMALS]
2380   Where is the lady of the house?
THE ANIMALS:
  Out of the house
  On a carouse
  Up chimney and away.
MEPHISTOPHELES:
  How long does she rampage today?
THE ANIMALS:
  Until we get our paws warm, anyway.
MEPHISTOPHELES [*to* FAUST]:
  How do you like these cunning creatures?
FAUST:
  Repulsive to the nth degree.
MEPHISTOPHELES:
  No, discourse such as this one features
  Is just the kind that most entrances me.

[*to the* ANIMALS]
2390   Now, you accursed puppets you,
  Why are you paddling in that broth, pray tell?
THE ANIMALS:
  We're cooking up some beggars' stew.
MEPHISTOPHELES:
  You'll have a good big clientele.
THE HE-MONKEY [*coming over and fawning on* MEPHISTOPHELES]:
  O roll the dice
  And make me nice
  And rich with gains!
  My lot is bad,
  But if I had
  Some money, I'd have brains.
MEPHISTOPHELES:
2400   How happy would this monkey be
  If he could play the lottery!

[*Meanwhile the young monkeys have been playing with a large globe and now roll it forward.*]

THE HE-MONKEY:
>   That is the world;
>   Spun and twirled,
>   It never ceases;
>   It rings like glass,
>   But hollow, alas,
>   It breaks to pieces.
>   Here it gleams bright,
>   And here more bright,
2410 >   Alive am I.
>   Dear son, I say
>   Keep far away,
>   For you must die.
>   It's made of clay,
>   And splinters fly.

MEPHISTOPHELES:
>   And why the sieve?

THE HE-MONKEY [*takes it down*]:
>   I'd know you if
>   You were a thief.[20]

[*He runs to the* SHE-MONKEY *and has her look through it.*]
>   Look through the sieve:
2420 >   You see the thief
>   And name him not?

MEPHISTOPHELES [*going over to the fire*]:
>   And why the pot?

THE HE-MONKEY AND THE SHE-MONKEY:
>   The silly sot!
>   Not know the pot,
>   Not know the kettle?

MEPHISTOPHELES:
>   Uncivil beast!

THE HE-MONKEY:
>   Here, take the whisk
>   And sit on the settle.

[*He has* MEPHISTOPHELES *sit down.*]

FAUST [*has all this time been standing in front of a mirror, now going up to it, now stepping back away from it*]:
>   What do I see with form divine
2430 >   Upon this magic mirror shine?
>   O Love, lend me the swiftest of your pinions
>   And take me off to her dominions!

---

[20] **why . . . thief:** Thieves were supposed to be recognizable as such when viewed through a sieve.

Unless I stand right here in this one place
And do not venture to go near,
I see her misted only and unclear—
A woman of the utmost grace!
Can any woman be so fair?
In this recumbent body do I face
The essence of all heavens here?

2440 Is there on earth the like of it?

MEPHISTOPHELES:

It's natural, if a god will six whole days expend
And then himself shout bravo! in the end,
That something smart must come of it.
Go right ahead and gaze your fill;
Just such a sweetheart I can well provide,
And lucky is the man who will
Then take her with him as his bride.

[FAUST *keeps right on looking into the mirror.* MEPHISTOPHELES *sprawls on the settle and toys with the whisk as he goes on speaking.*]

I sit here like a king upon his throne,
I hold a scepter, and I lack a crown alone.

[*The* ANIMALS, *who have been going through all kinds of odd motions helter-skelter, bring* MEPHISTOPHELES *a crown amid loud cries.*]

THE ANIMALS:

2450 O just be so good
As with sweat and blood
To glue this crown and lime it.

[*They handle the crown clumsily and break it in two pieces, then hop around with the pieces.*]

Now it is done!
We talk, look, and run,
We listen and rhyme it—

FAUST [*toward the mirror*]:

I'm going crazy here, I feel!

MEPHISTOPHELES [*pointing to the* ANIMALS]:

My own head now almost begins to reel.

THE ANIMALS:

If we have luck
And don't get stuck

2460 We'll make sense yet!

FAUST [*as before*]:

My heart is catching fire within!
Let's get away from here, and fast!

MEPHISTOPHELES [*in his previous posture*]:

This much you'll have to grant at least:
As poets they are genuine.

[*The kettle, which the* SHE-MONKEY *has left unwatched, begins to boil over. A great flame flashes up the chimney. Down through the flame comes the* WITCH *with hideous screams.*]

THE WITCH:

> Ow! Ow! Ow! Ow!
> Damnable brute! Accursed sow!
> Neglect the kettle, scorch your mate!
> Accursed beast!

[*catching sight of* FAUST *and* MEPHISTOPHELES]

> What have we here?
2470
> Who are you here?
> What do you want?
> Who has sneaked in?
> Flames and groans
> Consume your bones!

[*She dips the skimmer into the kettle and scoops flames at* FAUST, MEPHISTOPHELES, *and the* ANIMALS. *The* ANIMALS *whimper.*]

MEPHISTOPHELES [*reverses the whisk he is holding and goes smashing the glasses and pots*]:

> Crash! And smash!
> There goes your trash!
> Your glassware's done!
> It's all in fun,
> I'm only beating time,
2480
> Carrion, to your rhyme.

[*as the* WITCH *falls back in fury and horror*]

> You recognize me, Bone-bag? Skeleton?
> You know your master and your lord?
> What keeps me now from going on
> To pulverize you and your monkey horde!
> For my red coat you have such small respect?
> My rooster feather you don't recognize?
> Is my face hidden? Or do you expect
> I'll state my name and enterprise?

THE WITCH:

> O Sir, forgive this rude salute from me!
2490
> And yet no horse hoof do I see;
> And then where is your raven pair?

MEPHISTOPHELES:

> This time I'll let you get away with it.
> It has been quite some while, I will admit,
> Since last we met. And to be fair,
> The culture that has licked the world up slick
> Has even with the Devil turned the trick.
> The northern phantom is no longer to be found;

Where will you see horns, tail, or claws around?
As for the foot, which I can't do without,
2500   It would work me much social harm, I fear;
And so, like many a young man, I've gone about
With padded calves this many a long year.

THE WITCH [*dancing*]:

I'll lose my mind for jubilation
To see Squire Satan back in circulation!

MEPHISTOPHELES:

Woman, I forbid that appellation!

THE WITCH:

Why? What harm has it ever done?

MEPHISTOPHELES:

It's long since passed to fable books and vanished.
Yet people are no better off. The Evil One
They're rid of, but their evils are not banished.
2510   Just call me Baron, that will do.
I am a cavalier like any cavalier.
You do not doubt my noble blood, and you
Can see the coat of arms that I wear here.

[*He makes an indecent gesture.*]

THE WITCH [*laughing immoderately*]:

Ha! Ha! Just like you, that I'll swear!
Oh you're a rogue, just as you always were!

MEPHISTOPHELES [*to* FAUST]:

Learn this, my friend! This is the way
To handle witches any day.

THE WITCH:

Now, gentlemen, how can I be of use?

MEPHISTOPHELES:

A good glass of the well-known juice,
2520   But of your oldest, is what I'm after;
It's years that put the powers in those brews.

THE WITCH:

Why, sure! Here is a bottle on my shelf
From which I sometimes take a nip myself
And which no longer has a trace of stink.
I'll gladly pour you out a little glass.

[*softly*]

But if this man here unprepared should drink,
You know he'll die before two hours pass.

MEPHISTOPHELES:

He's a good friend, and I mean things to thrive with him;
Give him the best your kitchen offers, serve him well.

2530 So draw your circle, speak your spell,
And fill his cup right to the brim.

[*With bizarre gestures the* WITCH *describes a circle and places strange things inside it. Meanwhile the glasses begin to ring and the kettle to boom and make music. Finally she fetches a great book and disposes the monkeys within the circle to serve her as a lectern and to hold torches. She beckons* FAUST *to come to her.*]

FAUST [*to* MEPHISTOPHELES]:
Now tell me, what is all this leading to?
These frantic motions and this wild ado
And all of this disgusting stuff
I've known and hated long enough.

MEPHISTOPHELES:
On, nonsense! It's just for the fun of it!
And don't be such a prig! As a physician,
She needs to hocus-pocus just a bit
So that the juice can work on your condition.

[*He gets* FAUST *into the circle.*]

THE WITCH [*begins to declaim with great bombast out of a book*]:
2540 This must ye ken!
From one take ten;
Skip two; and then
Even up three,
And rich you'll be.
Leave out the four.
From five and six,
Thus says the witch,
Make seven and eight,
And all is straight.
2550 And nine is one,
And ten is none.
This is the witch's one-times-one!

FAUST:
I think the hag's in fever and delirium.

MEPHISTOPHELES:
Oh, there is lots more still to come.
As I well know, the whole book's in that vein.
I've wasted much time going through its pages,
For total paradox will still remain
A mystery alike to fools and sages.
My friend, the art is old and new.
2560 For ages it has been the thing to do,
By Three and One, and One and Three,
To broadcast error in guise of verity.
And so they teach and jabber unperturbed;

With fools, though, who is going to bother?
Man has a way of thinking, when he hears a word,
That certainly behind it lies some thought or other.

THE WITCH [*continues*]:
The lofty force
Of wisdom's source
Is from the whole world hidden.
2570   Once give up thinking,
And in a twinkling
It's granted you unbidden.

FAUST:
What nonsense is she spouting now before us?
My head is going to split before too long.
I feel as if I'm listening to a chorus
Of fools a hundred thousand strong.

MEPHISTOPHELES:
Enough, O worthy Sibyl! Pray, no more!
Bring on your potion now, and pour
A goblet quickly to the brim;
2580   My friend is safe, your drink won't injure him.
He is a man of many titles,
And many a dram has warmed his vitals.

[*With many ceremonies the* WITCH *pours out the drink in a goblet. As* FAUST *raises it to his mouth a little flame arises.*]
Just drink it down. Go on! You'll love
The way it makes your heart soar higher.
What! With the Devil hand-in-glove
And boggle at a little fire?

[*The* WITCH *dissolves the circle.* FAUST *steps forth.*]
Come right on out! You must not rest.

THE WITCH:
And may the dram do you much good!

MEPHISTOPHELES [*to the* WITCH]:
If you have any favor to request,
2590   Just tell me on Walpurgis,[21] if you would.

THE WITCH:
Here is a spell; say it occasionally
And you'll see strange results without a doubt.

MEPHISTOPHELES [*to* FAUST]:
Just come along, entrust yourself to me.
You must perspire now necessarily

---

[21]Walpurgis: The Bloksberg, highest peak of the Harz Mountains, was the traditional scene of devils' orgies on St. Walpurga's Night, April 30.

To get the force to penetrate both in and out.
I'll teach you later all the joys of indolence,
And soon to your heart's pleasure you'll commence
To feel how Cupid rises up and hops about.

FAUST:

Just one more quick look in the mirror there!
2600   That womanly form was O! So fair!

MEPHISTOPHELES:

No, no! For soon, alive before you here
The paragon of women shall appear.

[*aside*]

With that drink in you, you will find
All women Helens to your mind.

A Street

FAUST:

Fair lady, may I be so free
As to offer my arm and company?

MARGARET:

I'm neither a lady nor fair, and may
Go unescorted on my way.

[*She disengages herself and goes on.*]
FAUST:

By heaven, but that child is sweet!
2610   Like none I ever chanced to meet.
So virtuous and modest, yes,
But with a touch of spunkiness.
Her lips so red, her cheek so bright,
I never shall forget the sight.
The shy way she cast down her eye
Has pressed itself deep in my heart;
And then the quick and short reply,
That was the most delightful part!

[*Enter* MEPHISTOPHELES.]
You must get me that girl, you hear?

MEPHISTOPHELES:

Which one?

FAUST:

2620   She just went by me here.

MEPHISTOPHELES:

That one? She just came from the priest,
He absolved her from her sins and all;
I stole up near the confessional.
She's just a simple little thing,

Went to confession just for nothing.
On such as she I have no hold.

FAUST:

And yet she's past fourteen years old.

MEPHISTOPHELES:

Why, you talk just like Jack the Rake
Who wants all flowers to bloom for his sake
2630   And fancies that no honor is,
Or favor, but the picking's his.
It doesn't always work that way.

FAUST:

Dear Master Laudable, I say
Don't bother me with your legality!
And I am telling you outright,
Unless that creature of delight
Lies in my arms this very night,
At midnight we part company.

MEPHISTOPHELES:

Remember there are limits! I
2640   Need fourteen days at least to try
And find an opportunity.

FAUST:

Had I but seven hours clear,
I wouldn't need the Devil near
To lead that girl astray for me.

MEPHISTOPHELES:

You're talking like a Frenchman. Wait!
And don't be put out or annoyed:
What good's a thing too soon enjoyed?
The pleasure is not half so great
As when you first parade the doll
2650   Through every sort of folderol
And knead and pat and shape her well,
The way that all French novels tell.

FAUST:

I've appetite enough without it.

MEPHISTOPHELES:

With no more joking now about it:
I'm telling you that pretty child
Will not be hurriedly beguiled.
There's nothing to be gained by force;
To cunning we must have recourse.

FAUST:

Get me some of that angel's attire!
2660   Lead me to her place of rest!
Get me the kerchief from her breast,

A garter for my love's desire!
MEPHISTOPHELES:
　　Just so you see that I do heed
　　Your pain and serve your every need,
　　We shall not waste a single minute.
　　I'll take you to her room and put you in it.
FAUST:
　　And shall I see her? have her?
MEPHISTOPHELES:
　　　　　　　　　　No!
　　She'll be at a neighbor's when we go.
　　And all alone there you can dwell
2670　Upon the fragrance of her cell
　　And hope for future joys as well.
FAUST:
　　Can we go now?
MEPHISTOPHELES:
　　　　　　It's too soon yet.
FAUST:
　　Get me a gift for her, and don't forget.

　　　　　　　　　　　　　　　　[*Exit.*]

MEPHISTOPHELES:
　　What! Gifts so soon! That's fine! He'll be right in his glory!
　　I know a lot of pretty places
　　Where there are buried treasure cases;
　　I must go through my inventory!

　　　　　　　　　　　　　　　　[*Exit.*]

Evening

A small, neat room. MARGARET *braiding her hair and doing it up.*
MARGARET:
　　I'd give a good deal if I knew
　　Who was that gentleman today!
2680　He had a very gallant way
　　And comes of noble lineage too.
　　That much I could read from his face—
　　Or he'd not be so bold in the first place.

　　　　　　　　　　　　　　　　[*Exit.*]

[*Enter* FAUST *and* MEPHISTOPHELES.]
MEPHISTOPHELES:
　　Come on! But softly. In you go!
FAUST [*after a silence*]:
　　I beg you, leave me here alone.
MEPHISTOPHELES [*peering about*]:
　　Not every girl's this neat, you know?

　　　　　　　　　　　　　　　　[*Exit.*]

FAUST [*looking all around*]:
Welcome, lovely twilight gloom
That hovers in this sacred room!
Seize on my heart, sweet love pangs who
2690   Both live and languish on hope's own dew.
How everything here is imbued
With stillness, order, and content!
Here in this poverty, what plenitude!
Here in this prison, what ravishment!

[*He throws himself into the leather armchair beside the bed.*]
O you who have both joy and sorrow known
From times gone by, clasp me too in your arms!
How often at this patriarchal throne
Children have gathered round about in swarms!
Perhaps my sweetheart, plump-cheeked, used to stand
2700   Here grateful for a Christmas present and
Devoutly kiss her grandsire's withered hand.
I feel your spirit, maiden, playing
About me, breathing order, plenitude,
And every day in mother-fashion saying
The cloth upon the table must be fresh renewed
And underfoot clean sand be strewed.
Dear hand! so godlike! In it lies
What turns a cottage to a paradise.
And here!

[*He lifts the bed curtains.*]
                What chill of rapture seizes me!
2710   Here I could linger on for hours.
Here, Nature, you with your creative powers
From light dreams brought the angel forth to be;
Here lay the child, her bosom warm
With life; here tenderly there grew
With pure and sacred help from you
The godlike image of her form.
        And you? What purpose brought you here?
How I am touched with shame sincere!
What do you want? Why is your heart so sore?
2720   O sorry Faust! I know you now no more.
        Does magic haze surround me everywhere?
I pressed for pleasure with no least delay,
And in a love dream here I melt away!
Are we the toys of every breath of air?
        If she this moment now were to come by,
What punishment your impudence would meet!
The loud-mouth lummox — O how small! — would lie

Dissolved in shame before her feet.

[*Enter* MEPHISTOPHELES.]
MEPHISTOPHELES:
Quick now! I see her at the gate.
FAUST:
2730   Away! And never to come back!
MEPHISTOPHELES:
Here is a casket of some weight,
I took it elsewhere from a rack.
Just put it in her clothespress there,
It'll make her head swim, that I'll swear.
I put some little baubles in it
To bait another bauble and win it.
A girl's a girl and play is play.
FAUST:
I wonder . . . should I?
MEPHISTOPHELES:
             You delay?
You wouldn't maybe want to keep the baubles?
2740   In that case I advise Your Lust
To save my pretty daytime, just
Don't bother me with further troubles.
You are not miserly, I trust!
I scratch my head, I rub my hands —

[*He puts the casket in the clothespress and pushes the lock shut again.*]
Off and away now!
To get that lovely child to play now
Into your heart's desires and plans.
And you stand all
Poised to proceed to lecture hall,
2750   And as if in the flesh, and grey,
Physics and Metaphysics led the way.
Come on!

                                              [*Exeunt.*]

[*Enter* MARGARET *with a lamp.*]
MARGARET:
It's close in here, there is no air.

[*She opens the window.*]
And yet it's not so warm out there.
I feel so odd, I can't say how —
I do wish Mother would come home now.
I'm chilled all over, and shivering!
I'm such a foolish, timid thing!

[*She begins to sing as she undresses.*]

There was a king of Thule
2760   True even to the grave,
To whom a golden goblet
His dying mistress gave.
    Naught did he hold more dear,
He drained it every feast;
And from his eye a tear
Welled each time as he ceased.
    When life was nearly done,
His towns he totaled up,
Begrudged his heir not one,
2770   But did not give the cup.
    There with his vassals all
At royal board sat he
In high ancestral hall
Of his castle by the sea.
    The old toper then stood up,
Quaffed off his last life-glow,
And flung the sacred cup
Down to the flood below.
    He saw it fall, and drink,
2780   And sink deep in the sea;
Then did his eyelids sink,
And no drop more drank he.

[*She opens the clothespress to put her clothes away and catches sight of the jewel casket.*]
How did this pretty casket get in here?
I locked the press, I'm sure. How queer!
What can it have inside it? Can it be
That someone left it as security
For money Mother has provided?
Here on a ribbon hangs a little key—
I think I'll have a look inside it!
2790   What's this? O Lord in heaven! See!
I've never seen the like in all my days!
A noble lady with such jewelry
Could walk with pride on holidays.
I wonder how this chain would look on me?
Such glorious things! Whose could they be?

[*She puts it on and steps up to the mirror.*]
If just these earrings could be mine!
One looks so different in them right away.
What good does beauty do, young thing? It may
Be very well to wonder at,
2800   But people let it go at that;

They praise you half in pity.
Gold serves all ends,
On gold depends
Everything. Ah, we poor!

Promenade

FAUST *pacing up and down in thought.* MEPHISTOPHELES *comes to him.*
MEPHISTOPHELES:
　　Now by the element of hell! By love refused!
　　I wish I knew a stronger oath that could be used!
FAUST:
　　What's this? What's griping you so badly?
　　I've never seen a face the like of this!
MEPHISTOPHELES:
　　Why, I'd surrender to the Devil gladly
2810　　If I were not the Devil as it is!
FAUST:
　　Have you gone off your head? I grant
　　It suits you, though, to rave and rant.
MEPHISTOPHELES:
　　Just think, those jewels for Gretchen that I got,
　　Some priest has made off with the lot! —
　　Her mother got to see the things,
　　Off went her dire imaginings;
　　That woman's got some sense of smell,
　　She has prayerbook-sniffing on the brain,
　　A whiff of any item, and she can tell
2820　　Whether the thing is sacred or profane.
　　That jewelry she spotted in a minute
　　As having no great blessing in it.
　　"My child," she cried, "ill-gotten good
　　Ensnares the soul, consumes the blood.
　　Before Our Lady we will lay it,
　　With heaven's manna she'll repay it."²²
　　Margretlein pulled a pouty face,
　　Called it a gift horse, and in any case
　　She thought he wasn't godless, he
2830　　Who sneaked it in so cleverly.
　　The mother had a priest drop by;
　　No sooner did he the trick espy
　　Than his eyes lit up with what he saw.
　　"This shows an upright mind," quoth he,
　　"Self-conquest gains us victory.

---

²² **heaven's . . . it**: Revelation 2:17: "To him that overcometh will I give to eat of the hidden manna."

The church has a good healthy maw,
She's swallowed up whole countries, still
She never yet has eaten her fill.
The church, dear ladies, alone has health
2840   For digestion of ill-gotten wealth."

FAUST:
That's nothing but the usual game,
A king and a Jew can do the same.

MEPHISTOPHELES:
Then up he scooped brooch, chain, and rings
As if they were just trivial things
With no more thanks, if's, and's, or but's
Than if they were a bag of nuts,
Promised them celestial reward—
All edified, they thanked him for it.

FAUST:
And Gretchen?

MEPHISTOPHELES:
Sits lost now in concern,
2850   Not knowing yet which way to turn;
Thinks day and night about the gems,
But more of him from whom the present stems.

FAUST:
I hate to see the dear girl worry.
Get her a new set in a hurry.
The first one wasn't too much anyway.

MEPHISTOPHELES:
My gentleman finds this mere child's play.

FAUST:
And here's the way I want it. Go
Make friends there with that neighbor. Show
You're not a devil made of sugar water,
2860   Get those new gems and have them brought her.

MEPHISTOPHELES:
Sir, I obey with all my heart.

[*Exit* FAUST.]

This fool in love will huff and puff
The sun and moon and stars apart
To get his sweetheart pastime stuff.

[*Exit.*]

The Neighbor's House

MARTHA *alone.*

MARTHA:
Now God forgive my husband, he
Has not done the right thing by me.

Way off into the world he's gone,
And leaves me on the straw alone.
Yet he surely had no cause on my part,
2870   God knows I loved him with all my heart.

[*She weeps.*]
He could be dead! — If I just knew for sure!
Or had a statement with a signature!

[*Enter* MARGARET.]
MARGARET:
Dame Martha!
MARTHA:
What is it, Gretelchen?
MARGARET:
My knees are sinking under me.
I've found one in my press again,
Another casket, of ebony,
And this time it's a gorgeous set
Far richer than the first one yet.
MARTHA:
This time you mustn't tell your mother,
2880   Off it would go to church just like the other.
MARGARET:
O look at them! Just see! Just see!
MARTHA [*putting them on her*]:
You *are* a lucky creature!
MARGARET:
Unfortunately
In church or on the street I do not dare
Be seen in them, or anywhere.
MARTHA:
You just come over frequently,
Put on the jewels in secret here,
Walk by the mirror an hour or so in privacy,
And we'll enjoy them, never fear.
There'll come a chance, a holiday, before we're done,
2890   Where you can show them to the people one by one,
A necklace first, pearl ear-drops next; your mother
Won't notice it, or we'll make up some thing or other.
MARGARET:
But who could bring both caskets here?
There's something not quite right . . .

[*A knock.*]
Oh, dear!
Could that be Mother coming here?

MARTHA [*looking through the blinds*]:
> It's a strange gentleman—Come in!

[MEPHISTOPHELES *steps in.*]
MEPHISTOPHELES:
> I'm so free as to step right in,
> The ladies must excuse my liberty.

[*Steps back respectfully before* MARGARET.]
> I wish to see Dame Martha Schwerdtlein, if I may.
MARTHA:
2900   Right here! What might the gentleman have to say?
MEPHISTOPHELES [*aside to her*]:
> I know you now, that is enough for me.
> You have distinguished company.
> Forgive my freedom, I shall then
> Return this afternoon again.
MARTHA [*aloud*]:
> Child, think of it! The gentleman takes
> You for some lady! For mercy's sakes!
MARGARET:
> I'm just a poor young girl; I find
> The gentleman is far too kind.
> These gems do not belong to me.
MEPHISTOPHELES:
2910   Oh, it's not just the jewelry.
> She has a quick glance, and a way!
> I am delighted I may stay.
MARTHA:
> What is your errand then? I'm very—
MEPHISTOPHELES:
> I wish my tidings were more merry.
> I trust you will not make me rue this meeting:
> Your husband is dead and sends you greeting.
MARTHA:
> He's dead! That faithful heart! Oh, my!
> My husband's dead! Oh! I shall die!
MARGARET:
> Dear lady, Oh! Do not despair!
MEPHISTOPHELES:
2920   Now listen to the sad affair.
MARGARET:
> I hope I never, never love.
> Such loss as this I would die of.
MEPHISTOPHELES:
> Glad must have sad, sad must have glad, as always.

MARTHA:

O tell me all about his dying!

MEPHISTOPHELES:

At Padua, by Saint Anthony's
They buried him, and he is lying
In ground well sanctified and blest
At cool and everlasting rest.

MARTHA:

And there is nothing else you bring?

MEPHISTOPHELES:

2930　Yes, one request and solemn enterprise:
Three hundred Masses for him you should have them sing.
My pockets are quite empty otherwise.

MARTHA:

What, not a luck-piece, or a trinket such
As any journeyman deep in his pack would hoard
As a remembrance token stored
And sooner starve or beg than use it!

MEPHISTOPHELES:

Madam, it grieves me very much;
Indeed he did not waste his money or lose it.
And much did he his failings then deplore,
2940　Yes, and complained of his hard luck still more.

MARGARET:

To think that human fortunes so miscarry!
Many's the Requiem I'll pray for him, I'm sure.

MEPHISTOPHELES:

Ah, you deserve now very soon to marry,
A child of such a kindly nature.

MARGARET:

It's not yet time for that. Oh, no!

MEPHISTOPHELES:

If not a husband, then meanwhile a beau.
It's one of heaven's greatest graces
To hold so dear a thing in one's embraces.

MARGARET:

It's not the custom here for one.

MEPHISTOPHELES:

2950　Custom or not, it still is done.

MARTHA:

But tell me more!

MEPHISTOPHELES:

　　　　　　　I stood at his bedside—
Half-rotten straw it was and little more
Than horse manure; but in good Christian style he died,

Yet found he had still further items on his score.
"How I detest myself!" he cried with dying breath,
"For having left my business and my wife!
Ah, that remembrance is my death.
If she would just forgive me in this life!"—

MARTHA [*weeping*]:

The good man! I long since forgave.

MEPHISTOPHELES:

2960   "God knows, though, she was more to blame than I."

MARTHA:

It's a lie! And he with one foot in the grave!

MEPHISTOPHELES:

Oh, he was talking through his hat
There at the end, if I am half a judge.
"I had no time to sit and yawn," he said,
"First children and then earning children's bread,
Bread in the widest sense, at that,
And could not even eat my share in peace."

MARTHA:

Did he forget my love, how I would drudge
Both day and night and never cease?

MEPHISTOPHELES:

2970   No, he remembered that all right.
"As I put out from Malta," he went on,
"I prayed for wife and children fervently;
Then heaven too disposed things favorably
So our ship took a Turkish galleon
With treasure for the great Sultan aboard.
Then bravery came in for reward
And I got, as was only fair,
My own well calculated share."

MARTHA:

What! Where? Do you suppose he buried it?

MEPHISTOPHELES:

2980   Who knows where the four winds have carried it?
A pretty girl took him in tow when he
Was roaming Naples there without a friend;
She showed him so much love and loyalty
He bore the marks right to his blessed end.

MARTHA:

The rogue! He robbed his children like a thief!
And all that misery and grief
Could not prevent the shameful life he led.

MEPHISTOPHELES:

But that, you see, is why he's dead.

2990 Were I in your place now, you know,
I'd mourn him for a decent year and then
Be casting round meanwhile to find another beau.
MARTHA:
Oh Lord, the kind my first man was,
I'll never in this world find such again.
There never was a fonder fool than mine.
Only, he liked the roving life too much,
And foreign women, and foreign wine,
And then, of course, those devilish dice.
MEPHISTOPHELES:
Well, well, it could have worked out fine
If he had only taken such
3000 Good care on his part to be nice.
I swear on those terms it is true
I would myself exchange rings with you.
MARTHA:
Oh, the gentleman has such joking ways!
MEPHISTOPHELES [*aside*]:
It's time for me to be pushing onward!
She'd hold the very Devil to his word.

[*to* GRETCHEN]
How are things with your heart these days?
MARGARET:
What do you mean, Sir?
MEPHISTOPHELES [*aside*]:
                    O you innocents!
Ladies, farewell!
MARGARET:
                    Farewell.
MARTHA:
                              One word yet! What I crave is
Some little piece of evidence
3010 Of when and how my sweetheart died and where his grave is.
I've always been a friend of orderliness,
I'd like to read his death note in the weekly press.
MEPHISTOPHELES:
Good woman, what two witnesses report
Will stand as truth in any court.
I have a friend, quite serious,
I'll bring him to the judge with us.
I'll go and get him.
MARTHA:
                    Do that! Do!

MEPHISTOPHELES:

This lady will be with you too?

A splendid lad, much traveled. He

3020   Shows ladies every courtesy.

MARGARET:

The gentleman would make me blush for shame.

MEPHISTOPHELES:

Before no earthly king that one could name.

MARTHA:

Out in the garden to the rear

This afternoon we'll expect both of you here.

A Street

FAUST:

How is it? Will it work? Will it succeed?

MEPHISTOPHELES:

Ah, bravo! I find you aflame indeed.

Gretchen is yours now pretty soon.

You meet at neighbor Martha's house this afternoon.

The woman is expressly made

3030   To work the pimp and gypsy trade!

FAUST:

Good!

MEPHISTOPHELES:

Ah, but something is required of us.

FAUST:

One good turn deserves another.

MEPHISTOPHELES:

We will depose some testimony or other

To say her husband's bones are to be found

In Padua in consecrated ground.

FAUST:

Fine! First we'll need to do some journey-going.

MEPHISTOPHELES:

Sancta simplicitas! For that we need not fuss.

Just testify, and never mind the knowing.

FAUST:

Think of a better plan, or nothing doing.

MEPHISTOPHELES:

3040   O saintly man! and sanctimonious!

False witness then you never bore

In all your length of life before?

Have you not with great power given definition

Of God, the world, and all the world's condition,

Of man, man's heart, man's mind, and what is more,
With brazen brow and with no lack of breath?
And when you come right down to it,
You knew as much about them, you'll admit,
As you know of this Mister Schwerdtlein's death!

FAUST:

3050   You are a liar and a sophist too.

MEPHISTOPHELES:

Or would be, if I didn't know a thing or two.
Tomorrow will you not deceive
Poor Gretchen and then make her believe
The vows of soul-felt love you swear?

FAUST:

And from my heart.

MEPHISTOPHELES:

                All good and fair!
Then comes eternal faith, and love still higher,
Then comes the super-almighty desire —
Will that be heartfelt too, I inquire?

FAUST:

Stop there! It will! — If I have feeling,
3060   And for this feeling, for this reeling
Seek a name, and finding none,
With all my senses through the wide world run,
And clutch at words supreme, and claim
That boundless, boundless is the flame
That burns me, infinite and never done,
Is that a devilish, lying game?

MEPHISTOPHELES:

I still am right!

FAUST:

                Mark this and heed it,
And spare me further waste of throat and lung:
To win an argument takes no more than a tongue,
3070   That's all that's needed.
But come, this chatter fills me with disgust,
For you are right, primarily because I must.

A Garden

MARGARET *on* FAUST's *arm*, MARTHA *with* MEPHISTOPHELES, *strolling up and down.*

MARGARET:

I feel, Sir, you are only sparing me
And shaming me by condescending so.
A traveler, from charity,

Will often take things as they go.
I realize my conversation can
Not possibly amuse such an experienced man.

FAUST:

One glance of yours, one word delights me more
3080   Than all of this world's wisdom-store.

[*He kisses her hand.*]

MARGARET:

How can you kiss it? It must seem to you
So coarse, so rough a hand to kiss.
What kinds of tasks have I not had to do!
You do not know how strict my mother is.

[*They pass on.*]

MARTHA:

And so, Sir, you are traveling constantly?

MEPHISTOPHELES:

Business and duty keep us on our way.
Many a place one leaves regretfully,
But then one simply cannot stay.

MARTHA:

It may well do while in one's prime
3090   To rove about the world as a rolling stone,
But then comes the unhappy time,
And dragging to the grave, a bachelor, alone,
Was never good for anyone.

MEPHISTOPHELES:

Ah, such with horror I anticipate.

MARTHA:

Then act, dear Sir, before it is too late.

[*They pass on.*]

MARGARET:

But out of sight is out of mind!
Your courtesy comes naturally;
But you have friends in quantity
Who are more clever than my kind.

FAUST:

3100   Dear girl, believe me, clever in that sense
Means usually a close self-interest.

MARGARET:

Really?

FAUST:

To think simplicity and innocence
Are unaware their sacred way is best,

That lowliness and sweet humility
Are bounteous Nature's highest gifts —

MARGARET:

Think only for a moment's time of me,
I shall have time enough to think of you.

FAUST:

Then you are much alone?

MARGARET:

Yes, our house is a little one,
3110 And yet it must be tended to.
We have no maid, hence I must cook and sweep and knit
And sew, and do the errands early and late;
And then my mother is a bit
Too strict and strait.
And yet she has no need to scrimp and save this way;
We could live better far than others, you might say;
My father left a sizeable estate,
A house and garden past the city gate.
But I have rather quiet days of late.
3120 My brother is a soldier,
My little sister died;
The child did sometimes leave me with my patience tried,
And yet I'd gladly have the trouble back again,
She was so dear to me.

FAUST:

                              An angel, if like you.

MARGARET:

I brought her up; she dearly loved me too.
She was born following my father's death.
Mother we thought at her last breath,
She was so miserable, but then
She slowly, slowly got her strength again.
3130 It was impossible for her to nurse
The little mite herself, of course,
And so I raised her all alone
On milk and water; she became my own.
In my arms, in my lap she smiled,
Wriggled, and grew up to be a child.

FAUST:

You must have known the purest happiness.

MARGARET:

But many trying hours nonetheless.
At night her little cradle used to stand
Beside my bed, and she had but to stir
3140 And I was there at hand,

Sometimes to feed her, sometimes to comfort her,
Sometimes when she would not be still, to rise
And pace the floor with her to soothe her cries,
And yet be at the washtub early, do
The marketing and tend the hearth fire too,
And every morrow like today.
One's spirits are not always cheerful, Sir, that way;
Yet food is relished better, as is rest.

[*They pass on.*]

MARTHA:

3150   Poor women! They are badly off indeed,
A bachelor is hard to change, they say.

MEPHISTOPHELES:

Someone like you is all that I would need
To set me on a better way.

MARTHA:

But is there no one, Sir, that you have found?
Speak frankly, is your heart in no wise bound?

MEPHISTOPHELES:

The proverb says: A wife and one's own household
Are worth their weight in pearls and gold.

MARTHA:

But I mean, have you felt no inclination?

MEPHISTOPHELES:

I have met everywhere with much consideration.

MARTHA:

But has your heart in no case been impressed?

MEPHISTOPHELES:

3160   With ladies one must not presume to jest.

MARTHA:

Oh, you misunderstand me!

MEPHISTOPHELES:

                                What a shame! I find
I understand — that you are very kind.

[*They pass on.*]

FAUST:

And so you did, my angel, recognize
Me in the garden here at the first look?

MARGARET:

Did you not see how I cast down my eyes?

FAUST:

And you forgive the liberty I took
And all my impudence before
When you had just left the cathedral door?

MARGARET:

    I was confused, the experience was all new.

3170   No one could say bad things of me.

    Ah, thought I, could he possibly

    Have noted something brazen or bold in you?

    He seemed to think here was a girl he could

    Treat in just any way he would.

    I must confess that then I hardly knew

    What soon began to argue in your favor;

    But I was angry with myself, however,

    For not becoming angrier with you.

FAUST:

    My darling!

MARGARET:

              Wait!

[*She picks a star flower and plucks the petals off it one by one.*]

FAUST:

                 What is it? A bouquet?

MARGARET:

3180   No, just a game.

FAUST:

              What?

MARGARET:

                You'd laugh at me if I should say.

[*She murmurs something as she goes on plucking.*]

FAUST:

    What are you murmuring?

MARGARET [*half aloud*]:

                He loves me — loves me not.

FAUST:

    You lovely creature of the skies!

MARGARET [*continuing*]:

    Loves me — not — loves me — not —

[*with delight as she reaches the last petal*]

    He loves me!

FAUST:

           Yes, my child! And let this language of

    The flowers be your oracle. He loves you!

    Do you know what that means? He loves you!

[*He takes both her hands.*]

MARGARET:

    I'm trembling!

FAUST:

    O do not tremble! Let this glance
    And let this pressure of my hands
3190   Say what is inexpressible:
    To yield oneself entirely and to feel
    A rapture that must be everlasting!
    Eternal! — Its end would be despair.
    No! Without end! Without end!

[MARGARET *presses his hands, disengages herself, and runs off. He stands in thought for a moment, then follows her.*]

MARTHA [*coming along*]:

    It's getting dark.

MEPHISTOPHELES:

               We must be on our way.

MARTHA:

    I'd ask you gentlemen to stay,
    But this is such a wicked neighborhood.
    It seems that no one has a thing to do
    Or put his mind to
3200   But watch his neighbor's every move and stir.
    No matter what one does, there's always talk.
    What of our couple?

MEPHISTOPHELES:

             They've flown up the arbor walk.
    The wanton butterflies!

MARTHA:

             He seems to take to her.

MEPHISTOPHELES:

    And she to him. Such is the world's old way.

A Summer House

MARGARET *comes running in, hides behind the door, puts her finger to her lips, and peeps through the crack.*

MARGARET:

    He's coming!

[FAUST *comes along.*]

FAUST:

             Little rogue, to tease me so!
    I'll catch you!

[*He kisses her.*]

MARGARET [*embracing him and returning his kiss*]:

             From my heart I love you so!

[MEPHISTOPHELES *knocks.*]

FAUST [*stamping his foot*]:
>Who's there?

MEPHISTOPHELES:
>>A friend!

FAUST:
>>>A beast!

MEPHISTOPHELES:
>>>>It's time for us to go.

[MARTHA *comes along.*]

MARTHA:
>Yes, it is late, Sir.

FAUST:
>>>May I not escort you, though?

MARGARET:
>My mother would—farewell!

FAUST:
>>>>Ah, must I leave you then?

3210 Farewell!

MARTHA:
>>Adieu!

MARGARET:
>>>But soon to meet again!

>>>>>[*Exeunt* FAUST *and* MEPHISTOPHELES.]

>Dear Lord! What things and things there can
>Come to the mind of such a man!
>I stand abashed, and for the life of me
>Cannot do other than agree.
>A simple child, I cannot see
>Whatever it is he finds in me.

>>>>>>[*Exit.*]

Forest and Cavern

FAUST:
>Spirit sublime, thou gavest me, gavest me all
>For which I asked. Thou didst not turn in vain
>Thy countenance upon me in the fire.
3220 >Thou gavest me glorious Nature for my kingdom,
>And power to feel it and enjoy it. No
>Cold, marveling observation didst thou grant me,
>Deep vision to her very heart thou hast
>Vouchsafed, as into the heart of a friend.
>Thou dost conduct the ranks of living creatures
>Before me and teachest me to know my brethren
>In quiet bush, in air, and in the water.
>And when the storm in forest roars and snarls,

And the giant fir comes crashing down, and, falling,
3230   Crushes its neighbor boughs and neighbor stems,
And hills make hollow thunder of its fall,
Then dost thou guide me to safe caverns, showest
Me then unto myself, and my own bosom's
Profound and secret wonders are revealed.
And when before my sight the pure moon rises
And casts its mellow comfort, then from crags
And rain-sprent bushes there come drifting toward me
The silvery forms from ages now gone by,
Allaying meditation's austere pleasure.
3240   That no perfection is to man allotted,
I now perceive. Along with this delight
That brings me near and nearer to the gods,
Thou gavest me this companion whom I can
No longer do without, however he
Degrades me to myself or insolently
Turns thy gifts by a breath to nothingness.
Officiously he fans a frantic fire
Within my bosom for that lovely girl.
Thus from desire I stagger to enjoyment
3250   And in enjoyment languish for desire.

[*Enter* MEPHISTOPHELES.]
MEPHISTOPHELES:

Won't you have had enough of this life presently?
How can it in the long run do for you?
All well and good to try it out and see,
But then go on to something new!

FAUST:

I do wish you had more to do
Than pester me on a good day.

MEPHISTOPHELES:

All right, then, I won't bother you.
You dare not mean that anyway.
In you, friend, gruff, uncivil, and annoyed,
3260   There's nothing much to lose, indeed.
The whole day long you keep my time employed!
But from my master's nose it's hard to read
What pleases him and what one should avoid.

FAUST:

Now there is just the proper tone!
He wants my thanks for having been annoying.

MEPHISTOPHELES:

What kind of life would you now be enjoying,

Poor son of earth, without the help I've shown?
But I have long since cured you anyhow
From gibberish your imagination talked,
3270   And if it weren't for me you would have walked
Right off this earthly globe by now.
Why should you mope around and stare
Owl-like at cave and rocky lair?
Why suck up food from soggy moss and trickling stone
Just like a toad all, all alone?
A fine sweet pastime! That stick-in-the-mud
Professor still is in your blood.

FAUST:

Can you conceive the fresh vitality
This wilderness existence gives to me?
3280   But if you could conceive it, yes,
You would be devil enough to block my happiness.

MEPHISTOPHELES:

A superterrestrial delight!
To lie around on dewy hills at night,
Clasp earth and heaven to you in a rapture,
Inflate yourself to deity's great size,
Delve to earth's core by impulse of surmise,
All six days' creation in your own heart capture,
In pride of power enjoy I know not what,
In ecstasy blend with the All there on the spot,
3290   The son of earth dissolved in vision,
And then the lofty intuition —

[*with a gesture*]

To end — just how, I must not mention.

FAUST:

O vile!

MEPHISTOPHELES:

That does not please you much; meanwhile
You have the right to speak your moral "Vile!"
Before chaste ears one must not talk about
What chaste hearts cannot do without.
All right: occasional pleasure of a lie
To yourself, is something I will not deny;
But you won't last long in that vein.
3300   Soon you will be elsewhere attracted,
Or if it goes too long, distracted
To madness or to anguished pain.
Enough of this! Your sweetheart sits there in her room,
Around her everything is gloom.

You never leave her thoughts, and she
Loves you just overwhelmingly.
Passion came to flood first on your part,
As melting snow will send a brooklet running high;
You poured all that into her heart,
3310   And now your brook is running dry.
It seems to me, instead of playing king
In woodland wilds, so great a lord
Might help the childish little thing
And give her loving some reward.
Time hangs upon her like a pall,
She stands by the window, watches the clouds along
And past the ancient city wall.
"If I were a little bird!" so goes her song
Half the night and all day long.
3320   Sometimes cheerful, mostly sad and of
No further power of tears,
Then calm again, so it appears,
And always in love.

FAUST:

Serpent! Serpent!

MEPHISTOPHELES [*aside*]:

Admit I've got you there!

FAUST:

Infamous being! Begone! And do not dare
So much as speak that lovely creature's name!
Do not arouse desire in me to where
Half-maddened senses burst in open flame!

MEPHISTOPHELES:

3330   What, then? She thinks you fled from her,
And more or less that's just what did occur.

FAUST:

I am near her, and even if I were
Afar, I could not lose her or forget;
The very body of the Lord, when her
Lips touch it, rouses envy and regret.

MEPHISTOPHELES:

My friend, I've often envied you indeed
The twin roes[23] that among the lilies feed.

FAUST:

Pander, begone!

---

[23] the twin roes: An allusion to the Song of Solomon, 4:5: "Thy two breasts are like two young roes that are
twins, which feed among the lilies."

MEPHISTOPHELES:

               Fine! I laugh while you rail.

    The God that created girls and boys

3340   Saw that the noblest power He enjoys

    Was seeing that occasion should not fail.

    Come on, then! What a shame this is!

    You're going to your sweetheart's room

    And not off to your doom.

FAUST:

    What if I do find heaven in her arms?

    What if in her embrace my spirit warms?

    Do I not still feel her distress?

    Am I not still the fugitive, the homeless,

    The monster without rest or purpose sweeping

3350   Like a cataract from crag to crag and leaping

    In frenzy of desire to the abyss?

    While at one side, she, with her childlike mind,

    Dwells in a cottage on the Alpine slope

    With all her quiet life confined

    Within her small world's narrow scope.

    And I, the God-detested,

    Had not enough, but wrested

    The crag away and scattered

    Its ruins as they shattered

3360   To undermine her and her peace as well!

    The victim you demanded, fiend of hell!

    Help, Devil, make this time of anguish brief!

    Let it be soon if it must be!

    Let her fate crash in ruins over me,

    Together let us come to grief.

MEPHISTOPHELES:

    Ah, now it seethes again and glows!

    Go in and comfort her, you lout!

    A head like yours beholds the close

    Of doom as soon as he sees no way out.

3370   Hurrah for men that bravely dare!

    You're half bedeviled anyway;

    There's nothing sillier in the world, I say,

    Than being a devil in despair.

Gretchen's Room

GRETCHEN *at her spinning wheel, alone.*

GRETCHEN:

    My peace is gone,

My heart is sore,
I'll find it never
And nevermore.
      When he does not come
I live in a tomb,
3380   The world is all
Bitter as gall.
      O, my poor head
Is quite distraught,
And my poor mind
Is overwrought.
      My peace is gone,
My heart is sore,
I'll find it never
And nevermore.
3390   I look from my window
Only to greet him,
I leave the house
Only to meet him.
      His noble gait
And form and guise,
The smile of his mouth,
The spell of his eyes,
      The magic in
Those words of his,
3400   The clasp of his hand,
And oh! — his kiss.
      My peace is gone,
My heart is sore,
I'll find it never
And nevermore.
      My bosom aches
To feel him near,
Oh, could I clasp
And hold him here
3410   And kiss and kiss him
Whom I so cherish,
Beneath his kisses
I would perish!

Martha's Garden
MARGARET:
      Promise me, Henry!
FAUST:
                        If I can!

MARGARET:

    About religion, what do you feel now, say?

    You are a good, warmhearted man,

    And yet I fear you're not inclined that way.

FAUST:

    Leave that, my child! That I love you, you feel;

    For those I love, my flesh and blood I'd give,

3420   And no one's church or feelings would I steal.

MARGARET:

    But that is not enough! One must believe!

FAUST:

    Must one?

MARGARET:

            O, if I had some influence!

    You do not even revere the sacraments.

FAUST:

    I do revere them.

MARGARET:

              But without desire.

    It's long since you have gone to Mass or to confession.

    Do you believe in God?

FAUST:

             My darling, who can say:

    I believe in God?

    Ask priest or sage you may,

    And their replies seem odd

3430   Mockings of the asker.

MARGARET:

            Then you do not believe?

FAUST:

    My answer, dear one, do not misconceive!

    Who can name

    Him, or proclaim:

    I believe in Him?

    Who is so cold

    As to make bold

    To say: I do not believe in Him?

    The all-embracing,

    The all-sustaining,

3440   Does He not hold and sustain

    You, me, Himself?

    Does heaven not arch high above us?

    Does earth not lie firm here below?

    And do not everlasting stars

    Rise with a kindly glance?

    Do I not gaze into your eyes,

And do not all things crowd
Into your head and heart,
Working in eternal mystery
3450   Invisibly visible at your side?
Let these things fill your heart, vast as they are,
And when you are entirely happy in that feeling,
Then call it what you will:
Heart, Fortune, Love, or God!
I have no name for it.
Feeling is everything,
Names are sound and smoke
Obscuring heaven's glow.

MARGARET:
That is all very good and fair;
3460   The priest says much the same, although
He used a different wording as he spoke.

FAUST:
It is said everywhere
By all hearts underneath the sky of day,
Each heart in its own way;
So why not I in mine?

MARGARET:
It sounds all right when you express it so;
There's something not quite right about it, though;
You have no Christianity.

FAUST:
Dear child!

MARGARET:
It has this long time troubled me
3470   To find you keep the company you do.

FAUST:
How so?

MARGARET:
The person whom you have with you,
In my profoundest being I abhor,
And nothing in my life before
So cut me to the heart
As this man's face when he came near.

FAUST:
My darling, have no fear.

MARGARET:
His presence roils my blood, yet for my part,
People otherwise win my heart;
Much as I yearn to have you near,
3480   This person inspires in me a secret fear,

And if I take him for a scoundrel too,
God forgive me for the wrong I do!

FAUST:

Such queer fish also have to be.

MARGARET:

To live with him would never do for me!
Let him but so much as appear,
He looks about with such a sneer
And half enraged;
Nothing can keep his sympathy engaged;
Upon his brow it's written clear
3490   That he can hold no person dear.
In your embrace I feel so free,
So warm, so yielded utterly;
His presence chokes me, chills me through and through.

FAUST:

O you intuitive angel, you!

MARGARET:

This so overwhelms me, that when
He joins us, be it where it may,
It seems that I no longer love you then.
With him there, I could never pray.
This eats my very heart; and you,
3500   Henry, must feel the same thing too.

FAUST:

This is a matter of antipathy.

MARGARET:

I must be going.

FAUST:

                    O, when will it be
That I may for a little hour rest
In your embrace in quiet, breast to breast?

MARGARET:

If I but slept alone, this very night
I'd leave the door unbolted, you realize,
But Mother's sleep is always light,
And if she took us by surprise,
I would die on the spot, I think.

FAUST:

3510   There is no need for that, my dear!
Here is a little phial. A mere
Three drops into her drink
Will shroud up Nature in deep sleep.

MARGARET:

What will I not do for your sake?

It will not harm her, though, to take?

FAUST:
Would I propose it, Love, if that were so?

MARGARET:
I look at you, dear man, and do not know
What so compels me to your will;
Already I have done so much for you
3520   That there is little left for me to do.

[*Exit.*]

[*Enter* MEPHISTOPHELES.]

MEPHISTOPHELES:
The little monkey's gone?

FAUST:
                                    You spied again?

MEPHISTOPHELES:
                                                        I could

Not help but hear it word for word:
Professor had his catechism heard;
I hope it does you lots of good.
Girls have a way of wanting to find out
Whether a man's conventionally devout.
They think: he gave in there, he'll truckle to us, no doubt.

FAUST:
You, monster, do not realize
How this good loyal soul can be
3530   So full of faith and trust —
Which things alone suffice
To make her bliss — and worry holily
For fear she must look on her best beloved as lost.

MEPHISTOPHELES:
You supersensual sensual wooer,
A girl has got you on a puppet wire.

FAUST:
You misbegotten thing of filth and fire!

MEPHISTOPHELES:
She's mighty clever too at physiognomy:
When I am present, she feels — how, she's not just sure,
My mask bodes meaning at a hidden level;
3540   She thinks beyond a doubt I'm a "Genie,"
And possibly the very Devil.
Tonight, then —?

FAUST:
                            What is that to you?

MEPHISTOPHELES:
I have my pleasure in it too!

At the Well

GRETCHEN *and* LIESCHEN *with pitchers.*

LIESCHEN:

About Barbie, I suppose you've heard?

GRETCHEN:

I get out very little. Not a word.

LIESCHEN:

Why, Sibyl was telling me today.
She's finally gone down Fools' Way.
That's what grand airs will do!

GRETCHEN:

How so?

LIESCHEN:

It stinks!
She's feeding two now when she eats and drinks.

GRETCHEN:

3550   Ah!

LIESCHEN:

Serves her right! And long enough
She hung around that fellow. All that stuff!
It was walk and jaunt
Out to the village and dancing haunt,
And everywhere she had to shine,
Always treating her to pastry and wine;
She got to think her good looks were so fine
She lost her self-respect and nothing would do
But she accepted presents from him too.
It was kiss and cuddle, and pretty soon
3560   The flower that she had was gone.

GRETCHEN:

O the poor thing!

LIESCHEN:

Is it pity that you feel!
When our kind sat at the spinning wheel
And our mothers wouldn't let us out at night,
There she was with her lover at sweet delight
Down on the bench in the dark entryway
With never an hour too long for such play.
So let her go now with head bowed down
And do church penance in a sinner's gown!

GRETCHEN:

But surely he'll take her as his wife!

LIESCHEN:

3570   He'd be a fool! A chipper lad

Finds fun is elsewhere to be had.
Besides, he's gone.

GRETCHEN:

O, that's not fair!

LIESCHEN:

If she gets him, she'll find it bad.
The boys will rip her wreath, and what's more,
They'll strew chopped straw around her door![24]

[*Exit.*]

GRETCHEN [*walking home*]:
How firmly I could once inveigh
When any young girl went astray!
For others' sins I could not find
Words enough to speak my mind!
3580   Black as it was, blacker it had to be,
And still it wasn't black enough for me.
I thanked my stars and was so game,
And now I stand exposed to shame!
Yet all that led me to this pass
Was so good, and so dear, alas!

Zwinger[25]

In a niche of the wall a statue of the Mater dolorosa[26] *with jugs of flowers in front of it.*
GRETCHEN [*puts fresh flowers in the jugs*]:
O deign
Amid your pain
To look in mercy on my grief
    With sword thrust through
3590   The heart of you,
You gaze up to your Son in death.
    To Him on high
You breathe your sigh
For His and your distressful grief.
    Who knows
What throes
Wrack me, flesh and bone?
What makes my poor heart sick with fear

---

[24] **strew . . . door!**: A traditional way of punishing promiscuous girls.

[25] *Zwinger:* An untranslatable term for the open space between the last houses of a town and the inside of the city walls, sometimes the open space between two parallel city walls. Gretchen has sought the most out-of-the-way spot in the city for her private devotions.

[26] *Mater dolorosa:* A statue of Mary, the mother of Jesus, in an attitude of grief as she beholds the crucifixion; in accordance with Luke 2:35 her visible heart is pierced with a sword. The text that follows freely adapts the famous thirteenth-century hymn *Stabat mater dolorosa.*

And what it is I plead for here,
3600 Only you know, you alone!
      No matter where I go,
I know such woe, such woe
Here within my breast!
I am not quite alone,
Alas! I weep, I moan,
My heart is so distressed.
      The flowerpots at my window
Had only tears for dew
When early in the morning
3610 I picked these flowers for you.
      When bright into my room
The early sun had come,
Upon my bed in gloom
I sat, with sorrow numb.
      Help! Rescue me from shame and death!
O deign
Amid your pain
To look in mercy on my grief!

Night

The street in front of GRETCHEN's *door.* VALENTINE, *a soldier,* GRETCHEN's *brother.*
VALENTINE:
      When I used to be in a merry crowd
3620 Where many a fellow liked to boast,
And lads in praise of girls grew loud
And to their fairest raised a toast
And drowned praise in glasses' overflow,
Then, braced on my elbows, I
Would sit with calm assurance by
And listen to their braggadocio;
Then I would stroke my beard and smile
And take my brimming glass in hand
And say: "To each his own! Meanwhile
3630 Where is there one in all the land
To hold a candle or compare
With my sister Gretel anywhere?"
Clink! Clank! the round of glasses went;
"He's right!" some shouted in assent,
"The glory of her sex!" cried some,
And all the braggarts sat there dumb.
But now!—I could tear my hair and crawl
Right up the side of the smooth wall!—

Now every rascal that comes near
3640　Can twit me with a jibe or sneer!
With every chance word dropped I sweat
Like one who has not paid a debt.
I'd knock the whole lot down if I
Could only tell them that they lie.
　　　What have we here? Who's sneaking along?
There are two of them, if I'm not wrong.
If he's the one, I'll grab his hide,
He won't get out of here alive!

[*Enter* FAUST *and* MEPHISTOPHELES.]
FAUST:
How from the window of that sacristy
3650　The vigil lamp casts forth its flickering light
Sidewise faint and fainter down the night,
And darkness closes around totally.
So in my heart the darkness reigns.
MEPHISTOPHELES:
And I feel like a cat with loving-pains
That sneaks up fire escapes and crawls
And slinks along the sides of walls;
I feel so cozy at it, and so right,
With a bit of thievery, a bit of rutting to it.
Through all my limbs I feel an ache for
3660　The glorious Walpurgis Night.
Day after tomorrow brings us to it;
Then one knows what he stays awake for.
FAUST:
Will it come to the top, that treasure
I see glimmering over there?
MEPHISTOPHELES:
You very soon will have the pleasure
Of lifting the pot to upper air.
Just recently I took a squint:
It's full of ducats shiny from the mint.
FAUST:
Not a jewel, not a ring
3670　To add to others of my girl's?
MEPHISTOPHELES:
I do believe I saw a string
Of something that looked much like pearls.
FAUST:
That's good. I really hate to go
Without a gift to take with me.

MEPHISTOPHELES:
>You needn't fuss and trouble so
>About enjoying something free.
>But now that all the stars are in the sky,
>You'll hear a real art work from me:
>I'll sing her a moral lullaby
3680
>To befool her the more certainly.

[*He sings to the zither.*]
>What dost thou here
>With dawn so near,
>O Katie dear,
>Outside your sweetheart's door?
>Maiden, beware
>Of entering there
>Lest forth you fare
>A maiden nevermore.
>   Maidens, take heed!
3690
>Once do the deed,
>And all you need
>Is: Good night, you poor things!
>If you're in love,
>To no thief give
>The thing you have
>Except with wedding rings.

VALENTINE [*steps forward*]:
>Who is it you're luring? By the Element!
>You accursed rat-catcher, you!
>To the Devil first with the instrument!
3700
>Then to the Devil with the singer too!

MEPHISTOPHELES:
>The zither's smashed, there's nothing left of it.

VALENTINE:
>And next there is a skull to split!

MEPHISTOPHELES [*to* FAUST]:
>Don't flinch, Professor, and don't fluster!
>Come close in by me, and don't tarry.
>Quick! Whip out your feather duster!
>Just thrust away and I will parry.

VALENTINE:
>Then parry this!

MEPHISTOPHELES:
>   Why not?

VALENTINE:
>   This too!

MEPHISTOPHELES:
    Of course!

VALENTINE:
          I think the Devil fights in you!
    What's this? My hand is going lame.

MEPHISTOPHELES [*to* FAUST]:
3710   Thrust home!

VALENTINE [*falls*]:
        O!

MEPHISTOPHELES:
        There, the lummox is quite tame.
    Come on! It's time for us to disappear.
    Soon they will raise a murderous hue and cry.
    With the police I always can get by,
    But of the court of blood I stand in fear.

MARTHA [*at the window*]:
    Come out! Come out!

GRETCHEN [*at the window*]:
        Bring out a light!

MARTHA [*as before*]:
    They swear and scuffle, shout and fight.

PEOPLE:
    Here's one already dead!

MARTHA [*coming out*]:
    Where are the murderers? Have they fled?

GRETCHEN [*coming out*]:
    Who's lying here?

PEOPLE:
        Your mother's son.

GRETCHEN:
3720   Almighty God! I am undone!

VALENTINE:
    I'm dying! That's a tale
    Soon told and sooner done.
    Why do you women stand and wail?
    Come close and hear me, everyone!

[*They all gather around him.*]
    My Gretchen, see! too young you are
    And not yet wise enough by far,
    You do not manage right.
    In confidence I'll tell you more:
    You have turned out to be a whore,
3730   And being one, be one outright.

GRETCHEN:
    My brother! God! What do you mean?

VALENTINE:

> Leave our Lord God out of this farce. What's done
> Is done, alas! and cannot be undone.
> And what comes next will soon be seen.
> You started secretly with one,
> It won't be long till others come,
> And when a dozen more have had you,
> The whole town will have had you too.
>   When shame is born, she first appears
> 3740   Stealthily amid the world
> And with the veil of darkness furled
> About her head and ears.
> First one would gladly slay her outright.
> But as she grows and waxes bold,
> She walks quite naked in the daylight,
> But is no fairer to behold.
> The uglier her visage grows,
> The more by open day she goes.
>   The time already I foresee
> 3750   When all the decent citizenry
> Will from you, harlot, turn away
> As from a plague corpse in their way.
> Your heart will sink within you when
> They look you in the eye! No more
> Golden chains will you wear then!
> Or stand by the altar in church as before!
> No more in collars of fine lace
> Will you come proudly to the dancing place!
> Off to a dismal corner you will slouch
> 3760   Where the beggars and the cripples crouch.[27]
> And even though God may forgive,
> Accursed here on earth you still will live.

MARTHA:

> Commend your soul to God! Will you
> Take blasphemy upon you too?

VALENTINE:

> If I could reach your withered skin and bone,
> You shameless, pandering, old crone,
> I do believe that I could win
> Full pardon for my every sin!

---

[27] **No more . . . crouch:** As Goethe had observingly read, a Frankfurt police ordinance of the fifteenth century forbade promiscuous women to wear jewelry, silk, satin, or damask, and denied them the use of a pew in church. This latter requirement would force them to remain at the rear with the "beggars and the cripples."

GRETCHEN:
    My brother! What pain of hell for me!
VALENTINE:
3770   I tell you, let your weeping be!
    When you gave up your honor, you gave
    The fiercest heart-stab I could know.
    Now through the sleep of death I go
    To God, a soldier true and brave.

        [*Dies.*]

Cathedral

Service, organ, and choir. GRETCHEN *among many people. An* EVIL SPIRIT *behind* GRETCHEN.
EVIL SPIRIT:
    How different, Gretchen, it was
    When still full of innocence
    You approached this altar,
    From your little dog-eared prayer book
    Murmuring prayers,
    Half childish play,
3780   Half God in heart!
    Gretchen!
    Where are your thoughts?
    Within your heart
    What deed of crime?
    Do you pray for your mother's soul that slept
    Away unto the long, long pain because of you?
    Whose blood is on your doorstep?
    —And underneath your heart
    Does not a new life quicken,
3790   Tormenting itself and you
    With its premonitory presence?
GRETCHEN:
    Alas! Alas!
    If I could be rid of the thoughts
    That rush this way and that way
    Despite my will!
CHOIR:
    Dies irae, dies illa
    solvet saeclum in favilla.[28]

---

[28] *Dies . . . favilla:* The opening of the greatest of medieval hymns, the *Dies irae*, composed before 1250, probably by Thomas of Celano, and used in masses of the dead: "The day of wrath, that day / Shall dissolve the world in fire." Through nineteen three-line stanzas the hymn describes the end of the world and the Last Judgment.

[*The organ sounds.*]

EVIL SPIRIT:

> Wrath seizes you!
3800 > The trumpet sounds!
> The graves shudder!
> And your heart
> From ashen rest,
> For flames of torment
> Once more reconstituted,
> Quakes forth.

GRETCHEN:

> If I were out of here!
> I feel as if the organ were
> Stifling my breath,
3810 > As if the choir dissolved
> My inmost heart.

CHOIR:

> *Judex ergo cum sedebit,*
> *quidquid latet adparebit,*
> *nil inultum remanebit.*[29]

GRETCHEN:

> I cannot breathe!
> The pillars of the wall
> Imprison me!
> The vaulted roof
> Crushes me! — Air!

EVIL SPIRIT:

3820 > Concealment! Sin and shame
> Are not concealed.
> Air? Light?
> Woe to you!

CHOIR:

> *Quid sum miser tunc dicturus?*
> *Quem patronum rogaturus?*
> *Cum vix justus sit securus.*[30]

EVIL SPIRIT:

> The clarified avert
> Their countenances from you.
> The pure shudder to reach

---

[29] *Judex . . . remanebit:* "Therefore when the Judge shall sit, / Whatever is hidden shall appear, / Nothing shall remain unavenged."

[30] *Quid . . . securus:* "What shall I, wretched, say? / What patron shall I call upon? / When scarcely the just man is safe."

3830   Out hands to you.
Woe!

CHOIR:

Quid sum miser tunc dicturus?

GRETCHEN:

Neighbor! Your smelling-bottle!

[*She falls in a faint.*]

Walpurgis Night

The Harz Mountains. Vicinity of Schierke and Elend.[31]

MEPHISTOPHELES:

Now don't you long for broomstick-transportation?
I'd like the toughest he-goat there can be.
We're far yet, by this route, from destination.

FAUST:

Since my legs still are holding out so sturdily,
This knotty stick will do for me.
Why take a short cut anyway?

3840   Slinking through this labyrinth of alleys,
Then climbing cliffs above these valleys
Where streams plunge down in everlasting spray,
Such is the spice of pleasure on this way!
Springtime over birches weaves its spell,
It's sensed already by the very pine;
Why should it not affect our limbs as well?

MEPHISTOPHELES:

There's no such feeling in these limbs of mine!
Within me all is winter's chill;
On my path I'd prefer the frost and snow.

3850   How drearily the reddish moon's disc, still
Not full, is rising with belated glow
And giving such bad light that any step now
Will have us bumping into rock or tree!
I'll call a will-o'-the-wisp,[32] if you'll allow.

---

[31] **Harz . . . Elend:** Saint Walpurgis (Walpurga, Walburga, Valburg, d. 780) was a niece of Saint Boniface and herself a missionary to Germany. By coincidence, her church calendar day, April 30, fell together with the pagan festivals on the eve of May Day, the end of winter and the beginning of summer. Under the Christian dispensation, those festivals, like the Halloween festivals (Oct. 31) at the end of summer and the beginning of winter, passed into folklore as devils' orgies. Folklore further localized those orgies on the Brocken, highest peak of the Harz Mountains in central Germany. From the village of Elend a two- or three-hour walk leads past the village of Schierke to a desolate plateau and finally to the top of the Brocken.

[32] **will-o'-the-wisp:** (*ignus fatuus,* Jack-o'-Lantern) A conglomeration of phosphorescent gas from decayed vegetation in swamps. By night it resembles an eerily swaying lantern.

I see one burning merrily.
Hey, there, my friend! May I request your flare?
Why flash for nothing over there?
Just be so good and light our way up here.

WILL-O'-THE-WISP:
I hope sheer awe will give me mastery
3860 Over my natural instability;
Most commonly we go a zigzag career.

MEPHISTOPHELES:
Ho, ho! It's man you want to imitate!
Now in the Devil's name, go straight!
Or else I'll blow your flicker-life right out.

WILL-O'-THE-WISP:
You are the master here beyond a doubt,
And so I'll do my best to serve you nicely.
Remember, though! The mountain is magic-mad tonight,
And if you want a will-o'-the-wisp to lend you light
You mustn't take these matters too precisely.

[FAUST, MEPHISTOPHELES, WILL-O'-THE-WISP *in alternating song.*]
3870   Having entered, as it seems,
Realms of magic and of dreams,
Guide us well so that we may
Get along our upward way
Through the vast and empty waste.
        Tree after tree, with what mad haste
They rush past us as we go,
See the boulders bending low,
And the rocks of long-nosed sort,
How they snore and how they snort.
3880   Athwart the turf, the stones athwart,
Brook and brooklet speeds along.
Is it rustling? Is it song?
Do I hear love's sweet lament
Singing of days from heaven sent?
What we hope and what we love!
And the echo is retold
Like a tale from times of old.
        To-whit! To-whoo! it sounds away,
Screech owl, plover, and the jay;
3890   Have all these stayed wide awake?
Are those efts amid the brake?
Long of haunch and thick of paunch!
And the roots that wind and coil
Snakelike out of stone and soil
Knot the bonds of wondrous snares,

Scare us, take us unawares;
Out of tough and living gnarls
Polyp arms reach out in snarls
For the traveler's foot. Mice scurry

3900   Thousand-colored by drove and flurry
Through the moss and through the heather!
And the fireflies in ascent
Densely swarm and swirl together,
Escort to bewilderment.
        Have we stopped or are we trying
To continue onward flying?
Everything is whirling by,
Rocks and trees are making faces,
Wandering lights in many places

3910   Bloat and bulge and multiply.

MEPHISTOPHELES:

Grab my cloak-end and hold tight.
Here's a sort of medium height
Which for our amazement shows
How Mammon in the mountain glows.

FAUST:

How oddly in the valley bottoms gleams
A dull glow like the break of day,
And even in the chasm's deepest seams
It probes and gropes its searching way.
There steam puffs forth, there vapor twines,

3920   Here through the mist the splendor shines,
Now dwindling to a slender thread,
Now gushing like a fountainhead.
It fans out in a hundred veins
A long stretch of the valley run,
Then where the narrow pass constrains
Its course, it merges into one.
There sparks are gusting high and higher
Like golden sand strewn on the night.
Look! There along its entire height

3930   The cliff-face kindles into fire.

MEPHISTOPHELES:

Has not Sir Mammon done some fine contriving
To illuminate his palace hall?
You're lucky to have seen it all.
But now I scent the boisterous guests arriving.

FAUST:

How the wind's bride rides the air!
How she beats my back with cuff and blow!

MEPHISTOPHELES:
>   Grab on to this cliff's ancient ribs with care
>   Or she will hurl you to the chasm far below.
>   A mist has thickened the night.
3940
>   Hark! Through the forests, what a crashing!
>   The startled owls fly up in fright.
>   Hark! The splitting and the smashing
>   Of pillars in the greenwood hall!
>   Boughs strain and snap and fall.
>   The tree trunks' mighty moaning!
>   The tree roots' creaking and groaning!
>   In fearful entanglement they all
>   Go tumbling to their crushing fall,
>   And through the wreckage-littered hollows
3950
>   The hissing wind howls and wallows.
>   Do you hear voices there on high?
>   In the distance, or nearby?
>   Yes, the mountain all along
>   Is bathed in frenzied magic song.

WITCHES [*in chorus*]:
>   The witches to the Brocken ride,
>   The stubble is yellow, the corn is green.
>   There with great crowds up every side,
>   Seated on high, Lord Urian° is seen.   the Devil
>   And on they go over stock and stone,
3960
>   The he-goat st——s from the f——ts of the crone.[33]

A VOICE:
>   Old Baubo[34] by herself comes now,
>   Riding on a farrow sow.

CHORUS:
>   Pay honor where honor is due!
>   Dame Baubo, up and on with you!
>   A mother astride a husky sow,
>   The whole witch crew can follow now.

A VOICE:
>   Which way did *you* come?

A VOICE:
>   By Ilsenstein crest.
>   And I took a peep in an owlet's nest:
>   What eyes she made at me!

---

[33] "The he-goat stinks from the farts of the crone."

[34] **Old Baubo:** In Greek mythology, an obscene and bestial nurse of Demeter.

A VOICE:

                              O go to hell!

3970   Why must you drive so hard!

A VOICE:

    She skinned me alive,
    I'll never survive!

WITCHES [*chorus*]:

    The way is broad, the way is long,
    O what a mad and crazy throng!
    The broomstick scratches, the pitchfork pokes,
    The mother bursts open, the infant chokes.

WITCHMASTERS [*semi-chorus*]:

    We creep along like a snail in his house,
    The women are always up ahead.
    For traveling to the Devil's house,

3980   Women are a thousand steps ahead.

THE OTHER HALF:

    Why, that's no cause for sorry faces!
    Women need the thousand paces;
    But let them hurry all they can,
    One jump is all it takes a man.

A VOICE [*above*]:

    Come on along from Felsensee there, you!

VOICES [*from below*]:

    We'd like to make the top there too.
    We wash and are as clean as clean can be,
    And still the same sterility.

BOTH CHORUSES:

    The wind has died, the star has fled,

3990   The dull moon hides, and in its stead
    The whizzings of our magic choir
    Strike forth a thousand sparks of fire.

A VOICE [*from below*]:

    Wait! Wait! Or I'll get left!

A VOICE [*from above*]:

    Who's calling from that rocky cleft?

A VOICE [*from below*]:

    Take me with you! Take me with you!
    Three hundred years I have been climbing
    And still can't make the top, I find.
    I'd like to be with my own kind.

BOTH CHORUSES:

    A broom or stick will carry you,

4000   A pitchfork or a he-goat too;
    Whoever cannot fly today

Is lost forever, you might say.

HALF-WITCH [*below*]:

Here all these years I've minced along;
How did the others get so far ahead?
I have no peace at home, and yet
Can't get in here where I belong.

CHORUS OF WITCHES:

The salve puts courage in a hag,
A sail is made from any rag,
For a ship any trough will do;
4010   None flies unless today he flew.

BOTH CHORUSES:

And when the topmost peak we round
Just coast along and graze the ground,
So far and wide the heath will be
Hid by your swarm of witchery.

[*They alight.*]

MEPHISTOPHELES:

They push and shove, they bustle and gab,
They hiss and swirl, they hustle and blab!
They glow, shed sparks, and stink and burn!
The very witches' element!
Hold tight to me, or we'll be swept apart in turn.
4020   Where are you?

FAUST:

                    Here!

MEPHISTOPHELES:

                        What? Swept so far so soon?
I must invoke my house-right and call the tune.
Squire Voland° comes! Give ground, sweet rabble, ground!   the Devil
Grab on to me, Professor! In one bound
We'll give this mob the slip quite easily;
It's too mad even for the likes of me.
There's something shining with a very special flare
Down in those bushes. Curiosity
Impels me. Come! We'll drop in there.

FAUST:

You Spirit of Contradiction! Be my guiding light!
4030   I think it was a move that made good sense:
We travel to the Brocken on Walpurgis Night
To isolate ourselves up here by preference.

MEPHISTOPHELES:

Just see the jolly fires! Why here
A club has gathered for good cheer.

In little circles one is not alone.

FAUST:

I'd rather be up there, I own.
I see the glow and twisting smoke.
The crowd streams toward the Evil One;
There many a riddle must be undone.

MEPHISTOPHELES:

4040 And many a riddle also spun.
But let the great world revel away,
Here where it's quiet we shall stay.
It is a usage long since instituted
That in the great world little worlds are constituted.
I see young witches naked and bare,
And old ones clothed more prudently;
For my sake, show them courtesy,
The effort is small, the jest is rare.
I hear some tuning up of instruments.
4050 Damned whine and drone! One must get used to it.
Come on! Come on! Now there's no help for it,
I'll go in first and prepare your entrance,
And you will owe me for another work of mine.
This is no little space, you must admit, my friend.
Look, and your eye can hardly see the end.
A hundred bonfires burn there in a line;
There's dancing, chatting, cooking, drinking, making love;
What better things than these can you think of?

FAUST:

In which of your roles will you now appear,
4060 Magician or Devil, to introduce me here?

MEPHISTOPHELES:

Most commonly I go incognito,
But on such gala days one lets one's Orders show.
I have no Garter to distinguish me,
But here the cloven hoof is held in dignity.
You see that snail that's creeping toward us there
Its feelers have already spied
My presence somehow in the air;
I couldn't hide here even if I tried.
Come on! We'll stroll along from fire to fire,
4070 I'll be the wooer and you can be the squire.

[*to some people who are sitting around some dying embers*]
Old gentlemen, what are you doing here?
I'd praise you if I found you in the midst of cheer

Surrounded by the noise and youthful riot;
Alone at home we get our fill of quiet.

GENERAL:

Who can put any faith in nations,
Do for them all you may have done?
With women and with populations
Youth is always number one.

PRIME MINISTER:

They're too far off the right course now today,
4080   I still stick with the men of old;
For frankly, when we had our way,
That was the actual Age of Gold.

PARVENU:

We weren't so stupid either, you'll allow,
And often did what we should not;
But everything is topsy-turvy now
Just when we'd like to keep the things we've got.

AUTHOR:

Where can you read a publication
With even a modicum of sense?
As for the younger generation,
4090   They are the height of impudence.

MEPHISTOPHELES [*who suddenly looks very old*]:

I feel men ripe for doomsday, now my legs
Are climbing Witches' Hill in their last climb;
And since my cask is running dregs,
The world is also running out of time.

HUCKSTER WITCH:

O Sirs, don't pass me by this way!
Don't miss this opportunity!
Just give my wares some scrutiny,
All sorts of things are on display.
Across the earth you will not find
4100   A booth like this; no item here, not one
But what has good sound mischief done
At some time to the world and human kind.
No dagger here but what has dripped with gore,
No cup but what has served to pour
Consuming poison in some healthy frame,
No jewel but what has misled to her shame
Some lovely girl, no sword but of the kind
That stabbed an adversary from behind.

MEPHISTOPHELES:

Cousin, you're out of date in times like these.

4110   What's done is past, what's past is done.
          Get in a stock of novelties!
          With us it's novelties or none.
FAUST:
          If I don't lose my mind! But I declare
          This really is what I would call a fair!
MEPHISTOPHELES:
          The whole mad rout is pushing on above;
          You're being shoved, though you may think you shove.
FAUST:
          Now who is that?
MEPHISTOPHELES:
                        Observe her with some care,
          For that is Lilith.[35]
FAUST:
                    Who?
MEPHISTOPHELES:
                              Adam's first wife.
          Beware of her resplendent hair,
4120   The one adornment that she glories in,
          Once she entraps a young man in that snare,
          She won't so quickly let him out again.
FAUST:
          That old witch with the young one sitting there,
          They've kicked their heels around, that pair!
MEPHISTOPHELES:
          No rest for them today. Ah! They're beginning
          Another dance. Come on! Let's get into the swing.
FAUST [*dancing with the* YOUNG WITCH]:
          A lovely dream once came to me;
          In it I saw an apple tree,
          Two lovely apples shone upon it,
4130   They charmed me so, I climbed up on it.
THE BEAUTY:
          Apples always were your craze
          From Paradise to present days.
          I feel joy fill me through and through
          To think my garden bears them too.
MEPHISTOPHELES [*with the* OLD WITCH]:
          A dismal dream once came to me;
          In it I saw a cloven tree,

---

[35] **Lilith:** In Hebrew folklore, Adam's first wife, before Eve, in Genesis 1; she refused to be subordinate to Adam and retreated to the Red Sea where she haunted lonely places and attacked children.

It had a black, almighty hole;
Yet black as it was, it charmed my soul.

THE OLD WITCH:

I proffer now my best salute

4140   To the Knight with the Horse's Hoof!
So if your cork will do, go to it,
Unless large bung won't let you do it.

PROKTOPHANTASMIST:[36]

Accursed mob! This is presumptuous!
Was it not long since proved to you
Ghosts do not have the same feet humans do?
And here you dance just like the rest of us!

THE BEAUTY [*dancing*]:

And what does *he* want at our ball?

FAUST [*dancing*]:

Oh, he turns up just anywhere at all.
What others dance, he must evaluate.

4150   If there's a step about which he can't prate,
It's just as if the step had not occurred.
It bothers him the most when we go forward.
If you would run in circles round about
The way he does in his old mill,
He'd call it good and sing its praises still,
Especially if his opinion were sought out.

PROKTOPHANTASMIST:

But you're still here! Oh! This is insolent!
Begone! Why, we brought in Enlightenment!
This Devil's pack, with them all rules are flouted.

4160   We are so clever, yet there is no doubt about it:
There's still a ghost at Tegel. How long have I swept
Illusions out, and still I find they're kept.

THE BEAUTY:

Then go away and let us have the field.

PROKTOPHANTASMIST:

I tell you spirits to your faces
I will not stand for any traces
Of spirit despotism I can't wield.

[*The dancing goes on.*]

I just can't win today, no matter what I do.
But I can always take a trip;

---

[36] Proktophantasmist: This character is a parody of Friedrich Nicolai (1733–1811), an aging rationalist and leader of the Berlin Enlightenment who had written a parody of Goethe's novel, *The Sorrows of Young Werther*.

And I still hope, before I'm done, to slip
4170   One over on the devils and the writers too.
MEPHISTOPHELES:
    Down in the nearest puddle he will plump,
    That is the best assuagement he can find;
    If leeches feast upon his rump,
    He will be cured of ghosts and his own mind.

[*to* FAUST, *who has left the dance*]
    Why do you leave that pretty girl
    Who in the dance so sweetly sang?
FAUST:
    Because a little red mouse sprang
    Out of her mouth while she was singing.
MEPHISTOPHELES:
    What's wrong with that? The mouse was still not grey.
4180   Why raise such questions and be bringing
    Them to a trysting hour anyway?
FAUST:
    Then I saw—
MEPHISTOPHELES:
                What?
FAUST:
                    Mephisto, do you see
    A pale girl standing over there alone?
    She drags herself but slowly from the place
    And seems to move with shackled feet.
    I must confess she has the sweet
    Look of my kindly Gretchen's face.
MEPHISTOPHELES:
    Let that be! That bodes well for no one.
    It is a magic image, lifeless, an eidolon.
4190   Encounters with such are not good;
    The fixed stare freezes human blood
    And one is turned almost to stone—
    You've heard of the Medusa,[37] I suppose.
FAUST:
    Indeed, a corpse's eyes are those,
    Unshut by loving hand. That is the breast
    That Gretchen offered for my rest,
    That is the dear, sweet body I have known.

---

[37] the Medusa: Greek mythological figure whose hair was made of serpents; turned men into stone by looking at them. She was slain by Perseus, who cut off her head.

MEPHISTOPHELES:

> You easily misguided fool, that's magic art.
> She looks to every man like his own sweetheart.

FAUST:

4200
> What suffering! And what delight!
> My eyes can not shift from that sight.
> How oddly round that lovely throat there lies
> A single band of scarlet thread
> No broader than a knife has bled.

MEPHISTOPHELES:

> Quite right! And I can see it likewise.
> Beneath her arm she also carries that same head
> Since Perseus cut it off for her.
> And you crave for illusion still!
> Come, let us climb that little hill,

4210
> The Prater[38] is no merrier,
> And if I haven't been misled,
> I actually see a theater.
> What's being given?

SERVIBILIS:

>   A minute yet before it starts.
> A new play, last of seven in a row;
> That is the number given in these parts.
> A dilettant made up the show,
> And dilettanti take the parts.
> Forgive me, Sirs, if I now disappear;
> I just delight in running up the curtain.

MEPHISTOPHELES:

4220
> I'm glad to find you on the Blocksberg here,
> It's just where you belong, that's certain.

ARIEL:

> If mind or Nature gave you wings
>   And any wing discloses,
> Follow where my leading brings
>   You to the Hill of Roses.

ORCHESTRA [*pianissimo*]:

> Gauze of mist and cloud-bank's edge
>   Are touched with streaks of dawn.
> Breeze in branch and wind in sedge,
>   And everything is gone.

---

[38] **The Prater:** Famous park in Vienna.

Gloomy Day[39]

A field.

FAUST: In misery! Desperate! Long wandering pitifully upon the earth and now in prison! Locked up as a wrongdoer for ghastly torments in a jail, that lovely, unfortunate creature! To come to this! To this! — Perfidious, worthless Spirit, and this you kept from me! — Stand there, yes, stand there! Roll those devilish eyes furiously in your head! Stand and defy me with your unbearable presence! In prison! In irrevocable misery! Delivered over to evil spirits and to judging, heartless humanity! And meanwhile you lull me with insipid dissipations, conceal her increasing misery from me, and let her go helpless to destruction!

MEPHISTOPHELES: She is not the first.

FAUST: Cur! Monster of abomination! — Turn him, Infinite Spirit, turn the worm back into his canine form, the way he used to like to trot along in front of me often in time of night, and roll at the feet of the harmless traveler, and cling to the shoulders of one who fell. Turn him back into his favorite shape, so he can crawl on his belly in the sand up to me and I can kick him, the reprobate! — Not the first! — Grief! Grief beyond the grasp of any human soul, that more than one creature has sunk to the depths of such misery, that the first did not atone for the guilt of all the others in her writhing and deathly agony before the eyes of Eternal Forgiveness! It grinds through my marrow and my life, the misery of this one alone; you grin complacently over the fate of thousands!

MEPHISTOPHELES: Now we are once again at the limit of our wits, where the minds of you mortals go overboard. Why do you make common cause with us if you can't go through with it? You want to fly and are not proof to dizziness? Did we force ourselves on you, or you on us?

FAUST: Do not bare your ravening fangs at me that way! I loathe it! — Great and glorious Spirit who didst deign to appear to me, who knowest my heart and my soul, why dost thou forge me together with this infamous associate who gloats on harm and revels in destruction?

MEPHISTOPHELES: Are you through?

FAUST: Save her! Or woe to you! The ghastliest of curses upon you unto millennia!

MEPHISTOPHELES: I cannot loose the avenger's bonds, nor open his locks. — Save her! — Who was it plunged her into ruin? I or you? [FAUST *gazes wildly about.*] So you reach for thunderbolts? Lucky they were not given to you miserable mortals! To pulverize an innocent person in his path is the way of the tyrant, in order to relieve his feelings.

FAUST: Take me there! She shall be free!

MEPHISTOPHELES: And the risk you run? Remember: blood-guilt from your hand still lies upon the city. Over the place where the slain man fell hover avenging spirits in wait for the returning murderer.

---

[39] Scene 22, "Walpurgis-Night's Dream," a puzzling scene seldom included in dramatic productions of *Faust,* has been omitted.

FAUST: This yet from you? A world of murder and death upon you, monster! Take me there, I say, and set her free!

MEPHISTOPHELES: I will take you, and what I *can* do: hear! Do I have all power in heaven and on earth? The jailer's senses I will becloud, *you* get possession of his keys and lead her out yourself with your human hand. I will stand watch! The magic horses are ready, I will carry you away. This much I can do.

FAUST: Up and away!

Night, Open Country

FAUST, MEPHISTOPHELES, *rushing on black horses.*

FAUST:

 What are they doing yonder on Gallows Rock?

MEPHISTOPHELES:

4400 I don't know what they're brewing or doing.

FAUST:

 They soar and swoop, bending and stooping.

MEPHISTOPHELES:

 A crew of witches.

FAUST:

 They strew and bless.

MEPHISTOPHELES:

 On past! On past!

Dungeon

FAUST *in front of a little iron door, with a bunch of keys and a lamp.*

FAUST:

 A horror long unfamiliar over me crawls,
 Grief seizes me, grief common to human kind.
 She is imprisoned in these clammy walls,
 Her crime a fond illusion of the mind.
 You shrink back from her door
4410 Afraid to see her once more!
 On! Delay brings Death up from behind.

[*He seizes the lock.*]
[*Singing is heard from inside.*]

 My mother, the whore,
 She murdered me!
 My father, the rogue,
 He has eaten me!
 Little sister has laid
 My bones away
 In a place of cool, cool shade.
 And I am turned into a woodland bird;
4420 Fly away! Fly away!

FAUST [*unlocking the door*]:
> She does not dream her lover can thus hear
> Her clanking chains, her rustling straw so near.

[*He enters.*]
MARGARET [*cowering on her pallet*]:
> They're coming. O how bitter it is to die!
FAUST [*softly*]:
> Be still! Be still! I come to set you free.
MARGARET [*throwing herself at his feet*]:
> If you are human, feel my misery.
FAUST:
> You'll wake the jailer with your cry!

[*He takes hold of the chains to unlock them.*]
MARGARET [*on her knees*]:
> Who was it, headsman, who could give
> You so much power!
> You take me at the midnight hour.
4430
> Have pity on me, let me live!
> Is tomorrow morning not time enough?

[*She stands up.*]
> Am I not still so young, so young!
> To die so soon!
> And I was beautiful, and that was my undoing.
> My friend was near, now he is near no more.
> My wreath lies torn, the flowers scattered that I wore.
> O do not seize me so violently!
> What have I done to you? O pity me!
> Let me not in vain implore,
4440
> I never saw you in my life before!
FAUST:
> Will I survive such misery!
MARGARET:
> I am now wholly in your might.
> First let me nurse my child again.
> I fondled it all through the night;
> They took it from me just to cause me pain,
> And now they say that I have slain
> My child. Now I shall never more be glad.
> And they sing songs about me! How can they be
> So wicked! So runs an ancient story, but who bade
4450
> Them make that tale fit me!
FAUST [*falling on his knees*]:
> A lover at your feet implores
> You to come forth out of these woeful doors.

MARGARET [*kneels with him*]:
    O let us kneel and call upon the saints in prayer!
    Look! Underneath that stair,
    Beneath that threshold there,
    Hell seethes! Beneath the floor
    The Evil One
    Makes ghastly noise
    Of tumult and uproar!
FAUST [*loudly*]:
4460   Gretchen! Gretchen!
MARGARET [*attentively*]:
    That was my beloved's voice!

[*She jumps up. Her chains fall off.*]
    Where is he? I heard him calling me.
    No one can stop me. I am free!
    To his arms I will fly,
    And at his heart I'll lie!
    Gretchen, he called! He stood there at that door.
    And through the howling din of hell's uproar,
    Through the wrath of devils' mocking noise
    I recognized that sweet, that loving voice.
FAUST:
4470   I *am* here!
MARGARET:
           You! O say that once again!

[*embracing him*]
    It *is* he! Where is anguish now, or pain?
    Where is my prison's agony?
    You come to set me free!
    And I am saved! —
    There is the street once more where I
    That first time saw you passing by.
    There is the cheerful garden too
    With Martha and me waiting for you.
FAUST [*trying to lead her away*]:
    Come with me! Come with me!
MARGARET:
               O tarry!
4480   I gladly tarry where you tarry.

[*caressing him*]
FAUST:
    Hurry!
    Unless you hurry,
    It will cost us a bitter price.

MARGARET:

    What! Can you no longer kiss?
    So briefly gone, so soon returned,
    My friend, and kissing all unlearned?
    Why am I frightened with such strange alarms,
    When from your words, your glances, overwhelmingly
    I once felt all of heaven in your arms,
4490   When you would kiss as though to stifle me?
    Kiss me now, or
    I will kiss you!

[*She embraces him.*]

    Alas! your lips are cold,
    And dumb.
    What has become
    Of your loving?
    Who has robbed me of it?

[*She turns away from him.*]

FAUST:

    Come! Follow me! My darling, be bold!
    I'll love you with a passion thousandfold,
4500   Only come with me! That's all I'd have you do!

MARGARET [*turning toward him*]:

    But is it you? But is it really you?

FAUST:

    It is! But come with me!

MARGARET:

                  You loose my chain,
    And take me back into your arms again.
    How is it that you do not shrink from me? —
    Do you know who it is, my friend, you're setting free?

FAUST:

    Come! Come! Deep night will soon be done.

MARGARET:

    I sent my mother to her death,
    I drowned my child — the one
    Born to both you and me — yes, to you too.
4510   It *is* you! I can not believe it yet.
    Give me your hand! It is no dream!
    Your dear hand! — O! But it is wet!
    Wipe it off. But still I seem
    To see blood on it.
    My God! What have you done!
    Put up your sword,
    That much I ask!

FAUST:
>O let the past be past and done
>Or you will be my death.

MARGARET:
4520
>No, you must stay alive!
>The graves I will describe for you,
>And you must see to them
>This coming morning;
>The best spot give to my mother,
>And next to her my brother;
>Bury me off a little way,
>But not too far away;
>And the babe at my right breast.
>No one else will lie by me!—
4530
>To nestle at your side so lovingly,
>That was a rapture sweet and blest!
>But for me that will never come again.
>It seems as if I had to force my way to you,
>As if you spurned me away from you;
>Yet it is you, and your look is so winsome.

FAUST:
>If you feel it is I, then come!

MARGARET:
>Out there?

FAUST:
>To freedom.

MARGARET:
>If the grave is there,
>If Death is waiting, come!
4540
>From there to my eternal bed
>But not one step beyond—
>You go? O Henry, if I could go too!

FAUST:
>You can! If you but will! There is the door.

MARGARET:
>I cannot go! For me hope is no more.
>What good is flight? They only hunt me down.
>It is so wretched to have to beg,
>And with an evil conscience too!
>It is so wretched to wander far from home,
>And they would catch me anyway!

FAUST:
4550
>I will stay with you.

MARGARET:
>O quick! O quick!

Save your poor child.
Go up the path
That skirts the brook
And across the bridge
To the woods beyond,
Left, where the plank is
In the pond.
Catch it quick!
4560   It tries to rise,
It struggles still!
Save it! Save it!

FAUST:

Control yourself!
One step, and you are free!

MARGARET:

If only we were past the hill!
There sits my mother on a stone,
And I am cold with dread!
There sits my mother on a stone
And shakes her head.
4570   She does not beckon, does not nod, her head sinks lower,
She slept so long, she wakes no more.
She slept so we might love.
O those were happy times!

FAUST:

If all things fail that I can say,
Then I must carry you away.

MARGARET:

No, let me go! I will not suffer violence!
Let go the hand that murderously holds me so fast!
I did all things to please you in the past.

FAUST:

The day shows grey. My love! My love!

MARGARET:

4580   Yes, daylight penetrates. The final day.
It was to be my wedding day.
Tell no one you have been with Gretchen.
Alas! rough hands
Have ripped the wreath I wore.
And we shall meet once more,
But not at the dance.
The crowd wells forth, it swells and grows
And overflows
The streets, the square;

4590 The staff is broken, the death knell fills the air.[40]
How I am seized and bound!
I am already at the block.
The neck of every living soul around
Foresenses the ax blade and its shock.
The crowd is silent as a tomb.

FAUST:
Would I were never born!

[MEPHISTOPHELES *appears outside.*]

MEPHISTOPHELES:
Up! Or it is your doom.
Useless dallying! Shilly-shallying!
My horses shudder outside the door,[41]
4600 It is the break of day.

MARGARET:
What rises out of the floor?
He! He! Send him away!
What does he want in this sacred place?[42]
He comes for me!

FAUST:
                    You shall live!

MARGARET:
Judgment of God! Myself to Thee I give!

MEPHISTOPHELES [*to* FAUST]:
Come on! Come on! Or I'll leave you here with her.

MARGARET:
Father, I am Thine! Deliver me!
You angels! Sacred hosts, descend!
Guard me about, protect me and defend!
4610 Henry! I shudder to behold you.

MEPHISTOPHELES:
She is condemned!

A VOICE [*from above*]:
                    Is saved!

MEPHISTOPHELES [*to* FAUST]:
                    Hither to me!

---

[40] **staff . . . air:** The judge broke a wand as a way to symbolize a death sentence.

[41] **My . . . door:** They are magic horses of the night and cannot bear the light of day.

[42] **sacred place:** A condemned person's place of confinement was inaccessible to evil spirits; that Mephistopheles dares intrude is a sign of his desperation lest he lose Faust.

[*disappears with* FAUST.]

A VOICE [*from within, dying away*]:
   Henry! Henry!

FROM THE SECOND PART OF THE TRAGEDY

Act One

Pleasant Region

FAUST *reclining on flowery greensward, restless, trying to sleep. Twilight. A ring of spirits hovering and flitting, graceful tiny forms.*
ARIEL[43] [*song accompanied by Aeolian harps*]:
   When the blossoms of the spring
   Float as rain down to the earth,
   When green fields are shimmering
   For all who are of this world's birth,
   Elfins of high spirit race
   Haste to help where help they can;
   Be he holy, be he base,
4620   They grieve for the grieving man.
   You airy hoverers where this head now lies,
   Reveal yourselves in noble elfin guise,
   Assuage the frantic turmoil of his soul,
   Withdraw the fiery bitter arrows of remorse,
   From horror lived through, purge and make him whole.
   Four are the watches of night's course,
   Be prompt to keep them gladly and in full.
   First, on cool pillows let his head be laid,
   Then bathe him in the Lethe of the dew;
4630   Lithe shall his strained and stiffened limbs be made
   And rest deliver him to day, all new.
   Perform the fairest elfin rite,
   Restore him to the holy light.
CHORUS [*singly, by twos, and in combination, alternately and together*]:
   When the air lies warm and calm
   Over green-hemmed field and dale,
   Twilight wafts a fragrant balm,
   Wafts sweet mists in veil on veil,
   Whispers softly of sweet peace,
   Rocks the heart to childlike rest,
4640   Grants this weary man's eyes ease,
   Shuts the portals of the west.
   Night has come with total dark,

---

[43] Ariel and the Elves symbolize the curative powers of Nature.

Holily star moves to star,
Sovereign fire and feeble spark
Glitters near and glows afar,
Glitters here lake-mirrored, glows
High up in the clear of night;
Sealing joy in deep repose,
Reigns the moon in fullest light.

4650   Now these hours are snuffed out,
Pain and joy have died away;
Health is certain; banish doubt,
Put your trust in coming day.
Green dawn valleys, hills are pillows
Fluffed for shadowed rest and sweet,
Harvestwards in silver billows
Sway and surge the tides of wheat.

Wish on wishes to obtain,
Look to skies all bright aloft.
4660   Lightest fetters still restrain,
Sleep is seed coat: sluff it off!
Though the many shrink and waver,
Do not tarry to make bold;
All things tend in that man's favor
Who perceives and takes swift hold.

[*Tremendous tumult proclaims the approach of the sun.*]
ARIEL:

Hark! the horal tempest nears!
Sounding but to spirit ears
Where the newborn day appears.
Cliff gates, rasping, open; under
4670   Phoebus' chariot wheels rolls thunder;
What mighty din the daylight brings!
Drumrolls pounding, trumpets sounding,
Eyesight-dazzling, ear-astounding,
Unheard be such unheard things.[44]
Into headed flowers dart!
Lie there still in deepest part,
Under leaves, in clefts of rock:
Deafness comes of such a shock!

FAUST:

Life's pulse, renewed in vigor, throbs to greet
4680   Aethereal dawning of the gentle light.

---

[44] Cliff . . . things: Because such sounds ("sounding but to spirit ears") would, if received by physical ears, drive the hearer to madness, if not annihilate him.

New-quickened, Earth, thou breathest at my feet,
Thou who wert also constant through the night;
Already thou conferrest joy once more
And rousest resolution of great might
To strive for highest being evermore.
　　　In shimmering dawn revealed the world now lies,
The thousand voices of the forest soar,
A radiance streams in glory from the skies
Though mists in valleys still are drifted deep,
4690　And branches fresh with life emerge and rise
From fragrant glens where they were drowned in sleep;
By dull depths yielded up, hue clears on hue
Where pearls from glistening bloom and petal weep,
And paradise emerges to my view.
　　　Lift up your eyes! — Each giant mountain height
Proclaims the solemnest of hours anew.
They soonest catch the everlasting light
Which will thereafter unto us descend.
Now down the Alpine lawns steep-sloping, bright
4700　New radiance and clarity extend
And step by step their last objectives gain.
The sun comes forth! But when I that way tend,
I am struck blind, I turn aside in pain.
　　　So is it with our yearning hopes that tried
And finally their utmost wish attain
When portals of fulfillment open wide.
And now as those eternal depths upraise
Flame so tremendous, we stand terrified;
We sought to set the torch of life ablaze
4710　And find ourselves engulfed in seas of fire!
Is it great love, or hate, whose burning gaze
Strikes now a mighty grief, now vast desire,
Till we turn backwards to the earth and run
And veil ourselves in youth's soft cloud attire?
　　　Behind me only be the shining sun!
The cataract that through the cleft rock roars
To ever mounting rapture has me won;
From plunge to plunge it overflows and pours
Itself in thousands and uncounted streams
4720　While high in air mist-veil on mist-veil soars.
But O how glorious through the storm there gleams
The changeless, ever changeful rainbow bent,
Sometimes distinct, sometimes with shattered beams,
Dispensing showers of cool and fragrant scent.
Man's effort is there mirrored in that strife.

Reflect and by reflection comprehend:
There in that rainbow's radiance *is* our life.[45]

Act Five[46]

Open Country
A TRAVELER:

Those dark lindens, well I know them,
Standing in their strength of age;
Once again I pass below them
After such long pilgrimage.
Here, then, is the place at last;
That same cottage sheltered me,
On those dunes I once was cast
11050   By the tempest-ridden sea.
I should like to bless my hosts,
Such a kindly, sturdy pair,
Who were old then on these coasts,
All too old still to be there.
What good folk they used to be!
Shall I knock? Call out? — Good greeting!
If your hospitality
Still brings good to strangers meeting.

BAUCIS [*a little old woman, very ancient*]:
Welcome, comer, softly speak,
11060   Do not break my husband's rest;
From his sleep the old man, weak,
Draws brief waking's rapid zest.

TRAVELER:
Tell me, Mother, is it you
Who once saved the young man's life?
To whom now fresh thanks are due,
Both to husband and to wife?
Are you Baucis, who to my
Half-dead lips new life once gave?

[*The husband appears.*]

---

[45] Behind me . . . our life: The complex thought may be paraphrased: Humankind is no match for the sun; its vital force is more appropriately symbolized by the cataract that rushes onward because its nature is to rush onward; human achievement is a by-product like the rainbow, sometimes realized in full, more often realized only in segments of its shattered arch.

[46] After a series of symbolic adventures, including a marriage to Helen of Troy, a visit to the underworld realm of the Mothers, and the experience of a new classical golden age, Faust, now an old man of 100 years, has reached the final days of his life. Yet he is still an active man, as the development project he undertakes in this act indicates.

You Philemon, who saved my

11070 Drowning treasure from the wave?
By the flames of your quick fire,
By your bell's sweet silver sound,
That adventure grim and dire
Safe conclusion from you found.
   Let me step down here a way,
Gazing on the boundless sea;
Let me kneel and let me pray,
For my heart oppresses me.

[*He walks forward on the dune.*]
PHILEMON [*to* BAUCIS]:
Hurry now to set the table

11080 Underneath the garden trees.
Let him go, he is not able
To believe what his eye sees.

[*standing next to the* TRAVELER]
That by which you were mistreated,
Wave on wild wave foaming, lies—
See you!—as a garden treated,
As a scene from Paradise.
Aging, I was not on hand
To be helpful as before;
While my strength waned, waves were banned

11090 Far out from the former shore.
Clever lords set daring wights
Dredging ditches, damming, diking,
Curbing ocean's sovereign rights,
Ruling it to their own liking.
Field on field, see! green and sweet,
Meadow, garden, forest, town.—
Come, however, come and eat,
For the sun will soon be down.—
Sails loom there against the west

11100 Seeking port and safe repair;
Like the birds, they know their nest,
For the harbor now is there.
Thus at furthest range of sight
Lies the blue fringe of the main,
All the rest to left and right
Is a thickly peopled plain.

[*In the garden. The three at table.*]

BAUCIS:

> You are silent? do not eat
> Though your lips are starved for food?

PHILEMON:

> He is marveling at the feat;
11110 > Tell him how those matters stood.

BAUCIS:

> As for marvels, this was one!
> Even now it troubles me;
> For the whole affair was done
> Not as rightful things should be.

PHILEMON:

> Should the Emperor be to blame
> If he let him have this shore?
> Did a herald not proclaim
> That with trumpets at our door?
> Near our dunes they first were seen;
11120 > Swiftly tents and shacks appeared.
> But amid the verdant green
> Soon a palace was upreared.

BAUCIS:

> Daytimes, noisy varlets might
> Vainly hack and delve away;
> Where the flamelets swarmed by night
> Stood a dike the following day.
> Human sacrifices bled,
> Nighttime heard them shriek and wail,
> Seawards rolled the tides of red,
11130 > Morning saw a new canal.
> Godless is he, and he still
> Wants our cottage, wants our trees,
> As a swaggering neighbor, will
> Have us as dependencies.

PHILEMON:

> Yet he offered us a fine
> Homestead on the new-made land.

BAUCIS:

> Trust no bottom dredged from brine,
> On your headland make your stand!

PHILEMON:

> To our chapel come away
11140 > Final sunlight to behold,
> Let us sound the bells and pray
> Kneeling to the God of old.

Palace

Spacious ornamental garden; a large, straight canal. FAUST *in extreme old age, walking and meditating.*

LYNCEUS THE TOWER WARDEN [*through a speaking-trumpet*]:

>   The sun sinks down, the final ships
>   Are moving briskly into port.
>   One mighty barque makes for the slips
>   On the canal close by your court.
>   The colored ensigns flutter faster,
>   The sturdy masts stand tall and straight,
>   The boatman hails you as his master,
> 11150   And Fortune hails you as most great.

[*The little bell rings out on the dune.*]

FAUST [*starting up*]:

>   Accursed bell! In profanation,
>   Like spiteful shot it wounds my ear;
>   Before me lies my vast creation,
>   Vexation dogs me at the rear;
>   The envious sound reminds me still
>   Complete possession is not mine,
>   The brown hut on the linden hill,
>   The moldering church is still not mine.
>   If I desired its coolness, I
> 11160   Would seek its alien shade with fear,
>   A thorn to my foot, a thorn to my eye.
>   Would I were far away from here!

TOWER WARDEN [*as above*]:

>   How gaily comes the boat with sails
>   Before the gentle evening gales.
>   How swift its course looms up with hoard
>   Of boxes, bales, and chests aboard.

[*A splendid ship richly and colorfully laden with produce of foreign climes.* MEPHISTOPHELES. *The* THREE MIGHTY MEN.]

CHORUS:

>   And so we land,
>   And so we meet.
>   Our master and
> 11170   Our lord we greet.

[*They disembark; the wares are brought ashore.*]

MEPHISTOPHELES:

>   So we have proved ourselves, content
>   If we our master's praises earn.
>   We had but two ships when we went
>   But now have twenty on return.

The mighty things that we have wrought
Show by the cargo we have brought.
Free ocean is mind's liberation:
Who there cares for deliberation!
What counts is sudden grasp and grip
11180 To catch a fish or catch a ship,
And once you have control of three,
A fourth is hooked quite easily;
The fifth is in a sorry plight
For you have might and therefore right.
"What" is the question, never "How."
If I don't mix up stern and bow,
Then business, war, and piracy
Are an unsevered trinity.

THE THREE MIGHTY MEN:
No thanks we get!
11190 We get no thanks!
Our master thinks
Our cargo stinks.
He makes a face,
He takes no pleasure
For all we bring
Him royal treasure.

MEPHISTOPHELES:
Expect no more.
What do you care?
After all,
11200 You got your share.

THE MEN:
That was only
In sport. Now we
Demand to share
Equally.

MEPHISTOPHELES:
First arrange
In hall on hall
These costly items
One and all.
Once he sees
11210 The precious sight,
Once he reckons
Costs aright,
He won't skimp
You in the least,
He'll give the fleet

Feast on feast.
The gay birds come with morning's tide
And for them I can best provide.

[*The cargo is removed.*]
MEPHISTOPHELES [*to* FAUST]:
    With solemn brow, with somber glance
11220   You take these noble gifts of Chance;
    Your wisdom has been glorified,
    The shore and ocean are allied,
    In swift career from shore the sea
    Accepts your vessels willingly;
    Admit that now your arm extends
    From here to earth's extremest ends.
    Here it began, on this spot stood
    The very first poor shack of wood;
    A little ditch was scraped in loam
11230   Where now the oar leaps swift with foam.
    Your own high thought, your servers' toil
    Have won the prize from sea and soil.
    From here . . .

FAUST:
              O be that "here" accursed!
    It's just the thing I mind the worst.
    I must tell you as my ally
    I cannot bear it, I am maimed
    In heart, blow after blow, thereby,
    And telling you, I am ashamed.
    Those old folks up there ought to move,
11240   I'd like those lindens for my seat;
    Those few trees not my own disprove
    My worldwide claims and spell defeat.
    There for the prospect I would now
    Build scaffolding from bough to bough
    And open vistas looking on
    All the things that I have done,
    And have in one view all combined
    This masterpiece of human mind,
    With shrewd sense spurring active feats
11250   Throughout far nations' dwelling seats.
        This is the torment of the rack,
    In wealth perceiving what we lack.
    The sound of bells, the lindens' bloom
    Give me the sense of church and tomb;
    The will that nothing could withstand
    Is broken here upon this sand.

What can I do about it? Tell
Me! I am frantic from that bell.

MEPHISTOPHELES:

Such nuisance cannot help but gall

11260   You, that is only natural.
Who would deny it? Far and near
That jangling grates on every ear.
And that damned ding-dong-diddle, why!
It shrouds the cheerful evening sky,
It butts in on your every turn
From baby-bath to funeral urn,
As if between the ding and dong
Life were a mere dream all along.

FAUST:

Resistance, stubborn selfishness

11270   Can spoil the lordliest success,
Until in angry pain one must
Grow tired at last of being just.

MEPHISTOPHELES:

Why should you fuss about things here
When colonizing's your career?

FAUST:

Then go and get them off my path! —
You know the pretty homestead where
I mean to move the aged pair.

MEPHISTOPHELES:

We'll move them out to their new ground
Before there's time to look around.

11280   For any violence that's done
A pretty place will soon atone.

[*He gives a shrill whistle.*]

[*Enter the* THREE MIGHTY MEN.]

Come! Do as your lord bids you do.
Tomorrow he will feast the crew.

THE THREE:

The old man met us with a slight.
A nice feast is no more than right.

[*Exeunt.*]

MEPHISTOPHELES [*ad spectatores*]:

What happed of old now haps anew:
For there was Naboth's vineyard too. (I Kings 21)[47]

---

[47] **what . . . too:** See I Kings 21. When Naboth refused to sell his vineyard to King Ahab, Queen Jezebel had Naboth arrested and killed.

Deep Night

LYNCEUS THE TOWER WARDEN [*on the watchtower, singing*]:
  For sight I was born,
  For viewing was set;
11290 To watchtower sworn,
  I love the world yet.
  I gaze out afar,
  I see what is near,
  The moon and the star,
  The forest and deer.
  Thus splendors of ages
  On all sides I view;
  As I found them all good,
  So I find myself too.
11300 You fortunate eyes,
  For all you have seen,
  Whatever it was,
  It still was so fine!

 [*A pause.*]
    Not alone for my delight
  Am I stationed here so high;
  In the darkness of the night
  Monstrous horror strikes my eye!
  I see sparks that dart and blow
  Through the linden trees' twin night,
11310 Strong and stronger twists the glow
  As the wind's draft fans it bright.
  Hah! the cottage is on fire!
  Walls that moist and mossy stand;
  Speedy rescue they require
  And no rescue is at hand.
  Oh! those kindly aged folk,
  Always careful with their fire,
  Now are victims of the smoke
  In disaster dread and dire!
11320 Flames flame up, red stands the shape
  Of that black and mossy shell;
  If those good folk could escape
  From that wildly burning hell!
  Tongues of lightning lightly leap,
  Through the leaves and branches sweep;
  Withered boughs, they flare and burn,
  Falling with a sudden blaze.
  Must my eyes so much discern?

Alas for my far-sighted gaze!
11330   Now the chapel goes down crashing,
Crushed by weight of limb and bough,
Pointed flames go writhing, flashing
To the highest treetops now.
Scarlet burns each hollow tree
To the very roots at last.

[*A long pause. Song.*]
What was once a joy to see
After centuries has passed.
FAUST [*on the balcony, toward the dunes*]:
Above me what a whimpering dirge.
The word is here, the sound is late;
11340   My warder wails; my deep thoughts urge
That this deed was precipitate.
But if the lindens have been wrecked
And left as charred stumps hideously,
A lookout I shall soon erect
To face out toward infinity.
I also see the new house where
In peace the aged couple stays,
Who, sensing my kind wish and care,
Will now enjoy their latter days.
MEPHISTOPHELES AND THE THREE [*below*]:
11350   We come at a good rapid trot,
But go off well, the thing did not.
We rapped, we knocked, we rapped again,
And still they would not let us in.
We battered and we knocked away,
The rotten door fell in and lay;
We shouted out in threat and call
But found they heard us not at all.
As happens in such cases, they
Just would not hear, would not obey;
11360   We had no time to waste or spare
And soon we cleared them out of there.
The couple's sufferings were slight,
And all they did was die of fright.
A stranger there put up a show
Of force and had to be laid low.
Amid the brief course of the match
Some scattered coals got in the thatch,
And now the fire is blazing free
To the cremation of all three.

FAUST:

11370   To all my words then you were deaf!
I wanted an exchange, not theft.
Upon this ruthless action be
My curse! Share in it equally!

CHORUS:

The ancient saying still makes sense:
Bow willingly to violence;
But if you bravely make resistance,
Risk house and home—and your existence.

[*Exeunt.*]

FAUST [*on the balcony*]:

The stars conceal their gaze and shining,
The fire sinks smoldering and declining;
11380   A faint gust fans it fitfully
And wafts its smoke and scent to me.
Too rashly bidden, too rashly done!—
What glides so spectrally toward me?

Midnight

Enter FOUR GREY WOMEN.

THE FIRST:

My name is Want.

THE SECOND:

My name is Guilt.

THE THIRD:

My name is Care.

THE FOURTH:

My name is Distress.

THREE [*together*]:

The door is fast-bolted, we cannot get in,
The owner is wealthy, we'll never get in.

WANT:

Here I turn to shadow.

GUILT:

Here I have no place.

DISTRESS:

From me is averted the much-pampered face.

CARE:

11390   You sisters, you can not and may not get in,
But Care through the keyhole will make her way in.

[CARE *disappears.*]

WANT:

O sisters, grey sisters, away let us glide.

GUILT:

I'll be your ally and walk close at your side.

DISTRESS:

And close on your footsteps will follow Distress.

THE THREE:

Hard rides now the cloud, disappears now the star,

From behind, from behind, from afar, from afar

There comes now our brother, and his name is—Death.

[*Exeunt.*]

FAUST [*in the palace*]:

Four I saw come, but only three go hence,

And of their speech I could not catch the sense.

11400   "Distress" I heard, and like caught breath

A gloomy rhyme-word followed—"Death."

It sounded hollow, hushed with ghostly fear.

I've still not fought my way into the clear.

If I could sweep my path from magic free

And quite unlearn the spells of sorcery,

If I could face you, Nature, as a man,

It then would be worth while to be a man.

    Such was I once, before I cursed to doom

Both myself and the world in that dark room.

11410   The air so teems with monsters ghostly shaped

That no one knows how they can be escaped.

If *one* day laughs amid sweet reason's light,

Dreams weave us round with cobwebs that same night.

If vernal fields make our glad hearts beat faster,

A bird croaks; and what does he croak? Disaster.

Ensnared by superstition soon and late,

It works and shows itself and hints our fate,

And daunted we stand helpless in the gloom.

    The door creaks, yet no one comes in the room.

[*shaken*]

11420   Is someone here?

CARE:

              Well may you ask. I am.

FAUST:

And you, who are you then?

CARE:

                But here I am.

FAUST:

Go back, then!

CARE:

           I am in my proper station.

FAUST [*angered at first, then appeased; to himself*]:
>   Then watch yourself and speak no incantation.

CARE:
>   If no ear for me were found,
>   In the heart I still would sound.
>   In my ever changeful guise
>   Fearful force I exercise,
>   On the highroad, on the sea
>   Bearing you dread company,

11430
>   Ever found though sought for never,
>   Cursed and yet cajoled forever.
>   But have you never yet known Care?

FAUST:
>   I have but raced on through the world;
>   I seized on every pleasure by the hair;
>   What did not satisfy, I let go by,
>   And what eluded me, I let it be.
>   I have but craved, accomplished my delight,
>   Then wished anew, and so with main and might
>   Stormed through my life; first grandly and with passion,

11440
>   But now more wisely, in more prudent fashion.
>   I know enough about the world of men,
>   The prospect yonder is beyond our ken;
>   A fool is he who that way blinks his eyes
>   And fancies kindred beings in the skies.
>   Let him stand firm here and here look around:
>   This world is not mute if the man is sound.
>   Why need he stray off to eternity!
>   What he knows here is certainty.
>   So let him walk along his earthly day:

11450
>   If spirits haunt him, let him go his way,
>   Find joy and torment in his forward stride,
>   And at each moment be unsatisfied.

CARE:
>   One whom I can once possess
>   Finds the whole world profitless;
>   Eternal gloom descends and lies,
>   For him suns neither set nor rise;
>   With external senses whole,
>   Darkness dwells within his soul,
>   On the earth there is no treasure

11460
>   He can grasp or own with pleasure,
>   He starves in plenty, and for him
>   Weal and woe become mere whim;
>   Be it bliss or be it sorrow,

He postpones it till the morrow;
Living in the future ever,
He succeeds in no endeavor.

FAUST:

Stop! You will not succeed with me!
I will not hear such folly. Hence!
Hearing this evil litany
11470   Could addle wisest men's good sense.

CARE:

Whether he should go or stay,
His decision seeps away;
At broad highways' midmost he
Gropes by half-steps hesitantly.
He gets deep and deeper lost,
Sees all things as purpose-crossed,
Burdening himself and others,
Breathing deeply as he smothers,
Neither dead nor yet alive,
11480   Succumb he can't, nor yet survive.
Galling "O, I should!" combined
With his painful "Never mind . . . ,"
Liberated and suppressed,
Semi-sleeping with no rest,
He is fixed in place and groomed
For the hell to which he's doomed.

FAUST:

Unholy specters! Thus you have betrayed
The race of humans time and time again,
And out of days of mere indifference made
11490   A filthy snarl and tangled net of pain.
From demons one can scarcely be quite free,
Not to be broken are the spirit ties,
And yet your power, great as it may be,
O Care, I will not recognize.

CARE:

Then feel it now, as I behind
Me leave my curse and turn from you.
Since human beings all their lives are blind,
Now, Faustus, be you just so too!

[*She breathes upon him. Exit.*]

FAUST [*blinded*]:

The night seems deep and deeper to be sinking,
11500   Bright light still shines within myself alone.
I hasten to enact what I am thinking;
No will imposes save the master's own.

Up, servers, from your couches, every man,
And gladly see the boldness of my plan!
Take up your tools, swing shovel now and spade!
Bring instantly to flower the lands surveyed.
Strict ordering and swift diligence
Will yield the fairest recompense.
In this great task one mind commands
11510   Sufficiently a thousand hands.

Great Forecourt of the Palace

Torches.

MEPHISTOPHELES [*as Foreman leading the way*]:
    This way! This way! Come on! Come on!
    You shambling lemur batches,[48]
    You semi-natures made of bone
    And frazzled sinew patches.
LEMURS [*in chorus*]:
    We come at call, we are on hand,
    And as we heard by half,
    There is, they say, a spacious land
    That we're supposed to have.
        Sharp-pointed stakes, here's your supply,
11520   Here is the measuring chain;
    The summons was for us, but why,
    Quite slips our minds again.
MEPHISTOPHELES:
    No fussing now for elegance,
    Just go by your own measurements;
    The tallest should lie down upon the ground,
    The rest can lift the sod up all around.
    Just sink the longish trench four-sided
    With which our forebears were provided.
    Out of the palace to the narrow home,
11530   That is the sorry end to which we come.
LEMURS [*digging and making droll gestures*]:
    When I was young and lived and loved,
    Methought that was full sweet,
    When frolic rang and mirth was loud
    There I would stir my feet.
        Now spiteful Age has struck at me
    And hit me with his crutch;

---

[48] shambling . . . batches: Roman spirits of the unrighteous dead, represented as skeletons held together by their funeral wrappings.

I stumbled on a yawning grave—
Why must they open such!

FAUST [*coming from the palace and groping his way by the doorposts*]:

O how this clang of spades delights my soul!

11540 These are the many who perform my toil
And reconcile the earth with its own soil
And for the waves set up a goal
And gird tight limits round the sea.

MEPHISTOPHELES [*aside*]:

And yet all your activity
Serves us, with dam and dike creation;
For Neptune the great water devil
You are preparing one big revel.
You all are lost in every wise—
The elements are our allies,

11550 And things head for annihilation.

FAUST:

Foreman!

MEPHISTOPHELES:

Here!

FAUST:

By any means you may,
Get workmen here by throngs and hordes,
Incite with strictness and rewards,
Entice them, urge them, give them pay!
I want to have reports each day of how
The trench proceeds that we are starting now.

MEPHISTOPHELES [*half-aloud*]:

They talked no trench when last they gave
Reports to me, but of a grave.

FAUST:

A swamp there by the mountain lies,

11560 Infecting everything attained;
If that foul pool could once be drained,
The feat would outstrip every prize.
For many millions I shall open spaces
Where they, not safe but active-free, have dwelling places.
Verdant the fields and fruitful; man and beast
Alike upon that newest earth well pleased,
Shall settle soon the mighty strength of hill
Raised by a bold and busy people's will,
And here inside, a land like Paradise.

11570 Then let the outer flood to dike's rim rise,
And as it eats and seeks to crush by force,
The common will will rush to stem its course.

To this opinion I am given wholly
And this is wisdom's final say:
Freedom and life belong to that man solely
Who must reconquer them each day.
Thus child and man and old man will live here
Beset by peril year on busy year.
Such in their multitudes I hope to see
11580   On free soil standing with a people free.
Then to that moment I could say:
Linger on, you are so fair!
Nor can the traces of my earthly day
In many aeons pass away. —
Foresensing all the rapture of that dream,
This present moment gives me joy supreme.

[FAUST *sinks back; the* LEMURS *take hold of him and lay him down on the ground.*]
MEPHISTOPHELES:
No joy could sate him, no bliss could satisfy,
He chased his changeful vision to the last;
This final moment, paltry, void, and dry,
11590   The poor wretch wants to hold it fast.
Time masters him who could withstand
My power, the old man lies here on the sand.
The clock has stopped —
CHORUS:
Has stopped. As death-still as the midnight.
The clock hand falls.
MEPHISTOPHELES:
It falls. And "it is finished."[49]
CHORUS:
And all is over.
MEPHISTOPHELES:
Over! Stupid word!
Does it make sense?
Over, and sheerest naught, total indifference!
All this creating comes to what?
To make things as if they were not.
11600   "A thing is over now!" What does that mean?
The same as if the thing had never been,
Yet circles round and round as if it *were*.
Eternal Emptiness I still prefer.

---

[49] "it is finished": A parody of Christ's last words on the Cross. (John 19:30)

Burial

LEMUR [*solo*]:

    O, who so badly built this house
    With shovel and with spade?

LEMURS [*chorus*]:

    For you, mute guest in hempen shroud,
    It's far too finely made.

LEMUR [*solo*]:

    And who so badly decked the hall?
    Of tables, chairs, not any?

LEMURS [*chorus*]

11610   The lease was short-termed. After all,
    Believers are so many.

MEPHISTOPHELES:

    Here lies the body; if the spirit strays,
    I'll soon confront it with that blood-signed scroll—
    They have so many methods nowadays
    To cheat the Devil of a soul.
    Our old way seems to give offense,
    Our new way they do not condone;
    Once I'd have done it all alone,
    Where now I have to have assistants.

11620   We're badly off on every score.
    Old rights, time-honored ways of yore—
    There's nothing left that you can trust.
    Time was, a soul rode up the final gasp;
    Then as with quickest mouse I'd make a thrust
    And whoops! there she would be tight in my grasp.
    Now they hang back, won't leave the dismal place,
    Inside the filthy corpse they tarry late;
    The elements in mutual hate
    Expel them finally by sheer disgrace.

11630   And if I fret for days and hours now,
    There still are questions of When? Where? and How?
    Old Death has lost his rapid strength; about
    The very Whether? there has long been doubt.
    On dead-stiff limbs I've doted often, then
    A false alarm and off they walked again.

[*Fantastic and imperious conjuring gestures.*]

    Come on, then! On the double! All of you
    Lords of the straight, lords of the crooked horn,
    Chips off the ancient block, you devils born,
    And bring the jaws of hell up with you too.

11640   For hell has many, many sets of jaws,

By different ranks and standings it devours,
But we won't haggle over rules and laws
From now on in this final game of ours.

[*The hideous jaws of hell open on the left.*]
The eyeteeth gape; up from the vaulted pit
There seethes a tide of flame in raging flow,
And through the steam-clouds in the back of it
I see the fiery city all aglow.
The red tide breaks in surges to the very teeth,
The damned swim, hoping rescue, up the bath;
11650   But the hyena champs them back beneath
And they retrace in pain their burning path.
There's much more off in nooks you may perceive,
The scariest things jammed in the tightest space!
It's good to scare the sinners: they believe
It's only an imaginary place.

[*to the* FAT DEVILS *with short, straight horns*]
You paunchy rascals with the cheeks that burn,
All fattened up on brimstone, how you glow!
Short dumpy things with necks that cannot turn,
Watch for a gleam of phosphor here below:
11660   That will be Soul, or Psyche with the wings;[50]
Once they're pulled off, she's just a nasty worm;
I'll set my seal on her, then off she slings
Down to the whirlwind and the fiery storm!
      Those nether regions watch with care,
You lard-guts! Duty bids you so.
For if she deigns to dwell down there
We do not just exactly know.
The navel's where she likes to hide—
Watch there, she might whisk past you to one side.

[*to the* LEAN DEVILS *with long, crooked horns*]
11670   You fancy bucks, you giant fuglemen,
Keep sawing air, don't stop from first to last.
With arms and sharp claws spread, be ready when
The fluttering thing on fleeing wing comes past.
She surely must find her old house a bore;
Then too, the "genius"[51] also wants to soar.

[*Glory from above, on the right.*]

---

[50] **Psyche . . . wings:** *Psyche,* the Greek word for *soul,* represented as a butterfly.

[51] **"genius":** The spirit that inhabits the human body.

THE HEAVENLY HOST:
　　Follow, you envoys
　　Of celestial joys
　　In unhurried flight:
　　Sinners forgiving,
11680　Dust to make living;
　　Down from above
　　Tokens of love
　　To all creatures giving
　　In hovering flight.

MEPHISTOPHELES:
　　Discords I hear and mawkish whimpering
　　Coming from topside with unwelcome light.
　　It's that half-boy-half-maiden simpering
　　In which a canting taste takes such delight.
　　In our depravity, you know, we meant
11690　And planned destruction for the human race;
　　The most disgraceful thing we could invent
　　Would, in *their* worship, be in place.
　　　　Just see the minions mince and charm!
　　They've snitched a lot of souls in just this wise
　　By turning our own weapons to our harm;
　　They're devils too, though in disguise.
　　To lose out now would mean eternal shame;
　　Up to that grave, then, and cling fast to same!

CHORUS OF ANGELS [*strewing roses*]:
　　Refulgence of roses
11700　Fragrance expending!
　　Tremulous, swaying,
　　Life-force conveying,
　　Branchlet-bewisped
　　Buds now unclasped,
　　Bloom fullest and best.
　　　　Springtime arise,
　　Crimson and green;
　　Bring Paradise
　　To him at his rest.

MEPHISTOPHELES [*to the* SATANS]:
11710　Why do you duck and wince? Is that hell's play?
　　Stand firm and let them strew away.
　　Back to your stations, gawks, and stay!
　　They fancy they are going to snow
　　Hot devils under with their posy show.
　　Your breath will melt and shrivel that away.
　　Now blow, you puff-cheeks! There! Enough! Enough!

You've bleached and blanched them with your huff and puff. —
Don't blow so lustily, shut snout and nose!
O, now you've overblown your blows.

11720   You must learn when to stop! When will you learn!
They're shriveled, but they're going to scorch and burn!
As bright and poisonous flames they're drifting near!
Stand firm against them, crowd together here!
All courage vanishes, strength ebbs away.
The devils scent strange fires' caressing play.

ANGELS [*chorus*]:
Blossoms of joy,
Flames of high gladness,
Love they expend,
Bliss they portend,
11730   Heart as it may:
Truth in their words,
Clear aetherwards
Eternal hordes,
Limitless day!

MEPHISTOPHELES:
O curses on this ninny band!
Upon their heads the Satans stand.
The louts turn cartwheels down the path
And plop ass-backwards into hell.
Take comfort from your well deserved hot bath!
11740   *I'm* staying on here for a spell. —

[*knocking aside the drifting roses*]
Will-o'-the-wisps, begone! Shine as you will,
Once caught, you're little turds of jelly still.
Why flutter so? Just go away! And quick!
Like pitch and sulphur to my neck they stick!

ANGELS [*chorus*]:
What you may not possess
You must abjure;
What gives your heart distress
You must not endure.
If it crowds in by force,
11750   We must take valiant course.
Love only lovers
Brings to the door.

MEPHISTOPHELES:
My head and liver burn, my heart is rent.
A super-devilish element!
Worse stinging far than hell's own fire. —
That's why you lift laments so dire,

Unhappy lovers, who forever crane
Your necks to look at loved ones who disdain.
    Me too! But what makes my head that way tend?
11760 Am I not sworn to fight them to the end?
I used to find them such a hateful sight.
Has something alien pierced me through and through?
I love to have these darling boys in view.
What keeps me now from cursing them tonight?
If *I* am gulled at this late date,
Who will then as "the Fool" be styled?
These handsome rascals that I hate
Seem just too lovely, and I am beguiled. —
    Now pretty lads, come tell me true:
11770 Are you too not of Lucifer's family?
You're just so nice, I'd like a kiss from you,
I feel you're just the thing for me.
It comes so cozily, so naturally,
As if we'd met a thousand times before,
So kitten-sly and raffishly;
With every glance you charm me more and more.
Come closer, grant me just one glance!

ANGELS:
But why do you fall back when we advance?
We move up closer; meet us if you can.

[*The* ANGELS, *moving about, come to occupy the entire space.*]
MEPHISTOPHELES [*who is forced into the proscenium*]:
11780 You call *us* spirits damned, but you
Are the real witch-masters tried and true,
For you seduce both maid and man. —
O cursed adventure! Do you claim
This is the element of love?
My entire body is aflame,
I hardly feel the burning from above. —
You hover to and fro; come down and stir
Your lovely limbs in ways a trifle worldlier.
Your seriousness is most becoming for a while,
11790 But just for once I'd like to see you smile;
That would give me a pleasure unsurpassed.
I mean the kind of looks that lovers cast.
A flicker of the lips, and there we'll have it.
I like you best, there, lad so slim and tall,
But clergy-looks don't go with you at all.
Give me a glance that's just the least bit avid.
Then, too, you could more decent-nakedly appear;
Those flowing robes are all too morals-emphasizing —

They turn their backs—a glimpse now from the rear!—
11800   The little monkeys are so appetizing!
CHORUS OF ANGELS:
Turn, flames of love,
Toward clarity;
Be the self-damned saved
By verity;
Self-redeemed be they
From evil's sway,
Blessed to be
In the totality.
MEPHISTOPHELES [*getting control of himself*]:
What is this!—I am raw with sores all round,
11810   A very Job, shocked at the state he's in
And yet triumphant as he looks within
Himself and trusts himself and his own kin;
My noble devil parts are safe and sound,
The love infection breaks out through the skin.
Now that the cursed flames are out, I call
Down curses, as you well deserve, on one and all!
CHORUS OF ANGELS:
Sacred ardors!
Whom you surround
Has full life found
11820   With the good, in bliss.
Ascend up allied
And praises wreathe,
In air purified
The spirit may breathe!

[*They ascend, bearing with them* FAUST's *immortal part.*]
MEPHISTOPHELES [*looking about*]:
What's this?—Now where can they have gone?
You juveniles have caught me by surprise
And off to heaven with the booty flown.
So that's why they were nibbling at this grave!
They've made off with my great and unique prize,
11830   The soul which he to me once pledged and gave,
They've smuggled it away, that's what they've done.
     To whom can I go for redress?
Who will get me my well-earned right?
You have been fooled in your old days. Confess,
However, you deserve your sorry plight.
I have outrageously mismanaged,
A mighty outlay—shamefully!—is lost,
Absurd amour and common lust have managed

To catch the canny Devil to his cost.
11840 But if the one of wise experience got
Himself involved in that mad, childish game,
Still, slight the folly was most surely not
Which caught him at the last and overcame.

Mountain Gorges

Forest, cliff, wilderness. Holy anchorites,[52] *disposed up the mountainside, stationed in the ravines.*

CHORUS AND ECHO:
Woodlands, they falter toward it,
Cliffsides, they weigh against it,
Root-snarls, they clutch into it,
Tree dense to tree up along it.
Waves in a foaming welter,
Nethermost cave yields shelter.
11850 Lions in silence rove
Friendly and tame around,
Reverencing holy ground,
Love's holy treasure-trove.

PATER ECSTATICUS[53] [*floating up and down*]:
Ecstasy's ceaseless fire,
Love's bond of hot desire,
Seething heart of pain,
Foaming joy divine.
Arrows, transfix me!
Lances, enforce me!
11860 Cudgels, batter me!
Lightning bolts, shatter me!
So the All may utterly
Abolish the Nullity,
Gleam the fixed star above,
Essence of endless love.

PATER PROFUNDUS[54] [*lower region*]:
As rocky chasms here beneath
On deeper chasms base their thrusts,
As countless brooklets, shining, seethe
In downward leaps and foaming gusts,

---

[52] **Holy anchorites:** Hermits of the early Christian centuries who withdrew into the wilderness to devote their entire existence to the adoration of God. Goethe here makes them symbols of intense aspiration utterly possessed by love.

[53] **Pater Ecstaticus:** The title given to Saint Anthony; this spirit is mystical with a longing for the infinite.

[54] **Pater Profundus:** The title of St. Bernard of Clairvaux; a spirit of the lower region (profundus), this spirit is earthy and sense-bound.

11870   As upward to the air above
The tall tree in its power strains,
Just so, it is almighty Love
That forms all things and all sustains.
There is a roaring all around
As if woods were billows under gales,
And yet there falls with gracious sound
The wealth of waters to the vales,
As if bound to bring moisture there;
The lightning flash of flaming dart
11880   That struck to purify the air
And purge infection from its heart—
All are Love's messengers proclaiming
Creation's ceaseless workings multifold.
May my soul also know such flaming,
Where spirit, now perplexed and cold,
In gross net of the senses caught,
Is riveted in chains that smart.
O God! Assuage and calm my thought,
Illuminate my needy heart!

PATER SERAPHICUS[55] [*middle region*]:
11890   What cloud of dawning at this minute
Parts the pine trees' floating hair?
Do I guess what lives within it?
Here is a youthful spirit choir.

CHORUS OF BLESSED BOYS:[56]
Tell us, Father, where we wander,
Tell us, kind man, who we are.
Happy are we, and so tender
Is the life that we all bear.

PATER SERAPHICUS:
Children, you were midnight-born[57]
Sense and spirit half attained;
11900   From your parents you were torn,
For the angels you were gained.
One who loves, before your faces
You feel present; draw, then, near;
Rugged earthways left no traces
On you as you now appear.
Come you down, and with the loan
Of my earthly-bounded eyes,

---

[55] **Pater Seraphicus:** The title of St. Francis of Assisi; this spirit is self-denying and concerned for others.

[56] **Chorus . . . boys:** The souls of the infant dead.

[57] **midnight-born:** Children born at midnight were thought to have little chance of living.

Using them as if your own,
View the land that round you lies.

[*He takes them into himself.*]
11910   These are trees; these, cliffsides jutting;
That, a waterfall that plunges,
By its awesome down-course cutting
Short the steep path as it lunges.
BLESSED BOYS [*from within*]:
This is mighty to behold,
But a place in which to grieve,
Chills us with a terror cold.
Good man, kind man, let us leave.
PATER SERAPHICUS:
Rise to higher spheres; mature
Unobserved by any eyes,
11920   As, in ways forever pure,
God's own presence fortifies.
For throughout free air above
Spirits taste no other food
Than revelation of eternal Love
Which nurtures to beatitude.
CHORUS OF BLESSED BOYS [*circling about the highest peaks*]:
Gladly entwine
Hands in a ring,
With feelings divine
Dance and sing.
11930   Trust in the lore
Divinely told,
Him you adore
You shall behold.
ANGELS [*soaring in the higher atmosphere, bearing the immortal part of* FAUST]:
Delivered is he now from ill,
Whom we a spirit deemed:
"Who strives forever with a will,
By us can be redeemed."
And if in him the higher Love
Has had a share, to meet him
11940   Will come the blessed host above
And warmly greet him.
THE YOUNGER ANGELS:
Loving-holy penitents,
By the roses that they rained,
Helped us to the triumph gained
In this task of eminence,
Helped to win this treasured soul.

Demons yielded from their goal,
Devils at our onslaught fled.
Spirits felt Love's pain instead
11950   Of their usual hellish anguish;
Bitter pangs could even vanquish
The arch-Satan's self. Exult!
Joyous is the high result!

THE MORE PERFECTED ANGELS:

Earth remnants still arrest us,
Hard to endure;
Were he made of asbestos,
He is not pure.[58]
When once strong spirit force
Subsumes man's elements,
11960   No angels can divorce
The quintessence
Of dual self made one;
The two parts allied
Eternal Love alone
Can then divide.

THE YOUNGER ANGELS:

Misted at rocky height
Spirits appear
Moving closer in sight
As they haste along.
11970   The cloudlets grow more clear,
I see a lively throng
Of blessed boys,
From earth's oppression free,
Joined in a ring,
Glad with the joys
Of spheres so beauteously
Decked with new spring.
With these let him begin,
And, rising with them, win
11980   Perfection gradually.

THE BLESSED BOYS:

With joy we receive
Him in pupa stage;
In him we achieve
Angelic pledge.
Unravel the cocoon strands

---

[58] **Were he . . . pure:** Although asbestos is an unburnable material, it is nonetheless material and thus not spiritual.

Around him rife.
Great he already stands
With holy life.
DOCTOR MARIANUS[59] [*in the highest, purest cell*]:
The prospect here is free,
11990 The mind uplifting.
There ladies move past me
Upward drifting.
The Glorious One beneath
Her starry wreath
In splendor there is seen,
All Heaven's Queen.

[*enraptured*]
    Highest mistress of the world,
Admit me, in this blue
Tent of heaven here unfurled,
12000 To thy mystery's view.
What earnestly and tenderly
Stirs men's hearts, approve,
And all things they bring to thee
In holy joy of love.
    Courage fights invincibly
Till thou bidd'st it cease,
Ardor mellows suddenly
As thou givest peace.
Virgin pure in fairest sense,
12010 Mother, of all honor worth,
Queen in eminence,
Of gods the peer by birth.
    Around her dense-
ly gather clouds,
Penitents
In gentle crowds
About her knees,
Bright aether breathing,
Mercy beseeching.
12020   To thee, inviolate,
It is not denied
That the easily misled
Should in thee confide.
    In their weakness swept away,
Hard they are to save;

---

[59] Doctor Marianus: A teacher of the cult of the Virgin Mary.

Who of his own power may
Wrest chains from lust's slave?
Whose foot will not fail him fast
On the slippery path?
12030   Who is not deceived at last
By a cozening breath?

[*The* MATER GLORIOSA *soars forth.*]
CHORUS OF FEMALE PENITENTS:
Thou soarest on high
To eternal realms.
O hear our cry!
Peerless art thou,
Merciful art thou!
MAGNA PECCATRIX (St. Luke 7:36):[60]
By the love which at the feet
Of thy transfigured Son God-born
Shed tears as though of balsam sweet
12040   Despite the Pharisee's high scorn;
By the alabaster ointment box
Shedding fragrance down on Him,
By the hair and flowing locks
Which then dried each sacred limb—
MULIER SAMARITANA (St. John 4):[61]
By the well whereto were driven
Abram's herds, and by the well-dips
Whence a cooling drink was given
To the Saviour's thirsting lips;
By the spring of purity
12050   Which from thence outpours and flows
Ever clear and copiously
As through all the worlds it goes—
MARIA AEGYPTIACA [*Acta Sanctorum*]:[62]
By the consecrated tomb
Where the Lord was laid of yore,
By the arm that beckoned doom,
Thrusting me back from the door;
By the forty-year repentance
That I lived in desert waste,

---

[60] **Magna Peccatrix:** The "greatly sinful woman" who washed Jesus' feet at the house of the Pharisee.

[61] **Mulier Samaritana:** The "woman of Samaria" who drew water for Jesus to drink.

[62] **Maria Aegyptiaca:** Mary of Egypt was forbidden to enter the Church of the Holy Sepulchre in Jerusalem and did penance in the desert for forty-eight years.

By the blessed farewell sentence
12060 That upon the sand I traced —
ALL THREE:
Thou who never dost deny
Help to those whose sins are great,
And eternally on high
Dost repentance elevate,
Grant to this good soul as well,
Who did only once transgress,
Hardly knowing that she fell —
Grant remission limitless.
UNA POENITENTIUM, ONCE NAMED GRETCHEN [*nestling close*]:
Deign, O deign,
12070 Amid thy reign
In radiance,
To look in mercy on my joy.
My once beloved,
No more troubled,
Joins me in joy.
BLESSED BOYS [*drawing near in a circling movement*]:
So soon he has outgrown us
In might of limb;
Reward will soon be shown us
For care of him.
12080 Too little time we sojourned
For life to reach us,
But those things he has learned,
And he will teach us.
A PENITENT, ONCE NAMED GRETCHEN:
Amid the noble choir of Heaven
He hardly knows that self of his,
He guesses not the new life given,
Yet of the holy host he is.
See how he wrests himself out free
Of his integument of earth,
12090 How in ethereal raiment he
Shows youthful vigor in new birth.
Vouchsafe to me to be his guide,
His eyes still dazzle with new day.
MATER GLORIOSA:
Rise, and in higher spheres abide;
He will sense you and find the way.
DOCTOR MARIANUS [*prostrate on his face, in adoration*]:
Gaze upward to that saving glance;
Toward beatitude,

Gentle penitents, advance,
Be changed with gratitude.
12100   Let every better sense be keen
To do thee service duly;
Virgin, Mother, and our Queen,
Goddess, help us truly.

CHORUS MYSTICUS:
All transitory
Things represent;
Inadequates here
Become event,
Ineffables here,
Accomplishment;
12110   The Eternal-Feminine
Draws us onward.[63]

---

[63] All . . . onward: These lines can be interpreted as follows. All transitory things are—as in Plato's doctrine—imperfect reflections of divine realities. Humankind's utmost striving while on earth is necessary, but it requires the complement of heavenly assistance. Transition from earthly form into eternal form is accomplished, but no words are adequate to describe it. The Eternal-Feminine is the unfailing inspiration, the moving force giving impetus in earthly life as in the life hereafter to strive from lesser stages upward toward infinite perfection. That perfection is Love; in Dante's final line of the *Paradiso,* "the Love that moves the sun and the other stars."

Heroes and Heroines

The great revolutions of the late eighteenth century—the American Revolution, the French Revolution, and the Industrial Revolution—caused social turmoil that spurred a new interest in heroes. As the old European aristocracy was displaced by a new class, the middle class or bourgeoisie, despairingly described by Mr. Turveydrop in Dickens's *Bleak House* as a "race of weavers," there arose a longing for the great man who could give shape and direction to the age. The opening line, however ironic, of Byron's MOCK-EPIC[1] *Don Juan* (1818) might be taken as a mantra of the times: "I want a hero."

HERO WORSHIP

The great man—the Romantic hero is nearly always a man—might be a revolutionary like George Washington or Simón Bolívar, the Latin American liberator, who led the overthrow of old regimes, or he might be the strong man like Napoleon, who brought order out of revolutionary chaos. Romantic writers sought heroes among such mythic and legendary rebels as Prometheus and Don Juan and among historical figures, from Alexander and Julius Caesar to Peter the Great of Russia and Frederick of Prussia. Composers wrote symphonies to heroism, like Beethoven's Third, "The Eroica," which celebrated Napoleon, and grand operas, which reached their apotheosis in Richard Wagner's *Ring* cycle (1874), reviving the heroes of Germanic mythology. In its arts and ideology, the nineteenth century would become what one twentieth-century critic has characterized

---

[1] **mock-epic:** A poem, such as Pope's *Rape of the Lock,* that treats a commonplace subject using the form and conventions of the epic.

as "a century of hero-worship." And even if sometimes the search failed to turn up a hero, the belief in heroes and the ongoing watch for them would, as Thomas Carlyle asserted in *On Heroes, Hero-Worship, and The Heroic in History* (1841), save the century from destruction: "For myself in these days, I seem to see in this indestructibility of Hero-worship the everlasting adamant lower than which the confused wreck of revolutionary things cannot fall. . . . That man, in some sense or other, worships Heroes; that we all of us reverence and must ever reverence Great Men: this is, to me, the living rock amid all rushings-down whatsoever;—the one fixed point in modern revolutionary history."

FAUST, THE DIVIDED ROMANTIC HERO

Both rebel and ruler, the **ROMANTIC HERO** lives in contradiction. As a revolutionary, like Byron's Cain or Shelley's Prometheus, he is an outsider, even an outlaw, who challenges the divine and social order of things. His isolation, however, involves him in a contradiction, for it cuts him off from those he hopes to lead. **Zarathustra**, Nietzsche's prophet of the **SUPERMAN** in *Thus Spoke Zarathustra* (1883–84), is spurned by the people to whom he preaches in the marketplace. Dostoevsky's Christ in *"The Grand Inquisitor"* demands too much when he calls for mankind to sacrifice comfort and security and choose freedom instead. These heroes cannot be both above the world and in the world at the same time. Faust is also caught in this Romantic contradiction. He describes himself as a divided man: "Two souls abide, alas, within my breast," he laments, "And each one seeks for riddance from the other." On one hand he yearns for supernatural knowledge and on the other he desires to be immersed in worldly experience. By mastering medicine, law, science, and theology, he isolates himself from the rest of mankind and by seeking forbidden knowledge he becomes an intellectual outlaw, yet he also hopes to participate in the common human experience. **Gerard de Nerval** in his "Observations on Goethe's Faust" characterizes Faust's situation when he observes "his is all the grandeur and strength of

zah-ruh-THOOS-truh

p. 201

zhuh-RAR duh
nur-VAHL

p. 188

Jacques-Louis David, *Napolean at St. Bernhard*. Painting
Napolean embodied the heroic ideals of the early nineteenth century, and paintings such as this depicted him as a noble, confident warrior. (Kunsthistorisches Museum)

For myself in these days, I seem to see in this indestructibility of Hero-worship the everlasting adamant lower than which the confused wreck of revolutionary things cannot fall. . . . That man, in some sense or other, worships Heroes; that we all of us reverence and must ever reverence Great Men; this is, to me, the living rock amid all rushings-down whatsoever, — the one fixed point in modern revolutionary history.

– Thomas Carlyle, *Heroes and Hero-Worship*

sten-DAWL

p. 190

the human race, his is also all its weaknesses." Goethe's version of the Faust story does not emphasize Faust's heresy, and it does not end with the hero condemned to hell. Faust's desire to know and experience everything, his "striving," is his great virtue and the source of his ultimate redemption. But it is also his "tragedy" in that it leads to the death and suffering of Margaret and her family; even his redemptive final project to reclaim the marshes and develop housing for common people makes martyrs of Baucis and Philemon. The play forces one to consider the costs of heroism and progress and to recognize the tragic dimensions of experience.

NAPOLEON

If Faust is the great literary hero, then Napoleon is the defining historical hero of the century, receiving high praise and blame from many writers. A man of immense ambition, Napoleon was the most admired and feared military commander of his time. He conquered an empire that stretched across Europe, from the Iberian peninsula to the Russian border, and even reached into parts of North Africa. An outsider and upstart from Corsica, a rebel from "the people," Napoleon fit the **ROMANTIC** model of the hero who would oppose the old regime and institute governmental reforms to bring order and progress to France and the continent. Even his enemies revered him as a master of military strategy and as the ruler who rescued the French Revolution from the anarchy of the Reign of Terror. Yet in the end Napoleon's promise was blighted by his imperial designs, and the other nations of Europe eventually banded together to defeat and exile him, making him an international outlaw. He ended his days alone on St. Helena Island in the South Atlantic, where he died in 1821, but lived on in the imagination of such nineteenth-century writers as Lord Byron, **Stendhal**, and Tolstoy.[2]

Byron's Napoleon, like Faust, is a man of extremes and contradictions, a hero who rejects human limitations and "aspire[s]/ Beyond the fitting medium of desire." In **Childe Harold's** ruminations on Napoleon, Byron transforms the emperor into a

---

[2] Stendhal: The pen name of French novelist Marie Henri Beyle (1783–1842), a soldier in Napoleon's army during the Italian campaign in 1800 and again during the Russian campaign in 1812. He treats Napoleon as a heroic figure in his novel *The Red and the Black* (1831). **Leo Tolstoy** (1828–1910): Russian novelist (p. 617) who studies Napoleon's "heroism" in *War and Peace* (1865–69), his novel about Napoleon's Russian campaign.

BYRONIC HERO,[3] a type of literary outlaw he popularized in poems celebrating such "mixt and extreme" figures as Cain and Don Juan. Byron's Napoleon assumes a godlike role and scornfully looks down on mankind. A restless, "unquiet" spirit, he is both the conqueror and the captive of those who elevate and ultimately humiliate him, simultaneously heroic leader and outlaw.

Pierre-Dominique **Toussaint-Louverture,** leader of a slave rebellion in Haiti in the 1790s and self-proclaimed ruler of the island in 1801, was often called "the black Napoleon." His skills as a military strategist and government administrator, as well as his ultimate fate—dying in exile in a French prison in 1803—link his life story with that of the revolutionary emperor. Both were "upstarts" who had risen to positions of power. As a former slave who liberated his country from slavery, Toussaint-Louverture assumed especially heroic stature in the eyes of the abolitionists who sought to end slavery in the Caribbean and the southern United States. **John Greenleaf Whittier,** perhaps the most influential poet among the American abolitionists, celebrated Toussaint-Louverture as a martyred hero of the movement. In his poem "Toussaint L'Ouverture," from his *Voices of Freedom* collection (1846), he describes the rebel general as he leads the slaves to freedom, declaring "The yoke is spurned, the chain is broken;/ . . . No more the mocking White shall rest/ His foot upon the Negro's breast." Whittier ends the poem celebrating "one of earth's great spirits."

too-SEHNG
loo-vehr-TOOR

p. 193

In her immensely popular abolitionist novel *Uncle Tom's Cabin* (1851), **Harriet Beecher Stowe's** hero dies a martyr's death from torture while refusing to tell what he knows about escaped slaves. He also refrains from condemning the barbarism of his cruel master, Simon Legree. His death is the archetype of Christian martyrdom.

p. 194

ARGUING ABOUT HEROISM

The celebration of heroes such as Toussaint-Louverture and Napoleon in the literature and art of the nineteenth century was part of a larger discussion about the nature and consequences of

---

[3] Byronic hero: A type of hero based on the heroes in Lord Byron's long poems, figures like Childe Harold, Manfred, and Cain. The Byronic hero is an outsider, even an outlaw—a proud, moody, and defiant man who seems burdened by an unnamed sense of guilt or misery.

I want a hero.

— Byron, *Don Juan*

p. 393

heroism. While Carlyle worshipped heroes as the saviors of the time, the Faustian figures in nineteenth-century literature often descended into self-destructive obsessions and madness. **Mary Shelley's** Victor Frankenstein dies pursuing the monster he created; Herman Melville's Captain Ahab in *Moby-Dick* (1851) is destroyed by the white whale; Ibsen's Halvard Solness in *Master Builder* (1892) falls from the grandiose tower he has constructed. And in *War and Peace* (1865–69), a novel about Napoleon's Russian campaign and the century's most sustained treatment of the subject of heroism, Tolstoy set out to prove that great men do not determine history. The real heroes of that novel are the Russian peasants, the anonymous instruments of the historical forces that ultimately defeat the arrogant strong man.

To the dominant bourgeoisie of the later nineteenth century, the heroic virtues of the old aristocracy had become suspect. Strength, nobility, and military prowess had been devalued, and more domestic qualities like thrift, honesty, and industry gained stature. Friedrich Nietzsche, however, writing at the end of the century, attacked these newer virtues, calling them "slave morality." In a wishful prophesy **Nietzsche** predicted the arrival of a race of Supermen who would reject such Christian virtues and adopt a harsh and ruthless heroic ethic in their place.

NEE-chuch (NEE-chee)

HEROIC OPPORTUNITIES FOR WOMEN

Heroes of the nineteenth century, both literary and historical, are nearly always men. The women in these heroes' world, such as Faust's Margaret, are sacrificed to the man's striving. Most women of the time were relegated to the separate, domestic sphere of marriage and housekeeping. The many female protagonists in the novels of the period only occasionally challenge this separation and seek to enter the public realm where heroism is possible. More often they are forced into a kind of martyrdom, having to suppress their energy or direct it against themselves. **George Eliot** (the pen name of Marian Evans) wrote about women who refused to accept relegation to a private sphere but who were ultimately frustrated in their aspirations for a public life. In another age they might have been heroines, women of action like Saint Teresa of Avila, who in the sixteenth century founded nunneries and reformed the Carmelite Order of

p. 202

Japanese Samurai Armor
Samurai lived by a very strict code and, accordingly, wore ornate, specially designed armor. (Art Resource)

the Catholic Church. Dorothea Brooke, the protagonist of Eliot's epic novel *Middlemarch* (1871–72), dreams of expressing her spirituality by building houses for the poor, but her public ambitions are thwarted by a patriarchal society, and she is also trapped in a stultifying marriage.

REVIVING THE WAY OF THE SAMURAI

p. 204

boo-shee-DOH

Nineteenth-century Japanese society was, in many ways, even more constrained with rules and conventions than was Europe's. By the end of the century, however, Japan had been opened to the West and its traditions were changing. **Inazo Nitobé's** characterization of the Japanese in terms of **Bushido**, the traditional code of the SAMURAI, both recalls the heroic virtues of the warrior class and suggests the ways in which they were altered by the bourgeois culture of the time. Nitobé, a Japanese Christian, relates samurai virtues to Western ethics and softens them with the Christian ideals of love and compassion. Nitobé has been contrasted with Nietzsche—while Nietzsche rejects Christian virtues for the Supermen of his future society, Nitobé calls on those values to soften the warrior culture he celebrates.

■ CONNECTIONS

Goethe, *Faust* **(p. 29); Pushkin,** *The Bronze Horseman* **(p. 339); Chekhov,** *The Cherry Orchard* **(p. 708).** The Faustian hero reappears in Pushkin's *Bronze Horseman,* in which Peter the Great's scheme to build St. Petersburg on the sea, a project like Faust's housing development, brings suffering as well as success. Are Goethe's and Pushkin's views on heroism identical? Like Faust and Peter the Great, Lopahin in *The Cherry Orchard* is also a developer, but he is thoroughly bourgeois and seems to possess none of the heroic qualities of the Romantic idealists and nation builders. Can you account for this changed attitude in Chekhov's play?

Conrad, *Heart of Darkness* **(Book 6).** The apparent Romantic hero in *Heart of Darkness* is Kurtz, the extraordinary European who sets out to Africa with the heroic mission of civilizing the "dark continent." By the end of the novella, the reality of Africa has overwhelmed his Romantic idealism and he succumbs to "the horror." Is Conrad suggesting that heroism is no longer possible? Does he offer an alternative view of heroism to that represented by Kurtz?

Flaubert, "A Simple Heart" (p. 439). Like George Eliot, Flaubert uses the genre of the saint's life, with some irony, as one of the models for his biography of Félicité in "A Simple Heart." Does his story suggest that Flaubert subscribes to Eliot's view that there are no possibilities for heroism for a woman in the nineteenth century?

In the World, **"Emancipation" (p. 814).** Consider Uncle Tom's death in relation to the materials in the *In the World* section on emancipation. From what perspective could Tom's death be considered heroic? Do nineteenth-century ideas of heroism include an ideal of martyrdom? Could Tom be said to be "emancipated"?

Melville, "Bartleby the Scrivener" (p. 851); Lu Xun, "The Story of Ah Q.," (Book 6). Consider two figures who have been described as antiheroes in light of nineteenth-century ideas about heroism: Melville's Bartleby and Lu Xun's Ah Q. In what ways do they invert those ideas? Is there anything heroic in the lives of Bartleby or Ah Q?

■ PRONUNCIATION

Bushido: boo-shee-DOH
Gerard de Nerval: zhuh-RAR duh nur-VAHL
Niebelungenlied: nee-buh-LOONG-un-leed
Nietzsche: NEE-chuch (NEE-chee)
Stendhal: sten-DAWL
Toussaint-Louverture: too-SEHNG loo-vehr-TOOR
Zarathustra: zah-ruh-THOOS-truh

GERARD DE NERVAL (GERARD LABRUNIE)
1808–1855

After his mother died in 1810, Gerard de Nerval was sent from Paris to the countryside where he was raised in the household of a great-uncle, an idyllic time that he remembered longingly in his troubled later life. He returned to Paris to attend college, and there he became one of a circle of writers and artists that included his close friend, Théophile Gautier. His failed relationship with Jenny Colon, an actress, cast a shadow over his life, becoming an obsession that shows up in many of his literary works. Haunted by mental illness, de Nerval was in and out of mental hospitals in the later years of his life, which ended when he hanged himself from a lamppost in Paris in 1855.

De Nerval is best known for his story "Aurelia" (1853–54) and for "Les Chimères" (1854), a sonnet sequence that also draws heavily on his personal life. Among his other works are stories in the manner of E. T. A. Hoffmann and an adaptation of Goethe's *Faust*.

> This passion for knowledge and for immortality, Faust possesses to the highest degree. Often this raises him to the level of a god.
> – GERARD DE NERVAL

FROM

∾ Observations on Goethe's Faust

Translated by Howard E. Hugo

Where else has the sublime character of Faust been better set forth than in this work, in these lofty meditations whose brilliance my weak prose could never grasp? Every generous mind has experienced something of this condition of the human spirit, aiming without respite toward some divine revelation — tugging, so to speak, at the whole length of its chain until that moment when cold reality comes to disenchant the audacity of its illusions and its hopes; and, like the voice of God, dashes it back to the world of dust.

This passion for knowledge and for immortality, Faust possesses to the highest degree. Often this raises him to the level of a god or to the concept we have of deity. Yet everything about him is natural and probable. If his is all the grandeur and strength of the human race, his are also all its weaknesses. When he asked Hell for the help that Heaven denied him, doubtlessly his first thought was for these seeming and apparent boons, and for universal wisdom. By good deeds he hoped to sanctify such diabolic treasures; and via knowledge he hoped to receive absolution from God for his audacity. All that was necessary to upset these dreams, was his love for a young girl. Here was that apple from the Garden of Eden which, in lieu of knowledge and life, gave him the satisfaction of the moment and an eternity of torture.

Manfred and Don Juan[1] are the two dramatic characters who come closest to Faust. But what a difference! Manfred is remorse personified. Still, he has a fantastic quality about him hard for us to accept on rational grounds. Everything about him, both his strength and his weaknesses, is raised to a superhuman plane. He inspires astonishment within us at the same time that he arouses no interest. No one has participated in either his joys or his sorrows. This observation is still more applicable to Don Juan. If Faust and Manfred have given us certain delineations of a type of human perfection, then Don Juan can be nothing more than a type of demoralization, dedicated in the long run to the spirit of evil. We feel that both these qualities are worthy of each other. Yet the result is the same for all three of these heroes. Love for women finally defeats them! . . .

What a parallel is to be drawn between these three different, yet so great, creations! . . . I dare not allow myself to be forced to continue it! Given that Faust is quite superior to the other two; again, how much Margareta surpasses Don Juan's vulgar conquests and that imagined Astarte of Manfred!

---

[1] Manfred and Don Juan: The heroes of two long poems by Lord Byron, *Manfred* (1817) and *Don Juan* (1819–24).

GEORGE GORDON, LORD BYRON
1788–1824

The most notorious of the English **ROMANTIC** poets, Lord Byron was viewed in his own time, particularly in Europe, as the model Romantic bard. The heroes of his poems—Childe Harold, Manfred, Don Juan, and others—became versions of the **"BYRONIC HERO,"** a moody and restless wanderer, haunted by an unnamed guilt in his mysterious past. Byron himself, in his own time, was assumed to be the source for these tormented figures. His life does provide much to support that hypothesis. A nobleman who assumed his title at age ten, he dissipated much of his inheritance in riotous living; carried on a scandalous affair with his half-sister, Augusta Leigh; separated from his wife, Annabella Milbanke, after a year of marriage; and fathered an illegitimate child by poet Percy Bysshe Shelley's wife's sister, Claire Clairmont. Serving a brief stint in the House of Lords, Byron was committed to liberal causes; he was also a devoted friend and a generous master to his dependents. He cultivated a reputation for himself as a kind of hero, fashioning himself as a world traveler, swimming across the Hellespont, the strait between the European and Asian parts of Turkey, and fighting for Greek independence from the Turks. In the latter cause Byron died, at only 36 years of age.

Childe Harold's Pilgrimage (1812, 1816, 1818), a narrative based on Byron's own travels throughout Europe, was an overnight sensation. After

Traveler Gazing over the Mist

This image depicts the Romantic archetype of a solitary man contemplating a vastness. (Hamburger Kunstahlle)

the first cantos appeared in 1812, Byron claimed he "awoke one morning and found myself famous." The melancholy, worldly, and cosmopolitan traveler Childe Harold, who narrates the poem, gives a Byronic cast to the places and people he meets. Even Napoleon, in the excerpt that follows, takes on the contradictory characteristics of the Byronic hero. Published in 1816, this part of *Childe Harold* was written after Napoleon's defeat at the Battle of Waterloo in 1815, after which Napoleon was forced into exile on the island of St. Helena in the South Atlantic.

FROM

∾ Childe Harold's Pilgrimage

FROM CANTO 3

Napoleon

36

There sunk the greatest, nor the worst of men,
Whose spirit antithetically mixt
One moment of the mightiest, and again
On little objects with like firmness fixt,
Extreme in all things! hadst thou been betwixt,
Thy throne had still been thine, or never been;
For daring made thy rise as fall: thou seek'st
Even now to re-assume the imperial mien,
And shake again the world, the Thunderer of the scene!

37

10   Conqueror and captive of the earth art thou!
She trembles at thee still, and thy wild name
Was ne'er more bruited in men's minds than now
That thou art nothing, save the jest of Fame,
Who wooed thee once, thy vassal, and became
The flatterer of thy fierceness, till thou wert
A god unto thyself; nor less the same
To the astounded kingdoms all inert,
Who deem'd thee for a time whate'er thou didst assert.

38

Oh, more or less than man — in high or low,
20   Battling with nations, flying from the field;
Now making monarchs' necks thy footstool, now
More than thy meanest soldier taught to yield;

An empire thou couldst crush, command, rebuild,
But govern not thy pettiest passion, nor,
However deeply in men's spirits skill'd,
Look through thine own, nor curb the lust of war,
Nor learn that tempted Fate will leave the loftiest star.

39

Yet well thy soul hath brook'd the turning tide
With that untaught innate philosophy,
30   Which, be it wisdom, coldness, or deep pride,
Is gall and wormwood to an enemy.
When the whole host of hatred stood hard by,
To watch and mock thee shrinking, thou hast smiled
With a sedate and all-enduring eye;—
When Fortune fled her spoil'd and favourite child,
He stood unbowed beneath the ills upon him piled.

40

Sager than in thy fortunes; for in them
Ambition steel'd thee on too far to show
That just habitual scorn which could contemn
40   Men and their thoughts; 'twas wise to feel, not so
To wear it ever on thy lip and brow,
And spurn the instruments thou wert to use
Till they were turn'd unto thine overthrow:
'Tis but a worthless world to win or lose;
So hath it proved to thee, and all such lot who choose.

41

If, like a tower upon a headlong rock,
Thou hadst been made to stand or fall alone,
Such scorn of man had help'd to brave the shock;
But men's thoughts were the steps which paved thy throne,
50   *Their* admiration thy best weapon shone;
The part of Philip's son° was thine, not then   Alexander the Great
(Unless aside thy purple had been thrown)
Like stern Diogenes[1] to mock at men;
For sceptred cynics earth were far too wide a den.

42

But quiet to quick bosoms is a hell,
And *there* hath been thy bane; there is a fire

---

[1]Diogenes (c. 412–323 B.C.E.): Greek Cynic philosopher. His philosophy so impressed Alexander that the ruler declared, "If I were not Alexander, I should wish to be Diogenes."

And motion of the soul which will not dwell
In its own narrow being, but aspire
Beyond the fitting medium of desire;
60   And, but once kindled, quenchless evermore,
Preys upon high adventure, nor can tire
Of aught but rest; a fever at the core,
Fatal to him who bears, to all who ever bore.

43

This makes the madmen who have made men mad
By their contagion; Conquerors and Kings,
Founders of sects and systems, to whom add
Sophists, Bards, Statesmen, all unquiet things
Which stir too strongly the soul's secret springs,
And are themselves the fools to those they fool;
70   Envied, yet how unenviable! what stings
Are theirs! One breast laid open were a school
Which would unteach mankind the lust to shine or rule:

44

Their breath is agitation, and their life
A storm whereon they ride, to sink at last,
And yet so nurs'd and bigotted to strife,
That should their days, surviving perils past,
Melt to calm twilight, they feel overcast
With sorrow and supineness, and so die;
Even as a flame unfed, which runs to waste
80   With its own flickering, or a sword laid by
Which eats into itself, and rusts ingloriously.

45

He who ascends to mountain-tops, shall find
The loftiest peaks most wrapt in clouds and snow;
He who surpasses or subdues mankind,
Must look down on the hate of those below.
Though high *above* the sun of glory glow,
And far *beneath* the earth and ocean spread,
Round him are icy rocks, and loudly blow
Contending tempests on his naked head,
90   And thus reward the toils which to those summits led.

John Greenleaf Whittier
1807–1892

One of the most popular American poets of his time, Whittier was often linked with Longfellow as a poet for all seasons. A Quaker with deep religious and social convictions, Whittier gave up a career as a journalist to work toward the abolition of slavery. Much of his literary work, particularly in the middle years of his life, was devoted to promoting the abolitionist cause. "Toussaint L'Ouverture," the poem from which the passage that follows is taken, was written in 1846 for the volume *Songs of Freedom* and celebrates the life and martyrdom of Toussaint-Louverture.

> And men shall learn
> to speak of thee
> As one of earth's
> great spirits
> – WHITTIER, of
> Toussaint
> L'Ouverture

FROM

Toussaint L'Ouverture

Sleep calmly in thy dungeon-tomb,
    Beneath Besançon's[1] alien sky,
Dark Haytien! — for the time shall come,
Yea, even now is nigh, —
When, everywhere, thy name shall be
Redeemed from *color's infamy;*
And men shall learn to speak of thee
As one of earth's great spirits, born
In servitude, and nursed in scorn,
Casting aside the weary weight
And fetters of its low estate,
In that strong majesty of soul
    Which knows no color, tongue, or clime, —
Which still hath spurned the base control
    Of tyrants through all time!
Far other hands than mine may wreath
The laurel round the brow of death,
And speak thy praise as one whose word
A thousand fiery spirits stirred, —
Who crushed his foeman as a worm, —
Whose step on human hearts fell firm: —
Be mine the better task to find
A tribute for thy lofty mind,
Amidst whose gloomy vengeance shone

---

[1]Besançon: City in east-central France where Toussaint-Louverture was imprisoned and buried.

Some milder virtues all thine own, —
Some gleams of feeling, pure and warm,
Like sunshine on a sky of storm, —
Proofs that the Negro's heart retains
Some nobleness amidst its chains, —
That kindness to the wronged is never
    Without its excellent reward, —
Holy to human-kind, and ever
    Acceptable to God.

❧ HARRIET BEECHER STOWE
1811–1896

> Daughter of the influential Congregational clergyman Lyman Beecher, Harriet Beecher Stowe is best known for *Uncle Tom's Cabin* (1851), her best-selling abolitionist novel. Although a New Englander by birth, she learned about slavery firsthand during two decades spent in Cincinnati, a border town between the North and the South and an important station of the Underground Railway. Her novel, more than 300,000 copies of which were sold in a single year, galvanized support for the abolitionist cause. By the time of her death in 1896, Stowe, who spent the remainder of her life after 1850 in New England, had published twelve novels and numerous articles.
>
>   The following excerpt describes the final hours of Uncle Tom's life. Although he knows the whereabouts of two fugitive slaves, Tom refuses to reveal that information in spite of being tortured by his cruel master, Simon Legree, and Legree's two goons, the slaves Sambo and Quimbo. Tom, who has been a spiritual guide to his fellow slaves, accepts his suffering and death as his Christian duty.

FROM

❧ Uncle Tom's Cabin

THE DEATH OF TOM

Tom's whole soul overflowed with compassion and sympathy for the poor wretches by whom he was surrounded. To him it seemed as if his life sorrows were now over, and as if, out of that strange treasury of peace and joy, with which he had been endowed from above, he longed to pour out something for the relief of their woes.

It is true, opportunities were scanty; but, on the way to the fields, and back again, and during the hours of labor, chances fell in his way of extending a helping hand to the weary, the disheartened and discouraged. The poor, worn-down, brutalized creatures, at first, could scarce comprehend this; but, when it was continued week after week, and month after month, it began to awaken long-silent chords in their benumbed hearts. Gradually and imperceptibly the strange, silent, patient man, who was ready to bear every one's burden and sought help from none,—who stood aside for all, and came last, and took least, yet was foremost to share his little all with any who needed,—the man who, in cold nights, would give up his tattered blanket to add to the comfort of some woman who shivered with sickness, and who filled the baskets of the weaker ones in the field, at the terrible risk of coming short in his own measure,—and who, though pursued with unrelenting cruelty by their common tyrant, never joined in uttering a word of reviling or cursing,—this man, at last, began to have a strange power over them; and, when the more pressing season was past, and they were allowed again their Sundays for their own use, many would gather together to hear from him of Jesus. They would gladly have met to hear, and pray, and sing, in some place, together; but Legree would not permit it, and more than once broke up such attempts, with oaths and brutal execrations,—so that the blessed news had to circulate from individual to individual. Yet who can speak the simple joy with which some of these poor outcasts, to whom life was a joyless journey to a dark unknown, heard of a compassionate Redeemer and a heavenly home? It is the statement of missionaries, that, of all races of the earth, none have received the Gospel with such eager docility as the African. The principle of reliance and unquestioning faith, which is its foundation, is more a native element in this race than any other; and it has often been found among them, that a stray seed of truth, borne on some breeze of accident into hearts the most ignorant, has sprung up into fruit, whose abundance has shamed that of higher and more skillful culture. . . .

The hunt was long, animated, and thorough, but unsuccessful; . . .

"Now, Quimbo," said Legree, as he stretched himself down in the sitting-room, "you jest go and walk that Tom up here, right away! The old cuss is at the bottom of this yer whole matter; and I 'll have it out of his old black hide, or I 'll know the reason why."

Sambo and Quimbo, both, though hating each other, were joined in one mind by a no less cordial hatred of Tom. Legree had told them, at first, that he had bought him for a general overseer, in his absence; and this had begun an ill will, on their part, which had increased, in their debased and servile natures, as they saw him becoming obnoxious to their master's displeasure. Quimbo, therefore, departed, with a will, to execute his orders.

Tom heard the message with a forewarning heart; for he knew all the plan of the fugitives' escape, and the place of their present concealment; he knew the deadly character of the man he had to deal with, and his despotic power. But he felt strong in God to meet death, rather than betray the helpless.

He set his basket down by the row, and, looking up, said, "Into thy hands I commend my spirit! Thou hast redeemed me, O Lord God of truth!" and then quietly yielded himself to the rough, brutal grasp with which Quimbo seized him.

"Ay, ay!" said the giant, as he dragged him along; "ye 'll cotch it, now! I 'll boun' Mas'r's back 's up *high*! No sneaking out, now! Tell ye, ye 'll get it, and no mistake! See how ye 'll look, now, helpin' Mas'r's niggers to run away! See what ye 'll get!"

The savage words none of them reached that ear! — a higher voice there was saying, "Fear not them that kill the body, and, after that, have no more that they can do." Nerve and bone of that poor man's body vibrated to those words, as if touched by the finger of God; and he felt the strength of a thousand souls in one. As he passed along, the trees and bushes, the huts of his servitude, the whole scene of his degradation, seemed to whirl by him as the landscape by the rushing car. His soul throbbed, — his home was in sight, — and the hour of release seemed at hand.

"Well, Tom!" said Legree, walking up, and seizing him grimly by the collar of his coat, and speaking through his teeth, in a paroxysm of determined rage, "do you know I 've made up my mind to KILL you?"

"It 's very likely, Mas'r," said Tom, calmly.

"I *have*," said Legree, with grim, terrible calmness, "*done — just — that — thing*, Tom, unless you 'll tell me what you know about these yer gals!"

Tom stood silent.

"D' ye hear?" said Legree, stamping, with a roar like that of an incensed lion. "Speak!"

"*I han't got nothing to tell, Mas'r*," said Tom, with a slow, firm, deliberate utterance.

"Do you dare to tell me, ye old black Christian, ye don't *know*?" said Legree.

Tom was silent.

"Speak!" thundered Legree, striking him furiously. "Do you know anything?"

"I know, Mas'r; but I can't tell anything. *I can die!*"

Legree drew in a long breath; and, suppressing his rage, took Tom by the arm, and, approaching his face almost to his, said in a terrible voice, "Hark 'e Tom — ye think, 'cause I 've let you off before, I don't mean what I say; but, this time, I 've *made up my mind,* and counted the cost. You 've always stood it out agin me: now, I 'll *conquer ye or kill ye!* — one or t' other. I 'll count every drop of blood there is in you, and take 'em, one by one, till ye give up!"

Tom looked up to his master, and answered, "Mas'r, if you was sick, or in trouble, or dying, and I could save ye, I 'd *give* ye my heart's blood; and, if taking every drop of blood in this poor old body would save your precious soul, I 'd give 'em freely, as the Lord gave his for me. Oh, Mas'r! don't bring this great sin on your soul! It will hurt you more than 't will me! Do the worst you can, my troubles 'll be over soon; but, if ye don't repent, yours won't *never* end!"

Like a strange snatch of heavenly music, heard in the lull of a tempest, this burst of feeling made a moment's blank pause. Legree stood aghast, and looked at Tom; and there was such a silence that the tick of the old clock could be heard, measuring, with silent touch, the last moments of mercy and probation to that hardened heart.

It was but a moment. There was one hesitating pause, — one irresolute, relenting thrill,—and the spirit of evil came back, with sevenfold vehemence; and Legree, foaming with rage, smote his victim to the ground.

Scenes of blood and cruelty are shocking to our ear and heart. What man has nerve to do, man has not nerve to hear. What brother-man and brother-Christian must suffer, cannot be told us, even in our secret chamber, it so harrows up the soul! And yet, oh, my country! these things are done under the shadow of thy laws! O Christ! thy church sees them, almost in silence!

But, of old, there was One whose suffering changed an instrument of torture, degradation, and shame, into a symbol of glory, honor, and immortal life; and, where his spirit is, neither degrading stripes, nor blood, nor insults, can make the Christian's last struggle less than glorious.

Was he alone, that long night, whose brave, loving spirit was bearing up, in that old shed, against buffeting and brutal stripes?

Nay! There stood by him One,—seen by him alone,—"like unto the Son of God."

The tempter stood by him, too,—blinded by furious, despotic will,—every moment pressing him to shun that agony by the betrayal of the innocent. But the brave, true heart was firm on the Eternal Rock. Like his Master, he knew that, if he saved others, himself he could not save; nor could utmost extremity wring from him words, save of prayer and holy trust.

"He's most gone, Mas'r," said Sambo, touched, in spite of himself, by the patience of his victim.

"Pay away, till he gives up! Give it to him!—give it to him!" shouted Legree. "I'll take every drop of blood he has, unless he confesses!"

Tom opened his eyes, and looked upon his master. "Ye poor miserable crittur!" he said, "there an't no more ye can do! I forgive ye, with all my soul!" and he fainted entirely away.

"I b'lieve, my soul, he's done for, finally," said Legree, stepping forward, to look at him. "Yes, he is! Well, his mouth's shut up, at last,—that's one comfort!"

Yes, Legree; but who shall shut up that voice in thy soul? that soul, past repentance, past prayer, past hope, in whom the fire that never shall be quenched is already burning!

Yet Tom was not quite gone. His wondrous words and pious prayers had struck upon the hearts of the imbruted blacks, who had been the instruments of cruelty upon him; and, the instant Legree withdrew, they took him down, and, in their ignorance, sought to call him back to life,—as if *that* were any favor to him.

"Sartin, we's been doin' a dreful wicked thing!" said Sambo; "hopes Mas'r 'll have to 'count for it, and not we."

They washed his wounds,—they provided a rude bed, of some refuse cotton, for him to lie down on; and one of them, stealing up to the house, begged a drink of brandy of Legree, pretending that he was tired, and wanted it for himself. He brought it back and poured it down Tom's throat.

"Oh, Tom!" said Quimbo, "we's been awful wicked to ye!"

"I forgive ye, with all my heart!" said Tom, faintly.

"Oh, Tom! do tell us who is *Jesus,* anyhow?" said Sambo, — "Jesus, that 's been a standin' by you so, all this night? — Who is he?"

The word roused the failing, fainting spirit. He poured forth a few energetic sentences of that wondrous One, — his life, his death, his everlasting presence, and power to save.

They wept, — both the two savage men.

"Why didn't I never hear this before?" said Sambo; "but I do believe! — I can't help it! Lord Jesus, have mercy on us!"

"Poor critturs!" said Tom, "I 'd be willin' to bar all I have, if it 'll only bring ye to Christ! O Lord! give me these two more souls, I pray!"

That prayer was answered.

❧ FRIEDRICH NIETZSCHE
1844–1900

NEE-chuh (NEE-chee)

Once the sin against God was the greatest sin; but God died, and these sinners died with him. To sin against earth is now the most dreadful thing.

– *Thus Spoke Zarathustra,* I,3

Friedrich **Nietzsche** is one of the most controversial and influential nineteenth-century philosophers. Born in Prussia, the son of a Lutheran minister, Nietzsche went to the Universities of Bonn and Leipzig before becoming, in 1869, a professor of classical philology at the University of Basel in Switzerland, a post he held for ten years. In his early works, *The Birth of Tragedy from the Spirit of Music* (1872) and *Untimely Meditations* (1873–76), Nietzsche wrote, in part, as an apostle of the composer Richard Wagner. But he broke with Wagner at the end of the decade and, after resigning from the university, went on in the 1880s to write the works on which his reputation is based: *The Gay Science* (1882), *Thus Spoke Zarathustra* (1883–84), *Beyond Good and Evil* (1886), and *The Genealogy of Morals* (1887). In 1889 he suffered a mental breakdown and was largely incapacitated during the last decade of his life.

An evolutionary thinker, Nietzsche replaced the Darwinian struggle for existence with a struggle for power. His ideal was the SUPERMAN *(Übermensch),* a superior man who unites the Dionysian (passion) and the Apollonian (reason), creatively employing both to become a higher type of human being. Such fulfillment, Nietzsche thought, was thwarted by both ENLIGHTENMENT rationalism, which encouraged conformity, and Christianity, which promoted weakness and failure. The Superman, by contrast, celebrated the passions and the body as well as the mind, affirming this world and the present moment rather than otherworldly consolation, thus taking responsibility for his own freedom and destiny. The passage from *The Gay Science* describes the new age that Nietzsche envisages and the men who will prepare the way for the Superman. The selec-

Zoroaster or Zarathustra Educating His People
This illustration comes from a series of late-nineteenth-century collectors' cards found in French bouillon-cube containers. Zoraster, or Zarathustra, was an ancient figure who preached a dualistic, good-versus-evil, apocalyptic philosophy. He is credited with founding Zoroastrianism, thought by some to be the first monotheistic religion. It is still practiced by a small community today. (Art Archive)

tion from *Thus Spoke Zarathustra* picks up after Zarathustra has spent ten years in the wilderness and has returned to society as a prophet, bringing news of the Superman and seeking the men who will prepare the way for him. He will discover, however, that those in the marketplace are not ready to hear his message. Nietzsche's use of literary forms to communicate philosophical ideas was a practice adopted by such later philosophers as Sartre and Camus, who developed their philosophical

The secret of the greatest fruitfulness and the greatest enjoyment of existence is: to *live dangerously*!
– *The Gay Science*, 283

statements in novels and plays. The influence of Nietzsche's ideas on twentieth-century writers, especially the EXISTENTIALISTS, was profound.

A note on the translation: Walter Kauffmann avoids the biblical rhetoric often used by Nietzsche's translators. His strategy reduces the shock effect of Nietzsche's assertions and gives the ideas more direct statement. Consistent with this strategy, he renders the concept by which Nietzsche is best known as *overman* rather than *superman*.

FROM

 # The Gay Science

Translated by Walter Kaufmann

[283]

Preparatory men. I welcome all signs that a more manly, a warlike, age is about to begin, an age which, above all, will give honor to valor once again. For this age shall prepare the way for one yet higher, and it shall gather the strength which this higher age will need one day—this age which is to carry heroism into the pursuit of knowledge and *wage wars* for the sake of thoughts and their consequences. To this end we now need many preparatory valorous men who cannot leap into being out of nothing—any more than out of the sand and slime of our present civilization and metropolitanism: men who are bent on seeking for that aspect in all things which must be *overcome;* men characterized by cheerfulness, patience, unpretentiousness, and contempt for all great vanities, as well as by magnanimity in victory and forbearance regarding the small vanities of the vanquished; men possessed of keen and free judgment concerning all victors and the share of chance in every victory and every fame; men who have their own festivals, their own weekdays, their own periods of mourning, who are accustomed to command with assurance and are no less ready to obey when necessary, in both cases equally proud and serving their own cause; men who are in greater danger, more fruitful, and happier! For, believe me, the secret of the greatest fruitfulness and the greatest enjoyment of existence is: to *live dangerously!* Build your cities under Vesuvius[1]! Send your ships into uncharted seas! Live at war with your peers and yourselves! Be robbers and conquerors, as long as you cannot be rulers and owners, you lovers of knowledge! Soon the age will be past when you could be satisfied to live like shy deer, hidden in the woods! At long last the pursuit of knowledge will reach out for its due: it will want to *rule* and *own*, and you with it!

---

[1]**Vesuvius:** Volcano near Naples in Italy; an eruption of Vesuvius buried the city of Pompeii in 79 B.C.E.

FROM

∾ Thus Spoke Zarathustra: First Part

Translated by Walter Kaufmann

3

When Zarathustra came into the next town, which lies on the edge of the forest, he found many people gathered together in the market place; for it had been promised that there would be a tightrope walker. And Zarathustra spoke thus to the people:

"*I teach you the overman.* Man is something that shall be overcome. What have you done to overcome him?

"All beings so far have created something beyond themselves; and do you want to be the ebb of this great flood and even go back to the beasts rather than overcome man? What is the ape to man? A laughingstock or a painful embarrassment. And man shall be just that for the overman: a laughingstock or a painful embarrassment. You have made your way from worm to man, and much in you is still worm. Once you were apes, and even now, too, man is more ape than any ape.

"Whoever is the wisest among you is also a mere conflict and cross between plant and ghost. But do I bid you become ghosts or plants?

"Behold, I teach you the overman. The overman is the meaning of the earth. Let your will say: the overman *shall be* the meaning of the earth! I beseech you, my brothers, *remain faithful to the earth,* and do not believe those who speak to you of otherworldly hopes! Poison-mixers are they, whether they know it or not. Despisers of life are they, decaying and poisoned themselves, of whom the earth is weary: so let them go.

"Once the sin against God was the greatest sin; but God died, and these sinners died with him. To sin against the earth is now the most dreadful thing, and to esteem the entrails of the unknowable higher than the meaning of the earth.

"Once the soul looked contemptuously upon the body, and then this contempt was the highest: she wanted the body meager, ghastly, and starved. Thus she hoped to escape it and the earth. Oh, this soul herself was still meager, ghastly, and starved: and cruelty was the lust of this soul. But you, too, my brothers, tell me: what does your body proclaim of your soul? Is not your soul poverty and filth and wretched contentment?

"Verily, a polluted stream is man. One must be a sea to be able to receive a polluted stream without becoming unclean. Behold, I teach you the overman: he is this sea; in him your great contempt can go under.

"What is the greatest experience you can have? It is the hour of the great contempt. The hour in which your happiness, too, arouses your disgust, and even your reason and your virtue.

"The hour when you say, 'What matters my happiness? It is poverty and filth and wretched contentment. But my happiness ought to justify existence itself.'

"The hour when you say, 'What matters my reason? Does it crave knowledge as the lion his food? It is poverty and filth and wretched contentment.'

"The hour when you say, 'What matters my virtue? As yet it has not made me rage. How weary I am of my good and my evil! All that is poverty and filth and wretched contentment.'

"The hour when you say, 'What matters my justice? I do not see that I am flames and fuel. But the just are flames and fuel.'

"The hour when you say, 'What matters my pity? Is not pity the cross on which he is nailed who loves man? But my pity is no crucifixion.'

"Have you yet spoken thus? Have you yet cried thus? Oh, that I might have heard you cry thus!

'Not your sin but your thrift cries to heaven; your meanness even in your sin cries to heaven.

"Where is the lightning to lick you with its tongue? Where is the frenzy with which you should be inoculated?

"Behold, I teach you the overman: he is this lightning, he is this frenzy."

When Zarathustra had spoken thus, one of the people cried: "Now we have heard enough about the tightrope walker; now let us see him too!" And all the people laughed at Zarathustra. But the tightrope walker, believing that the word concerned him, began his performance.

✎ GEORGE ELIOT (MARIAN EVANS)
1819–1880

Here and there is born a Saint Theresa, foundress of nothing, whose loving heart-beats and sobs after an unattained goodness tremble off and are dispersed among hindrances, instead of centering in some long-recognisable deed.

– ELIOT, Prelude to
Middlemarch

A native of rural Nottinghamshire in England, Marian Evans, who as a novelist used the pen name George Eliot, moved to London as a young woman, where she became one of the leading intellectuals of her day. In 1846 she translated Friedrich Strauss's *Das Leben Jesu (The Life of Jesus)*, which sought to reconcile Christianity with science; she wrote reviews and essays for the *Westminster Review,* the leading radical journal of the day; and she entered into a lifelong relationship with George Lewes, a critic and essayist, who could not divorce his insane first wife. At 37, encouraged by Lewes, Eliot began writing fiction and soon became one of the most important novelists of her day. Her fiction often recalls the rural life she knew as a child. *Middlemarch* (1871–72), her masterpiece, sub-titled "A Study of Provincial Life," traces the interconnected lives of village people, showing how their aspirations are thwarted by the mores of their closed world and by their own failings. The novel's heroine, Dorothea Brooke, wants to improve the world by building houses for the poor, but her marriage and the restrictions placed on women in her society deny her the opportunity for such public action. In the preface to the novel, Eliot compares such women with Saint Teresa of Avila (1515–1582), the Spanish mystic who founded nunneries and reformed the Carmelite Order. Women of the nineteenth century, Eliot suggests, are denied the chance that St. Teresa was given to do public works.

FROM

∾ Middlemarch

PRELUDE

Who that cares much to know the history of man, and how the mysterious mixture behaves under the varying experiments of Time, has not dwelt, at least briefly, on the life of Saint Theresa, has not smiled with some gentleness at the thought of the little girl walking forth one morning hand-in-hand with her still smaller brother, to go and seek martyrdom in the country of the Moors? Out they toddled from rugged Avila, wide-eyed and helpless-looking as two fawns, but with human hearts, already beating to a national idea; until domestic reality met them in the shape of uncles, and turned them back from their great resolve. That child-pilgrimage was a fit beginning. Theresa's passionate, ideal nature demanded an *epic* life: what were many-volumed romances of chivalry and the social conquests of a brilliant girl to her? Her flame quickly burned up that light fuel; and, fed from within, soared after some illimitable satisfaction, some object which would never justify weariness, which would reconcile self-despair with the rapturous consciousness of life beyond self. She found her epos in the reform of a religious order.

That Spanish woman who lived three hundred years ago, was certainly not the last of her kind. Many Theresas have been born who found for themselves no epic life wherein there was a constant unfolding of far-resonant action; perhaps only a life of mistakes, the offspring of a certain spiritual grandeur ill-matched with the meanness of opportunity; perhaps a tragic failure which found no sacred poet and sank unwept into oblivion. With dim lights and tangled circumstance they tried to shape their thought and deed in noble agreement; but after all, to common eyes their struggles seemed mere inconsistency and formlessness; for these later-born Theresas were helped by no coherent social faith and order which could perform the function of knowledge for the ardently willing soul. Their ardour alternated between a vague ideal and the common yearning of womanhood; so that the one was disapproved as extravagance, and the other condemned as a lapse.

Some have felt that these blundering lives are due to the inconvenient indefiniteness with which the Supreme Power has fashioned the natures of women: if there were one level of feminine incompetence as strict as the ability to count three and no more, the social lot of women might be treated with scientific certitude. Meanwhile the indefiniteness remains, and the limits of variation are really much wider than any one would imagine from the sameness of women's coiffure and the favourite love-stories in prose and verse. Here and there a cygnet is reared uneasily among the ducklings in the brown pond, and never finds the living stream in fellowship with its own oary-footed kind. Here and there is born a Saint Theresa, foundress of nothing, whose loving heart-beats and sobs after an unattained goodness tremble off and are dispersed among hindrances, instead of centering in some long-recognisable deed.

∾ INAZO NITOBÉ
1862–1933

A Soldier in Full Armour, Nineteenth Century
Depictions of samurai often focused on their stylish armor and their proud warrior's disposition. (National Trust Photographic Library/John Hammond)

Professor, internationalist, and interpreter of Japan to the West, Inazo Nitobé drew on his extensive knowledge of Western literature and philosophy to explain — by contrast and comparison — his native culture. Educated at the Sapporo Agricultural School and the University of Tokyo, with graduate study done at Johns Hopkins University and the University of Halle, in Germany, where he received his Ph.D. in 1890, Nitobé began his professional career as a professor of agricultural economics. When illness forced him to resign in 1897 and to come to America, he wrote his best-known work, *Bushido: The Soul of Japan* (1899), in English to explain the Japanese psyche to the West. Nitobé used *Bushido* — the traditional ethical system of the SAMURAI, which taught rectitude, benevolence, honor, loyalty, and self-control as its primary virtues — to structure his account of the Japanese mind. Even though feudalism had been officially abolished in Nitobé's native country, many of its qualities remained in Japanese culture. There was, in fact, a revived interest in Bushido as modernization took place, and the classic work on the subject, *Hagakare (Bushido, the Way of the Samarai)* by Tsunetomo Yamamoto (1659–1719), which had been underground for two centuries, was published for the first time for the general reader in 1906. Nitobé, in the final chapter of his book, explains the contemporary appeal of Bushido as a counter to Western materialism. However, he recognized that the age of military heroism was past and, as a Japanese Christian, he believed that Japan would integrate the virtues of Bushido with Christian individualism.

A note on the text: Written in English to explain Japan to the West, *Bushido: The Soul of Japan* went through numerous editions in the first two decades of the twentieth century.

FROM

∾ Bushido: The Soul of Japan

Principalities and powers are arrayed against the Precepts of Knighthood. Already, as Veblen[1] says, "the decay of the ceremonial code—or, as it is otherwise called, the vulgarization of life—among the industrial classes proper, has become one of the chief enormities of latter-day civilization in the eyes of all persons of delicate sensibilities." . . .

The state built upon the rock of Honour and fortified by the same—shall we call it the *Ehrenstaat*,[2] or, after the manner of Carlyle, the Heroarchy?—is fast falling into the hands of quibbling lawyers and gibbering politicians armed with logic-chopping engines of war. The words which a great thinker used in speaking of Theresa and Antigone may aptly be repeated of the samurai, that "the medium in which their ardent deeds took shape is forever gone."[3]

Alas for knightly virtues! alas for samurai pride! Morality ushered into the world with the sound of bugles and drums, is destined to fade away as "the captains and the kings depart."

If history can teach us anything, the state built on martial virtues—be it a city like Sparta or an Empire like Rome—can never make on earth a "continuing city." Universal and natural as is the fighting instinct in man, fruitful as it has proved to be of noble sentiments and manly virtues, it does not comprehend the whole man. Beneath the instinct to fight there lurks a diviner instinct—to love. We have seen that Shintoism, Mencius, and Wan Yang Ming,[4] have all clearly taught it; but Bushido and all other militant types of ethics, engrossed, doubtless, with questions of immediate practical need, too often forgot duly to emphasize this fact. Life has grown larger in these latter times. Callings nobler and broader than a warrior's claim our attention today. With an enlarged view of life, with the growth of democracy, with better knowledge of other peoples and nations, the Confucian idea of benevolence— dare I also add the Buddhist idea of pity?—will expand into the Christian conception of love. Men have become more than subjects, having grown to the estate of citizens; nay, they are more than citizens—being men. Though war clouds hang heavy upon our horizon, we will believe that the wings of the angel of peace can disperse them. The history of the world confirms the prophecy that "the meek shall inherit the earth."[5] A nation that sells its birthright of peace, and backslides from the front rank of industrialism into the file of filibusterism, makes a poor bargain indeed!

---

[1] **Veblen:** Thornstein Veblen (1857–1929), American economist and social scientist.

[2] ***Ehrenstaat:*** A German term coined by Nitobé, meaning the country of honor.

[3] **"the medium . . . forever gone.":** Nitobé does not identify the thinker he is quoting here, but the point being made is similar to that of George Eliot in the previous selection.

[4] **Shintoism . . . Ming:** Shintoism is the traditional religion of Japan; Mencius (c. 371–288 B.C.E.) was a classical Confucian philosopher (Book 1); Wan Yang Ming (1472–1529) was a Chinese philosopher and reformer of neo-Confucianism.

[5] **"the meek . . . earth":** Matthew 5:5.

When the conditions of society are so changed that they have become not only adverse but hostile to Bushido, it is time for it to prepare for an honourable burial. It is just as difficult to point out when chivalry dies, as to determine the exact time of its inception. Dr. Miller says that chivalry was formally abolished in the year 1559, when Henry II. of France was slain in a tournament. With us, the edict formally abolishing feudalism in 1871 was the signal to toll the knell of Bushido. The edict, issued five years later, prohibiting the wearing of swords, rang out the old, "the unbought grace of life, the cheap defence of nations, the nurse of manly sentiment and heroic enterprise," it rang in the new age of "sophisters, economists, and calculators."

It has been said that Japan won her late war with China by means of Murata guns and Krupp cannon; it has been said the victory was the work of a modern school-system; but these are less than half-truths. Does ever a piano, be it of the choicest workmanship of Ehrbar or Steinway burst forth into the Rhapsodies of Liszt or the Sonatas of Beethoven, without a master's hand? Or, if guns win battles, why did not Louis Napoleon beat the Prussians with his *Mitrailleuse*,[6] or the Spaniards with their Mausers the Filipinos, whose arms were no better than the old-fashioned Remingtons? Needless to repeat what has grown a trite saying, — that it is the spirit that quickeneth, without which the best of implements profiteth but little. The most improved guns and cannon do not shoot of their own accord; the most modern educational system does not make a coward a hero. No! What won the battles on the Yalu, in Corea and Manchuria,[7] were the ghosts of our fathers, guiding our hands and beating in our hearts. They are not dead, those ghosts, the spirits of our warlike ancestors. To those who have eyes to see, they are clearly visible. Scratch a Japanese of the most advanced ideas, and he will show a samurai. The great inheritance of honour, of valour, and of all martial virtues is, as Professor Cramb[8] very fitly expresses it, "but ours on trust, the fief inalienable of the dead and of the generations to come," and the summons of the present is to guard this heritage, nor to bate one jot of the ancient spirit; the summons of the future will be so to widen its scope to apply it in all walks and relations of life.

It has been predicted — and predictions have been corroborated by the events of the last half-century — that the moral system of Feudal Japan, like its castles and its armouries, will crumble into dust, and new ethics rise phoenix-like to lead New Japan in her path of progress. Desirable and probable as the fulfilment of such a prophecy is, we must not forget that a phoenix rises only from its own ashes, and that it is not a bird of passage, neither does it fly on pinions borrowed from other birds. "The Kingdom of God is within you."[9] It does not come rolling down the mountains, however lofty; it does not come sailing across the seas, however broad. "God has granted," says the Koran, "to every people a prophet in its own tongue."

---

[6] *Mitrailleuse:* Machine guns.

[7] Yalu . . . Manchuria: In the China-Japanese War of 1894–95, Japan claimed victory after pushing China out of Korea and gaining temporary control of the Yalu River dividing Korea from Manchuria.

[8] Professor Cramb: John A. Cramb (1862–1913), British historian who advocated a policy of military strength.

[9] "The Kingdom . . . you": Luke 17:21.

The seeds of the Kingdom, as vouched for and apprehended by the Japanese mind, blossomed in Bushido. Now its days are closing—sad to say, before its full fruition—and we turn in every direction for other sources of sweetness and light, of strength and comfort, but among them there is as yet nothing found to take its place. The profit-and-loss philosophy of utilitarians and materialists finds favour among logic-choppers with half a soul. The only other ethical system which is powerful enough to cope with utilitarianism and materialism is Christianity, in comparison with which Bushido, it must be confessed, is like "a dimly burning wick" which the Messiah was proclaimed not to quench, but to fan into a flame. Like His Hebrew precursors, the prophets—notably Isaiah, Jeremiah, Amos, and Habakkuk—Bushido laid particular stress on the moral conduct of rulers and public men and of nations, whereas the ethics of Christ, which deal almost solely with individuals and His personal followers, will find more and more practical application as individualism, in its capacity of a moral factor, grows in potency. The domineering, self-assertive, so-called master-morality of Nietzsche, itself akin in some respects to Bushido, is, if I am not greatly mistaken, a passing phase or temporary reaction against what he terms, by morbid distortion, the humble, self-denying slave-morality of the Nazarene.

Christianity and materialism (including utilitarianism)—or will the future reduce them to still more archaic forms of Hebraism and Hellenism?—will divide the world between them. Lesser systems of morals will ally themselves to either side for their preservation. On which side will Bushido enlist? Having no set dogma or formula to defend, it can afford to disappear as an entity; like the cherry blossom, it is willing to die at the first gust of the morning breeze. But a total extinction will never be its lot. Who can say that stoicism[10] is dead? It is dead as a system; but it is alive as a virtue: its energy and vitality are still felt through many channels of life—in the philosophy of Western nations, in the jurisprudence of all the civilized world. Nay, wherever man struggles to raise himself above himself, wherever his spirit masters his flesh by his own exertions, there we see the immortal discipline of Zeno at work.

Bushido as an independent code of ethics may vanish, but its power will not perish from the earth; its schools of martial prowess or civic honour may be demolished, but its light and its glory will long survive their ruins. Like its symbolic flower, after it is blown to the four winds, it will still bless mankind with the perfume with which it will enrich life. Ages after, when its customaries will have been buried and its very name forgotten, its fragrance will come floating in the air as from a far-off, unseen hill, "the wayside gaze beyond";—then in the beautiful language of the Quaker poet,

> "The traveller owns the grateful sense
> Of sweetness near, he knows not whence,
> And, pausing, takes with forehead bare
> The benediction of the air."

---

[10] stoicism: Philosophical school of classical Greece and Rome, founded by Zeno of Citium (c. 334–c. 262 B.C.E.), that taught the virtues of endurance, virtuous living, and self-reliance.

⟨⟨ WILLIAM BLAKE

1757–1827

Perhaps no writer of the early nineteenth century represents the revolt against the empirical philosophy of the ENLIGHTENMENT more than the English poet, printmaker, and visionary William Blake. Imbued with the spirit of the age of revolution and Romanticism, Blake strenuously condemns what he deems the slavish following of religious, social, and aesthetic conventions that stifled individual freedom and creativity in his day, and defiantly declares his personal independence from them: "I must create my own system or be enslav'd by another man's." Blake believed that God resides within each human being, and it was his goal to use his imaginative works to free other people and enable them to see the divine spirit within themselves and so to build up a world of beauty, joy, peace, and freedom. He stated this goal poetically in the preface to *Milton*, one of his longer visionary works:

> I will not cease from Mental Flight,
> Nor shall my sword sleep in my hand
> Till we have built Jerusalem,
> In England's green and pleasant land.

Although his contemporaries largely neglected Blake's work, his fiery celebration of the imagination, his revolt against Neoclassical standards, and his exuberant energy and spirit of reform have earned him a reputation as one of the most important Romantic poets.

The Visionary Engraver. William Blake was born in London on November 28, 1757, the son of a shopkeeper. He grew up in London, where he very early displayed a talent for drawing and a proclivity for visionary encounters with a world beyond the senses. When he was eight years old, for example, his father reprimanded Blake for telling him about seeing bright winged angels in a tree, and throughout his life Blake reported conversing with angels and other visitors from the spirit world who often guided his work. Never receiving a formal education, Blake received instruction in drawing from Henry Parr's school and at age fourteen was apprenticed as an engraver with James Basire, engraver for the Society of Antiquaries. There he exercised his talents on drawing likenesses from relics of ancient kings and queens and of biblical figures, such as Joseph of Arimathea, while reading extensively and trying his hand at poetry. One project in particular, the engravings for Jacob Bryant's *New System or Analysis of Ancient Mythology* (1774–76), introduced Blake to ancient myths from around the world. Bryant's comparative approach to mythology and his attempt to show that myths as varied as those from Egypt, Greece, and Rome might all derive from the same origin may have influenced Blake in later years as he developed his own mythology. Certainly, as we learn from *A Descriptive Catalogue*, Blake followed Bryant in believing that "[t]he antiquities of every Nation under

www For links to more information about Blake and a quiz on his poetry, see *World Literature Online* at bedfordstmartins.com/worldlit.

William Blake, "The Tyger," 1794

Blake produced twenty-eight copies of Songs of Innocence and Experience, *which combined engraving, watercolor, and poetry to create what some have called "composite art," as can be seen in a page from the work reproduced here. (The Pierpont Morgan Library/Art Resource)*

Heaven are the same thing, as Jacob Bryant and all antiquaries have proved."

After his seven-year apprenticeship to Basire and a brief stint studying at the Royal Academy of Art, for whose conventions he developed a strong distaste, Blake set up as an engraver in London, where he associated with Henry Fuseli and John Flaxman, fellow artists who both encouraged and influenced Blake's highly idiosyncratic work. In 1782, Blake married Catherine Boucher, who assisted him in his various activities, which in addition to writing and engraving his own works included giving lessons in drawing and doing commercial engraving. After the death of Blake's younger brother, Robert, in 1787, Blake reported having conversations with his spirit, crediting him with having inspired Blake in his visionary works. In 1800 Blake accepted the generosity of William Hayley, a conventional poet and patron of the arts, who encouraged the Blakes to move to a cottage at Felpham, on the Sussex seacoast. Hayley provided Blake with the means to pursue his own work, but he tried to tether Blake's imagination and direct him toward more publicly acceptable, conventional tastes. As a result of his quarreling with Hayley, whom he called the "Enemy of my Spiritual Life while he pretends to be the Friend of my Corporeal," Blake returned to 17 South Molton Street, London, in 1803, having narrowly escaped from being prosecuted for sedition for reportedly inveighing against the king as he removed a drunken soldier, John Scofield, from his garden at Felpham.

To the end of his life, Blake managed to eke out a living with commercial engraving and printing projects, but he continued to apply his fullest energies to his longer prophetic works, including *Jerusalem* and *The Four Zoas,* even after the dismal failure of an exhibition of his work in 1809. The visionary poet and artist was somewhat vindicated in his later years, having attracted the devotion and critical praise of younger artists such as John Varley, John Linnel, and Samuel Palmer, who helped support the impoverished poet. Turning in his old age primarily to painting and drawing, Blake completed superb illustrations for the works of Virgil and Dante and for the Book of Job. He died on August 12, 1827, reportedly singing with joy.

Songs of Innocence and Experience.   Blake's first publication was a collection of lyrical poems written just before and during his apprenticeship to Basire. The only work of Blake's printed by conventional means, *Poetical Sketches* (1783) contains verses on traditional topics, such as the seasons, love, and poetry. Nonetheless, in these poems we see the beginnings of that sublime tone, subtle irony, and deviation from convention that characterize Blake's mature work. Moreover, as in "How sweet I roam'd from field to field," some of the poetry anticipates Blake's concern with the distinction between innocence and experience that informs his first major work, *Songs of Innocence and Experience* (1794). Blake produced the original twenty-eight copies of the combined *Songs of Innocence and Experience* using the innovative method of relief etching that he himself had developed and which he used for all of his subsequent publications. In these works, Blake combines engraving, watercolor, and poetry to create what some critics call his "composite art," a multimedia presentation of his poetry that aims to achieve a profound impression on the reader and gives the works a sense of fluidity and process.

In 1789 Blake completed *Songs of Innocence,* which appears to present from the resilient and hopeful view of a child the social and moral problems that had been plaguing London. By 1794, Blake had added the companion poems of *Songs of Experience,* which treat the same topics but from the more critical (some would say cynical) and sinister perspective of an adult. Although some equate innocence with childhood and experience with adulthood, these two categories more accurately represent, in Blake's terms, "two contrary states of the human soul," for either perspective is available to the human consciousness regardless of age. Indeed, Blake's masterful irony disturbs even the pleasant and joyful surfaces of *Songs of Innocence* with the potential for a more sinister account of what takes place in each poem. In "The Chimney Sweeper," for example, little

Tom Dacre's dream may be enough to keep him "happy & warm," but the moral slogan of the last line—"So if all do their duty, they need not fear harm"—reminds us of the innumerable tracts, tales, and poems written in Blake's day to enjoin working people to submit cheerfully to a life of labor. The poem anticipates the radical protest of its companion poem in *Songs of Experience,* in which the young chimney sweeper is aware of the hypocrisy of his parents, who would sell him into slavery and then congratulate themselves on having done their duty to "God & his Priest & King." Although Blake disdained the Enlightenment rationalism of Voltaire and Rousseau, as is evident in "Mock on Mock on Voltaire Rousseau," Blake's satire, directed at the hypocrisy and moral turpitude of those who uncritically follow the crowd, shows some similarities with that of his Enlightenment adversaries.

Prophetic Works.   If *Songs of Innocence and Experience* presents a society parasitic upon genius, innocence, and those whose spirit and energy are as yet unfettered by religious, social, political, and moral convention, it also celebrates the vitality, imagination, and independence of those who challenge the institutions that create the "mind-forg'd manacles." Because Blake saw his work as "an endeavor to restore what the ancients

William Blake, "The Lamb," 1794
(Art Resource)

call the golden age," what he hoped to do through his unique combination of poetic and visual art was to awaken the vital poetic genius within all human beings. Thus, from *Songs of Innocence and Experience* to *The Four Zoas*, Blake challenges readers to become active participants in the construction of meaning. Moreover, writing in the age of the French Revolution, the age of political radicals such as Mary Wollstonecraft, William Godwin, and Thomas Paine, Blake's call for imaginative freedom is also a call for political and social freedom, including the freedom of women from subordination to men and the freedom of slaves, as articulated in one of his early myths, *Visions of the Daughters of Albion* (1791–92). Throughout his increasingly arcane "Lambeth prophecies," such as *America* (1793), *Europe* (1794), *The Book of Urizen* (1794), and *The Book of Los* (1795), Blake attacked the moral authoritarianism, religious falsehood, and materialism of his time. In the longer prophecies, such as *Milton* (1804), *Jerusalem* (1804), and *The Four Zoas* (c. 1797–1804), which remained incomplete at his death, Blake further elaborated his complex myth and envisioned a world set free from its political, social, and religious fetters by the power of the imagination. The biblical rhetoric and diction, the formal experimentalism, and the private myth-making that Blake undertook in these later works also appeared in *The Marriage of Heaven and Hell* (1793), one of Blake's earliest, most important, and most accessible prophetic works.

The Marriage of Heaven and Hell.   This poem might be described as a compendium of Blake's ideas, displayed in a literary-aesthetic form that defies categorization. In addition to the colored plates and the "illuminated printing" of this work, *The Marriage of Heaven and Hell* involves a hybridization of many literary forms including biblical prophecy, satire, autobiography, aphorism, lyric, and prose. The poem is a direct satire of Emanuel Swedenborg's *Heaven and Hell*, in which Swedenborg[1] anticipates in "memorable relations" the eventual reconciliation of good and evil. Indeed, Blake's poem challenges the very system of binary oppositions upon which Swedenborg's doctrine is based. Nothing, in Blake's view, is either good or bad except as the beholder makes it so. As in "The Tyger," from *Songs of Experience*, Blake shows here that the hand that framed the tiger also framed the lamb, and he subjects the binary system underlying the Western valuation of good and evil to a devastating critique. Indeed, the prophetic bard in this poem positions himself squarely opposite the empiricist and rationalist intellectual tradition of the Enlightenment, attacks the system-builders who have relied upon reason alone to construct their vision of the world, and denounces those who have perverted the dynamic, imaginative vision of prophecy by changing it into fixed forms of religious doctrine. Here Blake shows his utter disdain, even contempt, for anything that is static or frozen into convention and custom, a point poignantly expressed in his claim that "without

---

[1]Swedenborg (1688–1772): Emanuel Swedenborg, Swedish scientist and mystic respected for his engineering skills and works on natural philosophy, as well as for his spiritual and religious teachings—*Heaven and Hell* (1758), *Divine Love and Wisdom* (1763), and *Divine Providence* (1764).

contraries there is no progression." Thus, the "marriage" of the title is ironic, for Blake's poem ultimately advocates not reconciliation but ongoing dialectic; "opposition," as he puts it, "is true friendship."

Although Blake's philosophy admits of few generalizations, *The Marriage of Heaven and Hell* shows that Blake sees the material world as the product of the Fall. He recognizes that only through acknowledging the Fall and embracing the body, rather than denying it as orthodox Christianity would, can human beings be redeemed. Like the utopian socialist Fourier, Blake believes that the repression of desire poisons both the body and the mind or spirit: "He who desires but acts not breeds pestilence." Blake recognizes the interdependence of mind and body, and condemns that form of religion that outlaws the body and in so doing cuts off the spirit from the primary source of its energy.

The major agency of repression is reason, represented in Blake's later prophecies by Urizen, a figure who represents the withering of faculties that occurs when one accepts the limits of the five senses. As Blake puts it in Plate 14, "man has closed himself up, till he sees all things thro' narrow chinks of his cavern." Here we encounter the major paradox of Blake's thought. Although the five senses impose limits upon reason, which in turn becomes the "outward circumference of energy," it is only through the full and active engagement of the senses that we may recognize our true spiritual existence. In *Europe,* for example, Blake writes that "Five windows light the cavern'd Man." These windows are the five senses that are "the chief inlets of Soul in this age." That is, the senses in this life are remnants of the "enlarg'd and numerous senses" of our spiritual life. Thus, we must learn to use them to their fullest, for they bring a clarity of vision that finally frees us from the limits of empiricism. It is Blake's hope in *The Marriage of Heaven and Hell* and in later works to engage readers' faculties to their fullest and so cleanse their perceptions so that everyone will see "the infinite in every thing."

■ CONNECTIONS

Voltaire, *Candide;* Denis Diderot, *Supplement to Bougainville's Travels* (both Book 4). Poems such as "London," "Holy Thursday," and *The Marriage of Heaven and Hell* are ruthless satires on what Blake saw as the repressive institutions of Europe, including organized religion and marriage. Voltaire and Diderot also attack the corruption and hypocrisy of European institutions, and Diderot targets marriage and sexual mores in Europe in particular as sources of repression and hypocrisy. Although Blake is known as a Romantic and a critic of the Enlightenment faith in reason, in which ways does his work participate in the Enlightenment critique of society? What makes Blake's work Romantic?

Charles Baudelaire, "The Albatross," p. 418; Emily Dickinson, "They Shut me up in Prose," p. 914; Yeats, "The Second Coming," (Book 6). Rebelling against tradition, celebrating innovation and imagination, and inventing new poetic forms, Blake's illuminated works set him apart from the mainstream poets of his time. Ironically, his prophetic claims for poets distanced him from his contemporaries but profoundly influenced later writers and artists. Baudelaire, Dickinson, and Yeats make similar claims for poets. What image of poets or artists emerges from these writers' works? How do culture, gender, and historical circumstance figure into each writer's view of the role of the poet in society?

Ghalib, *Poems*, p. 965. Blake is well known for combining spiritual intensity with social criticism and for his mastery of irony. Moreover, despite its engagement with the world, Blake's poetry, as in "The Tyger," evokes a sense of the infinite by means of a generative, but elusive, symbolism. Ghalib's *ghazals* also are known for their passionate intensity, their ironic treatment of love and the world, and their fusion of the spiritual and the worldly. How do Blake and Ghalib use symbolism and irony to infuse ordinary or familiar objects with a spiritual power or presence? What symbols or ideas do these poets share? What about their work is culturally specific?

■ **FURTHER RESEARCH**

Biography
Ackroyd, Peter. *Blake.* 1996.
Erdman, David V. *Blake: Prophet Against Empire.* 1954; revised 1964.

Criticism
Clark, Steve, and David Worrall, eds. *Blake in the Nineties.* 1999.
Eaves, Morris. *William Blake's Theory of Art.* 1982.
Essick, Robert. *William Blake, Printmaker.* 1980.
Frye, Northrop. *Fearful Symmetry.* 1947.
Mellor, Anne. *Blake's Human Form Divine.* 1974.
Mitchell, W. J. T. *Blake's Composite Art.* 1978.

∽ How sweet I roam'd from field to field

How sweet I roam'd from field to field,
   And tasted all the summer's pride,
'Till I the prince of love° beheld,   Eros or Cupid
   Who in the sunny beams did glide!

He shew'd me lilies for my hair,
   And blushing roses for my brow;
He led me through his gardens fair,
   Where all his golden pleasures grow.

"How sweet I roam'd from field to field" **and** *"To the Muses."* These two short lyric poems were written before 1783, very early in Blake's poetic career. Written in rhymed tetrameter quatrains (stanzas of four lines each, with four stressed syllables in each line), they anticipate the form Blake uses for most of *Songs of Innocence and Experience.* Both poems make classical allusions and introduce conventional elegiac themes that were familiar to readers of late-eighteenth-century British poetry. "How sweet I roam'd from field to field" demonstrates Blake's adept handling of irony and introduces what would become a recurrent motif in his work—the cruel delight of a master depriving someone of his or her freedom—a matter of no small importance in the age of revolution and agitation for the abolition of slavery.

With sweet May dews my wings were wet,
10   And Phoebus[1] fir'd my vocal rage;
He caught me in his silken net,
    And shut me in his golden cage.

He loves to sit and hear me sing,
    Then, laughing, sports and plays with me;
Then stretches out my golden wing,
    And mocks my loss of liberty.

---

[1] Phoebus: Phoebus Apollo, "the bright one"; the Greek god of music, prophecy, and poetry.

∾ To the Muses

Whether on Ida's[1] shady brow,
    Or in the chambers of the East,
The chambers of the sun, that now
    From antient melody have ceas'd;

Whether in Heav'n ye wander fair,
    Or the green corners of the earth,
Or the blue regions of the air,
    Where the melodious winds have birth;

Whether on chrystal[2] rocks ye rove,
10   Beneath the bosom of the sea
Wand'ring in many a coral grove,
    Fair Nine,[3] forsaking Poetry!

How have you left the antient love
    That bards of old enjoy'd in you!
The languid strings do scarcely move!
    The sound is forc'd, the notes are few!

TO THE MUSES

[1] Ida: A mountain in Phrygia, associated with many events in classical mythology and the Trojan War.

[2] Blake's nonstandard spellings and inconsistent spelling will be retained throughout; obvious slips have been silently corrected.

[3] Fair Nine: The nine Muses, daughters of Zeus and Mnemosyne (memory), who inspired writers, poets, musicians, and other creative artists.

FROM

Songs of Innocence

INTRODUCTION

Piping down the valleys wild
Piping songs of pleasant glee
On a cloud I saw a child.
And he laughing said to me.

Pipe a song about a Lamb;
So I piped with merry chear,
Piper pipe that song again —
So I piped, he wept to hear.

Drop thy pipe thy happy pipe
10 Sing thy songs of happy chear,
So I sung the same again
While he wept with joy to hear

Piper sit thee down and write
In a book that all may read —
So he vanish'd from my sight.
And I pluck'd a hollow reed.

And I made a rural pen,
And I stain'd the water clear,
And I wrote my happy songs
20 Every child may joy to hear

Songs of Innocence and Experience. Blake completed and published **Songs of Innocence** in 1789. *Songs of Experience* was not finished until four years later, at which time Blake combined the two works under a joint title and added a subtitle: *The Songs of Innocence and Experience: Showing the Contrary States of the Human Soul.* The subtitle as well as the pairing of poems — e.g., "The Lamb" and "The Tyger," the two Chimney Sweeper poems, and the two Holy Thursday poems — suggests that readers should read them together, as the different perspectives they present are like a dialogue. As becomes clear when reading, though the childlike perspective of the *Songs of Innocence* presents a brighter, more hopeful and joyful perspective on life, the world the speakers occupy is as freighted with wickedness, hypocrisy, and exploitation as the one presented by the more seasoned, realistic, or cynical speakers of *Songs of Experience.* Blake's masterful irony disturbs the pleasant and joyful surfaces of *Songs of Innocence*, enabling the reader to construct a more troubled account

THE LAMB

    Little Lamb who made thee
    Dost thou know who made thee
Gave thee life & bid thee feed.
By the stream & o'er the mead;
Gave thee clothing of delight,
Softest clothing wooly bright;
Gave thee such a tender voice,
Making all the vales rejoice!
    Little Lamb who made thee
10   Dost thou know who made thee

    Little Lamb I'll tell thee,
    Little Lamb I'll tell thee!
He is called by thy name,
For he calls himself a Lamb:
He is meek & he is mild,
He became a little child:
I a child & thou a lamb,
We are called by his name.
    Little Lamb God bless thee.
20   Little Lamb God bless thee.

THE LITTLE BLACK BOY.

My mother bore me in the southern wild,
And I am black, but O! my soul is white;
White as an angel is the English child:
But I am black as if bereav'd of light.

My mother taught me underneath a tree
And sitting down before the heat of day,
She took me on her lap and kissed me,
And pointing to the east began to say.

Look on the rising sun: there God does live
10 And gives his light, and gives his heat away.

---

of what takes place in each poem. In some of the illustrated poems such as "The Tyger," Blake also develops ironic tension between the poem and the visual art. In Blake's drawing, the tiger has a sheepish demeanor. In the text, the tiger is associated with a sublime terror. Through these contradictions Blake leaves it to readers to effect their own resolutions or to recognize that reality is indeed a construct of their own imaginative vision.

And flowers and trees and beasts and men receive
Comfort in morning joy in the noon day.

And we are put on earth a little space,
That we may learn to bear the beams of love,
And these black bodies and this sun-burnt face
Is but a cloud, and like a shady grove.

For when our souls have learn'd the heat to bear
The cloud will vanish we shall hear his voice.
Saying: come out from the grove my love & care,
20 And round my golden tent like lambs rejoice.

Thus did my mother say and kissed me,
And thus I say to little English boy.
When I from black and he from white cloud free,
And round the tent of God like lambs we joy:

I'll shade him from the heat till he can bear,
To lean in joy upon our fathers knee.
And then I'll stand and stroke his silver hair,
And be like him and he will then love me.

THE CHIMNEY SWEEPER

When my mother died I was very young,
And my father sold me while yet my tongue,
Could scarcely cry weep weep weep weep.
So your chimneys I sweep & in soot I sleep.

Theres little Tom Dacre, who cried when his head
That curl'd like a lambs back, was shav'd, so I said.
Hush Tom never mind it, for when your head's bare,
You know that the soot cannot spoil your white hair.

And so he was quiet, & that very night,
10 As Tom was a sleeping he had such a sight,
That thousands of sweepers Dick, Joe Ned & Jack
Were all of them lock'd up in coffins of black

And by came an Angel who had a bright key,
And he open'd the coffins & set them all free.

Then down a green plain leaping laughing they run
And wash in a river and shine in the Sun.

Then naked & white, all their bags left behind,
They rise upon clouds, and sport in the wind.
And the Angel told Tom if he'd be a good boy,
20 He'd have God for his father & never want joy.

And so Tom awoke and we rose in the dark
And got with our bags & our brushes to work.
Tho' the morning was cold, Tom was happy & warm,
So if all do their duty, they need not fear harm.

HOLY THURSDAY

Twas on a Holy Thursday[1] their innocent faces clean
The children walking two & two in red & blue & green
Grey headed beadles walkd before with wands as white as snow
Till into the high dome of Pauls[2] they like Thames[3] waters flow

O what a multitude they seemd these flowers of London town
Seated in companies they sit with radiance all their own
The hum of multitudes was there but multitudes of lambs
Thousands of little boys & girls raising their innocent hands

Now like a mighty wind they raise to heaven the voice of song
10 Or like harmonious thunderings the seats of heaven among
Beneath them sit the aged men wise guardians[4] of the poor
Then cherish pity, lest you drive an angel from your door

---

[1] **Holy Thursday:** Normally designates Ascension Day, the fortieth day after Easter. The annual charity-school services, to which this poem refers, were held on the first Thursday in May, unless that day fell on Ascension Day. Thus, Blake is being ironic here.

[2] **Pauls:** St. Paul's Cathedral in London.

[3] **Thames:** River that runs through London.

[4] **wise guardians:** The overseers or governors of the charity schools.

FROM

∾ Songs of Experience

INTRODUCTION

Hear the voice of the Bard!
Who Present, Past, & Future sees
Whose ears have heard,
The Holy Word,
That walk'd among the ancient trees.

Calling the lapsed Soul
And weeping in the evening dew;
That might controll,
The starry pole;
10 And fallen fallen light renew!

O Earth O Earth return!
Arise from out the dewy grass;
Night is worn,
And the morn
Rises from the slumberous mass.

Turn away no more:
Why wilt thou turn away
The starry floor
The watry shore
20 Is giv'n thee till the break of day.

EARTH'S ANSWER

Earth rais'd up her head,
From the darkness dread & drear.
Her light fled:
Stony dread!
And her locks cover'd with grey despair.

Prison'd on watry shore
Starry Jealousy does keep my den
Cold and hoar

Weeping o'er
10 I hear the Father of the ancient men

Selfish father of men
Cruel jealous selfish fear
Can delight
Chain'd in night
The virgins of youth and morning bear.

Does spring hide its joy
When buds and blossoms grow?
Does the sower?
Sow by night?
20 Or the plowman in darkness plow?

Break this heavy chain,
That does freeze my bones around
Selfish! vain,
Eternal bane!
That free Love with bondage bound.

HOLY THURSDAY

Is this a holy thing to see,
In a rich and fruitful land,
Babes reducd to misery,
Fed with cold and usurous hand?

Is that trembling cry a song?
Can it be a song of joy?
And so many children poor?
It is a land of poverty!

And their sun does never shine.
10 And their fields are bleak & bare.
And their ways are fill'd with thorns.
It is eternal winter there.

For where-e'er the sun does shine,
And where-e'er the rain does fall:
Babe can never hunger there,
Nor poverty the mind appall.

THE CHIMNEY SWEEPER

A little black thing among the snow:
Crying weep, weep, in notes of woe!
Where are thy father & mother? say?
They are both gone up to the church to pray.

Because I was happy upon the heath,
And smil'd among the winters snow:
They clothed me in the clothes of death,
And taught me to sing the notes of woe.

And because I am happy, & dance & sing,
10 They think they have done me no injury:
And are gone to praise God & his Priest & King
Who make up a heaven of our misery.

THE SICK ROSE

O Rose thou art sick.
The invisible worm,
That flies in the night
In the howling storm:

Has found out thy bed
Of crimson joy:
And his dark secret love
Does thy life destroy.

THE TYGER

Tyger Tyger, burning bright,
In the forests of the night;
What immortal hand or eye,
Could frame thy fearful symmetry?

In what distant deeps or skies
Burnt the fire of thine eyes!
On what wings dare he aspire?
What the hand, dare sieze the fire?

And what shoulder, & what art,
10 Could twist the sinews of thy heart?

And when thy heart began to beat,
What dread hand? & what dread feet?

What the hammer? what the chain,
In what furnace was thy brain?
What the anvil? what dread grasp,
Dare its deadly terrors clasp?

When the stars threw down their spears
And water'd heaven with their tears:
Did he smile his work to see?
20 Did he who made the Lamb make thee?

Tyger, Tyger burning bright,
In the forests of the night:
What immortal hand or eye,
Dare frame thy fearful symmetry?

LONDON

I wander thro' each charter'd⁵ street,
Near where the charter'd Thames does flow.
And mark in every face I meet
Marks of weakness, marks of woe.

In every cry of every Man,
In every Infants cry of fear,
In every voice: in every ban,
The mind-forg'd manacles I hear

How the Chimney-sweepers cry
10 Every blackning Church appalls,
And the hapless Soldiers sigh,
Runs in blood down Palace walls

But most thro' midnight streets I hear
How the youthful Harlots curse
Blasts the new-born Infants tear
And blights with plagues the Marriage hearse

---

⁵London's charters granted certain liberties and privileges to its citizens and also demarcated the rights of property.

෴ The Marriage of Heaven and Hell

Plate 2[1]

THE ARGUMENT.

Rintrah[2] roars & shakes his fires in the burdend air;
Hungry clouds swag on the deep

Once meek, and in a perilous path,
The just man kept his course along
The vale of death.
Roses are planted where thorns grow.
And on the barren heath
Sing the honey bees.

Then the perilous path was planted:
10 And a river, and a spring
On every cliff and tomb;
And on the bleached bones
Red clay brought forth.

Till the villain left the paths of ease,
To walk in perilous paths, and drive
The just man into barren climes.

Now the sneaking serpent walks
In mild humility.

The Marriage of Heaven and Hell. Composed between 1790 and 1793, *Marriage* is a satiric but visionary poem that alludes directly to the Swedish mystic Emanuel Swedenborg's *Heaven and Hell* (1758). While Blake accepted some of Swedenborg's mystical theology—that Christ was human, for example—he disagreed with and in this poem ridicules Swedenborg's dualism. Not only did Swedenborg accept the duality of body and soul, but as a predestinarian he believed that people were damned or saved at birth, and he condemned the "sins" of the flesh, believing that spiritual redemption came only when the hell of physical desire was subsumed into or married to the heaven of spiritual love.

For Blake, such dualism and the damnation of the body lead to hell on earth, because the suppression of desire breeds hypocrisy, repression, and the constriction of the imagination. In some ways like Diderot's *Supplement to Bougainville's Travels*, *The Marriage of Heaven and Hell* celebrates the emancipation of the body and soul from the bounded circumstances of religious and civil law, but Blake's poem also combines that freedom with the divinity of humanity and the freedom of the creative imagination.

---

[1] The plate numbers refer to Blake's artwork, not reproduced in this edition, on which the text appears.

[2] Rintrah: A mythic figure in Blake's works who represents the angry prophet, like Isaiah. The imagery of this section draws in part upon Isaiah 34 and 35, which Blake mentions in the following section.

And the just man rages in the wilds
20   Where lions roam.

Rintrah roars & shakes his fires in the burdend air;
Hungry clouds swag on the deep.

Plate 3

As a new heaven is begun, and it is now thirty-three years[3] since its advent: the Eternal Hell revives. And lo! Swedenborg is the Angel sitting at the tomb; his writings are the linen clothes folded up.[4] Now is the dominion of Edom, & the return of Adam into Paradise; see Isaiah XXXIV & XXXV Chap:[5]

Without Contraries is no progression. Attraction and Repulsion, Reason and Energy, Love and Hate, are necessary to Human existence.

From these contraries spring what the religious call Good & Evil. Good is the passive that obeys Reason[.] Evil is the active springing from Energy.

Good is Heaven. Evil is Hell.

Plate 4

THE VOICE OF THE DEVIL

All Bibles or sacred codes. have been the causes of the following Errors.

1. That Man has two real existing principles Viz: a Body & a Soul.

2. That Energy. calld Evil. is alone from the Body. & that Reason. calld Good. is alone from the Soul.

3. That God will torment Man in Eternity for following his Energies. But the following Contraries to these are True

1 Man has no Body distinct from his Soul for that calld Body is a portion of Soul discernd by the five Senses, the chief inlets of Soul in this age

2 Energy is the only life and is from the Body and Reason is the bound or outward circumference of Energy.

3 Energy is Eternal Delight

---

[3] **As . . . years:** Emanuel Swedenborg (1688–1772), whose works Blake parodies here, predicted that the Last Judgment would occur in 1757, the year of Blake's birth. Writing in 1790, Blake thus refers to his own birth and sets up Swedenborg as a kind of John the Baptist and himself as a kind of Christ, who was crucified and resurrected at age 33.

[4] **Angel . . . up:** Blake alludes here to the resurrection of Christ as described in Matthew 28:1–7 and John 20:1–10.

[5] **Now . . . Chap:** In Genesis 27–28 and 36, Edom refers to Esau, the son of Isaac, at the time he will triumph over his deceitful brother Jacob, who had tricked their father into giving him Esau's rightful blessing. Isaiah 34 and 35 describe God's judgment upon the wicked descendants of Edom and the redemption of the just. The symbolic density here is typical of *The Marriage of Heaven and Hell,* where Blake condenses biblical allusions into a myth that resonates politically to the moment and promise of the French Revolution, and psychologically to the possibility for the imaginative and spiritual redemption of the individual.

Plate 5

Those who restrain desire, do so because theirs is weak enough to be restrained; and the restrainer or reason usurps its place & governs the unwilling.

And being restraind it by degrees becomes passive till it is only the shadow of desire.

The history of this is written in Paradise Lost. & the Governor or Reason is call'd Messiah.

And the original Archangel or possessor of the command of the heavenly host, is calld the Devil or Satan and his children are call'd Sin & Death[6]

But in the Book of Job Miltons Messiah is call'd Satan.[7]

For this history has been adopted by both parties

It indeed appear'd to Reason as if Desire was cast out, but the Devils account is, that the Messi[PL 6]ah fell. & formed a heaven of what he stole from the Abyss

This is shewn in the Gospel, where he prays to the Father to send the comforter or Desire that Reason may have Ideas to build on, the Jehovah of the Bible being no other than he, who dwells in flaming fire. Know that after Christs death, he became Jehovah.

But in Milton; the Father is Destiny, the Son, a Ratio of the five senses.[8] & the Holy-ghost, Vacuum!

Note. The reason Milton wrote in fetters when he wrote of Angels & God, and at liberty when of Devils & Hell, is because he was a true Poet and of the Devils party without knowing it

A MEMORABLE FANCY.

As I was walking among the fires of hell, delighted with the enjoyments of Genius; which to Angels look like torment and insanity. I collected some of their Proverbs: thinking that as the sayings used in a nation, mark its character, so the Proverbs of Hell, shew the nature of Infernal wisdom better than any description of buildings or garments.

When I came home; on the abyss of the five senses, where a flat sided steep frowns over the present world. I saw a mighty Devil folded in black clouds, hovering on the sides of the rock, with cor[PL 7]roding fires he wrote the following sentence now percieved by the minds of men, & read by them on earth.

How do you know but ev'ry Bird that cuts the airy way,
Is an immense world of delight, clos'd by your senses five?

---

[6] See *Paradise Lost* 2.758–69.

[7] Because God allows Satan to punish the just man Job, as Milton's Messiah punishes Satan in Book 6 of *Paradise Lost.*

[8] Ratio . . . senses: i.e., reduced from the senses; an example of Blake's impatience with the empiricism of John Locke and his followers.

Proverbs of Hell.

In seed time learn, in harvest teach, in winter enjoy.
Drive your cart and your plow over the bones of the dead.
The road of excess leads to the palace of wisdom.
Prudence is a rich ugly old maid courted by Incapacity.
He who desires but acts not, breeds pestilence.
The cut worm forgives the plow.
Dip him in the river who loves water.
A fool sees not the same tree that a wise man sees.
He whose face gives no light, shall never become a star.
10 Eternity is in love with the productions of time.
The busy bee has no time for sorrow.
The hours of folly are measur'd by the clock, but of wisdom: no clock can measure.
All wholsom food is caught without a net or a trap.
Bring out number weight & measure in a year of dearth.
No bird soars too high. if he soars with his own wings.
A dead body. revenges not injuries.
The most sublime act is to set another before you.
If the fool would persist in his folly he would become wise
Folly is the cloke of knavery.
20 Shame is Prides cloke.

Plate 8

Prisons are built with stones of Law, Brothels with bricks of Religion.
The pride of the peacock is the glory of God.
The lust of the goat is the bounty of God.
The wrath of the lion is the wisdom of God.
The nakedness of woman is the work of God.
Excess of sorrow laughs. Excess of joy weeps.
The roaring of lions, the howling of wolves, the raging of the stormy sea, and the
    destructive sword. are portions of eternity too great for the eye of man.
The fox condemns the trap, not himself.
Joys impregnate. Sorrows bring forth.
30 Let man wear the fell of the lion. woman the fleece of the sheep.
The bird a nest, the spider a web, man friendship.
The selfish smiling fool. & the sullen frowning fool. shall be both thought wise. that
    they may be a rod.
What is now proved was once, only imagin'd.
The rat, the mouse, the fox, the rabbet; watch the roots, the lion, the tyger, the
    horse, the elephant, watch the fruits.
The cistern contains: the fountain overflows
One thought. fills immensity.

Always be ready to speak your mind, and a base man will avoid you.

Every thing possible to be believ'd is an image of truth.

The eagle never lost so much time. as when he submitted to learn of the crow.

Plate 9

40 The fox provides for himself. but God provides for the lion.

Think in the morning, Act in the noon, Eat in the evening, Sleep in the night.

He who has sufferd you to impose on him knows you.

As the plow follows words, so God rewards prayers.

The tygers of wrath are wiser than the horses of instruction

Expect poison from the standing water.

You never know what is enough unless you know what is more than enough.

Listen to the fools reproach! it is a kingly title!

The eyes of fire, the nostrils of air, the mouth of water, the beard of earth.

The weak in courage is strong in cunning.

50 The apple tree never asks the beech how he shall grow, nor the lion. the horse, how
      he shall take his prey.

The thankful reciever bears a plentiful harvest.

If others had not been foolish, we should be so.

The soul of sweet delight, can never be defil'd,

When thou seest an Eagle, thou seest a portion of Genius. lift up thy head!

As the catterpiller chooses the fairest leaves to lay her eggs on, so the priest lays his
      curse on the fairest joys.

To create a little flower is the labour of ages.

Damn. braces: Bless relaxes.

The best wine is the oldest. the best water the newest.

Prayers plow not! Praises reap not!

60 Joys laugh not! Sorrows weep not!

Plate 10

The head Sublime, the heart Pathos, the genitals Beauty, the hands & feet
      Proportion.

As the air to a bird or the sea to a fish, so is contempt to the contemptible.

The crow wish'd every thing was black, the owl, that every thing was white.

Exuberance is Beauty.

If the lion was advise'd by the fox. he would be cunning.

Improve[me]nt makes strait roads, but the crooked roads without Improvement,
      are roads of Genius.

Sooner murder an infant in its cradle than nurse unacted desires

Where man is not nature is barren.

Truth can never be told so as to be understood, and not be believ'd.

70   Enough! or Too Much

Plate 11

The ancient Poets animated all sensible objects with Gods or Geniuses, calling them by the names and adorning them with the properties of woods, rivers, mountains, lakes, cities, nations, and whatever their enlarged & numerous senses could percieve.

And particularly they studied the genius of each city & country. placing it under its mental deity.

Till a system was formed, which some took advantage of & enslav'd the vulgar by attempting to realize or abstract the mental deities from their objects; thus began Priesthood.

Choosing forms of worship from poetic tales.

And at length they pronouncd that the Gods had orderd such things.

Thus men forgot that All deities reside in the human breast.

Plate 12

A MEMORABLE FANCY.

The Prophets Isaiah and Ezekiel dined with me, and I asked them how they dared so roundly to assert. that God spake to them; and whether they did not think at the time, that they would be misunderstood, & so be the cause of imposition.

Isaiah answer'd. I saw no God, nor heard any, in a finite organical perception; but my senses discover'd the infinite in every thing, and as I was then perswaded, & remain confirm'd; that the voice of honest indignation is the voice of God, I cared not for consequences but wrote.

Then I asked: does a firm perswasion that a thing is so, make it so?

He replied. All poets believe that it does, & in ages of imagination this firm perswasion removed mountains; but many are not capable of a firm perswasion of any thing.

Then Ezekiel said. The philosophy of the east taught the first principles of human perception some nations held one principle for the origin & some another, we of Israel taught that the Poetic Genius (as you now call it) was the first principle and all the others merely derivative, which was the cause of our despising the Priests & Philosophers of other countries, and prophecying that all Gods [PL 13] would at last be proved to originate in ours & to be the tributaries of the Poetic Genius, it was this. that our great poet King David desired so fervently & invokes so patheticly, saying by this he conquers enemies & governs kingdoms; and we so loved our God. that we cursed in his name all the deities of surrounding nations, and asserted that they had rebelled; from these opinions the vulgar came to think that all nations would at last be subject to the jews.

This said he, like all firm perswasions, is come to pass, for all nations believe the jews code and worship the jews god, and what greater subjection can be

I heard this with some wonder, & must confess my own conviction. After dinner I ask'd Isaiah to favour the world with his lost works, he said none of equal value was lost. Ezekiel said the same of his.

I also asked Isaiah what made him go naked and barefoot three years? he answerd, the same that made our friend Diogenes the Grecian.[9]

I then asked Ezekiel. why he eat dung, & lay so long on his right & left side?[10] he answerd. the desire of raising other men into a perception of the infinite   this the North American tribes practise. & is he honest who resists his genius or conscience. only for the sake of present ease or gratification?

Plate 14

The ancient tradition that the world will be consumed in fire at the end of six thousand years is true. as I have heard from Hell.

For the cherub with his flaming sword is hereby commanded to leave his guard at tree of life, and when he does, the whole creation will be consumed, and appear infinite. and holy whereas it now appears finite & corrupt.

This will come to pass by an improvement of sensual enjoyment.

But first the notion that man has a body distinct from his soul, is to be expunged; this I shall do, by printing in the infernal method, by corrosives, which in Hell are salutary and medicinal, melting apparent surfaces away, and displaying the infinite which was hid.[11]

If the doors of perception were cleansed every thing would appear to man as it is, infinite.

For man has closed himself up, till he sees all things thro' narrow chinks of his cavern.

Plate 15

A MEMORABLE FANCY

I was in a Printing house in Hell & saw the method in which knowledge is transmitted from generation to generation.

In the first chamber was a Dragon-Man, clearing away the rubbish from a caves mouth; within, a number of Dragons were hollowing the cave,

In the second chamber was a Viper folding round the rock & the cave, and others adorning it with gold silver and precious stones.

In the third chamber was an Eagle with wings and feathers of air, he caused the inside of the cave to be infinite, around were numbers of Eagle like men, who built palaces in the immense cliffs.

In the fourth chamber were Lions of flaming fire raging around & melting the metals into living fluids.

---

[9] Isaiah . . . Grecian: Isaiah had walked naked as a portent and warning to Egypt and Ethiopia (Isaiah 20:3); Diogenes (c. 400–325 B.C.E.) was a Greek philosopher of the Cynic school, which denounced the artificial comforts of civilization in favor of an austere simplicity.

[10] Ezekial . . . side: See Ezekiel 4:4–6 and 12.

[11] printing . . . hid: Here and in the section that follows Blake describes the process of "illuminated printing," the method of relief etching that he developed for producing his prophetic works.

In the fifth chamber were Unnam'd forms, which cast the metals into the expanse.

There they were reciev'd by Men who occupied the sixth chamber, and took the forms of books & were arranged in libraries.

Plate 16

The Giants who formed this world into its sensual existence and now seem to live in it in chains, are in truth. the causes of its life & the sources of all activity, but the chains are, the cunning of weak and tame minds. which have power to resist energy, according to the proverb, the weak in courage is strong in cunning.

Thus one portion of being, is the Prolific. the other, the Devouring: to the devourer it seems as if the producer was in his chains, but it is not so, he only takes portions of existence and fancies that the whole.

But the Prolific would cease to be Prolific unless the Devourer as a sea recieved the excess of his delights.

Some will say, Is not God alone the Prolific? I answer, God only Acts & Is, in existing beings or Men.

These two classes of men are always upon earth, & they should be enemies; whoever tries [PL 17] to reconcile them seeks to destroy existence.

Religion is an endeavour to reconcile the two.

Note. Jesus Christ did not wish to unite but to seperate them, as in the Parable of sheep and goats! & he says I came not to send Peace but a Sword.[12]

Messiah or Satan or Tempter was formerly thought to be one of the Antediluvians[13] who are our Energies.

A MEMORABLE FANCY[14]

An Angel came to me and said   O pitiable foolish young man! O horrible! O dreadful state! consider the hot burning dungeon thou art preparing for thyself to all eternity, to which thou art going in such career.

I said, perhaps you will be willing to shew me my eternal lot & we will contemplate together upon it and see whether your lot or mine is most desirable

So he took me thro' a stable & thro' a church & down into the church vault at the end of which was a mill: thro' the mill we went, and came to a cave. down the winding cavern we groped our tedious way till a void boundless as a nether sky appeard beneath us. & we held by the roots of trees and hung over this immensity, but I said, if you please we will commit ourselves to this void, and see whether providence is here also, if you will not I will? but he answerd, do not presume O youngman but as we here remain behold thy lot which will soon appear when the darkness passes away

---

[12] See Matthew 10:34 for the parable of sheep and goats; Matthew 25:33 for Christ bearing the sword.

[13] Antediluvians: Those who lived before the great flood.

[14] This section is a Swiftean parody of the abstract and rationalistic theology that Blake believes perverts the perception of divinity or spiritual reality in his time.

So I remaind with him sitting in the twisted [PL 18] root of an oak. he was suspended in a fungus which hung with the head downward into the deep;

By degrees we beheld the infinite Abyss, fiery as the smoke of a burning city; beneath us at an immense distance was the sun, black but shining[;] round it were fiery tracks on which revolv'd vast spiders, crawling after their prey; which flew or rather swum in the infinite deep, in the most terrific shapes of animals sprung from corruption. & the air was full of them, & seemd composed of them; these are Devils. and are called Powers of the air, I now asked my companion which was my eternal lot? he said, between the black & white spiders

But now, from between the black & white spiders a cloud and fire burst and rolled thro the deep   blackning all beneath, so that the nether deep grew black as a sea & rolled with a terrible noise: beneath us was nothing now to be seen but a black tempest, till looking east between the clouds & the waves, we saw a cataract of blood mixed with fire and not many stones throw from us appeard and sunk again the scaly fold of a monstrous serpent[.] at last to the east, distant about three degrees appeard a fiery crest above the waves[.] slowly it reared like a ridge of golden rocks till we discoverd two globes of crimson fire, from which the sea fled away in clouds of smoke, and now we saw, it was the head of Leviathan, his forehead was divided into streaks of green & purple like those on a tygers forehead: soon we saw his mouth & red gills hang just above the raging foam tinging the black deep with beams of blood, advancing toward [PL 19] us with all the fury of a spiritual existence.

My friend the Angel climb'd up from his station into the mill; I remain'd alone, & then this appearance was no more, but I found myself sitting on a pleasant bank beside a river by moon light hearing a harper who sung to the harp, & his theme was, The man who never alters his opinion is like standing water, & breeds reptiles of the mind.

But I arose, and sought for the mill, & there I found my Angel, who surprised asked me, how I escaped?

I answerd. All that we saw was owing to your metaphysics: for when you ran away, I found myself on a bank by moonlight hearing a harper, But now we have seen my eternal lot, shall I shew you yours? he laughd at my proposal; but I by force suddenly caught him in my arms, & flew westerly thro' the night, till we were elevated above the earths shadow: then I flung myself with him directly into the body of the sun, here I clothed myself in white, & taking in my hand Swedenborgs volumes sunk from the glorious clime, and passed all the planets till we came to saturn, here I staid to rest & then leap'd into the void, between saturn & the fixed stars.[15]

Here said I! is your lot, in this space, if space it may be calld, Soon we saw the stable and the church, & I took him to the altar and open'd the Bible, and lo! it was a deep pit, into which I descended driving the Angel before me, soon we saw seven houses of brick,[16] one we enterd; in it were a [PL 20] number of monkeys,

---

[15] saturn . . . stars: In the Ptolemaic cosmos, Saturn was the most distant planet, beyond which was a band of fixed stars. Swedenborg believed that the stars were inhabited by spirits and angels.

[16] seven houses of brick: Perhaps the seven churches in Asia to which John addresses the prophecy of Revelation (Revelation 1:4).

baboons, & all of that species chaind by the middle, grinning and snatching at one another, but witheld by the shortness of their chains: however I saw that they sometimes grew numerous, and then the weak were caught by the strong and with a grinning aspect, first coupled with & then devourd, by plucking off first one limb and then another till the body was left a helpless trunk. this after grinning & kissing it with seeming fondness they devourd too; and here & there I saw one savourily picking the flesh off of his own tail; as the stench terribly annoyd us both we went into the mill, & I in my hand brought the skeleton of a body, which in the mill was Aristotles Analytics.[17]

So the Angel said: thy phantasy has imposed upon me & thou oughtest to be ashamed.

I answerd: we impose on one another, & it is but lost time to converse with you whose works are only Analytics

Opposition is true Friendship.

Plate 21

I have always found that Angels have the vanity to speak of themselves as the only wise; this they do with a confident insolence sprouting from systematic reasoning;

Thus Swedenborg boasts that what he writes is new; tho' it is only the Contents or Index of already publish'd books

A man carried a monkey about for a shew, & because he was a little wiser than the monkey, grew vain, and conciev'd himself as much wiser than seven men. It is so with Swedenborg; he shews the folly of churches & exposes hypocrites, till he imagines that all are religious. & himself the single [PL 22] one on earth that ever broke a net.

Now hear a plain fact: Swedenborg has not written one new truth: Now hear another: he has written all the old falshoods.

And now hear the reason. He conversed with Angels who are all religious, & conversed not with Devils who all hate religion, for he was incapable thro' his conceited notions.

Thus Swedenborgs writings are a recapitulation of all superficial opinions, and an analysis of the more sublime, but no further.

Have now another plain fact: Any man of mechanical talents may from the writings of Paracelsus or Jacob Behmen,[18] produce ten thousand volumes of equal value with Swedenborg's. and from those of Dante or Shakespear, an infinite number.

But when he has done this, let him not say that he knows better than his master, for he only holds a candle in sunshine.

---

[17] **Analytics:** Treatises on logic and science.

[18] **Paracelsus** (c. 1493–1541): Swiss physician and alchemist associated with the occult sciences and the pursuit of the elixir of life; **Jacob Behmen:** Jakob Böhme (1575–1624), a German mystic and theosophist whose work influenced Blake.

A Memorable Fancy

Once I saw a Devil in a flame of fire. who arose before an Angel that sat on a cloud. and the Devil utterd these words.

The worship of God is. Honouring his gifts in other men each according to his genius. and loving the [PL 23] greatest men best, those who envy or calumniate great men hate God, for there is no other God.

The Angel hearing this became almost blue but mastering himself he grew yellow, & at last white pink & smiling, and then replied,

Thou Idolater, is not God One? & is not he visible in Jesus Christ? and has not Jesus Christ given his sanction to the law of ten commandments and are not all other men fools, sinners, & nothings?

The Devil answer'd; bray a fool in a morter with wheat. yet shall not his folly be beaten out of him: if Jesus Christ is the greatest man, you ought to love him in the greatest degree; now hear how he has given his sanction to the law of ten commandments: did he not mock at the sabbath, and so mock the sabbaths God? murder those who were murderd because of him? turn away the law from the woman taken in adultery? steal the labor of others to support him? bear false witness when he omitted making a defence before Pilate? covet when he pray'd for his disciples, and when he bid them shake off the dust of their feet against such as refused to lodge them? I tell you, no virtue can exist without breaking these ten commandments. Jesus was all virtue, and acted from im[PL 24]pulse. not from rules.

When he had so spoken: I beheld the Angel who stretched out his arms embracing the flame of fire & he was consumed and arose as Elijah.[19]

Note. This Angel, who is now become a Devil, is my particular friend: we often read the Bible together in its infernal or diabolical sense which the world shall have if they behave well

I have also: The Bible of Hell: which the world shall have whether they will or no.

One Law for the Lion & Ox is Oppression

Plate 25

A Song of Liberty[20]

1. The Eternal Female groand! it was heard over all the Earth:
2. Albions[21] coast is sick silent; the American meadows faint!
3. Shadows of Prophecy shiver along by the lakes and the rivers and mutter across the ocean? France rend down thy dungeon;[22]
4. Golden Spain burst the barriers of old Rome;
5. Cast thy keys O Rome[23] into the deep down falling, even to eternity down falling,

---

[19] Angel . . . Elijah: See 2 Kings 2:11 where Elijah, riding on a fiery chariot, rises on a whirlwind of flame.
[20] Blake bound this poem, etched in 1792, to some of the versions of *The Marriage of Heaven and Hell*. Capturing the revolutionary spirit of the time, this symbolic narrative describes the birth of the spirit of revolution, later called Orc in Blake's mythology, and his struggle with the forces of tyranny, later embodied more fully in Blake's myth as Urizen.   [21] Albions: England.   [22] France . . . dungeon: An allusion to the storming of the Bastille on July 14, 1789, which marked the beginning of the French Revolution.   [23] Cast . . . Rome: The power and authority of the Roman Catholic Pope.

6. And weep

7. In her trembling hands she took the new born terror howling:

8. On those infinite mountains of light now barr'd out by the atlantic sea,[24] the new born fire stood before the starry king!

9. Flag'd with grey brow'd snows and thunderous visages the jealous wings wav'd over the deep.

10. The speary hand burned aloft, unbuckled was the shield, forth went the hand of jealousy among the flaming hair, and [PL 26] hurl'd the new born wonder thro' the starry night.

11. The fire, the fire, is falling!

12. Look up! look up! O citizen of London. enlarge thy countenance; O Jew, leave counting gold! return to thy oil and wine; O African! black African! (go. winged thought widen his forehead.)

13. The fiery limbs, the flaming hair, shot like the sinking sun into the western sea.

14. Wak'd from his eternal sleep, the hoary element roaring fled away:

15. Down rushd beating his wings in vain the jealous king; his grey brow'd councellors, thunderous warriors, curl'd veterans, among helms, and shields, and chariots[,] horses, elephants: banners, castles, slings and rocks,

16. Falling, rushing, ruining! buried in the ruins, on Urthona's[25] dens.

17. All night beneath the ruins, then their sullen flames faded emerge round the gloomy king,

18. With thunder and fire: leading his starry hosts thro' the waste wilderness [PL 27] he promulgates his ten commands,[26] glancing his beamy eyelids over the deep in dark dismay,

19. Where the son of fire in his eastern cloud, while the morning plumes her golden breast,

20. Spurning the clouds written with curses, stamps the stony law to dust, loosing the eternal horses from the dens of night, crying

Empire is no more! and now the lion & wolf shall cease.[27]

CHORUS

Let the Priests of the Raven of dawn, no longer in deadly black. with hoarse note curse the sons of joy. Nor his accepted brethren whom, tyrant, he calls free: lay the bound or build the roof. Nor pale religious letchery call that virginity, that wishes but acts not!

For every thing that lives is Holy

---

[24] **atlantic sea:** Atlantis; here as a prelapsarian utopia of freedom.   [25] **Urthona:** "Earth Owner"; in later works Urthona is a spirit of imagination and creativity. His confinement here symbolizes the collapse of creative power and liberty under the "mind forg'd manacles" of political and religious dogma.   [26] **ten commands:** The Ten Commandments of Moses, associated here with the demise of true religious inspiration and the formation of religious institutions and reductive forms of sectarianism.   [27] **lion . . . cease:** See Isaiah 65:17–25; the creation of the New Jerusalem will bring in a time when "the wolf and the lamb shall feed together, / the lion shall eat straw like the ox; / and dust shall be the serpent's food." Compare also Blake's concluding apothegm to Plate 24: "One Law for the Lion & Ox is Oppression."

❧ WILLIAM WORDSWORTH
1770–1850

William Wordsworth
Befitting his role as Romantic poet, Wordsworth here appears withdrawn and deep in thought, his head resting in his hand. (Corbis)

Few poets embody the **ROMANTIC** spirit of the age so much as the English poet William Wordsworth. Although he completed most of his great poetry between 1793 and 1807, Wordsworth continued writing until his death in 1850. Spanning the period from the **FRENCH REVOLUTION** until well into the **VICTORIAN** era, Wordsworth's poetic output offers a unique record of the transformations in political and poetic sentiment in the nineteenth century. A self-conscious reformer in his youth, Wordsworth supported the early stages of the French Revolution, hoping that it would inspire England to take steps toward political reform. That spirit of reform carried over into his early poetry, in which he rejected elaborate poetic diction and the stale personifications of neoclassical poetry, using instead the plain language of everyday speech in poems that focused on the feelings and dignity of common people. For many literary historians, 1798, the year in which Wordsworth and Samuel Taylor Coleridge published *Lyrical Ballads,* stands as the inaugural year of Romantic poetry in England. In Wordsworth's middle and later years, his enthusiasm for political reform began to wane, but he continued to write important and innovative poetry, and eventually became England's poet laureate. Though younger poets, notably Lord Byron, Percy Bysshe Shelley, and Robert Browning,[1] berated Wordsworth for his political conservatism, he had ardent supporters throughout the nineteenth and twentieth centuries and undoubtedly remains one of the most influential British poets from the nineteenth century.

Early Childhood.   William Wordsworth was born April 7, 1770, in the small Cumberland village of Cockermouth near the English Lake District. The son of a lawyer who managed the vast estates of the Earl of Lonsdale, Wordsworth at first enjoyed a pleasant childhood along the banks of River Derwent. When he was seven years old, however, his mother died and the family, including his three brothers and his sister, Dorothy, went to live among different relatives. William went with his brother Richard to Hawkshead, Lancashire, to live with Anne Tyson while they attended grammar school. During these formative days, which he remembers fondly in his great work *The Prelude* (1805 and 1850),

---

[1] **Lord Byron** (1788–1824): English Romantic poet most widely known throughout Europe, satirized Wordsworth and other Lake School poets in *English Bards and Scotch Reviewers* (1809) and in *Don Juan* (1819–24). **Percy Bysshe Shelley** (1792–1822): Author of *Prometheus Unbound* (1820) and *Adonais* (1821), among many other poems, criticized Wordsworth in his sonnet "To Wordsworth" (1816). **Robert Browning** (1812–1889): Master of the dramatic monologue and author of *The Ring and the Book* (1868–69), among many other poems, lamented Wordsworth's political shift to the right in "The Lost Leader" (1845).

Wordsworth spent much of his free time roaming the surrounding countryside and hills.

Cambridge and France. Wordsworth's father died in 1783, and although he had left an estate of nearly 5,000 pounds claimed against the Earl of Lonsdale, the Earl withheld payment, leaving the Wordsworth children dependent on their uncles. In 1787, Wordsworth entered St. John's College, Cambridge, taking a minimal interest in his courses while pursuing a broad range of independent reading in the classics, Italian, and contemporary English literature. Leaving Cambridge in January 1791, Wordsworth took a degree without distinction and disappointed his uncles' hopes that he would take a position in the church. The summer before taking his degree, Wordsworth had traveled to France and toured on foot through the Swiss and Italian Alps with his friend Robert Jones. France in the summer of 1790 was in a ferment of revolutionary hope and fear; as Wordsworth writes in *The Prelude,* Book 9, "The land all swarmed with passion" and the people were "risen up / Fresh as the morning star." The Revolution had begun a year before with the storming of the Bastille on July 14, 1789, and sympathizers with the revolutionary principles saw in France the possibility for the overthrow of absolutism. A new age and spirit was being born; Book 10 of *The Prelude* expresses Wordsworth's sense of hope in those early years of the Revolution: "Bliss was it in that dawn to be alive."

   Wordsworth returned to France in 1791 when a more somber mood hung over the Revolution. With Louis XVI under house arrest and division within the National Assembly, Paris was in confusion. Although Wordsworth was not in France during the executions of Louis and Marie Antoinette in January and October 1793, respectively, Wordsworth felt from England the shock that jarred all of Europe at the Reign of Terror that followed shortly thereafter. During the Reign of Terror—a series of trials and summary executions aimed at quelling anti-republican sentiment and eliminating traitors—more than 2,600 people were executed in fifteen months. In the words of Wordsworth's *Prelude,* Book 10, it was "A woeful time for them whose hopes did still / Outlast the shock." Although some European intellectuals continued to support the Revolution even through the shadow of the guillotine, seeing violence as an unfortunate but necessary stage of radical transformation, the Reign of Terror largely tempered or extinguished altogether the hopes that before had been so profound. In *Ode: Intimations of Immortality,* Wordsworth uses the form of the ODE[2] to focus on the theme of loss of innocence. The

www For links to more information about Wordsworth and a quiz on his poetry and information about his Twenty-first-century relevance, see *World Literature Online* at bedfordstmartins .com/worldlit.

---

[2] **ode:** An elevated form of lyric poem, generally focused on a single theme, using varied metric and rhyme patterns. The Pindaric, or regular ode is structured by three-strophe divisions, modulating between the strophe, antistrophe, and epode, which vary in tone; the Horatian ode uses only one stanza type, but with variation introduced within each stanza; and the irregular ode, sometimes called the English ode, introduces wide variety among stanza forms, rhyme schemes, and metrical patterns. Wordsworth's *Ode: Intimations of Immortality* is an irregular ode.

speaker's struggle to find "abundant recompense" from that loss serves as a metaphor for the struggle of many Europeans whose vision of an egalitarian society gave way to disenchantment in the violent wake of the Revolution.

Grasmere.   During the turbulent years of the Revolution, Wordsworth was in England, taking walking tours, drifting in and out of London's radical circles (which included William Godwin and Mary Wollstonecraft), visiting his friends and family, and finally setting up a home with his sister Dorothy Wordsworth, first at Racedown in 1795, later at Alfoxden in 1798, and finally at Grasmere in the heart of the English Lake District in 1799 after a brief trip to Germany. In 1797, while at Racedown, Wordsworth began his famous friendship and collaboration with Samuel Taylor Coleridge. In 1798, Wordsworth and Coleridge published *Lyrical Ballads;* "Lines Composed a Few Miles above Tintern Abbey," included in the selection that follows, was published as the final poem in that collection.

"Tintern Abbey" and the later *Ode: Intimations of Immortality* (composed between 1802 and 1804) are more highly stylized than most of the poems in *Lyrical Ballads,* but both demonstrate Wordsworth's intense interest in exploring the relationships between feeling and consciousness, mind and nature, the past and present. In their philosophical musing and their displaced grappling with the great concerns of the Revolution, "Tintern Abbey" and *Ode* mark the beginning and end of one of Wordsworth's most productive phases, 1798 to 1802. He continued to write poetry—including what some think to be his greatest work, the fourteen-book *Prelude*—for almost another forty years. Having established a home at Grasmere with his wife, Mary Hutchinson, and his sister, Wordsworth set up a thriving poetic "cottage industry." Between 1798 and 1850, he published several volumes of poetry, including *Poems in Two Volumes* in 1807, *The Excursion* in 1814, and *Yarrow Revisited, and Other Poems* in 1835. *The Prelude,* Wordsworth's heavily revised autobiographical poem of epic proportions, remained unpublished until shortly after his death on April 23, 1850.

Nature and Philosophy.   Often erroneously called a "nature poet" (in the sense of a poet who merely describes the natural world and the landscape), Wordsworth primarily writes of the relationship between mind and nature, what he sees as the reciprocal interaction between nature and human consciousness. Looking forward to a long philosophical poem that he and Coleridge had projected as his life's goal, Wordsworth delineated what turned out to be the subject matter for almost all of his poems, and especially *The Prelude.* In the "Prospectus to *The Recluse*," Wordsworth dismisses the typical mythological subject matter of epic

Tintern Abbey, 1869 ▶
This cathedral was the inspiration for and namesake of "Lines Composed a Few Miles above Tintern Abbey." (Library of Congress)

poems and turns his attention instead to "the Mind of Man— / My haunt, and the main region of my song." What he hopes to show in the course of this work is

> How exquisitely the individual Mind
> (And the progressive powers perhaps no less
> Of the whole species) to the external World
> Is fitted:—and how exquisitely, too—
> Theme this but little heard of among men
> The external World is fitted to the Mind.

The primary experience of nature, in both its beautiful and terrifying aspects, Wordsworth believes, is vitally important for sustaining and invigorating the spiritual strength and creative power of human beings through later times of trial, loss, and confinement in places that offer less inspiration. The sustenance that these moments of contact with nature offer, however, depends on a reciprocating power—rendered variously as a "wise passiveness" and an "auxiliar light"—from the heart and mind of the person encountering nature. These moments of intensive and reflexive experience become for Wordsworth "spots of time" with a "fructifying virtue," a dialogue that generates in the individual the power to awaken new feelings from memories at a later time.

Loss and Recompense.   Critics often describe the Wordsworthian encounter with nature as a dialectical process, an interaction between two apparently discordant and separate entities that produces a kind of unity between them. This process, which runs through European Romanticism, drives the experience of the speaker of "Tintern Abbey" as the discontinuity between the present and past experience of the landscape at first opens a disturbing gap between the present and the past self. But that gap allows him to find a new strength. "Tintern Abbey" begins with the speaker returning to a scene that he had previously visited. Looking out over the landscape, he superimposes the remembered landscape upon what he sees. The composite landscape that results points to certain losses and gains that the poet has experienced over time. In *The Prelude,* Wordsworth describes the experience this way:

> so wide appears
> The vacancy between me and those days
> Which yet have such self-presence in my mind
> That sometimes when I think of them I seem
> Two consciousnesses—conscious of myself,
> And of some other being.

That other being, as we see in "Tintern Abbey" and in *Ode,* may be variously the natural child, the naive "roe" bounding among the hills, as Wordsworth did at Hawkshead; or the political child, an equally naive tourist or spectator of the Revolution who remains innocent of the blood of kings and commoners. In these two poems—in their celebration of childhood, their failure to recuperate a lost innocence, and their attempt to find compensation in an understanding of that loss—Wordsworth captures what William Hazlitt calls the "spirit of the age" of post-Revolutionary Romanticism.

■ CONNECTIONS

Matsuo Bashō, *Narrow Road through the Backcountry* (Book 4). Wordsworth's poetry marks a new appreciation for and self-conscious reflection about nature and the human place in the environment in nineteenth-century England. Similarly, Bashō's *Narrow Road through the Deep Interior* inaugurates a new feeling for nature in Japan. Both writers are credited with advancing new literary forms and introducing complex ideas in a simple and economical style. In what way do these writers create a sense of place and reflect on consciousness and nature? How do their styles reinforce their ideas about the good life?

William Blake, *Songs of Innocence and Experience*, p. 216. In *Ode: Intimations of Immortality* and in "Tintern Abbey," Wordsworth explores the gap between childhood experience and adult consciousness, between experience and memory, joy and sorrow. Similarly, Blake's *Songs* depict what he calls the "contrary states of the soul," which he figures as the difference between a joyful acceptance of the world in all its promise and wonder and a self-conscious, ironic understanding of the world's contradictions and hypocrisy. Wordsworth is often seen as a poet of the country and Blake as a poet of the city, but are there similarities in their work? What in their work allows one to call each of these poets "Romantic"?

Walt Whitman, *Song of Myself*, p. 882. The mountains and waters of the Lake District, the valley of the Wye, and the English rural countryside celebrated in Wordsworth's poetry have become symbols of England and part of the English national identity. Similarly, the urban and rural scenes of Whitman's *Song of Myself* have long been identified with America and the American national identity. What is it in the work of these two poets that clearly marks them each as an English or an American poet? And in what ways does their poetry transcend national boundaries and cultural specificity?

■ FURTHER RESEARCH

Biography
Gill, Stephen. *William Wordsworth: A Life*. 1990.

Criticism
Campbell, Patrick, ed. *Wordsworth and Coleridge: Lyrical Ballads: Critical Perspectives*. 1991.
Cronin, Richard, ed. *1798: The Year of the Lyrical Ballads*. 1998.
Glen, Heather. *Vision and Disenchantment: Blake's Songs and Wordsworth's Lyrical Ballads*. 1983.
Hartman, Geoffrey H. *Wordworth's Poetry, 1787–1814*. 1964.
Jacobus, Mary. *Tradition and Experiment in Wordsworth's Lyrical Ballads*. 1976.
Parrish, Stephen Maxfield. *The Art of the Lyrical Ballads*. 1973.

FROM

○ᑛ Lyrical Ballads

Expostulation and Reply

"Why William, on that old grey stone,
Thus for the length of half a day,
Why William, sit you thus alone,
And dream your time away?

"Where are your books? that light bequeath'd
To beings else forlorn and blind!
Up! Up! and drink the spirit breath'd
From dead men to their kind.

"You look round on your mother earth,
10 As if she for no purpose bore you;
As if you were her first-born birth,
And none had lived before you!"

One morning thus, by Esthwaite lake,
When life was sweet I knew not why,

Lyrical Ballads. Many critics see this poetry volume as the beginning of Romanticism in English poetry. It was published in 1798 and went into a second edition, with the addition of Wordsworth's famous Preface, in 1800. While Wordsworth wrote most of the poems contained in the collection, Samuel Taylor Coleridge's contributions include the first version of his famous *The Rime of the Ancient Mariner* as well as some short poems, including "The Mad Mother" and "The Nightingale." Wordsworth and Coleridge conceived of *Lyrical Ballads* as an experiment to see how far poetry could use the "real language of men in a state of vivid sensation" to convey the importance of ordinary actions and incidents. Hence, Wordsworth's poems in *Lyrical Ballads* describe "incidents and situations from common life" and attempt to invoke the noble simplicity of the rustics and common people who inhabit his poems. Rejecting the stilted poetic diction of Neoclassical poets such as Alexander Pope, Wordsworth attempted to capture — in a "purified" form — the natural rhythms and inflections of rustic life, where, it was thought, people had more direct access to the permanent truths and noble feelings of nature itself. As he wrote in one of the poems in the collection, "One impulse from a vernal wood / May teach you more of man, / Of moral evil and of good, / Than all the sages can."

   Lyrical Ballads was praised by a few discriminating readers, such as William Hazlitt, as the sign of a new spirit of poetry, but many critics trained in the Neoclassical principles of the eighteenth century delivered mixed reviews of the book. Nonetheless, even those critics who objected to the lowly subject matter of the collaboration and its outright dismissal of poetic decorum acknowledged that the poems contained a depth of feeling that was admirable and new.

To me my good friend Matthew spake,
And thus I made reply.

"The eye it cannot chuse but see,
We cannot bid the ear be still;
Our bodies feel, where'er they be,
20 Against, or with our will.

"Nor less I deem that there are powers,
Which of themselves our minds impress,
That we can feed this mind of ours,
In a wise passiveness.

"Think you, mid all this mighty sum
Of things for ever speaking,
That nothing of itself will come,
But we must still be seeking?

"—Then ask not wherefore, here, alone,
30 Conversing as I may,
I sit upon this old grey stone,
And dream my time away."

THE TABLES TURNED

An Evening Scene, on the Same Subject

Up! up! my friend, and clear your looks,
Why all this toil and trouble?
Up! up! my friend, and quit your books,
Or surely you'll grow double.

The sun above the mountain's head,
A freshening lustre mellow,
Through all the long green fields has spread,
His first sweet evening yellow.

Books! 'tis a dull and endless strife,
10 Come, hear the woodland linnet,
How sweet his music; on my life
There's more of wisdom in it.

And hark! how blithe the throstle sings!
And he is no mean preacher;

Come forth into the light of things,
Let Nature be your teacher.

She has a world of ready wealth,
Our minds and hearts to bless—
Spontaneous wisdom breathed by health,
20   Truth breathed by cheerfulness.

One impulse from a vernal wood
May teach you more of man;
Of moral evil and of good,
Than all the sages can.

Sweet is the lore which nature brings;
Our meddling intellect
Misshapes the beauteous forms of things;
—We murder to dissect.

Enough of science and of art;
30   Close up these barren leaves;
Come forth, and bring with you a heart
That watches and receives.

[“I wandered lonely as a Cloud”]

I wandered lonely as a Cloud
That floats on high o'er Vales and Hills,
When all at once I saw a crowd
A host of dancing Daffodils;
Along the Lake, beneath the trees,
Ten thousand dancing in the breeze.

The waves beside them danced, but they
Outdid the sparkling waves in glee:—
A Poet could not but be gay
10   In such a laughing company:
I gazed—and gazed—but little thought
What wealth the shew to me had brought:

For oft when on my couch I lie
In vacant or in pensive mood,
They flash upon that inward eye
Which is the bliss of solitude,
And then my heart with pleasure fills,
And dances with the Daffodils.

LINES COMPOSED A FEW MILES ABOVE TINTERN ABBEY[1]

Five years have past; five summers, with the length
Of five long winters! and again I hear
These waters,[2] rolling from their mountain-springs
With a soft inland murmur. — Once again
Do I behold these steep and lofty cliffs,
That on a wild secluded scene impress
Thoughts of more deep seclusion; and connect
The landscape with the quiet of the sky.
The day is come when I again repose
10 Here, under this dark sycamore, and view
These plots of cottage-ground, these orchard-tufts,
Which at this season, with their unripe fruits,
Are clad in one green hue, and lose themselves
'Mid groves and copses. Once again I see
These hedge-rows, hardly hedge-rows, little lines
Of sportive wood run wild: these pastoral farms,
Green to the very door; and wreaths of smoke
Sent up, in silence, from among the trees!
With some uncertain notice, as might seem
20 Of vagrant dwellers in the houseless woods,
Or of some Hermit's cave, where by his fire
The Hermit sits alone.
                                    These beauteous forms,
Through a long absence, have not been to me
As is a landscape to a blind man's eye:
But oft, in lonely rooms, and 'mid the din
Of towns and cities, I have owed to them
In hours of weariness, sensations sweet,
Felt in the blood, and felt along the heart;
And passing even into my purer mind,
30 With tranquil restoration: — feelings too
Of unremembered pleasure: such, perhaps,
As have no slight or trivial influence
On that best portion of a good man's life,
His little, nameless, unremembered, acts
Of kindness and of love. Nor less, I trust,
To them I may have owed another gift,
Of aspect more sublime; that blessed mood,
In which the burden of the mystery,

---

[1]Tintern Abbey: Then as now, a ruined monastery in Monmouthshire.

[2]These waters: The Wye, a river that runs through Wales and western England.

In which the heavy and the weary weight
40   Of all this unintelligible world,
Is lightened:—that serene and blessed mood,
In which the affections gently lead us on,—
Until, the breath of this corporeal frame
And even the motion of our human blood
Almost suspended, we are laid asleep
In body, and become a living soul:
While with an eye made quiet by the power
Of harmony, and the deep power of joy,
We see into the life of things.
                                        If this
50   Be but a vain belief, yet, oh! how oft—
In darkness and amid the many shapes
Of joyless daylight; when the fretful stir
Unprofitable, and the fever of the world,
Have hung upon the beatings of my heart—
How oft, in spirit, have I turned to thee,
O sylvan Wye! thou wanderer through the woods,
How often has my spirit turned to thee!

        And now, with gleams of half-extinguished thought,
With many recognitions dim and faint,
60   And somewhat of a sad perplexity,
The picture of the mind revives again:
While here I stand, not only with the sense
Of present pleasure, but with pleasing thoughts
That in this moment there is life and food
For future years. And so I dare to hope,
Though changed, no doubt, from what I was when first
I came among these hills; when like a roe
I bounded o'er the mountains, by the sides
Of the deep rivers, and the lonely streams,
70   Wherever nature led: more like a man
Flying from something that he dreads, than one
Who sought the thing he loved. For nature then
(The coarser pleasures of my boyish days,
And their glad animal movements all gone by)
To me was all in all.—I cannot paint
What then I was. The sounding cataract
Haunted me like a passion: the tall rock,
The mountain, and the deep and gloomy wood,
Their colours and their forms, were then to me
80   An appetite; a feeling and a love,

That had no need of a remoter charm,
By thought supplied, nor any interest
Unborrowed from the eye. — That time is past,
And all its aching joys are now no more,
And all its dizzy raptures. Not for this
Faint I, nor mourn nor murmur; other gifts
Have followed; for such loss, I would believe,
Abundant recompense. For I have learned
To look on nature, not as in the hour
90 Of thoughtless youth; but hearing oftentimes
The still, sad music of humanity,
Nor harsh nor grating, though of ample power
To chasten and subdue. And I have felt
A presence that disturbs me with the joy
Of elevated thoughts; a sense sublime
Of something far more deeply interfused,
Whose dwelling is the light of setting suns,
And the round ocean and the living air,
And the blue sky, and in the mind of man:
100 A motion and a spirit, that impels
All thinking things, all objects of all thought,
And rolls through all things. Therefore am I still
A lover of the meadows and the woods,
And mountains; and of all that we behold
From this green earth; of all the mighty world
Of eye, and ear, — both what they half create,
And what perceive; well pleased to recognize
In nature and the language of the sense,
The anchor of my purest thoughts, the nurse,
110 The guide, the guardian of my heart, and soul
Of all my moral being.
                                   Nor perchance,
If I were not thus taught, should I the more
Suffer my genial[3] spirits to decay:
For thou art with me here upon the banks
Of this fair river; thou my dearest Friend,[4]
My dear, dear Friend; and in thy voice I catch
The language of my former heart, and read
My former pleasures in the shooting lights
Of thy wild eyes. Oh! yet a little while

---

[3] genial: Creative and generative of both imaginative works and social feeling.

[4] my dearest Friend: Dorothy Wordsworth, the poet's sister.

120 May I behold in thee what I was once,
My dear, dear Sister! and this prayer I make,
Knowing that Nature never did betray
The heart that loved her; 'tis her privilege,
Through all the years of this our life, to lead
From joy to joy: for she can so inform
The mind that is within us, so impress
With quietness and beauty, and so feed
With lofty thoughts, that neither evil tongues,
Rash judgements, nor the sneers of selfish men,
130 Nor greetings where no kindness is, nor all
The dreary intercourse of daily life,
Shall e'er prevail against us, or disturb
Our cheerful faith, that all which we behold
Is full of blessings. Therefore let the moon
Shine on thee in thy solitary walk;
And let the misty mountain-winds be free
To blow against thee: and, in after years,
When these wild ecstasies shall be matured
Into a sober pleasure; when thy mind
140 Shall be a mansion for all lovely forms,
Thy memory be as a dwelling-place
For all sweet sounds and harmonies; oh! then,
If solitude, or fear, or pain, or grief,
Should be thy portion, with what healing thoughts
Of tender joy wilt thou remember me,
And these my exhortations! Nor, perchance—
If I should be where I no more can hear
Thy voice, nor catch from thy wild eyes these gleams
Of past existence—wilt thou then forget
150 That on the banks of this delightful stream
We stood together; and that I, so long
A worshipper of Nature, hither came
Unwearied in that service: rather say
With warmer love—oh! with far deeper zeal
Of holier love. Nor wilt thou then forget,
That after many wanderings, many years
Of absence, these steep woods and lofty cliffs,
And this green pastoral landscape, were to me
More dear, both for themselves and for thy sake!

ᴖ Ode: Intimations of Immortality

The Child is Father of the Man;
And I could wish my days to be
Bound each to each by natural piety.[1]

1

There was a time when meadow, grove, and stream,
The earth, and every common sight,
   To me did seem
  Apparelled in celestial light,
The glory and the freshness of a dream.
It is not now as it hath been of yore;—
  Turn wheresoe'er I may,
   By night or day,
The things which I have seen I now can see no more.

2

10   The Rainbow comes and goes,
   And lovely is the Rose;
   The Moon doth with delight
Look round her when the heavens are bare;
   Waters on a starry night
   Are beautiful and fair;
  The sunshine is a glorious birth;
  But yet I know, where'er I go,
That there hath past away a glory from the earth.

"Ode: Intimations of Immortality." Wordsworth wrote this poem between 1802 and 1804; it was published in 1807 as "Ode" in a collection of Wordsworth's entitled *Poems in Two Volumes*. It is one of Wordsworth's greatest and most important poems, a philosophical meditation on the gradual and apparently inevitable subordination of the soul to natural, domestic, and social experience after birth into bodily form. A story of innocence and experience comparable to Blake's *Songs*, "Ode" tracks the development of a spiritually enlightened child as he succumbs to the customs, habits, and diversions of the material and social influences that shape his mind and, in a memorable phrase, "fit his tongue / To dialogues of business, love, or strife." Eventually, however, as in "Tintern Abbey," the poem offers philosophical compensation for the loss of spiritual immediacy or transparency. That compensation is the "philosophical mind," which in its "obstinate questionings" about the nature of reality and spiritual existence provides reassuring evidence of life after death. The poem is divided into three parts, strophes 1–4, 5–8, and 9–11, which modulate through belatedness or loss, to an analysis of the process of acculturation, to a recuperation of hope and a sense of the afterlife.

---

[1] These are the final lines from an earlier poem, "My Heart Leaps Up."

3

Now, while the birds thus sing a joyous song,
20   And while the young lambs bound
        As to the tabor's sound,
To me alone there came a thought of grief:
A timely utterance gave that thought relief,
        And I again am strong:
The cataracts blow their trumpets from the steep;
No more shall grief of mine the season wrong;
I hear the Echoes through the mountains throng,
The Winds come to me from the fields of sleep,
        And all the earth is gay;
30   Land and sea
      Give themselves up to jollity,
        And with the heart of May
      Doth every Beast keep holiday;—
        Thou Child of Joy,
Shout round me, let me hear thy shouts, thou happy Shepherd-boy!

4

Ye blessèd Creatures, I have heard the call
    Ye to each other make; I see
The heavens laugh with you in your jubilee;
    My heart is at your festival,
40   My head hath its coronal,
The fulness of your bliss, I feel—I feel it all.
      Oh evil day! if I were sullen
      While Earth herself is adorning,
        This sweet May-morning,
      And the Children are culling
        On every side,
      In a thousand valleys far and wide,
      Fresh flowers: while the sun shines warm,
And the Babe leaps up on his Mother's arm:—
50   I hear, I hear, with joy I hear!
      —But there's a Tree, of many, one,
A single Field which I have looked upon,
Both of them speak of something that is gone:
      The Pansy at my feet
      Doth the same tale repeat:
Whither is fled the visionary gleam?
Where is it now, the glory and the dream?

5

Our birth is but a sleep and a forgetting:
The Soul that rises with us, our life's Star,
60　　　Hath had elsewhere its setting,
　　　　　And cometh from afar:
　　　Not in entire forgetfulness,
　　　And not in utter nakedness,
But trailing clouds of glory do we come
　　　From God, who is our home:
Heaven lies about us in our infancy!
Shades of the prison-house begin to close
　　　Upon the growing Boy,
　　　　　But He
70　Beholds the light, and whence it flows,
　　　He sees it in his joy;
The Youth, who daily farther from the east
　　　Must travel, still is Nature's Priest,
　　　And by the vision splendid
　　　Is on his way attended;
At length the Man perceives it die away,
And fade into the light of common day.

6

Earth fills her lap with pleasures of her own;
Yearnings she hath in her own natural kind,
80　And, even with something of a Mother's mind,
　　　And no unworthy aim,
　　　The homely Nurse doth all she can
To make her Foster-child, her Inmate Man,
　　　Forget the glories he hath known,
And that imperial palace whence he came.

7

Behold the Child among his new-born blisses,
A six years' Darling of a pigmy size!
See, where 'mid work of his own hand he lies,
Fretted by sallies of his mother's kisses,
90　With light upon him from his father's eyes!
See, at his feet, some little plan or chart,
Some fragment from his dream of human life,
Shaped by himself with newly-learnèd art;

A wedding or a festival,
A mourning or a funeral;
　　And this hath now his heart,
　　And unto this he frames his song:
　　　Then will he fit his tongue
To dialogues of business, love, or strife;
100　　　But it will not be long
　　　Ere this be thrown aside,
　　　And with new joy and pride
The little Actor cons another part;
Filling from time to time his "humorous stage"[2]
With all the Persons, down to palsied Age,
That Life brings with her in her equipage;
　　　As if his whole vocation
　　　Were endless imitation.

8

Thou, whose exterior semblance doth belie
110　　　Thy Soul's immensity;
Thou best Philosopher, who yet dost keep
Thy heritage, thou Eye among the blind,
That, deaf and silent, read'st the eternal deep,
Haunted for ever by the eternal mind,—
　　　Mighty Prophet! Seer blest!
　　　On whom those truths do rest,
Which we are toiling all our lives to find,
In darkness lost, the darkness of the grave;
Thou, over whom thy Immortality
120 Broods like the Day, a Master o'er a Slave,
A Presence which is not to be put by;
Thou little Child, yet glorious in the might
Of heaven-born freedom on thy being's height,
Why with such earnest pains dost thou provoke
The years to bring the inevitable yoke,
Thus blindly with thy blessedness at strife?
Full soon thy Soul shall have her earthly freight,
And custom lie upon thee with a weight,
Heavy as frost, and deep almost as life!

---

[2] "humorous stage": From a sonnet dedicated to Fulke Greville in Elizabethan poet Samuel Daniel's *Musophilus* (1599).

9

130   O joy! that in our embers
       Is something that doth live,
       That nature yet remembers
       What was so fugitive!
The thought of our past years in me doth breed
Perpetual benediction: not indeed
For that which is most worthy to be blest;
Delight and liberty, the simple creed
Of Childhood, whether busy or at rest,
With new-fledged hope still fluttering in his breast: —
140   Not for these I raise
       The song of thanks and praise;
       But for those obstinate questionings
       Of sense and outward things,
       Fallings from us, vanishings;
       Blank misgivings of a Creature
Moving about in worlds not realized,
High instincts before which our mortal Nature
Did tremble like a guilty Thing surprised:
       But for those first affections,
150   Those shadowy recollections,
       Which, be they what they may,
Are yet the fountain light of all our day,
Are yet a master light of all our seeing;
       Uphold us, cherish, and have power to make
Our noisy years seem moments in the being
Of the eternal Silence: truths that wake,
       To perish never;
Which neither listlessness, nor mad endeavour,
       Nor Man nor Boy,
160 Nor all that is at enmity with joy,
Can utterly abolish or destroy!
       Hence in a season of calm weather
       Though inland far we be,
Our Souls have sight of that immortal sea
       Which brought us hither,
       Can in a moment travel thither,
And see the Children sport upon the shore,
And hear the mighty waters rolling evermore.

10

Then sing, ye Birds, sing, sing a joyous song!
170   And let the young Lambs bound
           As to the tabor's sound!
We in thought will join your throng,
           Ye that pipe and ye that play,
           Ye that through your hearts today
           Feel the gladness of the May!
What though the radiance which was once so bright
Be now for ever taken from my sight,
           Though nothing can bring back the hour
Of splendour in the grass, of glory in the flower;
180   We will grieve not, rather find
           Strength in what remains behind;
           In the primal sympathy
           Which having been must ever be;
           In the soothing thoughts that spring
           Out of human suffering;
           In the faith that looks through death,
In years that bring the philosophic mind.

11

And O, ye Fountains, Meadows, Hills, and Groves,
Forebode not any severing of our loves!
190 Yet in my heart of hearts I feel your might;
I only have relinquished one delight
To live beneath your more habitual sway.
I love the Brooks which down their channels fret,
Even more than when I tripped lightly as they;
The innocent brightness of a new-born Day
           Is lovely yet;
The Clouds that gather round the setting sun
Do take a sober colouring from an eye
That hath kept watch o'er man's mortality;
200 Another race hath been, and other palms are won.
Thanks to the human heart by which we live,
Thanks to its tenderness, its joys, and fears,
To me the meanest flower that blows can give
Thoughts that do often lie too deep for tears.

❧ SAMUEL TAYLOR COLERIDGE
1772–1834

Coleridge had one of the most lively and fertile minds of his generation. Like **Goethe** and Goethe's Faust, Coleridge took all of human knowledge for his inquiry, including the classics, history, religion, philosophy, music, art, theology, and literary criticism. Providing the intellectual bridge between **GERMAN ROMANTICISM**[1] and the England of his day, Coleridge developed key ideas concerning the godlike role of the artist, the centrality of the creative imagination, the fundamental structure of reality, and the mythic connection between consciousness and nature. His search for a comprehensive system that would unite the individual with nature began with a cognitive principle; he wanted to establish that the mind does not simply "collect" sensations and reflect upon them—the mechanism of **"ASSOCIATIONISM"**[2]—but that it also actively, creatively, shapes perception. Although we do not entirely create our realities— **"IDEALISM"**[3]—we certainly qualify and formulate our sensations, and this kind of mental activity was integral to Coleridge's conviction that art, in its broadest function, "is the mediatress between, and reconciler of, nature and man."

p. 23

Henry Meyer, *Portrait of Samuel Taylor Coleridge.* Engraving. Drawing by Charles Robert Leslie *Portrait of Coleridge as a young man. (The Bridgeman Art Library)*

Similar to the tales of E. T. A. Hoffmann[4] in Germany, Coleridge's most spectacular poems tap into another facet of **ROMANTICISM**—the flirtation with Gothic realities. Whether or not poems like "The Ancient Mariner" and "Kubla Khan" originated in Coleridge's use of opium, to which he was addicted, with brilliant imagery and metaphor they describe the dreamlike reveries of the subconscious and the mystery of the spirit world.

Experiments during Coleridge's Early Years. Born October 21, 1772, Samuel Taylor Coleridge was the son of a clergyman and schoolmaster who died when Coleridge was nine. Shortly thereafter Coleridge was sent to Christ's Hospital in London, where he received a classical education and dabbled in metaphysics, theology, and social satire. After a year at Jesus College, Cambridge, he enlisted in the Light Dragoons, a cavalry unit, under the name of Silas Tompkin Comberbach, but he was

---

[1] German Romanticism: In addition to German Romantic poets such as Friedrich Hölderlin (1770–1843), Novalis (1772–1801), and Heinrich Heine (1797–1856), Germany produced Romantic theorists such as Friedrich Schlegel (1772–1829), F. W. J. Schelling (1775–1854), and August Wilhelm Schlegel (1767–1845), who believed that the ancient Christian myth needed to be replaced with a more modern one.

[2] associationism: The belief that our views of reality are built from bits and pieces of sensations joined together through patterns of association.

[3] idealism: Philosophical idealism in its various forms holds that objects of perception are in reality mental constructs and not the material objects themselves.

[4] E. T. A. Hoffmann: (1776–1822) Writer of tales of fantasy and the dark regions of the human spirit.

Max Beerbohm, *Samuel Taylor Coleridge, Table Talking*, 1904 *Coleridge's conversations were known for their brilliance and charm—they were recorded and published—but this engraving, meant ironically, shows Coleridge literally boring his audience to sleep. (The Bridgeman Art Library)*

Coleridge is a cloud-circled meteor of the air, a hooded eagle among blinking owls.

– PERCY SHELLEY

ill-suited for military life and returned to Cambridge. In 1794 he met Robert Southey,[5] and together they made plans to establish a utopian society called a Pantisocracy, in which everyone would share power and be equal, on the banks of the Susquehanna River in America. Coleridge agreed to marry Sarah Fricker as part of the scheme to populate the colony. When the Pantisocracy plans fell through, Coleridge nevertheless married Sarah in 1795, after having left Cambridge without a degree. Following the birth of their first son, David Hartley[6]—named after Coleridge's favorite philosopher at the time—they moved to a cottage at Nether Stowey.

In 1797 a close friendship arose between Coleridge and William Wordsworth that would significantly change their personal and professional lives. Coleridge's admiration for Wordsworth was initially unqualified: "Wordsworth is a very great man, the only man to whom *at all times* and *in all modes of excellence* I feel myself inferior." Their long conversations and periods of creativity led to the publication of *Lyrical Ballads* in 1798, a book that changed the course of English literature and ushered in an era of imaginative genius that would later be called Romanticism. In that same year, an annuity of 150 pounds from Josiah and Tom Wedgwood—from a family famous for pottery—allowed Coleridge to concentrate on his writing. Coleridge wrote his best poems and, in fact, most of his poems during the period of 1798 to 1802. In September 1798, Wordsworth and his sister, Dorothy, journeyed with Coleridge to Germany, where Coleridge's study of German philosophy, especially Kant,[7] profoundly influenced his ideas about nature and the imagination.

---

[5] Robert Southey: (1774–1843) At one time the poet laureate of England.

[6] David Hartley: (1705–1757) The founder of Associationist psychology.

[7] Kant: Immanuel Kant (1724–1804) was an influential German philosopher who believed that reason shaped perception.

Opium Provides Some Relief.   Laudanum, a derivative of opium, was prescribed for Coleridge's poor health, particularly for the painful attacks of rheumatism he suffered. During the winter of 1800 to 1801 Coleridge became convinced that he had a debilitating addiction to opium, which he was taking in heavy doses. This recognition contributed to periods of depression and Coleridge's own uncertainty about his worth as a person, a writer, and a thinker. A journey to Malta and other parts of Europe in 1804 was designed as a rest cure for his mind and body. Coleridge returned to England, however, even more addicted to opium, estranged from his wife, and plagued by financial problems.

Coleridge's mental and physical health led to his tendency to leave written works unfinished. His friend Charles Lamb called him a "damaged archangel," and he and other friends doubted that Coleridge lived up to his grand potential. Nevertheless, the quantity and variety of his writing, including notebooks and marginalia, is impressive. Because of financial need in 1808, he gave a series of public lectures on poetry and drama that he would continue for the next few years. His lectures on Shakespeare are particularly important for their insights into Shakespeare's characters. Coleridge also wrote for newspapers, and his periodical, *The Friend,* lasted for more than a year. A play, *Remorse,* was successfully produced in 1813. Finally in 1816, relief came to Coleridge in the person of James Gillman, a Highgate doctor who took Coleridge into his home and looked after his health by controlling his addiction. There Coleridge spent the last eighteen years of his life actively writing plays and essays devoted to religious and social subjects. His most important piece of prose, *Biographia Literaria,* a mixture of autobiography, criticism, and philosophy, was published in 1817. Even his conversations, known for their brilliance and charm, were recorded and published. Americans Ralph Waldo Emerson and James Fenimore Cooper[8] made the pilgrimage to England to talk with him. Percy Shelley, a younger Romantic poet, said, "Coleridge is a cloud-circled meteor of the air, a hooded eagle among blinking owls."

Writing the Mysteries of Life.   In *Biographia Literaria,* Coleridge describes the plan for *Lyrical Ballads:* Wordsworth was to write poems that would "give the charm of novelty to things of every day" and direct the mind "to the loveliness and the wonders of the world before us." Coleridge would choose "persons and characters supernatural" for poems that would contain "a semblance of truth sufficient to procure for these shadows of imagination that willing suspension of disbelief for the moment, which constitutes poetic faith." The original edition of *Lyrical Ballads* began with Coleridge's "Rime of the Ancient Mariner" and concluded with Wordsworth's "Tintern Abbey."

> Coleridge . . . may be regarded as the leading English representative of the European reactions against the eighteenth century. . . . There was at this time a new spirit afloat, a sense that there were spiritual needs, and unseen realities, which had been unrecognized in the religious, ethical, political and aesthetic teachings of the immediate past. The new demand was for an interpretation of the whole range of human experience which should be richer, more deeply satisfying, than the old, dry, superficial rationalism.
>
> – BASIL WILLEY, 1966

---

[8] Ralph Waldo Emerson and James Fenimore Cooper: **Emerson** (1803–1882) was a philosopher and poet with interests similar to Coleridge's; Emerson was associated with Transcendentalism, a nineteenth-century movement in American thought. **Cooper** (1789–1851) became famous for his frontier novels, such as *The Last of the Mohicans* (1826).

Combining lyrical verse with the ballad in "Ancient Mariner" indicates Coleridge's interest in capturing elemental experience in a poem that combines polite poetic form with a popular story. "Ancient Mariner," the only imitation of a genuine folk ballad in the collection, is largely responsible for Coleridge's poetic fame, along with two other poems of the supernatural, "Kubla Khan" and "Christabel," which are unfinished. These poems reveal the poet's interest in exotic travelogues and the mysterious, supernatural world of the **Gothic**.[9]

"The Ancient Mariner."   Coleridge gleaned some of the details in this poem from accounts of voyages around Cape Horn and in the Pacific; his descriptions of phosphorescence at night and other travel details ring strikingly true. The poem draws on the traditions of Ahasuarus, the Wandering Jew,[10] and the Flying Dutchman[11]—the man who after committing a sin must wander the earth and tell his story to others, presumably to save them from a similar fate. It is not farfetched to see in the ancient mariner's solitary lifestyle Coleridge's own propensity for wandering and solitude. In fact, the major images of the poem—sea, calm, wind, murder, bird, sailing, snakes—are metaphors for inner states of the mind or psyche, so that the poem can be read as both a literal voyage and an allegory of the mind or soul.

When writer and critic Anna Barbauld accused the poem of having no moral, Coleridge replied that he thought the poem had too much of a moral and concluded: "It ought to have had no more moral than the Arabian Nights' tale of the merchant's sitting down to eat dates by the side of a well, and throwing the shells aside, and lo! a genie starts up, and says he *must* kill the aforesaid merchant, *because* one of the date shells had, it seems, put out the eye of the genie's son." (*Table Talk*)

"Kubla Khan."   Coleridge claimed that he composed this poem, named for the grandson of Genghis Khan,[12] in an opium dream that was interrupted by a visitor, an explanation that has caused a great deal of controversy. The first two-thirds of the poem have elements of fantastical writing: an exotic location, dreamlike imagery with sexual overtones, an elusive situation, and lush sound patterns. The symbolism of the "deep romantic chasm" is not only mysterious and erotic but also connotes danger with the "Ancestral voices prophesying war!"

---

[9] Gothic: The Gothic movement of the nineteenth century is known for its exploration of horror and mystery and its use of ghosts and haunted houses.

[10] Ahasuarus, the Wandering Jew: Many legends down through the ages revolve around a person who rejected Jesus on the last day of his life and was doomed to wander the earth in penance until Judgement Day. He is called the Wandering Jew; one of his names is Ahasuarus.

[11] the Flying Dutchman: The legend of the Flying Dutchman is a variant of the guilt and penance motif; the name refers to the captain of a ship who is guilty of a curse or vow and must captain his ship crewed by dead men until doomsday.

[12] Genghis Khan: (1162?–1227) Great Mongol conqueror of central Asia.

A concern with nature shows up in many of Coleridge's poems, but a higher priority is given to the inner life, the nature of introspection, the formative importance of the imagination, and the sinuous motion of moods and dreams—much of which we would now call psychology. Like other Romantics such as E. T. A. Hoffmann and Novalis, Coleridge explored the shadowy valleys of faith and despair, lofty creation and cataclysmic destruction.

www For links to more information about Coleridge and a quiz on his poetry, see *World Literature Online* at bedfordstmartins .com/worldlit.

■ CONNECTIONS

E. T. A. Hoffmann "The Mines of Falun," p. 298. European Romantic writers made use of dark and mysterious experiences to suggest that there were as yet unexplored dimensions of the psyche that might be a threat to ordinary consciousness. Hoffmann's use of underground images in "The Mines of Falun" to indicate that his protagonist Elis might be personally overwhelmed by his experiences of the underworld can be compared with Coleridge's uses of the Gothic in his poems. How does Coleridge portray the strength of the unconscious in "Kubla Khan"?

Leo Tolstoy *The Death of Ivan Ilych*, p. 623. Some nineteenth-century writers portrayed the middle class as dangerously preoccupied with superficial, materialistic concerns. Tolstoy presents Ivan Ilych as someone who needs to be awakened, jolted into consciousness. How does Coleridge present the wedding guest in "The Rime of the Ancient Mariner," and what role does death play in getting his attention?

Federico Garcia Lorca "Lament for Ignacio Sanchez Mejias," (Book 6). One way that writers protested against the scientific materialism of the nineteenth century was to portray nature as alive and conscious. In "Lament for Ignacio Sanchez Mejias," Lorca depicts a sympathetic nature to support the grief involved with Mejias's death. How does Coleridge's animate, almost surreal, nature in "The Rime of the Ancient Mariner" accentuate the need for a change of consciousness?

■ FURTHER RESEARCH

Biography
Ashton, Rosemary. *The Life of Samuel Taylor Coleridge: A Critical Biography*. 1996.
Davidson, Graham. *Coleridge's Career*. 1990.
Holmes, Richard. *Coleridge: Early Visions*. 1989.
Roe, Nicholas. *Wordsworth and Coleridge: The Radical Years*. 1988.

Criticism
Bate, Walter Jackson. *Coleridge*. 1968.
Beer, John. *Coleridge's Poetic Intelligence*. 1975.
Campbell, P., ed. *Wordsworth and Coleridge: Lyrical Ballads: Critical Perspectives*. 1991.
Lowes, John Livingston. *The Road to Xanadu*. 1927.

❧ Kubla Khan

In Xanadu did Kubla Khan[1]
A stately pleasure-dome decree:
Where Alph,[2] the sacred river, ran
Through caverns measureless to man
    Down to a sunless sea.
So twice five miles of fertile ground
With walls and towers were girdled round:
And here were gardens bright with sinuous rills,
Where blossomed many an incense-bearing tree;
10 And here were forests ancient as the hills,
Enfolding sunny spots of greenery.

But oh! that deep romantic chasm which slanted
Down the green hill athwart a cedarn cover!
A savage place! as holy and enchanted
As e'er beneath a waning moon was haunted
By woman wailing for her demon-lover!
And from this chasm, with ceaseless turmoil seething,
As if this earth in fast thick pants were breathing,

"Kubla Khan." First published as an unfinished poem in *Lyrical Ballads* (1798), the complete title of Coleridge's dream poem is "Kubla Khan or, A Vision in a Dream, A Fragment." In a preface to the poem, Coleridge explains how in 1797 he took opium for poor health and fell asleep while reading Samuel Purchas' *Purchas His Pilgrimage* (1613), which was about Kubla Khan. He describes the composition in the third person: "On awakening he appeared to himself to have a distinct recollection of the whole, and taking his pen, ink, and paper, instantly and eagerly wrote down the lines that are here preserved. At this moment he was unfortunately called out by a person on business from Porlock, and detained by him above an hour, and on his return to his room, found, to his no small surprise and mortification, that though he still retained some vague and dim recollection of the general purport of the vision, yet, with the exception of some eight or ten scattered lines and images, all the rest had passed away like the images on the surface of a stream into which a stone has been cast. . . ." "Kubla Khan" is typically grouped with two other Coleridge poems, "The Rime of the Ancient Mariner" and "Christabel," because all three are deeply symbolic poems, drawing upon the interest that people of Coleridge's day had in the exotic and foreign. On one level "Kubla Khan" is about the unconscious, sacred origin of the creativity which erupts like a fountain and then returns to the earth, a process with strong sexual overtones. The poem is also about the precocious, dangerous poet with "flashing eyes" and "floating hair"—the outsider or revolutionary. These levels of meaning, and others, are sustained by a rich variety of sounds, the music of the poem, made up principally of alliteration and end rime.

[1] Kubla Khan: Mongol emperor (1215?–1294).
[2] Alph: Perhaps the Alpheus River, but certainly a primordial river.

A mighty fountain momently was forced;
20 Amid whose swift half-intermitted burst
Huge fragments vaulted like rebounding hail,
Or chaffy grain beneath the thresher's flail:
And 'mid these dancing rocks at once and ever
It flung up momently the sacred river.
Five miles meandering with a mazy motion
Through wood and dale the sacred river ran,
Then reached the caverns measureless to man,
And sank in tumult to a lifeless ocean:
And 'mid this tumult Kubla heard from far
30 Ancestral voices prophesying war!
    The shadow of the dome of pleasure
    Floated midway on the waves;
    Where was heard the mingled measure
    From the fountain and the caves.
It was a miracle of rare device,
A sunny pleasure-dome with caves of ice!
    A damsel with a dulcimer
    In a vision once I saw:
    It was an Abyssinian maid,
40   And on her dulcimer she played,
    Singing of Mount Abora.
    Could I revive within me,
    Her symphony and song,
    To such a deep delight 'twould win me,
That with music loud and long,
I would build that dome in air,
That sunny dome! those caves of ice!
And all who heard should see them there,
And all should cry, Beware! Beware!
50 His flashing eyes, his floating hair!
Weave a circle round him thrice,
And close your eyes with holy dread,
For he on honey-dew hath fed,
And drunk the milk of Paradise.

10

∾ The Rime of the Ancient Mariner

In Seven Parts

Facile credo, plures esse Naturas invisibiles quam visibles in rerum universitate. Sed horum omnium familiam quis nobis enarrabit? et gradus et cognationes et discrimina et singulorum munera? Quid agunt? quae loca habitant? Harum rerum notitiam semper ambivit ingenium humanum, nunquam attigit. Juvat, interea, non diffiteor, quandoque in animo, tanquam in tabulâ, majoris et melioris mundi imaginem contemplari: ne mens assuefacta hodiernae vitae minutiis se contrahat nimis, et tota subsidat in pusillas cogitationes. Sed veritati interea invigilandum est, modusque servandus, ut certa ab incertis, diem a nocte, distinguamus.

— T. Burnet, Archaeol. Phil. *p. 68.*[1]

Argument

How a Ship having passed the Line was driven by storms to the cold Country towards the South Pole; and how from thence she made her course to the tropical Latitude of the Great Pacific Ocean; and of the strange things that befell; and in what manner the Ancyent Marinere came back to his own Country.

Part 1

It is an ancient Mariner,
And he stoppeth one of three.
"By thy long gray beard and glittering eye,
Now wherefore stopp'st thou me?

An ancient Mariner meeteth three Gallants bidden to a wedding-feast, and detaineth one.

"The Rime of the Ancient Mariner." This poem, first published in *Lyrical Ballads* (1798), hinges on a transformation of consciousness through the agency of a spirit world. The mariner, without attention or deliberate thought, kills an albatross, one of God's creatures. He then must learn the consequences of this act while developing a different way of perceiving the natural world. After his initiation, the mariner feels compelled to tell his story to others; it is important to appreciate why he chooses the wedding guest. Insofar as the tale about the albatross, the suffering of the sailors, and the spiritual agency become in the poet's hands a vivid, moving experience, the mariner's story becomes a potential rite of transformation not only for his listener but for the reader as well.

---

[1]Latin epigraph: "I readily believe that there are more invisible than visible Natures in the universe. But who will explain for us the family of all these beings, and the ranks and relations and distinguishing features and functions of each? What do they do? What places do they inhabit? The human mind has always sought the knowledge of these things, but never attained it. Meanwhile I do not deny that it is helpful sometimes to contemplate in the mind, as on a tablet, the image of a greater and better world, lest the intellect, habituated to the petty things of daily life, narrow itself and sink wholly into trivial thoughts. But at the same time we must be watchful for the truth and keep a sense of proportion, so that we may distinguish the certain from the uncertain, day from night." [Thomas Burnet, 1692]

"The Bridegroom's doors are opened wide,
And I am next of kin,
The guests are met, the feast is set:
May'st hear the merry din."

He holds him with his skinny hand;
10   "There was a ship," quoth he.
"Hold off! unhand me, gray-beard loon!"
Eftsoons° his hand dropt he.   at once

He holds him with his glittering eye—
The Wedding-Guest stood still,
And listens like a three years' child.
The Mariner hath his will.

The Wedding-Guest sat on a stone:
He cannot choose but hear;
And thus spake on that ancient man,
20   The bright-eyed Mariner.

"The ship was cheered, the harbor cleared,
Merrily did we drop
Below the kirk,° below the hill,   church
Below the light-house top.

"The sun came up upon the left,
Out of the sea came he!
And he shone bright, and on the right
Went down into the sea.

"Higher and higher every day,
30   Till over the mast at noon²—"
The Wedding-Guest here beat his breast,
For he heard the loud bassoon.

The bride hath paced into the hall,
Red as a rose is she;
Nodding their heads before her goes
The merry minstrelsy.

The Wedding-Guest he beat his breast,
Yet he cannot choose but hear;

The Wedding-Guest is spellbound by the eye of the old seafaring man and constrained to hear his tale.

The Mariner tells how the ship sailed southward with a good wind and fair weather, till it reached the Line.

The Wedding-Guest heareth the bridal music; but the Mariner continueth his tale.

---

² over the mast at noon: The sun is straight up at noon at the equator.

And thus spake on that ancient man,
40 The bright-eyed Mariner.

"And now the Storm-blast came, and he   *The ship driven by a storm*
Was tyrannous and strong: *toward the south pole.*
He struck with his o'ertaking wings,
And chased us south along.

"With sloping masts and dipping prow,
As who pursued with yell and blow
Still treads the shadow of his foe,
And forward bends his head,
The ship drove fast, loud roared the blast,
50 And southward aye we fled.

"And now there came both mist and snow,
And it grew wondrous cold:
And ice, mast-high, came floating by,
As green as emerald.

"And through the drifts the snowy clifts   *The land of ice, and of fearful*
Did send a dismal sheen: *sounds where no living thing*
Nor shapes of men nor beasts we ken —   *was to be seen.*
The ice was all between.

"The ice was here, the ice was there,
60 The ice was all around:
It cracked and growled, and roared and howled,
Like noises in a swound!°   swoon

"At length did cross an Albatross,   *Till a great sea-bird called the*
Through the fog it came;   *Albatross, came through the*
As if it had been a Christian soul,   *snow-fog, and was received with*
We hailed it in God's name.   *great joy and hospitality.*

"It ate the food it ne'er had eat,
And round and round it flew.
The ice did split with a thunder-fit;
70 The helmsman steered us through!

"And a good south wind sprung up behind;   *And lo! the Albatross proveth a*
The Albatross did follow,   *bird of good omen, and*
And every day, for food or play,   *followeth the ship as it returned*
Came to the mariners' hollo!   *northward through fog and*
                                              floating ice.

"In mist or cloud, on mast or shroud,
It perched for vespers nine;
Whiles all the night, through fog-smoke white,
Glimmered the white moon-shine."

"God save thee, ancient Mariner!
80 From the fiends, that plague thee thus! —
Why look'st thou so?"— "With my cross-bow
I shot the Albatross!"

*The ancient Mariner
inhospitably killeth the pious
bird of good omen.*

PART 2

"The Sun now rose upon the right:[3]
Out of the sea came he,
Still hid in mist, and on the left
Went down into the sea.

"And the good south wind still blew behind,
But no sweet bird did follow,
Nor any day for food or play
90 Came to the mariners' hollo!

"And I had done a hellish thing,
And it would work 'em woe:
For all averred, I had killed the bird
That made the breeze to blow.
Ah, wretch! said they, the bird to slay,
That made the breeze to blow!

*His shipmates cry out against
the ancient Mariner, for killing
the bird of good luck.*

"Nor dim nor red, like God's own head,
The glorious Sun uprist:
Then all averred, I had killed the bird
100 That brought the fog and mist.
Twas right, said they, such birds to slay,
That bring the fog and mist.

*But when the fog cleared off they
justify the same, and thus make
themselves accomplices in the
crime.*

"The fair breeze blew, the white foam flew,
The furrow followed free;
We were the first that ever burst
Into that silent sea.

*The fair breeze continues; the
ship enters the Pacific Ocean,
and sails northward, even till it
reaches the Line.*

"Down dropt the breeze, the sails dropt down,
Twas sad as sad could be;

*The ship hath been suddenly
becalmed.*

---

[3] **Sun . . . right:** Having rounded Cape Horn, the ship heads north with the sunrise on the right side.

And we did speak only to break
110   The silence of the sea!

"All in a hot and copper sky,
The bloody Sun, at noon,
Right up above the mast did stand,
No bigger than the Moon.

"Day after day, day after day,
We stuck, nor breath nor motion;
As idle as a painted ship
Upon a painted ocean.

"Water, water, everywhere,   *And the Albatross begins to be*
120   And all the boards did shrink;   *avenged.*
Water, water, everywhere,
Nor any drop to drink.

"The very deep did rot: O Christ!
That ever this should be!
Yea, slimy things did crawl with legs
Upon the slimy sea.

"About, about, in reel and rout   *A Spirit had followed them; one*
The death-fires⁴ danced at night;   *of the invisible inhabitants of this*
The water, like a witch's oils,   *planet, neither departed souls*
130   Burnt green, and blue and white.   *nor angels; concerning whom the*
                                                       learned Jew, Josephus, and the
                                                       Platonic Constantinopolitan,
                                                       Michael Psellus, may be consulted.

"And some in dreams assured were   *They are very numerous, and*
Of the Spirit that plagued us so;   *there is no climate or element*
Nine fathom deep he had followed us   *without one or more.*
From the land of mist and snow.

"And every tongue, through utter drought,
Was withered at the root;
We could not speak, no more than if
We had been choked with soot.

"Ah! well-a-day! what evil looks   *The shipmates, in their sore dis-*
140   Had I from old and young!   *tress, would fain throw the whole*
Instead of the cross, the Albatross   *guilt on the ancient Mariner: in*
About my neck was hung.   *sign whereof they hang the dead*
                                                       sea-bird round his neck.

---

⁴ death-fires: The corposant, or St. Elmo's fire, on the ship's rigging.

PART 3

"There passed a weary time. Each throat
Was parched, and glazed each eye.
A weary time! a weary time!
How glazed each weary eye,
When looking westward, I beheld
A something in the sky.

The ancient Mariner beholdeth
a sign in the element afar off.

"At first it seemed a little speck,
150 And then it seemed a mist;
It moved and moved, and took at last
A certain shape, I wist.°

knew

"A speck, a mist, a shape, I wist!
And still it neared and neared:
As if it dodged a water-sprite,
It plunged and tacked and veered.

"With throats unslaked, with black lips baked,
We could nor laugh nor wail;
Through utter drought all dumb we stood!
160 I bit my arm, I sucked the blood,
And cried, A sail! a sail!

At its nearer approach, it
seemeth him to be a ship; and at
a dear ransom he freeth his
speech from the bonds of thirst.

"With throats unslaked, with black lips baked,
Agape they heard me call:
Gramercy!⁵ they for joy did grin,
And all at once their breath drew in,
As they were drinking all.

A flash of joy;

"See! see! (I cried) she tacks no more!
Hither to work us weal°
Without a breeze, without a tide,
170 She steadies with upright keel!

benefit

And horror follows. For can it be
a ship that comes onward
without wind or tide?

"The western wave was all aflame,
The day was well nigh done!
Almost upon the western wave
Rested the broad bright Sun;
When that strange shape drove suddenly
Betwixt us and the Sun.

---

⁵ **Gramercy!**: French *grand-merci*, "great thanks."

"And straight the Sun was flecked with bars,
(Heaven's Mother send us grace!)
As if through a dungeon-grate he peered
180 With broad and burning face.

It seemeth him but the skeleton of a ship.

"Alas! (thought I, and my heart beat loud)
How fast she nears and nears!
Are those her sails that glance in the Sun,
Like restless gossameres?[6]

"Are those her ribs through which the Sun
Did peer, as through a grate?
And is that Woman all her crew?
Is that a Death? and are there two?
Is Death that woman's mate?

And its ribs are seen as bars on the face of the setting Sun. The Specter-Woman and her Deathmate, and no other on board the skeleton-ship.

190 "Her lips were red, her looks were free,
Her locks were yellow as gold:
Her skin was as white as leprosy,
The Night-mare Life-in-Death was she,
Who thicks man's blood with cold.

Like vessel, like crew!

"The naked hulk alongside came,
And the twain were casting dice;
'The game is done! I've won! I've won!'
Quoth she, and whistles thrice.

Death and Life-in-Death have diced for the ship's crew, and she (the latter) winneth the ancient Mariner.

"The Sun's rim dips; the stars rush out:
200 At one stride comes the dark;
With far-heard whisper, o'er the sea,
Off shot the specter-bark.

No twilight within the courts of the Sun.

"We listened and looked sideways up!
Fear at my heart, as at a cup,
My life-blood seemed to sip!
The stars were dim, and thick the night,
The steersman's face by his lamp gleamed white;
From the sails the dew did drip —
Till clomb above the eastern bar
210 The hornéd Moon, with one bright star
Within the nether tip.

At the rising of the Moon,

"One after one, by the star-dogged Moon,
Too quick for groan or sigh,

One after another,

---

[6] **gossameres:** A film of cobwebs.

Each turned his face with a ghastly pang,
And cursed me with his eye.

"Four times fifty living men,
(And I heard nor sigh nor groan)
With heavy thump, a lifeless lump
They dropt down one by one.

220 "The souls did from their bodies fly—
They fled to bliss or woe!
And every soul, it passed me by
Like the whizz of my cross-bow!"

His shipmates drop down dead.

But Life-in-Death begins her work on the ancient Mariner.

Part 4

"I fear thee, ancient Mariner!
I fear thy skinny hand!
And thou art long, and lank, and brown,
As is the ribbed sea-sand.

The Wedding-Guest feareth that a Spirit is talking to him;

"I fear thee and thy glittering eye,
And thy skinny hand, so brown."—
230 "Fear not, fear not, thou Wedding-Guest!
This body dropt not down.

But the ancient Mariner assureth him of his bodily life, and proceedeth to relate his horrible penance.

"Alone, alone, all, all alone,
Alone on a wide, wide sea!
And never a saint took pity on
My soul in agony.

"The many men, so beautiful!
And they all dead did lie:
And a thousand thousand slimy things
Lived on; and so did I.

He despiseth the creatures of the calm.

240 "I looked upon the rotting sea,
And drew my eyes away;
I looked upon the rotting deck,
And there the dead men lay.

And envieth that they should live, and so many lie dead.

"I looked to heaven, and tried to pray;
But or ever a prayer had gusht,
A wicked whisper came, and made
My heart as dry as dust.

"I closed my lids, and kept them close,
 And the balls like pulses beat;
250 For the sky and the sea, and the sea and the sky
 Lay like a load on my weary eye,
 And the dead were at my feet.

"The cold sweat melted from their limbs,
 Nor rot nor reek did they:
 The look with which they looked on me
 Had never passed away.

*But the curse liveth for him in
the eye of the dead men.*

"An orphan's curse would drag to hell
 A spirit from on high;
 But oh! more horrible than that
260 Is a curse in a dead man's eye!
 Seven days, seven nights, I saw that curse,
 And yet I could not die.

"The moving Moon went up the sky,
 And nowhere did abide:
 Softly she was going up,
 And a star or two beside—

*In his loneliness and fixedness
he yearneth towards the
journeying Moon, and the stars
that still sojourn, yet still move
onward; and everywhere the
blue sky belongs to them, and is
their appointed rest, and their
native country and their own
natural homes, which they enter
unannounced, as lords that are
certainly expected, and yet there
is a silent joy at their arrival.*

"Her beams bemocked the sultry main,
 Like April hoar-frost spread;
 But where the ship's huge shadow lay,
270 The charméd water burnt alway
 A still and awful red.

"Beyond the shadow of the ship,
 I watched the water-snakes:
 They moved in tracks of shining white,
 And when they reared, the elfish light
 Fell off in hoary flakes.

*By the light of the Moon he
beholdeth God's creatures of the
great calm.*

"Within the shadow of the ship
 I watched their rich attire:
 Blue, glossy green, and velvet black,
280 They coiled and swam; and every track
 Was a flash of golden fire.

"O happy living things! no tongue
 Their beauty might declare:
 A spring of love gushed from my heart,

*Their beauty and their
happiness.*

And I blessed them unaware;
Sure my kind saint took pity on me,
And I blessed them unaware.

He blesseth them in his heart.

"The selfsame moment I could pray;
And from my neck so free
290 The Albatross fell off, and sank
Like lead into the sea."

The spell begins to break.

PART 5

"Oh sleep! it is a gentle thing,
Beloved from pole to pole!
To Mary Queen the praise be given!
She sent the gentle sleep from Heaven,
That slid into my soul.

"The silly° buckets on the deck,
That had so long remained,
I dreamt that they were filled with dew;
300 And when I awoke, it rained.

unused

*By grace of the holy Mother, the
ancient Mariner is refreshed
with rain.*

"My lips were wet, my throat was cold,
My garments all were dank;
Sure I had drunken in my dreams,
And still my body drank.

"I moved, and could not feel my limbs:
I was so light—almost
I thought that I had died in sleep,
And was a blessed ghost.

"And soon I heard a roaring wind:
310 It did not come anear;
But with its sound it shook the sails,
That were so thin and sere.

*He heareth sounds and seeth
strange sights and commotions
in the sky and the elements.*

"The upper air burst into life!
And a hundred fire-flags sheen,[7]
To and fro they were hurried about!
And to and fro, and in and out,
The wan stars danced between.

---

[7] Sheen: Shone; these are the Southern Lights.

"And the coming wind did roar more loud,
And the sails did sigh like sedge;
320 And the rain poured down from one black cloud;
The Moon was at its edge.

"The thick black cloud was cleft, and still
The Moon was at its side:
Like waters shot from some high crag,
The lightning fell with never a jag,
A river steep and wide.

"The loud wind never reached the ship,
Yet now the ship moved on!
Beneath the lightning and the Moon
330 The dead men gave a groan.

The bodies of the ship's crew are inspired, and the ship moves on;

"They groaned, they stirred, they all uprose,
Nor spake, nor moved their eyes;
It had been strange, even in a dream,
To have seen those dead men rise.

"The helmsman steered, the ship moved on;
Yet never a breeze up blew;
The mariners all 'gan work the ropes,
Where they were wont to do;
They raised their limbs like lifeless tools—
340 We were a ghastly crew.

"The body of my brother's son
Stood by me, knee to knee:
The body and I pulled at one rope,
But he said nought to me."

"I fear thee, ancient Mariner!"
"Be calm, thou Wedding-Guest!
'Twas not those souls that fled in pain,
Which to their corses° came again,   corpses
But a troop of spirits blest:

But not by the souls of the men, nor by demons of earth or middle air, but by a blessed troop of angelic spirits, sent down by the invocation of the guardian saint.

350 "For when it dawned—they dropped their arms,
And clustered round the mast;
Sweet sounds rose slowly through their mouths,
And from their bodies passed.

"Around, around, flew each sweet sound,
Then darted to the Sun;
Slowly the sounds came back again,
Now mixed, now one by one.

"Sometimes a-dropping from the sky
I heard the skylark sing;
360 Sometimes all little birds that are,
How they seemed to fill the sea and air
With their sweet jargoning!°

warbling

"And now 'twas like all instruments,
Now like a lonely flute;
And now it is an angel's song,
That makes the heavens be mute.

"It ceased; yet still the sails made on
A pleasant noise till noon,
A noise like of a hidden brook
370 In the leafy month of June,
That to the sleeping woods all night
Singeth a quiet tune.

"Till noon we quietly sailed on,
Yet never a breeze did breathe:
Slowly and smoothly went the ship,
Moved onward from beneath.

"Under the keel nine fathom deep,
From the land of mist and snow,
The Spirit slid: and it was he
380 That made the ship to go.
The sails at noon left off their tune,
And the ship stood still also.

*The lonesome Spirit from the
south pole carries on the ship as
far as the Line, in obedience to
the angelic troop, but still
requireth vengeance.*

"The Sun, right up above the mast,
Had fixed her to the ocean:
But in a minute she 'gan stir,
With a short uneasy motion—
Backwards and forwards half her length
With a short uneasy motion.

"Then like a pawing horse let go,
390 She made a sudden bound:

It flung the blood into my head,
And I fell down in a swound.

"How long in that same fit I lay,
I have not[8] to declare;
But ere my living life returned,
I heard, and in my soul discerned,
Two voices in the air.

"'Is it he?' quoth one, 'Is this the man?
By Him who died on cross,
400   With his cruel bow he laid full low
The harmless Albatross.

"'The Spirit who bideth by himself
In the land of mist and snow,
He loved the bird that loved the man
Who shot him with his bow.'

"The other was a softer voice,
As soft as honey-dew:
Quoth he, 'The man hath penance done,
And penance more will do.'"

PART 6

FIRST VOICE

410   "'But tell me, tell me! speak again,
Thy soft response renewing—
What makes that ship drive on so fast?
What is the ocean doing?'

SECOND VOICE

"'Still as a slave before his lord,
The ocean hath no blast;
His great bright eye most silently
Up to the Moon is cast—

"'If he may know which way to go;
For she guides him smooth or grim.

*The Polar Spirit's fellow
demons, the invisible
inhabitants of the element, take
part in his wrong; and two of
them relate, one to the other
that penance long and heavy for
the ancient Mariner hath been
accorded to the Polar Spirit,
who returneth southward.*

---

[8] I have not: That is, "I do not know."

420 See, brother, see! how graciously
     She looketh down on him.'

FIRST VOICE

" 'But why drives on that ship so fast,
     Without or wave or wind?'

SECOND VOICE

" 'The air is cut away before,
     And closes from behind.'
     " 'Fly, brother, fly! more high, more high!
     Or we shall be belated:
     For slow and slow that ship will go,
     When the Mariner's trance is abated.'

*The Mariner hath been cast into
a trance; for the angelic power
causeth the vessel to drive
northward faster than human
life could endure.*

430 "I woke, and we were sailing on
     As in a gentle weather:
     'Twas night, calm night, the moon was high;
     The dead men stood together.

*The supernatural motion is
retarded; the Mariner awakes,
and his penance begins anew.*

     "All stood together on the deck,
     For a charnel-dungeon fitter:
     All fixed on me their stony eyes,
     That in the Moon did glitter.

     "The pang, the curse, with which they died,
     Had never passed away:
440 I could not draw my eyes from theirs,
     Nor turn them up to pray.

     "And now this spell was snapt: once more
     I viewed the ocean green,
     And looked far forth, yet little saw
     Of what had else been seen —

The curse is finally expiated.

     "Like one, that on a lonesome road
     Doth walk in fear and dread,
     And having once turned round, walks on,
     And turns no more his head;
450 Because he knows, a frightful fiend
     Doth close behind him tread.

     "But soon there breathed a wind on me,
     Nor sound nor motion made:

Its path was not upon the sea,
In ripple or in shade.

"It raised my hair, it fanned my cheek
Like a meadow-gale of spring—
It mingled strangely with my fears,
Yet it felt like a welcoming.

460   "Swiftly, swiftly flew the ship,
Yet she sailed softly too:
Sweetly, sweetly blew the breeze—
On me alone it blew.

"Oh! dream of joy! is this indeed
The light-house top I see?
Is this the hill? is this the kirk?
Is this mine own countree?

*And the ancient Mariner
beholdeth his native country.*

"We drifted o'er the harbor-bar,
And I with sobs did pray—
470   O let me be awake, my God!
Or let me sleep alway.

"The harbor-bay was clear as glass,
So smoothly it was strewn!
And on the bay the moonlight lay,
And the shadow of the Moon.

"The rock shone bright, the kirk no less,
That stands above the rock:
The moonlight steeped in silentness
The steady weathercock.

480   "And the bay was white with silent light
Till, rising from the same,
Full many shapes, that shadows were,
In crimson colors came.

*The angelic spirits leave the
dead bodies,*

"A little distance from the prow
Those crimson shadows were:
I turned my eyes upon the deck—
Oh, Christ! what saw I there!

"Each corse lay flat, lifeless and flat,
And, by the holy rood!°

cross

490 A man all light, a seraph-man,[9]
On every corse there stood.

"This seraph-band, each waved his hand,
It was a heavenly sight!
They stood as signals to the land,
Each one a lovely light;

"This seraph-band, each waved his hand,
No voice did they impart—
No voice; but oh! the silence sank
Like music on my heart.

500 "But soon I heard the dash of oars,
I heard the Pilot's cheer;
My head was turned perforce away,
And I saw a boat appear.

"The Pilot and the Pilot's boy,
I heard them coming fast:
Dear Lord in Heaven! it was a joy
The dead men could not blast.

"I saw a third—I heard his voice:
It is the Hermit good!
510 He singeth loud his godly hymns
That he makes in the wood.
He'll shrieve my soul, he'll wash away
The Albatross's blood."

PART 7

"This Hermit good lives in that wood
Which slopes down to the sea.
How loudly his sweet voice he rears!
He loves to talk with marineres
That come from a far countree.

The Hermit of the wood,

"He kneels at morn, and noon, and eve—
520 He hath a cushion plump:
It is the moss that wholly hides
The rotted old oak-stump.

---

[9] **Seraph-man:** The highest rank of angels.

"The skiff-boat neared: I heard them talk,
'Why, this is strange, I trow!
Where are those lights so many and fair,
That signal made but now?'

"'Strange, by my faith!' the Hermit said—
'And they answered not our cheer!
The planks looked warped! and see those sails,
530 How thin they are and sere!
I never saw aught like to them,
Unless perchance it were

Approacheth the ship with wonder.

"'Brown skeletons of leaves that lag
My forest-brook along;
When the ivy-tod° is heavy with snow,
And the owlet whoops to the wolf below,
That eats the she-wolf's young.'

clump

"'Dear Lord! it hath a fiendish look—
(The Pilot made reply)
540 I am a-feared'—'Push on, push on!'
Said the Hermit cheerily.

"The boat came closer to the ship,
But I nor spake nor stirred;
The boat came close beneath the ship,
And straight a sound was heard.

"Under the water it rumbled on,
Still louder and more dread:
It reached the ship, it split the bay;
The ship went down like lead.

The ship suddenly sinketh.

550 "Stunned by that loud and dreadful sound,
Which sky and ocean smote,
Like one that hath been seven days drowned
My body lay afloat;
But swift as dreams, myself I found
Within the Pilot's boat.

The ancient Mariner is saved in the Pilot's boat.

"Upon the whirl, where sank the ship,
The boat spun round and round;
And all was still, save that the hill
Was telling of the sound.

560 "I moved my lips — the Pilot shrieked
     And fell down in a fit;
     The holy Hermit raised his eyes,
     And prayed where he did sit.

     "I took the oars: the Pilot's boy,
     Who now doth crazy go,
     Laughed loud and long, and all the while
     His eyes went to and fro.
     'Ha! ha!' quoth he, 'full plain I see,
     The Devil knows how to row.'

570 "And now, all in my own countree,
     I stood on the firm land!
     The Hermit stepped forth from the boat,
     And scarcely he could stand.

     "'O shrieve me, shrieve me, holy man!'
     The Hermit crossed his brow.
     'Say quick,' quoth he, 'I bid thee say —
     What manner of man art thou?'

The ancient Mariner earnestly entreateth the Hermit to shrieve him; and the penance of life falls on him.

     "Forthwith this frame of mine was wrenched
     With a woful agony,
580 Which forced me to begin my tale;
     And then it left me free.

     "Since then, at an uncertain hour,
     That agony returns;
     And till my ghastly tale is told,
     This heart within me burns.

And ever and anon throughout his future life an agony constraineth him to travel from land to land,

     "I pass, like night, from land to land;
     I have strange power of speech;
     That moment that his face I see,
     I know the man that must hear me:
590 To him my tale I teach.

     "What loud uproar bursts from that door!
     The wedding-guests are there:
     But in the garden-bower the bride
     And bride-maids singing are:
     And hark the little vesper bell,
     Which biddeth me to prayer!

"O Wedding-Guest! this soul hath been
Alone on a wide, wide sea:
So lonely 'twas, that God himself
600 Scarce seeméd there to be.

"Oh sweeter than the marriage-feast,
'Tis sweeter far to me,
To walk together to the kirk
With a goodly company! —

"To walk together to the kirk,
And all together pray,
While each to his great Father bends,
Old men, and babes, and loving friends,
And youths and maidens gay!

610 "Farewell, farewell! but this I tell
To thee, thou Wedding-Guest!
He prayeth well, who loveth well
Both man and bird and beast.

And to teach by his own example love and reverence to all things that God made and loveth.

"He prayeth best, who loveth best
All things both great and small;
For the dear God who loveth us,
He made and loveth all."

The Mariner, whose eye is bright,
Whose beard with age is hoar,
620 Is gone: and now the Wedding-Guest
Turned from the bridegroom's door.

He went like one that hath been stunned,
And is of sense forlorn:
A sadder and a wiser man,
He rose the morrow morn.

✏ JOHN KEATS
1795–1821

During his brief life of twenty-six years, John Keats wrote a handful of lyrics, odes, and narrative poems that have placed him among the elite European Romantic poets. Using sensuous imagery to reflect the elusive Romantic quest for the beautiful, Keats's poetry explores the tragic discrepancy between the promise of the imaginary and the disappointment of the real. For Keats, every encounter with imagined beauty leaves us even more forlorn when we inevitably sink back into the misery and suffering of everyday life. As he puts it at the conclusion of "Ode to a Nightingale," "the fancy cannot cheat so well / As she is fam'd to do." Questioning the value of poetry to improve our lot, Keats dedicated himself to the craft of writing with a self-conscious conviction and passionate intensity that resulted in some of the most celebrated poems in the English language. Embracing the transitory, the changeable, and the elusive in his work, Keats, paradoxically, left a seemingly permanent legacy of well-crafted verse that, like his celebrated Grecian urn, continues to "tease us out of thought" and inspire in readers a palpable joy.

Portrait of John Keats, after a painting by W. Hilton.
Keats lived to be only 26, when he died of tuberculosis. This portrait evokes his inquisitive nature. (Corbis)

Unpromising Origins.   Keats was born in London in 1795, the son of a stable boy, Thomas Keats, who had worked his way to chief ostler of the stables and married the manager's daughter, Frances Jennings. Thomas Keats died in an accident in 1804, leaving his wife alone with eight-year-old John, his two younger brothers, George and Tom, and a younger sister, Frances Mary, known as Fanny. His mother's unsuccessful second marriage brought further demise to the family, and the children were left with their maternal grandmother for a while. After Frances finally returned to her children, the young Keats had to nurse her through her death by tuberculosis, a disease that would eventually take his brother Tom in 1818 and Keats himself in 1821.

Education.   Keats's early education was at a school in Enfield, where the headmaster's son, Charles Cowden Clarke, took a particular interest in him and greatly encouraged his literary interests. Keats was pulled out of school when his grandmother appointed an unimaginative tea merchant named Richard Abbey to be his guardian. Abbey guided Keats into medical studies. Although Keats spent four years as an apprentice and continued in medicine at Guy's Hospital in London in 1815, he soon abandoned medicine for poetry, having met Leigh Hunt (1784–1859), a political radical, critic, poet, and editor of *The Examiner*. Encouraged by Hunt and a circle of reform-minded writers who would eventually become known as the "Cockney School," Keats decided to devote himself fully to poetry.

Keats was twenty-two when Hunt sponsored his first book of poems in 1817. This volume included "On First Looking into Chapman's Homer"

www   For links to more information about Keats and a quiz on his poetry and his twenty-first-century relevance, see *World Literature Online* at bedfordstmartins .com/worldlit.

Keats . . . saw life as a process in which no fixed order, no clear "balance of good and evil," was discernible. For him life was a mystery, a mist, a chaos in which pleasure and pain were inextricably entangled.

— ANNE MELLOR,
English Romantic Irony

and "Sleep and Poetry," poems that revealed Keats's talent and his seriousness about poetry as a vocation.

Troubles at Home and with the Critics.   Following Milton's example of using classical themes for long poems, Keats undertook an overly ambitious project, *Endymion,* which was published in 1818. *Endymion* contains some 4,000 lines of rich, almost luxuriant images of a mortal named Endymion who searches for and eventually finds a goddess symbolizing beauty.

The work drew some rancorous criticism from Tory reviewers, including John Gibson Lockhart (1794–1854) writing in *Blackwood's Magazine.* Lockhart ridiculed the poem for its politics and poetics, coining the term "Cockney School" to refer to Keats's lack of high birth and formal education and as an epithet for Leigh Hunt and his circle, which included the literary critic and essayist William Hazlitt (1778–1830) and the painter Benjamin Robert Haydon (1786–1846). In the same year Keats also had family problems. His brother George and his wife emigrated to Kentucky and lost their money in a bad investment. Keats was left to care for his younger brother, Tom, who had contracted tuberculosis and was slowly wasting away, dying in December of that year. Keats himself went on a walking tour of northern England and returned with a severe sore throat, a warning sign of tuberculosis.

Annus Mirabilis.   But in the same winter of 1818, Keats fell in love with Fanny Brawne. In the latter part of 1819 they became engaged, but they were never married. In this bittersweet time of family loss and hardship, his own economic poverty, and his devotion to Fanny Brawne, Keats, within a nine-month period — January to September 1819 — wrote the great poems of his career: "The Eve of St. Agnes," "La Belle Dame sans Merci: A Ballad," six magnificent odes, "Lamia," and a number of fine sonnets.

In an early poem, "Sleep and Poetry," Keats had set up a program for his own development as a poet, which was modeled after the careers of epic poets such as Virgil and Milton. He was to begin with pastoral poems: "First the realm I'll pass / Of Flora, and old Pan: sleep in the grass, / Feed upon apples red, and strawberries, / And choose each pleasure that my fancy sees." Eventually he would grow beyond these poems: "Yes, I must pass them for a nobler life, / Where I may find the agonies, the strife / Of human hearts." Keats mastered the first stage, that of creating pictures and delighting in the sensuous surface of reality. Although he was rapidly maturing as a writer, he did not live long enough to fulfill completely his goal of dealing with the dark or painful complexities of human experience.

In February 1820, Keats coughed up blood. The tuberculosis that had claimed both his mother and brother threatened his life. Advised to go to a warmer climate for the winter, Keats suffered through his last months in Italy. He died in Rome on February 23, 1821.

Negative Capability. Keats's letters provide us with a picture of his broad interests, both personal and intellectual. In his correspondence he talks about people, the cultural scene in London, the nature and role of the poet, his family, his love for Fanny Brawne, his ideas about life and death. One of his ideas he termed *negative capability:* "that is when man is capable of being in uncertainties, Mysteries, doubts, without any irritable reaching after fact & reason" (To George & Tom Keats, 1817). Keats questions whether logic or a philosophical system can finally satisfy or explain the intricacies of the human spirit. An individual can appreciate the flux of life only by remaining content with half-knowledge, contradictory knowledge, without grasping after answers, the comfort of rational certainties. Only then does it become possible to imaginatively sympathize with the changing variety of life. Shakespeare, for example, was willing to submerge his own self in order to enter into the diverse characters of his plays. Following this idea, Keats maintained that a poet should have no identity: "it is not itself—it has no self—it is every thing and nothing—It has no character—it enjoys light and shade; it lives in gusto, be it foul or fair, high or low, rich or poor, mean or elevated—It has as much delight in conceiving an Iago as an Imogen" (to Richard Woodhouse, 1818).

In his letters, Keats develops Romantic notions about the importance of beauty and intensity in poetry: "the excellence of every Art is its intensity, capable of making all disagreeables evaporate, from their being in close relationship with Beauty & Truth" (to George & Tom Keats, 1817). There is a kind of truth in art that is different from logical truth or scientific truth: "The Imagination may be compared to Adam's dream—he awoke and found it truth . . . I have never yet been able to perceive how any thing can be known for truth by consecutive reasoning. . . . However it may be, O for a Life of Sensations rather than of Thoughts!" (To Benjamin Bailey, 1817). In poetry, the truth of the imagination is accessed by way of images, and Keats's own poems illustrate this.

"La Belle Dame sans Merci: A Ballad" picks up the motif of the *femme fatale* who exacts a stern price for her sexual favors. Rich details are used to create the otherworldly reality of the seduction scenes; the connection between sex and death is a lingering byproduct of the experience. One of Keats's constant themes is the suffering that an awareness of mortality brings to the sensitive young poet. In "Ode to Autumn," the season itself is experienced in all of its ripeness and "mellow fruitfulness," but the underlying recognition is that winter death is just moments away. Keats captures the delicious indolence of the season in the second stanza with a personification of Autumn lost in the reveries of harvest. A variation on this theme is developed in his "Ode to a Nightingale," where sensuous image is piled on sensuous image. The poet requests a drink that will release him from worldly cares, "where but to think is to be full of sorrow." Again tempted by death, the poet vows to use poetry, not drunkenness, to join the nightingale, which becomes a symbolic "immortal Bird" whose song resounds through the centuries and in faraway lands. Having lost his separate identity in the union with the imaginary

[Keats's poetry] explores the way we prove the essential truths of life upon our pulses, a metaphor that suggests a link between the avenues of sense perception and the higher faculties of heart and head.

– STUART SPERRY,
Keats the Poet, 1973

. . . if Poetry comes
not as naturally as
the Leaves to a tree it
had better not come
at all . . ."

– KEATS, Letter to
John Taylor, 1818

nightingale, the speaker enters a world of pure imagination, where his senses are suspended so that he can only "guess" what lies beneath his feet. In this moment the poet longs for self-extinction, to stay forever in this moment when dream takes the place of the real. The connection is broken, however, and the speaker, somewhat disoriented, returns to the world of suffering, only to question which world is more real.

The scenes of lovers on an urn in "Ode on a Grecian Urn" provide another occasion to lament the transience of youth and to celebrate timeless art, which creates the illusion of holding on to life's sweetness. In the final stanza, the poet is able to admit the limitations of art with the words "Cold pastoral!" The last two lines of the poem involving beauty and truth have inspired innumerable readings of their meaning or meanings. In a letter to Bailey (November 22, 1817), Keats wrote: "I am certain of nothing but of the holiness of the Heart's affections and the truth of Imagination—What the imagination seizes as Beauty must be truth."

■ CONNECTIONS

Ghalib, *Poems*, p. 965. Keats believed that poetry should be marked by passionate intensity, and his poems often present a deeply felt modulation between joy and sorrow, fulfillment and loss, desire and despair. So, too, Ghalib's *ghazals* present an impassioned negotiation between despair and desire, as they explore the troubled pleasures of worldly and spiritual love. Compare Keats's imaginative moments of reverie and his poems of longing to similar moments in Ghalib's *ghazals*. What can be said to be universal or at least shared about their work? What is culturally specific?

Charles Baudelaire, *Poems*, p. 412. For Keats, as he writes in "Ode to a Nightingale," the world is a place of "weariness," "fever," and "fret"— "Where but to think is to be full of sorrow." Although he worried that poets might only further vex the world, he believed that poetry should be salutary—that it should find joy in melancholy, beauty in the mundane. Similarly, though perhaps even more skeptically than Keats, Baudelaire sought to find beauty and the ideal in his poetic engagement with the sordid and miserable details of the world. How are Baudelaire's and Keats's views of the role of the poet and poetry similar? To what degree does Baudelaire represent a turn toward a more realistic grappling with the changing conditions of nineteenth-century Europe?

Alexander Pushkin, "The Bronze Horseman," p. 337; William Butler Yeats, "Sailing to Byzantium," (Book 6). Keats's "Ode on a Grecian Urn" contrasts the transience of life with the permanence of art—a common motif in Romantic and post-Romantic poetry, including that of Pushkin and Yeats. How do the poems named here present an opposition between the world of mutability and the world of art? How do Pushkin and Yeats modify the theme as it is treated in Keats's poem?

■ FURTHER RESEARCH

Biography
Bate, Walter Jackson. *John Keats.* 1963.
Motion, Andrew. *Keats.* 1998.
Ward, Aileen. *John Keats.* 1963.

Criticism

Bloom, Harold, ed. *John Keats.* 1985.

De Almeida, Hermione, ed. *Critical Essays on John Keats.* 1990.

McFarland, Thomas. *The Masks of Keats: The Endeavour of a Poet.* 2000.

Roe, Nicholas. *John Keats and the Culture of Dissent.* 1997.

Ryan, Robert M. and Ronald A. Sharp, eds. *The Persistence of Poetry: Bicentennial Essays on Keats.* 1998.

Vendler, Helen. *The Odes of John Keats.* 1983.

❧ On First Looking into Chapman's Homer

Much have I travell'd in the realms of gold,[1]
  And many goodly states and kingdoms seen;
  Round many western islands have I been
Which bards in fealty to Apollo[2] hold.
Oft of one wide expanse had I been told
  That deep-brow'd Homer ruled as his demesne;
  Yet did I never breathe its pure serene
Till I heard Chapman speak out loud and bold:
Then felt I like some watcher of the skies
10 When a new planet swims into his ken;[3]
Or like stout Cortez[4] when with eagle eyes
  He star'd at the Pacific — and all his men
Look'd at each other with a wild surmise —
  Silent, upon a peak in Darien.[5]

"On First Looking into Chapman's Homer." In October 1816, Keats spent an evening with his former teacher Charles Cowden Clarke, who had introduced him to George Chapman's seventeenth-century translations of the *Iliad* and *Odyssey.* Cowden Clarke noted that Keats left late and returned before breakfast the next morning with the sonnet completed. It was first published in the *Examiner* in December 1816. It is Keats's inaugural poem, announcing his dedication to a life of poetry and comparing his discovery of his vocation to the momentous "discoveries" of Herschel and Balboa, whom Keats mistakes as Cortez.

---

[1] realms of gold: Douglas Bush links this phrase to Apollo's "Western halls of gold," though they possibly allude to El Dorado, the legendary city of gold; some critics have suggested Keats may also be referring to the gilded pages of bound books.

[2] Apollo: The god of poetry and inspiration in Greek mythology.

[3] new planet . . . ken: Most likely alludes to the discovery of Uranus by the astronomer F. W. Herschel in 1781.

[4] Cortez: Keats here mistakes Hernando Cortez (1485–1547) for Balboa (1475–1517), who actually reached the Pacific when crossing through Panama in 1513.

[5] Darien: A mountain range in eastern Panama; Keats uses the word to mean Panama itself.

❧ La Belle Dame sans Merci:[1] A Ballad

1

O what can ail thee, knight-at-arms,
    Alone and palely loitering?
The sedge has withered from the lake,
    And no birds sing.

2

O what can ail thee, knight-at-arms,
    So haggard and so woe-begone?
The squirrel's granary is full,
    And the harvest's done.

3

I see a lily on thy brow,
10   With anguish moist and fever dew,
And on thy cheek a fading rose
    Fast withereth too.

4

"I met a lady in the meads°   *meadows*
    Full beautiful—a faery's child,
Her hair was long, her foot was light,
    And her eyes were wild.

5

"I made a garland for her head,
    And bracelets too, and fragrant zone;°   *girdle*

"La Belle Dame sans Merci." Composed in April 1819, this poem was first published in the *Indicator* on May 10, 1820. The title alludes to a ballad of the same title written by French medieval poet Alain Chartier (1385?–1433?). Keats uses a modified form of the ballad stanza to construct a dialogue between two speakers about the forlorn knight's encounter with a femme fatale. As in "Ode to a Nightingale," the encounter with this mysterious beauty, an embodiment of all the knight could dream for, is followed by disappointment and loss.

---

[1] La . . . Merci: "The Beautiful Lady without Pity," the title of a medieval poem by Alain Chartier.

She looked at me as she did love,
20   And made sweet moan.

6

"I set her on my pacing steed,
      And nothing else saw all day long,
For sidelong would she bend and sing
      A faery's song.

7

"She found me roots of relish sweet,
      And honey wild, and manna dew,
And sure in language strange she said
      'I love thee true.'

8

"She took me to her elfin grot,°   grotto
30   And there she wept and sighed full sore,
And there I shut her wild wild eyes
      With kisses four.

9

"And there she lulléd me asleep,
      And there I dreamed—Ah! woe betide!
The latest dream I ever dreamt
      On the cold hill side.

10

"I saw pale kings and princes too,
      Pale warriors, death-pale were they all;
They cried, 'La Belle Dame sans Merci
40   Hath thee in thrall!'

11

"I saw their starved lips in the gloom°   twilight
      With horrid warning gapéd wide,
And I awoke, and found me here,
      On the cold hill's side.

12

"And this is why I sojourn here,
       Alone and palely loitering,
Though the sedge is withered from the lake,
       And no birds sing."

∽   Ode to a Nightingale

1

My heart aches, and a drowsy numbness pains
       My sense, as though of hemlock I had drunk,
Or emptied some dull opiate to the drains
       One minute past, and Lethe-wards[1] had sunk:
'Tis not through envy of thy happy lot,
       But being too happy in thine happiness,—
              That thou, light-wingéd Dryad° of the trees,   wood nymph
                     In some melodious plot
       Of beechen green, and shadows numberless,
10   Singest of summer in full-throated ease.

2

O, for a draught of vintage! that hath been
       Cool'd a long age in the deep-delvéd earth,
Tasting of Flora and the country green,
       Dance, and Provençal song, and sunburnt mirth!
O for a beaker full of the warm South,
       Full of the true, the blushful Hippocrene,[2]

"Ode to a Nightingale." Keats composed this poem on scraps of paper in May 1819 while listening one morning after breakfast to the song of a nightingale. It is interesting to think of the poem in terms of the imaginative sympathy that Keats believed was one of the gifts of a true poet. He describes that capacity in a letter to Benjamin Bailey dated 22 November 1817, where he says, "if a Sparrow come before my Window I take part in its existence and pick about the Gravel." Here, of course, the Nightingale represents the ideal, or Beauty, and the annihilation of the poet's bodily senses in his identification with the bird enables him to experience a world of beauty from which he inevitably must be separated.

ODE TO A NIGHTINGALE

[1] **Lethe-wards:** Lethe is the river of forgetfulness in Greek mythology.

[2] **Hippocrene:** Fountain of the Muses on Mt. Helicon in Greece.

With beaded bubbles winking at the brim,
  And purple-stainéd mouth;
That I might drink, and leave the world unseen,
20   And with thee fade away into the forest dim:

3

Fade far away, dissolve, and quite forget
  What thou among the leaves hast never known,
The weariness, the fever, and the fret
  Here, where men sit and hear each other groan;
Where palsy shakes a few, sad, last gray hairs,
  Where youth grows pale, and spectre-thin, and dies;
    Where but to think is to be full of sorrow
      And leaden-eyed despairs,
  Where Beauty cannot keep her lustrous eyes,
30   Or new Love pine at them beyond to-morrow.

4

Away! away! for I will fly to thee,
  Not charioted by Bacchus and his pards,°   leopards
But on the viewless wings of Poesy,
  Though the dull brain perplexes and retards:
Already with thee! tender is the night,
  And haply° the Queen-Moon is on her throne,   perhaps
    Cluster'd around by all her starry Fays;°   fairies
      But here there is no light,
  Save what from heaven is with the breezes blown
40   Through verdurous glooms and winding mossy ways.

5

I cannot see what flowers are at my feet,
  Nor what soft incense hangs upon the boughs,
But, in embalméd darkness, guess each sweet
  Wherewith the seasonable month endows
The grass, the thicket, and the fruit-tree wild;
  White hawthorn, and the pastoral eglantine;
    Fast fading violets cover'd up in leaves;
      And mid-May's eldest child,
  The coming musk-rose, full of dewy wine,
50   The murmurous haunt of flies on summer eves.

6

Darkling° I listen; and, for many a time   in the dark
    I have been half in love with easeful Death,
Call'd him soft names in many a muséd rhyme,
    To take into the air my quiet breath;
Now more than ever seems it rich to die,
    To cease upon the midnight with no pain,
        While thou art pouring forth thy soul abroad
        In such an ecstasy!
    Still wouldst thou sing, and I have ears in vain —
60   To thy high requiem become a sod.

7

Thou wast not born for death, immortal Bird!
    No hungry generations tread thee down;
The voice I hear this passing night was heard
    In ancient days by emperor and clown:
Perhaps the self-same song that found a path
    Through the sad heart of Ruth,[3] when, sick for home,
    She stood in tears amid the alien corn;
        The same that oft-times hath
    Charm'd magic casements, opening on the foam
70   Of perilous seas, in faery lands forlorn.

8

Forlorn! the very word is like a bell
    To toll me back from thee to my sole self!
Adieu! the fancy cannot cheat so well
    As she is fam'd to do, deceiving elf.
Adieu! adieu! thy plaintive anthem fades
    Past the near meadows, over the still stream,
        Up the hill-side; and now 'tis buried deep
        In the next valley-glades:
    Was it a vision, or a waking dream?
80   Fled is that music: — Do I wake or sleep?

---

[3] Ruth: From the Book of Ruth in the Bible.

ॐ Ode on a Grecian Urn

1

Thou still unravish'd bride of quietness,
    Thou foster-child of silence and slow time,
Sylvan historian, who canst thus express
    A flowery tale more sweetly than our rhyme:
What leaf-fring'd legend haunts about thy shape
      Of deities or mortals, or of both,
        In Tempe or the dales of Arcady?[1]
    What men or gods are these? What maidens loth?
What mad pursuit? What struggle to escape?
10   What pipes and timbrels?° What wild ecstasy?   *tambourines*

2

Heard melodies are sweet, but those unheard
    Are sweeter; therefore, ye soft pipes, play on;
Not to the sensual ear, but, more endear'd,
    Pipe to the spirit ditties of no tone:
Fair youth, beneath the trees, thou canst not leave
    Thy song, nor ever can those trees be bare;
      Bold lover, never, never canst thou kiss,
Though winning near the goal—yet, do not grieve;
      She cannot fade, though thou hast not thy bliss,
20   For ever wilt thou love, and she be fair!

"Ode on a Grecian Urn." Composed in 1819, this ode was first published in the *Annals of the Fine Arts* on January 15, 1820. Through the figure of the urn, a complex artifact of Keats's synthetic imagination, the poem captures the generative power of the otherwise static work of art—"cold pastoral." As in "Ode to the Nightingale" where the poet's imagination overflows with activity when his senses are suspended, here the "unheard melodies," that is, imagined melodies, are far sweeter than heard ones, just as the poet's imaginative response to the static figures painted on the vase bring them to life. The lovers are poised at the threshold of ecstasy, at the point just before anticipation and desire give way to consummation. These figures, then, are an image of Keats's sense of longing for the beautiful, a longing that for him invited the production of works of art. Despite Keats's desire for a "life of Sensations" "Ode on a Grecian Urn" suggests that the anticipation of sensation was for him a more profound, certainly a more stimulating experience than sensation itself. Nonetheless, the poem abounds in rich, sensuous detail and imagery.

---

[1] **Tempe:** A lovely valley in Greece near Mount Olympus; **Arcady:** Region in the Peloponnese, here symbolizing rural beauty.

3

Ah, happy, happy boughs! that cannot shed
    Your leaves, nor ever bid the spring adieu;
And, happy melodist, unweariéd,
    For ever piping songs for ever new:
More happy love! more happy, happy love!
    For ever warm and still to be enjoy'd,
        For ever panting, and for ever young;
All breathing human passion far above,
    That leaves a heart high-sorrowful and cloy'd,
30   A burning forehead, and a parching tongue.

4

Who are these coming to the sacrifice?
    To what green altar, O mysterious priest,
Lead'st thou that heifer lowing at the skies,
    And all her silken flanks with garlands drest?
What little town by river or sea shore,
    Or mountain-built with peaceful citadel,
        Is emptied of this folk, this pious morn?
And, little town, thy streets for evermore
    Will silent be; and not a soul to tell
40   Why thou art desolate, can e'er return.

5

O Attic² shape! Fair attitude! with brede°   *pattern*
    Of marble men and maidens overwrought,
With forest branches and the trodden weed;
    Thou, silent form, dost tease us out of thought
As doth eternity: Cold pastoral!
    When old age shall this generation waste,
        Thou shalt remain, in midst of other woe
        Than ours, a friend to man, to whom thou say'st,
"Beauty is truth, truth beauty,"³ — that is all
50   Ye know on earth, and all ye need to know.

---

² Attic: Attica, the region in Greece where Athens is located.

³ Beauty . . . beauty: The first published version of this poem, appearing in *Annals of the Fine Arts,* does not have this phrase in quotation marks; the second version, published in *Lamia, Isabella, The Eve of St. Agnes, and Other Poems* (1820), which Keats saw into press, does. The last two lines of this poem have presented a textual and critical problem for scholars and critics.

❧ Ode to Autumn

1

Season of mists and mellow fruitfulness,
    Close bosom-friend of the maturing sun;
Conspiring with him how to load and bless
    With fruit the vines that round the thatch-eves run;
To bend with apples the moss'd cottage-trees,
    And fill all fruit with ripeness to the core;
        To swell the gourd, and plump the hazel shells
    With a sweet kernel; to set budding more,
And still more, later flower for the bees,
10 Until they think warm days will never cease,
        For Summer has o'er-brimm'd their clammy cells.

2

Who hath not seen thee oft amid thy store?
    Sometimes whoever seeks abroad may find
Thee sitting careless on a granary floor,
    Thy hair soft-lifted by the winnowing wind;
Or on a half-reap'd furrow sound asleep,
    Drows'd with the fume of poppies, while thy hook
        Spares the next swath and all its twinéd flowers:
And sometimes like a gleaner thou dost keep
20   Steady thy laden head across a brook;
    Or by a cyder-press, with patient look,
        Thou watchest the last oozings hours by hours.

3

Where are the songs of Spring? Ay, where are they?
    Think not of them, thou hast thy music too,—
While barréd clouds bloom the soft-dying day,
    And touch the stubble-plains with rosy hue;

"Ode to Autumn." Keats had been taking a Sunday's walk along the stubble fields near Winchester when he was so "struck," to use his word, by the beauty of the scene that he was moved to compose this poem about the season. Its rich bounty of sensuous details and images captures the fullness of the season just after harvest time. Keats has created a timeless image in the second stanza where he personifies Autumn as a drowsy farmhand sated from the harvest feast, lounging absentmindedly by the cider press.

Then in a wailful choir the small gnats mourn
　　Among the river sallows,° borne aloft　　　　　　　　　　　　　　　　willows
　　　　Or sinking as the light wind lives or dies;
30　And full-grown lambs loud bleat from hilly bourn;
　　Hedge-crickets sing; and now with treble soft
　　The red-breast whistles from a garden-croft;[1]
　　　And gathering swallows twitter in the skies.

---

[1] garden-croft: Enclosed farmland.

ᖴ E. T. A. HOFFMANN
1776–1822

Although Ernst Theodor Amadeus Hoffmann made his living as a lawyer, he is remembered today for his tales of fantasy and the supernatural. Although he is not as well known in North America as Edgar Allan Poe, people have glimpsed the eerie beauty of his work through Tchaikovsky's[1] *Nutcracker Suite.* Hoffmann's tales such as "The Nutcracker and the King of the Mice" and "The Mines of Falun" exemplify two important aspects of ROMANTICISM. Hoffmann drew on his own native northern- and central-European folk traditions, such as the sinister sandman who visits fretful children and the earth spirits who haunt mines, and recognized them as an imaginative source as rich as Greek and Roman mythology. Along with the Grimm brothers, Jacob and Wilhelm,[2] Hoffmann was part of Romanticism's "re-discovery" of folklore in the nineteenth century, which was characterized by a search for indigenous roots and a valuation of common people, who were idealized as living close to nature and portrayed as harboring beliefs in fairies and magic toadstools.

Hoffmann's tales also explore the uncanny and the grotesque, identifying the supernatural as an important aspect of nature. This acknowledgment of the supernatural is a direct reaction against the rationalism and common sense of the Enlightenment world of the eighteenth century. Hoffmann's ghosts, apparitions, and dreams are always more worthy of attention than the pronouncements of respectable burghers (merchants); the supernatural calls out to Hoffmann's heroes and heroines powerfully because it is a manifestation of repressed guilt or a neglected longing in their hearts. Although related to the medieval castles,

---

[1] Tchaikovsky: Peter Ilich Tchaikovsky (1840–93), a Russian composer.

[2] Grimm brothers, Jacob and Wilhelm: (1785–1863) and (1786–1859) Linguists and folklorists famous for *Grimm's Fairy Tales* (1812–15).

haunted graveyards, and moldy dungeons of the **GOTHIC** novel, Hoffmann's stories portrayed a disturbing realm of fantasy that was just around the corner from ordinary reality.

www For links to more information about Hoffmann and a quiz on "The Mines of Falun," see *World Literature Online* at bedfordstmartins .com/worldlit.

The Consolation of Fantasy.   Hoffmann's works often center on a lonely young person such as Elis Froebom in "The Mines of Falun." Hoffmann's parents separated soon after his birth in 1776, in Königsberg in East Prussia, and he grew up with a fragile mother unable to cope with her circumstances, an ailing grandmother, and a stern uncle. Hoffmann spoke of these years as "an arid heath, without blossom or flower." Fortunately, one cheerful unmarried aunt loved him, and his playmate Theodor von Hippel would prove a staunch friend for all his days. And Hoffmann discovered an emotional outlet and solace in music. Although gifted in many arts—acting, painting, stage design, and literature—music was Hoffmann's first and enduring love. In homage to Wolfgang Amadeus Mozart,[3] the eighteenth-century Austrian composer, Hoffmann changed his baptismal name from Wilhelm to Amadeus.

Despite this artistic bent, the young Hoffmann chose the profession of law. He did well at the university and seemed destined for a comfortable government career, but in 1796, after a scandalous love affair with a married cousin, he fled to Glogau in what is now Poland. This episode was the first of many disruptions in Hoffmann's life. Like Edgar Allan Poe,[4] his spiritual heir, and like many of his fictional characters, Hoffmann was someone who naturally sought out chaos, who subconsciously invited upheaval as soon as he found himself in a settled situation.

Hoffmann was transferred in 1800 to the pleasant Polish city of Posen, where he pursued the arts while serving on the Prussian Polish High Court. When he married Michalina Roher Trzynska, the proper daughter of a civil official, he seemed to have at last entered respectable adulthood. But very soon thereafter, in 1802, Hoffmann upset the peace when he drew a widely circulated cartoon of the imperious local commanding general as a drummer boy beating a fierce tattoo on a teapot with a kitchen spoon. He was punished with a transfer to the tiny village of Plock, deep in central Poland. In April 1804, Theodor von Hippel, titled and wealthy, reappeared in Hoffmann's life and, as he would on many successive occasions, pulled strings to help Hoffmann. This time he got Hoffmann transferred to Warsaw, a vibrant center of art and culture where he thrived. He established an orchestra in his spare time and began composing innovative music. Although seldom performed today, his pieces suggest bold aural images and emotions; Richard Wagner,[5] the nineteenth-century German composer, learned much from him.

When Napoleon defeated the Prussians in 1806, Hoffmann's idyll shattered. In 1807 he was deported to Berlin for refusing to take a French oath of allegiance. While his wife remained stranded in Warsaw, their

---

[3] Wolfgang Amadeus Mozart: Brilliant Austrian composer (1756–1791) of symphonies and operas.

[4] Edgar Allan Poe: American poet and fiction writer (1809–1849) known for his stories of the supernatural.

[5] Richard Wagner: German composer (1813–1883) known for his operas featuring Germanic mythology.

child died in an epidemic. Although the trauma of separation and grief seems to have killed their love, they remained together. The couple eked out a grim living in Berlin until 1808, when Hoffmann was made director of a musical theater in Bamberg, where he began writing short stories.

The Ebb and Flow of Romance.   Hoffmann once wrote that the greatness of Beethoven,[6] whose musical career spanned this period, came from "endless longing that is the very essence of romanticism"; in midlife Hoffmann tasted that "essence" for himself, falling wildly in love with a sixteen-year-old music student. When she married in 1812, Hoffmann left the city. From then on he turned more and more to writing fiction, with hopeless love as one of his recurring themes.

For the next two years, through the dreary confusion of the Napoleonic wars, Hoffmann and his long-suffering wife drifted back and forth between Dresden and Leipzig. He took such a keen interest in closely observing battles that he once got shot; his Battle Symphony sought to depict musically the Battle of Dresden.[7] Even in his composing, Hoffmann was growing more and more attracted to storytelling. His first book, *Fantasy-pieces in the Style of Callot (Fantasiestucke in Callots Manier)*, was published in 1814. In that same year, with von Hippel's help, Hoffmann found work at the Supreme Court in Berlin, where he lived until his death in 1822. Always conscientious about his legal duties, Hoffmann managed at the same time to lead a pleasurable life and to write prolifically. His novel, *The Devil's Elixir (Die Elixiere des Teufels)*, appeared in 1816. At the end of his life, Hoffmann got into another faceoff with authority when the king of Prussia appointed him head of a commission to sniff out traitors. Hoffmann, who championed free speech, kept declaring suspects innocent, even when he personally disliked them. His last years were spent in ill health aggravated by alcoholism and near-bankruptcy.

"The Mines of Falun."   This work of short fiction and additional short stories came out in separate volumes under the general title *The Serapion Brotherhood (Die Serapionsbruder)* between 1819 and 1821. The full, translated name of Hoffmann's novel *Kater Murr* (1820–22) is *Tomcat Murr's Opinions on Life, Together with a Fragmentary Biography of Kapellmeister Johann Kreisler;* in it the autobiography of a cat is alternated with a biography of the musician Kreisler. Three of Hoffmann's writings were turned into an operatic masterpiece by Jacques Offenbach,[8] *The Tales of Hoffmann (Les Contes d'Hoffmann*, 1881).

In "The Mines of Falun" (1819, 1821), the uncanny impinges subtly upon a quite solid nineteenth-century Europe of commerce and pleasure,

---

[6] **Beethoven:** German composer (1770–1827) known for his grand emotional symphonies; his Fifth Symphony is perhaps the most popular classical symphony in the West.

[7] **Battle of Dresden:** This battle in August 1813 was Napoleon's last great victory before his defeat in October of the same year.

[8] **Jacques Offenbach:** French composer (1819–1880) of operettas.

with the East India Company, sailors' carouses, actual Swedish mines, and explanations of profit-sharing. Like many Romantic protagonists, Elis Froebom is alone in a crowd, emotionally unfulfilled; like **Goethe's** p. 29 Faust who thirsts for "the breasts of life," Elis cannot quench his desire with liquor or a woman's love. Like Faust's, his dissatisfaction with his present calling seems darkly linked with family history and old guilts; he miraculously survived the storm in which his father drowned, and his mother died during his last voyage. In time Elis encounters a series of father and mother figures, some of whom exact revenge for Elis's carefree life as a sailor and his attempts to lead a normal life.

In his first conversation with the mysterious Torbern, Elis dwells on his longing for the nurturing mother he has lost, tipping off Torbern that he could be a potential follower of that sternest of mothers, the Metal Queen. While ordinary people content themselves pottering about on the surface of the female earth, the queen reserves her real secrets for those who dare a descent into Her darkness. As in **Keats**'s "Lamia," "Hyperion," p. 281 and "La Belle Dame sans Merci," **Coleridge's** "Christabel," many of Poe's p. 255 tales, and a number of other Romantic texts written by men, a fear of women permeates this work.

The memory of Elis's beloved mother evokes racking guilt in him. Ulla, the "bright angel," first arouses his desires, but then her father plays a trick on him that drives him in despair toward the mine and to his second vision of the Metal Queen. She snares him in a marriage promise that will mean his death. As for the queen herself, merely to look upon her is to be bound to her, and to look away from her means the reluctant beholder will be turned to stone — an allusion to the Greek Gorgon Medusa.[9] Hoffmann's suggestions about sexuality in this no-exit tale are grim indeed.

■ CONNECTIONS

John Keats, "La Belle Dame," p. 286. Nineteenth-century Romanticism revived the role of the *femme fatale* in literature. In Keats's poem "La Belle Dame sans Merci," the nature of the fatal woman, other than her seductive appeal, is rather ambiguous. In "The Mines of Falun," does Hoffmann link the Metal Queen to some aspect of Elis's psyche, to some deep need?

Sigmund Freud (Book 6). A number of nineteenth-century writers were attracted to the dark, irrational side of consciousness. Freud believed that the unconscious was filled with repressed sexual energy. How does Hoffmann's tale seem to anticipate Freud's ideas about the sexual nature of the unconscious?

Adrienne Rich, *Poems* (Book 6). The exploration of the hidden depths of the unconscious in literature is often dramatized by a descent into the underworld. Adrienne Rich in her poem "Diving into the Wreck" uses an underwater exploration of a sunken wreck to symbolize her descent into the unconscious. How is Hoffmann's use of the mine similar to Rich's use of the underwater wreck?

---

[9] **Medusa:** One of three Gorgon sisters in Greek mythology who had snakes for hair; anyone who looked at her was turned to stone.

■ **FURTHER RESEARCH**

Biography
Bleiler, E. F. *The Best Tales of Hoffmann.* 1963.

History & Culture
Kayser, Wolfgang. *The Grotesque in Art and Literature.* 1981.

Criticism
McGlathery, James. *Mysticism and Sexuality: E. T. A. Hoffmann.* 1981.

∽ The Mines of Falun

Translated by E. F. Bleiler

One bright, sunny day in July the whole population of Goethaborg was assembled at the harbour. A fine East Indiaman, happily returned from her long voyage, was lying at anchor, with her long, homeward-bound pennant and the Swedish flag fluttering gaily in the azure sky. Hundreds of boats, skiffs, and other small craft, thronged with rejoicing seafolk, were going to and fro on the mirroring waters of the Goethaelf, and the cannon of Masthuggetorg thundered their far-echoing greeting out to sea. The gentlemen of the East India Company were walking up and down on the quay, reckoning up, with smiling faces, the plentiful profits they had netted, and rejoicing at the yearly increasing success of their hazardous enterprise and at the growing commercial importance of their good town of Goethaborg. For the same reasons everybody looked at these brave adventurers with pleasure and pride, and shared their rejoicing; for their success brought sap and vigour into the whole life of the place.

The crew of the East Indiaman, about a hundred strong, landed in a number of boats (gaily dressed with flags for the occasion) and prepared to hold their Hoensning. That is the name of the feast which the sailors hold on such occasions; it often goes on for several days. Musicians went before them in strange, gay dresses; some played lustily on violins, oboes, fifes, and drums, while others sang merry songs. After them came the crew, walking two and two; some, with gay ribbons on their hats and jackets, waved fluttering streamers; others danced and skipped; and all of them shouted and cheered at the tops of their voices, till the sounds of merriment rang far and wide.

The Mines of Falun. In this story, Hoffmann is playing on very old beliefs about mines; myths from widely separated cultures view miners and metalsmiths as people who have made pacts with the local earth goddess. Like Faust, Elis learns that quests cannot be abandoned simply because one decides it is better to lead a normal life. Nature, the rich mother and mistress who "lays bare her most secret treasures," demands absolute loyalty; she is both nurturer and devourer, and her rules are not human rules. The journey into the mines becomes a journey into the inner darkness of the individual, where that which has been hidden or denied has the power to seduce and destroy. We use E. F. Bleiler's standard translation of "The Mines of Falun" with our footnotes.

Thus the gay procession passed through the streets, and on to the suburb of Haga, where a feast was ready for them in a tavern.

Here the best of "Oel" flowed in rivers and bumper after bumper was quaffed. Women joined them, as is always the case when sailors come home from a long voyage; dancing began, and wilder and wilder grew the revel, and louder and louder the din.

One sailor only—a slender, handsome lad of about twenty or a little less—had slipped away and was sitting alone outside, on the bench at the door of the tavern.

Two or three of his shipmates came out to him, and one of them cried, laughing loudly:

"Now then, Elis Froebom! are you going to be a donkey, as usual, and sit out here sulking instead of joining the sport like a man? Why, you might as well part company from the old ship altogether, and set sail on your own hook as fight shy of the Hoensning. One would think you were a regular long-shore landlubber, and had never been afloat on blue water. All the same, you've got as good pluck as any sailor that walks a deck—ay, and as cool and steady a head in a gale of wind as ever I came athwart; but you see, you can't take your liquor! You'd sooner keep the ducats in your pocket than serve them out to the land-sharks ashore here. Here, lad! take a drink of that; or Naecken, the sea-devil, and all the Troll will be foul of your hawse[1] before you know where you are!"

Elis Froebom jumped up quickly from the bench, glared angrily at his shipmates, took the tumbler—which was filled to the brim with brandy—and emptied it at a draught; then he said:

"You see I can take my glass with any man of you, Ivens; and you can ask the captain if I'm a good sailor or not; so stow away that long tongue of yours and sheer off! I don't care about all this drink and row here; and what I'm doing out here by myself's no business of yours; you have nothing to do with it."

"All right, my hearty!" answered Ivens. "I know all about it. You're one of these Nerica men—and a moony lot the whole cargo of them are too. They're the sort that would rather sit and pipe their eye about nothing particular than take a good glass and see what the women at home are made of, after a twelve-month's cruise! But just you belay there a bit. Steer full and bye, and stand off and on, and I'll send somebody out to you that'll cut you adrift in a pig's whisper from that old bench where you've cast your anchor."

They went, and presently a very pretty girl came out of the tavern and sat down bedside the melancholy Elis, who was still sitting, silent and thoughtful, on the bench. From her dress and general appearance there could be no doubt as to her calling. But the life she was leading had not yet quite marred the delicacy of the wonderfully tender features of her beautiful face; there was no trace of repulsive boldness about the expression of her dark eyes—rather a quiet, melancholy longing.

"Aren't you coming to join your shipmates, Elis?" she said. "Now that you're back safe and sound, after all you've gone through on your long voyage, aren't you glad to be home in the old country again?"

---

[1] hawse: The part of a ship's bow where anchor-cables are fastened.

The girl spoke in a soft, gentle voice, putting her arms about him. Elis Froebom looked into her eyes as if roused from a dream. He took her hand; he pressed her to his breast. It was evident that what she had said had made its way to his heart.

"Ah!" he said, as if collecting his thoughts, "it's no use talking about enjoying myself I can't join in all that riot and uproar; there's no pleasure in it, for me. You go back. Sing and shout like the rest of them, if you can, and let gloomy, melancholy Elis stay out here by himself; he would only spoil your pleasure. Wait a minute, though! I like you, and I want you to think of me sometimes, when I'm away on the sea again."

With that he took two shining ducats out of his pocket and a beautiful Indian handkerchief from his breast, and gave them to the girl. Her eyes streamed with tears; she rose, laid the money on the bench, and said:

"Oh, keep your ducats; they only make me miserable; but I'll wear the handkerchief in remembrance of you. You're not likely to find me next year when you hold your Hoensning in the Haga."

And she crept slowly away down the street, with her hands pressed to her face.

Elis fell back into his gloomy reveries. At length, as the uproar in the tavern grew loud and wild, he cried:

"Oh, I wish I were deep, deep beneath the sea! for there's nobody left in the wide, wide world that I can be happy with now!"

A deep, harsh voice spoke, close behind him: "You must have been most unfortunate, youngster, to wish to die, just when life should be opening before you."

Elis looked round, and saw an old miner leaning with folded arms against the boarded wall of the tavern, looking down at him with a grave, penetrating stare.

As Elis looked at him, a feeling came to him as if some familiar figure had suddenly come into the deep, wild solitude in which he had thought himself lost. He pulled himself together, and told the old miner that his father had been a stout sailor, but had perished in the storm from which he himself had been saved as if by a miracle; that his two soldier brothers had died in battle, and he had supported his mother with the liberal pay he drew for sailing to the East Indies. He said he had been obliged to follow the life of a sailor, having been brought up to it from childhood, and it had been a great piece of good fortune that he got into the service of the East India Company. This voyage, the profits had been greater than usual, and each of the crew had been given a sum of money over and above his pay; so that he had hastened, in the highest spirits, with his pockets full of ducats, to the little cottage where his mother lived. But strange faces looked at him from the windows, and a young woman who opened the door to him at last told him in a cold, harsh tone that his mother had died three months earlier, and that he would find the few bits of things that were left, after paying the funeral expenses, waiting for him at the Town Hall.

The death of his mother broke his heart. He felt alone in the world—as much so as if he had been wrecked on some lonely reef, helpless and miserable. All his life at sea seemed to him to have been a mistaken, purposeless driving. And when he thought of his mother, perhaps badly looked after by strangers, he thought it a wrong and horrible thing that he should have gone to sea at all, instead of staying at home and taking proper care of her. His comrades had dragged him to the Hoensning in spite of himself, and he had thought too that the uproar and even the drink might deaden his pain; but instead of that, all the veins in his breast seemed to be bursting, and he felt as if he would bleed to death.

"Well," said the old miner, "you'll soon be off to sea again, Elis, and then your sorrow will soon be over. Old folks must die; there's no help for that. She has only gone from this miserable world to a better."

"Ah!" said Elis, "it is just because nobody believes in my sorrow, and that they all think me a fool to feel it — I say it's that which is driving me out of the world! I won't go to sea any more; I'm sick of living altogether. When the ship used to go flying along through the water, with all sails set, spreading like wings, the waves playing and dashing in exquisite music, and the wind singing in the rigging, my heart used to bound. Then I could hurrah and shout on deck like the best of them. And when I was on lookout duty of dark, quiet nights, I used to think about getting home, and how glad my dear old mother would be to have me back. I could enjoy a Hoensning like the rest of them then. And when I had shaken the ducats into mother's lap and given her the handkerchiefs and all the other pretty things I had brought home, her eyes would sparkle with pleasure, and she would clap her hands for joy, and run out and in, and fetch me ale which she had kept for my homecoming. And when I sat with her evenings, I would tell her of all the strange folks I had seen, and their ways and customs, and about the wonderful things I had come across in my long voyages. This delighted her; and she would tell me of my father's wonderful cruises in the far North, and lots of strange sailor's yarns which I had heard a hundred times but never could hear too often. Ah! who will give me that happiness back again? What should I do among my shipmates? They would only laugh at me. Where should I find any heart for my work? There would be no purpose to it."

"It gives me real satisfaction to listen to you, youngster," said the old miner. "I have been observing you, without your knowledge, for the last hour or two, and have had my own enjoyment in doing so. All that you have said and done has shown me that you have a very thoughtful mind, and a character and nature pious, simple, and sincere. Heaven could have given you no more precious gifts; but you were never in all your born days in the least cut out for a sailor. How could the wild, unsettled sailor's life suit a meditative, melancholy Neriker like you? — for I can see that you come from Nerica by your features and whole appearance. You are right to say good-bye to that life forever. But you're not going to walk about idle, with your hands in your pockets? Take my advice, Elis Froebom. Go to Falun, and be a miner. You are young and strong. You'll soon be a first-class pick-hand; then a hewer; presently a surveyor, and so get higher and higher. You have a lot of ducats in your pocket. Take care of them; invest them; add more to them. Very likely you'll soon get a 'Hemmans' of your own, and then a share in the works. Take my advice, Elis Froebom; be a miner."

The old man's words caused him a sort of fear.

"What?" he cried. "Would you have me leave the bright, sunny sky that revives and refreshes me, and go down into that hell-like abyss, and dig and tunnel like a mole for metals and ores, merely to gain a few wretched ducats? Oh, never!"

"The usual thing," said the old man. "People despise what they have had no chance of knowing anything about! As if all the constant wearing, petty anxieties inseparable from business up here on the surface, were nobler than the miner's work. To his skill, knowledge, and untiring industry Nature lays bare her most secret treasures. You speak of gain with contempt, Elis Froebom. Well, there's something infinitely higher in question here, perhaps: the mole tunnels the ground from blind instinct; but it may be, in the deepest depths, by the pale glimmer of the mine candle, men's eyes get to see clearer, and at length, growing stronger and stronger, acquire the power of reading in the stones, the gems, and the minerals, the mirroring of secrets which are hidden above the clouds. You know nothing about mining, Elis. Let me tell you a little."

He sat down on the bench beside Elis, and began to describe the various processes minutely, placing all the details before him in the clearest and brightest colours. He talked of the mines of Falun, in which he said he had worked since he was a boy; he described the great main-shaft, with its dark brown sides; he told how incalculably rich the mine was in gems of the finest water. More and more vivid grew his words, more and more glowing his face. He went, in his description, through the different shafts as if they had been the alleys of some enchanted garden. The jewels came to life, the fossils began to move; the wondrous pyrosmalite and the almandine[2] flashed in the light of the miner's candles; the rock crystals glittered, and darted their rays.

Elis listened intently. The old man's strange way of speaking of all these subterranean marvels as if he were standing in the midst of them impressed him deeply. His breast felt stifled; it seemed to him as if he were already down in these depths with the old man, and would never look upon the friendly light of day again. And yet it seemed as though the old man were opening to him a new and unknown world, to which he really properly belonged, and that he had somehow felt all the magic of that world in mystic forebodings since his boyhood.

"Elis Froebom," said the old man at last, "I have laid before you all the glories of a calling for which Nature really destined you. Think the subject over well, and then act as your better judgment counsels you."

He rose quickly from the bench and strode away without any goodbye to Elis, without looking at him even. Soon he disappeared from his sight.

Meanwhile quietness had set in in the tavern. The strong ale and brandy had got the upper hand. Many of the sailors had gone away with the girls; others were lying snoring in corners. Elis—who could go no more to his old home—asked for, and was given, a little room to sleep in.

Scarcely had he thrown himself, worn and weary as he was, upon his bed, when dreams began to wave their pinions over him. He thought he was sailing in a beautiful vessel on a sea calm and clear as a mirror, with a dark, cloudy sky vaulted overhead. But when he looked down into the sea he presently saw that what he had thought was water was a firm, transparent, sparkling substance, in the shimmer of which the ship, in a wonderful manner, melted away, so that he found himself standing upon this floor of crystal, with a vault of black rock above him, for that was rock

---

[2] Pyrosmalite and almandine: Varieties of brightly colored crystals.

which he had taken at first for clouds. Impelled by some power unknown to him he stepped onward, but at that moment everything around him began to move, and wonderful plants and flowers, of glittering metal, came shooting up out of the crystal mass he was standing on, and entwined their leaves and blossoms in the loveliest manner. The crystal floor was so transparent that Elis could distinctly see the roots of these plants. But soon, as his glance penetrated deeper and deeper, he saw, far, far down in the depths, innumerable beautiful maidens, embracing each other with white, gleaming arms; and it was from their hearts that the roots, plants, and flowers were growing. And when these maidens smiled, a sweet sound rang all through the vault above, and the wonderful metal-flowers shot up higher and waved their leaves and branches in joy. An indescribable sense of rapture came upon the lad; a world of love and passionate longing awoke in his heart.

"Down, down to you!" he cried, and threw himself with outstretched arms down upon the crystal ground. But it gave way under him, and he seemed to be floating in shimmering ether.

"Ha! Elis Froebom; what do you think of this world of glory?" a strong voice cried. It was the old miner. But as Elis looked at him, he seemed to expand into gigantic size, and to be made of glowing metal. Elis was beginning to be terrified; but a brilliant light came darting like a sudden lightning flash out of the depths of the abyss, and the earnest face of a grand, majestic woman appeared. Elis felt the rapture of his heart swelling and swelling into destroying pain. The old man had hold of him, and cried:

"Take care, Elis Froebom! That is the queen. You may look up now."

He turned his head involuntarily, and saw the stars of the night sky shining through a cleft in the vault overhead. A gentle voice called his name as if in inconsolable sorrow. It was his mother's. He thought he saw her form up at the cleft. But it was a young and beautiful woman who was calling him, and stretching her hands down into the vault.

"Take me up!" he cried to the old man. "I tell you I belong to the upper world, and its familiar, friendly sky."

"Take care, Froebom," said the old man solemnly; "be faithful to the queen, whom you have devoted yourself to."

But now, when he looked down again into the immobile face of the majestic woman, he felt that his personality dissolved away into glowing molten stone. He screamed aloud in nameless fear and awoke from this dream of wonder, whose rapture and terror echoed deep within his being.

"I suppose I could scarcely help dreaming all this extraordinary stuff," he said to himself, as he collected his senses with difficulty; "the old miner told me so much about the glories of the subterranean world that of course my head's quite full of it. But I never in my life felt as I do now. Perhaps I'm still dreaming. No, no; I suppose I must be a little out of sorts. Let's get into the open air. The fresh sea breeze'll soon set me all right."

He pulled himself together, and ran to the Klippa Haven, where the uproar of the Hoensning was breaking out again. But he soon found that all enjoyment passed him by, that he couldn't hold any thought fast in his mind, that presages and wishes to which he could give no name went crossing each other in his mind. He thought of his dead mother with the bitterest sorrow; but then, again, it seemed to him that what he most longed for was to see that girl again—the one whom he gave the handkerchief to—who had spoken so nicely to him the evening before. And yet he was afraid that if she were to come to meet him out of some street, she would turn out in the end to be the old miner. And he was afraid of *him;* though, at the same time, he would have liked to hear more from him of the wonders of the mine.

Driven hither and thither by all these fancies, he looked down into the water, and then he thought he saw the silver ripples hardening into the sparkling glimmer in which the grand ships melted away, while the dark clouds, which were beginning to gather and obscure the blue sky, seemed to sink down and thicken into a vault of rock. He was in his dream again, gazing into the immobile face of the majestic woman, and the devouring pain of passionate longing took possession of him as before.

His shipmates roused him from his reverie to go and join one of their processions, but an unknown voice seemed to whisper in his ear:

"What are you doing here? Away, away! Your home is in the mines of Falun. There all the glories which you saw in your dream are waiting for you. Away, away to Falun!"

For three days Elis hung and loitered about the streets of Goethaborg, constantly haunted by the wonderful images of his dream, continually urged by the unknown voice. On the fourth day he was standing at the gate through which the road to Gefle goes, when a tall man walked through it, passing him. Elis fancied he recognized in this man the old miner, and he hastened on after him, but could not overtake him.

He followed him on and on, without stopping.

He knew he was on the road to Falun, and this circumstance quieted him in a curious way; for he felt certain that the voice of destiny had spoken to him through the old miner, and that it was he who was now leading him on to his appointed place and fate.

And in fact, many times—particularly if there was any uncertainty about the road—he saw the old man suddenly appear out of some ravine, or from thick bushes, or gloomy rocks, stalk away before him, without looking round, and then disappear again.

At last, after journeying for many weary days, Elis saw in the distance two great lakes with a thick vapour rising between them. As he mounted the hill to westward, he saw some towers and black roofs rising through the smoke. The old man appeared before him, grown to gigantic size, pointed with outstretched hand towards the vapour, and disappeared again among the rocks.

"There lies Falun," said Elis, "the end of my journey."

He was right; for people, coming up from behind him, said the town of Falun lay between the lakes Runn and Warpann, and that the hill he was ascending was the Guffrisberg, where the main shaft of the mine was.

He went bravely on. But when he came to the enormous gulf, like the jaws of hell itself, the blood curdled in his veins, and he stood as if turned to stone at the sight of this colossal work of destruction.

The main shaft of the Falun mines is some twelve hundred feet long, six hundred feet broad, and a hundred and eighty feet deep. Its dark brown sides go, at first for the most part, perpendicularly down, till about halfway they are sloped inwards towards the center by enormous accumulations of stones and refuse. In these, and on the sides, there peeped out here and there timberings of old shafts, formed of strong shores set close together and strongly rabbeted at the ends, in the way that log houses are built. Not a tree, not a blade of grass to be seen in all the bare, blank, crumbling congeries of stony chasms; the pointed, jagged, indented masses of rock tower aloft all round in wonderful forms, often like monstrous animals turned to stone, often like colossal human beings. In the abyss itself lie in wild confusion — pell-mell — stones, slag, and scoria, and an eternal, stupefying sulphurous vapour rises from the depths, as if the hell-broth, whose reek poisons and kills all the green gladsomeness of nature, were being brewed down below. One would think this was where Dante went down and saw the Inferno, with all its horror and immitigable pain.

As Elis looked down into this monstrous abyss, he remembered what an old sailor, one of his shipmates, had told him once. This shipmate of his, at a time when he was down with fever, thought the sea had suddenly all gone dry, and the boundless depths of the abyss had opened under him, so that he saw all the horrible creatures of the deep twining and writhing about in dreadful contortions among thousands of extraordinary shells and groves of coral, till they died, and lay dead, with their mouths all gaping. The old sailor said that to see such a vision meant death, ere long, in the waves; and in fact very soon he did fall overboard, no one knew exactly how, and was drowned without possibility of rescue. Elis thought of that: for indeed the abyss seemed to him to be a good deal like the bottom of the sea run dry; and the black rocks, and the blue and red slag and scoria, were like horrible monsters shooting out polyp-arms at him. Two or three miners happened just then to be coming up from work in the mine, and in their dark mining clothes, with their black, grimy faces, they were much like ugly, diabolical creatures of some sort, slowly and painfully crawling and forcing their way up to the surface.

Elis felt a shudder of dread go through him, and — what he had never experienced in all his career as a sailor — he became giddy. Unseen hands seemed to be dragging him down into the abyss.

He closed his eyes and ran a few steps away from it, and it was not till he began climbing up the Guffrisberg again, far from the shaft, and could look up at the bright, sunny sky, that he quite lost the feeling of terror which had taken possession of him. He breathed freely once more, and cried, from the depths of his heart:

"Lord of my Life! what are the dangers of the sea compared with the horror which dwells in that awful abyss of rock? The storm may rage, the black clouds may come whirling down upon the breaking billows, but the beautiful, glorious sun soon gets the mastery again and the storm is past. But never does the sun penetrate into these black, gloomy caverns; never a freshening breeze of spring can revive the heart down there. No! I shall not join you, black earthworms! Never could I bring myself to lead that terrible life."

He resolved to spend that night in Falun, and set off back to Goethaborg the first thing in the morning.

When he got to the market place, he found a crowd of people there. A train of miners with their mine candles in their hands, and musicians before them, was halted before a handsome house. A tall, slightly built middle-aged man came out, looking around him with kindly smiles. It was easy to see by his frank manner, his open brow, and his bright, dark-blue eyes that he was a genuine Dalkarl. The miners formed a circle around him, and he shook them each cordially by the hand, saying kindly words to them all.

Elis learned that this was Pehrson Dahlsjoe, Alderman, and owner of a fine "Fraelse" at Stora-Kopparberg. "Fraelse" is the name given in Sweden to landed property leased out for the working of the lodes of copper and silver contained in it. The owners of these lands have shares in the mines and are responsible for their management.

Elis was told, further, that the Assizes were just over that day, and that then the miners went round in procession to the houses of the aldermen, the chief engineers and the minemasters, and were hospitably entertained.

When he looked at these fine, handsome fellows, with their kindly, frank faces, he forgot all about the earthworms he had seen coming up the shaft. The healthy gladsomeness which broke out afresh in the whole circle, as if new-fanned by a spring breeze, when Pehrson Dahlsjoe came out, was of a different sort from the senseless noise and uproar of the sailors' Hoensning. The manner in which these miners enjoyed themselves went straight to the serious Elis's heart. He felt indescribably happy; but he could scarce restrain his tears when some of the young pickmen sang an ancient ditty in praise of the miner's calling, and of the happiness of his lot, to a simple melody which touched his heart and soul.

When this song was ended, Pehrson Dahlsjoe opened his door, and the miners all went into his house one after another. Elis followed involuntarily and stood at the threshold, so that he could see the whole spacious room where the miners took their places on benches. Then the doors at the side opposite to him opened, and a beautiful young lady in evening dress came in. She was in the full glory of the freshest bloom of youth, tall and slender with dark hair in many curls, and a bodice fastened with rich clasps. The miners all stood up, and a low murmur of pleasure ran through their ranks. "Ulla Dahlsjoe!" they said. "What a blessing Heaven has bestowed on our hearty alderman in her!" Even the oldest miners' eyes sparkled when she gave them her hand in kindly greeting, as she did to them all. Then she brought beautiful silver tankards, filled them with splendid ale (such as Falun is famous for), and handed them to the guests with a face beaming with kindness and hospitality.

When Elis saw her a lightning flash seemed to go through his heart, kindling all the heavenly bliss, the love-longings, the passionate ardour lying hidden and imprisoned there. For it was Ulla Dahlsjoe who had held out the hand of rescue to him in his mysterious dream. He thought he understood now the deep significance of that dream, and, forgetting the old miner, praised the stroke of fortune which had brought him to Falun.

Alas! he felt he was but an unknown, unnoticed stranger, standing there on the doorstep miserable, comfortless, alone—and he wished he had died before he saw Ulla, as he now must perish for love and longing. He could not move his eyes from the beautiful creature, and as she passed close to him, he pronounced her name in a low, trembling voice. She turned and saw him standing there with a face as red as fire, unable to utter a syllable. So she went up to him and said, with a sweet smile:

"I suppose you are a stranger, friend, since you are dressed as a sailor. Well! why are you standing at the door? Come in and join us."

Elis felt as if in the blissful paradise of some happy dream, from which he would presently waken to inexpressible wretchedness. He emptied the tankard which she had given him; and Pehrson Dahlsjoe came up, and after kindly shaking hands with him, asked him where he came from and what had brought him to Falun.

Elis felt the warming power of the noble liquor in his veins, and looking Dahlsjoe in the eye, he felt happy and courageous. He told him he was a sailor's son and had been at sea since his childhood, had just come home from the East Indies and found his mother dead; that he was now alone in the world; that the wild sea life had become altogether distasteful to him; that his keenest inclination led him to a miner's calling, and that he wished to get employment as a miner here in Falun. The latter statement, quite the reverse of his recent determination, escaped him involuntarily; it was as if he could not have said anything else to the alderman, as if it were the most ardent desire of his soul, although he had not known it himself till now.

Pehrson Dahlsjoe looked at him long and carefully, as if he would read his heart; then he said:

"I cannot suppose, Elis Froebom, that it is mere thoughtless fickleness and the love of change that lead you to give up the calling you have followed hitherto, nor that you have omitted to weigh maturely and consider all the difficulties and hardships of the miner's life before making up your mind to take to it. It is an old belief with us that the mighty elements with which the miner has to deal, and which he controls so bravely, destroy him unless he strains all his being to keep command of them — if he gives place to other thoughts which weaken that vigour which he has to reserve wholly for his constant conflict with Earth and Fire. But if you have properly tested the sincerity of your inward call and it has withstood the trial, you are come in a good hour. Workmen are wanted in my part of the mine. If you like, you can stay here with me, and tomorrow the Captain will take you down with him, and show you what to do."

Elis's heart swelled with gladness at this. He thought no more of the terror of the awful, hell-like abyss into which he had looked. The thought that he was going to see Ulla every day and live under the same roof with her filled him with rapture and delight. He gave way to the sweetest hopes.

Pehrson Dahlsjoe told the miners that a young hand had applied for employment, and presented him to them then and there. They all looked approvingly at the well-knit lad, and thought he was quite cut out for a miner, what with his light, powerful figure, his industry and straightforwardness.

One of the men, well advanced in years, came and shook hands with him cordially, saying he was Head Captain in Pehrson Dahlsjoe's part of the mine, and would be very glad to give him any help and instruction in his power. Elis had to sit down beside this man, who at once began, over his tankard of ale, to describe with much minuteness the sort of work which Elis would have to commence with.

Elis remembered the old miner whom he had seen at Goethaborg, and strangely enough found he was able to repeat nearly all that he had told him.

"Ay," cried the Head Captain. "Where can you have learned all that? It's most surprising! There can't be a doubt that you will be the finest pickman in the mine in a very short time."

Ulla—going back and forth among the guests and attending to them—often nodded kindly to Elis, and told him to be sure and enjoy himself. "You're not a stranger now, you know," she said, "but one of the household. You have nothing more to do with the treacherous sea—the rich mines of Falun are your home."

A heaven of bliss and rapture dawned upon Elis at these words of Ulla's. It was evident that she liked to be near him; and Pehrson Dahlsjoe watched his quiet earnestness of character with manifest approval.

But Elis's heart beat violently when he stood again by the reeking hell-mouth, and went down the mine with the Captain, in his miner's clothes, with the heavy, iron-shod Dalkarl shoes on his feet. Hot vapours soon threatened to suffocate him, and then presently the candles flickered in the cutting draughts of cold air that blew in the lower levels. They went down deeper and deeper, on iron ladders at last scarcely a foot wide; and Elis found that his sailor's adroitness at climbing was not of the slightest service to him there.

They got to the lowest depths of the mine at last, and the Captain showed him what work he was to do.

Elis thought of Ulla. Like some bright angel he saw her hovering over him, and he forgot all the terror of the abyss, and the hardness of the labour.

It was clear in all his thoughts that it was only if he devoted himself with all the power of his mind, and with all the exertion which his body would endure, to mining work here with Pehrson Dahlsjoe, that there was any possibility of his fondest hopes being some day realized. Wherefore it came about that he was as good at his work as the most practiced hand in an incredibly short space of time.

Staunch Pehrson Dahlsjoe got to like this good, industrious lad better and better every day, and often told him plainly that he had found in him one whom he regarded as a dear son as well as a first-class mine-hand. Also Ulla's regard for him became more and more unmistakable. Often, when he was going to his work and there was any prospect of danger, she would enjoin him with tears in her eyes to be sure to take care of himself. And she would come running to meet him when he came back, and always had the finest of ale or some other refreshment ready for him. His heart danced for joy one day when Pehrson said to him that as he had brought a good sum of money with him, there could be no doubt that—with his habits of economy and industry—he would soon have a Hemmans, or perhaps even a Fraelse; and then not a mineowner in all Falun would refuse if he asked for his daughter. Elis would have liked to tell him at once how unspeakably he loved Ulla, and how all his hopes of happiness were based upon her. But unconquerable shyness and the doubt whether Ulla really liked him—though he often thought she did—sealed his lips.

One day it chanced that Elis was at work in the lowest depths of the mine, shrouded in thick, sulphurous vapour, so that his candle only shed a feeble glimmer and he could scarcely distinguish the run of the lode. Suddenly he heard—as if coming from some still deeper cutting—a knocking as if somebody was at work with a pick-hammer. As that sort of work was scarcely possible at such a depth, and as he knew nobody was down there that day but himself—because the Captain had all the men employed in another part of the mine—this knocking and hammering struck him as strange and uncanny. He stopped working and listened to the hollow sounds, which seemed to come nearer and nearer. All at once he saw, close by him, a black shadow and—as a keen draught of air blew away the sulphur vapour—the old miner whom he had seen in Goethaborg.

"Good luck," he cried, "good luck to Elis Froebom, down here among the stones! What do you think of the life, comrade?"

Elis would have liked to ask in what wonderful way the old man had got into the mine; but he kept striking his hammer on the rocks with such force that the sparks went whirling all round, and the mine rang as if with distant thunder. Then he cried, in a terrible voice:

"There's a grand run of trap[3] just here; but a scurvy, ignorant scoundrel like you sees nothing in it but a narrow streak of 'trumm' not worth a beanstalk. Down here you're a sightless mole, and you'll always be a mere abomination to the Metal Prince. You're of no use up above either—trying to get hold of the pure Regulus; which you never will—hey! You want to marry Pehrson Dahlsjoe's daughter; that's what you've taken to mine work for, not from any love of it. Mind what you're after, doubleface; take care that the Metal Prince, whom you are trying to deceive, doesn't take you and dash you down so that the sharp rocks tear you limb from limb. And Ulla will never be your wife; that much I tell you."

Elis's anger was kindled at the old man's insulting words.

"What are you doing," he cried, "here in my master, Herr Pehrson Dahlsjoe's shaft, where I am doing my duty and working as hard at it as I can? Be off out of this the way you came, or we'll see which of us two will dash the other's brains out down here."

With which he placed himself in a threatening attitude and swung his hammer about the old man's ears; he only gave a sneering laugh, and Elis saw with terror how he swarmed up the narrow ladder rungs like a squirrel, and disappeared amongst the black labyrinths of the chasms.

The young man felt paralyzed in all his limbs; he could not go on with his work, but went up. When the old Head Captain—who had been busy in another part of the mine—saw him, he cried:

"For God's sake, Elis, what has happened to you? You're as pale as death. I suppose it's the sulphur gas; you're not accustomed to it yet. Here, take a drink, my lad; that'll do you good."

Elis took a good mouthful of brandy out of the flask which the Head Captain handed to him; and then, feeling better, told him what had happened down in the mine, as also how he had made the uncanny old miner's acquaintance in Goethaborg.

---

[3] **Trap:** A kind of igneous rock that is crushed and used to make roadbeds.

The Head Captain listened silently; then dubiously shook his head and said:

"That must have been old Torbern that you met, Elis; and I see now that there really is something in the tales that people tell about him. More than one hundred years ago, there was a miner here of the name of Torbern. He seems to have been one of the first to bring mining into a flourishing condition at Falun here, and in his time profits far exceeded anything that we know of now. Nobody at that time knew so much about mining as Torbern, who had great scientific skill and thoroughly understood all the ins and outs of the business. The richest lodes seemed to disclose themselves to him, as if he was endowed with higher powers peculiar to himself; and as he was a gloomy, meditative man, without wife or child—with no regular home, indeed—and very seldom came up to the surface, it couldn't fail that a story soon went about that he was in compact with the mysterious power which dwells in the bowels of the earth and creates metals. Disregarding Torbern's solemn warnings— for he always prophesied that some calamity would happen as soon as the miners' impulse to work ceased to be sincere love for the marvellous metals and ores— people went on enlarging the excavations more and more for the sake of mere profit, till on St. John's Day[4] of the year 1678, came the terrible landslip and subsidence which formed our present enormous main shaft, laying waste the whole of the works, as they were then, in the process. It was only after many months' labour that several of the shafts were with much difficulty put into workable order again. Nothing was seen or heard of Torbern. There seemed to be no doubt that he had been at work down below at the time of the catastrophe, so that there could be no question what his fate had been. But not long after, particularly when the work was beginning to go better again, the miners said they had seen old Torbern in the mine, and that he had given them valuable advice and pointed out rich lodes to them. Others had come across him at the top of the main shaft, walking round it, sometimes lamenting, sometimes shouting in wild anger. Other young fellows have come here in the way you yourself did, saying that an old miner had advised them to take to mining and shown them the way to Falun. This always happened when there was a scarcity of hands; very likely it was Torbern's way of helping on the cause. But if it really was he whom you had those words with in the mine, and if he spoke of a fine run of trap there isn't a doubt that there must be a grand vein of ore thereabouts, and we must see tomorrow if we can come across it. Of course you remember that we call rich veins of the kind 'trap-runs,' and that a 'trumm' is a vein which goes subdividing into several smaller ones, and probably gets lost altogether."

When Elis, tossed hither and thither by various thoughts went into Pehrson Dahlsjoe's, Ulla did not come to meet him as usual. She was sitting with downcast looks and—as he thought—eyes which had been weeping; and beside her was a handsome young fellow, holding her hand and trying to say all sorts of kind and amusing things to which she seemed to pay little attention. Pehrson Dahlsjoe took Elis—who, seized by gloomy presentiments, was keeping a dark glance riveted on the pair—into another room, and said:

---

[4] **Saint John's Day:** June 24, near the summer solstice; in old European folklore, it was thought to be a good day for discovering buried treasure.

"Well, Elis, you will soon have it in your power to give me a proof of your regard and sincerity. I have always looked upon you as a son, but you will soon take the place of one altogether. The man whom you see in there is a well-to-do merchant, Eric Olavsen by name, from Goethaborg. I am giving him my daughter for his wife, at his desire. He will take her to Goethaborg, and then you will be left alone with me, my only support in my declining years. Well, you say nothing? You turn pale? I trust this step doesn't displease you, and that now that I'm going to lose my daughter you are not going to leave me too? But I hear Olavsen mentioning my name; I must go in."

With which he went back to the room.

Elis felt a thousand red-hot irons tearing at his heart. He could find no words, no tears. In wild despair he ran out, out of the house, away to the great mine shaft.

That monstrous chasm had a terrible appearance by day; but now, when night had fallen and the moon was just peeping down into it, the desolate crags looked like a numberless horde of horrible monsters, the dire brood of hell, rolling and writhing in wildest confusion all about its reeking sides and clefts, and flashing up fiery eyes and shooting forth glowing claws to clutch the race of mortals.

"Torbern, Torbern," Elis cried in a terrible voice which made the rocks re-echo. "Torbern, I am here; you were not wrong—I was a wretched fool to fix my hopes on any earthly love, up on the surface here. My treasure, my life, everything for me, is down below. Torbern! take me down with you! Show me the richest veins, the lodes of ore, the glowing metal! I will dig and bore, and toil and labour. Never, never more will I come back to see the light of day. Torbern! Torbern! take me down to you!"

He took his flint and steel from his pocket, lighted his candle, and went quickly down the shaft, into the deep cutting where he had been on the previous day, but he saw nothing of the old man. But what was his amazement when, at the deepest point, he saw the vein of metal with the utmost clearness and distinctness, so that he could trace every one of its ramifications and its risings and fallings. But as he kept his gaze fixed more and more firmly on this wonderful vein, a dazzling light seemed to come shining through the shaft, and the walls of rock grew transparent as crystal. That mysterious dream which he had had in Goethaborg came back upon him. He was looking upon those Elysian Fields of glorious metallic trees and plants on which, by way of fruits, buds, and blossoms, hung jewels streaming with fire. He saw the maidens and he looked on the face of the mighty queen. She put out her arms, drew him to her, and pressed him to her breast. Then a burning ray darted through his heart, and all his consciousness was merged in a feeling of floating in waves of some blue, transparent, glittering mist.

"Elis Froebom! Elis Froebom!" a powerful voice from above cried out, and the reflection of torches began shining in the shaft. It was Pehrson Dahlsjoe who had come down with the Captain to search for the lad, who had been seen running in the direction of the main shaft like a mad creature.

They found him standing as if turned to stone, with his face pressed against the cold, hard rock.

"What are you doing down here in the nighttime, you foolish fellow?" cried Pehrson. "Pull yourself together, and come up with us. Who knows what good news you may hear."

Elis went up in profound silence after Dahlsjoe, who did not cease to rate him soundly for exposing himself to such danger. It was broad daylight when they got to the house.

Ulla threw herself into Elis's arms with a great cry and called him the fondest names, and Pehrson said to him:

"You foolish fellow! How could I help seeing, long ago, that you were in love with Ulla, and that it was on her account, in all probability, that you were working so hard in the mine? Neither could I help seeing that she was just as fond of you. Could I wish for a better son-in-law than a fine, hearty, hard-working, honest miner — than just yourself, Elis? What vexed me was that you never would speak."

"We scarcely knew ourselves," said Ulla, "how fond we were of each other."

"However that may be," said Pehrson, "I was annoyed that Elis didn't tell me openly and candidly of his love for you, and that was why I made up the story about Eric Olavsen, which was so nearly being the death of you, you silly fellow. Not but what I wished to try you, Ulla, into the bargain. Eric Olavsen has been married for many a day, and I give my daughter to you, Elis Froebom, for, I say again, I couldn't wish for a better son-in-law."

Tears of joy and happiness ran down Elis's cheeks. The highest bliss which his imagination had pictured had come to pass so suddenly and unexpectedly that he could scarcely believe it was anything but another blissful dream. The work people came to dinner, at Dahlsjoe's invitation, in honour of the event. Ulla had dressed in her prettiest attire, and looked more charming than ever, so that they all cried, over and over again, "Eh! what a sweet and charming creature Elis has for his wife! May God bless them and make them happy!"

Yet the terror of the previous night still lay upon Elis's pale face, and he often stared about him as if he were far away from all that was going on round him. "Elis, darling, what is the matter?" Ulla asked anxiously. He pressed her to his heart and said, "Yes, yes, you are my own, and all is well." But in the midst of all his happiness he often felt as though an icy hand clutched at his heart, and a dismal voice asked him:

"Is it your highest aim to be engaged to Ulla? Wretched fool! Have you not looked upon the face of the queen?"

He felt himself overpowered by an indescribable feeling of anxiety. He was haunted and tortured by the thought that one of the workmen would suddenly assume gigantic proportions, and to his horror he would recognize in him Torbern, come to remind him, in a terrible manner, of the subterranean realm of gems and metals to which he had devoted himself.

And yet he could see no reason why the spectral old man should be hostile to him, or what connection there was between his mining work and his love.

Pehrson, seeing Elis's disordered condition, attributed it to the trouble he had gone through and his nocturnal visit to the mine. Not so Ulla, who, seized by a secret presentiment, implored her lover to tell her what terrible thing had happened to him to tear him away from her so entirely. This almost broke his heart. It was in vain that he tried to tell her of the wonderful face which had revealed itself to him in the depths of the mine. Some unknown power seemed to seal his lips forcibly; he felt as though the terrible face of the queen were looking out from his heart, so that if he mentioned her, everything about him would turn to stone, to dark, black rock, as at the sight of the Medusa's frightful head. All the glory and magnificence which had filled him with rapture in the abyss appeared to him now as a pandemonium of immitigable torture, deceptively decked out to allure him to his ruin.

Dahlsjoe told him he must stay at home for a few days to shake off the sickness which he seemed to have fallen into. And during this time Ulla's affection, which now streamed bright and clear from her candid, childlike heart, drove away the memory of his fateful adventure in the mine depths. Joy and happiness brought him back to life and to belief in his good fortune, and in the impossibility of its being ever interfered with by any evil power.

When he went down the pit again, everything appeared quite different to what it used to be. The most glorious veins lay clear and distinct before his eyes. He worked twice as zealously as before; he forgot everything else. When he got to the surface again, it cost him an effort to remember Pehrson Dahlsjoe, even his Ulla. He felt as if divided into two halves, as if his better self, his real personality, went down to the central point of the earth, and there rested in bliss in the queen's arms, whilst *he* went to his dark dwelling in Falun. When Ulla spoke of their love, and the happiness of their future life together, he would begin to talk of the splendours of the depths, and the inestimably precious treasures that lay hidden there, and in so doing would get entangled in such wonderful, incomprehensible sayings that alarm and terrible anxiety took possession of the poor child, who could not divine why Elis should be so completely altered from his former self. He kept telling the Captain and Dahlsjoe himself with the greatest delight, that he had discovered the richest veins and the most magnificent trap-runs, and when these turned out to be nothing but unproductive rock, he would laugh contemptuously and say that none but he understood the secret signs, the significant writing, fraught with hidden meaning, which the queen's own hand had inscribed on the rocks, and that it was sufficient to understand those signs without bringing to light what they indicated.

The old Captain looked sorrowfully at Elis, who spoke, with wild gleaming eyes of the glorious paradise which glowed down in the depths of the earth. "That terrible old Torbern has been at him," he whispered in Dahlsjoe's ear.

"Pshaw! don't believe these miners' yarns," cried Dahlsjoe. "He's a deep-thinking serious fellow, and love has turned his head, that's all. Wait till the marriage is over, then we'll hear no more of the trap-runs, the treasures, and the subterranean paradise."

The wedding day fixed by Dahlsjoe came at last. For a few days previously Elis had been more tranquil, more serious, more sunk in deep reflection than ever. But, on the other hand, never had he shown such affection for Ulla as at this time. He could not leave her for a moment, and never went down the mine at all. He seemed to have forgotten his restless excitement about mining work, and never a word of the subterranean kingdom crossed his lips. Ulla was all rapture. Her fear lest the dangerous powers of the subterranean world, of which she had heard old miners speak, had been luring him to his destruction, had left her; and Dahlsjoe too said, laughing to the Captain, "You see, Elis was only a little light-headed for love of my Ulla."

Early on the morning of the wedding day, which was St. John's Day as it chanced, Elis knocked at the door of Ulla's room. She opened it, and started back terrified at the sight of Elis, dressed in his wedding clothes, deadly pale, with dark gloomy fire sparkling in his eyes.

"I only want to tell you, my beloved Ulla," he said, in a faint, trembling voice, "that we are just arrived at the summit of the highest good fortune which it is possible for mortals to attain. Everything has been revealed to me in the night which is just over. Down in the depths below, hidden in chlorite and mica, lies the cherry-coloured sparkling almandine, on which the tablet of our lives is graven. I have to give it to you as a wedding present. It is more splendid than the most glorious blood-red carbuncle,[5] and when, united in truest affection, we look into its streaming splendour together, we shall see and understand the peculiar manner in which our hearts and souls have grown together into the wonderful branch which shoots from the queen's heart, at the central point of the globe. All that is necessary is that I go and bring this stone to the surface, and that I will do now, as fast as I can. Take care of yourself meanwhile, darling. I will be back in a little while."

Ulla implored him with bitter tears to give up all idea of such a dreamlike undertaking, for she felt a strong presentiment of disaster; but Elis declared that without this stone he should never know a moment's peace or happiness, and that there was not the slightest danger of any kind. He pressed her fondly to his heart, and was gone.

The guests were all assembled to accompany the bridal pair to the church of Copparberg, where they were to be married, and a crowd of girls, who were to be the bridesmaids and walk in procession before the bride (as is the custom of the place), were laughing and playing round Ulla. The musicians were tuning their instruments to begin a wedding march. It was almost noon, but Elis had not made his appearance. Suddenly some miners came running up, horror in their pale faces, with the news that there had been a terrible catastrophe, a subsidence of the earth, which had destroyed the whole of Pehrson Dahlsjoe's part of the mine.

"Elis! oh, Elis! you are gone!" screamed Ulla, wildly, and fell as if dead. Then for the first time Dahlsjoe learned from the Captain that Elis had gone down the main shaft in the morning. Nobody else had been in the mine, the rest of the men having been invited to the wedding. Dahlsjoe and all the others hurried off to search, at the imminent danger of their own lives. In vain! Elis Froebom was not to be found. There could be no question but that the earth-fall had buried him in the rock. And thus came desolation and mourning upon the house of brave Pehrson Dahlsjoe, at the moment when he thought he was assured of peace and happiness for the remainder of his days.

Long had stout Pehrson Dahlsjoe been dead, his daughter Ulla long lost sight of and forgotten. Nobody in Falun remembered them. More than fifty years had gone by since Froebom's luckless wedding day, when it chanced that some miners who

---

[5] carbuncle: Any of several kinds of red gemstones.

were making a connection passage between two shafts found, at a depth of three hundred yards, buried in vitriolated water, the body of a young miner, which seemed when they brought it to the daylight to be turned to stone.

The young man looked as if he were lying in a deep sleep, so perfectly preserved were the features of his face, so wholly without trace of decay his new suit of miner's clothes, and even the flowers in his breast. The people of the neighbourhood all collected round the young man, but no one recognized him or could say who he had been, and none of the workmen missed any comrade.

The body was going to be taken to Falun, when out of the distance an old, old woman came creeping slowly and painfully up on crutches.

"Here's the old St. John's Day grandmother!" the miners said. They had given her this name because they had noticed that every year she came up to the main shaft on Saint John's Day, and looked down into its depths, weeping, lamenting, and wringing her hands as she crept round it, then went away again.

The moment she saw the body she threw away her crutches, lifted her arms to Heaven, and cried, in the most heart-rending way.

"Oh! Elis Froebom! Oh, my sweet, sweet bridegroom!"

And she huddled down beside the body, took the stone hands and pressed them to her heart, chilled with age, but throbbing still with the fondest love, like some naphtha flame under the surface ice.

"Ah!" she said, looking round at the spectators, "nobody, nobody among you remembers poor Ulla Dahlsjoe, this poor boy's happy bride fifty long years ago. When I went away, in my terrible sorrow and despair, to Ornaes, old Torbern comforted me, and told me I should see my poor Elis, who was buried in the rock upon our wedding day, once more here upon earth. And I have come every year and looked for him. And now this blessed meeting has been granted me this day. Oh, Elis! Elis! my beloved husband!"

She wound her arms about him as if she would never part from him more, and the people all stood around in the deepest emotion.

Fainter and fainter grew her sobs and sighs, till they ceased to be audible.

The miners closed around. They would have raised poor Ulla, but she had breathed out her life upon her bridegroom's body. The spectators noticed now that it was beginning to crumble into dust. The appearance of petrifaction had been deceptive.

In the church of Copparberg, where they were to have been married fifty years earlier, the miners laid in the earth the ashes of Elis Froebom, and with them the body of her who had been thus "Faithful unto death."

❧ HEINRICH HEINE
1797–1856

HINE-rik HIGH-nuh

p. 321

LOH-ruh-ligh

Heinrich Heine is one of the most influential German writers of the nineteenth century. Best known for his lyric poetry and literary criticism, Heine also wrote political and narrative poetry, plays, and many influential essays on German and French politics and culture. While Austrian composer Franz Schubert (1797–1828) and German composer Robert Schumann (1810–1856) set to music many of Heine's lyrics from the early *Book of Songs* (***Buch de Lieder,*** 1827), writers such as Karl Marx and Sigmund Freud drew on his political poems and critical essays in their treatises on political economy and psychoanalytic theory, respectively. Heine's early lyric poetry, such as "A Spruce Is Standing Lonely" and **"The Lorelei,"** draws on ROMANTIC themes such as exile and longing, and literary conventions such as the BALLAD form,[1] but he would soon subvert what he saw as the sentimentality and naiveté of the Romantic vision. Later poems such as "The Migratory Rats" and "The Silesian Weavers" sustain the irony of his earlier work and register the alienation and fears of nineteenth-century Europeans caught up in the turbulence of political, social, and economic revolutions. The body of Heine's poetry enacts the struggle, undertaken in the larger culture of Europe in the nineteenth century, between Romanticism and REALISM.[2] The aims of prosperity and progress held by the generation of the young century were tempered by the stark realities of reactionary and revolutionary politics, industrialization and commercialism, urbanization and an increase in the population, and the consequent alienation and disillusion that many people felt.

Patrons and Patriarchs.   Heinrich Heine was born in 1797 at Düsseldorf, a small German city near the Rhine River. He was the son of German-Jewish drape merchants, whose modest success was overshadowed by the immense wealth of Heinrich's domineering millionaire uncle, Salomon Heine. Salomon played a strong role in Heine's development, financing a failed business venture and providing for his nephew's university education in law at the Universities of Bonn, Göttingen, and Berlin. At Bonn, Heine studied with the Romantic philosopher-critic

Portrait of Heinrich Heine. Engraving
Heine was known for his youthful looks and well-kept appearance. (Bibliothèque Nationale, Paris)

---

[1] **ballad form:** A fairly simple verse designed to be sung, which generally tells a dramatic tale or simple story; ballads are associated with the oral traditions or folklore of common people. The folk ballad usually consists of four lines of alternating tetrameter (four accented syllables) and trimeter (three accented syllables), following a rhyme scheme of *abab* or *abcb*.

[2] **Realism:** The attempt in literature to conform the depiction of characters and settings as closely as possible to one's experience of the real world; beginning in about the middle of the nineteenth century, writers in France, England, and the United States deliberately rejected the hyperbole and sentimentality of previous novels and attempted to produce fiction that closely resembled reality.

Arthur W. Schlegel;[3] there too, against his uncle's and his mother's wishes, Heine delved into literary studies by translating sections of **Byron's** *Childe Harold* and *Manfred,* writing his own ballads and lyrics, and sketching out plans for a volume of verse. At Berlin, Heine met Rhal Varnhagen von Ense, a wealthy patron of the arts, at whose salon he found inspiration to pursue a career in literature. During that time he undertook a literary pilgrimage to meet the great German writer Goethe, to whom he sent his first collection of original poems.

p. 189

The Self-Conscious Romantic.   After returning to Göttingen, where he received a law degree in 1825, Heine was determined to pursue a literary career. Supported by his uncle, Heine traveled throughout Germany, England, France, and Italy, writing some prose pieces, including *The Harz Journey,* as well as poetry, including the series of poems in *The Homecoming* and *The North Sea Poems.* Heine published these and other poems in his first collection, *The Book of Songs,* in 1827. This volume includes many romantic lyrics about lost love, alluding to Heine's early and disappointed love for his cousins Amalie and Therese. The lovelorn speaker of these lyrics typifies the Romantic convention of the forlorn speaker caught up in bittersweet disappointment and longing that Heine would later reject. In these verses, however, Heine already begins to display the self-conscious irony that characterizes his later work. The volume was immediately successful in Germany and abroad, and the love lyrics have been favorably compared with those of the **Renaissance** poet Petrarch (1304–1374), whose romantic sonnets in vernacular Italian represent some of the greatest love lyrics in European poetry.

After the **Revolution of 1830**[4] in France, frustrated by his unsuccessful attempts to find a position in civil service at home, Heine turned to Paris as a place more suitable to his liberal ideals than was the politically conservative, increasingly nationalistic Germany. Like the English poet Lord Byron who left England in 1816 never to return, Heine moved to Paris in May 1831, never to reside in Germany again. In the 1830s Heine wrote three seminal essays on French and German culture, which appeared first as a series of newspaper articles: "French Affairs" (1832), "The Romantic School" (1833–35) and "Concerning the History of Religion and Philosophy in Germany" (1834–35). "The Romantic School," a penetrating essay on GERMAN ROMANTICISM, traces the origins of the movement to its roots in the Catholicism of the Middle Ages and critically describes

www For links to more information about Heine and a quiz on his poetry, see *World Literature Online* at bedfordstmartins .com/worldlit.

---

[3] **Arthur W. Schlegel:** (1767–1845) An important German Romantic literary critic and translator of Shakespeare, associated with the "Jena Circle," which included his younger brother Friedrich Schlegel, also a literary critic.

[4] **Revolution of 1830:** After the death of Louis XVIII (r. 1814–24), Charles X (r. 1824–30) succeeded to the French throne and immediately began to undermine the liberal reforms guaranteed under his predecessor and to grant privileges to his ultraroyalist supporters. In July 1830, Charles's opponents took to the streets of Paris, Charles abdicated the throne, and the bankers and industrialists brought in King Louis Philippe (r. 1830–48), who promised to preserve the reforms Charles had tried to dissolve.

He was a fine
man . . . one would
have said a German
Apollo, to see his
high white forehead,
pure as a marble
table, which was
shadowed with great
masses of brown
hair.

– THÉOPHILE GAUTIER

its idealistic tendencies in terms that anticipate Marx's famous critique of German idealism in *The German Ideology.*[5] Heine hoped to correct what he saw as the misrepresentations of German culture presented in Madame de Staël's[6] important book *Of Germany* (1813). *"Concerning the History of Religion and Philosophy in Germany"* is a critique of contemporary German politics that cites the potential and outlines the process which Germany could reform itself according to liberal ideas that had begun with the Reformation[7] of the sixteenth century and continued through the philosophy of the Enlightenment to the modern critical philosophy of Heine's own day.

The Political and Poetical Reformer.   While immersed in the writing of these essays, in 1834 Heine moved in with his companion, Crescence Eugénie Mirat, the daughter of a Parisian shopkeeper, whom he married in August 1841. (Eugénie is known by her nickname "Mathilde" in Heine's poetry.) Shortly thereafter, Heine made a last trip to Germany to visit his mother and uncle, seeing both for the last time. Upon returning to Paris, he met Karl Marx and began writing two long political poems: *Germany—A Winter's Tale,* a scathing critique of reactionary politics, nationalism, and censorship in Germany, and *Atta Troll: A Midsummer Night's Dream* (1843–45), a satiric fable attacking self-righteous radicals and ridiculing the shallow character of polemical verse, which he described as "rhymed newspaper articles." Having earlier acquainted himself with the utopian socialism of Saint-Simon (1760–1825)[8] and the modest democratic reforms in France under King Louis Philippe (r. 1830–48), Heine believed in and hoped for political and social transformation in the service of egalitarian reform. In *Travel Pictures* (1826–27), Heine had expressed that the "great task" of his day was "emancipation," and the long political poems demonstrate his ongoing commitment to freedom. Although he contributed occasional political satires and poems, including "The Silesian Weavers," to Marx's *Yearbooks* and *Forward!* in the 1840s, Heine was not a partisan poet, and *Germany* and *Atta Troll* show that he was capable of attacking extremism in any form, whether reactionary or revolutionary.

Germany was banned in its home country when it was published in 1844 as part of Heine's second major collection of poetry, *New Poems.* As

---

[5] *The German Ideology:* An unpublished treatise written by German philosopher Karl Marx (1818–1883) in 1845–46 that launched a radical critique of the idealistic tendencies of German philosophy and set up the basis for Marx's materialist theories.

[6] Madame de Staël: (1766–1817) Novelist, literary critic, and essayist, the Genevan-born Germaine Necker, later Madame de Staël, was one of the most important women of letters in Europe in the early nineteenth century.

[7] Reformation: The challenge to the Catholic Church initiated by such sixteenth-century reformers as Martin Luther and John Calvin.

[8] Saint-Simon: (1760–1825) Claude-Henri de Rouvroy, Comte de Saint-Simon, was an early utopian socialist whose writings advocated a restructuring of society that would improve the welfare of all citizens by entrusting power to industry and science.

far as the authorities in the German states were concerned, Heine was a revolutionary and Francophile (literally, "lover of France"). Nonetheless, the book sold out and went quickly into a second edition. In December 1844 Heine's uncle Salomon died, leaving the allowance to which Heine had grown accustomed in question. After a prolonged and bitter battle between Heine and his cousin Karl the allowance was restored. By this time Heine began to show signs of the debilitating spinal paralysis, attributed to syphilis, that finally confined him to bed—what he called his "mattress grave"—from 1848 to the end of his life. Though bedridden, in his last years Heine continued writing and published two more major collections of verse, *Romanzero* (1851) and *Poems 1853 and 1854* (1854). He died in February 1856.

> Freedom is a new religion, the religion of our age.
>
> – HEINRICH HEINE

Anti-Romantic Irony. While Heine's poetry drew on the ideas of Romantic theorists such as Schlegel and on the popular ballad and folk forms of the Romantic poets, from the very beginning Heine was skeptical of what he saw as the naive and simplistic idealism of the Romantic school, which projected human fulfillment onto some endlessly deferred horizon. Heine instead was inclined to face head-on the contradictions and disappointments of reality. Nonetheless, as Jeffrey Sammons points out in a biography of the writer, "it did not occur to him, at least at the outset, that genuine poetry could be about the real" and so the poems that appeared in *Tragedies with a Lyrical Intermezzo* (1823), *Travel Pictures* (1826–27), and *The Book of Songs* (1827), his first collection, invoked Romantic themes, such as the Romantic treatment and contrasting of the ideal and the real; the sorrows of unrequited love; and the longing for self-annihilation; but Heine undercut them with an ironic sense of those subjects' futility. Sammons calls the tension between the ideal and the real in Heine's early poems, such as "The Grenadiers" and "The Lorelei," as "Heine's anti-Romantic irony."

The lyrical elegance, simple diction, and dreamlike quality of the poems in *The Book of Songs* enchanted readers, who recognized in Heine an extraordinary talent. Many of the lyric poems, such as "The Lorelei," are well known as popular songs in Germany even today. Franz Schubert set six of Heine's poems from the "Homecoming" section to music for his *Swansong* in 1828. More than 3,000 musical versions of Heine's verses exist today. The first stanza of "You are like a flower," which has been set to music more than 200 times, is quoted below in its original form. Heine's supple use of poetic devices, including alliteration, assonance, enjambment, caesura, trimeter, and half rhymes, creates a rich and self-sustaining melody of its own:

> Du bist wie eine Blume,
> So hold und schön und rein;
> Ich schau' dich an, und Wehmut
> Schleicht mir ins Herz hinein.

The lines in English may be rendered: "You are like a flower / So sweet and lovely and pure; / I look at you, and melancholy / Steals into my very heart." The translation inevitably loses some of the grace of Heine's finely wrought quatrain.

The Poetry of Life.   While Heine's attention to political and social events kept him occupied with prose works during the 1830s, he continued to write poetry during these years and completed a manuscript collection by 1838 that, in expanded form, would become *New Poems,* published in 1844. This collection was followed by two other major works that confirmed his reputation as one of Germany's greatest poets, a master of technique and self-conscious irony—*Romanzero* (1851) and *Poems of 1853 and 1854* (1854). In these volumes the ironic tone of the early work deepens and the Romantic themes often give way to overtly political poems, such as "The Silesian Weavers" and "The Slave Ship." These two collections also contain some of Heine's most moving poetry, written while he was wasting away in his "mattress grave," about human suffering, which is not naturalized as a necessary condition but seen as a result of historical forces and human cruelty. *Romanzero* also contains Heine's "Hebrew Melodies," in which Heine movingly engages his Jewish heritage with a mixture of admiration and distance. Heine once wrote that "the poetry of life is greater than the poetry of death"; the poetry he wrote as he lay dying may be said to be the poetry of life, inasmuch as it bears down unflinchingly upon the beauty as well as the cruelty of life, its promise as well as its disappointment. To the end, Heine kept up his uncompromising power to "Cast a cold eye / On life, on death," as William Butler Yeats wrote in "Under Ben Bulben."

■ CONNECTIONS

Olaudah Equiano, *The Interesting Narrative of the Life of Olaudah Equiano, or Gustavus Vassa the African;* **Harriet Jacobs,** *Incidents in the Life of a Slave Girl* (both Book 4). Heine's "The Slave Ship" is a satirical poem that criticizes slavery and the slave trade by creating an ironic juxtaposition between the captain's businesslike calculations and the reader's understanding of the horrors onboard the slave ship. How effective is Heine's satire as a form of criticism and how do his techniques in the poem compare with those used by Equiano or Jacobs in their slave narratives?

William Blake, "Holy Thursday," "London," and *The Marriage of Heaven and Hell,* **p. 208.** Heine, like William Blake, is a master of irony, which both poets use to launch devastating critiques against their respective societies. Like Blake, too, Heine extends irony to his stanzaic forms and language, using deceptively simple meter and diction that undercut the seriousness of his themes. Compare Blake's and Heine's use of irony in their poetry of social protest.

Baudelaire, *Poems,* **p. 412.** Heine's poetry presents a tension between a longing for the ideal and a calculated and open-eyed engagement with the harsher aspects of the world. Even his love poetry is marked by sadness and a sense of impossibility. Like Heine's, Baudelaire's work marks a transition between Romantic idealism and a dogged engagement with the more difficult elements of everyday reality that we associate with Realism. To what extent may Heine and Baudelaire be considered Romantic poets?

■ **FURTHER RESEARCH**

Biography
Kossoff, Philip. *Valiant Heart*. 1983.
Sammons, Jeffrey L. *Heinrich Heine: A Modern Biography*. 1979.

Criticism
Franklin, Ursula. *Exiles and Ironists*. 1988.
Sammons, Jeffrey L. *Heinrich Heine, The Elusive Poet*. 1969.

■ **PRONUNCIATION**

Heinrich Heine: HINE-rik HIGH-nuh
Lorelei: LOH-ruh-ligh

A Spruce Is Standing Lonely

Translated by P. G. L. Webb

A spruce is standing lonely
in the North on a barren height.
He drowses; ice and snowflakes
wrap him in a blanket of white.

He dreams about a palm tree
in a distant, eastern land,
that languishes lonely and silent
upon the scorching sand.

"A Spruce Is Standing Lonely." Originally published in 1823 in what Heine titled the "Lyrical Intermezzo"—a section of poems placed between two tragedies, *Almansor* and *William Ratcliff*—the poem reappeared under the same heading in *Book of Songs* (1827). Like many of the verses from Heine's early period, this poem has often been set to music—more than 100 times, in fact.

∾ The Grenadiers

Translated by Louis Untermeyer

Toward France there wandered two grenadiers;
    In Russia they had been taken.
And as they reached the German frontiers,
    Body and spirit were shaken.

For there they learned the tragic tale
    That France had been lost and forsaken;
The Army had suffered to no avail,
    And the Emperor, the Emperor was taken!

They wept together, those two grenadiers;
10   To one thing their thoughts kept returning.
Alas, said one, half choked with tears,
    That old wound of mine keeps burning.

The other said, This is the end;
    With you I'd gladly perish.
But there's the homeland to defend,
    And wife and child to cherish.

What matters wife? What matters child?
    With far greater cares I am shaken.
Let them go and beg with hunger wild.
20   My Emperor, my Emperor is taken!

And, brother, this my only prayer,
    Now I am dying, grant me:
You'll bear my body to France, and there
    In the soil of France you'll plant me.

The cross of honor with crimson band
    Lay on my heart that bound me;

"The Grenadiers." The grenadiers of this poem are two French soldiers on their way home after Napoleon's army suffered catastrophic defeat in the Russian campaign of 1812–13. Napoleon was captured in October 1813 by forces of a European coalition, including Prussia, Britain, Austria, and Sweden, and sentenced to exile on the island of Elba. He eventually escaped and returned to France, where he revitalized his forces and was finally defeated at the Battle of Waterloo in 1815. The young Heine admired Napoleon for his liberal ideals, tactical genius, and heroic spirit, but like other writers who admired these qualities in Napoleon he was critical of the revolutionary emperor's despotism.

Then put the musket in my hand
    And strap my saber round me.

Then I will lie and listen and wait,
30   A sentinel, down in the grass there,
Till I hear the roar of the guns and the great
    Thunder of hoofs as they pass there.

The Emperor will come and the columns will wave;
    The swords will be flashing and rending;
And I will arise, full-armed, from the grave,
    My Emperor, my Emperor defending!

∾ The Minnesingers

Translated by Louis Untermeyer

Come the minnesingers, raising
    Dust and laughter and lament.
Here's a contest that's amazing;
    Here's a curious tournament.

Wild and ever restless Fancy
    Is the minnesinger's horse,
Art his shield, the Word his lance; he
    Bears them lightly round the course.

Many women pleased and pleasant,
10   Smile and drop a flower down;
But the right one's never present
    With the rightful laurel-crown.

Other fighters nimbly canter
    To the lists, care-free and whole;
But we minnesingers enter
    With a death-wound in our soul.

"The Minnesingers." This ballad celebrates the power of poetry through the medieval figures of minnesingers, German minstrels of the twelfth through fourteenth centuries, here depicted in a contest to the death for the love of a lady they will never see. The poem questions the minnesingers' power even as it praises it, rather like **Charles Baudelaire's "The Albatross,"** which compares the poet to a beautiful bird whose long wings make it appear awkward when grounded on the deck of a ship.

And the one who wrings the inmost
    Song-blood from his burning breast,
He's the victor; he shall win most
20   Praise and smiles and all the rest.

❧ The Lorelei

Translated by Felix Pollak

I don't know the reason why
I should be feeling so sad;
A tale of times gone by
Keeps running through my head.

The air is cool, day is sinking,
And quiet flows the Rhine;
The mountain peak is glinting
In the evening's parting shine.

The loveliest maiden is sitting
10 Above there, wondrously fair;
Her golden jewels aglitter,
She is combing her golden hair.

The comb she is holding is golden,
She is singing a song so weird,
So eerie and so bold,
As never an ear has heard.

In his little craft the boatman
Is seized by a woeful love;
He sees not the cliffs approaching,
20 His eyes are fastened above.

I fancy the waves will cover
Both boatman and boat before long;

"The Lorelei." Originally published as one of the poems in *Travel Pictures,* "The Lorelei" is based on Heine's return home from Berlin in the late spring of 1823. Written in ballad form, the poem tells the story of the sirenlike temptress whose enchanting song draws a distracted boatman to his death. The "Lurlei" was a hazardous rock between St. Goar and Oberwesel on the Rhine River. This poem is still well known in Germany today in the version set to music in 1837 by the composer Friedrich Silcher (1789–1860).

And that was done to her lover
By the Lorelei and her song.

ॐ   ## The Silesian Weavers

Translated by Aaron Kramer

In gloomy eyes there wells no tear.
Grinding their teeth, they are sitting here:
Germany, your shroud's on our loom;
And in it we weave the threefold doom.
    We're weaving; we're weaving.

Doomed be the God who was deaf to our prayer
In winter's cold and hunger's despair.
All in vain we hoped and bided;
He only mocked us, hoaxed, derided—
10   We're weaving; we're weaving.

Doomed be the king, the rich man's king,
Who would not be moved by our suffering,
Who tore the last coin out of our hands,
And let us be shot by his bloodthirsty bands—
    We're weaving; we're weaving.

Doomed be the fatherland, false name,
Where nothing thrives but disgrace and shame,
Where flowers are crushed before they unfold,
Where the worm is quickened by rot and mold—
20   We're weaving; we're weaving.

The loom is creaking, the shuttle flies;
Nor night nor day do we close our eyes.
Old Germany, your shroud's on our loom,

"The Silesian Weavers." Published in Karl Marx's *Forward!* in 1844, this poem commemorates the June 1844 revolt of the destitute weavers from Peterswaldau in Silesia, then part of Prussia, against their employers. The rebellion was quickly and brutally suppressed by Prussian troops. Heine's poem was a rallying point for German workers for many years. One of the earliest German workers' revolts, this action by the weavers contributed to the growing dissension that culminated in the revolutions that swept Europe in 1848, which limited the powers of the Prussian king to which the poem refers, Friedrich Wilhelm IV.

And in it we weave the threefold doom;
 We're weaving; we're weaving.

 # The Asra

Translated by Ernst Feise

Daily went the Sultan's beauteous
Daughter walking for her pleasure
In the evening at the fountain
Where the splashing waters whiten.

Daily stood the youthful bondsman
In the evening at the fountain
Where the splashing waters whiten,
Daily he grew pale and paler.

Then one evening stepped the princess
10 Up to him with sudden questions:
"You must tell me what your name is,
What your country is, your kinfolk."

And the bondsman said: "Mohamet
Is my name, I am from Yemen,
And my kinsmen are the Asra,
They who die when love befalls them."

"The Asra." The story on which this poem is based appears in *On Love* by the French writer Stendhal, the author of *The Red and the Black* (1830). The poem, written in the ballad form, describes the hopeless love of a member of the Asra, a legendary tribe of slaves who are doomed to die when they fall in love. Invoking the exotic setting of the Arabic world to intensify the theme of unrequited love, "The Asra" is a good example of Romantic Orientalism (compare Coleridge's "Kubla Khan"). The impossibility of the love between the slave and the Sultan's daughter is underscored not only by the curse upon the Asra, but by the class difference between the bondsman (slave) and the princess. In three stanzas Heine creates a condensed portrait of the tragedy of desire with overtones of political or social critique that might be compared with the *ghazals* of Ghalib.

The Slave Ship

Translated by Aaron Kramer

1

The supercargo Mynher van Koek
Sits in his cabin, counting;
He calculates his lading bills
And sees the profits mounting.

"The rubber's good, the pepper's good:
Three hundred barrels and sacks;
I've gold dust and rare ivory—
But best is my cargo of blacks.

I bought them on the Senegal,
10   Six hundred heads—all told.
Their flesh is hard, their sinews taut
As the finest iron mold.

Whiskey, beads, and trinkets of steel
Were all the fortune I spent—
Should half of my cargo stay alive
I'll make eight hundred percent.

Should only three hundred blacks remain
When I get to Rio de Janeiro,
I'll make three hundred ducats apiece
20   From the house of Gonzales Perreiro."

But all at once Mynher van Koek
Was roused from his reflection;
The ship surgeon, van der Smissen by name,
Returned from his tour of inspection.

"The Slave Ship." Heine's final collection of poems, *Poems of 1853 and 1854,* contained this poem and was published in 1854, the year France finally banned slavery in its colonies. The "supercargo" was generally the business director for the ship, but here it apparently refers to the captain, Mynher van Koek. He and the ship's physician, van der Smissen, calculate their profit and loss in language that commodifies the human beings their ship carries. The furious dance the slaves are forced to perform creates a grotesque spectacle of the master-slave relationship.

He's a skinny thing—red warts on his nose;
"Now tell me," the captain cries,
"Tell me, ship surgeon, how do you find
My dear black merchandise?"

The doctor nods his thanks, and says:
30 "That's what I've come to announce—
Tonight the rate of mortality
Significantly mounts.

A daily average of two have died,
But seven went today:
Four men, three women—I entered the loss
In the records right away.

I looked the corpses over well,
For many a time these knaves
Pretend to be dead, because they hope
40 We'll toss them out on the waves.

I took the irons off the dead,
And, as usual, gave an order
Early this morning, that every corpse
Should be cast out into the water.

Sharkfish, whole battalions of them,
Shot swiftly up from the brine;
They love the Negro meat so well!
They're pensioners of mine.

Since first our ship put out to sea
50 They've stubbornly pursued;
These monsters catch the corpses' scent
With a sniffing hunger for food.

It's a comical thing to see the sharks
Go snapping after the dead!
One of them tears at the rags, and one
At the legs, and one at the head.

When everything's swallowed, they cheerfully stir
Around the vessel's planks,
And gape at me with sated eyes
60 As though to express their thanks."

But, sighing, the captain interrupts:
"How can I end this curse?
"How can I keep the rate of death
From getting worse and worse?"

"Through their own fault," the surgeon sneers,
"Many succumb to death;
The air in the hold of the ship is foul
From their offensive breath.

And many die because they're sad,
70 For they're kept in a boredom that kills;
A bit of music, dancing, and air,
Will cure them of all their ills."

"Splendid advice!" the captain cries,
"My dear old van der Smissen's
More clever than Aristotle[1] was,
Who gave Alexander lessons.

The Tulip Society's president
Has more than an average mind,
But when it comes to reasoning
80 You leave him far behind.

Music! Music! The blacks shall dance
Here on the deck of the ship;
And whomever the hopping can't amuse,
Let him be cured by the whip!"

2

Many thousands of stars look out
From the high blue tent of the skies:
Longingly radiant, large and bright,
Like lovely ladies' eyes.

They gaze down into the endless sea
90 With its phosphorous purple hue;

---

[1]**Aristotle:** (384–322 B.C.E.) Greek philosopher who started a school at the Lyceum in Athens and tutored **Alexander the Great**, who became leader of the Macedonians in 336 B.C.E. Aristotle's works, mainly collated from his students' notes, include *The Poetics, The Physics, The Nichomachean Ethics,* and *Politics.*

Soft in the night the sleepless waves
Voluptuously coo.

There's not a sail on the slave ship now;
It drifts unrigged and bare;
But lanterns glitter along the deck,
And music's in the air.

The helmsman plays a violin,
The doctor's trumpet sounds,
The cook plays flute, while a cabin boy
100   Stands at the drum, and pounds.

A hundred Negroes, women and men,
Are whirling around—insane—
Shouting and hopping; at every leap
A rhythmic clatter of chains.

They stamp the boards with blusterous joy,
And many a naked beau
Embraces his beautiful Negro lass—
Between them a sigh of woe.

The hangman is *maître des plaisirs:*
110   And, swinging left and right,
He's whipped the sluggish dancers on,
Driven them to delight.

And diddle-dum-dee and shnedderedeng!
The noise allures from the deep
The monsters of the water world
That were lying sound asleep.

Many hundreds of sharks come close
With sleepy, half-shut eyes;
They stare up at the reveling ship
120   In wonder and surprise.

They know it's not their breakfast time,
And open wide their jaws—
Revealing rows of shiny teeth
As huge and sharp as saws.

And diddle-dum-dee and shnedderedeng—
No end to the exultations.

The sharkfish bite themselves in the tail —
So great is their impatience.

I think they don't like music much,
130   Like many of their gang.
"Trust no music-hating beast!"
Albion's bard[2] once sang.

And shnedderedeng diddle-dum-dee —
There's never an end to the dance!
Mynher van Koek, at the bow of the ship,
Prayerfully folds his hands:

"Take pity, O Lord, in the name of Christ,
And let these sinners live!
You know they're stupid as cows, O Lord,
140   And if they enrage you — forgive!

Spare their lives in the name of Christ
Who died for us all on the cross!
For unless three hundred heads remain
I'll suffer a terrible loss."

---

[2] **Albion's bard:** Refers to William Shakespeare; the quoted phrase in the previous line alludes to Lorenzo's speech from *The Merchant of Venice* V.i.83–87: "The man that hath no music in himself, / Nor is moved with concord of sweet sounds. . . . / Let no such man be trusted."

ℭ The Migratory Rats

Translated by Ernst Feise

There are two kinds of rat,
The hungry and the fat;
The fat ones happily stay at home,
But the hungry ones set out to roam.

"The Migratory Rats." Unpublished in Heine's lifetime, this poem lashes out equally at revolutionaries and their political opponents. Harkening back to the ambiguities of his earlier political poems, *Atta Troll: A Midsummer Night's Dream* and *Germany—A Winter's Tale,* Heine's mastery of irony in *Rats* creates a charged atmosphere of disgust and contempt in the tension between these caricatures of political extremism.

They wander thousands of miles,
They have no domiciles;
Straight on they move in a furious run,
They cannot be stopped by rain or sun.

No mountains they cannot skim,
10   No lakes too broad for their swim!
Many get drowned or break their necks,
But those who survive pass over the wrecks.

These queer peculiar louts
Grow whiskers above their snouts;
As radical egalitarians they wear
In ratty fashion close-cropped their hair.

This fierce and radical squad
Knows no eternal God;
Unbaptized they leave their numerous broods,
20   They keep their women as common goods.

A sensuous mob, they think
Only of food and drink;
They ignore, since food is their only goal,
The immortality of the soul.

For such a brutal rat
Fears neither hell nor cat;
No goods, nor money they ever acquire,
To redivide the world they desire.

Approaching I see the foe
30   Of wandering rats, oh woe!
They come, already they are at our heels,
Their number is legion, I hear their squeals.

O woe! now we are lost!
At our portal their awful host!
The council and mayor shake their heads,
They despair of warding off those reds.

The burghers take up arms,
The blackfrocks ring the alarms;
The palladium of public morality,
40   Property, is in jeopardy.

No ringing of bells, no priestly pleas,
No wise and august council decrees,
Not even cannons of wildest gage
Will help you, my children, against their rage.

∿ Morphine

Translated by Ernst Feise

Great is the likeness of those beauteous two,
The youthful brothers, though the one appears
Much paler than the other, also much
More stern, yes, I might almost say much more
Aristocratic than that one who clasped me
Tenderly in his arm — How sweetly gentle
Was then his smile, his glance so full of bliss!
Thus it would happen that his wreath of poppies,
His head encircling, grazed my forehead also
10   And with strange fragrance banished all the pain
Out of my soul — Yet such a kind reprieve
It lasts but a short while, because completely
Restored can I be only when his brother,
The stern and pallid one, inverts his torch. —
Oh, sleep is good, death better — to be sure,
The best of all were not to have been born.

"Morphine." One of Heine's last poems, this was written while his own death was imminent and was not published in his lifetime. The "youthful brothers" are Sleep and Death.

✍ ALEXANDER PUSHKIN
1799–1837

ah-lik-SAHN-dur
POOSH-kin

on-YAY-gin
p. 189

The three great Romantic writers in Russia during the early nineteenth century were Nikolai Gogol, Mikhail Lermontov,[1] and **Alexander Pushkin.** Pushkin holds the place in Russian literature that Shakespeare and Goethe occupy in the literature of their countries. Because of its formal and stylistic diversity, range, and innovation, like Shakespeare's and Goethe's, Pushkin's work does not easily fall into a single category. Indeed, his greatest work, *Eugene Onegin,* a novel written in verse and modeled on **Byron's** *Don Juan,* combines features of the Romantic lyric but looks forward to the shift toward Realism in its depiction of character and its straightforward plot. *Onegin,* like Pushkin's other works, celebrates in true Romantic form the genius and independence of the "natural man" who does not hesitate to challenge conventional authority and power.

Early Life.   **Alexander Pushkin** was born in Moscow in 1799; his father was a minor writer and his mother the granddaughter of an Ethiopian slave in the court of Peter the Great who eventually became a landowner and a general. Pushkin was proud of both his boyar ancestry—the aristocratic class below the ruling princes at the time—on his father's side and his African ancestry on his mother's, and he honored the latter in *The Negro of Peter the Great,* a novel that remained incomplete at his death in 1837. Trained at home to read and speak French, as most aristocratic children were in early-nineteenth-century Russia, Pushkin in his youth wrote poetry in French rather than his native Russian. Eventually he attended the lycée at Tsarskoe Selo, a highly selective and elite school that specialized in turning the sons of aristocrats into soldiers and civil servants. While at school, Pushkin wrote poetry, a comic play, a novel, and a short story—in Russian now—exercising early his talent to explore, master, and even parody the dominant forms of literature.

> [Pushkin's] preoccupation with Peter the Great and his epoch made him the progenitor of a Russian national mythology that shaped the historical discourse of generations of Russian writers and intellectuals.
>
> – SVETLANA EVDOKIMOVA, historian, 1999

Exile and Poetry.   Steeped in the ENLIGHTENMENT tradition of political and social thought that was standard fare at the lycée, Pushkin graduated in 1817 and took a position with the Foreign Office in St. Petersburg. Two poems that he wrote during this early period, "Freedom" (1817) and "The Village" (1819), show Pushkin's flirtation with revolutionary ideas—especially sympathy for the plight of serfs, a qualified attack on Tsar Alexander's despotism, and a more general (and less threatening) love of freedom. This dalliance, however, along with his membership in a revolutionary group called The Green Lamp, ultimately led to his exile in the

---

[1]Nikolai Gogol, Mikhail Lermontov: Nikolai Vasilyevich **Gogol** (1809–1852), Russian fiction writer whose most important novel is *Dead Souls* (1842); Mikhail Yurevich **Lermontov** (1814–1841), Russian poet and novelist who like Pushkin was an admirer of Lord Byron; his most famous novel is *A Hero of Our Time* (1840).

south, in Ekaterinoslav, under charges of circulating seditious literature. Pushkin was taken in by the Raevsky family, who introduced him to the work of Byron. During the early 1820s, Pushkin, who was now with General Raevsky in Kishinev and eventually Odessa, on the Black Sea, found himself in a rich cultural ferment of Romanian, Greek, Jewish, Armenian, and even Gypsy traditions. In Odessa there were many Greek refugees in exile from their country, now under the domination of the Ottoman Empire. Like Byron and Shelley in England, Pushkin grew sympathetic to the revolt of the Greeks against the occupying Ottomans. Indeed, Byron's work became increasingly important to Pushkin as he finished some of the most important poems of his southern cycle—*The Prisoner of the Caucasus* (1822), *The Fountain of Bakhchisarai* (1823), and *The Gipsies* (1824)—and began writing *Eugene Onegin*. With the publication of these narrative poems, Pushkin's genius was immediately recognized. The free form and rebel heroes of the poems, their interest in "natural man," and their disenchantment with authoritarian rule clearly set Pushkin among the great Romantics of his age.

Pardon and Patronage.   In 1824, after a disagreement with the governor, Pushkin was again exiled, this time to his mother's estate at Mikhailovskoye, where he continued to work on *Eugene Onegin* and completed a second masterpiece, *Boris Godunov* (1825), a tragedy written in verse. Consistent with Pushkin's opposition to French classicism and his quest for freer form, *Boris Godunov* rejects the strict "unities" of French classical tragedy[2] in favor of a Shakespearean openness. Because of the unconventional form, the play, like Byron's *Manfred*, remained popular as a closet drama but was not produced until 1870. In 1825, following Tsar Alexander's death and the **DECEMBRIST REVOLT**,[3] Pushkin met with the new tsar, Nicholas, who extended both a pardon and patronage to Pushkin. Pushkin thought his work would now be free from censorship, but Nicholas objected to portions of *Boris Godunov*. In 1831, Pushkin married Natalia Goncharov, whose love of court society and flirtatiousness led six years later to Pushkin's death in a duel with one of her suitors, a French émigré named Baron d'Anthes.

Eugene Onegin.   Begun in 1823 and published in chapter form through 1830, this work, like Byron's *Don Juan*, grew by accretion. It is the story of the love between a young man who has left St. Petersburg to live on the estate of his uncle and the young Tatanya, the daughter of a nearby

Orest Admamovic Kiprenski, *Portrait of Pushkin*.
Pushkin was the great-grandson of an Ethiopian slave in the court of Peter the Great, and this portrait of the revered poet hints at his African ancestry. (Art Resource)

www   For links to more information about Pushkin and a quiz on *The Bronze Horseman*, see *World Literature Online* at bedfordstmartins .com/worldlit.

---

[2] **the unities:** In French Neoclassical criticism, critics argued that playwrights must observe the unities of time, place, and action: the events depicted on stage should not exceed a period of 24 hours, they should be limited to one place, and they should all center around a single action, with little or no digression into subplots.

[3] **Decembrist revolt:** After the death of Tsar Alexander I (r. 1801–1825), a group of liberal officers, many of whom had served in the Napoleonic Wars, rebelled in the month of December against the heir, Nicholas I (r. 1825–1855), in hopes of bringing to power a ruler who would guarantee them a constitutional monarchy; they were crushed by Nicholas, who subjected them to severe punishment in order to dim the hopes of any other reform-minded Russians.

yiv-GYAY-nee

family. The episodes of *Onegin* often leave the two main characters aside to pursue other—some might say digressive—themes and scenes, including stories about minor characters, descriptions of places, and observations on literature. In these stanzas, the verse novel offers a detailed panorama of Russian culture in the early nineteenth century, including the politics of the Decembrist revolt and the influence of European literature on early Russian Romanticism.

The Little Plays.   During the 1830s, Pushkin began publishing a series of "little plays," dramatic narrative poems that treat important cultural moments or ideas. *The Stone Guest* retells the story of Don Juan, and *Mozart and Salieri* depicts Salieri's fabled jealousy of Mozart, a theme revived in our time by Peter Shaffer's *Amadeus.* Pushkin identifies Mozart's work with spontaneity and genius, in contrast to the studied craftsmanship of Salieri's[4] work, which cannot reach the same creative heights and so frustrates the otherwise competent musician. In addition, Pushkin wrote during the 1830s a number of short stories and novellas, including *The Queen of Spades* (1834) and *The Captain's Daughter* (1836), the latter of which returns to a historical event, the Pugachev rebellion, for a story that objectively depicts the land-owning classes in the nineteenth century.

The *Bronze Horseman* (completed in 1833 and published in 1837), included in the selection here, is one of Pushkin's literary treatments of Tsar Peter the Great, the horseman of the bronze statue. The story takes place during the great flood of St. Petersburg in 1824 and poignantly sets up a contrast between Peter's greatness and the incidents in the life of the petty clerk **Yevgeni.** Pushkin praises the building of St. Petersburg, the work and vision of Tsar Peter, in response to those who questioned the wisdom of building on such a desolate site constantly threatened by the sea. In the poem, the destructive potential of the sea suggests a severe historical necessity that threatens to desolate the works of human creativity and craft. Once for Pushkin an image of freedom, as it is in Byron's poetry, the sea here becomes a predatory beast that feeds upon the city.

The Bronze Horseman.   In this narrative poem, Yevgeni, a prototype of the ubiquitous clerks that one finds in Gogol and Dostoevsky, loses all that he loves in the flood. In his bitter disappointment, he castigates Peter, the city's founder, by scorning the statue of the Bronze Horseman, which seems to come to life and chase him through the city. Yevgeni's vision of ruin contrasts with Peter's vision for the city as he studies the bleak Baltic coastland upon which he, Faust-like, wants to found a city to mark both his own greatness and the greatness of his nation. Peter's reclamation of the barren land stands as a heroic act of imagination and power. But the triumph of human creativity over natural forces

---

[4] Salieri: (1750–1825) Italian-born composer and music teacher whose pupils included the great Romantic composers Ludwig von Beethoven (1770–1827) and Franz Schubert (1797–1828).

John H. Clark, *View of the Palace of Peter the Great and the Senate House at St. Petersburg,*
1815. Etching
This majestic statue in St. Petersburg of Peter the Great atop his horse, also known as the
Bronze Horseman, was the inspiration for the Pushkin poem of the same name. (The
Bridgeman Art Library)

ultimately fails, and Yevgeni and others like him must bear the burden of
Peter's lack of total mastery. The opposition between Yevgeni and Peter
also has a political dimension, for it roused early critics to see the poem as
an opposition between the individual and the state—hence the original
censorship imposed by Tsar Nicholas. Critics disagree over which character represents the hero: Peter or Yevgeni. Is Peter a creative genius who
defies natural desolation and realizes his vision in the building of the city,
or is he a despot whose overreaching ambition leads to the desolation of
the small people like Yevgeni? Is Yevgeni simply the common person outdone by greater human, political, and natural powers, or is he a hero who
despite his weakness challenges these powers, a spokesperson for the
oppressed masses whose helpless defiance nonetheless foreshadows a
revolution?

■ CONNECTIONS

Coleridge, *The Rime of the Ancient Mariner,* **p. 262.** Pushkin's *Bronze Horseman,* like
Coleridge's *Rime,* invokes the supernatural in a tale that depicts the psychological
consequences of acts of separation and traumatic encounters with forces outside
one's control. Both Coleridge and Pushkin make an effort, as Coleridge put it, to
induce in their readers a "willing suspension of disbelief for the moment" to make

their stories plausible. How do these poems negotiate the line between fantasy and realism?

Goethe, *Faust*, p. 29. In the background of Pushkin's *Bronze Horseman* is Peter the Great's reclamation of land that allowed for the building of St. Petersburg. In the poem, the tsar's great project has indirectly led to the utter ruin of Yevgeni. In *Faust, Part II,* Faust begins his own project of reclamation and development, dismissing as insignificant the cost to the cottagers Philemon and Baucis. Goethe seems to reward Faust for his developer's vision, just as Pushkin in the introduction to his poem praises Peter for his. Does each poem nonetheless raise questions about the costs of visionary projects that involve the reclamation of land and the disruption of the lives of common people? Is Pushkin's praise more qualified than Goethe's?

Takenishi, "The Rite" (Book 6). In a general sense, Pushkin's *Bronze Horseman* explores the unexpected costs involved in the triumph of human ingenuity and technology (art or *techne*) over nature. Takenishi's "Rite" offers a testimonial to those who grievously suffered as a result of what is often touted as one of the great achievements of twentieth-century science — the harnessing of the atom. How do these two apparently very different works from different time periods and cultures lead us to consider the consequences of progress and perhaps to question our faith in technology?

■ **FURTHER RESEARCH**

Biography
Feinstein, Elaine. *Pushkin: A Biography.* 1999.
Sandler, Stephanie. *Distant Pleasures.* 1989.
Troyat, Henry. *Pushkin.* 1936; rpt. 1971.

Criticism
Arndt, Walter. *Pushkin Threefold: Narrative, Lyric, Polemic and Ribald Verse.* 1972.
Bethea, David M., ed. *Pushkin Today.* 1993.
Briggs, A. D. P. *Alexander Pushkin: A Critical Study.* 1983.
Evdokimova, Svetlana. *Pushkin's Historical Imagination.* 1999.
Lednicki, Waclaw. *Pushkin's Bronze Horseman: The Story of a Masterpiece.* 1955.
Todd, William M. "Pushkin" in *Handbook of Russian Literature,* ed. Victor Terras.
     1985.

■ **PRONUNCIATION**

Alexander Pushkin: ah-lik-SAHN-dur POOSH-kin
Onegin: on-YAY-gin
Neva: NYEH-vuh
Yevgeni: yiv-GYAY-nee

ᘏ The Bronze Horseman

Translated by D. M. Thomas

A TALE OF ST. PETERSBURG

Introduction

On a shore washed by desolate waves, *he*[1] stood,
Full of high thoughts, and gazed into the distance.
The broad river rushed before him; a wretched skiff
Sped on it in solitude. Here and there,
Like black specks on the mossy, marshy banks,
Were huts, the shelter of the hapless Finn;
And forest, never visited by rays
Of the mist-shrouded sun, rustled all round.

And he thought: From here we will outface the Swede;
10 To spite our haughty neighbour I shall found
A city here.[2] By nature we are fated
To cut a window through to Europe,
To stand with a firm foothold on the sea.
Ships of every flag, on waves unknown

"The Bronze Horseman." One of a series of dramatic narrative poems or "little plays," Pushkin completed this poem in 1833 and published it in 1837. *The Bronze Horseman* tells the story of a poor clerk, Yevgeni, whose life falls to pieces during the great flood of St. Petersburg in 1824. The catastrophe that befalls Yevgeni, who may symbolize the hundreds like him who suffered from the flood, is a re-evaluation of Tsar Peter the Great's monumental achievement of building St. Petersburg. While praising Peter for his vision, the poem evokes our sympathy for Yevgeni, whose condemnation of the tsar brings to life the statue commemorating his founding of St. Petersburg. Yet Yevgeni's disrespect for the tsar is an act that sets him apart from the community. As many critics have observed, the poem dramatizes the tension between the powerful and the weak, the visionary leader and the long-suffering bureaucrat, questioning the Faustian ideology of progress as well as the human desire to exercise dominion over nature. But the poem also leaves open the possibility that Yevgeni's dire circumstances may be punishment for his act of separation from his community. The line drawn between hero and villain is blurred; is Peter the Great the hero or is Yevgeni? Or is it impossible to make such distinctions? Pushkin's genius invites readers to arrive at their own resolutions.

---

[1] *he:* Peter I, the Great (1672–1725), tsar of Russia from 1682 to 1725, who led the Westernization of Russia, often by stern measures.

[2] With the aid of Italian and French architects, in 1703 Peter began to construct St. Petersburg, or Petrograd; the new city was a monument to Peter's plans for Westernizing Russia and a symbol of strength against longtime foes, including Sweden, just across the Baltic.

To them, will come to visit us, and we
Shall revel in the open sea.

A hundred years have passed, and the young city,
The grace and wonder of the northern lands,
Out of the gloom of forests and the mud
20 Of marshes splendidly has risen; where once
The Finnish fisherman, the sad stepson
Of nature, standing alone on the low banks,
Cast into unknown waters his worn net,
Now huge harmonious palaces and towers
Crowd on the bustling banks; ships in their throngs
Speed from all ends of the earth to the rich quays;
The Neva[3] is clad in granite; bridges hang
Poised over her waters; her islands are covered
With dark-green gardens, and before the younger
30 Capital, ancient Moscow has grown pale,
Like a widow in purple before a new empress.

I love you, Peter's creation, I love your stern
Harmonious look, the Neva's majestic flow,
Her granite banks, the iron tracery
Of your railings, the transparent twilight and
The moonless glitter of your pensive nights,
When in my room I write or read without
A lamp, and slumbering masses of deserted
Streets shine clearly, and the Admiralty spire
40 Is luminous, and, without letting in
The dark of night to golden skies, one dawn
Hastens to relieve another, granting
A mere half-hour to night. I love
The motionless air and frost of your harsh winter,
The sledges coursing along the solid Neva,
Girls' faces brighter than roses, and the sparkle
And noise and sound of voices at the balls,
And, at the hour of the bachelor's feast, the hiss
Of foaming goblets and the pale-blue flame
50 Of punch. I love the warlike energy
Of Mars' Field,[4] the uniform beauty of the troops

---

[3] **The Neva:** The river that runs through St. Petersburg into the Baltic; the poem is based on the devastating flood of 1824 when the Neva overflowed its banks.

[4] **Mars' Field:** The parade grounds in St. Petersburg.

Of infantry and of the horses, tattered
Remnants of those victorious banners in array
Harmoniously swaying, the gleam of those
Bronze helmets, shot through in battle. O martial
Capital,[5] I love the smoke and thunder
Of your fortress, when the empress of the north
Presents a son to the royal house, or when
Russia celebrates another victory
60 Over the foe, or when the Neva, breaking
Her blue ice, bears it to the seas, exulting,
Scenting spring days.

          Flaunt your beauty, Peter's
City, and stand unshakeable like Russia,
So that even the conquered elements may make
Their peace with you; let the Finnish waves
Forget their enmity and ancient bondage,
And let them not disturb with empty spite
Peter's eternal sleep!

          There was a dreadful time—the memory of it
70 Is still fresh . . . I will begin my narrative
Of it for you, my friends. My tale will be sad.

1

November over darkened Petrograd.
With a roar of waves splashing against the edges
Of her shapely bounds, the Neva tossed
Like a sick man in his restless bed.
It was already late and dark; against
The window angrily the rain was beating,
And the wind blew, howling sadly. At that time
Came young Yevgeni home, from friends . . . We'll call
80 Our hero by this name. It's pleasant, and
Has long been congenial to my pen.
We do not need his surname, though perhaps
In times gone by it shone, under the pen
Of Karamzin,[6] rang forth in our native legends;

---

[5] Capital: St. Petersburg was capital of Russia from 1712 to 1914, when the capital moved to Moscow.

[6] Karamzin: Nikolai Mikhailovich Karamzin (1766–1825), Russian writer and historian, author of the *History of the Russian State* (1818–24).

But now it is forgotten by the world
And fame. Our hero lives in Kolomna,[7] works
Somewhere, avoids the paths of the famous, mourns
Neither dead relatives nor the forgotten past.

    And so, having come home, Yevgeni tossed
90 His cloak aside, undressed, lay down. But for
A long time could not fall asleep, disturbed
By divers thoughts. What did he think about?
About the fact that he was poor, by toil
Would have to earn honour and independence;
That God might have granted him more brains and money;
That there are lazy devils, after all,
For whom life is so easy! That he had been
A clerk for two years; he also thought the weather
Was not becoming any calmer; that
100 The river was still rising; as like as not,
The bridges on the Neva had been raised,
And for two or three days he would be cut off
From Parasha. At that point Yevgeni sighed
From his heart, and fell to dreaming like a poet.
    "Get married? Me? Why not! It would be hard,
Of course; but then, I'm young and healthy, ready
To toil day and night; somehow or other
I'll fix myself a humble, simple shelter
Where Parasha and I can live in quiet.
110 After a year or two I'll get a job,
And Parasha will bring up our children . . . Then
We shall begin to live, and thus we'll go
Hand in hand to the grave, and our grandchildren
Will bury us . . ."

    Thus he dreamed. And he felt sad that night,
And wished the wind would not howl gloomily,
The rain not beat so angrily at the window . . .

    At last he closed his sleepy eyes. And now
The foul night thins, and the pale day draws on . . .
The dreadful day!

120   All night the Neva rushed
Towards the sea against the storm, unable
To overcome the madness of the winds . . .

---

[7] **Kolomna**: At the time, an outlying suburb of Petersburg.

She could no longer carry on the struggle . . .
By morning, throngs of people on her banks
Admired the spray, the mountains and the foam
Of maddened waters. But harried by the gale
Out of the gulf, the Neva turned back, angry,
Turbulent, and swamped the islands. The weather
Raged more fiercely, Neva swelled up and roared,
130 Bubbling like a cauldron; suddenly
Hurled herself on the city like a beast.
Everything ran before her, everything
Suddenly became deserted — suddenly
The waters flowed into the cellars underground,
The canals surged up to the railings,
And Petropolis floated up, like Triton,[8]
Plunged to the waist in water.

Siege! Assault! The sly waves climb like thieves
Through the windows. Scudding boats smash the panes
140 With their sterns. Hawkers' trays, fragments of huts,
Beams, roofs, the wares of thrifty trading,
The chattels of pale poverty, bridges swept
Away by the storm, coffins from the buried
Cemetery — all float along the streets!

The people gaze upon the wrath of God
And await their doom. Alas! All's swept away:
Shelter and food — where shall they find them?

In that dread year the late Tsar in his glory
Still ruled Russia. He came out on to the balcony,
150 Sad, troubled, and said: "Tsars cannot master
The divine elements." He sat down and with thoughtful
Sorrowful eyes gazed on the dire disaster:
The squares like lakes; broad rivers of streets
Pouring into them. The palace a sad island.
The Tsar spoke — from end to end of the city,
Along streets near and far, a dangerous journey
Through the storm waters, generals set off
To save the people, drowning in their homes.

There, in Peter's square, where in the corner
160 A new house towers, where over the lofty porch

---

[8] Triton: A sea god, son of the chief god of the sea, Poseidon, and Amphitrite, a sea goddess; Triton calmed the waters by sounding a conch shell.

Two guardian lions stand like living creatures
With upraised paw—there sat, astride the marble
Beast, hatless, his arms crossed tightly,
Motionless and fearfully pale, Yevgeni.
He was afraid, poor fellow, not for himself.
He did not hear the greedy billow rise,
Lapping his soles; he did not feel the rain
Lashing his face, nor the wind, wildly howling,
Tear his hat from his head. His desperate gaze
170 Was fixed on one distant point. Like mountains,
There the waves rose up from the seething depths,
And raged, there the storm howled, there wreckage
Rushed to and fro . . . God, God! There—
Alas!—so close to the waves, almost by the gulf
Itself, is an unpainted fence and a willow
And a small ramshackle house: there they live,
A widow and her daughter, Parasha, his dream . . .
Or is all this a dream? Is all our life
Nothing but an empty dream, heaven's jest?

180   And he, as though bewitched, as if riveted
To the marble, cannot get down! Around him
Is water and nothing else! And, his back turned
To him, in unshakeable eminence, over
The angry river, the turbulent Neva, stands
The Image, with outstretched arm, on his bronze horse.

2

But now, satiated with destruction, wearied
By her insolent violence, the Neva drew back,
Revelling in the chaos she had caused,
And carelessly abandoning her booty.
190 Thus a marauder, bursting into a village with
His savage band, smashes, slashes, shatters,
And robs; shrieks, gnashing of teeth, violence,
Oaths, panic, howls! And weighed down by their plunder,
Fearing pursuit, exhausted, the robbers leave
For home, dropping their plunder on the way.

The water fell, the roadway was visible,
And my Yevgeni, in hope and fear and grief,
Hastened with sinking heart to the scarcely abated
River. But full of their victory the waves
200 Still seethed angrily, as though beneath them

Fires were smouldering; foam still covered them,
And heavily the Neva breathed, like a horse
Galloping home from battle. Yevgeni looks:
He sees a boat; he runs towards his find;
Shouts to the ferryman—and for ten kopecks
The carefree ferryman rows him across the billows.

     And long the experienced oarsman struggled with
The stormy waves, and all the time the skiff
Was on the point of plunging with its rash crew
210 To the depths, between the ranges of the waves
—And at last he reached the bank.
                       The wretched man
Runs down a familiar street to familiar places.
He gazes, and can recognize nothing.
A dreadful vision! All is piled up before him:
This has been hurled down, that has been torn away;
The little houses have become twisted, others
Have completely collapsed, others have been shifted
By the waves; all around, as on a battlefield,
Corpses are strewn. Yevgeni rushes headlong,
220 Remembering nothing, exhausted by torments,
To the place where fate awaits him with unknown tidings,
As with a sealed letter. And now he is
Already rushing through the suburb, and here
Is the bay, and close by is the house . . .
What is this? . . .
              He stopped. Went back and turned.
Looked . . . walked forward . . . looked again.
Here is the place where their house stood;
Here is the willow. There were gates here—swept
Away, evidently. But where is the house?
230 And, full of gloomy anxiety, he walks, he walks
Around, talks loudly to himself—and then,
Striking his forehead with his hand, he laughed.

     Darkness fell upon the city, shaking
With terror; long its people did not sleep,
But talked among themselves of the past day.

     Dawn's light shone over the pale capital
And found no trace of the disaster; loss
Was covered by a purple cloak. And life
Resumed its customary order. People
240 Walked coldly, impassively, along cleared streets.

Government officials, leaving their night's shelter,
Went to their jobs. The indomitable tradesman
Opened his cellar looted by the Neva,
Hoping to make good his loss at his neighbour's expense.
Boats were being hauled away from courtyards.

      Already Count Khvostov,[9] beloved of heaven,
Was singing the disaster of Neva's banks
In his immortal verses.

               But my poor, poor
Yevgeni! . . . Alas! his confused mind could not endure
250 The shocks he had suffered. His ears still heard
The boom of Neva and the winds. Silently
He wandered round, filled with dreadful thoughts.
Some sort of dream tormented him. A week,
A month, went by—still he did not go home.
When the time ran out, his landlord leased
His abandoned nook to a poor poet. Yevgeni
Did not come to collect his belongings. He grew
A stranger to the world. All day he wandered
On foot, and slept at night on the embankment;
260 He fed on scraps handed to him through windows.
Tattered and mouldy grew his shabby clothes.
Children threw stones at him. Often the whips
Of coachmen lashed him, for he could not find his way;
It seemed he noticed nothing, deafened by
An inner turmoil. And so he dragged out his life,
Neither beast nor man, neither this nor that,
Not of the living world nor of the dead . . .

      Once he was sleeping on the Neva banks.
The days of summer were declining towards autumn.
270 A sickly wind was breathing. The sullen wave
Splashed against the embankment, reproachfully
Grumbling and beating against the smooth steps,
Like a petitioner at the door of judges
Who keep turning him away. The poor wretch woke.
It was dark: rain dripped, the wind howled gloomily;
A distant watchman traded cries with it.
Yevgeni started up; recalled his nightmare;

---

[9] Count Khvostov: A minor poet and contemporary of Pushkin.

Hastily he set off wandering, until
He suddenly stopped—and slowly began to cast
280 His eyes around, with wild fear on his face.
He found himself at the foot of the pillars of
The great house. Over the porch the lions stood
On guard, like living creatures, with their paws
Upraised; and eminently dark and high
Above the railed-in rock, with arm outstretched,
The Image, mounted on his horse of bronze.
        Yevgeni shuddered. Terribly his thoughts
Grew clear in him. He recognized the place
Where the flood played, where greedy waves had pressed,
290 Rioting round him angrily, and the lions,
And the square, and him who motionlessly
Held aloft his bronze head in the darkness,
Him by whose fateful will the city had
Been founded on the sea . . . How terrible
He was in the surrounding murk! What thought
Was on his brow, what strength was hidden in him!
And in that steed what fire! Where do you gallop,
Proud steed, and where will you plant your hoofs?
O mighty master of fate! was it not thus,
300 Towering on the precipice's brink,
You reared up Russia with your iron curb?

        The poor madman walked around the pedestal
Of the Image, and brought wild looks to bear
On the countenance of the lord of half the world.
His breast contracted, his brow was pressed against
The cold railings, his eyes were sealed by mist,
Flames ran through his heart, his blood boiled.
Sombrely he stood before the statue;
His teeth clenched, his hands tightened, trembling
310 With wrath, possessed by a dark power, he whispered:
"All right then, wonder-worker, just you wait!"
And suddenly set off running at breakneck speed.
It seemed to him that the face of the dead Tsar,
Momentarily flaring up with rage,
Was slowly turning . . . Across the empty square
He runs, and hears behind him—like the rumble
Of thunder—the clash and clangor of hoofs
Heavily galloping over the shaking square.
And lit by the pale moonlight, stretching out
320 His hand aloft, the Bronze Horseman rushes

After him on his ponderously galloping mount;
And all night long, wherever the madman ran,
The Bronze Horseman followed with a ringing clatter.

And from that time, whenever his wanderings took him
Into that square, confusion appeared on his face.
Hastily he would press his hand to his heart,
As though to ease its torment, he would doff
His tattered cap, he would not raise his troubled
Eyes, and would go on by some roundabout way.

330   A small island can be seen off-shore. Sometimes
A fisherman out late will moor there with
His net and cook his meagre supper. Or
Some civil servant, boating on a Sunday,
Will pay a visit to the barren island.
No grass grows, not a blade. The flood, in sport,
Had driven a ramshackle little house there.
Above the water it had taken root
Like a black bush. Last spring a wooden barge
Carried away the wreckage. By the threshold
340 They found my madman, and on that very spot
For the love of God they buried his cold corpse.

⌇ CHARLES DARWIN
1809–1882

We think of Charles Darwin and evolution as being synonymous, but evolution was a concept with considerable currency before Darwin came along. His grandfather, Erasmus Darwin (1731–1802), a physician, poet, and naturalist, anticipated some of the concepts of evolution in his writings in the late eighteenth century. The French naturalist Jean Lamarck (1744–1829) had published his evolutionary theory in 1801, arguing that all life forms emerged from a gradual process of modification, passing on acquired characteristics from one generation to the next. Geologists, especially Darwin's friend and mentor Charles Lyell (1797–1875), reconstructed the calendar of the earth's history and attributed changes in the earth's forms to gradual and uniform processes. At the same time that Darwin produced *The Origin of Species* (1859) his fellow scientist Alfred Russel Wallace (1823–1913) proposed a similar theory, and he should be remembered as the co-originator of the theory of evolution. Darwin, whose works cross several scientific disciplines—geology, botany, zoology, paleontology, anthropology, and psychology—described the mechanisms of evolution, the struggle for existence, and natural selection, and developed an overarching theory that brought disciplines together and opened up new directions in many other fields of study, especially in the social sciences.

Charles Darwin, 1855
This photograph of Darwin was taken four years before The Origin of Species *was published. (Corbis)*

Although Darwin's work created some controversy when it originally appeared and is still resisted in some quarters, the more important phenomenon is the quickness and ease with which his ideas were accepted in the scientific disciplines in which he worked and the broad influence they have had outside the natural sciences. By the end of the century there were evolutionary theories explaining economic, social, and political development as well as evolutionary accounts of the natural world. Even religion was described as having evolved from primitive superstition to ever greater and more scientific understandings of the universe. Darwin brought about what Thomas Kuhn in *The Structure of Scientific Revolutions* (1962) has characterized as a "paradigm shift"—he changed the way we see the world.

The Voyage of the *Beagle*. Charles Darwin was born into a prominent and intellectual family: his paternal grandfather, Erasmus Darwin, was a scientist, and his maternal grandfather, Josiah Wedgwood, was a potter. Though he set out to follow his grandfather Erasmus by studying medicine at Edinburgh University, he left Edinburgh before completing his courses, transferring to Cambridge where he studied for the clergy. When he completed his degree in 1831, however, he was saved from a stint in a country parish by an opportunity to serve as a ship's naturalist on the HMS *Beagle*. For the next five years, Darwin sailed around the world, spending most of the time in southern latitudes, keeping notes of his observations and discoveries. He was especially interested in variations

www For links to more information about Darwin and a quiz on *The Origin of Species,* see *World Literature Online* at bedfordstmartins .com/worldlit.

349

HMS *Beagle* in the Straits of Magellan
This artist's rendering of the HMS Beagle *shows what the ship looked like that carried Darwin and a crew of seventy-three men around the Madeira, Canary, and Cape Verde islands. (Hulton / Archive)*

he found in animals of the same species as he traveled from one place to another and in the unusual species on such isolated islands as the Galapagos Islands, off the coast of Ecuador. After publishing his findings in *Journal of Researches into Geology and Natural History, of the Various Countries Visited by HMS* Beagle (1839), Darwin was recognized as an important natural scientist. He was named secretary of the British Geological Society and became a close friend of Charles Lyell, the most prominent geologist of the period. While Darwin worked on geological topics—a book on coral reefs, for example, published in 1842—he was beginning to develop his theory of natural selection.

Origin of Species.   In 1839 Darwin married his cousin, Emma Wedgwood, and moved to the country. There, protecting his frail health, he became a kind of scientific recluse, carrying out his experiments and developing his theory. By 1855 he was ready to start on the work that would make the case for natural selection. When he learned in 1858 that a younger scientist, Alfred Russel Wallace, had reached similar conclusions and was preparing a paper to propose his theory, Darwin consulted with Lyell, who arranged a meeting of the Linnean Society where both Wallace and Darwin could present summaries of their ideas. The challenge from Wallace spurred Darwin's work on his book, which appeared in 1859 under the title *On the Origin of Species by Means of Natural Selection, or the Preservation of Favoured Races in the Struggle for Life.* The first edition sold out on the day of publication, and the book, with Darwin's continuing revisions and responses to criticism, went through several more editions during his lifetime. Darwin completed several other works during the two final decades of his life, most notable among them *The Variation of Animals and Plants under Domestication* (1868); *The Descent of Man, and Selection in Relation to Sex* (1871), which applied the principles stated in *Origin* to the development of mankind; *The Expression of Emotions in Man and Animals* (1872); and several books on botanical topics. Darwin died in 1882 and was buried in Westminster Abbey, near the resting place of his scientific predecessor Isaac Newton.

Since Copernicus shunted people off from the center of the universe to a minor planet of a fifth-rate star, no scientific discovery had been so staggering to the popular mind as Darwin's.

– PHILIP APPLEMAN, critic, 1979

Darwin and Malthus.   Darwin had been inspired, in part, by Thomas Malthus's *Essay on Population* (1798). Malthus proposed the concept of survival of the fittest to explain social and economic issues. He argued that a competitive life-and-death struggle in society was inevitable, because as the population increased exponentially, the food supply grew only incrementally. Thus, the struggle for survival that ensued was proved mathematically. Malthus elevated scarcity to a natural law that would be used to justify poverty and to replace the traditional religious doctrine of charity with the doctrine of laissez-faire,[1] which called for the natural laws of competition and struggle to operate unimpeded.

Controversy over Evolution.   Malthus's ideas were controversial, and he was attacked as being cruel and heartless. When Darwin and his fellow geologists and biologists extended Malthusian concepts to issues that had formerly come under religious authority—the age of the earth, the processes of creation, the ancestry of mankind, and the meaning and purpose of life—the controversy became even more intense. In its full title, *Origin* more than raised these issues; it offered a secular and mechanistic explanation to replace theological notions of divine intelligence and design in the natural world. Critics charged that Darwin's was a godless and violent universe, ruled by chance, without purpose or meaning. However, Darwin was not ready to enter into public debate. His health and temperament were not suited to such controversy, but many of his supporters willingly took on the opposition, especially Thomas Henry Huxley (1825–1895), who earned the nickname "Darwin's Bulldog" for his spirited and tenacious advocacy of Darwin's ideas.

Darwin's Rhetoric.   Darwin's very reticence, however, probably contributed to the acceptance and broad influence of his ideas; he presented himself as a scientist rather than a debater. When other scientists objected to his ideas or interpretations of the data, Darwin responded by modifying his ideas, elucidating the data more fully, or clarifying his explanations in the many later editions of his work. *Origin,* with its detailed accounts of variations in particular species and its presentation of myriad examples, is often characterized as "boring." Darwin is remembered for the comprehensive theory that he proposed, but in his writing he gives precedence to the facts, not theory. When he does take on the controversial issues raised by his work—whether there is, for example, evidence of design in the natural world—he asks whether the data provide support for such conclusions and he seeks an answer that does not go beyond the evidence at hand. "My theology is a simple muddle," he wrote in 1870. "I cannot look at the universe as the result of blind chance, yet I can see no evidence of beneficent design, or indeed of design of any kind, in the details."

> My theology is a simple muddle. I cannot look at the universe as the result of blind chance, yet I can see no evidence of beneficent design, or indeed of design of any kind, in the details.
>
> – CHARLES DARWIN

---

[1] *laissez-faire:* French for "let them do"; doctrine in classical economics that asserts the economy should operate on its own, without interference from the government.

The muddle, however, is a fitting conclusion to the struggle of an honest observer to remain true to his experience. Darwin convinces by the very plainness of his rhetoric. He does on occasion construct his argument more imaginatively, especially in the famous metaphors of the tree of life and the tangled bank, both of which appear in the following selections. The ambiguities in these images, however, complicate as much as they clarify Darwin's vision of the natural world. Critics ask whether the tree, alive only at its growing tips, is an adequate representation of Darwin's sense of the history of the natural world and whether the "tangle" on Darwin's bank is to be taken as a sign of order or disorder in the natural scheme of things. Readers may also be left with a muddle, but it is one that is part of a process of discovery that answers some questions and introduces new realms of inquiry.

■ CONNECTIONS

In the World: **Science and Creation, p. 380; Tagore,** *Broken Ties,* **p. 986.** The controversy raised by *The Origin of Species* is represented by Bishop Wilberforce's attack on Darwin included in *In the World:* Science and Creation. Several other selections in that section address the relationship between science and religion in somewhat broader terms. In which ways can Darwinism be reconciled with a religious point of view? How do Hindus in Rabindranath Tagore's *Broken Ties* respond to Western scientific positivism?

Pope, *Essay on Man* **(Book 4).** In *Essay on Man,* Alexander Pope develops the traditional hierarchical worldview known as "the great chain of being." Consider Darwin's theory of natural selection in relation to this traditional view. How do the two theories differ? In what do they agree?

Pardo Bazan, "The Oldest Story," p. 699; Machado de Assis, "Adam and Eve," **p. 922; Stanton,** *The Woman's Bible,* **p. 400.** The story of Adam and Eve, the classic Western story of mankind's origins, is critiqued in Elizabeth Cady Stanton's exegesis of Genesis (see *In the World:* Science and Creation) and also in two short stories, "The Oldest Story" by Emilia Pardo Bazan and "Adam and Eve" by Machado de Assis. Are these critiques developed from a "scientific" perspective? What might Darwin have said about the Genesis story?

■ FURTHER RESEARCH

Biography
Barlow, Nora, ed. *The Autobiography of Charles Darwin, 1809–1882: With Original Omissions Restored.* 1958.
DeBeer, Gavin. *Charles Darwin: A Scientific Biography.* 1964.

Criticism
Appleman, Philip, ed. *Darwin: A Norton Critical Edition.* 1970; 1979. Includes selections from Darwin's work, background materials, and critical essays on Darwin.
Barzun, Jacques. *Darwin, Marx, Wagner: Critique of a Heritage.* 1941.
Ghiselin, Michael T. *The Triumph of Darwinian Method.* 1984.
Hyman, Stanley Edgar. *The Tangled Bank: Darwin, Marx, Fraser and Freud as Imaginative Writers.* 1962.
Levine, George. *Darwin and the Novelists.* 1988.
Norris, Margot. *Beasts of the Modern Imagination: Darwin, Nietzsche, Kafka, Ernst and Lawrence.* 1985.

∾ The Origin of Species

FROM STRUGGLE FOR EXISTENCE

The Term, Struggle for Existence, Used in a Large Sense

I should premise that I use this term in a large and metaphorical sense including dependence of one being on another, and including (which is more important) not only the life of the individual, but success in leaving progeny. Two canine animals, in a time of dearth, may be truly said to struggle with each other which shall get food and live. But a plant on the edge of a desert is said to struggle for life against the drought, though more properly it should be said to be dependent on the moisture. A plant which annually produces a thousand seeds, of which only one of an average comes to maturity, may be more truly said to struggle with the plants of the same and other kinds which already clothe the ground. The mistletoe is dependent on the apple and a few other trees, but can only in a far-fetched sense be said to struggle with these trees, for, if too many of these parasites grow on the same tree, it languishes and dies. But several seedling mistletoes, growing close together on the same branch, may more truly be said to struggle with each other. As the mistletoe is disseminated by birds, its existence depends on them; and it may methodically be said to struggle with other fruit-bearing plants, in tempting the birds to devour and thus disseminate its seeds. In these several senses, which pass into each other, I use for convenience' sake the general term of Struggle for Existence.

Geometrical Ratio of Increase

A struggle for existence inevitably follows from the high rate at which all organic beings tend to increase. Every being, which during its natural lifetime produces several eggs or seeds, must suffer destruction during some period of its life, and during some season or occasional year, otherwise, on the principle of geometrical increase, its numbers would quickly become so inordinately great that no country could support the product. Hence, as more individuals are produced than can possibly survive, there must in every case be a struggle for existence, either one individual with another of the same species, or with the individuals of distinct species, or with the physical conditions of life. It is the doctrine of Malthus[1] applied with manifold force

---

The Origin of Species. Darwin's seminal work prompted immediate controversy with scientists and nonscientists alike. The selection here presents Darwin's discussion of the central concept of his work, the principle of natural selection, and the mechanism that enables it: the struggle for existence. The excerpts are taken from the sixth edition of *Origin* (1872), the last published during Darwin's lifetime. His revisions and additions show him as a scientist responding to criticisms of his work and indicating changes and refinements in his thinking.

---

[1] **Malthus:** Thomas Malthus (1766–1834) explained economic competition through the concept of the struggle for existence in *An Essay on the Principle of Population* (1798).

to the whole animal and vegetable kingdoms; for in this case there can be no artificial increase of food, and no prudential restraint from marriage. Although some species may be now increasing, more or less rapidly, in numbers, all cannot do so, for the world would not hold them.

There is no exception to the rule that every organic being naturally increases at so high a rate, that, if not destroyed, the earth would soon be covered by the progeny of a single pair. Even slow-breeding man has doubled in twenty-five years, and at this rate, in less than a thousand years, there would literally not be standing-room for his progeny. Linnæus[2] has calculated that if an annual plant produced only two seeds—and there is no plant so unproductive as this—and their seedlings next year produced two, and so on, then in twenty years there should be a million plants. The elephant is reckoned the slowest breeder of all known animals, and I have taken some pains to estimate its probable minimum rate of natural increase; it will be safest to assume that it begins breeding when thirty years old, and goes on breeding till ninety years old, bringing forth six young in the interval, and surviving till one hundred years old; if this be so, after a period of from 740 to 750 years there would be nearly nineteen million elephants alive, descended from the first pair.

But we have better evidence on this subject than mere theoretical calculations, namely, the numerous recorded cases of the astonishingly rapid increase of various animals in a state of nature, when circumstances have been favourable to them during two or three following seasons. Still more striking is the evidence from our domestic animals of many kinds which have run wild in several parts of the world; if the statements of the rate of increase of slow-breeding cattle and horses in South America, and latterly in Australia, had not been well authenticated, they would have been incredible. So it is with plants; cases could be given of introduced plants which have become common throughout whole islands in a period of less than ten years. Several of the plants, such as the cardoon and a tall thistle, which are now the commonest over the whole plains of La Plata, clothing square leagues of surface almost to the exclusion of every other plant, have been introduced from Europe; and there are plants which now range in India, as I hear from Dr. Falconer, from Cape Comorin to the Himalaya, which have been imported from America since its discovery. In such cases, and endless others could be given, no one supposes, that the fertility of the animals or plants has been suddenly and temporarily increased in any sensible degree. The obvious explanation is that the conditions of life have been highly favourable, and that there has consequently been less destruction of the old and young, and that nearly all the young have been enabled to breed. Their geometrical ratio of increase, the result of which never fails to be surprising, simply explains their extraordinarily rapid increase and wide diffusion in their new homes.

In a state of nature almost every full-grown plant annually produces seed, and amongst animals there are very few which do not annually pair. Hence we may confidently assert, that all plants and animals are tending to increase at a geometrical ratio,—that all would rapidly stock every station in which they could anyhow

---

[2] Linnæus: Carolus Linnæus (1707–1778); Swedish botanist who developed the modern system of classification for plants and animals.

exist,—and that this geometrical tendency to increase must be checked by destruction at some period of life. Our familiarity with the larger domestic animals tends, I think, to mislead us: we see no great destruction falling on them, but we do not keep in mind that thousands are annually slaughtered for food, and that in a state of nature an equal number would have somehow to be disposed of.

The only difference between organisms which annually produce eggs or seeds by the thousand, and those which produce extremely few, is, that the slow-breeders would require a few more years to people, under favourable conditions, a whole district, let it be ever so large. The condor lays a couple of eggs and the ostrich a score, and yet in the same country the condor may be the more numerous of the two; the Fulmar petrel lays but one egg, yet it is believed to be the most numerous bird in the world. One fly deposits hundreds of eggs, and another, like the hippobosca, a single one; but this difference does not determine how many individuals of the two species can be supported in a district. A large number of eggs is of some importance to those species which depend on a fluctuating amount of food, for it allows them rapidly to increase in number. But the real importance of a large number of eggs or seeds is to make up for much destruction at some period of life; and this period in the great majority of cases is an early one. If an animal can in any way protect its own eggs or young, a small number may be produced, and yet the average stock be fully kept up; but if many eggs or young are destroyed, many must be produced, or the species will become extinct. It would suffice to keep up the full number of a tree, which lived on an average for a thousand years, if a single seed were produced once in a thousand years, supposing that this seed were never destroyed, and could be ensured to germinate in a fitting place. So that, in all cases, the average number of any animal or plant depends only indirectly on the number of its eggs or seeds.

In looking at Nature, it is most necessary to keep the foregoing considerations always in mind—never to forget that every single organic being may be said to be striving to the utmost to increase in numbers; that each lives by a struggle at some period of its life; that heavy destruction inevitably falls either on the young or old, during each generation or at recurrent intervals. Lighten any check, mitigate the destruction ever so little, and the number of the species will almost instantaneously increase to any amount.

From Natural Selection;
or the Survival of the Fittest

The affinities of all the beings of the same class have sometimes been represented by a great tree. I believe this simile largely speaks the truth. The green and budding twigs may represent existing species; and those produced during former years may represent the long succession of extinct species. At each period of growth all the growing twigs have tried to branch out on all sides, and to overtop and kill the surrounding twigs and branches, in the same manner as species and groups of species have at all times overmastered other species in the great battle for life. The limbs divided into great branches, and these into lesser and lesser branches, were themselves once, when the tree was young, budding twigs, and this connection of

the former and present buds by ramifying branches may well represent the classification of all extinct and living species in groups subordinate to groups. Of the many
twigs which flourished when the tree was a mere bush, only two or three, now grown
into great branches, yet survive and bear the other branches; so with the species
which lived during long-past geological periods, very few have left living and modified descendants. From the first growth of the tree, many a limb and branch has
decayed and dropped off; and these fallen branches of various sizes may represent
those whole orders, families, and genera which have now no living representatives,
and which are known to us only in a fossil state. As we here and there see a thin
straggling branch springing from a fork low down in a tree, and which by some
chance has been favoured and is still alive on its summit, so we occasionally see an
animal like the Ornithorhynchus or Lepidosiren,[3] which in some small degree con-
nects by its affinities two large branches of life, and which has apparently been saved
from fatal competition by having inhabited a protected station. As buds give rise by
growth to fresh buds, and these, if vigorous, branch out and overtop on all sides
many a feebler branch, so by generation I believe it has been with the great Tree of
Life, which fills with its dead and broken branches the crust of the earth, and covers
the surface with its ever-branching and beautiful ramifications.

From Recapitulation and Conclusion

As this whole volume is one long argument, it may be convenient to the reader to
have the leading facts and inferences briefly recapitulated.

   That many and serious objections may be advanced against the theory of
descent with modification through variation and natural selection, I do not deny. I
have endeavored to give to them their full force. Nothing at first can appear more
difficult to believe than that the more complex organs and instincts have been perfected, not by means superior to, though analogous with, human reason, but by the
accumulation of innumerable slight variations, each good for the individual possessor. Nevertheless, this difficulty, though appearing to our imagination insuperably
great, cannot be considered real if we admit the following propositions, namely, that
all parts of the organisation and instincts offer, at least, individual differences — that
there is a struggle for existence leading to the preservation of profitable deviations of
structure or instinct — and, lastly, that gradations in the state of perfection of each
organ may have existed, each good of its kind. The truth of these propositions cannot, I think, be disputed.

   Under domestication we see much variability, caused, or at least excited, by
changed conditions of life; but often in so obscure a manner, that we are tempted to
consider the variations as spontaneous. Variability is governed by many complex
laws, — by correlated growth, compensation, the increased use and disuse of parts,
and the definite action of the surrounding conditions. There is much difficulty in
ascertaining how largely our domestic productions have been modified; but we may

---

[3] Ornithorhynchus: Duck-billed platypus. **Lepidosiren:** South American lungfish.

safely infer that the amount has been large, and that modifications can be inherited for long periods. As long as the conditions of life remain the same, we have reason to believe that a modification, which has already been inherited for many generations, may continue to be inherited for an almost infinite number of generations. On the other hand, we have evidence that variability when it has once come into play, does not cease under domestication for a very long period; nor do we know that it ever ceases, for new varieties are still occasionally produced by our oldest domesticated productions.

Variability is not actually caused by man; he only unintentionally exposes organic beings to new conditions of life, and then nature acts on the organisation and causes it to vary. But man can and does select the variations given to him by nature, and thus accumulates them in any desired manner. He thus adapts animals and plants for his own benefit or pleasure. He may do this methodically, or he may do it unconsciously by preserving the individuals most useful or pleasing to him without any intention of altering the breed. It is certain that he can largely influence the character of a breed by selecting, in each successive generation, individual differences so slight as to be inappreciable except by an educated eye. This unconscious process of selection has been the great agency in the formation of the most distinct and useful domestic breeds. That many breeds produced by man have to a large extent the character of natural species, is shown by the inextricable doubts whether many of them are varieties or aboriginally distinct species.

There is no reason why the principles which have acted so efficiently under domestication should not have acted under nature. In the survival of favoured individuals and races, during the constantly-recurrent Struggle for Existence, we see a powerful and ever-acting form of Selection. The struggle for existence inevitably follows from the high geometrical ratio of increase which is common to all organic beings. This high rate of increase is proved by calculation, — by the rapid increase of many animals and plants during a succession of peculiar seasons, and when naturalised in new countries. More individuals are born than can possibly survive. A grain in the balance may determine which individuals shall live and which shall die, — which variety or species shall increase in number, and which shall decrease, or finally become extinct. As the individuals of the same species come in all respects into the closest competition with each other, the struggle will generally be most severe between them; it will be almost equally severe between the varieties of the same species, and next in severity between the species of the same genus. On the other hand the struggle will often be severe between beings remote in the scale of nature. The slightest advantage in certain individuals, at any age or during any season, over those with which they come into competition, or better adaptation in however slight a degree to the surrounding physical conditions, will, in the long run, turn the balance.

With animals having separated sexes, there will be in most cases a struggle between the males for the possession of the females. The most vigorous males, or those which have most successfully struggled with their conditions of life, will generally leave most progeny. But success will often depend on the males having special weapons, or means of defense, or charms; and a slight advantage will lead to victory.

As geology plainly proclaims that each land has undergone great physical changes, we might have expected to find that organic beings have varied under nature, in the same way as they have varied under domestication. And if there has been any variability under nature, it would be an unaccountable fact if natural selection had not come into play. It has often been asserted, but the assertion is incapable of proof, that the amount of variation under nature is a strictly limited quantity. Man, though acting on external characters alone and often capriciously, can produce within a short period a great result by adding up mere individual differences in his domestic productions; and every one admits that species present individual differences. But, besides such differences, all naturalists admit that natural varieties exist, which are considered sufficiently distinct to be worthy of record in systematic works. No one has drawn any clear distinction between individual differences and slight varieties; or between more plainly marked varieties and sub-species, and species. On separate continents, and on different parts of the same continent when divided by barriers of any kind, and on outlying islands, what a multitude of forms exist, which some experienced naturalists rank as varieties, others as geographical races or sub-species, and others as distinct, though closely allied species!

If then, animals and plants do vary, let it be ever so slightly or slowly, why should not variations or individual differences, which are in any way beneficial, be preserved and accumulated through natural selection, or the survival of the fittest? If man can by patience select variations useful to him, why, under changing and complex conditions of life, should not variations useful to nature's living products often arise, and be preserved or selected? What limit can be put to this power, acting during long ages and rigidly scrutinising the whole constitution, structure, and habits of each creature, — favouring the good and rejecting the bad? I can see no limit to this power, in slowly and beautifully adapting each form to the most complex relations of life. The theory of natural selection, even if we look no farther than this, seems to be in the highest degree probable. I have already recapitulated, as fairly as I could, the opposed difficulties and objections: now let us turn to the special facts and arguments in favour of the theory.

On the view that species are only strongly marked and permanent varieties, and that each species first existed as a variety, we can see why it is that no line of demarcation can be drawn between species, commonly supposed to have been produced by special acts of creation, and varieties which are acknowledged to have been produced by secondary laws. On this same view we can understand how it is that in a region where many species of a genus have been produced, and where they now flourish, these same species should present many varieties; for where the manufactory of species has been active, we might expect, as a general rule, to find it still in action; and this is the case if varieties be incipient species. Moreover, the species of the larger genera, which afford the greater number of varieties or incipient species, retain to a certain degree the character of varieties; for they differ from each other by a less amount of difference than do the species of smaller genera. The closely allied species also of the larger genera apparently have restricted ranges, and in their affinities they are clustered in little groups round other species — in both respects resembling varieties. These are strange relations on the view that each species was independently created, but are intelligible if each existed first as a variety.

As each species tends by its geometrical rate of reproduction to increase inordinately in number; and as the modified descendants of each species will be enabled to increase by as much as they become more diversified in habits and structure, so as to be able to seize on many and widely different places in the economy of nature, there will be a constant tendency in natural selection to preserve the most divergent offspring of any one species. Hence, during a long-continued course of modification, the slight differences characteristic of varieties of the same species, tend to be augmented into the greater differences characteristic of the species of the same genus. New and improved varieties will inevitably supplant and exterminate the older, less improved, and intermediate varieties; and thus species are rendered to a large extent defined and distinct objects. Dominant species belonging to the larger groups within each class tend to give birth to new and dominant forms; so that each large group tends to become still larger, and at the same time more divergent in character. But as all groups cannot thus go on increasing in size, for the world would not hold them, the more dominant groups beat the less dominant. This tendency in the large groups to go on increasing in size and diverging in character, together with the inevitable contingency of much extinction, explains the arrangement of all the forms of life in groups subordinate to groups, all within a few great classes, which has prevailed throughout all time. This grand fact of the grouping of all organic beings under what is called the Natural System, is utterly inexplicable on the theory of creation.

As natural selection acts solely by accumulating slight, successive, favourable variations, it can produce no great or sudden modifications; it can act only by short and slow steps. Hence, the canon of "Natura non facit saltum,"[4] which every fresh addition to our knowledge tends to confirm, is on this theory intelligible. We can see why throughout nature the same general end is gained by an almost infinite diversity of means, for every peculiarity when once acquired is long inherited, and structures already modified in many different ways have to be adapted for the same general purpose. We can, in short, see why nature is prodigal in variety, though niggard in innovation. But why this should be a law of nature if each species has been independently created no man can explain.

Many other facts are, as it seems to me, explicable on this theory. How strange it is that a bird, under the form of a woodpecker, should prey on insects on the ground; that upland geese which rarely or never swim, should possess webbed feet; that a thrushlike bird should dive and feed on sub-aquatic insects; and that a petrel should have the habits and structure fitting it for the life of an auk! and so in endless other cases. But on the view of each species constantly trying to increase in number, with natural selection always ready to adapt the slowly varying descendants of each to any unoccupied or ill-occupied place in nature, these facts cease to be strange, or might even have been anticipated.

---

[4] "Natura . . . saltum": Nature does not make leaps; i.e., there are no gaps in nature.

We can to a certain extent understand how it is that there is so much beauty throughout nature; for this may be largely attributed to the agency of selection. That beauty, according to our sense of it, is not universal, must be admitted by every one who will look at some venomous snakes, at some fishes, and at certain hideous bats with a distorted resemblance to the human face. Sexual selection has given the most brilliant colours, elegant patterns, and other ornaments to the males, and sometimes to both sexes of many birds, butterflies, and other animals. With birds it has often rendered the voice of the male musical to the female, as well as to our ears. Flowers and fruit have been rendered conspicuous by brilliant colours in contrast with the green foliage, in order that the flowers may be readily seen, visited and fertilised by insects, and the seeds disseminated by birds. How it comes that certain colours, sounds, and forms should give pleasure to man and the lower animals, — that is, how the sense of beauty in its simplest form was first acquired, — we do not know any more than how certain odours and flavours were first rendered agreeable.

As natural selection acts by competition, it adapts and improves the inhabitants of each country only in relation to their co-inhabitants; so that we need feel no surprise at the species of any one country, although on the ordinary view supposed to have been created and specially adapted for that country, being beaten and supplanted by the naturalised productions from another land. Nor ought we to marvel if all the contrivances in nature be not, as far as we can judge, absolutely perfect, as in the case even of the human eye; or if some of them be abhorrent to our ideas of fitness. We need not marvel at the sting of the bee, when used against an enemy, causing the bee's own death; at drones being produced in such great numbers for one single act, and being then slaughtered by their sterile sisters; at the astonishing waste of pollen by our fir-trees; at the instinctive hatred of the queenbee for her own fertile daughters; at the ichneumonidæ[5] feeding within the living bodies of caterpillars; or at other such cases. The wonder indeed is, on the theory of natural selection, that more cases of the want of absolute perfection have not been detected.

The complex and little known laws governing the production of varieties are the same, as far as we can judge, with the laws which have governed the production of distinct species. In both cases physical conditions seem to have produced some direct and definite effect, but how much we cannot say. Thus, when varieties enter any new station, they occasionally assume some of the characters proper to the species of that station. With both varieties and species, use and disuse seem to have produced a considerable effect; for it is impossible to resist this conclusion when we look, for instance, at the logger-headed duck, which has wings incapable of flight, in nearly the same condition as in the domestic duck; or when we look at the burrowing tucu-tucu, which is occasionally blind, and then at certain moles, which are habitually blind and have their eyes covered with skin; or when we look at the blind animals inhabiting the dark caves of America and Europe. With varieties and species, correlated variation seems to have played an important part, so that when one part has been modified other parts have been necessarily modified. With both varieties and species, reversions to long-lost characters occasionally occur. How

---

[5] ichneumonidæ: A type of parasitic wasp.

inexplicable on the theory of creation is the occasional appearance of stripes on the shoulders and legs of the several species of the horse-genus and of their hybrids! How simply is this fact explained if we believe that these species are all descended from a striped progenitor, in the same manner as the several domestic breeds of the pigeon are descended from the blue and barred rock-pigeon!

On the ordinary view of each species having been independently created, why should specific characters, or those by which the species of the same genus differ from each other, be more variable than generic characters in which they all agree? Why, for instance, should the colour of a flower be more likely to vary in any one species of a genus, if the other species possess differently coloured flowers, than if all possessed the same coloured flowers? If species are only well-marked varieties, of which the characters have become in a high degree permanent, we can understand this fact; for they have already varied since they branched off from a common progenitor in certain characters, by which they have come to be specifically distinct from each other; therefore these same characters would be more likely again to vary than the generic characters which have been inherited without change for an immense period. It is inexplicable on the theory of creation why a part developed in a very unusual manner in one species alone of a genus, and therefore, as we may naturally infer, of great importance to that species, should be eminently liable to variation, but, on our view, this part has undergone, since the several species branched off from a common progenitor, an unusual amount of variability and modification, and therefore we might expect the part generally to be still variable. But a part may be developed in the most unusual manner, like the wing of a bat, and yet not be more variable than any other structure, if the part be common to many subordinate forms, that is, if it has been inherited for a very long period; for in this case, it will have been rendered constant by long-continued natural selection.

Glancing at instincts, marvellous as some are, they offer no greater difficulty than do corporeal structures on the theory of the natural selection of successive slight, but profitable modifications. We can thus understand why nature moves by graduated steps in endowing different animals of the same class with their several instincts. I have attempted to show how much light the principle of gradation throws on the admirable architectural powers of the hivebee. Habit no doubt often comes into play in modifying instincts; but it certainly is not indispensable, as we see in the case of neuter insects, which leave no progeny to inherit the effects of long-continued habit. On the view of all the species of the same genus having descended from a common parent, and having inherited much in common, we can understand how it is that allied species, when placed under widely different conditions of life, yet follow nearly the same instincts, why the thrushes of tropical and temperate South America, for instance, line their nests with mud like our British species. On the view of instincts having been slowly acquired through natural selection, we need not marvel at some instincts being not perfect and liable to mistakes, and at many instincts causing other animals to suffer.

If species be only well-marked and permanent varieties, we can at once see why their crossed offspring should follow the same complex laws in their degrees and kinds of resemblance to their parents,—in being absorbed into each other by successive crosses, and in other such points,—as do the crossed offspring of acknowledged varieties. This similarity would be a strange fact, if species had been independently created and varieties had been produced through secondary laws.

If we admit that the geological record is imperfect to an extreme degree, then the facts, which the record does give, strongly support the theory of descent with modifications. New species have come on the stage slowly and at successive intervals; and the amount of change, after equal intervals of time, is widely different in different groups. The extinction of species and of whole groups of species which has played so conspicuous a part in the history of the organic world, almost inevitably follows from the principle of natural selection; for old forms are supplanted by new and improved forms. Neither single species nor groups of species reappear when the chain of ordinary generation is once broken. The gradual diffusion of dominant forms, with the slow modification of their descendants, causes the forms of life, after long intervals of time, to appear as if they had changed simultaneously throughout the world. The fact of the fossil remains of each formation being in some degree intermediate in character between the fossils in the formations above and below, is simply explained by their intermediate position in the chain of descent. The grand fact that all extinct beings can be classed with all recent beings, naturally follows from the living and the extinct being the offspring of common parents. As species have generally diverged in character during their long course of descent and modification, we can understand why it is that the more ancient forms, or early progenitors of each group, so often occupy a position in some degree intermediate between existing groups. Recent forms are generally looked upon as being, on the whole, higher in the scale of organisation than ancient forms; and they must be higher, in so far as the later and more improved forms have conquered the older and less improved forms in the struggle for life; they have also generally had their organs more specialised for different functions. This fact is perfectly compatible with numerous beings still retaining simple and but little improved structures, fitted for simple conditions of life; it is likewise compatible with some forms having retrograded in organisation, by having become at each stage of descent better fitted for new and degraded habits of life. Lastly, the wonderful law of the long endurance of allied forms on the same continent,—of marsupials in Australia, of edentata in America, and other such cases,—is intelligible, for within the same country the existing and the extinct will be closely allied by descent.

Looking to geographical distribution, if we admit that there has been during the long course of ages much migration from one part of the world to another, owing to former climatal and geographical changes and to the many occasional and unknown means of dispersal, then we can understand, on the theory of descent with modification, most of the great leading facts in Distribution. We can see why there should be so striking a parallelism in the distribution of organic beings throughout space, and in their geological succession throughout time; for in both cases the beings have been connected by the bond of ordinary generation, and the means of modification have been the same. We see the full meaning of the wonderful fact, which has struck every traveller, namely, that on the same continent, under the most diverse conditions, under heat and cold, on mountain and lowland, on deserts and marshes, most of the inhabitants within each great class are plainly related; for they are the descendants of the same progenitors and early colonists. On this same principle of former migration, combined in most cases with modification, we can understand, by the aid of the Glacial period, the identity of some few plants, and the close alliance of many others, on the most distant mountains, and in the northern and southern temperate zones; and likewise the close alliance of some of the inhabitants of the sea in the northern and southern temperate latitudes, though separated by the whole intertropical ocean. Although two countries may present physical conditions as closely similar as the same species ever require, we need feel no surprise at their inhabitants being widely different, if they have been for a long period completely sundered from each other; for as the relation of organism to organism is the most important of all relations, and as the two countries will have received colonists at various periods and in different proportions, from some other country or from each other, the course of modification in the two areas will inevitably have been different.

On this view of migration, with subsequent modification, we see why oceanic islands are inhabited by only few species, but of these, why many are peculiar or endemic forms. We clearly see why species belonging to those groups of animals which cannot cross wide spaces of the ocean, as frogs and terrestrial mammals, do not inhabit oceanic islands; and why, on the other hand, new and peculiar species of bats, animals which can traverse the ocean, are found on islands far distant from any continent. Such cases as the presence of peculiar species of bats on oceanic islands and the absence of all other terrestrial mammals, are facts utterly inexplicable on the theory of independent acts of creation.

The existence of closely allied or representative species in any two areas, implies, on the theory of descent with modification, that the same parent-forms formerly inhabited both areas; and we almost invariably find that wherever many closely allied species inhabit two areas, some identical species are still common to both. Wherever many closely allied yet distinct species occur, doubtful forms and varieties belonging to the same groups likewise occur. It is a rule of high generality that the inhabitants of each area are related to the inhabitants of the nearest source whence immigrants might have been derived. We see this in the striking relation of nearly all plants and animals of the Galapagos archipelago, of Juan Fernandez, and of the other American islands, to the plants and animals of the neighbouring American mainland; and of those of the Cape de Verde Archipelago, and of the other African islands to the African mainland. It must be admitted that these facts receive no explanation on the theory of creation.

The fact, as we have seen, that all past and present organic beings can be arranged within a few great classes, in groups subordinate to groups, and with the extinct groups often falling in between the recent groups, is intelligible on the theory of natural selection with its contingencies of extinction and divergence of character. On these same principles we see how it is, that the mutual affinities of the forms within each class are so complex and circuitous. We see why certain characters are far more serviceable than others for classification;—why adaptive characters, though of paramount importance to the beings, are of hardly any importance in classification; why characters derived from rudimentary parts, though of no service to the beings, are often of high classificatory value; and why embryological characters are often the most valuable of all. The real affinities of all organic beings, in contradistinction to their adaptive resemblances, are due to inheritance or community of descent. The Natural System is a genealogical arrangement, with the acquired grades of difference, marked by the terms, varieties, species, genera, families, &c.; and we have to discover the lines of descent by the most permanent characters whatever they may be and of however slight vital importance.

The similar framework of bones in the hand of a man, wing of a bat, fin of the porpoise, and leg of the horse, — the same number of vertebra forming the neck of the giraffe and of the elephant, — and innumerable other such facts, at once explain themselves on the theory of descent with slow and slight successive modifications. The similarity of pattern in the wing and in the leg of a bat, though used for such different purpose, — in the jaws and legs of a crab, — in the petals, stamens, and pistils of a flower, is likewise, to a large extent, intelligible on the view of the gradual modification of parts or organs, which were aboriginally alike in an early progenitor in each of these classes. On the principle of successive variations not always supervening at an early age, and being inherited at a corresponding not early period of life, we clearly see why the embryos of mammals, birds, reptiles, and fishes should be so closely similar, and so unlike the adult forms. We may cease marvelling at the embryo of an airbreathing mammal or bird having branchial slits and arteries running in loops, like those of a fish which has to breathe the air dissolved in water by the aid of well-developed branchiæ.

Disuse, aided sometimes by natural selection, will often have reduced organs when rendered useless under changed habits or conditions of life; and we can understand on this view the meaning of rudimentary organs. But disuse and selection will generally act on each creature, when it has come to maturity and has to play its full part in the struggle for existence, and will thus have little power on an organ during early life; hence the organ will not be reduced or rendered rudimentary at this early age. The calf, for instance, has inherited teeth, which never cut through the gums of the upper jaw, from an early progenitor having well-developed teeth; and we may believe, that the teeth in the mature animal were formerly reduced by disuse, owing to the tongue and palate, or lips, having become excellently fitted through natural selection to browse without their aid; whereas in the calf, the teeth have been left unaffected, and on the principle of inheritance at corresponding ages have been inherited from a remote period to the present day. On the view of each organism with all its separate parts having been specially created, how utterly inexplicable is it that organs bearing the plain stamp of inutility, such as the teeth in the embryonic calf or the shrivelled wings under the soldered wing-covers of many beetles, should so frequently occur. Nature may be said to have taken pains to reveal her scheme of modification, by means of rudimentary organs, of embryological and homologous structures, but we are too blind to understand her meaning.

I have now recapitulated the facts and considerations which have thoroughly convinced me that species have been modified, during a long course of descent. This has been effected chiefly through the natural selection of numerous successive, slight, favourable variations; aided in an important manner by the inherited effects of the use and disuse of parts; and in an unimportant manner, that is in relation to adaptive structures, whether past or present, by the direct action of external conditions, and by variations which seem to us in our ignorance to arise spontaneously. It appears that I formerly underrated the frequency and value of these latter forms of variation, as leading to permanent modifications of structure independently of natural selection. But as my conclusions have lately been much misrepresented, and it has been stated that I attribute the modification of species exclusively to natural selection, I may be permitted to remark that in the first edition of this work, and subsequently, I placed in a most conspicuous position—namely, at the close of the Introduction—the following words: "I am convinced that natural selection has been the main but not the exclusive means of modification." This has been of no avail. Great is the power of steady misrepresentation; but the history of science shows that fortunately this power does not long endure.

It can hardly be supposed that a false theory would explain, in so satisfactory a manner as does the theory of natural selection, the several large classes of facts above specified. It has recently been objected that this is an unsafe method of arguing; but it is a method used in judging of the common events of life, and has often been used by the greatest natural philosophers. The undulatory theory of light has thus been arrived at; and the belief in the revolution of the earth on its own axis was until lately supported by hardly any direct evidence. It is no valid objection that science as yet throws no light on the far higher problem of the essence or origin of life. Who can explain what is the essence of the attraction of gravity? No one now objects to following out the results consequent on this unknown element of attraction; notwithstanding that Leibnitz formerly accused Newton of introducing "occult qualities and miracles into philosophy."

I see no good reason why the views given in this volume should shock the religious feelings of any one. It is satisfactory, as showing how transient such impressions are, to remember that the greatest discovery ever made by man, namely, the law of the attraction of gravity, was also attacked by Leibnitz,[6] "as subversive of natural, and inferentially of revealed, religion." A celebrated author and divine has written to me that "he has gradually learnt to see that it is just as noble a conception of the Deity to believe that He created a few original forms capable of self-development into other and needful forms, as to believe that He required a fresh act of creation to supply the voids caused by the action of His laws."

Why, it may be asked, until recently did nearly all the most eminent living naturalists and geologists disbelieve in the mutability of species? It cannot be asserted that organic beings in a state of nature are subject to no variation; it cannot be proved that the amount of variation in the course of long ages is a limited quality; no clear distinction has been, or can be, drawn between species and well-marked varieties. It cannot be maintained that species when intercrossed are invariably sterile, and varieties invariably fertile; or that sterility is a special endowment and sign of creation. The belief that species were immutable productions was almost unavoidable as long as the history of the world was thought to be of short duration; and now

---

[6] **Leibnitz:** Gottfried Wilhelm Leibnitz (1646–1716); German philosopher and mathematician.

that we have acquired some idea of the lapse of time, we are too apt to assume, without proof, that the geological record is so perfect that it would have afforded us plain evidence of the mutation of species, if they had undergone mutation.

But the chief cause of our natural unwillingness to admit that one species has given birth to clear and distinct species, is that we are always slow in admitting great changes of which we do not see the steps. The difficulty is the same as that felt by so many geologists, when Lyell[7] first insisted that long lines of inland cliffs had been formed, the great valleys excavated, by the agencies which we see still at work. The mind cannot possibly grasp the full meaning of the term of even a million years; it cannot add up and perceive the full effects of many slight variations, accumulated during an almost infinite number of generations.

Although I am fully convinced of the truth of the views given in this volume under the form of an abstract, I by no means expect to convince experienced naturalists whose minds are stocked with a multitude of facts all viewed, during a long course of years, from a point of view directly opposite to mine. It is so easy to hide our ignorance under such expressions as the "plan of creation," "unity of design," &c., and to think that we give an explanation when we only re-state a fact. Any one whose disposition leads him to attach more weight to unexplained difficulties than to the explanation of a certain number of facts will certainly reject the theory. A few naturalists, endowed with much flexibility of mind, and who have already begun to doubt the immutability of species, may be influenced by this volume; but I look with confidence to the future, — to young and rising naturalists, who will be able to view both sides of the question with impartiality. Whoever is led to believe that species are mutable will do good service by conscientiously expressing his conviction; for thus only can the load of prejudice by which this subject is overwhelmed be removed.

Several eminent naturalists have of late published their belief that a multitude of reputed species in each genus are not real species; but that other species are real, that is, have been independently created. This seems to me a strange conclusion to arrive at. They admit that a multitude of forms, which till lately they themselves thought were special creations, and which are still thus looked at by the majority of naturalists, and which consequently have all the external characteristic features of true species, — they admit that these have been produced by variation, but they refuse to extend the same view to other and slightly different forms. Nevertheless they do not pretend that they can define, or even conjecture, which are the created forms of life, and which are those produced by secondary laws. They admit variation as a *vera causa*[8] in one case, they arbitrarily reject it in another, without assigning any distinction in the two cases. The day will come when this will be given as a curious illustration of the blindness of preconceived opinion. These authors seem no more startled at a miraculous act of creation than at an ordinary birth. But do they really believe

---

[7] **Lyell:** Charles Lyell (1797–1875); English geologist best known for *Principles of Geology* (1830–33).

[8] *vera causa:* True cause.

that at innumerable periods in the earth's history certain elemental atoms have been commanded suddenly to flash into living tissues? Do they believe that at each supposed act of creation one individual or many were produced? Were all the infinitely numerous kinds of animals and plants created as eggs or seed, or as full grown? and in the case of mammals, were they created bearing the false marks of nourishment from the mother's womb? Undoubtedly some of these same questions cannot be answered by those who believe in the appearance or creation of only a few forms of life, or of some one form alone. It has been maintained by several authors that it is as easy to believe in the creation of a million beings as of one; but Maupertuis'[9] philosophical axiom "of least action" leads the mind more willingly to admit the smaller number; and certainly we ought not to believe that innumerable beings within each great class have been created with plain, but deceptive, marks of descent from a single parent.

As a record of a former state of things, I have retained in the foregoing paragraphs, and elsewhere, several sentences which imply that naturalists believe in the separate creation of each species; and I have been much censured for having thus expressed myself. But undoubtedly this was the general belief when the first edition of the present work appeared. I formerly spoke to very many naturalists on the subject of evolution, and never once met with any sympathetic agreement. It is probable that some did then believe in evolution, but they were either silent, or expressed themselves so ambiguously that it was not easy to understand their meaning. Now things are wholly changed, and almost every naturalist admits the great principle of evolution. There are, however, some who still think that species have suddenly given birth, through quite unexplained means, to new and totally different forms: but, as I have attempted to show, weighty evidence can be opposed to the admission of great and abrupt modifications. Under a scientific point of view, and as leading to further investigation, but little advantage is gained by believing that new forms are suddenly developed in an inexplicable manner from old and widely different forms, over the old belief in the creation of species from the dust of the earth.

It may be asked how far I extend the doctrine of the modification of species. The question is difficult to answer, because the more distinct the forms are which we consider, by so much the arguments in favour of community of descent become fewer in number and less in force. But some arguments of the greatest weight extend very far. All the members of whole classes are connected together by a chain of affinities, and all can be classed on the same principle, in groups subordinate to groups. Fossil remains sometimes tend to fill up very wide intervals between existing orders.

Organs in a rudimentary condition plainly show that an early progenitor had the organ in a fully developed condition; and this in some cases implies an enormous amount of modification in the descendants. Throughout whole classes various structures are formed on the same pattern, and at a very early age the embryos

---

[9] Maupertuis: Pierre Louis Moreau de Maupertuis (1698–1759), French mathematician and astronomer who supported the work of Isaac Newton.

closely resemble each other. Therefore I cannot doubt that the theory of descent with modification embraces all the members of the same great class or kingdom. I believe that animals are descended from at most only four or five progenitors, and plants from an equal or lesser number.

Analogy would lead me one step farther, namely, to the belief that all animals and plants are descended from some one prototype. But analogy may be a deceitful guide. Nevertheless all living things have much in common, in their chemical composition, their cellular structure, their laws of growth, and their liability to injurious influences. We see this even in so trifling a fact as that the same poison often similarly affects plants and animals; or that the poison secreted by the gall-fly produces monstrous growths on the wild rose or oak-tree. With all organic beings excepting perhaps some of the very lowest, sexual production seems to be essentially similar. With all, as far as is at present known the germinal vesicle is the same; so that all organisms start from a common origin. If we look even to the two main divisions— namely, to the animal and vegetable kingdoms—certain low forms are so far intermediate in character that naturalists have disputed to which kingdom they should be referred. As Professor Asa Gray[10] has remarked, "the spores and other reproductive bodies of many of the lower algae may claim to have first a characteristically animal, and then an unequivocally vegetable existence." Therefore, on the principle of natural selection with divergence of character, it does not seem incredible that, from such low and intermediate form, both animals and plants may have been developed; and, if we admit this, we must likewise admit that all the organic beings which have ever lived on this earth may be descended from some one primordial form. But this inference is chiefly grounded on analogy and it is immaterial whether or not it be accepted. No doubt it is possible, as Mr. G. H. Lewes[11] has urged, that at the first commencement of life many different forms were evolved; but if so we may conclude that only a very few have left modified descendants. For, as I have recently remarked in regard to the members of each great kingdom, such as the Vertebrata, Articulata, &c., we have distinct evidence in their embryological homologous and rudimentary structures that within each kingdom all the members are descended from a single progenitor.

When the views advanced by me in this volume, and by Mr. Wallace,[12] or when analogous views on the origin of species are generally admitted, we can dimly foresee that there will be a considerable revolution in natural history. Systematists will be able to pursue their labours as at present; but they will not be incessantly haunted by the shadowy doubt whether this or that form be a true species. This, I feel sure and I speak after experience, will be no slight relief: The endless disputes whether or not some fifty species of British brambles are good species will cease. Systematists will have only to decide (not that this will be easy) whether any form be sufficiently

---

[10] **Asa Gray:** (1810–1888) American botanist and taxonomist.

[11] **G. H. Lewes:** (1817–1878) English critic and author who wrote mainly on philosophical and scientific topics.

[12] **Wallace:** Alfred Russel Wallace (1823–1913); English naturalist who developed the concept of evolution at about the same time as Darwin; published in *Contributions to the Theory of Natural Selection* (1870).

constant and distinct from other forms, to be capable of definition; and if definable, whether the differences be sufficiently important to deserve a specific name. This latter point will become a far more essential consideration than it is at present; for differences, however slight, between any two forms if not blended by intermediate gradations, are looked at by most naturalists as sufficient to raise both forms to the rank of species.

Hereafter we shall be compelled to acknowledge that the only distinction between species and well-marked varieties is, that the latter are known, or believed, to be connected at the present day by intermediate gradations, whereas species were formerly thus connected. Hence, without rejecting the consideration of the present existence of intermediate gradations between any two forms we shall be led to weigh more carefully and to value higher the actual amount of difference between them. It is quite possible that forms now generally acknowledged to be merely varieties may hereafter be thought worthy of specific names; and in this case scientific and common language will come into accordance. In short, we shall have to treat species in the same manner as those naturalists treat genera, who admit that genera are merely artificial combinations made for convenience. This may not be a cheering prospect; but we shall at least be free from the vain search for the undiscovered and undiscoverable essence of the term species.

The other and more general departments of natural history will rise greatly in interest. The terms used by naturalists, of affinity, relationship, community of type, paternity, morphology, adaptive characters, rudimentary and aborted organs, &c., will cease to be metaphorical, and will have a plain signification. When we no longer look at an organic being as a savage looks at a ship, as something wholly beyond his comprehension; when we regard every production of nature as one which has had a long history; when we contemplate every complex structure and instinct as the summing up of many contrivances, each useful to the possessor, in the same way as any great mechanical invention is the summing up of the labour, the experience, the reason and even the blunders of numerous workmen; when we thus view each organic being, how far more interesting — I speak from experience — does the study of natural history become!

A grand and almost untrodden field of inquiry will be opened, on the causes and laws of variation, on correlation, on the effects of use and disuse, on the direct action of external conditions, and so forth. The study of domestic productions will rise immensely in value. A new variety raised by man will be a more important and interesting subject for study than one more species added to the infinitude of already recorded species. Our classifications will come to be, as far as they can be so made, genealogies; and will then truly give what may be called the plan of creation. The rules for classifying will no doubt become simpler when we have a definite object in view. We possess no pedigrees or armorial bearings; and we have to discover and trace the many diverging lines of descent in our natural genealogies, by characters of any kind which have long been inherited. Rudimentary organs will speak infallibly with respect to the nature of long-lost structures. Species and groups of species which are called aberrant, and which may fancifully be called living fossils, will aid us in forming a picture of the ancient forms of life. Embryology will often reveal to us the structure, in some degree obscured, of the prototype of each great class.

When we feel assured that all the individuals of the same species, and all the closely allied species of most genera, have within a not very remote period descended from one parent, and have migrated from some one birth-place; and when we better know the many means of migration, then, by the light which geology now throws, and will continue to throw, on former changes of climate and of the level of the land, we shall surely be enabled to trace in an admirable manner the former migrations of the inhabitants of the whole world. Even at present, by comparing the differences between the inhabitants of the sea on the opposite sides of a continent, and the nature of the various inhabitants on that continent, in relation to their apparent means of immigration, some light can be thrown on ancient geography.

The noble science of Geology loses glory from the extreme imperfection of the record. The crust of the earth with its imbedded remains must not be looked at as a well-filled museum, but as a poor collection made at hazard and at rare intervals. The accumulation of each great fossiliferous formation will be recognised as having depended on an unusual concurrence of favourable circumstances, and the blank intervals between the successive stages as having been of vast duration. But we shall be able to gauge with some security the duration of these intervals by a comparison of the preceding and succeeding organic forms. We must be cautious in attempting to correlate as strictly contemporaneous two formations, which do not include many identical species, by the general succession of the forms of life. As species are produced and exterminated by slowly acting and still existing causes, and not by miraculous acts of creation; and as the most important of all causes of organic change is one which is almost independent of altered and perhaps suddenly altered physical conditions, namely, the mutual relation of organism to organism, — the improvement of one organism entailing the improvement or the extermination of others; it follows, that the amount of organic change in the fossils of consecutive formations probably serves as a fair measure of the relative though not actual lapse of time. A number of species, however, keeping in a body might remain for a long period unchanged, whilst within the same period several of these species by migrating into new countries and coming into competition with foreign associates, might become modified; so that we must not overrate the accuracy of organic change as a measure of time.

In the future I see open fields for far more important researches. Psychology will be securely based on the foundation already well laid by Mr. Herbert Spencer,[13] that of the necessary acquirement of each mental power and capacity by gradation. Much light will be thrown on the origin of man and his history.

Authors of the highest eminence seem to be fully satisfied with the view that each species has been independently created. To my mind it accords better with what we know of the laws impressed on matter by the Creator, that the production and extinction of the past and present inhabitants of the world should have been due to

---

[13] Herbert Spencer: (1820–1903) English philosopher who sought to interpret all phenomena according to the principle of evolutionary progress. He helped to popularize Darwin's ideas, especially in *First Principles* (1862).

secondary causes, like those determining the birth and death of the individual. When I view all beings not as special creations, but as the lineal descendants of some few beings which lived long before the first bed of the Cambrian system was deposited, they seem to me to become ennobled. Judging from the past, we may safely infer that not one living species will transmit its unaltered likeness to a distant futurity. And of the species now living very few will transmit progeny of any kind to a far distant futurity; for the manner in which all organic beings are grouped, shows that the greater number of species in each genus, and all the species in many genera, have left no descendants, but have become utterly extinct. We can so far take a prophetic glance into futurity as to foretell that it will be the common and widely-spread species, belonging to the larger and dominant groups within each class, which will ultimately prevail and procreate new and dominant species. As all the living forms of life are the lineal descendants of those which lived long before the Cambrian epoch, we may feel certain that the ordinary succession by generation has never once been broken, and that no cataclysm has desolated the whole world. Hence we may look with some confidence to a secure future of great length. And as natural selection works solely by and for the good of each being, all corporeal and mental endowments will tend to progress towards perfection.

It is interesting to contemplate a tangled bank, clothed with many plants of many kinds, with birds singing on the bushes, with various insects flitting about, and with worms crawling through the damp earth, and to reflect that these elaborately constructed forms, so different from each other, and dependent upon each other in so complex a manner, have all been produced by laws acting around us. These laws, taken in the largest sense, being Growth with Reproduction; Inheritance which is almost implied by reproduction; Variability from the indirect and direct action of the conditions of life, and from use and disuse: a Ratio of Increase so high as to lead to a Struggle for Life, and as a consequence to Natural Selection, entailing Divergence of Character and the Extinction of less-improved forms. Thus, from the war of nature, from famine and death, the most exalted object which we are capable of conceiving, namely, the production of the higher animals, directly follows. There is grandeur in this view of life, with its several powers, having been originally breathed by the Creator into a few forms or into one; and that, whilst this planet has gone cycling on according to the fixed law of gravity, from so simple a beginning endless forms most beautiful and most wonderful have been, and are being evolved.

ꙮ The Descent of Man

FROM GENERAL SUMMARY AND CONCLUSION

The main conclusion here arrived at, and now held by many naturalists who are well competent to form a sound judgment, is that man is descended from some less highly organized form. The grounds upon which this conclusion rests will never be shaken, for the close similarity between man and the lower animals in embryonic development, as well as in innumerable points of structure and constitution, both of high and of the most trifling importance, — the rudiments which he retains, and the abnormal reversions to which he is occasionally liable, — are facts which cannot be disputed. They have long been known, but until recently they told us nothing with respect to the origin of man. Now when viewed by the light of our knowledge of the whole organic world, their meaning is unmistakable. The great principle of evolution stands up clear and firm, when these groups or facts are considered in connection with others, such as the mutual affinities of the members of the same group, their geographical distribution in past and present times, and their geological succession. It is incredible that all these facts should speak falsely. He who is not content to look, like a savage, at the phenomena of nature as disconnected, cannot any longer believe that man is the work of a separate act of creation. He will be forced to admit that the close resemblance of the embryo of man to that, for instance, of a dog — the construction of his skull, limbs, and whole frame on the same plan with that of other mammals, independently of the uses to which the parts may be put — the occasional re-appearance of various structures, for instance of several muscles, which man does not normally possess, but which are common to the Quadrumana[1] — and a crowd of analogous facts — all point in the plainest manner to the conclusion that man is the co-descendant with other mammals of a common progenitor.

We have seen that man incessantly presents individual differences in all parts of his body and in his mental faculties. These differences or variations seem to be induced by the same general causes, and to obey the same laws as with the lower animals. In both cases similar laws of inheritance prevail. Man tends to increase at a greater rate than his means of subsistence; consequently he is occasionally subjected to a severe struggle for existence, and natural selection will have effected whatever lies within its scope. A succession of strongly-marked variations of a similar nature

---

The Descent of Man. In 1871, Darwin extended his evolutionary hypothesis to human beings. Although this argument was implicit in *Origin* and at the crux of the many objections to that earlier work, in *Descent* Darwin deals explicitly with the issue of man's ancestry and explains how human intelligence, morality, and spirituality could result from an evolutionary process. These selections are taken from the second edition of the work, published in 1874.

---

[1] Quadrumana: An order of apes.

is by no means requisite; slight fluctuating differences in the individual suffice for the work of natural selection; not that we have any reason to suppose that in the same species, all parts of the organisation tend to vary to the same degree. We may feel assured that the inherited effects of the long-continued use or disuse of parts will have done much in the same direction with natural selection. Modifications formerly of importance, though no longer of any special use, are long-inherited. When one part is modified, other parts change through the principle of correlation, of which we have instances in many curious cases of correlated monstrosities. Something may be attributed to the direct and definite action of the surrounding conditions of life, such as abundant food, heat or moisture; and lastly, many characters of slight physiological importance, some indeed of considerable importance, have been gained through sexual selection. . . .

By considering the embryological structure of man,—the homologies which he presents with the lower animals,—the rudiments which he retains,—and the reversions to which he is liable, we can partly recall in imagination the former condition of our early progenitors; and can approximately place them in their proper place in the zoological series. We thus learn that man is descended from a hairy, tailed quadruped, probably arboreal in its habits, and an inhabitant of the Old World. This creature, if its whole structure had been examined by a naturalist, would have been classed amongst the Quadrumana, as surely as the still more ancient progenitor of the Old and New World monkeys. The Quadrumana and all the higher mammals are probably derived from an ancient marsupial animal, and this through a long series of diversified forms, from some amphibian-like creature, and this again from some fish-like animal. In the dim obscurity of the past we can see that the early progenitor of all the Vertebrata must have been an aquatic animal provided with branchiæ, with the two sexes united in the same individual, and with the most important organs of the body (such as the brain and heart) imperfectly or not at all developed. This animal seems to have been more like the larvæ of the existing marine Ascidians than any other known form.

The high standard of our intellectual powers and moral disposition is the greatest difficulty which presents itself, after we have been driven to this conclusion on the origin of man. But every one who admits the principle of evolution, must see that the mental powers of the higher animals, which are the same in kind with those of man, though so different in degree, are capable of advancement. Thus the interval between the mental powers of one of the higher apes and of a fish, or between those of an ant and scale-insect, is immense; yet their development does not offer any special difficulty; for with our domesticated animals, the mental faculties are certainly variable, and the variations are inherited. No one doubts that they are of the utmost importance to animals in a state of nature. Therefore the conditions are favourable for their development through natural selection. The same conclusion may be extended to man; the intellect must have been all-important to him, even at a very remote period, as enabling him to invent and use language, to make weapons, tools, traps, &c., whereby with the aid of his social habits, he long ago became the most dominant of all living creatures.

A great stride in the development of the intellect will have followed, as soon as the half-art and half-instinct of language came into use; for the continued use of language will have reacted on the brain and produced an inherited effect; and this again will have reacted on the improvement of language. As Mr. Chauncey Wright[2] has well remarked, the largeness of the brain in man relatively to his body, compared with the lower animals, may be attributed in chief part to the early use of some simple form of language,—that wonderful engine which affixes signs to all sorts of objects and qualities, and excites trains of thought which would never arise from the mere impression of the senses, or if they did arise could not be followed out. The higher intellectual powers of man, such as those of ratiocination, abstraction, self-consciousness, &c., probably follow from the continued improvement and exercise of the other mental faculties.

The development of the moral qualities is a more interesting problem. The foundation lies in the social instincts, including under this term the family ties. These instincts are highly complex, and in the case of the lower animals give special tendencies towards certain definite actions; but the more important elements are love, and the distinct emotion of sympathy. Animals endowed with the social instincts take pleasure in one another's company, warn one another of danger, defend and aid one another in many ways. These instincts do not extend to all the individuals of the species, but only to those of the same community. As they are highly beneficial to the species, they have in all probability been acquired through natural selection.

A moral being is one who is capable of reflecting on his past actions and their motives—of approving of some and disapproving of others; and the fact that man is the one being who certainly deserves this designation, is the greatest of all distinctions between him and the lower animals. But in the fourth chapter I have endeavoured to shew that the moral sense follows, firstly, from the enduring and ever-present nature of the social instincts; secondly, from man's appreciation of the approbation and disapprobation of his fellows; and thirdly, from the high activity of his mental faculties, with past impressions extremely vivid; and in these latter respects he differs from the lower animals. Owing to this condition of mind, man cannot avoid looking both backwards and forwards, and comparing past impressions. Hence after some temporary desire or passion has mastered his social instincts, he reflects and compares the now weakened impression of such past impulses with the ever-present social instincts; and he then feels that sense of dissatisfaction which all unsatisfied instincts leave behind them, he therefore resolves to act differently for the future,—and this is conscience. Any instinct, permanently stronger or more enduring than another, gives rise to a feeling which we express by saying that it ought to be obeyed. A pointer dog, if able to reflect on his past conduct, would say to himself, I ought (as indeed we say of him) to have pointed at that hare and not have yielded to the passing temptation of hunting it.

---

[2] Mr. Chauncey Wright: "On the Limits of Natural Selection," in the "North American Review," Oct. 1870, p. 295. [Darwin]

Social animals are impelled partly by a wish to aid the members of their community in a general manner, but more commonly to perform certain definite actions. Man is impelled by the same general wish to aid his fellows; but has few or no special instincts. He differs also from the lower animals in the power of expressing his desires by words, which thus become a guide to the aid required and bestowed. The motive to give aid is likewise much modified in man: it no longer consists solely of a blind instinctive impulse, but is much influenced by the praise or blame of his fellows. The appreciation and the bestowal of praise and blame both rest on sympathy; and this emotion, as we have seen, is one of the most important elements of the social instincts. Sympathy, though gained as an instinct, is also much strengthened by exercise or habit. As all men desire their own happiness, praise or blame is bestowed on actions and motives, according as they lead to this end; and as happiness is an essential part of the general good, the greatest-happiness principle indirectly serves as a nearly safe standard of right and wrong. As the reasoning powers advance and experience is gained, the remoter effects of certain lines of conduct on the character of the individual, and on the general good, are perceived; and then the self-regarding virtues come within the scope of public opinion, and receive praise, and their opposites blame. But with the less civilised nations reason often errs, and many bad customs and base superstitions come within the same scope, and are then esteemed as high virtues, and their breach as heavy crimes.

The moral faculties are generally and justly esteemed as of higher value than the intellectual powers. But we should bear in mind that the activity of the mind in vividly recalling past impressions is one of the fundamental though secondary bases of conscience. This affords the strongest argument for educating and stimulating in all possible ways the intellectual faculties of every human being. No doubt a man with a torpid mind, if his social affections and sympathies are well developed, will be led to good actions, and may have a fairly sensitive conscience. But whatever renders the imagination more vivid and strengthens the habit of recalling and comparing past impressions, will make the conscience more sensitive, and may even somewhat compensate for weak social affections and sympathies.

The moral nature of man has reached its present standard, partly through the advancement of his reasoning powers and consequently of a just public opinion, but especially from his sympathies having been rendered more tender and widely diffused through the effects of habit, example, instruction, and reflection. It is not improbable that after long practice virtuous tendencies may be inherited. With the more civilised races, the conviction of the existence of an all-seeing Deity has had a potent influence on the advance of morality. Ultimately man does not accept the praise or blame of his fellows as his sole guide, though few escape this influence, but his habitual convictions, controlled by reason, afford him the safest rule. His conscience then becomes the supreme judge and monitor. Nevertheless the first foundation or origin of the moral sense lies in the social instincts, including sympathy; and these instincts no doubt were primarily gained, as in the case of the lower animals, through natural selection.

The belief in God has often been advanced as not only the greatest, but the most complete of all the distinctions between man and the lower animals. It is however impossible, as we have seen, to maintain that this belief is innate or instinctive in man. On the other hand a belief in all-pervading spiritual agencies seems to be universal; and apparently follows from a considerable advance in man's reason, and from a still greater advance in his faculties of imagination, curiosity, and wonder. I am aware that the assumed instinctive belief in God has been used by many persons as an argument for His existence. But this is a rash argument, as we should thus be compelled to believe in the existence of many cruel and malignant spirits, only a little more powerful than man; for the belief in them is far more general than in a beneficent Deity. The idea of a universal and beneficent Creator does not seem to arise in the mind of man, until he has been elevated by long-continued culture.

He who believes in the advancement of man from some low organised form, will naturally ask how does this bear on the belief in the immortality of the soul. The barbarous races of man, as Sir J. Lubbock[3] has shewn, possess no clear belief of this kind; but arguments derived from the primeval beliefs of savages are, as we have just seen, of little or no avail. Few persons feel any anxiety from the impossibility of determining at what precise period in the development of the individual, from the first trace of a minute germinal vesicle, man becomes an immortal being; and there is no greater cause for anxiety because the period cannot possibly be determined in the gradually ascending organic scale.[4]

I am aware that the conclusions arrived at in this work will be denounced by some as highly irreligious; but he who denounces them is bound to shew why it is more irreligious to explain the origin of man as a distinct species by descent from some lower form, through the laws of variation and natural selection, than to explain the birth of the individual through the laws of ordinary reproduction. The birth both of the species and of the individual are equally parts of that grand sequence of events, which our minds refuse to accept as the result of blind chance. The understanding revolts at such a conclusion, whether or not we are able to believe that every slight variation of structure, — the union of each pair in marriage, — the dissemination of each seed, — and other such events, have all been ordained for some special purpose.

Sexual selection has been treated at great length in this work; for, as I have attempted to shew, it has played an important part in the history of the organic world. I am aware that much remains doubtful, but I have endeavoured to give a fair view of the whole case. In the lower divisions of the animal kingdom, sexual selection seems to have done nothing: such animals are often affixed for life to the same spot, or have the sexes combined in the same individual, or what is still more important, their perceptive and intellectual faculties are not sufficiently advanced to allow

---

[3] Sir J. Lubbock: Sir John Lubbock (1834–1913); English naturalist and anthropologist; author of *Prehistoric Times* (1865).

[4] Few persons . . . scale: The Rev. J. A. Picton gives a discussion to this effect in his "New Theories and the Old Faith," 1870. [Darwin]

of the feelings of love and jealousy, or of the exertion of choice. When, however, we come to the Arthropoda and Vertebrata, even to the lowest classes in these two great Sub-Kingdoms, sexual selection has effected much. . . .

The belief in the power of sexual selection rests chiefly on the following considerations. Certain characters are confined to one sex; and this alone renders it probable that in most cases they are connected with the act of reproduction. In innumerable instances these characters are fully developed only at maturity, and often during only a part of the year, which is always the breeding-season. The males (passing over a few exceptional cases) are the more active in courtship; they are the better armed, and are rendered the more attractive in various ways. It is to be especially observed that the males display their attractions with elaborate care in the presence of the females; and that they rarely or never display them excepting during the season of love. It is incredible that all this should be purposeless. Lastly we have distinct evidence with some quadrupeds and birds, that the individuals of one sex are capable of feeling a strong antipathy or preference for certain individuals of the other sex.

Bearing in mind these facts, and the marked results of man's unconscious selection, when applied to domesticated animals and cultivated plants, it seems to me almost certain that if the individuals of one sex were during a long series of generations to prefer pairing with certain individuals of the other sex, characterised in some peculiar manner, the offspring would slowly but surely become modified in this same manner. I have not attempted to conceal that, excepting when the males are more numerous than the females, or when polygamy prevails, it is doubtful how the more attractive males succeed in leaving a large number of offspring to inherit their superiority in ornaments or other charms than the less attractive males; but I have shewn that this would probably follow from the females, — especially the more vigorous ones, which would be the first to breed, — preferring not only the more attractive but at the same time the more vigorous and victorious males.

Although we have some positive evidence that birds appreciate bright and beautiful objects, as with the bower-birds of Australia, and although they certainly appreciate the power of song, yet I fully admit that it is astonishing that the females of many birds and some mammals should be endowed with sufficient taste to appreciate ornaments, which we have reason to attribute to sexual selection; and this is even more astonishing in the case of reptiles, fish, and insects. But we really know little about the minds of the lower animals. It cannot be supposed, for instance, that male birds of paradise or peacocks should take such pains in erecting, spreading, and vibrating their beautiful plumes before the females for no purpose. We should remember the fact given on excellent authority in a former chapter, that several pea-hens, when debarred from an admired male, remained widows during a whole season rather than pair with another bird.

Nevertheless I know of no fact in natural history more wonderful than that of the female Argus pheasant should appreciate the exquisite shading of the ball-and-socket ornaments and the elegant patterns on the wing-feathers of the male. He who thinks that the male was created as he now exists must admit that the great plumes, which prevent the wings from being used for flight, and which are displayed during courtship and at no other time in a manner quite peculiar to this one species, were given to him as an ornament. If so, he must likewise admit that the female was created and endowed with the capacity of appreciating such ornaments. I differ only in the conviction that the male Argus pheasant acquired his beauty gradually, through the preference of the females during many generations for the more highly ornamented males; the æsthetic capacity of the females having been advanced through exercise or habit, just as our own taste is gradually improved. In the male through the fortunate chance of a few feathers being left unchanged, we can distinctly trace how simple spots with a little fulvous shading on one side may have been developed by small steps into the wonderful ball-and-socket ornaments; and it is probable that they were actually thus developed.

Everyone who admits the principle of evolution, and yet feels great difficulty in admitting that female mammals, birds, reptiles, and fish, could have acquired the high taste implied by the beauty of the males, and which generally coincides with our own standard, should reflect that the nerve-cells of the brain in the highest as well as in the lowest members of the Vertebrate series, are derived from those of the common progenitor of this great Kingdom. For we can thus see how it has come to pass that certain mental faculties, in various and widely distinct groups of animals, have been developed in nearly the same manner and to nearly the same degree.

The reader who has taken the trouble to go through the several chapters devoted to sexual selection, will be able to judge how far the conclusions at which I have arrived are supported by sufficient evidence. If he accepts these conclusions he may, I think, safely extend them to mankind; but it would be superfluous here to repeat what I have so lately said on the manner in which sexual selection apparently has acted on man, both on the male and female side, causing the two sexes to differ in body and mind, and the several races to differ from each other in various characters, as well as from their ancient and lowly-organised progenitors.

He who admits the principle of sexual selection will be led to the remarkable conclusion that the nervous system not only regulates most of the existing functions of the body, but has indirectly influenced the progressive development of various bodily structures and of certain mental qualities. Courage, pugnacity, perseverance, strength and size of body, weapons of all kinds, musical organs, both vocal and instrumental, bright colours and ornamental appendages, have all been indirectly gained by the one sex or the other, through the exertion of choice, the influence of love and jealousy, and the appreciation of the beautiful in sound, colour, or form; and these powers of the mind manifestly depend on the development of the brain.

Man scans with scrupulous care the character and pedigree of his horses, cattle, and dogs before he matches them; but when he comes to his own marriage he rarely, or never, takes any such care. He is impelled by nearly the same motives as the lower animals, when they are left to their own free choice, though he is in so far superior to them that he highly values mental charms and virtues. On the other hand he is strongly attracted by mere wealth or rank. Yet he might by selection do something not only for the bodily constitution and frame of his offspring, but for their intellectual and moral qualities. Both sexes ought to refrain from marriage if they are in any marked degree inferior in body or mind; but such hopes are Utopian and will never be even partially realised until the laws of inheritance are thoroughly known. Everyone does good service, who aids toward this end. When the principles of breeding and inheritance are better understood, we shall not hear ignorant members of our legislature rejecting with scorn a plan for ascertaining whether or not consanguineous marriages are injurious to man.

The advancement of the welfare of mankind is a most intricate problem: all ought to refrain from marriage who cannot avoid abject poverty for their children; for poverty is not only a great evil, but tends to its own increase by leading to recklessness in marriage. On the other hand, as Mr. Galton[5] has remarked, if the prudent avoid marriage, whilst the reckless marry, the inferior members tend to supplant the better members of society. Man, like every other animal, has no doubt advanced to his present high condition through a struggle for existence consequent on his rapid multiplication; and if he is to advance still higher, it is to be feared that he must remain subject to a severe struggle. Otherwise he would sink into indolence, and the more gifted men would not be more successful in the battle of life than the less gifted. Hence our natural rate of increase, though leading to many and obvious evils, must not be greatly diminished by any means. There should be open competition for all men; and the most able should not be prevented by laws or customs from succeeding best and rearing the largest number of offspring. Important as the struggle for existence has been and even still is, yet as far as the highest part of man's nature is concerned there are other agencies more important. For the moral qualities are advanced, either directly or indirectly, much more through the effects of habit, the reasoning powers, instruction, religion, &c., than through natural selection; though to this latter agency may be safely attributed the social instincts, which afforded the basis for the development of the moral sense.

---

[5] **Mr. Galton:** Sir Francis Galton (1822–1911); English scientist, founder of eugenics, the science of human improvement by genetic control, and Charles Darwin's cousin. He opposed the theory of acquired characteristics.

Science and Creation

When Darwin published *The Origin of Species* in 1859, he aggravated a controversy that had been building for at least half a century. As scientists sought to explain more and more phenomena by natural causes, they challenged supernatural explanations and brought science into conflict with religion. "Religion," the evolutionary English philosopher Herbert Spencer asserted, "has been impelled by science to give up one after another of its dogmas, of those assumed cognitions which it could not substantiate." The two cutting-edge sciences of the nineteenth century, geology and biology, were in the frontline of the assault. Geologists sought to separate geological theory from the Bible and to establish nature as the sole source of truths about the history of the earth. Charles Lyell,[1] Darwin's friend and mentor, argued that past changes in the earth were not caused by catastrophes like Noah's flood but by the same processes that could be observed operating in the present. This principle and others like it challenged the notion of divine intervention. Biologists attributed the extinction of some species and the emergence of others to natural causes, explanations that seemed to call into question the biblical account of creation. Darwin brought together many of the ideas of geologists and biologists and integrated them into a coherent theory that revealed the natural mechanisms by which life evolved. In doing so, he became the representative of Science and its challenges to religion. The texts chosen for this section discuss the

---

[1] **Charles Lyell:** (1797–1875) English geologist whose *Principles of Geology* (1830–33) gained general acceptance for the theory of uniformitarianism, the theory that earth changes are caused by forces that have operated uniformly from the origin of the earth to the present time.

THE LION OF THE SEASON.

ALARMED FLUNKEY. "MR. G G-G-O-O-O-RILLA!"

"The Lion of the Season," 1861

This satiric cartoon was published while the controversy over Darwin's Origin of Species was raging. (Art Resource)

Religion has been impelled by science to give up one after another of its dogmas, of those assumed cognitions which it could not substantiate.

– HERBERT SPENCER, 1862

impact of science in the nineteenth century on literature and religion, especially religious doctrines about the creation of life.

EVOLUTION AND CREATION

The theory of evolution particularly challenged three doctrines of creation held by many orthodox Christians. Evolution's account of slow and continual modifications to biological species applied geological uniformitarianism to biology, confirmed the geologist's account of the history of the earth, and discredited the Bible-based calendar that dated creation at about 4000 B.C.E.[2] It also challenged the doctrine of a permanent and fixed creation that was based on the creation narrative in Genesis, which describes all species being created at one time. Darwin contended that creation is an ongoing process, a continuous struggle out of which the surviving species emerge like the victors of a battle. Finally, evolution called into question the notion of the "special creation" of mankind by God and argued instead that humans were animals that had developed over time from lower forms. That man should be a younger cousin of the ape was probably the idea most offensive to the church and its adherents.

p. 385

p. 389

The theory of evolution led many religious people to doubt their faith; it also raised doubts about science. The excerpt from Bishop Samuel Wilberforce's review of *The Origin of Species* is representative of the reaction of many religious people to Darwin's ideas. Although Wilberforce claims to be responding to *Origin* "solely on scientific grounds," his objections really go back to what he considers its incompatibility with Scripture. Alfred, Lord Tennyson was also distressed by the religious implications of the new sciences. In *In Memoriam* (1850), he records his doubts after learning that the fossil record indicates that many species have become extinct, which suggests to him that there is no God who cares about the life or death of individual creatures, and that in a "Nature, red in tooth and claw," the only laws seem to be those of chance and the struggle for existence. As Tennyson and many others saw it, the scientific worldview destroyed the possibility

---

[2] Bible . . . B.C.E.: In the mid seventeenth century, Archbishop James Ussher (1581–1656) constructed a calendar based on Scripture that dated creation at 4004 B.C.E. It was incorporated into many editions of the Bible and adopted by many Christians.

of a personal God, and it lacked the beauty and harmony associated with divine creation.

SCIENCE AND LITERATURE

Even writers who had no particular religious objections to science nonetheless found its impact unsettling. For some Romantics, science, with its crude physical view of reality, undermined the imagination. The protagonist of Mary Shelley's *Frankenstein* (1818), scientist Victor Frankenstein, pieces together a creature from body parts dug up from graves and galvanizes it to life. But disgusted by the crudity of his creation, he rejects and abandons it. The story, read variously as a parable about the responsibility of the artist, about childbirth and parenthood, and about the inevitable frustrations of the creative process, is also a commentary on the limitations of science. Edgar Allan Poe's **"Sonnet — To Science"** describes the chilling effect of the "dull realities" of science on the imagination. Later in the century, however, these dull realities would show up in the novels of REALISTS who consciously tried to faithfully depict the physical world around them. Émile Zola, leader of the NATURALISTS[3] in France, based his whole aesthetic on an evolutionary perspective. In the passage from the Preface to the second edition of *Thérèse Raquin,* Zola defends his novel from critics who attacked its morality. He explains that his characters are creatures determined by physical laws, animals reacting instinctively to the physical and hereditary forces that work on them.

p. 393

p. 396

p. 398

tay-REZ rah-KANG

SCIENCE AND THE CREATION STORY

Some religions responded to the challenges brought by science by attempting to adapt religion to the new ideas. Some theologians sought to elucidate Christian doctrine and the Bible in the new light of science, using both the Scriptures and nature as sources of revelation. These commentators developed, for example, natural explanations for the miracles recorded in the Bible. At the same time, "higher criticism," a movement to apply historical, linguistic, and critical theories to the interpretation of Scripture, looked on biblical

---

[3] Naturalists: A school of Realist writers led by Émile Zola, who formulated Naturalism's main tenets, which applied science to literary theory and characterized human beings as physical creatures whose lives were determined by heredity, environment, and physical instincts.

p. 400

p. 406
hee-RAH-tah
aht-soo-TAH-neh

p. 408

p. 409
hoo-SHUR

stories as myths containing symbolic but not literal truth. In developing *The Woman's Bible,* Elizabeth Cady Stanton and her colleagues relied on the work and methods of these biblical reinterpreters to challenge patriarchial readings of Scripture, especially the story of the Garden of Eden. **Hirata Atsutane**, part of the NEO-SHINTO revival in Japan, objected to similar license taken by those who reinterpreted Shintoism's sacred texts as myths. He might be described as a Shinto fundamentalist, although his argument for the literal truth of the Shinto creation story is based on the proposition that similar stories are found in many other world religions. On the other hand, **Syed Ahmed Khan,** an Islamic scholar, argues that there can be no differences between science and religion since both are devoted to discovering the truth. Science simply reveals the truths about God's creation. **Hu Shi**, a Chinese BUDDHIST writing in the early twentieth century under the influence of Western ideas, dismisses traditional religion and derives his philosophy of life from science alone.

■ CONNECTIONS

Goethe, *Faust,* **p. 29.** Goethe was a scientist as well as a poet and dramatist. Do you find evidence of a scientific point of view in *Faust*? Could Faust's agreement with Mephistopheles be said to arise from a scientific curiosity? Think about Faust's project to drain the marshes. Could it be considered a "scientific" endeavor? How does it contribute to Faust's redemption?

Tagore, *Broken Ties,* **p. 986.** In *Broken Ties,* Western scientific "atheism," represented by Jagomohan, who subscribes to the views of the Utilitarian philosophers Jeremy Bentham and John Stuart Mill, confronts Eastern spirituality, here represented by Harimohan, a Hindu traditionalist, and Lilananda Swami. What does the story suggest are the positive and negative aspects of each point of view? Is the conflict between them resolved by the end of the story?

Pardo Bazan, "The Oldest Story," p. 699; Machado de Assis, "Adam and Eve," **p. 922.** Elizabeth Cady Stanton's feminist commentary on Genesis relates to two other "reinterpretations" of the Adam and Eve story, those of Emilia Pardo Bazan in "The Oldest Story" and Machado de Assis in "Adam and Eve." Do any of these works reflect the influence of science on religious belief in the nineteenth century?

■ PRONUNCIATION

Chang Chün-mai: jahng-jwen-MIGH
Hamadryad: ham-uh-DRIGH-ad
Hirata Atsutane: hee-RAH-tah aht-soo-TAH-neh
Hu Shi: hoo-SHUR
Liang Ch'i-ch'ao: lyahng-chee-CHOW
Naiad: NIGH-yad
Takami-musubi: tah-KAH-mee moo-SOO-bee
Shakyamuni: shuk-yuh-MOO-nee
Wu Chih-hui: woo-zhur-HWAY

❧ SAMUEL WILBERFORCE
1805–1873

An Anglican minister and Bishop of Oxford, Wilberforce was an amateur naturalist, but his review of *The Origin of Species* in the conservative *Quarterly Review* (1860) reflected more his view that the Bible is the divinely inspired word of God than it did his scientific interests. At a meeting of the British Association for the Advancement of Science on June 30, 1860, Wilberforce concluded a violent attack on *Origin* by asking Thomas Henry Huxley, Darwin's most eloquent spokesman, whether it was from his grandfather or his grandmother that he claimed descent from an ape. According to an eyewitness, Huxley responded: "A man has no reason to be ashamed of having an ape for his grandfather. If there were an ancestor whom I should feel shame in recalling, it would be a *man,* a man of restless and versatile intellect, who, not content with an equivocal success in his own sphere of activity, plunges into scientific questions with which he has no real acquaintance, only to obscure

Evolution is, in truth, an ingenious theory for diffusing throughout creation the working and so the personality of the Creator. And thus . . . such views really tend inevitably to banish from the mind most of the peculiar attributes of the Almighty.

– SAMUEL WILBERFORCE

MONKEYANA.

"Am I a Man and a Brother?" Cartoon published in *Punch,* London, 1861

Many were offended by Darwin's suggestion that human beings and monkeys shared ancestry. (Art Resource)

them by an aimless rhetoric, and distract the attention of his hearers from the real point at issue by eloquent digressions, and skilled appeals to religious prejudice."

FROM

✑ Review of *Origin of Species*, 1860

On what then is the new theory based? We say it with unfeigned regret, in dealing with such a man as Mr. Darwin, on the merest hypothesis, supported by the most unbounded assumptions. . . .

. . . Place the first beginning where you will, that beginning *must* contain the apparent history of a *past,* which existed only in the mind of the Creator. If, with Mr. Darwin, to escape the difficulty of supposing the first man at his creation to possess in that framework of his body "false marks of nourishment from his mother's womb," with Mr. Darwin you consider him to have been an improved ape, you only carry the difficulty up from the first man to the first ape; if, with Mr. Darwin, in violation of all observation, you break the barrier between the classes of vegetable and animal life, and suppose every animal to be an "improved" vegetable, you do but carry your difficulty with you into the vegetable world; for, how could there be seeds if there had been no plants to seed them? and if you carry up your thoughts through the vista of the Darwinian eternity up to the primaeval fungus, still the primaeval fungus must have had humus, from which to draw into its venerable vessels the nourishment of its archetypal existence, and that humus must itself be a "false mark" of a pre-existing vegetation. . . .

Our readers will not have failed to notice that we have objected to the views with which we have been dealing solely on scientific grounds. We have done so from our fixed conviction that it is thus that the truth or falsehood of such arguments should be tried. We have no sympathy with those who object to any facts or alleged facts in nature, or to any inference logically deduced from them, because they believe them to contradict what it appears to them is taught by Revelation. We think that all such objections savour of a timidity which is really inconsistent with a firm and well-instructed faith. . . . He who is as sure as he is of his own existence that the God of Truth is at once the God of Nature and the God of Revelation, cannot believe it to be possible that His voice in either, rightly understood, can differ, or deceive His creatures. To oppose facts in the natural world because they seem to oppose Revelation, or to humour them so as to compel them to speak its voice, is, he knows, but another form of the ever-ready feebleminded dishonesty of lying for God, and trying by fraud or falsehood to do the work of the God of truth. It is with another and a nobler spirit that the true believer walks amongst the works of nature. The words graven on the everlasting rocks are the words of God, and they are graven by His hand. No more can they contradict His Word written in His book, than could the words of the old covenant graven by His hand on the stony tables contradict the writing of His hand in the volume of the new dispensation. There may be to man difficulty in rec-onciling all the utterances of the two voices. But what of that? He has learned already that here he knows only in part, and that the day of reconciling all apparent contra-dictions between what must agree is nigh at hand. He rests his mind in perfect quiet-ness on this assurance, and rejoices in the gift of light without a misgiving as to what it may discover. . . .

Mr. Darwin writes as a Christian, and we doubt not that he is one. We do not for a moment believe him to be one of those who retain in some corner of their hearts a secret unbelief which they dare not vent; and we therefore pray him to consider well the grounds on which we brand his speculations with the charge of such a tendency. First, then, he not obscurely declares that he applies his scheme of the action of the principle of natural selection to MAN himself, as well as to the animals around him. Now, we must say at once, and openly, that such a notion is absolutely incompatible not only with single expressions in the word of God on that subject of natural sci-ence with which it is not immediately concerned, but, which in our judgment is of far more importance, with the whole representation of that moral and spiritual con-dition of man which is its proper subject-matter. Man's derived supremacy over the earth; man's power of articulate speech; man's gift of reason; man's free-will and responsibility; man's fall and man's redemption; the incarnation of the Eternal Son; the indwelling of the Eternal Spirit,—all are equally and utterly irreconcilable with the degrading notion of the brute origin of him who was created in the image of God, and redeemed by the Eternal Son assuming to himself his nature. Equally inconsistent, too, not with any passing expressions, but with the whole scheme of God's dealing with man as recorded in His word, is Mr. Darwin's daring notion of man's further development into some unknown extent of powers, and shape, and size, through natural selection acting through that long vista of ages which he casts mistily over the earth upon the most favoured individuals of his species. We care not in these pages to push the argument further. We have done enough for our purpose in thus succinctly intimating its course. . . .

Nor can we doubt, secondly, that this view, which thus contradicts the revealed relation of creation to its Creator, is equally inconsistent with the fullness of His glory. It is, in truth, an ingenious theory for diffusing throughout creation the work-ing and so the personality of the Creator. And thus, however unconsciously to him who holds them, such views really tend inevitably to banish from the mind most of the peculiar attributes of the Almighty.

How, asks Mr. Darwin, can we possibly account for the manifest plan, order, and arrangement which pervade creation, except we allow to it this self-developing power through modified descent? . . .

How can we account for all this? By the simplest and yet the most comprehen-sive answer. By declaring the stupendous fact that all creation is the transcript in matter of ideas eternally existing in the mind of the Most High—that order in the utmost perfectness of its relation pervades His works, because it exists as in its cen-tre and highest fountain-head in Him the Lord of all. Here is the true account of the fact which has so utterly misled shallow observers, that Man himself, the Prince and Head of this creation, passes in the earlier stages of his being through phases of existence closely analogous, so far as his earthly tabernacle is concerned, to those in which the lower animals ever remain. At that point of being the development of the protozoa is arrested. Through it the embryo of their chief passes to the perfection of his earthly frame. But the types of those lower forms of being must be found in the animals which never advance beyond them—not in man for whom they are but the foundation for an after-development; whilst he too, Creation's crown and

Darwin ridiculed
Some of Darwin's critics were so distressed by his theory of evolution that they parodied him by depicting him as a monkey, or at least as a man willing to equate monkeys with people. (Hulton / Archive)

perfection, thus bears witness in his own frame to the law of order which pervades the universe. . . .

. . . We trust that he [Darwin] is mistaken in believing that he may count Sir C. Lyell as one of his converts. We know indeed the temptations which he can bring to bear upon his geological brother. The Lyellian hypothesis, itself not free from some of Mr. Darwin's faults, stands eminently in need for its own support of some such new scheme of physical life as that propounded here. Yet no man has been more distinct and more logical in the denial of the transmutation of species than Sir C. Lyell, and that not in the infancy of his scientific life, but in its full vigour and maturity. . . .

He [Lyell] shows the fallacy of Lamarck's reasoning,[1] and by anticipation confutes the whole theory of Mr. Darwin, when gathering clearly up into a few heads the recapitulation of the whole argument in favour of the reality of species in nature. . . .

We trust that Sir C. Lyell abides still by these truly philosophical principles; and that with his help and with that of his brethren this flimsy speculation may be as completely put down as was what in spite of all denials we must venture to call its twin though less-instructed brother, the "Vestiges of Creation."[2] In so doing they will assuredly provide for the strength and continually growing progress of British science. . . .

---

[1] **[Lyell] . . . reasoning:** Lyell challenged the theory of Jean Baptiste Lamarck (1744–1829), a French naturalist who argued that acquired characteristics can be passed on from one generation to the next. Lamarck's work was an important forerunner to Darwin's theory of evolution.

[2] **"Vestiges of Creation":** In *Vestiges of the Natural History of Creation* (1844) Robert Chambers (1802–1871) developed an evolutionary theory, but his work lacked evidence and was generally rejected by the scientific community.

ᘉ ALFRED, LORD TENNYSON
1809–1892

English poet laureate from 1850 until his death 42 years later, Tennyson was viewed in his own time as the spokesman of his age. His poems often made public issues out of his personal concerns. *In Memoriam* (1850), a series of elegies for Tennyson's close friend, Arthur Hallam, who died in 1833, chronicles the stages of the poet's long-continuing grief. Tennyson's faith that Hallam's death has some meaning is shaken by evidence from the fossil record, which reveals many extinct species from the past, suggesting that there is no God who cares about the life and death of individual creatures.

Science, and especially evolutionary theory, made it difficult for many in the nineteenth century to maintain their belief in traditional religion. The famous stanzas presented below, published a decade before

Though Nature, red
in tooth and claw
With ravine, shrieked
against his creed —
– TENNYSON, *In Memoriam*

Armillary sphere, heliocentric, c. 1810
This Italian sculpture shows an early understanding of the solar system. In the center is the sun, around which several rings revolve. The inner rings mark the orbits of Earth, Mars, and Jupiter, giving the planets' speed of rotation. The large outermost band is inscribed with the signs of the zodiac and months of the year. (Art Resource)

The Origin of Species appeared, indicate just how pervasive evolutionary theory was at the time. Tennyson was probably thinking specifically of the ideas of geologist Charles Lyell when he wrote these verses.

FROM

 *In Memoriam*

54

O yet we trust that somehow good
   Will be the final goal of ill,
   To pangs of nature, sins of will,
Defects of doubt, and taints of blood;

That nothing walks with aimless feet;
   That not one life shall be destroyed,

Or cast as rubbish to the void,
    When God hath made the pile complete;

That not a worm is cloven in vain;
10   That not a moth with vain desire
    Is shriveled in a fruitless fire,
Or but subserves another's gain.

Behold, we know not anything;
    I can but trust that good shall fall
    At last — far off — at last, to all,
And every winter change to spring.

So runs my dream; but what am I?
    An infant crying in the night;
    An infant crying for the light,
20 And with no language but a cry.

55

The wish, that of the living whole
    No life may fail beyond the grave,
    Derives it not from what we have
The likest God within the soul?

Are God and Nature then at strife,
    That Nature lends such evil dreams?
    So careful of the type° she seems,   *species*
So careless of the single life,

That I, considering everywhere
30   Her secret meaning in her deeds,
    And finding that of fifty seeds
She often brings but one to bear,

I falter where I firmly trod,
    And falling with my weight of cares
    Upon the great world's altar-stairs
That slope through darkness up to God,

I stretch lame hands of faith, and grope,
    And gather dust and chaff, and call
    To what I feel is Lord of all,
40 And faintly trust the larger hope.

56

"So careful of the type?" but no.
　　From scarpèd¹ cliff and quarried stone
　　She cries, "A thousand types are gone;
I care for nothing, all shall go.

"Thou makest thine appeal to me:
　　I bring to life, I bring to death;
　　The spirit does but mean the breath:
I know no more." And he, shall he,

Man, her last work, who seemed so fair,
50　　Such splendid purpose in his eyes,
　　Who rolled the psalm to wintry skies,　　　　　　temples
Who built him fanes° of fruitless prayer,

Who trusted God was love indeed
　　And love Creation's final law—
　　Though Nature, red in tooth and claw
With ravine, shrieked against his creed—

Who loved, who suffered countless ills,
　　Who battled for the True, the Just,
　　Be blown about the desert dust,
60 Or sealed within the iron hills?²

No more? A monster then, a dream,
　　A discord. Dragons of the prime,　　　　　　　　tore
　　That tare° each other in their slime,
Were mellow music matched° with him.　　　　　　compared

O life as futile, then, as frail!
　　O for thy voice to soothe and bless!
　　What hope of answer, or redress?
Behind the veil, behind the veil.

---

¹ scarpèd: Cut away to expose the layers of rock.
² sealed . . . hills: That is, as fossils.

✺ MARY SHELLEY
1797–1851

Her father was philosopher William Godwin and her mother was Mary Wollstonecraft, feminist author of *A Vindication of the Rights of Woman*. Mary Shelley's husband was poet Percy Bysshe Shelley.

Wollstonecraft died of complications in childbirth while delivering Mary. Godwin, a mentor to Percy Shelley, did not accept his daughter's liaison with the poet, which began when Mary, sixteen years old and pregnant, ran off with Shelley to Europe. The pair married two years later, after Shelley's estranged first wife committed suicide. Mary's years with Shelley were filled with turmoil and personal disaster. Three of their four children died in infancy, and Shelley drowned in 1822, leaving Mary an impoverished and bereft widow.

Mary Shelley wrote *Frankenstein* (1818) when she was nineteen and living with Shelley in Geneva, Switzerland. The four members of their household—the two Shelleys, Lord Byron, and doctor John William Polidori—set out to write ghost stories to share with one another. Mary Shelley's story, apparently, was the only one that was completed; it has become one of the best-known works in the English language. Although the popular imagination has often confused the novel's monster with his creator, Dr. Frankenstein, the central issue of the story—the power of science to play God—is still present in even the most casual of adaptations.

The following excerpt picks up when Dr. Frankenstein describes a confrontation with his creature in which the creature pleads for sympathy. That Shelley intended more than a simple ghost or horror story is apparent when the "monster" asserts to Frankenstein: "Remember, that I am thy creature; I ought to be thy Adam; but I am rather the fallen angel, whom thou drivest from joy for no misdeed," inviting comparisons to *Paradise Lost* and the Eden story in the Book of Genesis.

> Remember that I am thy creature; I ought to be thy Adam; but I am rather the fallen angel, whom thou drivest from joy for no misdeed.
>
> – MARY SHELLEY, *Frankenstein*

FROM

✺ Frankenstein

It was nearly noon when I arrived at the top of the ascent. For some time I sat upon the rock that overlooks the sea of ice. A mist covered both that and the surrounding mountains. Presently a breeze dissipated the cloud, and I descended upon the glacier. The surface is very uneven, rising like the waves of a troubled sea, descending low, and interspersed by rifts that sink deep. The field of ice is almost a league in width, but I spent nearly two hours in crossing it. The opposite mountain is a bare perpendicular rock. From the side where I now stood Montanvert[1] was exactly

---

[1] Montanvert: One of three large glaciers on **Mont Blanc**, a major peak in the Swiss Alps.

Illustration from
Frankenstein
c. mid 19th century
*This engraving shows
Frankenstein's
creature as a
handsome, well-built
figure with classical
features, quite
different from
twentieth-century
and present-day
renderings. Franken-
stein looks on in
horror at what he has
created from the
bones of the dead.
(The Bridgeman Art
Library)*

opposite, at the distance of a league; and above it rose Mont Blanc, in awful majesty. I remained in a recess of the rock, gazing on this wonderful and stupendous scene. The sea, or rather the vast river of ice, wound among its dependent mountains, whose aerial summits hung over its recesses. Their icy and glittering peaks shone in the sunlight over the clouds. My heart, which was before sorrowful, now swelled with something like joy; I exclaimed—"Wandering spirits, if indeed ye wander, and do not rest in your narrow beds, allow me this faint happiness, or take me, as your companion, away from the joys of life."

As I said this, I suddenly beheld the figure of a man, at some distance, advancing towards me with superhuman speed. He bounded over the crevices in the ice, among which I had walked with caution; his stature, also, as he approached, seemed to exceed that of man. I was troubled: a mist came over my eyes, and I felt a faintness seize me; but I was quickly restored by the cold gale of the mountains. I perceived, as the shape came nearer (sight tremendous and abhorred!) that it was the wretch whom I had created. I trembled with rage and horror, resolving to wait his approach, and then close with him in mortal combat. He approached; his countenance bespoke bitter anguish, combined with disdain and malignity, while its unearthly ugliness rendered it almost too horrible for human eyes. But I scarcely observed this; rage and hatred had at first deprived me of utterance, and I recovered only to over-whelm him with words expressive of furious detestation and contempt.

"Devil," I exclaimed, "do you dare approach me? and do not you fear the fierce vengeance of my arm wreaked on your miserable head? Begone, vile insect! or rather, stay, that I may trample you to dust! and, oh! that I could, with the extinction of your miserable existence, restore those victims whom you have so diabolically murdered!"

"I expected this reception," said the dæmon. "All men hate the wretched; how, then, must I be hated, who am miserable beyond all living things! Yet you, my creator, detest and spurn me, thy creature, to whom thou art bound by ties only dissoluble by the annihilation of one of us. You purpose to kill me. How dare you sport thus with life? Do your duty towards me, and I will do mine towards you and the rest of mankind. If you will comply with my conditions, I will leave them and you at peace; but if you refuse, I will glut the maw of death, until it be satiated with the blood of your remaining friends."

"Abhorred monster! fiend that thou art! the tortures of hell are too mild a vengeance for thy crimes. Wretched devil! you reproach me with your creation; come on, then, that I may extinguish the spark which I so negligently bestowed."

My rage was without bounds; I sprang on him, impelled by all the feelings which can arm one being against the existence of another.

He easily eluded me, and said—

"Be calm! I entreat you to hear me, before you give vent to your hatred on my devoted head. Have I not suffered enough, that you seek to increase my misery? Life, although it may only be an accumulation of anguish, is dear to me, and I will defend it. Remember, thou hast made me more powerful than thyself; my height is superior to thine; my joints more supple. But I will not be tempted to set myself in opposition to thee. I am thy creature, and I will be even mild and docile to my natural lord and king, if thou wilt also perform thy part, the which thou owest me. Oh, Frankenstein, be not equitable to every other, and trample upon me alone, to whom thy justice, and even thy clemency and affection, is most due. Remember, that I am thy creature; I ought to be thy Adam; but I am rather the fallen angel, whom thou drivest from joy for no misdeed. Every where I see bliss, from which I alone am irrevocably excluded. I was benevolent and good; misery made me a fiend. Make me happy, and I shall again be virtuous."

"Begone! I will not hear you. There can be no community between you and me; we are enemies. Begone, or let us try our strength in a fight, in which one must fall."

"How can I move thee? Will no entreaties cause thee to turn a favourable eye upon thy creature, who implores thy goodness and compassion? Believe me, Frankenstein: I was benevolent; my soul glowed with love and humanity: but am I not alone, miserably alone? You, my creator, abhor me; what hope can I gather from your fellow-creatures, who owe me nothing? They spurn and hate me. The desert mountains and dreary glaciers are my refuge. I have wandered here many days; the caves of ice, which I only do not fear, are a dwelling to me, and the only one which man does not grudge. These bleak skies I hail, for they are kinder to me than your fellow-beings. If the multitude of mankind knew of my existence, they would do as you do, and arm themselves for my destruction. Shall I not then hate them who abhor me? I will keep no terms with my enemies. I am miserable, and they shall share my wretchedness. Yet it is in your power to recompense me, and deliver them from an evil which it only remains for you to make so great, that not only you and your family, but thousands of others, shall be swallowed up in the whirlwinds of its rage. Let your compassion be moved, and do not disdain me. Listen to my tale: when you have heard that, abandon or commiserate me, as you shall judge that I deserve. But hear me. The guilty are allowed, by human laws, bloody as they are, to speak in their own defence before they are condemned. Listen to me, Frankenstein. You accuse me of murder; and yet you would, with a satisfied conscience, destroy your own creature. Oh, praise the eternal justice of man! Yet I ask you not to spare me: listen to me; and then, if you can, and if you will, destroy the work of your hands."

"Why do you call to my remembrance," I rejoined, "circumstances, of which I shudder to reflect, that I have been the miserable origin and author? Cursed be the day, abhorred devil, in which you first saw light! Cursed (although I curse myself) be the hands that formed you! You have made me wretched beyond expression. You have left me no power to consider whether I am just to you, or not. Begone! Relieve me from the sight of your detested form."

"Thus I relieve thee, my creator," he said, and placed his hated hands before my eyes, which I flung from me with violence; "thus I take from thee a sight which you abhor. Still thou canst listen to me, and grant me thy compassion. By the virtues that I once possessed, I demand this from you. Hear my tale; it is long and strange, and the temperature of this place is not fitting to your fine sensations; come to the hut upon the mountain. The sun is yet high in the heavens; before it descends to hide itself behind yon snowy precipices, and illuminate another world, you will have heard my story, and can decide. On you it rests, whether I quit for ever the neighbourhood of man, and lead a harmless life, or become the scourge of your fellow-creatures, and the author of your own speedy ruin."

⟡ EDGAR ALLAN POE
1809–1849

Although Poe has sometimes been dismissed as an amateur poet and creator of horror and science-fiction stories, he is the writer responsible for turning the short story into a serious art form, and he invented the detective story. He was particularly influential with the French Symbolists; Baudelaire called him "the most powerful writer of the age."

Poe's career as a journalist, editor, and writer, shadowed by his instability and alcoholism, ended abruptly in 1849 when he disappeared while on a journey from Richmond to Philadelphia. He was found unconscious a week later in Baltimore, where he died within a few days. The mystery surrounding his death continues to puzzle and intrigue his readers.

"Sonnet—To Science," written when Poe was twenty, is a young man's romantic musing on the effects of science on the imagination.

◠ Sonnet — To Science

Science! true daughter of Old Time thou art!
    Who alterest all things with thy peering eyes.
Why preyest thou thus upon the poet's heart,
    Vulture, whose wings are dull realities?
How should he love thee? or how deem thee wise?
    Who wouldst not leave him in his wandering
To seek for treasure in the jeweled skies,
    Albeit he soared with an undaunted wing?
10 Hast thou not dragged Diana[1] from her car?
    And driven the Hamadryad[2] from the wood
To seek a shelter in some happier star?
    Hast thou not torn the Naiad[3] from her flood,
The Elfin from the green grass, and from me
The summer dream beneath the tamarind tree?[4]

---

[1] **Diana:** Roman goddess of the hunt; her "car" is the moon.   [2] **Hamadryad:** A wood nymph who lives only as long as the tree of which she is the spirit lives.   [3] **Naiad:** A river nymph.   [4] **tamarind tree:** An Asian tree, suggesting the East's association with the imagination.

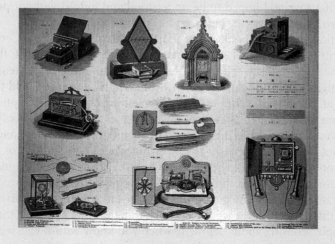

"The Electric Exhibition at the Crystal Palace," *The Illustrated London News,* 1882. Engraving *The Crystal Palace was a giant exhibition hall built in London for the Great Exhibition of 1851, which showcased Britain's industrial strength. The Electric Exhibition showcased newly invented electric tools. (The Bridgeman Art Library)*

ÉMILE ZOLA

1840–1902

French novelist, critic, and founder of the NATURALIST movement, Émile Zola applied the principles of scientific determinism to literature. In his *Rougon-Macquart* cycle of twenty novels (1871–1893), subtitled "The Natural and Social History of a Family Under the Second Empire," Zola performed a dissection of French society. His controversial work, which viewed human beings as creatures whose biological heredity determined their character, was often attacked as immoral or perverse. *Thérèse Raquin* (1867), an early novel, was the first in which Zola put his "experimental"—the term meant something like "empirical"—theory into practice. In the Preface to the second edition excerpted here, Zola explains his intent to those who he claims completely misunderstood the novel when it originally appeared.

Thérèse Raquin

Translated by Leonard Tancock

FROM

PREFACE TO THE SECOND EDITION

I was simple enough to suppose that this novel could do without a preface. Being accustomed to express my thoughts quite clearly and to stress even the minutest details of what I write, I hoped to be understood and judged without preliminary explanations. It seems I was mistaken.

The critics greeted this book with a churlish and horrified outcry. Certain virtuous people, in newspapers no less virtuous, made a grimace of disgust as they picked it up with the tongs to throw it into the fire. Even the minor literary reviews, the ones that retail nightly the tittle-tattle from alcoves and private rooms, held their noses and talked of filth and stench. I am not complaining about this reception; on the contrary I am delighted to observe that my colleagues have such maidenly susceptibilities. Obviously my work is the property of my judges and they can find it nauseating without my having any right to object, but what I do complain of is that not one of the modest journalists who blushed when they read *Thérèse Raquin* seems to have understood the novel. If they had, they might perhaps have blushed still more, but at any rate I should at the present moment be enjoying the deep satisfaction of having disgusted them for the right reason. Nothing is more annoying than hearing worthy people shouting about depravity when you know within yourself that they are doing so without any idea what they are shouting about.

So I am obliged to introduce my own work to my judges. I will do so in a few lines, simply to forestall any future misunderstanding.

In *Thérèse Raquin* my aim has been to study temperaments and not characters. That is the whole point of the book. I have chosen people completely dominated by their nerves and blood, without free will, drawn into each action of their lives by the inexorable laws of their physical nature. Thérèse and Laurent are human animals, nothing more. I have endeavoured to follow these animals through the devious working of their passions, the compulsion of their instincts, and the mental unbalance resulting from a nervous crisis. The sexual adventures of my hero and heroine are the satisfaction of a need, the murder they commit a consequence of their adultery, a consequence they accept just as wolves accept the slaughter of sheep. And finally, what I have had to call their remorse really amounts to a simple organic disorder, a revolt of the nervous system when strained to breaking-point. There is a complete absence of soul, I freely admit, since that is how I meant it to be.

I hope that by now it is becoming clear that my object has been first and foremost a scientific one. When my two characters, Thérèse and Laurent, were created, I set myself certain problems and solved them for the interest of the thing. I tried to explain the mysterious attraction that can spring up between two different temperaments, and I demonstrated the deep-seated disturbances of a sanguine nature brought into contact with a nervous one. If the novel is read with care, it will be seen that each chapter is a study of a curious physiological case. In a word, I had only one desire: given a highly-sexed man and an unsatisfied woman, to uncover the animal side of them and see that alone, then throw them together in a violent drama and note down with scrupulous care the sensations and actions of these creatures. I simply applied to two living bodies the analytical method that surgeons apply to corpses. . . .

❧ ELIZABETH CADY STANTON
1815–1902

Anna Elizabeth Klumpke, *Portrait of the Reformer Elizabeth Cady Stanton*

The women's rights activist and reformer Elizabeth Cady Stanton. (National Portrait Gallery, Smithsonian Institution/Art Resource)

Feminist and leader of the women's suffrage movement, Elizabeth Cady Stanton, with Lucretia Mott, convened the first women's rights convention in the United States at Seneca Falls, New York, in 1848. She also composed the Women's Bill of Rights that was adopted by the convention. In 1850, she and Susan B. Anthony began a forty-year collaboration as leaders of the suffrage movement. *The Woman's Bible* (1895), a project led by Stanton, sought to challenge patriarchal interpretation of Scripture by offering a feminist exegesis, or critical interpretation, of the Bible.

FROM

❧ The Woman's Bible

THE BOOK OF GENESIS.

Chapter I.

Genesis i: 26, 27, 28.

26 ¶ And God said, Let us make man in our image, after our likeness: and let them have dominion over the fish of the sea, and over the fowl of the air, and over the cattle, and over all the earth, and over every creeping thing that creepeth upon the earth.

27 So God created man in his *own* image, in the image of God created he him; male and female created he them.

28 And God blessed them, and God said unto them, Be fruitful, and multiply, and replenish the earth, and subdue it; and have dominion over the fish of the sea, and over the fowl of the air, and over every living thing that moveth upon the earth.

Here is the sacred historian's first account of the advent of woman; a simultaneous creation of both sexes, in the image of God. It is evident from the language that there was consultation in the Godhead, and that the masculine and feminine elements were equally represented. Scott[1] in his commentaries says, "this consultation of the Gods is the origin of the doctrine of the trinity." But instead of three male personages, as generally represented, a Heavenly Father, Mother, and Son would seem more rational.

The first step in the elevation of woman to her true position, as an equal factor in human progress, is the cultivation of the religious sentiment in regard to her dignity and equality, the recognition by the rising generation of an ideal Heavenly Mother, to whom their prayers should be addressed, as well as to a Father.

If language has any meaning, we have in these texts a plain declaration of the existence of the feminine element in the Godhead, equal in power and glory with the masculine. The Heavenly Mother and Father! God created man in his *own image, male and female.*" Thus Scripture, as well as science and philosophy, declares the eternity and equality of sex — the philosophical fact, without which there could have been no perpetuation of creation, no growth or development in the animal, vegetable, or mineral kingdoms, no awakening nor progressing in the world of thought. The masculine and feminine elements, exactly equal and balancing each other, are as essential to the maintenance of the equilibrium of the universe as positive and negative electricity, the centripetal and centrifugal forces, the laws of attraction which bind together all we know of this planet whereon we dwell and of the system in which we revolve.

In the great work of creation the crowning glory was realized, when man and woman were evolved on the sixth day, the masculine and feminine forces in the image of God, that must have existed eternally, in all forms of matter and mind. All the persons in the Godhead are represented in the Elohim[2] the divine plurality taking counsel in regard to this last and highest form of life. Who were the members of this high council, and whether a duality or a trinity? Verse 27 declares the image of God male and female. How then is it possible to make woman an afterthought? We find in verses 5–16 the pronoun "he" used. Should it not in harmony with verse 26 be "they," a dual pronoun? We may attribute this to the same cause as the use of "his" in verse 11 instead of "it." The fruit tree yielding fruit after "his" kind instead of after "its" kind. The paucity of a language may give rise to many misunderstandings.

The above texts plainly show the simultaneous creation of man and woman, and their equal importance in the development of the race. All those theories based on the assumption that man was prior in the creation, have no foundation in Scripture.

As to woman's subjection, on which both the canon and the civil law delight to dwell, it is important to note that equal dominion is given to woman over every living thing, but not one word is said giving man dominion over woman.

---

[1] Scott: Thomas Scott, author of a Bible commentary especially popular in the nineteenth century.

[2] Elohim: Plural Hebrew noun for "God" or "gods."

Here is the first title deed to this green earth giving alike to the sons and daughters of God. No lesson of woman's subjection can be fairly drawn from the first chapter of the Old Testament.

Chapter II.

Genesis ii: 21–25.

21 And the Lord God caused a deep sleep to fall upon Adam, and he slept; and he took one of his ribs, and closed up the flesh thereof.

22 And the rib which the Lord God had taken from man, made he a woman, and brought her unto the man.

23 And Adam said, This *is* now bone of my bone, and flesh of my flesh: she shall be called Woman, because she was taken out of man.

24 Therefore shall a man leave his father and his mother, and shall cleave unto his wife; and they shall be one flesh.

25 And they were both naked, the man and his wife, and were not ashamed.

As the account of the creation in the first chapter is in harmony with science, common sense, and the experience of mankind in natural laws, the inquiry naturally arises, why should there be two contradictory accounts in the same book, of the same event? It is fair to infer that the second version, which is found in some form in the different religions of all nations, is a mere allegory, symbolizing some mysterious conception of a highly imaginative editor.

The first account dignifies woman as an important factor in the creation, equal in power and glory with man. The second makes her a mere afterthought. The world in good running order without her. The only reason for her advent being the solitude of man.

There is something sublime in bringing order out of chaos; light out of darkness; giving each planet its place in the solar system; oceans and lands their limits; wholly inconsistent with a petty surgical operation, to find material for the mother of the race. It is on this allegory that all the enemies of women rest their battering rams, to prove her inferiority. Accepting the view that man was prior in the creation, some Scriptural writers say that as the woman was of the man, therefore, her position should be one of subjection. Grant it, then as the historical fact is reversed in our day, and the man is now of the woman, shall his place be one of subjection?

The equal position declared in the first account must prove more satisfactory to both sexes; created alike in the image of God — The Heavenly Mother and Father.

Thus, the Old Testament, "in the beginning," proclaims the simultaneous creation of man and woman, the eternity and equality of sex; and the New Testament echoes back through the centuries the individual sovereignty of woman growing out of this natural fact. Paul, in speaking of equality as the very soul and essence of Christianity, said, "There is neither Jew nor Greek, there is neither bond nor free, there is neither male nor female; for ye are all one in Christ Jesus."[3] With this recognition of the feminine element in the Godhead in the Old Testament, and this decla-

---

[3] "There . . . Jesus": Galatians 3:28.

ration of the equality of the sexes in the New, we may well wonder at the contemptible status woman occupies in the Christian Church of today.

All the commentators and publicists writing on woman's position, go through an immense amount of fine-spun metaphysical speculations, to prove her subordination in harmony with the Creator's original design.

It is evident that some wily writer, seeing the perfect equality of man and woman in the first chapter, felt it important for the dignity and dominion of man to effect woman's subordination in some way. To do this a spirit of evil must be introduced, which at once proved itself stronger than the spirit of good, and man's supremacy was based on the downfall of all that had just been pronounced very good. This spirit of evil evidently existed before the supposed fall of man, hence woman was not the origin of sin as so often asserted.

Chapter III.

Genesis iii: 1–24.

1 Now the serpent was more subtle than any beast of the field which the Lord God had made. And he said unto the woman, Yea, hath God said, Ye shall not eat of every tree of the garden?

2 And the woman said unto the serpent, We may eat of the fruit of the trees of the garden:

3 But of the fruit of the tree which *is* in the midst of the garden, God hath said Ye shall not eat of it, neither shall ye touch it, lest ye die.

4 And the serpent said unto the woman, Ye shall not surely die:

5 For God doth know that in the day ye eat thereof then your eyes shall be opened, and ye shall be as gods, knowing good and evil.

6 And when the woman saw that the tree *was* good for food, and that it *was* pleasant to the eyes, and a tree to be desired to make *one* wise, she took of the fruit thereof, and did eat and gave also unto her husband with her; and he did eat.

7 And the eyes of them both were opened, and they knew that they *were* naked; and they sewed fig leaves together, and made themselves aprons.

8 And they heard the voice of the Lord God walking in the garden in the cool of the day; and Adam and his wife hid themselves from the presence of the Lord God amongst the trees in the garden.

9 And the Lord God called unto Adam, and said unto him, Where *art* thou?

10 And he said, I heard thy voice in the garden, and I was afraid, because I *was* naked; and I hid myself.

11 And he said, Who told thee that thou *wast* naked? Hast thou eaten of the tree, whereof I commanded thee that thou shouldst not eat?

12 And the man said, The woman whom thou gavest *to be* with me, she gave me of the tree, and I did eat.

13 And the Lord God said unto the woman, What *is* this *that* thou hast done? And the woman said, The serpent beguiled me, and I did eat.

14 And the Lord God said unto the serpent, Because thou hast done this, thou *art* cursed above all cattle, and above every beast of the field; upon thy belly shalt thou go, and dust shalt thou eat all the days of thy life:

15 And I will put enmity between thee and the woman, and between thy seed and her seed; it shall bruise thy head and thou shalt bruise his heel.

16 Unto the woman he said, I will greatly multiply thy sorrow and thy conception; in sorrow thou shalt bring forth children: and thy desire *shall be* to thy husband, and he shall rule over thee.

17 And unto Adam he said, Because thou hast hearkened unto the voice of thy wife, and hast eaten of the tree, of which I commanded thee, saying, Thou shalt not eat of it; cursed *is* the ground for thy sake; in sorrow shalt thou eat *of* it all the days of thy life;

18 Thorns also and thistles shall it bring forth to thee; and thou shalt eat the herb of the field;

19 In the sweat of thy face shalt thou eat bread till thou return unto the ground; for out of it wast thou taken; for dust thou *art,* and unto dust shalt thou return.

20 And Adam called his wife's name Eve; because she was the mother of all living.

21 Unto Adam also and to his wife did the Lord God make coats of skins and clothed them.

22 ⁋ And the Lord God said, Behold the man is become as one of us, to know good and evil; and now, lest he put forth his hand, and take also of the tree of life, and eat, and live for ever;

23 Therefore the Lord God sent him forth from the garden of Eden, to till the ground from whence he was taken.

24 So he drove out the man: and he placed at the east of the garden of Eden cherubim, and a flaming sword which turned every way, to keep the way of the tree of life.

Adam Clarke,[4] in his commentaries, asks the question, "Is this an allegory?" He finds it beset with so many difficulties as an historical fact, that he inclines at first to regard it as a fable, a mere symbol, of some hidden truth. His mind seems more troubled about the serpent than any other personage in the drama. As snakes cannot walk upright, and have never been known to speak, he thinks this beguiling creature must have been an ourang-outang, or some species of ape. However, after expressing all his doubts, he rests in the assumption that it must be taken literally, and that with higher knowledge of the possibilities of all living things, many seeming improbabilities will be fully realized.

A learned professor in Yale College,[5] before a large class of students, expressed serious doubts as to the forbidden fruit being an apple, as none grew in that latitude. He thinks it must have been a quince. If the serpent and the apple are to be withdrawn thus recklessly from the tableaux, it is feared that with advancing civilization the whole drama may fall into discredit. Scientists tells us that "the missing link" between the ape and man, has recently been discovered, so that we can now trace back an unbroken line of ancestors to the dawn of creation.

As out of this allegory grows the doctrines of original sin, the fall of man, and woman the author of all our woes, and the curses on the serpent, the woman, and the man; the Darwinian theory of the gradual growth of the race from a lower to a

---

[4] **Adam Clarke:** (1760–1832) Author of a popular Bible commentary published in 1811.

[5] **learned . . . College:** Daniel Cady Eaton, Professor of Botany. [Stanton]

higher type of animal life, is more hopeful and encouraging. However, as our chief interest is in woman's part in the drama, we are equally pleased with her attitude, whether as a myth in an allegory, or as the heroine of an historical occurrence.

In this prolonged interview, the unprejudiced reader must be impressed with the courage, the dignity, and the lofty ambition of the woman. The tempter evidently had a profound knowledge of human nature, and saw at a glance the high character of the person he met by chance in his walks in the garden. He did not try to tempt her from the path of duty by brilliant jewels, rich dresses, worldly luxuries or pleasures, but with the promise of knowledge, with the wisdom of the Gods. Like Socrates or Plato, his powers of conversation and asking puzzling questions, were no doubt marvellous, and he roused in the woman that intense thirst for knowledge, that the simple pleasures of picking flowers and talking with Adam did not satisfy. Compared with Adam she appears to great advantage through the entire drama.

The curse pronounced on woman is inserted in an unfriendly spirit to justify her degradation and subjection to man. With obedience to the laws of health, diet, dress, and exercise, the period of maternity should be one of added vigor in both body and mind, a perfectly natural operation should not be attended with suffering. By the observance of physical and psychical laws the supposed curse can be easily transformed into a blessing. Some churchmen speak of maternity as a disability, and then chant the Magnificat[6] in all their cathedrals round the globe. Through all life's shifting scenes, the mother of the race has been the greatest factor in civilization.

We hear the opinion often expressed, that woman always has, and always will be in subjection. Neither assertion is true. She enjoyed unlimited individual freedom for many centuries, and the events of the present day all point to her speedy emancipation. Scientists now give 85,000 years for the growth of the race. They assign 60,000 to savagism, 20,000 to barbarism, and 5,000 to civilization. Recent historians tell us that for centuries woman reigned supreme. That period was called the Matriarchate. Then man seized the reins of government, and we are now under the Patriarchate. But we see on all sides new forces gathering, and woman is already abreast with man in art, science, literature, and government. The next dynasty, in which both will reign as equals, will be the Amphiarchate, which is close at hand.

Psychologists tell us of a sixth sense now in process of development, by which we can read each other's mind and communicate without speech. The Tempter might have had that sense, as he evidently read the minds of both the creature and the Creator, if we are to take this account as literally true, as Adam Clarke advises.

---

[6] **Magnificat:** Words spoken by Mary in Luke 1:46–55, beginning "My soul doth magnify the Lord . . ."

HIRATA ATSUTANE
1776–1843

A leader of the NEO-SHINTO revival in early nineteenth century Japan, **Hirata Atsutane** set out to prove, sometimes by unbelievable arguments, the superiority of Shinto to other beliefs, especially CONFUCIANISM and BUDDHISM. A physician who had studied Dutch medical texts, Hirata admired Western science and theology, though he harshly criticized Western nations. His chauvinistic treatment of Shinto, and hence Japan, helped prepare the way for the rise of Japanese nationalism at the end of the century. In the selection that follows, Hirata argues for the truth of the Shinto creation story, basing his claim on the replication of similar stories in other world religions. Like Western fundamentalists, he rejects the treatment of such stories as myths, insisting instead on their literal truth.

Kawahara Keiga,
Visit to Shinto Temple,
c. 1800. Watercolor

Shintoism, a Japanese folk religion, enjoyed a revival in neo-Shintoism in the early nineteenth century. (The Art Archive/ Rijksmuseum voor Volkenkunde Leiden (Leyden)/Dagli Orti)

The Creator God

[FROM *KODŌ TAII*
IN *HIRATA ATSUTANE ZENSHŪ*, I, 27–28]

If we examine the origins of the name Mi-musubi given to two of the gods, it is clear from facts recorded in the annals of the divine age that the name stems from their miraculous creative power. We are also informed by the positive declaration of the gods of the sun and the moon that Takami-musubi[1] must be credited with the cre-

---

[1] **Takami-musubi:** Hirata usually does not distinguish between the two "Musubi" gods, Takami-musubi and Kami-musubi, but tends to regard them as two aspects of one god. [Translator]

ation of Heaven and earth, that he is a god of incomparable power, and that he without doubt resides in Heaven and reigns over the world. Despite the pellucidly clear nature of these truths, scholars whose minds have become damaged by Chinese and Indian learning (as well as people who in their ignorance display impious disbelief) do not understand that the very fact of their own birth is immediately attributable to the creative power of this god. They persist in their skepticism and declare that the ancient truths are merely legends peculiar to Japan which they refuse to believe. These truths, however, are by no means confined to Japan. In many other countries it is believed that the seed of man and all other things owe their existence to the powers of this god.

As proof of this we may cite different foreign traditions. In the ancient Chinese legends, where this god is referred to as Shang Ti or T'ien Ti, it is recorded that he resides in Heaven and reigns over the world, and that man was created by him. Moreover, the legend states that it was Shang Ti who implanted in men's hearts such true principles as humanity, righteousness, decorum, and wisdom. This legend is preserved in general form in ancient works like the *Book of Odes,* the *Book of Documents,* and the *Analects,*[2] as all can plainly see who take the trouble to look. However, since the Chinese are of an irreverent disposition, some perverted scholars assert that the ancient legends are merely parables, and voice other such theories. I have elsewhere dealt with this matter in detail.

In the ancient Indian legends the god Musubi is called Brahma the Creator. Here again we find him described as residing in the extremely lofty heaven of the thirty-three devas,[3] and it is stated that he reigns over the world and that the heavens and earth, man and all things were created by him. The most ancient traditions have it that no god is as holy as he. However, in later times a man named Shākyamuni[4] appeared who invented what he called Buddhism, a religion to suit his own tastes. He deceived men with his so-called divine powers, which were actually a kind of black magic. The false opinion was spread that Buddha was more sacred than Brahma, and even learned priests were deceived by the lie. No one now is left in India who knows the truth.

Far to the west of India there are numerous other countries, and in each of them there are traditions of a god of Heaven who created the heavens and earth, man and all things. This may be known from reading Dutch books.

Thus, in all countries, as if by common consent, there are traditions of a divine being who dwells in Heaven and who created all things. These traditions have sometimes become distorted, but when we examine them they afford proof of the authenticity of the ancient traditions of the Imperial Land. There are many gods, but this god stands at the center of them and is holiest of all.

---

[2] *Book of Odes . . . Analects:* **Book of Odes** (*Shih Ching*) and **Book of Documents** (*Shu Ching*) are two of the five Confucian classics that make up the earliest works of Chinese literature. *Odes* is a collection of songs and poems from central China dating from the eleventh to the fifth centuries B.C.E. *Documents,* sometimes called *Classic of History,* is a collection of documents from 2357 to 631 B.C.E. **Analects,** a collection of the sayings and short dialogues of Confucius, dates from the seventh century B.C.E.

[3] devas: Angels.   [4] Shākyamuni: The Buddha.

SYED AHMED KHAN
1817–1898

A Muslim from northern India, Syed Ahmed Khan is sometimes considered the father of modern Muslim education. Grandson of a prime minister to the Mughal emperor, he served in government himself and was a subjudge for the East India Company, the British colonial agency in India. He had great respect for Western learning, especially the natural sciences, and for the British, and he founded several schools that combined Western and Islamic studies. As an interpreter of the Qur'an, he relied on his own judgment to form his views on the text rather than deferring to traditional authorities. His assertion that nothing in the Qur'an contradicted the laws of nature reflects his independence as a scriptural interpreter and earned him and his followers the title *Necharis,* or Naturists.

Page of naskhi script
of the Qur'ān written
by Ismail al-Zuhdi,
with floral illumi-
nations, 1802
*Much Muslim art
focuses on the Qur'an
itself. This Ottoman-
era page from the
Qur'ān displays
delicate, ornate floral
designs. (The
Bridgeman Art
Library)*

The Qur'ān and Science

The Qur'ān does not prove that the earth is stationary, nor does it prove that the earth is in motion. Similarly it can not be proved from the Qur'ān that the sun is in motion, nor can it be proved from it that the sun is stationary. The Holy Qur'ān was not concerned with these problems of astronomy; because the progress in human knowledge was to decide such matters itself. The Qur'ān had a much higher and a far nobler purpose in view. It would have been tantamount to confusing the simple Bedouins by speaking to them about such matters and to throwing into perplexity even the learned, whose knowledge and experience had not yet made the necessary progress, by discussing such problems. The real purpose of a religion is to improve morality; by raising such questions that purpose would have been jeopardized. In spite of all this I am fully convinced that the Work of God and the Word of God can never be antagonistic to each other; we may, through the fault of our knowledge, sometimes make mistakes in understanding the meaning of the Word.

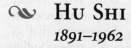 # HU SHI

1891–1962

A leader in the literary revolution of the early twentieth century in China, **Hu Shi** promoted vernacular writing and Western science as the bases for modern Chinese culture. Educated in the United States, he returned to China a disciple of pragmatist John Dewey, who took the position that the validity of a proposition could be judged by its consequences. Hu Shi took part in a vigorous debate in China in the 1920s over whether science could provide a philosophy of life and take the place of traditional metaphysics.

FROM

Hu Shih wen-cun, Collection II, Chapter I

The Chinese people's philosophy of life has not yet been brought face to face with science. At this moment we painfully feel that science has not been sufficiently promoted, that scientific education has not been developed, and that the power of science has not been able to wipe out the black smoke that covers the whole country. To our amazement there are still prominent scholars [like Liang Ch'i-ch'ao][1] who shout, "European science is bankrupt," blame the cultural bankruptcy of Europe on science, deprecate it, score the sins of the scientists' philosophy of life, and do not want science to exert any influence on a philosophy of life. Seeing this, how can those who believe in science not worry? How can they help crying out loud to defend science? This is the motive which has given rise to this big battle of "science versus philosophy of life." We must understand this motive before we can see the position the controversy occupies in the history of Chinese thought. . . .

Chang Chün-mai's[2] chief point is that "the solution of problems pertaining to a

---

[1] **Liang Ch'i-ch'ao:** (1873–1929) Confucian scholar who reinterpreted the Confucian classics in an attempt to utilize tradition as a justification for sweeping innovations in Chinese culture, education, and the civil service system.

[2] **Chang Chün-mai:** (1886–?) Student of Liang Ch'i-ch'ao who argued for the necessity of metaphysics underlying a philosophy of life.

philosophy of life cannot be achieved by science." In reply to him, we should make clear what kind of philosophy of life has been produced when science was applied to problems pertaining to a philosophy of life. In other words, we should first describe what a scientific philosophy of life is and then discuss whether such a philosophy of life can be established, whether it can solve the problems pertaining to a philosophy of life, and whether it is a plague on Europe and poison to the human race, as Liang Ch'i-ch'ao has said it is. I cannot help feeling that in this discussion consisting of a quarter of a million words, those who fight for science, excepting Mr. Wu Chih-hui,[3] share a common error, namely, that of not stating in concrete terms what a scientific philosophy of life is, but merely defending in an abstract way the assertion that science *can* solve the problems of a philosophy of life. . . . They have not been willing publicly to admit that the concrete, purely materialistic, and purely mechanistic philosophy of life is the scientific philosophy of life. We say they have not been willing; we do not say they have not dared. We merely say that with regard to the scientific philosophy of life, the defenders of science do not believe in it as clearly and firmly as does Mr. Wu Chih-hui and therefore they cannot publicly defend their view. . . .

In a word, our future war plan should be to publicize our new belief, to publicize what we believe to be the new philosophy of life. The basic ideas of this new philosophy of life have been declared by Mr. Wu. We shall now summarize these general ideas, elaborate and supplement them to some extent, and present here an outline of this new philosophy of life:

1. On the basis of our knowledge of astronomy and physics, we should recognize that the world of space is infinitely large.

2. On the basis of our geological and paleontological knowledge, we should recognize that the universe extends over infinite time.

3. On the basis of all our verifiable scientific knowledge, we should recognize that the universe and everything in it follow natural laws of movement and change — "natural" in the Chinese sense of "being so of themselves" — and that there is no need for the concept of a supernatural Ruler or Creator.

4. On the basis of the biological sciences, we should recognize the terrific wastefulness and brutality in the struggle for existence in the biological world, and consequently the untenability of the hypothesis of a benevolent Ruler who "possesses the character of loving life."

5. On the basis of the biological, physiological, and psychological sciences, we should recognize that man is only one species in the animal kingdom and differs from the other species only in degree but not in kind.

6. On the basis of the knowledge derived from anthropology, sociology, and the biological sciences, we should understand the history and causes of the evolution of living organisms and of human society.

7. On the basis of the biological and psychological sciences, we should recognize that all psychological phenomena are explainable through the law of causality.

---

[3] Wu Chih-hui: (1865–1953) Chinese philosopher who advocated a rigorously materialistic point of view.

8. On the basis of biological and historical knowledge, we should recognize that morality and religion are subject to change, and that the causes of such change can be scientifically discovered.

9. On the basis of our newer knowledge of physics and chemistry, we should recognize that matter is not dead or static but living and dynamic.

10. On the basis of biological and sociological knowledge, we should recognize that the individual—the "small self"—is subject to death and extinction, but mankind—the "Large Self"—does not die and is immortal, and should recognize that to live for the sake of the species and posterity is religion of the highest kind; and that those religions which seek a future life either in Heaven or the Pure Land, are selfish religions.

This new philosophy of life is a hypothesis founded on the commonly accepted scientific knowledge of the last two or three hundred years. We may confer on it the honorable title of "scientific philosophy of life." But to avoid unnecessary controversy, I propose to call it merely "the naturalistic philosophy of life."

ℂ CHARLES BAUDELAIRE
1821–1867

Studio of Goupil,
Charles Baudelaire,
Photograph
*Baudelaire's
confrontational
poetry finds beauty in
things conventionally
deemed perverse,
horrible, and
repulsive. Images of
Baudelaire, such as
this portrait, often
indicate his contempt
for the viewer and
society. (Corbis)*

One of the most important and influential French poets of the nineteenth century, **Charles Baudelaire** took the poetry of his country in a new direction. Like the German poet Heinrich Heine (1797–1856), Baudelaire rejected many of the tenets of the **ROMANTIC** school and cultivated a more impersonal, critically distanced voice in his work. While not completely abandoning the idealism of his Romantic predecessors and contemporaries, Baudelaire embraced the brute realities of life in poetry that is as concrete as it is shocking. Baudelaire believed that human beings were naturally wicked, inevitably drawn to and fascinated with crime and deviance; his poetry confronts readers as hypocrites and presents them with sometimes repugnant spectacles of the beauty inherent in things conventionally deemed perverse, horrible, and repulsive. Beauty itself, as he writes in "Hymn to Beauty," partakes of both the "infernal and the divine," and it bestows upon us both "kindnesses and crimes." Although Baudelaire's honest exploration of taboo subjects subjected him and his work to public condemnation, the poet's grasp of what he called the "primeval perversity of man" marked a change in literary sensibility in nineteenth-century Europe, pointing to the **MODERNISM** of the next century. The dynamic tension between the ideal and the real in Baudelaire's poetry, his conscientious craftsmanship, and his engagement with the most sordid details of human life exerted a profound influence on late nineteenth-century and modernist poetry in Europe and beyond, including that of T. S. Eliot (1888–1965), Paul Valéry (1871–1945), and Rainer Maria Rilke (1875–1926). In the words of French **SYMBOLIST**[1] poet Paul Verlaine (1844–1896), "the profound originality of Charles Baudelaire is to represent powerfully and essentially modern man. . . ."

The School Years.   Charles Baudelaire was born in Paris in 1821 into a family of respectable means. His father, François Baudelaire, died in 1825, after which Charles was raised by his mother, Caroline Defayis, and stepfather, Jacques Aupic, a military officer whom the boy deeply resented. In 1832, after moving to Lyons with his family, Baudelaire attended school at Collège de Lyon, and later, after returning to Paris in 1836, at Lycée Louis-le-Grand, where he developed a keen interest in modern literature. Despite winning several academic prizes, while at lycée Baudelaire began to develop the deep sense of boredom, or **ENNUI**, that later became a major theme in his poetry. Having been expelled from the lycée for his

---

[1] Symbolist: Generally refers to a movement among poets in France anticipated in the work of Charles Baudelaire (1821–1867) and Arthur Rimbaud (1854–1891) but practiced self-consciously by Stéphane Mallarmé (1842–1898), Paul Verlaine (1844–1896), and Jules Laforgue (1860–1887), who sought to effect the fluidity and evocative harmony of music in their work—to capture tones, fragrances, sensations, and intuitions rather than concrete images or rational ideas.

troublesome behavior, Baudelaire took his *baccalauréat* examinations at another school, the Collège Saint Louis, in 1839 and was faced with choosing a career. Against his stepfather's wishes, the young Baudelaire plunged into a life of literature and art in the Latin Quarter, at that time a student ghetto of cheap lodgings, cafés, bars, and brothels. Here Baudelaire devoured the new literature that was coming out, absorbed himself in the new art, and, when not carousing, wrote poetry.

The Latin Quarter.   In 1841, two years after he took his examinations, Baudelaire's mother and General Aupick put him on a ship bound for Calcutta as a means to reform his bad behavior. The twenty-year-old Baudelaire was not happy to be away from his friends and he returned to France on another vessel, having refused to reboard his ship when it reached Saint-Denis de la Réunion, off the coast of Madagascar in the Indian Ocean. Returning to his unconventional life and now determined more than ever to be a writer, Baudelaire immersed himself in the bars and cafés of the Latin Quarter, where he began writing some of the poems that would appear in his most important work, *The Flowers of Evil* (*Les fleurs du mal,* 1857). He also began his relationship with Jeanne Duval, a Creole woman with whom he lived on and off for many years and who is the "black Venus" of his poems. Upon turning twenty-one in 1842 Baudelaire received a tightly restricted inheritance from his father and began frequenting art galleries and museums. Baudelaire's *Salons* (1845, 1846, and 1859) and his essays on the paintings of Eugène Delacroix and Constantin Guys, among others, represent a formidable body of art criticism. In the midst of the Revolution of 1848, Baudelaire discovered the works of Edgar Allan Poe, with whom he strongly identified and whose formalist poetic principles Baudelaire found strikingly similar to his own. Baudelaire at the time was known in literary and artistic circles as an art critic and obscure poet. With his translations of Poe, appearing from 1856 to 1865, he began to catch the attention of the broader public.

Poet of Evil.   The appearance in June 1857 of *The Flowers of Evil,* the first collection of Baudelaire's poetry, earned him almost immediate notoriety; the book was immediately condemned by reviewers and French officials, who ordered the book seized on the grounds that it offended public and religious morals. Like Gustave Flaubert, who had been acquitted earlier in the year on charges of obscenity for *Madame Bovary,* Baudelaire was brought to trial, in August 1857. Although he was acquitted on charges of blasphemy, he had to pay a fine for violating public morality and leave out six poems from all subsequent editions of the book. In 1862 Baudelaire published twenty prose poems that formed the basis of a posthumously published collection of fifty such poems called *Paris Spleen.* In that same year he suffered a stroke that he rightly interpreted as a portent of his death. From 1864 to March 1866, suffering from poor health and living in poverty, Baudelaire gave a few lectures in Belgium and in 1865 arranged to publish a new collection titled *The Waifs of Charles Baudelaire,* which contained some new poems as well as the ones that had been banned in France. In June 1866, after suffering a

www   For links to more information about Baudelaire and a quiz on his poetry, see *World Literature Online* at bedfordstmartins.com/worldlit.

But with Baudelaire, French poetry at length passes beyond our frontiers. It is read throughout the world; it takes its place as the characteristic poetry of modernity; it encourages imitation, it enriches countless minds.

– PAUL VALÉRY, poet and critic, 1962

Jean Beraud, *Boulevard des Capuchines and the Théâtre du Vaudeville in 1889*. Painting
Baudelaire sought to help his readers transcend what he called spleen—*the restless*
malaise affecting modern life. His experience of that life was Paris, with its bourgeois
lifestyle and busy street life. (Giraudon/Art Resource)

> Baudelaire is indeed
> the greatest exem-
> plar in *modern* poetry
> in any language, for
> his verse and lan-
> guage is the nearest
> thing to a complete
> renovation that we
> have experienced.
> But his renovation
> of an attitude
> towards life is no
> less radical and no
> less important.
>
> – T. S. Eliot

debilitating stroke two months before, Baudelaire returned to Paris,
where he died on August 31, 1867.

Ennui. Edgar Allan Poe's rejection of the role of inspiration in poetic
composition and his focus on deliberate craftsmanship appealed to
Baudelaire, who spoke of his own writing as a "travail," a labor. Although
Baudelaire shared in the Romantic poets' quest for beauty, he believed
that it would be found not in airy flights of the imagination but, paradoxically, in the midst of the most revolting realities. He dismissed the
Romantic idea of nature as a ground of human goodness and purity,
believing that nature—human nature, in particular—is composed of
more evil than good; as he puts it in *The Painter of Modern Life*, "Evil happens without effort, naturally; Good is always the product of some art." A
poet of the city rather than of the country, Baudelaire believed that carefully wrought works of art, not solitary Romantic reveries in the countryside, would liberate human beings from the melancholic inertia that he
called *ennui*. For Baudelaire, ennui—profound boredom and apathy
associated with blindly following custom and convention—was the
worst crime of all.

Flowers of Evil.   Baudelaire's poetry places the real and the ideal in a tense balance, projecting, as in "The Voyage," the ideal of perfection onto a future just out of reach while immersing the reader in the repetition of human imperfection. In this poem as in "The Swan," Baudelaire's work anticipates that of the Symbolist school of poets, a group that included Stéphane Mallarmé (1842–1898), Paul Verlaine (1844–1896), Arthur Rimbaud (1854–1891), and Jules Laforgue (1860–1887). The Symbolists sought to create a language imitating the qualities of music by freeing poetry from the conventional structures and forms of versification (verse-writing) adhered to by their predecessors. By means of symbols—signs or images that serve as points of convergence—Symbolists hoped to evoke a sense of the beautiful and of unity among all things. For these poets, the symbol, like music, should remain elusive and ambiguous; as a means of evading or denying the referential function of language, the symbol evokes language's mystery. Some of Baudelaire's poems, particularly "Correspondences," place special emphasis on symbols. Nevertheless, even as Baudelaire approaches the infinite and the beautiful—often figured by the Symbolists as the *azure,* the deep blue of the open sky—he draws the reader to horrific details of the real.

Flowers of Evil to *Paris Spleen.*   In *The Flowers of Evil,* Baudelaire's first collection of poetry, published in 1857, the pursuit of the ideal involves a deliberately shocking embrace of what conventional society deems unsavory, even repulsive. In "To the Reader," Baudelaire declares himself the poet of evil and promises to hold up a mirror to what hypocrites refuse to confront. In stark, sensuous detail, as in "Carrion," which describes a decaying corpse, Baudelaire pushes toward the extreme limits of human experience. *The Flowers of Evil* explores the sordid and the grotesque partly to shock its readers and partly to move them to find beauty in the ugliness of their everyday lives. In a collection of prose poems written in the last two decades of his life, *Paris Spleen* (1862), Baudelaire softens the imagery and tone of his work while still addressing the distemper of modern urban life. In prose poems that strive for the effect of music, Baudelaire captures the despair as well as the pleasure of melancholy and solitude as the solitary poet moves among crowds of strangers in the city. In these poems, perhaps even more than in *The Flowers of Evil,* Baudelaire foretells of the experience of alienation that writers of the early twentieth century would elaborate on.

■ CONNECTIONS

Heinrich Heine, p. 316. Baudelaire's poetry comprises Romantic idealism and dogged realism — a longing for the infinite grounded in a tough-minded grasp of the ways of the world. In its engagement with the harsher aspects of everyday reality, Heine's sensibility in many ways parallels Baudelaire's. To what degree are Heine and Baudelaire Romantic poets? What in their poetry suggests a critical distance from Romanticism?

T. S. Eliot: *The Love Song of J. Alfred Prufrock* and *The Wasteland,* (Book 6). Many readers of Baudelaire, including T. S. Eliot himself, saw in Baudelaire's writing a precursor to modernist sensibilities. What aspects of Baudelaire's poetry does Eliot draw upon in his own work? How does Eliot's verse differ from Baudelaire's?

Gabriel Garcia Marquez, "A Very Old Man with Enormous Wings," (Book 6). Baudelaire's "The Albatross" describes the unsympathetic, even hostile, reaction of the poet's contemporaries to an early literary manifestation of the alienation found in post-nineteenth-century poems and stories. Marquez's "A Very Old Man with Enormous Wings" invokes a metaphor similar to the albatross—an earthbound angel as an object of curiosity, mockery, and scorn—to describe the fate of religious idealism, among other things, in the modern world. How does Baudelaire's poem anticipate Marquez's story? How does the short story elaborate on the possibilities of Baudelaire's metaphor for the modern reader?

■ **FURTHER RESEARCH**

Biography
Pichois, Claude. *Baudelaire.* 1989.
Starkie, Enid. *Baudelaire.* 1953.

Criticism
Bloom, Harold, ed. *Charles Baudelaire.* 1987.
Evans, Margery A. *Baudelaire and Intertextuality: Poetry at the Crossroads.* 1993.
Hyslop, Lois Boe. *Charles Baudelaire Revisited.* 1992.
Peyre, Henry, ed. *Baudelaire: A Collection of Critical Essays.* 1962.
Porter, Laurence M. *The Crisis of French Symbolism.* 1990.

■ **PRONUNCIATION**

Charles Baudelaire: SHARL boh-duh-LARE

꩜ To the Reader

Translated by Stanley Kunitz

Ignorance, error, cupidity, and sin
Possess our souls and exercise our flesh;
Habitually we cultivate remorse
As beggars entertain and nurse their lice.

Our sins are stubborn. Cowards when contrite
We overpay confession with our pains,

The Flowers of Evil. Baudelaire divided the poems in this work, first published in 1857, into five thematic sections: Spleen and the Ideal, Flowers of Evil, Revolt, Wine, and Death. The first edition contained one hundred poems, plus "To the Reader," a prefatory poem set apart from the rest that serves as an overture to the volume. In the book's second edition, published in 1861, Baudelaire cut six poems (by court order), added thirty-five new poems, modified some of the originals, and rearranged all the poems under the first-edition headings, adding a new section titled Parisian Scenes. Modern editors tend to follow the groupings of the 1861 edition, as is done here.

And when we're back again in human mire
Vile tears, we think, will wash away our stains.

Thrice-potent Satan in our cursèd bed
10   Lulls us to sleep, our spirit overkissed,
Until the precious metal of our will
Is vaporized — that cunning alchemist!

Who but the Devil pulls our waking-strings!
Abominations lure us to their side;
Each day we take another step to hell,
Descending through the stench, unhorrified.

Like an exhausted rake who mouths and chews
The martyrized breast of an old withered whore
We steal, in passing, whatever joys we can,
20   Squeezing the driest orange all the more.

Packed in our brains incestuous as worms
Our demons celebrate in drunken gangs,
And when we breathe, that hollow rasp is Death
Sliding invisibly down into our lungs.

If the dull canvas of our wretched life
Is unembellished with such pretty ware
As knives or poison, pyromania, rape,
It is because our soul's too weak to dare!

But in this den of jackals, monkeys, curs,
30   Scorpions, buzzards, snakes, — this paradise
Of filthy beasts that screech, howl, grovel, grunt —
In this menagerie of mankind's vice

There's one supremely hideous and impure!
Soft-spoken, not the type to cause a scene,

"To the Reader" establishes a kinship in crime between the poet and the reader, whom the poem's speaker refers to as *"Hypocrite lecteur — mon semblable — mon frère"* ("Hypocrite reader — my double — my brother"). A litany of vices form a common bond between himself and the reader, but *ennui* — profound and melancholic apathy or boredom — is singled out as the foremost of these sins. Ennui, like its companion condition, spleen, stifles imagination and action, leaving its victims helplessly mired in hypocritical lethargy. One might compare Blake's proverb from *The Marriage of Heaven and Hell:* "Sooner murder an infant in its cradle than nurse unacted desires." "To the Reader" introduces the themes and motifs that appear throughout the collection, much as an overture does for a symphony, and deliberately aims to entice complicit readers into the heart of the book and provoke them to willful action.

He'd willingly make rubble of the earth
And swallow up creation in a yawn.

 # The Albatross

Translated by Richard Wilbur

Often, for pastime, mariners will ensnare
The albatross, that vast sea-bird who sweeps
On high companionable pinion where
Their vessel glides upon the bitter deeps.

Torn from his native space, this captive king
Flounders upon the deck in stricken pride,
And pitiably lets his great white wing
Drag like a heavy paddle at his side.

This rider of winds, how awkward he is, and weak!
10 How droll he seems, who lately was all grace!
A sailor pokes a pipestem into his beak;
Another, hobbling, mocks his trammeled pace.

The Poet is like this monarch of the clouds,
Familiar of storms, of stars, and of all high things;
Exiled on earth amidst its hooting crowds,
He cannot walk, borne down by his giant wings.

"**The Albatross.**" The majority of poems in *The Flowers of Evil* fall under the heading of "Spleen and the Ideal," an epithet that sets up the opposition between the melancholic bitterness and the hopeful striving for beauty and joy that permeate Baudelaire's poetry. This duality surfaces clearly in "Hymn to Beauty," in which beauty, whether derived from heaven or hell, may redeem the speaker from the drudgery of everyday routine. Similarly, "The Albatross" pits the ideal flights of the poet against the banality of other human beings. Here the poet appears as an outsider whose creative powers are out of place in the busy world that taunts him; the awkward figure of the albatross is much like Gabriel Garcia Marquez's angel who is treated like a circus animal in "The Old Man with Enormous Wings." In both works, imaginative creations and spirituality are treated like idle amusements and commodities.

    "Spleen and the Ideal" also contains poems addressed to Jeanne Duval, Baudelaire's Creole mistress, such as "Her Hair." The escape into exotic beauty in that poem, made ironic by the concession that such love is won by the constant supply of sapphires, pearls, and rubies, contrasts dramatically with the grotesque central image of "Carrion," a notorious Baudelaire poem wherein the speaker finds beauty in a bloated corpse. Also under "Spleen and the Ideal" are the four poems titled "Spleen," which nuance Baudelaire's understanding of that notion. Like its twin, ennui, spleen is variously identified with paralysis of the soul, torpor, melancholy, and boredom. Spleen and the ideal appear in Baudelaire's work as "contrary states of the soul," to borrow Blake's phrase.

❧ Correspondences

Translated by Richard Wilbur

Nature is a temple whose living colonnades
Breathe forth a mystic speech in fitful sighs;
Man wanders among symbols in those glades
Where all things watch him with familiar eyes.

Like dwindling echoes gathered far away
Into a deep and thronging unison
Huge as the night or as the light of day,
All scents and sounds and colors meet as one.

Perfumes there are as sweet as the oboe's sound,
10 Green as the prairies, fresh as a child's caress,
— And there are others, rich, corrupt, profound

And of an infinite pervasiveness,
Like myrrh, or musk, or amber, that excite
The ecstasies of sense, the soul's delight.

❧ Hymn to Beauty

Translated by Dorothy Martin

From heaven or hell, O Beauty, come you hence?
Out from your gaze, infernal and divine,
Pours blended evil and beneficence,
And therefore men have likened you to wine.

Sunset and dawn within your eyes are fair;
Stormlike you scatter perfume into space;
Your kiss, a philtre from an amphora rare,
Charms boys to courage and makes heroes base.

Whence come you, from what spheres, or inky deeps,
10 With careless hand joy and distress to strew?
Fate, like a dog at heel, behind you creeps;
You govern all things here, and naught you rue.

You walk upon the dead with scornful glances,
Among your gems Horror is not least fair;

Murder, the dearest of your baubles, dances
Upon your haughty breast with amorous air.

Mothlike around your flame the transient, turning,
Crackles and flames and cries, "Ah, heavenly doom!"
The quivering lover o'er his mistress yearning
20 Is but a dying man who woos his tomb.

From heaven or the abyss? Let questioning be,
O artless monster wreaking endless pain,
So that your smile and glance throw wide to me
An infinite that I have loved in vain.

From Satan or from God? Holy or vile?
Let questioning rest. O soft-eyed sprite, my queen,
O rhythm, perfume, light — so you beguile
Time from his slothfulness, the world from spleen.

∾ Her Hair

Translated by Doreen Bell

O fleece, that down the neck waves to the nape!
O curls! O perfume nonchalant and rare!
O ecstacy! To fill this alcove shape
With memories that in these tresses sleep,
I would shake them like pennons in the air!

Languorous Asia, burning Africa,
And a far world, defunct almost, absent,
Within your aromatic forest stay!
As other souls on music drift away,
10 Mine, o my love! still floats upon your scent.

I shall go there where, full of sap, both tree
And man swoon in the heat of southern climes;
Strong tresses, be the swell that carries me!
I dream upon your sea of ebony
Of dazzling sails, of oarsmen, masts and flames:

A sun-drenched and reverberating port,
Where I imbibe colour and sound and scent;
Where vessels, gliding through the gold and moire,

Open their vast arms as they leave the shore
20 To clasp the pure and shimmering firmament.

I'll plunge my head, enamoured of its pleasure,
In this black ocean where the other hides;
My subtle spirit then will know a measure
Of fertile idleness and fragrant leisure,
Lulled by the infinite rhythm of its tides!

Pavilion, of blue-shadowed tresses spun,
You give me back the azure from afar;
And where the twisted locks are fringed with down
Lurk mingled odours I grow drunk upon
30 Of oil of coconut, of musk and tar.

A long time! always! my hand in your hair
Will sow the stars of sapphire, pearl, ruby,
That you be never deaf to my desire,
My oasis and gourd whence I aspire
To drink deep of the wine of memory!

✺ Carrion

Translated by Richard Howard

Remember, my soul, the thing we saw
    that lovely summer day?
On a pile of stones where the path turned off
    the hideous carrion —

legs in the air, like a whore — displayed
    indifferent to the last,
a belly slick with lethal sweat
    and swollen with foul gas.

the sun lit up that rottenness
10   as though to roast it through,
restoring to Nature a hundredfold
    what she had here made one.

And heaven watched the splendid corpse
    like a flower open wide —
you nearly fainted dead away
    at the perfume it gave off.

Flies kept humming over the guts
    from which a gleaming clot
of maggots poured to finish off
20   what scraps of flesh remained.

The tide of trembling vermin sank,
    then bubbled up afresh
as if the carcass, drawing breath,
    by *their* lives lived again

and made a curious music there—
    like running water, or wind,
or the rattle of chaff the winnower
    loosens in his fan.

Shapeless—nothing was left but a dream
30   the artist had sketched in,
forgotten, and only later on
    finished from memory.

Behind the rocks an anxious bitch
    eyed us reproachfully,
waiting for the chance to resume
    her interrupted feast.

—Yet you will come to this offence,
    this horrible decay,
you, the light of my life, the sun
40   and moon and stars of my love!

Yes, you will come to this, my queen,
    after the sacraments,
when you rot underground among
    the bones already there.

But as their kisses eat you up,
    my Beauty, tell the worms
I've kept the sacred essence, saved
    the form of my rotted loves!

∾ Spleen

Translated by Kenneth O. Hanson

Old Pluvius,[1] month of rains, in peevish mood
Pours from his urn chill winter's sodden gloom
On corpses fading in the near graveyard,
On foggy suburbs pours life's tedium.

My cat seeks out a litter on the stones,
Her mangy body turning without rest.
An ancient poet's soul in monotones
Whines in the rain-spouts like a chilblained ghost.

A great bell mourns, a wet log wrapped in smoke
10 Sings in falsetto to the wheezing clock,
While from a rankly perfumed deck of cards

(A dropsical old crone's fatal bequest)
The Queen of Spades, the dapper Jack of Hearts
Speak darkly of dead loves, how they were lost.

---

[1] Pluvius: From the Latin, *pluvia,* meaning rain, Pluvius is month five of the French revolutionary calendar, extending from January 20 to February 18.

∾ Spleen

Translated by Sir John Squire

When the low heavy sky weighs like a lid
Upon the spirit aching for the light
And all the wide horizon's line is hid
By a black day sadder than any night;

When the changed earth is but a dungeon dank
Where batlike Hope goes blindly fluttering
And, striking wall and roof and mouldered plank,
Bruises his tender head and timid wing;

When like grim prison bars stretch down the thin,
10 Straight, rigid pillars of the endless rain,

And the dumb throngs of infamous spiders spin
Their meshes in the caverns of the brain,

Suddenly, bells leap forth into the air,
Hurling a hideous uproar to the sky
As 'twere a band of homeless spirits who fare
Through the strange heavens, wailing stubbornly.

And hearses, without drum or instrument,
File slowly through my soul; crushed, sorrowful,
Weeps Hope, and Grief, fierce and omnipotent,
20 Plants his black banner on my drooping skull.

 ## The Swan

Translated by Kate Flores

To Victor Hugo

1

Andromache,[1] I think of you! — This little stream,
Poor wretched mirror resplendent once
With all the grandeur of your widow's grief,
This deceptive Simoïs,[2] heightened with your tears,

Has suddenly, as I wandered through the new Carrousel,
Restored a fertile memory of mine.

"The Swan." This poem, added to the second edition of 1861, appears in the Parisian Scenes section of *The Flowers of Evil*, a new section whose verses have been described as being more compassionate and sympathetic toward human suffering than the poems written earlier. Like the other poems in Parisian Scenes, such as "The Little Old Women" and "Parisian Dream," "The Swan" addresses life in the capital city. Its nostalgia seems almost Romantic as the speaker laments the loss of "Old Paris" and compares his regret to that of exiles and victims of violent change, such as Andromache, an African slave, and shipwrecked sailors. The hard edge of Baudelaire's imagery is evident when "The Swan" is read together with Wordsworth's "Lines Written a Few Miles above Tintern Abbey."

---

[1] Andromache: Wife of the Trojan hero Hector and mother of Astyanax, both of whom were killed by the Greeks; after the fall of Troy, Andromache was taken as a slave by Pyrrhus (Neoptolomus), the son of her husband's killer, Achilles; Pyrrhus eventually gave Andromache to Helenus, Hector's brother, who had also been taken by the Greeks.

[2] Simoïs: A river in the vicinity of Troy.

—Old Paris is no more (the contours of a city
Change, alas! more quickly than a mortal heart);

Only in spirit do I see that regiment of booths,
10   That array of makeshift capitals and posts,
The turf, the rough stones greened by the puddle waters,
And, gleaming in the cases, the jumbled bric-a-brac.

There at one time a menagerie stood;
There I saw one morning, at the hour when, under cold clear skies,
The working world awakes, and the cleaners of the streets
Hurl into the quiet air a dismal hurricane,

A swan who had escaped his cage,
And, padding the dry pavement with his webbed feet,
Trailed his snowy plumage along the scraggly ground.
20   Beside a waterless gutter the creature opened his beak

And tremulously bathing his wings in the dust, cried,
His heart full of the lovely lake of his birth:
"Water, when the deluge? Tempests, when do you thunder?"
I can see that hapless one, strange and fatal myth,

Toward the heavens, sometimes, like Ovid's man,
Toward the heavens ironical and cruelly blue,
Bend his thirsting head upon his convulsive neck,
As though addressing reproaches unto God!

2

Paris changes! but my melancholy alters not a whit!
30   New palaces, scaffoldings, stocks,
Old neighborhoods to me are all allegory now,
And now my cherished remembrances are heavier than rocks!

Thus before this Louvre an image dejects me:
I think of my glorious swan, with his mad gestures,
Like the exiled, ridiculous and sublime,
And wrung by a truceless yearning! and then of you,

Andromache, fallen from a mighty husband's arms,
A lowly creature, beneath the hand of supernal Pyrrhus,
Bending down distraught beside an empty tomb;
40   Widow of Hector, alas! and wife to Helenus!

I think upon the Negress, tubercular and wasted,
Groveling in the mud, and seeking, with haggard eye,
Beyond the massive wall of mist,
Magnificent Africa's absent coconut palms;

Of all who have lost what cannot ever be regained,
Not ever! of those who drink their fill of tears
And suckle of Sorrow like a good she-wolf!
Of scrawny orphans desiccating like flowers!

Thus in the forest of my spirit's exile
50 An old Remembrance echoes full blast like a horn!
I think upon sailors forgotten on isles,
Of the captured, the defeated! . . . and of so many more!

❧ The Voyage

Translated by Barbara Gibbs

TO MAXIME DU CAMP

1

To the child, in love with maps and pictures,
The universe is vast as his appetite.
Ah how immense the world is by lamplight!
How small the world is in recollection!

One morning we set out, our brains full of fire,
Our hearts swollen with rancor and harsh longing,

"The Voyage." Added in the second edition of 1861, this is the final poem of the collection and appears under the heading Death. If "To the Reader" provides the overture to the symphony of poems in *The Flowers of Evil*, "The Voyage" serves as the book's grand finale. A poem that Baudelaire claimed was written to subvert the idea of progress that was driving the engines of business and industry in the nineteenth century, "The Voyage" ends up celebrating the infinitude of human desire. The imagination of the child "in love with maps and pictures" leads him or her on a series of voyages undertaken solely for the sake of movement. At each stop along the journey, no matter how exotic the place, how totally different in culture and geography, the traveler finds the same demons that haunted him or her at home — greed, cruelty, and the familiar enemies, ennui and spleen. Yet the traveler is driven on by a sense of restlessness, the kind of striving Goethe made a virtue of in *Faust.* "The Voyage" brings out the underside of infinite desire, as the endless quest for the new generates bitter disappointment and frustration. "The Voyage" may be compared with the prose poem "Anywhere out of this world," from Baudelaire's *Paris Spleen,* which offers another perspective on infinite, aimless desire.

And we go, following the wave's rhythm,
Cradling our infinite on the seas' finite:

Some are glad to leave a squalid birthplace,
10 Or their abhorred cradles; some, astrologers
Drowned in a woman's eyes, their tyrannical
Circe[1] of the dangerous perfumes.

Not to be turned to beasts, they make themselves
Drunk on space and light and the flaming skies;
The frost that bites them, the suns that tan them,
Slowly wear away the marks of kisses.

But the true travelers are those who leave
For leaving's sake; light hearts like balloons,
They never swerve from their fatality,
20 And say, without knowing why: "Let us go on!"

Those whose desires have the shape of clouds,
Who dream, like a recruit of the cannon,
Of boundless, changing, unknown pleasures
Whose name the human mind has never known!

2

We imitate—horror!—the top and ball,
Waltzing and skipping; even in our sleep
Curiosity torments and rolls us
Like a merciless Angel whipping suns.

Strange lot, in which the goal displaces itself,
30 And being nowhere may be anywhere!
In which Man, whose hope never flags, goes always
Running like a madman in search of rest!

Our soul's a ship seeking its Icaria;[2]
A voice shouts from the bridge: "Open your eyes!"
From the top, ardent and mad, another cries:
"Love . . . glory . . . happiness!" Hell is a sandbar!

---

[1] **Circe:** The island sorceress in *The Odyssey* who changed men and women into beasts.

[2] **Icaria:** An island in the Aegean named after Icarus, the boy who fell to the sea having flown too close to the sun when he and his father, Daedalus, escaped prison on waxen wings. In French literature, Icaria is associated with utopian quests, as in Étienne Cabet's *Voyage to Icaria* (1840).

Each island signaled by the man on watch
Is an Eldorado[3] promised by Fate;
Imagination, preparing her feast,
40 Sees only a reef in the dawning light.

Poor lover of chimerical countries!
Must we toss him in chains, or in the sea, this
Inventor of Americas, this drunken
Sailor whose vision poisons the abyss?

Such is the old vagrant who paws the mud
And dreams, nose in air, of dazzling Edens;
His bewitched eye beholds a Capua[4]
All around, where the candle lights a hovel.

3

Marvelous travelers! What noble tales
50 We read in your eyes profound as oceans!
Show us your chests of splendid memories,
Astounding jewels, made of wind and stars.

We will sail without steam or canvas!
Enliven the boredom of our prisons;
Pass across our spirits, stretched like canvases,
Your memories in their frames of horizons.

Tell us, what have you seen?

4

                    "We have seen stars
And billows; and we have also seen sands;
And, despite shocks and unforeseen disasters,
60 We were often bored, as you were here.

The sun's splendor above violet seas,
The splendor of cities in the setting sun,
Made our hearts burn with restless ardor
To plunge into a sky of seductive light.

---

[3] **Eldorado:** Legendary city of gold that enflamed the colonial quests of Spanish conquistadors in the sixteenth century.

[4] **Capua:** A city in southern Italy notorious for its luxury and libertinism.

The richest cities, the noblest landscapes,
Never possess the mysterious
Attraction of those chance makes out of clouds.
And desire kept us forever anxious.

— Enjoyment augments the strength of desire.
70 Desire, ancient tree that thrives on pleasure,
All the while your bark thickens and hardens,
Your branches would look more closely on the sun!

When will you stop growing, great tree, longer
Lived than the cypress? — Yet we were careful
To cull a few sketches for your album,
Brothers who think all that's exotic fair!

We bowed before idols with trunks, and
Thrones constellated with shining jewels,
And carven palaces whose fairy pomp
80 Would make your bankers ruinous dreams.

Costumes like a drunkenness for the eyes
We say; women with painted teeth and nails,
And skilled fakirs whom the snake caresses."

5
And then, after that what?

6
                    "O childish brains!

Lest we forget the most important thing,
Everywhere, without wishing to, we viewed,
From top to bottom of the fatal ladder,
The dull pageant of everlasting sin:

Woman, conceited slave, neither amused
90 Nor disgusted by her self-worship;
Man, hot, gluttonous tyrant, hard and grasping,
Slave of a slave, gutter in the sewer;

The hangman enjoying, the martyr sobbing,
The fete that spices and perfumes the blood;
The despot unnerved by power's poison,
The mob in love with the brutalizing whip;

A great many religions like our own,
All scaling heaven; Holiness seeking
Its pleasure in nails and haircloth, as a
100 Delicate wallows in a feather bed;

Babbling Mankind, drunk with its own genius,
And mad as it ever was, crying out
To God, in its furious agony:
'O my fellow, my master, I curse thee!'

And the less stupid, bold lovers of Madness,
Fleeing the herd fenced in by Destiny,
To take refuge in a vast opium!
— Thus the everlasting news of the whole globe."

7

A bitter knowledge we gain by traveling!
110 The world, monotonous and small, today,
Yesterday, tomorrow, reflects our image:
Dreadful oasis in a waste of boredom!

Shall we depart or stay? Stay if you can;
Depart if you must. Some run, others crouch
To deceive the watchful, deadly foe, Time!
There are those, alas! who run without rest,

Like the wandering Jew[5] and the apostles,
Whom nothing suffices, carriage or ship,
To flee that base retiary; others
120 Wear him out without leaving their cradles.

When at last he has his foot on our backs,
Then we'll be able to hope and cry: on!
Just as we used to set out for China,
Eyes fixed on the horizon and hair streaming,

We will embark on the sea of Darkness
With the joyous hearts of young passengers;
Listen to those charming, mournful voices
Singing: "Come this way, who desire to eat

---

[5] **The wandering Jew:** A legendary Jew, condemned to roam the world until Judgment Day for mocking Christ on his way to the Crucifixion.

The perfumed Lotus![6] Here are gathered the
130 Miraculous fruits your hearts hunger for;
Come and grow drunk on the strange mildness
Of this afternoon without an ending."

We know the ghost by its familiar speech;
Our Pylades stretch out their arms to us.
"To renew your heart, swim towards your Electra!"[7]
Cries she whose knees we kissed in former days.

8

Death, old captain, it's time to weigh anchor!
This country bores us, O Death! Let us set sail!
If the sea and sky are as black as ink,
140 Our hearts, you know well, are bursting with rays!

Pour your poison on us; let it comfort
Us! We long, so does this fire burn our brains,
To dive into the gulf, Hell or Heaven,
What matter? Into the Unknown in search of the *new!*

---

[6] Lotus: The fabled plant that induces a state of blissful indolence and forgetfulness; an allusion to the land of the Lotus-eaters in Book 9 of *The Odyssey,* in which voices of the dead lured the sailors to this land of happy stupor.

[7] Electra: Pylades was the loyal friend of Orestes, son of King Agamemnon and his faithless wife Clytemnestra; Electra, Orestes' sister, saved her brother from being murdered by Aegisthus, their mother's lover, who helped her kill Agamemnon when he returned to Mycenae after the Trojan War. Electra eventually married Pylades; both symbolize the faithful companion.

FROM

∾ Paris Spleen

Translated by Louise Varèse

TO EVERY MAN HIS CHIMERA

Under a vast gray sky, on a vast and dusty plain without paths, without grass, without a nettle or a thistle, I came upon several men bent double as they walked.

Each one carried on his back an enormous Chimera[1] as heavy as a sack of flour, as a sack of coal, as the accoutrement of a Roman foot-soldier.

But the monstrous beast was no inanimate weight; on the contrary, it hugged and bore down heavily on the man with its elastic and powerful muscles; it clutched at the breast of its mount with enormous claws; and its fabulous head overhung the man's forehead like those horrible helmets with which ancient warriors tried to strike terror into their enemies.

I questioned one of these men and asked him where they were going like that. He replied that he did not know and that none of them knew; but that obviously they must be going somewhere since they were impelled by an irresistible urge to go on.

A curious thing to note: not one of these travelers seemed to resent the ferocious beast hanging around his neck and glued to his back; apparently they considered it a part of themselves. All those worn and serious faces showed not the least sign of despair; under the depressing dome of the sky, with their feet deep in the dust of the earth as desolate as the sky, they went along with the resigned look of men who are condemned to hope forever.

Short Poems in Prose or *Paris Spleen.*   After Baudelaire's death, a small collection, grown to fifty prose poems in all, appeared under this title. The poet's prose poems had been written over the last two decades of his life and had previously appeared occasionally in periodicals and in a smaller collection of twenty poems. In these poems, Baudelaire took pains to capture the experience of life in Paris in a form particularly suited to what Baudelaire called "the intersection of . . . innumerable connections." He described the prose poem as "musical, but without rhythm or rhyme, flexible and uneven enough to adapt itself to the lyrical impulses of the soul, to the undulations of reverie, to the jolts of the mind." Part of the new experience of the city was the encounter with what Walter Benjamin in a famous essay on Baudelaire describes as "the amorphous crowd of passers-by, the people in the street." Also novel was the voyeuristic experience of looking out windows and capturing momentary glimpses of anonymous lives, a phenomenon captured in Baudelaire's "Windows" that has become a recurrent motif in photography and film. For some critics, including Benjamin, Baudelaire is the quintessential poet of the city, and nowhere does this aspect of his work come through better than in the prose poems of *Paris Spleen.*

---

[1]Chimera: In Greek mythology, a monster with the head of a lion, the body of a goat, and the tail of a serpent; a chimera suggests a foolish or unlikely fantasy.

And the procession passed by me and disappeared in the haze of the horizon just where the rounded surface of the planet prevents man's gaze from following.

And for a few moments I persisted in trying to understand this mystery; but soon irresistible indifference descended upon me, and I was more cruelly oppressed by its weight than those men had been by their crushing Chimeras.

CROWDS

It is not given to every man to take a bath of multitude; enjoying a crowd is an art; and only he can relish a debauch of vitality at the expense of the human species, on whom, in his cradle, a fairy has bestowed the love of masks and masquerading, the hate of home, and the passion for roaming.

Multitude, solitude: identical terms, and interchangeable by the active and fertile poet. The man who is unable to people his solitude is equally unable to be alone in a bustling crowd.

The poet enjoys the incomparable privilege of being able to be himself or someone else, as he chooses. Like those wandering souls who go looking for a body, he enters as he likes into each man's personality. For him alone everything is vacant; and if certain places seem closed to him, it is only because in his eyes they are not worth visiting.

The solitary and thoughtful stroller finds a singular intoxication in this universal communion. The man who loves to lose himself in a crowd enjoys feverish delights that the egoist locked up in himself as in a box, and the slothful man like a mollusk in his shell, will be eternally deprived of. He adopts as his own all the occupations, all the joys and all the sorrows that chance offers.

What men call love is a very small, restricted, feeble thing compared with this ineffable orgy, this divine prostitution of the soul giving itself entire, all its poetry and all its charity, to the unexpected as it comes along, to the stranger as he passes.

It is a good thing sometimes to teach the fortunate of this world, if only to humble for an instant their foolish pride, that there are higher joys than theirs, finer and more uncircumscribed. The founders of colonies, shepherds of peoples, missionary priests exiled to the ends of the earth, doubtlessly know something of this mysterious drunkenness; and in the midst of the vast family created by their genius, they must often laugh at those who pity them because of their troubled fortunes and chaste lives.

WINDOWS

Looking from outside into an open window one never sees as much as when one looks through a closed window. There is nothing more profound, more mysterious, more pregnant, more insidious, more dazzling than a window lighted by a single candle. What one can see out in the sunlight is always less interesting than what goes on behind a window pane. In that black or luminous square life lives, life dreams, life suffers.

Across the ocean of roofs I can see a middle-aged woman, her face already lined, who is forever bending over something and who never goes out. Out of her face, her dress and her gestures, out of practically nothing at all, I have made up this woman's story, or rather legend, and sometimes I tell it to myself and weep.

If it had been an old man I could have made up his just as well.

And I go to bed proud to have lived and to have suffered in someone besides myself.

Perhaps you will say "Are you sure that your story is the real one?" But what does it matter what reality is outside myself, so long as it has helped me to live, to feel that I am, and what I am?

ANYWHERE OUT OF THE WORLD[1]

Life is a hospital where every patient is obsessed by the desire of changing beds. One would like to suffer opposite the stove, another is sure he would get well beside the window.

It always seems to me that I should be happy anywhere but where I am, and this question of moving is one that I am eternally discussing with my soul.

"Tell me, my soul, poor chilly soul, how would you like to live in Lisbon? It must be warm there, and you would be as blissful as a lizard in the sun. It is a city by the sea; they say that it is built of marble, and that its inhabitants have such a horror of the vegetable kingdom that they tear up all the trees. You see it is a country after my own heart; a country entirely made of mineral and light, and with liquid to reflect them."

My soul does not reply.

"Since you are so fond of being motionless and watching the pageantry of movement, would you like to live in the beatific land of Holland? Perhaps you could enjoy yourself in that country which you have so long admired in paintings on museum walls. What do you say to Rotterdam,[2] you who love forests of masts, and ships that are moored on the doorsteps of houses?"

My soul remains silent.

"Perhaps you would like Batavia[3] better? There, moreover, we should find the wit of Europe wedded to the beauty of the tropics."

Not a word. Can my soul be dead?

"Have you sunk into so deep a stupor that you are happy only in your unhappiness? If that is the case, let us fly to countries that are the counterfeits of Death. I know just the place for us, poor soul. We will pack up our trunks for Torneo.[4] We will go still farther, to the farthest end of the Baltic Sea; still farther from life if possible;

---

[1] Anywhere . . . World: The title derives from Thomas Hood's *Bridge of Sighs,* a poem referred to in Poe's *Poetic Principle.*

[2] Rotterdam: Major port town of the Netherlands.

[3] Batavia: Name given by the Dutch to the capital city of the Dutch East Indies; it is now Jakarta, the capital of Indonesia.

[4] Torneo: Tornio, a city in Finland at the northern tip of the Gulf of Bothnia.

we will settle at the Pole. There the sun only obliquely grazes the earth, and the slow alternations of daylight and night abolish variety and increase that other half of nothingness, monotony. There we can take deep baths of darkness, while sometimes for our entertainment, the Aurora Borealis will shoot up its rose-red sheafs like the reflections of the fireworks of hell!"

At last my soul explodes! "Anywhere! Just so it is out of the world!"

☙ GUSTAVE FLAUBERT
1821–1880

Perhaps more than any other writer of the nineteenth century, **Gustave Flaubert** can be described as the exemplar of **REALISM.** *Madame Bovary* (1856), his masterwork, models the objective narrative technique and commonplace subject matter of the Realists, and Flaubert's statements about writing articulate the basic concepts of Realist literary theory. Realists worldwide—from Guy de Maupassant and Émile Zola in France to Henry James in America and Ivan Turgenev[1] in Russia—modeled their work on Flaubert's and took instruction from his principles for writing fiction. He was, in Henry James's phrase, the "novelist's novelist." Vladimir Nabokov[2] summarized Flaubert's achievement and influence in the following terms: "Ponder most carefully the following fact: a master of Flaubert's artistic power manages to transform what he has conceived as a sordid world inhabited by frauds and philistines and mediocrities and brutes and wayward ladies into one of the most perfect pieces of fiction known, and this he achieves by bringing all the parts into harmony, by the inner force of style, by all such devices of form as the counterpoint of transition from one theme to another, of foreshadowing and echoes. Without Flaubert there would have been no Marcel Proust in France, no James Joyce in Ireland. Chekhov in Russia would not have been quite Chekhov.[3] So much for Flaubert's literary influence."

goo-STAHV floh-BARE

www For links to more information about Flaubert and a quiz on "A Simple Heart," see *World Literature Online* at bedfordstmartins .com/worldlit.

---

[1] **Maupassant . . . Turgenev:** Leading Realist novelists of the late nineteenth century. **Guy de Maupassant** (1850–1893), French writer of short stories and sometimes novelist; **Henry James** (1843–1916), American novelist and critic best known for *The Portrait of a Lady* (1881); **Émile Zola** (1840–1902), French novelist, leader of the Naturalists, and author of many novels, including *Nana* (1880) and *Germinal* (1885), see p. 398; **Ivan Turgenev** (1818–1883), Russian novelist, dramatist, and short-story writer; author of *Fathers and Sons* (1861) and other works.

[2] **Vladimir Nabokov:** (1899–1977) Russian American novelist best known for *Lolita* (1955).

[3] **Proust . . . Chekhov:** Modern Realist writers. **Marcel Proust** (1877–1922), French novelist whose series of novels entitled *À la recherche du temps perdu* (*Remembrance of Things Past*, 1913–1927) are an extended interior monologue on time and memory. **James Joyce** (1882–1941), Irish novelist best known for *Ulysses* (1922), see Book 6; **Anton Chekhov** (1860–1904), Russian dramatist and writer of short stories, see p. 702.

J. Lemot, *Gustave
Flaubert Dissecting
Madame Bovary,
Parodie,* 1869
*Flaubert strove for
economy of expression
and absolute
concreteness in his
work, in which he
aimed to be "as
precise as the
language of science."*
Madame Bovary *is
parodied here as
being overly
clinical—Flaubert is
depicted in this
engraving as a
surgeon dissecting his
patient. (The
Bridgeman Art
Library)*

An Uneventful Life.   Born into a medical family in Rouen in 1821, Flaubert claimed that his clinical powers of observation were the result of having a "doctor's eye." He saw the provincial life of his native Normandy as diseased, afflicted by stultifying conventionality. As a schoolboy he compiled lists of *idées recues,* or received ideas, to mock the banality of bourgeois life, and for relief from provincial tedium, he began writing exotic romantic stories, including *The Memoirs of a Fool,* written at age sixteen, recounting his secret love for an older married woman. He escaped Normandy by going to Paris to study law, but after failing his examinations and suffering a nervous breakdown he withdrew from the university and returned home in 1846. Although he took occasional trips to Paris and traveled to Greece, North Africa, and the Middle East, Flaubert spent the rest of his uneventful life on the family estate in Normandy, living with his mother and niece, and writing. He devoted himself to his art, laboring several years over each of his books as he searched for just the right word or detail to develop a story. He never married.

Realism and Objectivity.   Flaubert's first work was the extravagant early narrative *The Temptation of St. Anthony,* the manuscript of which a friend advised him to burn, suggesting that he try instead to write a more "down to earth" novel based on an actual case. The actual case he had in mind was that of a local doctor's wife who had deceived her husband. Convinced, Flaubert began writing *Madame Bovary,* his first published novel. Writing the novel took five years and forced its author into very disciplined habits of composition. Flaubert strove to attain complete objectivity in the presentation of his story, eliminating all commentary by the author and hiding his attitude toward the characters and their story. "The author, in his work," he wrote, "must be like God in the Universe, present everywhere and visible nowhere." Although he was contemptuous of the bourgeois provincialism of his characters and of Emma Bovary's romantic delusions, Flaubert attempted to enter sympathetically into her world and to record the story of her adulteries with absolute objectivity. He measured his success as an artist by his capacity to enter "at every moment into skins which are antipathetic to me." He claimed victory in this struggle when he asserted, "I am Madame Bovary." As his heroine he could be everywhere in his novel, yet visible nowhere.

Le Seul Mot Juste.   Flaubert sought absolute economy of expression and precise concreteness for his novel, with each detail contributing to a unity of tone. He wanted his style to be "as rhythmical as verse and as precise as the language of science." The subject matter of the story, he believed, was not important. The important thing was to choose *le seul mot juste*—the one right word. "The only truth in this world," Flaubert asserted, "is in the well-made sentence." But many of Flaubert's contemporary readers were unimpressed by the stylistic merit of the novel and believed that the subject matter was in fact important. They were outraged by Emma's adulteries. After the novel appeared in 1856, the French government brought charges against the author for "outraging public morals and religion." At trial Flaubert narrowly escaped conviction, and in the process he gained public notoriety.

Flaubert, the "novelist's novelist."

– HENRY JAMES

Romantic Indulgence and Realist Restraint.   Flaubert's achievements as a Realist were not easily come by, for his Romantic impulses were strong. Unlike Dickens, Balzac, and Dostoevsky,[4] who infused their realistic depiction of urban life with a personal, Romantic mythology within a single work, Flaubert satisfied his dual inclinations in separate works, alternating between writing excessive and indulgent romances and carefully controlled realistic novels.

In his next novel, *Salammbô* (1863), Flaubert returned to Romantic excesses. A historical novel that takes place in ancient Carthage, it indulges in lush orientalism, describing the unrestrained indulgences of its Eastern setting in extravagant language. *A Sentimental Education* (1869) was a return to the Realist style of *Madame Bovary*. An account of the passion of its young hero, Frederic Moreau, for an older woman, the novel is set against a very detailed historical account of the period preceding the coup d'état of 1851 when Louis Napoleon dissolved the Second Republic and declared the Second Empire. Flaubert had reworked this novel several times, beginning it many years earlier in *The Memoirs of a Fool*. Similarly, his Romantic next book, *The Temptation of St. Anthony* (1874), was one that he had rewritten at different stages of his life. His changing religious views can be traced in its various versions, from early antireligious nihilism to a later respect for religion in the final published version.

A Realistic Saint's Life.   Flaubert's last published collection, *Three Tales* (1877), reveals both sides of the author's character in its sharply contrasting stories: "A Simple Heart," "The Legend of St. Julian Hospitaller," and "Herodias." As different as these three stories are from one another, they are all, like *The Temptation of St. Anthony*, saints' lives.[5] "A Simple Heart," closest to *Madame Bovary* in subject matter and technique, shows Flaubert's ability to sympathize with his provincial characters and to understand their lives from the inside. **Félicité**'s life, unlike Emma Bovary's, is not sordid; rather, it is a triumph of the commonplace, a simple life that achieves saintly dignity.

fay-lee-see-TAY

"A Simple Heart" follows many of the conventions of the traditional saint's tale. The course of Félicité's life structures the story, which begins with her childhood and ends with her beatific death. Her life, like that of

---

[4] Dickens . . . Dostoevsky: Nineteenth-century novelists sometimes described as Romantic Realists. They authored detailed accounts of urban life but did not adopt the purely objective point of view of Flaubert and later Realists. Rather they used detail to develop mythic versions of the cities they wrote about: **Charles Dickens** (1812–1870) of London, in such novels as *Bleak House* (1853), see p. 670; **Honoré de Balzac** (1799–1850) of Paris, in such novels as *Le Père Goriot* (1835); **Fyodor Dostoevsky** (1821–1881) of St. Petersburg, in *Crime and Punishment* (1866) and other novels, see p. 462.

[5] saints' lives: Biographies of saints, celebrating their lives and devoted to their glorification. Especially popular in the Middle Ages, these works typically included accounts of the conversion, temptations, miracles, and death — often by martyrdom — of saints.

pong lay-VEK

oh-BANG

a saint, is a series of trials. She is orphaned as a child and mistreated by the family that takes her in. Later, her lover betrays her, and those she loves most—Virginie, her nephew, her mistress, and even her parrot—die and leave her alone. She performs heroic acts, such as fending off a bull, and suffers persecution when she is beaten on the road. Her death, on a saint's day, is marked by a beatific vision.

Félicité's is also a realistic story. Writing of Normandy, where he lived nearly all his life, Flaubert describes in precise detail the small provincial town of **Pont-l'Évêque** and the surrounding countryside. "A Simple Heart," like *Madame Bovary*, is a story of disillusionment, as everything that Félicité holds dear is lost or taken away. Her life seems to belie her name, which means happiness, for it is a recitation of suffering and loss. The vision at the end of her life that commingles her downtrodden parrot and the Holy Spirit seems to be the culmination of the absurd and the pathetic, as it appears to be merely the delusion of an illiterate peasant. Viewed from the outside, Félicité's life lacks the deep meaning assigned to saints' lives.

But in perceiving Félicité's innocence, Flaubert reveals the spirituality of this most common life. We may recognize Madame **Aubain**'s selfishness and contempt for her servant, but Félicité is innocent of such awareness, and when she loses her mistress, she loses much of the meaning of her life. Flaubert's objectivity makes us aware of both Mme. Aubain's coldness and her importance to Félicité. Likewise, on the surface, Félicité's love for Loulou, her parrot, appears comic and grotesque, but viewed from the sympathetic interior understanding that Flaubert achieves, her power to love the bird defines her saintliness. In the drab, gray world of the sculleries and the Norman countryside in which Félicité lives, the parrot is an exotic touch of color and becomes the central image in the spiritual vision that ultimately focuses her life.

The literary model of the saint's life is an implied Romantic contrast with the seeming triviality and absurdity of Félicité's life. Flaubert's identification with his character is what closes the gap between the ideal and the absurd. It is this gap—between ideal perfection and imperfect reality—and writers' encounters with it in their experience that informed the idealism of the early Romantics and the Realism of their successors.

■ CONNECTIONS

Pushkin, *The Bronze Horseman*, p. 339. Both Pushkin's *Bronze Horseman* and Flaubert's "Simple Heart" are about common people, but Pushkin's is a Romantic story, Flaubert's a Realistic. Pushkin places Yevgeni in extraordinary circumstances; Flaubert describes the everyday life of Félicité. How do these two approaches affect the reader's attitude toward the protagonists? Are the authors' opinions of their characters apparent?

Mahfouz, "Zaabalawi" (Book 6). Both "A Simple Heart" and Mahfouz's "Zaabalawi" are stories of spiritual quests, though Félicité's search is neither as conscious nor as public as the narrator's in Mahfouz's story. Both tales end in ironic ambiguity: The reader is left wondering how seriously to take Félicité's parrot, and the protagonist of "Zaabalawi" is still searching for Zaabalawi at the end of his story. What are the stages of the two quests and how successful was each character in finding what he or she was searching for?

■ FURTHER RESEARCH

Biography

Sartre, Jean-Paul. *The Family Idiot: Gustave Flaubert.* Tr. Carol Cosman. 1981.

Criticism

Brombert, Victor. *The Novels of Flaubert.* 1966.
Cortland, Peter. *A Reader's Guide to Flaubert.* 1968.
Culler, Jonathan. *Flaubert: The Uses of Uncertainty.* 1974.
Giraud, Raymond, ed. *Flaubert: A Collection of Critical Essays.* 1964.
Israel-Pelletier, Aimée. *Flaubert's Straight and Suspect Saints: The Unity of* Trois Contes. 1991. Includes a chapter on "A Simple Heart."
Schor, Naomi, and Henry F. Majewski. *Flaubert and Postmodernism.* 1984. Includes two essays on the novellas.

Related Works

Barnes, Julian. *Flaubert's Parrot.* 1984. A contemporary novel based on Flaubert's life and the themes of "A Simple Heart."

■ PRONUNCIATION

Aubain: oh-BANG
Félicité: fay-lee-see-TAY
Gustave Flaubert: goo-STAHV floh-BARE
Pont-l'Évêque: pong lay-VEK

◌ A Simple Heart

Translated by Arthur McDowall

1

Madame Aubain's servant Félicité was the envy of the ladies of Pont-l'Évêque[1] for half a century.

She received a hundred francs a year. For that she was cook and general servant, and did the sewing, washing, and ironing; she could bridle a horse, fatten poultry, and churn butter — and she remained faithful to her mistress, unamiable as the latter was.

"A Simple Heart." First published in *Three Tales* (1877), this story illustrates Flaubert's ability to combine sympathic interior understanding of his characters with a controlled, objective narration. The story, Ezra Pound remarked, "contains all that anyone knows about writing." Flaubert objectively presents the triviality and absurdity of Félicité's life, but in his identification with his simple heroine he reveals her saintly innocence.

First published in London in 1923, Arthur McDowall's restrained translation is still an effective rendering of Flaubert's prose. McDowall sought to capture the rhythm and precision of Flaubert's style while "keeping close to the letter." The notes are the editors'.

---

[1] Pont-l'Évêque: A village in Normandy.

Mme. Aubain had married a gay bachelor without money who died at the beginning of 1809, leaving her with two small children and a quantity of debts. She then sold all her property except the farms of Toucques and Geffosses, which brought in five thousand francs a year at most, and left her house in Saint-Melaine for a less expensive one that had belonged to her family and was situated behind the market.

This house had a slate roof and stood between an alley and a lane that went down to the river. There was an unevenness in the levels of the rooms which made you stumble. A narrow hall divided the kitchen from the "parlour" where Mme. Aubain spent her day, sitting in a wicker easy chair by the window. Against the panels, which were painted white, was a row of eight mahogany chairs. On an old piano under the barometer a heap of wooden and cardboard boxes rose like a pyramid. A stuffed armchair stood on either side of the Louis-Quinze chimney-piece, which was in yellow marble with a clock in the middle of it modelled like a temple of Vesta.[2] The whole room was a little musty, as the floor was lower than the garden.

The first floor began with "Madame's" room: very large, with a pale-flowered wall-paper and a portrait of "Monsieur" as a dandy of the period. It led to a smaller room, where there were two children's cots without mattresses. Next came the drawing-room, which was always shut up and full of furniture covered with sheets. Then there was a corridor leading to a study. The shelves of a large bookcase were respectably lined with books and papers, and its three wings surrounded a broad writing-table in darkwood. The two panels at the end of the room were covered with pen-drawings, water-colour landscapes, and engravings by Audran,[3] all relics of better days and vanished splendour. Félicité's room on the top floor got its light from a dormer-window, which looked over the meadows.

She rose at daybreak to be in time for Mass, and worked till evening without stopping. Then, when dinner was over, the plates and dishes in order, and the door shut fast, she thrust the log under the ashes and went to sleep in front of the hearth with her rosary in her hand. Félicité was the stubbornest of all bargainers; and as for cleanness, the polish on her saucepans was the despair of other servants. Thrifty in all things, she ate slowly, gathering off the table in her fingers the crumbs of her loaf—a twelve-pound loaf expressly baked for her, which lasted for three weeks.

At all times of year she wore a print handkerchief fastened with a pin behind, a bonnet that covered her hair, grey stockings, a red skirt, and a bibbed apron—such as hospital nurses wear—over her jacket.

Her face was thin and her voice sharp. At twenty-five she looked like forty. From fifty onwards she seemed of no particular age; and with her silence, straight figure, and precise movements she was like a woman made of wood, and going by clockwork.

---

[2] Vesta: The Roman goddess of the hearth.

[3] Audran: Gérard Audran (1640–1703) made engravings of famous paintings for use in home decoration.

2

She had had her love-story like another.

Her father, a mason, had been killed by falling off some scaffolding. Then her mother died, her sisters scattered, and a farmer took her in and employed her, while she was still quite little, to herd the cows at pasture. She shivered in rags and would lie flat on the ground to drink water from the ponds; she was beaten for nothing, and finally turned out for the theft of thirty sous which she did not steal. She went to another farm, where she became dairy-maid; and as she was liked by her employers her companions were jealous of her.

One evening in August (she was then eighteen) they took her to the assembly at Colleville. She was dazed and stupefied in an instant by the noise of the fiddlers, the lights in the trees, the gay medley of dresses, the lace, the gold crosses, and the throng of people jigging all together. While she kept shyly apart a young man with a well-to-do air, who was leaning on the shaft of a cart and smoking his pipe, came up to ask her to dance. He treated her to cider, coffee, and cake, and bought her a silk handkerchief; and then, imagining she had guessed his meaning, offered to see her home. At the edge of a field of oats he pushed her roughly down. She was frightened and began to cry out; and he went off.

One evening later she was on the Beaumont road. A big hay-wagon was moving slowly along; she wanted to get in front of it, and as she brushed past the wheels she recognized Theodore. He greeted her quite calmly, saying she must excuse it all because it was "the fault of the drink." She could not think of any answer and wanted to run away.

He began at once to talk about the harvest and the worthies of the commune, for his father had left Colleville for the farm at Les Écots, so that now he and she were neighbours. "Ah!" she said. He added that they thought of settling him in life. Well, he was in no hurry; he was waiting for a wife to his fancy. She dropped her head; and then he asked her if she thought of marrying. She answered with a smile that it was mean to make fun of her.

"But I am not, I swear!"—and he passed his left hand round her waist. She walked in the support of his embrace; their steps grew slower. The wind was soft, the stars glittered, the huge wagon-load of hay swayed in front of them, and dust rose from the dragging steps of the four horses. Then, without a word of command, they turned to the right. He clasped her once more in his arms, and she disappeared into the shadow.

The week after Theodore secured some assignations with her.

They met at the end of farmyards, behind a wall, or under a solitary tree. She was not innocent as young ladies are—she had learned knowledge from the animals—but her reason and the instinct of her honour would not let her fall. Her resistance exasperated Theodore's passion; so much so that to satisfy it—or perhaps quite artlessly,—he made her an offer of marriage. She was in doubt whether to trust him, but he swore great oaths of fidelity.

Soon he confessed to something troublesome; the year before his parents had bought him a substitute for the army, but any day he might be taken again, and the idea of serving was a terror to him. Félicité took this cowardice of his as a sign of affection, and it redoubled hers. She stole away at night to see him, and when she reached their meeting-place Theodore racked her with his anxieties and urgings.

At last he declared that he would go himself to the prefecture for information, and would tell her the result on the following Sunday, between eleven and midnight.

When the moment came she sped towards her lover. Instead of him she found one of his friends.

He told her that she would not see Theodore any more. To ensure himself against conscription he had married an old woman, Madame Lehoussais, of Toucques, who was very rich.

There was an uncontrollable burst of grief. She threw herself on the ground, screamed, called to the God of mercy, and moaned by herself in the fields till daylight came. Then she came back to the farm and announced that she was going to leave; and at the end of the month she received her wages, tied all her small belongings with a handkerchief, and went to Pont-l'Évêque.

In front of the inn there she made inquiries of a woman in a widow's cap, who, as it happened, was just looking for a cook. The girl did not know much, but her willingness seemed so great and her demands so small that Mme. Aubain ended by saying:

"Very well, then, I will take you."

A quarter of an hour afterwards Félicité was installed in her house.

She lived there at first in a tremble, as it were, at "the style of the house" and the memory of "Monsieur" floating over it all. Paul and Virginie, the first aged seven and the other hardly four, seemed to her beings of a precious substance; she carried them on her back like a horse; it was a sorrow to her that Mme. Aubain would not let her kiss them every minute. And yet she was happy there. Her grief had melted in the pleasantness of things all round.

Every Thursday regular visitors came in for a game of boston,[4] and Félicité got the cards and foot-warmers ready beforehand. They arrived punctually at eight and left before the stroke of eleven.

On Monday mornings the dealer who lodged in the covered passage spread out all his old iron on the ground. Then a hum of voices began to fill the town, mingled with the neighing of horses, bleating of lambs, grunting of pigs, and the sharp rattle of carts along the street. About noon, when the market was at its height, you might see a tall, hook-nosed old countryman with his cap pushed back making his appearance at the door. It was Robelin, the farmer of Geffosses. A little later came Liébard, the farmer from Toucques—short, red, and corpulent—in a grey jacket and gaiters shod with spurs.

Both had poultry or cheese to offer their landlord. Félicité was invariably a match for their cunning, and they went away filled with respect for her.

At vague intervals Mme. Aubain had a visit from the Marquis de Gremanville, one of her uncles, who had ruined himself by debauchery and now lived at Falaise

---

[4] boston: Card game similar to whist, named after the birthplace of the American Revolution, to which the technical terms in the game refer.

on his last remaining morsel of land. He invariably came at the luncheon hour, with a dreadful poodle whose paws left all the furniture in a mess. In spite of efforts to show his breeding, which he carried to the point of raising his hat every time he mentioned "my late father," habit was too strong for him; he poured himself out glass after glass and fired off improper remarks. Félicité edged him politely out of the house—"You have had enough, Monsieur de Gremanville! Another time!"—and she shut the door on him.

She opened it with pleasure to M. Bourais, who had been a lawyer. His baldness, his white stock, frilled shirt, and roomy brown coat, his way of rounding the arm as he took snuff—his whole person, in fact, created that disturbance of mind which overtakes us at the sight of extraordinary men.

As he looked after the property of "Madame" he remained shut up with her for hours in "Monsieur's" study, though all the time he was afraid of compromising himself. He respected the magistracy immensely, and had some pretensions to Latin.

To combine instruction and amusement he gave the children a geography book made up of a series of prints. They represented scenes in different parts of the world: cannibals with feathers on their heads, a monkey carrying off a young lady, Bedouins in the desert, the harpooning of a whale, and so on. Paul explained these engravings to Félicité; and that, in fact, was the whole of her literary education. The children's education was undertaken by Guyot, a poor creature employed at the town hall, who was famous for his beautiful hand and sharpened his penknife on his boots.

When the weather was bright the household set off early for a day at Geffosses Farm.

Its courtyard is on a slope, with the farmhouse in the middle, and the sea looks like a grey streak in the distance.

Félicité brought slices of cold meat out of her basket, and they breakfasted in a room adjoining the dairy. It was the only surviving fragment of a country house which was now no more. The wallpaper hung in tatters, and quivered in the draughts. Mme. Aubain sat with bowed head, overcome by her memories; the children became afraid to speak. "Why don't you play, then?" she would say, and off they went.

Paul climbed into the barn, caught birds, played at ducks and drakes over the pond, or hammered with his stick on the big casks which boomed like drums. Virginie fed the rabbits or dashed off to pick cornflowers, her quick legs showing their embroidered little drawers.

One autumn evening they went home by the fields. The moon was in its first quarter, lighting part of the sky; and mist floated like a scarf over the windings of the Toucques. Cattle, lying out in the middle of the grass, looked quietly at the four people as they passed. In the third meadow some of them got up and made a half-circle in front of the walkers. "There's nothing to be afraid of," said Félicité, as she stroked the nearest on the back with a kind of crooning song; he wheeled round and the others did the same. But when they crossed the next pasture there was a formidable bellow. It was a bull, hidden by the mist. Mme. Aubain was about to run. "No! no! don't go so fast!" They mended their pace, however, and heard a loud breathing behind them which came nearer. His hoofs thudded on the meadow grass like hammers; why, he was galloping now! Félicité turned round, and tore up clods of earth with both hands and threw them in his eyes. He lowered his muzzle, waved his horns, and quivered with fury, bellowing terribly. Mme. Aubain, now at the end of the pasture with her two little ones, was looking wildly for a place to get over the high bank. Félicité was retreating, still with her face to the bull, keeping up a shower of clods which blinded him, and crying all the time, "Be quick! be quick!"

Mme. Aubain went down into the ditch, pushed Virginie first and then Paul, fell several times as she tried to climb the bank, and managed it at last by dint of courage.

The bull had driven Félicité to bay against a rail-fence; his slaver was streaming into her face; another second, and he would have gored her. She had just time to slip between two of the rails, and the big animal stopped short in amazement.

This adventure was talked of at Pont-l'Évêque for many a year. Félicité did not pride herself on it in the least, not having the barest suspicion that she had done anything heroic.

Virginie was the sole object of her thoughts, for the child developed a nervous complaint as a result of her fright, and M. Poupart, the doctor, advised sea-bathing at Trouville. It was not a frequented place then. Mme. Aubain collected information, consulted Bourais, and made preparations as though for a long journey.

Her luggage started a day in advance, in Liébard's cart. The next day he brought round two horses, one of which had a lady's saddle with a velvet back to it, while a cloak was rolled up to make a kind of seat on the crupper of the other. Mme. Aubain rode on that, behind the farmer. Félicité took charge of Virginie, and Paul mounted M. Lechaptois' donkey, lent on condition that great care was taken of it.

The road was so bad that its five miles took two hours. The horses sank in the mud up to their pasterns, and their haunches jerked abruptly in the effort to get out; or else they stumbled in the ruts, and at other moments had to jump. In some places Liébard's mare came suddenly to a halt. He waited patiently until she went on again, talking about the people who had properties along the road, and adding moral reflections to their history. So it was that as they were in the middle of Toucques, and passed under some windows bowered with nasturtiums, he shrugged his shoulders and said: "There's a Mme. Lehoussais lives there; instead of taking a young man she . . ." Félicité did not hear the rest; the horses were trotting and the donkey galloping: They all turned down a bypath; a gate swung open and two boys appeared; and the party dismounted in front of a manure-heap at the very threshold of the farmhouse door.

When Mme. Liébard saw her mistress she gave lavish signs of joy. She served her a luncheon with a sirloin of beef, tripe, black-pudding, a fricassee of chicken, sparkling cider, a fruit tart, and brandied plums; seasoning it all with compliments to Madame, who seemed in better health; Mademoiselle, who was "splendid" now; and Monsieur Paul, who had "filled out" wonderfully. Nor did she forget their deceased grandparents, whom the Liébards had known, as they had been in the service of the family for several generations. The farm, like them, had the stamp of antiquity. The beams on the ceiling were worm-eaten, the walls blackened with smoke, and the window-panes grey with dust. There was an oak dresser laden with every sort of useful article—jugs, plates, pewter bowls, wolf-traps, and sheep-shears; and a huge syringe made the children laugh. There was not a tree in the three courtyards without mushrooms growing at the bottom of it or a tuft of mistletoe on its boughs. Several of them had been thrown down by the wind. They had taken root again at the middle; and all were bending under their wealth of apples. The thatched roofs, like brown velvet and of varying thickness, withstood the heaviest squalls. The cart-shed, however, was falling into ruin. Mme. Aubain said she would see about it, and ordered the animals to be saddled again.

It was another half-hour before they reached Trouville. The little caravan dismounted to pass Écores—it was an overhanging cliff with boats below it—and three minutes later they were at the end of the quay and entered the courtyard of the Golden Lamb, kept by good Mme. David.

From the first days of their stay Virginie began to feel less weak, thanks to the change of air and the effect of the sea-baths. These, for want of a bathing-dress, she took in her chemise; and her nurse dressed her afterwards in a coastguard's cabin which was used by the bathers.

In the afternoons they took the donkey and went off beyond the Black Rocks, in the direction of Hennequeville. The path climbed at first through ground with dells in it like the green sward of a park, and then reached a plateau where grass fields and arable lay side by side. Hollies rose stiffly out of the briary tangle at the edge of the road; and here and there a great withered tree made zigzags in the blue air with its branches.

They nearly always rested in a meadow, with Deauville on their left, Havre on their right, and the open sea in front. It glittered in the sunshine, smooth as a mirror and so quiet that its murmur was scarcely to be heard; sparrows chirped in hiding and the immense sky arched over it all. Mme. Aubain sat doing her needlework; Virginie plaited rushes by her side; Félicité pulled up lavender, and Paul was bored and anxious to start home.

Other days they crossed the Toucques in a boat and looked for shells. When the tide went out sea-urchins, starfish, and jelly-fish were left exposed; and the children ran in pursuit of the foam-flakes which scudded in the wind. The sleepy waves broke on the sand and unrolled all along the beach; it stretched away out of sight, bounded on the land-side by the dunes which parted it from the Marsh, a wide meadow shaped like an arena. As they came home that way, Trouville, on the hill-slope in the background, grew bigger at every step, and its miscellaneous throng of houses seemed to break into a gay disorder.

On days when it was too hot they did not leave their room. From the dazzling brilliance outside light fell in streaks between the laths of the blinds. There were no sounds in the village; and on the pavement below not a soul. This silence round them deepened the quietness of things. In the distance, where men were caulking, there was a tap of hammers as they plugged the hulls, and a sluggish breeze wafted up the smell of tar.

The chief amusement was the return of the fishing-boats. They began to tack as soon as they had passed the buoys. The sails came down on two of the three masts;

and they drew on with the foresail swelling like a balloon, glided through the splash of the waves, and when they had reached the middle of the harbour suddenly dropped anchor. Then the boats drew up against the quay. The sailors threw quivering fish over the side; a row of carts was waiting, and women in cotton bonnets darted out to take the baskets and give their men a kiss.

One of them came up to Félicité one day, and she entered the lodgings a little later in a state of delight. She had found a sister again — and then Nastasie Barette, "wife of Leroux," appeared, holding an infant at her breast and another child with her right hand, while on her left was a little cabin boy with his hands on his hips and a cap over his ear.

After a quarter of an hour Mme. Aubain sent them off; but they were always to be found hanging about the kitchen, or encountered in the course of a walk. The husband never appeared.

Félicité was seized with affection for them. She bought them a blanket, some shirts, and a stove; it was clear that they were making a good thing out of her. Mme. Aubain was annoyed by this weakness of hers, and she did not like the liberties taken by the nephew, who said "thee" and "thou" to Paul. So as Virginie was coughing and the fine weather gone, she returned to Pont-l'Évêque.

There M. Bourais enlightened her on the choice of a boys' school. The one at Caen was reputed to be the best, and Paul was sent to it. He said his good-byes bravely, content enough at going to live in a house where he would have companions.

Mme. Aubain resigned herself to her son's absence as a thing that had to be. Virginie thought about it less and less. Félicité missed the noise he made. But she found an occupation to distract her; from Christmas onward she took the little girl to catechism every day.

3

After making a genuflexion at the door she walked up between the double rows of chairs under the lofty nave, opened Mme. Aubain's pew, sat down, and began to look about her. The choir stalls were filled with the boys on the right and the girls on the left, and the curé stood by the lectern. On a painted window in the apse the Holy Ghost looked down upon the Virgin. Another window showed her on her knees before the child Jesus, and a group carved in wood behind the altar-shrine represented St. Michael overthrowing the dragon.

The priest began with a sketch of sacred history. The Garden, the Flood, the Tower of Babel, cities in flames, dying nations, and overturned idols passed like a dream before her eyes; and the dizzying vision left her with reverence for the Most High and fear of his wrath. Then she wept at the story of the Passion. Why had they crucified Him, when He loved the children, fed the multitudes, healed the blind, and had willed, in His meekness, to be born among the poor, on the dung-heap of a stable? The sowings, harvests, wine-presses, all the familiar things that the Gospel speaks of, were a part of her life. They had been made holy by God's passing; and she loved the lambs more tenderly for her love of the Lamb, and the doves because of the Holy Ghost.

She found it hard to imagine Him in person, for He was not merely a bird, but a flame as well, and a breath at other times. It may be His light, she thought, which flits at night about the edge of the marshes, His breathing which drives on the clouds, His voice which gives harmony to the bells; and she would sit rapt in adoration, enjoying the cool walls and the quiet of the church.

Of doctrines she understood nothing—did not even try to understand. The curé discoursed, the children repeated their lesson, and finally she went to sleep, waking up with a start when their wooden shoes clattered on the flagstones as they went away.

It was thus that Félicité, whose religious education had been neglected in her youth, learned the catechism by dint of hearing it; and from that time she copied all Virginie's observances, fasting as she did and confessing with her. On Corpus Christi Day they made a festal altar together.

The first communion loomed distractingly ahead. She fussed over the shoes, the rosary, the book and gloves; and how she trembled as she helped Virginie's mother to dress her!

All through the mass she was racked with anxiety. She could not see one side of the choir because of M. Bourais but straight in front of her was the flock of maidens, with white crowns above their hanging veils, making the impression of a field of snow; and she knew her dear child at a distance by her dainty neck and thoughtful air. The bell tinkled. The heads bowed, and there was silence. As the organ pealed, singers and congregation took up the "Agnus Dei";[5] then the procession of the boys began, and after them the girls rose. Step by step, with their hands joined in prayer, they went towards the lighted altar, knelt on the first step, received the sacrament in turn, and came back in the same order to their places. When Virginie's turn came Félicité leaned forward to see her; and with the imaginativeness of deep and tender feeling it seemed to her that she actually was the child; Virginie's face became hers, she was dressed in her clothes, it was her heart beating in her breast. As the moment came to open her mouth she closed her eyes and nearly fainted.

She appeared early in the sacristy next morning for Monsieur the curé to give her the communion. She took it with devotion, but it did not give her the same exquisite delight.

Mme. Aubain wanted to make her daughter into an accomplished person; and as Guyot could not teach her music or English she decided to place her in the Ursuline Convent at Honfleur as a boarder. The child made no objection. Félicité sighed and thought that Madame lacked feeling. Then she reflected that her mistress might be right; matters of this kind were beyond her.

So one day an old spring-van drew up at the door, and out of it stepped a nun to fetch the young lady. Félicité hoisted the luggage on to the top, admonished the driver, and put six pots of preserves, a dozen pears, and a bunch of violets under the seat.

At the last moment Virginie broke into a fit of sobbing; she threw her arms

---

[5] "Agnus Dei": A prayer to Christ, addressed to the "Lamb of God."

round her mother, who kissed her on the forehead, saying over and over "Come, be brave! be brave!" The step was raised, and the carriage drove off.

Then Mme. Aubain's strength gave way; and in the evening all her friends—the Lormeau family, Mme. Lechaptois, the Rochefeuille ladies, M. de Houppeville, and Bourais—came in to console her.

To be without her daughter was very painful for her at first. But she heard from Virginie three times a week, wrote to her on the other days, walked in the garden, and so filled up the empty hours.

From sheer habit Félicité went into Virginie's room in the mornings and gazed at the walls. It was boredom to her not to have to comb the child's hair now, lace up her boots, tuck her into bed—and not to see her charming face perpetually and hold her hand when they went out together. In this idle condition she tried making lace. But her fingers were too heavy and broke the threads; she could not attend to anything, she had lost her sleep, and was, in her own words, "destroyed."

To "divert herself" she asked leave to have visits from her nephew Victor.

He arrived on Sundays after mass, rosy-cheeked, bare-chested, with the scent of the country he had walked through still about him. She laid her table promptly and they had lunch, sitting opposite each other. She ate as little as possible herself to save expense, but stuffed him with food so generous that at last he went to sleep. At the first stroke of vespers she woke him up, brushed his trousers, fastened his tie, and went to church, leaning on his arm with maternal pride.

Victor was always instructed by his parents to get something out of her—a packet of moist sugar, it might be, a cake of soap, spirits, or even money at times. He brought his things for her to mend and she took over the task, only too glad to have a reason for making him come back.

In August his father took him off on a coasting voyage. It was holiday time, and she was consoled by the arrival of the children. Paul, however, was getting selfish, and Virginie was too old to be called "thou" any longer; this put a constraint and barrier between them.

Victor went to Morlaix, Dunkirk, and Brighton in succession and made Félicité a present on his return from each voyage. It was a box made of shells the first time, a coffee cup the next, and on the third occasion a large gingerbread man. Victor was growing handsome. He was well made, had a hint of a moustache, good honest eyes, and a small leather hat pushed backwards like a pilot's. He entertained her by telling stories embroidered with nautical terms.

On a Monday, July 14, 1819 (she never forgot the date), he told her that he had signed on for the big voyage and next night but one he would take the Honfleur boat and join his schooner, which was to weigh anchor from Havre before long. Perhaps he would be gone two years.

The prospect of this long absence threw Félicité into deep distress; one more good-bye she must have, and on the Wednesday evening, when Madame's dinner was finished, she put on her clogs and made short work of the twelve miles between Pont-l'Évêque and Honfleur.

When she arrived in front of the Calvary she took the turn to the right instead of the left, got lost in the timber-yards, and retraced her steps; some people to whom she spoke advised her to be quick. She went all round the harbour basin, full of ships, and knocked against hawsers; then the ground fell away, lights flashed across each other, and she thought her wits had left her, for she saw horses up in the sky.

Others were neighing by the quay-side, frightened at the sea. They were lifted by a tackle and deposited in a boat, where passengers jostled each other among cider casks, cheese baskets, and sacks of grain; fowls could be heard clucking, the captain swore; and a cabin-boy stood leaning over the bows, indifferent to it all. Félicité, who had not recognized him, called "Victor!" and he raised his head; all at once, as she was darting forwards, the gangway was drawn back.

The Honfleur packet, women singing as they hauled it, passed out of harbour. Its framework creaked and the heavy waves whipped its bows. The canvas had swung round, no one could be seen on board now, and on the moon-silvered sea the boat made a black speck which paled gradually, dipped, and vanished.

As Félicité passed by the Calvary she had a wish to commend to God what she cherished most, and she stood there praying a long time with her face bathed in tears and her eyes towards the clouds. The town was asleep, coastguards were walking to and fro; and water poured without cessation through the holes in the sluice, with the noise of a torrent. The clocks struck two.

The convent parlour would not be open before day. If Félicité were late Madame would most certainly be annoyed; and in spite of her desire to kiss the other child she turned home. The maids at the inn were waking up as she came in to Pont-l'Évêque.

So the poor slip of a boy was going to toss for months and months at sea! She had not been frightened by his previous voyages. From England or Brittany you came back safe enough; but America, the colonies, the islands — these were lost in a dim region at the other end of the world.

Félicité's thoughts from that moment ran entirely on her nephew. On sunny days she was harassed by the idea of thirst; when there was a storm she was afraid of the lightning on his account. As she listened to the wind growling in the chimney or carrying off the slates she pictured him lashed by that same tempest, at the top of a shattered mast, with his body thrown backwards under a sheet of foam; or else (with a reminiscence of the illustrated geography) he was being eaten by savages, captured in a wood by monkeys, or dying on a desert shore. And never did she mention her anxieties.

Mme. Aubain had anxieties of her own, about her daughter. The good sisters found her an affectionate but delicate child. The slightest emotion unnerved her. She had to give up the piano.

Her mother stipulated for regular letters from the convent. She lost patience one morning when the postman did not come, and walked to and fro in the parlour from her armchair to the window. It was really amazing; not a word for four days!

To console Mme. Aubain by her own example Félicité remarked:

"As for me, Madame, it's six months since I heard . . ."

"From whom, pray?"

"Why . . . from my nephew," the servant answered gently.

"Oh! your nephew!" And Mme. Aubain resumed her walk with a shrug of the shoulders, as much as to say: "I was not thinking of him! And what is more, it's absurd! A scamp of a cabin-boy—what does he matter? . . . whereas my daughter . . . why, just think!"

Félicité, though she had been brought up on harshness, felt indignant with Madame—and then forgot. It seemed the simplest thing in the world to her to lose one's head over the little girl. For her the two children were equally important; a bond in her heart made them one, and their destinies must be the same.

She heard from the chemist that Victor's ship had arrived at Havana. He had read this piece of news in a gazette.

Cigars—they made her imagine Havana as a place where no one does anything but smoke, and there was Victor moving among the negroes in a cloud of tobacco. Could you, she wondered, "in case you needed," return by land? What was the distance from Pont-l'Évêque? She questioned M. Bourais to find out.

He reached for his atlas and began explaining the longitudes; Félicité's consternation provoked a fine pedantic smile. Finally he marked with his pencil a black, imperceptible point in the indentations of an oval spot, and said as he did so, "Here it is." She bent over the map; the maze of coloured lines wearied her eyes without conveying anything; and on an invitation from Bourais to tell him her difficulty she begged him to show her the house where Victor was living. Bourais threw up his arms, sneezed, and laughed immensely: a simplicity like hers was a positive joy. And Félicité did not understand the reason; how could she when she expected, very likely, to see the actual image of her nephew—so stunted was her mind!

A fortnight afterwards Liébard came into the kitchen at market-time as usual and handed her a letter from her brother-in-law. As neither of them could read she took it to her mistress.

Mme. Aubain, who was counting the stitches in her knitting, put the work down by her side, broke the seal of the letter, started, and said in a low voice, with a look of meaning:

"It is bad news . . . that they have to tell you. Your nephew . . ."

He was dead. The letter said no more.

Félicité fell on to a chair, leaning her head against the wainscot; and she closed her eyelids, which suddenly flushed pink. Then with bent forehead, hands hanging, and fixed eyes, she said at intervals:

"Poor little lad! poor little lad!"

Liébard watched her and heaved sighs. Mme. Aubain trembled a little.

She suggested that Félicité should go to see her sister at Trouville. Félicité answered by a gesture that she had no need.

There was a silence. The worthy Liébard thought it was time for them to withdraw.

Then Félicité said:

"They don't care, not they!"

Her head dropped again; and she took up mechanically, from time to time, the long needles on her work-table.

Women passed in the yard with a barrow of dripping linen.

As she saw them through the window-panes she remembered her washing; she had put it to soak the day before, to-day she must wring it out; and she left the room.

Her plank and tub were at the edge of the Toucques. She threw a pile of linen on the bank, rolled up her sleeves, and taking her wooden beater dealt lusty blows whose sound carried to the neighbouring gardens. The meadows were empty, the river stirred in the wind; and down below long grasses wavered, like the hair of corpses floating in the water. She kept her grief down and was very brave until the evening; but once in her room she surrendered to it utterly, lying stretched on the mattress with her face in the pillow and her hands clenched against her temples.

Much later she heard, from the captain himself, the circumstances of Victor's end. They had bled him too much at the hospital for yellow fever. Four doctors held him at once. He had died instantly, and the chief had said:

"Bah! there goes another!"

His parents had always been brutal to him. She preferred not to see them again; and they made no advances, either because they forgot her or from the callousness of the wretchedly poor.

Virginie began to grow weaker.

Tightness in her chest, coughing, continual fever, and veinings on her cheek-bones betrayed some deep-seated complaint. M. Poupart had advised a stay in Provence. Mme. Aubain determined on it, would have brought her daughter home at once but for the climate of Pont-l'Évêque.

She made an arrangement with a job-master, and he drove her to the convent every Tuesday. There is a terrace in the garden, with a view over the Seine. Virginie took walks there over the fallen vine-leaves, on her mother's arm. A shaft of sunlight through the clouds made her blink sometimes, as she gazed at the sails in the distance and the whole horizon from the castle of Tancarville to the light-houses at Havre. Afterwards they rested in the arbour. Her mother had secured a little cask of excellent Malaga; and Virginie, laughing at the idea of getting tipsy, drank a thimble full of it, no more.

Her strength came back visibly. The autumn glided gently away. Félicité reassured Mme. Aubain. But one evening, when she had been out on a commission in the neighbourhood, she found M. Poupart's gig at the door. He was in the hall, and Mme. Aubain was tying her bonnet.

"Give me my foot-warmer, purse, gloves! Quicker, come!"

Virginie had inflammation of the lungs; perhaps it was hopeless.

"Not yet!" said the doctor, and they both got into the carriage under whirling flakes of snow. Night was coming on and it was very cold.

Félicité rushed into the church to light a taper. Then she ran after the gig, came up with it in an hour, and jumped lightly in behind. As she hung on by the fringes a thought came into her mind: "The courtyard has not been shut up; supposing burglars got in!" And she jumped down.

At dawn next day she presented herself at the doctor's. He had come in and started for the country again. Then she waited in the inn, thinking that a letter would come by some hand or other. Finally, when it was twilight, she took the Lisieux coach.

The convent was at the end of a steep lane. When she was about half-way up it she heard strange sounds—a death-bell tolling. "It is for someone else," thought Félicité, and she pulled the knocker violently.

After some minutes there was a sound of trailing slippers, the door opened ajar, and a nun appeared.

The good sister, with an air of compunction, said that "she had just passed away." On the instant the bell of St. Leonard's tolled twice as fast.

Félicité went up to the second floor.

From the doorway she saw Virginie stretched on her back, with her hands joined, her mouth open, and head thrown back under a black crucifix that leaned towards her, between curtains that hung stiffly, less pale than was her face. Mme. Aubain, at the foot of the bed which she clasped with her arms, was choking with sobs of agony. The mother superior stood on the right. Three candlesticks on the chest of drawers made spots of red, and the mist came whitely through the windows. Nuns came and took Mme. Aubain away.

For two nights Félicité never left the dead child. She repeated the same prayers, sprinkled holy water over the sheets, came and sat down again, and watched her. At the end of the first vigil she noticed that the face had grown yellow, the lips turned blue, the nose was sharper, and the eyes sunk in. She kissed them several times, and would not have been immensely surprised if Virginie had opened them again; to minds like hers the supernatural is quite simple. She made the girl's toilette, wrapped her in her shroud, lifted her down into her bier, put a garland on her head, and spread out her hair. It was fair, and extraordinarily long for her age. Félicité cut off a big lock and slipped half of it into her bosom, determined that she should never part with it.

The body was brought back to Pont-l'Évêque, as Mme. Aubain intended; she followed the hearse in a closed carriage.

It took another three-quarters of an hour after the mass to reach the cemetery. Paul walked in front, sobbing. M. Bourais was behind, and then came the chief residents, the women shrouded in black mantles, and Félicité. She thought of her nephew; and because she had not been able to pay these honours to him her grief was doubled, as though the one were being buried with the other.

Mme. Aubain's despair was boundless. It was against God that she first rebelled, thinking it unjust of Him to have taken her daughter from her — she had never done evil and her conscience was so clear! Ah, no! — she ought to have taken Virginie off to the south. Other doctors would have saved her. She accused herself now, wanted to join her child, and broke into cries of distress in the middle of her dreams. One dream haunted her above all. Her husband, dressed as a sailor, was returning from a long voyage, and shedding tears he told her that he had been ordered to take Virginie away. Then they consulted how to hide her somewhere.

She came in once from the garden quite upset. A moment ago — and she pointed out the place — the father and daughter had appeared to her, standing side by side, and they did nothing, but they looked at her.

For several months after this she stayed inertly in her room. Félicité lectured her gently; she must live for her son's sake, and for the other, in remembrance of "her."

"Her?" answered Mme. Aubain, as though she were just waking up. "Ah, yes! . . . yes! . . . You do not forget her!" This was an allusion to the cemetery, where she was strictly forbidden to go.

Félicité went there every day.

Precisely at four she skirted the houses, climbed the hill, opened the gate, and came to Virginie's grave. It was a little column of pink marble with a stone underneath and a garden plot enclosed by chains. The beds were hidden under a coverlet of flowers. She watered their leaves, freshened the gravel, and knelt down to break up the earth better. When Mme. Aubain was able to come there she felt a relief and a sort of consolation.

Then years slipped away, one like another, and their only episodes were the great festivals as they recurred—Easter, the Assumption, All Saints' Day. Household occurrences marked dates that were referred to afterwards. In 1825, for instance, two glaziers white-washed the hall; in 1827 a piece of the roof fell into the courtyard and nearly killed a man. In the summer of 1828 it was Madame's turn to offer the consecrated bread; Bourais, about this time, mysteriously absented himself; and one by one the old acquaintances passed away: Guyot, Liébard, Mme. Lechaptois, Robelin, and Uncle Gremanville, who had been paralysed for a long time.

One night the driver of the mail-coach announced the Revolution of July[6] in Pont-l'Évêque. A new sub-prefect was appointed a few days later—Baron de Larsonnière, who had been consul in America, and brought with him, besides his wife, a sister-in-law and three young ladies, already growing up. They were to be seen about on their lawn, in loose blouses, and they had a negro and a parrot. They paid a call on Mme. Aubain which she did not fail to return. The moment they were seen in the distance Félicité ran to let her mistress know. But only one thing could really move her feelings—the letters from her son.

He was swallowed up in a tavern life and could follow no career. She paid his debts, he made new ones; and the sighs that Mme. Aubain uttered as she sat knitting by the window reached Félicité at her spinning-wheel in the kitchen.

They took walks together along the espaliered wall, always talking of Virginie and wondering if such and such a thing would have pleased her and what, on some occasion, she would have been likely to say.

All her small belongings filled a cupboard in the two-bedded room. Mme. Aubain inspected them as seldom as she could. One summer day she made up her mind to it—and some moths flew out of the wardrobe.

Virginie's dresses were in a row underneath a shelf, on which there were three dolls, some hoops, a set of toy pots and pans, and the basin that she used. They took out her petticoats as well, and the stockings and handkerchiefs, and laid them out on the two beds before folding them up again. The sunshine lit up these poor things, bringing out their stains and the creases made by the body's movements. The air was warm and blue, a blackbird warbled, life seemed bathed in a deep sweetness. They found a little plush hat with thick, chestnut-coloured pile; but it was eaten all over by moths. Félicité begged it for her own. Their eyes met fixedly and filled with tears; at last the mistress opened her arms, the servant threw herself into them, and they embraced each other, satisfying their grief in a kiss that made them equal.

---

[6] **Revolution of July:** In 1830 the Bourbons were expelled and Louis Philippe became king of France.

It was the first time in their lives, Mme. Aubain's nature not being expansive. Félicité was as grateful as though she had received a favour, and cherished her mistress from that moment with the devotion of an animal and a religious worship.

The kindness of her heart unfolded.

When she heard the drums of a marching regiment in the street she posted herself at the door with a pitcher of cider and asked the soldiers to drink. She nursed cholera patients and protected the Polish refugees;[7] one of these even declared that he wished to marry her. They quarrelled, however; for when she came back from the Angelus one morning she found that he had got into her kitchen and made himself a vinegar salad which he was quietly eating.

After the Poles came father Colmiche, an old man who was supposed to have committed atrocities in '93.[8] He lived by the side of the river in the ruins of a pigsty. The little boys watched him through the cracks in the wall, and threw pebbles at him which fell on the pallet where he lay constantly shaken by a catarrh; his hair was very long, his eyes inflamed, and there was a tumour on his arm bigger than his head. She got him some linen and tried to clean up his miserable hole; her dream was to establish him in the bake-house, without letting him annoy Madame. When the tumour burst she dressed it every day; sometimes she brought him cake, and would put him in the sunshine on a truss of straw. The poor old man, slobbering and trembling, thanked her in his worn-out voice, was terrified that he might lose her, and stretched out his hands when he saw her go away. He died; and she had a mass said for the repose of his soul.

That very day a great happiness befell her; just at dinner-time appeared Mme. de Larsonnière's negro, carrying the parrot in its cage, with perch, chain, and padlock. A note from the baroness informed Mme. Aubain that her husband had been raised to a prefecture and they were starting that evening; she begged her to accept the bird as a memento and mark of her regard.

For a long time he had absorbed Félicité's imagination, because he came from America; and that name reminded her of Victor, so much so that she made inquiries of the negro. She had once gone so far as to say "How Madame would enjoy having him!"

The negro repeated the remark to his mistress; and as she could not take the bird away with her she chose this way of getting rid of him.

4

His name was Loulou. His body was green and the tips of his wings rose-pink; his forehead was blue and his throat golden.

But he had the tiresome habits of biting his perch, tearing out his feathers, sprinkling his dirt about, and spattering the water of his tub. He annoyed Mme. Aubain, and she gave him to Félicité for good.

---

[7] **Polish refugees:** After Russia suppressed the Polish uprisings in 1831, many Polish refugees came to France.

[8] **atrocities in '93:** The Reign of Terror during the French Revolution began in 1793.

She endeavoured to train him; soon he could repeat "Nice boy! Your servant, sir! Good morning, Marie!" He was placed by the side of the door, and astonished several people by not answering to the name Jacquot, for all parrots are called Jacquot. People compared him to a turkey and a log of wood, and stabbed Félicité to the heart each time. Strange obstinacy on Loulou's part!—directly you looked at him he refused to speak.

None the less he was eager for society; for on Sundays, while the Rochefeuille ladies, M. de Houppeville, and new familiars—Onfroy the apothecary, Monsieur Varin, and Captain Mathieu—were playing their game of cards, he beat the windows with his wings and threw himself about so frantically that they could not hear each other speak.

Bourais' face, undoubtedly, struck him as extremely droll. Directly he saw it he began to laugh—and laugh with all his might. His peals rang through the courtyard and were repeated by the echo; the neighbours came to their windows and laughed too; while M. Bourais, gliding along under the wall to escape the parrot's eye, and hiding his profile with his hat, got to the river and then entered by the garden gate. There was a lack of tenderness in the looks which he darted at the bird.

Loulou had been slapped by the butcher-boy for making so free as to plunge his head into his basket; and since then he was always trying to nip him through his shirt. Fabu threatened to wring his neck, although he was not cruel, for all his tattooed arms and large whiskers. Far from it; he really rather liked the parrot, and in a jovial humour even wanted to teach him to swear. Félicité, who was alarmed by such proceedings, put the bird in the kitchen. His little chain was taken off and he roamed about the house.

His way of going downstairs was to lean on each step with the curve of his beak, raise the right foot, and then the left; and Félicité was afraid that these gymnastics brought on fits of giddiness. He fell ill and could not talk or eat any longer. There was a growth under his tongue, such as fowls have sometimes. She cured him by tearing the pellicle off with her finger-nails. Mr. Paul was thoughtless enough one day to blow some cigar smoke into his nostrils, and another time when Mme. Lormeau was teasing him with the end of her umbrella he snapped at the ferrule. Finally he got lost.

Félicité had put him on the grass to refresh him, and gone away for a minute, and when she came back—no sign of the parrot! She began by looking for him in the shrubs, by the waterside, and over the roofs, without listening to her mistress's cries of "Take care, do! You are out of your wits!" Then she investigated all the gardens in Pont-l'Évêque, and stopped the passers-by. "You don't ever happen to have seen my parrot, by any chance, do you?" And she gave a description of the parrot to those who did not know him. Suddenly, behind the mills at the foot of the hill she thought she could make out something green that fluttered. But on the top of the hill there was nothing. A hawker assured her that he had come across the parrot just before, at Saint-Melaine, in Mère Simon's shop. She rushed there; they had no idea of what she meant. At last she came home exhausted, with her slippers in shreds and despair in her soul; and as she was sitting in the middle of the garden-seat at Madame's side, telling the whole story of her efforts, a light weight dropped on to her shoulder—it was Loulou! What on earth had he been doing? Taking a walk in the neighbourhood, perhaps!

She had some trouble in recovering from this, or rather never did recover. As the result of a chill she had an attack of quinsy,[9] and soon afterwards an earache. Three years later she was deaf; and she spoke very loud, even in church. Though Félicité's sins might have been published in every corner of the diocese without dishonour to her or scandal to anybody, his Reverence the priest thought it right now to hear her confession in the sacristy only.

Imaginary noises in the head completed her upset. Her mistress often said to her, "Heavens! how stupid you are!" "Yes, Madame," she replied, and looked about for something.

Her little circle of ideas grew still narrower; the peal of church-bells and the lowing of cattle ceased to exist for her. All living beings moved as silently as ghosts. One sound only reached her ears now—the parrot's voice.

Loulou, as though to amuse her, reproduced the click-clack of the turn-spit, the shrill call of a man selling fish, and the noise of the saw in the joiner's house opposite; when the bell rang he imitated Mme. Aubain's "Félicité! the door! the door!"

They carried on conversations, he endlessly reciting the three phrases in his repertory, to which she replied with words that were just as disconnected but uttered what was in her heart. Loulou was almost a son and a lover to her in her isolated state. He climbed up her fingers, nibbled at her lips, and clung to her kerchief; and when she bent her forehead and shook her head gently to and fro, as nurses do, the great wings of her bonnet and the bird's wings quivered together.

When the clouds massed and the thunder rumbled Loulou broke into cries, perhaps remembering the downpours in his native forests. The streaming rain made him absolutely mad; he fluttered wildly about, dashing up to the ceiling, upset everything, and went out through the window to dabble in the garden; but he was back quickly to perch on one of the fire-dogs[10] and hopped about to dry himself, exhibiting his tail and his beak in turn.

One morning in the terrible winter of 1837 she had put him in front of the fire-place because of the cold. She found him dead, in the middle of his cage: head downwards, with his claws in the wires. He had died from congestion, no doubt. But Félicité thought he had been poisoned with parsley, and though there was no proof of any kind her suspicions inclined to Fabu.

She wept so piteously that her mistress said to her, "Well, then, have him stuffed!"

She asked advice from the chemist, who had always been kind to the parrot. He wrote to Havre, and a person called Fellacher undertook the business. But as parcels sometimes got lost in the coach she decided to take the parrot as far as Honfleur herself.

Along the sides of the road were leafless apple-trees, one after the other. Ice covered the ditches. Dogs barked about the farms; and Félicité, with her hands under her cloak, her little black sabots[11] and her basket, walked briskly in the middle of the road.

She crossed the forest, passed High Oak, and reached St. Gatien.

---

[9] quinsy: Tonsillitis.   [10] fire-dogs: Andirons.   [11] sabots: Wooden shoes.

A cloud of dust rose behind her, and in it a mail-coach, carried away by the steep hill, rushed down at full gallop like a hurricane. Seeing this woman who would not get out of the way, the driver stood up in front and the postilion shouted too. He could not hold in his four horses, which increased their pace, and the two leaders were grazing her when he threw them to one side with a jerk of the reins. But he was wild with rage, and lifting his arm as he passed at full speed, gave her such a lash from waist to neck with his big whip that she fell on her back.

Her first act, when she recovered consciousness, was to open her basket. Loulou was happily none the worse. She felt a burn in her right cheek, and when she put her hands against it they were red; the blood was flowing.

She sat down on a heap of stones and bound up her face with her handkerchief. Then she ate a crust of bread which she had put in the basket as a precaution, and found a consolation for her wound in gazing at the bird.

When she reached the crest of Ecquemauville she saw the Honfleur lights sparkling in the night sky like a company of stars; beyond, the sea stretched dimly. Then a faintness overtook her and she stopped; her wretched childhood, the disillusion of her first love, her nephew's going away, and Virginie's death all came back to her at once like the waves of an oncoming tide, rose to her throat, and choked her.

Afterwards, at the boat, she made a point of speaking to the captain, begging him to take care of the parcel, though she did not tell him what was in it.

Fellacher kept the parrot a long time. He was always promising it for the following week. After six months he announced that a packing-case had started, and then nothing more was heard of it. It really seemed as though Loulou was never coming back. "Ah, they have stolen him!" she thought.

He arrived at last, and looked superb. There he was, erect upon a branch which screwed into a mahogany socket, with a foot in the air and his head on one side, biting a nut which the bird-stuffer—with a taste for impressiveness—had gilded.

Félicité shut him up in her room. It was a place to which few people were admitted, and held so many religious objects and miscellaneous things that it looked like a chapel and bazaar in one.

A big cupboard impeded you as you opened the door. Opposite the window commanding the garden a little round one looked into the court; there was a table by the folding-bed with a water-jug, two combs, and a cube of blue soap in a chipped plate. On the walls hung rosaries, medals, several benign Virgins, and a holy water vessel made out of cocoa-nut; on the chest of drawers, which was covered with a cloth like an altar, was the shell box that Victor had given her, and after that a watering-can, a toy-balloon, exercise-books, the illustrated geography, and a pair of young lady's boots; and, fastened by its ribbons to the nail of the looking-glass, hung the little plush hat! Félicité carried observances of this kind so far as to keep one of Monsieur's frock-coats. All the old rubbish which Mme. Aubain did not want any longer she laid hands on for her room. That was why there were artificial flowers along the edge of the chest of drawers and a portrait of the Comte d'Artois[12] in the little window recess.

---

[12] **Comte d'Artois:** Title of Charles X, the last of the Bourbon kings. He ruled between 1824 and 1830 and died in 1836 in exile.

With the aid of a bracket Loulou was established over the chimney, which jutted into the room. Every morning when she woke up she saw him there in the dawning light, and recalled old days and the smallest details of insignificant acts in a deep quietness which knew no pain.

Holding, as she did, no communication with anyone, Félicité lived as insensibly as if she were walking in her sleep. The Corpus Christi processions roused her to life again. Then she went round begging mats and candlesticks from the neighbours to decorate the altar they put up in the street.

In church she was always gazing at the Holy Ghost in the window, and observed that there was something of the parrot in him. The likeness was still clearer, she thought, on a crude colour-print representing the baptism of Our Lord. With his purple wings and emerald body he was the very image of Loulou.

She bought him, and hung him up instead of the Comte d'Artois, so that she could see them both together in one glance. They were linked in her thoughts; and the parrot was consecrated by his association with the Holy Ghost, which became more vivid to her eye and more intelligible. The Father could not have chosen to express Himself through a dove, for such creatures cannot speak; it must have been one of Loulou's ancestors, surely. And though Félicité looked at the picture while she said her prayers she swerved a little from time to time towards the parrot.

She wanted to join the Ladies of the Virgin, but Mme. Aubain dissuaded her.

And then a great event loomed up before them — Paul's marriage.

He had been a solicitor's clerk to begin with, and then tried business, the Customs, the Inland Revenue, and made efforts, even, to get into the Rivers and Forests. By an inspiration from heaven he had suddenly, at thirty-six, discovered his real line — the Registrar's Office. And there he showed such marked capacity that an inspector had offered him his daughter's hand and promised him his influence.

So Paul, grown serious, brought the lady to see his mother.

She sniffed at the ways of Pont-l'Évêque, gave herself great airs, and wounded Félicité's feelings. Mme. Aubain was relieved at her departure.

The week after came news of M. Bourais' death in an inn in Lower Brittany. The rumour of suicide was confirmed, and doubts arose as to his honesty. Mme. Aubain studied his accounts, and soon found out the whole tale of his misdoings — embezzled arrears, secret sales of wood, forged receipts, etc. Besides that he had an illegitimate child, and "relations with a person at Dozulé."

These shameful facts distressed her greatly. In March 1853 she was seized with a pain in the chest; her tongue seemed to be covered with film, and leeches did not ease the difficult breathing. On the ninth evening of her illness she died, just at seventy-two.

She passed as being younger, owing to the bands of brown hair which framed her pale, pock-marked face. There were few friends to regret her, for she had a stiffness of manner which kept people at a distance.

But Félicité mourned for her as one seldom mourns for a master. It upset her ideas and seemed contrary to the order of things, impossible and monstrous, that Madame should die before her.

Ten days afterwards, which was the time it took to hurry there from Besançon, the heirs arrived. The daughter-in-law ransacked the drawers, chose some furniture, and sold the rest; and then they went back to their registering.

Madame's armchair, her small round table, her foot-warmer, and the eight chairs were gone! Yellow patches in the middle of the panels showed where the engravings had hung. They had carried off the two little beds and the mattresses, and all Virginie's belongings had disappeared from the cupboard. Félicité went from floor to floor dazed with sorrow.

The next day there was a notice on the door, and the apothecary shouted in her ear that the house was for sale.

She tottered, and was obliged to sit down. What distressed her most of all was to give up her room, so suitable as it was for poor Loulou. She enveloped him with a look of anguish when she was imploring the Holy Ghost, and formed the idolatrous habit of kneeling in front of the parrot to say her prayers. Sometimes the sun shone in at the attic window and caught his glass eye, and a great luminous ray shot out of it and put her in an ecstasy.

She had a pension of three hundred and eighty francs a year which her mistress had left her. The garden gave her a supply of vegetables. As for clothes, she had enough to last her to the end of her days, and she economized in candles by going to bed at dusk.

She hardly ever went out, as she did not like passing the dealer's shop, where some of the old furniture was exposed for sale. Since her fit of giddiness she dragged one leg; and as her strength was failing Mère Simon, whose grocery business had collapsed, came every morning to split the wood and pump water for her.

Her eyes grew feeble. The shutters ceased to be thrown open. Years and years passed, and the house was neither let nor sold.

Félicité never asked for repairs because she was afraid of being sent away. The boards on the roof rotted; her bolster was wet for a whole winter. After Easter she spat blood.

Then Mère Simon called in a doctor. Félicité wanted to know what was the matter with her. But she was too deaf to hear, and the only word which reached her was "pneumonia." It was a word she knew, and she answered softly "Ah! like Madame," thinking it natural that she should follow her mistress.

The time for the festal shrines[13] was coming near. The first one was always at the bottom of the hill, the second in front of the post-office, and the third towards the middle of the street. There was some rivalry in the matter of this one, and the women of the parish ended by choosing Mme. Aubain's courtyard.

The hard breathing and fever increased. Félicité was vexed at doing nothing for the altar. If only she could at least have put something there! Then she thought of the parrot. The neighbours objected that it would not be decent. But the priest gave her

---

[13] **time . . . shrines:** At the festival for the local saint's day, a procession would proceed through a series of shrines.

permission, which so intensely delighted her that she begged him to accept Loulou, her sole possession, when she died.

From Tuesday to Saturday, the eve of the festival, she coughed more often. By the evening her face had shrivelled, her lips stuck to her gums, and she had vomitings; and at twilight next morning, feeling herself very low, she sent for a priest.

Three kindly women were round her during the extreme unction. Then she announced that she must speak to Fabu. He arrived in his Sunday clothes, by no means at his ease in the funereal atmosphere.

"Forgive me," she said, with an effort to stretch out her arm; "I thought it was you who had killed him."

What did she mean by such stories? She suspected him of murder — a man like him! He waxed indignant, and was on the point of making a row.

"There," said the women, "she is no longer in her senses, you can see it well enough!"

Félicité spoke to shadows of her own from time to time. The women went away, and Mère Simon had breakfast. A little later she took Loulou and brought him close to Félicité with the words:

"Come, now, say good-bye to him!"

Loulou was not a corpse, but the worms devoured him; one of his wings was broken, and the tow was coming out of his stomach. But she was blind now; she kissed him on the forehead and kept him close against her cheek. Mère Simon took him back from her to put him on the altar.

5

Summer scents came up from the meadows; flies buzzed; the sun made the river glitter and heated the slates. Mère Simon came back into the room and fell softly asleep.

She woke at the noise of bells; the people were coming out from vespers. Félicité's delirium subsided. She thought of the procession and saw it as if she had been there.

All the school children, the church-singers, and the firemen walked on the pavement, while in the middle of the road the verger armed with his hallebard and the beadle with a large cross advanced in front. Then came the schoolmaster, with an eye on the boys, and the sister, anxious about her little girls; three of the daintiest, with angelic curls, scattered rose-petals in the air; the deacon controlled the band with outstretched arms; and two censer-bearers turned back at every step towards the Holy Sacrament, which was borne by Monsieur the curé, wearing his beautiful chasuble, under a canopy of dark-red velvet held up by four churchwardens. A crowd of people pressed behind, between the white cloths covering the house walls, and they reached the bottom of the hill.

A cold sweat moistened Félicité's temples. Mère Simon sponged her with a piece of linen, saying to herself that one day she would have to go that way.

The hum of the crowd increased, was very loud for an instant and then went further away.

A fusillade shook the window-panes. It was the postilions saluting the monstrance.[14] Félicité rolled her eyes and said as audibly as she could: "Does he look well?" The parrot was weighing on her mind.

Her agony began. A death-rattle that grew more and more convulsed made her sides heave. Bubbles of froth came at the corners of her mouth and her whole body trembled.

Soon the booming of the ophicleides,[15] the high voices of the children, and the deep voices of the men were distinguishable. At intervals all was silent, and the tread of feet, deadened by the flowers they walked on, sounded like a flock pattering on grass.

The clergy appeared in the courtyard. Mère Simon clambered on to a chair to reach the attic window, and so looked down straight upon the shrine. Green garlands hung over the altar, which was decked with a flounce of English lace. In the middle was a small frame with relics in it; there were two orange-trees at the corners, and all along stood silver candlesticks and china vases, with sunflowers, lilies, peonies, foxgloves, and tufts of hortensia. This heap of blazing colour slanted from the level of the altar to the carpet which went on over the pavement; and some rare objects caught the eye. There was a silver-gilt sugar-basin with a crown of violets; pendants of Alençon stone glittered on the moss, and two Chinese screens displayed their landscapes. Loulou was hidden under roses, and showed nothing but his blue forehead, like a plaque of lapis lazuli.

The churchwardens, singers, and children took their places round the three sides of the court. The priest went slowly up the steps, and placed his great, radiant golden sun[16] upon the lace. Everyone knelt down. There was a deep silence; and the censers glided to and fro on the full swing of their chains.

An azure vapour rose up into Félicité's room. Her nostrils met it; she inhaled it sensuously, mystically; and then closed her eyes. Her lips smiled. The beats of her heart lessened one by one, vaguer each time and softer, as a fountain sinks, an echo disappears; and when she sighed her last breath she thought she saw an opening in the heavens, and a gigantic parrot hovering above her head.

---

[14] monstrance: The container for the consecrated host.

[15] ophicleides: A deep-toned brass wind instrument.

[16] golden sun: The monstrance.

❧ FYODOR DOSTOEVSKY
1821–1881

Perov Vasilij, *Portrait of Fyodor Dostoevsky* *Dostoevsky's inquisitive and serious nature is evident in this painting. (Art Resource)*

Like other writers of Russia's Golden Age of Literature, Dostoevsky was concerned about the challenges his divided homeland was facing: some intellectuals and artists felt that Russia, with its remote geographical location, was out of the political and social mainstream of Europe. It was lagging behind the technical and democratic times, they thought, and should hasten the process of Westernization. The progressive winds blowing over Russia carried with them socialist ideas about atheism, revolution, and social progress. After his experiences with liberal political movements as a young man, Dostoevsky began to question whether human beings were essentially rational and could act reasonably according to an ideology or if there was a dark force within them shaping behavior. In his characters he examined the boundaries of reason and the shadowy side of human consciousness. Eventually he embraced orthodox ideas about sin, penance, and forgiveness, and sided with populist, or SLAVOPHILE,[1] ideas about peasants and nationalism, Christianity, and Russia's destiny. Because of his honest and detailed depictions of Russian life, Dostoevsky is usually classified as a Realist novelist, along with Honoré de Balzac, Gustave Flaubert (p. 435), George Eliot (p. 202), Charles Dickens (p. 670), and Leo Tolstoy (p. 617), but this label is too limiting for his genius.

FYOH-dore
mik-AIL-oh-vitch
duh-stah-YEV-skee

The Young Radical. Fyodor Mikhailovich Dostoevsky was born October 30, 1821, in Moscow. His father was a doctor at a public hospital for the poor, where the family lived. This setting provided an early introduction to pain and suffering for the young Fyodor. His mother was sickly and died when he was sixteen. That same year he was enrolled at the Military Engineer's school in St. Petersburg. En route to the school he saw a government courier beat his coachman with his fists. "This revolting scene remained in my memory for the rest of my life," he wrote in 1876. During his five years of study in St. Petersburg his primary interest was literature.

Fyodor's retired father, who had had a reputation for brutality, was murdered by the peasants on his small estate while his son was away. Dostoevsky resigned his military commission in 1844, and, with some inherited money from his father, devoted himself to writing. The result was the publication of *Poor Folk* in 1846, which portrayed the lives of the lower classes. It was a big success, especially with Belinski,[2] the most important

---

[1] **Slavophile:** Someone who admires Slavs, the dominant Russian ethnicity; in nineteenth-century Russia this term meant someone who believed in the national traditions of Russia and felt that Russia had the one true religion, and someone who felt destined to export Russian teachings and to establish the kingdom of God on earth.

[2] **Belinski:** Vissarion Grigoryevich Belinsky (1811–1848), an influential critic who believed that Western reforms would benefit Russia and bring it into the modern age.

critic of the time and a champion of literary Realism and Western culture. Dostoevsky immediately became a part of the young Russian literary set with utopian, revolutionary schemes.

In reaction to the **REVOLUTION OF 1848**[3] in France and out of fear that the winds of reform might make their way to Russia, Tsar Nicholas I had socialists, including Dostoevsky, rounded up and arrested in Moscow in 1849. They were tried and sentenced to death. In a prearranged sadistic plot devised to scare the young intellectuals, they were led blindfolded before a firing squad, and at the very last moment a reprieve was granted. Not surprisingly, Dostoevsky never forgot that moment either. He spent the next four years in penal servitude in Siberia. Released in 1854, he was assigned as a common soldier to a town on the Mongolian border where he married the consumptive widow of a customs official, a disastrous marriage that lasted until her death in 1864.

A Change of Mind and Heart.   While in prison, Dostoevsky underwent a profound conversion, replacing the progressive, revolutionary ideas of his youth with a more orthodox belief in the potential in human nature for evil, the cleansing benefits of suffering, the redemptive power of love, and a faith in the prophetic mission of the Russian peasant. He also experienced the first of the epileptic seizures that would haunt him the rest of his life. After nearly ten years of exile in Siberia, which is described in *The House of the Dead* (1862), Dostoevsky was finally permitted to return to European Russia and arrived in St. Petersburg in 1859. Three years after his first wife died and following a stormy affair, he married his stenographer, Anna Gregorievna Snitkin. They fled to Europe to avoid creditors, but eventually his wife brought some semblance of order and stability to his life. Dostoevsky's money problems resulted from his brother's debts and his own debilitating gambling; meanwhile he was writing some of the finest novels of the Western world, such as *Crime and Punishment* (1866) and *The Idiot* (1868). During the last ten years of his life he enjoyed comparatively easy circumstances along with popularity and respect. *A Raw Youth* was published in 1875, and from 1876 to 1880 he wrote *The Diary of a Writer*, a monthly journal. The climax of his writing career was a novel he had worked on for years, *The Brothers Karamazov* (1880), which was a huge success. Less than a year after its publication Dostoevsky died, on January 28, 1881.

Ideas of Flesh and Blood.   Dostoevsky's novels are like laboratories where the major ideas of Europeans in the second half of the nineteenth century are dissected. The ideas are not examined abstractly as, say, in a philosophical treatise, but are embodied in flesh and blood individuals— that is, as lived ideas. Berdyaev writes that ideas for Dostoevsky "are fiery billows, never frozen categories . . . they are the destiny of living being, its burning motive-power." Typically, characters in Dostoevsky's major

www   For links to more information about Dostoevsky, a quiz on *Notes from Underground,* and a quiz on *The Brothers Karamazov,* see *World Literature Online* at bedfordstmartins .com/worldlit.

---

[3] **Revolution of 1848:** Often called the February Revolution, when the French monarchy of Louis Philippe was overthrown and the Second Republic was established.

novels are in crisis, usually because of a crime or an immoral act they've committed. Rarely are his characters seen in the context of ordinary, everyday situations, the humdrum of work or play, complacency or habit—such as we might find in Anton Chekhov's[4] short stories. Dostoevsky tends to place his protagonists in margins between freedom and captivity, love and hate, crime and forgiveness, sin and salvation, life and death. Through these intense conflicts Dostoevsky bypasses mundane concerns in order to explore the ultimate questions of existence. Even though his own inner conflicts and spiritual odyssey became the basis for a number of his fictional heroes, it would be a mistake to read Dostoevsky's novels as solely autobiographical.

The Major Novels.   In 1864 Dostoevsky used a vulgar persona to chastise Russian intellectuals in the short novel *Notes from Underground*, which initiated the period of his major novels and exhibits some of his favorite literary techniques. The title has also been translated as *Voices from Under the Floorboards*, suggesting that "underground" refers to not only a political or social position but a psychological or emotional space as well. In it a man with a wounded ego explores his own inner darkness in a tortured confessional monologue while indicting simplistic theories of social progress and the overzealous application of science to human beings. *Notes* was followed by *Crime and Punishment* in 1866, a novel that on one level is a psychological detective story in which an intelligent but desperate student murders a despicable old moneylender in order to steal enough money to continue his education. For much of the book the student, Raskolnikov, plays cat and mouse with Inspector Porfiry and his own conscience. Interwoven with the realistic, grim portraits of poor, disenfranchised urban life is the idea that, through the suffering it causes him, Raskolnikov's crime provides the occasion for his own redemption as assisted by Sonia, a saintly prostitute. In *The Idiot* (1868), Dostoevsky projects the spiritual insights of his own epileptic experiences onto his hero, Prince Myshkin, a fascinating mixture of goodness and innocence. *The Possessed* (1871) is a direct attack on the youthful revolutionaries who would use political philosophies from the West to reform Russia; indirectly Dostoevsky was answering Turgenev,[5] whose sympathies appeared to be with the Westernizers in *Fathers and Sons*. Although Dostoevsky's characters often get caught up in debating contemporary issues, it is usually the internal, psychological debate, the conflict of consciousness or conscience, that interests Dostoevsky.

The *Brothers Karamazov*, from which the selected passage, "The Grand Inquisitor," is taken, is a story of parricide. In a strangely modern family configuration, father Karamazov has one son by his first wife, two sons by his second wife, and one illegitimate son by a simpleminded

---

[4] Anton Chekhov: Chekhov (1860–1904) often used everyday settings for his characters. See p. 1187.

[5] Turgenev: Ivan Turgenev (1818–1883) looked favorably on embracing Western ideas to modernize Russia. *Fathers and Sons* was published in 1861.

peasant. The boys' mothers die and the sons are raised by relatives so that the father can pursue his crude, hedonistic ways. They grow up to be very different in personality and interests but nevertheless representative of the diverse, conflicting parts of Dostoevsky himself and contemporary society. Dmitri is passionate and tempestuous like his father. Alyosha is both innocent and saintly. The illegitimate Smerdyakov is degenerate, an epileptic who eventually kills his father. Ivan is the intellectual, torn between doubt and faith, hope and nihilism, reflecting most directly Dostoevsky's own inner division. Ivan struggles with the idea of a loving God who could permit extensive suffering on earth, especially that of innocent children. All the brothers in their own ways live life passionately.

"The Grand Inquisitor" and *Notes from Underground*.   Ivan reads "The Grand Inquisitor" to Alyosha, a work he calls his "poem in prose." Set in Spain during the INQUISITION,[6] the piece describes two kinds of Christianity: the Grand Inquisitor represents the institution of Christianity: all the structures of the church that seek to justify their own existence through the manipulation and redemption of the laity. Jesus represents another kind of Christianity: a radical kind of freedom that demands from individuals personal responsibility and choice. Dostoevsky did not intend Ivan's prose poem to be a series of answers that prescribe a course of action. As a literary gem, it is meant to raise questions and stimulate multiple interpretations. Part of Dostoevsky's genius was that he went beyond the usual boundaries of nineteenth-century consciousness and called into question the institutions and programs of Western culture, exposing a spiritual wasteland that would plague the sensibilities of modern writers.

In *Notes from Underground,* Dostoevsky created a startlingly new voice in literature, a narrator who thoroughly examines his attitudes and opinions until he arrives at a state of hyperconsciousness and inaction, living a life of deep despair and humiliation. Unlike the form of nineteenth-century Romanticism that sought elevated states of being in order to mystically experience nature, the underground man says, "to be hyperconscious is a disease." Nevertheless his despair brings an odd kind of enjoyment; as he explains, "enjoyment here consisted precisely in the hyperconsciousness of one's own degradation; it was from feeling oneself that one had reached the last barrier, that it was nasty. . . ." Acute sensitivity is preferable to decency, normalcy, and conformity.

Other confessional works of Western literature stress individualism and honesty but arrive at radically different conclusions than those of the underground man. St. Augustine's (354–430) *Confessions* deals with the baseness of human beings but offers conversion to Christianity as a salvation. Like the underground man, Jean-Jacques Rousseau (1712–1778)

> For Dostoevsky, the ultimate realities are not the external forms of life, flesh and blood men, but their inner depths, the destiny of the human spirit. Reality is the relations of man with God and with Satan, reality is the ideas by which man lives.
>
> – NICHOLAS BERDYAEV, critic, 1957

---

[6] Inquisition: Formal tribunal set up in the thirteenth century by the Roman Catholic Church to identify and punish heretics. Punishments included burning at the stake.

On the furthest horizon Dostoevsky has lit beacons of such radiant brilliance that they seem to us not terrestrial fires, but stars in heaven; but he, all the while, is at our sides, guiding their rays into our breasts — their cruelly healing lancets of light, more searing than molten steel. At every palpitation of our hearts, he says to us: "Yes, I know; and I know more, and much else besides." Amidst the roar of the maelstrom calling us, amidst the yawn of the chasm enticing us, rises the sound of his pipes, the sanity-destroying pipes of the deep. And inexorably he stands before us, with his penetrating, enigmatic gaze, the sombre and keen-eyed guide through the labyrinth of our souls, simultaneously guiding and spying upon us.

– VYACHESLAV IVANOV, critic, 1960

begins his *Confessions* with the idea that one can speak truthfully only about one's self, but then Rousseau argues that humans are naturally good and that his depravity is caused by society. Dostoevsky's narrator refuses the consolation of Christianity, and at some length he rejects any social philosophy that seeks to provide a rational explanation for human behavior. Comparing mechanistic social theories to an anthill or a piano key, he maintains that individuals will commit the most irrational acts to betray what he calls the "laws of nature, the conclusions of natural science, of mathematics."

Dostoevsky believed that the intellectual fashions of Western Europe were invading Russia and infecting its indigenous lifestyle, the Russian homeland, and spirituality. Pinning the idea of "the sublime and the beautiful" on German philosopher Immanuel Kant (1724–1804), for example, Dostoevsky warns that vague, rational ideals detract from lived experience. Speaking through his narrator, Dostoevsky insists, "We have almost reached the point of almost looking at actual 'real life' as an effort, almost as hard work, and we are all privately agreed that it is better in books." In *Notes from Underground*, rational perfection is symbolized by the Crystal Palace, a building constructed of glass and steel for a London exposition in 1851; Dostoevsky thought that such engineering marvels might satisfy material needs at the expense of the human spirit.

Dostoevsky should not, however, be wholly identified with the protagonist of *Notes*, an unreliable narrator who after all is attempting to justify his misery. The underground man takes a stand on the side of willfulness and freedom of choice — anything to contradict the abstract certainty of 2 + 2 = 4. This extreme individuality may result in wretchedness, absurdity, and shame, but it is nevertheless the highest good. In Part One of the novel the narrator's thoughts may be sympathetic, but his personal life is severely limited. Part Two is a retrospective assessment of the price the narrator has paid for hyperconsciousness. During a period of twenty years Dostoevsky's monologist slowly withdrew from human relationships: He shunned his fellow employees, he rejected his friends, and he was rejected by them. Most important, he stimulated love in Liza, a prostitute, and then declined her love. If there is any remedy for his degradation and sad solipsism, it is love; to love is to be released from the bondage of self-pity, to become involved in life. Liza, the model sinner stripped of all social respectability, nevertheless represents potential redemption for the underground man.

With this narrator and the worldview of *Notes from Underground*, Dostoevsky is a precursor to twentieth-century Existentialist writers and philosophers, for whom heightened self-consciousness is a precondition for estrangement from middle-class society. It is one of the great ironies of the modern world that sensitivity and awareness do not necessarily bring consolation, understanding, and a faith in God's goodness, but perhaps isolation and confusion. In *Notes from Underground*, as in Dostoevsky's other major works, there is only one answer to this existential predicament — love.

■ CONNECTIONS

Henrik Ibsen, *Hedda Gabler,* **p. 561.** Nineteenth-century writers criticized the middle-class institutions of marriage and religion. Ibsen portrayed marriage as enslaving, especially for women. How does Dostoevsky's Inquisitor represent religious bondage rather than spiritual freedom?

Rabindranath Tagore, *Broken Ties,* **p. 986.** A favorite theme in nineteenth-century literature and philosophy is the conflict between reason and religion. Tagore projects this conflict geographically, using Europe to represent skeptical reason and India, personal faith. How does Dostoevsky's underground man represent the dangers of rationalism?

Albert Camus, *The Guest* **(Book 6).** The *outsider* as hero originated in nineteenth-century Romanticism. Camus's Daru is the model twentieth-century outsider, the man who does not fit in and must follow his own values. How does Dostoevsky anticipate the existential hero with the underground man's extreme self-consciousness and unwillingness to conform to society's mainstream?

■ FURTHER RESEARCH

Biography
Magarshack, David. *Dostoevsky.* 1963.
Terras, F. M. *Dostoevsky: Life, Work, and Criticism.* 1984.

Historical Background
Mirsky, Dmitri. *History of Russian Literature.* 1963. Contains a broad overview of
    Russian literature and a literary context for Dostoevsky.

Criticism
Amoia, Alba della Fazia. *Fyodor Dostoevsky.* 1993. A good general introduction to
    Dostoevsky's writings.
Berdyaev, Nicholas. *Dostoevsky: An Interpretation.* 1957. This work is particularly
    interested in Dostoevsky's version of Christianity.
Ivanov, Vyacheslav. *Freedom and the Tragic Life: A Study in Dostoevsky.* 1952. Focuses on
    philosophical issues.
Jones, Malcolm, and Garth M. Terry, eds. *New Essays on Dostoevsky.* 1983.
Simmons, Ernest J. *Dostoevsky: The Making of a Novelist.* 1950. Describes the influ-
    ences that shaped Dostoevsky's maturation as a writer.
Wellek, Rene, ed. *Dostoevsky: A Collection of Critical Essays.* 1962.

■ PRONUNCIATION

Fyodor Mikhailovich Dostoevsky: FYOH-dore mik-AIL-oh-vitch duh-stah-YEV-skee

❧ Notes from Underground

Translated by Ralph E. Matlaw

PART ONE

Underground[1]

I

I am a sick man . . . I am a spiteful man. I am an unpleasant man. I think my liver is diseased. However, I don't know beans about my disease, and I am not sure what is bothering me. I don't treat it and never have, though I respect medicine and doctors. Besides, I am extremely superstitious, let's say sufficiently so to respect medicine. (I am educated enough not to be superstitious, but I am.) No, I refuse to treat it out of spite. You probably will not understand that. Well, but *I* understand it. Of course, I can't explain to you just whom I am annoying in this case by my spite. I am perfectly well aware that I cannot "get even" with the doctors by not consulting them. I know better than anyone that I thereby injure only myself and no one else. But still, if I don't treat it, it is out of spite. My liver is bad, well then—let it get even worse!

Notes from Underground. In Part One of this short novel, the narrator provides the intellectual context for his anger, suffering, and inaction. After an introduction, he explains the reasons for his suffering in sections numbered II through IV. Sections V and VI deal with the nature of a problematic mind—that is, a mind suffering from endless vacillation. Sections VII to IX are a critique of rational social theories that seem to provide either prescriptions or limitations for human behavior, symbolized by the anthill, the chicken coop, and the Crystal Palace. As he attempts to validate the irrational in human beings—that which is unpredictable and imaginative—the narrator addresses an audience, or "gentlemen," at times as an imaginary informal jury and at others as an internal critic of his interior monologue.

In Part Two, the narrator tells of three experiences that illustrate his previous theorizing: the incident with the officer, the dinner for Zverkov, and the affair with the prostitute, Liza, who interestingly represents a kind of Christlike love. Ironically, the narrator becomes trapped by his circular reasoning. His ultimate treatment of Liza is the culminating reflection of his endless philosophizing and his abject condition as a human being.

We have chosen Ralph E. Matlaw's translation of *Notes from Underground* (1960) because it does an excellent job of approximating Dostoevsky's use of idiomatic speech in this work. We have provided the footnotes.

---

[1] Underground: The author of these notes and the "Notes" themselves are, of course, imaginary. Nevertheless, such persons as the writer of these notes, not only may, but positively must, exist in our society, considering those circumstances under which our society was in general formed. I wanted to expose to the public more clearly than it is done usually, one of the characters of the recent past. He is one of the representatives of the current generation. In this excerpt, entitled "Underground," this person introduces himself, his views, and, as it were, tries to explain the reasons why he appeared and was bound to appear in our midst. In the folllowing excerpt, the actual notes of this person about several events in his life, will appear. [Dostoevsky]

I have been living like that for a long time now—twenty years. I am forty now. I used to be in the civil service, but no longer am. I was a spiteful official. I was rude and took pleasure in being so. After all, I did not accept bribes, so I was bound to find a compensation in that, at least. (A bad joke but I will not cross it out. I wrote it thinking it would sound very witty; but now that I see myself that I only wanted to show off in a despicable way, I will purposely not cross it out!) When petitioners would come to my desk for information I would gnash my teeth at them, and feel intense enjoyment when I succeeded in distressing some one. I was almost always successful. For the most part they were all timid people—of course, they were petitioners. But among the fops there was one officer in particular I could not endure. He simply would not be humble, and clanked his sword in a disgusting way. I carried on a war with him for eighteen months over that sword. At last I got the better of him. He left off clanking it. However, that happened when I was still young. But do you know, gentlemen, what the real point of my spite was? Why, the whole trick, the real vileness of it lay in the fact that continually, even in moments of the worst spleen, I was inwardly conscious with shame that I was not only not spiteful but not even an embittered man, that I was simply frightening sparrows at random and amusing myself by it. I might foam at the mouth, but bring me some kind of toy, give me a cup of tea with sugar, and I would be appeased. My heart might even be touched, though probably I would gnash my teeth at myself afterward and lie awake at night with shame for months after. That is the way I am.

I was lying when I said just now that I was a spiteful official. I was lying out of spite. I was simply indulging myself with the petitioners and with the officer, but I could never really become spiteful. Every moment I was conscious in myself of many, very many elements completely opposite to that. I felt them positively teeming in me, these opposite elements. I knew that they had been teeming in me all my life, begging to be let out, but I would not let them, would not let them, purposely would not let them out. They tormented me till I was ashamed; they drove me to convulsions, and finally, they bored me, how they bored me! Well, are you not imagining, gentlemen, that I am repenting for something now, that I am asking your forgiveness for something? I am sure you are imagining that. However, I assure you it does not matter to me if you are.

Not only could I not become spiteful, I could not even become anything: neither spiteful nor kind, neither a rascal nor an honest man, neither a hero nor an insect. Now, I am living out my life in my corner, taunting myself with the spiteful and useless consolation that an intelligent man cannot seriously become anything and that only a fool can become something. Yes, an intelligent man in the nineteenth century must and morally ought to be pre-eminently a characterless creature; a man of character, an active man is pre-eminently a limited creature. That is the conviction of my forty years. I am forty years old now, and forty years, after all, is a whole lifetime; after all, that is extreme old age. To live longer than forty years is bad manners; it is vulgar, immoral. Who does live beyond forty? Answer that, sincerely and honestly. I will tell you who do: fools and worthless people do. I tell all old men that to their face, all those respectable old men, all those silver-haired and reverend old men! I tell the whole world that to its face. I have a right to say so, for I'll go on living to sixty myself. I'll live till seventy! Till eighty! Wait, let me catch my breath.

No doubt you think, gentlemen, that I want to amuse you. You are mistaken in that, too. I am not at all such a merry person as you imagine, or as you may imagine; however, if irritated by all this babble (and I can feel that you are irritated) you decide to ask me just who I am—then my answer is, I am a certain low-ranked civil servant. I was in the service in order to have something to eat (but only for that reason), and when last year a distant relation left me six thousand roubles in his will I immediately retired from the service and settled down in my corner. I used to live in this corner before, but now I have settled down in it. My room is a wretched horrid one on the outskirts of town. My servant is an old country-woman, spiteful out of stupidity, and, moreover, she always smells bad. I am told that the Petersburg climate is bad for me, and that with my paltry means it is very expensive to live in Petersburg. I know all that better than all these sage and experienced counsellors and monitors. But I am going to stay in Petersburg. I will not leave Petersburg! I will not leave because . . . Bah, after all it does not matter in the least whether I leave or stay.

But incidentally, what can a decent man speak about with the greatest pleasure?

Answer: About himself.

Well, then, I will talk about myself.

II

Now I want to tell you, gentlemen, whether you care to hear it or not, why I could not even become an insect. I tell you solemnly that I wanted to become an insect many times. But I was not even worthy of that. I swear to you, gentlemen, that to be hyperconscious is a disease, a real positive disease. Ordinary human consciousness would be too much for man's everyday needs, that is, half or a quarter of the amount which falls to the lot of a cultivated man of our unfortunate nineteenth century, especially one who has the particular misfortune to inhabit Petersburg, the most abstract and intentional city in the whole world. (There are intentional and unintentional cities.) It would have been quite enough, for instance, to have the consciousness by which all so-called straightforward persons and men of action live. I'll bet you think I am writing all this to show off, to be witty at the expense of men of action; and what is more, that out of ill-bred showing-off, I am clanking a sword, like my officer. But, gentlemen, whoever can pride himself on his diseases and even show off with them?

However, what am I talking about? Everyone does that. They do pride themselves on their diseases, and I, perhaps, more than any one. There is no doubt about it: my objection was absurd. Yet just the same, I am firmly convinced not only that a great deal of consciousness, but that any consciousness is a disease. I insist on it. Let us drop that, too, for a minute. Tell me this: why did it happen that at the very, yes, at the very moment when I was most capable of recognizing every refinement of "all the sublime and beautiful," as we used to say at one time, I would, as though purposely, not only feel but do such hideous things, such that—well, in short, such as everyone probably does but which, as though purposely, occurred to me at the very time when I was most conscious that they ought not to be done. The more conscious

I was of goodness, and of all that "sublime and beautiful,"[2] the more deeply I sank into my mire and the more capable I became of sinking into it completely. But the main thing was that all this did not seem to occur in me accidentally, but as though it had to be so. As though it were my most normal condition, and not in the least disease or depravity, so that finally I even lost the desire to struggle against this depravity. It ended by my almost believing (perhaps actually believing) that probably this was really my normal condition. But at first, in the beginning, that is, what agonies I suffered in that struggle! I did not believe that others went through the same things, and therefore I hid this fact about myself as a secret all my life. I was ashamed (perhaps I am even ashamed now). I reached the point of feeling a sort of secret abnormal, despicable enjoyment in returning home to my corner on some disgusting Petersburg night, and being acutely conscious that that day I had again done something loathsome, that what was done could never be undone, and secretly, inwardly gnaw, gnaw at myself for it, nagging and consuming myself till at last the bitterness turned into a sort of shameful accursed sweetness, and finally into real positive enjoyment! Yes, into enjoyment, into enjoyment! I insist upon that. And that is why I have started to speak, because I keep wanting to know for a fact whether other people feel such an enjoyment. Let me explain: the enjoyment here consisted precisely in the hyperconsciousness of one's own degradation; it was from feeling oneself that one had reached the last barrier, that it was nasty, but that it could not be otherwise; that you no longer had an escape; that you could never become a different person; that even if there remained enough time and faith for you to change into something else you probably would not want to change; or if you did want to, even then you would do nothing; because perhaps in reality there was nothing for you to change into. And the worst of it, and the root of it all, was that it all proceeded according to the normal and fundamental laws of hyperconsciousness, and with the inertia that was the direct result of those laws, and that consequently one could not only not change but one could do absolutely nothing. Thus it would follow, as the result of hyperconsciousness, that one is not to blame for being a scoundrel, as though that were any consolation to the scoundrel once he himself has come to realize that he actually is a scoundrel. But enough. Bah, I have talked a lot of nonsense, but what have I explained? Can this enjoyment be explained? But I will explain it! I will get to the bottom of it! That is why I have taken up my pen.

To take an instance, I am terribly vain. I am as suspicious and touchy as a hunchback or a dwarf. But to tell the truth, there have been moments when if someone had happened to slap my face I would, perhaps, have even been glad of that. I say, very seriously, that I would probably have been able to discover a peculiar sort of enjoyment even in that—the enjoyment, of course, of despair; but in despair occur the most intense enjoyments, especially when one is very acutely conscious of one's hopeless position. As for the slap in the face—why then the consciousness of being beaten to a pulp would positively overwhelm one. The worst of it is, no matter how I

---

[2] **"Sublime and beautiful"**: Two books by European philosophers contain this or something close to this highly abstract phrase: Edmund Burke's *Philosophical Inquiry into the Origin of Our Ideas of the Sublime and Beautiful* (1756) and Immanuel Kant's *Observations on the Feeling of the Beautiful and Sublime* (1756).

tried, it still turned out that I was always the most to blame in everything, and what is most humiliating of all, to blame for no fault of my own but, so to say, through the laws of nature. In the first place, to blame because I am cleverer than any of the people surrounding me. (I have always considered myself cleverer than any of the people surrounding me, and sometimes, would you believe it, I have even been ashamed of that. At any rate, all my life, I have, as it were, looked away and I could never look people straight in the eye.) To blame, finally, because even if I were magnanimous, I would only have suffered more from the consciousness of all its uselessness. After all, I would probably never have been able to do anything with my magnanimity — neither to forgive, for my assailant may have slapped me because of the laws of nature, and one cannot forgive the laws of nature; nor to forget, for even if it were the laws of nature, it is insulting all the same. Finally, even if I had wanted to be anything but magnanimous, had desired on the contrary to revenge myself on the man who insulted me, I could not have revenged myself on anyone for anything because I would certainly never have made up my mind to do anything, even if I had been able to. Why would I not have made up my mind? I want to say a few words about that in particular.

III

After all, people who know how to revenge themselves and to take care of themselves in general, how do they do it? After all, when they are possessed, let us suppose, by the feeling of revenge, then for the time there is nothing else but that feeling left in their whole being. Such a man simply rushes straight toward his object like an infuriated bull with its horns down, and nothing but a wall will stop him. (By the way: facing the wall, such people — that is, the straightforward persons and men of action — are genuinely nonplussed. For them a wall is not an evasion, as for example for us people who think and consequently do nothing; it is not an excuse for turning aside, an excuse for which our kind is always very glad, though we scarcely believe in it ourselves, usually. No, they are nonplussed in all sincerity. The wall has for them something tranquilizing, morally soothing, final — maybe even something mysterious . . . but of the wall later.) Well, such a direct person I regard as the real normal man, as his tender mother nature wished to see him when she graciously brought him into being on the earth. I envy such a man till I am green in the face. He is stupid. I am not disputing that, but perhaps the normal man should be stupid, how do you know? Perhaps it is very beautiful, in fact. And I am all the more convinced of that suspicion, if one can call it so, by the fact that if, for instance, you take the antithesis of the normal man, that is, the hyperconscious man, who has come, of course, not out of the lap of nature but out of a retort (this is almost mysticism, gentlemen, but I suspect this, too), this retort-made man is sometimes so nonplussed in the presence of his antithesis that with all his hyperconsciousness he genuinely thinks of himself as a mouse and not a man. It may be a hyperconscious mouse, yet it is a mouse, while the other is a man, and therefore, etc. And the worst is, he himself, his very own self, looks upon himself as a mouse. No one asks him to do so. And that is an important point. Now let us look at this mouse in action. Let us suppose, for instance, that it feels insulted, too (and it almost always does feel insulted), and wants to revenge itself too. There may even be a greater accumulation of spite in it than in *l'homme de la nature et de la vérité*.[3] The base, nasty desire to repay with spite whoever has offended it, rankles perhaps even more nastily in it than in *l'homme de la nature et de la vérité*, because *l'homme de la nature et de la vérité* through his innate stupidity looks upon his revenge as justice pure and simple; while in consequence of his hyperconsciousness the mouse does not believe in the justice of it. To come at last to the deed itself, to the very act of revenge. Apart from the one fundamental nastiness the unfortunate mouse succeeds in creating around it so many other nastinesses in the form of doubts and questions, adds to the one question so many unsettled questions, that there inevitably works up around it a sort of fatal brew, a stinking mess, made up of its doubts, agitations, and lastly of the contempt spat upon it by the straightforward men of action who stand solemnly about it as judges and arbitrators, laughing at it till their healthy sides ache. Of course the only thing left for it is to dismiss all that with a wave of its paw, and, with a smile of assumed contempt in which it does not even believe itself, creep ignominiously into its mouse-hole. There, in its nasty, stinking, underground home our insulted, crushed, and ridiculed mouse promptly becomes absorbed in cold, malignant, and, above all, everlasting spite. For forty years together it will remember its injury down to the smallest, most shameful detail, and every time will add, of itself, details still more shameful, spitefully teasing and irritating itself with its own imagination. It will be ashamed of its own fancies, but yet it will recall everything, it will go over it again and again, it will invent lies against itself pretending that those things might have happened, and will forgive nothing. Maybe it will begin to revenge itself, too, but, as it were, piecemeal, in trivial ways, from behind the stove, incognito, without believing either in its own right to vengeance, or in the success of its revenge, knowing beforehand that from all its efforts at revenge it will suffer a hundred times more than he on whom it revenges itself, while he, probably will not even feel it. On its deathbed it will recall it all over again, with interest accumulated over all the years. But it is just in that cold, abominable half-despair, half-belief, in that conscious burying oneself alive for grief in the underworld for forty years, in that hyperconsciousness and yet to some extent doubtful hopelessness of one's position, in that hell of unsatisfied desires turned inward, in that fear of oscillations, of resolutions taken for ever and regretted again a minute later—that the savor of that strange enjoyment of which I have spoken lies. It is so subtle, sometimes so difficult to analyze consciously, that somewhat limited people, or simply people with strong nerves, will not understand anything at all in it. "Possibly," you will add on your own account with a grin, "people who have never received a slap in the face will not understand it either," and in that way you will politely hint to me that I, too, perhaps, have been slapped in the face in my life, and so I speak as an expert. I'll bet that you are thinking that. But set your minds at rest, gentlemen, I have not received a slap in the face, though it doesn't matter to me at all what you may think about it. Possibly, I

---

[3] *l'homme de la nature et de la vérité*: French for "the man of nature and truth." The man living close to nature is inherently good, an idea made famous by Jean-Jacques Rousseau's *Confessions* (1781–88).

even myself regret that I have given so few slaps in the face during my life. But enough, not another word on the subject of such extreme interest to you.

I will continue calmly about people with strong nerves who do not understand a certain refinement of enjoyment. Though in certain circumstances these gentlemen bellow their loudest like bulls, though this, let us suppose, does them the greatest honor, yet, as I have already said, confronted with the impossible they at once resign themselves. Does the impossible mean the stone wall? What stone wall? Why, of course, the laws of nature, the conclusions of natural science, of mathematics. As soon as they prove to you, for instance, that you are descended from a monkey, then it is no use scowling, accept it as a fact. When they prove to you that in reality one drop of your own fat must be dearer to you than a hundred thousand of your fellow creatures, and that this conclusion is the final solution of all so-called virtues and duties and all such ravings and prejudices, then you might as well accept it, you can't do anything about it, because two times two is a law of mathematics. Just try refuting it.

"But really," they will shout at you, "there is no use protesting; it is a case of two times two makes four! Nature does not ask your permission, your wishes, and whether you like or dislike her laws does not concern her. You are bound to accept her as she is, and consequently also all her conclusions. A wall, you see, is a wall — etc. etc." Good God! but what do I care about the laws of nature and arithmetic, when, for some reason, I dislike those laws and the fact that two times two makes four? Of course I cannot break through a wall by battering my head against it if I really do not have the strength to break through it, but I am not going to resign myself to it simply because it is a stone wall and I am not strong enough.

As though such a stone wall really were a consolation, and really did contain some word of conciliation, if only because it is as true as two times two makes four. Oh, absurdity of absurdities! How much better it is to understand it all, to be conscious of it all, all the impossibilities and the stone walls, not to resign yourself to a single one of those impossibilities and stone walls if it disgusts you to resign yourself; to reach, through the most inevitable, logical combinations, the most revolting conclusions on the everlasting theme that you are yourself somehow to blame even for the stone wall, though again it is as clear as day you are not to blame in the least, and therefore grinding your teeth in silent impotence sensuously to sink into inertia, brooding on the fact that it turns out that there is even no one for you to feel vindictive against, that you have not, and perhaps never will have, an object for your spite, that it is a sleight-of-hand, a bit of juggling, a card-sharper's trick, that it is simply a mess, no knowing what and no knowing who, but in spite of all these uncertainties, and jugglings, still there is an ache in you, and the more you do not know, the worse the ache.

IV

"Ha, ha, ha! Next you will find enjoyment in a toothache," you cry with a laugh.

"Well? So what? There is enjoyment even in a toothache," I answer. I had a toothache for a whole month and I know there is. In that case, of course, people are not spiteful in silence, they moan; but these are not sincere moans, they are malicious moans, and the maliciousness is the whole point. The sufferer's enjoyment finds expression in those moans; if he did not feel enjoyment in them he would not moan. It is a good example, gentlemen, and I will develop it. The moans express in the first place all the aimlessness of your pain, which is so humiliating to your consciousness; the whole legal system of Nature on which you spit disdainfully, of course, but from which you suffer all the same while she does not. They express the consciousness that you have no enemy, but that you do have a pain; the consciousness that in spite of all the dentists in the world you are in complete slavery to your teeth; that if someone wishes it, your teeth will leave off aching, and if he does not, they will go on aching another three months; and that finally if you still disagree and still protest, all that is left you for your own gratification is to thrash yourself or beat your wall with your fist as hard as you can, and absolutely nothing more. Well then, these mortal insults, these jeers on the part of someone unknown, end at last in an enjoyment which sometimes reaches the highest degree of sensuality. I beg you, gentlemen, to listen sometimes to the moans of an educated man of the nineteenth century who is suffering from a toothache, particularly on the second or third day of the attack, when he has already begun to moan not as he moaned on the first day, that is, not simply because he has a toothache, not just as any coarse peasant might moan, but as a man affected by progress and European civilization, a man who is "divorced from the soil and the national principles," as they call it these days. His moans become nasty, disgustingly spiteful, and go on for whole days and nights. And, after all, he himself knows that he does not benefit at all from his moans; he knows better than anyone that he is only lacerating and irritating himself and others in vain; he knows that even the audience for whom he is exerting himself and his whole family now listen to him with loathing, do not believe him for a second, and that deep down they understand that he could moan differently, more simply, without trills and flourishes, and that he is only indulging himself like that out of spite, out of malice. Well, sensuality exists precisely in all these consciousnesses and infamies. "It seems I am troubling you, I am lacerating your hearts, I am keeping everyone in the house awake. Well, stay awake then, you, too, feel every minute that I have a toothache. I am no longer the hero to you now that I tried to appear before, but simply a nasty person, a scoundrel. Well, let it be that way, then! I am very glad that you see through me. Is it nasty for you to hear my foul moans? Well, let it be nasty. Here I will let you have an even nastier flourish in a minute. . . ." You still do not understand, gentlemen? No, it seems our development and our consciousness must go further to understand all the intricacies of this sensuality. You laugh? I am delighted. My jokes, gentlemen, are of course in bad taste, uneven, involved, lacking self-confidence. But of course that is because I do not respect myself. Can a man with consciousness respect himself at all?

V

Come, can a man who even attempts to find enjoyment in the very feeling of self-degradation really have any respect for himself at all? I am not saying this now from any insipid kind of remorse. And, indeed, I could never endure to say, "Forgive me, Daddy, I won't do it again," not because I was incapable of saying it, but, on the contrary, perhaps just because I was too capable of it, and in what a way, too! As though on purpose I used to get into trouble on occasions when I was not to blame in the faintest way. That was the nastiest part of it. At the same time I was genuinely touched and repentant, I used to shed tears and, of course, tricked even myself, though it was not acting in the least and there was a sick feeling in my heart at the time. For that one could not even blame the laws of nature, though the laws of nature have offended me continually all my life more than anything. It is loathsome to remember it all, but it was loathsome even then. Of course, in a minute or so I would realize with spite that it was all a lie, a lie, an affected, revolting lie, that is, all this repentance, all these emotions, these vows to reform. And if you ask why I worried and tortured myself that way, the answer is because it was very dull to twiddle one's thumbs, and so one began cutting capers. That is really it. Observe yourselves more carefully, gentlemen, then you will understand that that's right! I invented adventures for myself and made up a life, so as to live at least in some way. How many times it has happened to me—well, for instance, to take offence at nothing, simply on purpose; and one knows oneself, of course, that one is offended at nothing, that one is pretending, but yet one brings oneself, at last, to the point of really being offended. All my life I have had an impulse to play such pranks, so that in the end, I could not control it in myself. Another time, twice, in fact, I tried to force myself to fall in love. I even suffered, gentlemen, I assure you. In the depth of my heart I did not believe in my suffering, there was a stir of mockery, but yet I did suffer, and in the real, regular way I was jealous, I was beside myself, and it was all out of boredom, gentlemen, all out of boredom; inertia overcame me. After all, the direct, legitimate, immediate fruit of consciousness is inertia, that is, conscious thumb twiddling. I have referred to it already, I repeat, I repeat it emphatically: all straightforward persons and men of action are active just because they are stupid and limited. How can that be explained? This way: as a result of their limitation they take immediate and secondary causes for primary ones, and in that way persuade themselves more quickly and easily than other people do that they have found an infallible basis for their activity, and their minds are at ease and that, you know, is the most important thing. To begin to act, you know, you must first have your mind completely at ease and without a trace of doubt left in it. Well, how am I, for example, to set my mind at rest? Where are the primary causes on which I am to build? Where are my bases? Where am I to get them from? I exercise myself in the process of thinking, and consequently with me every primary cause at once draws after itself another still more primary, and so on to infinity. That is precisely the essence of every sort of consciousness and thinking. It must be a case of the laws of nature again. In what does it finally result? Why, just the same. Remember I spoke just now of vengeance. (I am sure you did not grasp that.) I said that a man revenges himself because he finds justice in it. Therefore he has found a primary cause, found a basis, to wit, justice. And so he is completely set at rest, and consequently he carries out his revenge calmly and successfully, as he is convinced that he is doing a just and honest thing. But, after all, I see no justice in it, I find no sort of virtue in it either, and consequently if I attempt to revenge myself, it would only be out of spite. Spite, of course, might overcome everything, all my doubts, and could consequently serve quite successfully in a place of a primary cause, precisely because it is not a cause. But what can be done if I do not even have spite (after all, I began with that just now)? Again, in consequence of those accursed laws of consciousness, my spite is subject to chemical disintegration. You look into it, the object flies off into air, your reasons evaporate, the criminal is not to be found, the insult becomes fate rather than an insult, something like the toothache, for which no one is to blame, and consequently there is only the same outlet left again—that is, to beat the wall as hard as you can. So you give it up as hopeless because you have not found a fundamental cause. And try letting yourself be carried away by your feelings, blindly, without reflection, without a primary cause, repelling consciousness at least for a time; hate or love, if only not to sit and twiddle your thumbs. The day after tomorrow, at the latest, you will begin despising yourself for having knowingly deceived yourself. The result—a soap-bubble and inertia. Oh, gentlemen, after all, perhaps I consider myself an intelligent man only because all my life I have been able neither to begin nor to finish anything. Granted, granted I am a babbler, a harmless annoying babbler, like all of us. But what is to be done if the direct and sole vocation of every intelligent man is babble, that is, the intentional pouring of water through a sieve?

VI

Oh, if I had done nothing simply out of laziness! Heavens, how I would have respected myself then. I would have respected myself because I would at least have been capable of being lazy; there would at least have been in me one positive quality, as it were, in which I could have believed myself. Question: Who is he? Answer: A loafer. After all, it would have been pleasant to hear that about oneself! It would mean that I was positively defined, it would mean that there was something to be said about me. "Loafer"—why, after all, it is a calling and an appointment, it is a career, gentlemen. Do not joke, it is so. I would then, by rights, be a member of the best club, and would occupy myself only in continually respecting myself. I knew a gentleman who prided himself all his life on being a connoisseur of Lafitte. He considered this as his positive virtue, and never doubted himself. He died, not simply with a tranquil but with a triumphant conscience, and he was completely right. I should have chosen a career for myself then too: I would have been a loafer and a glutton, not a simple one, but, for instance, one in sympathy with everything good and beautiful. How do you like that? I have long had visions of it. That "sublime and beautiful" weighs heavily on my mind at forty. But that is when I am forty, while then—oh, then it would have been different! I would have found myself an appropriate occupation, namely, to drink to the health of everything sublime and beautiful. I would have seized every opportunity to drop a tear into my glass and then to drain it to all that is sublime and beautiful. I would then have turned everything into the sublime and the beautiful; I would have sought out the sublime and the beautiful in the nastiest, most unquestionable trash. I would have become as tearful as a wet sponge. An artist, for instance, paints Ge's picture.[4] At once I drink to the health of

---

[4] **Ge's picture:** N. N. Ge's painting, *Last Supper,* was exhibited in 1863. This sentence seems to indicate that an artist painted a picture of Ge.

the artist who painted Ge's picture, because I love all that is "sublime and beautiful." An author writes "Whatever You Like"[5]; at once I drink to the health of "Whatever You Like" because I love all that is "sublime and beautiful." I would demand respect for doing so, I would persecute anyone who would not show me respect. I would live at ease, I would die triumphantly—why, after all, it is charming, perfectly charming! And what a belly I would have grown, what a triple chin I would have established, what a red nose I would have produced for myself, so that every passer-by would have said, looking at me: "Here is an asset! Here is something really positive!" And, after all, say what you like, it is very pleasant to hear such remarks about oneself in this negative age, gentlemen.

VII

But these are all golden dreams. Oh, tell me, who first declared, who first proclaimed, that man only does nasty things because he does not know his own real interests; and that if he were enlightened, if his eyes were opened to his real normal interests, man would at once cease to do nasty things, would at once become good and noble because, being enlightened and understanding his real advantage, he would see his own advantage in the good and nothing else, and we all know that not a single man can knowingly act to his own disadvantage. Consequently, so to say, he would begin doing good through necessity. Oh, the babe! Oh, the pure, innocent child! Why, in the first place, when in all these thousands of years has there ever been a time when man has acted only for his own advantage? What is to be done with the millions of facts that bear witness that men, *knowingly,* that is, fully understanding their real advantages, have left them in the background and have rushed headlong on another path, to risk, to chance, compelled to this course by nobody and by nothing, but, as it were, precisely because they did not want the beaten track, and stubbornly, wilfully, went off on another difficult, absurd way seeking it almost in the darkness. After all, it means that this stubbornness and willfulness were more pleasant to them than any advantage. Advantage! What is advantage? And will you take it upon yourself to define with perfect accuracy in exactly what the advantage of man consists of? And what if it so happens that a man's advantage *sometimes* not only may, but even must, consist exactly in his desiring under certain conditions what is harmful to himself and not what is advantageous. And if so, if there can be such a condition then the whole principle becomes worthless. What do you think—are there such cases? You laugh; laugh away, gentlemen, so long as you answer me: Have man's advantages been calculated with perfect certainty? Are there not some which not only have been included but cannot possibly be included under any classification? After all, you, gentlemen, so far as I know, have taken your whole register of human advantages from the average of statistical figures and scientific-economic formulas. After all, your advantages are prosperity, wealth, freedom, peace—and so on, and so on. So that a man who, for instance, would openly and knowingly oppose that whole list would, to your thinking, and indeed to mine too, of course, be an

---

[5] **"Whatever You Like":** Title of an article written by M. E. Shchedrin in 1863.

obscurantist or an absolute madman, would he not? But, after all, here is something amazing: why does it happen that all these statisticians, sages, and lovers of humanity, when they calculate human advantages invariably leave one out? They don't even take it into their calculation in the form in which it should be taken, and the whole reckoning depends upon that. There would be no great harm to take it, this advantage, and to add it to the list. But the trouble is, that this strange advantage does not fall under any classification and does not figure in any list. For instance, I have a friend. Bah, gentlemen! But after all he is your friend, too; and indeed there is no one, no one, to whom he is not a friend! When he prepares for any undertaking this gentleman immediately explains to you, pompously and clearly, exactly how he must act in accordance with the laws of reason and truth. What is more, he will talk to you with excitement and passion of the real normal interests of man; with irony he will reproach the short-sighted fools who do not understand their own advantage, for the true significance of virtue; and, within a quarter of an hour, without any sudden outside provocation, but precisely through that something internal which is stronger than all his advantages, he will go off on quite a different tack—that is, act directly opposite to what he has just been saying himself, in opposition to the laws of reason, in opposition to his own advantage—in fact, in opposition to everything. I warn you that my friend is a compound personality, and therefore it is somehow difficult to blame him as an individual. The fact is, gentlemen, it seems that something that is dearer to almost every man than his greatest advantages must really exist, or (not to be illogical) there is one most advantageous advantage (the very one omitted of which we spoke just now) which is more important and more advantageous than all other advantages, for which, if necessary, a man is ready to act in opposition to all laws, that is, in opposition to reason, honor, peace, prosperity—in short, in opposition to all those wonderful and useful things if only he can attain that fundamental, most advantageous advantage which is dearer to him than all.

"Well, but it is still advantage just the same," you will retort. But excuse me, I'll make the point clear, and it is not a case of a play on words, but what really matters is that this advantage is remarkable from the very fact that it breaks down all our classifications, and continually shatters all the systems evolved by lovers of mankind for the happiness of mankind. In short, it interferes with everything. But before I mention this advantage to you, I want to compromise myself personally, and therefore I boldly declare that all these fine systems—all these theories for explaining to mankind its real normal interests, so that inevitably striving to obtain these interests, it may at once become good and noble—are, in my opinion, so far, mere logical exercises! Yes, logical exercises. After all, to maintain even this theory of the regeneration of mankind by means of its own advantage, is, after all, to my mind almost the same thing as—as to claim, for instance, with Buckle,[6] that through civilization mankind becomes softer, and consequently less bloodthirsty, and less fitted for warfare. Logically it does not seem to follow from his arguments. But man is so fond of

---

[6] **Buckle:** Thomas Buckle, in *History of Civilization in England* (1857–61), maintains that the advancement of civilization brings the end of warfare.

systems and abstract deductions that he is ready to distort the truth intentionally, he is ready to deny what he can see and hear just to justify his logic. I take this example because it is the most glaring instance of it. Only look about you: blood is being spilled in streams, and in the merriest way, as though it were champagne. Take the whole of the nineteenth century in which Buckle lived. Take Napoleon—both the Great and the present one. Take North America—the eternal union. Take farcical Schleswig-Holstein.[7] And what is it that civilization softens in us? Civilization only produces a greater variety of sensations in man—and absolutely nothing more. And through the development of this variety, man may even come to find enjoyment in bloodshed. After all, it has already happened to him. Have you noticed that the subtlest slaughterers have almost always been the most civilized gentlemen, to whom the various Attilas and Stenka Razins[8] could never hold a candle, and if they are not so conspicuous as the Attilas and Stenka Razins it is precisely because they are so often met with, are so ordinary, and have become so familiar to us. In any case if civilization has not made man more bloodthirsty, it has at least made him more abominably, more loathsomely bloodthirsty than before. Formerly he saw justice in bloodshed and with his conscience at peace exterminated whomever he thought he should. And now while we consider bloodshed an abomination, we nevertheless engage in this abomination and even more than ever before. Which is worse? Decide that for yourselves. It is said that Cleopatra[9] (pardon the example from Roman history) was fond of sticking gold pins into her slave-girls' breasts and derived enjoyment from their screams and writhing. You will say that that occurred in comparatively barbarous times; that these are barbarous times too, because (also comparatively speaking) pins are stuck in even now; that even though man has now learned to see more clearly occasionally than in barbarous times, he is still far from having *accustomed* himself to act as reason and science would dictate. But all the same you are fully convinced that he will inevitably accustom himself to it when he gets completely rid of certain old bad habits, and when common sense and science have completely re-educated human nature and turned it in a normal direction. You are confident that man will then refrain from erring *intentionally*, and will, so to say, willy-nilly, not want to set his will against his normal interests. More than that: Then, you say, science itself will teach man (though to my mind that is a luxury) that he does not really have either caprice or will of his own and that he has never had it, and that he himself is something like a piano key or an organ stop, and that, moreover, laws of nature exist in this world, so that everything he does is not done by his will at all, but is done by itself, according to the laws of nature. Consequently we have only to discover these laws of nature, and man will no longer be responsible for his actions and life will become exceedingly easy for him. All human actions will then, of course, be tabulated according to these laws, mathematically, like tables of loga-

---

[7] **Schleswig-Holstein:** Region in northern Germany contested by Denmark and Prussia in the eighteenth and nineteenth centuries.

[8] **Attilas . . . Razins:** Stenka Razin was the head of a Russian peasant revolt in 1670. Attila (d. 453), leader of the Huns, led a number of raids against the Roman empire.

[9] **Cleopatra:** (69 B.C.E.–30 B.C.E.) Queen of Egypt and the mistress of both Julius Caesar and Marc Antony.

rithms up to 108,000, and entered in a table; or, better still, there would be published certain edifying works like the present encyclopedic lexicons, in which everything will be so clearly calculated and designated that there will be no more incidents or adventures in the world.

Then—it is still you speaking—new economic relations will be established, all ready-made and computed with mathematical exactitude, so that every possible question will vanish in a twinkling, simply because every possible answer to it will be provided. Then the crystal palace[10] will be built. Then—well, in short, those will be halcyon days. Of course there is no guaranteeing (this is my comment now) that it will not be, for instance, terribly boring then (for what will one have to do when everything is calculated according to the table?) but on the other hand everything will be extraordinarily rational. Of course boredom may lead you to anything. After all, boredom even sets one to sticking gold pins into people, but all that would not matter. What is bad (this is my comment again) is that for all I know people will be thankful for the gold pins then. After all, man is stupid, phenomenally stupid. Or rather he is not stupid at all, but he is so ungrateful that you could not find another like him in all creation. After all, it would not surprise me in the least, if, for instance, suddenly for no reason at all, general rationalism in the midst of the future, a gentleman with an ignoble, or rather with a reactionary and ironical, countenance were to arise and, putting his arms akimbo, say to us all. "What do you think, gentlemen, hadn't we better kick over all that rationalism at one blow, scatter it to the winds, just to send these logarithms to the devil, and to let us live once more according to our own foolish will!" That again would not matter; but what is annoying is that after all he would be sure to find followers—such is the nature of man. And all that for the most foolish reason, which, one would think, was hardly worth mentioning: that is, that man everywhere and always, whoever he may be, has preferred to act as he wished and not in the least as his reason and advantage dictated. Why, one may choose what is contrary to one's own interests, and sometimes one *positively ought* (that is my idea). One's own free unfettered choice, one's own fancy, however wild it may be, one's own fancy worked up at times to frenzy—why that is that very "most advantageous advantage" which we have overlooked, which comes under no classification and through which all systems and theories are continually being sent to the devil. And how do these sages know that man must necessarily need a rationally advantageous choice? What man needs is simply *independent* choice, whatever that independence may cost and wherever it may lead. Well, choice, after all, the devil only knows . . .

VIII

"Ha! ha! ha! But after all, if you like, in reality, there is no such thing as choice," you will interrupt with a laugh. "Science has even now succeeded in analyzing man to such an extent that we know already that choice and what is called freedom of will are nothing other than—"

---

[10] **crystal palace:** Constructed of glass and steel, the crystal palace was exhibited at an exposition in London in 1851; at the time it was an architectural marvel of near perfection.

Wait, gentlemen, I meant to begin with that myself. I admit that I was even frightened. I was just going to shout that after all the devil only knows what choice depends on, and that perhaps that was a very good thing, but I remembered the teaching of science—and pulled myself up. And here you have begun to speak. After all, really, well, if some day they truly discover a formula for all our desires and caprices—that is, an explanation of what they depend upon, by what laws they arise, just how they develop, what they are aiming at in one case or another and so on, and so on, that is, a real mathematical formula—then, after all, man would most likely at once stop to feel desire, indeed, he will be certain to. For who would want to choose by rule? Besides, he will at once be transformed from a human being into an organ stop or something of the sort; for what is a man without desire, without free will, and without choice, if not a stop in an organ? What do you think? Let us consider the probability—can such a thing happen or not?

"H'm!" you decide. "Our choice is usually mistaken through a mistaken notion of our advantage. We sometimes choose absolute nonsense because in our stupidity we see in that nonsense the easiest means for attaining an advantage assumed beforehand. But when all that is explained and worked out on paper (which is perfectly possible, for it is contemptible and senseless to assume in advance that man will never understand some laws of nature), then, of course, so-called desires will not exist. After all, if desire should at any time come to terms completely with reason, we shall then, of course, reason and not desire, simply because, after all, it will be impossible to retain reason and *desire* something senseless, and in that way knowingly act against reason and desire to injure ourselves. And as all choice and reasoning can really be calculated, because some day they will discover the laws of our so-called free will—so joking aside, there may one day probably be something like a table of desires so that we really shall choose in accordance with it. After all, if, for instance, some day they calculate and prove to me that I stuck my tongue out at someone because I could not help sticking my tongue out at him and that I had to do it in that particular way, what sort of *freedom* is left me, especially if I am a learned man and have taken my degree somewhere? After all, then I would be able to calculate my whole life for thirty years in advance. In short, if that comes about, then, after all, we could do nothing about it. We would have to accept it just the same. And, in fact, we ought to repeat to ourselves incessantly that at such and such a time and under such and such circumstances, Nature does not ask our leave; that we must accept her as she is and not as we imagine her to be, and if we really aspire to tables and indices and well, even—well, let us say to the chemical retort, then it cannot be helped. We must accept the retort, too, or else it will be accepted without our consent."

Yes, but here I come to a stop! Gentlemen, you must excuse me for philosophizing; it's the result of forty years underground! Allow me to indulge my fancy for a minute. You see, gentlemen, reason, gentlemen, is an excellent thing, there is no disputing that, but reason is only reason and can only satisfy man's rational faculty, while will is a manifestation of all life, that is, of all human life including reason as well as all impulses. And although our life, in this manifestation of it, is often worthless, yet it is life nevertheless and not simply extracting square roots. After all, here I, for instance, quite naturally want to live, in order to satisfy all my faculties for life, and not simply my rational faculty, that is, not imply one-twentieth of all my faculties for life. What does reason know? Reason only knows what it has succeeded in learning (some things it will perhaps never learn; while this is nevertheless no comfort, why not say so frankly?) and human nature acts as a whole, with everything that is in it, consciously or unconsciously, and, even if it goes wrong, it lives. I suspect, gentlemen, that you are looking at me with compassion; you repeat to me that an enlightened and developed man, such, in short, as the future man will be, cannot knowingly desire anything disadvantageous to himself, that this can be proved mathematically. I thoroughly agree, it really can—by mathematics. But I repeat for the hundredth time, there is one case, one only, when man may purposely, consciously, desire what is injurious to himself, what is stupid, very stupid—simply in order *to have the right* to desire for himself even what is very stupid and not to be bound by an obligation to desire only what is rational. After all, this very stupid thing, after all, this caprice of ours, may really be more advantageous for us, gentlemen, than anything else on earth, especially in some cases. And in particular it may be more advantageous than any advantages even when it does us obvious harm, and contradicts the soundest conclusions of our reason about our advantage—because in any case it preserves for us what is most precious and most important—that is, our personality, our individuality. Some, you see, maintain that this really is the most precious thing for man; desire can, of course, if it desires, be in agreement with reason; particularly if it does not abuse this practice but does so in moderation, it is both useful and sometimes even praiseworthy. But very often, and even most often, desire completely and stubbornly opposes reason, and . . . and . . . and do you know that that, too, is useful and sometimes even praiseworthy? Gentlemen, let us suppose that man is not stupid. (Indeed, after all, one cannot say that about him anyway, if only for the one consideration that, if man is stupid, then, after all, who is wise?) But if he is not stupid, he is just the same monstrously ungrateful! Phenomenally ungrateful. I even believe that the best definition of man is—a creature that walks on two legs and is ungrateful. But that is not all, that is not his worst defect; his worst defect is his perpetual immorality, perpetual—from the days of the Flood to the Schleswig-Holstein period of human destiny. Immorality, and consequently lack of good sense; for it has long been accepted that lack of good sense is due to no other cause than immorality. Try it, and cast a look upon the history of mankind. Well, what will you see? Is it a grand spectacle? All right, grand, if you like. The Colossus of Rhodes,[11] for instance, that is worth something. Mr. Anaevsky[12] may well testify that some say it is the work of human hands, while others maintain that it was created by Nature herself. Is it variegated? Very well, it may be variegated too. If one only took the dress uniforms, military and civilian, of all peoples in all ages—that alone is worth something, and if you take the undress uniforms you will never get to the end

---

[11] **Colossus of Rhodes:** Large statue of Helios, the sun god, erected in the harbor of the island of Rhodes about 280 B.C.E.; considered one of the seven wonders of the world.

[12] **Anaevsky:** A. E. Anaevsky, a Russian literary critic.

of it; no historian could keep up with it. Is it monotonous? Very well. It may be monotonous, too; they fight and fight; they are fighting now, they fought first and they fought last—you will admit that it is almost too monotonous. In short, one may say anything about the history of the world—anything that might enter the most disordered imagination. The only thing one cannot say is that it is rational. The very word sticks in one's throat. And, indeed, this is even the kind of thing that continually happens. After all, there are continually turning up in life moral and rational people, sages, and lovers of humanity, who make it their goal for life to live as morally and rationally as possible, to be, so to speak, a light to their neighbors, simply in order to show them that it is really possible to live morally and rationally in this world. And so what? We all know that those very people sooner or later toward the end of their lives have been false to themselves, playing some trick, often a most indecent one. Now I ask you: What can one expect from man since he is a creature endowed with such strange qualities? Shower upon him every earthly blessing, drown him in bliss so that nothing but bubbles would dance on the surface of his bliss, as on a sea; give him such economic prosperity that he would have nothing else to do but sleep, eat cakes, and busy himself with ensuring the continuation of world history and even then man, out of sheer ingratitude, sheer libel, would play you some loathsome trick. He would even risk his cakes and would deliberately desire the most fatal rubbish, the most uneconomical absurdity, simply to introduce into all this positive rationality his fatal fantastic element. It is just his fantastic dreams, his vulgar folly, that he will desire to retain, simply in order to prove to himself (as though that were so necessary) that men still are men and not piano keys, which even if played by the laws of nature themselves threaten to be controlled so completely that soon one will be able to desire nothing but by the calendar. And, after all, that is not all: even if man really were nothing but a piano key, even if this were proved to him by natural science and mathematics, even then he would not become reasonable, but would purposely do something perverse out of sheer ingratitude, simply to have his own way. And if he does not find any means he will devise destruction and chaos, will devise sufferings of all sorts, and will thereby have his own way. He will launch a curse upon the world, and, as only man can curse (it is his privilege, the primary distinction between him and other animals) then, after all, perhaps only by his curse will he attain his object, that is, really convince himself that he is a man and not a piano key! If you say that all this, too, can be calculated and tabulated, chaos and darkness and curses, so that the mere possibility of calculating it all beforehand would stop it all, and reason would reassert itself— then man would purposely go mad in order to be rid of reason and have his own way! I believe in that, I vouch for it, because, after all, the whole work of man seems really to consist in nothing but proving to himself continually that he is a man and not an organ stop. It may be at the cost of his skin! But he has proved it; he may become a caveman, but he will have proved it. And after that can one help sinning, rejoicing that it has not yet come, and that desire still depends on the devil knows what!

You will shout at me (that is, if you will still favor me with your shout) that, after all, no one is depriving me of my will, that all they are concerned with is that my will should somehow of itself, of its own free will, coincide with my own normal interests, with the laws of nature and arithmetic.

Bah, gentlemen, what sort of free will is left when we come to tables and arithmetic, when it will all be a case of two times two makes four? Two times two makes four even without my will. As if free will meant that!

IX

Gentlemen, I am joking, of course, and I know myself that I'm joking badly, but after all you know, one can't take everything as a joke. I am, perhaps, joking with a heavy heart. Gentlemen, I am tormented by questions; answer them for me. Now you, for instance, want to cure men of their old habits and reform their will in accordance with science and common sense. But how do you know, not only that it is possible, but also that it is *desirable,* to reform man in that way? And what leads you to the conclusion that it is so *necessary* to reform man's desires? In short, how do you know that such a reformation will really be advantageous to man? And to go to the heart of the matter, why are you *so sure* of your conviction that not to act against his real normal advantages guaranteed by the conclusions of reason and arithmetic is always advantageous for man and must be a law for all mankind? After all, up to now it is only your supposition. Let us assume it to be a law of logic, but perhaps not a law of humanity at all. You gentlemen perhaps think that I am mad? Allow me to defend myself. I agree that man is pre-eminently a creative animal, predestined to strive consciously toward a goal, and to engage in engineering; that is, eternally and incessantly, to build new roads, *wherever they may lead.* But the reason why he sometimes wants to swerve aside may be precisely that he is *forced* to make that road, and perhaps, too, because however stupid the straightforward practical man may be in general, the thought nevertheless will sometimes occur to him that the road, it would seem, almost always does lead *somewhere,* and that the destination it leads to is less important than the process of making it, and that the chief thing is to save the well-behaved child from despising engineering, and so giving way to the fatal idleness, which, as we all know, is the mother of all vices. Man likes to create and build roads, that is beyond dispute. But why does he also have such a passionate love for destruction and chaos? Now tell me that! But on that point I want to say a few special words myself. May it not be that he loves chaos and destruction (after all, he sometimes unquestionably likes it very much, that is surely so) because he is instinctively afraid of attaining his goal and completing the edifice he is constructing? How do you know, perhaps he only likes that edifice from a distance, and not at all at close range, perhaps he only likes to build it and does not want to live in it, but will leave it, when completed, *aux animaux domestiques*[13] — such as the ants, the sheep, and so on, and so on. Now the ants have quite a different taste. They have an amazing edifice of that type, that endures forever — the anthill.

With the anthill, the respectable race of ants began and with the anthill they will probably end, which does the greatest credit to their perseverence and staidness. But

---

[13] *aux animaux domestiques:* French for "to domestic animals."

man is a frivolous and incongruous creature, and perhaps, like a chessplayer, loves only the process of the game, not the end of it. And who knows (one cannot swear to it), perhaps the only goal on earth to which mankind is striving lies in this incessant process of attaining, or in other words, in life itself, and not particularly in the goal which of course must always be two times two makes four, that is a formula, and after all, two times two makes four is no longer life, gentlemen, but is the beginning of death. Anyway, man has always been somehow afraid of this two times two makes four, and I am afraid of it even now. Granted that man does nothing but seek that two times two makes four, that he sails the oceans, sacrifices his life in the quest, but to succeed, really to find it—he is somehow afraid, I assure you. He feels that as soon as he has found it there will be nothing for him to look for. When workmen have finished their work they at least receive their pay, then go to the tavern, then they wind up at the police station—and there is an occupation for a week. But where can man go? Anyway, one can observe a certain awkwardness about him every time he attains such goals. He likes the process of attaining, but does not quite like to have attained, and that, of course, is terribly funny. In short, man is a comical creature; there seems to be a kind of pun in it all. But two times two makes four is, after all, something insufferable. Two times two makes four seems to me simply a piece of insolence. Two times two makes four is a fop standing with arms akimbo barring your path and spitting. I admit that two times two makes four is an excellent thing, but if we are going to praise everything, two times two makes five is sometimes also a very charming little thing.

And why are you so firmly, so triumphantly convinced that only the normal and the positive—in short, only prosperity—is to the advantage of man? Is not reason mistaken about advantage? After all, perhaps man likes something besides prosperity? Perhaps he likes suffering just as much? Perhaps suffering is just as great an advantage to him as prosperity? Man is sometimes fearfully, passionately in love with suffering and that is a fact. There is no need to appeal to universal history to prove that; only ask yourself, if only you are a man and have lived at all. As far as my own personal opinion is concerned, to care only for prosperity seems to me somehow even ill-bred. Whether it's good or bad, it is sometimes very pleasant to smash things, too. After all, I do not really insist on suffering or on prosperity either. I insist on my caprice, and its being guaranteed to me when necessary. Suffering would be out of place in vaudevilles, for instance; I know that. In the crystal palace it is even unthinkable; suffering means doubt, means negation, and what would be the good of a crystal palace if there could be any doubt about it? And yet I am sure man will never renounce real suffering, that is, destruction and chaos. Why, after all, suffering is the sole origin of consciousness. Though I stated at the beginning that consciousness, in my opinion, is the greatest misfortune for man, yet I know man loves it and would not give it up for any satisfaction. Consciousness, for instance, is infinitely superior to two times two makes four. Once you have two times two makes four, there is nothing left to do or to understand. There will be nothing left but to bottle up your five senses and plunge into contemplation. While if you stick to consciousness, even though you attain the same result, you can at least flog yourself at times, and that will, at any rate, liven you up. It may be reactionary, but corporal punishment is still better than nothing.

X

You believe in a crystal edifice that can never be destroyed; that is, an edifice at which one would neither be able to stick out one's tongue nor thumb one's nose on the sly. And perhaps I am afraid of this edifice just because it is of crystal and can never be destroyed and that one could not even put one's tongue out at it even on the sly.

You see, if it were not a palace but a chicken coop and rain started, I might creep into the chicken coop to avoid getting wet, and yet I would not call the chicken coop a palace out of gratitude to it for sheltering me from the rain. You laugh, you even say that in such circumstances a chicken coop is as good as a mansion. Yes, I answer, if one had to live simply to avoid getting wet.

But what is to be done if I have taken it into my head that this is not the only object in life, and that if one must live one may as well live in a mansion. That is my choice, my desire. You will only eradicate it when you have changed my desire. Well, do change it, tempt me with something else, give me another ideal. But in the meantime, I will not take a chicken coop for a palace. Let the crystal edifice even be an idle dream, say it is inconsistent with the laws of nature and that I have invented it only through my own stupidity, through some old-fashioned irrational habits of my generation. But what do I care if it is inconsistent? Does it matter at all, since it exists in my desires, or rather exists as long as my desires exist? Perhaps you are laughing again? Laugh away; I will put up with all your laughter rather than pretend that I am satisfied when I am hungry. I know, anyway, that I will not be appeased with a compromise, with an endlessly recurring zero, simply because it is consistent with the laws of nature and *really* exists. I will not accept as the crown of my desires a block of buildings with apartments for the poor on a lease of a thousand years and, to take care of any contingency, a dentist's shingle hanging out. Destroy my desires, eradicate my ideals, show me something better, and I will follow you. You may say, perhaps, that it is not worth your getting involved in it; but in that case, after all, I can give you the same answer. We are discussing things seriously; but if you won't deign to give me your attention, then, after all, I won't speak to you, I do have my underground.

But while I am still alive and have desires I would rather my hand were withered than to let it bring one brick to such a building! Don't remind me that I have just rejected the crystal edifice for the sole reason that one cannot put out one's tongue at it. I did not say it at all because I am so fond of putting my tongue out. Perhaps the only thing I resented was that of all your edifices up to now, there has not been a single one at which one could not put out one's tongue. On the contrary, I would let my tongue be cut off out of sheer gratitude if things could be so arranged that I myself would lose all desire to put it out. What do I care that things cannot be so arranged, and that one must be satisfied with model apartments? Why then am I made with such desires? Can I have been made simply in order to come to the conclusion that the whole way I am made is a swindle? Can this be my whole purpose? I do not believe it.

But do you know what? I am convinced that we underground folk ought to be kept in tow. Though we may be able to sit underground forty years without speaking, when we do come out into the light of day and break out we talk and talk and talk.

XI

The long and the short of it is, gentlemen, that it is better to do nothing! Better conscious inertia! And so hurrah for underground!

Though I have said that I envy the normal man to the point of exasperation, yet I would not care to be in his place as he is now (though I will not stop envying him. No, no; anyway the underground life is more advantageous!) There, at any rate, one can—Bah! But after all, even now I am lying! I am lying because I know myself as surely as two times two makes four, that it is not at all underground that is better, but something different, quite different, for which I long but which I cannot find! Damn underground!

I will tell you another thing that would be better, and that is, if I myself believed even an iota of what I have just written. I swear to you, gentlemen, that I do not really believe one thing, not even one word, of what I have just written. That is, I believe it, perhaps, but at the same time, I feel and suspect that I am lying myself blue in the face.

"Then why have you written all this?" you will say to me.

"I ought to put you underground for forty years without anything to do and then come to you to find out what stage you have reached! How can a man be left alone with nothing to do for forty years?"

"Isn't that shameful, isn't that humiliating?" you will say, perhaps, shaking your heads contemptuously. "You long for life and try to settle the problems of life by a logical tangle. And how tiresome, how insolent your outbursts are, and at the same time, how scared you are! You talk nonsense and are pleased with it; you say impudent things and are constantly afraid of them and apologizing for them. You declare that you are afraid of nothing and at the same time try to ingratiate yourself with us. You declare that you are gnashing your teeth and at the same time you try to be witty so as to amuse us. You know that your witticisms are not witty, but you are evidently well satisfied with their literary value. You may perhaps really have suffered, but you have no respect whatsoever for your own suffering. You may be truthful in what you have said but you have no modesty; out of the pettiest vanity you bring your truth to public exposure, to the market place, to ignominy. You doubtlessly mean to say something, but hide your real meaning for fear, because you lack the resolution to say it, and only have a cowardly impudence. You boast of consciousness, but you are unsure of your ground, for though your mind works, yet your heart is corrupted by depravity, and you cannot have a full, genuine consciousness without a pure heart. And how tiresome you are, how you thrust yourself on people and grimace! Lies, lies, lies!"

Of course I myself have made up just now all the things you say. That, too, is from underground. For forty years I have been listening to your words there through a crack under the floor. I have invented them myself. After all there was nothing else

I could invent. It is no wonder that I have learned them by heart and that it has taken a literary form.

But can you really be so credulous as to think that I will print all this and give it to you to read too? And another problem; why do I really call you "gentlemen," why do I address you as though you really were my readers? Such declarations as I intend to make are never printed nor given to other people to read. Anyway, I am not strong-minded enough for that, and I don't see why I should be. But you see a fancy has occurred to me and I want to fulfill it at all costs. Let me explain.

Every man has some reminiscences which he would not tell to everyone, but only to his friends. He has others which he would not reveal even to his friends, but only to himself, and that in secret. But finally there are still others which a man is even afraid to tell himself, and every decent man has a considerable number of such things stored away. That is, one can even say that the more decent he is, the greater the number of such things in his mind. Anyway, I have only lately decided to remember some of my early adventures. Till now I have always avoided them, even with a certain uneasiness. Now, however, when I am not only recalling them, but have actually decided to write them down, I want to try the experiment whether one can be perfectly frank, even with oneself, and not take fright at the whole truth. I will observe, parenthetically, that Heine[14] maintains that a true autobiography is almost an impossibility, and that man is bound to lie about himself. He considers that Rousseau certainly told lies about himself in his confessions, and even intentionally lied, out of vanity. I am convinced that Heine is right; I understand very well that sometimes one may, just out of sheer vanity, attribute regular crimes to oneself, and indeed I can very well conceive that kind of vanity. But Heine judged people who made their confessions to the public. I, however, am writing for myself, and wish to declare once and for all that if I write as though I were addressing readers, that is simply because it is easier for me to write in that way. It is merely a question of form, only an empty form—I shall never have readers. I have made this plain already.

I don't wish to be hampered by any restrictions in compiling my notes. I shall not attempt any system or method. I will jot things down as I remember them.

But here, perhaps, someone will take me at my word and ask me: if you really don't count on readers, why do you make such compacts with yourself—and on paper too—that is, that you won't attempt any system or method, that you will jot things down as you remember them, etc., etc.? Why do you keep explaining? Why do you keep apologizing?

Well, there it is, I answer.

Incidentally, there is a whole psychological system in this. Or, perhaps, I am simply a coward. And perhaps also, that I purposely imagine an audience before me in order to conduct myself in a more dignified manner while I am jotting things down. There are perhaps thousands of reasons.

And here is still something else. What precisely is my object in writing? If it is

---

[14] **Heine:** Heinrich Heine (1797–1856), German poet who accused Rousseau of lying in *Confessions*.

not for the public, then after all, why should I not simply recall these incidents in my own mind without putting them down on paper?

Quite so; but yet it is somehow more dignified on paper. There is something more impressive in it; I will be able to criticize myself better and improve my style. Besides, perhaps I will really get relief from writing. Today, for instance, I am particularly oppressed by a certain memory from the distant past. It came back to my mind vividly a few days ago, and since then, has remained with me like an annoying tune that one cannot get rid of. And yet I must get rid of it. I have hundreds of such memories, but at times some single one stands out from the hundreds and oppresses me. For some reason I believe that if I write it down I will get rid of it. Why not try?

Besides, I am bored, and I never do anything. Writing will really be a sort of work. They say work makes man kindhearted and honest. Well, here is a chance for me, anyway.

It is snowing today. A wet, yellow, dingy snow. It fell yesterday too and a few days ago. I rather think that I remembered that incident which I cannot shake off now, apropos of the wet snow. And so let it be a story apropos of the wet snow.

PART TWO

Apropos of the Wet Snow

> When from the gloom of corruption
> I delivered your fallen soul
> With the ardent speech of conviction;
> And, full of profound torment,
> Wringing your hands, you cursed
> The vice that ensnared you;
> When, with memories punishing
> Forgetful conscience
> You told me the tale
> Of all that happened before me,
> And suddenly, covering your face,
> Full of shame and horror,
> You tearfully resolved,
> Outraged, shocked. . . .
> *Etc., etc., etc.*
> FROM THE POETRY OF N. A. NEKRASOV.[15]

I

At that time I was only twenty-four. My life was even then gloomy, disorganized, and solitary to the point of savagery. I made friends with no one and even avoided talking, and hid myself in my corner more and more. At work in the office I even tried never to look at anyone, and I was very well aware that my colleagues looked upon me, not only as a crank, but looked upon me—so I always thought—seemed to

---

[15] Nekrasov: Russian poet Nikolay A. Nekrasov (1821–1878).

look upon me with a sort of loathing. I sometimes wondered why no one except me thought that he was looked upon with loathing. One of our clerks had a repulsive, pock-marked face, which even looked villainous. I believe I would not have dared to look at anyone with such an unsightly face. Another had a uniform so worn that there was an unpleasant smell near him. Yet not one of these gentlemen was disconcerted either by his clothes or his face or in some moral sense. Neither of them imagined that he was looked at with loathing, and even if he had imagined it, it would not have mattered to him, so long as his superiors did not look at him in that way. It is perfectly clear to me now that, owing to my unbounded vanity and, probably, to the high standard I set for myself, I very often looked at myself with furious discontent, which verged on loathing, and so I inwardly attributed the same view to everyone. For instance, I hated my face; I thought it disgusting, and even suspected that there was something base in its expression and therefore every time I turned up at the office I painfully tried to behave as independently as possible so that I might not be suspected of being base, and to give my face as noble an expression as possible. "Let my face even be ugly," I thought, "but let it be noble, expressive, and, above all, *extremely* intelligent." But I was absolutely and painfully certain that my face could never express those perfections; but what was worst of all, I thought it positively stupid-looking. And I would have been quite satisfied if I could have looked intelligent. In fact, I would even have put up with looking base if, at the same time, my face could have been thought terribly intelligent.

Of course, I hated all my fellow-clerks, one and all, and I despised them all, yet at the same time I was, as it were, afraid of them. It happened at times that I even thought more highly of them than of myself. It somehow happened quite suddenly then that I alternated between despising them and thinking them superior to myself. A cultivated and decent man cannot be vain without setting an inordinately high standard for himself, and without despising himself at certain moments to the point of hatred. But whether I despised them or thought them superior I dropped my eyes almost every time I met anyone. I even made experiments whether I could face So-and-So's looking at me, and I was always the first to drop my eyes. This tormented me to the point of frenzy. I was also morbidly afraid of being ridiculous, and so I slavishly worshipped the conventional in everything external. I loved to fall into the common rut, and had a whole-hearted terror of any kind of eccentricity in myself. But how could I live up to it? I was morbidly cultivated as a cultivated man of our age should be. They were all dull, and as like one another as so many sheep. Perhaps I was the only one in the office who constantly thought that I was a coward and a slave, and I thought it precisely because I was cultivated. But I did not only think it, in actuality it was really so. I was a coward and a slave. I say this without the slightest embarrassment. Every decent man in our age must be a coward and a slave. That is his normal condition. I am profoundly convinced of that. He is made that way and is constructed for that very purpose. And not only at the present time owing to some casual circumstances, but always, at all times, a decent man must be a coward and a slave. That is the law of nature for all decent people on the earth. If any one of them happens to be brave about something, he need not be comforted or carried away by that; he will funk out just the same before something else. That is how it invariably and inevitably ends. Only asses and mules are brave, and even they are so only until they come up against the wall. It is not even worth while to pay attention to them. Because they don't mean anything at all.

Still another circumstance tormented me in those days: that no one resembled me and that I resembled no one else. "I am alone and they are *every one*," I thought—and pondered.

From that it can be seen that I was still an absolute child.

The very opposite sometimes happened. After all, how vile it sometimes seemed to have to go to the office; things reached such a point that I often came home ill. But all at once, for no rhyme or reason, there would come a phase of skepticism and indifference (everything happened to me in phases), and I would myself laugh at my intolerance and fastidiousness. I would reproach myself with being *romantic.* Sometimes I was unwilling to speak to anyone, while at other times I would not only talk, but even think of forming a friendship with them. All my fastidiousness would suddenly vanish for no rhyme or reason. Who knows, perhaps I never had really had it, and it had simply been affected, and gotten out of books. I have still not decided that question even now. Once I quite made friends with them, visited their homes, played preference,[16] drank vodka, talked of promotions . . . But here let me make a digression.

We Russians, speaking generally, have never had those foolish transcendental German, and still more, French, romantics on whom nothing produces any effect; if there were an earthquake, if all France perished at the barricades, they would still be the same, they would not even change for decency's sake, but would still go on singing their transcendental songs, so to speak, to the hour of their death, because they are fools. We, in Russia, have no fools; that is well known. That is what distinguishes us from foreign lands. Consequently those transcendental natures do not exist among us in their pure form. We only think they do because our "positivistic" journalists and critics of that time, always on the hunt for Kostanzhoglos and Uncle Peter Ivaniches[17] and foolishly accepting them as our ideal, slandered our romantics, taking them for the same transcendental sort that exists in Germany or France. On the contrary, the characteristics of our romantics are absolutely and directly opposed to the transcendental European type, and not a single European standard can be applied to them. (Allow me to make use of this word "romantic"—an old-fashioned and much-respected word which has done good service and is familiar to all.) The characteristics of our romantics are to understand everything, *to see everything and often to see it incomparably more clearly than our most positivistic minds see it;* to refuse to accept anyone or anything, but at the same time not to despise anything; to give way, to yield, from policy; never to lose sight of a useful practical goal (such as rent-free government quarters, pensions, decorations), to keep their eye on that object through all the enthusiasms and volumes of lyrical poems, and at the same time to preserve "the sublime and the beautiful" inviolate within them to the

---

[16] preference: A card game.

[17] Kostanzhoglos . . . Ivaniches: Characters in Part II of Gogol's *Dead Souls* and Goncharov's *The Same Old Story,* respectively. [Translator]

hour of their death, and also, incidentally, to preserve themselves wrapped in cotton, like some precious jewel if only for the benefit of "the sublime and the beautiful." Our romantic is a man of great breadth and the greatest rogue of all our rogues, I assure you. I can even assure you from experience. Of course all that occurs if he is intelligent. But what am I saying! The romantic is always intelligent, and I only meant to observe that although we have had foolish romantics they don't count, and they were only so because in the flower of their youth they degenerated completely into Germans, and to preserve their precious jewel more comfortably, settled some-where out there—by preference in Weimar or the Black Forest. I, for instance, gen-uinely despised my official work and did not openly abuse it simply through necessity because I was in it myself and got a salary for it. And, as a result, take note, I did not openly abuse it. Our romantic would rather go out of his mind (which inci-dentally happened very rarely) than abuse it, unless he had some other career in view; and he is never kicked out, unless, of course, he is taken to the lunatic asylum as "the King of Spain"[18] and then only if he went very mad. But after all, it is only the thin, fair people who go out of their minds in Russia. Innumerable romantics later in life rise to considerable rank in the service. Their versatility is remarkable! And what a faculty they have for the most contradictory sensations! I was comforted by those thoughts even in those days, and I am so still. That is why there are so many "broad natures" among us who never lose their ideal even in the depths of degradation; and though they never lift a finger for their ideal, though they are arrant thieves and rob-bers, yet they tearfully cherish their first ideal and are extraordinarily honest at heart. Yes, only among us can the most arrant rogue be absolutely and even loftily honest at heart without in the least ceasing to be a rogue. I repeat, our romantics, after all, frequently become such accomplished rascals (I use the term "rascals" affec-tionately), suddenly display such a sense of reality and practical knowledge, that their bewildered superiors and the public can only gape in amazement at them.

Their many-sidedness is really astounding, and goodness knows what it may turn itself into under future circumstances, and what lies in store for us later on. They are good stuff! I do not say this out of any foolish or boastful patriotism. But I feel sure that you are again imagining that I am joking. Or perhaps it's just the con-trary, and you are convinced that I really think so. Anyway, gentlemen, I shall wel-come both views as an honor and a special favor. And do forgive my digression.

I did not, of course, maintain a friendship with my comrades and soon was at loggerheads with them, and in my youthful inexperience I even gave up bowing to them, as though I had cut off all relations. That, however, only happened to me once. As a rule, I was always alone.

In the first place, at home, I spent most of my time reading. I tried to stifle all that was continually seething within me by means of external sensations. And the only source of external sensation possible for me was reading. Reading was a great help, of course, it excited, delighted, and tormented me. But at times it bored me

---

[18] **"the King of Spain":** The hero of Gogol's short story "Diary of a Madman" (1835) goes insane believing he is the king of Spain.

terribly. One longed for movement just the same, and I plunged all at once into dark, subterranean, loathsome—not vice but petty vice. My petty passions were acute, smarting, from my continual sickly irritability. I had hysterical fits, with tears and convulsions. I had no resource except reading—that is, there was then nothing in my surroundings which I could respect and which attracted me. I was overwhelmed with depression, too; I had an hysterical craving for contradictions and for contrast, and so I took to vice. I have not said all this to justify myself, after all—but no, I am lying. I did want to justify myself. I make that little observation for my own benefit, gentlemen. I don't want to lie. I vowed to myself I would not.

I indulged my vice in solitude at night, furtively, timidly, filthily, with a feeling of shame which never deserted me, even at the most loathsome moments, and which at such moments drove me to curses. Even then I already had the underground in my soul. I was terribly afraid of being seen, of being met, of being recognized. I visited various completely obscure places.

One night as I was passing a tavern, I saw through a lighted window some gentlemen fighting with billiard cues, and saw one of them thrown out of the window. At another time I would have felt very much disgusted, but then I was suddenly in such a mood that I actually envied the gentleman thrown out of the window, and I envied him so much that I even went into the tavern and into the billiard-room. "Perhaps," I thought, "I'll have a fight, too, and they'll throw me out of the window."

I was not drunk, but what is one to do—after all, depression will drive a man to such a pitch of hysteria. But nothing happened. It seemed that I was not even equal to being thrown out of the window and I went away without having fought.

An officer put me in my place from the very first moment.

I was standing by the billiard-table and in my ignorance blocking up the way, and he wanted to pass; he took me by the shoulders and without a word—without a warning or an explanation—moved me from where I was standing to another spot and passed by as though he had not noticed me. I could even have forgiven blows, but I absolutely could not forgive his having moved me and so completely failing to notice me.

Devil knows what I would then have given for a real regular quarrel—a more decent, a more *literary* one, so to speak. I had been treated like a fly. This officer was over six feet, while I am short and thin. But the quarrel was in my hands. I had only to protest and I certainly would have been thrown out of the window. But I changed my mind and preferred to beat a resentful retreat.

I went out of the tavern straight home, confused and troubled, and the next night I continued with my petty vices, still more furtively, abjectly, and miserably than before, as it were, with tears in my eyes—but still I did continue them. Don't imagine, though, that I funked out on the officer through cowardice. I have never been a coward at heart, though I have always been a coward in action. Don't be in a hurry to laugh. There is an explanation for it. I have an explanation for everything, you may be sure.

Oh, if only that officer had been one of the sort who would consent to fight a duel! But no, he was one of those gentlemen (alas, long extinct!) who preferred fighting with cues, or, like Gogol's Lieutenant Pirogov, appealing to the police. They did not fight duels and would have thought a duel with a civilian like me an utterly un-seemly procedure in any case—and they looked upon the duel altogether as some-thing impossible, something free-thinking and French, but they were quite ready to insult people, especially when they were over six feet.

I did not funk out through cowardice here but through unbounded vanity. I was not afraid of his six feet, not of getting a sound thrashing and being thrown out of the window; I would probably have had sufficient physical courage; but I lacked suf-ficient moral courage. What I was afraid of was that everyone present, from the inso-lent marker down to the lowest little stinking pimply clerk hanging around in a greasy collar, would jeer at me and fail to understand when I began to protest and to address them in literary language. For even now we cannot, after all, speak of the point of honor—not of honor, but of the point of honor (*point d'honneur*)—except in literary language. You cannot allude to the "point of honor" in ordinary language. I was fully convinced (the sense of reality, in spite of all romanticism!) that they would all simply split their sides with laughter and that the officer would not simply, that is, not uninsultingly, beat me, but would certainly prod me in the back with his knee, kick me round the billiard-table that way and only then perhaps have pity and throw me out of the window. Of course, this trivial incident could not have ended like that with me. I often met that officer afterward in the street and observed him very carefully. I am not quite sure whether he recognized me. I imagine not; I judge from certain signs. But I—I stared at him with spite and hatred and so it went on—for several years! My resentment even grew deeper with the years. At first I began making stealthy inquiries about this officer. It was difficult for me to do so, for I knew no one. But one day I heard someone call him by his name in the street when I was following him at a distance, just as though I were tied to him—and so I learned his surname. Another time I followed him to his flat, and for a few pennies learned from the porter where he lived, on which floor, whether he lived alone or with others, and so on—in fact, everything one could learn from a porter. One morning, though I had never tried to write anything before, it suddenly occurred to me to describe this officer in the form of an exposé, in a satire, in a tale. I wrote the tale with relish. I did expose him. I slandered him; at first I so altered his name that it could easily be recognized but on second thought I changed it, and sent the story to the *Annals of the Fatherland*. But at that time such exposés were not yet the fashion and my story was not printed. That was a great vexation to me. Sometimes I was positively choked with resentment. At last I decided to challenge my enemy to a duel. I composed a splendid, charming letter to him, imploring him to apologize to me, and hinting rather plainly at a duel in case of refusal. The letter was so composed that if the officer had had the least understanding of the "sublime and the beautiful" he would certainly have rushed to me to fling himself on my neck and to offer me his friendship. And how fine that would have been! How we would have gotten along! How we would have gotten along! "He could have shielded me with his higher rank, while I could have improved his mind with my culture, and, well—my ideas, and all sorts of things might have happened." Just think, this was two years after his insult to me, and my challenge was the most ridiculous anachronism, in spite of all the inge-nuity of my letter in disguising and explaining away the anachronism. But, thank

God (to this day I thank the Almighty with tears in my eyes), I did not send the letter to him. Cold shivers run down my back when I think of what might have happened if I had sent it. And all at once I revenged myself in the simplest way, by a stroke of genius! A brilliant thought suddenly dawned upon me. Sometimes on holidays I used to stroll along the sunny side of the Nevsky between three and four in the afternoon. That is, I did not stroll so much as experience innumerable torments, humiliations, and resentments; but no doubt that was just what I wanted. I used to wriggle like an eel among the passers-by in the most unbecoming fashion, continually moving aside to make way for generals, for officers of the Guards and the Hussars, or for ladies. In those minutes I used to feel a convulsive twinge at my heart, and hot all the way down my back at the mere thought of the wretchedness of my dress, of the wretchedness and vulgarity of my little wriggling figure. This was a regular martyrdom, a continual, intolerable humiliation at the thought, which passed into an incessant and direct sensation, that I was a fly in the eyes of this whole world, a nasty, disgusting fly—more intelligent, more cultured, more noble than any of them, of course, but a fly that was continually making way for everyone, insulted and humiliated by everyone. Why I inflicted this torment upon myself, why I went to the Nevsky, I don't know. I felt simply *drawn* there at every possible opportunity.

Already then I began to experience a rush of the enjoyment of which I spoke in the first chapter. After my affair with the officer I felt even more drawn there than before: it was on the Nevsky that I met him most frequently, it was *there* that I could admire him. He, too, went there chiefly on holidays. He, too, made way for generals and persons of high rank, and he, too, shifted among them like an eel; but people like me, or even neater than I, he simply walked over; he made straight for them as though there was nothing but empty space before him, and never, under any circumstances, moved aside. I gloated over my resentment watching him and—resentfully made way for him every time. It tormented me that even in the street I could not be on an even footing with him. "Why must you invariably be the first to move aside?" I kept asking myself in hysterical rage, waking up sometimes at three o'clock in the morning. "Why precisely you and not he? After all, there's no regulation about it; after all, there's no written law about it. Let the making way be equal as it usually is when refined people meet; he moves halfway and you move halfway; you pass with mutual respect." But that never happened, and I always made way, while he did not even notice I moved aside for him. And lo and behold the most astounding idea dawned upon me! "What," I thought, "if I meet him and—don't move aside? What if I don't move aside on purpose, even if I were to bump into him? How would that be?" This audacious idea little by little took such a hold on me that it gave me no peace. I dreamt of it continually, terribly, and I purposely went to the Nevsky more frequently in order to picture more vividly how I would do it when I did do it. I was delighted. This plan seemed to me more and more practical and possible. "Of course I will not really bump him," I thought, already more good-natured in my joy. "I will simply not turn aside, will bump against him, not very violently, but just shouldering each other—just as much as decency permits. I will bump him just as much as he bumps me." At last I made up my mind completely. But my preparations took a great deal of time. To begin with, when I carried out my plan I would have to look rather more decent, and I had to think of my clothes. "In any case, if, for instance, there were any sort of public scandal (and the public there is of the most *superflu*:[19] the Countess walks there; Prince D. walks there; the whole literary world is there), I would have to be well dressed; that inspires respect and of itself puts us in some way on equal footing in the eyes of high society." With that in mind I asked for my salary in advance, and bought at Churkin's a pair of black gloves and a decent hat. Black gloves seemed to me both more dignified and *bon ton*[20] than the lemon-colored ones which I had contemplated at first. "The color is too gaudy, it looks as though one were trying to be conspicuous," and I did not take the lemon-colored ones. I had gotten ready a good shirt, with the bone studs, long beforehand; but my overcoat very much delayed me. The coat in itself was a very good one, it kept me warm; but it was wadded and it had a raccoon collar which was the height of vulgarity. I had to change the collar at any sacrifice, and to have a beaver one like an officer's. For this purpose I began visiting the Gostiny Dvor and after several attempts I lit on a piece of cheap German beaver. Though these German beavers very soon wear out and look shabby, at first, when new, they look exceedingly well, and after all, I only needed it for one occasion. I asked the price; even so, it was too expensive. After thinking it over thoroughly I decided to sell my raccoon collar. The rest of the money—a considerable sum for me, I decided to borrow from Anton Antonich Syetochkin, my superior, an unassuming person, but grave and dependable. He never lent money to anyone, but I had, on entering the service, been specially recommended to him by an important personage who had got me my job. I was terribly worried. To borrow from Anton Antonich seemed to me monstrous and shameful. I did not sleep for two or three nights, and indeed I did not sleep well in general at that time, I was in a fever; I had a vague sinking at my heart or suddenly it would start to throb, throb, throb! Anton Antonich was at first surprised, then he frowned, then he reflected, and did after all lend me the money, receiving from me a written authorization to take from my salary a fortnight later the sum that he had lent me. In this way everything was at last ready. The handsome beaver was established in place of the mean-looking raccoon, and I began by degrees to get to work. It would never have done to act offhand, at random; the plan had to be carried out skillfully, by degrees. But I must confess that after many efforts I almost even began to despair; we could not run into each other and that is all there was to it. I made every preparation, I was quite determined—it seemed as though we would run into one another directly—and before I knew what I was doing I had stepped aside for him again and he had passed without noticing me. I even prayed as I approached him that God would grant me determination. One time I had made up my mind thoroughly, but it ended in my stumbling and falling at his feet because at the very last instant when I was only some six inches from him my courage failed me. He very calmly stepped over me, while I flew to one side like a ball. That night I was ill again, feverish and delirious. And suddenly it ended most happily. The night before I had made up my mind not to carry out my fatal plan and to abandon it all, and with that goal in mind

---

[19] *superflu:* French for "overly refined."   [20] *bon ton:* French for "good taste."

I went to the Nevsky for the last time, just to see how I would abandon it all. Suddenly, three paces from my enemy, I unexpectedly made up my mind—I closed my eyes, and we ran full tilt, shoulder to shoulder, into each other! I did not budge an inch and passed him on a perfectly equal footing! He did not even look round and pretended not to notice it; but he was only pretending, I am convinced of that. I am convinced of that to this day! Of course, I got the worst of it—he was stronger, but that was not the point. The point was that I had attained my goal, I had kept up my dignity. I had not yielded a step, and had put myself publicly on an equal social footing with him. I returned home feeling that I was perfectly avenged for everything. I was delighted. I was triumphant and sang Italian arias. Of course, I will not describe to you what happened to me three days later; if you have read my first chapter "Underground," you can guess for yourself. The officer was afterward transferred; I have not seen him now for fourteen years. What is the dear fellow doing now? Whom is he walking over?

II

But the period of my dissipation would end and I always felt terribly sick afterward. It was followed by remorse—I tried to drive it away; I felt too sick. By degrees, however, I grew used to that, too. I grew used to everything, that is, I did not really grow used to it, but rather I voluntarily resigned myself to enduring it. But I had a means of escape that reconciled everything—that was to find refuge in "the sublime and the beautiful," in dreams. Of course I was a terrible dreamer. I would dream for three months on end, tucked away in my corner, and you may believe me that at those moments I had no resemblance to the gentleman who, in his chicken-hearted anxiety, put a German beaver collar on his greatcoat. I suddenly became a hero. I would not have received my six-foot lieutenant even if he had called on me. I could not even picture him before me then. What were my dreams and how I could satisfy myself with them, it is hard to say now, but at the time I did satisfy myself with them, to some extent. Dreams were particularly sweet and vivid after a little vice; they came with remorse and with tears, with curses and transports. There were moments of such positive intoxication, of such happiness, that there was not the faintest trace of irony within me, on my honor. I had faith, hope, love. That is just it. I believed blindly at such times that by some miracle, through some external circumstance, all this would suddenly open out, expand; that suddenly a vista of suitable activity—beneficial, good, and above all, *ready-made* (what sort of activity I had no idea, but the great thing was that it should be all ready for me)—would rise up before me, and I should come out into the light of day, almost riding a white horse and crowned with laurel. I could not conceive of a secondary role for myself, and for that reason I quite contentedly played the lowest one in reality. Either to be a hero or to grovel in the mud—there was nothing between. That was my ruin, for when I was in the mud I comforted myself with the thought that at other times I was a hero, and I took refuge in this hero for the mud: for an ordinary man, say, it is shameful to defile himself, but a hero is too noble to be utterly defiled, and so he might defile himself. It is worth noting that these attacks of "the sublime and the beautiful" visited me even during the period of vice and just at the times when I had sunk to the very bottom.

They came in separate spurts, as though reminding me of themselves, but did not banish the vice by their appearance. On the contrary, they seemed to add a zest to it by contrast, and were only sufficiently present to serve as an appetizing sauce. That sauce was made up of contradictions and sufferings, of agonizing inward analysis, and all these torments and pin-pricks lent my vice a certain piquancy, even a significance—in short, completely fulfilled the function of a good sauce. There was even a certain depth of meaning in it. And I could hardly have restrained myself to the simple, vulgar, direct clerk-like vice and have endured all the filthiness of it. What could have attracted me about it then and have driven me at night into the street? No, I had a noble loophole for everything.

And what love, oh Lord, what love I felt at times in those dreams of mine! In those "flights into the sublime and the beautiful"; though it was fantastic love, though it was never applied to anything human in reality, yet there was so much of this love that afterward one did not even feel the impulse to apply it in reality; that would have been a superfluous luxury. Everything, however, always passed satisfactorily by a lazy and fascinating transition into the sphere of art; that is, into the beautiful forms of life, ready made, violently stolen from the poets and novelists and adapted to all sorts of needs and uses. I, for instance, was triumphant over everyone; everyone, of course, lay in the dust and was forced to recognize my superiority spontaneously, and I forgave them all. I, a famous poet, and a courtier, fell in love; I inherited countless millions and immediately devoted them to humanity, and at the same time I confessed before all the people my shameful deeds, which, of course, were not merely shameful, but contained an enormous amount of "the sublime and the beautiful," something in the Manfred[21] style. Everyone would weep and kiss me (what idiots they would be if they did not), while I would go barefoot and hungry preaching new ideas and fighting a victorious Austerlitz[22] against the reactionaries. Then a march would sound, an amnesty would be declared, the Pope would agree to retire from Rome to Brazil; then there would be a ball for the whole of Italy at the Villa Borghese[23] on the shores of Lake Como, Lake Como being for that purpose transferred to the neighborhood of Rome; then would come a scene in the bushes, etc., etc.—as though you did not know all about it! You will say that it is vulgar and base to drag all this into public after all the tears and raptures I have myself admitted. But why is it base? Can you imagine that I am ashamed of it all, and that is was stupider than anything in your life, gentlemen? And I can assure you that some of these fancies were by no means badly composed. Not everything took place on the shores of Lake Como. And yet you are right—it really is vulgar and base. And what is most base of all is that I have now started to justify myself to you. And even more base than that is my making this remark now. But that's enough, or, after all, there will be no end to it; each step will be more base than the last.

I could never stand more than three months of dreaming at a time without feeling an irresistible desire to plunge into society. To plunge into society meant to visit

---

[21] **Manfred:** The defiant hero of Byron's poem *Manfred* (1817).

[22] **Austerlitz:** Scene of Napoleon's victory over the Russian and Austrian armies in 1805.

[23] **Villa Borghese:** An elegant palace built by Cardinal Borghese.

my superior, Anton Antonich Syetochkin. He was the only permanent acquaintance I have had in my life, and I even wonder at the fact myself now. But I even went to see him only when that phase came over me, and when my dreams had reached such a point of bliss that it became essential to embrace my fellows and all mankind immediately. And for that purpose I needed at least one human being at hand who actually existed. I had to call on Anton Antonich, however, on Tuesday—his at-home day; so I always had to adjust my passionate desire to embrace humanity so that it might fall on a Tuesday. This Anton Antonich lived on the fourth floor in a house in Five Corners, in four low-pitched rooms of a particularly frugal and sallow appearance, one smaller than the next. He had two daughters and their aunt, who used to pour out the tea. Of the daughters one was thirteen and another fourteen, they both had snub noses, and I was terribly embarrassed by them because they were always whispering and giggling together. The master of the house usually sat in his study on a leather couch in front of the table, with some gray-headed gentleman, usually a colleague from our office or even some other department. I never saw more than two or three visitors there, and those always the same. They talked about the excise duty, about business in the senate, about salaries, about promotions, about His Excellency, and the best means of pleasing him, and so on, and so on. I had the patience to sit like a fool beside these people for four hours at a stretch, listening to them without knowing what to say to them or venturing to say a word. I became stupefied; several times I felt myself perspiring. I was overcome by a sort of paralysis; but that was pleasant and useful for me. On returning home I deferred for a time my desire to embrace all mankind.

I had, however, one other acquaintance of a sort, Simonov, who was an old schoolfellow. Indeed I had a number of schoolfellows in Petersburg, but I did not associate with them and had even given up nodding to them in the street. Perhaps I even transferred into the department I was in simply to avoid their company and to cut off at one stroke all connection with my hateful childhood. Curses on that school and all those terrible years of penal servitude! In short, I parted from my schoolfellows as soon as I got out into the world. There were two or three left to whom I nodded in the street. One of them was Simonov, who had been in no way distinguished at school, was of a quiet and even disposition; but I discovered in him a certain independence of character and even honesty. I don't even suppose that he was particularly limited. I had at one time spent some rather soulful moments with him, but these had not lasted long and had somehow been suddenly clouded over. He was evidently uncomfortable at these reminiscences, and was, it seemed, always afraid that I might take up the same tone again. I suspected that he had an aversion for me, but I still went on going to see him, not being completely certain of it.

And so on one occasion, on a Thursday, unable to endure my solitude and knowing that it was Thursday Anton Antonich's door would be closed, I thought of Simonov. Climbing up four floors to his place, I was thinking that I made the man uncomfortable and that it was a mistake to go to see him. But as it always happened that such reflections impelled me even more strongly, as though purposely, to put myself into a false position, I went in. It was almost a year since I had last seen Simonov.

III

I found two more of my old schoolfellows with him. They seemed to be discussing an important matter. All of them scarcely took any notice of my entrance, which was strange, for I had not seen them for years. Evidently they looked upon me as something on the level of a common fly. I had not been treated like that even at school, although everybody hated me there. I knew, of course, that they must despise me now for my lack of success in the service, and for having let myself sink so low, going about badly dressed and so on which seemed to them a sign of my inaptitude and insignificance. But nevertheless I had not expected such contempt. Simonov even seemed surprised at my turning up. Even in the old days he had always seemed surprised at my coming. All this disconcerted me; I sat down, feeling rather miserable, and began listening to what they were saying.

They were engaged in an earnest and even heated discussion about a farewell dinner these gentlemen wanted to arrange together the very next day for their friend Zverkov, an officer in the army, who was going away to a distant province. Monsieur Zverkov had been all the time at school with me too. I had begun to hate him particularly in the upper classes. In the lower classes he had simply been a pretty, playful boy whom everybody liked. I had hated him, however, even in the lower classes, just because he was a pretty and playful boy. He was always consistently poor in his work, and got worse and worse as he went on; nevertheless he was successfully graduated as influence was exerted on his behalf. During his last year at school he inherited an estate of two hundred serfs, and as almost all of us were poor he even started to boast before us. He was vulgar to the worst degree, but nevertheless he was a good-natured fellow, even when he boasted. In spite of superficial, fantastic and rhetorical notions of honor and dignity, all but a very few of us positively grovelled before Zverkov, and the more so the more he boasted. And they did not grovel for any advantage, but simply because he had been favored by the gifts of nature. Moreover, we came somehow to accept the idea that Zverkov was a specialist in regard to tact and good manners. That particularly infuriated me. I hated the sharp, self-confident tone of his voice, his admiration for his own witticisms, which were terribly stupid, though he was bold in his expressions; I hated his handsome but stupid face (for which I would, however, have gladly exchanged my *intelligent* one), and the free-and-easy military manners in fashion in the 'forties. I hated the way in which he used to talk of his future conquests of women (he did not venture to begin with women until he had officer's epaulettes and was looking forward to them with impatience), and boasted of the duels he would constantly be fighting. I remember how I, invariably so taciturn, suddenly attacked Zverkov, when one day he talked at a leisure moment with his schoolfellows of the affairs he would have in the future and growing as sportive as a puppy in the sun, he all at once declared that he would not leave a single village girl on his estate unnoticed, that that was his *droit de seigneur*,[24] and that if the peasants dared to protest he would have them all flogged and double their taxes,

---

[24] *droit de seigneur:* French for "the lord's right"; a feudal custom allowing a lord to spend the first night with a bride.

the bearded rascals. Our servile rabble applauded, but I attacked him, not at all out of compassion for the girls and their fathers, but simply because they were applauding such a beetle. I got the better of him on that occasion, but though Zverkov was stupid he was lively and impudent, and so laughed it off, and even in such a way that my victory was not really complete: the laugh was on his side. He got the better of me on several occasions afterward, but without malice, somehow just in jest, casually, in fun. I remained maliciously and contemptuously silent. When we left school he made advances to me; I did not rebuff them much, for I was flattered, but we soon parted naturally. Afterward I heard of his barrack-room success as a lieutenant, and of the *fast life* he was leading. Then there came other rumors—of his *successes* in the service. By then he no longer greeted me in the street, and I suspected that he was afraid of compromising himself by greeting a person as insignificant as I. I also saw him once in the theatre, in the third tier of boxes. By then he was a staff officer. He was twisting and twirling about, ingratiating himself with the daughters of an ancient general. In three years his looks had gotten considerably worse, though he was still rather handsome and smart. He had somehow swelled, started to put on weight. One could see that by the time he was thirty he would be completely fat. So it was, finally, to this Zverkov that my schoolfellows were going to give a dinner on his departure. They had kept up with him for those three years, though privately they did not consider themselves on an equal footing with him, I am convinced of that.

Of Simonov's two visitors, one was Ferfichkin, a Russianized German—a little fellow with the face of a monkey, a blockhead who was always deriding everyone, a very bitter enemy of mine from our days in the lower classes—a vulgar, impudent, boastful fellow, who affected a most sensitive feeling of personal honor, though, of course, he was a wretched little coward at heart. He was one of those admirers of Zverkov who made up to the latter out of calculation, and often borrowed money from him. Simonov's other visitor, Trudolyubov, was a person in no way remarkable—a military lad, tall with a cold face, quite honest. But he worshipped success of every sort, and was only capable of thinking of promotion. He was some distant relation of Zverkov and this, foolish as it seems, gave him a certain importance among us. He never thought me of any consequence whatever; while his behavior to me was not quite courteous, it was tolerable.

"Well then, with seven roubles each," said Trudolyubov, "twenty-one *roups* from the three of us, we can dine well. Zverkov, of course, won't pay."

"Of course not, since we are inviting him," Simonov decided.

"Can you imagine," Ferfichkin interrupted hotly and conceitedly, like some insolent flunky boasting of his master the general's decorations, "can you imagine that Zverkov will let us pay alone? He will accept from delicacy, but he will order *a half case* on his own."

"Why do we need half a case for the four of us?" observed Trudolyubov, taking notice only of the half case.

"So the three of us, with Zverkov for the fourth, twenty-one roubles, at the Hôtel de Paris at five o'clock tomorrow," Simonov, who had been asked to make the arrangements, concluded finally.

"How about twenty-one roubles?" I asked in some agitation, even offended, apparently; "if you count me it will be twenty-eight, not twenty-one roubles."

It seemed to me that to invite myself so suddenly and unexpectedly would be positively graceful, and that they would all be conquered at once and would look at me with respect.

"Do you want to join, too?" Simonov observed, with displeasure, and seemed to avoid looking at me. He knew me inside out.

It infuriated me that he knew me inside out.

"Why not? After all, I am an old schoolfellow of his too, I believe, and I must admit I feel offended that you have left me out," I said, boiling over again.

"And where were we to find you?" Ferfichkin put in roughly.

"You were never on good terms with Zverkov," Trudolyubov added, frowning. But I had already clutched at the idea and would not let go.

"I do not think that anyone has a right to judge that," I retorted in a shaking voice, as though God only knows what had happened. "Perhaps that is just my reason for wishing it now, that I have not always been on good terms with him."

"Oh, there's no making you out—with these refinements," Trudolyubov jeered.

"We'll put your name down," Simonov decided, addressing me. "Tomorrow at five o'clock at the Hotel de Paris."

"What about the money?" Ferfichkin began in an undertone, indicating me to Simonov, but he broke off, for even Simonov was embarrassed.

"That will do," said Trudolyubov, getting up. "If he wants to come so much, let him."

"But after all it's a private thing, between us friends," Ferfichkin said crossly, as he too picked up his hat. "It's not an official meeting. Perhaps we do not want you at all—"

They went away. Ferfichkin did not salute me in any way as he went out. Trudolyubov barely nodded. Simonov, with whom I remained alone, was in some state of vexed perplexity, and looked at me strangely. He did not sit down and did not ask me to.

"H'm—yes—tomorrow, then. Will you pay your share now? I just ask so as to know," he muttered in embarrassment.

I blazed up in anger but as I did so I remembered that I had owed Simonov fifteen roubles for ages—which I had, indeed, never forgotten, though I had not paid it.

"You will understand, Simonov, that I could have had no idea when I came here—I am very much vexed that I have forgotten—"

"All right, all right, it doesn't matter. You can pay tomorrow after the dinner. After all, I simply wanted to know—Please don't—"

He broke off and began pacing the room still more vexed. As he walked he began to thump with his heels and stomped even louder.

"Am I keeping you?" I asked, after two minutes of silence.

"Oh, no!" he said, starting, "that is—to be truthful—yes. I have to go and see someone—not far from here," he added in a sort of apologetic voice, somewhat ashamed.

"My goodness, but why didn't you say so?" I cried, seizing my cap with, incidentally, an astonishingly free-and-easy air, which was the last thing I would have expected of myself.

"After all, it's close by—not two paces away," Simonov repeated, accompanying me to the front door with a fussy air which did not suit him at all. "So five o'clock, punctually, tomorrow," he called down the stairs after me. He was very glad to get rid of me. I was in a fury.

"What possessed me, what possessed me to force myself upon them?" I gnashed my teeth, as I strode along the street. "For a scoundrel, a pig like that Zverkov! Of course, I had better not go; of course, I can just snap my fingers at them. I am not bound in any way. I'll send Simonov a note by tomorrow's post—"

But what made me furious was that I knew for certain that I would go, that I would purposely go; and the more tactless, the more ill-mannered my going would be, the more certainly I would go.

And there was even a positive obstacle to my going: I had no money. All I had altogether, was nine roubles. But I had to give seven of that to my servant, Apollon, for his monthly wages. That was all I paid him—he had to keep himself.

Not to pay him was impossible, considering his character. But I will talk about that fellow, about that plague of mine, another time.

However, I knew I would go after all and would not pay him his wages.

That night I had the most hideous dreams. No wonder; the whole evening I had been oppressed by memories of my days of penal servitude at school, and I could not shake them off. I was sent to the school by distant relations, upon whom I was dependent and of whom I have heard nothing since—they sent me there, a lonely, silent boy, already crushed by their reproaches, already troubled by doubt, and looking savagely at everything around him. My schoolfellows met me with spiteful and merciless jibes because I was not like any of them. But I could not endure their taunts; I could not give in to them as cheaply as they gave in to one another. I hated them from the first, and shut myself away from everyone in timid, wounded, and disproportionate pride. Their coarseness revolted me. They laughed cynically at my face, at my clumsy figure; and yet what stupid faces they themselves had. In our school the boys' faces somehow degenerated and grew stupider particularly. How many fine-looking boys came to us? In a few years they became repulsive looking. Even at sixteen I wondered at them morosely; even then I was struck by the pettiness of their thoughts, the stupidity of their pursuits, their games, their conversations. They had no understanding of such essential things, they took no interest in such striking, impressive subjects, that I could not help considering them inferior to myself. It was not wounded vanity that drove me to it, and for God's sake do not thrust upon me your hackneyed remarks, repeated to nausea, that "I was only a dreamer, while they even then understood real life." They understood nothing, they had no idea of real life, and I swear that that was what made me most indignant with them. On the contrary, the most obvious, striking reality they accepted with fantastic stupidity and even then had already begun to respect only success. Everything that was just, but oppressed and looked down upon, they laughed at cruelly and shamefully. They took rank for intelligence; even at sixteen they were already talking about a snug berth. Of course a great deal of it was due to their stupidity, to the bad examples that constantly surrounded them in their childhood and boyhood. They were monstrously depraved. Of course much of that, too, was superficial and much was only affected cynicism; of course there were glimpses of youth and freshness in them even beneath their depravity; but even that freshness was not attractive in them, and showed itself in a certain rakishness. I hated them terribly, though perhaps I was worse than any of them. They repaid me in kind, and not conceal their aversion for me. But by then I did not want them to like me; on the contrary, I continually longed for them to humiliate me. To escape from their derision I purposely began to make all the progress I could with my studies and forced my way to the very top. This impressed them. Moreover, they all began to grasp slowly that I was already reading books none of them could read, and understood things (not forming part of our school curriculum) of which they had not even heard. They took a savage and sarcastic view of it, but were morally impressed, especially as the teachers began to notice me on those grounds. The mockery ceased but the hostility remained, and cold and strained relations were formed between us. In the end I could not stand it myself; with years a craving for society, for friends, developed in me. I attempted to get on friendly terms with some of my schoolfellows; but somehow or other my intimacy with them was always strained and soon ended of itself. Once, indeed, I did have a friend. But I was already a tyrant at heart; I wanted to exercise unlimited power over him; I tried to instill into him a contempt for his surroundings; I required of him a disdainful and complete break with those surroundings. I frightened him with my passionate affection; I reduced him to tears, to convulsions. He was a simple and devoted soul; but when he submitted to me completely I began to hate him immediately and rejected him — as though all I needed him for was to win a victory over him, to subjugate him and nothing else. But I could not subjugate all of them; my friend was not at all like them either, he was, in fact, a rare exception. The first thing I did on leaving school was to give up the special job for which I had been destined so as to break all ties, to curse my past and scatter it to the winds — And goodness knows why, after all that, I should drag myself to that Simonov!

Early next morning I roused myself and jumped out of bed with excitement, as though it were all about to happen at once. But I believed that some radical change in my life was coming, and would inevitably come that day. Owing to its rarity, perhaps, any external event, however trivial, always made me feel as though some radical change in my life would occur immediately. I went to the office as usual, however, but slipped away home two hours early to get ready. The important thing, I thought, is not to be the first to arrive, or they will think I was overjoyed at coming. But there were thousands of such important points to consider, and they all agitated me to the point of impotence. I polished my boots a second time with my own hands; nothing in the world would have induced Apollon to clean them twice a day, as he considered that it was more than his duties required of him. I stole the brushes to clean them from the passage, so that he would not detect it and then start to despise me. Then I minutely examined my clothes, and found that everything looked old, worn, and threadbare. I had let myself get too slovenly. My uniform, perhaps, was in good shape, but I could hardly go out to dinner in my uniform. And the worst thing was that on the knee of my trousers was a big yellow stain. I had a foreboding that that stain would in itself deprive me of nine-tenths of my personal dignity. I knew, too, that it was stooping very low to think so. "But this is no time for thinking: now the real thing is beginning," I thought, and my heart sank. I knew, too, perfectly well even then, that I was monstrously exaggerating the facts. But how could I help it? I could not control myself and I was already shaking with fever. With despair I pictured to myself how coldly and disdainfully that "scoundrel" Zverkov would greet me; with what dull-witted, absolutely profound contempt the blockhead Trudolyubov would look at me; with what nasty insolence the beetle Ferfichkin would snigger at me in order to curry favor with Zverkov; how completely Simonov would take it all in, and how he would despise me for the abjectness of my vanity and faint-heartedness, and worst of all how paltry, *unliterary,* commonplace it would all be. Of course the best thing would be not to go at all. But that was the most impossible of all: once I feel impelled to do anything, I am completely drawn into it, head first. I would have jeered at myself ever afterward: "So you funked it, you funked the *real thing,* you funked it!" On the contrary, I passionately longed to show all that "rabble" that I was not at all such a coward as I pictured myself. What is more, even in the acutest paroxysm of this cowardly fever, I dreamed of getting the upper hand, of overcoming them, carrying them away, making them like me—if only for my "elevation of thought and unmistakable wit." They would abandon Zverkov, he would sit on one side, silent and ashamed, while I would crush Zverkov. Then, perhaps, I would be reconciled to him and toast our camaraderie; but what was most spiteful and insulting for me was that I knew even then, knew completely and for certain, that I needed nothing of all this really, that I did not really want to crush, to subdue, to attract them, and that I would be the first not to care a straw, really, for the result, even if I did achieve it. Oh, how I prayed to God for the day to pass quickly! In inexpressible anguish I went to the window, opened a pane, and looked out into the turbid darkness of the thickly falling wet snow.

At last my wretched little wall clock hissed out five. I seized my hat trying not to look at Apollon, who had been all day expecting his month's wages, but in his pride was unwilling to be the first to speak about it. I slipped past him and out the door, and jumping into a high-class sledge, on which I spent my last half-rouble, I drove up in grand style to the Hôtel de Paris.

IV

I had already known the day before that I would be the first to arrive. But it was no longer a question of precedence.

Not only were they not there, but I even had difficulty finding our room. The table had still not been completely set. What did it mean? After a good many questions I finally ascertained from the waiters that the dinner had been ordered not for five, but for six o'clock. This was confirmed at the buffet too. I even felt ashamed to go on questioning them. It was still only twenty-five minutes past five. If they changed the dinner hour they ought in any case to have let me know—that is what the post is for, and not to have subjected me to "shame" both in my own eyes and—well, before the waiters. I sat down: the servant began to set the table; I felt even more insulted when he was present. Toward six o'clock they brought in candles, though there were lamps burning in the room. It had not occurred to the waiter, however, to bring them in at once when I arrived. In the next room, two gloomy, angry-looking persons were eating their dinners in silence at two different tables. There was a great deal of noise, even shouting, in a room farther away; one could hear the laughter of a crowd of people, and nasty little shrieks in French; there were ladies at the dinner. In short, it was sickening. I rarely passed a more unpleasant time, so much so that when they did arrive all together punctually at six I was for the first moment overjoyed to see them, as though they were my deliverers, and almost forgot it was incumbent upon me to look insulted.

Zverkov walked in at the head of them; evidently he was the leading spirit. He and all of them were laughing; but, seeing me, Zverkov drew himself up, walked up to me unhurriedly with a slight, rather jaunty bend from the waist, and shook hands with me in a friendly but not over-friendly fashion, with a sort of circumspect courtesy almost like a general's as though in giving me his hand he were warding off something. I had imagined, on the contrary, that as soon as he came in he would immediately break into his former thin, shrieking laugh and fall to making his insipid jokes and witticisms. I had been preparing for them ever since the previous day, but I had never expected such condescension, such high-official courtesy. So, then, he felt himself immeasurably superior to me in every respect! If he had only meant to insult me by that high-official tone, it would still not have mattered, I thought — I could pay him back for it one way or another. But what if, in reality, without the least desire to be offensive, that sheep's-head had seriously acquired the notion that he was immeasurably superior to me and could only look at me in a patronizing way? The very supposition made me gasp.

"I was surprised to hear of your desire to join us," he began, lisping and drawling, which was something new. "You and I seem to have seen nothing of one another. You fight shy of us. You shouldn't. We are not such terrible people as you think. Well, anyway, I am glad to renew our acquaintance."

And he turned carelessly to put down his hat on the window sill.

"Have you been waiting long?" Trudolyubov inquired.

"I arrived punctually at five o'clock as I was informed yesterday," I answered aloud, with an irritability that promised an imminent explosion.

"Didn't you let him know that we had changed the hour?" said Trudolyubov to Simonov.

"No, I didn't. I forgot," the latter replied, with no sign of regret, and without even apologizing to me he went off to order the *hors d'ouevres*.

"So you've been here a whole hour? Oh, you poor fellow!" Zverkov cried ironically, for according to his notions this was bound to be extremely funny. That scoundrel Ferfichkin followed with his nasty little snigger like a puppy yapping. My position struck him, too, as extremely ludicrous and embarrassing.

"It isn't funny at all!" I cried to Ferfichkin, more and more irritated. "It wasn't my fault, but other people's. They neglected to let me know. It was — it was — it was simply absurd."

"It's not only absurd, but something else as well," muttered Trudolyubov, naïvely taking my part. "You are too complacent about it. It was simply rudeness—unintentional, of course. And how could Simonov—h'm!"

"If a trick like that had been played on me," observed Ferfichkin, "I would—"

"But you should have ordered yourself something," Zverkov interrupted, "or simply asked for dinner without waiting for us."

"You will allow that I might have done that without your permission," I rapped out. "If I waited, it was—"

"Let us sit down, gentlemen," cried Simonov, coming in. "Everything is ready; I can answer for the champagne; it is capitally chilled.—After all, I did not know your address. Where was I to look for you?" He suddenly turned to me, but again he seemed to avoid looking at me. Evidently he had something against me. He must have made up his mind after what happened yesterday.

Everybody sat down: I did the same. It was a round table. Trudolyubov was on my left, Simonov on my right. Zverkov was sitting opposite, Ferfichkin next to him, between him and Trudolyubov.

"Te-e-ell me, are you—in a government agency?" Zverkov went on, attending to me. Seeing that I was embarrassed, he seriously thought that he ought to be friendly to me, and, so to speak, cheer me up. "Does he want me to throw a bottle at his head or something?" I thought, in a fury. In my unaccustomed surroundings I was unnaturally quick to be irritated.

"In the N——— office," I answered jerkily, with my eyes on my plate.

"And—ha-ave you a go-od berth? Te-e-ll me, what ma-a-de you leave your former job?"

"What ma-a-de me was that I wanted to leave my original job," I drawled twice as much as he, hardly able to control myself. Ferfichkin snorted. Simonov looked at me ironically. Trudolyubov stopped eating and began looking at me with curiosity.

Zverkov was jarred but he pretended not to notice it.

"A-a-and the remuneration?"

"What remuneration?"

"I mean, your sa-a-lary?"

"Why are you cross-examining me?"

However, I told him at once what my salary was. I blushed terribly.

"It is not very handsome," Zverkov observed majestically.

"Yes, you can't afford to dine in restaurants on that," Ferfichkin added insolently.

"I think it's very low," Trudolyubov observed gravely.

"And how thin you have grown! How you have changed!" added Zverkov, with a shade of venom in his voice, scanning me and my attire with a sort of insolent compassion.

"Oh, spare his blushes," cried Ferfichkin, sniggering.

"My dear sir, permit me to tell you I am not blushing," I broke out at last; "do you hear? I am dining here, at this restaurant, at my own expense, at mine, not at other people's—note that, Monsieur Ferfichkin."

"Wha-at do you mean? Isn't everyone here dining at his own expense? You seem to be—" Ferfichkin let fly at me, turning as red as a lobster, and looking me in the face with fury.

"Tha-at's what I mean," I answered, feeling I had gone too far, "and I imagine it would be better to talk of something more intelligent."

"You intend to show off your intelligence, I suppose?"

"Don't disturb yourself, that would be quite out of place here."

"What are you clacking away like that for, my good sir, eh? Have you gone out of your wits in your *dumb*partment?"

"Enough, gentlemen, enough!" Zverkov cried, authoritatively.

"How stupid it is," muttered Simonov.

"It really is stupid. We have met here, a company of friends, for a farewell dinner to a good comrade and you are settling old scores," said Trudolyubov, rudely addressing himself to me alone. "Yesterday you invited yourself to join us, so don't disturb the general harmony."

"Enough, enough!" cried Zverkov. "Stop it, gentlemen, it's out of place. Better let me tell you how I nearly got married the day before yesterday . . ."

And then followed a burlesque narrative of how this gentleman had almost been married two days before. There was not a word about marriage, however, but the story was adorned with generals, colonels, and high courtiers while Zverkov practically took the lead among them. It was greeted with approving laughter; Ferfichkin even squealed.

No one paid any attention to me, and I sat crushed and humiliated.

"Good heavens, these are not the people for me!" I thought. "And what a fool I have made of myself before them! I let Ferfichkin go too far, though. The brutes imagine that it is an honor for me to sit down with them. They don't understand that I do them an honor. I to them and not they to me! I've grown thinner! My clothes! Oh, damn my trousers! Zverkov long ago noticed the yellow stain on the knee . . . But what's the use! I must get up at once, this very minute, take my hat and simply go without a word — out of contempt! And tomorrow I can send a challenge. The scoundrels! After all I don't care about the seven roubles. They may think . . . Damn it! I don't care about the seven roubles. I'll go this minute!"

Of course I remained.

I drank sherry and Lafitte by the glassful in my distress. Being unaccustomed to it, I quickly became intoxicated and my annoyance increased with the intoxication. I longed all at once to insult them all in a most flagrant manner and then go away. To seize the moment and show what I could do, so that they would say, "Though he is absurd, he's clever," and — and — in short, damn them all!

I scanned them all insolently with my dulled eyes. But they seemed to have forgotten me altogether. *They* were noisy, vociferous, cheerful. Zverkov kept talking. I began to listen. Zverkov was talking about some sumptuous lady whom he had at last led on to declaring her love (of course, he was lying like a horse), and how he had been helped in this affair by an intimate friend of his, a Prince Kolya, an officer in the Hussars, who had three thousand serfs.

"And yet, this Kolya, who has three thousand serfs, has not put in an appearance here tonight at all to see you off," I cut in suddenly. For a minute everyone was silent.

"You are drunk already." Trudolyubov deigned to notice me at last, glancing contemptuously in my direction. Zverkov, without a word, examined me as though I were a little beetle. I dropped my eyes. Simonov made haste to fill up the glasses with champagne.

Trudolyubov raised his glass, as did everyone else but me.

"Your health and good luck on the journey!" he cried to Zverkov. "To old times, gentlemen, to our future, hurrah!"

They all tossed off their glasses, and crowded round Zverkov to kiss him. I did not move; my full glass stood untouched before me.

"Why, aren't you going to drink it?" roared Trudolyubov, losing patience and turning menacingly to me.

"I want to make a toast separately, on my own account . . . and then I'll drink it, Mr. Trudolyubov."

"Disgusting crank!" muttered Simonov.

I drew myself up in my chair and feverishly seized my glass, prepared for something extraordinary, though I did not know myself precisely what I was going to say.

"*Silence!*" cried Ferfichkin, in French. "Now for a display of wit!"

Zverkov waited very gravely, knowing what was coming.

"Lieutenant Zverkov," I began, "let me tell you that I hate phrases, phrase-mongers and corseted waists — that's the first point, and there is a second one to follow it."

There was a general stir.

"The second point is: I hate dirty stories and people who tell dirty stories. Especially people who tell dirty stories!

"The third point: I love truth, sincerity, and honesty," I went on almost mechanically, for I was beginning to shiver with horror and had no idea how I came to be talking like this. "I love thought, Monsieur Zverkov; I love true comradeship, on an equal footing and not — h'm — I love — but, however, why not? I will drink to your health, too, Monsieur Zverkov. Seduce the Circassian[25] girls, shoot the enemies of the fatherland, and — and — to your health, Monsieur Zverkov!"

Zverkov got up from his seat, bowed to me, and said:

"I am very much obliged to you."

He was frightfully offended and even turned pale.

"Damn the fellow!" roared Trudolyubov, bringing his fist down on the table.

"Well, he ought to be punched in the nose for that," squealed Ferfichkin.

"We ought to turn him out," muttered Simonov.

"Not a word, gentlemen, not a movement!" cried Zverkov solemnly, checking the general indignation. "I thank you all, but I can show him for myself how much value I attach to his words."

"Mr. Ferfichkin, you will give me satisfaction tomorrow at the latest for your words just now!" I said aloud, turning with dignity to Ferfichkin.

"A duel, you mean? Certainly," he answered. But probably I was so ridiculous as I challenged him and it was so out of keeping with my appearance that everyone, including Ferfichkin, roared with laughter.

---

[25] **Circassian:** A region in the Caucasus.

"Yes, let him alone, of course! After all, he is completely drunk," Trudolyubov said with disgust.

"I will never forgive myself for letting him join us," Simonov muttered again.

"Now is the time to throw a bottle at their heads," I thought to myself. I picked up the bottle . . . and poured myself a full glass.

"No, I had better sit on to the end," I went on thinking; "you would be pleased, my friends, if I left. Nothing will induce me to go. I'll go on sitting here, and drinking to the end, on purpose, as a sign that I don't attach the slightest importance to you. I will go on sitting and drinking, because this is a public-house and I paid my entrance money. I'll sit here and drink, for I look upon you as so many pawns, as inanimate pawns. I'll sit here and drink—and sing if I want to, yes, sing, for I have the right to—to sing—h'm!"

But I did not sing. I simply tried not to look at any of them. I assumed most unconcerned attitudes and waited with impatience for them to speak *first,* of their own accord. But alas, they did not speak! And oh, how I wished, how I wished at that moment to be reconciled to them! It struck eight, at last nine. They moved from the table to the sofa. Zverkov stretched himself on a couch and put one foot on a round table. The wine was brought there. He did, as a matter of fact, order three bottles on his own account. He didn't, of course, invite me to join them. They all sat round him on the sofa. They listened to him, almost with reverence. It was evident that they were fond of him. "For what? For what?" I wondered. From time to time they were moved to drunken enthusiasm and kissed each other. They talked of the Caucasus, of the nature of true passion, of advantageous jobs in the service, of the income of a Hussar called Podkharzhevsky, whom none of them knew personally and rejoiced that he had a large income; of the extraordinary grace and beauty of a Princess D., whom none of them had ever seen; then it came to Shakespeare's being immortal.

I smiled contemptuously and walked up and down the other side of the room, opposite the sofa, along the wall, from the table to the stove and back again. I tried my very utmost to show them that I could do without them, and yet I purposely stomped with my boots, thumping with my heels. But it was all in vain. They paid no attention at all. I had the patience to walk up and down in front of them that way from eight o'clock till eleven, in one and the same place, from the table to the stove and from the stove back again to the table. "I walk up and down to please myself and no one can prevent me." The waiter who came into the room several times stopped to look at me. I was somewhat giddy from turning round so often; at moments it seemed to me that I was in delirium. During those three hours I was three times soaked with sweat, and then dry again. At times, with an intense, acute pang, I was stabbed to the heart by the thought that ten years, twenty years, forty years would pass, and that even in forty years I would remember with loathing and humiliation those filthiest, most ludicrous, and most terrible moments of my life. No one could have gone out of his way to degrade himself more shamelessly and voluntarily, and I fully realized it, fully, and yet I went on pacing up and down from the table to the stove. "Oh, if you only knew what thoughts and feelings I am capable of, how cultured I am!" I thought at moments, mentally addressing the sofa on which my enemies were sitting. But my enemies behaved as though I did not exist in the room.

Once—only once—they turned toward me, just when Zverkov was talking about Shakespeare, and I suddenly gave a contemptuous laugh. I snorted in such an effected and nasty way that they all at once broke off their conversation, and silently and gravely for two minutes watched me walking up and down from the table to the stove, *paying no attention whatsoever to them.* But nothing came of it; they said nothing, and two minutes later they ceased to notice me again. It struck eleven.

"Gentlemen," cried Zverkov, getting up from the sofa, "let us all go there *now!*"

"Of course, of course," the others said.

I turned sharply to Zverkov. I was so exhausted, so broken, that I would have cut my throat to put an end to it. I was in a fever; my hair, soaked with perspiration, stuck to my forehead and temples.

"Zverkov, I beg your pardon," I said abruptly and resolutely. "Ferfichkin, yours too, and everyone's, everyone's; I have insulted you all!"

"Aha! A duel is not in your line, old man," Ferfichkin hissed venomously.

It sent a deep pang to my heart.

"No, it's not the duel I am afraid of, Ferfichkin! I am ready to fight you tomorrow, after we are reconciled. I insist upon it, in fact, and you cannot refuse. I want to show you that I am not afraid of a duel. You will fire first and I will fire into the air."

"He is comforting himself," remarked Simonov.

"He's simply raving," declared Trudolyubov.

"But let us pass. Why are you barring our way? Well, what do you want?" Zverkov answered disdainfully. They were all flushed; their eyes were bright; they had been drinking heavily.

"I asked for your friendship, Zverkov; I insulted you, but—"

"Insulted? You-u insulted me-e-e! Permit me to tell you, sir, that you never, under any circumstances, could possibly insult *me.*"

"And that's enough of you. Out of the way!" concluded Trudolyubov. "Let's go."

"Olympia is mine, gentlemen, that's agreed!" cried Zverkov.

"We won't dispute your right, we won't dispute your right," the others answered, laughing.

I stood as though spat upon. The party went noisily out of the room. Trudolyubov struck up some stupid song. Simonov remained behind for a moment to tip the waiters. I suddenly went up to him.

"Simonov! give me six roubles!" I said, decisively and desperately.

He looked at me in extreme amazement, with dulled eyes. He, too, was drunk.

"You don't mean you are even coming with us *there*?"

"Yes."

"I've no money," he snapped out, and with a scornful laugh he went out of the room.

I clutched at his overcoat. It was a nightmare.

"Simonov! I saw you had money, why do you refuse me? Am I a scoundrel? Beware of refusing me; if you knew, if you knew why I am asking! Everything depends upon it! My whole future, my whole plans!"

Simonov pulled out the money and almost flung it at me.

"Take it, if you have no sense of shame!" he pronounced pitilessly, and ran to overtake them.

I was left alone for a moment. Disorder, the remains of dinner, a broken wine-glass on the floor, spilt wine, cigarette butts, intoxication and delirium in my brain, an agonizing misery in my heart and finally the waiter, who had seen and heard all and was looking inquisitively into my face.

"I am going *there*!" I shouted. "Either they will all fall down on their knees to beg for my friendship — or I will give Zverkov a slap in the face!"

V

"So this is it, so this is it at last, a clash with reality," I muttered as I ran headlong downstairs. "This, it seems, is very different from the Pope's leaving Rome and going to Brazil; this, it seems, is very different from the ball on the shores of Lake Como!"

"You are a scoundrel," flashed through my mind, "if you laugh at this now."

"No matter!" I cried, answering myself. "Now everything is lost!"

There was no trace of them left, but that made no difference — I knew where they had gone.

At the steps was standing a solitary night sledge-driver in a rough peasant coat, powdered over with the wet, and, as it were, warm snow that was still falling thickly. It was sultry and warm. The little shaggy piebald horse was also powdered with snow and was coughing, I remember that very well. I made a rush for the roughly made sledge; but as soon as I raised my foot to get into it, the recollection of how Simonov had just given me six roubles seemed to double me up and I tumbled into the sledge like a sack.

"No, I must do a great deal to make up for all that," I cried. "But I will make up for it or perish on the spot this very night. Start!"

We set off. There was an absolute whirl in my head.

"They won't go down on their knees to beg for my friendship. That is a mirage, a cheap mirage, revolting, romantic, and fantastical — that is another ball at Lake Como. And so I have to slap Zverkov's face! It is my duty to. And so it is settled; I am flying to give him a slap in the face. Hurry up!"

The cabby tugged at the reins.

"As soon as I go in I'll give it to him. Ought I to say a few words by way of preface before giving him the slap? No, I'll simply go in and give it to him. They will all be sitting in the drawing-room, and he with Olympia on the sofa. That damned Olympia! She laughed at my looks on one occasion and refused me. I'll pull Olympia's hair, pull Zverkov's ears! No, better one ear, and pull him by it round the room. Maybe they will all begin beating me and will kick me out. That is even very likely. No matter! Anyway, I will slap him first; the initiative will be mine; and according to the code of honor that is everything: he will be branded and no blows can wipe off the slap, nothing but a duel can. He will be forced to fight. And let them beat me then. Let them, the ungrateful wretches! Trudolyubov will beat me hardest, he is so strong; Ferfichkin is sure to catch hold from the side and tug at my hair. But no matter, no matter! That's what I am going for. The blockheads will be forced at last to see the tragedy of it all! When they drag me to the door I shall call out to them that in reality they are not worth my little finger." "Get on, driver, get on!" I cried to the driver. He started and flicked his whip, I shouted so savagely.

"We shall fight at daybreak, that's a settled thing. I am through with the Department. Ferfichkin called the Department 'Dumbpartment' before. But where can I get pistols? Nonsense! I'll call my salary in advance and buy them. And powder, and bullets? That's the second's business. And how can it all be done by daybreak? And where am I to get a second? I have no friends. Nonsense!" I cried, lashing myself more and more into a fury. "Nonsense! the first person I meet in the street is bound to be my second, just as he would be bound to pull a drowning man out of water. The strangest things may happen. Even if I were to ask the Director himself to be my second tomorrow, even he would be bound to consent, if only from a feeling of chivalry, and to keep the secret! Anton Antonich—"

The fact is that at that very minute the disgusting absurdity of my plans and the other side of the question were clearer and more vivid to my imagination than they could be to anyone on earth, but—

"Get on, driver, get on, you rascal, get on!"

"Ugh, sir!" said the son of toil.

Cold shivers suddenly ran down me.

"Wouldn't it be better . . . wouldn't it be better . . . to go straight home now? Oh, my God! Why, why did I invite myself to this dinner yesterday? But no, it's impossible. And my three hours' walk from the table to the stove? No, they, they and no one else must pay for walking up and down! They must wipe out this dishonor! Drive on!"

"And what if they hand me over to the police? They won't dare! They'll be afraid of the scandal. And what if Zverkov is so contemptuous that he refuses to fight a duel? That is even sure to happen, but in that case I'll show them—I will turn up at the posting station when he is setting off tomorrow—I'll catch him by the leg, I'll pull off his coat when he gets into the carriage. I'll get my teeth into his hand, I'll bite him. See to what lengths you can drive a desperate man! He may hit me on the head and they may pummel me from behind. I will shout to the whole crowd of spectators: "Look at this young puppy who is driving off to captivate the Circassian girls after letting me spit in his face!"

"Of course, after that everything will be over! The Department will have vanished off the face of the earth. I will be arrested. I will be tried, I will be dismissed from the service, thrown in prison, sent to Siberia, deported. Never mind! In fifteen years when they let me out of prison I will trudge off to him, a beggar in rags, I shall find him in some provincial city. He will be married and happy. He will have a grown-up daughter . . . I will say to him: 'Look, monster, at my hollow cheeks and my rags! I've lost everything—my career, my happiness, art, science, *the woman I loved*, and all through you. Here are pistols. I have come to discharge my pistol and—and I . . . forgive you.' Then I will fire into the air and he hear nothing more of me."

I was actually on the point of tears, though I knew perfectly well at that very moment that all this was out of Pushkin's *Silvio* and Lermontov's *Masquerade*.[26] And

---

[26] **Pushkin's *Silvio* and Lermontov's *Masquerade*:** Pushkin's short story (1830) and Lermontov's play (1835) are about issues of honor.

all at once I felt terribly ashamed, so ashamed that I stopped the sledge, stepped out of it and stood still in the snow in the middle of the street. The driver sighed and gazed at me in astonishment.

What was I to do? I could not go on there—that was clearly absurd, and I could not leave things as they were, because that would seem as though—"Heavens, how could I leave things! And after such insults!" "No!" I cried, throwing myself into the sledge again. "It is ordained! It is fate! Drive on, drive on to that place!"

And in my impatience I punched the sledge-driver on the back of the neck.

"What are you up to? What are you hitting me for?" the poor man shouted, but he whipped up his nag so that it began to kick out.

The wet snow was falling in big flakes; I unbuttoned myself. I did not care about it. I forgot everything else, for I had finally decided on the slap, and felt with horror that after all it was going to happen *now, at once,* that it would happen immediately and that *no force could stop it.* The deserted street lamps gleamed sullenly in the snowy darkness like torches at a funeral. The snow drifted under my greatcoat, under my coat, under my necktie, and melted there. I did not cover myself up—after all, all was already lost, anyway. At last we arrived. I jumped out, almost fainting, ran up the steps and began knocking and kicking at the door. My legs, particularly at the knee, felt terribly weak. The door was opened quickly as though they knew I was coming. As a matter of fact, Simonov had warned them that perhaps another would arrive, and this was a place in which one had to give notice and to observe certain precautions. It was one of the "millinery establishments" which were abolished by the police a long time ago. By day it really was a shop; but at night, if one had an introduction, one might visit it for other purposes.

I walked rapidly through the dark shop into the familiar drawing-room, where there was only one candle burning, and stopped in amazement; there was no one there.

"Where are they?" I asked somebody.

But by now, of course, they had separated.

Before me stood a person with a stupid smile, the "madam" herself, who had seen me before. A minute later a door opened and another person came in.

Paying no attention to anything, I strode about the room, and, I believe, I talked to myself. I felt as though I had been saved from death and was conscious of it, joyfully, all over: after all, I would have given that slap. I would certainly, certainly have given it! But now they were not here and—everything had vanished and changed! I looked round. I could not realize my condition yet. I looked mechanically at the girl who had come in and had a glimpse of a fresh, young, rather pale face, with straight, dark eyebrows, and with a grave, as it were, amazed glance, eyes that attracted me at once. I would have hated her if she had been smiling. I began looking at her more intently and, as it were, with effort. I had not fully collected my thoughts. There was something simple and good-natured in her face, but something strangely serious. I am sure that this stood in her way here, and that not one of those fools had noticed her. She could not, however, have been called a beauty, though she was tall, strong-looking, and well built. She was very simply dressed. Something loathsome stirred within me. I went straight up to her—

I happened to look at myself in the mirror. My harassed face struck me as extremely revolting, pale, spiteful, nasty, with disheveled hair. "No matter, I am glad of it," I thought; "I am glad that I shall seem revolting to her; I like that."

VI

. . . Somewhere behind a screen a clock began wheezing, as though under some great pressure, as though someone were strangling it. After an unnaturally prolonged wheezing there followed a shrill, nasty, and, as it were, unexpectedly rapid chime — as though someone were suddenly jumping forward. It struck two. I woke up, though I had not really been asleep but only lay semi-conscious.

It was almost completely dark in the narrow, cramped, low-pitched room, cluttered up with an enormous wardrobe and piles of cardboard boxes and all sorts of frippery and litter. The candle stump that had been burning on the table was going out and it gave a faint flicker from time to time. In a few minutes it would be completely dark.

I was not long in coming to myself; everything came back to my mind at once, without an effort, as though it had been in ambush to pounce upon me again. And, indeed, even while I was unconscious, a point continually seemed to remain in my memory that could not ever be forgotten, and around it my dreams moved drearily. But strange to say, everything that had happened to me during that day seemed to me now, on waking, to be in the far, far-away distant past, as though I had long, long ago lived all that down.

My head was heavy. Something seemed to be hovering over me, provoking me, rousing me, and making me restless. Misery and gall seemed to surge up in me again and to seek an outlet. Suddenly I saw beside me two wide-open eyes scrutinizing me curiously and persistently. The look in those eyes was coldly detached, sullen, utterly detached, as it were; it weighed heavily on me.

A grim idea came into my brain and passed all over my body, like some nasty sensation, such as one feels when one goes into a damp and mouldy cellar. It was somehow unnatural that those two eyes only now thought of beginning to examine me. I recalled, too, that during those two hours I had not said a single word to this creature, and had, in fact, considered it entirely unnecessary; it had even for some reason gratified me before. Now I suddenly realized vividly how absurd, revolting as a spider, was the idea of vice which, without love, grossly and shamelessly begins directly with that in which true love finds its consummation. For a long time we gazed at each other like that, but she did not drop her eyes before mine and did not change her expression, so that at last, somehow, I felt uncomfortable.

"What is your name?" I asked abruptly, to put an end to it quickly.

"Liza," she answered almost in a whisper, but somehow without any friendliness; she turned her eyes away.

I was silent.

"What weather today — the snow — it's abominable!" I said, almost to myself, putting my arm under my head despondently, and gazing at the ceiling.

She made no answer. This was all outrageous.

"Are you a local girl?" I asked a minute later, almost angrily, turning my head slightly toward her.

"No."

"Where do you come from?"

"From Riga," she answered reluctantly.

"Are you a German?"

"No, Russian."

"Have you been here long?"

"Where?"

"In this house?"

"A fortnight."

She spoke more and more jerkily. The candle went out: I could no longer distinguish her face.

"Have you a father and mother?"

"Yes — no — I have."

"Where are they?"

"There — in Riga."

"What are they?"

"Oh, nothing."

"Nothing? Why, what do they do?"

"Tradespeople."

"Have you always lived with them?"

"Yes."

"How old are you?"

"Twenty."

"Why did you leave them?"

"Oh, for no reason."

That answer meant "Let me alone; I feel wretched." We were silent.

God knows why I did not go away. I felt myself more and more wretched and dreary. The image of the previous day started to flit through my mind in confusion independently of my will. I suddenly recalled something I had seen that morning when, full of anxious thoughts, I was hurrying to the office.

"I saw them carrying a coffin out yesterday and they nearly dropped it," I suddenly said aloud with no desire at all to start a conversation, but just so, almost by accident.

"A coffin?"

"Yes, in the Haymarket; they were bringing it up out of a cellar."

"From a cellar?"

"Not from a cellar, but from a basement. Oh, you know — down below — from a house of ill-fame. It was filthy all round — eggshells, litter — a stench. It was loathsome."

Silence.

"A nasty day to be buried," I began, simply to avoid being silent.

"Nasty, in what way?"

"The snow, the wet." (I yawned.)

"It doesn't matter," she said suddenly, after a brief silence.

"No, it's abominable." (I yawned again.) "The grave diggers must have sworn at getting drenched by the snow. And there must have been water in the grave."

"Why would there be water in the grave?" she asked, with a sort of curiosity, but speaking even more harshly and abruptly than before. I suddenly began to feel provoked.

"Why, there must have been water at the bottom a foot deep. You can't dig a dry grave in Volkovo Cemetery."

"Why?"

"Why? Why, the place is waterlogged. It's a regular marsh. So they bury them in water. I've seen it myself—many times."

(I had never seen it at all, and I had never even been in Volkovo, but had only heard stories of it.)

"Do you mean to say it doesn't matter to you whether you die?"

"But why should I die?" she answered, as though defending herself.

"Why, some day you will die, and you will die just the same as that dead woman. She was—a girl like you. She died of consumption."

"The wench would have died in a hospital, too . . . (She knows all about it already; she said "wench," not "girl.")

"She was in debt to her madam," I retorted, more and more provoked by the discussion; "and went on earning money for her almost up to the very end, though she was in consumption. Some coachmen standing by were talking about her to some soldiers and telling them so. No doubt her former acquaintances. They were laughing. They were going to meet in a pot-house to drink to her memory." (I lied a great deal here.)

Silence followed, profound silence. She did not even stir.

"And is it better to die in a hospital?"

"Isn't it just the same? Besides, why should I die?" she added irritably.

"If not now, a little later."

"Why a little later?"

"Why, indeed? Now you are young, pretty, fresh, you fetch a high price. But after another year of this life you will be very different—you will fade."

"In a year?"

"Anyway, in a year you will be worth less," I continued malignantly. "You will go from here to something lower, another house; a year later—to a third, lower and lower, and in seven years you will come to a basement in the Haymarket. And that's if you are lucky. But it would be much worse if you got some disease, consumption, say—and caught a chill, or something or other. It's not easy to get over an illness in your way of life. If you catch anything you may not get rid of it. And so you would die."

"Oh, well, then I will die," she answered, quite vindictively, and she made a quick movement.

"But after all, it's a pity."

"For whom?"

"Pity for life."

Silence.

"Were you engaged? Eh?"

"What's that to you?"

"Oh, I am not cross-examining you. It's nothing to me. Why are you so cross? Of course you may have had your own troubles. What is it to me? I simply felt sorry."

"For whom?"

"Sorry for you."

"No need," she whispered hardly audibly, and again made a faint movement.

That incensed me at once. What! I was so gentle with her, and she—

"Why, what do you think? Are you on the right path, ah?"

"I don't think anything."

"That's what's wrong, that you don't think. Wake up while there is still time. And there is still time. You are still young, good-looking; you might love, be married, be happy—"

"Not all married women are happy," she snapped out in the rude, fast way she had spoken before.

"Not all, of course, but anyway it is much better than the life here. Infinitely better. Besides, with love one can live even without happiness. Even in sorrow life is sweet; life is sweet, however one lives. But here you have nothing except foulness. Phew!"

I turned away with disgust; I was no longer reasoning coldly. I began to feel myself what I was saying and warmed to the subject. I was already longing to expound the cherished *little ideas* I had brooded over in my corner. Something suddenly flared up in me. An object had "appeared" before me.

"Never mind my being here. I am not an example for you. I am, perhaps, even worse than you are. I was drunk when I came here, though," I hastened, however, to say in self-defense. "Besides, a man is no example for a woman. It's a different thing. I may degrade and defile myself, but I am not anyone's slave. I come and go, and there's an end to it. I shake it off, and I am a different man. But you are a slave from the start. Yes, a slave! You give up everything, your whole freedom. If you want to break your chains afterward, you won't be able to; you will be caught more and more in the snares. It is an accursed bondage. I know it. I won't mention anything else, maybe you won't understand it, but tell me: after all, surely you are in debt to your madam already? There, you see," I added, though she made no answer, but only listened in silence, entirely absorbed, "that's bondage for you! You will never buy your freedom. They will see to that. It's like selling your soul to the devil—

"And besides—perhaps I, too, am just as unfortunate, how do you know—and wallow in the mud on purpose, also out of misery? After all, men take to drink out of grief; well, maybe I am here out of grief. Come, tell me, what good is there here? Here you and I—were intimate—just now and did not say one word to one another all the time, and it was only afterward you began staring at me like a wild creature, and I at you. Is that loving? Is that how human beings are intimate? It's hideous, that's what it is!"

"Yes!" she assented sharply and hurriedly.

I was even amazed by the eagerness of this "yes." So the same thought may have been straying through her mind when she was staring at me just before. So she, too, was capable of certain thoughts? "Damn it all, this was curious, this was *kinship?*" I thought, almost rubbing my hands. And indeed how can one fail to manage a young soul like that?

The sport in it attracted me most.

She turned her head nearer to me, and it seemed to me in the darkness that she propped herself on her arm. Perhaps she was scrutinizing me. How I regretted that I could not see her eyes. I heard her deep breathing.

"Why did you come here?" I asked her, with a note of authority already in my voice.

"Oh, I don't know."

"But after all how nice it would be to be living in your own father's house! It's warm and free; you have a nest of your own."

"But what if it's worse than this?"

"I must take the right tone," flashed through my mind. "I may not get far with sentimentality."

But it was only a momentary thought. I swear she really did interest me. Besides, I was exhausted and moody. And after all, cunning so easily goes hand in hand with feeling.

"Who denies it?" I hastened to answer. "Anything may happen. I am, after all, convinced that someone has wronged you and is guiltier toward you than you toward them. After all, I know nothing of your story, but it's not likely, a girl like you has come here of her own inclination—"

"What kind of girl am I?" she whispered, hardly audible, but I heard it.

Damn it all, I was flattering her. That was abominable. But perhaps it was a good thing—She was silent.

"See, Liza, I will tell you about myself. If I had had a home from childhood, I shouldn't be what I am now. I often think about that. After all, no matter how bad it may be at home, at least they are your father and mother, and not enemies, strangers. Once a year, at least, they'll show their love for you. Anyway, you know you are at home. I grew up without a home; and perhaps that's why I've turned so—unfeeling."

I waited again.

"Perhaps she doesn't understand," I thought, "and, indeed, it is absurd, this moralizing."

"If I were a father and had a daughter, I believe I should love my daughter more than my sons, really," I began indirectly, as though talking of something else, in order to distract her attention. I confess I blushed.

"Why so?" she asked.

Ah! so she was listening!

"I don't know, Liza. I knew a father who was a stern, strict man, but he used to go down on his knees to his daughter, used to kiss her hands and feet, he couldn't make enough of her, really. When she danced at parties he used to stand for five hours at a stretch without taking his eyes off her. He was mad about her; I understand that! She would fall asleep tired at night, and he would get up to kiss her in her sleep and make the sign of the cross over her. He would go about in a dirty old coat, he was stingy to everyone else, but would spend his last penny for her, giving her expensive presents, and it was a delight to him when she was pleased with what he gave her. Fathers always love their daughters more than mothers do. Some girls live happily at home! And I believe I would never let my daughter marry."

"What next?" she said with a faint smile.

"I would be jealous, I really would. To think that she should kiss anyone else! That she should love a stranger more than her father! It's painful to imagine it. Of course, that's all nonsense, of course every father would be reasonable at last. But I believe before I would let her marry, I would worry myself to death; I would find fault with all her suitors. But I would end by letting her marry whom she herself loved. After all, the one whom the daughter loves always seems the worst to the father. That is always so. So many families get into trouble with that."

"Some are glad to sell their daughters, rather than to marry them honorably."

Ah! So that was it!

"Such a thing, Liza, happens in those accursed families in which there is neither love nor God," I retorted warmly, "and where there is no love, there is no sense either. There are such families, it's true, but I am not speaking of them. You must have seen wickedness in your own family, if you talk like that. You must have been genuinely unlucky. H'm!—that sort of thing mostly comes about through poverty."

"And is it any better among the rich? Even among the poor, honest people live happily."

"H'm—yes. Perhaps. Another thing, Liza, man only likes to count his troubles, but he does not count his joys. If he counted them up as he ought, he would see that every lot has enough happiness provided for it. And what if all goes well with the family, if the blessing of God is upon it, if the husband is a good one, loves you, cherishes you, never leaves you! There is happiness in such a family! Sometimes there is happiness even in the midst of sorrow; and indeed sorrow is everywhere. If you marry *you will find out for yourself.* But think of the first years of married life with one you love: what happiness, what happiness there sometimes is in it! And indeed it's the ordinary thing. In those early days even quarrels with one's husband end happily. Some women get up more quarrels with their husbands the more they love them. Indeed, I knew a woman like that: she seemed to say that because she loved him deeply, she would torment him out of love so that he'd feel it. Did you know that you may torment a man on purpose out of love? Women are particularly given to that, thinking to themselves, 'I will love him so much afterward, I will make so much of him, that it's no sin to torment him a little now.' And everyone in the house rejoices in the sight of you, and you are happy and gay and peaceful and honorable. Then there are some women who are jealous. If the husband goes off someplace—I knew one such woman, she couldn't restrain herself, but would jump up at night and would run off on the sly to find out where he was, whether he was with some other woman. That's already bad. And the woman knows herself it's wrong, and her heart fails her and she suffers, but, after all, she loves—it's all through love. And how sweet it is to make up after quarrels, to admit she was wrong, or to forgive him! And they are both so happy, all at once they become so happy, as though they had met anew, been married over again; as though their love had begun anew. And no one, no one should know what passes between husband and wife if they love one another. And no matter how their quarrels ended they ought not to call in even their own mothers to judge between them and tell tales of one another. They are their own judges. Love is a holy mystery and ought to be hidden from all other eyes, no matter what happens. That makes it holier and better. They respect one another more, and much is built on respect. And if once there has been love, if they have been married for love, why should love pass away? Surely one can keep it! It is rare that one cannot keep it. And if the husband is kind and straightforward, why should not love last? The first phase of married love will pass, it is true, but then there will come a love that is better still. Then there will be the union of souls, they will have everything in common, there will be no secrets between them. And once they have children, the most difficult times will seem to them happy, so long as there is love and courage. Even toil will be a joy, you may deny yourself bread for your children and even that will be a joy. After all, they will love you for it afterward; so you are laying by for your future. As the children grow up you feel that you are an example, a support for them; that even after you die your children will always cherish your thoughts and feelings, because they have received them from you, they will take on your semblance and likeness. So you see it is a great duty. How can it fail to draw the father and mother closer? People say it's a trial to have children. Who says that? It is heavenly joy! Are you fond of little children, Liza? I am awfully fond of them. You know—a little rosy baby boy at your bosom, and what husband's heart is not touched, seeing his wife nursing his child! A plump little rosy baby, sprawling and snuggling, chubby little hands and feet, clean tiny little nails, so tiny that it makes one laugh to look at them; eyes that look as if they understand everything. And while it sucks it clutches at your bosom with its little hand, plays. When its father comes up, the child tears itself away from the bosom, flings itself back, looks at its father, laughs, as though it were God knows how funny, and falls to sucking again. Or it will bite its mother's breast when it is cutting its little teeth while it looks sideways at her with its little eyes as though to say, 'Look, I am biting!' Is not all that a joy when they are all three together, husband, wife, and child? One can forgive a great deal for the sake of such moments. Yes, Liza, one must first learn to live oneself before one blames others!"

"It's by pictures, pictures like that one must get at you," I thought to myself, though I did not speak with real feeling, and all at once I flushed crimson. "What if she were suddenly to burst out laughing, what would I do then?" That idea drove me to fury. Toward the end of my speech I really was excited, and now my vanity was somehow wounded. The silence continued. I almost wanted to nudge her.

"Why are you . . ." she began, and stopped. But I understood: there was a quiver of something different in her voice, not abrupt, harsh, and unyielding as before, but something soft and shamefaced, so shamefaced that I suddenly felt ashamed and guilty.

"What?" I asked with tender curiosity.

"Why, you . . ."

"What?"

"Why you—speak exactly like a book," she said, and something sarcastic was heard in her voice.

That remark sent a pang to my heart. It was not what I was expecting.

I did not understand that she was hiding her feelings by sarcasm and that this is usually the last refuge of modest and chaste-souled people when the privacy of their soul is coarsely and intrusively invaded, and that their pride makes them refuse to surrender till the last moment and shrink from expressing their feelings to you. I ought to have guessed the truth for the timidity with which she had a number of times attempted her sarcasm, only bringing herself to utter it at last with an effort. But I did not guess, and a spiteful feeling took possession of me.

"Wait a bit!" I thought.

VII

"Oh, hush, Liza! How can you talk about my speaking like a book when it makes even me, an outsider, feel sick? Though I don't look at it as an outsider, for, indeed, all that has touched me to the heart. Is it possible, is it possible that you do not feel sick at being here yourself? Evidently habit does wonders! God knows what habit can do with anyone. Can you really and seriously think that you will never grow old, that you will always be good-looking, and that they will keep you here forever and ever? I say nothing of the filth here. Though let me tell you this about it; about your present life, I mean; even though you are young now, attractive, nice, with soul and feeling, yet you know, as soon as I came to myself just now, I felt at once sick at being here with you! After all, one can only come here when one is drunk. But if you were anywhere else, living as decent people live, I would perhaps be more than attracted by you, I would fall in love with you, would be glad of a look from you, let alone a word. I would hang about your door, would go down on my knees to you, we would become engaged and I would even consider it an honor to do so. I would not dare to have an impure thought about you. But here, after all, I know that I have only to whistle and you have to come with me whether you like it or not. I don't consult your wishes, but you mine. The lowest laborer hires himself as a workman but he doesn't make a slave of himself altogether; besides, he knows that he will be free again. But when will you be free? Only think what you are giving up here! What is it you are making a slave of? It is your soul, together with your body; you are selling your soul which you have no right to dispose of! You give your love to be outraged by every drunkard! Love! But after all, that's everything, but after all, it's a jewel, it's a maiden's treasure, love—why, after all a man would be ready to give his soul, to face death to gain that love. But how much is your love worth now? You can be bought, all of you, body and soul, and there is no need to strive for love when you can have everything without love. And after all, there is no greater insult for a girl than that, do you understand? To be sure, I have heard that they comfort you, poor fools, they let you have lovers of your own here. But after all, that's simply a farce, that's simply a sham, it's just laughing at you, and you are taken in by it! Why, do you suppose he really loves you, that lover of yours? I don't believe it. How can he love you when he knows that you may be called away from him any minute? He would be a vile fellow if he did! Would he have a grain of respect for you? What have you in common with him? He laughs at you and robs you—that is all his love amounts to! You are lucky if he does not beat you. Very likely he does beat you, too. Ask him, if you have one, whether he will marry you. He will laugh in your face, if he doesn't spit in it or give you a blow—yet he may not be worth a plugged nickel himself. And for what have you ruined your life, if you come to think of it? For the coffee they give you to drink and the plentiful meals? But after all, why do they feed you? An honest girl couldn't swallow the food, she would know why she was being fed. You are in debt here, and, of course, you will always be in debt, and you will go on in debt to the end, till the visitors here begin to scorn you. And that will soon happen, don't rely upon your youth—all that flies by, like an express train here, after all. You will be kicked out. And not simply kicked out; long before that they will begin to nag you, scold you, abuse you, as though you had not sacrificed your health for her, had not ruined your youth and your soul for her benefit, but as though you had ruined her, ravaged her, robbed her. And don't expect anyone to take your part; the others, your companions, will attack you, too, to win her favor, for all are in slavery here, and have lost all conscience and pity long ago. They have become utterly vile, and nothing on earth is viler, more loathsome, and more insulting than their abuse. And you are laying down everything here, everything unconditionally, youth and health and beauty and hope, and at twenty-two you will look like a woman of thirty-five, and you will be lucky if you are not diseased, pray to God for that! No doubt you are thinking now after all that you have a lark and no work to do! Yet there is no harder or more dreadful work in the world or ever has been. One would think that the heart alone would be worn out with tears. And you won't dare to say a word, not half a word, when they drive you away from here: you will go away as though you were to blame. You will change to another house, then to a third, then somewhere else, till you come down at last to the Haymarket. There you will be beaten at every turn; that is a courtesy there, the visitors there don't know how to be friendly without beating you. You don't believe that it is so hateful there? Go and look for yourself some time, you can see with your own eyes. Once, one New Year's Day, I saw a woman at a door. Her own kind had turned her out as a joke, to give her a taste of the frost because she had been howling too much, and they shut the door behind her. At nine o'clock in the morning she was already completely drunk, dishevelled, half-naked, covered with bruises, her face was powdered, but she had a black eye, blood was trickling from her nose and her teeth; some cabman had just beaten her. She was sitting on the stone steps, a salt fish of some sort was in her hand; she howling, wailing something about her 'fate' and beating with the fish on the steps, and cabmen and drunken soldiers were crowding in the doorway taunting her. You don't believe that you will ever be like that? I would not like to believe it, either, but how do you know, maybe ten years, eight years ago that very woman with that salt fish came here fresh as a little cherub, innocent, pure, knowing no evil, blushing at every word. Perhaps she was like you, proud, ready to take offence, not like the others; perhaps she looked like a queen, and knew what happiness was in store for the man who would love her and whom she would love. Do you see how it ended? And what if at that very minute when she was beating on the filthy steps with that fish, drunken and dishevelled—what if at that very minute she recalled the pure early days in her father's house, when she used to go to school and the neighbor's son watched for her on the way, declaring that he would love her as long as he lived, that he would devote his life to her, and when they vowed to love one another for ever and be married as soon as they were grown up! No, Liza, it would be a joy for you, a joy if you were to die soon of consumption in some corner, in some cellar like that woman just now. In the hospital, do you say? You will be lucky if they take you, but what if you are still of use to the madam here?

Consumption is a queer disease, it is not like fever. The patient goes on hoping till the last minute and says he is all right. He deludes himself. And that's just advantageous for your madam. Don't doubt it, that's how it is; you have sold your soul, and what is more you owe money, so you don't even dare to say a word. But when you are dying, everyone will abandon you, everyone will turn away from you, for then there will be nothing to get from you. What's more, they will reproach you for taking up space, for taking so long to die. You won't even be able to beg for a drink of water without getting abuse. 'Aren't you going to die, you foul wench; you won't let us sleep with your moaning, you make the gentlemen sick.' That's true. I have heard such things said myself. When you are really dying they will push you into the filthiest corner in the cellar; in the damp and darkness; what will your thoughts be, lying there alone? When you die, strange hands will lay you out, with grumbling and impatience; no one will bless you, no one will sigh for you, they will only want to get rid of you as soon as possible; they will buy a coffin, take you to the grave as they did that poor woman today, and celebrate your memory at the tavern. There is slush, filth, wet snow in the grave—no need to put themselves out for you: 'Let her down, Vanyukha; it's just like her "fate" after all, here she goes in, head first, the wench. Shorten the cord, you rascal.' 'It's all right as it is.' 'All right, is it? Why, she's on her side! Wasn't she a human being, too? Well, never mind, cover her up.' And they won't care to waste much time quarreling over you. They will scatter the wet blue clay as quickly as they can and go off to the tavern—and there your memory on earth will end; other women have children who visit their graves, fathers, husbands. While for you there will be neither tear, nor sigh, nor remembrance; no one, no one in the whole wide world will ever come to you; your name will vanish from the face of the earth as though you had never existed, had never been born at all! Nothing but filth and mud, no matter how much you knock on your coffin lid at night, when the dead arise, however you cry: 'Let me out, kind people, to live in the light of day! My life was no life at all; my life has been thrown away like a dirty rag; it was drunk away in the tavern at the Haymarket; let me out, kind people, to live in the world again!'"

And I worked myself up to such a pitch that I began to have a lump in my throat myself and—and suddenly I stopped, sat up in dismay, and bending over apprehensively, began to listen with a beating heart. I had reason to be worried.

I felt for some time that I was turning her soul upside down and breaking her heart, and the more I was convinced of it, the more I wanted to gain my end as quickly and as effectively as possible. The sport, the sport attracted me; yet it was not merely the sport.

I knew I was speaking stiffly, artificially, even bookishly, in short I did not know how to speak except "just like a book." But that did not bother me: after all I knew, I felt, that I would be understood and that this very bookishness would perhaps even be a help. But now, having achieved my effect, I was suddenly panic-stricken. No, I had never, never before witnessed such despair! She was lying face down, pressing her face deep into the pillow and clutching it in both hands. Her heart was being torn. Her youthful body was shuddering all over as though in convulsions. Suppressed sobs rent her bosom and suddenly burst out in weeping and wailing, then she pressed even deeper into the pillow: she did not want anyone here, not a single living soul, to know of her anguish and her tears. She bit the pillow, bit her hand till it bled (I saw that afterward), or, thrusting her fingers into her dishevelled hair, seemed rigid with the effort to restrain herself, holding her breath and clenching her teeth. I began to say something to her, to beg her to calm herself, but felt that I did not dare; and suddenly, all in a sort of chill, almost in terror, began fumbling in the dark, trying hurriedly to get dressed to go. It was dark: try as I would, I could not finish dressing quickly. Suddenly I felt a box of matches and a candlestick with a whole new candle in it. As soon as the room was lighted up, Liza sprang up, sat up in bed, and with a contorted face, with a half-insane smile, looked at me almost senselessly. I sat down beside her and took her hands; she came to herself, made a movement toward me, would have clasped me, but did not dare, and slowly bowed her head before me.

"Liza, my dear, I was wrong to— Forgive me," I began but she squeezed my hand in her fingers so tightly that I felt I was saying the wrong thing and stopped.

"This is my address, Liza, come to me."

"I will come," she whispered resolutely, her head still bowed.

"But now I am going, good-by—till we meet again."

I got up; she, too, stood up and suddenly flushed all over, shuddered, snatched up a shawl that was lying on a chair and muffled herself in it to her chin. As she did this she gave another sickly smile, blushed, and looked at me strangely. I felt wretched; I was in haste to get away—to disappear.

"Wait a minute," she said suddenly, in the passage just at the doorway, stopping me with her hand on my overcoat. She put down the candle hastily and ran off; evidently she had thought of something or wanted to show me something. As she ran away she flushed, her eyes shone, and a smile appeared on her lips—what was the meaning of it? Against my will I waited; she came back a minute later with an expression that seemed to ask forgiveness for something. In fact, it was not the same face, nor the same look it had been before: sullen, mistrustful, and obstinate. Her look was now imploring, soft, and at the same time trustful, caressing, timid. Children look that way at people they are very fond of, of whom they are asking a favor. Her eyes were a light hazel, they were lovely eyes, full of life, capable of expressing love as well as sullen hatred.

Making no explanation, as though I, as a sort of higher being, must understand everything without explanations, she held out a piece of paper to me. Her whole face was positively beaming at that instant with naïve, almost childish, triumph. I unfolded it. It was a letter to her from a medical student or someone of that sort—a very high-flown and flowery, but extremely respectful, declaration of love. I don't recall the words now, but I remember well enough that through the high-flown phrases there was apparent a genuine feeling, which cannot be feigned. When I had finished reading it I met her glowing, questioning, and childishly impatient eyes fixed upon me. She fastened her eyes upon my face and waited impatiently for what I would say. In a few words, hurriedly, but with a sort of joy and pride, she explained to me that she had been to a dance somewhere, in a private house, at some "very, very nice people's house, a *family* who *still know nothing,* absolutely nothing," for she had only come here so lately and it had all happened—and she hadn't made up her mind to stay and was certainly going away as soon as she had paid her debt—"and at that party there had been that student who had danced with her the whole evening, had talked to her, and it turned out that he had known her in the old days at Riga when he was a child, they had played together, but a very long time ago—and he knew her parents, but *about this* he knew nothing, nothing, nothing whatever, and had no suspicion! And the day after the dance (three days ago) he had sent her that letter through the friend with whom she had gone to the party—and—well, that was all."

She dropped her shining eyes with a sort of bashfulness as she finished.

The poor girl was keeping that student's letter as a treasure and had run to fetch it, her only treasure, because she did not want me to go away without knowing that she, too, was honestly and genuinely loved; that she, too, was addressed respectfully. No doubt that letter was destined to lie in her box and lead to nothing. But it doesn't matter, I am certain that she would guard it as a treasure all her life, as her pride and justification, and now at such a minute she had thought of that letter and brought it with naïve pride to raise herself in my eyes that I might see, that I, too, might think well of her. I said nothing, pressed her hand, and went out. I so longed to get away. I walked home all the way in spite of the fact that the wet snow was still falling in large flakes. I was exhausted, shattered, in bewilderment. But behind the bewilderment the truth was already gleaming. The loathsome truth!

VIII

It was some time, however, before I consented to recognize that truth. Waking up in the morning after some hours of heavy, leaden sleep, and immediately realizing all that had happened on the previous day, I was positively amazed at my last night's *sentimentality* with Liza, at all those "horrors and pity of yesterday." After all, to have such an attack of womanish hysteria, pah! I concluded. "And why did I force my address upon her? What if she comes? Let her come, though; it is all right—" But *obviously* that was not now the chief and the most important matter: I had to make haste and at all costs save my reputation in the eyes of Zverkov and Simonov as quickly as possible; that was the chief business. And I was so taken up that morning that I actually forgot all about Liza.

First of all I had to repay at once what I had borrowed the day before from Simonov. I resolved on a desperate course: to borrow fifteen roubles from Anton Antonich. As luck would have it he was in the best of humors that morning, and gave it to me at once, as soon as I asked. I was so delighted at this that, as I signed the I O U with a swaggering air, I told him *casually* that the night before "I had been making merry with some friends at the Hôtel de Paris; we were giving a farewell party to a comrade, in fact, I might say a friend of my childhood, and you know—a desperate rake, spoilt—of course, he belongs to a good family, and has considerable means, a brilliant career; he is witty, charming, carries on affairs with certain ladies, you understand; we drank an extra 'half-a-case' and—" And after all it went off all right; all this was said very lightly, unconstrainedly and complacently.

On reaching home I promptly wrote to Simonov.

To this hour I am lost in admiration when I recall the truly gentlemanly, good-humored, candid tone of my letter. With tact and good taste, and, above all, entirely without superfluous words, I blamed myself for all that had happened. I defended myself, "if only I may still be allowed to defend myself," by alleging that being utterly unaccustomed to wine, I had been intoxicated by the first glass which (I claimed) I had drunk before they arrived, while I was waiting for them at the Hotel de Paris between five and six o'clock. I particularly begged Simonov's pardon; I asked him also to convey my explanations to all the others, especially to Zverkov whom "I remember as though in a dream" I seem to have insulted. I added that I would have called upon all of them myself, but that my head ached, and that besides, I was rather ashamed. I was especially pleased with that "certain lightness," almost carelessness (strictly within the bounds of politeness, however), which was suddenly reflected in my style, and better than any possible arguments, gave them at once to understand that I took rather an independent view of "all that unpleasantness last night"; that I was by no means so utterly crushed as you, gentlemen, probably imagine; but on the contrary that I looked at it as a gentleman serenely respecting himself should. "On a young hero's past no censure is cast!"

"There is, after all, even an aristocratic playfulness about it!" I thought admiringly, as I read over the letter. "And it's all because I am a cultured and educated man! Others in my place would not have known how to extricate themselves, but here I have gotten out of it and am as gay as ever again, and all because I am a cultured and educated man of our day." And, indeed, perhaps, everything really was due to the wine yesterday. H'm! — well, no, it was not the wine. I drank nothing at all between five and six while I was waiting for them. I had lied to Simonov; lied shamelessly; and even now I wasn't ashamed —

Hang it all, though! The important thing was that I was rid of it.

I put six roubles in the letter, sealed it up, and asked Apollon to take it to Simonov. When he learned that there was money in the letter, Apollon became more respectful and agreed to take it. Toward evening I went out for a walk. My head was still aching and giddy, after yesterday. But as evening came on and the twilight grew thicker, my impressions changed and grew more and more confused and, after them, my thoughts. Something was not dead within me, in the depths of my heart and conscience it would not die, and it expressed itself as a burning anguish. For the most part I jostled my way through the most crowded business streets, along Meshchansky Street, along Sadovy Street and in the Yusupov Garden. I always particularly liked to stroll along these streets at dusk just when they become more crowded with people of all sorts, merchants and artisans going home from their day's work, with faces looking malicious out of anxiety. What I liked was just that cheap bustle, that bare, humdrum prosaic quality. On this occasion all that bustling in the streets irritated me more than ever. I could not make out what was wrong with me, I could not find the clue. Something was rising up, rising up continually in my soul, painfully, and refusing to be appeased. I returned home completely upset; it was just as though some crime were lying on my conscience.

The thought that Liza was coming worried me continually. It seemed queer to me that of all yesterday's memories, the memory of her tormented me as it were, particularly, quite separately, as it were. I had succeeded in forgetting everything else by evening time. I dismissed it all and was still perfectly satisfied with my letter to

Simonov. But on this point I was not satisfied at all. It was as though I were worried only by Liza. "What if she comes," I thought incessantly. "Well, so what, it's all right, let her come! H'm! it's horrid that she should see how I live for instance. Yesterday I seemed such a—hero to her, while now, h'm! It's horrid, though, that I have let myself sink so low, the room looks like a beggar's. And I brought myself to go out to dinner in such a suit! And my oilcloth sofa with the stuffing sticking out. And my robe, which will not cover me! What tatters. And she will see all this and she will see Apollon. That beast is certain to insult her. He will fasten upon her in order to be rude to me. And I, of course, will be panic-stricken as usual. I will begin to bow and scrape before her and to pull my robe around me, I will begin to smile, to lie. Oh, how foul! And it isn't the foulness of it that matters most! There is something more important, more loathsome, viler! Yes, viler! And to put on that dishonest lying mask again!"

When I reached that thought I flared up all at once.

"Why dishonest? How dishonest? I was speaking sincerely last night. I remember there was real feeling in me, too. What I wanted was to awake noble feelings in her. Her crying was a good thing, it will have a good effect."

Yet I could not feel at ease.

All that evening, even when I had come back home, even after nine o'clock, when I calculated that Liza could not possibly come, she still haunted me, and what was worse, she always came back to my mind in the same position. One moment out of all that had happened last night presented itself before me vividly: the moment when I struck a match and saw her pale, distorted face, with its tortured look. And what a pitiful, what an unnatural, what a distorted smile she had at that moment! But I did not know then that even fifteen years later I would still always picture Liza to myself with that pitiful, distorted, inappropriate smile which was on her face at that minute.

Next day I was ready again to look upon it all as nonsense, due to over-excited nerves, and, above all, as *exaggerated*. I always recognized that as a weak point of mine, and was sometimes very much afraid of it. "I exaggerate everything, that is where I go wrong," I repeated to myself every hour. But, nevertheless, Liza will very likely come still, nevertheless, was the refrain with which all my reflections ended then. I was so uneasy that I sometimes flew into a fury. "She'll come, she is certain to come!" I cried, running about the room, "if not today, she will come tomorrow; she'll seek me out! The damnable romanticism of these *pure hearts!* Oh, the vileness—oh, the silliness—oh, the stupidity of these 'wretched sentimental souls'! Why, how could one fail to understand? How could one possibly fail to understand?"

But at this point I stopped short, and even in great confusion.

"And how few, how few words," I thought, in passing, "were needed; how little of the idyllic (and affectedly, bookishly, artificially idyllic too) had sufficed to turn a whole human life at once according to my will. That's innocence for you! That's virgin soil for you!"

At times the thought occurred to me to go to her, "to tell her all" and beg her not to come to me. But this thought stirred such wrath in me that I believed I would have crushed that "damned" Liza if she had happened to be near me at the time. I would have insulted her, have spat at her, have turned her out, have struck her!

One day passed, however, a second and a third; she did not come and I began to grow calmer, I felt particularly bold and cheerful after nine o'clock, I even began sometimes to dream, and rather sweetly: I, for instance, became the salvation of Liza, simply through her coming to me and my talking to her. I develop her, educate her. Finally, I notice that she loves me, loves me passionately. I pretend not to understand (I don't know, however, why I pretend, just for effect, perhaps). At last all confusion, beautiful, trembling and sobbing, she flings herself at my feet and tells me that I am her savior, and that she loves me better than anything in the world. I am amazed, but—"Liza," I say, "can you really believe that I have noticed your love? I saw it all, I divined it, but I did not dare to approach you first, because I had an influence over you and was afraid that you would force yourself, out of gratitude, to respond to my love, would try to rouse in your heart a feeling which was perhaps absent, and I did not wish that because it would be—tyranny. It would be indelicate (in short, I launch off at that point into European, inexplicably lofty subtleties, à la George Sand),[27] but now, now you are mine, you are my creation, you are pure, you are beautiful, you are my beautiful wife.

> "And into my house come bold and free,
> Its rightful mistress there to be."[28]

Then we begin to live together happily, go abroad, etc., etc. In short, in the end it seemed vulgar to me myself, and I began to put out my tongue at myself.

Besides, they won't let her out, "the hussy!" I thought. After all, they don't let them go out very readily, especially in the evening (for some reason I fancied she would have to come in the evening, and precisely at seven o'clock). Though she did say she was not altogether a slave there yet, and had certain rights; so, h'm! Damn it all, she will come, she is sure to come!

It was a good thing, in fact, that Apollon distracted my attention at that time by his rudeness. He drove me beyond all patience! He was the bane of my life, the curse laid upon me by Providence. We had been squabbling continually for years, and I hated him. My God, how I hated him! I believe I had never hated anyone in my life as I hated him, especially at some moments. He was an elderly, dignified man, who worked part of his time as a tailor. But for some unknown reason, he despised me beyond all measure, and looked down upon me insufferably. Though indeed, he looked down upon everyone. Simply to glance at that flaxen, smoothly brushed head, at the tuft of hair he combed up on his forehead and oiled with sunflower oil, at that dignified mouth, always pursed, made one feel one was confronting a man who never doubted himself. He was an insufferable pedant, the greatest pedant I had met on earth, and with that had a vanity only befitting Alexander the Great. He was in love with every button on his coat, every nail on his fingers—absolutely in love with them, and he looked it! In his behavior to me he was an absolute tyrant, spoke very little to me, and if he chanced to glance at me he gave me a firm, majestically

---

[27] **George Sand:** The pseudonym for Aurore Dudevant (1804–1876), a female French novelist.

[28] **There to be:** The last lines of the poem used as an epigraph for Part II of *Notes*.

self-confident, and invariably ironical look that sometimes drove me to fury. He did his work with the air of doing me the greatest favor. Though he did scarcely anything for me, and did not, indeed, consider himself obliged to do anything, there could be no doubt that he looked upon me as the greatest fool on earth, and that the reason he did not "get rid of me" was simply that he could get wages from me every month. He consented "to do nothing" for me for seven roubles a month. Many sins should be forgiven me for what I suffered from him. My hatred reached such a point that sometimes his very walk almost threw me into convulsions. What I loathed particularly was his lisp. His tongue must have been a little too long or something of that sort, for he continually lisped, and seemed to be very proud of it, imagining that it greatly added to his dignity. He spoke in a slow, measured tone, with his hands behind his back and his eyes fixed on the ground. He maddened me particularly when he read the Psalms aloud to himself behind his partition. I waged many a battle over that reading! But he was awfully fond of reading aloud in the evenings, in a slow, even, chanting voice, as though over the dead. It is interesting that he has ended up that way. He hires himself out to read the Psalms over the dead, and at the same time he kills rats and makes shoe polish. But at that time I could not get rid of him, it was as though he were chemically combined with my existence. Besides, nothing would have induced him to consent to leave me. I could not live in a furnished room: my apartment was my privacy, my shell, my cave, in which I concealed myself from all mankind, and Apollon seemed to me, God only knows why, an integral part of that apartment, and for seven whole years I could not get rid of him.

For example, to be two or three days late with his wages was impossible. He would have made such a fuss, I would not have known where to hide my head. But I was so exasperated with everyone during that period, that I made up my mind for some reason and with some object to *punish* Apollon and not to pay him for a fortnight the wages I owed him. I had intended to do this for a long time, for the last two years, simply in order to teach him not to give himself airs with me, and to show him that if I liked I could withhold his wages. I decided to say nothing to him about it, and even to be silent purposely in order to conquer his pride and force him to be the first to speak of his wages. Then I would take the seven roubles out of a drawer, show him I have the money and have put it aside purposely, but that I don't want, I don't want, I simply don't want to pay him his wages, I don't want to just because that is *what I want*, because "I am master and it is for me to decide," because he has been disrespectful, because he is a ruffian; but if he were to ask respectfully I might be softened and give it to him, otherwise he might wait another fortnight, another three weeks, a whole month . . .

But no matter how angry I was, he always got the better of me. I could not even hold out for four days. He began as he always did begin such cases, for there had been such cases already, there had been attempts (and it may be observed I knew all this beforehand, I knew his nasty tactics by heart), to wit: he would begin by fixing upon me an exceedingly severe stare, keeping it up for several minutes at a time, particularly on meeting me or seeing me out of the house. If I held out and pretended not to notice these stares, he would, still in silence, proceed to further tortures. All at once, for no reason at all, he would softly and smoothly walk into my room when I was pacing up and down, or reading, stand at the door, one hand behind his back and one foot forward, and fix upon me a stare more than severe, utterly contemptuous. If I suddenly asked him what he wanted, he would not answer, but continue to stare at me persistently for some seconds longer, then, with a peculiar compression of his lips and a very significant air, deliberately turn round and deliberately go back to his room. Two hours later he would come out again and again present himself before me in the same way. It has happened that in my fury I did not even ask him what he wanted, but simply raised my head sharply and imperiously and began staring back at him. So we stared at one another for two minutes; at last he turned with deliberation and dignity and went back again for two hours.

If I were still not brought to reason by all this, but persisted in my revolt, he would suddenly begin sighing while he looked at me, long, deep sighs as though measuring by them the depths of my moral degradation, and, of course, it ended at last by his triumphing completely: I raged and shouted, but was still forced to do what he wanted.

This time the usual maneuvers of "severe staring" had scarcely begun when I lost my temper and flew at him in a fury. I was irritated beyond endurance even without him.

"Wait," I shouted in a frenzy, as he was slowly and silently turning with one hand behind his back, to go to his room. "Wait! Come back, come back, I tell you!" and I must have bawled so unnaturally, that he turned round and even looked at me with a certain amazement. However, he persisted in saying nothing, and that infuriated me.

"How dare you come and look at me like that without being sent for? Answer!"

After looking at me calmly for half a minute, he began turning round again.

"Wait!" I roared, running up to him. "Don't stir! There. Answer, now: what did you come in to look at?"

"If you have any order to give me at the moment, it is my duty to carry it out," he answered, after another silent pause, with a slow, measured lisp, raising his eyebrows and calmly twisting his head from one side to another, all this with exasperating composure.

"That's not it, that is not what I am asking you about, you torturer!" I shouted, shaking with anger. "I'll tell you myself, you torturer, why you came here: you see, I don't give you your wages, you are so proud you don't want to bow down and ask for it, and so you have come to punish me with your stupid stares, to torture me, and you have no sus-pic-ion, you torturer, how stupid it is—stupid, stupid, stupid, stupid!"

He would have turned round again without a word, but I seized him.

"Listen," I shouted to him. "Here's the money, do you see, here it is" (I took it out of the table drawer) "here's the whole seven roubles but you are not going to have it, you . . . are . . . not . . . going . . . to . . . have it until you come respectfully with bowed head to beg my pardon. Do you hear?"

"That cannot be," he answered, with the most unnatural self-confidence.

"It will be so," I said. "I give you my word of honor, it will be!"

"And there's nothing for me to beg your pardon for," he went on, as though he had not noticed my exclamations at all. "Why, besides, you called me a 'torturer,' for which I can summon you at the police station at any time for insulting behavior."

"Go, summon me," I roared, "go at once, this very minute, this very second! You are a torturer all the same! A torturer! A torturer!" But he merely looked at me, then turned, and regardless of my loud calls to him, he walked to his room with an even step and without looking round.

"If it had not been for Liza nothing of this would have happened," I decided inwardly. Then, after waiting a minute, I myself went behind the screen with a dignified and solemn air, though my heart was beating slowly and violently.

"Apollon," I said quietly and emphatically, though I was breathless, "go at once without a minute's delay and fetch the police officer."

He had meanwhile settled himself at his table, put on his spectacles and taken up something to tailor. But, hearing my order, he burst into a guffaw.

"At once, go this minute! Go on, or else you can't imagine what will happen."

"You are certainly not in your right mind," he observed, without even raising his head, lisping as deliberately as ever and threading his needle. "Whoever heard of a man sending for the police against himself? And as for being frightened—you are upsetting yourself about nothing, for nothing will come of it."

"Go!" I shrieked, grabbing him by the shoulder. I felt that in another minute I would hit him.

But I did not notice that suddenly the door from the passage softly and slowly opened at that instant and a figure came in, stopped short, and began staring at us in amazement. I glanced, nearly died with shame, and rushed back to my room. There, clutching at my hair with both hands, I leaned my head against the wall and stood motionless in that position.

Two minutes later I heard Apollon's deliberate footsteps.

"There is *some woman* asking for you," he said, looking at me with peculiar severity. Then he stood aside and let in—Liza. He would not go away, but stared at us sarcastically.

"Go away, go away," I commanded in desperation. At that moment my clock began whirring and wheezing and struck seven.

IX

And into my house come bold and free,
   Its rightful mistress there to be.

    From the same poetic work

I stood before her crushed, crestfallen, revoltingly embarrassed, and I believe I smiled as I did my utmost to wrap myself in the skirts of my ragged wadded robe—just exactly as I had imagined the scene not long before in a fit of depression. After standing over us for a couple of minutes Apollon went away, but that did not make me more comfortable. What made it worse was that suddenly, she, too, became embarrassed, more so, in fact, than I would have expected. At the sight of me, of course.

"Sit down," I said mechanically, moving a chair up to the table, and I sat down on the sofa. She obediently sat down at once and gazed at me open-eyed, evidently expecting something from me at once. This naïveté of expectation drove me to fury, but I restrained myself.

She ought to have tried not to notice, as though everything had been as usual, while instead she . . . and I dimly felt that I would make her pay dearly for *all this.*

"You have found me in a strange position, Liza," I began, stammering and knowing that this was the wrong way to begin.

"No, no, don't imagine anything," I cried, seeing that she had suddenly flushed. "I am not ashamed of my poverty. On the contrary, I look on my poverty with pride. I am poor but honorable. One can be poor and honorable," I muttered. "However — would you like tea?"

"No —" she was beginning.

"Wait a minute."

I leapt up and ran to Apollon. I had to get out of the room somehow.

"Apollon," I whispered in feverish haste, flinging down before him the seven roubles which had remained all the time in my clenched fist, "here are your wages. You see I give them to you; but for that you must come to my rescue: bring me tea and a dozen rusks from the restaurant. If you won't go, you'll make a man miserable! You don't know what this woman is. This is — everything! You may be imagining something, but you don't know what a woman she is!"

Apollon, who had already sat down to his work and put on his spectacles again, at first glanced askance at the money without speaking or putting down his needle; then, without paying the slightest attention to me, or making any answer, he went on busying himself with his needle, which he had not yet threaded. I waited before him for several minutes with my arms crossed *à la Napoléon.* My temples were moist with sweat. I was pale, I felt it. But, thank God, he must have been moved to pity, looking at me. Having threaded his needle, he deliberately got up from his seat, deliberately moved back his chair, deliberately took off his spectacles, deliberately counted the money, and finally asking me over his shoulder: "Shall I get a whole pot?" deliberately walked out of the room. As I was going back to Liza, the thought occurred to me on the way: shouldn't I run away just as I was in my robe, no matter where, and let come what may?

I sat down again. She looked at me uneasily. For some minutes we were silent.

"I will kill him," I shouted suddenly, striking the table with my fist so that the ink spurted out of the inkstand.

"What are you saying!" she cried, starting.

"I will kill him! kill him!" I shrieked, suddenly striking the table in absolute frenzy, and at the same time fully understanding how stupid it was to be in such a frenzy.

"You don't know, Liza, what that torturer is to me. He is my torturer. He has gone now to fetch some rusks; he —"

And suddenly I burst into tears. It was an hysterical attack. How ashamed I felt in the midst of my sobs; but still I could not restrain them.

She was frightened. "What is the matter? What is wrong?" she shrieked, fussing around me.

"Water, give me water, over there!" I muttered in a faint voice, though I was inwardly conscious that I could easily have done without water and without muttering in a faint voice. But I was what is called *putting it on,* to save appearances, though the attack was a genuine one.

She gave me water, looking at me in bewilderment. At that moment Apollon brought in the tea. It suddenly seemed to me that this commonplace and prosaic tea was terribly undignified and paltry after all that had happened, and I blushed. Liza even looked at Apollon with alarm. He went out without a glance at us.

"Liza, do you despise me?" I asked, looking at her fixedly, trembling with impatience to know what she was thinking.

She was embarrassed and did not know what to answer.

"Drink your tea," I said to her angrily. I was angry with myself, but, of course, it was she who would have to pay for it. A horrible spite against her suddenly surged up in my heart; I believe I could have killed her. To revenge myself on her I swore inwardly not to say a word to her all the time. "She is the cause of it all," I thought.

Our silence lasted for five minutes. The tea stood on the table; we did not touch it. I had got to the point of purposely refraining from beginning to drink in order to embarrass her further; it was awkward for her to begin alone. Several times she glanced at me with mournful perplexity. I was obstinately silent. I was, of course, myself the chief sufferer, because I was fully conscious of the disgusting meanness of my spiteful stupidity, and yet at the same time I absolutely could not restrain myself.

"I want to—get away—from there altogether," she began, to break the silence in some way, but, poor girl, that was just what she ought not to have spoken about at such a moment, stupid enough even without that to a man so stupid as I was. My heart positively ached with pity for her tactless and unnecessary straightforwardness. But something hideous at once stifled all compassion in me: it even provoked me to greater venom. Let the whole world go to pot. Another five minutes passed.

"Perhaps I am in your way?" she began timidly, hardly audibly, and was getting up.

But as soon as I saw this first impulse of wounded dignity I positively trembled with spite, and at once burst out.

"Why did you come to me, tell me that, please?" I began, gasping for breath and regardless of all logical connection in my words. I longed to have it all out at once, at one burst: I did not even trouble how to begin.

"Why did you come? Answer, answer," I cried, hardly knowing what I was doing. "I'll tell you, my good girl, why you came. You came because I talked *fine sentiments* to you then. So now you are soft as butter and longing for fine sentiments again. So you may as well know, know that I was laughing at you then. And I am laughing at you now. Why are you shuddering? Yes, I was laughing at you! I had been insulted just before, at dinner, by the fellows who came that evening before me. I came to you, meaning to thrash one of them, an officer; but I didn't succeed. I didn't find him; I had to avenge the insult on someone to get my own back again; you turned up, I vented my spleen on you and laughed at you. I had been humiliated, so I wanted to humiliate; I had been treated like a rag, so I wanted to show my power. That's what it was, and you imagined I had come there on purpose to save you, didn't you? Did you imagine that? Did you imagine that?"

I knew that she would perhaps get muddled and not grasp all the details, but I knew, too, that she would grasp the gist of it very well. And so, indeed, she did. She turned white as a handkerchief, tried to say something, and distorted her mouth painfully but she sank on a chair as though she had been felled by an ax. And all the time afterward she listened to me with her lips parted and her eyes wide open, shuddering with awful terror. The cynicism, the cynicism of my words overwhelmed her—

"Save you!" I went on, jumping up from my chair and running up and down the room before her. "Save you from what? But perhaps I am worse than you myself. Why didn't you throw it in my teeth when I was giving you that sermon: 'But you, what did you come here for yourself? Was it to read us a sermon?' Power, power was what I wanted then, sport was what I wanted, I wanted to wring out your tears, your humiliation, your hysteria—that was what I wanted then! After all, I couldn't keep it up then, because I am a wretch, I was frightened, and, the devil knows why, gave you my address in my folly. Afterward, before I got home, I was cursing and swearing at you because of that address. I hated you already because of the lies I had told you. Because I only like to play with words, to dream in my mind, but, do you know, what I really want is that you would all go to hell, that is what I want. I want peace; yes, I'd sell the whole world for a farthing right now, so long as I was left in peace. Is the world to go to pot, or am I to go without my tea? I say let the world go to pot as long as I get my tea every time. Did you know that, or not? Well, anyway, I know that I am a blackguard, a scoundrel, an egotist, a sluggard. Here I have been shuddering for the last three days at the thought of your coming. And do you know what has worried me particularly for these three days? That I posed as such a hero to you then, and now you would see me in a wretched torn robe, a beggar, an abomination. I told you just now that I was not ashamed of my poverty; you may as well know that I am ashamed of it; I am more ashamed of it than of anything, more afraid of it than of being found out if I were a thief, because I am as vain as though I had been skinned and the very air blowing on me hurt. Surely by now even you must have realized that I will never forgive you for having found me in this wretched robe, just as I was flying at Apollon like a spiteful sheep-dog at his lackey, and the lackey was jeering at him! And I shall never forgive you for the tears I could not help shedding before you just now, like some silly woman put to shame! And for what I am confessing to you now, I shall never forgive *you,* either! Yes—you must answer for it all because you turned up like this, because I am a blackguard, because I am the nastiest, stupidest, pettiest, absurdest, and most envious of all worms on earth, none of whom is a bit better than I am, but who, the devil only knows why, are never embarrassed; while I will always be insulted by every louse, that is my doom! And what is it to me that you don't understand a word of this! And what do I care, what do I care about you, and whether you go to ruin there or not? Do you understand how I will hate you now after saying this, for having been here and listening? After all, a man speaks out like this once in a lifetime and then it is in hysterics! What more do you want? Why, after all, do you still stand there in front of me? Why do you torment me? Why don't you go?"

But at this point a strange thing happened.

I was so accustomed to think and imagine everything from books, and to picture everything in the world to myself just as I had made it up in my dreams beforehand, that I could not even take in this strange circumstance all at once. What happened was this: Liza, wounded and crushed by me, understood a great deal more than I imagined. She understood from all this what a woman understands first of all, if she feels genuine love, that is, that I was myself unhappy.

The frightened and wounded expression on her face was followed first by a look of sorrowful perplexity. When I began to call myself a scoundrel and a blackguard and my tears flowed (that tirade was accompanied throughout by tears) her whole face worked convulsively. She was on the point of getting up and stopping me; when I finished she took no notice of my shouting: "Why are you here, why don't you go away?" but realized only that it must have been very bitter to me to say all this. Besides, she was so crushed, poor girl; she considered herself infinitely beneath me; how could she feel anger or resentment? Suddenly she leapt up from her chair with an irresistible impulse and held out her hands, yearning toward me, though still timid and not daring to stir. At this point there was an upheaval in my heart too. Then she suddenly rushed to me, threw her arms round me, and burst into tears. I, too, could not restrain myself, and sobbed as I never had before.

"They won't let me—I can't be—good!" I managed to say, then I went to the sofa, fell on it, face downward, and sobbed on it for a quarter of an hour in genuine hysterics. She knelt near me, put her arms round me, and stayed motionless in that position.

But the trouble was that the hysterics could not go on for ever. And (after all, I am writing the loathsome truth) lying face downward on the sofa with my face thrust into my nasty leather pillow, I began by degrees to be aware of a far-away, involuntary, but irresistible feeling that after all it would be awkward for me to raise my head now and look Liza straight in the face. Why was I ashamed? I don't know, but I was ashamed. In my overwrought brain the thought also occurred that our parts were after all completely reversed now, that she was now the heroine, while I was just a crushed and humiliated creature as she had been before me that night— four days before . . . And all this came into my mind during the minutes I was lying face down on the sofa!

My God! surely I was not envious of her then?

I don't know, to this day I cannot decide, and at the time, of course, I was still less able to understand what I was feeling than now. I cannot get on without domineering and tyrannizing over someone, after all, but—but, after all, there is no explaining anything by reasoning and consequently it is useless to reason.

I conquered myself, however, and raised my head—I had to do so sooner or later—and I am convinced to this day that it was just because I was ashamed to look at her that another feeling was suddenly kindled and flamed up in my heart—a feeling of mastery and possession. My eyes gleamed with passion, and I gripped her hands tightly. How I hated her and how I was drawn to her at that minute! The one feeling intensified the other. It was almost like an act of vengeance! At first there was a look of amazement, even of terror, on her face, but only for one instant. She warmly and rapturously embraced me.

X

A quarter of an hour later I was rushing up and down the room in frenzied impatience, from minute to minute I went up to the screen and peeped through the crack at Liza. She was sitting on the floor with her head leaning against the bed, and must have been crying. But she did not go away, and that irritated me. This time she understood it all. I had insulted her once and for all, but—there's no need to describe it. She realized that my outburst of passion had been simply revenge, a new humiliation for her and that to my earlier, almost generalized hatred was added now a *personal, envious* hatred—though I do not maintain positively that she understood all this distinctly; but she certainly did fully understand that I was a despicable man, and what was worse, incapable of loving her.

I know I shall be told that this is incredible; that it is incredible to be as spiteful and stupid as I was; it may be added it was strange that I would not love her, or at any rate, appreciate her love. Why is it strange? In the first place, by then I was incapable of love, for, I repeat, with me loving meant tyrannizing and showing my moral superiority. I have never in my life ever been able to imagine any other sort of love, and have nowadays come to the point of sometimes thinking that love really consists in the right—freely given by the beloved object—to be tyrannized over. Even in my underground dreams I did not imagine love in any form except as a struggle. I always began it with hatred and ended it with moral subjugation, and afterward I could never imagine what to do with the subjugated object. And what is there incredible in that, since I had so succeeded in corrupting myself morally, since I was so out of touch with "real life," that I had just thought of reproaching her and putting her to shame for having come to me to hear "fine sentiments," and I did not even guess that she had come not at all to hear fine sentiments, but to love me, because to a woman true resurrection, true salvation from any sort of ruin, and true moral regeneration is contained in love and can only show itself in that form. I no longer hated her so much, however, when I was running about the room and peeping through the crack in the screen. I was only insufferably oppressed by her being here. I wanted her to disappear. I wanted "peace," I wanted to be left alone in my underground world. "Real life" oppressed me with its novelty so much that I could hardly breathe.

But several minutes passed and she still remained without stirring, as though she were unconscious. I had the shamelessness to tap softly at the screen as though to remind her. She started, sprang up, and flew to seek her shawl, her hat, her coat, just as though she were making her escape from me. Two minutes later she came from behind the screen and looked with heavy eyes at me. I gave a spiteful grin, which was forced, however, to *keep up appearances,* and I turned away from her look.

"Good-bye," she said, going toward the door.

I ran up to her, seized her hand, opened it, thrust something in it—and closed it again. Then I turned immediately and hurriedly rushed to the other corner of the room, to avoid seeing, anyway—

I meant to lie a moment ago—to write that I did this accidentally, not knowing what I was doing, through foolishness, through losing my head. But I don't want to lie, and so I will say straight out that I opened her hand and put the money in it—from spite. It came into my head to do so while I was running up and down the room and she was sitting behind the screen. But I can say this for certain: though I did that cruel thing purposely, it was not an impulse from the heart, but came from my evil brain. This cruelty was so affected, so purposely made up, so completely a product of the brain, of *books,* that I could not even keep it up for a minute—first I rushed to the corner to avoid seeing her, and then in shame and despair rushed after Liza. I opened the door in the passage and began listening.

"Liza! Liza!" I cried on the stairs, but in a low voice, not boldly.

There was no answer, but it seemed to me I heard her footsteps, lower down on the stairs.

"Liza!" I cried, more loudly.

No answer. But at that minute I heard the stiff outer glass door open heavily with a creak and slam violently. The roar echoed up the stairs.

She had gone. I went back to my room in hesitation. I felt horribly oppressed.

I stood still at the table beside the chair on which she had sat and looked aimlessly before me. A minute passed. Suddenly I started; straight before me on the table I saw—in short, I saw a crumpled blue five-rouble note, the one I had thrust into her hand a minute before. It was the same note; it could be no other, there was no other in the apartment. So she had managed to fling it from her hand on the table at the moment when I had rushed into the farther corner.

So what? I might have expected that she would do that. Might I have expected it? No, I was such an egotist, I was so lacking in respect for people in actuality, that I could not even imagine she would do so. I could not endure it. A moment later I flew like a madman to get dressed, flinging on what I could at random and ran headlong after her. She could not have got two hundred paces away when I ran out into the street.

It was a still night and the snow was coming down in masses and falling almost perpendicularly, blanketing the pavement and the empty street. There was no one in the street, no sound was to be heard. The street lamps gave a disconsolate and useless glimmer. I ran two hundred paces to the intersection and stopped short. Where had she gone? And why was I running after her?

Why? To fall down before her, to sob with remorse, to kiss her feet, to beg her forgiveness! I longed for that. My whole heart was being rent to pieces, and never, never will I recall that minute with indifference. But—what for? I thought. Would I not begin to hate her, perhaps, even tomorrow, just because I had kissed her feet today? Would I give her happiness? Had I not again recognized that day, for the hundredth time, what I was worth? Would I not torment her?

I stood in the snow, gazing into the troubled darkness and pondered this.

"And will it not be better? *Will it not be better?*" I fantasized afterward at home, stifling the living pang of my heart with fantastic dreams. "Will it not be better that she carry the outrage with her forever? Outrage—why, after all, that is purification: it is the most stinging and painful consciousness! Tomorrow I would have defiled her soul and have exhausted her heart, while now the feeling of humiliation will never die in her, and however loathsome the filth awaiting her, that outrage will elevate and purify her—by hatred—h'm!—perhaps by forgiveness also. But will all that make things easier for her, though? . . ."

And, indeed, I will at this point ask an idle question on my own account: which is better—cheap happiness or exalted sufferings? Well, which is better?

So I dreamed as I sat at home that evening, almost dead with the pain in my soul. Never yet had I endured such suffering and remorse, but could there possibly have been the faintest doubt when I ran out from my lodging that I would turn back halfway? I never met Liza again and I have heard nothing about her. I will add, too, that for a long time afterward I remained pleased with the *phrase* about the utility of outrage and hatred, in spite of the fact that I almost fell ill from misery.

Even now, many years later, I somehow remember all this as very bad. I have many bad memories now, but—hadn't I better end my "Notes" here? I believe I made a mistake in beginning to write this *story;* so it's hardly literature so much as corrective punishment. After all, to tell long stories, for example, showing how I have ruined my life by morally rotting in my corner, through lack of fitting environment, through divorce from reality, and vainglorious spite in my underground world, would certainly not be interesting; a novel needs a hero, and all the traits of an anti-hero are *expressly* gathered together here, and what matters most, it all produces an unpleasant impression, for we are all divorced from life, we are all cripples, every one of us, more or less. We are so far divorced from it that we immediately feel a sort of loathing for actual "real life," and so cannot even stand to be reminded of it. After all, we have reached the point of almost looking at actual "real life" as an effort, almost as hard work, and we are all privately agreed that it is better in books. And why do we sometimes fret, why are we perverse and ask for something else? We don't know why ourselves. It would be worse for us if our capricious requests were granted. Come, try, come give anyone of us, for instance, a little more independence, untie our hands, widen the spheres of our activity, relax the controls and we—yes, I assure you—we would immediately beg to be under control again. I know that you will very likely be angry with me for that, and will begin to shout and stamp your feet. "Speak for yourself," you will say, "and for your miseries in your underground holes, but don't dare to say 'all of us.'" Excuse me, gentlemen, after all I do not mean to justify myself with that "all of us." As for what concerns me in particular I have only, after all, in my life carried to an extreme what you have not dared to carry halfway, and what's more, you have taken your cowardice for good sense, and have found comfort in deceiving yourselves. So that perhaps, after all, there is more "life" in me than in you. Look into it more carefully! After all, we don't even know where living exists now, what it is, and what it is called! Leave us alone without books and we will be lost and in a confusion at once—we will not know what to join, what to cling to, what to love and what to hate, what to respect and what to despise. We are even oppressed by being men— men with real *individual* body and blood. We are ashamed of it, we think it a disgrace and try to contrive to be some sort of impossible generalized man. We are still-born, and for many years we have not been begotten by living fathers, and that suits us better and better. We are developing a taste for it. Soon we shall somehow contrive to be born from an idea. But enough; I don't want to write more from "underground" . . .

The "notes" of this paradoxalist do not end here, however. He could not resist and continued them. But it also seems to me that we may stop here.

❧ The Brothers Karamazov

Translated by Constance Garnett

THE GRAND INQUISITOR

"*. . . Do you know, Alyosha—don't laugh! I made a poem about a year ago. If you can waste another ten minutes on me, I'll tell it to you.*"

"*You wrote a poem?*"

"*Oh, no, I didn't write it,*" laughed Ivan, "*and I've never written two lines of poetry in my life. But I made up this poem in prose and I remembered it. I was carried away when I made it up. You will be my first reader—that is, listener. Why should an author forego even one listener?*" smiled Ivan. "*Shall I tell it to you?*"

"*I am all attention,*" said Alyosha.

"*My poem is called 'The Grand Inquisitor'; it's a ridiculous thing, but I want to tell it to you.*"

"Even this must have a preface—that is, a literary preface," laughed Ivan, "and I am a poor hand at making one. You see, my action takes place in the sixteenth century, and at that time, as you probably learnt at school, it was customary in poetry to bring down heavenly powers on earth. Not to speak of Dante, in France clerks, as well as the monks in the monasteries, used to give regular performances in which the Madonna, the saints, the angels, Christ, and God Himself were brought on the stage.

"The Grand Inquisitor." The setting for Ivan's prose poem is Seville, Spain, at the height of the Inquisition in the sixteenth century, when the Roman Catholic hierarchy attempted to purge heretics and Protestant sympathizers from the church. In the poem Jesus has finally returned to earth to heal and comfort his people after fifteen centuries. He is immediately arrested and isolated by the Grand Inquisitor. In a persuasive and moving monologue, the Inquisitor explains to Jesus why the church as an institution had to betray his original mission and enslave people by exploiting "miracle, mystery, and authority." According to the Inquisitor, the masses were incapable of handling the freedom intended by Jesus and were willing to exchange it for bread and the illusion of freedom. The Inquisitor vacillates between powerful apologist for institutional cynicism and lonely, disillusioned atheist. In a perfect response to the Inquisitor's degradation, Jesus kisses him on the lips and departs.

Following "The Grand Inquisitor" in the novel is a discussion with a Father Zossima, a true holy man who acts as a foil to the Inquisitor. Father Zossima preaches unconditional love for our fallen world: "Love all God's creation, the whole and every grain of sand in it. Love every leaf, every ray of God's light. Love the animals, love the plants, love everything. If you love everything, you will perceive the divine mystery in things. Once you perceive it, you will begin to comprehend it better every day. And you will come at last to love the whole world with an all-embracing love." In contrast to Father Zossima, the Inquisitor represents the corruption of the spirit through institutional authority.

The translation of "The Grand Inquisitor" by Constance Garnett, first published as a part of *The Brothers Karamazov* in 1912, quickly became the standard translation of this work. The editors provided the footnotes.

In those days it was done in all simplicity. In Victor Hugo's 'Notre Dame de Paris' an edifying and gratuitous spectacle was provided for the people in the Hotel de Ville of Paris in the reign of Louis XI in honor of the birth of the dauphin. It was called *Le bon jugement de la très sainte et gracieuse Vierge Marie,*[1] and she appears herself on the stage and pronounces her *bon jugement.* Similar plays, chiefly from the Old Testament, were occasionally performed in Moscow, too, up to the times of Peter the Great. But besides plays there were all sorts of legends and ballads scattered about the world, in which the saints and angels and all the powers of Heaven took part when required. In our monasteries the monks busied themselves in translating, copying, and even composing such poems—and even under the Tatars. There is, for instance, one such poem (of course, from the Greek), 'The Wanderings of Our Lady Through Hell,' with descriptions as bold as Dante's. Our Lady visits Hell, and the Archangel Michael leads her through the torments. She sees the sinners and their punishment. There she sees among others one noteworthy set of sinners in a burning lake; some of them sink to the bottom of the lake so that they can't swim out, and 'these God forgets'—an expression of extraordinary depth and force. And so Our Lady, shocked and weeping, falls before the throne of God and begs for mercy for all in Hell—for all she has seen there, and indiscriminately. Her conversation with God is immensely interesting. She beseeches Him, she will not desist, and when God points to the hands and feet of her Son, nailed to the Cross, and asks, 'How can I forgive His tormentors?' she bids all the saints, all the martyrs, all the angels and archangels to fall down with her and pray for mercy on all without distinction. It ends by her winning from God a respite of suffering every year from Good Friday till Trinity day, and the sinners at once raise a cry of thankfulness from Hell, chanting, 'Thou art just, O Lord, in this judgment.' Well, my poem would have been of that kind if it had appeared at that time. He comes on the scene in my poem, but He says nothing, only appears and passes on. Fifteen centuries have passed since He promised to come in His glory, fifteen centuries since His prophet wrote, 'Behold, I come quickly';[2] 'Of that day and that hour knoweth no man, neither the Son, but the Father,'[3] as He Himself predicted on earth. But humanity awaits him with the same faith and with the same love. Oh, with greater faith, for it is fifteen centuries since man has ceased to see signs from Heaven.

> No signs from Heaven come today
> To add to what the heart doth say.

There was nothing left but faith in what the heart doth say. It is true there were many miracles in those days. There were saints who performed miraculous cures; some holy people, according to their biographies, were visited by the Queen of Heaven herself. But the devil did not slumber, and doubts were already arising among men of the truth of these miracles. And just then there appeared in the north of Germany a terrible new heresy. 'A huge star like to a torch' (that is, to a church) 'fell on the sources of the waters and they became bitter.' These heretics began blasphemously

---

[1] *Le bon . . . Marie:* The good judgment of the saintly and gracious Virgin Mary.   [2] "Behold . . . quickly": Revelations 22:7.   [3] "Of . . . Father": Mark 13:32.

denying miracles. But those who remained faithful were all the more ardent in their faith. The tears of humanity rose up to Him as before, awaiting His coming, loved Him, hoped for Him, yearned to suffer and die for Him as before. And so many ages mankind had prayed with faith and fervor, 'O Lord our God, hasten Thy coming,' so many ages called upon Him, that in His infinite mercy He deigned to come down to His servants. Before that day He had come down, He had visited some holy men, martyrs, and hermits, as is written in their 'Lives.' Among us, Tyutchev,[4] with absolute faith in the truth of his words, bore witness that

> Bearing the Cross, in slavish dress,
> Weary and worn, the Heavenly King
> Our mother, Russia, came to bless,
> And through our land went wandering.

And that certainly was so, I assure you.

"And behold, He deigned to appear for a moment to the people, to the tortured, suffering people, sunk in iniquity, but loving Him like children. My story is laid in Spain, in Seville, in the most terrible time of the Inquisition, when fires were lighted every day to the glory of God, and 'in the splendid *auto da fé*[5] the wicked heretics were burnt.' Oh, of course, this was not the coming in which He will appear according to His promise at the end of time in all His heavenly glory, and which will be sudden 'as lightning flashing from east to west.'[6] No, He visited His children only for a moment, and there where the flames were crackling round the heretics. In His infinite mercy He came once more among men in that human shape in which He walked among men for three years fifteen centuries ago. He came down to the 'hot pavement' of the southern town in which on the day before almost a hundred heretics had, *ad majorem gloriam Dei,*[7] been burnt by the cardinal, the Grand Inquisitor, in a magnificent *auto da fé,* in the presence of the king, the court, the knights, the cardinals, the most charming ladies of the court, and the whole population of Seville.

"He came softly, unobserved, and yet, strange to say, every one recognized Him. That might be one of the best passages in the poem. I mean, why they recognized Him. The people are irresistibly drawn to Him, they surround Him, they flock about Him, follow Him. He moves silently in their midst with a gentle smile of infinite compassion. The sun of love burns in His heart, light and power shine from His eyes, and their radiance, shed on the people, stirs their hearts with responsive love. He holds out His hands to them, blesses them, and a healing virtue comes from contact with Him, even with His garments. An old man in the crowd, blind from childhood, cries out, 'O Lord, heal me and I shall see Thee!' and, as it were, scales fall from his eyes and the blind man sees Him. The crowd weeps and kisses the earth under His feet. Children throw flowers before Him, sing, and cry hosannah. 'It is He — it is He!' all repeat. 'It must be He, it can be no one but Him!' He stops at the steps of the Seville cathedral at the moment when the weeping mourners are bringing in a little

---

[4] **Tyutchev:** A Russian poet (1803–1873).   [5] ***auto da fé:*** Literally, "act of faith"; indicates the burning of a heretic.
[6] **as . . . west:** Matthew 24:27.   [7] ***ad . . . Dei:*** "For the greater glory of God," the Jesuits' motto.

open white coffin. In it lies a child of seven, the only daughter of a prominent citizen. The dead child lies hidden in flowers. 'He will raise your child,' the crowd shouts to the weeping mother. The priest, coming to meet the coffin, looks perplexed and frowns, but the mother of the dead child throws herself at His feet with a wail. 'If it is Thou, raise my child!' she cries, holding out her hands to Him. The procession halts, the coffin is laid on the steps at His feet. He looks with compassion, and His lips once more softly pronounce, 'Maiden, arise!'[8] and the maiden arises. The little girl sits up in the coffin and looks round, smiling with wide-open wondering eyes, holding a bunch of white roses they had put in her hand.

"There are cries, sobs, confusion among the people, and at that moment the cardinal himself, the Grand Inquisitor, passes by the cathedral. He is an old man, almost ninety, tall and erect, with a withered face and sunken eyes, in which there is still a gleam of light. He is not dressed in his gorgeous cardinal's robes, as he was the day before, when he was burning the enemies of the Roman Church—at that moment he was wearing his coarse, old, monk's cassock. At a distance behind him come his gloomy assistants and slaves and the 'holy guard.' He stops at the sight of the crowd and watches it from a distance. He sees everything; he sees them set the coffin down at His feet, sees the child rise up, and his face darkens. He knits his thick grey brows and his eyes gleam with a sinister fire. He holds out his finger and bids the guards take Him. And such is his power, so completely are the people cowed into submission and trembling obedience to him, that the crowd immediately makes way for the guards, and in the midst of deathlike silence they lay hands on Him and lead Him away. The crowd instantly bows down to the earth, like one man, before the old inquisitor. He blesses the people in silence and passes on. The guards lead their prisoner to the close, gloomy, vaulted prison in the ancient palace of the Holy Inquisition and shut Him in it. The day passes and is followed by the dark, burning 'breathless' night of Seville. The air is 'fragrant with laurel and lemon.' In the pitch darkness the iron door of the prison is suddenly opened and the Grand Inquisitor himself comes in with a light in his hand. He is alone; the door is closed at once behind him. He stands in the doorway and for a minute or two gazes into His face. At last he goes up slowly, sets the light on the table and speaks.

"'Is it Thou? Thou?' but receiving no answer, he adds at once, 'Don't answer, be silent. What canst Thou say, indeed? I know too well what Thou wouldst say. And Thou hast no right to add anything to what Thou hadst said of old. Why, then, art Thou come to hinder us? For Thou hast come to hinder us, and Thou knowest that. But dost Thou know what will be tomorrow? I know not who Thou art and care not to know whether it is Thou or only a semblance of Him, but tomorrow I shall condemn Thee and burn Thee at the stake as the worst of heretics. And the very people who have today kissed Thy feet, tomorrow at the faintest sign from me will rush to heap up the embers of Thy fire. Knowest Thou that? Yes, maybe Thou knowest it,' he added with thoughtful penetration, never for a moment taking his eyes off the Prisoner."

---

[8] "Maiden, arise!": Mark 5:41.

"I don't quite understand, Ivan. What does it mean?" Alyosha, who had been listening in silence, said with a smile. "Is it simply a wild fantasy, or a mistake on the part of the old man — some impossible *quid pro quo*?"[9]

"Take it as the last," said Ivan, laughing, "if you are so corrupted by modern realism and can't stand anything fantastic. If you like it to be a case of mistaken identity, let it be so. It is true," he went on, laughing, "the old man was ninety, and he might well be crazy over his set idea. He might have been struck by the appearance of the Prisoner. It might, in fact, be simply his ravings, the delusion of an old man of ninety, overexcited by the *auto da fé* of a hundred heretics the day before. But does it matter to us after all whether it was a mistake of identity or a wild fantasy? All that matters is that the old man should speak out, should speak openly of what he has thought in silence for ninety years."

"And the Prisoner too is silent? Does He look at him and not say a word?"

"That's inevitable in any case," Ivan laughed again. "The old man has told Him He hasn't the right to add anything to what He has said of old. One may say it is the most fundamental feature of Roman Catholicism, in my opinion at least. 'All has been given by Thee to the Pope,' they say, 'and all, therefore, is still in the Pope's hands, and there is no need for Thee to come now at all. Thou must not meddle for the time, at least.' That's how they speak and write, too — the Jesuits, at any rate. I have read it myself in the works of their theologians. 'Hast Thou the right to reveal to us one of the mysteries of that world from which Thou hast come?' my old man asks Him, and answers the question for Him. 'No, Thou has not; that Thou mayest not add to what has been said of old, and mayest not take from men the freedom which Thou didst exalt when Thou wast on earth. Whatsoever Thou revealest anew will encroach on men's freedom of faith; for it will be manifest as a miracle, and the freedom of their faith was dearer to Thee than anything in those days fifteen hundred years ago. Didst Thou not often say then, "I will make you free"?[10] But now Thou hast seen these "free" men,' the old man adds suddenly, with a pensive smile. 'Yes, we've paid dearly for it,' he goes on, looking sternly at Him, 'but at last we have completed that work in Thy name. For fifteen centuries we have been wrestling with Thy freedom, but now it is ended and over for good. Dost Thou not believe that it's over for good? Thou lookest meekly at me and deignest not even to be wroth with me. But let me tell Thee that now, today, people are more persuaded than ever that they have perfect freedom, yet they have brought their freedom to us and laid it humbly at our feet. But that has been our doing. Was this what Thou didst? Was this Thy freedom?'"

"I don't understand again," Alyosha broke in. "Is he ironical, is he jesting?"

"Not a bit of it! He claims it as a merit for himself and his Church that at last they have vanquished freedom and have done so to make men happy. 'For now' (he is speaking of the Inquisition, of course) 'for the first time it has become possible to think of the happiness of men. Man was created a rebel; and how can rebels be happy? Thou wast warned,' he says to Him. 'Thou hast had no lack of admonitions,

---

[9] *quid pro quo*: Misunderstanding. [10] "I . . . free": For example, John 8:36.

and warnings, but Thou didst not listen to those warnings; Thou didst reject the only way by which men might be made happy. But, fortunately, departing Thou didst hand on the work to us. Thou hast promised, Thou hast established by Thy word, Thou hast given to us the right to bind and to unbind, and now, of course, Thou canst not think of taking it away. Why, then, hast Thou come to hinder us?'"

"And what's the meaning of 'no lack of admonitions and warnings'?" asked Alyosha.

"Why, that's the chief part of what the old man must say.

"'The wise and dread Spirit, the spirit of self-destruction and nonexistence,' the old man goes on, 'the great spirit talked with Thee in the wilderness, and we are told in the books that he "tempted" Thee.¹¹ Is that so? And could anything truer be said than what he revealed to Thee in three questions and what Thou didst reject, and what in the books is called "the temptation"? And yet if there has ever been on earth a real stupendous miracle, it took place on that day, on the day of the three temptations. The statement of those three questions was itself the miracle. If it were possible to imagine simply for the sake of argument that those three questions of the dread spirit had perished utterly from the books, and that we had to restore them and to invent them anew, and to do so had gathered together all the wise men of the earth—rulers, chief priests, learned men, philosophers, poets—and had set them the task to invent three questions, such as would not only fit the occasion, but express in three words, three human phrases, the whole future history of the world and of humanity—dost Thou believe that all the wisdom of the earth united could have invented anything in depth and force equal to the three questions which were actually put to Thee then by the wise and mighty spirit in the wilderness? From those questions alone, from the miracle of their statement, we can see that we have here to do not with the fleeting human intelligence, but with the absolute and eternal. For in those three questions the whole subsequent history of mankind is, as it were, brought together into one whole, and foretold, and in them are united all the unsolved historical contradictions of human nature. At the time it could not be so clear, since the future was unknown; but now that fifteen hundred years have passed, we see that everything in those three questions was so justly divined and foretold, and has been so truly fulfilled, that nothing can be added to them or taken from them.

"'Judge Thyself who was right—Thou or he who questioned Thee then? Remember the first question; its meaning, in other words, was this: "Thou wouldst go into the world, and art going with empty hands, with some promise of freedom which men in their simplicity and their natural unruliness cannot even understand, which they fear and dread—for nothing has ever been more insupportable for a man and a human society than freedom. But seest Thou these stones in this parched and barren wilderness? Turn them into bread, and mankind will run after Thee like a flock of sheep, grateful and obedient, though forever trembling, lest Thou withdraw Thy hand and deny them Thy bread." But Thou wouldst not deprive man of freedom and didst reject the offer, thinking, what is that freedom worth, if obedience is

---

¹¹**he "tempted" Thee:** The story of Satan's temptation of Jesus is told in Matthew 4:1–11 and in Luke 4:1–13.

bought with bread? Thou didst reply that man lives not by bread alone. But dost Thou know that for the sake of that earthly bread the spirit of the earth will rise up against Thee and will strive with Thee and overcome Thee, and all will follow him, crying, "Who can compare with this beast? He has given us fire from heaven!"[12] Dost Thou know that the ages will pass, and humanity will proclaim by the lips of their sages that there is no crime, and therefore no sin; there is only hunger? "Feed men, and then ask of them virtue!" that's what they'll write on the banner which they will raise against Thee, and with which they will destroy Thy temple. Where Thy temple stood will rise a new building; the terrible tower of Babel[13] will be built again, and though, like the one of old, it will not be finished, yet Thou mightest have prevented that new tower and have cut short the sufferings of men for a thousand years; for they will come back to us after a thousand years of agony with their tower. They will seek us again, hidden underground in the catacombs, for we shall be again perse-cuted and tortured. They will find us and cry to us, "Feed us, for those who have promised us fire from heaven haven't given it!" And then we shall finish building their tower, for he finishes the building who feeds them. And we alone shall feed them in Thy name, declaring falsely that it is in Thy name. Oh, never, never can they feed themselves without us! No science will give them bread so long as they remain free. In the end they will lay their freedom at our feet, and say to us, "Make us your slaves, but feed us." They will understand themselves, at last, that freedom and bread enough for all are inconceivable together, for never, never will they be able to share between them! They will be convinced, too, that they can never be free, for they are weak, vicious, worthless, and rebellious. Thou didst promise them the bread of Heaven, but, I repeat again, can it compare with earthly bread in the eyes of the weak, ever-sinful, and ignoble race of man? And if for the sake of the bread of Heaven thousands and tens of thousands shall follow Thee, what is to become of the millions and tens of thousands of millions of creatures who will not have the strength to forego the earthly bread for the sake of the heavenly? Or dost Thou care only for the tens of thousands of the great and strong, while the millions, numerous as the sands of the sea, who are weak but love Thee, must exist only for the sake of the great and strong? No, we care for the weak, too. They are sinful and rebellious, but in the end they too will become obedient. They will marvel at us and look on us as gods, because we are ready to endure the freedom which they have found so dreadful and to rule over them — so awful it will seem to them to be free. But we shall tell them that we are Thy servants and rule them in Thy name. We shall deceive them again, for we will not let Thee come to us again. That deception will be our suf-fering, for we shall be forced to lie.

"'This is the significance of the first question in the wilderness, and this is what Thou hast rejected for the sake of that freedom which Thou hast exalted above everything. Yet in this question lies hidden the great secret of this world. Choosing "bread," Thou wouldst have satisfied the universal and everlasting craving of humanity — to find someone to worship. So long as man remains free he strives for nothing so incessantly and so painfully as to find someone to worship. But man

---

[12] **"Who can . . . heaven.":** Revelations, 13:4, 13.   [13] **tower of Babel:** Genesis 11.

seeks to worship what is established beyond dispute, so that all men would agree at once to worship it. For these pitiful creatures are concerned not only to find what one or the other can worship, but to find something that all would believe in and worship; what is essential is that all may be *together* in it. This craving for *community* of worship is the chief misery of every man individually and of all humanity from the beginning of time. For the sake of common worship they've slain each other with the sword. They have set up gods and challenged one another, "Put away your gods and come and worship ours, or we will kill you and your gods!" And so it will be to the end of the world, even when gods disappear from the earth; they will fall down before idols just the same. Thou didst know, Thou couldst not but have known, this fundamental secret of human nature, but Thou didst reject the one infallible banner which was offered Thee to make all men bow down to Thee alone—the banner of earthly bread; and Thou hast rejected it for the sake of freedom and the bread of Heaven. Behold what Thou didst further. And all again in the name of freedom! I tell Thee that man is tormented by no greater anxiety than to find someone quickly to whom he can hand over the gift of freedom with which the ill-fated creature is born. But only one who can appease their conscience can take over their freedom. In bread there was offered Thee an invincible banner; give bread, and man will worship Thee, for nothing is more certain than bread. But if someone else gains possession of his conscience—oh! then he will cast away Thy bread and follow after him who has ensnared his conscience. In that Thou wast right. For the secret of man's being is not only to live but to have something to live for. Without a stable conception of the object of life, man would not consent to go on living, and would rather destroy himself than remain on earth, though he had bread in abundance. That is true. But what happened? Instead of taking men's freedom from them, Thou didst make it greater than ever! Didst Thou forget that man prefers peace, and even death, to freedom of choice in the knowledge of good and evil? Nothing is more seductive for man than his freedom of conscience, but nothing is a greater cause of suffering. And behold, instead of giving a firm foundation for setting the conscience of man at rest forever, Thou didst choose all that is exceptional, vague, and enigmatic; Thou didst choose what was utterly beyond the strength of men, acting as though Thou didst not love them at all—Thou who didst come to give Thy life for them! Instead of taking possession of man's freedom, Thou didst increase it, and burdened the spiritual kingdom of mankind with its sufferings forever. Thou didst desire man's free love, that he should follow Thee freely, enticed and taken captive by Thee. In place of the rigid, ancient law, man must hereafter with free heart decide for himself what is good and what is evil, having only Thy image before him as his guide. But didst Thou not know he would at last reject even Thy image and Thy truth, if he is weighed down with the fearful burden of free choice? They will cry aloud at last that the truth is not in Thee, for they could not have been left in greater confusion and suffering than Thou hast caused, laying upon them so many cares and unanswerable problems.

"'So that, in truth, Thou didst Thyself lay the foundation for the destruction of Thy kingdom, and no one is more to blame for it. Yet what was offered Thee? There are three powers, three powers alone, able to conquer and to hold captive forever the conscience of these impotent rebels for their happiness—those forces are miracle, mystery, and authority. Thou hast rejected all three and hast set the example for doing so. When the wise and dread spirit set Thee on the pinnacle of the temple and said to Thee, "If Thou wouldst know whether Thou art the Son of God then cast Thyself down, for it is written: the angels shall hold him up lest he fall and bruise himself, and Thou shalt know then whether Thou art the Son of God and shalt prove then how great is Thy faith in Thy Father." But Thou didst refuse and wouldst not cast Thyself down. Oh! of course, Thou didst proudly and well like God; but the weak, unruly race of men, are they gods? Oh, Thou didst know then that in taking one step, in making one movement to cast Thyself down, Thou wouldst be tempting God and have lost all Thy faith in Him, and wouldst have been dashed to pieces against that earth which Thou didst come to save. And the wise spirit that tempted Thee would have rejoiced. But I ask again, are there many like Thee? And couldst Thou believe for one moment that men, too, could face such a temptation? Is the nature of men such that they can reject miracle, and at the great moments of their life, the moments of their deepest, most agonizing spiritual difficulties, cling only to the free verdict of the heart? Oh, Thou didst know that Thy deed would be recorded in books, would be handed down to remote times and the utmost ends of the earth, and Thou didst hope that man, following Thee, would cling to God and not ask for a miracle. But Thou didst not know that when man rejects miracle he rejects God too; for man seeks not so much God as the miraculous. And as man cannot bear to be without the miraculous, he will create new miracles of his own for himself, and will worship deeds of sorcery and witchcraft, though he might be a hundred times over a rebel, heretic, and infidel. Thou didst not come down from the Cross when they shouted to Thee, mocking and reviling Thee, "Come down from the Cross and we will believe that Thou art He."[14] Thou didst not come down, for again Thou wouldst not enslave man by a miracle, and didst crave faith given freely, not based on miracle. Thou didst crave for free love and not the base raptures of the slave before the might that has overawed him forever. But Thou didst think too highly of men therein, for they are slaves, of course, though rebellious by nature. Look round and judge; fifteen centuries have passed; look upon them. Whom hast Thou raised up to Thyself? I swear, man is weaker and baser by nature than Thou hast believed him! Can he, can he do what Thou didst? By showing him so much respect, Thou didst, as it were, cease to feel for him, for Thou didst ask far too much from him—Thou who hast loved him more than Thyself! Respecting him less, Thou wouldst have asked less of him. That would have been more like love, for his burden would have been lighter. He is weak and vile. What though he is everywhere now rebelling against our power, and proud of his rebellion? It is the pride of a child and a schoolboy. They are little children rioting and barring out the teacher at school. But their childish delight will end; it will cost them dear. They will cast down temples and drench the earth with blood. But they will see at last, the foolish children, that, though they are rebels, they are impotent rebels, unable to keep up their own rebellion. Bathed in their foolish tears, they will recognize at last that He who created them rebels must have meant to

---

[14] "Come . . . He": Mark 15:32.

mock at them. They will say this in despair, and their utterance will be a blasphemy which will make them more unhappy still, for man's nature cannot bear blasphemy, and in the end always avenges it on itself. And so unrest, confusion, and unhappiness—that is the present lot of man after Thou didst bear so much for their freedom! Thy great prophet tells in vision and in image that he saw all those who took part in the first resurrection and that there were of each tribe twelve thousand. But if there were so many of them, they must have been not men but gods. They had borne Thy cross, they had endured scores of years in the barren, hungry wilderness, living upon locusts and roots—and Thou mayest indeed point with pride at those children of freedom, of free love, of free and splendid sacrifice for Thy name. But remember that they were only some thousands; and what of the rest? And how are the other weak ones to blame, because they could not endure what the strong have endured? How is the weak soul to blame that it is unable to receive such terrible gifts? Canst Thou have simply come to the elect and for the elect? But if so, it is a mystery and we cannot understand it. And if it is a mystery, we too have a right to preach a mystery, and to teach them that it's not the free judgment of their hearts, not love, that matters, but a mystery which they must follow blindly, even against their conscience. So we have done. We have corrected Thy work and have founded it upon *miracle, mystery,* and *authority.* And men rejoiced that they were again led like sheep, and that the terrible gift that had brought them such suffering was, at last, lifted from their hearts. Were we right teaching them this? Speak! Did we not love mankind, so meekly acknowledging their feebleness, lovingly lightening their burden, and permitting their weak nature even sin with our sanction? Why hast Thou come now to hinder us? And why dost Thou look silently and searchingly at me with Thy mild eyes? Be angry. I don't want Thy love, for I love Thee not. And what use is it for me to hide anything from Thee? Don't I know to Whom I am speaking? All that I can say is known to Thee already. And is it for me to conceal from Thee our mystery? Perhaps it is Thy will to hear it from my lips. Listen, then. We are not working with Thee, but with *him*—that is our mystery. It's long—eight centuries—since we have been on *his* side and not on Thine. Just eight centuries ago, we took from him what Thou didst reject with scorn, that last gift he offered Thee, showing Thee all the kingdoms of the earth.[15] We took from him Rome and the sword of Cæsar, and proclaimed ourselves sole rulers of the earth, though hitherto we have not been able to complete our work. But whose fault is that? Oh, the work is only beginning, but it has begun. It has long to await completion and the earth has yet much to suffer, but we shall triumph and shall be Cæsars, and then we shall plan the universal happiness of man. But Thou mightest have taken even the sword of Cæsar. Why didst Thou reject that last gift? Hadst Thou accepted that last counsel of the mighty spirit, Thou wouldst have accomplished all that man seeks on earth—that is, someone to worship, someone to keep his conscience, and some means of uniting all in one unanimous and harmonious ant heap, for the craving for universal unity is the third and last anguish of men. Mankind as a whole has always striven to organize a universal

---

[15] **that last gift . . . earth:** In 401, Pope Innocent I claimed authority over the Roman Church, establishing an institution competitive with the Roman Empire.

state. There have been many great nations with great histories, but the more highly they were developed the more unhappy they were, for they felt more acutely than other people the craving for world-wide union. The great conquerors, Timours and Genghis Khans,[16] whirled like hurricanes over the face of the earth, striving to subdue its people, and they too were but the unconscious expression of the same craving for universal unity. Hadst Thou taken the world and Cæsar's purple, Thou wouldst have founded the universal state and have given universal peace. For who can rule men if not he who holds their conscience and their bread in his hands? We have taken the sword of Cæsar, and in taking it, of course, have rejected Thee and followed *him*. Oh, ages are yet to come of the confusion of free thought, of their science and cannibalism. For having begun to build their tower of Babel without us, they will end, of course, with cannibalism. But then the beast will crawl to us and lick our feet and spatter them with tears of blood. And we shall sit upon the beast and raise the cup, and on it will be written, "Mystery." But then, and only then, the reign of peace and happiness will come for men. Thou art proud of Thine elect, but Thou hast only the elect, while we give rest to all. And besides, how many of those elect, those mighty ones who could become elect, have grown weary waiting for Thee, and have transferred and will transfer the powers of their spirit and the warmth of their heart to the other camp, and end by raising their *free* banner against Thee. Thou didst Thyself lift up that banner. But with us all will be happy and will no more rebel, nor destroy one another as under Thy freedom. Oh, we shall persuade them that they will only become free when they renounce their freedom to us and submit to us. And shall we be right or shall we be lying? They will be convinced that we are right, for they will remember the horrors of slavery and confusion to which Thy freedom brought them. Freedom, free thought and science, will lead them into such straits and will bring them face to face with such marvels and insoluble mysteries that some of them, the fierce and rebellious, will destroy themselves; others, rebellious but weak, will destroy one another, while the rest, weak and the unhappy, will crawl fawning to our feet and whine to us: "Yes, you were right, you alone possess His mystery, and we come back to you, save us from ourselves!"

"'Receiving bread from us, they will see clearly that we take the bread made by their hands from them, to give it to them, without any miracle. They will see that we do not change the stones to bread, but in truth they will be more thankful for taking it from our hands than for the bread itself! For they will remember only too well that in old days, without our help, even the bread they made turned to stones in their hands, while since they have come back to us, the very stones have turned to bread in their hands. Too, too well they know the value of complete submission! And until men know that, they will be unhappy. Who is most to blame for their not knowing it, speak? Who scattered the flock and sent it astray on unknown paths? But the flock will come together again and will submit once more, and then it will be once for all. Then we shall give them the quiet humble happiness of weak creatures such as they are by nature. Oh, we shall persuade them at last not to be proud, for Thou didst lift

---

[16]**Timours . . . Khans:** Timour, or Timur (c. 1336–1405), and Genghis Khan (c. 1167–1227) were Mongol conquerors.

them up and thereby taught them to be proud. We shall show them that they are weak, that they are only pitiful children, but that childlike happiness is the sweetest of all. They will become timid and will look to us and huddle close to us in fear, as chicks to the hen. They will marvel at us and will be awe-stricken before us, and will be proud at our being so powerful and clever, that we have been able to subdue such a turbulent flock of thousands of millions. They will tremble impotently before our wrath, their minds will grow fearful, they will be quick to shed tears like women and children, but they will be just as ready at a sign from us to pass to laughter and rejoicing, to happy mirth and childish song. Yes, we shall set them to work, but in their leisure hours we shall make their life like a child's game, with children's songs and innocent dance. Oh, we shall allow them even sin; they are weak and helpless, and they will love us like children because we allow them to sin. We shall tell them that every sin will be expiated, if it is done with our permission, that we allow them to sin because we love them, and the punishment for these sins we take upon ourselves. And we shall take it upon ourselves, and they will adore us as their saviors who have taken on themselves their sins before God. And they will have no secrets from us. We shall allow or forbid them to live with their wives and mistresses, to have or not to have children—according to whether they have been obedient or disobedient—and they will submit to us gladly and cheerfully. The most painful secrets of their conscience, all, all they will bring to us, and we shall have an answer for all. And they will be glad to believe our answer, for it will save them from the great anxiety and terrible agony they endure at present in making a free decision for themselves. And all will be happy, all the millions of creatures, except the hundred thousand who rule over them. For only we, we who guard the mystery, shall be unhappy. There will be thousands of millions of happy babes, and a hundred thousand sufferers who have taken upon themselves the curse of the knowledge of good and evil. Peacefully they will die, peacefully they will expire in Thy name, and beyond the grave they will find nothing but death. But we shall keep the secret, and for their happiness we shall allure them with the reward of heaven and eternity. Though if there were anything in the other world, it certainly would not be for such as they. It is prophesied that Thou wilt come again in victory, Thou wilt come with Thy chosen, the proud and strong, but we will say that they have only saved themselves, but we have saved all. We are told that the harlot who sits upon the beast, and holds in her hands the *mystery,* shall be put to shame, that the weak will rise up again, and will rend her royal purple and will strip naked her loathsome body.[17] But then I will stand up and point out to Thee the thousand millions of happy children who have known no sin. And we who have taken their sins upon us for their happiness will stand up before Thee and say: "Judge us if Thou canst and darest." Know that I fear Thee not. Know that I too have been in the wilderness, I too have lived on roots and locusts, I too prized the freedom with which Thou hast blessed men, and I too was striving to stand among Thy elect, among the strong and powerful, thirsting "to make up the number." But I awakened and would not serve madness. I turned back and joined the ranks of those *who have*

---

[17] **the harlot . . . body:** The Whore of Babylon in Revelation 17.

corrected Thy work. I left the proud and went back to the humble, for the happiness of the humble. What I say to Thee will come to pass, and our dominion will be built up. I repeat, tomorrow Thou shalt see that obedient flock who at a sign from me will hasten to heap up the hot cinders about the pile on which I shall burn Thee for coming to hinder us. For if anyone has ever deserved our fires, it is Thou. Tomorrow I shall burn Thee. *Dixi.*'"[18]

Ivan stopped. He was carried away as he talked and spoke with excitement; when he had finished, he suddenly smiled.

Alyosha had listened in silence; toward the end he was greatly moved and seemed several times on the point of interrupting, but restrained himself. Now his words came with a rush.

"But . . . that's absurd!" he cried, flushing. "Your poem is in praise of Jesus, not in blame of Him—as you meant it to be. And who will believe you about freedom? Is that the way to understand it? That's not the idea of it in the Orthodox Church . . . That's Rome, and not even the whole of Rome, it's false—those are the worst of the Catholics, the Inquisitors, the Jesuits! . . . And there could not be such a fantastic creature as your Inquisitor. What are these sins of mankind they take on themselves? Who are these keepers of the mystery who have taken some curse upon themselves for the happiness of mankind? When have they been seen? We know the Jesuits, they are spoken ill of, but surely they are not what you describe? They are not that at all, not at all. . . . They are simply the Romish army for the earthly sovereignty of the world in the future, with the Pontiff of Rome for Emperor . . . that's their ideal, but there's no sort of mystery or lofty melancholy about it. . . . It's simple lust of power, of filthy earthly gain, of domination—something like a universal serfdom with them as masters—that's all they stand for. They don't even believe in God, perhaps. Your suffering inquisitor is a mere fantasy."

"Stay, stay," laughed Ivan, "how hot you are! A fantasy you say, let it be so! Of course it's a fantasy. But allow me to say: Do you really think that the Roman Catholic movement of the last centuries is actually nothing but the lust of power, of filthy earthly gain? Is that Father Païssy's teaching?"

"No, no, on the contrary, Father Païssy did once say something the same as you . . . but of course it's not the same, not a bit the same," Alyosha hastily corrected himself.

"A precious admission, in spite of your 'not a bit the same.' I ask you why your Jesuits and inquisitors have united simply for vile material gain? Why can there not be among them one martyr oppressed by great sorrow and loving humanity? You see, only suppose that there was one such man among all those who desire nothing but filthy material gain—if there's only one like my old inquisitor, who had himself eaten roots in the desert and made frenzied efforts to subdue his flesh to make himself free and perfect. But yet all his life he loved humanity, and suddenly his eyes were opened, and he saw that it is no great moral blessedness to attain perfection and freedom, if at the same time one gains the conviction that billions of God's creatures

---

[18] *Dixi:* The closing word for a religious pronouncement, meaning "I have spoken."

have been created as a mockery, that they will never be capable of using their freedom, that these poor rebels can never turn into giants to complete the tower, that it was not for such geese that the great idealist dreamt his dream of harmony. Seeing all that, he turned back and joined — the clever people. Surely that could have happened?"

"Joined whom, what clever people?" cried Alyosha, completely carried away. "They have no such great cleverness and no mysteries and secrets. . . . Perhaps nothing but atheism, that's all their secret. Your inquisitor does not believe in God, that's his secret!"

"What if it is so! At last you have guessed it. It's perfectly true that that's the whole secret, but isn't that suffering, at least for a man like that, who has wasted his whole life in the desert and yet could not shake off his incurable love of humanity? In his old age he reached the clear conviction that nothing but the advice of the great dread spirit could build up any tolerable sort of life for the feeble, unruly, 'incomplete, empirical creatures created in jest.' And so, convinced of this, he sees that he must follow the counsel of the wise spirit, the dread spirit of death and destruction, and therefore accept lying and deception, and lead men consciously to death and destruction, and yet deceive them all the way so that they may not notice where they are being led, that the poor, blind creatures may at least on the way think themselves happy. And note, the deception is in the name of Him in Whose ideal the old man had so fervently believed all his life long. Is not that tragic? And if only one such stood at the head of the whole army 'filled with the lust of power only for the sake of filthy gain' — would not one such be enough to make a tragedy? More than that, one such standing at the head is enough to create the actual leading idea of the Roman Church with all its armies and Jesuits, its highest idea. I tell you frankly that I firmly believe that there has always been such a man among those who stood at the head of the movement. Who knows, there may have been some such even among the Roman Popes. Who knows, perhaps the spirit of that accursed old man who loves mankind so obstinately in his own way is to be found even now in a whole multitude of such old men, existing not by chance but by agreement, as a secret league formed long ago for the guarding of the mystery, to guard it from the weak and the unhappy, so as to make them happy. No doubt it is so, and so it must be indeed. I fancy that even among the Masons there's something of the same mystery at the bottom, and that that's why the Catholics so detest the Masons as their rivals breaking up the unity of the idea, while it is so essential that there should be one flock and one shepherd. . . . But from the way I defend my idea I might be an author impatient of your criticism. Enough of it."

"You are perhaps a Mason yourself!" broke suddenly from Alyosha. "You don't believe in God," he added, speaking this time very sorrowfully. He fancied besides that his brother was looking at him ironically. "How does your poem end?" he asked, suddenly looking down. "Or was it the end?"

"I meant it to end like this: When the Inquisitor ceased speaking, he waited some time for his Prisoner to answer him. His silence weighed down upon him. He saw the Prisoner had listened intently all the time, looking gently in his face and evidently not wishing to reply. The old man longed for Him to say something, however bitter and terrible. But He suddenly approached the old man in silence and softly kissed him on his bloodless, aged lips. That was all his answer. The old man shuddered. His lips moved. He went to the door, opened it, and said to him: 'Go, and come no more. . . . Come not at all, never, never!' And he let him out into the dark alleys of the town. The Prisoner went away."

"And the old man?"

"The kiss glows in his heart, but the old man adheres to his idea."

"And you with him, you too?" cried Alyosha, mournfully.

Ivan laughed.

"Why, it's all nonsense, Alyosha. It's only a senseless poem of a senseless student, who could never write two lines of verse. Why do you take it so seriously? Surely you don't suppose I am going straight off to the Jesuits, to join the men who are correcting His work? Good Lord, it's no business of mine. I told you, all I want is to live on to thirty, and then . . . dash the cup to the ground!"

"But the little sticky leaves, and the precious tombs, and the blue sky, and the woman you love! How will you live, how will you love them?" Alyosha cried sorrowfully. "With such a hell in your heart and your head, how can you? No, that's just what you are going away for, to join them . . . if not, you will kill yourself, you can't endure it!"

"There is a strength to endure everything," Ivan said with a cold smile.

"What strength?"

"The strength of the Karamazovs—the strength of the Karamazov baseness."

"To sink into debauchery, to stifle your soul with corruption, yes?"

"Possibly even that . . . only perhaps till I am thirty I shall escape it, and then—"

"How will you escape it? By what will you escape it? That's impossible with your ideas."

"In the Karamazov way, again."

"'Everything is lawful,' you mean? Everything is lawful, is that it?"

Ivan scowled, and all at once turned strangely pale.

"Ah, you've caught up yesterday's phrase, which so offended Miüsov—and which Dmitri pounced upon so naïvely and paraphrased!" he smiled queerly. "Yes, if you like, 'everything is lawful' since the word has been said. I won't deny it. And Mitya's version isn't bad."

Alyosha looked at him in silence.

"I thought that going away from here I have you at least," Ivan said suddenly, with unexpected feeling; "but now I see that there is no place for me even in your heart, my dear hermit. The formula, 'all is lawful,' I won't renounce—will you renounce me for that, yes?"

Alyosha got up, went to him, and softly kissed him on the lips.

"That's plagiarism," cried Ivan, highly delighted. "You stole that from my poem. Thank you, though. Get up, Alyosha, it's time we were going, both of us."

They went out, but stopped when they reached the entrance of the restaurant.

"Listen, Alyosha," Ivan began in a resolute voice, "if I am really able to care for the sticky little leaves, I shall only love them remembering you. It's enough for me that you are somewhere here, and I shan't lose my desire for life yet. Is that enough for you? Take it as a declaration of love if you like. And now you go to the right and I to the left. And it's enough, do you hear—enough! I mean even if I don't go away tomorrow (I think I certainly shall go) and we meet again, don't say a word more on these subjects. I beg that particularly. And about Dmitri, too, I ask you especially never speak to me again," he added, with sudden irritation; "it's all exhausted, it has all been said over and over again, hasn't it? And I'll make you one promise in return for it. When, at thirty, I want to 'dash the cup to the ground,' wherever I may be I'll come to have one more talk with you, even though it were from America—you may be sure of that. I'll come on purpose. It will be very interesting to have a look at you, to see what you'll be by that time. It's rather a solemn promise, you see. And we really may be parting for seven years or ten. Come, go now to your Pater Seraphicus, he is dying. If he dies without you, you will be angry with me for having kept you. Good-bye, kiss me once more; that's right, now go."

❧ HENRIK IBSEN
1828–1906

HEN-rik IB-sin

Recalling his childhood in Skien, a logging village in rural Norway, **Henrik Ibsen** described the view from the window of his room as "only buildings, nothing green." And the structures that he particularly remembered—the church, the jail with its pillory, and the madhouse—may have been the models for the institutions that constrain and oppress the characters in his great social dramas, plays that dissect the institutions of Europe in the late nineteenth century.

Often called the "father of the modern drama," Ibsen is best known for realistic plays such as *A Doll's House* (1879), *An Enemy of the People* (1882), and *Hedda Gabler* (1890). These plays explore the ways in which bourgeois values and social conventions deny individuals opportunities for growth and fulfillment. Very different from the romantic comedies and melodramas that were the standard theatrical fare at the time, Ibsen's plays often shocked nineteenth-century audiences, who went to the theater to be amused. But the productions moved other playwrights and changed the course of drama, influencing especially such modern dramatists as George Bernard Shaw in England and Eugene O'Neill and Arthur Miller[1] in the United States—heirs to a dramatic tradition Shaw called "**IBSENISM**."

More than any one man, it is he [Ibsen] who had made us "our world," that is to say, "our modernity."

– EZRA POUND

---

[1]**Shaw . . . Miller: George Bernard Shaw** (1856–1950), Anglo-Irish playwright, critic, and social commentator, author of numerous plays, including *The Devil's Disciple* (1897), *Major Barbara* (1905), and *Man and Superman* (1905). **Eugene O'Neill** (1888–1953), American Playwright, author of *Ah, Wilderness!* (1933), *Long Day's Journey into Night* (1956), and many other plays. **Arthur Miller** (b. 1915), American playwright best known for *Death of a Salesman* (1949) and *The Crucible* (1953).

Early Poverty and Apprenticeship in the Theater.   Born the son of a prosperous businessman in Skien in 1828, Ibsen learned early the precariousness of bourgeois respectability. When he was nine, his father's business failed and the family was cast into poverty and forced to move ignominiously out of town. At fifteen, he left home to become a druggist's apprentice at Grimstad, where he spent six years and fathered an illegitimate child — a buried secret in Ibsen's life much like those that show up in many of his plays. He moved to Christiania (now Oslo) in 1850 with hopes of entering the university, but he failed part of the entrance examinations and went to work in a theater instead. And it was in the theater — as producer, director, and writer — that Ibsen would spend the next fourteen years learning his true craft.

Henrik Ibsen, c. 1900
This photograph shows off Ibsen's trademark full white beard and small spectacles. (Austrian Archives/Corbis)

Escape to Southern Europe.   In 1864 Ibsen fled the literal darkness and bourgeois oppression of Norway to take up residence in Italy and Germany, where he lived for the next twenty-seven years, returning to Norway only twice for brief vacations before ultimately going back to his native country. In Italy and Germany he wrote his great social dramas, or "problem plays," beginning in 1877 with *The Pillars of Society*, which stripped the veil of hypocrisy from community leaders to expose the rot underneath. That play was followed by the scandalous *A Doll's House* (1879) and *Ghosts* (1881). All three plays present the pillars of village life — the church, marriage, and family — as oppressive and hypocritical institutions and bring to light secrets that threaten to destroy the plays' protagonists. *The Wild Duck* (1884), *An Enemy of the People* (1882), and *Rosmersholm* (1882) are studies of characters who are afraid to tell the truth. The human psychological dimension becomes increasingly important for Ibsen, especially in such later plays as *The Lady from the Sea* (1888), *Hedda Gabler* (1890), and *The Master Builder* (1892), which explore the effects on women of their subordinate role in society and men's aggressive dominance.

Mythological and Symbolic Plays.   Although best known for his realistic social dramas, Ibsen was also a writer of symbol and mythology. Much of his early work was devoted to historical and mythological subjects, culminating in *Brand* (1865) and *Peer Gynt* (1867), two dramatic poems that through Nordic folklore comment indirectly on contemporary Norway. In his plays of the late 1890s, such as *John Gabriel Borkman* (1896) and *When We Dead Awaken* (1899), Ibsen turned to a more symbolic and visionary style. In these less realistic works Ibsen can be considered father to such modern symbolic dramatists as William Butler Yeats and Tennessee Williams.[2]

Ibsen returned to Norway in 1891 and spent the last fifteen years of his life in Christiania, where he died in 1906. Appropriately, his dying word was *tvertimod,* meaning "on the contrary."

www   For links to more information about Ibsen, a quiz on *Hedda Gabler,* and the twenty-first-century relevance of this play, see *World Literature Online* at bedfordstmartins.com/worldlit.

---

[2]Yeats . . . Williams: **William Butler Yeats** (1865–1939), Irish poet and playwright who drew on Irish mythology, folklore, and Japanese *Nō* drama to shape his symbolic plays; see Book 6. **Tennessee Williams** (1914–1983), American playwright best known for *The Glass Menagerie* (1945) and *A Streetcar Named Desire* (1947).

The Method of the Social Dramas.   In nearly all of Ibsen's social plays one finds a hero or heroine constrained by social institutions—the church, marriage, and middle-class respectability. These characters are not simply victims of social forces, however; through bad choices, mistakes, and personal weaknesses they suppress guilty secrets or tell lies and contribute to creating their difficulties. The plays almost always center on a moment of crisis when a secret or lie is revealed and the hero or heroine must choose how to meet the revelation.

In composing his plays, Ibsen employed the stylistic conventions of "the well-made play"[3]: a single, central situation carefully constructed to build to a climactic crisis, unity of time and place, and realistic dialogue and stage settings. Ibsen's middle-class audiences could believe they were observing their own lives or the lives of people like themselves when watching one of his dramas. In his choice of subject matter, in the tragic seriousness of many of the situations he explored, however, Ibsen broke the mold of the well-made play. He also strayed from convention in his treatment of female characters.

Ibsen's Feminism.   Many of Ibsen's unforgettable characters are women whose marriages deny them opportunities for personal growth. In *A Doll's House,* Nora Helmer is trapped in a patriarchal marriage, her husband treating her like a doll rather than an adult with human aspirations and feelings. Suffocated by this stultifying relationship, Nora decides to leave her husband and children to seek self-fulfillment. The play ends as she leaves, slamming the door behind her. Nora's was a shocking but comic ending, for Nora and the audience assume that she will find a more enriching life outside of her marriage. But for many of the female characters in Ibsen's social dramas, the outcome is less liberating. Mrs. Alving in *Ghosts,* for example, brings about her own unhappiness and her son's destruction by maintaining a front of respectability to hide the corruption in her marriage.

Hedda Gabler.   One of Ibsen's later social dramas, *Hedda Gabler,* also exposes the oppression of bourgeois marriage. Hedda, the daughter of a general, comes from the disappearing aristocratic-officer class, but her father has died and left her without the resources to maintain an aristocratic lifestyle. In her late twenties and at the edge of spinsterhood, she

agrees to marry **Jørgen Tesman,** an academic from the bourgeoisie whose plans for supporting her in the style to which she is accustomed depend on his securing a professorship. Hedda tolerates the fatuous, sentimental, and tedious Tesman with the consolation that he will provide

---

[3] **"The well-made play":** The plays of Augustin Eugène Scribe (1791–1861) and his followers established the rules for "the well-made play." It was to be carefully constructed around a single situation that built, scene by scene, to a climactic revelation. The situation usually involved a misunderstanding, a secret, or a suppressed document that, when discovered, prompted a reversal and a dénouement. The dialogue was colloquial and realistic, and the subject matter, commonplace and trivial.

her with money and a fine house where she can entertain in style. When Tesman is disappointed in his plans for a professorship, Hedda is in turn denied her social compensations.

Bourgeois marriage offers Hedda no rewards. She is oppressed by Tesman's relatives, encumbered by the thought of children, and bored with her husband's academic obsessions. Lacking opportunities for happiness in her marriage, Hedda turns to manipulating others—becoming a meddling matchmaker with Thea Elvsted, a flirtatious tease with Judge Brack, and a taunting temptress with **Eilert Løvborg**.

AY-lert LOWV-borg

Ibsen structures the play around a series of shifting triangles. Hedda interferes in the relationships between Thea and Løvborg and between Tesman and Løvborg, and she is haunted by Tesman's past relationship with Thea and her own with Løvborg. In the present, Judge Brack tries to triangulate Hedda's marriage, and Mademoiselle Diana, though she never appears onstage, complicates both Hedda's and Thea's relationship with Løvborg. Hedda's meddling may begin in idle curiosity about Thea's marriage, but it quickly develops into destructive manipulation as Hedda causes Løvborg such distress that he turns to drink and she destroys his fragile relationship with Thea, symbolized by her destruction of the manuscript that the couple had worked on together. By this point in the play Hedda has become incapable of any affirming, creative acts, and she cannot acknowledge the child in her own womb. The logic of her life and her actions has become totally negative. Nevertheless, Hedda's final action in the play is shocking and unsettling, made even more so by Judge Brack's famous and banal closing observation: "God—people—people don't do things like that."

■ CONNECTIONS

Goethe, *Faust*, p. 29. Like *Faust*, *Hedda Gabler* is concerned with the way social conventions and institutions frustrate individual fulfillment. Both *Faust*'s Margaret and Ibsen's Hedda are victims of male domination, and both die as a result of their predicament. Despite its celebration of the eternal feminine, *Faust* is firmly grounded in a male consciousness. The feminine is useful in defining Faust's incompleteness, but the play does not get inside a feminine point of view. It remains a male quest story. *Hedda Gabler,* despite Ibsen's claim that he did not understand the women's movement, tells its story from a woman's point of view. In what ways are Margaret and Hedda oppressed? What marks *Faust* as a man's story and *Hedda Gabler* as a woman's story?

Higuchi Ichiyo, "The Thirteenth Night," p. 1107. Like Thea Elvsted, Oseki in Higuchi Ichiyo's "Thirteenth Night" decides to leave her husband and child because she doesn't want to live in domestic oppression. Thea seeks creative fulfillment in collaborating with Lovborg on his manuscript. How are we to understand this collaboration and Thea's later alliance with Tesman? Has Thea simply found another kind of subservience? Or is writing, as the link between Løvborg's manuscript and a child suggests, a creative and fulfilling alternative to homemaking? Why is Hedda unable to find a fulfilling way to live? Does Oseki have any choices besides her marriage? Why does she return to it?

Camus, *The Stranger* and "The Myth of Sisyphus" (Book 6). In Act 4 of *Hedda Gabler,* Hedda refers several times to the "absurdity" of her situation, and when she

A Doll's House, Ghosts, and *Hedda Gabler* provided resonant theatrical images that participated in the cultural redefinition of women's place in European society.

– CHARLES R. LYONS, critic, 1991

first hears of Løvborg's suicide she is struck by the "courage" of his act. Is Hedda speaking as an existentialist at this point in the play, seeing her life as absurd and admiring Løvborg's capacity to make life and death choices? Is her own suicide a courageous and heroic act?

■ FURTHER RESEARCH

Biography
Meyer, Michael. *Ibsen: A Biography.* 1971.

Criticism
Bryan, George B. *An Ibsen Companion.* 1984.
Downs, Brian. *Ibsen: The Intellectual Background.* 1948; *A Study of Six Plays by Ibsen.* 1950.
Johnston, Brian. *The Ibsen Cycle: The Design of the Plays from* Pillars of Society *to* When We Dead Awaken. 1992.
McFarlane, James. *The Cambridge Companion to Ibsen.* 1994.
Shaw, George Bernard. *The Quintessence of Ibsenism.* 1891.
Templeton, Joan. *Ibsen's Women.* 1997.
Thomas, David. *Henrik Ibsen.* 1983.

On *A Doll's House*
Durbach, Errol. A Doll's House: *Ibsen's Myth of Transformation.* 1991.
Mitchell, Hayley R., ed. *Readings on* A Doll's House. 1999. A collection of critical essays on the play.

■ PRONUNCIATION

Henrik Ibsen: HEN-rik IB-sin
Eilert Løvborg: AY-lert LOWV-borg
Jørgen Tesman: YOR-gun TES-mahn

ᘉ Hedda Gabler

Translated by Nicholas Rudall

ACT 1

A large, substantial, and tastefully furnished drawing room decorated in dark colors. In the back of the room a wide doorway with its curtains drawn, revealing an antechamber decorated in a similar style. On the right we can see part of the front room. A folding door leads to the hall. On the left is a glass door (French window), also with its curtains drawn. Through it can be seen

---

Hedda Gabler. Published in 1890, this play was first performed in Germany in 1891. That production and six others in the same year failed to engage the sympathy of their audiences. Only the London production of 1891, praised by Henry James and George Bernard Shaw, who said he "had never had a more tremendous sensation in a theatre," was a success. Since then *Hedda* has become perhaps the most performed of Ibsen's plays.

One of Ibsen's later works, this drama shares a realistic setting and an apparent concern with social issues with his earlier "problem plays," works like *A Doll's House* (1879), *Ghosts* (1881), and *The*

part of the veranda and some trees covered with autumn leaves. In the front of the drawing room is an oval table with a tablecloth on it and chairs around it. On the right, near the wall, a large dark porcelain stove, a tall armchair, a footstool, and two small side tables. Also on the right is a sofa with a small round table in front of it. On the left is another sofa. A piano is up center. On either side of the large door are two stands with terra cotta and majolica ornaments. In the rear room can be seen a sofa, a table, and one or two chairs. Above the sofa hangs a portrait of a handsome elderly man in the uniform of a general. Over the table is a hanging lamp with a glass shade. Many bouquets of flowers are arranged about the drawing room in their vases. Other bouquets are still on the tables. The rooms are thickly carpeted. It is early morning. The sun is shining in through the French windows.

 Miss Tesman comes in from the hall. She is wearing a hat and carrying a parasol. She is followed by Berte who is carrying a bouquet wrapped in papers. Miss Tesman is a woman of about sixty-five, pleasant and handsome. She is wearing a simple but well-made grey outfit. Berte, who is middle aged, is plain and rather countrified in her appearance.

CHARACTERS

JØRGEN TESMAN, *a research fellow in the history of culture*	MRS. ELVSTED
	JUDGE BRACK
HEDDA GABLER, *his wife*	EILERT LØVBORG
MISS JULIANA (JULIE) TESMAN, *his aunt*	BERTE, *the housekeeper*

MISS TESMAN: *(inside doorway, listens, and whispers)* My goodness—I don't think they're even up yet.

BERTE: That's what I told you, miss. The boat got in so late last night. And then . . . Heavens! All the stuff she wanted unpacked before she went to bed.

MISS TESMAN: Well, let them sleep. But . . . *(opening French windows)* good, fresh, morning air . . . that we can give them when they come down.

BERTE: *(by the table—at a loss—flowers in hand)* Please, miss. I don't see anywhere to put these. I think I'd better put them over here. *(puts flowers on piano)*

MISS TESMAN: Well, well, my dear Berte, so you've got yourself a new mistress now. Lord knows it was hard for me to let you go.

BERTE: *(near tears)* It was hard for me too, miss. What can I say? All those happy years I spent with you and Miss Rina.

MISS TESMAN: We must all take what comes, Berte. That's all there is to it. Jørgen can't do without you, you know. He can't, it's as simple as that. You've looked after him since he was a little boy.

Wild Duck (1884). *Hedda,* however, does not focus on a defined social problem; instead it is especially interested in the psychology of its complex and manipulative central figure. After her father's death, Hedda can no longer afford to live in the aristocratic manner to which she has become accustomed. Powerless to direct the course of her life, she succumbs to marriage with a tedious academic who lacks the resources to allow her to be the grand hostess she wants to be. So Hedda amuses herself by meddling destructively in others' lives. When Judge Brack discerns that her machinations brought about Løvborg's suicide, Hedda is completely in the judge's control and can no longer play the evasive flirt with him. Rather than suffer the judge's blackmail, she chooses to escape.

 This Nicholas Rudall translation renders the play in a contemporary idiom for the American stage.

BERTE: Yes, but, miss, I can't stop thinking about Miss Rina. Poor thing—lying there, completely helpless. And that new girl looking after her. She won't know how to take proper care of an invalid. I know she won't.

MISS TESMAN: Yes, she will. I'll teach her. But of course I'll do most of it myself. So don't you worry about my poor sister.

BERTE: Well, there's something else too, miss. I'm very much afraid that I won't please the young mistress.

MISS TESMAN: Oh well, at first there may be a thing or two, but . . .

BERTE: Because I'm sure she's very particular.

MISS TESMAN: Naturally! General Gabler's daughter. What a life she had when the general was still alive. Do you remember when she went riding with her father? Galloping along in that long black riding outfit. And that feather in her hat.

BERTE: Oh, yes, I remember . . . very well. But I never dreamed that she and young Mr. Tesman would make a go of it.

MISS TESMAN: No more did I. But while I think of it, it isn't *Mr.* Tesman any more. From now on you must call him Dr. Tesman.

BERTE: Yes, the young mistress did say something about that last night. Right away. As soon as they were inside the door. Is it true then, miss?

MISS TESMAN: It is indeed. They gave him his doctor's degree! Just think of that. Abroad, during the trip, you know. I hadn't heard a word about it until last night down on the pier.

BERTE: Well, he's so clever, he is. He could be anything he wanted. But I never thought he'd turn his hand to curing people.

MISS TESMAN: Oh, he's not that kind of doctor. *(nods significantly)* And, well, I'm not supposed to say, but pretty soon you may have to call him something even grander than doctor.

BERTE: Oh, good heavens, what could that be, miss?

MISS TESMAN: *(smiles)* Wouldn't you like to know! *(moved)* Oh, dear God, if only his father could look up from his grave and see what his son has become. . . . *(looking around)* Berte! What's all this? Why have you taken the slipcovers off the furniture?

BERTE: She told me to. Doesn't like covers on chairs, she said.

MISS TESMAN: Are they going to make this their living room then?

BERTE: It seemed like it. Mrs. Tesman did the talking. Mr. Tes—Doctor Tesman didn't say anything about it.

(George Tesman enters inner room from right, singing to himself. Carries an empty unstrapped suitcase. He is a youngish-looking man of thirty-three. Blond hair. Beard. Carelessly dressed in comfortable lounging clothes.)

MISS TESMAN: Good morning, good morning, Jørgen.

TESMAN: *(in doorway)* Aunt Julie. Dearest Aunt Julie. You came all the way out here and so early in the morning.

MISS TESMAN: Well, I just had to drop by and see how you were.

TESMAN: And I'm sure you didn't get a full night's sleep.

MISS TESMAN: Oh, that doesn't bother me.

TESMAN: But you got home all right? After meeting us? How?

MISS TESMAN: Of course I did . . . but thank you. The Judge was good enough to see me home.

TESMAN: We were sorry we couldn't give you a ride in the carriage. But, well, you saw for yourself . . . Hedda had all those boxes.

MISS TESMAN: Yes, she did. Quite a collection, really.

BERTE: Should I go and ask Mrs. Tesman if there's anything I could help her with?

TESMAN: No, thank you, Berte, you'd better not. She said she would ring if she wanted anything.

BERTE: *(going off right)* All right then.

TESMAN: One moment. . . . You could take this with you. *(hands her the suitcase)*

BERTE: I'll put it in the attic. *(exits by hall door)*

TESMAN: Just think, Aunt Julie, that suitcase was stuffed full with my papers. You wouldn't believe the things I found in the libraries. Old documents, notes, papers that no one knew anything about.

MISS TESMAN: Yes, well then, Jørgen, you didn't waste any time on your honeymoon.

TESMAN: No, I didn't. But take your hat off. My goodness! Here, let me help you with the ribbon.

MISS TESMAN: *(as he does so)* Ah, dear God, this is just like the old days—when you were still at home with us.

TESMAN: *(inspecting the hat)* An elegant hat you've got here.

MISS TESMAN: I bought it to please Hedda.

TESMAN: Hedda? What made you . . .

MISS TESMAN: So she won't be ashamed to be seen going out with me.

TESMAN: *(patting her cheek)* You think of everything, don't you. *(puts hat down on a chair by the table)* Now then—over here, by me, on the sofa . . . we'll sit and chat for a while until Hedda comes. *(They sit. She places her parasol on the corner of the sofa.)*

MISS TESMAN: *(taking his hands and looking in his eyes)* It's so good to have you back again, Jørgen. Right here next to me. Jochum's little boy.

TESMAN: For me, too, Aunt Julie. To see you again. You have been mother and father to me.

MISS TESMAN: Yes. I know that there will always be a place in your heart for those two old aunts of yours.

TESMAN: But Aunt Rina . . . how is she? Any better?

MISS TESMAN: Oh, no . . . we can't expect her to ever get better, poor thing. She lies there day after day, year after year. May the good Lord let me keep her a little while longer. Because I just wouldn't know what to do with myself if she . . . especially now when I don't have you to look after any more.

TESMAN: *(patting her cheek)* There, there, come now!

MISS TESMAN: *(changing her tone)* But you're a married man now, Jørgen. To think it was you who walked off with Hedda Gabler. The beautiful Hedda Gabler. And with all those infatuated young men she had.

TESMAN: *(hums a little, smiles complacently)* Yes . . . I have a suspicion that I have several friends who'd like to change places with me.

MISS TESMAN: And that honeymoon! What was it, five? no, nearly six months!

TESMAN: Yes, but I had my research to do, too, of course. The libraries, all those books to read.

MISS TESMAN: Yes, of course. *(confidentially, lowering her voice)* But now listen, Jørgen, don't you . . . don't you have something . . . special . . . to tell me?

TESMAN: About the trip?

MISS TESMAN: Yes.

TESMAN: No, I can't think of anything—apart from what I wrote in my letters. I got my doctor's degree there—but I told you that yesterday.

MISS TESMAN: Yes, I know, but I mean . . . what I'm saying is, don't you have any . . . any expectations?

TESMAN: Expectations?

MISS TESMAN: My goodness, Jørgen. This is your old aunt you're talking to.

TESMAN: Well, naturally I have expectations.

MISS TESMAN: Yes.

TESMAN: Well, I do expect, with some confidence, to be made a professor one day soon.

MISS TESMAN: Oh, a professor . . . yes.

TESMAN: In fact, I am sure of it. But dear Aunt Julie—you know that as well as I do.

MISS TESMAN: *(with a little laugh)* Of course I do. *(changing the subject)* But we were talking about the trip. It must have cost a fortune.

TESMAN: Well, the fellowship was fairly substantial. It helped a great deal.

MISS TESMAN: But I just don't see how you could make it do for both of you.

TESMAN: No, I suppose that is difficult to understand.

MISS TESMAN: Especially traveling with a lady. That makes it much more expensive, doesn't it?

TESMAN: Yes, of course—a little more. But Hedda simply had to have this trip. She *had* to. There was no saying no to her.

MISS TESMAN: No, no, I dare say you're right. A honeymoon abroad seems to be quite the thing these days. But tell me, what do you think of the house? Have you had a good look round?

TESMAN: Indeed I have. I've been up since dawn.

MISS TESMAN: And. . . ? Well, what do you think of it?

TESMAN: I love it. It's quite, quite wonderful. The only thing is . . . I don't know what we'll do with two empty rooms . . . the ones between the back parlor and Hedda's bedroom.

MISS TESMAN: *(with a small laugh)* Oh, my dear Jørgen, you'll know what to do with them . . . when the time comes.

TESMAN: Yes, of course, you're quite right. As my library grows, hmm?

MISS TESMAN: Yes, quite so. It was your library I was thinking of.

TESMAN: I'm really most happy for Hedda—for her most of all. Before we got married she used to say that this was the only house for her. Secretary Falk's town house was the only one.

MISS TESMAN: And to think it came up for sale as soon as you'd left. You were lucky.

TESMAN: Yes, very. Very lucky.

MISS TESMAN: But it will be expensive, my dear Jørgen. It's so big. Terribly expensive.

TESMAN: *(somewhat crestfallen)* Yes, I suppose so. Yes.

MISS TESMAN: Oh, my Lord, yes.

TESMAN: How much do you think? I mean, roughly, hmm?

MISS TESMAN: Well, you won't know till all the bills come in.

TESMAN: Judge Brack was very helpful. He managed to get us very reasonable terms. At least that's what he wrote to Hedda.

MISS TESMAN: Well, let's not worry about it. I've put down a little deposit for you to cover the carpets and the furniture.

TESMAN: Aunt Julie! You can't! Where could you. . . ?

MISS TESMAN: I took a mortgage on my pension.

TESMAN: *(getting up)* What? But that is yours! Yours and Aunt Rina's.

MISS TESMAN: I couldn't think of what else to do.

TESMAN: *(in front of her)* But that was so . . . so foolish of you. Your pension! It's all the two of you have to live on.

MISS TESMAN: Now calm down, there's a good boy. It's only a formality. That's what Judge Brack said. He was kind enough to arrange the whole thing. Just a formality . . . those were his very words.

TESMAN: That's all well and good. But I . . .

MISS TESMAN: You'll have your own salary now. And if we have to put a little money down now, at the beginning . . . well, it's a pleasure to help out.

TESMAN: Aunt Julie, Aunt Julie, Aunt Julie, when will you stop making sacrifices for me?

MISS TESMAN: *(gets up, puts hands on his shoulders)* What else do I have? You're my only joy. If I can make life a little easier for you, what else is there? You have no father, no mother to help you. And now we are almost there, Jørgen! It's been very hard, I know, at times. But now, my dear, dear boy, you have reached the end.

TESMAN: Yes, when I think of it, I can't believe how everything has turned out.

MISS TESMAN: And those who were against you — all those who stood in your way — they've just . . . disappeared. Gone. Lost. They have *lost*, Jørgen. And the one who was the greatest danger to you, where is he? He fell the hardest. He made his bed and he must lie in it . . . fool that he is.

TESMAN: What have you heard . . . since I went away? Is there any news about Eilert?

MISS TESMAN: Only that he's supposed to have published a new book.

TESMAN: Eilert Løvborg? When? Just recently now?

MISS TESMAN: That's what I heard. But there can't be much to it. I shouldn't think but when your book comes out . . . that will be something different. What are you writing about?

TESMAN: The Middle Ages . . . the cottage industries of the Brabant[1] . . . in that period.

---

[1] **Brabant:** A medieval dukedom located in what is now Belgium and the Netherlands.

MISS TESMAN: To be able to write about things like that. I don't know how you do it.

TESMAN: Well, the actual publication may not be for some time yet. I have a good deal of material to put in order.

MISS TESMAN: Yes, you collect and you organize. You do it so well. You're my brother's son, Jørgen.

TESMAN: I'm ready, anxious really, to get started. Especially now, here, in the quiet and comfort of this house.

MISS TESMAN: And best of all, dear boy . . . you have your Hedda . . . the wife of your dreams.

TESMAN: Yes, Hedda. My Hedda . . . that's the most wonderful part of it all. *(looking toward doorway)* I think I hear her coming now.

HEDDA: *(Enters from left inner room. Twenty-nine years old. Noble. Elegant. Pale complexion. Steel grey eyes, expressing cold clear calm. Attractive brown hair. Tasteful, loose-fitting gown.)*

MISS TESMAN: *(going to her)* Good morning, my dear Hedda—it's so good to see you.

HEDDA: *(extending her hand)* Good morning, dear Miss Tesman. Well, you are here early. It is so kind of you to come.

MISS TESMAN: Not at all. *(slightly embarrassed)* And did the bride have a good night's sleep in her new house?

HEDDA: I slept quite adequately, thank you.

TESMAN: Listen to that. Adequately, she says. Hedda! You were sleeping like a log when I got up.

HEDDA: Fortunately. But of course it takes time, Miss Tesman, to get used to new surroundings. *(looking to left)* Oh, look at that, the maid has left the doors wide open. The sunlight is just flooding in.

MISS TESMAN: *(going to doors)* Well, then, we can close them.

HEDDA: No, don't! *(to Tesman)* Would you draw the curtains, my dear. It will give a softer light.

TESMAN: *(by door)* Yes, of course, my dear. There now. *(closes curtains)* You have the shade and the fresh air.

HEDDA: Yes, we really need the fresh air in here. With all these flowers. Well, won't you sit down, Miss Tesman.

MISS TESMAN: Oh, no, thank you. I just wanted to see if everything was all right. *(looking around)* And thank goodness it is. So I'll be on my way. My sister's just lying there waiting for me, poor thing.

TESMAN: Give her my love and tell her I'll come and see her later today.

MISS TESMAN: Of course I will. . . . But *(reaching in her bag)* I almost forgot. . . . I have something for you, Jørgen. . . . Ah, here we are!

TESMAN: What is it, Aunt Julie, hmm?

MISS TESMAN: *(bringing out a flat parcel wrapped in newspaper)* Here you are, my dear. Take a look.

TESMAN: *(opening package)* Well, well, well, you kept them for me! Aunt Julie! *(kissing her)* Hedda, isn't that sweet now?

HEDDA: *(by the sideboard)* Yes, dear, what is it?

TESMAN: My old slippers. Look . . . my slippers.

HEDDA: Yes, they were a frequent conversation piece during our trip.

TESMAN: Well, I missed them. *(going to Hedda, smiling)* These are the famous slippers. Look.

HEDDA: *(moving to stove)* I don't care to, thank you.

TESMAN: *(following)* No, no. Aunt Rina embroidered these for me. Ill as she was. They mean a lot to me. Fond memories!

HEDDA: *(at the table)* But not for me.

MISS TESMAN: No, not for Hedda, Jørgen.

TESMAN: But I just thought . . . well, Hedda's part of the family now, and . . .

HEDDA: *(interrupting)* We are not going to get on with that new maid, Tesman.

MISS TESMAN: Berte! But why?

TESMAN: Yes, my dear, why do you say that?

HEDDA: Look! Here. . . . She's left her old hat here on the chair.

TESMAN: *(shocked and dropping the slippers)* But, Hedda!

HEDDA: What if someone were to come in and see it. . . !

TESMAN: No, no, Hedda. That's Aunt Julie's hat.

HEDDA: Really.

MISS TESMAN: Yes, it is. And one thing it's not is old, Mrs. Tesman.

HEDDA: I hadn't really looked at it very closely, Miss Tesman.

MISS TESMAN: *(tying the ribbons)* As a matter of fact, this is the first time I've worn it. The first.

TESMAN: And it's an elegant hat. Very attractive.

MISS TESMAN: It isn't so special, Jørgen. *(looks around)* And my parasol. . . ? Ah, here it is. *(picks it up)* This is mine, too. *(mutters)* Not Berte's.

TESMAN: New hat. New parasol. *(clicks through teeth)* Tut, tut, tut. What do you think of that, Hedda, hmm?

HEDDA: Very nice.

TESMAN: Yes, very nice, very nice. But before you go, take a good look at Hedda. Isn't she beautiful?

MISS TESMAN: As always, Jørgen. As always. Hedda has always been beautiful. *(she nods and starts out right)*

TESMAN: *(following)* Yes, but now there's a kind of aura about her . . . a kind of glow. She . . . she . . . filled out . . . blossomed on our honeymoon together.

HEDDA: Stop it! *(crossing room)*

MISS TESMAN: *(stopping)* Filled out.

TESMAN: Of course, you can't really see it when she's wearing that dressing gown. But I, who have the opportunity to . . .

HEDDA: *(by the doors, impatiently)* You have no opportunity, for anything.

TESMAN: It must have been the mountain air, down in the Tyrol.

HEDDA: *(curtly)* I'm just as I was when I left.

TESMAN: Yes, that's what you say. But I don't think you're right. What do you think, Aunt Julie?

MISS TESMAN: *(gazing at her, hands folded)* She is lovely—lovely—lovely. *(goes to her, takes her face in her hands, bends it down, and kisses her hair)* God bless you and keep you, Hedda Tesman—For Jørgen's sake.

HEDDA: *(gently freeing herself)* There, there. Please now . . .

MISS TESMAN: *(with quiet feeling)* I won't let a day go by without looking in on the two of you.

TESMAN: Oh, please do, please do, Aunt Julie.

MISS TESMAN: Goodbye. Goodbye.

(She exits by hall door. Tesman accompanies her, leaving the door half open. Tesman is heard thanking her for his slippers and reminding her to greet Aunt Rina. At the same time Hedda moves about the room, raising her arms, clenching her fists in quiet anger. She opens the curtains, stands by the door looking out. Tesman reenters and closes the door behind him.)

TESMAN: *(picking up his slippers)* What are you looking at, Hedda?

HEDDA: *(calm, controlled)* The leaves—they've already turned—yellow and withered.

TESMAN: *(wraps up slippers, put them on the table)* Yes, well, we're in September already.

HEDDA: *(restless again)* Yes . . . to think . . . we're already in . . . September.

TESMAN: Didn't Aunt Julie seem a bit strange to you . . . hmm? Almost a little . . . cold? What do you think was bothering her?

HEDDA: I hardly know her. Isn't she always like that?

TESMAN: No, not like she was today.

HEDDA: *(leaving door)* Was she upset about the hat, do you think?

TESMAN: No, I don't think so. Not really. Perhaps just a little at first. . . .

HEDDA: But it wasn't particularly polite, was it? To leave her hat just lying around in our living room. One just doesn't do that.

TESMAN: I can assure you she won't do it again.

HEDDA: Well, I'll make it up to her somehow.

TESMAN: Yes, Hedda, it would be nice if you did that.

HEDDA: When you go to see them later, why don't you ask her to come back this evening?

TESMAN: Yes. Yes, I will. Thank you. And there is one other thing you could do . . . it would make her very happy. . . .

HEDDA: Yes?

TESMAN: If you could stop calling her Miss Tesman . . . call her by her first name. For my sake, Hedda, dear?

HEDDA: No. That I just can't do. I told you this once before. I'll try to call her Aunt. That will have to do.

TESMAN: Well, I suppose that's all right. I was just thinking . . . now that you're part of the family . . .

HEDDA: *(with a short laugh as she goes to the doorway)* I don't know about that.

TESMAN: *(short pause)* Is something the matter, hmm? Hedda?

HEDDA: I'm just looking at my old piano. It doesn't really go with the rest of the furniture.

TESMAN: When I get my first paycheck I promise you we'll trade it in for a new one.

HEDDA: No, I don't want to do that. I can't part with it. We can put it in there, in the inner room. And we can get another, a new one for in here. Whenever that's convenient, I mean.

TESMAN: *(slightly taken aback)* Yes, well, of course, we could do that.

HEDDA: *(picking up bouquet from piano)* These flowers weren't here last night.

TESMAN: I expect Aunt Julie brought them for you.

HEDDA: *(examining them)* There's a visiting card. *(takes it out and reads it)* "Will be back later today." Can you guess who it's from?

TESMAN: No. Who? Hmm?

HEDDA: "Mrs. Thea Elvsted."

TESMAN: Oh, really? The . . . uh . . . sheriff's wife. Miss Rysing, I think her name was.

HEDDA: Yes, that's right. She was always showing off her hair . . . I remember. An annoying habit. She was an old flame of yours, wasn't she?

TESMAN: Oh, not for long. And it was long before I met you, Hedda. But, she's here in town, hmm? I wonder why.

HEDDA: It's strange that she'd call on us. I've hardly seen her since we were at school together.

TESMAN: Yes. No, I haven't seen her, either . . . oh, since God knows when. I don't know how she can stand living out there—I mean, out in the back woods, hmm?

HEDDA: *(thinks a minute, then bursts out)* Wait a minute—isn't it . . . somewhere near there that he . . . that Eilert Løvborg lives?

TESMAN: Yes, I think so. Somewhere near there.

(Berte enters)

BERTE: Excuse me, ma'am. She's back again. The lady who brought you the flowers this morning. The ones in your hand, ma'am.

HEDDA: Oh, is she? Well, show her in, please.

(Berte opens the door for Mrs. Elvsted and exits. Mrs. Elvsted is of slight build. Soft, pretty features. Large blue eyes, frightened look. Hair is white/gold. Abundant and wavy. A couple of years younger than Hedda. She wears a dark visiting dress, tasteful, slightly out of style.)

HEDDA: *(walks to her, warmly)* Good morning, my dear Mrs. Elvsted. How lovely to see you again.

MRS. ELVSTED: *(nervous, struggling to control it)* Yes, it's been a long time . . . since we met.

TESMAN: *(giving his hand)* And, indeed, since *we* met, hmm?

HEDDA: Thank you for the lovely flowers.

MRS. ELVSTED: Oh, don't mention it. . . . I . . . I was going to come yesterday afternoon. But then I heard that you were still on your way home.

TESMAN: You've just arrived in town, hmm?

MRS. ELVSTED: Yes. Yesterday afternoon. I was about in despair when I found that you weren't at home.

HEDDA: In despair? Why?

TESMAN: My dear Miss Rysing . . . I mean, Mrs. Elvsted . . .

HEDDA: There's nothing wrong, I hope.

MRS. ELVSTED: Well, yes, there is. And I couldn't think of anyone else to turn to.

HEDDA: *(putting flowers down)* Come . . . let's sit down . . . here on the sofa.

MRS. ELVSTED: Oh, I couldn't . . . I'm really too . . .

HEDDA: Of course you can. Come on.

(she draws Mrs. Elvsted down on the sofa and sits beside her)

TESMAN: Well now, Mrs. . . . uh . . . what is it, Mrs. Elvsted?

HEDDA: Has something happened? Something at home?

MRS. ELVSTED: Well, yes . . . and no. It's very difficult. I don't want you to misunderstand.

HEDDA: Well, in that case, just simply say what's on your mind, Mrs. Elvsted.

MRS. ELVSTED: Yes. Yes, of course. Well, the thing is — perhaps you already know. Eilert Løvborg has come back.

HEDDA: Løvborg . . .

TESMAN: *(overlapping)* Eilert Løvborg. Well, well. He's come back, Hedda.

HEDDA: I can hear perfectly well.

MRS. ELVSTED: He's been here a week already. A whole week . . . in the city. It's not a safe place for him. Especially alone. There are people here who would just use him, given the chance.

HEDDA: But my dear Mrs. Elvsted — why is he a concern of yours?

MRS. ELVSTED: *(glances quickly and anxiously at her)* He was the children's tutor.

HEDDA: Your children?

MRS. ELVSTED: I have none. My husband's.

HEDDA: Your stepchildren.

MRS. ELVSTED: Yes.

TESMAN: *(with some hesitation)* But was he — I don't know quite how to put this — was he responsible enough — I mean in his work habits — to be teaching children?

MRS. ELVSTED: For the past two years his behavior has been beyond reproach.

TESMAN: Well, that's good news, isn't it, Hedda?

HEDDA: I heard.

MRS. ELVSTED: Beyond reproach. I can assure you. Without question. But now . . . knowing that he's back . . . in the city. And with so much money in his pockets . . . I am frightened to death for him.

TESMAN: But why didn't he stay with you and your husband, hmm?

MRS. ELVSTED: After his book came out, he just couldn't stay with us. He was always on edge.

TESMAN: Yes, Aunt Julie was saying that he'd published a new book.

MRS. ELVSTED: Yes, a very big new book. It's a cultural history, I believe . . . with an analysis of the progress of civilization. It came out about two weeks ago. It's already a success — the sales are good and the response so very favorable.

TESMAN: Is that so? It must be something he had lying around from a few years ago. In better days.

MRS. ELVSTED: No. You mean from his earlier work?

TESMAN: Yes.

MRS. ELVSTED: No. It was written when he was staying with us. During this past year.

TESMAN: Well, now. That's very good news, Hedda, isn't it, hmm?

MRS. ELVSTED: Yes, I just hope things don't change.

HEDDA: Have you seen him since you came to town?

MRS. ELVSTED: No, not yet. It was hard to find his address. But this morning I finally found out where he was living.

HEDDA: *(looks at her closely)* Isn't it rather strange that your husband—hmm? I mean . . .

MRS. ELVSTED: *(interrupting)* My husband. . . ? What do you mean. . . ?

HEDDA: *(also overlapping)* That your husband sends you into town on such an errand? Not to come and look after his friend himself?

MRS. ELVSTED: No, no, my husband doesn't have time for things like that. And I had—I had some shopping to do anyway.

HEDDA: *(slight smile)* Of course, I understand.

MRS. ELVSTED: *(getting up; restless)* Mr. Tesman, please, this is very important. Please be kind to Eilert Løvborg if he comes to visit you. And he will. I'm sure of that. You were such good friends in the past. And you both do the same kind of work—so I gather—the same kind of research.

TESMAN: We used to, at any rate.

MRS. ELVSTED: And that's why it's so important—why I ask you to—to keep an eye on him. You will do that, Mr. Tesman, won't you? You promise?

TESMAN: I'll be only too pleased to, Mrs. Rysing.

HEDDA: Elvsted.

TESMAN: I'll do all that I can. I promise. You can count on me.

MRS. ELVSTED: *(pressing his hands)* Thank you. You're very kind. Thank you. Thank you. *(nervously)* You see, my husband is not very fond of him.

HEDDA: You ought to drop him a note, Tesman. He might not come by on his own.

TESMAN: Yes, that sounds like a good idea, Hedda. I'll do that, hmm?

HEDDA: And the sooner the better. You could do it now, I think?

MRS. ELVSTED: *(pleading)* Yes, could you? If you could . . .

TESMAN: I'll do it right away. Do you have his address, Mrs. . . . . Mrs. Elvsted?

MRS. ELVSTED: Yes. *(takes slip of paper from her bag and gives it to him)* Here it is.

TESMAN: Very good. Well, then, if you'll excuse me—I'll go in. *(looking around)* My slippers. Ah, here they are. *(leaving with parcel)*

HEDDA: Write him a nice, warm, friendly letter, Tesman. A long one.

TESMAN: I will. I will. Don't worry.

MRS. ELVSTED: But please don't mention my name. Don't say that I . . .

TESMAN: Of course not. That goes without saying, hmm? *(leaves, into inner room)*

HEDDA: *(Going to her. Smiles. Low voice.)* There! We just killed two birds with one stone.

MRS. ELVSTED: What do you mean?

HEDDA: You didn't see that I wanted him out of the room?

MRS. ELVSTED: Yes, to write the letter.

HEDDA: But I also wanted to talk to you alone.

MRS. ELVSTED: *(flustered)* You mean about this . . . this same thing.

HEDDA: Precisely.

MRS. ELVSTED: *(nervous)* But there's nothing more to say, Mrs. Tesman. There really isn't.

HEDDA: Oh, yes, there is. There's a lot more to say. I can see that. Now come. Sit here. *(makes her sit in an easy chair by the stove and seats herself on ottoman)* We'll have a nice, quiet, confidential talk. Just the two of us.

MRS. ELVSTED: *(anxious, looks at watch)* But my dear Mrs. Tesman—I'm sorry, but I really must be going.

HEDDA: Oh, there's plenty of time. Now then. Tell me about yourself, how things are going at home.

MRS. ELVSTED: That's the last thing I want to talk about.

HEDDA: But you can talk to me. After all, we were at school together.

MRS. ELVSTED: Yes, but you were a year ahead of me. I was terribly afraid of you in those days.

HEDDA: Afraid of me?

MRS. ELVSTED: Terribly. For one thing, you used to pull my hair—whenever we passed on the stairs.

HEDDA: Did I really?

MRS. ELVSTED: Yes, and there was one time when you told me you were going to burn it off.

HEDDA: I was just teasing—we were always teasing.

MRS. ELVSTED: I know, but I was so . . . so silly in those days. And anyway, we've just drifted so far apart—since then. We've moved in such different circles.

HEDDA: All the more reason to get close again. Listen. At school we were quite good friends, really—we called each other by our first names.

MRS. ELVSTED: No, I don't think we did. I think you're mistaken.

HEDDA: No, I'm sure of it. I remember it quite clearly. And we were friends then and we must be friends now. Just as we were. *(moves ottoman closer)* There now! *(kisses her cheek)* You must call me Hedda.

MRS. ELVSTED: *(pressing and patting her hand)* Oh, you're so kind to me. It's not at all what I'm used to.

HEDDA: It will be just like the old days. And I'll call you Thora.

MRS. ELVSTED: It's Thea, actually.

HEDDA: Oh, yes, of course. That's what I meant. . . . Thea. *(looks at her)* So you're not used to kindness, Thea, is that it? In your own home?

MRS. ELVSTED: A home! If I had a home. . . . But I don't. I never had.

HEDDA: *(looking around)* I thought it might be something like this.

MRS. ELVSTED: *(helplessly, looking straight ahead)* Yes—yes—yes.

HEDDA: I'm not sure if I remember correctly—but didn't you go to your husband's—to the Elvsteds as a governess at first?

MRS. ELVSTED: Yes, that was my position. But his wife, his first wife, was already very ill, practically bedridden. So I had to take charge of the whole house—everything.

HEDDA: And in the end—afterwards—you became his wife.

MRS. ELVSTED: *(dully)* Yes. I did.

HEDDA: Let's see, how long ago was that?

MRS. ELVSTED: Since my marriage?

HEDDA: Yes.

MRS. ELVSTED: Five years.

HEDDA: That's right. It must be.

MRS. ELVSTED: Oh, those five years. Or at least the past two or three. If you only knew, Mrs. Tesman.

HEDDA: *(taps her hand slightly)* Mrs. Tesman? Hedda! Hedda!

MRS. ELVSTED: Yes, all right, I'm sorry. I'll try. . . . If only you knew, Hedda, if only you could just understand. . . .

HEDDA: *(casually)* Eilert Løvborg lived up there near you too, didn't he? During the past two or three years.

MRS. ELVSTED: Eilert Løvborg? *(looks at her uncertainly)* Yes. Yes, he did.

HEDDA: Did you know him before—when he lived in town?

MRS. ELVSTED: Oh, not really. Hardly at all. I mean, I knew his name, of course.

HEDDA: But up there—you must have seen him quite often. . . ?

MRS. ELVSTED: Yes. He came to the house every day. He was tutoring the children, you know. Because, well, what with everything else—I couldn't do it myself.

HEDDA: Of course not. And your husband? He must have to be away from home quite often?

MRS. ELVSTED: Well, yes, Mrs. Tes— Hedda, as a public official he has to travel all over the district.

HEDDA: Thea—my poor, sweet Thea—now you must tell me everything—just as it is.

MRS. ELVSTED: I—no—you had better ask the questions.

HEDDA: Well, what sort of man is your husband? I mean—to be with, live with. . . . What's he like? Is he good to you?

MRS. ELVSTED: *(evasively)* I'm sure he thinks he does everything for the best.

HEDDA: But he's rather too old for you, isn't he? At least twenty years older than you, I believe.

MRS. ELVSTED: *(irritated)* That's true. Along with everything else. If the truth be told, I . . . I—he disgusts me. We have not a thing in common. Not a single thing.

HEDDA: But he must be fond of you. I mean, in his own way.

MRS. ELVSTED: I don't know. I think he thinks of me as . . . useful to him. I don't spend much money. I'm . . . inexpensive.

HEDDA: More fool you.

MRS. ELVSTED: *(shaking her head)* There's no option. Not with him. He thinks only of himself—and perhaps the children. A little.

HEDDA: And Eilert Løvborg, Thea?

MRS. ELVSTED: Eilert Løvborg? What makes you say that?

HEDDA: Well, when he sends you all the way to town to look after him . . . it seems to me. . . . *(smiles, almost imperceptibly)* Besides, that's what you told my husband. . . .

MRS. ELVSTED: Did I? *(nervous gesture)* Yes, I suppose I did. *(quiet outburst)* No—I might as well tell you here and now. . . . It's bound to come out anyway sooner or later.

HEDDA: But my dear Thea. . . ?

MRS. ELVSTED: All right. My husband doesn't know that I'm here.

HEDDA: What? He doesn't know?!

MRS. ELVSTED: No. He wasn't home. He's gone away again—oh, I couldn't stand it any longer, Hedda. It . . . it's become impossible. I'm all alone up there. I packed a few of my things—just those that I needed—I said nothing to anyone. And I left.

HEDDA: Just like that.

MRS. ELVSTED: Yes. And I took the first train to town.

HEDDA: But my dear Thea . . . how could you bring yourself to do a thing like that?

MRS. ELVSTED: *(rises, pauses)* What else could I do?

HEDDA: But what will he say. . . ? When you go back home.

MRS. ELVSTED: *(by table, looks at her)* Go back? To him?

HEDDA: Yes.

MRS. ELVSTED: I'll never go back.

HEDDA: *(rises, approaches slowly)* So you've left him. For good.

MRS. ELVSTED: Yes. There was nothing else to do.

HEDDA: But . . . to go away, so—so openly.

MRS. ELVSTED: You can't keep a thing like that secret.

HEDDA: But what do you think people will say, Thea?

MRS. ELVSTED: God knows, they can say what they like. *(Sitting on sofa. Sad. Tired.)* I only did what I had to do.

HEDDA: *(brief silence)* What do you intend to do now? Will you find work?

MRS. ELVSTED: I don't know yet. All I know is, I have to live here, near Eilert Løvborg, if I am to live at all.

HEDDA: *(moves chair from table, sits beside her, strokes her hands)* Thea—tell me— how did this—this friendship between you and Eilert Løvborg—how did it begin?

MRS. ELVSTED: It just happened. Little by little. I had some sort of power over him, I suppose.

HEDDA: Oh?

MRS. ELVSTED: He gave up his old habits. Not because I asked him to. I couldn't do that. But he knew that they upset me. So he just stopped.

HEDDA: *(quickly hiding a scornful smile)* So you have—rehabilitated him, as they say. My dear Thea!

MRS. ELVSTED: That's what he says. And he has done something for me. He's made me feel like a human being again. Taught me to think—to understand things that before . . . so many things . . .

HEDDA: A tutor to you as well as to the children?

MRS. ELVSTED: No, not exactly. But he'd talk to me—for hours. About so many things. And then it became truly beautiful. I was so happy—he let me share in his work. He let me help him.

HEDDA: He did?

MRS. ELVSTED: Yes. When he was writing the book—we—we would work on it together.

HEDDA: Like the best of friends!

MRS. ELVSTED: Yes. Oh, yes. That's how he felt, too. Oh, Hedda, just think—I ought to be so happy. But I'm not. I'm so afraid it won't last.

HEDDA: You don't trust him any more than that?

MRS. ELVSTED: There's always been the shadow of another woman. She stands between Eilert Løvborg and me.

HEDDA: *(very intent)* Who?

MRS. ELVSTED: I don't know. A shadow from his past. Someone he can't forget.

HEDDA: What has he told you—about this?

MRS. ELVSTED: He brought it up only once—in passing. That's all.

HEDDA: And what did he say?

MRS. ELVSTED: He said that when they broke up she threatened to kill him. With a gun.

HEDDA: *(cold, restrained)* Nonsense. Not here! People just don't do that sort of thing.

MRS. ELVSTED: No. That's true. That's why I thought it might just have been that singer he used to—the one with the red hair—?

HEDDA: That's possible.

MRS. ELVSTED: People said she carried a gun.

HEDDA: It was probably her. It must have been.

MRS. ELVSTED: *(wringing her hands)* She's come back—oh, Hedda—that's what I've heard. She's come back. I'm in despair, Hedda!

HEDDA: Shhh! *(glances at inner room)* Here's Tesman—*(gets up and whispers)* Not a word! To anybody.

MRS. ELVSTED: *(jumps up)* No! No, of course!

(Tesman enters, letter in hand, from right)

TESMAN: There we are—all finished.

HEDDA: Good. Mrs. Elvsted was just leaving. If you wait a moment I'll walk you to the gate.

TESMAN: Hedda, dear—do you think Berte could take care of this?

HEDDA: *(takes letter)* I'll see to it.

(Berte enters from hall)

BERTE: Judge Brack is here. He wonders if he might see you both, ma'am?

HEDDA: Yes. Ask the Judge to come in. And—here—put this in the mailbox, would you?

BERTE: *(takes letter)* Yes, ma'am.

(Opens door for Judge Brack. Exits. Judge Brack is forty-five. Thickset. Well built. Brisk. Graceful. Round face. Distinguished profile. Short hair, mostly black. Well groomed. Eyes bright, sparkling. Thick eyebrows and moustache. Well-tailored walking suit. Pince-nez on string, which he lets fall on occasion.)

JUDGE BRACK: *(hat in hand, bowing)* May one pay one's respects so early in the morning?

HEDDA: One certainly may.

TESMAN: *(shakes hand)* You're always welcome here. *(introducing him)* Judge Brack—Mrs. Rysing.

HEDDA: *(quiet groan)* Ahh. . . .

BRACK: *(bows)* Delighted!

HEDDA: *(looks at him and laughs)* It's a pleasure to see you in daylight, Judge Brack.

BRACK: Have I changed?

HEDDA: A bit younger, I think.

BRACK: Thank you.

TESMAN: But look at my Hedda, hmm? Doesn't she have a kind of glow to her, hmm? She's positively . . .

HEDDA: Stop it. Please don't talk about me that way. You might thank the Judge for all the trouble he's gone to.

BRACK: Nonsense. It was a pleasure.

HEDDA: Thank you. You are a true friend. But I'm sorry, Thea, I know you have to leave. Excuse me; I'll be right back.

(Mutual goodbyes. Mrs. Elvsted and Hedda exit right.)

BRACK: Well, your wife is reasonably satisfied, I take it.

TESMAN: Oh, yes. We can't thank you enough. Of course, I understand that there are still some minor adjustments to be made. And we still need one or two things for the house. A few small purchases. Here and there.

BRACK: Oh? Really?

TESMAN: But we don't want to bother you with such things. Hedda said she'd take care of them. But . . . do sit down, hmm?

BRACK: Thank you. Just for a moment. *(sits by table)* There *is* something I need to talk to you about, Tesman.

TESMAN: Hmm? Oh, yes, I see. *(sits)* The time for serious financial advice. Ready for the lecture.

BRACK: Oh, no—the financial arrangements are, um . . . there's no great rush as far as the money's concerned. . . . Although I wish we could have been a little more economical.

TESMAN: That, my dear Judge, was not possible. It's all in Hedda's hands and, well, you know how she is. I couldn't let her live like a grocer's wife, now, could I?

BRACK: No. No. I understand. That *is* the problem, I suppose.

TESMAN: Besides—fortunately, it can't be long before I get my appointment.

BRACK: Well, you know, these things can take time.

TESMAN: Have you heard something? Is there any news, hmm?

BRACK: No, I've heard nothing. But—by the way—I do have something to tell you.

TESMAN: Oh?

BRACK: Your old friend Eilert Løvborg is back in town.

TESMAN: I know.

BRACK: Oh? Who told you?

TESMAN: The lady who was just here.

BRACK: Oh, I see. What was her name again? I didn't quite catch . . .

TESMAN: Mrs. Elvsted.

BRACK: Ah, yes, the sheriff's wife. Yes, he was living near them for a while.

TESMAN: And, um—so I gather—he's reformed, completely changed his ways.

BRACK: Yes, that's what they're saying.

TESMAN: And he's published a new book, hmm?

BRACK: Yes.

TESMAN: And it's caused quite a sensation.

BRACK: An extraordinary sensation.

TESMAN: Who'd have thought? Well, that's just marvelous. Isn't it? He was so very talented. I was afraid that he was done for. Finished.

BRACK: Yes. That's what everybody thought.

TESMAN: But what will he do now? Hmm? How can he possibly make a living?

(Hedda enters during Tesman's last words)

HEDDA: *(to Brack, laughing, touch of sarcasm)* Tesman is always worrying about how people are going to make a living.

TESMAN: Yes, well, my dear, we are talking about poor Eilert Løvborg.

HEDDA: *(quick glance)* Oh, really? *(sits in easy chair at stove)* What's the matter with him?

TESMAN: Well, I'm sure he's spent his inheritance—run through it long ago. And he can't write a new book every year, can he now? So I was asking how he could possibly survive.

BRACK: Perhaps I can shed a little light on that.

TESMAN: Oh?

BRACK: First, he has relatives of some considerable influence.

TESMAN: Yes, but they washed their hands of him a long time ago.

BRACK: All the same, they used to think of him as the great hope of that family.

TESMAN: Used to, but he put an end to that himself.

HEDDA: Who can say? *(smiles)* I hear that the Elvsteds have—rehabilitated him.

BRACK: Second, there's his book—

TESMAN: Well, I hope they can help him find *something* to do. I just wrote him a letter. Hedda, I asked him to come by this evening.

BRACK: Oh. That's a pity. You're supposed to join me for dinner at the club, Tesman. You'd forgotten. We talked about it last night on the pier.

HEDDA: Had you forgotten, Tesman?

TESMAN: Yes. I'm sorry. It slipped my mind.

BRACK: Well, I'm sure he won't come. So that's that!

TESMAN: Why? What makes you say that?

BRACK: *(gets up, hesitates, hands on back of chair)* My dear Tesman—and, indeed, you too, Mrs. Tesman—I cannot, in good conscience, allow us to go any further without telling you—the fact is . . . the fact . . .

HEDDA: It's Eilert Løvborg, isn't it?

TESMAN: The fact is—? Judge, please continue.

BRACK: You must face the fact that—that your appointment may not come through as quickly as you'd hoped. Or expected.

TESMAN: *(getting up quickly)* Why? Why? Has something gone wrong?

BRACK: There is a strong possibility that the appointment will be made only after a competition is held.

TESMAN: A competition? Hedda! Just think of that.

HEDDA: *(leaning back in her chair)* Yes. Yes, I see.

TESMAN: But with whom? Not with—

BRACK: Yes. With Eilert Løvborg.

TESMAN: *(striking his hands together)* No. That is out of the question. Quite impossible.

BRACK: All the same—it may well happen.

TESMAN: Yes, but, Judge, that would be unbelievably unfair. *(gesturing with his arms)* Cruel, even! After all, I'm a married man! We got married because the position was virtually promised. We went into debt. Borrowed money from Aunt Julie. The position was—was, well, virtually promised to me.

BRACK: Well, I'm sure that you'll get it in the end. But there will be a competition.

HEDDA: *(motionless in the armchair)* Just think, Tesman—a duel to the death.

TESMAN: How can you sit there—as if you didn't care. . . ?

HEDDA: Oh, I care. I care deeply. I can't wait to see how it turns out.

BRACK: In any case, Mrs. Tesman, now you know how things stand. That's a minor relief to me. *(smiles)* What I mean is—those "few things" you were going to buy? That little threat is out of the question, hmm?

HEDDA: This changes nothing.

BRACK: I see. Well, that's something else again. . . . Goodbye. *(to Tesman)* When I take my afternoon walk, I'll call for you.

TESMAN: What? Oh, yes, please do. Yes—I'm sorry, I'm afraid I'm a little bit lost at the moment.

HEDDA: *(remains seated, gives her hand)* Goodbye, Judge. Come back soon, won't you?

BRACK: I will. Thank you. Goodbye. Goodbye.

TESMAN: *(accompanying him only to door)* Goodbye, my dear Judge. You must excuse me. . . .

(Brack exits)

TESMAN: Oh, Hedda, Hedda. One should never live in a dream world.

HEDDA: Do *you* do that?

TESMAN: Well, yes—of course. I can't deny it. To get married—to set up a home—on the strength of a mere promise.

HEDDA: Perhaps you're right.

TESMAN: Well, at least we *have* a home—a nice, comfortable home. The home that we *both* dreamed of, Hedda. That we set our hearts on.

HEDDA: *(rises slowly, wearily)* Yes, that was part of our agreement—that we'd maintain a life of elegant respectability—live here—

TESMAN: I know, I know. Dearest Hedda—I have longed to see you, as the lady of this house, entertaining a select circle of our friends. Yes, well—for a while we'll just have to be by ourselves. Perhaps we'll see Aunt Julie once in a while. That's all. But I wanted it to be so different—for you, so very different.

HEDDA: I suppose a butler is now out of the question.

TESMAN: I'm afraid so. No, there's not a chance of that, under the circumstances.

HEDDA: And my horse, my own riding horse . . .

TESMAN: *(aghast)* The horse!

HEDDA: I suppose that is out of the question.

TESMAN: Good Lord—no—that goes without saying.

HEDDA: *(crossing room)* Well, at least I have one thing left to keep me amused.

TESMAN: *(smiling)* Well, thank heaven for that. What is it, my love, hmm?

HEDDA: *(in the doorway, with veiled scorn)* My pistols, Jørgen.

TESMAN: *(afraid)* Your pistols.

HEDDA: *(cold stare)* General Gabler's pistols. *(she exits through inner door)*

TESMAN: *(to doorway, calling after her)* No, Hedda! For heaven's sake. . . . Please! Don't touch them! Leave them alone. For my sake, Hedda. Please.

ACT 2

The same room, but the piano has been removed. In its place is an elegant little writing table. A small table, new sofa. Most of the flowers have been removed. Mrs. Elvsted's bouquet is on the center table. It is afternoon. Hedda is dressed to receive callers. She stands alone near the open French windows, loading a revolver. The other is lying in an open case on the desk.

HEDDA: *(looking into garden, calls out)* Good afternoon, Judge! Welcome back!

BRACK: *(from garden)* Thank you, Mrs. Tesman.

HEDDA: *(raises pistol)* Judge Brack, your time has come!

BRACK: *(still in garden)* No! No! No! Don't point it at me.

HEDDA: That's what you get for sneaking in round the back. *(fires)*

BRACK: *(nearer)* Are you out of your mind?

HEDDA: Oh, dear—I didn't hit you, did I?

BRACK: *(still outside)* Stop it. Stop this nonsense.

HEDDA: All right. Do come in.

BRACK: *(Dressed for dinner. Enters, carrying a light overcoat.)* Good God, woman! Are you still playing your ridiculous games? What are you shooting at?

HEDDA: Oh, I was just firing into the blue of the sky.

BRACK: *(gently taking the gun)* If you'll permit me, Mrs. Tesman. *(looks at it)* Ah, yes, I remember this very well. *(looks around)* Where is the case? Ah, here we are. *(puts gun in case, closes it)* We'll have no more of that nonsense this afternoon.

HEDDA: Well, what in God's name am I supposed to do with myself?

BRACK: No visitors?

HEDDA: *(closing glass door)* No. Not one. I suppose all our friends are still out of town.

BRACK: And Tesman? Not at home?

HEDDA: *(at writing table, puts pistol case in drawer)* No. After lunch he went off to see his aunts. He didn't expect you back so soon.

BRACK: I should have thought of that. That was stupid of me.

HEDDA: *(turning to him)* Stupid? Why?

BRACK: If I'd known, I'd have come by even earlier.

HEDDA: *(crossing room)* If you had, you wouldn't have found anyone at home. I was in my room, getting dressed.

BRACK: Ah! And there isn't a small crack in the door for us to—to converse through?

HEDDA: You forgot to see to that.

BRACK: Also stupid of me.

HEDDA: So we'll have to stay right here. And wait. . . . I don't think Tesman will be back for a while.

BRACK: I can be very patient.

(Hedda sits on sofa. Brack puts overcoat on nearby chair—sits. Keeps his hat. Brief pause. They look at one another.)

HEDDA: Well?

BRACK: *(imitates her tone)* Well?

HEDDA: I said it first.

BRACK: All right. *(leans forward)* Let's have a nice, quiet chat, Mrs.—Hedda Gabler. *(leans back)*

HEDDA: It seems like a lifetime since we last talked together. Doesn't it? I don't mean last night or this morning. That meant nothing.

BRACK: You mean—just the two of us. Alone.

HEDDA: Something like that.

BRACK: I missed you. Every day you were gone.

HEDDA: I felt the same way.

BRACK: Did you? Honestly? I thought you were having a marvelous time.

HEDDA: Marvelous.

BRACK: That's what Tesman said in his letters.

HEDDA: Oh, yes. It was marvelous for him. He loved poking around in collections of old books. Copying his—his parchments, or whatever you call them.

BRACK: *(with a smile)* But that's what he does. Isn't it? Partly, anyway.

HEDDA: Yes. That's what he does. And there's nothing wrong with it—but what about *me*? Oh, Judge—you just don't know. I'm so terribly bored.

BRACK: *(sympathetically)* Are you? In all seriousness?

HEDDA: You must understand—to go away for months on end. No one to talk to. No one who knew our circle of friends, or who was interested in my kind of life.

BRACK: Yes, I believe I would have been bored, too.

HEDDA: And the most unbearable thing of all—

BRACK: What?

HEDDA: To be with the same person . . . all the . . . everlastingly.

BRACK: Morning, noon, and night. Yes—I do understand. At every conceivable hour.

HEDDA: I said everlastingly.

BRACK: I understand. Still, Tesman is such a good man—I should have thought.

HEDDA: My dear Judge—Tesman is an academic.

BRACK: True.

HEDDA: And academics are not the most entertaining traveling companions. Not in the long run, anyway.

BRACK: Not even the academic one loves?

HEDDA: Don't use that nauseating word.

BRACK: *(puzzled)* I don't understand, Mrs. Tesman.

HEDDA: *(half laughing, half annoyed)* You should try it sometime. Listening to the cultural history of civilization. Morning, noon, and night.

BRACK: Everlastingly.

HEDDA: Yes. Yes! And the Middle Ages, and the cottage industries of the Brabant—Oh, God!

BRACK: *(looks at her closely)* Then how . . . how did you . . . I mean . . .

HEDDA: Why did I choose Jørgen Tesman?

BRACK: If you want to put it that way, yes.

HEDDA: Oh, come now. Do you really find that so strange?

BRACK: Well, yes—and in some ways, no.

HEDDA: I was tired of the dance. Tired. My time was over. *(with a shudder)* No, I don't want to say that. I don't want to think it.

BRACK: No. There's no reason to. None at all.

HEDDA: Oh, reasons—reasons. *(watching him)* And, anyway, Jørgen Tesman is a perfectly respectable young man.

BRACK: Perfectly. And absolutely dependable.

HEDDA: And there's nothing about him that one could call slightly—ridiculous?

BRACK: Ridiculous. . . . No. I wouldn't say that.

HEDDA: And what's more—he works unbelievably hard on his research. There's no doubt about that. In time he may go very far.

BRACK: I assumed that you, like everyone else, believed in him, believed indeed that he would become an eminent scholar.

HEDDA: *(tired)* Yes, I did. And then when he insisted that he wanted to take care of me—provide for me. What could I do but accept?

BRACK: No, of course—if you look at it that way. . . .

HEDDA: That was more than my other admirers were willing to do for me.

BRACK: *(laughs)* Well, I can't speak for all of them. . . . But as far as I am concerned—I've always had a great deal of respect for the institution of marriage. Always—in general, that is, Mrs. Tesman.

HEDDA: *(teasing)* Well, I never really had any high hopes for you.

BRACK: All I want is a close circle of intimate friends—I want to be of use—I want to help—to come and go simply as a friend—a trusted friend.

HEDDA: You mean, of the master of the house.

BRACK: *(bowing slightly)* To be perfectly honest—I meant the lady. But the master, too, of course. That kind of triangle of friends—*à trois,* shall we say—can be wonderfully satisfying for all concerned.

HEDDA: Yes, there were many times that I wanted someone else with us. Oh, those endless conversations in the railway carriages. Just the two of us.

BRACK: Fortunately, the wedding trip is over.

HEDDA: *(shaking her head)* No, there's a long way to go. I've just come to the first stop on the line.

BRACK: Well, at the station you get out, move around, and . . .

HEDDA: I'll never get out.

BRACK: Never?

HEDDA: No. There's always someone who . . .

BRACK: *(laughs)* Looks at one's legs, is that it?

HEDDA: Yes. Exactly.

BRACK: But, after all, what's the . . .

HEDDA: *(cutting him off)* Never. That's not for me. I shall keep my seat. I will not move. Just the two of us.

BRACK: But what if a third party were to come in and join you?

HEDDA: Ah! That would be quite different.

BRACK: A friend. A trusted friend.

HEDDA: An entertaining friend. Full of life.

BRACK: And not an academic.

HEDDA: *(with a sigh)* Yes. Oh, yes, that would be a relief.

BRACK: *(hearing door open)* We are now *à trois*.

HEDDA: *(quietly)* And the train goes on.

(Tesman enters. Grey walking suit. Felt hat. Pile of books in hands. Others in his pockets.)

TESMAN: *(to table, breathing with the weight)* Oh, this is quite a load to carry. . . . And it's so hot out. *(puts books down)* I'm sweating—oh, Judge! I'm sorry. I didn't know you were here. Berte didn't tell me.

BRACK: *(rises)* I came in through the garden.

HEDDA: What are all those books?

TESMAN: *(stands leafing through some of them)* New publications—in my special field.

HEDDA: Special field.

BRACK: Yes, Mrs. Tesman—special field.

(they smile)

HEDDA: What do you need them for?

TESMAN: My dear Hedda, as a specialist I need every book, every article that's published in my field. I have to keep up with all the current literature.

HEDDA: I'm sure you're right.

TESMAN: *(searching through)* Look. Here's Løvborg's new book. Did you want to see it, Hedda? *(offers it)*

HEDDA: No—thank you. Perhaps later.

TESMAN: I took a quick look at it on the way home.

BRACK: And what do you—as a specialist—what do you think of it?

TESMAN: It's actually quite remarkable. Serious, thoughtful, precise. He's never written like this before. *(gathers books)* But—if you'll excuse me—I'll take these into the study. I can't wait to cut the pages.[2] And then I'll change for dinner. We're not late, are we?

BRACK: No. Not at all. There's plenty of time.

TESMAN: Well, in that case, I won't rush. *(starts out, stops in doorway)* Oh, by the way, Hedda — Aunt Julie won't be coming over this evening.

HEDDA: Oh, really? Is she still upset about the hat?

TESMAN: Oh, no! Aunt Julie's not like that. Really, Hedda! No. It's Aunt Rina — she's very ill.

HEDDA: Isn't she always?

TESMAN: Yes, but today she really took a turn for the worse.

HEDDA: Then she's right to stay with her. I'll just have to put up with it. That's all.

TESMAN: Aunt Julie was, in fact, delighted with her visit this morning. She thought you looked the picture of health.

HEDDA: *(under her breath, rising)* Oh, these infernal aunts.

TESMAN: Hmm?

HEDDA: *(to French doors)* Nothing.

TESMAN: Oh, well, all right. Excuse me — *(exits right)*

BRACK: What happened with the hat?

HEDDA: Oh, nothing — it was — Miss Tesman — this morning. She'd put her hat down on that chair. *(she smiles)* And I pretended to think it was the maid's.

BRACK: *(shaking his head)* My dear Hedda — how could you do that? She's such a sweet lady.

HEDDA: *(nervous — pacing)* Sometimes I can't help myself. I just do things . . . all of a sudden . . . on a whim. *(sits in armchair by stove)* Oh, I can't explain it.

BRACK: You're not really happy. . . . *(behind his chair)* That's the truth, isn't it?

HEDDA: *(staring straight ahead)* I know of no reason why I should be happy — do you?

BRACK: Well, yes — among other things — you have the home that you always wanted.

HEDDA: Ah, you too! You too believe this house was my one great passion. *(looks at him, laughs)*

BRACK: You mean, it wasn't true?

HEDDA: Perhaps there was some truth in it.

BRACK: And?

HEDDA: Tesman used to escort me home last summer — after our dinner parties —

BRACK: Unfortunately, I had to take a different path.

HEDDA: Yes, you took quite a different path last summer.

BRACK: *(laughs)* Mrs. Tesman! Shame on you. . . . Anyway, go on about Tesman.

HEDDA: We passed by here one evening and — Tesman was a nervous wreck as usual, trying to think of something to talk about — and I felt sorry for him — for this intellectual. . . .

---

[2] **cut the pages:** In the nineteenth century, books were often sold with the large folios that came from the printer folded but uncut; the reader was expected to separate the pages by cutting them along the folds.

BRACK: Honestly? *(doubting smile)* Did you?

HEDDA: I really did. So, there was this awkward silence—and again, just on a whim—I broke it by saying that I'd like to live in this house.

BRACK: Just like that?

HEDDA: Just like that.

BRACK: And then?

HEDDA: And then, my whimsicality had its consequences.

BRACK: As it often does, Mrs. Tesman. For all of us.

HEDDA: Thank you. So you see, Tesman and I found each other in our common passion for the house of Senator Falk. Then there was the engagement and the wedding and the honeymoon and—all the rest of it. . . . I was going to say I've made my bed—now I must lie in it. . . .

BRACK: Priceless, Hedda. Priceless. *(pause)* But then, this house means virtually nothing to you?

HEDDA: Oh, God, no.

BRACK: Not even now? After all, we've done what you asked for—it's elegant, comfortable.

HEDDA: *(expression of disgust)* All the rooms reek of lavender and rose petals. Perhaps that's Aunt Julie's fault. She brought it with her.

BRACK: *(laughing)* No, I think that's a bouquet from the late Mrs. Falk.

HEDDA: Yes, there is a smell of mortality about it. Like a corsage the morning after. *(hands behind her neck, leaning back, looks at him)* Oh, Judge—you cannot conceive how unutterably bored I shall be out here.

BRACK: There must be something you can do to make life more interesting—let us call it a . . . distraction.

HEDDA: Something . . . to bring me pleasure.

BRACK: Precisely.

HEDDA: I can't imagine what that could be. However, I often wonder whether— *(interrupting herself)* But it won't come to anything either.

BRACK: Who can say? Tell me what it is.

HEDDA: I wonder whether I couldn't get Tesman interested in a political career.

BRACK: *(laughs)* Tesman! No, my dear, a political life is not for him. He's entirely unsuited.

HEDDA: I'm sure you're right. But all the same, couldn't I ease him in that direction? Make him take it up?

BRACK: No doubt. But what would be your satisfaction if he were to fail? Why would you have him do that?

HEDDA: Because I'm bored. . . . I've told you. *(after a pause)* Do you think it absolutely impossible for Tesman to become, say, a cabinet minister?

BRACK: Hmm. You see, my dear Hedda, for him to acquire such a position he would have to be a comparatively wealthy man.

HEDDA: *(rising impatiently)* Yes. That's it exactly. This . . . this poverty that I've come into. *(crosses room)* That's what makes my life so miserable. So totally . . . absurd. Yes. For that's what it is.

BRACK: I disagree. I don't think it's that at all.

HEDDA: What then?

BRACK: I don't think you've ever lived through anything that . . . that has challenged you.

HEDDA: Anything truly serious, you mean?

BRACK: You could put it that way. But it may be about to happen.

HEDDA: If you mean this wretched business about the professorship—that's Tesman's problem, not mine. I shan't give it a second thought.

BRACK: No, it's not that. Suppose—to put it as delicately as possible, you were to find yourself carrying a greater responsibility? Some new claim upon our little Mrs. Tesman?

HEDDA: *(angry)* Be quiet! You will never see anything like that happen. Never.

BRACK: *(cautiously)* We'll talk about that in a year's time . . . hmm? At the most.

HEDDA: *(curtly)* I have no plans of that kind, Judge Brack. Nothing that will lay claim to me.

BRACK: Ah. But shouldn't you? After all, most women have the need, the desire . . .

HEDDA: I told you to be quiet. *(by the door)* I have often thought that I have only one need, one desire.

BRACK: *(approaching her)* And what is that—if I may be so bold?

HEDDA: To bore myself to death. There. Now you know. *(turns, looks back at room, and laughs)* You see! Here's the proof. Our professor!

BRACK: *(softly, in a warning voice)* Now, now, Hedda!

(Tesman, in evening dress with hat and gloves, enters from inner room)

TESMAN: Hedda? Any word from Eilert Løvborg? Hmm?

HEDDA: No. Nothing yet.

TESMAN: Well, I expect he'll be here soon.

HEDDA: Do you really think he'll come?

TESMAN: Certain of it. *(to Brack)* I feel sure that what you told us this morning . . . was just gossip—rumor.

BRACK: You think so?

TESMAN: That's what Aunt Julie thinks, at any rate. She's absolutely certain that he won't stand in my way. Think of that.

BRACK: Ah, well. That's good to hear.

TESMAN: *(Puts hat and gloves on chair, right. To Brack.)* But, if you don't mind, I'd like to wait for him as long as possible.

BRACK: There's plenty of time. There'll be no one there until seven or seven-thirty.

TESMAN: So, in the meantime, we can keep Hedda company, hmm? While we wait.

HEDDA: *(takes Brack's hat and coat to sofa)* If worst comes to worst, Mr. Løvborg can stay and talk to me.

BRACK: *(trying to take his hat and coat)* Allow me, Mrs. Tesman. What do you mean—if worst comes to worst?

HEDDA: If he doesn't want to go with you and Tesman.

TESMAN: *(looking at her, dubious)* Now, Hedda, dear—I don't think that would be, um, proper, do you? After all, Aunt Julie isn't going to be coming.

HEDDA: No, but Mrs. Elvsted will be here. The three of us will have tea together.

TESMAN: Yes, well, I'm sure that will be all right.

BRACK: *(smiling)* It's probably the safest thing to do, anyway.

HEDDA: What do you mean?

BRACK: Well, if you remember, Mrs. Tesman, you always used to . . . show a certain disdain for my parties. You said they were only fit for gentlemen — gentlemen of the highest principles.

HEDDA: No doubt Mr. Løvborg's principles are high enough now. The reformed sinner . . .

(Berte appears at hall door)

BERTE: There's a gentleman at the door, ma'am. He's asking if you're at home.

HEDDA: Show him in.

TESMAN: *(quietly)* I'm sure that's him. Think of that!

(Eilert Løvborg enters from the hall. He is slim, wiry. Same age as Tesman but looks older, haggard. Tired. His hair and beard are dark brown. Face long, pale, patches of color on the cheekbones. Dressed in new black visiting suit. Dark gloves, silk hat. Stops at door, makes a quick bow. Seems embarrassed.)

TESMAN: *(shaking him by the hand, warmly)* Well, well, my dear Eilert — it's been such a long time.

LØVBORG: *(subdued voice)* Thank you for your letter, Tesman. *(going to her)* And may I shake your hand, too, Mrs. Tesman?

HEDDA: *(taking his hand)* I am pleased to see you, Mr. Løvborg. *(motioning an introduction)* I don't know whether you two gentlemen . . .

LØVBORG: *(slight bow)* Judge Brack, I believe.

BRACK: *(slight bow)* Yes — it's been quite some time.

TESMAN: *(placing his hands on Løvborg's shoulders)* Now then, I want you to feel right at home here. He must — mustn't he, Hedda? Especially since I hear you're coming back to live in town, hmm?

LØVBORG: Yes. Yes, I am.

TESMAN: Well, that makes sense, hmm, Hedda? Listen, I've just got a copy of your new book — haven't had time to read it yet.

LØVBORG: Save yourself the trouble.

TESMAN: Why? What do you mean?

LØVBORG: There's nothing much to it, really.

TESMAN: Good heavens, man — how can you say that?

BRACK: But it's been received very well, I gather. Much praised.

LØVBORG: Well, that's all I really wanted. So I put nothing into the book that was even remotely controversial.

BRACK: Very clever.

TESMAN: Well, but, my dear Eilert . . .

LØVBORG: No. You see, I intend to get this new appointment — make a fresh start.

TESMAN: *(slightly embarrassed)* Yes. Yes. I see. There is that to consider.

LØVBORG: *(smiling, lays down hat, and takes a packet wrapped in paper from his coat pocket)* Now, when this is published, Tesman, you will have to read it. This is the real book. I have put myself — all of myself — into these pages.

TESMAN: Indeed? And what is it?

LØVBORG: The sequel.

TESMAN: To what?

LØVBORG: The book.

TESMAN: Your new one?

LØVBORG: Of course.

TESMAN: Yes, but I thought that you had already—in your analysis—covered contemporary history.

LØVBORG: I have. This one deals with the future of civilization.

TESMAN: Yes, but we can know nothing about the future.

LØVBORG: No, but there are one or two things that one can say about it, nonetheless. *(opens packet)* Take a look—

TESMAN: That's not your handwriting, is it?

LØVBORG: I dictated it. *(flipping through pages)* It's in two parts. The first is an analysis of potential civilizing forces. And the second *(running through the end pages)* is a projection of the probable lines of development.

TESMAN: That's so very strange. I would never have thought of writing anything like that.

HEDDA: *(at glass door, drumming on window pane)* Probably not.

LØVBORG: *(replacing manuscript in package and laying it on table)* I had hoped that I might read you some of it this evening.

TESMAN: That was very good of you, Løvborg. But this evening . . . *(looks to Brack)* I don't see how we can. . . .

LØVBORG: Well then, some other time. It can wait.

BRACK: You see, I'm giving a small dinner party this evening—mainly in Tesman's honor.

LØVBORG: *(looking for hat)* Then I won't detain you.

BRACK: No, no. It would be delightful if you'd join us.

LØVBORG: *(curtly)* No, that's not possible. But thank you.

BRACK: Oh, come along. It's a small intimate gathering. We shall have a "gay old time" as Hed—Mrs. Tesman would say.

LØVBORG: I'm sure you will. However, it's not . . .

BRACK: And you could bring the manuscript with you and read it to Tesman later—at my house. I could give you a room to yourselves.

TESMAN: That's very kind of you. What do you think, Eilert? Why don't you, hmm?

HEDDA: I think it's clear, Tesman, that Mr. Løvborg would prefer not to go. I'm sure he is more inclined to stay here and have supper with me.

LØVBORG: With you, Mrs. Tesman? *(looking at her)*

HEDDA: And Mrs. Elvsted.

LØVBORG: Ah—*(passing it off lightly)* Yes, I happened to see her for a moment this morning.

HEDDA: Did you? Well, she is coming this evening. So, you see, you must stay, Mr. Løvborg. Otherwise, she will have no one to see her home.

LØVBORG: I suppose that's true. Thank you, Mrs. Tesman—in that case, I shall stay.

HEDDA: Then will you please excuse me for a moment—I have to speak to the maid. (*Goes to hall door. Rings bell. Enter Berte. Hedda whispers to her, points to inner room. Berte nods and leaves.*)

TESMAN: (*during this exchange*) Tell me, Eilert—this new field of yours—this analysis of the future—is that what you are going to lecture about?

LØVBORG: Yes.

TESMAN: When I was at the bookstore, they told me you are going to give a series of lectures in the autumn.

LØVBORG: That is my intention, yes. I hope, Tesman, that will not upset you in any way.

TESMAN: No. No. Not in the least. But, um . . .

LØVBORG: I quite understand that it can bring you no pleasure.

TESMAN: (*uncomfortable*) Well, I could hardly expect you—out of consideration for me—to, um . . .

LØVBORG: I shall wait, however, until you have received your appointment.

TESMAN: You'll wait? Yes, but . . . but aren't you going to comp—aren't you going to apply for the position?

LØVBORG: No. It's only the moral victory that I care for.

TESMAN: Good Lord. . . . Aunt Julie was right after all. I knew it—Hedda! Just think. Eilert has no intention of standing in our way.

HEDDA: Our way? (*coldly*) Please leave me out of this. (*She goes to door of inner room. Berte is placing a tray with decanter and glasses on the table. Hedda nods approval and comes back again. Berte leaves.*)

TESMAN: (*during the above*) And you, Judge Brack, hmm? What do you have to say about this?

BRACK: Well, a moral victory . . . yes . . . a moral victory has its virtues, but all the same . . .

TESMAN: Yes, of course—but all the same . . .

HEDDA: (*looking at Tesman with a cold smile*) You look as though you've been struck by lightning.

TESMAN: Yes, well, so I have, I almost think.

BRACK: Don't you see, Mrs. Tesman? A thunderstorm has just passed over us.

HEDDA: (*indicating inner room*) Will you take a glass of cold punch, gentlemen?

BRACK: A glass of punch? (*looking at his watch*) Yes. Thank you. That would be a pleasure.

TESMAN: Excellent idea, Hedda! Just the thing! Now that the weight has been taken off my mind. . . .

HEDDA: Won't you join them, Mr. Løvborg?

LØVBORG: (*gesture of refusal*) No. No, thank you. Nothing for me.

BRACK: Good heavens, man—cold punch! It's not poison.

LØVBORG: No—not for others.

HEDDA: I will keep Mr. Løvborg company while you take your drink.

TESMAN: Yes. Yes, Hedda dear, do—thank you.

(*He and Brack exit. They drink punch, smoke, and engage in animated conversation during the following scene. Løvborg remains standing by the stove. Hedda goes to the writing table.*)

HEDDA: *(raising her voice a little)* Would you care to look at some photographs, Mr. Løvborg? Tesman and I took a trip through the Tyrol[3] on our way home. *(Picks up album, places it on table by sofa, and sits in corner. Løvborg approaches, stops, and looks at her. Then he takes chair and seats himself to her left, with his back to the inner room.)*

HEDDA: *(opening album)* You see this mountain range, Mr. Løvborg? It's the Ortler group. Tesman has written the name underneath: "The Ortlers—near Meran."

LØVBORG: *(who has never taken his eyes off her—softly and slowly)* Hedda—Gabler!

HEDDA: *(glancing quickly at him)* Ah—shhh!

LØVBORG: *(again, softly)* Hedda Gabler.

HEDDA: *(looking at album)* That *was* my name—in the old days—when we two knew each other.

LØVBORG: And now I must learn never to say Hedda Gabler again—never—as long as I live.

HEDDA: Yes, you must. *(still turning the pages)* And I think you should practice it. The sooner the better.

LØVBORG: *(indignant)* Hedda Gabler—married! And married to Jørgen Tesman.

HEDDA: Yes. . . . So it goes.

LØVBORG: Oh, Hedda—Hedda—how could you throw yourself away?

HEDDA: *(looking at him sharply)* I won't allow this!

LØVBORG: What do you mean?

(Tesman enters, goes to sofa)

HEDDA: *(hears him coming and says unconcernedly)* And this is the view from the Val D'Ampezzo, Mr. Løvborg. Just look at that. *(looks affectionately up at Tesman)* What's the name of these mountains, darling?

TESMAN: Let me see. Oh. Those are the Dolomites.

HEDDA: Yes, of course. Those are the Dolomites, Mr. Løvborg.

TESMAN: Hedda, my dear, would you like a glass of punch? Just for yourself, hmm? I just came to ask.

HEDDA: Yes, I would, and perhaps some petits-fours.

TESMAN: Cigarettes?

HEDDA: No.

TESMAN: Right. *(Goes into inner room and exits right. Brack occasionally watches Hedda and Løvborg.)*

LØVBORG: *(softly, as before)* Hedda, tell me—how could you do this?

HEDDA: *(apparently absorbed in album as before)* If you persist in being so familiar with me, I shall leave.

LØVBORG: But we are alone—may I not. . . ?

HEDDA: You may think it but not say it.

---

[3] **the Tyrol:** An area in the Austrian and Italian Alps. The Ortler Group and the Dolomites are mountain ranges in the area. Meran, a city in the Austrian Tyrol in 1890, is now Merano, Italy. The Val D'Ampezzo (Ampezzo Valley) is a tourist spot in the area. The Brenner Pass is on the main route into Austria.

LØVBORG: I understand. I must not invade the world of Jørgen Tesman—the man you love.

HEDDA: *(smiles)* Love? *(laughs to herself)*

LØVBORG: You don't love him, then?

HEDDA: I will never be unfaithful to him. Never. Remember that.

LØVBORG: Hedda, answer me one thing—

HEDDA: Shhh!

(Tesman enters with small tray)

TESMAN: Here you are. They look tempting, don't they? *(puts tray on table)*

HEDDA: Why did you bring it yourself?

TESMAN: It gives me pleasure to wait on you, Hedda.

HEDDA: Why have you poured out two glasses? Mr. Løvborg said he wouldn't have any.

TESMAN: No. It was for Mrs. Elvsted. She'll be here soon, won't she?

HEDDA: Yes . . . Mrs. Elvsted . . . very soon, I expect.

TESMAN: You'd forgotten, eh?

HEDDA: We were so absorbed in the photographs. *(showing him one)* Do you remember this little village?

TESMAN: Let me see . . . yes. That's just below the Brenner Pass. We spent the night there.

HEDDA: And met that party of tourists.

TESMAN: That's right. That was the place. You'd have enjoyed being with us, Eilert, wouldn't he, hmm? *(returns to Brack)*

LØVBORG: Answer me this one thing, Hedda.

HEDDA: Yes.

LØVBORG: Was there no love—no flicker of love in your friendship for me?

HEDDA: I wonder if there was. I suppose I feel that we were very close—two very intimate friends. *(she smiles)* You in particular were always very—frank.

LØVBORG: You made me so.

HEDDA: When I look back on it, I think . . . I feel . . . there was something very beautiful—fascinating—even daring in that intimacy . . . that secret friendship of ours. No one ever knew.

LØVBORG: Yes, yes, Hedda. I feel it, too. I used to come to your father's house, in the afternoon. He'd sit by the window reading the papers, with his back to us.

HEDDA: And we sat on the sofa in the corner.

LØVBORG: With the same magazine on the table in front of us.

HEDDA: There being no photographs.

LØVBORG: No—and then, Hedda, I told you—confessed to you—things about myself . . . that no one else knew. At least not then. I sat there and told you openly about my—awful destructive life. About the lost days and nights. Hedda, Hedda, what power did you have over me, that you could force me to tell you those things?

HEDDA: Do you think I had power over you?

LØVBORG: What else could I think? The way you phrased your questions . . . so evasive . . . so ambiguous. . . .

HEDDA: Which you understood so clearly.

LØVBORG: How could you sit there and question me like that? Question me quite frankly. . . .

HEDDA: But evasively . . . as you pointed out.

LØVBORG: Yes, but frankly, nevertheless. Question after question — about all sorts of things.

HEDDA: And how could you answer, Mr. Løvborg?

LØVBORG: That is what I don't understand, when I look back on it. Hedda, I ask you again — was there no love, no love at all? When you made me confess to you — did you ever feel that you could absolve me of my sins? Tell me, did you?

HEDDA: No, not quite.

LØVBORG: Then why did you do it?

HEDDA: Don't you see, a young girl — given such a chance, without anyone knowing . . .

LØVBORG: Yes?

HEDDA: Could not resist looking in on a world which . . . which . . .

LØVBORG: Well?

HEDDA: Which is absolutely forbidden to her.

LØVBORG: So that was it?

HEDDA: Partly. Partly — at least I think so.

LØVBORG: But friendship . . . that is the reason for being. Why did that have to die for us?

HEDDA: The fault was yours.

LØVBORG: It was you who left me.

HEDDA: Yes, when that friendship threatened to become something more serious. *(pauses)* You had no shame. How could you think of breaking that trust — of dishonoring me?

LØVBORG: *(with clenched fists)* Then why didn't you go through with it? Why didn't you shoot me down?

HEDDA: The scandal. I was afraid of the scandal.

LØVBORG: Yes. Yes, Hedda, you were always a coward at heart.

HEDDA: A terrible coward. *(changing her tone)* Which was lucky for you. But now you have all the comfort and consolation you need. At the Elvsteds.

LØVBORG: I know that Thea has spoken to you.

HEDDA: And perhaps you have told her something about us?

LØVBORG: No. Not a word. She's too stupid to understand things like that.

HEDDA: Stupid?

LØVBORG: Yes. Stupid . . . about things like that.

HEDDA: And I am a coward. *(leans toward him and without looking him in the eye, says softly)* But now I shall tell you something — in confidence.

LØVBORG: *(eagerly)* Yes?

HEDDA: The fact that I did not shoot you down — that was . . .

LØVBORG: Yes?

HEDDA: That was not what made me a coward — that night.

LØVBORG: *(looks at her a moment, understands, and whispers passionately)* Oh,

Hedda! Hedda Gabler! I begin to see now what made us such close friends. You and I—! You, too, had this passion for life—

HEDDA: *(softly, with a quick glance)* Take care! Don't think it for a moment!

(It is growing dark. Berte opens the hall door.)

HEDDA: *(snaps the album shut and calls out)* Well! At last—my dear Thea! Do come in.

(Mrs. Elvsted enters in evening dress. The door is closed behind her.)

HEDDA: *(on sofa, stretches her arms toward her)* Thea, darling, you can have no idea how I've been longing for this!

(Mrs. Elvsted makes a slight gesture of greeting to the other men. Goes to take Hedda's hand. Løvborg rises. He and Mrs. Elvsted greet each other with a silent nod.)

MRS. ELVSTED: Shall I go in and see your husband for a moment?

HEDDA: Oh no, there's no need. Leave them alone; they'll be going out shortly.

MRS. ELVSTED: They're not staying?

HEDDA: No, they're going out to dinner.

MRS. ELVSTED: *(to Løvborg)* Are you going with them?

LØVBORG: No.

HEDDA: Mr. Løvborg will stay with us.

MRS. ELVSTED: *(about to set a chair by his side)* Oh, how nice it is here!

HEDDA: No, Thea, my love. Not there. Come over here by me. I shall sit between you.

MRS. ELVSTED: Just as you please.

(Mrs. Elvsted sits on sofa on Hedda's right. Løvborg reseats himself on his chair.)

LØVBORG: *(after short pause, to Hedda)* Isn't she lovely to look at?

HEDDA: *(stroking her hair)* Only to look at?

LØVBORG: Yes. You see, we are real friends—she and I. We have absolute trust in each other. We can sit and talk with perfect frankness.

HEDDA: No evasion? Nor circumspection, Mr. Løvborg?

LØVBORG: No—

MRS. ELVSTED: *(softly, clinging to Hedda)* I'm so very happy, Hedda. Not only this, but he says that I am an inspiration to him, too.

HEDDA: *(looks and smiles)* Ah! Does he say that?

LØVBORG: And then again, Mrs. Tesman, she is so brave.

MRS. ELVSTED: Brave? Heavens, do you think I'm brave?

LØVBORG: Very—where your friendship with me is concerned.

HEDDA: Yes—courage. If only one had courage!

LØVBORG: And what then? What would it mean?

HEDDA: Then life would be worth living. In spite of everything. *(quickly changes the subject)* Now, Thea, you must have a glass of cold punch.

MRS. ELVSTED: No, thank you. I never take any.

HEDDA: And you, Mr. Løvborg?

LØVBORG: No, nor I, thank you.

MRS. ELVSTED: No, he never does, either.

HEDDA: *(looks straight at him)* But if I say you shall?

LØVBORG: It would be no use.

HEDDA: *(laughs)* Then I have no power over you?

LØVBORG: Not where that is concerned, no.

HEDDA: I think you should—I'm quite serious—for your own sake.

MRS. ELVSTED: Hedda, please!

LØVBORG: What do you mean?

HEDDA: Well, perhaps it's more for other people.

LØVBORG: How so?

HEDDA: Yes. You see, people might very well be suspicious of you . . . that deep down you really did not trust yourself—that your courage was only skin deep.

MRS. ELVSTED: *(softly)* Oh, please, Hedda.

LØVBORG: People can think what they like—at least for now.

MRS. ELVSTED: *(joyfully)* Yes, yes, let them—

HEDDA: I saw it in Judge Brack a moment ago. It was written all over his face.

LØVBORG: What did you see?

HEDDA: Contempt. In his smile. When you were afraid to join them in there.

LØVBORG: Afraid? The fact is—I chose to stay here and talk with you.

MRS. ELVSTED: There's nothing wrong with that, Hedda.

HEDDA: But the Judge could not know that. In fact, I saw him look at Tesman and smile when you were afraid to join them for their wretched little dinner party.

LØVBORG: You say "afraid" again. Do you think I was afraid?

HEDDA: *I* don't. But that's what Judge Brack thought.

LØVBORG: He can think what he likes.

HEDDA: Then you're not going with them?

LØVBORG: I'm staying here with you and Thea.

MRS. ELVSTED: Hedda, please . . . you must believe him.

HEDDA: *(smiles and nods her approval)* Strong as a rock! A man of principle—now and forever. Yes, that's how a man should be. *(to Mrs. Elvsted, touching her lightly)* What did I tell you this morning? There was no reason to be so upset.

LØVBORG: What do you mean, "upset"?

MRS. ELVSTED: *(terrified)* Hedda! Oh, Hedda!

HEDDA: You can see for yourself. You were in a state of mortal panic—and there was no need—*(changing the subject)* There—you see. Now we can just enjoy ourselves. The three of us.

LØVBORG: Can you explain yourself, please, Mrs. Tesman?

MRS. ELVSTED: Oh, my God, Hedda . . . what are you doing? Why. . . ?

HEDDA: Don't get excited. That loathsome Judge Brack is watching you.

LØVBORG: In mortal panic—on my account?

MRS. ELVSTED: *(softly, pitifully)* Oh, Hedda—now you've ruined everything.

LØVBORG: *(Looks at her for a moment. His face is drawn.)* So that was our friendship. That was your trust in me.

MRS. ELVSTED: *(imploringly)* You are my dearest friend—please, let me explain . . .

LØVBORG: *(takes glass of punch, raises it to his lips, says in husky voice)* Thea, your health! *(empties glass, takes a second)*

MRS. ELVSTED: *(softly)* Hedda, Hedda, how could you do this?

HEDDA: Me? How could I do it? You don't seem to understand.

LØVBORG: And to you, Mrs. Tesman. Your health. Thanks to you for the truth. Here's to truth. *(empties glass and is about to refill it)*

HEDDA: *(lays her hand on his arm)* No more, hmm? That's enough for now. Remember, you're going out to dinner.

MRS. ELVSTED: No. No.

HEDDA: Shhh! They're watching you.

LØVBORG: *(puts glass down)* Now, Thea—tell me the truth.

MRS. ELVSTED: Yes.

LØVBORG: Did your husband know that you had followed me?

MRS. ELVSTED: *(nervous hands)* Oh, Hedda—do you know what he's asking?

LØVBORG: Did he know? Did you arrange to come into town and look after me? Perhaps it was the sheriff's idea? Maybe he needed help at the office, or perhaps he missed me at the card table?

MRS. ELVSTED: *(softly, agonized)* Oh, Løvborg, Løvborg.

LØVBORG: *(about to fill another glass)* Well, here's one for old Sheriff Elvsted.

HEDDA: *(stopping him)* No more just now. You have to read your manuscript to Tesman.

LØVBORG: *(putting down the glass)* Thea, I apologize. There was no reason to take it this way. It was stupid of me. Don't be angry. You are still the dearest of friends. You shall see—you and the others—that if I fell once—that is over. I am on my feet again. Because of you, Thea.

MRS. ELVSTED: *(very happy)* Thank God. Thank God.

(Brack has risen and looked at his watch. He and Tesman enter.)

BRACK: *(takes hat and coat)* Well, Mrs. Tesman, it's time for us to leave.

HEDDA: Yes, I suppose it is.

LØVBORG: *(rising)* For me, too, Judge.

MRS. ELVSTED: *(softly, imploring)* Løvborg, don't go. Don't do it.

HEDDA: *(overlapping, pinching her arm)* They can hear you.

MRS. ELVSTED: *(suppresses a cry of pain)*

LØVBORG: You were kind enough to invite me.

BRACK: So, you're coming after all?

LØVBORG: Yes, if you don't mind.

BRACK: I'd be delighted.

LØVBORG: *(to Tesman, putting manuscript in his overcoat)* I would like to show you one or two things before I send this off to the printers.

TESMAN: Excellent, excellent. That would be delightful. Oh, um, Hedda—how is Mrs. Elvsted to get home?

HEDDA: We'll manage, I'm sure.

LØVBORG: *(looking at the ladies)* Mrs. Elvsted? Oh, of course, I'll come and fetch her. At ten o'clock—or thereabouts. Is that all right, Mrs. Tesman?

HEDDA: Yes, that's perfect. Thank you.

TESMAN: Good. That's settled. I shall probably be home somewhat later, my dear.

HEDDA: You may stay as long as you please.

MRS. ELVSTED: *(concealing her anxiety)* Well then, Mr. Løvborg, I shall wait for you here.

LØVBORG: *(hat in hand)* Please do, Mrs. Elvsted.

BRACK: It's time for the group tour to leave the station. I hope we'll have a "gay old time"—as a certain beautiful lady puts it.

HEDDA: That certain lady would like to be there, but sight unseen.

BRACK: Why unseen?

HEDDA: To listen to all those risqué conversations, Judge.

BRACK: *(laughing)* I would advise the lady against it.

TESMAN: *(also laughing)* Hedda—you ought to be ashamed of yourself.

BRACK: Well, goodbye. We must go. Goodbye.

LØVBORG: *(bowing)* At about ten o'clock, then.

(The men leave. Berte enters inner hall with lighted lamp. Places it on dining room table and leaves.)

MRS. ELVSTED: *(pacing around the room)* Hedda, Hedda, what is going to happen?

HEDDA: At ten o'clock he will be here. I can see him now—in the glow of victory—unafraid. *(smiles)* With vine leaves in his hair.

MRS. ELVSTED: Please, God . . .

HEDDA: And then, you see—he will be in control once again. He will be a free man once and for all.

MRS. ELVSTED: Oh God, if only he did come back like that—as you see him now.

HEDDA: He will. As I see him. Not any other way. *(goes to her)* You may keep your doubts. *I* believe in him. Now let's try to . . .

MRS. ELVSTED: What are you hiding from me, Hedda? There's something you want.

HEDDA: Yes, there is. I want—for once in my life—to have power over another human being. To change his destiny.

MRS. ELVSTED: And you haven't that power?

HEDDA: I do not. And I never have.

MRS. ELVSTED: Not over your husband.

HEDDA: That's hardly worth the trouble. You don't understand. Life has made me poor—and you—you are rich. *(takes her in her arms)* Perhaps I should burn off your hair after all.

MRS. ELVSTED: Don't. Please. Stop it. Sometimes you frighten me, Hedda.

BERTE: *(in the doorway)* Tea is ready in the dining room, ma'am.

HEDDA: Thank you. We're coming.

MRS. ELVSTED: No, no. I'd rather go. I'd like to leave right away.

HEDDA: Nonsense. You'll have more tea. Now don't be silly. And then—at ten o'clock—Eilert Løvborg will be here, with vine leaves in his hair.

(she takes Mrs. Elvsted, almost by force, to the doorway)

ACT 3

The same room. The curtains are drawn. A lamp, half turned down, on the table. The stove, door open, has the remains of a fire.

Mrs. Elvsted, wrapped in a large shawl, feet on footrest, sits close to the stove in an armchair. Hedda is asleep on the sofa, covered with a blanket.

Mrs. Elvsted sits up in her chair, listens. Settles back. Speaks softly to herself.

MRS. ELVSTED: Oh, God, God, God. Where is he?

(Berte slips in by hall door, letter in hand)

MRS. ELVSTED: *(turns, whispers)* Has anyone come?

BERTE: *(softly)* Yes. A girl brought this letter.

MRS. ELVSTED: *(holds out hand)* A letter? Give it to me!

BERTE: It's for Dr. Tesman, ma'am.

MRS. ELVSTED: Oh, I see.

BERTE: It was Miss Tesman's girl that brought it. I'll put it on the table.

MRS. ELVSTED: Yes, do.

BERTE: *(putting letter down)* I think I'd better put out the lamp—it's beginning to smoke.

MRS. ELVSTED: Yes, put it out. It will be light soon.

BERTE: *(putting out light)* It's light already, ma'am.

MRS. ELVSTED: Is it? And no one's come back yet?

BERTE: Lord bless you—I knew how it would be.

MRS. ELVSTED: What do you mean?

BERTE: Well, when I saw that a certain person had come back into town—well, when he went out with them. We've heard a lot about that gentleman, I can tell you.

MRS. ELVSTED: Not so loud. You'll wake Mrs. Tesman.

BERTE: *(looks at her, sighs)* No, no. Let her sleep, poor thing. Shall I put some wood on the fire?

MRS. ELVSTED: No, thanks, not for me.

BERTE: Very good, ma'am. *(exits quietly)*

HEDDA: *(awakened by shutting of door)* What's that?

MRS. ELVSTED: That was only the servant.

HEDDA: *(looking about her)* Oh, we're in here! I'd forgotten. *(sits up, stretches)* What time is it?

MRS. ELVSTED: *(looks at watch)* It's past seven.

HEDDA: When did Tesman come home?

MRS. ELVSTED: He didn't.

HEDDA: He's not home yet?

MRS. ELVSTED: *(rising)* No one has come.

HEDDA: And we sat here waiting until four o'clock.

MRS. ELVSTED: *(wringing her hands)* Oh God, I can't get him out of my mind.

HEDDA: *(yawning and covering her mouth with her hand)* We should have saved ourselves the trouble.

MRS. ELVSTED: Were you able to get any sleep?

HEDDA: Oh yes. I slept quite well. And you?

MRS. ELVSTED: I couldn't sleep at all, Hedda. Not for a moment.

HEDDA: *(crosses to her)* There, there. There's nothing to worry about. I know exactly what happened.

MRS. ELVSTED: What? What has happened? Tell me.

HEDDA: Well, of course they kept on drinking at the Judge's—for hours upon hours.

MRS. ELVSTED: Yes. Yes. I'm sure you're right—and then what do you—

HEDDA: So, you see, Tesman didn't like to come home and wake everyone up—ringing the doorbell in the middle of the night. *(laughs)* He probably didn't want anyone to see him either—in the condition he was in.

MRS. ELVSTED: But—where could he have gone?

HEDDA: To his aunt's house, I expect. He must have slept there. They keep his old room ready for him.

MRS. ELVSTED: No, he can't have stayed there. There's a letter for him—from Miss Tesman. It's over there.

HEDDA: Really? *(looks at the address)* Yes. It's from Aunt Julie. Well, he must have spent the night at Judge Brack's. And Eilert Løvborg is there too, with vine leaves in his hair, reading aloud.

MRS. ELVSTED: Hedda, you're just saying that—to make me feel better. You don't really believe it.

HEDDA: You really are a little fool, Thea.

MRS. ELVSTED: I'm sorry. I know. I know.

HEDDA: You look so tired.

MRS. ELVSTED: I am. I'm desperately tired.

HEDDA: Then listen to me. Go into my room and lie down on the bed for a while.

MRS. ELVSTED: No, no. I really couldn't sleep.

HEDDA: Of course you can.

MRS. ELVSTED: But your husband will be home soon, I'm sure. And when he does I must know.

HEDDA: I'll tell you as soon as he comes in.

MRS. ELVSTED: You promise?

HEDDA: I promise. Now go and get some sleep.

MRS. ELVSTED: Thank you. I'll try. *(goes to back room)*

(Hedda goes to glass doors, opens the curtains. Broad daylight. Takes hand mirror, arranges her hair. Goes to hall door, rings bell. Berte appears.)

BERTE: Yes, ma'am.

HEDDA: Put some more wood on the stove. I'm freezing.

BERTE: It will warm up in a minute. *(puts log on, stands listening)* That was the doorbell, wasn't it, ma'am?

HEDDA: Well, go and answer it. I'll do the fire.

BERTE: It will soon get going. *(leaves)*

(Hedda kneels, puts log on fire. Tesman enters, tired, serious. Tiptoes to doorway. About to slip in through curtains.)

HEDDA: *(at stove, does not look up)* Good morning.

TESMAN: *(turns)* Hedda! *(going to her)* Good heavens, you're up early!

HEDDA: Yes. I am.

TESMAN: I was sure you'd be still asleep. Fancy that, hmm? Hedda?

HEDDA: Don't talk so loud. Mrs. Elvsted is resting in my room.

TESMAN: Has she been here all night?

HEDDA: Yes. You see, no one came to fetch her.

TESMAN: Yes. Yes, of course.

HEDDA: *(closes stove, rises)* Well — did you enjoy yourselves at Judge Brack's?

TESMAN: Were you worried about me, hmm?

HEDDA: No. That wouldn't have occurred to me. I asked if you enjoyed yourself.

TESMAN: Yes — I did — in a way. Particularly at the beginning of the evening, when Eilert read me part of his book. We were at least an hour too early for dinner, if you can imagine that. Anyway, Brack had a few arrangements to make and so Eilert read to me.

HEDDA: *(seated by the table)* Well — what do you have to tell me. . . ?

TESMAN: *(sitting on footstool near stove)* Oh, Hedda — you can't imagine what that book is going to be like. It is — and I believe this totally — one of the most extraordinary things that has ever been written. Just think!

HEDDA: Yes. Yes, but I don't care about that. . . .

TESMAN: I have to admit — confess, even — that when he had finished reading an awful feeling came over me.

HEDDA: Awful? What do you mean?

TESMAN: I felt jealous. That this man was capable of writing such a profound book. Just think, Hedda.

HEDDA: Oh, I am. I am thinking.

TESMAN: It makes it all the more painful that — with all his gifts — he is nonetheless beyond saving.

HEDDA: You mean that he has more courage than the rest of you?

TESMAN: No, that's not it at all. I mean that he is incapable of any restraint — any control.

HEDDA: Then what happened? In the end?

TESMAN: Well, to be blunt about it — I think it can only be described as debauched.

HEDDA: Were there vine leaves in his hair?

TESMAN: What? Vine leaves? No, I saw nothing of the kind. He made a long, rambling speech — in honor of the woman who had "inspired him in his work." That was his exact phrase.

HEDDA: Did he say who she was?

TESMAN: No. He didn't. But I couldn't help thinking it was Mrs. Elvsted. You can be sure of that.

HEDDA: Well — where was he when you left him?

TESMAN: On his way back to town. We left the party together — those of us who were still there. Brack came with us to get a breath of fresh air. And then we decided we had better take Eilert home. He'd had far more than was good for him.

HEDDA: So I gather.

TESMAN: But now comes the strange part of it, Hedda—sad would be a better word. I am almost ashamed to tell you—for Løvborg's sake—

HEDDA: Go on.

TESMAN: Well, as we were getting closer to town, I fell behind the others a little. Just for a minute or two . . . I don't know. . . .

HEDDA: Yes? Yes—and then?

TESMAN: And then as I tried to catch up—what do you think I saw lying by the side of the road?

HEDDA: How could I—what did you find?

TESMAN: You mustn't tell a soul, Hedda. Never. You give me your word. For Løvborg's sake. *(takes packet, wrapped in paper, from his pocket)* This. This is what I found. Fancy that.

HEDDA: Isn't that what he had with him yesterday?

TESMAN: Yes. This is the manuscript. All of it. It's irreplaceable. And he just dropped it. And didn't notice. Just think, Hedda—so utterly careless. . . .

HEDDA: *(interrupting)* But why didn't you give it back to him at once?

TESMAN: I couldn't. Not in the state he was in.

HEDDA: Did you tell any of the others that you had found it?

TESMAN: No, of course not. You must understand, surely—for Løvborg's sake. I couldn't do that to him.

HEDDA: So no one knows that you have the manuscript.

TESMAN: No. And that's the way it must be.

HEDDA: Then what did you say to him afterward?

TESMAN: I didn't speak to him again. When we actually got into town, he and two or three others just disappeared—gave us the slip, as a matter of fact—if you can imagine.

HEDDA: I see. They must have taken him home, then.

TESMAN: I would think so. Brack went home, too.

HEDDA: And where have you been since then?

TESMAN: I went home with one of the other guests—delightful man—and had morning coffee with him. Or should I say late-night coffee, hmm? But I'm going to take a little rest. And later, when Løvborg has had a chance to sleep it off, I shall take this back to him.

HEDDA: *(holds out hand for package)* No, don't give it to him. Not yet. There's no hurry. Let me read it first.

TESMAN: No, my darling, I can't. I really can't do that.

HEDDA: Why not?

TESMAN: No. Just think how he'll feel when he wakes up. And no manuscript. He'll be absolutely distraught. There is no other copy. He told me.

HEDDA: *(looking at him carefully)* Can it not be reproduced? Written over again?

TESMAN: No, I'm sure that would not be possible. It's a question of inspiration, quite frankly.

HEDDA: Yes. Yes, I suppose it does depend on that. *(lightly)* Oh, by the way, there's a letter for you.

TESMAN: Oh, good heavens.

HEDDA: *(handing it to him)* It came early this morning.

TESMAN: It's from Aunt Julie. What can be the matter? *(puts packet on footstool and opens letter, reads)* Hedda! Oh, Hedda—she says that Aunt Rina is dying.

HEDDA: Well, we were expecting that.

TESMAN: She says that if I want to see her again, I had better hurry. I'll run over there right away.

HEDDA: *(suppressing a smile)* You'll run?

TESMAN: Oh, Hedda—please, my love—would you come with me? If only you could . . .

HEDDA: *(Rises, tired. Rejects the idea.)* No. Please don't ask me to. I can't bear to be near the presence of sickness and death. I can't. I hate it—the ugliness of it all.

TESMAN: Very well, then, um— *(bustling around)* My hat—coat . . . it must be in the hall. I hope I shall be in time, Hedda, hmm?

HEDDA: Perhaps if you were to run . . .

(Berte appears at door)

BERTE: Judge Brack is here. He wants to know if he can come in.

TESMAN: Right now? No, I can't possibly see him.

HEDDA: I can. Ask him to come in.

(Berte leaves)

HEDDA: *(quickly whispering)* The manuscript . . . *(she picks it up)*

TESMAN: Yes. Give it to me.

HEDDA: No. No, I'll keep it until you come back. *(she places it in the bookcase)*

(Tesman, standing, but in a hurry, cannot get his gloves on. Judge Brack enters.)

HEDDA: *(nods a greeting)* You're up with the dawn, I must say.

BRACK: Yes. Aren't I? *(to Tesman)* You're on your way out?

TESMAN: Yes. I must rush off to Aunt Rina. She's very weak. I'm sorry to say she won't survive this time.

BRACK: Oh dear, I'm sorry to hear it. Then, please, don't let me detain you—at such a difficult time.

TESMAN: Yes, I must rush off. Goodbye, then—goodbye. *(exits)*

HEDDA: *(approaching him)* Well, Judge Brack, it seems you made quite a night of it.

BRACK: I can assure you, dear Mrs. Tesman, that I did not get undressed.

HEDDA: Ah. You, too?

BRACK: As you can see. But did Tesman tell you about our adventures last night?

HEDDA: Oh yes, he bored me with the details—he had coffee somewhere or other.

BRACK: Yes, I've heard about that already. Eilert Løvborg was not with them?

HEDDA: No—they'd taken him home some time before that.

BRACK: Was Tesman with them?

HEDDA: No. It was some of the others, I gather.

BRACK: Jørgen Tesman is such an innocent. *(smiles)* Really he is.

HEDDA: Yes. *(looking at him)* That he is. Then there was something else?

BRACK: I think perhaps there was.

HEDDA: Please sit down, my dear Judge. Make yourself comfortable. And tell me what happened. *(She sits at left of table. Brack sits near her on long side of table.)*

HEDDA: Now, then?

BRACK: I had particular reasons for keeping track of my guests last night—at least some of my guests.

HEDDA: Eilert Løvborg in particular, perhaps?

BRACK: Frankly, yes.

HEDDA: That's very interesting. Please go on.

BRACK: Do you know where he—and one or two of the others—ended up last night?

HEDDA: If it's not somewhere unmentionable, then tell me.

BRACK: Oh no, it's not at all like that. Well, they put in an appearance at a particularly lively party.

HEDDA: Just lively, or could you call it a wild party?

BRACK: That would be accurate, I think.

HEDDA: Go on. Tell me more.

BRACK: Løvborg, and, indeed, some of the others, had been invited beforehand. I knew all about it. But, of course, he had declined; since, as you know, he has become a new man.

HEDDA: At the Elvsteds, yes, he has. So he went after all, then?

BRACK: Well, you see, my dear Mrs. Tesman. . . . Unfortunately, when he was at my party—how shall I put it—the spirit moved him . . .

HEDDA: Yes, I heard that he found inspiration.

BRACK: Of a most vehement kind. Well, I expect that changed his mind. We men are not always so strong—so principled—as we ought to be.

HEDDA: You, I'm sure, are an exception, Judge Brack. But Løvborg—what happened—?

BRACK: To make a long story short, he ended up in Mademoiselle Diana's apartment.

HEDDA: Mademoiselle Diana?

BRACK: It was she who was giving the party—to a select circle of her male admirers and female friends.

HEDDA: Does she have auburn hair?

BRACK: She does.

HEDDA: She's an entertainer—a chanteuse?

BRACK: Yes, when she has the time. Actually, she's more of a huntress than a singer. She hunts men. You must have heard of her, Mrs. Tesman. Eilert Løvborg was one of her more enthusiastic admirers—before he became a new man.

HEDDA: What happened in the end?

BRACK: Well, it wasn't very friendly—at least, so I've heard. After a most tender beginning, it seems that they actually came to blows. . . .

HEDDA: She and Løvborg?

BRACK: Yes. He accused her of stealing. He claimed he'd lost a wallet—and one or two other things as well. In short, he seems to have made a rather ugly scene.

HEDDA: So what happened then?

BRACK: I gather that there was a general free-for-all, in which not only the gentlemen but the ladies too took part. Fortunately, the police arrived before it went much further.

HEDDA: The police were there?

BRACK: Yes. I'm sure it will prove an expensive evening for Mr. Løvborg. The man is quite mad.

HEDDA: Why did you say "expensive"?

BRACK: I'm told he was quite violent—he struck a policeman in the face and tore the coat off his back. So he was taken into custody, along with the others.

HEDDA: How did you find all of this out?

BRACK: From the police. I went down to the station.

HEDDA: (gazing straight ahead) So that is what happened. There were no vine leaves in his hair.

BRACK: Vine leaves, Mrs. Tesman?

HEDDA: (changing tone) Judge—tell me . . . why did you—what was the real reason for your tracking him down like that?

BRACK: Well, in the first place, it would be of some importance to me if—during the course of the trial—it should emerge that Løvborg created this disturbance after leaving a party at my house.

HEDDA: Will it come to trial, then?

BRACK: Of course. However, that is of marginal concern to me. I "tracked him down" because I thought that as a friend of the family, I ought to supply you and Tesman with a full account of his nocturnal adventures.

HEDDA: Why did you think so, Judge Brack?

BRACK: Why? Because I have a shrewd suspicion that he intends to use you both as a sort of front—

HEDDA: Oh, how can you think such a thing?

BRACK: I'm not completely blind, my dear Hedda. Mark my words. Mrs. Elvsted will not be going home for some time.

HEDDA: Well, even if there *is* something between them, I should think there are plenty of other places where they could meet.

BRACK: Perhaps, but not a single home. It will be as it was before. Every respectable house will be closed to Eilert Løvborg.

HEDDA: As should mine, you mean?

BRACK: Yes. I must confess that it would be painful for me if this—this person were given free access to your home. He would be out of place—an intruder, even— if he managed to force his way into—

HEDDA: Into our little *ménage à trois.*

BRACK: Precisely. It would mean, quite simply, that I should find myself without a home.

HEDDA: (smiles) You want to be the one cock of the walk—that is what you want, hmm?

BRACK: (nods and lowers his voice) Yes, that is what I want. And I shall fight for it— with every weapon I can find.

HEDDA: *(smile fades)* You can be a dangerous man, Judge Brack—when the need arises.

BRACK: Do you think so?

HEDDA: I'm beginning to. In fact, I feel quite relieved that—you have no hold over me.

BRACK: *(with an ambiguous laugh)* Well, Mrs. Tesman, perhaps you're right to feel that way. Otherwise, who knows what I might be capable of?

HEDDA: That sounds like a threat.

BRACK: Oh, no, not at all. If our ménage is to exist, it must be unforced—spontaneous.

HEDDA: There I agree with you.

BRACK: Well, I have said all that I had to say. I should be getting back to town. Good-bye, Mrs. Tesman. *(going to glass door)*

HEDDA: Are you going through the garden?

BRACK: Yes, it's quicker.

HEDDA: And, of course, it's the back way.

BRACK: Exactly. I have no objections to that. In fact, it can be an exhilarating place to be.

HEDDA: During target practice, you mean?

BRACK: *(in doorway, laughing)* Ah, but people don't shoot their tame poultry.

HEDDA: *(also laughing)* No. Not when there's only one cock of the walk.

(They nod goodbye. He goes. She closes the door.)

(Hedda is serious. Stands, looks out, then goes to look through curtain of middle doorway. Takes Løvborg's package out of bookcase. Starts to look at it. Berte is heard, speaking loudly, in the doorway. Hedda turns, listens. Locks package in drawer, puts key on inkstand. Løvborg, with greatcoat and hat in hand, rushes in, confused, irritated.)

LØVBORG: *(turning back)* I must and I will come in. *(closes door, sees Hedda, gains control, bows)*

HEDDA: *(at writing table)* Well, Mr. Løvborg, isn't it rather late—to be calling for Thea?

LØVBORG: On the contrary. It's rather early to be calling on you. Please forgive me.

HEDDA: How do you know she is still here?

LØVBORG: They told me at her lodgings that she had not yet come home.

HEDDA: *(going to oval table)* And when they told you that, did you notice anything— anything strange?

LØVBORG: *(looking at her)* What do you mean, "strange"?

HEDDA: I mean, did they seem to think it odd?

LØVBORG: *(finally understanding)* Ah yes, of course. I'm dragging her down with me. No, in fact, I didn't notice anything. I suppose Tesman is not yet up?

HEDDA: No. I don't think so.

LØVBORG: When did he come home?

HEDDA: Very late.

LØVBORG: Did he say anything?

HEDDA: Yes. I gather you had a particularly lively evening at Judge Brack's.

LØVBORG: Is that all?

HEDDA: There was more, I believe—but I was so dreadfully sleepy.

(Mrs. Elvsted enters)

MRS. ELVSTED: *(going to him)* Ah, Løvborg—at last.

LØVBORG: Yes—at last. And too late.

MRS. ELVSTED: *(looking at him)* Why too late?

LØVBORG: It's too late for everything now. It's all over.

MRS. ELVSTED: No. No. Don't say that.

LØVBORG: That is what you will say, too, when I tell you . . .

MRS. ELVSTED: Then I don't *want* to hear. Nothing!

HEDDA: Perhaps you would like to speak to her alone—? I'll leave you.

LØVBORG: *(rudely)* No, stay—you too. Please. Please stay.

MRS. ELVSTED: I will *not* listen. Not to anything.

LØVBORG: I don't want to talk about what happened last night. It's not that.

MRS. ELVSTED: What, then?

LØVBORG: I've come to tell you that we must not see each other again.

MRS. ELVSTED: But why?

HEDDA: *(involuntarily—to self)* I knew it.

LØVBORG: You can be of no more service to me, Thea.

MRS. ELVSTED: How can you stand there and say that! No more service! Look, I can help you now—still—as I did before. We can work together. I know we can.

LØVBORG: I have no more work to do.

MRS. ELVSTED: *(in despair)* Then what am I to do with my life?

LØVBORG: You must go on as before—as if you'd never met me.

MRS. ELVSTED: I can't. You know I can't.

LØVBORG: You must try, Thea. You must go back home again.

MRS. ELVSTED: *(angry, protesting)* Never. Never. Not in this life. Wherever you are, there I will be also. I will not be driven out like this. I will be with you when the book is published.

HEDDA: *(half-whisper, in suspense)* Yes—the book.

LØVBORG: Yes—my book and Thea's. For that is what it is.

MRS. ELVSTED: I believe that. I feel it. And that is why I have a right to be with you when it is published. I want to see you glowing, once again, with pride and self-respect. And the happiness—oh, the happiness—I must share that with you.

LØVBORG: Thea, our book will never be published.

HEDDA: Ah.

MRS. ELVSTED: Never be published . . .

LØVBORG: No. Never.

MRS. ELVSTED: *(agonized, fearing the worst)* Løvborg—what have you done with the manuscript?

HEDDA: *(looks anxiously at him)* Yes—the manuscript . . .

MRS. ELVSTED: Where is it?

LØVBORG: Thea—don't ask me about it.

MRS. ELVSTED: Yes. Yes, I must know. I demand to know. Now.

LØVBORG: The manuscript—yes. Well, if—I have torn it into a thousand pieces.

MRS. ELVSTED: *(shrieks)* No! No!

HEDDA: *(involuntarily)* But that's not true.

LØVBORG: *(looks at her)* Not true, do you think?

HEDDA: *(collecting herself)* I—well, if you say so. It sounded so improbable.

LØVBORG: It's true, all the same.

MRS. ELVSTED: *(wringing her hands)* Oh, God, God. Hedda—he's torn his own work to pieces.

LØVBORG: My life is in pieces. Why not my work?

MRS. ELVSTED: When? Last night?

LØVBORG: Yes. I've told you. I tore it into a thousand pieces. And I scattered them on the waters of the fjord—far out where the water is sea-cold. Let them drift upon it—drift with the current and the wind. Soon they will sink—deep—then deeper and deeper, as I shall sink, Thea.

MRS. ELVSTED: You don't know what you've done. Do you know how I feel—how I shall feel to my dying day? It is as if you had killed a newborn child.

LØVBORG: I understand. It *is* like the death of a child.

MRS. ELVSTED: How could you? It was mine, too.

HEDDA: *(almost inaudibly)* The child—

MRS. ELVSTED: *(breathing heavily)* Then it is finished. Well, I will go now, Hedda.

HEDDA: Will you leave town?

MRS. ELVSTED: I don't know what I shall do. I see nothing. Nothing but darkness. *(exits by hall door)*

HEDDA: *(stands waiting)* Are you not going to see her home, Mr. Løvborg?

LØVBORG: I? Through the streets? In broad daylight? With people staring at us walking together? Is that what you suggest?

HEDDA: Of course, I don't know what else happened last night. But is the situation so irretrievable?

LØVBORG: Last night was just the beginning of the end. I know that. And the strange thing is that that sort of life has no appeal for me now. But she has broken my courage. I have no strength left for life.

HEDDA: *(looking straight ahead)* That simple, pretty nothing of a woman has changed a man's destiny. *(looking at him)* But how could you treat her so cruelly?

LØVBORG: Don't say that it was cruel.

HEDDA: You destroyed something that had lived in her soul for months. That wasn't cruel?

LØVBORG: Hedda, I can tell the truth to you.

HEDDA: The truth?

LØVBORG: First, you must promise, you must give me your word, that Thea will never know what I am about to tell you.

HEDDA: I give you my word.

LØVBORG: So. In the first place, what I said just now is untrue.

HEDDA: About the manuscript?

LØVBORG: Yes. I did not tear it to pieces. I did not throw it into the fjord.

HEDDA: Then—but where is it?

LØVBORG: I have destroyed it all the same—totally destroyed it, Hedda.

HEDDA: I don't understand.

LØVBORG: Thea said that what I had done was like killing a child.

HEDDA: Yes.

LØVBORG: But for a man to kill his child is—that is not the worst thing he can do to it.

HEDDA: Not the worst?

LØVBORG: No. I wanted to spare Thea from hearing that.

HEDDA: Then what is the worst?

LØVBORG: Let us think of a man who comes home, in the early hours of the morning, comes home to the mother of his child—he's been drinking heavily, the night was a debauch, and he says to her: "Listen—I've been out all night, here, there, and everywhere. . . . Look, I took the child with me—and he's lost. Completely lost. God knows where he is—God knows who may have their hands on him.

HEDDA: Yes, but after all, this was not a child—it was only a book, a manuscript.

LØVBORG: But Thea's soul was in that book.

HEDDA: Yes, I understand.

LØVBORG: Then you can understand that there is no future for us together.

HEDDA: Then where will you go from here?

LØVBORG: Nowhere. I will try to make an end of it all—as quickly as possible.

HEDDA: *(moving closer)* Eilert Løvborg, I want you to listen to me. When the time comes . . . will you not do it beautifully?

LØVBORG: Beautifully. *(smiles at her)* With vine leaves in my hair? That was your fantasy—a long time ago.

HEDDA: No. No. No more. The vine leaves have withered. But beautifully, nevertheless. For once. . . . You must go now. Goodbye. You must never come here again.

LØVBORG: Goodbye, Mrs. Tesman. Give Jørgen Tesman my love. *(he starts to leave)*

HEDDA: Wait. I want to give you something to take with you—a memento. *(Goes to drawer, takes out pistol case. Returns to Løvborg with one of the pistols.)*

LØVBORG: *(looks at her)* This—is this the memento?

HEDDA: *(nodding slowly)* Do you recognize it? It was aimed at you once.

LØVBORG: You should have used it then.

HEDDA: Take it—it's for you to use now.

LØVBORG: *(puts pistol in breast pocket)* I thank you.

HEDDA: Beautifully, Eilert Løvborg. Promise me that.

LØVBORG: Goodbye, Hedda Gabler. *(exits)*

(Hedda listens for a while. Goes to drawer, takes out manuscript. Takes out a few sheets. Looks at them. Sits in armchair by stove, package in her lap. Opens the stove, after a while, then unwraps whole package.)

HEDDA: *(throws a sheaf into the stove and whispers)* Thea, Thea, I am burning your child. It burns. Hair on fire. *(throws more on)* Your child and Eilert Løvborg's child. *(throws rest in)* It burns—I am burning your child.

ACT 4

The same day. It is evening. In darkness. The back room is lit by a hanging lamp. The curtains over the glass door are closed. Hedda, dressed in black, walks about the room. She goes to the back room and disappears for a moment. A few chords are heard on the piano. Then she returns.

Berte enters from the inner room. She places a lighted lamp on the table in front of the corner settee. Her eyes are red with weeping. Black ribbons in her cap. She exits quietly. Hedda goes to the curtains and looks into the darkness.

Miss Tesman enters in mourning, with bonnet and veil. Hedda goes to her, holding out her hands.

MISS TESMAN: Yes, Hedda, here I am—in my grief. I'm alone now. My poor sister has found peace at last.

HEDDA: I had heard—as you can see. Tesman sent word.

MISS TESMAN: Yes, he promised he would. But all the same I felt I had to come myself. To bring the news of death to this house of life.

HEDDA: That was most kind of you.

MISS TESMAN: She shouldn't have left us now. This is not the time for Hedda's house to be a house of mourning.

HEDDA: *(changing the subject)* She died quite peacefully, I gather, Miss Tesman?

MISS TESMAN: Oh, the end was so calm, so . . . so beautiful. And she was able to see Jørgen for the last time—she was able to say goodbye to him. I know that made her very happy. Content. Has he not come home yet?

HEDDA: No. He said in the note that he might be detained. Won't you sit down?

MISS TESMAN: No, thank you, my dear, dear Hedda. I would like to—but I have so much to do. I must prepare my dear sister for her eternal sleep. She shall go to her grave looking her best.

HEDDA: Can I be of any help?

MISS TESMAN: Oh, I wouldn't think of it. Hedda Tesman must have nothing to do with the sadness of death. And she must not even think about it, either—not at this time.

HEDDA: One is not always mistress of one's own thoughts. . . .

MISS TESMAN: *(continuing)* That is the way of the world. At home we shall be sewing the shroud; and here they'll be sewing other things—and soon, too, thank God.

(Tesman enters)

HEDDA: Ah, you've come home at last.

TESMAN: You here, Aunt Julie? And with Hedda? Fancy that.

MISS TESMAN: I was just going, my dear boy. Well, have you done all that you promised?

TESMAN: No. I'm sorry. I'm afraid I forgot half of it. I'll come to see you tomorrow. My brain is spinning today—can't keep my thoughts straight.

MISS TESMAN: Oh, Jørgen, my dear, dear Jørgen. You mustn't take it like this.

TESMAN: How? What do you mean?

MISS TESMAN: Even in your grief you must find happiness. You must be happy that she is at rest.

TESMAN: Oh, yes, yes, you're thinking of Aunt Rina.

HEDDA: You will feel lonely now, Miss Tesman.

MISS TESMAN: I expect so. At first. But that won't last too long, I hope. One must go on. I'm sure I'll find someone to take poor Rina's little room.

TESMAN: Really? Who do you think will take it?

MISS TESMAN: Oh, there's always someone who needs looking after, isn't there? Unfortunately.

HEDDA: Would you really take all that on yourself once again?

MISS TESMAN: All that! Heaven forgive you, child—it was no trouble at all for me.

HEDDA: But a complete stranger—how would you—

MISS TESMAN: One soon makes friends—particularly when someone is not well and needs you. I have to have someone to live for. I have to. But perhaps there'll soon be something to keep an old aunt busy in this house. And I thank heaven for it.

HEDDA: Don't worry about anything here.

TESMAN: Yes, just think what a wonderful time we three could have if—

HEDDA: If?

TESMAN: *(uneasily)* Oh, nothing. Everything will be fine. Let's hope so, hmm?

MISS TESMAN: Well, I'm sure you two want to talk to each other. *(smiling)* And perhaps Hedda has something special to tell you, Jørgen. So, goodbye. I must go home to Rina. *(stops at door)* To Rina. Isn't it strange? She's with me still, and with my poor brother as well.

TESMAN: Yes, just think of that, Aunt Julie. Yes.

(Miss Tesman leaves)

HEDDA: *(looks coldly at Tesman)* I almost believe you are more upset at Aunt Rina's death than Aunt Julie is.

TESMAN: It's not only that. I am very worried about Eilert Løvborg.

HEDDA: *(quickly)* Is there any news?

TESMAN: I went to his rooms this afternoon. I wanted to tell him that his manuscript was safe.

HEDDA: Well, did you see him?

TESMAN: No. He wasn't in. But afterward I met Mrs. Elvsted. And she told me he had been here early this morning.

HEDDA: Yes. As soon as you'd left.

TESMAN: He said that he'd torn his manuscript to pieces?

HEDDA: Yes—that's what he said.

TESMAN: God! He must have been completely out his mind. I suppose you thought it best not to give it back to him?

HEDDA: He did not get it.

TESMAN: But of course you told him that we had it.

HEDDA: No. *(quickly)* Did you tell Mrs. Elvsted?

TESMAN: No. I thought it better not to. But you should have told him, Hedda. Just think. He must be absolutely distraught. What if he should do himself some harm? Give me the manuscript, Hedda. I shall take it to him right away. Where is it?

HEDDA: *(cold, unmoved, leaning on armchair)* I have not got it.

TESMAN: Have not got it? What are you talking about?

HEDDA: I have burnt it—every single word of it.

TESMAN: *(horrified)* Burnt it! Burnt Eilert's manuscript!

HEDDA: Don't shout. The servant will hear you.

TESMAN: Burnt it. Good God. . . . No. No. That's impossible.

HEDDA: It is true, nevertheless.

TESMAN: Do you understand what you've done, Hedda? Apart from everything else, it was stolen. Stolen. Do you understand? Judge Brack will tell you what that means.

HEDDA: I think it would be wise not to speak of it again—neither to Judge Brack nor to anyone else.

TESMAN: It's unheard of—how could you do such a thing? What got into you? What made you think of it? Answer me that . . .

HEDDA: *(almost imperceptible smile)* I did it for your sake, Jørgen.

TESMAN: For me?!

HEDDA: This morning—what you told me about what he had read to you—

TESMAN: Yes, yes—what then?

HEDDA: You admitted that you had feelings of jealousy.

TESMAN: Yes, but that was natural. I didn't mean anything by it.

HEDDA: No matter. I couldn't bear the idea of you living in someone else's shadow.

TESMAN: *(half doubting, half overjoyed)* Oh, Hedda, Hedda. Is this true? But you . . . you've never shown your love to me like that. Never.

HEDDA: Well, I may as well tell you . . . at this time—at this time—I'm . . . *(breaks off)* No. No. You can ask Aunt Julie. She will tell you soon enough.

TESMAN: I think I understand. Hedda . . . is it true? Oh, Hedda!

HEDDA: Quiet. The servant will hear.

TESMAN: *(laughing)* The servant. Oh, Hedda, don't be so absurd. It's only Berte. I'll tell her myself.

HEDDA: *(hands knotted in desperation)* This is killing me—killing me, all this.

TESMAN: What? What is it, Hedda?

HEDDA: *(cold, in control)* All this—this absurdity. *(spelling it out)* This absurdity, Jørgen.

TESMAN: This absurdity! That I'm so happy at the news! What's absurd about that? But I won't say anything. I won't say anything to Berte.

HEDDA: Oh, why not that, too?

TESMAN: No. No, not yet. But I must tell Aunt Julie. Did you realize that you called me Jørgen a moment ago? Oh, Hedda, Aunt Julie will be so happy.

HEDDA: When she learns that I have burnt Eilert Løvborg's manuscript—for your sake?

TESMAN: That's not—look, as for the manuscript, of course no one must know about that. I'm talking about a different fire—your love for me. That is what I must share with Aunt Julie. I wonder, does this often happen when a marriage is so young?

HEDDA: Perhaps you should ask Aunt Julie that question, too.

TESMAN: I will—sometime soon, I will *(looks weary and worried again)* But the manuscript—it . . . The manuscript! Good God, it's terrible to think of what will happen to Eilert now.

(Mrs. Elvsted, dressed as in Act 1, enters by hall door)

MRS. ELVSTED: *(greets them hurriedly, evidently agitated)* My dear Hedda, please forgive my coming back.

HEDDA: What is the matter with you, Thea?

TESMAN: Is it Eilert Løvborg again?

MRS. ELVSTED: Yes. I'm very afraid that something awful has happened to him.

HEDDA: *(taking her arm)* Do you think so?

TESMAN: Good Lord, Mrs. Elvsted. Why do you think that?

MRS. ELVSTED: I went back to my boarding house, and I overheard some people talking about him—just as I came in. The stories that are going around—it's hard to believe.

TESMAN: Yes, I've heard a few things, too. But I can swear that he went straight home to bed last night.

HEDDA: Well, what did they say at the boarding house?

MRS. ELVSTED: Well, I didn't really hear anything at all—not clearly. Perhaps they did not know anything definite—or else . . . In any case, they stopped talking when they saw me, and I didn't have the courage to ask.

TESMAN: *(pacing uneasily)* Well, let's hope, Mrs. Elvsted, let's hope that there was a misunderstanding.

MRS. ELVSTED: No. No. I'm sure that they were talking about him—I'm sure. I think, in fact, that I heard the hospital mentioned—

TESMAN: The hospital?

HEDDA: Surely not!

MRS. ELVSTED: It terrified me. I went to his lodgings and asked for him there.

HEDDA: You actually had the courage to go there?

MRS. ELVSTED: What else could I do? Just not knowing—I couldn't bear that any longer.

TESMAN: But you didn't find him.

MRS. ELVSTED: No. And the people there knew nothing about him. They said he hadn't been home since yesterday afternoon.

TESMAN: Since yesterday—fancy that. But how could they say that?

MRS. ELVSTED: I know something terrible has happened to him. I can feel it.

TESMAN: Hedda, my dear—how would it be if I were to go and make some inquiries. . . ?

HEDDA: No, no, you must not get involved in this.

(Judge Brack, hat in hand, enters through hall door which Berte opens. He looks grave. Bows in silence.)

TESMAN: *(while Judge is in hallway)* Is that you, Judge?

BRACK: Yes. It was imperative that I should see you this evening.

TESMAN: You've heard the news about Aunt Rina?

BRACK: Yes, that among other things.

TESMAN: It's sad, isn't it?

BRACK: Well, my dear Tesman, that depends on how you look at it.

TESMAN: *(looks at him inquiringly)* Has—has anything else happened?

BRACK: Yes.

HEDDA: *(in suspense)* Is it upsetting, Judge Brack?

BRACK: That, too, depends on how you look at it, Mrs. Tesman.

MRS. ELVSTED: *(unable to restrain her anxiety)* It's Eilert Løvborg, isn't it? Something has happened to him.

BRACK: *(quick glance at her)* What makes you say that, madam? Have you already heard something?

MRS. ELVSTED: *(in confusion)* No, nothing. I've heard nothing, but . . .

TESMAN: For God's sake, tell us!

BRACK: *(shrugs shoulders)* Well, I regret to have to tell you that Eilert Løvborg has been taken to the hospital. He is lying on the point of death.

MRS. ELVSTED: *(screams)* Oh, God! Oh, God!

TESMAN: To the hospital! At the point of death.

HEDDA: *(quickly)* So soon.

MRS. ELVSTED: *(wailing)* We parted in anger, Hedda!

HEDDA: *(whispers)* Thea, Thea—be careful.

MRS. ELVSTED: *(ignoring her)* I must go to him—I must see him while he's still alive.

BRACK: It is useless, madam. No one can be admitted.

MRS. ELVSTED: Tell me—please—tell me, what happened to him? What is it?

TESMAN: *(to Brack)* Are you implying that he—that he himself—

HEDDA: Yes. yes. I'm sure of it.

TESMAN: Hedda—how can you. . . ?

BRACK: *(looking right at her)* Unfortunately, Mrs. Tesman, your guess was quite correct.

MRS. ELVSTED: It's awful—awful—awful—

TESMAN: He did it, then. Himself. Fancy that.

HEDDA: Shot himself.

BRACK: Another correct guess, Mrs. Tesman.

MRS. ELVSTED: *(trying to regain composure)* When did it happen, Mr. Brack?

BRACK: This afternoon, between three and four.

TESMAN: But—oh, my God—where was he? Where did he do it?

BRACK: *(hesitant)* Where—I suppose it must have been at his lodgings—

MRS. ELVSTED: No, that's impossible. I was there between six and seven.

BRACK: Then it must have been somewhere else. I really don't know. All I know is that he found . . . he had shot himself—in the heart.

MRS. ELVSTED: Oh, my God—that he should die like that!

HEDDA: *(to Brack)* Was it in the heart?

BRACK: Yes—that's what I said.

HEDDA: Not in the temple?

BRACK: In the heart, Mrs. Tesman.

HEDDA: Well, that too has its beauty.

BRACK: What do you mean, Mrs. Tesman?

HEDDA: Oh, nothing. Nothing.

TESMAN: And the wound is—is critical, you say.

BRACK: Absolutely mortal. The end has probably come by this time.

MRS. ELVSTED: Yes, I know it—I know it. The end . . . Oh, Hedda!

TESMAN: How did you learn all of this?

BRACK: *(quickly)* From one of the police. A man I had dealt with before.

HEDDA: *(in a clear voice)* At last an act that has some meaning.

TESMAN: *(terrified)* Good God, Hedda, what are you saying?

HEDDA: I mean that there is beauty in this act.

BRACK: Ah, Mrs. Tesman—

TESMAN: Beauty! How can—

MRS. ELVSTED: Oh, Hedda, where in God's name is the beauty?

HEDDA: Eilert Løvborg has settled his account with life. He made a choice. He had the courage to do it—to do the one thing that had to be done.

MRS. ELVSTED: No, that is not how it happened. You can't think that. It was beyond reason. He must have been out of control.

TESMAN: Utterly distraught.

HEDDA: I do not believe that. He chose—

MRS. ELVSTED: No. He was out of his mind. Just as he was when he tore up his manuscript.

BRACK: The manuscript? Did he tear it up?

MRS. ELVSTED: Yes. Last night.

TESMAN: *(whispers)* Oh, Hedda, we shall never get over this.

BRACK: That's quite extraordinary.

TESMAN: *(pacing)* I can't accept the idea of Løvborg's—of him taking leave of this life. And then not to leave behind him the book that would have made his name immortal—

MRS. ELVSTED: Oh, if only it could be put together again.

TESMAN: Yes. Yes, if only it could. I would give anything—anything.

MRS. ELVSTED: Perhaps it can, Mr. Tesman.

TESMAN: What do you mean?

MRS. ELVSTED: *(searches in the pocket of her dress)* Look at these. I kept them. These are his notes—he would write down his ideas and then dictate to me.

HEDDA: *(stepping forward)* Ah—

TESMAN: And you kept them—all of them?

MRS. ELVSTED: Yes, they're all here. I brought them with me when I—when I left home. They're all here.

TESMAN: Let me see them.

MRS. ELVSTED: *(handing the bundle of papers)* They're in no particular order, I'm afraid—all mixed up.

TESMAN: But just think if we could make something out of them! Perhaps if the two of us worked on it together.

MRS. ELVSTED: Yes. Oh, yes. We have to at least try.

TESMAN: We shall do more than that—we shall do it. For me there will be nothing else but that. That will be my life.

HEDDA: You, Jørgen? Your life?

TESMAN: Yes. Every moment that I can spare. My own research must wait. Hedda— you understand, don't you? I owe this to Eilert Løvborg. I owe it to his memory.

HEDDA: Perhaps.

TESMAN: And so, my dear Mrs. Elvsted, that is what we shall do. We shall give our minds to it. Totally. There is no use in brooding over what can never be changed. We must try to control our grief—as far as that is possible—and . . .

MRS. ELVSTED: Yes. Yes, Mr. Tesman. I will do the best I can.

TESMAN: Well, then, be good enough to come with me. I can't wait to begin. We must look through the notes together. But I don't think we should sit in here. No. Let's go in there—into the back room. Excuse me, my dear Judge. Come with me, Mrs. Elvsted.

MRS. ELVSTED: Oh, if only it were possible.

(They go into the back room. Mrs. Elvsted takes off her cloak and hat. They sit at the table under the hanging lamp and begin an eager examination of the papers. Hedda crosses to the stove and sits in the armchair. Brack goes to her.)

HEDDA: *(in a low voice)* Oh, what a feeling of freedom it gives one—this act of Eilert Løvborg's.

BRACK: Freedom, Mrs. Tesman? Well, of course, it is a release for him.

HEDDA: I mean for me. It gives me a sense of freedom to know that an act of deliberate courage is still possible in this world—an act that was both spontaneous and beautiful.

BRACK: *(smiling)* My dear Mrs. Tesman . . .

HEDDA: Oh, I know what you're going to say. You, too, are a specialist. You, too— like . . .

BRACK: *(looking at her)* Perhaps Eilert Løvborg meant more to you than you are willing to admit. Am I wrong?

HEDDA: I do not answer such questions. All I know is that Eilert Løvborg had the courage to live his life as he chose. And then the last, great act—an act of beauty. He had the will, he had the strength to turn away from the banquet of life—so early.

BRACK: I am sorry, Mrs. Tesman, but I'm afraid I must shatter that comfortable illusion.

HEDDA: Illusion?

BRACK: Yes—which could not have lasted very long in any case.

HEDDA: What do you mean?

BRACK: Eilert Løvborg did shoot himself—but it was not a matter of choice.

HEDDA: Not a matter of choice?

BRACK: No. It did not happen in quite the same way as I described.

HEDDA: *(in suspense)* You were hiding something. What was it?

BRACK: Well, for poor Mrs. Elvsted's sake, I . . . idealized the facts somewhat.

HEDDA: What are the facts?

BRACK: First, Løvborg is already dead.

HEDDA: At the hospital?

BRACK: Yes—without gaining consciousness.

HEDDA: And what else have you kept hidden?

BRACK: It did not happen at his lodgings.

HEDDA: That makes no difference.

BRACK: Perhaps. But I have to tell you that Løvborg was found shot—in . . . in Mademoiselle Diana's boudoir.

HEDDA: (makes a half attempt to rise) That's impossible. He can't have been there again today.

BRACK: He was there this afternoon. He went there—so I understand—to demand the return of something that they had taken from him. He talked, somewhat wildly, about a child—a lost child—

HEDDA: Oh . . . then that was why.

BRACK: I felt sure he meant his manuscript, but now I gather he destroyed it himself. I suppose it must have been his wallet.

HEDDA: Yes. I suppose so. And it was there that he was found.

BRACK: Yes. With a pistol in his breast pocket—it had been fired. And the bullet had passed through his chest and lodged in a vital part.

HEDDA: In the heart—

BRACK: No—in the bowels.

HEDDA: (looks at him with an expression of loathing) That too. Oh, what is it that makes everything I touch turn ugly and mean?

BRACK: There is one last thing, Mrs. Tesman—one last unpleasant feature.

HEDDA: And what is that?

BRACK: This pistol that he had—

HEDDA: (breathless) Well, what about it?

BRACK: He must have stolen it.

HEDDA: (leaps up) Stolen it! That is simply not true. He did not steal it.

BRACK: No other explanation is possible. He must have stolen it. Shh!

(Tesman and Mrs. Elvsted have risen from the table and entered the drawing room)

TESMAN: (papers in both hands) Hedda, my dear, it's almost impossible to read under that lamp—just think.

HEDDA: I am. I am thinking.

TESMAN: Would you mind if we sat at your writing table?

HEDDA: If you like. (quickly) No, wait. Let me clear it first.

TESMAN: Oh, don't bother. There's plenty of room.

HEDDA: No. Let me clear it. Please! I'll take these things and put them on the piano. There.

(She has taken something, covered with sheet music, from under the bookcase. She puts more music sheets upon it, takes it into the other room. Tesman lays the scraps of paper on the writing table and moves the lamp from the corner table. He and Mrs. Elvsted sit down and get on with their work. Hedda returns.)

HEDDA: (behind Mrs. Elvsted's chair, gently ruffling her hair) Well, my lovely Thea, how is it? How is this memorial to Eilert Løvborg?

MRS. ELVSTED: (looking at her) Oh, it will be dreadfully difficult to put it in order.

TESMAN: But we must do it. I am determined. Besides, it's something I'm good at—working on other people's papers, setting them in order.

(Hedda goes to the stove, sits. Brack stands over her.)

HEDDA: *(whispers)* What did you say about the pistol?

BRACK: *(softly)* That he must have stolen it.

HEDDA: Why stolen it?

BRACK: Because every other explanation ought to be unthinkable, Mrs. Tesman.

HEDDA: Indeed?

BRACK: *(glares at her)* Of course, Eilert Løvborg was here this morning, wasn't he?

HEDDA: Yes.

BRACK: Were you alone with him?

HEDDA: Some of the time.

BRACK: Did you leave the room at any time while he was here?

HEDDA: No.

BRACK: Try to remember. Were you out of the room—even for a moment?

HEDDA: Perhaps, yes, just for a moment. I was in the hallway.

BRACK: And where was your pistol case during that time?

HEDDA: It was locked up—in the—

BRACK: Well, where, Mrs. Tesman?

HEDDA: The case was on the writing table.

BRACK: Have you looked at it since then—to see whether both pistols are there?

HEDDA: No. I haven't.

BRACK: Well, there is no need. I saw the pistol that was found in Løvborg's pocket. I recognized it at once. I had seen it yesterday afternoon—and on other previous occasions.

HEDDA: Do you have it with you?

BRACK: No. The police have it.

HEDDA: And what will they do?

BRACK: They will try to find the owner.

HEDDA: And do you think they will succeed?

BRACK: *(bending over her and whispering)* No, Hedda Gabler—not so long as I say nothing.

HEDDA: *(looks at him, frightened)* And if you do say nothing—what then?

BRACK: *(shrugs his shoulders)* There is always the possibility that the pistol was stolen.

HEDDA: *(strongly)* Death rather than that.

BRACK: *(smiling)* Words, Mrs. Tesman, mere words. People don't do things like that.

HEDDA: *(ignoring him)* What if the pistol was not stolen? And what if the owner were discovered? What then?

BRACK: Well, Hedda, then there is the scandal.

HEDDA: The scandal!

BRACK: Yes. The scandal which frightens you to death. You see, you would be brought before the court. You and Mademoiselle Diana. She would have to explain what happened—whether the death was accidental or whether it was murder. Did the pistol go off as he was trying to take it out of his pocket, let us say, to threaten her? Or did she tear it out of his hand, shoot him, and then carefully replace it in his pocket? That would not be impossible—she is, I gather, quite capable of looking after herself.

HEDDA: The whole thing is unspeakably sordid. But it has nothing to do with *me!*

BRACK: No. But you would have to answer the question—why did you give the pistol to Eilert Løvborg? And when that fact is revealed, what conclusions will people draw? What will they think?

HEDDA: That thought had not entered my mind. *(bows her head)*

BRACK: Fortunately, there is no danger of that happening—so long as I say nothing.

HEDDA: *(looking up at him)* So, Judge Brack, I am in your power after all. From now on, I am at your disposal.

BRACK: *(whispers softly)* Dearest Hedda—believe me, I shall not take the slightest advantage of—

HEDDA: Nevertheless, I am in your power. I am subject to your will, your whim. I am a mere slave, a slave. *(rises quickly)* No. No. That is a thought that I cannot bear. Never.

BRACK: *(half-mocking look)* People usually get used to the inevitable.

HEDDA: *(looking at him)* Perhaps. *(Goes to writing table. Suppresses an involuntary smile. Imitates Tesman's vocal mannerisms.)* Well? Getting on, Jørgen, hmm?

TESMAN: Heaven knows. In any case, there's months of work here.

HEDDA: Just think. *(runs her hands through Mrs. Elvsted's hair)* Doesn't it seem strange to you, Thea? To be sitting here with Tesman, I mean—just as you must have sat with Eilert Løvborg.

MRS. ELVSTED: If only I could inspire your husband now—as I did then.

HEDDA: Oh, that will come—in time.

TESMAN: Yes, do you know, Hedda, I can almost feel something of the sort. Yes. But—won't you go and sit with Brack for a while?

HEDDA: Is there nothing I can do to help?

TESMAN: No, nothing. Not a thing. I trust you to keep Hedda company, my dear Brack.

BRACK: *(with a glance at her)* With the very greatest of pleasure.

HEDDA: Thank you. But I'm feeling rather tired this evening. I will go in and lie down on the sofa for a while.

TESMAN: Yes, do, my dear, hmm?

(Hedda leaves. Closes curtains. After a pause she is heard playing a dance on the piano.)

MRS. ELVSTED: *(getting up)* Oh, what is that?

TESMAN: *(runs to doorway)* Hedda, my dearest—please, no music. Not of that kind. Not tonight. Think of Aunt Rina. And of Eilert, too.

HEDDA: *(puts her head out between curtains)* And of Aunt Julie. And of everyone else. After this I shall be quiet.

TESMAN: It's really not good for her to see us at work like this. I'll tell you what, Mrs. Elvsted. There's an empty room at Aunt Julie's. You can take it. And I will come over in the evenings and we can work there.

HEDDA: *(still in the other room)* I can hear what you're saying, Tesman. And how am I going to get through the evenings, here in this house?

TESMAN: Oh, I'm sure Judge Brack will be kind enough to drop in occasionally—
even though I shall be out.

BRACK: *(in chair, calls out happily)* Oh, every evening, Mrs. Tesman, every evening.
And with the greatest of pleasure. We two will get on wonderfully together.

HEDDA: *(in clear voice)* Yes, I'm sure you flatter yourself that we will, Judge Brack.
Now that you are the one cock of the walk.

(A shot. The three rise to their feet.)

TESMAN: Oh, my God—what is she—

*(Runs in, opens curtains. Mrs. Elvsted follows. Screams, confusion. Berte enters through the
dining room door.)*

TESMAN: Shot herself! In the temple!

BRACK: God—people—people don't do things like that.

ᰢ Leo Tolstoy
1828–1910

Leo Tolstoy was the most famous Russian of his time. With the publication of two grand novels, *War and Peace* (1862–69) and *Anna Karenina*
(1877), Tolstoy held a place of elevated importance in European literary
circles, but he gained worldwide fame when he turned his attention to the
political and spiritual issues of his day, writing nonfiction books and
pamphlets that criticized the Russian Tsarist regime and charted a new
spirituality for his followers. During the last years of Tolstoy's life, people
came from all over the world to visit him at his country estate. Like Dostoevsky, Tolstoy rejected the Western materialism and secularism that
appeared to be a byproduct of modern science, believing that Russia's salvation lay in a reformation of Christian values. It is deceptive, however, to
characterize Tolstoy as a great novelist who turned into a moralist. His
whole life was a struggle between the body and the spirit, between reason
and faith. As a Romantic, he celebrated the lives and simple values of
peasants, people who lived close to the earth and close to their hearts. In
contrast, his aristocratic background seemed hollow and hypocritical.
Nevertheless, he was attracted to the benefits of the city, to books and literate conversation, as well as to the decadent pleasures provided by urban
life. As Tolstoy tried to reconcile his life with his art, he reflected a larger
nineteenth-century dichotomy between rational ENLIGHTENMENT ideals,
which could transform society, and the fresh vision of ROMANTICISM,
which could inflame the imagination of individuals, promote the irrational, and reject society.

LEE-oh TOLE-stoy

**Count Leo Tolstoy,
circa 1880**

*This photograph of
Tolstoy at age fifty-
two was taken soon
after he had completed*
Anna Karenina.
(Library of
Congress)

www   For links to more information about Tolstoy, a quiz on *The Death of Ivan Ilych,* and the twenty-first-century relevance of *Ivan Ilych,* see *World Literature Online* at bedfordstmartins .com/worldlit.

The Aristocrat with Peasant Sympathies.   Tolstoy was born on August 28, 1828, to Count Nikolaj Tolstoy and his wife, the former Princess Volkonsky, on the large country estate of Yasnaya Polyana, some 120 miles south of Moscow. The deaths of his mother when he was two, his father when he was nine, and a guardian aunt when he was thirteen left Tolstoy on his own at an early age. Later, with his primary attention on wine, women, and gambling, Tolstoy failed several courses at the University of Kazan, where he studied Asian languages and law. He left the university in 1847 without a degree and returned to Yasnaya Polyana, where he tried to improve the living conditions of the serfs on his family's estate. Frustrated by the suspicion of the peasants concerning making changes, Leo and his brother Nikolai journeyed to Caucasus, in Southern Russia, where Leo joined the army in 1851. Fighting first against Muslims and then against the French and English in the **CRIMEAN WAR** (1853–56),[1] Tolstoy turned his experiences into *Sevastopol Sketches* (1855), which along with an earlier work, *Childhood* (1852), brought him national recognition.

Two Epic Novels.   Uneasy with literary society in Russia, Tolstoy visited Europe, where he became convinced that Westernization would not solve his homeland's problems. He returned to Russia and continued writing at Yasnaya Polyana, establishing a progressive school there for the children of his illiterate workers. At age thirty-four he married Sofia, the eighteen-year-old, high-strung daughter of a court doctor. During the early years of his marriage, from 1863 to 1869, he wrote the monumental *War and Peace.* Focusing on the invasion of Russia by Napoleon in 1812, it is the panoramic, epic-like sweep of this work, its vibrant world of characters and settings, that establish it as one of the greatest novels ever written.

When Sofia insisted that they winter in Moscow, Leo became a census taker and for the first time confronted the appalling poverty and degradation of the poor working classes in Moscow's slums—men, women, and children who were being ground down by a kind of slave labor in the factories. Tolstoy's own luxurious lifestyle deeply troubled his conscience, and he was determined to simplify his way of life. He cut wood, swept floors, and plowed fields. He made his own leather boots, wore a peasant blouse and trousers, and went barefoot in the summer. He drank a brew of barley and acorns rather than coffee and set to work writing *Anna Karenina* (1875–77). In this novel of contemporary manners, Anna and Vronsky's illicit love is successful initially in defying the conventional codes of marriage, but the power of social mores eventually crushes it.

A Spiritual Crisis.   After completing *Anna Karenina,* Tolstoy was exhausted; he suffered a profound psychological and moral crisis concern-

---

[1] **Crimean War:** Although the Crimean War (1853–56) began as a conflict between Russia and the Ottoman empire, France and Britain won it with an extended siege of Russia's Black Sea naval base, Sevastopol, in the Crimea.

ing the futility of material success and the relentless movement of time toward death. He was rich and famous, but he questioned the value of his greatest novels. His autobiography, *A Confession* (1879), written in the tradition of both St. Augustine's[2] and Rousseau's[3] *Confessions,* describes this crisis of faith and includes a poignant fable about a traveler on the steppes who is attacked by a furious wild beast: "To save himself the traveler gets into a waterless well; but at the bottom of it he sees a dragon with jaws wide open to devour him. The unhappy man dares not get out for fear of the wild beast, and dares not descend for fear of the dragon, so he catches hold of the branch of a wild plant growing in a crevice of the well. His arms grow tired, and he feels that he must soon perish . . . he sees two mice, one black and one white, gradually making their way round the stem of the wild plant on which he is hanging, nibbling it through. The plant will soon give way and break off, and he will fall into the jaws of the dragon . . . still hanging, he looks around him, and, finding some drops of honey on the leaves of the wild plant, he stretches out his tongue and licks them." The beast of time pursues mortals into the dragon of death, while day and night eat away at man's hold on life.

According to the fable, death should compel us to savor the drops of honey available in the present moment, but Tolstoy's experience with death brought despair. In addition to the family he lost as a young boy, death had claimed his brother, his son Petya, who died in 1873, and his beloved Aunt Toinette, who died the following year. Tolstoy turned to religion: He studied the Scriptures and the history of Christianity. He wrestled with the concept of God. He emulated the piety of Russian peasants and took to visiting monasteries, the most notable of which is the Optina Monastery, made famous by Dostoevsky in *The Brothers Karamazov.* The New Testament's Sermon on the Mount and especially Matthew 5:39—"Do not resist evil"—became Tolstoy's program for moral and spiritual reform. He was attracted by the Beatitudes, the idea of dispossession of goods, pacifism, and strict self-control. Tolstoy's daring, courageous experiment was to take Jesus' Sermon on the Mount seriously and actually try to live by it. By stripping Christianity free of institutions, priesthood, and ritual, Tolstoy hoped to re-create a basic, moral Christianity that he hoped would liberate Russians from a corrupt religion controlled by the bureaucracy of the church.

Tolstoy's Mission of Nonviolence.   After *Anna Karenina* and his moral crisis of 1878, Tolstoy was no longer interested in literature as art, only in literature as message. Writing fiction was less important to him than producing a series of books and pamphlets explaining his own version of Jesus' teachings. *What I Believe* (1883) examines Jesus' pacifism, his instructions to resist not evil with evil, to turn the other cheek, and to

> Great writers are not necessarily authoritative; many a wonderful writer, like Chekhov, has been essentially impersonal . . . the ability to be nothing in himself, substantially nothing but his own characters. But the two most towering Russian writers, Dostoevsky and Tolstoy, have tried to be "heroes" in Carlyle's sense— evangelists and founders of a new belief.
>
> – ALFRED KAZIN

---

[2] **St. Augustine:** (354–430) An influential Catholic theologian from Hippo, North Africa, who wrote *Confessions* (c. 401) to tell the story of his conversion.

[3] **Rousseau:** (1812–1878), A French writer who wrote his *Confessions* (published 1781–88) to illustrate the importance of the individual and the self's particular genius.

love one's enemies. *What Then Must We Do* (1884) looks at the plight of the impoverished classes in Moscow, deplores the evils of money, and prescribes a return to the land. In *The Kingdom of God Is Within You* (1894), Tolstoy expresses his opposition to religious ritual and the abuses of church power. His particular form of Christian anarchy is summed up in five commandments: Do not be angry at anyone; Do not commit adultery; Do not swear any oaths; Do not repay evil with evil; Love your enemies and be good to both enemies and friends. Tolstoy also expressed his beliefs in works of fiction, including several short stories and one rather propagandistic novel, *The Resurrection* (1900), in which Prince Nekhludov comes to terms with the consequences of his promiscuity and the burdens of wealth through a spiritual resurrection.

Tolstoy's war on Orthodoxy led to his excommunication from the Russian Church in 1901. But outside Russia his reputation grew. Christians, Jews, Muslims, and BUDDHISTS from all over the world came to Yasnaya Polyana to sit at his feet. Mahatma Gandhi,[4] who became internationally famous for using the principles of nonviolence to liberate India from Great Britain in 1947, first came to know Tolstoy through *The Kingdom of God Is Within You,* and the two men corresponded. In both South Africa and India, Gandhi used Tolstoy's principles to mount campaigns of civil disobedience against unjust laws. Although his doctrine of nonviolence did not appeal to Russian Marxists, Tolstoy's ideas helped shape the twentieth-century practices of not only Gandhi but also Martin Luther King Jr. and Dorothy Day,[5] the founder of the Catholic Worker movement in New York City. For his part, Tolstoy admired the transcendental writings of Emerson and Thoreau[6] in America, and he looked to such European novelists and essayists as Goethe, Dickens, and Montaigne[7] for inspiration. He was familiar with Buddhist writings, the Qur'an,[8] and the Daoism (Taoism) of Laozi (Lao Tzu).[9]

Because Tolstoy not only wrote about the moral principles of the "good life," but earnestly attempted to incorporate his teachings into daily living while also admitting his failures and shortcomings, he gained world credibility, popularity, and a large personal following. But life at

---

[4] **Mahatma Gandhi:** (1869–1948) Hindu nationalist reformer known for his spiritual principles and practices. His use of civil disobedience contributed to India's independence from Great Britain. He was assassinated by a Hindu radical.

[5] **King Jr. . . . Day: Martin Luther King Jr.** (1929–1968) Civil rights leader who was assassinated. His speeches and sermons continue to provide inspiration and hope for minorities in the United States. **Dorothy Day** (1897–1980) was a nonviolent social radical who founded the Catholic Worker Movement, which clothes and feeds the poor in New York City and elsewhere.

[6] **Emerson and Thoreau: Ralph Waldo Emerson** (1803–1882) was an American philosopher who drew attention to the sacredness of nature. **Henry David Thoreau** (1817–1862) was a naturalist who wrote about the spirit of nature and believed that wilderness was important for urban America.

[7] **Montaigne:** Michel Montaigne (1533–1592) was the French father of the modern essay.

[8] **Qur'an:** Qur'an is the sacred scriptures of Islam.

[9] **Daoism of Laozi:** Laozi (seventh or fifth century B.C.E.) was the Chinese founder of Daoism, a religious philosophy devoted to following the *dao,* or path.

home was neither easy nor tranquil with this secular saint. Tolstoy's wife, Sofia, became increasingly jealous of his fame, and when he threatened to give up his financial holdings and distribute them to the poor, Sofia protested on behalf of herself and their thirteen children. On November 8, 1910, deeply troubled by his failure to live up to his own ideals, Tolstoy wrote Sofia a farewell letter and secretly departed Yasnaya Polyana. Falling ill on a train, he spent his final days in a station master's house at Astapovo. Sofia did not see her husband of forty-eight years until after he had slipped into a coma. He died on November 20.

Tolstoy's Development as a Writer.   Tolstoy's most famous work, *War and Peace,* is a long, historical novel about the invasion of Russia by Napoleon's army in 1812. Scholars have criticized Tolstoy's portrait of Napoleon and the author's fatalistic theory of history, wherein events are determined by Providence or Destiny. Within the vast panorama of history, heroes and empires emerge and disappear, but the values of love, marriage, and family endure. In the novel, epic battle scenes and military heroes are juxtaposed with scenes of social life in Moscow and St. Petersburg. And the heart of the novel is its detailed evocation of Russian life, which, episode after episode, builds into a coherent picture of a nineteenth-century world. For the hero, Pierre Bezukhov, the search for self-respect leads finally to the comfort of domestic values; in the end love, marriage, and family are the real victors.

Tolstoy's other monumental work, *Anna Karenina,* is a novel centered on social mores. Although at first Anna and Vronsky exhibit courage and magnitude in their illicit love affair, they are ultimately incapable of preserving their relationship in the face of social disapproval. The once-radiant Anna becomes wretchedly unhappy and tragically ends her life in suicide. Since the writing of *Anna Karenina,* there have been radical changes surrounding sexuality, marriage, and divorce that may make Anna's dilemma seem less immediate and intense than it was in Tolstoy's day. Tolstoy's own representative in the novel is Levin, who finds meaning in useful work. Tolstoy later repudiated his two magnificent classics in *What Is Art?* (1897), condemning art for art's sake. In their abundant, realistic detail those novels are aligned with works by nineteenth-century Realists such as French novelist Gustave Flaubert (1821–1880), but the mature Tolstoy questioned whether detail and in-depth portraits of characters obscured the message of his writings.

The Death of Ivan Ilych.   Like Rousseau in France and Thoreau in the United States, Tolstoy came to believe that personal salvation lay in a simple, natural life lived apart from the destructive influences of cities. The corruption inherent in the values of urban officialdom is aptly illustrated by the following selection, *The Death of Ivan Ilych* (1886), which belongs to the second major period of Tolstoy's life when, after his spiritual crisis, he focused on reconciling life, literature, and morality. The story's plot is simple and straightforward; as indicated by its title, there is no suspense about the outcome. Ivan Ilych is a judge, a public official, who is making his way up the social and institutional ladder when one day he has a minor accident while fixing a curtain and his life is radically turned around. As he grows weaker, slowly dying, he experiences all the loneliness and isolation that he has sown in the bureaucratic handling of his clientele as well as his own family. At the very end, he experiences a transformation that allows him to let go of his wasted life.

Critic Vladimir Lakshin summed up Tolstoy's place among Russia's literary masters: "We like Chekhov, admire Dostoevsky, love Pushkin, but Tolstoy? As a combination artist, philosopher, public figure, and human being, he is *neobychny* [unparalleled; incomparable]."

■ CONNECTIONS

Ibsen, *Hedda Gabler*, p. 561. Realist writers in the second half of the nineteenth century showed how social conditions influenced their characters' behavior. Ibsen's Hedda Gabler is a product of a small, backward Norwegian town of the 1860s. How does Tolstoy's Ivan Ilych reflect the social values of his time and place?

William Wordsworth, Poems, p. 236. As more and more people moved to cities in the nineteenth century, Romantic writers painted the country and nature with a sentimental brush: Living close to nature was more moral, more authentic, and less corrupt than life in the city. Wordsworth's poems not only idealize the natural life but also link it to childhood. How does Tolstoy's characterization of the servant Gerasim represent a life lived close to nature?

T. S. Eliot, *The Waste Land* (Book 6). In the early twentieth century, the modern city, by its size and heterogeneity, came to symbolize the loss of roots and the loss of identity. T. S. Eliot's *Waste Land* treats the modern city as a kind of spiritual death. How do Ivan Ilych's choices isolate him and cut him off from influences that would otherwise nurture him?

■ FURTHER RESEARCH

Biography
Simmons, Ernest J. *Leo Tolstoy*. 1946.
Troyat, Henri. *Tolstoy*. 1967.
Wilson, A. N. *Tolstoy*. 1988.

Criticism
Bilbajons, Rimvydas. *Tolstoy's Aesthetics and His Art*. 1991.
Christian, R. F. *Tolstoy: A Critical Introduction*. 1969.
Greenwood, E. B. *Tolstoy: The Comprehensive Vision*. 1975.
Matlaw, Ralph. *Tolstoy: A Collection of Critical Essays*. 1967.
Rahv, Philip. *Image and Idea*. 1949. Contains an individual chapter on *The Death of Ivan Ilych*.

■ PRONUNCIATION

Leo Tolstoy: LEE-oh TOLE-stoy
Fëdor Vasilievich: FYOH-dore vah-SEE-lyi-vich
Peter Ivanovich: PEE-tur ee-VAH-nuh-vich
Praskovya Fëdorovna Golovina: prah-SKOH-vyah FYOH-duh-ruv-nah
    guh-lah-VYEEN-ah
Ivan Egorovich Shebek: ee-VAHN yi-GOH-ruh-vich SHEH-bek
Schwartz: SHVARTS
Gerasim: gi-RAH-seem

Ilya Epimovich Golovin: ee-LYAH yeh-PEE-muh-vich guh-lah-VEEN
Leshchetitsky: leesh-chee-TIT-skee, lyee-shyee-TIT-skee
Vladimir Ivanovich: vlah-DEE-mere ee-VAH-nuh-vich
Dmitri Ivanovich Petrishchev: DMEE-tree ee-VAH-nuh-vich pee-TREESH-chef
Adrienne Lecouvreur: ah-dree-EN luh-koov-RUR

❧ The Death of Ivan Ilych

Translated by David Magarshack

I

During an interval in the Melvinski trial in the large building of the Law Courts, the members and public prosecutor met in Ivan Egorovich Shebek's private room, where the conversation turned on the celebrated Krasovski case. Fëdor Vasilievich warmly maintained that it was not subject to their jurisdiction, Ivan Egorovich maintained the contrary, while Peter Ivanovich, not having entered into the discussion at the start, took no part in it but looked through the *Gazette* which had just been handed in.

"Gentlemen," he said, "Ivan Ilych has died!"

"You don't say so!"

"Here, read it yourself," replied Peter Ivanovich, handing Fëdor Vasilievich the paper still damp from the press. Surrounded by a black border were the words: "Praskovya Fëdorovna Golovina, with profound sorrow, informs relatives and friends of the demise of her beloved husband Ivan Ilych Golovin, Member of the Court of Justice, which occurred on February the 4th of this year 1882. The funeral will take place on Friday at one o'clock in the afternoon."

Ivan Ilych had been a colleague of the gentlemen present and was liked by them all. He had been ill for some weeks with an illness said to be incurable. His post had been kept open for him, but there had been conjectures that in case of his death Alexeev might receive his appointment, and that either Vinnikov or Shtabel would succeed Alexeev. So on receiving the news of Ivan Ilych's death the first thought of each of the gentlemen in that private room was of the changes and promotions it might occasion among themselves or their acquaintances.

"I shall be sure to get Shtabel's place or Vinnikov's," thought Fëdor Vasilievich. "I was promised that long ago, and the promotion means an extra eight hundred rubles a year for me besides the allowance."

"Now I must apply for my brother-in-law's transfer from Kaluga," thought Peter Ivanovich. "My wife will be very glad, and then she won't be able to say that I never do anything for her relations."

"I thought he would never leave his bed again," said Peter Ivanovich aloud. "It's very sad."

"But what really was the matter with him?"

"The doctors couldn't say—at least they could, but each of them said something different. When last I saw him I thought he was getting better."

"And I haven't been to see him since the holidays. I always meant to go."

"Had he any property?"

"I think his wife had a little—but something quite trifling."

"We shall have to go to see her, but they live so terribly far away."

"Far away from you, you mean. Everything's far away from your place."

"You see, he never can forgive my living on the other side of the river," said Peter Ivanovich, smiling at Shebek. Then, still talking of the distances between different parts of the city, they returned to the Court.

Besides considerations as to the possible transfers and promotions likely to result from Ivan Ilych's death, the mere fact of the death of a near acquaintance aroused, as usual, in all who heard of it the complacent feeling that, "it is he who is dead and not I."

Each one thought or felt, "Well, he's dead but I'm alive!" But the more intimate of Ivan Ilych's acquaintances, his so-called friends, could not help thinking also that they would now have to fulfil the very tiresome demands of propriety by attending the funeral service and paying a visit of condolence to the widow.

Fëdor Vasilievich and Peter Ivanovich had been his nearest acquaintances. Peter Ivanovich had studied law with Ivan Ilych and had considered himself to be under obligations to him.

Having told his wife at dinner-time of Ivan Ilych's death and of his conjecture that it might be possible to get her brother transferred to their circuit, Peter Ivanovich sacrificed his usual nap, put on his evening clothes, and drove to Ivan Ilych's house.

At the entrance stood a carriage and two cabs.[1] Leaning against the wall in the hall downstairs near the cloak-stand was a coffin-lid covered with cloth of gold, ornamented with gold cord and tassels, that had been polished up with metal powder. Two ladies in black were taking off their fur cloaks. Peter Ivanovich recognized one of them as Ivan Ilych's sister, but the other was a stranger to him. His colleague Schwartz was just coming downstairs, but on seeing Peter Ivanovich enter he stopped and winked at him, as if to say: "Ivan Ilych has made a mess of things—not like you and me."

Schwartz's face with his Piccadilly whiskers[2] and his slim figure in evening dress, had as usual an air of elegant solemnity which contrasted with the playfulness of his character and had a special piquancy here, or so it seemed to Peter Ivanovich.

Peter Ivanovich allowed the ladies to precede him and slowly followed them upstairs. Schwartz did not come down but remained where he was, and Peter Ivanovich understood that he wanted to arrange where they should play bridge that evening. The ladies went upstairs to the widow's room, and Schwartz with seriously compressed lips but a playful look in his eyes, indicated by a twist of his eyebrows the room to the right where the body lay.

---

[1] **cabs:** Horse-drawn cabs. [2] **Piccadilly whiskers:** Side whiskers.

Peter Ivanovich, like everyone else on such occasions, entered feeling uncertain what he would have to do. All he knew was that at such times it is always safe to cross oneself. But he was not quite sure whether one should make obeisances while doing so. He therefore adopted a middle course. On entering the room he began crossing himself and made a slight movement resembling a bow. At the same time, as far as the motion of his head and arm allowed, he surveyed the room. Two young men— apparently nephews, one of whom was a high-school pupil—were leaving the room, crossing themselves as they did so. An old woman was standing motionless, and a lady with strangely arched eyebrows was saying something to her in a whisper. A vigorous, resolute Church Reader, in a frock-coat, was reading something in a loud voice with an expression that precluded any contradiction. The butler's assistant, Gerasim, stepping lightly in front of Peter Ivanovich, was strewing something on the floor. Noticing this, Peter Ivanovich was immediately aware of a faint odour of a decomposing body.

The last time he had called on Ivan Ilych, Peter Ivanovich had seen Gerasim in the study. Ivan Ilych had been particularly fond of him and he was performing the duty of a sick nurse.

Peter Ivanovich continued to make the sign of the cross slightly inclining his head in an intermediate direction between the coffin, the Reader, and the icons on the table in a corner of the room. Afterwards, when it seemed to him that this movement of his arm in crossing himself had gone on too long, he stopped and began to look at the corpse.

The dead man lay, as dead men always lie, in a specially heavy way, his rigid limbs sunk in the soft cushions of the coffin, with the head forever bowed on the pillow. His yellow waxen brow with bald patches over his sunken temples was thrust up in the way peculiar to the dead, the protruding nose seeming to press on the upper lip. He was much changed and had grown even thinner since Peter Ivanovich had last seen him, but, as is always the case with the dead, his face was handsomer and above all more dignified than when he was alive. The expression on the face said that what was necessary had been accomplished, and accomplished rightly. Besides this there was in that expression a reproach and a warning to the living. This warning seemed to Peter Ivanovich out of place, or at least not applicable to him. He felt a certain discomfort and so he hurriedly crossed himself once more and turned and went out of the door—too hurriedly and too regardless of propriety, as he himself was aware.

Schwartz was waiting for him in the adjoining room with legs spread wide apart and both hands toying with his top-hat behind his back. The mere sight of that playful, well-groomed, and elegant figure refreshed Peter Ivanovich. He felt that Schwartz was above all these happenings and would not surrender to any depressing influences. His very look said that this incident of a church service for Ivan Ilych could not be a sufficient reason for infringing the order of the session—in other words, that it would certainly not prevent his unwrapping a new pack of cards and shuffling them that evening while a footman placed four fresh candles on the table: in fact, that there was no reason for supposing that this incident would hinder their spending the evening agreeably. Indeed he said this in a whisper as Peter Ivanovich passed him, proposing that they should meet for a game at Fëdor Vasilievich's. But apparently Peter Ivanovich was not destined to play bridge that evening. Praskovya Fëdorovna (a short, fat woman who despite all efforts to the contrary had continued to broaden steadily from her shoulders downwards and who had the same extraordinarily arched eyebrows as the lady who had been standing by the coffin), dressed all in black, her head covered with lace, came out of her own room with some other ladies, conducted them to the room where the dead body lay, and said: "The service will begin immediately. Please go in."

Schwartz, making an indefinite bow, stood still, evidently neither accepting nor declining this invitation. Praskovya Fëdorovna, recognizing Peter Ivanovich, sighed, went close up to him, took his hand, and said: "I know you were a true friend to Ivan Ilych . . ." and looked at him awaiting some suitable response. And Peter Ivanovich knew that, just as it had been the right thing to cross himself in that room, so what he had to do here was to press her hand, sigh, and say, "Believe me. . . ." So he did all this and as he did it felt that the desired result had been achieved: that both he and she were touched.

"Come with me. I want to speak to you before it begins," said the widow. "Give me your arm."

Peter Ivanovich gave her his arm and they went to the inner rooms, passing Schwartz, who winked at Peter Ivanovich compassionately.

"That does for our bridge! Don't object if we find another player. Perhaps you can cut in when you do escape," said his playful look.

Peter Ivanovich sighed still more deeply and despondently, and Praskovya Fëdorovna pressed his arm gratefully. When they reached the drawing-room, upholstered in pink cretonne and lighted by a dim lamp, they sat down at the table — she on a sofa and Peter Ivanovich on a low pouffe, the springs of which yielded spasmodically under his weight. Praskovya Fëdorovna had been on the point of warning him to take another seat, but felt that such a warning was out of keeping with her present condition and so changed her mind. As he sat down on the pouffe Peter Ivanovich recalled how Ivan Ilych had arranged this room and had consulted him regarding this pink cretonne with green leaves. The whole room was full of furniture and knick-knacks, and on her way to the sofa the lace of the widow's black shawl caught on the carved edge of the table. Peter Ivanovich rose to detach it, and the springs of the pouffe, relieved of his weight, rose also and gave him a push. The widow began detaching her shawl herself, and Peter Ivanovich again sat down, suppressing the rebellious springs of the pouffe under him. But the widow had not quite freed herself and Peter Ivanovich got up again, and again the pouffe rebelled and even creaked. When this was all over she took out a clean cambric handkerchief and began to weep. The episode with the shawl and the struggle with the pouffe had cooled Peter Ivanovich's emotions and he sat there with a sullen look on his face. This awkward situation was interrupted by Sokolov, Ivan Ilych's butler, who came to report that the plot in the cemetery that Praskovya Fëdorovna had chosen would cost two hundred rubles. She stopped weeping and, looking at Peter Ivanovich with the air of a victim, remarked in French that it was very hard for her.

Peter Ivanovich made a silent gesture signifying his full conviction that it must indeed be so.

"Please smoke," she said in a magnanimous yet crushed voice, and turned to discuss with Sokolov the price of the plot for the grave.

Peter Ivanovich while lighting his cigarette heard her inquiring very circumstantially into the prices of different plots in the cemetery and finally decide which she would take. When that was done she gave instructions about engaging the choir. Sokolov then left the room.

"I look after everything myself," she told Peter Ivanovich, shifting the albums that lay on the table; and noticing that the table was endangered by his cigarette-ash, she immediately passed him an ash-tray, saying as she did so: "I consider it an affectation to say that my grief prevents my attending to practical affairs. On the contrary, if anything can—I won't say console me, but—distract me, it is seeing to everything concerning him." She again took out her handkerchief as if preparing to cry, but suddenly, as if mastering her feeling, she shook herself and began to speak calmly. "But there is something I want to talk to you about."

Peter Ivanovich bowed, keeping control of the springs of the pouffe, which immediately began quivering under him.

"He suffered terribly the last few days."

"Did he?" said Peter Ivanovich.

"Oh, terribly! He screamed unceasingly, not for minutes but for hours. For the last three days he screamed incessantly. It was unendurable. I cannot understand how I bore it; you could hear him three rooms off. Oh, what I have suffered!"

"Is it possible that he was conscious all that time?" asked Peter Ivanovich.

"Yes," she whispered. "To the last moment. He took leave of us a quarter of an hour before he died, and asked us to take Volodya away."

The thought of the sufferings of this man he had known so intimately, first as a merry little boy, then as a school-mate, and later as a grown-up colleague, suddenly struck Peter Ivanovich with horror, despite an unpleasant consciousness of his own and this woman's dissimulation. He again saw that brow, and that nose pressing down on the lip, and felt afraid for himself.

"Three days of frightful suffering and then death! Why, that might suddenly, at any time, happen to me," he thought, and for a moment felt terrified. But—he did not himself know how—the customary reflection at once occurred to him that this had happened to Ivan Ilych and not to him, and that it should not and could not happen to him, and that to think that it could would be yielding to depression which he ought not to do, as Schwartz's expression plainly showed. After which reflection Peter Ivanovich felt reassured, and began to ask with interest about the details of Ivan Ilych's death, as though death was an accident natural to Ivan Ilych but certainly not to himself.

After many details of the really dreadful physical sufferings Ivan Ilych had endured (which details he learnt only from the effect those sufferings had produced on Praskovya Fëdorovna's nerves) the widow apparently found it necessary to get to business.

"Oh, Peter Ivanovich, how hard it is! How terribly, terribly hard!" and she again began to weep.

Peter Ivanovich sighed and waited for her to finish blowing her nose. When she had done so he said, "Believe me . . ." and she again began talking and brought out what was evidently her chief concern with him — namely, to question him as to how she could obtain a grant of money from the government on the occasion of her husband's death. She made it appear that she was asking Peter Ivanovich's advice about her pension, but he soon saw that she already knew about that to the minutest detail, more even than he did himself. She knew how much could be got out of the government in consequence of her husband's death, but wanted to find out whether she could not possibly extract something more. Peter Ivanovich tried to think of some means of doing so, but after reflecting for a while and, out of propriety, condemning the government for its niggardliness, he said he thought that nothing more could be got. Then she sighed and evidently began to devise means of getting rid of her visitor. Noticing this, he put out his cigarette, rose, pressed her hand, and went out into the anteroom.

In the dining-room where the clock stood that Ivan Ilych had liked so much and had bought at an antique shop, Peter Ivanovich met a priest and a few acquaintances who had come to attend the service, and he recognized Ivan Ilych's daughter, a handsome young woman. She was in black and her slim figure appeared slimmer than ever. She had a gloomy, determined, almost angry expression, and bowed to Peter Ivanovich as though he were in some way to blame. Behind her, with the same offended look, stood a wealthy young man, an examining magistrate, whom Peter Ivanovich also knew and who was her fiancé, as he had heard. He bowed mournfully to them and was about to pass into the death-chamber, when from under the stairs appeared the figure of Ivan Ilych's schoolboy son, who was extremely like his father. He seemed a little Ivan Ilych, such as Peter Ivanovich remembered when they studied law together. His tear-stained eyes had in them the look that is seen in the eyes of boys of thirteen or fourteen who are not pure-minded. When he saw Peter Ivanovich he scowled morosely and shamefacedly. Peter Ivanovich nodded to him and entered the death-chamber. The service began: candles, groans, incense, tears, and sobs. Peter Ivanovich stood looking gloomily down at his feet. He did not look once at the dead man, did not yield to any depressing influence, and was one of the first to leave the room. There was no one in the anteroom, but Gerasim darted out of the dead man's room, rummaged with his strong hands among the fur coats to find Peter Ivanovich's and helped him on with it.

"Well, friend Gerasim," said Peter Ivanovich, so as to say something. "It's a sad affair, isn't it?"

"It's God's will. We shall all come to it some day," said Gerasim, displaying his teeth — the even, white teeth of a healthy peasant — and, like a man in the thick of urgent work, he briskly opened the front door, called the coachman, helped Peter Ivanovich into the sledge, and sprang back to the porch as if in readiness for what he had to do next.

Peter Ivanovich found the fresh air particularly pleasant after the smell of incense, the dead body, and carbolic acid.

"Where to, sir?" asked the coachman.

"It's not too late even now. . . . I'll call round on Fëdor Vasilievich."

He accordingly drove there and found them just finishing the first rubber, so that it was quite convenient for him to cut in.

II

Ivan Ilych's life had been most simple and most ordinary and therefore most terrible.

He had been a member of the Court of Justice, and died at the age of forty-five. His father had been an official who after serving in various ministries and departments in Petersburg had made the sort of career which brings men to positions from which by reason of their long service they cannot be dismissed, though they are obviously unfit to hold any responsible position, and for whom therefore posts are specially created, which though fictitious carry salaries of from six to ten thousand rubles that are not fictitious, and in receipt of which they live on to a great age.

Such was the Privy Councillor and superfluous member of various superfluous institutions, Ilya Epimovich Golovin.

He had three sons, of whom Ivan Ilych was the second. The eldest son was following in his father's footsteps only in another department, and was already approaching that stage in the service at which a similar sinecure would be reached. The third son was a failure. He had ruined his prospects in a number of positions and was now serving in the railway department. His father and brothers, and still more their wives, not merely disliked meeting him, but avoided remembering his existence unless compelled to do so. His sister had married Baron Greff, a Petersburg official of her father's type. Ivan Ilych was *le phénix de la famille*[3] as people said. He was neither as cold and formal as his elder brother nor as wild as the younger, but was a happy mean between them—an intelligent, polished, lively, and agreeable man. He had studied with his younger brother at the School of Law, but the latter had failed to complete the course and was expelled when he was in the fifth class. Ivan Ilych finished the course well. Even when he was at the School of Law he was just what he remained for the rest of his life: a capable, cheerful, good-natured, and sociable man, though strict in the fulfillment of what he considered to be his duty: and he considered his duty to be what was so considered by those in authority. Neither as a boy nor as a man was he a toady, but from early youth was by nature attracted to people of high station as a fly is drawn to the light, assimilating their ways and views of life and establishing friendly relations with them. All the enthusiasms of childhood and youth passed without leaving much trace on him; he succumbed to sensuality, to vanity, and latterly among the highest classes to liberalism, but always within limits which his instinct unfailingly indicated to him as correct.

At school he had done things which had formerly seemed to him very horrid and made him feel disgusted with himself when he did them; but when later on he

---

[3] *Le . . . famille:* French for "the phoenix of the family"; that is, a prodigy.

saw that such actions were done by people of good position and that they did not regard them as wrong, he was able not exactly to regard them as right, but to forget about them entirely or not be at all troubled at remembering them.

Having graduated from the School of Law and qualified for the tenth rank of the civil service, and having received money from his father for his equipment, Ivan Ilych ordered himself clothes at Scharmer's, the fashionable tailor, hung a medallion inscribed *respice finem*[4] on his watch-chain, took leave of his professor and the prince who was patron of the school, had a farewell dinner with his comrades at Donon's first-class restaurant, and with his new and fashionable portmanteau, linen, clothes, shaving and other toilet appliances, and a travelling rug, all purchased at the best shops, he set off for one of the provinces where, through his father's influence, he had been attached to the Governor as an official for special service.

In the province Ivan Ilych soon arranged as easy and agreeable a position for himself as he had had at the School of Law. He performed his official tasks, made his career, and at the same time amused himself pleasantly and decorously. Occasionally he paid official visits to country districts, where he behaved with dignity both to his superiors and inferiors, and performed the duties entrusted to him, which related chiefly to the sectarians,[5] with an exactness and incorruptible honesty of which he could not but feel proud.

In official matters, despite his youth and taste for frivolous gaiety, he was exceedingly reserved, punctilious, and even severe; but in society he was often amusing and witty, and always good-natured, correct in his manner, and *bon enfant*,[6] as the governor and his wife—with whom he was like one of the family—used to say of him.

In the province he had an affair with a lady who made advances to the elegant young lawyer, and there was also a milliner; and there were carousals with aides-de-camp who visited the district, and after-supper visits to a certain outlying street of doubtful reputation; and there was too some obsequiousness to his chief and even to his chief's wife, but all this was done with such a tone of good breeding that no hard names could be applied to it. It all came under the heading of the French saying: "*Il faut que jeunesse se passe.*"[7] It was all done with clean hands, in clean linen, with French phrases, and above all among people of the best society and consequently with the approval of people of rank.

So Ivan Ilych served for five years and then came a change in his official life. The new and reformed judicial institutions were introduced, and new men were needed. Ivan Ilych became such a new man. He was offered the post of examining magistrate, and he accepted it though the post was in another province and obliged him to give up the connexions he had formed and to make new ones. His friends met to give

---

[4] *respice finem*: Latin for "regard the end."

[5] sectarians: The Old Believers, a sect that broke away from the Russian Orthodox Church in the seventeenth century; members were subject to numerous legal restrictions.

[6] *bon enfant*: French for "good child."

[7] *"Il faut . . . passe"*: French for "Youth must have its way."

him a send-off; they had a group-photograph taken and presented him with a silver cigarette-case, and he set off to his new post.

As examining magistrate Ivan Ilych was just as *comme il faut*[8] and decorous a man, inspiring general respect and capable of separating his official duties from his private life, as he had been when acting as an official on special service. His duties now as examining magistrate were far more interesting and attractive than before. In his former position it had been pleasant to wear an undress uniform made by Scharmer, and to pass through the crowd of petitioners and officials who were timorously awaiting an audience with the governor, and who envied him as with free and easy gait he went straight into his chief's private room to have a cup of tea and a cigarette with him. But not many people had then been directly dependent on him—only police officials and the sectarians when he went on special missions—and he liked to treat them politely, almost as comrades, as if he were letting them feel that he who had the power to crush them was treating them in this simple, friendly way. There were then but few such people. But now, as an examining magistrate, Ivan Ilych felt that everyone without exception, even the most important and self-satisfied, was in his power, and that he need only write a few words on a sheet of paper with a certain heading, and this or that important, self-satisfied person would be brought before him in the role of an accused person or a witness, and if he did not choose to allow him to sit down, would have to stand before him and answer his questions. Ivan Ilych never abused his power; he tried on the contrary to soften its expression, but the consciousness of it and of the possibility of softening its effect, supplied the chief interest and attraction of his office. In his work itself, especially in his examinations, he very soon acquired a method of eliminating all considerations irrelevant to the legal aspect of the case, and reducing even the most complicated case to a form in which it would be presented on paper only in its externals, completely excluding his personal opinion of the matter, while above all observing every prescribed formality. The work was new and Ivan Ilych was one of the first men to apply the new Code of 1864.[9]

On taking up the post of examining magistrate in a new town, he made new acquaintances and connexions, placed himself on a new footing, and assumed a somewhat different tone. He took up an attitude of rather dignified aloofness towards the provincial authorities, but picked out the best circle of legal gentlemen and wealthy gentry living in the town and assumed a tone of slight dissatisfaction with the government, of moderate liberalism, and of enlightened citizenship. At the same time, without at all altering the elegance of his toilet, he ceased shaving his chin and allowed his beard to grow as it pleased.

Ivan Ilych settled down very pleasantly in this new town. The society there, which inclined towards opposition to the Governor, was friendly, his salary was larger, and he began to play *vint* [a form of bridge], which he found added not a little

---

[8] *comme il faut:* French for "as it should be."

[9] Code of 1864: After the emancipation of the serfs in 1861, the entire Russian legal system was reformed in 1864.

to the pleasure of life, for he had a capacity for cards, played good-humouredly, and calculated rapidly and astutely, so that he usually won.

After living there for two years he met his future wife, Praskovya Fëdorovna Mikhel, who was the most attractive, clever, and brilliant girl of the set in which he moved, and among other amusements and relaxations from his labours as examining magistrate, Ivan Ilych established light and playful relations with her.

While he had been an official on special service he had been accustomed to dance, but now as an examining magistrate it was exceptional for him to do so. If he danced now, he did it as if to show that though he served under the reformed order of things, and had reached the fifth official rank, yet when it came to dancing he could do it better than most people. So at the end of an evening he sometimes danced with Praskovya Fëdorovna, and it was chiefly during these dances that he captivated her. She fell in love with him. Ivan Ilych had at first no definite intention of marrying, but when the girl fell in love with him he said to himself: "Really, why shouldn't I marry?"

Praskovya Fëdorovna came of a good family, was not bad looking, and had some little property. Ivan Ilych might have aspired to a more brilliant match, but even this was good. He had his salary, and she, he hoped, would have an equal income. She was well connected, and was a sweet, pretty, and thoroughly correct young woman. To say that Ivan Ilych married because he fell in love with Praskovya Fëdorovna and found that she sympathized with his views of life would be as incorrect as to say that he married because his social circle approved of the match. He was swayed by both these considerations: the marriage gave him personal satisfaction, and at the same time it was considered the right thing by the most highly placed of his associates.

So Ivan Ilych got married.

The preparations for marriage and the beginning of married life, with its conjugal caresses, the new furniture, new crockery, and new linen, were very pleasant until his wife became pregnant—so that Ivan Ilych had begun to think that marriage would not impair the easy, agreeable, gay, and always decorous character of his life, approved of by society and regarded by himself as natural, but would even improve it. But from the first months of his wife's pregnancy, something new, unpleasant, depressing, and unseemly, and from which there was no way of escape, unexpectedly showed itself.

His wife, without any reason—*de gaieté de cœur*[10] as Ivan Ilych expressed it to himself—began to disturb the pleasure and propriety of their life. She began to be jealous without any cause, expected him to devote his whole attention to her, found fault with everything, and made coarse and ill-mannered scenes.

At first Ivan Ilych hoped to escape from the unpleasantness of this state of affairs by the same easy and decorous relation to life that had served him heretofore: he tried to ignore his wife's disagreeable moods, continued to live in his usual easy and pleasant way, invited friends to his house for a game of cards, and also tried going out to

---

[10] *de gaieté de coeur:* Literally, French for "out of gaiety of heart"; arbitrarily.

his club or spending his evenings with friends. But one day his wife began upbraiding him so vigorously, using such coarse words, and continued to abuse him every time he did not fulfill her demands, so resolutely and with such evident determination not to give way till he submitted—that is, till he stayed at home and was bored just as she was—that he became alarmed. He now realized that matrimony—at any rate with Praskovya Fëdorovna—was not always conducive to the pleasures and amenities of life, but on the contrary often infringed both comfort and propriety, and that he must therefore entrench himself against such infringement. And Ivan Ilych began to seek for means of doing so. His official duties were the one thing that imposed upon Praskovya Fëdorovna, and by means of his official work and the duties attached to it he began struggling with his wife to secure his own independence.

With the birth of their child, the attempts to feed it and the various failures in doing so, and with the real and imaginary illnesses of mother and child, in which Ivan Ilych's sympathy was demanded but about which he understood nothing, the need of securing for himself an existence outside his family life became still more imperative.

As his wife grew more irritable and exacting and Ivan Ilych transferred the centre of gravity of his life more and more to his official work, so did he grow to like his work better and became more ambitious than before.

Very soon, within a year of his wedding, Ivan Ilych had realized that marriage, though it may add some comforts to life, is in fact a very intricate and difficult affair towards which in order to perform one's duty, that is, to lead a decorous life approved of by society, one must adopt a definite attitude just as towards one's official duties.

And Ivan Ilych evolved such an attitude towards married life. He only required of it those conveniences—dinner at home, housewife, and bed—which it could give him, and above all that propriety of external forms required by public opinion. For the rest he looked for light-hearted pleasure and propriety, and was very thankful when he found them, but if he met with antagonism and querulousness he at once retired into his separate fenced-off world of official duties, where he found satisfaction.

Ivan Ilych was esteemed a good official, and after three years was made Assistant Public Prosecutor. His new duties, their importance, the possibility of indicting and imprisoning anyone he chose, the publicity his speeches received, and the success he had in all these things, made his work still more attractive.

More children came. His wife became more and more querulous and ill-tempered, but the attitude Ivan Ilych had adopted towards his home life rendered him almost impervious to her grumbling.

After seven years' service in that town he was transferred to another province as Public Prosecutor. They moved, but were short of money and his wife did not like the place they moved to. Though the salary was higher the cost of living was greater, besides which two of their children died and family life became still more unpleasant for him.

Praskovya Fëdorovna blamed her husband for every inconvenience they encountered in their new home. Most of the conversations between husband and wife, especially as to the children's education, led to topics which recalled former disputes, and those disputes were apt to flare up again at any moment. There remained only those rare periods of amorousness which still came to them at times but did not last long. These were islets at which they anchored for a while and then again set out upon that ocean of veiled hostility which showed itself in their aloofness from one another. This aloofness might have grieved Ivan Ilych had he considered that it ought not to exist, but he now regarded the position as normal, and even made it the goal at which he aimed in family life. His aim was to free himself more and more from those unpleasantnesses and to give them a semblance of harmlessness and propriety. He attained this by spending less and less time with his family, and when obliged to be at home he tried to safeguard his position by the presence of outsiders. The chief thing however was that he had his official duties. The whole interest of his life now centred in the official world and that interest absorbed him. The consciousness of his power, being able to ruin anybody he wished to ruin, the importance, even the external dignity of his entry into court, or meetings with his subordinates, his success with superiors and inferiors, and above all his masterly handling of cases, of which he was conscious—all this gave him pleasure and filled his life, together with chats with his colleagues, dinners, and bridge. So that on the whole Ivan Ilych's life continued to flow as he considered it should do—pleasantly and properly.

So things continued for another seven years. His eldest daughter was already sixteen, another child had died, and only one son was left, a schoolboy and a subject of dissension. Ivan Ilych wanted to put him in the School of Law, but to spite him Praskovya Fëdorovna entered him at the High School. The daughter had been educated at home and had turned out well: the boy did not learn badly either.

III

So Ivan Ilych lived for seventeen years after his marriage. He was already a Public Prosecutor of long standing, and had declined several proposed transfers while awaiting a more desirable post, when an unanticipated and unpleasant occurrence quite upset the peaceful course of his life. He was expecting to be offered the post of presiding judge in a University town, but Happe somehow came to the front and obtained the appointment instead. Ivan Ilych became irritable, reproached Happe, and quarrelled both with him and with his immediate superiors—who became colder to him and again passed him over when other appointments were made.

This was in 1880, the hardest year of Ivan Ilych's life. It was then that it became evident on the one hand that his salary was insufficient for them to live on, and on the other that he had been forgotten, and not only this, but that what was for him the greatest and most cruel injustice appeared to others a quite ordinary occurrence. Even his father did not consider it his duty to help him. Ivan Ilych felt himself abandoned by everyone, and that they regarded his position with a salary of 3,500 rubles as quite normal and even fortunate. He alone knew that with the consciousness of the injustices done him, with his wife's incessant nagging, and with the debts he had contracted by living beyond his means, his position was far from normal.

In order to save money that summer he obtained leave of absence and went with his wife to live in the country at her brother's place.

In the country, without his work, he experienced *ennui* for the first time in his life, and not only *ennui* but intolerable depression, and he decided that it was impossible to go on living like that, and that it was necessary to take energetic measures.

Having passed a sleepless night pacing up and down the veranda, he decided to go to Petersburg and bestir himself, in order to punish those who had failed to appreciate him and to get transferred to another ministry.

Next day, despite many protests from his wife and her brother, he started for Petersburg with the sole object of obtaining a post with a salary of five thousand rubles a year. He was no longer bent on any particular department, or tendency, or kind of activity. All he now wanted was an appointment to another post with a salary of five thousand rubles, either in the administration, in the banks, with the railways, in one of the Empress Marya's Institutions,[11] or even in the customs—but it had to carry with it a salary of five thousand rubles and be in a ministry other than that in which they had failed to appreciate him.

And this quest of Ivan Ilych's was crowned with remarkable and unexpected success. At Kursk an acquaintance of his, F. I. Ilyin, got into the first-class carriage, sat down beside Ivan Ilych, and told him of a telegram just received by the Governor of Kursk announcing that a change was about to take place in the ministry: Peter Ivanovich was to be superseded by Ivan Semënovich.

The proposed change, apart from its significance for Russia, had a special significance for Ivan Ilych, because by bringing forward a new man, Peter Petrovich, and consequently his friend Zachar Ivanovich, it was highly favourable for Ivan Ilych, since Zachar Ivanovich was a friend and colleague of his.

In Moscow this news was confirmed, and on reaching Petersburg Ivan Ilych found Zachar Ivanovich and received a definite promise of an appointment in his former department of Justice.

A week later he telegraphed to his wife: "Zachar in Miller's place. I shall receive appointment on presentation of report."

Thanks to this change of personnel, Ivan Ilych had unexpectedly obtained an appointment in his former ministry which placed him two stages above his former colleagues besides giving him five thousand rubles salary and three thousand five hundred rubles for expenses connected with his removal. All his ill humour towards his former enemies and the whole department vanished, and Ivan Ilych was completely happy.

He returned to the country more cheerful and contented than he had been for a long time. Praskovya Fëdorovna also cheered up and a truce was arranged between them. Ivan Ilych told of how he had been fêted by everybody in Petersburg, how all those who had been his enemies were put to shame and now fawned on him, how envious they were of his appointment, and how much everybody in Petersburg had liked him.

---

[11] **Empress Marya's Institutions:** Charitable institutions founded by the Empress Marya, wife of Paul I.

Praskovya Fëdorovna listened to all this and appeared to believe it. She did not contradict anything, but only made plans for their life in the town to which they were going. Ivan Ilych saw with delight that these plans were his plans, that he and his wife agreed, and that, after a stumble, his life was regaining its due and natural character of pleasant lightheartedness and decorum.

Ivan Ilych had come back for a short time only, for he had to take up his new duties on the 10th of September. Moreover, he needed time to settle into the new place, to move all his belongings from the province, and to buy and order many additional things: in a word, to make such arrangements as he had resolved on, which were almost exactly what Praskovya Fëdorovna too had decided on.

Now that everything had happened so fortunately, and that he and his wife were at one in their aims and moreover saw so little of one another, they got on together better than they had done since the first years of marriage. Ivan Ilych had thought of taking his family away with him at once, but the insistence of his wife's brother and her sister-in-law, who had suddenly become particularly amiable and friendly to him and his family, induced him to depart alone.

So he departed, and the cheerful state of mind induced by his success and by the harmony between his wife and himself, the one intensifying the other, did not leave him. He found a delightful house, just the thing both he and his wife had dreamt of. Spacious, lofty reception rooms in the old style, a convenient and dignified study, rooms for his wife and daughter, a study for his son — it might have been specially built for them. Ivan Ilych himself superintended the arrangements, chose the wall-papers, supplemented the furniture (preferably with antiques which he considered particularly *comme il faut*), and supervised the upholstering. Everything progressed and progressed and approached the ideal he had set himself: even when things were only half completed they exceeded his expectations. He saw what a refined and elegant character, free from vulgarity, it would all have when it was ready. On falling asleep he pictured to himself how the reception-room would look. Looking at the yet unfinished drawing-room he could see the fireplace, the screen, the what-not, the little chairs dotted here and there, the dishes and plates on the walls, and the bronzes, as they would be when everything was in place. He was pleased by the thought of how his wife and daughter, who shared his taste in this matter, would be impressed by it. They were certainly not expecting as much. He had been particularly successful in finding, and buying cheaply, antiques which gave a particularly aristocratic character to the whole place. But in his letters he intentionally understated everything in order to be able to surprise them. All this so absorbed him that his new duties — though he liked his official work — interested him less than he had expected. Sometimes he even had moments of absent-mindedness during the Court Sessions, and would consider whether he should have straight or curved cornices for his curtains. He was so interested in it all that he often did things himself, rearranging the furniture, or rehanging the curtains. Once when mounting a step-ladder to show the upholsterer, who did not understand, how he wanted the hangings draped, he made a false step and slipped, but being a strong and agile man he clung on and only knocked his side against the knob of the window frame. The bruised place was painful but the pain soon passed, and he felt particularly bright and well just then.

He wrote: "I feel fifteen years younger." He thought he would have everything ready by September, but it dragged on till mid-October. But the result was charming not only in his eyes but to everyone who saw it.

In reality it was just what is usually seen in the houses of people of moderate means who want to appear rich, and therefore succeed only in resembling others like themselves: there were damasks, dark wood, plants, rugs, and dull and polished bronzes—all the things people of a certain class have in order to resemble other people of that class. His house was so like the others that it would never have been noticed, but to him it all seemed to be quite exceptional. He was very happy when he met his family at the station and brought them to the newly furnished house all lit up, where a footman in a white tie opened the door into the hall decorated with plants, and when they went on into the drawing-room, and the study uttering exclamations of delight. He conducted them everywhere, drank in their praises eagerly, and beamed with pleasure. At tea that evening, when Praskovya Fëdorovna among other things asked him about his fall, he laughed and showed them how he had gone flying and had frightened the upholsterer.

"It's a good thing I'm a bit of an athlete. Another man might have been killed, but I merely knocked myself, just here; it hurts when it's touched, but it's passing off already—it's only a bruise."

So they began living in their new home—in which, as always happens, when they got thoroughly settled in they found they were just one room short—and with the increased income, which as always was just a little (some five hundred rubles) too little, but it was all very nice.

Things went particularly well at first, before everything was finally arranged and while something had still to be done: this thing bought, that thing ordered, another thing moved, and something else adjusted. Though there were some disputes between husband and wife, they were both so well satisfied and had so much to do that it all passed off without any serious quarrels. When nothing was left to arrange it became rather dull and something seemed to be lacking, but they were then making acquaintances, forming habits, and life was growing fuller.

Ivan Ilych spent his mornings at the law court and came home to dinner, and at first he was generally in a good humour, though he occasionally became irritable just on account of his house. (Every spot on the tablecloth or the upholstery, and every broken window-blind string, irritated him. He had devoted so much trouble to arranging it all that every disturbance of it distressed him.) But on the whole his life ran its course as he believed life should do: easily, pleasantly, and decorously.

He got up at nine, drank his coffee, read the paper, and then put on his undress uniform and went to the law courts. There the harness in which he worked had already been stretched to fit him and he donned it without a hitch: petitioners, inquiries at the chancery, the chancery itself, and the sittings public and administrative. In all this the thing was to exclude everything fresh and vital, which always disturbs the regular course of official business, and to admit only official relations with people, and then only on official grounds. A man would come, for instance, wanting some information. Ivan Ilych, as one in whose sphere the matter did not lie, would have nothing to do with him: but if the man had some business with him in his official capacity, something that could be expressed on officially stamped paper, he would do everything, positively everything he could within the limits of such relations, and in doing so would maintain the semblance of friendly human relations, that is, would observe the courtesies of life. As soon as the official relations ended, so did everything else. Ivan Ilych possessed this capacity to separate his real life from the official side of affairs and not mix the two, in the highest degree, and by long practice and natural aptitude had brought it to such a pitch that sometimes, in the manner of a virtuoso, he would even allow himself to let the human and official relations mingle. He let himself do this just because he felt that he could at any time he chose resume the strictly official attitude again and drop the human relation. And he did it all easily, pleasantly, correctly, and even artistically. In the intervals between the sessions he smoked, drank tea, chatted a little about politics, a little about general topics, a little about cards, but most of all about official appointments. Tired, but with the feelings of a virtuoso — one of the first violins who has played his part in an orchestra with precision — he would return home to find that his wife and daughter had been out paying calls, or had a visitor, and that his son had been to school, had done his homework with his tutor, and was duly learning what is taught at High Schools. Everything was as it should be. After dinner, if they had no visitors, Ivan Ilych sometimes read a book that was being much discussed at the time, and in the evening settled down to work, that is, read official papers, compared the depositions of witnesses, and noted paragraphs of the Code applying to them. This was neither dull nor amusing. It was dull when he might have been playing bridge, but if no bridge was available it was at any rate better than doing nothing or sitting with his wife. Ivan Ilych's chief pleasure was giving little dinners to which he invited men and women of good social position, and just as his drawing-room resembled all other drawing-rooms so did his enjoyable little parties resemble all other such parties.

Once they even gave a dance. Ivan Ilych enjoyed it and everything went off well, except that it led to a violent quarrel with his wife about the cakes and sweets. Praskovya Fëdorovna had made her own plans, but Ivan Ilych insisted on getting everything from an expensive confectioner and ordered too many cakes, and the quarrel occurred because some of those cakes were left over and the confectioner's bill came to forty-five rubles. It was a great and disagreeable quarrel. Praskovya Fëdorovna called him "a fool and an imbecile," and he clutched at his head and made angry allusions to divorce.

But the dance itself had been enjoyable. The best people were there, and Ivan Ilych had danced with Princess Trufonova, a sister of the distinguished founder of the Society "Bear my Burden."

The pleasures connected with his work were pleasures of ambition; his social pleasures were those of vanity; but Ivan Ilych's greatest pleasure was playing bridge. He acknowledged that whatever disagreeable incident happened in his life, the pleasure that beamed like a ray of light above everything else was to sit down to bridge with good players, not noisy partners, and of course to four-handed bridge (with five players it was annoying to have to stand out, though one pretended not to mind), to play a clever and serious game (when the cards allowed it) and then to have supper and drink a glass of wine. After a game of bridge, especially if he had won a little (to win a large sum was unpleasant), Ivan Ilych went to bed in specially good humour.

So they lived. They formed a circle of acquaintances among the best people and were visited by people of importance and by young folk. In their views as to their acquaintances, husband, wife, and daughter were entirely agreed, and tacitly and unanimously kept at arm's length and shook off the various shabby friends and relations who, with much show of affection, gushed into the drawing-room with its Japanese plates on the walls. Soon these shabby friends ceased to obtrude themselves and only the best people remained in the Golovins' set.

Young men made up to Lisa, and Petrishchev, an examining magistrate and Dmitri Ivanovich Petrishchev's son and sole heir, began to be so attentive to her that Ivan Ilych had already spoken to Praskovya Fëdorovna about it, and considered whether they should not arrange a party for them, or get up some private theatricals.

So they lived, and all went well, without change, and life flowed pleasantly.

IV

They were all in good health. It could not be called ill health if Ivan Ilych sometimes said that he had a queer taste in his mouth and felt some discomfort in his left side.

But this discomfort increased and, though not exactly painful, grew into a sense of pressure in his side accompanied by ill humour. And his irritability became worse and worse and began to mar the agreeable, easy, and correct life that had established itself in the Golovin family. Quarrels between husband and wife became more and more frequent, and soon the ease and amenity disappeared and even the decorum was barely maintained. Scenes again became frequent, and very few of those islets remained on which husband and wife could meet without an explosion. Praskovya Fëdorovna now had good reason to say that her husband's temper was trying. With characteristic exaggeration she said he had always had a dreadful temper, and that it had needed all her good nature to put up with it for twenty years. It was true that now the quarrels were started by him. His bursts of temper always came just before dinner, often just as he began to eat his soup. Sometimes he noticed that a plate or dish was chipped, or the food was not right, or his son put his elbow on the table, or his daughter's hair was not done as he liked it, and for all this he blamed Praskovya Fëdorovna. At first she retorted and said disagreeable things to him, but once or twice he fell into such a rage at the beginning of dinner that she realized it was due to some physical derangement brought on by taking food, and so she restrained herself and did not answer, but only hurried to get the dinner over. She regarded this self-restraint as highly praiseworthy. Having come to the conclusion that her husband had a dreadful temper and made her life miserable, she began to feel sorry for herself, and the more she pitied herself the more she hated her husband. She began to wish he would die; yet she did not want him to die because then his salary would cease. And this irritated her against him still more. She considered herself dreadfully unhappy just because not even his death could save her, and though she concealed her exasperation, that hidden exasperation of hers increased his irritation also.

After one scene in which Ivan Ilych had been particularly unfair and after which he had said in explanation that he certainly was irritable but that it was due to his not being well, she said that if he was ill it should be attended to, and insisted on his going to see a celebrated doctor.

He went. Everything took place as he had expected and as it always does. There was the usual waiting and the important air assumed by the doctor, with which he was so familiar (resembling that which he himself assumed in court), and the sounding and listening, and the questions which called for answers that were foregone conclusions and were evidently unnecessary, and the look of importance which implied that "if only you put yourself in our hands we will arrange everything—we know indubitably how it has to be done, always in the same way for everybody alike." It was all just as it was in the law courts. The doctor put on just the same air towards him as he himself put on towards an accused person.

The doctor said that so-and-so indicated that there was so-and-so inside the patient, but if the investigation of so-and-so did not confirm this, then he must assume that and that. If he assumed that and that, then . . . and so on. To Ivan Ilych only one question was important: was his case serious or not? But the doctor ignored that inappropriate question. From his point of view it was not the one under consideration; the real question was to decide between a floating kidney, chronic catarrh, or appendicitis. It was not a question of Ivan Ilych's life or death, but one between a floating kidney and appendicitis. And that question the doctor solved brilliantly, as it seemed to Ivan Ilych, in favour of the appendix, with the reservation that should an examination of the urine give fresh indications the matter would be reconsidered. All this was just what Ivan Ilych had himself brilliantly accomplished a thousand times in dealing with men on trial. The doctor summed up just as brilliantly, looking over his spectacles triumphantly and even gaily at the accused. From the doctor's summing up Ivan Ilych concluded that things were bad, but that for the doctor, and perhaps for everybody else, it was a matter of indifference, though for him it was bad. And this conclusion struck him painfully, arousing in him a great feeling of pity for himself and of bitterness towards the doctor's indifference to a matter of such importance.

He said nothing of this, but rose, placed the doctor's fee on the table, and remarked with a sigh: "We sick people probably often put inappropriate questions. But tell me, in general, is this complaint dangerous, or not? . . ."

The doctor looked at him sternly over his spectacles with one eye, as if to say: "Prisoner, if you will not keep to the questions put to you, I shall be obliged to have you removed from the court."

"I have already told you what I consider necessary and proper. The analysis may show something more." And the doctor bowed.

Ivan Ilych went out slowly, seated himself disconsolately in his sledge, and drove home. All the way home he was going over what the doctor had said, trying to translate those complicated, obscure, scientific phrases into plain language and find in them an answer to the question: "Is my condition bad? Is it very bad? Or is there as yet nothing much wrong?" And it seemed to him that the meaning of what the doctor had said was that it was very bad. Everything in the streets seemed depressing.

The cabmen, the houses, the passers-by, and the shops, were dismal. His ache, this dull gnawing ache that never ceased for a moment, seemed to have acquired a new and more serious significance from the doctor's dubious remarks. Ivan Ilych now watched it with a new and oppressive feeling.

He reached home and began to tell his wife about it. She listened, but in the middle of his account his daughter came in with her hat on, ready to go out with her mother. She sat down reluctantly to listen to this tedious story, but could not stand it long, and her mother too did not hear him to the end.

"Well, I am very glad," she said. "Mind now to take your medicine regularly. Give me the prescription and I'll send Gerasim to the chemist's." And she went to get ready to go out.

While she was in the room Ivan Ilych had hardly taken time to breathe, but he sighed deeply when she left it.

"Well," he thought, "perhaps it isn't so bad after all."

He began taking his medicine and following the doctor's directions, which had been altered after the examination of the urine. But then it happened that there was a contradiction between the indications drawn from the examination of the urine and the symptoms that showed themselves. It turned out that what was happening differed from what the doctor had told him, and that he had either forgotten, or blundered, or hidden something from him. He could not, however, be blamed for that, and Ivan Ilych still obeyed his orders implicitly and at first derived some comfort from doing so.

From the time of his visit to the doctor, Ivan Ilych's chief occupation was the exact fulfillment of the doctor's instructions regarding hygiene and the taking of medicine, and the observation of his pain and his excretions. His chief interests came to be people's ailments and people's health. When sickness, deaths, or recoveries were mentioned in his presence, especially when the illness resembled his own, he listened with agitation which he tried to hide, asked questions, and applied what he heard to his own case.

The pain did not grow less, but Ivan Ilych made efforts to force himself to think that he was better. And he could do this so long as nothing agitated him. But as soon as he had any unpleasantness with his wife, any lack of success in his official work, or held bad cards at bridge, he was at once acutely sensible of his disease. He had formerly borne such mischances, hoping soon to adjust what was wrong, to master it and attain success, or make a grand slam. But now every mischance upset him and plunged him into despair. He would say to himself: "There now, just as I was beginning to get better and the medicine had begun to take effect, comes this accursed misfortune, or unpleasantness. . . ." And he was furious with the mishap, or with the people who were causing the unpleasantness and killing him, for he felt that this fury was killing him but could not restrain it. One would have thought that it should have been clear to him that this exasperation with circumstances and people aggravated his illness, and that he ought therefore to ignore unpleasant occurrences. But he drew the very opposite conclusion: he said that he needed peace, and he watched for everything that might disturb it and became irritable at the slightest infringement of it. His condition was rendered worse by the fact that he read medical books and consulted doctors. The progress of his disease was so gradual that he could deceive himself when comparing one day with another—the difference was so slight. But when he consulted the doctors it seemed to him that he was getting worse, and even very rapidly. Yet despite this he was continually consulting them.

That month he went to see another celebrity, who told him almost the same as the first had done but put his questions rather differently, and the interview with this celebrity only increased Ivan Ilych's doubts and fears. A friend of a friend of his, a very good doctor, diagnosed his illness again quite differently from the others, and though he predicted recovery, his questions and suppositions bewildered Ivan Ilych still more and increased his doubts. A homeopathist diagnosed the disease in yet another way, and prescribed medicine which Ivan Ilych took secretly for a week. But after a week, not feeling any improvement and having lost confidence both in the former doctor's treatment and in this one's, he became still more despondent. One day a lady acquaintance mentioned a cure effected by a wonder-working icon. Ivan Ilych caught himself listening attentively and beginning to believe that it had occurred. This incident alarmed him. "Has my mind really weakened to such an extent?" he asked himself. "Nonsense! It's all rubbish. I mustn't give way to nervous fears but having chosen a doctor must keep strictly to his treatment. That is what I will do. Now it's all settled. I won't think about it, but will follow the treatment seriously till summer, and then we shall see. From now there must be no more of this wavering!" This was easy to say but impossible to carry out. The pain in his side oppressed him and seemed to grow worse and more incessant, while the taste in his mouth grew stranger and stranger. It seemed to him that his breath had a disgusting smell, and he was conscious of a loss of appetite and strength. There was no deceiving himself: something terrible, new, and more important than anything before in his life, was taking place within him of which he alone was aware. Those about him did not understand or would not understand it, but thought everything in the world was going on as usual. That tormented Ivan Ilych more than anything. He saw that his household, especially his wife and daughter who were in a perfect whirl of visiting, did not understand anything of it and were annoyed that he was so depressed and so exacting, as if he were to blame for it. Though they tried to disguise it he saw that he was an obstacle in their path, and that his wife had adopted a definite line in regard to his illness and kept to it regardless of anything he said or did. Her attitude was this: "You know," she would say to her friends, "Ivan Ilych can't do as other people do, and keep to the treatment prescribed for him. One day he'll take his drops and keep strictly to his diet and go to bed in good time, but the next day unless I watch him he'll suddenly forget his medicine, eat sturgeon—which is forbidden—and sit up playing cards till one o'clock in the morning."

"Oh, come, when was that?" Ivan Ilych would ask in vexation. "Only once at Peter Ivanovich's."

"And yesterday with Shebek."

"Well, even if I hadn't stayed up, this pain would have kept me awake."

"Be that as it may you'll never get well like that, but will always make us wretched."

Praskovya Fëdorovna's attitude to Ivan Ilych's illness, as she expressed it both to others and to him, was that it was his own fault and was another of the annoyances he caused her. Ivan Ilych felt that this opinion escaped her involuntarily—but that did not make it easier for him.

At the law courts too, Ivan Ilych noticed, or thought he noticed, a strange attitude towards himself. It sometimes seemed to him that people were watching him inquisitively as a man whose place might soon be vacant. Then again, his friends would suddenly begin to chaff him in a friendly way about his low spirits, as if the awful, horrible, and unheard-of thing that was going on within him, incessantly gnawing at him and irresistibly drawing him away, was a very agreeable subject for jests. Schwartz in particular irritated him by his jocularity, vivacity, and *savoir-faire,* which reminded him of what he himself had been ten years ago.

Friends came to make up a set and they sat down to cards. They dealt, bending the new cards to soften them, and he sorted the diamonds in his hand and found he had seven. His partner said "No trumps" and supported him with two diamonds. What more could be wished for? It ought to be jolly and lively. They would make a grand slam. But suddenly Ivan Ilych was conscious of that gnawing pain, that taste in his mouth, and it seemed ridiculous that in such circumstances he should be pleased to make a grand slam.

He looked at his partner Mikhail Mikhaylovich, who rapped the table with his strong hand and instead of snatching up the tricks pushed the cards courteously and indulgently towards Ivan Ilych that he might have the pleasure of gathering them up without the trouble of stretching out his hand for them. "Does he think I am too weak to stretch out my arm?" thought Ivan Ilych, and forgetting what he was doing he over-trumped his partner, missing the grand slam by three tricks. And what was most awful of all was that he saw how upset Mikhail Mikhaylovich was about it but did not himself care. And it was dreadful to realize why he did not care.

They all saw that he was suffering, and said: "We can stop if you are tired. Take a rest." Lie down? No, he was not at all tired, and he finished the rubber. All were gloomy and silent. Ivan Ilych felt that he had diffused this gloom over them and could not dispel it. They had supper and went away, and Ivan Ilych was left alone with the consciousness that his life was poisoned and was poisoning the lives of others, and that this poison did not weaken but penetrated more and more deeply into his whole being.

With this consciousness, and with physical pain besides the terror, he must go to bed, often to lie awake the greater part of the night. Next morning he had to get up again, dress, go to the law courts, speak, and write; or if he did not go out, spend at home those twenty-four hours a day each of which was a torture. And he had to live thus all alone on the brink of an abyss, with no one who understood or pitied him.

V

So one month passed and then another. Just before the New Year his brother-in-law came to town and stayed at their house. Ivan Ilych was at the law courts and Praskovya Fëdorovna had gone shopping. When Ivan Ilych came home and entered his study he found his brother-in-law there—a healthy, florid man—unpacking his portmanteau himself. He raised his head on hearing Ivan Ilych's footsteps and

looked up at him for a moment without a word. That stare told Ivan Ilych everything. His brother-in-law opened his mouth to utter an exclamation of surprise but
checked himself, and that action confirmed it all.

"I have changed, eh?"

"Yes, there is a change."

And after that, try as he would to get his brother-in-law to return to the subject
of his looks, the latter would say nothing about it. Praskovya Fëdorovna came home
and her brother went out to her. Ivan Ilych locked the door and began to examine
himself in the glass, first full face, then in profile. He took up a portrait of himself
taken with his wife, and compared it with what he saw in the glass. The change in
him was immense. Then he bared his arms to the elbow, looked at them, drew the
sleeves down again, sat down on an ottoman, and grew blacker than night.

"No, no, this won't do!" he said to himself, and jumped up, went to the table,
took up some law papers and began to read them, but could not continue. He unlocked the door and went into the reception-room, The door leading to the drawing-
room was shut. He approached it on tiptoe and listened.

"No, you are exaggerating!" Praskovya Fëdorovna was saying.

"Exaggerating! Don't you see it? Why, he's a dead man! Look at his eyes—
there's no light in them. But what is it that is wrong with him?"

"No one knows. Nikolaevich [that was another doctor] said something, but I
don't know what. And Leshchetitsky [this was the celebrated specialist] said quite
the contrary . . ."

Ivan Ilych walked away, went to his own room, lay down, and began musing:
"The kidney, a floating kidney." He recalled all the doctors had told him of how it
detached itself and swayed about. And by an effort of imagination he tried to catch
that kidney and arrest it and support it. So little was needed for this, it seemed to
him. "No, I'll go to see Peter Ivanovich again." [That was the friend whose friend was
a doctor.] He rang, ordered the carriage, and got ready to go.

"Where are you going, Jean?"[12] asked his wife, with a specially sad and exceptionally kind look.

This exceptionally kind look irritated him. He looked morosely at her.

"I must go to see Peter Ivanovich."

He went to see Peter Ivanovich, and together they went to see his friend, the doctor. He was in, and Ivan Ilych had a long talk with him.

Reviewing the anatomical and physiological details of what in the doctor's opinion was going on inside him, he understood it all.

There was something, a small thing, in the vermiform appendix. It might all
come right. Only stimulate the energy of one organ and check the activity of
another, then absorption would take place and everything would come right. He got
home rather late for dinner, ate his dinner, and conversed cheerfully, but could not
for a long time bring himself to go back to work in his room. At last, however, he
went to his study and did what was necessary, but the consciousness that he had put

---

[12] **Jean:** French version of Ivan.

something aside—an important, intimate matter which he would revert to when his work was done—never left him. When he had finished his work he remembered that this intimate matter was the thought of his vermiform appendix. But he did not give himself up to it, and went to the drawing-room for tea. There were callers there, including the examining magistrate who was a desirable match for his daughter, and they were conversing, playing the piano, and singing. Ivan Ilych, as Praskovya Fëdorovna remarked, spent that evening more cheerfully than usual, but he never for a moment forgot that he had postponed the important matter of the appendix. At eleven o'clock he said good-night and went to his bedroom. Since his illness he had slept alone in a small room next to his study. He undressed and took up a novel by Zola,[13] but instead of reading it he fell into thought, and in his imagination that desired improvement in the vermiform appendix occurred. There was the absorption and evacuation and the re-establishment of normal activity. "Yes, that's it!" he said to himself. "One need only assist nature, that's all." He remembered his medicine, rose, took it, and lay down on his back watching for the beneficent action of the medicine and for it to lessen the pain. "I need only take it regularly and avoid all injurious influences. I am already feeling better, much better." He began touching his side: it was not painful to the touch. "There, I really don't feel it. It's much better already." He put out the light and turned on his side. . . . "The appendix is getting better, absorption is occurring." Suddenly he felt the old, familiar, dull, gnawing pain, stubborn and serious. There was the same familiar loathsome taste in his mouth. His heart sank and he felt dazed. "My God! My God!" he muttered. "Again, again! and it will never cease." And suddenly the matter presented itself in a quite different aspect. "Vermiform appendix! Kidney!" he said to himself. "It's not a question of appendix or kidney, but of life and . . . death. Yes, life was there and now it is going, going and I cannot stop it. Yes. Why deceive myself? Isn't it obvious to everyone but me that I'm dying, and that it's only a question of weeks, days . . . it may happen this moment. There was light and now there is darkness. I was here and now I'm going there! Where?" A chill came over him, his breathing ceased, and he felt only the throbbing of his heart.

"When I am not, what will there be? There will be nothing. Then where shall I be when I am no more? Can this be dying? No, I don't want to!" He jumped up and tried to light the candle, felt for it with trembling hands, dropped candle and candlestick on the floor, and fell back on his pillow.

"What's the use? It makes no difference," he said to himself, staring with wide-open eyes into the darkness. "Death. Yes, death. And none of them know or wish to know it, and they have no pity for me. Now they are playing." (He heard through the door the distant sound of a song and its accompaniment.) "It's all the same to them, but they will die too! Fools! I first, and they later, but it will be the same for them. And now they are merry . . . the beasts!"

Anger choked him and he was agonizingly, unbearably miserable. "It is impossible that all men have been doomed to suffer this awful horror!" He raised himself.

---

[13] **Zola:** Émile Zola (1840–1902), a French novelist criticized by Tolstoy for his crude, naturalistic writing.

"Something must be wrong. I must calm myself—must think it all over from the beginning." And he again began thinking. "Yes, the beginning of my illness: I knocked my side, but I was still quite well that day and the next. It hurt a little, then rather more. I saw the doctors, then followed despondency and anguish, more doctors, and I drew nearer to the abyss. My strength grew less and I kept coming nearer and nearer, and now I have wasted away and there is no light in my eyes. I think of the appendix—but this is death! I think of mending the appendix, and all the while here is death! Can it really be death?" Again terror seized him and he gasped for breath. He leant down and began feeling for the matches, pressing with his elbow on the stand beside the bed. It was in his way and hurt him, he grew furious with it, pressed on it still harder, and upset it. Breathless and in despair he fell on his back, expecting death to come immediately.

Meanwhile the visitors were leaving. Praskovya Fëdorovna was seeing them off. She heard something fall and came in.

"What has happened?"

"Nothing. I knocked it over accidentally."

She went out and returned with a candle. He lay there panting heavily, like a man who has run a thousand yards, and stared upwards at her with a fixed look.

"What is it, Jean?"

"No . . . o . . . thing. I upset it." ("Why speak of it? She won't understand," he thought.)

And in truth she did not understand. She picked up the stand, lit his candle, and hurried away to see another visitor off. When she came back he still lay on his back, looking upwards.

"What is it? Do you feel worse?"

"Yes."

She shook her head and sat down.

"Do you know, Jean, I think we must ask Leshchetitsky to come and see you here."

This meant calling in the famous specialist, regardless of expense. He smiled malignantly and said "No." She remained a little longer and then went up to him and kissed his forehead.

While she was kissing him he hated her from the bottom of his soul and with difficulty refrained from pushing her away.

"Good-night. Please God you'll sleep."

"Yes."

VI

Ivan Ilych saw that he was dying, and he was in continual despair.

In the depth of his heart he knew he was dying, but not only was he not accustomed to the thought, he simply did not and could not grasp it.

The syllogism he had learnt from Kiezewetter's Logic:[14] "Caius is a man, men are

---

[14] **Kiezewetter's Logic:** Karl Kiezewetter (1706–1819) wrote a popular textbook, *Outline of Logic* (1796).

mortal, therefore Caius is mortal," had always seemed to him correct as applied to Caius, but certainly not as applied to himself. That Caius—man in the abstract—was mortal, was perfectly correct, but he was not Caius, not an abstract man, but a creature quite, quite separate from all others. He had been little Vanya, with a mamma and a papa, with Mitya and Volodya, with the toys, a coachman and a nurse, afterwards with Katenka and with all the joys, griefs, and delights of childhood, boyhood, and youth. What did Caius know of the smell of that striped leather ball Vanya had been so fond of? Had Caius kissed his mother's hand like that, and did the silk of her dress rustle so for Caius? Had he rioted like that at school when the pastry was bad? Had Caius been in love like that? Could Caius preside at a session as he did? "Caius really was mortal, and it was right for him to die; but for me, little Vanya, Ivan Ilych, with all my thoughts and emotions, it's altogether a different matter. It cannot be that I ought to die. That would be too terrible."

Such was his feeling.

"If I had to die like Caius I should have known it was so. An inner voice would have told me so, but there was nothing of the sort in me and I and all my friends felt that our case was quite different from that of Caius. And now here it is!" he said to himself. "It can't be. It's impossible! But here it is. How is this? How is one to understand it?"

He could not understand it, and tried to drive this false, incorrect, morbid thought away and to replace it by other proper and healthy thoughts. But that thought, and not the thought only but the reality itself, seemed to come and confront him.

And to replace that thought he called up a succession of others, hoping to find in them some support. He tried to get back into the former current of thoughts that had once screened the thought of death from him. But strange to say, all that had formerly shut off, hidden, and destroyed, his consciousness of death, no longer had that effect. Ivan Ilych now spent most of his time in attempting to re-establish that old current. He would say to himself: "I will take up my duties again—after all I used to live by them." And banishing all doubts he would go to the law courts, enter into conversation with his colleagues, and sit carelessly as was his wont, scanning the crowd with a thoughtful look and leaning both his emaciated arms on the arms of his oak chair; bending over as usual to a colleague and drawing his papers nearer he would interchange whispers with him, and then suddenly raising his eyes and sitting erect would pronounce certain words and open the proceedings. But suddenly in the midst of those proceedings the pain in his side, regardless of the stage the proceedings had reached, would begin its own gnawing work. Ivan Ilych would turn his attention to it and try to drive the thought of it away, but without success. *It* would come and stand before him and look at him, and he would be petrified and the light would die out of his eyes, and he would again begin asking himself whether *It* alone was true. And his colleagues and subordinates would see with surprise and distress that he, the brilliant and subtle judge, was becoming confused and making mistakes. He would shake himself, try to pull himself together, manage somehow to bring the sitting to a close, and return home with the sorrowful consciousness that his judicial labours could not as formerly hide from him what he wanted them to hide, and could not deliver him from *It*. And what was worst of all was that *It* drew his attention to itself not in order to make him take some action but only that he should look at *It*, look it straight in the face: look at it and without doing anything, suffer inexpressibly.

And to save himself from this condition Ivan Ilych looked for consolations—new screens—and new screens were found and for a while seemed to save him, but then they immediately fell to pieces or rather became transparent, as if *It* penetrated them and nothing could veil *It*.

In these latter days he would go into the drawing-room he had arranged—that drawing-room where he had fallen and for the sake of which (how bitterly ridiculous it seemed) he had sacrificed his life—for he knew that his illness originated with that knock. He would enter and see that something had scratched the polished table. He would look for the cause of this and find that it was the bronze ornamentation of an album, that had got bent. He would take up the expensive album which he had lovingly arranged, and feel vexed with his daughter and her friends for their untidiness—for the album was torn here and there and some of the photographs turned upside down. He would put it carefully in order and bend the ornamentation back into position. Then it would occur to him to place all those things in another corner of the room, near the plants. He could call the footman, but his daughter or wife would come to help him. They would not agree, and his wife would contradict him, and he would dispute and grow angry. But that was all right, for then he did not think about *It*. *It* was invisible.

But then, when he was moving something himself, his wife would say: "Let the servants do it. You will hurt yourself again." And suddenly *It* would flash through the screen and he would see it. It was just a flash, and he hoped it would disappear, but he would involuntarily pay attention to his side. "It sits there as before, gnawing just the same!" And he could no longer forget *It,* but could distinctly see it looking at him from behind the flowers. "What is it all for?"

"It really is so! I lost my life over that curtain as I might have done when storming a fort. Is that possible? How terrible and how stupid. It can't be true! It can't, but it is."

He would go to his study, lie down, and again be alone with *It:* face to face with *It*. And nothing could be done with *It* except to look at it and shudder.

VII

How it happened it is impossible to say because it came about step by step, unnoticed, but in the third month of Ivan Ilych's illness, his wife, his daughter, his son, his acquaintances, the doctors, the servants, and above all he himself, were aware that the whole interest he had for other people was whether he would soon vacate his place, and at last release the living from the discomfort caused by his presence and be himself released from his sufferings.

He slept less and less. He was given opium and hypodermic injections of morphine, but this did not relieve him. The dull depression he experienced in a somnolent condition at first gave him a little relief, but only as something new; afterwards it became as distressing as the pain itself or even more so.

Special foods were prepared for him by the doctors' orders, but all those foods became increasingly distasteful and disgusting to him.

For his excretions also special arrangements had to be made, and this was a torment to him every time—a torment from the uncleanliness, the unseemliness, and the smell, and from knowing that another person had to take part in it.

But just through this most unpleasant matter, Ivan Ilych obtained comfort. Gerasim, the butler's young assistant, always came in to carry the things out. Gerasim was a clean, fresh peasant lad, grown stout on town food and always cheerful and bright. At first the sight of him, in his clean Russian peasant costume, engaged in that disgusting task embarrassed Ivan Ilych.

Once when he got up from the commode too weak to draw up his trousers, he dropped into a soft armchair and looked with horror at his bare, enfeebled thighs with the muscles so sharply marked on them.

Gerasim with a firm light tread, his heavy boots emitting a pleasant smell of tar and fresh winter air, came in wearing a clean Hessian apron, the sleeves of his print shirt tucked up over his strong bare young arms; and refraining from looking at his sick master out of consideration for his feelings, and restraining the joy of life that beamed from his face, he went up to the commode.

"Gerasim!" said Ivan Ilych in a weak voice.

Gerasim started, evidently afraid he might have committed some blunder, and with a rapid movement turned his fresh, kind, simple young face which just showed the first downy signs of a beard.

"Yes, sir?"

"That must be very unpleasant for you. You must forgive me. I am helpless."

"Oh, why, sir," and Gerasim's eyes beamed and he showed his glistening white teeth, "what's a little trouble? It's a case of illness with you, sir."

And his deft strong hands did their accustomed task, and he went out of the room stepping lightly. Five minutes later he as lightly returned.

Ivan Ilych was still sitting in the same position in the armchair.

"Gerasim," he said when the latter had replaced the freshly-washed utensil. "Please come here and help me." Gerasim went up to him. "Lift me up. It is hard for me to get up, and I have sent Dmitri away."

Gerasim went up to him, grasped his master with his strong arms deftly but gently, in the same way that he stepped—lifted him, supported him with one hand, and with the other drew up his trousers and would have set him down again, but Ivan Ilych asked to be led to the sofa. Gerasim, without an effort and without apparent pressure, led him, almost lifting him, to the sofa and placed him on it.

"Thank you. How easily and well you do it all!"

Gerasim smiled again and turned to leave the room. But Ivan Ilych felt his presence such a comfort that he did not want to let him go.

"One thing more, please move up that chair. No, the other one—under my feet. It is easier for me when my feet are raised."

Gerasim brought the chair, set it down gently in place, and raised Ivan Ilych's legs on to it. It seemed to Ivan Ilych that he felt better while Gerasim was holding up his legs.

"It's better when my legs are higher," he said. "Place that cushion under them."

Gerasim did so. He again lifted the legs and placed them, and again Ivan Ilych felt better while Gerasim held his legs. When he set them down Ivan Ilych fancied he felt worse.

"Gerasim," he said. "Are you busy now?"

"Not at all, sir," said Gerasim, who had learnt from the townsfolk how to speak to gentlefolk.

"What have you still to do?"

"What have I to do? I've done everything except chopping the logs for tomorrow."

"Then hold my legs up a bit higher, can you?"

"Of course I can. Why not?" And Gerasim raised his master's legs higher and Ivan Ilych thought that in that position he did not feel any pain at all.

"And how about the logs?"

"Don't trouble about that, sir. There's plenty of time."

Ivan Ilych told Gerasim to sit down and hold his legs, and began to talk to him. And strange to say it seemed to him that he felt better while Gerasim held his legs up.

After that Ivan Ilych would sometimes call Gerasim and get him to hold his legs on his shoulders, and he liked talking to him. Gerasim did it all easily, willingly, simply, and with a good nature that touched Ivan Ilych. Health, strength, and vitality in other people were offensive to him, but Gerasim's strength and vitality did not mortify but soothed him.

What tormented Ivan Ilych most was the deception, the lie, which for some reason they all accepted, that he was not dying but was simply ill, and that he only need keep quiet and undergo a treatment and then something very good would result. He however knew that do what they would nothing would come of it, only still more agonizing suffering and death. This deception tortured him — their not wishing to admit what they all knew and what he knew, but wanting to lie to him concerning his terrible condition, and wishing and forcing him to participate in that lie. Those lies — lies enacted over him on the eve of his death and destined to degrade this awful, solemn act to the level of their visitings, their curtains, their sturgeon for dinner — were a terrible agony for Ivan Ilych. And strangely enough, many times when they were going through their antics over him he had been within a hairbreadth of calling out to them: "Stop lying! You know and I know that I am dying. Then at least stop lying about it!" But he had never had the spirit to do it. The awful, terrible act of his dying was, he could see, reduced by those about him to the level of a casual, unpleasant, and almost indecorous incident (as if someone entered a drawing-room diffusing an unpleasant odour) and this was done by that very decorum which he had served all his life long. He saw that no one felt for him, because no one even wished to grasp his position. Only Gerasim recognized it and pitied him. And so Ivan Ilych felt at ease only with him. He felt comforted when Gerasim supported his legs (sometimes all night long) and refused to go to bed, saying: "Don't you worry, Ivan Ilych. I'll get sleep enough later on," or when he suddenly became familiar and exclaimed: "If you weren't sick it would be another matter, but as it is, why should I grudge a little trouble?" Gerasim alone did not lie; everything showed that he alone understood the facts of the case and did not consider it necessary to disguise them, but simply felt sorry for his emaciated and enfeebled master. Once when Ivan Ilych was sending him away he even said straight out: "We shall all of us die, so why should I grudge a little trouble?"—expressing the fact that he did not think his work burdensome, because he was doing it for a dying man and hoped someone would do the same for him when his time came.

Apart from this lying, or because of it, what most tormented Ivan Ilych was that no one pitied him as he wished to be pitied. At certain moments after prolonged suffering he wished most of all (though he would have been ashamed to confess it) for someone to pity him as a sick child is pitied. He longed to be petted and comforted. He knew he was an important functionary, that he had a beard turning grey, and that therefore what he longed for was impossible, but still he longed for it. And in Gerasim's attitude towards him there was something akin to what he wished for, and so that attitude comforted him. Ivan Ilych wanted to weep, wanted to be petted and cried over, and then his colleague Shebek would come, and instead of weeping and being petted, Ivan Ilych would assume a serious, severe, and profound air, and by force of habit would express his opinion on a decision of the Court of Cassation and would stubbornly insist on that view. This falsity around him and within him did more than anything else to poison his last days.

VIII

It was morning. He knew it was morning because Gerasim had gone, and Peter the footman had come and put out the candles, drawn back one of the curtains, and begun quietly to tidy up. Whether it was morning or evening, Friday or Sunday, made no difference, it was all just the same: the gnawing, unmitigated, agonizing pain, never ceasing for an instant, the consciousness of life inexorably waning but not yet extinguished, the approach of that ever dreaded and hateful Death which was the only reality, and always the same falsity. What were days, weeks, hours, in such a case?

"Will you have some tea, sir?"

"He wants things to be regular, and wishes the gentlefolk to drink tea in the morning," thought Ivan Ilych, and only said "No."

"Wouldn't you like to move onto the sofa, sir?"

"He wants to tidy up the room, and I'm in the way. I am uncleanliness and disorder," he thought, and said only:

"No, leave me alone."

The man went on bustling about. Ivan Ilych stretched out his hand. Peter came up, ready to help.

"What is it, sir?"

"My watch."

Peter took the watch which was close at hand and gave it to his master.

"Half-past eight. Are they up?"

"No, sir, except Vladimir Ivanich" (the son) "who has gone to school. Praskovya Fëdorovna ordered me to wake her if you asked for her. Shall I do so?"

"No, there's no need to." "Perhaps I'd better have some tea," he thought, and added aloud: "Yes, bring me some tea."

Peter went to the door, but Ivan Ilych dreaded being left alone. "How can I keep him here? Oh yes, my medicine." "Peter, give me my medicine." "Why not? Perhaps it may still do me some good." He took a spoonful and swallowed it. "No, it won't help. It's all tomfoolery, all deception," he decided as soon as he became aware of the familiar, sickly, hopeless taste. "No, I can't believe in it any longer. But the pain, why this pain? If it would only cease just for a moment!" And he moaned. Peter turned towards him. "It's all right. Go and fetch me some tea."

Peter went out. Left alone Ivan Ilych groaned not so much with pain, terrible though that was, as from mental anguish. Always and for ever the same, always these endless days and nights. If only it would come quicker! If only *what* would come quicker? Death, darkness? . . . No, no! Anything rather than death!

When Peter returned with the tea on a tray, Ivan Ilych stared at him for a time in perplexity, not realizing who and what he was. Peter was disconcerted by that look and his embarrassment brought Ivan Ilych to himself.

"Oh, tea! All right, put it down. Only help me to wash and put on a clean shirt."

And Ivan Ilych began to wash. With pauses for rest, he washed his hands and then his face, cleaned his teeth, brushed his hair, and looked in the glass. He was terrified by what he saw, especially by the limp way in which his hair clung to his pallid forehead.

While his shirt was being changed he knew that he would be still more frightened at the sight of his body, so he avoided looking at it. Finally he was ready. He drew on a dressing-gown, wrapped himself in a plaid, and sat down in the armchair to take his tea. For a moment he felt refreshed, but as soon as he began to drink the tea he was again aware of the same taste, and the pain also returned. He finished it with an effort, and then lay down stretching out his legs, and dismissed Peter.

Always the same. Now a spark of hope flashes up, then a sea of despair rages, and always pain; always pain, always despair, and always the same. When alone he had a dreadful and distressing desire to call someone, but he knew beforehand that with others present it would be still worse. "Another dose of morphine—to lose consciousness. I will tell him, the doctor, that he must think of something else. It's impossible, impossible, to go on like this."

An hour and another pass like that. But now there is a ring at the door bell. Perhaps it's the doctor? It is. He comes in fresh, hearty, plump, and cheerful, with that look on his face that seems to say: "There now, you're in a panic about something, but we'll arrange it all for you directly!" The doctor knows this expression is out of place here, but he has put it on once for all and can't take it off—like a man who has put on a frock-coat in the morning to pay a round of calls.

The doctor rubs his hands vigorously and reassuringly.

"Brr! How cold it is! There's such a sharp frost; just let me warm myself!" he says, as if it were only a matter of waiting till he was warm, and then he would put everything right.

"Well now, how are you?"

Ivan Ilych feels that the doctor would like to say: "Well, how are our affairs?" but that even he feels that this would not do, and says instead: "What sort of a night have you had?"

Ivan Ilych looks at him as much as to say: "Are you really never ashamed of lying?" But the doctor does not wish to understand this question, and Ivan Ilych says: "Just as terrible as ever. The pain never leaves me and never subsides. If only something . . ."

"Yes, you sick people are always like that. . . . There, now I think I am warm enough. Even Praskovya Fëdorovna, who is so particular, could find no fault with my temperature. Well, now I can say good-morning," and the doctor presses his patient's hand.

Then, dropping his former playfulness, he begins with a most serious face to examine the patient, feeling his pulse and taking his temperature, and then begins the sounding and auscultation.

Ivan Ilych knows quite well and definitely that all this is nonsense and pure deception, but when the doctor, getting down on his knee, leans over him, putting his ear first higher then lower, and performs various gymnastic movements over him with a significant expression on his face, Ivan Ilych submits to it all as he used to submit to the speeches of the lawyers, though he knew very well that they were all lying and why they were lying.

The doctor, kneeling on the sofa, is still sounding him when Praskovya Fëdorovna's silk dress rustles at the door and she is heard scolding Peter for not having let her know of the doctor's arrival.

She comes in, kisses her husband, and at once proceeds to prove that she has been up a long time already, and only owing to a misunderstanding failed to be there when the doctor arrived.

Ivan Ilych looks at her, scans her all over, sets against her the whiteness and plumpness and cleanness of her hands and neck, the gloss of her hair, and the sparkle of her vivacious eyes. He hates her with his whole soul. And the thrill of hatred he feels for her makes him suffer from her touch.

Her attitude towards him and his disease is still the same. Just as the doctor had adopted a certain relation to his patient which he could not abandon, so had she formed one towards him—that he was not doing something he ought to do and was himself to blame, and that she reproached him lovingly for this—and she could not now change that attitude.

"You see he doesn't listen to me and doesn't take his medicine at the proper time. And above all he lies in a position that is no doubt bad for him—with his legs up."

She described how he made Gerasim hold his legs up.

The doctor smiled with a contemptuous affability that said: "What's to be done? These sick people do have foolish fancies of that kind, but we must forgive them."

When the examination was over the doctor looked at his watch, and then Praskovya Fëdorovna announced to Ivan Ilych that it was of course as he pleased, but she had sent today for a celebrated specialist who would examine him and have a consultation with Michael Danilovich (their regular doctor).

"Please don't raise any objections. I am doing this for my own sake," she said ironically, letting it be felt that she was doing it all for his sake and only said this to leave him no right to refuse. He remained silent, knitting his brows. He felt that he was so surrounded and involved in a mesh of falsity that it was hard to unravel anything.

Everything she did for him was entirely for her own sake, and she told him she was doing for herself what she actually was doing for herself, as if that was so incredible that he must understand the opposite.

At half-past eleven the celebrated specialist arrived. Again the sounding began and the significant conversations in his presence and in another room, about the kidneys and the appendix, and the questions and answers, with such an air of importance that again, instead of the real question of life and death which now alone confronted him, the question arose of the kidney and appendix which were not behaving as they ought to and would now be attacked by Michael Danilovich and the specialist and forced to amend their ways.

The celebrated specialist took leave of him with a serious though not hopeless look, and in reply to the timid question Ivan Ilych, with eyes glistening with fear and hope, put to him as to whether there was a chance of recovery, said that he could not vouch for it but there was a possibility. The look of hope with which Ivan Ilych watched the doctor out was so pathetic that Praskovya Fëdorovna, seeing it, even wept as she left the room to hand the doctor his fee.

The gleam of hope kindled by the doctor's encouragement did not last long. The same room, the same pictures, curtains, wall-paper, medicine bottles, were all there, and the same aching suffering body, and Ivan Ilych began to moan. They gave him a subcutaneous injection and he sank into oblivion.

It was twilight when he came to. They brought him his dinner and he swallowed some beef tea with difficulty, and then everything was the same again and night was coming on.

After dinner, at seven o'clock, Praskovya Fëdorovna came into the room in evening dress, her full bosom pushed up by her corset, and with traces of powder on her face. She had reminded him in the morning that they were going to the theatre. Sarah Bernhardt[15] was visiting the town and they had a box, which he had insisted on their taking. Now he had forgotten about it and her toilet offended him, but he concealed his vexation when he remembered that he had himself insisted on their securing a box and going because it would be an instructive and aesthetic pleasure for the children.

Praskovya Fëdorovna came in, self-satisfied but yet with a rather guilty air. She sat down and asked how he was, but, as he saw, only for the sake of asking and not in order to learn about it, knowing that there was nothing to learn — and then went on to what she really wanted to say: that she would not on any account have gone but that the box had been taken and Helen and their daughter were going, as well as Petrishchev (the examining magistrate, their daughter's fiancé) and that it was out of the question to let them go alone; but that she would have much preferred to

---

[15] **Sarah Bernhardt:** (1844–1923) A popular French actress.

sit with him for a while; and he must be sure to follow the doctor's orders while she was away.

"Oh, and Fëdor Petrovich" (the fiancé) "would like to come in. May he? And Lisa?"

"All right."

Their daughter came in in full evening dress, her fresh young flesh exposed (making a show of that very flesh which in his own case caused so much suffering), strong, healthy, evidently in love, and impatient with illness, suffering, and death, because they interfered with her happiness.

Fëdor Petrovich came in too, in evening dress, his hair curled *à la Capoul,*[16] a tight stiff collar round his long sinewy neck, an enormous white shirt-front and narrow black trousers tightly stretched over his strong thighs. He had one white glove tightly drawn on, and was holding his opera hat in his hand.

Following him the schoolboy crept in unnoticed, in a new uniform, poor little fellow, and wearing gloves. Terribly dark shadows showed under his eyes, the meaning of which Ivan Ilych knew well.

His son had always seemed pathetic to him, and now it was dreadful to see the boy's frightened look of pity. It seemed to Ivan Ilych that Vasya was the only one besides Gerasim who understood and pitied him.

They all sat down and again asked how he was. A silence followed. Lisa asked her mother about the opera-glasses, and there was an altercation between mother and daughter as to who had taken them and where they had been put. This occasioned some unpleasantness.

Fëdor Petrovich inquired of Ivan Ilych whether he had ever seen Sarah Bernhardt. Ivan Ilych did not at first catch the question, but then replied: "No, have you seen her before?"

"Yes, in *Adrienne Lecouvreur.*"[17]

Praskovya Fëdorovna mentioned some rôles in which Sarah Bernhardt was particularly good. Her daughter disagreed. Conversation sprang up as to the elegance and realism of her acting—the sort of conversation that is always repeated and is always the same.

In the midst of the conversation Fëdor Petrovich glanced at Ivan Ilych and became silent. The others also looked at him and grew silent. Ivan Ilych was staring with glittering eyes straight before him, evidently indignant with them. This had to be rectified, but it was impossible to do so. The silence had to be broken, but for a time no one dared to break it and they all became afraid that the conventional deception would suddenly become obvious and the truth become plain to all. Lisa was the first to pluck up courage and break that silence, but by trying to hide what everybody was feeling, she betrayed it.

"Well, if we are going it's time to start," she said, looking at her watch, a present from her father, and with a faint and significant smile at Fëdor Petrovich relating to something known only to them. She got up with a rustle of her dress.

---

[16] *à la Capoul:* "according to Capoul," a French style of curling hair.

[17] *Adrienne Lecouvreur:* A play by Eugène Scribe (1791–1861), a commercial playwright disliked by Tolstoy.

They all rose, said good-night, and went away.

When they had gone it seemed to Ivan Ilych that he felt better; the falsity had gone with them. But the pain remained—that same pain and that same fear that made everything monotonously alike, nothing harder and nothing easier. Everything was worse.

Again minute followed minute and hour followed hour. Everything remained the same and there was no cessation. And the inevitable end of it all became more and more terrible.

"Yes, send Gerasim here," he replied to a question Peter asked.

IX

His wife returned late at night. She came in on tiptoe, but he heard her, opened his eyes, and made haste to close them again. She wished to send Gerasim away and to sit with him herself, but he opened his eyes and said: "No, go away."

"Are you in great pain?"

"Always the same."

"Take some opium."

He agreed and took some. She went away.

Till about three in the morning he was in a state of stupefied misery. It seemed to him that he and his pain were being thrust into a narrow, deep black sack, but though they were pushed further and further in they could not be pushed to the bottom. And this, terrible enough in itself, was accompanied by suffering. He was frightened yet wanted to fall though the sack, he struggled but yet co-operated. And suddenly he broke through, fell, and regained consciousness. Gerasim was sitting at the foot of the bed dozing quietly and patiently, while he himself lay with his emaciated stockinged legs resting on Gerasim's shoulders; the same shaded candle was there and the same unceasing pain.

"Go away, Gerasim," he whispered.

"It's all right, sir. I'll stay a while."

"No. Go away."

He removed his legs from Gerasim's shoulders, turned sideways onto his arm, and felt sorry for himself. He only waited till Gerasim had gone into the next room and then restrained himself no longer but wept like a child. He wept on account of his helplessness, his terrible loneliness, the cruelty of man, the cruelty of God, and the absence of God.

"Why hast Thou done all this? Why hast Thou brought me here? Why, why dost Thou torment me so terribly?"

He did not expect an answer and yet wept because there was no answer and could be none. The pain again grew more acute, but he did not stir and did not call. He said to himself: "Go on! Strike me! But what is it for? What have I done to Thee? What is it for?"

Then he grew quiet and not only ceased weeping but even held his breath and became all attention. It was as though he were listening not to an audible voice but to the voice of his soul, to the current of thoughts arising within him.

"What is it you want?" was the first clear conception capable of expression in words, that he heard.

"What do you want? What do you want?" he repeated to himself.

"What do I want? To live and not to suffer," he answered.

And again he listened with such concentrated attention that even his pain did not distract him.

"To live? How?" asked his inner voice.

"Why, to live as I used to—well and pleasantly."

"As you lived before, well and pleasantly?" the voice repeated.

And in imagination he began to recall the best moments of his pleasant life. But strange to say none of those best moments of his pleasant life now seemed at all what they had then seemed—none of them except the first recollections of childhood. There, in childhood, there had been something really pleasant with which it would be possible to live if it could return. But the child who had experienced that happiness existed no longer, it was like a reminiscence of somebody else.

As soon as the period began which had produced the present Ivan Ilych, all that had then seemed joys now melted before his sight and turned into something trivial and often nasty.

And the further he departed from childhood and the nearer he came to the present the more worthless and doubtful were the joys. This began with the School of Law. A little that was really good was still found there—there was light-heartedness, friendship, and hope. But in the upper classes there had already been fewer of such good moments. Then during the first years of his official career, when he was in the service of the Governor, some pleasant moments again occurred: They were the memories of love for a woman. Then all became confused and there was still less of what was good; later on again there was still less that was good, and the further he went the less there was. His marriage, a mere accident, then the disenchantment that followed it, his wife's bad breath and the sensuality and hypocrisy: then that deadly official life and those preoccupations about money, a year of it, and two, and ten, and twenty, and always the same thing. And the longer it lasted the more deadly it became. "It is as if I had been going downhill while I imagined I was going up. And that is really what it was. I was going up in public opinion, but to the same extent life was ebbing away from me. And now it is all done and there is only death."

"Then what does it mean? Why? It can't be that life is so senseless and horrible. But if it really has been so horrible and senseless, why must I die and die in agony? There is something wrong!"

"Maybe I did not live as I ought to have done," it suddenly occurred to him. "But how could that be, when I did everything properly?" he replied, and immediately dismissed from his mind this, the sole solution of all the riddles of life and death, as something quite impossible.

"Then what do you want now? To live? Live how? Live as you lived in the law courts when the usher proclaimed 'The judge is coming!' The judge is coming, the judge!" he repeated to himself. "Here he is, the judge. But I am not guilty!" he exclaimed angrily. "What is it for?" And he ceased crying, but turning his face to the wall continued to ponder on the same question: Why, and for what purpose, is there all this horror? But however much he pondered he found no answer. And whenever the thought occurred to him, as it often did, that it all resulted from his not having lived as he ought to have done, he at once recalled the correctness of his whole life and dismissed so strange an idea.

X

Another fortnight passed. Ivan Ilych now no longer left his sofa. He would not lie in bed but lay on the sofa, facing the wall nearly all the time. He suffered ever the same unceasing agonies and in his loneliness pondered always on the same insoluble question: "What is this? Can it be that it is Death?" and the inner voice answered: "Yes, it is Death."

"Why these sufferings?" And the voice answered, "For no reason—they just are so." Beyond and besides this there was nothing.

From the very beginning of his illness, ever since he had first been to see the doctor, Ivan Ilych's life had been divided between two contrary and alternating moods: now it was despair and the expectation of this uncomprehended and terrible death, and now hope and an intently interested observation of the functioning of his organs. Now before his eyes there was only a kidney or an intestine that temporarily evaded its duty, and now only that incomprehensible and dreadful death from which it was impossible to escape.

These two states of mind had alternated from the very beginning of his illness, but the further it progressed the more doubtful and fantastic became the conception of the kidney, and the more real the sense of impending death.

He had but to call to mind what he had been three months before and what he was now, to call to mind with what regularity he had been going downhill, for every possibility of hope to be shattered.

Latterly during that loneliness in which he found himself as he lay facing the back of the sofa, a loneliness in the midst of a populous town and surrounded by numerous acquaintances and relations but that yet could not have been more complete anywhere—either at the bottom of the sea or under the earth—during that terrible loneliness Ivan Ilych had lived only in memories of the past. Pictures of his past rose before him one after another. They always began with what was nearest in time and then went back to what was most remote—to his childhood—and rested there. If he thought of the stewed prunes that had been offered him that day, his mind went back to the raw shrivelled French plums of his childhood, their peculiar flavour and the flow of saliva when he sucked their stones, and along with the memory of that taste came a whole series of memories of those days: his nurse, his brother, and their toys. "No, I mustn't think of that.... It is too painful," Ivan Ilych said to himself, and brought himself back to the present—to the button on the back of the sofa and the creases in its morocco. "Morocco is expensive, but it does not wear well: there had been a quarrel about it. It was a different kind of quarrel and a different kind of morocco that time when we tore father's portfolio and were punished, and mamma brought us some tarts...." And again his thoughts dwelt on his childhood, and again it was painful and he tried to banish them and fix his mind on something else.

Then again together with that chain of memories another series passed through his mind—of how his illness had progressed and grown worse. There also the further back he looked the more life there had been. There had been more of what was good in life and more of life itself. The two merged together. "Just as the pain went on getting worse and worse, so my life grew worse and worse," he thought. "There is one bright spot there at the back, at the beginning of life, and afterwards all becomes blacker and blacker and proceeds more and more rapidly—in inverse ratio to the square of the distance from death," thought Ivan Ilych. And the example of a stone falling downwards with increasing velocity entered his mind. Life, a series of increasing sufferings, flies further and further towards its end—the most terrible suffering. "I am flying. . . ." He shuddered, shifted himself, and tried to resist, but was already aware that resistance was impossible, and again with eyes weary of gazing but unable to cease seeing what was before them, he stared at the back of the sofa and waited—awaiting that dreadful fall and shock and destruction.

"Resistance is impossible!" he said to himself. "If I could only understand what it is all for! But that too is impossible. An explanation would be possible if it could be said that I have not lived as I ought to. But it is impossible to say that," and he remembered all the legality, correctitude, and propriety of his life. "That at any rate can certainly not be admitted," he thought, and his lips smiled ironically as if someone could see that smile and be taken in by it. "There is no explanation! Agony, death . . . What for?"

XI

Another two weeks went by in this way and during that fortnight an event occurred that Ivan Ilych and his wife had desired. Petrishchev formally proposed. It happened in the evening. The next day Praskovya Fëdorovna came into her husband's room considering how best to inform him of it, but that very night there had been a fresh change for the worse in his condition. She found him still lying on the sofa but in a different position. He lay on his back, groaning and staring fixedly straight in front of him.

She began to remind him of his medicines, but he turned his eyes towards her with such a look that she did not finish what she was saying; so great an animosity, to her in particular, did that look express.

"For Christ's sake let me die in peace!" he said.

She would have gone away, but just then their daughter came in and went up to say good morning. He looked at her as he had done at his wife, and in reply to her inquiry about his health said dryly that he would soon free them all of himself. They were both silent and after sitting with him for a while went away.

"Is it our fault?" Lisa said to her mother. "It's as if we were to blame! I am sorry for papa, but why should we be tortured?"

The doctor came at his usual time. Ivan Ilych answered "Yes" and "No," never taking his angry eyes from him, and at last said: "You know you can do nothing for me, so leave me alone."

"We can ease your sufferings."

"You can't even do that. Let me be."

The doctor went into the drawing-room and told Praskovya Fëdorovna that the case was very serious and that the only resource left was opium to allay her husband's sufferings, which must be terrible.

It was true, as the doctor said, that Ivan Ilych's physical sufferings were terrible, but worse than the physical sufferings were his mental sufferings, which were his chief torture.

His mental sufferings were due to the fact that that night, as he looked at Gerasim's sleepy, good-natured face with its prominent cheek-bones, the question suddenly occurred to him: "What if my whole life has really been wrong?"

It occurred to him that what had appeared perfectly impossible before, namely that he had not spent his life as he should have done, might after all be true. It occurred to him that his scarcely perceptible attempts to struggle against what was considered good by the most highly placed people, those scarcely noticeable impulses which he had immediately suppressed, might have been the real thing, and all the rest false. And his professional duties and the whole arrangement of his life and of his family, and all his social and official interests, might all have been false. He tried to defend all those things to himself and suddenly felt the weakness of what he was defending. There was nothing to defend.

"But if that is so," he said to himself, "and I am leaving this life with the consciousness that I have lost all that was given me and it is impossible to rectify it—what then?"

He lay on his back and began to pass his life in review in quite a new way. In the morning when he saw first his footman, then his wife, then his daughter, and then the doctor, their every word and movement confirmed to him the awful truth that had been revealed to him during the night. In them he saw himself—all that for which he had lived—and saw clearly that it was not real at all, but a terrible and huge deception which had hidden both life and death. This consciousness intensified his physical suffering tenfold. He groaned and tossed about, and pulled at his clothing which choked and stifled him. And he hated them on that account.

He was given a large dose of opium and became unconscious, but at noon his sufferings began again. He drove everybody away and tossed from side to side.

His wife came to him and said:

"Jean, my dear, do this for me. It can't do any harm and often helps. Healthy people often do it."

He opened his eyes wide.

"What? Take communion? Why? It's unnecessary! However . . ."

She began to cry.

"Yes, do, my dear. I'll send for our priest. He is such a nice man."

"All right. Very well," he muttered.

When the priest came and heard his confession, Ivan Ilych was softened and seemed to feel a relief from his doubts and consequently from his sufferings, and for a moment there came a ray of hope. He again began to think of the vermiform appendix and the possibility of correcting it. He received the sacrament with tears in his eyes.

When they laid him down again afterwards he felt a moment's ease, and the hope that he might live awoke in him again. He began to think of the operation that had been suggested to him. "To live! I want to live!" he said to himself.

His wife came in to congratulate him after his communion, and when uttering the usual conventional words she added:

"You feel better, don't you?"

Without looking at her he said "Yes."

Her dress, her figure, the expression of her face, the tone of her voice, all revealed the same thing. "This is wrong, it is not as it should be. All you have lived for and still live for is falsehood and deception, hiding life and death from you." And as soon as he admitted that thought, his hatred and his agonizing physical suffering again sprang up, and with that suffering a consciousness of the unavoidable, approaching end. And to this was added a new sensation of grinding shooting pain and a feeling of suffocation.

The expression of his face when he uttered that "yes" was dreadful. Having uttered it, he looked her straight in the eyes, turned on his face with a rapidity extraordinary in his weak state and shouted:

"Go away! Go away and leave me alone!"

XII

From that moment the screaming began that continued for three days, and was so terrible that one could not hear it through two closed doors without horror. At the moment he answered his wife he realized that he was lost, that there was no return, that the end had come, the very end, and his doubts were still unsolved and remained doubts.

"Oh! Oh! Oh!" he cried in various intonations. He had begun by screaming "I won't!" and continued screaming on the letter *O*.

For three whole days, during which time did not exist for him, he struggled in that black sack into which he was being thrust by an invisible, resistless force. He struggled as a man condemned to death struggles in the hands of the executioner, knowing that he cannot save himself. And every moment he felt that despite all his efforts he was drawing nearer and nearer to what terrified him. He felt that his agony was due to his being thrust into that black hole and still more to his not being able to get right into it. He was hindered from getting into it by his conviction that his life had been a good one. That very justification of his life held him fast and prevented his moving forward, and it caused him most torment of all.

Suddenly some force struck him in the chest and side, making it still harder to breathe, and he fell through the hole and there at the bottom was a light. What had happened to him was like the sensation one sometimes experiences in a railway carriage when one thinks one is going backwards while one is really going forwards and suddenly becomes aware of the real direction.

"Yes, it was all not the right thing," he said to himself, "but that's no matter. It can be done. But what *is* the right thing?" he asked himself, and suddenly grew quiet.

This occurred at the end of the third day, two hours before his death. Just then his schoolboy son had crept softly in and gone up to the bedside. The dying man was still screaming desperately and waving his arms. His hand fell on the boy's head, and the boy caught it, pressed it to his lips, and began to cry.

At that very moment Ivan Ilych fell through and caught sight of the light, and it was revealed to him that though his life had not been what it should have been, this could still be rectified. He asked himself, "What *is* the right thing?" and grew still, listening. Then he felt that someone was kissing his hand. He opened his eyes, looked at his son, and felt sorry for him. His wife came up to him and he glanced at her. She was gazing at him open-mouthed, with undried tears on her nose and cheek and a despairing look on her face. He felt sorry for her too.

"Yes, I am making them wretched," he thought. "They are sorry, but it will be better for them when I die." He wished to say this but had not the strength to utter it. "Besides, why speak? I must act," he thought. With a look at his wife he indicated his son and said: "Take him away . . . sorry for him . . . sorry for you too. . . ." He tried to add, "forgive me," but said "forgo" and waved his hand, knowing that He whose understanding mattered would understand.

And suddenly it grew clear to him that what had been oppressing him and would not leave him was all dropping away at once from two sides, from ten sides, and from all sides. He was sorry for them, he must act so as not to hurt them: release them and free himself from these sufferings. "How good and how simple!" he thought. "And the pain?" he asked himself. "What has become of it? Where are you, pain?"

He turned his attention to it.

"Yes, here it is. Well, what of it? Let the pain be."

"And death . . . where is it?"

He sought his former accustomed fear of death and did not find it. "Where is it? What death?" There was no fear because there was no death.

In place of death there was light.

"So that's what it is!" he suddenly exclaimed aloud. "What joy!"

To him all this happened in a single instant, and the meaning of that instant did not change. For those present his agony continued for another two hours. Something rattled in his throat, his emaciated body twitched, then the gasping and rattle became less and less frequent.

"It is finished!" said someone near him.

He heard these words and repeated them in his soul.

"Death is finished," he said to himself. "It is no more!"

He drew in a breath, stopped in the midst of a sigh, stretched out, and died.

Society and
Its Discontents

In *The Death of Ivan Ilych* Tolstoy describes the life, career, and death
of a nineteenth-century everyman. Ivan Ilych, whose Russian name
resembles the American name "John Doe," is a judge and civil
servant who has devoted himself to professional advancement, social
climbing, and decorum. Ivan is obsessed with success and doing the
proper thing. This superficial value system brings him external
rewards, but it does not provide him with inner satisfaction. His
marriage is unhappy, he is subject to occasional bouts of depression,
and he is totally unprepared to deal with his own death. In stages
ranging from boredom to depression, anger, self-pity, despair, and
finally, acceptance, he becomes aware of the seriousness of his condition. Facing death alone, he realizes that the values that have guided
him have made his life an "awful loneliness" based on lies and "the
absence of God."

Many of Tolstoy's contemporaries agreed that their time was a
godless and superficial one. Artists and writers in particular found
themselves at odds with the middle-class culture around them,
which they considered diseased and vacuous. This section presents
nineteenth-century writers' perceptions of their era's malady and
their expressions of social alienation.

THE SOCIAL DISEASE

Ivan Ilych's ailment might be equated with the nineteenth century's
dis-ease. Signs of material progress were ubiquitous: trains that
quadrupled the speed of travel; factories that produced all manner
of goods and made them available to vast numbers of people;
growing cities that offered new economic, educational, and cultural

> An individual in the
> bourgeois state of
> development while
> honest, industrious,
> and virtuous, is also
> not unapt to be a
> miracle of timid
> and shortsighted
> selfishness.
>
> – THEODORE
> ROOSEVELT, *Century
> Magazine*, 1886

Hetton Colliery

By the middle of the nineteenth century, signs of material progress in the industrializing world were abundant. Among them were mines, underground sites where workers extracted every type of mineral from the earth. England had a great wealth of coal beneath its surface, and collieries—coal mines and processing plants—were established over much of northern Britain. Thick, black smoke and a generally dreary appearance marked mining towns as symbols of the grittier aspects of the Industrial Revolution. (The Art Archive)

opportunities; overseas possessions supplying the new European economy with raw materials and foreign markets. Nevertheless, this material progress was attended by a haunting sense of loss. Peasants boarded the railways en route to a new beginning in the industrialized cities, leaving behind deserted rural villages. The celebrations of rural life in the poems of the early **ROMANTICS** were often odes to a disappearing way of life. The urban novelists of midcentury, Dickens in England, for example, and **Honoré de Balzac**[1] in France, reminded readers of the lost rural life by its very absence in their work. The scientific worldview that drove the Industrial Revolution displaced long-established traditions and beliefs and seemed to confirm Nietzsche's proposition that God was dead. Tolstoy was just one of many writers who considered the century itself diseased. In "The Scholar Gypsy" (1853), Matthew Arnold[2] refers to the "strange disease of modern life," a spiritual condition physically visible in the smoky cities, rampant with crowding, poverty, and illness. Karl Marx argued in *Capital* (1867) that physical and psychological illnesses of the time were an inevitable result of the division of labor inherent in the capitalist factory system. Dickens generalized Marx's analysis in *Little Dorrit* (1855), ascribing the mysterious "complaint" of the financier Merdle to greed and to a social system that reduced all human relationships to monetary exchanges.

oh-noh-RAY de bahl-ZAHK

THE DOMINANCE OF THE BOURGEOISIE

The economic and social changes in Europe brought about by the Industrial and French Revolutions of the late eighteenth century established the urban middle class, or the **BOURGEOISIE**, as the economically and politically dominant group in society. These powerful merchants and factory owners had displaced the landed feudal aristocracy and created a new value system. Devoted to making money, enforcing rules of social decorum, and reordering society to guarantee its position and power, the bourgeoisie tended to measure everything materialistically. Individual success was counted in monetary terms, and social progress was monitored by the gross national product. The arts were also commercialized; with the end of the patronage system, in which writers and artists had been supported by wealthy arts enthusiasts, artists instead had to sell their work and

boor-zhwah-ZEE

---

[1] Dickens . . . Balzac: **Charles Dickens** (1812–1870), English novelist, author of *Great Expectations, David Copperfield,* and many other novels, mainly about life in London. **Honoré de Balzac** (1799–1850), French novelist who wrote about life in Paris, especially in his series of novels entitled *The Human Comedy.*

[2] Matthew Arnold: (1822–1888) English poet, critic, and essayist; "The Scholar Gypsy" laments a lost time "when wits were fresh and clear."

live off the profits. Sales figures became measures of artistic merit. Even religion was reduced to the bottom line. Calvinistic Protestantism, the predominant religion of the new middle class, equated material success with spiritual providence.

SATIRIZING THE BOURGEOISIE AND SYMPATHIZING WITH THE POOR

Most poets, novelists, and painters maintained an uneasy relationship with the middle-class audience that supported their work. **Charles Dickens,** the most successful English writer of the century, was often considered a spokesman for the domestic virtues celebrated by the bourgeoisie. Nevertheless, he satirized superficial materialism in the character of Mr. Podsnap in *Our Mutual Friend* (1865), and analyzed the spiritual vacuity of middle-class culture in many of his other novels. In nearly all of his works he also attacked the neglect and exploitation of the poor by the institutions of bourgeois society. Jo, the illiterate street cleaner from *Bleak House* (1851), for example, is less well cared for than the domestic pets of the well-to-do.

p. 670

Gustave Flaubert,[3] the son of a physician, who scrutinized provincial middle-class life in *Madame Bovary* (1856) and other works, wrote in a letter to George Sand:[4] "Hatred of the Bourgeois is the beginning of virtue. But for me the term 'bourgeois' includes the bourgeois in overalls as well as the bourgeois who wears a frock coat. It is we, and we alone — that is the educated — who are the People, or, more accurately, the tradition of Humanity." Nineteenth-century artists had a love-hate relationship with their society and their times.

DIAGNOSING THE ILLNESS

p. 670

In the sonnet, "The world is too much with us" (1802–04), **William Wordsworth** succinctly states the opinion of many of his peers: Materialism has stunted spiritual awareness and severed mankind's connection to the natural world. Thomas Carlyle,[5] a Scottish

Portrait of Karl Marx, April 1882, Algiers
This is the last known photograph of the political philosopher. (Corbis)

---

[3] Gustave Flaubert: (1821–1880) French Realist novelist who was both fascinated and disgusted with the bourgeoisie. See p. 435.

[4] George Sand: Pen name of Amandine-Aurore-Lucie Dupin (1804–1876), French feminist and Romantic novelist notorious for her free lifestyle and her liaisons with the composer Chopin, the poet Musset, and others.

[5] Thomas Carlyle: (1795–1881) Scottish essayist, historian, biographer, and novelist, whose analysis of the "condition of England" is most fully developed in *Chartism* (1840) and *Past and Present* (1843).

philosophical essayist, detailed this diagnosis of the era in his analysis of what he called the "condition of England." Carlyle traced the cause to a mechanistic social system that reduced all human relations to economics, a "cash nexus" that cut mankind off from deeper spiritual truths. Danish philosopher and theologian **Søren Kierkegaard** believed that people were indeed suffering from a disease—despair. In *The Sickness Unto Death* (1849), he argued that despair was not restricted to the few people who were aware of its presence but was a general condition afflicting most of humanity. To become aware of one's condition was a positive step, however, for it instigated a search that ultimately would lead the seeker to God.

p. 675
SORE-in
KEER-kuh-gard

CLASS STRUGGLE

While many writers were looking to the past for refuge, **Karl Marx** and **Friedrich Engels,** MATERIALISTS who saw history as an economically determined series of class struggles, looked to the future. Their own time, they proposed, was caught in a struggle between the bourgeoisie and the remnants of the old FEUDAL ARISTOCRACY, which the bourgeoisie had dislodged from power. But the factory owners were also in conflict with the rising industrial PROLETARIAT, the workers who sold their labor to the employers for an hourly wage and operated the machines. These workers would ultimately defeat their employers, Marx and Engels contended. Their classic treatise concerning these class struggles is entitled *The Communist Manifesto* (1848).

p. 680

Friedrich Engels, Photograph
Engels was a German Socialist and the coauthor of The Communist Manifesto. *(Underwood & Underwood/Corbis)*

THE SAMURAI AND THE BOURGEOISIE

In Japan, a rising bourgeoisie struggled with an entrenched feudalism for more than two centuries. The Tokugawa SHOGUNATE that ruled from the early seventeenth century until 1868 had isolated Japan from the West in an attempt to curtail the power of the growing class of merchants and traders. A thriving bourgeois culture developed in the cities nevertheless, especially in Kyoto and in the capitol, Edo (Tokyo). The bourgeois arts, notably KABUKI, popular theater, and the woodcuts known as UKIYO-E, "pictures of the floating world," challenged the conventional arts of Japan's feudal aristocracy, such as the Nō drama and classical painting. Unlike the puritanical European middle class, the Japanese bourgeoisie openly celebrated the attractions of the floating world, the name given to the pleasure quarters of cities. Importing Western culture and ideas, however,

OO-kee-yoh EH

[The bourgeois] prefers comfort to pleasure, convenience to liberty, and a pleasant temperature to that deathly inner consuming fire.
– Hermann Hesse, *Steppenwolf,* 1927

p. 204

remained forbidden; those guilty of advocating contact with the West were subject to imprisonment.

After Commodore Perry's trade mission forced the opening of Japan to the West in 1854, the shogunate, a form of military government, rapidly lost power. The Constitution of 1868 established a government grounded in civil rights and promoted contact with the rest of the world. Although the Japanese were especially anxious to study Western science and to develop their nation industrially, they wanted somehow to preserve their traditional cultural and ethical values. The ethics that many Japanese affirmed were those of Bushido, the "way of the samurai" in traditional Japanese feudalism. Inazo Nitobé's 1899 best-seller, *Bushido: The Soul of Japan,* described Japanese culture in terms of the virtues of the samurai for Western audiences. In the passage from this work included in this section, Nitobé compares the samurai concept of honor and the Western utilitarian concept of honesty.

■ **CONNECTIONS**

Chekhov, *The Cherry Orchard,* p. 708; Flaubert, "A Simple Heart," p. 435; Pardo Bazán, "The Revolver," p. 696; Gilman, *The Yellow Wallpaper,* p. 941. Disease appears in many nineteenth-century works: in the situation of the Gaev family in *The Cherry Orchard,* which Leonid Andreyevich compares to an illness; in Virginie's sickness and death in "A Simple Heart"; in the heart condition of the widow in Emila Pardo Bazán's "Revolver"; in the insanity of the protagonist of Gilman's *Yellow Wallpaper.* In what ways might each of these illnesses be considered an example of Kierkegaard's "sickness unto death"?

Ibsen, *Hedda Gabler,* p. 561; Petronius, *The Satyricon* (Book 1). Consider Dickens' "Podsnaps," representatives of the self-satisfied, materialistic, conventional bourgeoisie whose type reappears in many literary works of the nineteenth century. What characteristics of this type do each of the following characters exhibit: Tesman, in Ibsen's *Hedda Gabler;* Madame Aubain, in Flaubert's "Simple Heart"; and Lopakhin, in Chekhov's *Cherry Orchard?* Could Trimalchio in Petronius' *Satyricon* be described as a kind of "Podsnap"?

Tagore, "Broken Ties," p. 986; Mori Ōgai, "The Dancing Girl," p. 1088; *In the World: East and West,* p. 1034. In Tagore's "Broken Ties," the atheistic Jagamohan who taunts his pious brother Harimohan recalls rebellious Western writers such as Flaubert and Nietzsche, who shocked the sensibilities of the conservative European middle class. The difference between the two brothers, broadly representative of the division between the materialistic West and the spiritual East (see *In the World: East and West*), defines the conflict inside Satish that ultimately leads to his illness and death. Toyotaro, the Japanese student in Mori Ōgai's "Dancing Girl," is similarly conflicted. Although he finds liberation in the culture of nineteenth-century Germany, which frees him from the rigid expectations he faced in Japan, the internal battle between the Japanese and Western parts of his personality leads to illness and unhappiness.

■ **PRONUNCIATION**

ukiyo-e: OO-kee-yoh EH

WILLIAM WORDSWORTH
1770–1850

One of Wordsworth's best-known poems, "The world is too much with us," treats the poet's great theme, the relationship between humankind and nature. Here Wordsworth suggests that by adopting materialistic values human beings have turned their backs on the sanctity of nature and can no longer connect with its spiritual power.

LES BONS BOURGEOIS.

N° 16.

Un jeune homme qui est l'espoir et l'orgueil de la famille Badinguet.

Honoré Daumier,
The Young Man Who Is the Hope and Pride of the Badinguet Family, **"Les Bons Bourgeois,"**
c. 1835–40
This midcentury color lithograph shows a mildly discontented family whose pride and joy is the youngster, who is dressed up as a Napolean-type figure. *(Archives Charmet)*

◈ The world is too much with us

The world is too much with us; late and soon,
Getting and spending, we lay waste our powers:
Little we see in nature that is ours;
We have given our hearts away, a sordid boon!
The Sea that bares her bosom to the moon;
The Winds that will be howling at all hours
And are up-gathered now like sleeping flowers;
For this, for everything, we are out of tune;
It moves us not. Great God! I'd rather be
A Pagan suckled in a creed outworn;
So might I, standing on this pleasant lea,
Have glimpses that would make me less forlorn;
Have sight of Proteus[1] rising from the sea;
Or hear old Triton[2] blow his wreathed horn.

---

[1] **Proteus:** In Greek mythology, an old man of the sea who could change his shape at will.

[2] **Triton:** Greek god of the sea.

◈ CHARLES DICKENS
1812–1870

> He never could make out why everybody was not quite satisfied, and he felt conscious that he set a brilliant social example in being particularly well satisfied with most things, and, above all other things, with himself.
>
> – Charles Dickens, *Our Mutual Friend*

The most important English novelist of the nineteenth century, Charles Dickens was a close observer of his times who provided a panorama of English society during the middle years of the century in his work. Dickens was a tireless advocate for the poor. His portrait of Jo in *Bleak House* (1851), a crossing-sweeper—a child who swept street crossings to rid them of muck—presents the boy as illiterate, neglected, and exploited by those above him.

"Podsnappery" comes from Dickens' last completed novel, *Our Mutual Friend* (1865), which dissects and analyzes English society. Podsnap is the consummate bourgeois, an insurance agent whose self-satisfaction, xenophobia, and complacency model the attitudes of the ascendant middle class, characterized by Matthew Arnold in *Culture and Anarchy* as "Philistines."

Marcus Stone, *Podsnappery*, 1864

Dickens's Podsnap is a self-satisfied, xenophobic, and complacent middle-class citizen.
This engraving from Our Mutual Friend *depicts the society of bourgeois luminaries who*
who share Podsnap's view of the world. (Courtesy of the Trustees of the Boston Public
Library)

∾ Our Mutual Friend

CHAPTER XI

Podsnappery

Mr. Podsnap was well to do, and stood very high in Mr. Podsnap's opinion. Beginning with a good inheritance, he had married a good inheritance, and had thriven exceedingly in the Marine Insurance way, and was quite satisfied. He never could make out why everybody was not quite satisfied, and he felt conscious that he set a brilliant social example in being particularly well satisfied with most things, and, above all other things, with himself.

Thus happily acquainted with his own merit and importance, Mr. Podsnap settled that whatever he put behind him he put out of existence. There was a dignified conclusiveness—not to add a grand convenience—in this way of getting rid of disagreeables, which had done much towards establishing Mr. Podsnap in his lofty place in Mr. Podsnap's satisfaction. "I don't want to know about it; I don't choose to discuss it; I don't admit it!" Mr. Podsnap had even acquired a peculiar flourish of his right arm in often clearing the world of its most difficult problems, by sweeping them behind him (and consequently sheer away) with those words and a flushed face. For they affronted him.

Mr. Podsnap's world was not a very large world, morally; no, nor even geographically: seeing that although his business was sustained upon commerce with other countries, he considered other countries, with that important reservation, a mistake, and of their manners and customs would conclusively observe, "Not English!," when, PRESTO! with a flourish of the arm, and a flush of the face, they were swept away. Elsewise, the world got up at eight, shaved close at a quarter-past, breakfasted at nine, went to the City¹ at ten, came home at half-past five, and dined at seven. Mr. Podsnap's notions of the Arts in their integrity might have been stated thus. Literature; large print, respectively descriptive of getting up at eight, shaving close at a quarter-past, breakfasting at nine, going to the City at ten, coming home at half-past five, and dining at seven. Painting and Sculpture; models and portraits representing Professors of getting up at eight, shaving close at a quarter-past, breakfasting at nine, going to the City at ten, coming home at half-past five, and dining at seven. Music; a respectable performance (without variations) on stringed and wind instruments, sedately expressive of getting up at eight, shaving close at a quarter-past, breakfasting at nine, going to the City at ten, coming home at half-past five, and dining at seven. Nothing else to be permitted to those same vagrants the Arts, on pain of excommunication. Nothing else To Be — anywhere!

As a so eminently respectable man, Mr. Podsnap was sensible of its being required of him to take Providence under his protection. Consequently he always knew exactly what Providence meant. Inferior and less respectable men might fall short of that mark, but Mr. Podsnap was always up to it. And it was very remarkable (and must have been very comfortable) that what Providence meant, was invariably what Mr. Podsnap meant.

These may be said to have been the articles of a faith and school which the present chapter takes the liberty of calling, after its representative man, Podsnappery. They were confined within close bounds, as Mr. Podsnap's own head was confined by his shirt-collar; and they were enunciated with a sounding pomp that smacked of the creaking of Mr. Podsnap's own boots.

---

¹ the City: The business district in London.

❧ Bleak House

[JO, THE CROSSING-SWEEPER]

Jo sweeps his crossing all day long. . . . He sums up his mental condition, when asked a question, by replying that he "don't know nothink." He knows that it's hard to keep the mud off the crossing in dirty weather, and harder still to live by doing it. Nobody taught him, even that much; he found it out.

Jo lives — that is to say, Jo has not yet died — in a ruinous place, known to the like of him by the name of Tom-all-Alone's. It is a black, dilapidated street, avoided by all decent people; where the crazy houses were seized upon, when their decay was far advanced, by some bold vagrants, who, after establishing their own possession, took to letting them out in lodgings. Now, these tumbling tenements contain, by night, a swarm of misery. As on the ruined human wretch, vermin parasites appear, so, these ruined shelters have bred a crowd of foul existence that crawls in and out of gaps in walls and boards; and coils itself to sleep, in maggot numbers, where the rain drips in; and comes and goes, fetching and carrying fever, and sowing more evil in its every footprint than Lord Coodle and Sir Thomas Doodle, and the Duke of Foodle, and all the fine gentlemen in office, down to Zoodle,[1] shall set right in five hundred years—though born expressly to do it.

Twice, lately, there has been a crash and a cloud of dust, like the springing of a mine, in Tom-all-Alone's; and, each time, a house has fallen. These accidents have made a paragraph in the newspapers, and have filled a bed or two in the nearest hospital. The gaps remain, and there are not unpopular lodgings among the rubbish. As several more houses are nearly ready to go, the next crash in Tom-all-Alone's may be expected to be a good one.

This desirable property is in Chancery,[2] of course. It would be an insult to the discernment of any man with half an eye, to tell him so. Whether "Tom" is the popular representative of the original plaintiff or defendant in Jarndyce and Jarndyce;[3] or, whether Tom lived here when the suit had laid the street waste, all alone, until other settlers came to join him; or, whether the traditional title is a comprehensive name for a retreat cut off from honest company and put out of the pale of hope; perhaps nobody knows. Certainly, Jo don't know.

"For *I* don't," says Jo, "*I* don't know nothink."

It must be a strange state to be like Jo! To shuffle through the streets, unfamiliar with the shapes and in utter darkness as to the meaning, of those mysterious symbols, so abundant over the shops, and the corner of streets, and on the doors, and in the windows! To see people read, and to see people write, and to see the postman deliver letters, and not to have the least idea of all that language—to be, to every scrap of it, stone blind and dumb! It must be very puzzling to see the good company going to the churches on Sundays, with their books in their hands and to think (for perhaps Jo *does* think, at odd times) what does it all mean, and if it means anything to anybody, how comes it that it means nothing to me? To be hustled, and jostled, and moved on; and really to feel that it would appear to be perfectly true that I have no business here, or there, or anywhere; and yet to be perplexed by the consideration that I *am* here somehow, too, and everybody overlooked me until I became the creature that I am! It must be a strange state, not merely to be told that I am scarcely human (as in the case of my offering myself for a witness), but to feel it of my own knowledge all my life! To see the horses, dogs, and cattle, go by me, and to know that in ignorance I belong to them, and not to the superior beings in my shape, whose

---

[1] **Coodle . . . Zoodle:** Here Dickens is satirizing politicians, all of whom ignore the plight of the poor.

[2] **Chancery:** The court that handles estates and processes wills. Since Tom-all-Alone's is "in Chancery," no clear ownership has been legally established and the property has been neglected.

[3] **Jarndyce and Jarndyce:** A case in Chancery.

delicacy I offend! Jo's ideas of a Criminal Trial, or a Judge, or a Bishop, or a Government, or that inestimable jewel to him (if he only knew it) the Constitution, should be strange! His whole material and immaterial life is wonderfully strange; his death, the strangest thing of all.

Jo comes out of Tom-all-Alone's, meeting the tardy morning which is always late in getting down there, and munches his dirty bit of bread as he comes along. His way lying through many streets, and the houses not yet being open, he sits down to breakfast on the door-step of the Society for the Propagation of the Gospel in Foreign Parts, and gives it a brush when he has finished, as an acknowledgment of the accommodation. He admires the size of the edifice, and wonders what it's all about. He has no idea, poor wretch, of the spiritual destitution of a coral reef in the Pacific, or what it costs to look up the precious souls among the cocoa-nuts and bread-fruit.

He goes to his crossing, and begins to lay it out for the day. The town awakes; the great tee-totum[4] is set up for its daily spin and whirl; all that unaccountable reading and writing, which has been suspended for a few hours, recommences. Jo, and the other lower animals, get on in the unintelligible mess as they can. It is market-day. The blinded oxen, over-goaded, over-driven, never guided, run into wrong places and are beaten out; and plunge, red-eyed and foaming, at stone walls; and often sorely hurt the innocent, and often sorely hurt themselves. Very like Jo and his order; very, very like!

A band of music comes and plays. Jo listens to it. So does a dog—a drover's dog, waiting for his master outside a butcher's shop, and evidently thinking about those sheep he has had upon his mind for some hours, and is happily rid of. He seems perplexed respecting three or four; can't remember where he left them; looks up and down the street, as half expecting to see them astray; suddenly pricks up his ears and remembers all about it. A thoroughly vagabond dog, accustomed to low company and public-houses; a terrific dog to sheep; ready at a whistle to scamper over their backs, and tear out mouthfuls of their wool; but an educated, improved, developed dog, who has been taught his duties and knows how to discharge them. He and Jo listen to the music, probably with much the same amount of animal satisfaction; likewise, as to awakened association, aspiration or regret, melancholy or joyful reference to things beyond the senses, they are probably upon a par. But, otherwise, how far above the human listener is the brute!

Turn that dog's descendants wild, like Jo, and in a very few years they will so degenerate that they will lose even their bark—but not their bite.

The day changes as it wears itself away, and becomes dark and drizzly. Jo fights it out, at his crossing, among the mud and wheels, the horses, whips, and umbrellas, and gets but a scanty sum to pay for the unsavoury shelter of Tom-all-Alone's. Twilight comes on; gas begins to start up in the shops; the lamplighter, with his ladder, runs along the margin of the pavement. A wretched evening is beginning to close in.

---

[4] tee-totum: A spinning top with letters on it used in games.

SØREN KIERKEGAARD
1813–1855

The Danish writer and religious philosopher Søren Kierkegaard is usually regarded as the founder of EXISTENTIALISM. He wrote treatises attacking the validity of systematic philosophical argument, asserting that existence and truth are ultimately subjective. *The Sickness Unto Death* (1849), one of his later works, addresses the isolation that each person must confront in his or her spirit. The despair at the heart of the human condition is the spur, Kierkegaard says, that prompts the individual to take responsibility for choosing to leap to God.

Woodcut of Søren Kierkegaard
Kierkegaard's physical appearance matched his eccentric demeanor. Later in life he suffered from a severely hunched back and walked with a cane. (Bettman/Corbis)

FROM

The Sickness unto Death

Translated by Howard V. Hong and Edna H. Hong

THE UNIVERSALITY OF THIS SICKNESS (DESPAIR)

Just as a physician might say that there very likely is not one single living human being who is completely healthy, so anyone who really knows mankind might say that there is not one single living human being who does not despair a little, who does not secretly harbor an unrest, an inner strife, a disharmony, an anxiety about an unknown something or a something he does not even dare to try to know, an anxiety about some possibility in existence or an anxiety about himself, so that, just as the physician speaks of going around with an illness in the body, he walks around with a sickness, carries around a sickness of the spirit that signals its presence at rare intervals in and through an anxiety he cannot explain. In any case, no human being ever lived and no one lives outside of Christendom who has not despaired, and no one in Christendom if he is not a true Christian, and insofar as he is not wholly that, he still is to some extent in despair.

Edvard Munch, *The Scream*, 1893 *This painting is known worldwide for its stark rendering of what Kierkegaard labeled "despair." (Art Resource)*

No doubt this observation will strike many people as a paradox, an overstatement, and also a somber and depressing point of view. But it is none of these things. It is not somber, for, on the contrary, it tries to shed light on what generally is left somewhat obscure; it is not depressing but instead is elevating, inasmuch as it views every human being under the destiny of the highest claim upon him, to be spirit; nor is it a paradox but, on the contrary, a consistently developed basic view, and therefore neither is it an overstatement.

However, the customary view of despair does not go beyond appearances, and thus it is a superficial view, that is, no view at all. It assumes that every man must himself know best whether he is in despair or not. Anyone who says he is in despair is regarded as being in despair, and anyone who thinks he is not is therefore regarded as not. As a result, the phenomenon of despair is infrequent rather than quite common. That one is in despair is not a rarity; no, it is rare, very rare, that one is in truth not in despair.

The common view has a very poor understanding of despair. Among other things, it completely overlooks (to name only this, which, properly understood, places thousands and thousands and millions in the category of despair), it completely overlooks that not being in despair, not being conscious of being in despair, is precisely a form of despair. In a much deeper sense, the position of the common view in interpreting despair is like that of the common view in determining whether a person is sick—in a much deeper sense, for the common view understands far less well what spirit is (and lacking this understanding, one cannot understand despair, either) than it understands sickness and health. As a rule, a person is considered to be healthy when he himself does not say that he is sick, not to mention when he himself says that he is well. But the physician has a different view of sickness. Why? Because the physician has a defined and developed conception of what it is to be healthy and ascertains a man's condition accordingly. The physician knows that just as there is merely imaginary sickness there is also merely imaginary health, and in the latter case he first takes measures to disclose the sickness. Generally speaking, the physician, precisely because he is a physician (well informed), does not have complete confidence in what a person says about his condition. If everyone's statement about his condition, that he is healthy or sick, were completely reliable, to be a physician would be a delusion. A physician's task is not only to prescribe remedies but also, first and foremost, to identify the sickness, and consequently his first task is to ascertain whether the supposedly sick person is actually sick or whether the supposedly healthy person is perhaps actually sick. Such is also the relation of the physician of the soul to despair. He knows what despair is; he recognizes it and therefore is satisfied neither with a person's declaration that he is not in despair nor with his declaration that he is. It must be pointed out that in a certain sense it is not even always the case that those who say they despair are in despair. Despair can be affected, and as a qualification of the spirit it may also be mistaken for and confused with all sorts of transitory states, such as dejection, inner conflict, which pass without developing into despair. But the physician of the soul properly regards these also as forms of despair; he sees very well that they are affectation. Yet this very affectation is despair: he sees very well that this dejection etc. are not of great significance, but precisely this—that it has and acquires no great significance—is despair.

The common view also overlooks that despair is dialectically different from what is usually termed a sickness, because it is a sickness of the spirit. Properly understood, this dialectic again brings thousands under the definition of despair. If at a given time a physician has made sure that someone is well, and that person later becomes ill, then the physician may legitimately say that this person at one time was healthy but now is sick. Not so with despair. As soon as despair becomes apparent, it is manifest that the individual was in despair. Hence, at no moment is it possible to decide anything about a person who has not been saved by having been in despair, for whenever that which triggers his despair occurs, it is immediately apparent that he has been in despair his whole life. On the other hand, when someone gets a fever, it can by no means be said that it is now apparent that he has had a fever all his life. Despair is a qualification of the spirit, is related to the eternal, and thus has something of the eternal in its dialectic.

Despair is not only dialectically different from a sickness, but all its symptoms are also dialectical, and therefore the superficial view is very easily deceived in determining whether or not despair is present. Not to be in despair can in fact signify precisely to be in despair, and it can signify having been rescued from being in despair. A sense of security and tranquillity can signify being in despair; precisely this sense of security and tranquillity can be the despair, and yet it can signify having conquered despair and having won peace. Not being in despair is not similar to not being sick, for not being sick cannot be the same as being sick, whereas not being in despair can be the very same as being in despair. It is not with despair as with a sickness, where feeling indisposed is the sickness. By no means. Here again the indisposition is dialectical. Never to have sensed this indisposition is precisely to be in despair.

This means and has its basis in the fact that the condition of man, regarded as spirit (and if there is to be any question of despair, man must be regarded as defined by spirit), is always critical. We speak of a crisis in relation to sickness but not in relation to health. Why not? Because physical health is an immediate qualification that first becomes dialectical in the condition of sickness, in which the question of a crisis arises. Spiritually, or when man is regarded as spirit, both health and sickness are critical; there is no immediate health of the spirit.

As soon as man ceases to be regarded as defined by spirit (and in that case there can be no mention of despair, either) but only as psychical-physical synthesis, health is an immediate qualification, and mental or physical sickness is the only dialectical qualification. But to be unaware of being defined as spirit is precisely what despair is. Even that which, humanly speaking, is utterly beautiful and lovable—a womanly youthfulness that is perfect peace and harmony and joy—is nevertheless despair. To be sure, it is happiness, but happiness is not a qualification of spirit, and deep, deep within the most secret hiding place of happiness there dwells also anxiety, which is despair; it very much wishes to be allowed to remain there, because for despair the most cherished and desirable place to live is in the heart of happiness. Despite its illusory security and tranquillity, all immediacy is anxiety and thus, quite consistently, is most anxious about nothing. The most gruesome description of something most terrible does not make immediacy as anxious as a subtle, almost carelessly, and yet deliberately and calculatingly dropped allusion to some indefinite something—in fact, immediacy is made most anxious by a subtle implication that it knows very well what is being talked about. Immediacy probably does not know it, but reflection never snares so unfailingly as when it fashions its snare out of nothing, and reflection is never so much itself as when it is—nothing. It requires extraordinary reflection, or, more correctly, it requires great faith to be able to endure reflection upon nothing—that is, infinite reflection. Consequently, even that which is utterly beautiful and lovable, womanly youthfulness, is still despair, is happiness. For that reason, it is impossible to slip through life on this immediacy. And if this happiness does succeed in slipping through, well, it is of little use, for it is despair. Precisely because the sickness of despair is totally dialectical, it is the worst misfortune never to have had that sickness: it is a true godsend to get it, even if it is the most dangerous of illnesses, if one does not want to be cured of it. Generally it is regarded as fortunate to be cured of a sickness; the sickness itself is the misfortune.

Therefore, the common view that despair is a rarity is entirely wrong; on the contrary, it is universal. The common view, which assumes that everyone who does not think or feel he is in despair is not or that only he who says he is in despair is, is totally false. On the contrary, the person who without affectation says that he is in despair is still a little closer, is dialectically closer, to being cured than all those who are not regarded as such and who do not regard themselves as being in despair. The physician of souls will certainly agree with me that, on the whole, most men live without ever becoming conscious of being destined as spirit—hence all the so-called security, contentment with life, etc., which is simply despair. On the other hand, those who say they are in despair are usually either those who have so deep a nature that they are bound to become conscious as spirit or those whom bitter experiences and dreadful decisions have assisted in becoming conscious as spirit: it is either the one or the other; the person who is really devoid of despair is very rare indeed.

There is so much talk about human distress and wretchedness—I try to understand it and have also had some intimate acquaintance with it—there is so much talk about wasting a life, but only that person's life was wasted who went on living so deceived by life's joys or its sorrows that he never became decisively and eternally conscious as spirit, as self or, what amounts to the same thing, never became aware and in the deepest sense never gained the impression that there is a God and that "he," he himself, his self, exists before this God—an infinite benefaction that is never gained except through despair. What wretchedness that so many go on living this way, cheated of this most blessed of thoughts! What wretchedness that we are engrossed in or encourage the human throng to be engrossed in everything else, using them to supply the energy for the drama of life but never reminding them of this blessedness. What wretchedness that they are lumped together and deceived instead of being split apart so that each individual may gain the highest, the only thing worth living for and enough to live in for an eternity. I think that I could weep an eternity over the existence of such wretchedness! And to me an even more horrible expression of this most terrible sickness and misery is that it is hidden—not only that the person suffering from it may wish to hide it and may succeed, not only that it can so live in a man that no one, no one detects it, no, but also that it can be so hidden in a man that he himself is not aware of it! And when the hourglass has run out, the hourglass of temporality, when the noise of secular life has grown silent and its restless or ineffectual activism has come to an end, when everything around you is still, as it is in eternity, then—whether you were man or woman, rich or poor, dependent or independent, fortunate or unfortunate, whether you ranked with royalty and wore a glittering crown or in humble obscurity bore the toil and heat of the day, whether your name will be remembered as long as the world stands and consequently as long as it stood or you are nameless and run nameless in the innumerable multitude, whether the magnificence encompassing you surpassed all human description or the most severe and ignominious human judgment befell you—eternity asks you and every individual in these millions and millions about only one thing: whether you have lived in despair or not, whether you have despaired in such a way that you did not realize that you were in despair, or in such a way that you covertly carried this sickness inside of you as your gnawing secret, as a fruit of sinful love under your heart, or in such a way that you, a terror to others, raged in despair. And if so, if you have lived in despair, then, regardless of whatever else you won or lost, everything is lost for you, eternity does not acknowledge you, it never knew you—or, still more terrible, it knows you as you are known and it binds you to yourself in despair.

❧ KARL MARX
1818–1883

FRIEDRICH ENGELS
1820–1895

"The philosophers have only *interpreted* the world; the point is to *change* it." Karl Marx, a doctor of philosophy from the University of Berlin, spent his lifetime studying the causes of human oppression and designing a social system called communism that he believed would put an end to it.

Marx was born in Prussia in 1818. After receiving his doctorate in 1841, he became editor of *Rheinische Zeitung,* a radical newspaper in Cologne. He met Friedrich Engels there, and married Jenny von Westphalen; both remained Marx's lifelong companions. He collaborated with Engels on *The German Ideology* in 1845 and 1846 and on *The Communist Manifesto* in 1848. Over the next twenty years, supported in part by Engels, Marx wrote his great work, *Capital.* He published the first volume in 1867, and Engels published the remaining two in 1885 and 1894, after Marx's death.

The Communist Manifesto, commissioned by the Communist League in London in 1847, is noteworthy for its tone. Part I, included here, announces the arrival of the world revolutionary movement. It portrays humankind as divided throughout history into opposing social classes, that have been narrowed down to two in the modern era: the bourgeoisie (the owners of the means of production) and the proletariat (those who must sell their labor in order to survive). It explains the dynamic of the Industrial Revolution. And it claims that the bourgeois revolution has gone out of control, until "what the bourgeoisie . . . produces, above all, is its own grave-diggers."

Part II, not included here, responds to concerns that the communists would abolish not only private property but also the family, education, marriage, national boundaries, and other "eternal truths," such as morality and religion. One by one, Engels demonstrates that these seemingly universal phenomena have a bourgeois character. Then he lists the measures the proletariat will take to bring about social justice once it comes to power. These include the abolition of private property, a graduated income tax, the centralization of credit, and equality of labor. The English translation by Samuel Moore done in 1888 was edited by Engels and published in London.

FROM

◌ The Communist Manifesto

Translated by Samuel Moore

I. BOURGEOIS AND PROLETARIANS[1]

The history of all hitherto existing society is the history of class struggles.

Freeman and slave, patrician and plebeian, lord and serf, guild-master and jour-neyman, in a word, oppressor and oppressed, stood in constant opposition to one another, carried on an uninterrupted, now hidden, now open fight, a fight that each time ended, either in a revolutionary re-constitution of society at large, or in the common ruin of the contending classes.

In the earlier epochs of history, we find almost everywhere a complicated arrangement of society into various orders, a manifold gradation of social rank. In ancient Rome we have patricians, knights, plebeians, slaves; in the Middle Ages, feu-dal lords, vassals, guild-masters, journeymen, apprentices, serfs; in almost all of these classes, again, subordinate gradations.

The modern bourgeois society that has sprouted from the ruins of feudal soci-ety has not done away with class antagonisms. It has but established new classes, new conditions of oppression, new forms of struggle in place of the old ones.

Our epoch, the epoch of the bourgeoisie, possesses, however, this distinctive fea-ture: It has simplified the class antagonisms: Society as a whole is more and more splitting up into two great hostile camps, into two great classes directly facing each other: Bourgeoisie and Proletariat.

From the serfs of the Middle Ages sprang the chartered burghers of the earliest towns. From these burgesses the first elements of the bourgeoisie were developed.

The discovery of America, the rounding of the Cape, opened up fresh ground for the rising bourgeoisie. The East-Indian and Chinese markets, the colonisation of America, trade with the colonies, the increase in the means of exchange and in com-modities generally, gave to commerce, to navigation, to industry, an impulse never before known, and thereby, to the revolutionary element in the tottering feudal soci-ety, a rapid development.

The feudal system of industry, under which industrial production was monopo-lised by closed guilds, now no longer sufficed for the growing wants of the new mar-kets. The manufacturing system took its place. The guild-masters were pushed on one side by the manufacturing middle class; division of labour between the different corporate guilds vanished in the face of division of labour in each single workshop.

Meantime the markets kept ever growing, the demand ever rising. Even manufac-ture no longer sufficed. Thereupon, steam and machinery revolutionised industrial

---

[1] **Bourgeois . . . Proletarians:** "By bourgeoisie is meant the class of modern Capitalists, owners of the means of social production and employers of wage-labour. By proletariat, the class of modern wage-labourers who, having no means of production of their own, are reduced to selling their labour-power in order to live." [Engels, 1888]

production. The place of manufacture was taken by the giant, Modern Industry, the place of the industrial middle class, by industrial millionaires, the leaders of whole industrial armies, the modern bourgeois.

Modern industry has established the world-market, for which the discovery of America paved the way. This market has given an immense development to commerce, to navigation, to communication by land. This development has, in its turn, reacted on the extension of industry; and in proportion as industry, commerce, navigation, railways extended, in the same proportion the bourgeoisie developed, increased its capital, and pushed into the background every class handed down from the Middle Ages.

We see, therefore, how the modern bourgeoisie is itself the product of a long course of development, of a series of revolutions in the modes of production and of exchange.

Each step in the development of the bourgeoisie was accompanied by a corresponding political advance of that class. An oppressed class under the sway of the feudal nobility, an armed and self-governing association in the mediaeval commune; here independent urban republic (as in Italy and Germany), there taxable "third estate" of the monarchy (as in France), afterwards, in the period of manufacture proper, serving either the semi-feudal or the absolute monarchy as a counterpoise against the nobility, and, in fact, corner-stone of the great monarchies in general, the bourgeoisie has at last, since the establishment of Modern Industry and of the world-market, conquered for itself, in the modern representative State, exclusive political sway. The executive of the modern State is but a committee for managing the common affairs of the whole bourgeoisie.

The bourgeoisie, historically, has played a most revolutionary part.

The bourgeoisie, wherever it has got the upper hand, has put an end to all feudal, patriarchal, idyllic relations. It has pitilessly torn asunder the motley feudal ties that bound man to his "natural superiors," and has left remaining no other nexus between man and man than naked self-interest, than callous "cash payment." It has drowned the most heavenly ecstasies of religious fervour, of chivalrous enthusiasm, of philistine sentimentalism, in the icy water of egotistical calculation. It has resolved personal worth into exchange value, and in place of the numberless indefeasible chartered freedoms, has set up that single, unconscionable freedom — Free Trade. In one word, for exploitation, veiled by religious and political illusions, it has substituted naked, shameless, direct, brutal exploitation.

The bourgeoisie has stripped of its halo every occupation hitherto honoured and looked up to with reverent awe. It has converted the physician, the lawyer, the priest, the poet, the man of science, into its paid wage-labourers.

The bourgeoisie has torn away from the family its sentimental veil, and has reduced the family relation to a mere money relation.

The bourgeoisie has disclosed how it came to pass that the brutal display of vigour in the Middle Ages, which Reactionists so much admire, found its fitting complement in the most slothful indolence. It has been the first to show what man's activity can bring about. It has accomplished wonders far surpassing Egyptian pyramids, Roman aqueducts, and Gothic cathedrals; it has conducted expeditions that put in the shade all former Exoduses of nations and crusades.

The bourgeoisie cannot exist without constantly revolutionising the instruments of production, and thereby the relations of production, and with them the whole relations of society. Conservation of the old modes of production in unaltered form, was, on the contrary, the first condition of existence for all earlier industrial classes. Constant revolutionising of production, uninterrupted disturbance of all social conditions, everlasting uncertainty and agitation distinguish the bourgeois epoch from all earlier ones. All fixed, fast-frozen relations, with their train of ancient and venerable prejudices and opinions, are swept away, all new-formed ones become antiquated before they can ossify. All that is solid melts into air, all that is holy is profaned, and man is at last compelled to face with sober senses, his real conditions of life, and his relations with his kind.

The need of a constantly expanding market for its product chases the bourgeoisie over the whole surface of the globe. It must nestle everywhere, settle everywhere, establish connexions everywhere.

The bourgeoisie has through its exploitation of the world-market given a cosmopolitan character to production and consumption in every country. To the great chagrin of Reactionists, it has drawn from under the feet of industry the national ground on which it stood. All old-established national industries have been destroyed or are daily being destroyed. They are dislodged by new industries, whose introduction becomes a life and death question for all civilised nations, by industries that no longer work up indigenous raw material, but raw material drawn from the remotest zones; industries whose products are consumed, not only at home, but in every quarter of the globe. In place of the old wants, satisfied by the productions of the country, we find new wants, requiring for their satisfaction the products of distant lands and climes. In place of the old local and national seclusion and self-sufficiency, we have intercourse in every direction, universal inter-dependence of nations. And as in material, so also in intellectual production. The intellectual creations of individual nations become common property. National one-sidedness and narrow-mindedness become more and more impossible, and from the numerous national and local literatures, there arises a world literature.

The bourgeoisie, by the rapid improvement of all instruments of production, by the immensely facilitated means of communication, draws all, even the most barbarian, nations into civilisation. The cheap prices of its commodities are the heavy artillery with which it batters down all Chinese walls, with which it forces the barbarians' intensely obstinate hatred of foreigners to capitulate. It compels all nations, on pain of extinction, to adopt the bourgeois mode of production; it compels them to introduce what it calls civilisation into their midst, *i.e.,* to become bourgeois themselves. In one word, it creates a world after its own image.

The bourgeoisie has subjected the country to the rule of the towns. It has created enormous cities, has greatly increased the urban population as compared with the rural, and has thus rescued a considerable part of the population from the idiocy of rural life. Just as it has made the country dependent on the towns, so it has made barbarian and semi-barbarian countries dependent on the civilised ones, nations of peasants on nations of bourgeois, the East on the West.

The bourgeoisie keeps more and more doing away with the scattered state of the population, of the means of production, and of property. It has agglomerated population, centralised means of production, and has concentrated property in a few hands. The necessary consequence of this was political centralisation. Independent, or but loosely connected provinces, with separate interests, laws, governments and systems of taxation, became lumped together into one nation, with one government, one code of laws, one national class-interest, one frontier and one customs-tariff.

The bourgeoisie, during its rule of scarce one hundred years, has created more massive and more colossal productive forces than have all preceding generations together. Subjection of Nature's forces to man, machinery, application of chemistry to industry and agriculture, steam-navigation, railways, electric telegraphs, clearing of whole continents for cultivation, canalisation of rivers, whole populations conjured out of the ground—what earlier century had even a presentiment that such productive forces slumbered in the lap of social labour?

We see then: The means of production and of exchange, on whose foundation the bourgeoisie built itself up, were generated in feudal society. At a certain stage in the development of these means of production and of exchange, the conditions under which feudal society produced and exchanged, the feudal organisation of agriculture and manufacturing industry, in one word, the feudal relations of property became no longer compatible with the already developed productive forces; they became so many fetters. They had to be burst asunder; they were burst asunder.

Into their place stepped free competition, accompanied by a social and political constitution adapted to it, and by the economical and political sway of the bourgeois class.

A similar movement is going on before our own eyes. Modern bourgeois society with its relations of production, of exchange and of property, a society that has conjured up such gigantic means of production and of exchange, is like the sorcerer, who is no longer able to control the powers of the nether world whom he has called up by his spells. For many a decade past the history of industry and commerce is but the history of the revolt of modern productive forces against modern conditions of production, against the property relations that are the conditions for the existence of the bourgeoisie and of its rule. It is enough to mention the commercial crises that by their periodical return put on its trial, each time more threateningly, the existence of the entire bourgeois society. In these crises a great part not only of the existing products, but also of the previously created productive forces, are periodically destroyed. In these crises there breaks out an epidemic that, in all earlier epochs, would have seemed an absurdity—the epidemic of over-production. Society suddenly finds itself put back into a state of momentary barbarism; it appears as if a famine, a universal war of devastation had cut off the supply of every means of subsistence; industry and commerce seem to be destroyed; and why? Because there is too much civilisation, too much means of subsistence, too much industry, too much commerce. The productive forces at the disposal of society no longer tend to further the development of the conditions of bourgeois property; on the contrary, they have become too powerful for these conditions, by which they are fettered, and so soon as they overcome these fetters, they bring disorder into the whole of bourgeois society, endanger the existence of bourgeois property. The conditions of bourgeois society are too narrow to comprise the wealth created by them. And how does the bourgeoisie get over these crises? On the one hand by enforced destruction of a mass of productive forces; on the other, by the conquest of new markets, and by the more thorough exploitation of the old ones. That is to say, by paving the way for more extensive and more destructive crises, and by diminishing the means whereby crises are prevented.

The weapons with which the bourgeoisie felled feudalism to the ground are now turned against the bourgeoisie itself.

But not only has the bourgeoisie forged the weapons that bring death to itself; it has also called into existence the men who are to wield those weapons—the modern working class—the proletarians.

In proportion as the bourgeoisie, *i.e.*, capital, is developed, in the same proportion is the proletariat, the modern working class, developed—a class of labourers, who live only so long as they find work, and who find work only so long as their labour increases capital. These labourers, who must sell themselves piece-meal, are a commodity, like every other article of commerce, and are consequently exposed to all the vicissitudes of competition, to all the fluctuations of the market.

Owing to the extensive use of machinery and to division of labour, the work of the proletarians has lost all individual character, and consequently, all charm for the workman. He becomes an appendage of the machine, and it is only the most simple, most monotonous, and most easily acquired knack, that is required of him. Hence, the cost of production of a workman is restricted, almost entirely, to the means of subsistence that he requires for his maintenance, and for the propagation of his race: But the price of a commodity, and therefore also of labour, is equal to its cost of production. In proportion, therefore, as the repulsiveness of the work increases, the wage decreases. Nay more, in proportion as the use of machinery and division of labour increases, in the same proportion the burden of toil also increases, whether by prolongation of the working hours, by increase of the work exacted in a given time or by increased speed of the machinery, etc.

Modern industry has converted the little workshop of the patriarchal master into the great factory of the industrial capitalist. Masses of labourers, crowded into the factory, are organised like soldiers. As privates of the industrial army they are placed under the command of a perfect hierarchy of officers and sergeants. Not only are they slaves of the bourgeois class, and of the bourgeois State; they are daily and hourly enslaved by the machine, by the over-looker, and, above all, by the individual bourgeois manufacturer himself. The more openly this despotism proclaims gain to be its end and aim, the more petty, the more hateful, and the more embittering it is.

The less the skill and exertion of strength implied in manual labour, in other words, the more modern industry becomes developed, the more is the labour of men superseded by that of women. Differences of age and sex have no longer any distinctive social validity for the working class. All are instruments of labour, more or less expensive to use, according to their age and sex.

No sooner is the exploitation of the labourer by the manufacturer, so far, at an end, that he receives his wages in cash, than he is set upon by the other portions of the bourgeoisie, the landlord, the shopkeeper, the pawnbroker, etc.

The lower strata of the middle class—the small tradespeople, shopkeepers, and retired tradesmen generally, the handicraftsmen and peasants—all these sink gradually into the proletariat, partly because their diminutive capital does not suffice for the scale on which Modern Industry is carried on, and is swamped in the competition with the large capitalists, partly because their specialised skill is rendered worthless by new methods of production. Thus the proletariat is recruited from all classes of the population.

The proletariat goes through various stages of development. With its birth begins its struggle with the bourgeoisie. At first the contest is carried on by individual labourers, then by the workpeople of a factory, then by the operatives of one trade, in one locality, against the individual bourgeois who directly exploits them. They direct their attacks not against the bourgeois conditions of production, but against the instruments of production themselves; they destroy imported wares that compete with their labour, they smash to pieces machinery, they set factories ablaze, they seek to restore by force the vanished status of the workman of the Middle Ages.

At this stage the labourers still form an incoherent mass scattered over the whole country, and broken up by their mutual competition. If anywhere they unite to form more compact bodies, this is not yet the consequence of their own active union, but of the union of the bourgeoisie, which class, in order to attain its own political ends, is compelled to set the whole proletariat in motion, and is moreover yet, for a time, able to do so. At this stage, therefore, the proletarians do not fight their enemies, but the enemies of their enemies, the remnants of absolute monarchy, the landowners, the non-industrial bourgeois, the petty bourgeoisie. Thus the whole historical movement is concentrated in the hands of the bourgeoisie; every victory so obtained is a victory for the bourgeoisie.

But with the development of industry the proletariat not only increases in number; it becomes concentrated in greater masses, its strength grows, and it feels that strength more. The various interests and conditions of life within the ranks of the proletariat are more and more equalised, in proportion as machinery obliterates all distinctions of labour, and nearly everywhere reduces wages to the same low level. The growing competition among the bourgeois, and the resulting commercial crises, make the wages of the workers ever more fluctuating. The unceasing improvement of machinery, ever more rapidly developing, makes their livelihood more and more precarious; the collisions between individual workmen and individual bourgeois take more and more the character of collisions between two classes. Thereupon the workers begin to form combinations (Trades Unions) against the bourgeois; they club together in order to keep up the rate of wages; they found permanent associations in order to make provision beforehand for these occasional revolts. Here and there the contest breaks out into riots.

Now and then the workers are victorious, but only for a time. The real fruit of their battles lies, not in the immediate result, but in the ever-expanding union of the workers. This union is helped on by the improved means of communication that are created by modern industry and that place the workers of different localities in contact with one another. It was just this contact that was needed to centralise the numerous local struggles, all of the same character, into one national struggle between classes. But every class struggle is a political struggle. And that union, to attain which the burghers of the Middle Ages, with their miserable highways, required centuries, the modern proletarians, thanks to railways, achieve in a few years.

This organisation of the proletarians into a class, and consequently into a political party, is continually being upset again by the competition between the workers themselves. But it ever rises up again, stronger, firmer, mightier. It compels legislative recognition of particular interests of the workers, by taking advantage of the divisions among the bourgeoisie itself. Thus the ten-hours' bill in England was carried.

Altogether collisions between the classes of the old society further, in many ways, the course of development of the proletariat. The bourgeoisie finds itself involved in a constant battle. At first with the aristocracy; later on, with those portions of the bourgeoisie itself, whose interests have become antagonistic to the progress of industry; at all times, with the bourgeoisie of foreign countries. In all these battles it sees itself compelled to appeal to the proletariat, to ask for its help, and thus, to drag it into the political arena. The bourgeoisie itself, therefore, supplies the proletariat with its own elements of political and general education, in other words, it furnishes the proletariat with weapons for fighting the bourgeoisie.

Further, as we have already seen, entire sections of the ruling classes are, by the advance of industry, precipitated into the proletariat, or are at least threatened in their conditions of existence. These also supply the proletariat with fresh elements of enlightenment and progress.

Finally, in times when the class struggle nears the decisive hour, the process of dissolution going on within the ruling class, in fact within the whole range of society, assumes such a violent, glaring character, that a small section of the ruling class cuts itself adrift, and joins the revolutionary class, the class that holds the future in its hands. Just as, therefore, at an earlier period, a section of the nobility went over to the bourgeoisie, so now a portion of the bourgeoisie goes over to the proletariat, and in particular, a portion of the bourgeois ideologists, who have raised themselves to the level of comprehending theoretically the historical movement as a whole.

Of all the classes that stand face to face with the bourgeoisie today, the proletariat alone is a really revolutionary class. The other classes decay and finally disappear in the face of Modern Industry; the proletariat is its special and essential product.

The lower middle class, the small manufacturer, the shopkeeper, the artisan, the peasant, all these fight against the bourgeoisie, to save from extinction their existence as fractions of the middle class. They are therefore not revolutionary, but conservative. Nay more, they are reactionary, for they try to roll back the wheel of history. If by chance they are revolutionary, they are so only in view of their impending transfer into the proletariat, they thus defend not their present, but their future interests, they desert their own standpoint to place themselves at that of the proletariat.

The "dangerous class,"[2] the social scum, that passively rotting mass thrown off by the lowest layers of old society, may, here and there, be swept into the movement by a proletarian revolution; its conditions of life, however, prepare it far more for the part of a bribed tool of reactionary intrigue.

In the conditions of the proletariat, those of old society at large are already virtually swamped. The proletarian is without property; his relation to his wife and children has no longer anything in common with the bourgeois family-relations; modern industrial labour, modern subjection to capital, the same in England as in France, in America as in Germany, has stripped him of every trace of national character. Law, morality, religion, are to him so many bourgeois prejudices, behind which lurk in ambush just as many bourgeois interests.

All the preceding classes that got the upper hand, sought to fortify their already acquired status by subjecting society at large to their conditions of appropriation. The proletarians cannot become masters of the productive forces of society, except by abolishing their own previous mode of appropriation, and thereby also every other previous mode of appropriation. They have nothing of their own to secure and to fortify; their mission is to destroy all previous securities for, and insurances of, individual property.

All previous historical movements were movements of minorities, or in the interests of minorities. The proletarian movement is the self-conscious, independent movement of the immense majority, in the interests of the immense majority. The proletariat, the lowest stratum of our present society, cannot stir, cannot raise itself up, without the whole superincumbent strata of official society being sprung into the air.

Though not in substance, yet in form, the struggle of the proletariat with the bourgeoisie is at first a national struggle. The proletariat of each country must, of course, first of all settle matters with its own bourgeoisie.

In depicting the most general phases of the development of the proletariat, we traced the more or less veiled civil war, raging within existing society, up to the point where that war breaks out into open revolution, and where the violent overthrow of the bourgeoisie lays the foundation for the sway of the proletariat.

Hitherto, every form of society has been based, as we have already seen, on the antagonism of oppressing and oppressed classes. But in order to oppress a class, certain conditions must be assured to it under which it can, at least, continue its slavish existence. The serf, in the period of serfdom, raised himself to membership in the commune, just as the petty bourgeois, under the yoke of feudal absolutism, managed to develop into a bourgeois. The modern labourer, on the contrary, instead of

---

[2] The "dangerous class": The German name for this underclass is *Lumpenproletariat.*

rising with the progress of industry, sinks deeper and deeper below the conditions of existence of his own class. He becomes a pauper, and pauperism develops more rapidly than population and wealth. And here it becomes evident, that the bourgeoisie is unfit any longer to be the ruling class in society, and to impose its conditions of existence upon society as an over-riding law. It is unfit to rule because it is incompetent to assure an existence to its slave within his slavery, because it cannot help letting him sink into such a state, that it has to feed him, instead of being fed by him. Society can no longer live under this bourgeoisie, in other words, its existence is no longer compatible with society.

The essential condition for the existence, and for the sway of the bourgeois class, is the formation and augmentation of capital; the condition for capital is wage-labour. Wage-labour rests exclusively on competition between the labourers. The advance of industry, whose involuntary promoter is the bourgeoisie, replaces the isolation of the labourers, due to competition, by their revolutionary combination, due to association. The development of Modern Industry, therefore, cuts from under its feet the very foundation on which the bourgeoisie produces and appropriates products. What the bourgeoisie, therefore, produces, above all, is its own grave-diggers. Its fall and the victory of the proletariat are equally inevitable.

❧ INAZO NITOBÉ
1862–1933

Inazo Nitobé's *Bushido: The Soul of Japan* (1899) sought to reveal the Japanese psyche to the West. *In the World:* Heroes and Heroines includes Inazo Nitobé's discussion of the heroic virtues of Japanese feudalism. In the passage excerpted here, Inazo Nitobé explains why the samurai have great difficulty adapting to middle-class ways by showing the antagonism between their traditional feudal ethics and the Western values of the marketplace. The text is from the 1905 Tokyo edition of *Bushido*.

For more on Inazo Nitobé, see p. 204.

It will be long before it will be recognized how many fortunes were wrecked in the attempt to apply Bushido ethics to business methods; but it was soon patent to every observing mind that the ways of wealth were not the ways of honor.

– INAZO NITOBÉ,
Bushido: The Soul of Japan

FROM

∾ Bushido: The Soul of Japan

Those who are well acquainted with our history will remember that only a few years after our treaty ports were opened to foreign trade, feudalism was abolished,[1] and when with it the samurai's fiefs were taken and bonds issued to them in compensation, they were given liberty to invest them in mercantile transactions. Now you may ask, "Why could they not bring their much boasted veracity into their new business relations and so reform the old abuses?" Those who had eyes to see could not weep enough, those who had hearts to feel could not sympathize enough, with the fate of many a noble and honest samurai who signally and irrevocably failed in his new and unfamiliar field of trade and industry, through sheer lack of shrewdness in coping with his artful plebeian rival. When we know that eighty percent of the business houses fail in so industrial a country as America, is it any wonder that scarcely one among a hundred samurai who went into trade could succeed in his new vocation? It will be long before it will be recognized how many fortunes were wrecked in the attempt to apply Bushido ethics to business methods; but it was soon patent to every observing mind that the ways of wealth were not the ways of honor. In what respects, then, were they different?

Of the three incentives to Veracity that Lecky[2] enumerates, viz: the industrial, the political, and the philosophical, the first was altogether lacking in Bushido. As to the second, it could develop little in a political community under a feudal system. It is in its philosophical, and as Lecky says, in its highest aspect, that Honesty attained elevated rank in our catalogue of virtues. With all my sincere regard for the high commercial integrity of the Anglo-Saxon race, when I ask for the ultimate ground, I am told that "Honesty is the best policy," that it *pays* to be honest. Is not this virtue, then, its own reward? If it is followed because it brings in more cash than falsehood, I am afraid Bushido would rather indulge in lies!

If Bushido rejects a doctrine of *quid pro quo* rewards, the shrewder tradesman will readily accept it. Lecky has very truly remarked that Veracity owes its growth largely to commerce and manufacture; as Nietzsche[3] puts it, "Honesty is the youngest of virtues"—in other words, it is the foster-child of industry, of modern industry. Without this mother, Veracity was like a blue-blood orphan whom only the most cultivated mind could adopt and nourish. Such minds were general among the samurai, but, for want of a more democratic and utilitarian foster-mother, the tender child failed to thrive.

---

[1] feudalism was abolished: In 1871 the new constitutional government of Japan abolished feudalism and offered payments to former samurai to help them take up a new way of life.

[2] Lecky: William Lecky (1838–1903), liberal British historian known for *History of the Rise and Influence of the Spirit of Rationalism in Europe* (1865) and *History of England in the Eighteenth Century* (1878–90).

[3] Nietzsche: Friedrich Nietzsche (1844–1900), German philosopher who often wrote in the sort of aphorisms that Nitobé quotes here. See p. 198.

∾ EMILIA PARDO BAZÁN
1852–1921

Emilia Pardo Bazán is Spain's foremost woman novelist. A contemporary of Benito Peréz Galdós,[1] with whom she had a discreet affair, Pardo Bazán scandalized the conservative Spain of her time by her involvement with both NATURALISM[2] and FEMINISM, and she displeased the male establishment with insistent demands that her literary achievements be acknowledged. Time has blunted the controversial edge of some of her intellectual positions and softened the scandal that some of her writings created when they first appeared. She is now recognized as one of the masters of Realist fiction, especially the short story, in which, as Walter Pattison points out, "there is no other Spaniard who is her equal."

Childhood and Education.   Born in Galicia, in the northwest corner of Spain, in 1852, Pardo Bazán was the only child of a well-to-do and prominent family in the remote region. A child prodigy who was able to read and write at age four, she was educated privately in Galicia for three years and later studied for three years at a fashionable French school in Madrid, where she began her lifelong involvement with France and its literature. Pardo Bazán credited her childhood reading as the real basis of her education. In her autobiography she tells of reading literary classics "four, five, or even six times over," and as an adolescent she could recite whole chapters of some books—most notably *Don Quixote, The Iliad, The Divine Comedy,* and the Bible—with complete accuracy. However, her parents prevented her from reading Alexandre Dumas, Eugène Sue, George Sand, Victor Hugo,[3] and other French ROMANTICS, a prohibition that made these writers even more attractive to her. French literature would become the major influence on her own writing.

Pardo Bazán's parents arranged their daughter's marriage at age sixteen to José Quiroga, a law student from an important family. In the political turmoil following the revolution of 1868, which forced the abdication

www For more information about Pardo Bazán and her work, see *World Literature Online* at bedfordstmartins .com/worldlit.

---

[1] **Benito Peréz Galdós:** (1843–1920) The most important Spanish novelist of the nineteenth century. His historical novels traced Spanish history from the Napoleonic period to the late nineteenth century, the time in which his masterwork, *Fortunata and Jacinta* (1886–87), is set.

[2] **Naturalism:** A literary school of the late nineteenth century led by Émile Zola (1840–1902) that sought to apply scientific objectivity to the novel. Influenced especially by Darwinism, the Naturalists created characters who were usually common people and whose lives were determined by heredity and environment. Because they allowed no idealization of character or situation, Naturalists were often attacked for obscenity for portraying human beings as instinctual animals.

[3] **Dumas . . . Hugo:** Leading writers of the French Romantic movement in the first half of the nineteenth century. Alexandre Dumas *pére* (1802–1870) is best known for *The Three Musketeers* (1844) and *The Count of Monte Cristo* (1844–45). Eugène Sue (1804–1859) authored *The Mysteries of Paris* (1843) and *The Wandering Jew* (1849). George Sand, the pen name of Amadine-Aurore-Lucie Dupin (1804–1876), wrote many novels and romances, including *Lélia* (1833) and *Mauprat* (1837). Victor Hugo (1802–1885) wrote *Notre Dame of Paris* (1831), commonly known as *The Hunchback of Notre Dame,* and *Les Misérables* (1862).

691

of Queen Isabella and heightened the struggle between conservative and democratic forces, Emilia's father, a Progressive deputy in the Cortes, the Spanish parliament, decided that it was prudent to leave Spain until things settled down. Pardo Bazán and her husband traveled with her parents to Paris, Vienna, Venice, Verona, Geneva, and London between 1871 and 1874, and the young author thus became familiar with the literary trends of other countries. By the time she returned to Spain Pardo Bazán knew other European literatures, especially that of France, better than her own. In 1876 her first child, Jaime, was born. Two more children, Blanca and Carmen, were born in 1879 and 1881.

Pardo Bazán's Writings.   Pardo Bazán's first publications were a prize-winning essay on Feijóo, an eighteenth-century Galician Benedictine (1876); articles on heat, light, and electricity (1876); and essays on Dante, Milton, and Darwin (1877). During the years of her children's infancy, she devoted herself to studying theology, philosophy, and the natural sciences. She would become a prolific commentator on many issues of the day.

Besides her nineteen novels, Pardo Bazán wrote twenty-one novellas, several important works of literary criticism, and nearly six hundred short stories. She also wrote numerous essays and articles, even cookbooks. She edited the literary journal *New Critical Theater* (1891–92) and a series of feminist books entitled *The Woman's Library*. In 1906 she succeeded in becoming the first woman president of the Madrid Athenaeum, an important literary society, and she held the chair of Romance Literature at the Central University of Madrid from 1916 until her death. She was never admitted to the Spanish Academy, an honor she sought for many years. Aside from her feminism, she was politically conservative and did not believe that democracy could solve Spain's problems. Her lifelong desire for an aristocratic title was gratified shortly before her death when the king of Spain named her a countess. She died in 1921.

Feminism.   Pardo Bazán may have been most at odds with traditional Spanish conservatism in her views on the rights of women. An outspoken advocate for more opportunities for women, she campaigned unsuccessfully to gain entry for herself and other women writers into the Royal Academy and successfully to be appointed a professor at the University of Madrid. She rejected the nearly universal assumption in Spain that the only role for women was marriage, and she had little respect for women whose lives were defined by that institution. Their "uselessness and intolerable insipidity," she asserted in *The Test* (*La prueba*, 1890) with characteristic bluntness, "was the combined product of a dull life, lack of education, narrowness of views, and frivolity." Many of her novels and stories, like those of Flaubert, Zola, and Ibsen,[4] were concerned with the

---

[4] **Flaubert . . . Ibsen:** Gustave Flaubert (1821–1880; see p. 435), French Realist novelist and author of *Madame Bovary* (1857); Émile Zola (1840–1902; see p. 398), French Realist whose theory of Naturalism was grounded in biological and environmental determinism and who was the author of *Germinal* (1885) and *Nana* (1880); Henrik Ibsen (1828–1906; see p. 556), Norwegian playwright whose realistic social-problem plays, such as *A Doll's House* (1879), changed the course of European drama in the late nineteenth century.

situation of women in nineteenth-century society. She blamed Spain's sexist institutions for denying women educational opportunities and recognition for their achievements, but she also found fault with women who acquiesced in their own oppression.

Early Naturalism.   Pardo Bazán's first novel, *Pascual López,* appeared in 1879, but it was her work in the 1880s that drew attention and controversy. To write *The Woman Orator* (*La tribuna,* 1883), a novel about women workers in a cigarette factory, Pardo Bazán spent several months observing these workers and familiarizing herself with their patterns of speech and behavior. The novel's detailed descriptions of the factory and the female workers as well as the workers' radical political opinions and its accurate rendering of the women's speech made it the first Spanish novel to treat proletarian characters sympathetically. An "obstetrical scene" at the end of the novel, in which the heroine's labor pains are described in graphic, though not clinical, detail, struck many readers as tasteless. *The House of Ulloa* (*Los pazos de Ulloa,* 1886), a story of the primitive and animalistic life in rural Galicia, generally considered Pardo Bazán's masterpiece, and *Mother Nature* (*La madre naturaleza,* 1887), a novel about an incestuous union in the same rural environment, were even more offensive to conservative Spanish tastes.

In these novels Pardo Bazán's characters are viewed externally and their lives seem to be biologically determined, signs of the influence of French Naturalism on the author's work. Like Zola, Pardo Bazán writes about common people, describing their lives in concrete physical detail and designing plots that often turn on sexual and biological issues. In many ways *Mother Nature* was a reworking of Zola's *The Transgression of Abbé Mouret* (1875); both are nineteenth-century versions of the Adam and Eve story. Pardo Bazán confirmed her reputation as a Naturalist with a critical work, *The Burning Question* (*La cuestión palpitante,* 1883), in which she discusses the French Naturalists, especially Zola and the Goncourt brothers.[5] Although she admired these writers, she also challenged their belief that scientific laws could govern thought and feeling and rejected their determinism and pessimism. Most of all she rejected the Naturalists' denial of the soul and of a spiritual dimension to life. Describing herself as a Realist in the preface to *A Wedding Journey* (1882), she asserted: "If all that has a true and effective existence is *real,* REALISM in art offers us a wider, more complete and perfect theory than *Naturalism.* It includes and encompasses the natural and the spiritual, the body and the soul, and it reconciles and brings into unison the opposition between Naturalism and rational Idealism." In spite of her protestations, she was regarded as one of the detested Naturalists by many conservative Spaniards. Her works were attacked as lecherous and profane, and her controversial literary reputation had repercussions in her personal life, reportedly contributing to her separation from her husband in 1885.

In the short story there is no other Spaniard who is her equal.

– WALTER PATTISON,
Emilia Pardo Bazán,
1971

---

[5] Goncourt brothers: Edmund Louis Antoine Huot de Goncourt (1822–1896) and Alfred Huot de Goncourt (1830–1870), French artists, art critics, and art historians who collaborated on several Naturalist novels, the best known being *Renée Mauperin* (1864).

Later Psychological Fiction.   Pardo Bazán's novels became increasingly psychological, influenced by the Russian Realists Dostoevsky, Tolstoy, and Turgenev,[6] about whom she wrote in *The Revolution and the Novel in Russia* (1887). Her last three novels, *The Chimera* (*La quimera*, 1905), *The Black Siren* (*La sirena negra*, 1908), and *Sweet Master* (*Dulce dueño*, 1911), deal with the psychology of religious experience; in all three works, the central figures undergo a religious conversion. Silvio Lago, a painter who is the hero of *The Chimera,* is particularly interesting, for his conversion enables him to transcend the Naturalism of his earlier work and add a spiritual dimension to his art.

The Short Stories.   Many of Pardo Bazán's short stories explore the psychological issues treated in her later novels and are surprisingly modern. Taking Guy de Maupassant,[7] whom she considered "the master of short story writers," as her mentor, Pardo Bazán sought to match his "impeccable execution, the simplicity of his recourses, his mastery of composition, and the sobriety of his style." She wanted to achieve similar succinctness and focus, using a single subject and creating a single effect, and she often used the device so frequent in Maupassant of the surprise ending. In "The Pearls," for example, a story that recalls Maupassant's "The Necklace," a husband gives his wife expensive pearls only to find them at the apartment of his best friend, with whom his wife has had an assignation. The irony and corrosive cynicism in many of Pardo Bazán's stories also calls to mind Maupassant.

Pardo Bazán also sought objectivity in her technique. Her stories are often told by a peripheral character within the tale who effaces the author as narrator. Both "The Revolver" and "The Oldest Story," two of Pardo Bazán's "feminist" stories included here, are narrated in this way. Pardo Bazán is thus also able to add a layer of irony to the stories: The older woman in "The Revolver" can observe the young widow and provide information that enables the reader to assess the reliability of her account, and the "March Hare" who retells the Genesis story leaves readers wondering whether they should entertain his version seriously or simply take it as the ravings of a madman. If these stories have a feminist argument to make about the abuses of patriarchy, they're not heavy-handed about it. Both the young widow and Eve collude in their victimization, and the ironies in their situations criticize both male and female gender roles.

---

[6] **Dostoevsky . . . Turgenev:** The great Russian Realists of the late nineteenth century. Fyodor Dostoevsky (1821–1881; see p. 462) composed the probing psychological novels *Crime and Punishment* (1866) and *The Brothers Karamazov* (1880); Leo Tolstoy (1828–1910; see p. 617) authored the panoramic novel of Napoleon's Russian campaign, *War and Peace* (1862–69), and *Anna Karenina* (1877); Ivan Turgenev (1818–1883) is best known for *Fathers and Sons* (1861).

[7] **Guy de Maupassant:** (1850–1893) French Realist writer and master of the short story form.

■ CONNECTIONS

In the World: Society and Its Discontents, p. 663; Chopin, "The Story of an Hour," p. 931; Gilman, *The Yellow Wallpaper,* p. 941; Conrad, *Heart of Darkness* (Book 6). Illness is often employed in literature as a metaphor for social discontent or psychological maladjustment. Consider the heart condition of the young widow in "The Revolver" in light of Kierkegaard's discussion of "the sickness unto death" (*In the World:* Society and Its Discontents). What might the widow's condition symbolize? Is her disease related to that of Mrs. Mallard in Chopin's "Story of an Hour," the woman in Gilman's *Yellow Wallpaper,* or Marlow in Conrad's *Heart of Darkness?*

Machado de Assis, "Adam and Eve," p. 922; Stanton, *The Woman's Bible,* p. 400. "The Oldest Story" is a feminist take on the Adam and Eve story from the Book of Genesis, a story also revised and retold in Machado de Assis's "Adam and Eve." Is Machado de Assis's version feminist? How do these stories compare with the original biblical tale and with Stanton's critique of Genesis?

The Arabian Nights (Book 2); Tagore, "The Hungry Stones," p. 977. A framed narrative — a story enclosed in another story or a larger contextualizing narrative — is a literary device with a long history, whose most elaborate instance is perhaps found in *The Arabian Nights,* in which Shahrazad's story frames the 1,001 nightly tales that she recounts for the sultan. The frame story can provide a moral, ironic, or historical perspective on the second story it contains. How does the Shahrazad frame story relate to one of the tales she tells? How does Tagore employ the frame story in "The Hungry Stones"? What does the frame story in "The Revolver" contribute to the story of the young widow?

■ FURTHER RESEARCH

Recent Translations of Pardo Bazán's Works
Borenstein, Walter, trans. *The Tribune of the People (La tribuna).* 1999.
Fedorchek, Robert M., trans. and ed. *"The White Horse" and Other Stories.* 1993.
O'Prey, Paul, and Lucia Graves, trans. *The House of Ulloa.* 1991.
Urruela, María Cristina, trans., and Joyce Tolliver, ed. *"Torn Lace" and Other Stories.*
      1996.

Critical Biography
Pattison, Walter T. *Emilia Pardo Bazán.* 1971.

❧ The Revolver

Translated by Angel Flores

In a burst of confidence, one of those provoked by the familiarity and companion-ship of bathing resorts, the woman suffering from heart trouble told me about her illness, with all the details of chokings, violent palpitations, dizziness, fainting spells, and collapses, in which one sees the final hour approach. . . . As she spoke, I looked her over carefully. She was a woman of about thirty-five or thirty-six, maimed by suffering; at least I thought so, but, on closer scrutiny, I began to suspect that there was something more than the physical in her ruin. As a matter of fact, she spoke and expressed herself like someone who had suffered a good deal, and I know that the ills of the body, when not of imminent gravity, are usually not enough to produce such a wasting away, such extreme dejection. And, noting how the broad leaves of the plane tree, touched with carmine by the artistic hand of autumn, fell to the ground majestically and lay stretched out like severed hands, I remarked, in order to gain her confidence, on the passing of all life, the melancholy of the transitoriness of every-thing . . .

"Nothing is anything," she answered, understanding at once that not curiosity but compassion was beckoning at the gates of her spirit. "Nothing is anything . . . unless we ourselves convert that nothing into something. Would to God we could see everything, always, with the slight but sad emotion produced in us by the fall of this foliage on the sand."

The sickly flush of her cheeks deepened, and then I realized that she had proba-bly been very beautiful, although her beauty was effaced and gone, like the colors of a fine picture over which is passed cotton saturated with alcohol. Her blond, silky hair showed traces of ash, premature gray hair. Her features had withered away; her complexion especially revealed those disturbances of the blood which are slow poi-sonings, decompositions of the organism. Her soft blue eyes, veined with black, must have once been attractive, but now they were disfigured by something worse

---

"The Revolver." First published in 1895, this story is one of Pardo Bazán's many feminist works. It employs a gun as a symbol of patriarchal tyranny, but Pardo Bazán is interested in far more than the weapon's FREUDIAN reference, the gun as phallic symbol. The story of a terrified widow is a FRAMED NARRATION in which an older woman narrator listens to the young widow confess her life story. The older woman observes the widow and confirms the truth of her narrative for the reader. There is irony in the revelation that the gun in the story was not loaded, suggesting that the power it represented was a sham. There are further ironies in the widow's confession that after her hus-band was killed she realized she still loved him, and in the setting of the spa, where she has come to treat the "bullet wound" that has left her with a heart condition.

The translation of "The Revolver" by Angel Flores done for a bilingual collection of Spanish stories was a rare translation of Pardo Bazán's work at the time it was published in 1960. Recent interest in women's writing has prompted the publication of two volumes of her stories in English translation since 1990.

than age; a kind of aberration, which at certain moments lent them the glitter of madness.

We grew silent: but my way of contemplating her expressed my pity so plainly that she, sighing for a chance to unburden her heavy heart, made up her mind, and stopping from time to time to breathe and regain her strength, she told me the strange story.

"When I married, I was very much in love. . . . My husband was, compared to me, advanced in years; he was bordering on forty, and I was only nineteen. My temperament was gay and lively; I retained a child-like disposition, and when he was not home I would devote my time to singing, playing the piano, chatting and laughing with girl-friends who came to see me and envied me my happiness, my brilliant marriage, my devoted husband, and my brilliant social position.

"This lasted a year—the wonderful year of the honeymoon. The following spring, on our wedding anniversary, I began to notice that Reinaldo's disposition was changing. He was often in a gloomy mood, and, without my knowing the cause, he spoke to me harshly, and had outbursts of anger. But it was not long before I understood the origins of his transformation: Reinaldo had conceived a violent, irrational jealousy, a jealousy without object or cause, which, for that very reason, was doubly cruel and difficult to cure.

"If we went out together, he was watchful lest people stare at me or tell me, in passing, one of those silly things people say to young women; if he went out alone, he was suspicious of what I was doing in the house, and of the people who came to see me; if I went out alone, his suspicions and suppositions were even more defamatory. . . .

"If I proposed, pleadingly, that we stay home together, he was watchful of my saddened expression, of my supposed boredom, of my work, of an instant when, passing in front of the window, I happened to look outside. . . . He was watchful, above all, when he noticed that my birdlike disposition, my good, child-like humor, had disappeared, and that on many afternoons, when I turned on the lights, he found my skin shining with the damp, ardent trace of tears. Deprived of my innocent amusements, now separated from my friends and relatives, and from my own family, because Reinaldo interpreted as treacherous artifices the desire to communicate and look at faces other than his, I often wept, and did not respond to Reinaldo's transports of passion with the sweet abandonment of earlier times.

"One day, after one of the usual bitter scenes, my husband said:

"'Flora, I may be a madman, but I am not a fool. I have alienated your love, and although perhaps you would not have thought of deceiving me, in the future, without being able to remedy it, you would. Now I shall never again be your beloved. The swallows that have left do not return. But because, unfortunately, I love you more each day, and love you without peace, with eagerness and fever, I wish to point out that I have thought of a way which will prevent questions, quarrels, or tears between us—and once and for all you will know what our future will be.'

"Speaking thus, he took me by the arm and led me toward the bedroom.

"I went trembling; cruel presentiments froze me. Reinaldo opened the drawer of the small inlaid cabinet where he kept tobacco, a watch, and handkerchiefs, and showed me a large revolver, a sinister weapon.

"'Here,' he said, 'is your guarantee that in the future your life will be peaceful and pleasant. I shall never again demand an accounting of how you spend your time, or of your friends, or of your amusements. You are free, free as the air. But the day I see something that wounds me to the quick ... that day, I swear by my mother! Without complaints or scenes, or the slightest sign that I am displeased, oh no, not that! I will get up quietly at night, take the weapon, put it to your temple, and you will wake up in eternity. Now you have been warned. ...'

"As for me, I was in a daze, unconscious. It was necessary to send for the doctor, inasmuch as the fainting spell lasted. When I recovered consciousness and remembered, the convulsion took place. I must point out that I have a mortal fear of firearms; a younger brother of mine died of an accidental shot. My eyes, staring wildly, would not leave the drawer of the cabinet that held the revolver.

"I could not doubt, from Reinaldo's tone and the look on his face, that he was prepared to carry out his threat, and knowing also how easily his imagination grew confused, I began to consider myself as dead. As a matter of fact, Reinaldo kept his promise, and left me complete mistress of myself, without directing the slightest censure my way, or showing, even by a look, that he was opposed to any of my wishes or disapproved of my actions; but this itself frightened me, because it indicated the strength and tyranny of a resolute will ... and, victim of a terror which every day grew more profound, I remained motionless, not daring to take a step. I would always see the steely reflection of the gun barrel.

"At night, insomnia kept my eyes open and I imagined I felt the metallic cold of a steel circle on my temple; or if I got to sleep, I woke up startled with palpitations that made my heart seem to leap from my breast, because I dreamed that an awful report was ripping apart the bones of my skull and blowing my brains out, dashing them against the wall ... And this lasted four years, four years without a single peaceful moment, when I never took a step without fearing that that step might give rise to tragedy."

"And how did that horrible situation end?" I asked, in order to bring her story to a close, because I saw her gasping for breath.

"It ended ... with Reinaldo, who was thrown by a horse, and had some internal injury, being killed on the spot.

"Then, and only then, I knew that I still loved him, and I mourned him quite sincerely, although he was my executioner, and a systematic one at that!"

"And did you pick up the revolver to throw it out the window?"

"You'll see," she murmured. "Something rather extraordinary happened. I sent Reinaldo's manservant to remove the revolver from my room, because in my dreams I continued to see the shot and feel the chill on my temple. ... And after he carried out the order, the manservant came to tell me: 'Señora, there was no cause for alarm. ... This revolver wasn't loaded.'

"'It wasn't loaded?'

"'No, Señora; and it looks to me as though it never was ... As a matter of fact, the poor master never got around to buying the cartridges. Why, I would even ask him at times if he wanted me to go to the gunsmith's and get them, but he didn't answer, and then he never spoke of the matter again.'

"And so," added the sufferer from heart disease, "an unloaded revolver shot me, not in the head, but in the center of my heart, and believe me when I tell you that, in spite of digitalis and baths and all the remedies, the bullet is unsparing. . . ."

ᖰ The Oldest Story

Translated by María Cristina Urruela

I once had an old friend, a man with a sense of humor and a bit of the March Hare or, as a classical author would say, someone crazed by his own caprice. He suffered from an illness that was quite the fashion fifty years ago but now is passé: a systematic loathing for everything having to do with religion, church, faith, and the clergy—a loathing that manifested itself in jokes that were rather Voltairean,[1] little stories as spicy as chili peppers, materialist arguments that were so innocent they were childlike, and crude sexual theories. All these were quite different from his true feelings and actions, since, despite his display of vulgar impiety, he was always a man of pure habits, kind heart, and consummate honesty.

One of the things that gave my friend the opportunity to rant was exegesis, meaning the interpretation—scathing, of course—of the sacred books. He was always going on and on about the Bible and arguing with Father Scío of San Miguel. He insisted that the priest should have been named not Father Scío but Father Nescío,[2] saying that it would be necessary to don spectacles to be able to see his learning and that the priest stumbled over himself continually within the murky mazes of those labyrinthine and nebulous texts which were as obscure as they were

---

"**The Oldest Story.**" First published in 1893, this work is a feminist retelling of the Eden story from the Book of Genesis. Pardo Bazán had already reinterpreted the story of Adam and Eve in the Naturalist novel *Mother Nature,* in which two innocents fall in love and then "fall" when they learn that they share the same father. In "The Oldest Story," Eve is exonerated from responsibility for the Fall, yet she nonetheless colludes with Adam when he uses her as a scapegoat and blames her for their transgression. This story, like "The Revolver," suggests that women are at least partly responsible for their victimization by men. Its narrator absolves herself from responsibility for this radical revision of Genesis by making it out to be something she was told by a male acquaintance, whom she says is something of a "March Hare." In a final twist, the male revisionist places a reflection of Eden deep in Eve's eyes that eternally attracts Adam's gaze.

"The Oldest Story," translated by María Christina Urruela, is from Joyce Tolliver's selection of Pardo Bazán's stories on feminist themes, *Torn Lace and Other Stories,* published in 1996.

---

[1] Voltairean: Resembling the satirical irreverence of Voltaire (1694–1778), who delighted in shocking his readers by attacking sacred cows.

[2] Father Nescío: Felipe Scío de San Miguel (1738–1796) was known for his biblical scholarship and his translation of the Bible. *Scio* is Latin for "I know"; *nescio* means "I do not know, I am ignorant." The Spanish word *necio* means stubborn or foolish, an ignoramus. [Translator]

ancient. My friend, without realizing that he was in the same position as Father Scío — indeed worse, for he lacked the theological and philological learning of that venerable biblical scholar — gamely "corrected" the priest's arguments, uttering odd absurdities that, taken in jest, helped us pass the long winter evenings in the village, when the rain soaks the earth and drips off the bare branches of the trees and the dogs howl fearfully, announcing imaginary perils.

On a night like this, after having gulped down the light milk punch we used to drink to ward off the cold, and with the card game in full force, my friend lit into the Book of Genesis and recast — in his own way — the story of Creation. Let nobody think that he revised it in the Darwinian sense; that would be too close to the Old Testament story of the Six Days, in which the creation of the universe ascends from the inorganic to the organic, from lower organisms to higher ones. No: Creation, according to my friend — who was so well-informed that no doubt he had conversed with the Creator Himself — took the form you will discover if you continue reading. All I am doing is transcribing the essence of the account — though I do not promise that the style is exactly right.

"On the first day God created man. Yes, man; Adam, made from the mud or clay of the amorphous planet. Now, do you think God experimented and tested and fumbled about, taking a week of practice, in order to end up with such a funny-looking creature as man? Certainly not. The only thing that explains and excuses man is that he sprang forth from the spark of improvisation, created when the Lord, on the spur of the moment, decided to condense the chaotic matter of space into spherical form.

"And He hatched man first, for a very simple reason: planning, as He did, that Adam would be lord and master of all creation, God thought it proper to give him a say in the constitution of His kingdoms and domains. In sum, God, in the role of a good father, wanted to make His creature happy by allowing him to speak up and state his preferences with his own big mouth.

"As Adam stirred, still aching from the pinches of the divine fingers that molded his form, he looked around: and as darkness still covered the face of the abyss, he felt sadness and fear, and he wanted to see, to take pleasure in the resplendent light. God pronounced the well-known *Fiat lux*,[3] and the glorious sun appeared in the firmament. Man saw, and his soul overflowed with joy.

"However, he soon noticed that what he saw was neither particularly varied nor very entertaining — an immense and barren expanse, sterile land on which the burning light of the sun flickered and rebounded like flaming arrows. Adam moaned softly, muttering that he was roasting and that the earth seemed like a wasteland to him. And without delay, God raised up vegetation, the soft velvety grass that covers the ground, the flowering shrubs that decorate and embellish it, and the majestic trees that cast their delightful shadows over it. When Adam observed that this enchanting mantle over the earth's surface was beginning to wilt, vast oceans appeared, along with rushing rivers, laughing fountains, and dew that fell in pearl droplets on

---

[3] *Fiat lux:* Latin for "Let there be light."

the fields. And when Adam complained that so much sun was bothering his eyes, our tireless God, instead of giving His handiwork tinted goggles, created nothing less than the moon and the stars and established the tranquil cycle of night and day.

"With all this, the first man was beginning to find Eden livable. He knew how to protect himself from the heat and how to shelter himself from the cold. God had satisfied his hunger and quenched his thirst right away, offering him delectable fruits and pure springs. Adam was able to wander freely in the thickets, the jungles, the valleys, the idyllic gardens, and the grottos of his privileged mansion. He was allowed to gather all the flowers, taste all the varied and sweet species of fruit, enjoy all the waters, lie down in all the soft beds of grass, and live without care or desire, letting the days of his eternal youth slip by in a world that was always young. Nonetheless, this idyllic good fortune was not enough for Adam: he missed having company, other living beings who would liven the confines of Paradise.

"And God, ever accommodating, hurried to surround Adam with a variety of animals. Some were graceful, gentle, handsome, and tame—like the pigeon and the turtledove; others friendly, playful, and mischievous—like the monkey and the cat. Still others were loyal and faithful, like the dog; and still others, like the lion, were beautiful and terrible in appearance—although for Adam they were all humble and tame, and he even had the tigers eating out of his hand. Since God wanted to make sure that Adam would never again feel lonely for want of other living beings to keep him company, He created animals by the millions and multiplied organisms, from the tiniest infusoria suspended in the air and water to the monstrous megatheres hiding deep in the jungles. He wanted Adam to find life everywhere, energetic, self-renewing, and full of passion: life that thrives in every clime and needs only the slightest spark of fire for its flame to be kindled.

"At first Adam was amused by these ragamuffins and played happily with them as if he were a child. Nonetheless, after a time, he realized that he was wearying of the inferior beings, just as he had wearied of the sun, the moon, the oceans, and the plants. As the sun rises and sets in an identical manner every day, so do creatures repeat the same antics, the same actions and movements—all predictable beforehand, depending on the species. The monkey will always imitate and grimace; the colt will leap and be graceful; the dog will be vigilant and devoted; the nightingale won't dream of changing his sonatas; as for the cat, that sluggard spends hours on end just purring, as we all know. And so Adam woke up one morning, thinking life was stupid and Paradise insipid.

"God is a quick study, and so He immediately realized that Adam was bored. He brought him to task, severely rebuking him. What did his lordship want? Didn't he have everything he could possibly desire? Didn't he enjoy supreme peace and enviable happiness in Eden? Didn't all creation obey him? Wasn't he now a very important person?

"Adam confessed with noble frankness that it was precisely that calm, that security that had him at his wit's end. He longed for something unexpected, for some kind of excitement, even if it cost him his peace and soporific serenity.

"And so God, regarding him with pity, came near him and subtly removed—not a rib, as most people would have it—but bits of his brain, a few smidgens of his heart, some nerve bundles, some fragments of bone, a few ounces of blood—in a word, a little bit of each part of him. And since God—having a choice—was not going to choose the worst parts, He of course took the very best bits, the most delicate and select bits—the very flower of the male, so to speak, from which to mold and create the female. So when Eve was finally created, Adam ended up less than he had been before, and, we must say, rather the worse for wear.

"For His part, God, knowing that He had in His hands the most exquisite essence of man, took great pains to mold it lovingly and give it shape. He didn't dare squeeze His fingers as tightly as when He had fashioned man. From His soft and enchanting caresses came those soft curves, those shapely and elegant contours that are such a contrast to the roughness and rigidity of the masculine form.

"When Eve was just right, God took her by the hand and presented her to Adam. Adam was enthralled and astounded by her and thought he must be in the presence of a celestial being, a luminous cherub. And for some days he continued to think this, never tiring of looking at her again and again, of admiring and flattering and buttering up the precious creature. It was in vain that Eve protested that she was made of the same clay as he; Adam didn't believe it. He swore that she came from another region, from the blue spaces where the stars spin, from the pure ether that holds the sun's orb, or perhaps from the ocean of light where spirits float before the throne of the Almighty. It is thought that it was about this time that Adam composed the first sonnet ever.

"This state of affairs lasted until Adam, without the need of any insinuations from the treacherous serpent, got an overwhelming craving for an apple that Eve guarded with great care. I know for a fact that Eve guarded it and that she didn't give it up so easily. This passage of the Scriptures is one of the most distorted. In the end, despite Eve's defense, Adam won out, since he was the stronger, and he wolfed down the apple. No sooner had the poorly chewed pieces of the fruit of perdition landed in his stomach than—oh wondrous change! incredible reversal!—instead of taking Eve for a seraph, he took her for a demon or a wild beast. Instead of thinking her pure and without blemish, he thought her a repository of all iniquity and evil. Instead of attributing to her his happiness and his ecstasy, he blamed her for his restlessness, for his sorrows, even for the banishment God imposed on them and for their eternal wanderings down that thorny, thistle-filled path.

"The fact is, by dint of hearing this so much, Eve came to believe it too. She acknowledged her blame, her memory of her origin escaped her, and she no longer dared claim that she was of the same substance as man—not better, not worse, but just a little more refined. And the myth of the Book of Genesis is repeated in the life of each and every Eve: Before the apple, Adam erects an altar to her and worships her on it. After the apple, he removes her from the altar, and then it's off to the stable with her, or to the dump . . .

"Nevertheless," my friend would add by way of a moral—after downing another glass of the mild punch—"since Eve was formed from Adam's most intimate essence, Adam, though heaping calumny on her, all the while goes after her like the rope after the bucket. He doesn't stop running after her until he has no breath left in his body and the roof of his mouth is cold. In truth, his wish has been granted:

Ever since God brought Eve to him, man has never been bored again, nor has he ever again enjoyed the peace and quiet of Eden. Banished from such a pleasant mansion, he can only catch a glimpse of it — for an instant — in the depths of Eve's eyes, where a reflection of its image remains."

❧ ANTON CHEKHOV
1860–1904

With highly refined writing skills, Anton Chekhov redefined both the drama and the short fiction of the nineteenth century and prepared both genres for the times ahead. In a letter to A. S. Suvorin, the editor of a Moscow newspaper, it is clear that Chekhov is charting a totally different course from the psychological treatments of Dostoevsky's novels or the epic landscapes of Tolstoy's *War and Peace,* a path down which generations of modern writers would follow the master. The correspondence contains a concise characterization of REALISM: "I think that it is not for writers to solve such questions as the existence of God, pessimism, etc. The writer's function is only to describe by whom, how, and under what conditions the questions of God and pessimism were discussed. The artist must be only an impartial witness of his characters and what they said, not their judge." In both his plays and his short stories, Chekhov wrote about ordinary people in ordinary situations, but the simplicity of his style is deceptive. In the small details, in the nuances of attitude and gesture, lie his genius for invoking, in all their beauty and sentiment, the profound ambiguities and complexities of human life. Chekhov was able to capture a uniquely "modern" consciousness: Self-knowledge is uncertain, and communication between individuals is always problematic and ambiguous. Missed communication is frequent in a rapidly changing society. Chekhov's writings reflect the uncertainty of ordinary life and the loss of faith in traditional beliefs at the turn of the century.

From Poverty to Short Stories.   **Anton Chekhov** was born at Taganrog on January 17, 1860. He attended a Greek preparatory school and later the Taganrog secondary school. His childhood was a time of poverty and beatings. Much later, in a letter to his close friend and publisher, Alexei Suvorin, Chekhov bitingly observed: "I acquired my belief in progress when still a child; I could not help believing in it, because the difference between the period when they flogged me and the period when they stopped flogging me was enormous." In 1879, three years after his father's grocery went bankrupt and the family relocated to Moscow to escape creditors, Anton enrolled in medical school and began to sell humorous, anecdotal, satiric stories to help support his family. During a visit to St. Petersburg in 1885, a year after receiving his medical degree, Chekhov

AHN-tone CHEK-uf

www For more information about Chekhov and *The Cherry Orchard,* see *World Literature Online* at bedfordstmartins .com/worldlit.

Chekhov Reading One of His Works

Chekhov is said to have written up to 300 stories in one year, often writing more than one a day. In this photograph he is reading to a group of attentive fans. (Art Resource)

> They are plays written on the simplest themes which in themselves are not interesting. But they are permeated by the eternal and he who feels this quality in them perceives that they are written for all eternity.
>
> – CONSTANTINE STANISLAVSKY, *My Life in Art*

discovered that he was famous. While still a student he had published almost 300 stories in the popular magazines of St. Petersburg and Moscow, and in 1886 *Motley Stories* was published, his first major collection. Chekhov was twenty-six years old. He described his writing technique: "I do not remember working more than a day on *any single* story of mine . . . I wrote my stories as reporters write their news about fires: mechanically, half-consciously, without worrying about either the reader or themselves." He would write 300 more short stories the following year. The young author wrote and wrote and wrote, learning a style that would be a trademark in many of his stories.

Setting New Standards in Both Fiction and Drama.   In 1888, Chekhov won the Pushkin Prize for the short story, "The Steppe." His fiction attracted the attention of Dmitri Grigorovich, an important novelist of the 1840s. Grigorovich introduced Chekhov to Alexei Suvorin, who would publish many of Chekhov's most famous stories in his newspaper, *Novoe Vremya (New Times)*. Suvorin even created a special literary supplement in the newspaper for Chekhov's work. Memorable short stories from that time are "Ward Number Six" and "A Lady with a Dog" and the novella, "The Duel." In 1887, Chekhov's first play, *Ivanov*, was produced in Moscow, launching his career. Thus Chekhov broke ground in two major literary forms and set standards of excellence for all writers who followed.

Nevertheless, Chekhov led the rather ordinary life of a Russian doctor of the late nineteenth century, with the exception of a strenuous trip he made in 1890 through Siberia to the penal colony on the island of Sakhalin. Chekhov made the trip on Tolstoy's suggestion and later described the inhumane conditions of the prisoners in *The Island of Sakhalin* (1894). In 1892 he purchased an estate fifty miles south of Moscow in the village of Melikhova, where he lived with his parents and spent his time writing, caring for patients, and contributing to local service projects. Chekhov had contracted tuberculosis when he was twenty-three, and in 1897, when his health began to fail, he was forced to sell the Melikhova estate and move to a warmer climate. He spent the rest of his life in Yalta, where he wrote some of his best plays and cultivated strong friendships with Tolstoy and Maxim Gorky.[1]

Chekhov's Most Famous Plays.
Chekhov's best dramas were written in the 1890s and early 1900s for the Moscow Art Theatre, which was directed by Constantine Stanislavsky,[2] one of the geniuses of modern theatre. In addition to *The Cherry Orchard* (1904), the plays of this period include *The Seagull* (1896), *Uncle Vanya* (1899), and *The Three Sisters* (1901). In 1901 Chekhov married an actress from the Moscow Art Theatre, Olga Leonardovna Knipper, and during the happy years of that union he wrote *The Cherry Orchard*, his masterpiece about the passing of the old order and the rise of the middle class. This play was produced on Chekhov's birthday, January 17, 1904. As it was also the twenty-fifth anniversary of his literary career, a grand celebration was planned for opening night. Nemirovich-Danchenko, the codirector of the theatre, paid the final tribute of the evening by saying to the playwright: "Our theatre is so much indebted to your talent, to your tender heart and pure soul, that you have every right to say 'This is my theatre.'" Chekhov died six months later, in Germany on July 2, 1904, at the Badenweiler spa in the Black Forest.

Themes and Artistry.
Although "The Beggar" and "The Bet" seem to bear the imprint of Tolstoy's nonviolent philosophy, Chekhov's stories and plays are rarely ideological in the sense that they can be neatly packaged by a moral or easily reduced to a philosophical statement. Chekhov's responses to the limited, often shallow perspectives of his characters do not reflect a particular political philosophy. Quick to deflate the arrogant and the pretentious, Chekhov was equally harsh with the crudities of life

It seems to me that in the presence of Anton Pavlovich everyone felt an unconscious desire to be simpler, more truthful, more himself, and I had many opportunities of observing how people threw off their attire of grand bookish phrases, fashionable expressions, and all the rest of the cheap trifles with which Russians in their anxiety to appear Europeans, adorn themselves. . . .

– MAXIM GORKY

---

[1] **Maxim Gorky:** (1868–1936) Russian novelist and playwright who was a political radical with deep sympathies for the lower classes. *The Lower Depths* is his best-known play outside of Russia. His nonfiction *Reminiscences* provides portraits of Tolstoy, Chekhov, and other contemporaries.

[2] **Constantine Stanislavsky:** (1863–1938) Brilliant Russian director and acting teacher and cofounder of the Moscow Art Theater.

lived close to the soil. Maxim Gorky summarizes Chekhov's attitudes towards his subjects: "Detesting all that was vulgar and unclean, he described the seamy side of life in the lofty language of the poet, with the gentle smile of the humorist, and the bitter inner reproach beneath the polished surface of his stories is scarcely noticeable. . . . No one ever understood the tragic nature of life's trifles so clearly and intuitively as Chekhov did, never before has a writer been able to hold up to human beings such a ruthlessly truthful picture of all that was shameful and pitiable in the dingy chaos of middle-class life."

It is often said that Chekhov's plays do not have a plot, and that this absence defines his approach to realism. Chekhov said that he wanted to show life as it is lived by ordinary people: "A play should be written in which people arrive, go away, have dinner, talk about the weather, and play cards. Life must be exactly as it is, and people as they are—not on stilts. . . . Let everything on the stage be just as complicated, and at the same time just as simple as it is in life."

Chekhov is a master stylist, able to evoke a whole scene or a character with just a few poignant details. He creates atmosphere and mood seemingly effortlessly, ranging over both urban and rural life. In a letter to his brother he talks about the use of suggestive detail to paint a scene: "You have to choose small details in describing nature, grouping them in such a way that if you close your eyes after reading it, you can picture the whole thing. For example, you'll get a picture of a moonlit night if you write that on the dam of the mill a piece of broken bottle flashed like a bright star and the black shadow of a dog or a wolf rolled by like a ball. . . ."

Chekhov's later work focuses on people's isolation, their inability to communicate with one another, and the oppressive boredom that grinds away at a person's vitality—the themes of his three masterpieces as well as of his first play, *Ivanov*. One of the later works, *Uncle Vanya* (1899), set in a country manor, is about disillusionment and fraud; nevertheless the devotion of Uncle Vanya and his niece, Sonia, brings some solace. *The Three Sisters* (1901), another play with very little action, explores the disappointments of love and the failure of three women to return to Moscow from the provinces. One of the sisters prophesies that "within another twenty-four or thirty years, everyone will work! Everyone!" an indictment of the leisure classes present in all of Chekhov's plays.

The Cherry Orchard.   This play in three acts is subtitled a comedy and concerns the rather purposeless existence of an ineffectual upper-class family unable to save its estate from a debtor's auction. Chekhov's major contribution to theatre may have been showing how drama is as much embedded in the internal struggles of characters as it is in outward action. Through the disposition of a bankrupt estate in *The Cherry Orchard* he depicts people trapped in their personalities and circumstances, incapable of either decisive action or expression of their true feelings.

The restrained drama of Chekhov's plays seldom reaches the scale of tragedy but more often than not touches on sentiment and comedy.

People make mistakes and suffer, but in the background is Chekhov's abiding faith in the quiet dignity of love and work, a life of simplicity and diligence. Maxim Gorky observed, "I have never known a man feel the importance of work as the foundation of all culture, so deeply, and for such varied reasons, as did Chekhov. . . . He loved to build, plant gardens, ornament the earth; he felt the poetry of labor. . . . Full of plans for the building of his house in Autka, he used to say: 'If every man did all he could on the piece of earth belonging to him, how beautiful would this world be!'"

■ CONNECTIONS

Goethe, *Faust,* p. 29. As the upper class lost its power and prestige to the middle class in the nineteenth century, the nobility of Europe were sometimes left without a significant role to play. Faust's project to drain the marshes can be contrasted with the impractical lives of the characters in *The Cherry Orchard*. How does Chekhov's belief in the redeeming nature of work offer an opportunity for his characters to find meaning in their lives? to find meaning for his characters?

Charlotte Perkins Gilman, *The Yellow Wallpaper,* p. 941. Central symbols take on a life of their own and reverberate throughout a text, providing unity as well as layered meaning. The yellow wallpaper in Gilman's text vibrantly relates the protagonist's state of mind. How does the cherry orchard reflect the states of mind of Chekhov's characters?

T. S. Eliot, *The Love Song of J. Alfred Prufrock* (Book 6). One effect of the new complexities of nineteenth-century life was psychological fragmentation — a split between mind and body, thought and feeling. Eliot illustrates such a division in his portrait of J. Alfred Prufrock, a man who seems incapable of making fundamental choices in his life and communicating with others. How do the difficulties of human communication affect human relationships in *The Cherry Orchard*?

■ FURTHER RESEARCH

Biography
Simmons, Ernest J. *Chekhov: A Biography*. 1962. Probably the best biography.

Criticism
Hahn, Beverly. *Chekhov: A Study of Major Stories and Plays*. 1977.
Jackson, R. L. *Chekhov: A Collection of Critical Essays*. 1967. Contains various perspectives on Chekhov's life and work.
Matlaw, Ralph E., ed. *Anton Chekhov's Short Stories: Texts of the Stories, Backgrounds, Criticism*. 1975. This Norton Critical Edition provides excellent translations of the major short stories and helpful background information.
Wellek, Rene, and N. D. Wellek. *Chekhov: New Perspectives*. 1984. A collection of contemporary criticism.

■ PRONUNCIATION

Anton Chekhov: AHN-tone CHEK-uf
Simon Panteleyevich: see-MYONE pahn-tyeh-LYAY-eh-vich
Lyubov Andreyevna: lyoo-BOHF ahn-DRAY-yev-nah
Yermolay Alexeyevich Lopakhin: yeer-moh-LIGH ah-lik-SYAY-yeh-vich lah-PAH-shin
Simeonov-Pishchik: YOH-nawf PEESH-chif
Peter (Pyotr) Sergeyevich Trofimov: PYOH-tur sir-GYAY-yeh-vich trah-FEE-muf

❧   The Cherry Orchard

Translated by David Magarshack

CHARACTERS

LYUBOV (LYUBA) ANDREYEVNA RANEVSKY,
   a landowner
ANYA, *her daughter, aged seventeen*
VARYA, *her adopted daughter, aged twenty-four*
LEONID ANDREYEVICH GAYEV, *Mrs. Ranevsky's brother*
YERMOLAY ALEXEYEVICH LOPAKHIN, *a businessman*
PETER (PYOTR) SERGEYEVICH TROFIMOV, *a student*

BORIS BORISOVICH SIMEONOV-PISHCHIK,
   a landowner
CHARLOTTE IVANOVNA, *a governess*
SIMON PANTELEYEVICH YEPIKHODOV, *a clerk*
DUNYASHA, *a maid*
FIRS, *a manservant, aged eighty-seven*
YASHA, *a young manservant*
A HIKER
A STATIONMASTER
A POST OFFICE CLERK
GUESTS *and* SERVANTS

The action takes place on MRS. RANEVSKY's *estate.*

ACT ONE

A room which is still known as the nursery. One of the doors leads to ANYA's *room. Daybreak; the sun will be rising soon. It is May. The cherry trees are in blossom, but it is cold in the orchard. Morning frost. The windows of the room are shut.*

Enter DUNYASHA, *carrying a candle, and* LOPAKHIN *with a book in his hand.*
LOPAKHIN: The train's arrived, thank goodness. What's the time?
DUNYASHA: Nearly two o'clock, sir. [*Blows out the candle.*] It's light already.

The Cherry Orchard. The arrival and departure of people frame the action, and at the play's center is the orchard. For Lyubov, Gayev, and the landowning elite, the cherry orchard symbolizes the privileges of money and tradition as well as an ignorance of the price the serf class had to pay for such unproductive, foolish luxury. The student Trofimov recognizes the burden of economic oppression represented by the orchard, and with youthful bombast champions work as the pathway to a new Russian Eden—a nineteenth-century "myth of progress." Between these two positions is Lopakhin, who embodies the crass materialism of the new, pragmatic middle class.

In a letter dated September 15, 1903, Chekhov chooses to describe *The Cherry Orchard* not as a tragedy of the old Russian aristocracy "but as comedy, in places even a farce." One meaning of *comedy* is a drama whose subject matter is commonplace, not sufficiently elevated to warrant the term *tragedy*; in this sense the characters in *The Cherry Orchard* are comedic. Social mores inhibit their communication, and their crippled wills prevent them from taking meaningful action. *Comedy* also means humor, and this play has its comic moments, however painful they might appear. With cultural pretensions, servants mimic the aristocrats, who in turn betray their own limitations with inappropriate gestures and remarks. Gayev, for example, dilutes his opinions with exclamations heard while playing billiards. Simeonov-Pishchik, a neighboring landowner, snatches Lyubov's medicines and swallows all the pills. Instead of talk of a match between Varya and Lopakhin, a relationship that would reconcile social classes and save the orchard, a conversation drifts to the weather and a broken thermometer. There is nothing comic, however, about the play's final scene, which overflows with pathos.

LOPAKHIN: How late was the train? Two hours at least. [*Yawns and stretches.*] What a damn fool I am! Came here specially to meet them at the station and fell asleep. . . . Sat down in a chair and dropped off. What a nuisance! Why didn't you wake me?

DUNYASHA: I thought you'd gone, sir. [*Listens.*] I think they're coming.

LOPAKHIN [*listening*]: No. . . . I should have been there to help them with the luggage and so on. [*Pause.*] Mrs. Ranevsky's been abroad for five years. I wonder what she's like now. . . . She's such a nice person. Simple, easy-going. I remember when I was a lad of fifteen, my late father—he used to keep a shop in the village—punched me in the face and made my nose bleed. We'd gone into the yard to fetch something, and he was drunk. Mrs. Ranevsky—I remember it as if it happened yesterday, she was such a young girl then and so slim—took me to the washstand in this very room, the nursery. "Don't cry, little peasant," she said, "it won't matter by the time you're wed." [*Pause.*] Little peasant . . . It's quite true my father was a peasant, but here I am wearing a white waistcoat and brown shoes. A dirty peasant in a fashionable shop. . . . Except, of course, that I'm a rich man now, rolling in money. But, come to think of it, I'm a plain peasant still. . . . [*Turns the pages of his book.*] Been reading this book and haven't understood a word. Fell asleep reading it.

Pause.

DUNYASHA: The dogs have been awake all night; they know their masters are coming.

LOPAKHIN: What's the matter, Dunyasha? Why are you in such a state?

DUNYASHA: My hands are shaking. I think I'm going to faint.

LOPAKHIN: A little too refined, aren't you, Dunyasha? Quite the young lady. Dress, hair. It won't do, you know. Remember your place!

Enter YEPIKHODOV *with a bunch of flowers; he wears a jacket and brightly polished high-boots which squeak loudly; on coming in, he drops the flowers.*

YEPIKHODOV [*picking up the flowers*]: The gardener sent these. Said to put them in the dining room. [*Hands the flowers to* DUNYASHA.]

LOPAKHIN: Bring me some kvass[1] while you're about it.

DUNYASHA: Yes, sir. [*Goes out.*]

YEPIKHODOV: Thirty degrees, morning frost, and the cherry trees in full bloom. Can't say I think much of our climate, sir. [*Sighs.*] Our climate isn't particularly accommodating, is it, sir? Not when you want it to be, anyway. And another thing. The other day I bought myself this pair of boots, and believe me, sir, they squeak so terribly that it's more than a man can endure. Do you happen to know of something I could grease them with?

LOPAKHIN: Go away. You make me tired.

YEPIKHODOV: Every day, sir, I'm overtaken by some calamity. Not that I mind. I'm used to it. I just smile. [DUNYASHA *comes in and hands* LOPAKHIN *the kvass.*] I'll be off. [*Bumps into a chair and knocks it over.*] There you are, sir. [*Triumphantly.*]

---

[1] kvass: Russian beer.

You see, sir, pardon the expression, this sort of circumstance . . . I mean to say . . . Remarkable! Quite remarkable! [*Goes out.*]

DUNYASHA: I simply must tell you, sir: Yepikhodov has proposed to me.

LOPAKHIN: Oh?

DUNYASHA: I really don't know what to do, sir. He's ever such a quiet fellow, except that sometimes he starts talking and you can't understand a word he says. It sounds all right and it's ever so moving, only you can't make head or tail of it. I like him a little, I think. I'm not sure though. He's madly in love with me. He's such an unlucky fellow, sir. Every day something happens to him. Everyone teases him about it. They've nicknamed him Twenty-two Calamities.

LOPAKHIN [*listens*]: I think I can hear them coming.

DUNYASHA: They're coming! Goodness, I don't know what's the matter with me. I've gone cold all over.

LOPAKHIN: Yes, they are coming all right. Let's go and meet them. Will she recognize me? We haven't seen each other for five years.

DUNYASHA [*agitated*]: I'm going to faint. Oh dear, I'm going to faint!

Two carriages can be heard driving up to the house. LOPAKHIN *and* DUNYASHA *go out quickly. The stage is empty. People can be heard making a noise in the adjoining rooms.* FIRS, *who has been to meet* MRS. RANEVSKY *at the station, walks across the stage hurriedly, leaning on a stick. He wears an old-fashioned livery coat and a top hat; he keeps muttering to himself, but it is impossible to make out a single word. The noise offstage becomes louder. A voice is heard: "Let's go through here."* MRS. RANEVSKY, ANYA, *and* CHARLOTTE, *with a lap dog on a little chain, all wearing traveling clothes,* VARYA, *wearing an overcoat and a head scarf,* GAYEV, SIMEONOV-PISHCHIK, LOPAKHIN, DUNYASHA, *carrying a bundle and an umbrella, and other servants with luggage walk across the stage.*

ANYA: Let's go through here. Remember this room, Mother?

MRS. RANEVSKY [*joyfully, through tears*]: The nursery!

VARYA: It's so cold. My hands are quite numb. [*To* MRS. RANEVSKY] Your rooms, the white one and the mauve one, are just as you left them, Mother dear.

MRS. RANEVSKY: The nursery! My dear, my beautiful room! I used to sleep here when I was a little girl. [*Cries.*] I feel like a little girl again now. [*Kisses her brother and* VARYA, *and then her brother again.*] Varya is the same as ever. Looks like a nun. And I also recognized Dunyasha. [*Kisses* DUNYASHA.]

GAYEV: The train was two hours late. How do you like that? What a way to run a railway!

CHARLOTTE [*To* PISHCHIK]: My dog also eats nuts.

PISHCHIK [*surprised*]: Good Lord!

All, except ANYA *and* DUNYASHA, *go out.*

DUNYASHA: We thought you'd never come. [*Helps* ANYA *off with her coat and hat.*]

ANYA: I haven't slept for four nights on our journey. Now I'm chilled right through.

DUNYASHA: You left before Easter. It was snowing and freezing then. It's different now, isn't it? Darling Anya! [*Laughs and kisses her.*] I've missed you so much, my darling, my precious! Oh, I must tell you at once! I can't keep it to myself a minute longer. . . .

ANYA [*apathetically*]: What is it this time?

DUNYASHA: Our clerk, Yepikhodov, proposed to me after Easter.

ANYA: Always the same. [*Tidying her hair.*] I've lost all my hairpins. [*She is so tired, she can hardly stand.*]

DUNYASHA: I don't know what to think. He loves me so much, so much!

ANYA [*tenderly, looking through the door into her room*]: My own room, my own windows, just as if I'd never been away! I'm home again! As soon as I get up in the morning, I'll run out into the orchard. . . . Oh, if only I could sleep. I didn't sleep all the way back, I was so worried.

DUNYASHA: Mr. Trofimov arrived the day before yesterday.

ANYA [*joyfully*]: Peter!

DUNYASHA: He's asleep in the bathhouse. He's been living there. Afraid of being a nuisance, he says. [*Glancing at her watch.*] I really ought to wake him, except that Miss Varya told me not to. "Don't you dare wake him!" she said.

VARYA *comes in with a bunch of keys at her waist.*

VARYA: Dunyasha, coffee quick! Mother's asking for some.

DUNYASHA: I won't be a minute! [*Goes out.*]

VARYA: Well, thank goodness you're all back. You're home again, my darling. [*Caressing her.*] My darling is home again! My sweet child is home again.

ANYA: I've had such an awful time!

VARYA: I can imagine it.

ANYA: I left before Easter. It was terribly cold then. All the way Charlotte kept talking and doing her conjuring tricks. Why did you force Charlotte on me?

VARYA: But you couldn't have gone alone, darling, could you? You're only seventeen!

ANYA: In Paris it was also cold and snowing. My French is awful. I found Mother living on the fourth floor. When I got there, she had some French visitors, a few ladies and an old Catholic priest with a book. The place was full of tobacco smoke and terribly uncomfortable. Suddenly I felt sorry for Mother, so sorry that I took her head in my arms, held it tightly, and couldn't let go. Afterwards Mother was very sweet to me. She was crying all the time.

VARYA [*through tears*]: Don't go on, Anya. Please don't.

ANYA: She'd already sold her villa near Mentone. She had nothing left. Nothing! I hadn't any money, either. There was hardly enough for the journey. Mother just won't understand! We had dinner at the station and she would order the most expensive things and tip the waiters a ruble each. Charlotte was just the same. Yasha, too, demanded to be given the same kind of food. It was simply awful! You see, Yasha is Mother's manservant. We've brought him back with us.

VARYA: Yes, I've seen the scoundrel.

ANYA: Well, what's been happening? Have you paid the interest on the mortgage?

VARYA: Heavens, no!

ANYA: Dear, oh dear . . .

VARYA: The estate will be up for sale in August.

ANYA: Oh dear!

LOPAKHIN [*puts his head through the door and bleats*]: Bah-h-h! [*Goes out.*]

VARYA [*through tears*]: Oh, I'd like to hit him! [*Shakes her fist.*]

ANYA [*gently embracing* VARYA]: Varya, has he proposed to you? [VARYA *shakes her head.*] But he loves you. Why don't you two come to an understanding? What are you waiting for?

VARYA: I don't think anything will come of it. He's so busy. He can't be bothered with me. Why, he doesn't even notice me. I wish I'd never known him. I can't stand the sight of him. Everyone's talking about our wedding, everyone's congratulating me, while there's really nothing in it. It's all so unreal. Like a dream. [*In a different tone of voice.*] You've got a new brooch. Like a bee, isn't it?

ANYA [*sadly*]: Yes, Mother bought it. [*Goes to her room, talking quite happily, like a child.*] You know, I went up in a balloon in Paris!

VARYA: My darling's home again! My dearest one's home again! [DUNYASHA *has come back with a coffeepot and is making coffee;* VARYA *is standing at the door of* ANYA'*s room.*] All day long, darling, I'm busy about the house, and all the time I'm dreaming, dreaming. If only we could find a rich husband for you! My mind would be at rest then. I'd go into a convent and later on a pilgrimage to Kiev . . . to Moscow. Just keep going from one holy place to another. On and on. . . . Wonderful!

ANYA: The birds are singing in the orchard. What's the time?

VARYA: It's past two. It's time you were asleep, darling. [*Goes into* ANYA'*s room.*] Wonderful!

Enter YASHA *with a traveling rug and a small bag.*

YASHA [*crossing the stage, in an affected genteel voice*]: May I be permitted to go through here?

DUNYASHA: I can hardly recognize you, Yasha. You've changed so much abroad.

YASHA: Hmmm . . . And who are you, may I ask?

DUNYASHA: When you left, I was no bigger than this. [*Shows her height from the floor with her hand.*] I'm Dunyasha, Fyodor Kozoedov's daughter. Don't you remember me?

YASHA: Mmmm . . . Juicy little cucumber! [*Looks round, then puts his arms around her; she utters a little scream and drops a saucer.* YASHA *goes out hurriedly.*]

VARYA [*in the doorway, crossly*]: What's going on there?

DUNYASHA [*in tears*]: I've broken a saucer.

VARYA: That's lucky.

ANYA [*coming out of her room*]: Mother must be told Peter's here.

VARYA: I gave orders not to wake him.

ANYA [*pensively*]: Father died six years ago. A month after that our brother, Grisha, was drowned in the river. Such a pretty little boy. He was only seven. Mother took it badly. She went away, went away never to come back. [*Shudders.*] Peter Trofimov was Grisha's tutor. He might remind her . . .

FIRS *comes in, wearing a jacket and a white waistcoat.*

FIRS [*walks up to the coffeepot anxiously*]: Madam will have her coffee here. [*Puts on white gloves.*] Is the coffee ready? [*Sternly, to* DUNYASHA.] You there! Where's the cream?

DUNYASHA: Oh dear! [*Goes out quickly.*]

FIRS [*fussing round the coffeepot*]: The nincompoop! [*Muttering to himself.*] She's
come from Paris. . . . Master used to go to Paris. . . . Aye, by coach. . . . [*Laughs.*]

VARYA: What are you talking about, Firs?

FIRS: Sorry, what did you say? [*Joyfully.*] Madam is home again! Home at last! I can
die happy now. [*Weeps with joy.*]

Enter MRS. RANEVSKY, GAYEV, *and* SIMEONOV-PISHCHIK, *the last one wearing a Russian long-
waisted coat of expensive cloth and wide trousers. As he enters,* GAYEV *moves his arms and body
as if he were playing billiards.*

MRS. RANEVSKY: How does it go now? Let me think. Pot the red in the corner. Double
into the middle pocket.

GAYEV: And straight into the corner! A long time ago, Lyuba, you and I slept in this
room. Now I'm fifty-one. . . . Funny, isn't it!

LOPAKHIN: Aye, time flies.

GAYEV: I beg your pardon?

LOPAKHIN: "Time flies," I said.

GAYEV: The place reeks of patchouli.[2]

ANYA: I'm off to bed. Good night, Mother. [*Kisses her mother.*]

MRS. RANEVSKY: My sweet little darling! [*Kisses her hands.*] You're glad to be home,
aren't you? I still can't believe it.

ANYA: Good night, Uncle.

GAYEV [*kissing her face and hands*]: God bless you. You're so like your mother! [*To his
sister*] You were just like her at that age, Lyuba.

ANYA *shakes hands with* LOPAKHIN *and* PISHCHIK. *Goes out and shuts the door behind her.*

MRS. RANEVSKY: She's terribly tired.

PISHCHIK: It was a long journey.

VARYA [*to* LOPAKHIN *and* PISHCHIK]: Well, gentlemen, it's past two o'clock. You
mustn't outstay your welcome, must you?

MRS. RANEVSKY [*laughs*]: You're just the same, Varya. [*Draws* VARYA *to her and kisses
her.*] Let me have my coffee first and then we'll all go. [FIRS *puts a little cushion
under her feet.*] Thank you, Firs dear. I've got used to having coffee. I drink it day
and night. Thank you, Firs, thank you, my dear old man. [*Kisses* FIRS.]

VARYA: I'd better make sure they've brought all the things in. [*Goes out.*]

MRS. RANEVSKY: Is it really me sitting here? [*Laughs.*] I feel like jumping about, waving my arms. [*Covers her face with her hands.*] And what if it's all a dream? God
knows, I love my country. I love it dearly. I couldn't look out of the train for crying. [*Through tears.*] But, I suppose I'd better have my coffee. Thank you, Firs,
thank you, dear old man. I'm so glad you're still alive.

FIRS: The day before yesterday . . .

GAYEV: He's a little deaf.

LOPAKHIN: At five o'clock I've got to leave for Kharkov. What a nuisance! I wish I

---

[2] **patchouli:** East Indian perfume.

could have had a good look at you, a good talk with you. You're still as magnificent as ever. . . .

PISHCHIK [*breathing heavily*]: Lovelier, I'd say. Dressed in the latest Paris fashion. If only I were twenty years younger—ho-ho-ho!

LOPAKHIN: This brother of yours says that I'm an ignorant oaf, a tightfisted peasant, but I don't mind. Let him talk. All I want is that you should believe in me as you used to, that you should look at me as you used to with those wonderful eyes of yours. Merciful heavens! My father was a serf of your father and your grandfather, but you, you alone, did so much for me in the past that I forgot everything, and I love you just as if you were my own flesh and blood, more than my own flesh and blood.

MRS. RANEVSKY: I can't sit still, I can't. . . . [*Jumps up and walks about the room in great agitation.*] This happiness is more than I can bear. Laugh at me if you like. I'm making such a fool of myself. Oh, my darling little bookcase . . . [*Kisses the bookcase.*] My sweet little table . . .

GAYEV: You know, of course, that Nanny died here while you were away.

MRS. RANEVSKY [*sits down and drinks her coffee*]: Yes, God rest her soul. They wrote to tell me about it.

GAYEV: Anastasy, too, is dead. Boss-eyed Peter left me for another job. He's with the Police Superintendent in town now. [*Takes a box of fruit drops out of his pocket and sucks one.*]

PISHCHIK: My daughter Dashenka—er—wishes to be remembered to you.

LOPAKHIN: I'd like to say something very nice and cheerful to you. [*Glances at his watch.*] I shall have to be going in a moment and there isn't much time to talk. As you know, your cherry orchard's being sold to pay your debts. The auction is on the twenty-second of August. But there's no need to worry, my dear. You can sleep soundly. There's a way out. Here's my plan. Listen carefully, please. Your estate is only about twelve miles from town, and the railway is not very far away. Now, all you have to do is break up your cherry orchard and the land along the river into building plots and lease them out for country cottages. You'll then have an income of at least twenty-five thousand a year.

GAYEV: I'm sorry, but what utter nonsense!

MRS. RANEVSKY: I don't quite follow you, Lopakhin.

LOPAKHIN: You'll be able to charge your tenants at least twenty-five rubles a year for a plot of about three acres. I bet you anything that if you advertise now, there won't be a single plot left by the autumn. They will all be snapped up. In fact, I congratulate you. You are saved. The site is magnificent and the river is deep enough for bathing. Of course, the place will have to be cleared, tidied up. . . . I mean, all the old buildings will have to be pulled down, including, I'm sorry to say, this house, but it isn't any use to anybody any more, is it? The old cherry orchard will have to be cut down.

MRS. RANEVSKY: Cut down? My dear man, I'm very sorry but I don't think you know what you're talking about. If there's anything of interest, anything quite remarkable, in fact, in the whole county, it's our cherry orchard.

LOPAKHIN: The only remarkable thing about this orchard is that it's very large. It only produces a crop every other year, and even then you don't know what to do with the cherries. Nobody wants to buy them.

GAYEV: Why, you'll find our orchard mentioned in the encyclopedia.

LOPAKHIN [*glancing at his watch*]: If we can't think of anything and if we can't come to any decision, it won't be only your cherry orchard but your whole estate that will be sold at auction on the twenty-second of August. Make up your mind. I tell you, there is no other way. Take my word for it. There isn't.

FIRS: In the old days, forty or fifty years ago, the cherries used to be dried, preserved, made into jam, and sometimes———

GAYEV: Do shut up, Firs.

FIRS: ———and sometimes cartloads of dried cherries were sent to Moscow and Kharkov. Fetched a lot of money, they did. Soft and juicy, those cherries were. Sweet and such a lovely smell . . . They knew the recipe then. . . .

MRS. RANEVSKY: And where's the recipe now?

FIRS: Forgotten. No one remembers it.

PISHCHIK [*to* MRS. RANEVSKY]: What was it like in Paris? Eh? Eat any frogs?

MRS. RANEVSKY: I ate crocodiles.

PISHCHIK: Good Lord!

LOPAKHIN: Till recently there were only the gentry and the peasants in the country. Now we have holiday-makers. All our towns, even the smallest, are surrounded by country cottages. I shouldn't be surprised if in twenty years the holiday-maker multiplies enormously. All your holiday-maker does now is drink tea on the veranda, but it's quite in the cards that if he becomes the owner of three acres of land, he'll do a bit of farming on the side, and then your cherry orchard will become a happy, prosperous, thriving place.

GAYEV [*indignantly*]: What nonsense!

Enter VARYA *and* YASHA.

VARYA: I've got two telegrams in here for you, Mother dear. [*Picks out a key and unlocks the old-fashioned bookcase with a jingling noise.*] Here they are.

MRS. RANEVSKY: They're from Paris. [*Tears the telegrams up without reading them.*] I've finished with Paris.

GAYEV: Do you know how old this bookcase is, Lyuba? Last week I pulled out the bottom drawer and saw some figures burned into it. This bookcase was made exactly a hundred years ago. What do you think of that? Eh? We ought really to celebrate its centenary. An inanimate object, but say what you like, it's a bookcase after all.

PISHCHIK [*amazed*]: A hundred years! Good Lord!

GAYEV: Yes, indeed. It's quite something. [*Feeling round the bookcase with his hands.*] Dear, highly esteemed bookcase, I salute you. For over a hundred years you have devoted yourself to the glorious ideals of goodness and justice. Throughout the hundred years your silent appeal to fruitful work has never faltered. It sustained [*through tears*] in several generations of our family, their courage and faith in a better future and fostered in us the ideals of goodness and social consciousness.

Pause.

LOPAKHIN: Aye. . . .

MRS. RANEVSKY: You haven't changed a bit, have you, darling Leonid?

GAYEV [*slightly embarrassed*]: Off the right into a corner! Pot into the middle pocket!

LOPAKHIN [*glancing at his watch*]: Well, afraid it's time I was off.

YASHA [*handing* MRS. RANEVSKY *her medicine*]: Your pills, ma'am.

PISHCHIK: Never take any medicines, dear lady. I don't suppose they'll do you much harm, but they won't do you any good either. Here, let me have 'em, my dear lady. [*Takes the box of pills from her, pours the pills into the palm of his hand, blows on them, puts them all into his mouth, and washes them down with kvass.*] There!

MRS. RANEVSKY [*alarmed*]: You're mad!

PISHCHIK: Swallowed the lot.

LOPAKHIN: The glutton!

All laugh.

FIRS: He was here at Easter, the gentleman was. Ate half a bucketful of pickled cucumbers, he did. . . . [*Mutters.*]

MRS. RANEVSKY: What is he saying?

VARYA: He's been muttering like that for the last three years. We've got used to it.

YASHA: Old age!

CHARLOTTE, *in a white dress, very thin and tightly laced, a lorgnette dangling from her belt, crosses the stage.*

LOPAKHIN: I'm sorry, Miss Charlotte, I haven't had the chance of saying how-do-you-do to you. [*Tries to kiss her hand.*]

CHARLOTTE [*snatching her hand away*]: If I let you kiss my hand, you'll want to kiss my elbow, then my shoulder . . .

LOPAKHIN: It's not my lucky day. [*They all laugh.*] My dear Charlotte, show us a trick, please.

MRS. RANEVSKY: Yes, do show us a trick, Charlotte.

CHARLOTTE: I won't. I'm off to bed. [*Goes out.*]

LOPAKHIN: We'll meet again in three weeks. [*Kisses* MRS. RANEVSKY'S *hand.*] Goodbye for now. I must go. [*To* GAYEV.] So long. [*Embraces* PISHCHIK.] So long. [*Shakes hands with* VARYA *and then with* FIRS *and* YASHA.] I wish I didn't have to go. [*To* MRS. RANEVSKY.] Let me know if you make up your mind about the country cottages. If you decide to go ahead, I'll get you a loan of fifty thousand or more. Think it over seriously.

VARYA [*angrily*]: For goodness' sake, go!

LOPAKHIN: I'm going, I'm going. . . . [*Goes out.*]

GAYEV: The oaf! However, I'm sorry. Varya's going to marry him, isn't she? He's Varya's intended.

VARYA: Don't say things you'll be sorry for, Uncle.

MRS. RANEVSKY: But why not, Varya? I should be only too glad. He's a good man.

PISHCHIK: A most admirable fellow, to tell the truth. My Dashenka—er—also says that—er—says all sorts of things. [*Drops off and snores, but wakes up immediately.*] By the way, my dear lady, you will lend me two hundred and forty rubles, won't you? Must pay the interest on the mortgage tomorrow.

VARYA [*terrified*]: We have no money; we haven't!

MRS. RANEVSKY: We really haven't any, you know.

PISHCHIK: Have a good look around—you're sure to find it. [*Laughs.*] I never lose hope. Sometimes I think it's all over with me, I'm done for, then—hey presto—they build a railway over my land and pay me for it. Something's bound to turn up, if not today, then tomorrow. I'm certain of it. Dashenka might win two hundred thousand. She's got a ticket in the lottery, you know.

MRS. RANEVSKY: Well, I've finished my coffee. Now to bed.

FIRS [*brushing* GAYEV's *clothes admonishingly*]: Put the wrong trousers on again, sir. What am I to do with you?

VARYA [*in a low voice*]: Anya's asleep. [*Opens a window quietly.*] The sun has risen. It's no longer cold. Look, Mother dear. What lovely trees! Heavens, what wonderful air! The starlings are singing.

GAYEV [*opens another window*]: The orchard's all white. Lyuba, you haven't forgotten, have you? The long avenue there—it runs on and on, straight as an arrow. It gleams on moonlit nights. Remember? You haven't forgotten, have you?

MRS. RANEVSKY [*looking through the window at the orchard*]: Oh, my childhood, oh, my innocence! I slept in this nursery. I used to look out at the orchard from here. Every morning happiness used to wake with me. The orchard was just the same in those days. Nothing has changed. [*Laughs happily.*] White, all white! Oh, my orchard! After the dark, rainy autumn and the cold winter, you're young again, full of happiness; the heavenly angels haven't forsaken you. If only this heavy load could be lifted from my heart; if only I could forget my past!

GAYEV: Well, and now they're going to sell the orchard to pay our debts. Funny, isn't it?

MRS. RANEVSKY: Look! Mother's walking in the orchard in . . . a white dress! [*Laughs happily.*] It *is* Mother!

GAYEV: Where?

VARYA: Really, Mother dear, what are you saying?

MRS. RANEVSKY: There's no one there. I just imagined it. Over there, on the right, near the turning to the summer house, a little white tree's leaning over. It looks like a woman. [*Enter* TROFIMOV. *He is dressed in a shabby student's uniform and wears glasses.*] What an amazing orchard! Masses of white blossom. A blue sky . . .

TROFIMOV: I say, Mrs. Ranevsky . . . [*She looks round at him.*] I've just come to say hello. I'll go at once. [*Kisses her hand warmly.*] I was told to wait till morning, but I—I couldn't, I couldn't.

MRS. RANEVSKY *gazes at him in bewilderment.*

VARYA [*through tears*]: This is Peter Trofimov.

TROFIMOV: Peter Trofimov. Your son Grisha's old tutor. I haven't changed so much, have I?

MRS. RANEVSKY *embraces him and weeps quietly.*

GAYEV [*embarrassed*]: There, there, Lyuba.

VARYA [*cries*]: I did tell you to wait till tomorrow, didn't I, Peter?

MRS. RANEVSKY: Grisha, my . . . little boy. Grisha . . . my son.

VARYA: It can't be helped, Mother. It was God's will.

TROFIMOV [*gently, through tears*]: Now, now . . .

MRS. RANEVSKY [*weeping quietly*]: My little boy died, drowned. Why? Why, my friend? [*More quietly.*] Anya's asleep in there and here I am shouting, making a noise. . . . Well, Peter? You're not as good-looking as you were, are you? Why not? Why have you aged so much?

TROFIMOV: A peasant woman in a railway carriage called me "a moth-eaten gentleman."

MRS. RANEVSKY: You were only a boy then. A charming young student. Now you're growing thin on top, you wear glasses. . . . You're not still a student, are you? [*Walks toward the door.*]

TROFIMOV: I expect I shall be an eternal student.

MRS. RANEVSKY [*kisses her brother and then* VARYA]: Well, go to bed now. You, Leonid, have aged too.

PISHCHIK [*following her*]: So, we're off to bed now, are we? Oh dear, my gout! I think I'd better stay the night here. Now, what about letting me have the—er—two hundred and forty rubles tomorrow morning, dear lady? Early tomorrow morning. . . .

GAYEV: He does keep on, doesn't he?

PISHCHIK: Two hundred and forty rubles—to pay the interest on the mortgage.

MRS. RANEVSKY: But I haven't any money, my dear man.

PISHCHIK: I'll pay you back, dear lady. Such a trifling sum.

MRS. RANEVSKY: Oh, all right. Leonid will let you have it. Let him have it, Leonid.

GAYEV: Let him have it? The hell I will.

MRS. RANEVSKY: What else can we do? Let him have it, please. He needs it. He'll pay it back.

MRS. RANEVSKY, TROFIMOV, PISHCHIK, *and* FIRS *go out.* GAYEV, VARYA, *and* YASHA *remain.*

GAYEV: My sister hasn't got out of the habit of throwing money about. [*To* YASHA] Out of my way, fellow. You reek of the hen house.

YASHA [*grins*]: And you, sir, are the same as ever.

GAYEV: I beg your pardon? [*To* VARYA] What did he say?

VARYA [*to* YASHA]: Your mother's come from the village. She's been sitting in the servants' quarters since yesterday. She wants to see you.

YASHA: Oh, bother her!

VARYA: You shameless bounder!

YASHA: I don't care. She could have come tomorrow, couldn't she? [*Goes out.*]

VARYA: Dear Mother is just the same as ever. Hasn't changed a bit. If you let her, she'd give away everything.

GAYEV: I suppose so. [*Pause.*] When a lot of remedies are suggested for an illness, it means that the illness is incurable. I've been thinking, racking my brains; I've got all sorts of remedies, lots of them, which, of course, means that I haven't got one. It would be marvelous if somebody left us some money. It would be marvelous if we found a very rich husband for Anya. It would be marvelous if one of us went to Yaroslavl to try our luck with our great-aunt, the Countess. She's very rich, you know. Very rich.

VARYA [*crying*]: If only God would help us.

GAYEV: Don't howl! Our aunt is very rich, but she doesn't like us. First, because my sister married a lawyer and not a nobleman. . . . [ANYA *appears in the doorway.*] She did not marry a nobleman, and she has not been leading an exactly blameless life, has she? She's a good, kind, nice person. I love her very much. But, however much you try to make allowances for her, you have to admit that she is an immoral woman. You can sense it in every movement she makes.

VARYA [*in a whisper*]: Anya's standing in the doorway.

GAYEV: I beg your pardon? [*Pause.*] Funny thing, there's something in my right eye. Can't see properly. On Thursday, too, in the district court . . .

ANYA *comes in.*

VARYA: Why aren't you asleep, Anya?

ANYA: I can't sleep, I can't.

GAYEV: My little darling! [*Kisses* ANYA's *face and hands.*] My dear child! [*Through tears.*] You're not my niece, you're my angel. You're everything to me. Believe me. Do believe me.

ANYA: I believe you, Uncle. Everyone loves you, everyone respects you, but, dear Uncle, you shouldn't talk so much. What were you saying just now about Mother, about your own sister? What did you say it for?

GAYEV: Well, yes, yes. [*He takes her hand and covers his face with it.*] You're quite right. It was dreadful. Dear God, dear God, help me! That speech I made to the bookcase today—it was so silly. The moment I finished it, I realized how silly it was.

VARYA: It's quite true, Uncle dear. You oughtn't to talk so much. Just don't talk, that's all.

ANYA: If you stopped talking, you'd feel much happier yourself.

GAYEV: Not another word. [*Kisses* ANYA's *and* VARYA's *hands.*] Not another word. Now to business. Last Thursday I was at the county court, and, well—er—I met a lot of people there, and we started talking about this and that, and—er—it would seem that we might manage to raise some money on a promissory note and pay the interest to the bank.

VARYA: Oh, if only God would help us!

GAYEV: I shall be there again on Tuesday, and I'll have another talk. [*To* VARYA.] For goodness' sake, don't howl! [*To* ANYA.] Your mother will have a talk with

Lopakhin. I'm sure he won't refuse her. After you've had your rest, you'll go to Yaroslavl to see your great-aunt, the Countess. That's how we shall tackle the problem from three different sides, and I'm sure we'll get it settled. The interest we shall pay. Of that I'm quite sure. [*Puts a fruit drop in his mouth.*] I give you my word of honor, I swear by anything you like, the estate will not be sold! [*Excitedly.*] Why, I'll stake my life on it! Here's my hand; call me a rotten scoundrel if I allow the auction to take place. I stake my life on it!

ANYA [*has regained her composure; she looks happy*]: You're so good, Uncle dear! So clever! [*Embraces him.*] I'm no longer worried now. Not a bit worried. I'm happy.

Enter FIRS.

FIRS [*reproachfully*]: Have you no fear of God, sir? When are you going to bed?

GAYEV: Presently, presently. Go away, Firs. Never mind, I'll undress myself this time. Well, children, bye-bye now. More about it tomorrow. Now you must go to bed. [*Kisses* ANYA *and* VARYA.] I'm a man of the eighties. People don't think much of that time, but let me tell you, I've suffered a great deal for my convictions during my life. It's not for nothing that the peasants love me. You have to know your peasant, you have to know how to————

ANYA: There you go again, Uncle.

VARYA: Please, Uncle dear, don't talk so much.

FIRS [*angrily*]: Sir!

GAYEV: I'm coming, I'm coming. You two go to bed. Off two cushions into the middle. Pot the white!

GAYEV *goes out,* FIRS *shuffling off after him.*

ANYA: I'm not worried any longer now. I don't feel like going to Yaroslavl. I don't like my great-aunt, but I'm no longer worried. I ought to thank Uncle for that. [*Sits down.*]

VARYA: I ought to go to bed, and I shall be going in a moment. I must tell you first that something unpleasant happened here while you were away. You know, of course, that only a few old servants live in the old servants' quarters: Yefimushka, Polia, Evstigney, and, well, also Karp. They had been letting some tramps sleep there, but I didn't say anything about it. Then I heard that they were telling everybody that I'd given orders for them to be fed on nothing but dried peas. I'm supposed to be a miser, you see. It was all that Evstigney's doing. Well, I said to myself, if that's how it is, you just wait! So I sent for Evstigney. [*Yawns.*] He comes. "What do you mean," I said, "Evstigney, you silly old fool?" [*Looks at* ANYA.] Darling! [*Pause.*] Asleep . . . [*Takes* ANYA *by the arm.*] Come to bed, dear. . . . Come on! [*Leads her by the arm.*] My darling's fallen asleep. Come along. [*They go out. A shepherd's pipe is heard playing from far away on the other side of the orchard.* TROFIMOV *walks across the stage and, catching sight of* VARYA *and* ANYA, *stops.*] Shh! She's asleep, asleep. Come along, my sweet.

ANYA [*softly, half asleep*]: I'm so tired. . . . I keep hearing harness bells. Uncle . . . dear . . . Mother and Uncle . . .

VARYA: Come on, my sweet, come on. . . .

They go into ANYA'*s room.*

TROFIMOV [*deeply moved*]: My sun! My spring!

Curtain.

ACT TWO

Open country. A small tumbledown wayside chapel. Near it, a well, some large stones, which look like old gravestones, and an old bench. A road can be seen leading to GAYEV'*s estate. On one side, a row of tall dark poplars; it is there that the cherry orchard begins. In the distance, some telegraph poles, and far, far away on the horizon, the outlines of a large town that is visible only in very fine, clear weather. The sun is about to set.* CHARLOTTE, YASHA, *and* DUNYASHA *are sitting on the bench;* YEPIKHODOV *is standing nearby and is playing a guitar; they all sit sunk in thought.* CHARLOTTE *wears a man's old peaked hat; she has taken a shotgun from her shoulder and is adjusting the buckle on the strap.*

CHARLOTTE [*pensively*]: I haven't a proper passport, I don't know how old I am, and I can't help thinking that I'm still a young girl. When I was a little girl, my father and mother used to travel the fairs and give performances — very good ones. I used to do the *salto mortale*[3] and all sorts of other tricks. When Father and Mother died, a German lady adopted me and began educating me. Very well. I grew up and became a governess, but where I came from and who I am, I do not know. Who my parents were, I do not know either. They may not even have been married. I don't know. [*Takes a cucumber out of her pocket and starts eating it.*] I don't know anything. [*Pause.*] I'm longing to talk to someone, but there is no one to talk to. I haven't anyone. . . .

YEPIKHODOV [*plays his guitar and sings*]: "What care I for the world and its bustle? What care I for my friends and my foes?". . . Nice to play a mandolin.

DUNYASHA: It's a guitar, not a mandolin. [*She looks at herself in a hand mirror and powders her face.*]

YEPIKHODOV: To a madman in love, it's a mandolin. [*Sings softly.*] "If only my heart was warmed by the fire of love requited."

YASHA *joins in.*

CHARLOTTE: How terribly these people sing! Ugh! Like hyenas.

DUNYASHA [*to* YASHA]: All the same, you're ever so lucky to have been abroad.

YASHA: Why, of course. Can't help agreeing with you there. [*Yawns, then lights a cigar.*]

YEPIKHODOV: Stands to reason. Abroad, everything's in excellent complexion. Been like that for ages.

YASHA: Naturally.

---

[3] *salto mortale:* Italian for "leap of death"; here, a standing somersault.

YEPIKHODOV: I'm a man of some education, I read all sorts of remarkable books, but what I simply can't understand is where it's all leading to. I mean, what do I really want—to live or to shoot myself? In any case, I always carry a revolver. Here it is. [*Shows them his revolver.*]

CHARLOTTE: That's done. Now I can go. [*Puts the shotgun over her shoulder.*] You're a very clever man, Yepikhodov. You frighten me to death. Women must be madly in love with you. Brrr! [*Walking away.*] These clever people are all so stupid. I've no one to talk to. Always alone, alone, I've no one, and who I am and what I am for is a mystery. [*Walks off slowly.*]

YEPIKHODOV: Strictly speaking, and apart from all other considerations, what I ought to say about myself, among other things, is that Fate treats me without mercy, like a storm a small boat. Even supposing I'm mistaken, why in that case should I wake up this morning and suddenly find a spider of quite enormous dimensions on my chest? As big as that. [*Uses both hands to show the spider's size.*] Or again, I pick up a jug of kvass and there's something quite outrageously indecent in it, like a cockroach. [*Pause.*] Have you ever read Buckle's *History of Civilization*?[4] [*Pause.*] May I have a word or two with you, Dunyasha?

DUNYASHA: Oh, all right. What is it?

YEPIKHODOV: I'd be very much obliged if you'd let me speak to you in private. [*Sighs.*]

DUNYASHA [*embarrassed*]: All right, only first bring me my cape, please. It's hanging near the wardrobe. It's so damp here.

YEPIKHODOV: Very well, I'll fetch it. . . . Now I know what to do with my revolver. [*Picks up his guitar and goes out strumming it.*]

YASHA: Twenty-two Calamities! A stupid fellow, between you and me. [*Yawns.*]

DUNYASHA: I hope to goodness he won't shoot himself. [*Pause.*] I'm ever so nervous. I can't help being worried all the time. I was taken into service when I was a little girl, and now I can't live like a peasant any more. See my hands? They're ever so white, as white as a young lady's. I've become so nervous, so sensitive, so like a lady. I'm afraid of everything. I'm simply terrified. So if you deceived me, Yasha, I don't know what would happen to my nerves.

YASHA [*kisses her*]: Little cucumber! Mind you, I expect every girl to be respectable. What I dislike most is for a girl to misbehave herself.

DUNYASHA: I've fallen passionately in love with you, Yasha. You're so educated. You can talk about anything.

Pause.

YASHA [*yawning*]: You see, in my opinion, if a girl is in love with somebody, it means she's immoral. [*Pause.*] It is so pleasant to smoke a cigar in the open air. [*Listens.*] Someone's coming. It's them. . . . [DUNYASHA *embraces him impulsively.*] Please go home and look as if you've been down to the river for a swim. Take that path or they'll think I had arranged to meet you here. Can't stand that sort of thing.

---

[4] *History of Civilization:* Henry Thomas Buckle's *History of Civilization in England* (1857–61), considered a very enlightened and progressive work in Chekhov's time.

DUNYASHA [*coughing quietly*]: Your cigar has given me an awful headache. [*Goes out.*]

YASHA *remains sitting near the chapel. Enter* MRS. RANEVSKY, GAYEV, *and* LOPAKHIN.

LOPAKHIN: You must make up your minds once and for all. There's not much time left. After all, it's quite a simple matter. Do you agree to lease your land for country cottages or don't you? Answer me in one word: yes or no. Just one word.

MRS. RANEVSKY: Who's been smoking such horrible cigars here? [*Sits down.*]

GAYEV: Now that they've built the railway, things are much more convenient. [*Sits down.*] We've been to town for lunch—pot the red in the middle! I really should have gone in to have a game first.

MRS. RANEVSKY: There's plenty of time.

LOPAKHIN: Just one word. [*Imploringly.*] Please give me your answer!

GAYEV [*yawns*]: I beg your pardon?

MRS. RANEVSKY [*looking in her purse*]: Yesterday I had a lot of money, but I've hardly any left today. My poor Varya! Tries to economize by feeding everybody on milk soup and the old servants in the kitchen on peas, and I'm just throwing money about stupidly. [*Drops her purse, scattering some gold coins.*] Goodness gracious, all over the place! [*She looks annoyed.*]

YASHA: Allow me to pick 'em up, madam. It won't take a minute. [*Starts picking up the coins.*]

MRS. RANEVSKY: Thank you, Yasha. Why on earth did I go out to lunch? That disgusting restaurant of yours with its stupid band, and those tablecloths smelling of soap. Why did you have to drink so much, Leonid? Or eat so much? Or talk so much? You did talk a lot again in the restaurant today and all to no purpose. About the seventies and the decadents[5] . . . And who to? Talking about the decadents to waiters!

LOPAKHIN: Aye. . . .

GAYEV [*waving his arm*]: I'm incorrigible, that's clear. [*Irritably to* YASHA.] What are you hanging around here for?

YASHA [*laughs*]: I can't hear your voice without laughing, sir.

GAYEV [*to his sister*]: Either he or I.

MRS. RANEVSKY: Go away, Yasha. Run along.

YASHA [*returning the purse to* MRS. RANEVSKY]: At once, madam. [*Is hardly able to suppress his laughter.*] This very minute. [*Goes out.*]

LOPAKHIN: The rich merchant Deriganov is thinking of buying your estate. I'm told he's coming to the auction himself.

MRS. RANEVSKY: Where did you hear that?

LOPAKHIN: That's what they're saying in town.

GAYEV: Our Yaroslavl great-aunt has promised to send us money, but when and how much we do not know.

LOPAKHIN: How much will she send? A hundred thousand? Two hundred?

---

[5] **decadents:** Late-nineteenth-century artists who explored the dark and macabre side of human experience.

MRS. RANEVSKY: Well, I hardly think so. Ten or fifteen thousand at most. We must be thankful for that.

LOPAKHIN: I'm sorry, but such improvident people as you, such peculiar, unbusinesslike people, I've never met in my life! You're told in plain language that your estate's going to be sold, and you don't seem to understand.

MRS. RANEVSKY: But what are we to do? Tell us, please.

LOPAKHIN: I tell you every day. Every day I go on repeating the same thing over and over again. You must let out the cherry orchard and the land for country cottages, and you must do it now, as quickly as possible. The auction is on top of you! Try to understand! The moment you decide to let your land, you'll be able to raise as much money as you like, and you'll be saved.

MRS. RANEVSKY: Country cottages, holiday-makers—I'm sorry, but it's so vulgar.

GAYEV: I'm of your opinion entirely.

LOPAKHIN: I shall burst into tears or scream or have a fit. I can't stand it. You've worn me out! [*To* GAYEV.] You're a silly old woman!

GAYEV: I beg your pardon?

LOPAKHIN: A silly old woman! [*He gets up to go.*]

MRS. RANEVSKY [*in dismay*]: No, don't go. Please stay. I beg you. Perhaps we'll think of something.

LOPAKHIN: What is there to think of?

MRS. RANEVSKY: Please don't go. I beg you. Somehow I feel so much more cheerful with you here. [*Pause.*] I keep expecting something to happen, as though the house was going to collapse on top of us.

GAYEV [*deep in thought*]: Cannon off the cushion. Pot into the middle pocket. . . .

MRS. RANEVSKY: I'm afraid we've sinned too much———

LOPAKHIN: You sinned!

GAYEV [*putting a fruit drop into his mouth*]: They say I squandered my entire fortune on fruit drops. [*Laughs.*]

MRS. RANEVSKY: Oh, my sins! . . . I've always thrown money about aimlessly, like a madwoman. Why, I even married a man who did nothing but pile up debts. My husband died of champagne. He drank like a fish. Then, worse luck, I fell in love with someone, had an affair with him, and it was just at that time—it was my first punishment, a blow that nearly killed me—that my boy was drowned in the river here. I went abroad, never to come back, never to see that river again. I shut my eyes and ran, beside myself, and *he* followed me—pitilessly, brutally. I bought a villa near Mentone because *he* had fallen ill. For the next three years I knew no rest, nursing him day and night. He wore me out. Everything inside me went dead. Then, last year, I had to sell the villa to pay my debts. I left for Paris, where he robbed me, deserted me, and went to live with another woman. I tried to poison myself. Oh, it was all so stupid, so shaming. . . . It was then that I suddenly felt an urge to go back to Russia, to my homeland, to my daughter. [*Dries her eyes.*] Lord, O Lord, be merciful! Forgive me my sins! Don't punish me any more! [*Takes a telegram from her pocket.*] I received this telegram from Paris today. He asks me to forgive him. He implores me to go back. [*Tears up the telegram.*] What's that? Music? [*Listens intently.*]

GAYEV: That's our famous Jewish band. Remember? Four fiddles, a flute, and a double bass.

MRS. RANEVSKY: Does it still exist? We ought to arrange a party and have them over to the house.

LOPAKHIN [*listening*]: I don't hear anything. [*Sings quietly.*] "And the Germans, if you pay 'em, will turn a Russian into a Frenchman." [*Laughs.*] I saw an excellent play at the theatre last night. It was very amusing.

MRS. RANEVSKY: I don't suppose it was amusing at all. You shouldn't be watching plays, but should be watching yourselves more often. What dull lives you live. What nonsense you talk.

LOPAKHIN: Perfectly true. Let's admit quite frankly that the life we lead is utterly stupid. [*Pause.*] My father was a peasant, an idiot. He understood nothing. He taught me nothing. He just beat me when he was drunk and always with a stick. As a matter of fact, I'm just as big a blockhead and an idiot myself. I never learnt anything, and my handwriting is so abominable that I'm ashamed to let people see it.

MRS. RANEVSKY: You ought to get married, my friend.

LOPAKHIN: Yes. That's true.

MRS. RANEVSKY: Married to our Varya. She's a nice girl.

LOPAKHIN: Aye. . . .

MRS. RANEVSKY: Her father was a peasant too. She's a hard-working girl, and she loves you. That's the important thing. Why, you've been fond of her for a long time yourself.

LOPAKHIN: Very well. I've no objection. She's a good girl.

Pause.

GAYEV: I've been offered a job in a bank. Six thousand a year. Have you heard, Lyuba?

MRS. RANEVSKY: You in a bank! You'd better stay where you are.

FIRS comes in carrying an overcoat.

FIRS [*to GAYEV*]: Please put it on, sir. It's damp out here.

GAYEV [*putting on the overcoat*]: You're a damned nuisance, my dear fellow.

FIRS: Come along, sir. Don't be difficult. . . . This morning, too, you went off without saying a word. [*Looks him over.*]

MRS. RANEVSKY: How you've aged, Firs!

FIRS: What's that, ma'am?

LOPAKHIN: Your mistress says you've aged a lot.

FIRS: I've been alive a long time. They were trying to marry me off before your dad was born. . . . [*Laughs.*] When freedom came,[6] I was already chief valet. I refused to accept freedom and stayed on with my master. [*Pause.*] I well remember how glad everyone was, but what they were glad about, they did not know themselves.

LOPAKHIN: It wasn't such a bad life before, was it? At least, they flogged you.

---

[6] When freedom came: Tsar Alexander emancipated the serfs in 1861.

FIRS [*not hearing him*]: I should say so. The peasants stuck to their masters and the masters to their peasants. Now everybody does what he likes. You can't understand nothing.

GAYEV: Shut up, Firs. I have to go to town tomorrow. I've been promised an introduction to a general who might lend us some money on a promissory note.

LOPAKHIN: Nothing will come of it. You won't pay the interest, either. You may be sure of that.

MRS. RANEVSKY: Oh, he's just imagining things. There aren't any generals.

Enter TROFIMOV, ANYA, *and* VARYA.

GAYEV: Here they are at last.

ANYA: There's Mother.

MRS. RANEVSKY [*affectionately*]: Come here, come here, my dears. [*Embracing* ANYA *and* VARYA.] If you only knew how much I love you both. Sit down beside me. That's right.

All sit down.

LOPAKHIN: Our eternal student is always walking about with the young ladies.

TROFIMOV: Mind your own business.

LOPAKHIN: He's nearly fifty and he's still a student.

TROFIMOV: Do drop your idiotic jokes.

LOPAKHIN: Why are you so angry, you funny fellow?

TROFIMOV: Well, stop pestering me.

LOPAKHIN [*laughs*]: Tell me, what do you think of me?

TROFIMOV: Simply this: You're a rich man and you'll soon be a millionaire. Now, just as a beast of prey devours everything in its path and so helps to preserve the balance of nature, so you, too, perform a similar function.

They all laugh.

VARYA: You'd better tell us about the planets, Peter.

MRS. RANEVSKY: No, let's carry on with what we were talking about yesterday.

TROFIMOV: What was that?

GAYEV: Pride.

TROFIMOV: We talked a lot yesterday, but we didn't arrive at any conclusion. As you see it, there's something mystical about the proud man. You may be right for all I know. But try to look at it simply, without being too clever. What sort of pride is it, is there any sense in it, if, physiologically, man is far from perfect? If, in fact, he is, in the vast majority of cases, coarse, stupid, and profoundly unhappy? It's time we stopped admiring ourselves. All we must do is — work!

GAYEV: We're going to die all the same.

TROFIMOV: Who knows? And what do you mean by "we're going to die"? A man may possess a hundred senses. When he dies, he loses only the five we know. The other ninety-five live on.

MRS. RANEVSKY: How clever you are, Peter!

LOPAKHIN [*ironically*]: Oh, frightfully!

TROFIMOV: Mankind marches on, perfecting its powers. Everything that is incomprehensible to us now, will one day become familiar and comprehensible. All we have to do is to work and do our best to assist those who are looking for truth. Here in Russia only a few people are working so far. The vast majority of the educated people I know, do nothing. They aren't looking for anything. They are quite incapable of doing any work. They call themselves intellectuals, but speak to their servants as inferiors and treat the peasants like animals. They're not particularly keen on their studies, they don't do any serious reading, they are bone idle, they merely talk about science, and they understand very little about art. They are all so solemn, they look so very grave, they talk only of important matters, they philosophize. Yet anyone can see that our workers are abominably fed, sleep on bare boards, thirty and forty to a room—bedbugs everywhere, stench, damp, moral turpitude. It's therefore obvious that all our fine phrases are merely a way of deluding ourselves and others. Tell me, where are all those children's crèches[7] people are talking so much about? Where are the reading rooms? You find them only in novels. Actually, we haven't any. All we have is dirt, vulgarity, brutality. I dislike and I'm frightened of all these solemn countenances, just as I'm frightened of all serious conversations. Why not shut up for once?

LOPAKHIN: Well, I get up at five o'clock in the morning, I work from morning till night, and I've always lots of money on me—mine and other people's—and I can see what the people around me are like. One has only to start doing something to realize how few honest, decent people there are about. Sometimes when I lie awake, I keep thinking: Lord, you've given us vast forests, boundless plains, immense horizons, and living here, we ourselves ought really to be giants——

MRS. RANEVSKY: You want giants, do you? They're all right only in fairy tales. Elsewhere they frighten me. [YEPIKHODOV *crosses the stage in the background, playing his guitar. Pensively.*] There goes Yepikhodov.

ANYA [*pensively*]: There goes Yepikhodov.

GAYEV: The sun's set, ladies and gentlemen.

TROFIMOV: Yes.

GAYEV [*softly, as though declaiming*]: Oh, nature, glorious nature! Glowing with eternal radiance, beautiful and indifferent, you, whom we call Mother, uniting in yourself both life and death, you—life-giver and destroyer . . .

VARYA [*imploringly*]: Darling Uncle!

ANYA: Uncle, again!

TROFIMOV: You'd far better pot the red in the middle.

GAYEV: Not another word! Not another word!

They all sit deep in thought. Everything is still. The silence is broken only by the subdued muttering of FIRS. *Suddenly a distant sound is heard. It seems to come from the sky, the sound of a breaking string, slowly dying away, melancholy.*

---

[7] children's crèches: Day nurseries.

MRS. RANEVSKY: What's that?

LOPAKHIN: I don't know. I expect a bucket must have broken somewhere far away in a coal mine, but somewhere a very long distance away.

GAYEV: Perhaps it was a bird, a heron or something.

TROFIMOV: Or an eagle-owl.

MRS. RANEVSKY [*shudders*]: It makes me feel dreadful for some reason.

Pause.

FIRS: Same thing happened before the misfortune: the owl hooted and the samovar kept hissing.

GAYEV: Before what misfortune?

FIRS: Before they gave us our freedom.

Pause.

MRS. RANEVSKY: Come, let's go in, my friends. It's getting dark. [*To* ANYA.] There are tears in your eyes. What's the matter, darling? [*Embraces her.*]

ANYA: It's nothing, Mother. Nothing.

TROFIMOV: Someone's coming.

A HIKER *appears. He wears a shabby white peaked cap and an overcoat; he is slightly drunk.*

HIKER: Excuse me, is this the way to the station?

GAYEV: Yes, follow that road.

HIKER: I'm greatly obliged to you sir. [*Coughs.*] Glorious weather . . . [*Declaiming.*] Brother, my suffering brother, come to the Volga, you whose groans . . . [*To* VARYA.] Mademoiselle, won't you give thirty kopecks to a starving Russian citizen?

VARYA, *frightened, utters a little scream.*

LOPAKHIN [*angrily*]: There's a limit to the most disgraceful behavior.

MRS. RANEVSKY [*at a loss*]: Here, take this. [*Looks for some money in her purse.*] No silver. Never mind, have this gold one.

HIKER: Profoundly grateful to you, ma'am. [*Goes out.*]

Laughter.

VARYA [*frightened*]: I'm going away. I'm going away. Good heavens, Mother dear, there's no food for the servants in the house, and you gave him a gold sovereign!

MRS. RANEVSKY: What's to be done with a fool like me? I'll give you all I have when we get home. You'll lend me some more money, Lopakhin, won't you?

LOPAKHIN: With pleasure.

MRS. RANEVSKY: Let's go in. It's time. By the way, Varya, we've found you a husband here. Congratulations.

VARYA [*through tears*]: This isn't a joking matter, Mother.

LOPAKHIN: Okhmelia, go to a nunnery![8]

---

[8] Okhmelia, go to a nunnery!: Lopakhin is quoting lines from Shakespeare's *Hamlet* in which Hamlet taunts Ophelia (Okhmelia).

GAYEV: Look at my hands. They're shaking. It's a long time since I had a game of billiards.

LOPAKHIN: Okhmelia, O nymph, remember me in your prayers!

MRS. RANEVSKY: Come along, come along, it's almost supper time.

VARYA: That man frightened me. My heart's still pounding.

LOPAKHIN: Let me remind you, ladies and gentlemen: The cherry orchard is up for sale on the twenty-second of August. Think about it! Think!

They all go out except TROFIMOV *and* ANYA.

ANYA [*laughing*]: I'm so glad the hiker frightened Varya. Now we are alone.

TROFIMOV: Varya's afraid we might fall in love. That's why she follows us around for days on end. With her narrow mind she cannot grasp that we are above love. The whole aim and meaning of our life is to bypass everything that is petty and illusory, that prevents us from being free and happy. Forward! Let us march on irresistibly toward the bright star shining there in the distance! Forward! Don't lag behind, friends!

ANYA [*clapping her hands excitedly*]: You talk so splendidly! [*Pause.*] It's so heavenly here today!

TROFIMOV: Yes, the weather is wonderful.

ANYA: What have you done to me, Peter? Why am I no longer as fond of the cherry orchard as before? I loved it so dearly. I used to think there was no lovelier place on earth than our orchard.

TROFIMOV: The whole of Russia is our orchard. The earth is great and beautiful. There are lots of lovely places on it. [*Pause.*] Think, Anya: your grandfather, your great-grandfather, and all your ancestors owned serfs. They owned living souls. Can't you see human beings looking at you from every cherry tree in your orchard, from every leaf and every tree trunk? Don't you hear their voices? To own living souls—that's what has changed you all so much, you who are living now and those who lived before you. That's why your mother, you yourself, and your uncle no longer realize that you are living on borrowed capital, at other people's expense, at the expense of those whom you don't admit farther than your entrance hall. We are at least two hundred years behind the times. We haven't got anything at all. We have no definite attitude toward our past. We just philosophize, complain of depression, or drink vodka. Isn't it abundantly clear that before we start living in the present, we must atone for our past, make an end of it? And atone for it we can only by suffering, by extraordinary, unceasing labor. Understand that, Anya.

ANYA: The house we live in hasn't really been ours for a long time. I'm going to leave it. I give you my word.

TROFIMOV: If you have the keys of the house, throw them into the well and go away. Be free as the wind.

ANYA [*rapturously*]: How well you said it!

TROFIMOV: Believe me, Anya, believe me! I'm not yet thirty, I'm young, I'm still a student, but I've been through hell more than once. I'm driven from pillar to post.

In winter I'm half-starved, I'm ill, worried, poor as a beggar. You can't imagine the terrible places I've been to! And yet, always, every moment of the day and night, my heart was full of ineffable visions of the future. I feel, I'm quite sure, that happiness is coming, Anya. I can see it coming already.

ANYA [*pensively*]: The moon is rising.

YEPIKHODOV *can be heard playing the same sad tune as before on his guitar. The moon rises. Somewhere near the poplars* VARYA *is looking for* ANYA *and calling, "Anya, where are you?"*

TROFIMOV: Yes, the moon is rising. [*Pause.*] There it is—happiness! It's coming nearer and nearer. Already I can hear its footsteps, and if we never see it, if we never know it, what does that matter? Others will see it.

VARYA [*offstage*]: Anya, where are you?

TROFIMOV: That Varya again! [*Angrily.*] Disgusting!

ANYA: Never mind, let's go to the river. It's lovely there.

TROFIMOV: Yes, let's.

They go out.

VARYA [*offstage*]: Anya! Anya!

Curtain.

ACT THREE

The drawing room, separated by an archway from the ballroom. A candelabra is alight. The Jewish band can be heard playing in the entrance hall. It is the same band that is mentioned in Act Two. Evening. In the ballroom people are dancing the Grande Ronde. SIMEONOV-PISHCHIK's *voice can be heard crying out, "Promenade à une paire!" They all come out into the drawing room:* PISHCHIK *and* CHARLOTTE *the first couple,* TROFIMOV *and* MRS. RANEVSKY *the second,* ANYA *and a* POST OFFICE CLERK *the third,* VARYA *and the* STATIONMASTER *the fourth, and so on.* VARYA *is quietly crying and dries her eyes as she dances. The last couple consists of* DUNYASHA *and a partner. They walk across the drawing room.* PISHCHIK *shouts, "Grande Ronde balancez!" and "Les cavaliers à genoux et remerciez vos dames!"*[9]

FIRS, *wearing a tailcoat, brings in soda water on a tray.* PISHCHIK *and* TROFIMOV *come into the drawing room.*

PISHCHIK: I've got high blood-pressure. I've had two strokes already, and I find dancing hard work. But, as the saying goes, if you're one of a pack, wag your tail, whether you bark or not. As a matter of fact, I'm as strong as a horse. My father, may he rest in peace, liked his little joke, and speaking about our family pedigree, he used to say that the ancient Simeonov-Pishchiks came from the horse that Caligula had made a senator. [*Sits down.*] But you see, the trouble is that I

---

[9] "Grande . . . dames!": The instructions for the French dance are: "Promenade à une paire!" or, walk in pairs; "Grande Ronde, balancez!" or, grand round and swing; and "Les cavaliers à genoux et remerciez vous dames," gentlemen, kneel and thank your ladies.

have no money. A hungry dog believes only in meat. [*Snores, but wakes up again at once.*] I'm just the same. All I can think of is money.

TROFIMOV: There really is something horsy about you.

PISHCHIK: Well, a horse is a good beast. You can sell a horse.

From an adjoining room comes the sound of people playing billiards. VARYA *appears in the ball-room under the archway.*

TROFIMOV [*teasing her*]: Mrs. Lopakhin! Mrs. Lopakhin!

VARYA [*angrily*]: Moth-eaten gentleman!

TROFIMOV: Well, I am a moth-eaten gentleman and proud of it.

VARYA [*brooding bitterly*]: We've hired a band, but how we are going to pay for it, I don't know. [*Goes out.*]

TROFIMOV [*to* PISHCHIK]: If the energy you have wasted throughout your life looking for money to pay the interest on your debts had been spent on something else, you'd most probably have succeeded in turning the world upside down.

PISHCHIK: Nietzsche,[10] the famous philosopher—a great man, a man of great intellect—says in his works that there's nothing wrong about forging bank notes.

TROFIMOV: Have you read Nietzsche?

PISHCHIK: Well, actually, Dashenka told me about it. I don't mind telling you, though, that in my present position I might even forge bank notes. The day after tomorrow I've got to pay three hundred and ten rubles. I've already got one hundred and thirty. [*Feels his pockets in alarm.*] My money's gone, I've lost my money! [*Through tears.*] Where is it? [*Happily.*] Ah, here it is, in the lining. Lord, the shock brought me out in a cold sweat!

Enter MRS. RANEVSKY *and* CHARLOTTE.

MRS. RANEVSKY [*hums a popular Georgian dance tune*]:[11] Why is Leonid so late? What's he doing in town? [*To* DUNYASHA] Offer the band tea, please.

TROFIMOV: I don't suppose the auction has taken place.

MRS. RANEVSKY: What a time to have a band! What a time to give a party! Oh, well, never mind. [*Sits down and hums quietly.*]

CHARLOTTE [*hands* PISHCHIK *a pack of cards*]: Here's a pack of cards. Think of a card.

PISHCHIK: All right.

CHARLOTTE: Now shuffle the pack. That's right. Now give it to me. Now, then, my dear Mr. Pishchik, *eins, zwei, drei!*[12] Look in your breast pocket. Is it there?

PISHCHIK [*takes the card out of his breast pocket*]: The eight of spades! Absolutely right! [*Surprised.*] Good Lord!

CHARLOTTE [*holding a pack of cards on the palm of her hand, to* TROFIMOV]: Tell me, quick, what's the top card?

TROFIMOV: Well, let's say the queen of spades.

---

[10] Nietzsche: Friedrich Nietzsche (1844–1900), a German philosopher known for his iconoclastic ideas; see p. 198.

[11] Georgian dance tune: The *Lezginka*—music for a courtship dance from the Caucasus mountains.

[12] *eins, zwei, drei!*: German for "one, two, three."

CHARLOTTE: Here it is. [*To* PISHCHIK]: What's the top card now?

PISHCHIK: The ace of hearts.

CHARLOTTE: Here you are! [*Claps her hands and the pack of cards disappears.*] What lovely weather we're having today. [*A mysterious female voice, which seems to come from under the floor, answers: "Oh yes, glorious weather, madam!"*] You're my ideal, you're so nice! [*The voice: "I like you very much too, madam."*]

STATIONMASTER [*clapping his hands*]: Bravo, Madam Ventriloquist!

PISHCHIK [*looking surprised*]: Good Lord! Enchanting, Miss Charlotte, I'm simply in love with you.

CHARLOTTE: In love! Are you sure you can love? *Guter Mensch, aber schlecter Musikant.*[13]

TROFIMOV [*claps* PISHCHIK *on the shoulder*]: Good old horse!

CHARLOTTE: Attention, please. One more trick. [*She takes a rug from a chair.*] Here's a very good rug. I'd like to sell it. [*Shaking it.*] Who wants to buy it?

PISHCHIK [*surprised*]: Good Lord!

CHARLOTTE: *Eins, zwei, drei!* [*Quickly snatching up the rug, which she had let fall, she reveals* ANYA *standing behind it.* ANYA *curtseys, runs to her mother, embraces her, and runs back to the ballroom, amid general enthusiasm.*]

MRS. RANEVSKY [*applauding*]: Bravo, bravo!

CHARLOTTE: Now, once more. *Eins, zwei, drei!* [*Lifts the rug; behind it stands* VARYA, *who bows.*]

PISHCHIK [*surprised*]: Good Lord!

CHARLOTTE: The end! [*Throws the rug over* PISHCHIK, *curtseys, and runs off to the ballroom.*]

PISHCHIK [*running after her*]: The hussy! What a woman, eh? What a woman! [*Goes out.*]

MRS. RANEVSKY: Still no Leonid. I can't understand what he can be doing in town all this time. It must be over now. Either the estate has been sold or the auction didn't take place. Why keep us in suspense so long?

VARYA [*trying to comfort her*]: I'm certain Uncle must have bought it.

TROFIMOV [*sarcastically*]: Oh, to be sure!

VARYA: Our great-aunt sent him power of attorney to buy the estate in her name and transfer the mortgage to her. She's done it for Anya's sake. God will help us and Uncle will buy it. I'm sure of it.

MRS. RANEVSKY: Your great-aunt sent fifteen thousand to buy the estate in her name. She doesn't trust us—but the money wouldn't even pay the interest. [*She covers her face with her hands.*] My whole future is being decided today, my future. . . .

TROFIMOV [*teasing* VARYA]: Mrs. Lopakhin!

VARYA [*crossly*]: Eternal student! Expelled twice from the university, weren't you?

MRS. RANEVSKY: Why are you so cross, Varya? He's teasing you about Lopakhin. Well, what of it? Marry Lopakhin if you want to. He is a nice, interesting man. If you don't want to, don't marry him. Nobody's forcing you, darling.

---

[13] *Guter . . . Musikant:* German for "Good man, but a bad musician."

VARYA: I regard such a step seriously, Mother dear. I don't mind being frank about it: He is a nice man, and I like him.

MRS. RANEVSKY: Well, marry him. What are you waiting for? That's what I can't understand.

VARYA: But, Mother dear, I can't very well propose to him myself, can I? Everyone's been talking to me about him for the last two years. Everyone! But he either says nothing or makes jokes. I quite understand. He's making money. He has his business to think of, and he hasn't time for me. If I had any money, just a little, a hundred rubles, I'd give up everything and go right away as far as possible. I'd have gone into a convent.

TROFIMOV: Wonderful!

VARYA [*to* TROFIMOV]: A student ought to be intelligent! [*In a gentle voice, through tears.*] How plain you've grown, Peter! How you've aged! [*To* MRS. RANEVSKY, *no longer crying.*] I can't live without having something to do, Mother! I must be doing something all the time.

Enter YASHA.

YASHA [*hardly able to restrain his laughter*]: Yepikhodov's broken a billiard cue! [*Goes out.*]

VARYA: What's Yepikhodov doing here? Who gave him permission to play billiards? Can't understand these people! [*Goes out.*]

MRS. RANEVSKY: Don't tease her, Peter. Don't you see she is unhappy enough already?

TROFIMOV: She's a bit too conscientious. Pokes her nose into other people's affairs. Wouldn't leave me and Anya alone all summer. Afraid we might have an affair. What business is it of hers? Besides, the idea never entered my head. Such vulgarity is beneath me. We are above love.

MRS. RANEVSKY: So, I suppose I must be beneath love. [*In great agitation.*] Why isn't Leonid back? All I want to know is: Has the estate been sold or not? Such a calamity seems so incredible to me that I don't know what to think. I'm completely at a loss. I feel like screaming, like doing something silly. Help me, Peter. Say something. For God's sake, say something!

TROFIMOV: What does it matter whether the estate's been sold today or not? The estate's been finished and done with long ago. There's no turning back. The road to it is closed. Stop worrying, my dear. You mustn't deceive yourself. Look the truth straight in the face for once in your life.

MRS. RANEVSKY: What truth? You can see where truth is and where it isn't, but I seem to have gone blind. I see nothing. You boldly solve all important problems, but tell me, dear boy, isn't it because you're young, isn't it because you haven't had the time to live through the consequences of any of your problems? You look ahead boldly, but isn't it because you neither see nor expect anything terrible to happen to you, because life is still hidden from your young eyes? You're bolder, more honest, you see much deeper than any of us, but think carefully, try to understand our position, be generous even a little, spare me. I was born here, you know. My father and mother lived here, and my grandfather also. I love this house. Life has no meaning for me without the cherry orchard, and if it has to be sold, then let me be sold with it. [*Embraces* TROFIMOV *and kisses him on the forehead.*] Don't you see, my son was drowned here. [*Weeps.*] Have pity on me, my good, kind friend.

TROFIMOV: You know I sympathize with you with all my heart.

MRS. RANEVSKY: You should have put it differently. [*Takes out her handkerchief. A telegram falls on the floor.*] My heart is so heavy today. You can't imagine how heavy. I can't bear this noise. The slightest sound makes me shudder. I'm trembling all over. I'm afraid to go to my room. I'm terrified to be alone. . . . Don't condemn me, Peter. I love you as my own son. I'd gladly let Anya marry you, I swear I would. Only, my dear boy, you must study, you must finish your course at the university. You never do anything. You just drift from one place to another. That's what's so strange. Isn't that so? Isn't it? And you should do something about your beard. Make it grow, somehow. [*Laughs.*] You are funny!

TROFIMOV [*picking up the telegram*]: I have no wish to be handsome.

MRS. RANEVSKY: That telegram's from Paris. I get one every day. Yesterday and today. That wild man is ill again, in trouble again. He asks me to forgive him. He begs me to come back to him, and I really think I ought to be going back to Paris to be near him for a bit. You're looking very stern, Peter. But what's to be done, my dear boy? What am I to do? He's ill. He's lonely. He's unhappy. Who'll look after him there? Who'll stop him from doing something silly? Who'll give him his medicine at the right time? And, why hide it? Why be silent about it? I love him. That's obvious. I love him. I love him. He's a millstone round my neck and he's dragging me down to the bottom with him, but I love the millstone, and I can't live without it. [*Presses* TROFIMOV'*s hand.*] Don't think badly of me, Peter. Don't say anything. Don't speak.

TROFIMOV [*through tears*]: For God's sake—forgive my being so frank, but he left you penniless!

MRS. RANEVSKY: No, no, no! You mustn't say that. [*Puts her hands over her ears.*]

TROFIMOV: Why, he's a scoundrel, and you're the only one who doesn't seem to know it. He's a petty scoundrel, a nonentity.

MRS. RANEVSKY [*angry but restraining herself*]: You're twenty-six or twenty-seven, but you're still a schoolboy—a sixth-grade schoolboy!

TROFIMOV: What does that matter?

MRS. RANEVSKY: You ought to be a man. A person of your age ought to understand people who are in love. You ought to be in love yourself. You ought to fall in love. [*Angrily.*] Yes! Yes! And you're not so pure either. You're just a prude, a ridiculous crank, a freak!

TROFIMOV [*horrified*]: What is she saying?

MRS. RANEVSKY: "I'm above love!" You're not above love, you're simply what Firs calls a nincompoop. Not have a mistress at your age!

TROFIMOV [*horrified*]: This is terrible! What is she saying? [*Walks quickly into the ballroom, clutching his head.*] It's dreadful! I can't! I'll go away! [*Goes out but immediately comes back.*] All is at an end between us! [*Goes out into the hall.*]

MRS. RANEVSKY [*shouting after him*]: Peter, wait! You funny boy, I was only joking. Peter!

Someone can be heard running rapidly up the stairs and then suddenly falling downstairs with a crash. ANYA *and* VARYA *scream, followed immediately by laughter.*

MRS. RANEVSKY: What's happened?

ANYA [*laughing, runs in*]: Peter's fallen down the stairs! [*Runs out.*]

MRS. RANEVSKY: What an eccentric! [*The* STATIONMASTER *stands in the middle of the ballroom and recites "The Fallen Woman"[5] by Alexey Tolstoy. The others listen. But he has hardly time to recite a few lines when the sound of a waltz comes from the entrance hall, and the recitation breaks off. Everyone dances.* TROFIMOV, ANYA, VARYA, *and* MRS. RANEVSKY *enter from the hall.*] Well, Peter dear, you pure soul, I'm sorry. . . . Come, let's dance. [*Dances with* TROFIMOV.]

ANYA *and* VARYA *dance together.* FIRS *comes in and stands his walking stick near the side door.* YASHA *has also come in from the drawing room and is watching the dancing.*

YASHA: Well, Grandpa!

FIRS: I'm not feeling too well. We used to have generals, barons, and admirals at our dances before, but now we send for the post office clerk and the stationmaster. Even they are not too keen to come. Afraid I'm getting weak. The old master, the mistress's grandfather that is, used to give us powdered sealing wax for medicine. It was his prescription for all illnesses. I've been taking sealing wax every day for the last twenty years or more. That's perhaps why I'm still alive.

YASHA: You make me sick, Grandpa. [*Yawns*]. I wish you was dead.

FIRS: Ugh, you nincompoop! [*Mutters.*]

TROFIMOV *and* MRS. RANEVSKY *dance in the ballroom and then in the drawing room.*

MRS. RANEVSKY: *Merci.* I think I'll sit down a bit. [*Sits down.*] I'm tired.

Enter ANYA.

ANYA [*agitated*]: A man in the kitchen said just now that the cherry orchard has been sold today.

MRS. RANEVSKY: Sold? Who to?

ANYA: He didn't say. He's gone away now.

ANYA *dances with* TROFIMOV; *both go off to the ballroom.*

YASHA: Some old man gossiping, madam. A stranger.

FIRS: Master Leonid isn't here yet. Hasn't returned. Wearing his light autumn overcoat. He might catch cold. Oh, these youngsters!

MRS. RANEVSKY: I shall die! Yasha, go and find out who bought it.

YASHA: But he's gone, the old man has. [*Laughs.*]

MRS. RANEVSKY [*a little annoyed*]: Well, what are you laughing at? What are you so pleased about?

YASHA: Yepikhodov's a real scream. Such a fool. Twenty-two Calamities!

---

[4] "The Fallen Woman": A sentimental poem by a distant relative of Leo Tolstoy.

MRS. RANEVSKY: Firs, where will you go if the estate's sold?

FIRS: I'll go wherever you tell me, ma'am.

MRS. RANEVSKY: You look awful! Are you ill? You'd better go to bed.

FIRS: Me to bed, ma'am? [*Ironically.*] If I goes to bed, who's going to do the waiting? Who's going to look after everything? I'm the only one in the whole house.

YASHA [*to* MRS. RANEVSKY]: I'd like to ask you a favor, madam. If you go back to Paris, will you take me with you? It's quite impossible for me to stay here. [*Looking round, in an undertone.*] You know perfectly well yourself what an uncivilized country this is—the common people are so immoral—and besides, it's so boring here, the food in the kitchen is disgusting, and on top of it, there's that old Firs wandering about, muttering all sorts of inappropriate words. Take me with you, madam, please!

Enter PISHCHIK.

PISHCHIK: May I have the pleasure of a little dance, fair lady? [MRS. RANEVSKY *goes with him.*] I'll have one hundred and eighty rubles off you all the same, my dear, charming lady. . . . I will, indeed. [*They dance.*] One hundred and eighty rubles. . . .

They go into the ballroom.

YASHA [*singing softly*]: "Could you but feel the agitated beating of my heart."

In the ballroom a woman in a gray top hat and check trousers can be seen jumping about and waving her arms. Shouts of "Bravo, Charlotte! Bravo!"

DUNYASHA [*stops to powder her face*]: Miss Anya told me to join the dancers because there are lots of gentlemen and very few ladies. But dancing makes me dizzy and my heart begins beating so fast. I say, Firs, the post office clerk said something to me just now that quite took my breath away.

The music becomes quieter.

FIRS: What did he say to you?

DUNYASHA: "You're like a flower," he said.

YASHA [*yawning*]: What ignorance! [*Goes out.*]

DUNYASHA: Like a flower! I'm ever so delicate, and I love people saying nice things to me!

FIRS: You'll come to a bad end, my girl. Mark my words.

Enter YEPIKHODOV.

YEPIKHODOV: You seem to avoid me, Dunyasha. Just as if I was some insect. [*Sighs.*] Oh, life!

DUNYASHA: What do you want?

YEPIKHODOV: No doubt you may be right. [*Sighs.*] But, of course, if one looks at things from a certain point of view, then, if I may say so and if you'll forgive my frankness, you have reduced me absolutely to a state of mind. I know what Fate has in store for me. Every day some calamity overtakes me, but I got used to it so long ago that I just look at my Fate and smile. You gave me your word, and though I——

DUNYASHA: Let's talk about it some other time. Leave me alone now. Now, I am dreaming. [*Plays with her fan.*]

YEPIKHODOV: Every day some calamity overtakes me, and I—let me say it quite frankly—why, I just smile, laugh even.

Enter VARYA *from the ballroom.*

VARYA: Are you still here, Simon! What an ill-mannered fellow you are, to be sure! [*To* DUNYASHA.] Be off with you, Dunyasha. [*To* YEPIKHODOV.] First you go and play billiards and break a cue, and now you wander about the drawing room as if you were a guest.

YEPIKHODOV: It's not your place to reprimand me, if you don't mind my saying so.

VARYA: I'm not reprimanding you. I'm telling you. All you do is drift about from one place to another without ever doing a stroke of work. We're employing an office clerk, but goodness knows why.

YEPIKHODOV [*offended*]: Whether I work or drift about, whether I eat or play billiards, is something which only people older than you, people who know what they're talking about, should decide.

VARYA: How dare you talk to me like that? [*Flaring up.*] How dare you? I don't know what I'm talking about, don't I? Get out of here! This instant!

YEPIKHODOV [*cowed*]: Express yourself with more delicacy, please.

VARYA [*beside herself*]: Get out of here this minute! Out! [*He goes toward the door, and she follows him.*] Twenty-two Calamities! Don't let me see you here again! Never set foot here again! [YEPIKHODOV *goes out. He can be heard saying behind the door:* "I'll lodge a complaint."] Oh, so you're coming back, are you? [*Picks up the stick which* FIRS *has left near the door.*] Come on, come on, I'll show you! Coming, are you? Well, take that! [*Swings the stick as* LOPAKHIN *comes in.*]

LOPAKHIN: Thank you very much!

VARYA [*angrily and derisively*]: I'm so sorry!

LOPAKHIN: It's quite all right. Greatly obliged to you for the kind reception.

VARYA: Don't mention it. [*Walks away, then looks round and inquires gently.*] I didn't hurt you, did I?

LOPAKHIN: Oh no, not at all. There's going to be an enormous bump on my head for all that.

Voices in the ballroom: "Lopakhin's arrived. Lopakhin!"

PISHCHIK: Haven't heard from you or seen you for ages, my dear fellow! [*Embraces* LOPAKHIN.] Do I detect a smell of brandy, dear boy? We're doing very well here, too.

Enter MRS. RANEVSKY.

MRS. RANEVSKY: Is it you, Lopakhin? Why have you been so long? Where's Leonid?

LOPAKHIN: He came back with me. He'll be here in a moment.

MRS. RANEVSKY [*agitated*]: Well, what happened? Did the auction take place? Speak, for heaven's sake!

LOPAKHIN [*embarrassed, fearing to betray his joy*]: The auction was over by four o'clock. We missed our train and had to wait till half past nine. [*With a deep sigh.*] Oh dear, I'm afraid I feel a little dizzy.

Enter GAYEV. *He carries some parcels in his right hand and wipes away his tears with his left.*

MRS. RANEVSKY: What's the matter, Leonid? Well! [*Impatiently, with tears.*] Quick, tell me for heaven's sake!

GAYEV [*doesn't answer, only waves his hand resignedly to* FIRS, *weeping*]: Here, take these—anchovies, Kerch herrings . . . I've had nothing to eat all day. I've had a terrible time. [*The door of the billiard room is open; the click of billiard balls can be heard and* YASHA's *voice: "Seven and eighteen!"* GAYEV's *expression changes. He is no longer crying.*] I'm awfully tired. Come and help me change, Firs.

GAYEV *goes off through the ballroom to his own room, followed by* FIRS.

PISHCHIK: Well, what happened at the auction? Come, tell us!

MRS. RANEVSKY: Has the cherry orchard been sold?

LOPAKHIN: It has.

MRS. RANEVSKY: Who bought it?

LOPAKHIN: I bought it. [*Pause.* MRS. RANEVSKY *is crushed; she would have collapsed on the floor if she had not been standing near an armchair.* VARYA *takes the keys from her belt, throws them on the floor in the center of the drawing room, and goes out.*] I bought it! One moment, please, ladies and gentlemen. I feel dazed. I can't talk. . . . [*Laughs.*] Deriganov was already there when we got to the auction. Gayev had only fifteen thousand, and Deriganov began his bidding at once with thirty thousand over and above the mortgage. I realized the position at once and took up his challenge. I bid forty. He bid forty-five. He kept raising his bid by five thousand and I by adding another ten thousand. Well, it was soon over. I bid ninety thousand on top of the arrears, and the cherry orchard was knocked down to me. Now the cherry orchard is mine! Mine! [*Laughs loudly.*] Merciful heavens, the cherry orchard's mine! Come on, tell me, tell me I'm drunk. Tell me I'm out of my mind. Tell me I'm imagining it all. [*Stamps his feet.*] Don't laugh at me! If my father and my grandfather were to rise from their graves and see what's happened, see how their Yermolay, their beaten and half-literate Yermolay, Yermolay who used to run around barefoot in winter, see how that same Yermolay bought this estate, the most beautiful estate in the world! I've bought the estate where my father and grandfather were slaves, where they weren't even allowed inside the kitchen. I must be dreaming. I must be imagining it all. It can't be true. It's all a figment of your imagination, shrouded in mystery. [*Picks up the keys, smiling affectionately.*] She's thrown down the keys. Wants to show she's no longer the mistress here. [*Jingles the keys.*] Oh well, never mind. [*The band is heard tuning up.*] Hey you, musicians, play something! I want to hear you. Come, all of you! Come and watch Yermolay Lopakhin take an axe to the cherry orchard. Watch the trees come crashing down. We'll cover the place with country cottages, and our grandchildren and great-grandchildren will see a new life springing up here. Strike up the music! [*The band plays.* MRS. RANEVSKY *has sunk into a chair and is weeping bitterly. Reproachfully.*] Why did you not listen to me? You poor dear, you will never get it back now. [*With tears.*] Oh, if only all this could be over soon, if only our unhappy, disjointed life could somehow be changed soon.

PISHCHIK [*takes his arm, in an undertone*]: She's crying. Let's go into the ballroom. Let's leave her alone. Come on. [*Takes his arm and leads him away to the ballroom.*]

LOPAKHIN: What's the matter? You there in the band, play up, play up! Let's hear you properly. Let's have everything as I want it now. [*Ironically.*] Here comes the new landowner, the owner of the cherry orchard! [*Knocks against a small table accidentally and nearly knocks over the candelabra.*] I can pay for everything!

LOPAKHIN *goes out with* PISHCHIK. *There is no one left in the ballroom except* MRS. RANEVSKY, *who remains sitting in a chair, hunched up and crying bitterly. The band plays quietly.* ANYA *and* TROFIMOV *come in quickly.* ANYA *goes up to her mother and kneels in front of her.* TROFIMOV *remains standing by the entrance to the ballroom.*

ANYA: Mother, Mother, why are you crying? My dear, good, kind Mother, my darling Mother, I love you; God bless you, Mother. The cherry orchard is sold. It's gone. That's true, quite true, but don't cry, Mother. You still have your life ahead of you, and you've still got your kind and pure heart. . . . Come with me, darling. Come. Let's go away from here. We shall plant a new orchard, an orchard more splendid than this one. You will see it, you will understand, and joy, deep, serene joy, will steal into your heart, sink into it like the sun in the evening, and you will smile, Mother! Come, darling! Come!

Curtain.

ACT FOUR

The scene is the same as in the first act. There are no curtains at the windows or pictures on the walls. Only a few pieces of furniture are left. They have been stacked in one corner as if for sale. There is a feeling of emptiness. Near the front door and at the back of the stage, suitcases, traveling bags, etc., are piled up. The door on the left is open and the voices of VARYA *and* ANYA *can be heard.* LOPAKHIN *stands waiting.* YASHA *is holding a tray with glasses of champagne. In the entrance hall* YEPIKHODOV *is tying up a box. There is a constant murmur of voices offstage, the voices of peasants who have come to say good-bye.* GAYEV'S *voice is heard: "Thank you, my dear people, thank you."*

YASHA: The peasants have come to say good-bye. In my opinion, sir, the peasants are decent enough fellows, but they don't understand a lot.

The murmur of voices dies away. MRS. RANEVSKY *and* GAYEV *come in through the entrance hall; she is not crying, but she is pale. Her face is quivering. She cannot speak.*

GAYEV: You gave them your purse, Lyuba. You shouldn't. You really shouldn't!

MRS. RANEVSKY: I—I couldn't help it. I just couldn't help it.

Both go out.

LOPAKHIN [*calling through the door after them*]: Please take a glass of champagne. I beg you. One glass each before we leave. I forgot to bring any from town, and I could find only one bottle at the station. Please! [*Pause.*] Why, don't you want any? [*Walks away from the door.*] If I'd known, I wouldn't have bought it. Oh well, I don't think I'll have any, either. [YASHA *puts the tray down carefully on a chair.*] You'd better have some, Yasha.

YASHA: Thank you, sir. To those who're going away! And here's to you, sir, who're staying behind! [*Drinks.*] This isn't real champagne. Take it from me, sir.

LOPAKHIN: Paid eight rubles a bottle. [*Pause.*] Damn cold here.

YASHA: The stoves haven't been lit today. We're leaving, anyway. [*Laughs.*]

LOPAKHIN: What's so funny?

YASHA: Oh, nothing. Just feeling happy.

LOPAKHIN: It's October, but it might just as well be summer: it's so sunny and calm. Good building weather. [*Glances at his watch and calls through the door.*] I say, don't forget the train leaves in forty-seven minutes. In twenty minutes we must start for the station. Hurry up!

TROFIMOV *comes in from outside, wearing an overcoat.*

TROFIMOV: I think it's about time we were leaving. The carriages are at the door. Where the blazes could my galoshes have got to? Disappeared without a trace. [*Through the door.*] Anya, I can't find my galoshes! Can't find them!

LOPAKHIN: I've got to go to Kharkov. I'll leave with you on the same train. I'm spending the winter in Kharkov. I've been hanging about here too long. I'm worn out with having nothing to do. I can't live without work. Don't know what to do with my hands. They just flop about as if they belonged to someone else.

TROFIMOV: Well, we'll soon be gone and then you can resume your useful labors.

LOPAKHIN: Come on, have a glass of champagne.

TROFIMOV: No, thank you.

LOPAKHIN: So you're off to Moscow, are you?

TROFIMOV: Yes. I'll see them off to town, and I'm off to Moscow tomorrow.

LOPAKHIN: I see. I suppose the professors have stopped lecturing while you've been away. They're all waiting for you to come back.

TROFIMOV: Mind your own business.

LOPAKHIN: How many years have you been studying at the university?

TROFIMOV: Why don't you think of something new for a change? This is rather old, don't you think? —and stale. [*Looking for his galoshes.*] I don't suppose we shall ever meet again, so let me give you a word of advice as a farewell gift: Don't wave your arms about. Get rid of the habit of throwing your arms about. And another thing: To build country cottages in the hope that in the fullness of time vacationers will become landowners is the same as waving your arms about. Still, I like you in spite of everything. You've got fine sensitive fingers, like an artist's, and you have a fine sensitive soul.

LOPAKHIN [*embraces him*]: My dear fellow, thanks for everything. Won't you let me lend you some money for your journey? You may need it.

TROFIMOV: Need it? Whatever for?

LOPAKHIN: But you haven't any, have you?

TROFIMOV: Oh, but I have. I've just got some money for a translation. Got it here in my pocket. [*Anxiously.*] Where could those galoshes of mine have got to?

VARYA [*from another room*]: Oh, take your filthy things! [*Throws a pair of galoshes onto the stage.*]

TROFIMOV: Why are you so cross, Varya? Good heavens, these are not my galoshes!

LOPAKHIN: I had about three thousand acres of poppy sown last spring. Made a clear profit of forty thousand. When my poppies were in bloom, what a beautiful sight they were! Well, so you see, I made forty thousand and I'd be glad to lend you some of it because I can afford to. So why be so high and mighty? I'm a peasant. . . . I'm offering it to you without ceremony.

TROFIMOV: Your father was a peasant, my father was a pharmacist, all of which proves exactly nothing. [LOPAKHIN *takes out his wallet.*] Put it back! Put it back! If you offered me two hundred thousand, I wouldn't accept it. I'm a free man. Everything you prize so highly, everything that means so much to all of you, rich or poor, has no more power over me than a bit of fluff blown about in the air. I can manage without you. I can pass you by. I'm strong and proud. Mankind is marching toward a higher truth, toward the greatest happiness possible on earth, and I'm in the front ranks!

LOPAKHIN: Will you get there?

TROFIMOV: I will. [*Pause.*] I will get there or show others the way to get there.

The sound of an axe striking a tree can be heard in the distance.

LOPAKHIN: Well, good-bye, my dear fellow. Time to go. You and I are trying to impress one another, but life goes on regardless. When I work hard for hours on end, I can think more clearly, and then I can't help feeling that I, too, know what I live for. Have you any idea how many people in Russia exist goodness only knows why? However, no matter. It isn't they who make the world go round. I'm told Gayev has taken a job at the bank at six thousand a year. He'll never stick to it. Too damn lazy.

ANYA [*in the doorway*]: Mother asks you not to begin cutting the orchard down till she's gone.

TROFIMOV: Really, haven't you any tact at all? [*Goes out through the hall.*]

LOPAKHIN: Sorry, I'll see to it at once, at once! The damned idiots! [*Goes out after* TROFIMOV.]

ANYA: Has Firs been taken to the hospital?

YASHA: I told them to this morning. They must have taken him, I should think.

ANYA [*to* YEPIKHODOV, *who is crossing the ballroom*]: Please find out if Firs has been taken to the hospital.

YASHA [*offended*]: I told Yegor this morning. I haven't got to tell him a dozen times, have I?

YEPIKHODOV: Old man Firs, if you want my final opinion, is beyond repair, and it's high time he was gathered to his fathers. So far as I'm concerned, I can only envy him. [*Puts a suitcase on a hatbox and squashes it.*] There, you see! I knew it. [*Goes out.*]

YASHA [*sneeringly*]: Twenty-two Calamities!

VARYA [*from behind the door*]: Has Firs been taken to the hospital?

ANYA: He has.

VARYA: Why didn't they take the letter for the doctor?

ANYA: We'd better send it on after him. [*Goes out.*]

VARYA [*from the next room*]: Where's Yasha? Tell him his mother's here. She wants to say good-bye to him.

YASHA [*waves his hand impatiently*]: Oh, that's too much!

All this time DUNYASHA *has been busy with the luggage. Now that* YASHA *is alone, she goes up to him.*

DUNYASHA: You haven't even looked at me once, Yasha. You're going away, leaving me behind. [*Bursts out crying and throws her arms around his neck.*]

YASHA: Must you cry? [*Drinks champagne.*] I'll be back in Paris in a week. Tomorrow we catch the express and off we go! That's the last you'll see of us. I can hardly believe it, somehow. *Vive la France!* I hate it here. It doesn't suit me at all. It's not the kind of life I like. I'm afraid it can't be helped. I've had enough of all this ignorance. More than enough. [*Drinks champagne.*] So what's the use of crying? Behave yourself and you won't end up crying.

DUNYASHA [*powdering her face, looking in a hand mirror*]: Write to me from Paris, please. I did love you, Yasha, after all. I loved you so much. I'm such an affectionate creature, Yasha.

YASHA: They're coming here. [*Busies himself around the suitcases, humming quietly.*]

Enter MRS. RANEVSKY, GAYEV, ANYA, *and* CHARLOTTE.

GAYEV: We ought to be going. There isn't much time left. [*Looking at* YASHA.] Who's smelling of pickled herrings here?

MRS. RANEVSKY: In another ten minutes we ought to be getting into the carriages. [*Looks round the room.*] Good-bye, dear house, good-bye, old grandfather house! Winter will pass, spring will come, and you won't be here any more. They'll have pulled you down. The things these walls have seen! [*Kisses her daughter affectionately.*] My precious one, you look radiant. Your eyes are sparkling like diamonds. Happy? Very happy?

ANYA: Oh yes, very! A new life is beginning, Mother!

GAYEV [*gaily*]: It is, indeed. Everything's all right now. We were all so worried and upset before the cherry orchard was sold, but now, when everything has been finally and irrevocably settled, we have all calmed down and even cheered up. I'm a bank official now, a financier. Pot the red in the middle. As for you, Lyuba, say what you like, but you too are looking a lot better. There's no doubt about it.

MRS. RANEVSKY: Yes, my nerves are better, that's true. [*Someone helps her on with her hat and coat.*] I sleep well. Take my things out, Yasha. It's time. [*To* ANYA.] We'll soon be seeing each other again, darling. I'm going to Paris. I'll live there on the money your great-aunt sent from Yaroslavl to buy the estate — three cheers for Auntie! — but the money won't last long, I'm afraid.

ANYA: You'll come home soon, Mother, very soon. I'm going to study, pass my school exams, and then I'll work and help you. We shall read all sorts of books together, won't we, Mother? [*Kisses her mother's hands.*] We shall read during the autumn evenings. We'll read lots and lots of books, and a new, wonderful world will open up to us. [*Dreamily.*] Oh, do come back, Mother!

MRS. RANEVSKY: I'll come back, my precious. [*Embraces her daughter.*]

Enter LOPAKHIN. CHARLOTTE *quietly hums a tune.*

GAYEV: Happy Charlotte! She's singing!

CHARLOTTE [*picks up a bundle that looks like a baby in swaddling clothes*]: My darling baby, go to sleep, my baby. [*A sound of a baby crying is heard.*] Hush, my sweet, my darling boy. [*The cry is heard again.*] Poor little darling, I'm so sorry for you! [*Throws the bundle down.*] So you will find me another job, won't you? I can't go on like this.

LOPAKHIN: We'll find you one, don't you worry.

GAYEV: Everybody's leaving us. Varya's going away. All of a sudden, we're no longer wanted.

CHARLOTTE: I haven't anywhere to live in town. I must go away. [*Sings quietly.*] It's all the same to me. . . .

Enter PISHCHIK.

LOPAKHIN: The nine days' wonder!

PISHCHIK [*out of breath*]: Oh dear, let me get my breath back! I'm all in. Dear friends . . . a drink of water, please.

GAYEV: Came to borrow some money, I'll be bound. Not from me this time. Better make myself scarce. [*Goes out.*]

PISHCHIK: Haven't seen you for ages, dearest lady. [*To* LOPAKHIN.] You here too? Glad to see you . . . man of immense intellect. . . . Here, that's for you, take it. [*Gives* LOPAKHIN *money.*] Four hundred rubles. That leaves eight hundred and forty I still owe you.

LOPAKHIN [*puzzled, shrugging his shoulders*]: I must be dreaming. Where did you get it?

PISHCHIK: One moment . . . Terribly hot . . . Most extraordinary thing happened. Some Englishmen came to see me. They found some kind of white clay on my land. [*To* MRS. RANEVSKY.] Here's four hundred for you too, beautiful ravishing lady. [*Gives her the money.*] The rest later. [*Drinks some water.*] Young fellow in the train just now was telling me that some — er — great philosopher advises people to jump off roofs. "Jump!" he says, and that'll solve all your problems. [*With surprise.*] Good Lord! More water, please.

LOPAKHIN: Who were these Englishmen?

PISHCHIK: I let them a plot of land with the clay on a twenty-four years' lease. And now you must excuse me, my friends. I'm in a hurry. Must be rushing off somewhere else. To Znoykov's, to Kardamonov's . . . Owe them all money. [*Drinks.*] Good-bye. I'll look in on Thursday.

MRS. RANEVSKY: We're just leaving for town. I'm going abroad tomorrow.

PISHCHIK: What? [*In a worried voice.*] Why are you going to town? Oh! I see! The furniture, the suitcases . . . Well, no matter. [*Through tears.*] No matter. Men of immense intellect, these Englishmen. . . . No matter. . . . No matter. I wish you all the best. May God help you. . . . No matter. Everything in this world comes to an end. [*Kisses* MRS. RANEVSKY's *hand.*] When you hear that my end has come, remember the—er—old horse and say: Once there lived a man called Simeonov-Pishchik; may he rest in peace. Remarkable weather we've been having. . . . Yes. [*Goes out in great embarrassment, but immediately comes back and says, standing in the doorway.*] My Dashenka sends her regards. [*Goes out.*]

MRS. RANEVSKY: Well, we can go now. I'm leaving with two worries on my mind. One concerns Firs. He's ill. [*With a glance at her watch.*] We still have about five minutes.

ANYA: Firs has been taken to the hospital, Mother. Yasha sent him off this morning.

MRS. RANEVSKY: My other worry concerns Varya. She's used to getting up early and working. Now that she has nothing to do, she's like a fish out of water. She's grown thin and pale, and she's always crying, poor thing. [*Pause.*] You must have noticed it, Lopakhin. As you very well know, I'd always hoped to see her married to you. Indeed, everything seemed to indicate that you two would get married. [*She whispers to* ANYA, *who nods to* CHARLOTTE, *and they both go out.*] She loves you, you like her, and I simply don't know why you two always seem to avoid each other. I don't understand it.

LOPAKHIN: To tell you the truth, neither do I. The whole thing's odd somehow. If there's still time, I'm ready even now. . . . Let's settle it at once and get it over. I don't feel I'll ever propose to her without you here.

MRS. RANEVSKY: Excellent! Why, it shouldn't take more than a minute. I'll call her at once.

LOPAKHIN: And there's champagne here too. Appropriate to the occasion. [*Looks at the glasses.*] They're empty. Someone must have drunk it. [YASHA *coughs.*] Lapped it up, I call it.

MRS. RANEVSKY [*excitedly*]: Fine! We'll go out. Yasha, *allez!*[15] I'll call her. [*Through the door.*] Varya, leave what you're doing and come here for a moment. Come on.

MRS. RANEVSKY *goes out with* YASHA.

LOPAKHIN [*glancing at his watch*]: Aye. . . .

Pause. Behind the door suppressed laughter and whispering can be heard. Enter VARYA.

VARYA [*spends a long time examining the luggage*]: Funny, can't find it.

LOPAKHIN: What are you looking for?

VARYA: Packed it myself, and can't remember.

Pause.

LOPAKHIN: Where are you going now, Varya?

VARYA: Me? To the Ragulins'. I've agreed to look after their house—to be their housekeeper, I suppose.

---

[15] *allez!:* French for "go!"

LOPAKHIN: In Yashnevo, isn't it? About fifty miles from here. [*Pause.*] Aye. . . . So life's come to an end in this house.

VARYA [*examining the luggage*]: Where can it be? Must have put it in the trunk. Yes, life's come to an end in this house. It will never come back.

LOPAKHIN: I'm off to Kharkov by the same train. Lots to see to there. I'm leaving Yepikhodov here to keep an eye on things. I've given him the job.

VARYA: Have you?

LOPAKHIN: This time last year it was already snowing, you remember. Now it's calm and sunny. A bit cold, though. Three degrees of frost.

VARYA: I haven't looked. [*Pause.*] Anyway, our thermometer's broken.

Pause. A voice from outside, through the door: "Mr. Lopakhin!"

LOPAKHIN [*as though he had long been expecting this call*]: Coming! [*Goes out quickly.*]

VARYA sits down on the floor, lays her head on a bundle of clothes, and sobs quietly. The door opens and MRS. RANEVSKY comes in cautiously.

MRS. RANEVSKY: Well? [*Pause.*] We must go.

VARYA [*no longer crying, dries her eyes*]: Yes, it's time, Mother dear. I'd like to get to the Ragulins' today, I only hope we don't miss the train.

MRS. RANEVSKY [*calling through the door*]: Anya, put your things on!

Enter ANYA, followed by GAYEV and CHARLOTTE. GAYEV wears a warm overcoat with a hood. SERVANTS and COACHMEN come in. YEPIKHODOV is busy with the luggage.

MRS. RANEVSKY: Now we can be on our way.

ANYA [*joyfully*]: On our way. Oh, yes!

GAYEV: My friends, my dear, dear friends, leaving this house for good, how can I remain silent, how can I, before parting from you, refrain from expressing the feelings which now pervade my whole being———

ANYA [*imploringly*]: Uncle!

VARYA: Uncle dear, please don't.

GAYEV [*dejectedly*]: Double the red into the middle. . . . Not another word!

Enter TROFIMOV, followed by LOPAKHIN.

TROFIMOV: Well, ladies and gentlemen, it's time to go.

LOPAKHIN: Yepikhodov, my coat!

MRS. RANEVSKY: Let me sit down a minute. I feel as though I've never seen the walls and ceilings of this house before. I look at them now with such eagerness, with such tender emotion. . . .

GAYEV: I remember when I was six years old sitting on this window sill on Trinity Sunday and watching Father going to church.

MRS. RANEVSKY: Have all the things been taken out?

LOPAKHIN: I think so. [*To YEPIKHODOV as he puts on his coat.*] Mind, everything's all right here, Yepikhodov.

YEPIKHODOV [*in a hoarse voice*]: Don't you worry, sir.

LOPAKHIN: What's the matter with your voice?

YEPIKHODOV: I've just had a drink of water and I must have swallowed something.

YASHA [*contemptuously*]: What ignorance!

MRS. RANEVSKY: There won't be a soul left in this place when we've gone.

LOPAKHIN: Not till next spring.

VARYA pulls an umbrella out of a bundle of clothes with such force that it looks as if she were going to hit someone with it; LOPAKHIN pretends to be frightened.

VARYA: Good heavens, you didn't really think that———

TROFIMOV: Come on, let's get into the carriages! It's time. The train will be in soon.

VARYA: There are your galoshes, Peter. By that suitcase. [*Tearfully.*] Oh, how dirty they are, how old. . . .

TROFIMOV [*putting on his galoshes*]: Come along, ladies and gentlemen.

Pause.

GAYEV [*greatly put out, afraid of bursting into tears*]: Train . . . station . . . in off into the middle pocket . . . double the white into the corner.

MRS. RANEVSKY: Come along!

LOPAKHIN: Is everyone here? No one left behind? [*Locks the side door on the left.*] There are some things in there. I'd better keep it locked. Come on!

ANYA: Good-bye, old house! Good-bye, old life!

TROFIMOV: Welcome new life!

TROFIMOV goes out with ANYA. VARYA casts a last look round the room and goes out unhurriedly. YASHA and CHARLOTTE, carrying her lap dog, go out.

LOPAKHIN: So, it's till next spring. Come along, ladies and gentlemen. Till we meet again. [*Goes out.*]

MRS. RANEVSKY and GAYEV are left alone. They seem to have been waiting for this moment. They fling their arms around each other, sobbing quietly, restraining themselves, as though afraid of being overheard.

GAYEV [*in despair*]: My sister! My sister!

MRS. RANEVSKY: Oh, my dear, my sweet, my beautiful orchard! My life, my youth, my happiness, good-bye! . . .

ANYA [*offstage, happily, appealingly*]: Mo-ther!

TROFIMOV [*offstage, happily, excited*]: Where are you?

MRS. RANEVSKY: One last look at the walls and the windows. Mother loved to walk in this room.

GAYEV: My sister, my sister!

ANYA [*offstage*]: Mo-ther!

TROFIMOV [*offstage*]: Where are you?

MRS. RANEVSKY: We're coming.

They go out. The stage is empty. The sound of all the doors being locked is heard, then of carriages driving off. It grows quiet. The silence is broken by the muffled noise of an axe striking a tree, sounding forlorn and sad. Footsteps can be heard. FIRS appears from the door on the right. He is dressed, as always, in a jacket and white waistcoat. He is wearing slippers. He looks ill.

FIRS [*walks up to the door and tries the handle*]: Locked! They've gone. [*Sits down on the sofa.*] Forgot all about me. Never mind. Let me sit down here for a bit.

Forgotten to put on his fur coat, the young master has. Sure of it. Gone off in his light overcoat. [*Sighs anxiously.*] I should have seen to it. . . . Oh, these youngsters! [*Mutters something which cannot be understood.*] My life's gone just as if I'd never lived. . . . [*Lies down.*] I'll lie down a bit. No strength left. Nothing's left. Nothing. Ugh, you — nincompoop! [*Lies motionless.*]

A distant sound is heard, which seems to come from the sky, the sound of a breaking string, slowly dying away, melancholy. It is followed by silence, broken only by the sound of an axe striking a tree far away in the orchard.
Curtain.

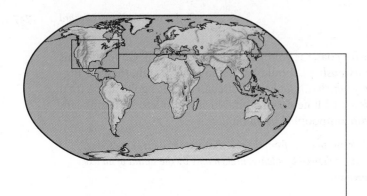

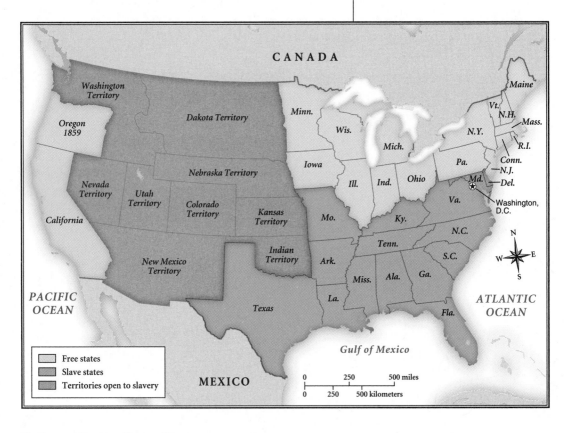

The Status of American Slavery, 1861

By 1861, the issue of slavery had become so explosive that the Southern states had seceded from the Union. Slavery was legal not only in the South, however; Delaware, Maryland, Missouri, and Kentucky all permitted it, as did the western territories.

THE AMERICAS
From Independence to Emancipation

🌾 Although inspired by the ideals of the European Enlightenment, the American Revolution was a kind of revolution different from the uprisings that occurred throughout Europe in the nineteenth century. The American Revolution sought to free America from the rule of the British monarchy and to install a democratic form of government, but unlike the French Revolution, it was also a war of independence. As a refusal to live under colonialism, the American Revolution would inspire similar efforts in many countries, especially in Latin America where Simón Bolívar (1783–1830) led revolutionary struggles that expelled Spain from the modern countries of Venezuela, Columbia, Ecuador, Peru, Bolivia, and Panama. Although Bolívar was successful in ousting Spain, his Napoleonic dream of uniting Latin American nations in a democratic federation was frustrated by ambitious tyrants who fought among themselves. In 1810, Miguel Hidalgo (1753–1811) launched the movement that would eventually free Mexico from Spanish rule, but the process of achieving genuine independence for that country would take more than a century.

SEEKING CULTURAL INDEPENDENCE

The American Revolution was the most successful of these revolts, in that it separated the United States from Britain and led to the establishment of a long-lasting constitutional government. Freeing American culture from European influence was a greater challenge. The U.S. Constitution was based on ideals promoted by the Enlightenment philosophers of France and England, and the former colonies were indebted to European military leaders, such as the French general Lafayette (1757–1834) and the Polish general Kosciusko (1746–1817), who had joined the

www For more information about the culture and context of the Americas in the nineteenth century, see *World Literature Online* at bedfordstmartins.com/worldlit.

East River Bridge (Brooklyn Bridge), 1870
*The Brooklyn Bridge was one of the great American technological marvels of the
nineteenth century. Comprising thousands of steel suspension cables, the elegant bridge
connecting Brooklyn and downtown Manhattan was a bold representation of America's
economic and industrial growth. (Library of Congress)*

upstarts' struggle out of a devotion to liberty. American writers of the post-
revolutionary period were similarly indebted to Europeans. James Fenimore
Cooper (1789–1851), author of what are known as the Leatherstocking novels about
the American frontier, was often called "the American Scott" because his works
seemed to do for American history what Sir Walter Scott had done for Scotland's.
Nathaniel Hawthorne's (1804–1864) supernatural and symbolic stories about New
England were compared with the works of European Gothic and supernatural
storytellers such as E. T. A. Hoffmann. Some literary historians would claim that
America did not produce a distinctively American literature until Mark Twain
published *Huckleberry Finn* in 1884, and at least one art historian has claimed that
American painting did not achieve a uniquely American point of view until the
work of Jackson Pollock in the 1930s and 1940s.

   Whatever their stylistic indebtedness to European art and literature, however,
American artists and writers did possess their own distinctly American subject
matter. The physical presence of a frontier of wilderness provided Americans with
a unique experience of mystery, beckoning, and challenge not available to European writers and artists, and much of the American art of the nineteenth century is
imaginatively caught up in its existence. Also, the Puritan heritage of many early

American writers, such as Hawthorne and Herman Melville (1819–1891), found expression in a biblically based mythology of the new nation. Perhaps the most authentically American voice prior to Mark Twain's was that of Walt Whitman (p. 877). His *Song of Myself* announces itself as a poem in the ROMANTIC vein, taking as its subject the poet himself. It is very different, however, from Wordsworth's autobiographical Romantic epic, *The Prelude* (written in 1805 but not published until 1850), which was subtitled "Growth of a Poet's Mind." In that work, Wordsworth writes of his personal, subjective experience; in *Song of Myself,* Whitman makes his personal experience the basis for a celebration of the richness and diversity of America. His song becomes America's song, and its catalogs of the country's landscape and people established Whitman's reputation abroad as "the poet of democracy." Standing on the Pacific coast, the poet marvelled at the breadth and size of America and at its non-Eurocentric perspective, in which a person could face west and look toward the East.

SLAVERY AND EMANCIPATION

The other great struggle in nineteenth-century America was an internal one—the fight against slavery. European travelers to the United States were fond of pointing out the hypocrisy of the institution of slavery in a nation that boasted of its commitment to liberty. Although American opposition to slavery began as an attempt to realize the principles of the Declaration of Independence and the U.S. Constitution, the abolition movement also belonged to a worldwide effort. When the French revolutionaries declared the "rights of man," they encouraged people everywhere to consider the injustice of slavery. Toussaint-Louverture, the "black Napoleon" of the French colony of Haiti, where slaves far outnumbered European colonists, led a revolt to free the slaves and secure independence for the island. In the nations liberated by Simón Bolívar in Latin America, new constitutions often included a provision prohibiting slavery. The movements to end slavery in the British colonies and the United States had their first successes in 1807 and 1808, when Britain and the United States stopped participating in the slave trade. Britain abolished slavery in its colonies in 1833; it took a war to prompt President Lincoln, the "Great Emancipator," to issue the Emancipation Proclamation in 1862. The Civil War (1861–65) was fought to abolish slavery, preserve the Union, and eliminate the feudal agricultural economy of the South that not only enslaved its workers but was also an impediment to the industrial and economic development of the nation as a whole. Unlike most wars of liberation during the nineteenth century, the Civil War was started by the conservatives, the South. However, the war's outcomes—national unity, a free economy, and the expansion of democracy—were those sought by liberal movements elsewhere.

LITERATURE OF EMANCIPATION

Besides the works of abolitionist authors such as Harriet Beecher Stowe (1811–1896), whose *Uncle Tom's Cabin* (1852) is a classic of the antislavery movement, the literary legacy of slavery is a large number of SLAVE NARRATIVES—autobiographical stories telling of the captivity, escape, and ultimate freedom of slaves—and sorrow songs, or spirituals. Using imagery that drew on everyday experience as well as the Bible to evoke the slave's situation and express the meaning of freedom, these spirituals contain some of the most moving poetry of the century.

Among the many American slave narratives, usually published with the aid of Northern abolitionists, are the autobiographies of Frederick Douglass (1817–1895), the activist, journalist, and public servant whose essay on Abraham Lincoln appears in *In the World:* Emancipation, and Harriet Jacobs (p. 754), who published her narrative under the pen name Linda Brent. Excerpts from a British slave narrative, that of Mary Prince, a slave from the British West Indies, is also included in *In the World:* Emancipation.

WOMEN'S RIGHTS

When two American abolitionists, Elizabeth Cady Stanton (1815–1902) and Lucretia Mott (1793–1880) (p. 827), attended the World Anti-Slavery Convention in London in 1840 and saw women delegates denied the right to speak simply because they were women, they returned home determined to take up the cause of women's oppression. They convened a conference at Seneca Falls, New York, in 1848, beginning the American women's rights movement. A "Declaration of Sentiments and Resolutions," based on the Declaration of Independence and drafted by Stanton and Mott, was adopted by those present at the meeting. Ironically, considering the meeting was convened because of Stanton and Mott's experience at an antislavery convention, the Seneca Falls assembly also narrowly passed a resolution calling for women's suffrage only after Frederick Douglass spoke movingly for it from the floor.

The women's rights movement inspired a literature of liberation by Realist writers in the second half of the century. Most literature about women in the first half of the century affirmed domestic virtues, the qualities desired in a wife and mother. In novels that are often considered to continue that tradition, Louisa May Alcott (1832–1888), best known for *Little Women* (1868–69), actually challenged it. Many of Alcott's heroines are working women, such as Jo March in *Little Women*, who writes for a living before succumbing to a conventional marriage. In *Work* (1873), Alcott's heroine suffers twenty years of exploitation and unequal treatment in the labor market before she becomes a spokesperson for women's rights. In addition to exposing the hardships faced by independent women, many writers of

Nineteenth-Century Americas: The Haitian Revolution

In 1789, the year of the French Revolution, St. Domingue, now Haiti, was France's most prosperous colony. It produced two-fifths of the world's sugar and half the world's coffee, and it accounted for forty percent of French overseas trade. Its population of more than half a million included about 25,000 white colonists, an equal number of free citizens of mixed descent, or *gens de couleur* as they were known, and more than 500,000 slaves of African descent. The struggle for liberty, fraternity, and equality in France was translated into a slave rebellion in this colonial context.

In the wake of the violence in France, white small holders (*petits blancs* who worked small farms) and large plantation owners *(grands blancs)* in St. Domingue marshaled their slaves into fighting forces and struggled against each other for political control of the colony. However, when the French National Assembly granted political rights to propertied *gens de couleur* in 1790, the whites banded together to prevent racial equality, and the political struggle turned into a racial war. Slaves originally mobilized to fight for their white masters chose to fight for their own emancipation. After 1893, led by Pierre-Dominique Toussaint-Louverture, the slaves defeated one opponent after another—the white plantation owners and small holders, invading forces of Spanish and English troops, and Napoleon's army of 44,000, led by the emperor's brother-in-law, General Charles Victor Emmanuel Leclerc. Toussaint-Louverture had become governor general of the colony in 1797, and although he was captured by trickery during the Napoleonic campaign and imprisoned in France, where he died in captivity, he had led the colony to independence, which was declared by his successor Jean-Jacques Dessalines on January 1, 1804.

Although France managed to hold on to Martinique and Guadeloupe, its other Caribbean colonies, the Haitian Revolution redefined the aims of the French Revolution for the Western Hemisphere. It spurred on antislavery movements that led to the abolition of the slave trade in the British colonies in 1808 and in the French colonies in 1818 and slavery itself in those colonies in 1834 and 1838. It also encouraged abolitionists in the United States and linked emancipation with the causes of freedom and democracy in the West. Convinced that the example of Haiti would bring about more revolutions, slaveholders throughout the Americas developed what historian Anthony Maingot has called a "terrified consciousness."

Francois-Dominique Toussaint-Louverture Declaring the Constitution of the Republic of Haiti, July 1, 1801. Toussaint-Louverture, the "black Napolean," is shown here with Haiti's constitution in hand. The presence of God and the bishop in this engraving is an expression of the divine source and inspiration of the document. (The Bridgeman Art Library)

the late nineteenth century, in America and elsewhere, also attacked patriarchal oppression in marriage. The heroine in Charlotte Perkins Gilman's (c. 1860–1935) (p. 941) *The Yellow Wallpaper* (1892) is driven to madness by the oppressive regimen prescribed by her physician and her husband. Kate Chopin's (1851–1904) (p. 931) Mrs. Mallard, in "The Story of an Hour" (1894), experiences an hour of joyous freedom before receiving the fatal news that her husband is in fact alive and has not been killed in a train crash.

❧ HARRIET A. JACOBS (LINDA BRENT)
c. 1813–1897

Among white residents of the United States and Canada in the eighteenth and nineteenth centuries, the Romantic impulse often took the form of dreams of starting life anew in the great western territories, places for the most part not yet inscribed with European ideas and codes of behavior. The North American West was for many the symbolic land of promise and self-fulfillment, and the early history of the United States is still often popularly imagined as the story of pioneers of European origin "winning" the West as they "redeemed" it from native peoples and from its own wildness.

This perspective was not shared by all living in North America at the time. For the enslaved African American people of the South, the direction of hope, the crucial journey, lay not to the west but to the north, toward the free states, and more particularly toward Canada after the Fugitive Slave Law of 1850 subjected runaway slaves within U.S. borders to deportation. In words that appeared to be about patient endurance and the sufferings of biblical peoples, spirituals and work songs encoded enslaved singers' longing for the journey north and even actual information about how to get there; for example, the "sweet chariot" that swings low to carry us home and the "drinking gourd" people are urged to follow are both references to the Big Dipper, an easily recognizable constellation whose lines point to the North Star, an indispensable guide to those traveling north under cover of night. Harriet Jacobs was one of the many slaves who made that journey and wrote about it. To protect those who had helped her to escape, she used the pseudonym "Linda Brent" and changed the names of almost all the people and places figuring in her life in the South. Her account of her life, of her years in slavery and hiding, and her ultimate escape, is one of the great SLAVE NARRATIVES.[1]

---

[1]**slave narratives:** Autobiographical narratives by former slaves describing their life and mistreatment under slavery, attempts to escape, and ultimate success in escaping to the North. The narratives, which employed many devices from popular fiction, were accompanied by testimonials to their authenticity.

Slavery and Sexual Oppression.   Jacobs was born into slavery in about 1813 in Edenton, North Carolina. She was orphaned early; her maternal grandmother, Molly Horniblow ("Aunt Martha"), was a freedwoman who made her living as a baker. When Jacobs was eleven, her first mistress died, and she was bequeathed to the three-year-old daughter of Dr. James Norcom ("Dr. Flint"). Norcom soon began a dogged campaign of sexual harassment against Jacobs. Although he threatened, cajoled, and gave her both presents and beatings, she resisted or evaded all his attempts at seduction and rape. When he forbade her to marry the African American freedman whom she loved, she exercised an option of resistance and took for her lover another influential white man, the young lawyer Samuel Treadwell Sawyer ("Mr. Sands"), by whom she bore two children, Joseph and Louisa Matilda. She explains the psychology that prompts her to accept the sympathetic Sawyer, but she acknowledges that the relationship is "sinful."

In 1835, Dr. Norcom punished Jacobs for continuing to refuse him by exiling her to his plantation, where slaves were treated more brutally than in town; next, he threatened to bring her children to the plantation and make them suffer particularly hard enslavement. Jacobs reasoned that if she were to disappear, Norcom would find her motherless children a mere burden and might sell them to an agent secretly representing their white father, whom she hoped would then free them.

Disappearance and Escape.   For nearly seven years, while most people believed her dead or fled to the North, Jacobs hid in a cramped crawl space in the attic of her grandmother's house, afraid to reveal her presence even to her own children. Sawyer was indeed able to purchase Joseph and Louisa Matilda, but he never got around to the crucial legal matter of setting them free.

Jacobs at last escaped by boat in 1842 to New York City where she worked as a nursemaid for the family of the editor Nathaniel Parker Willis.[2] There, she met Frederick Douglass, the most prominent writer and orator who had escaped slavery, and Amy Post[3] and Lydia Maria Child,[4] writers active in the causes of abolition and women's rights. There, too, she was at last reunited with her children. Her son Joseph became a sailor, a livelihood that kept him out of slavery's reach, but Jacobs and Louisa Matilda were traced to New York by the vengeful Norcom and his adult daughter. The Norcoms threatened to reclaim Jacobs and her daughter until Willis's wife purchased Jacobs and set her free.

Writing Her Autobiography.   Jacobs's friends urged her to tell her story, but for some time she held back because of the pain and shame of

www For more information about Jacobs and *Incidents in the Life of a Slave Girl,* see *World Literature Online* at bedfordstmartins .com/worldlit.

---

[2] **Nathaniel Parker Willis:** (1806–1867) American poet, travel writer, playwright, magazine editor, and critic.

[3] **Amy Post:** (1802–1889) Quaker abolitionist and feminist.

[4] **Lydia Maria Child:** (1802–1880) Novelist, social critic, abolitionist, and feminist; author of *The Frugal House-wife* (1829), *The Mother's Book* (1831), and several historical novels about life in New England.

With Frederick
Douglass's account
of his life, [*Incidents in
the Life of a Slave Girl*]
is one of the two
archetypes in the
genre of the slave
narrative.

– JEAN FAGAN YELLIN,
for her edition of the
book, 1987

revealing the sexual history so central to that telling. (It is worthwhile to remember that more than 140 years later, it is still hard for women and men to speak about histories of rape and childhood sexual abuse.) Above all, Jacobs feared her daughter Louisa Matilda's reaction to her story, especially because Jacobs's grandmother, who was supportive in all else, had condemned Jacobs for becoming Sawyer's lover and getting pregnant by him. Finally Jacobs agreed to write her autobiography, hoping that she might galvanize women to oppose the evils of slavery. With some help from editor Lydia Maria Child—whose work on the text was demonstrably that of an editor, not a ghostwriter—Jacobs brought out *Incidents in the Life of a Slave Girl* in 1861. Once Louisa Matilda knew the story, she embraced her mother along with her history, rejoicing in Jacobs's courage.

After the Civil War, Jacobs did relief work for freed slaves in the South and raised money for that cause in England. Toward the latter part of her life, she ran a boardinghouse in Cambridge, Massachusetts; she died in 1897. Louisa Matilda Jacobs continued her mother's work in relief and civil rights.

The Slave Narrative.   The slave narrative, most fully developed as a literary genre in the United States in the first half of the nineteenth century, emerged out of a rich blend of African, American, and European sources: the argument-by-storytelling and the rhythmic power of African tribal oratory; the verisimilitude of Realism; the melodramatic formulations and personal pleas to "Dear Reader" of the sentimental novel; the hairbreadth escapes of the picaresque tradition. This is not to say that the narratives' narrow escapes, hideous suffering, and heartfelt pleas were not genuine, but that the narrators had learned the means of their telling from oral and written expressions they had previously encountered.

The real people behind these narratives share with the fictional personae of contemporary European-American Romantic literature the determination of the individual to speak one's own name and insist on one's own identity through acts of open rebellion or carefully masked defiance against a larger society. A number of prominent white abolitionists in the United States and in England were themselves writers of Romantic fiction and poetry and felt able to sympathize with the African American writers on the ground of shared struggles against a dominant society that discouraged freedom. Many, such as Harriet Beecher Stowe,[5] John Greenleaf Whittier,[6] and Lydia Maria Child, helped to sponsor the lectures and publications of former slaves who had escaped to the North. But as Frederick Douglass, the author of the best known of all slave narratives, would remark in 1855, the free person, however sympathetic,

---

[5] Harriet Beecher Stowe: (1811–1896) Abolitionist and novelist best known for *Uncle Tom's Cabin* (1852).

[6] John Greenleaf Whittier: (1807–1892) Quaker poet who was an important spokesperson for the abolitionist movement; see p. 193.

Advertisement for Capture of Harriet Jacobs, July 4, 1835 *Placed on Independence Day, this ad was submitted by James Norcom, Harriet Jacobs's master. After she fled Norcom's plantation, Jacobs spent seven years hiding in the crawl space of her grandmother's attic before escaping to the North. (Courtesy of the North Carolina Office of Archives and History)*

$100 REWARD

WILL be given for the apprehension and delivery of my Servant Girl HARRIET. She is a light mulatto, 21 years of age, about 5 feet 4 inches high, of a thick and corpulent habit, having on her head a thick covering of black hair that curls naturally, but which can be easily combed straight. She speaks easily and fluently, and has an agreeable carriage and address. Being a good seamstress, she has been accustomed to dress well, has a variety of very fine clothes, made in the prevailing fashion, and will probably appear, if abroad, tricked out in gay and fashionable finery. As this girl absconded from the plantation of my son without any known cause or provocation, it is probable she designs to transport herself to the North.

The above reward, with all reasonable charges, will be given for apprehending her, or securing her in any prison or jail within the U. States.

All persons are hereby forewarned against harboring or entertaining her, or being in any way instrumental in her escape, under the most rigorous penalties of the law.

JAMES NORCOM.

Edenton, N. C. June 30

"cannot see things in the same light with the slave, because he does not, and cannot, look from the same point from which the slave does."

The Slave Narrative as African American Literature.   After the Civil War, many scholars came to regard slave narratives as political propaganda, ephemeral literature of little value except as curiosities. In the last decades of the twentieth century, the recovery and rereading of slave narratives was an important project of historians, anthropologists, folklorists, musicologists, and people in quest of the African American vision of the antebellum South. Literary critics have come to appreciate the narratives for their literary worth and to realize their profound influence on African American writing. As Rosa Bontemps remarked in 1966, "From the narrative came the spirit and vitality and the angle of vision responsible for the most effective prose writing by African American writers from

Northerners know nothing at all about slavery. They think it is perpetual bondage only. They have no conception of the depth of *degradation* involved in that word, SLAVERY.

— A WOMAN OF NORTH CAROLINA, quoted on the title page of the first edition of *Incidents*

William Wells Brown[7] to Charles W. Chesnutt,[8] from W. E. B. DuBois[9] to Richard Wright,[10] Ralph Ellison,[11] and James Baldwin.[12]" Bontemps's observation has been corroborated by African American writing of recent decades; many readers have found their way back to the slave narrative through Alex Haley's *Roots,* Toni Morrison's *Beloved,* or similar works.

Features of the Slave Narrative.   The slave narratives produced in the United States—more than 6,000 existing book-length narratives, Works Progress Administration interviews, and occasional essays, it has been estimated—vary greatly. But as James Olney and other scholars have pointed out, these texts share certain features of form and structure. For example, the authors often give accounts of how they learned to read and write and of the crucial role literacy plays in resisting slavery; they often include descriptions of slave auctions and feature an account of one spectacularly brutal master or overseer. Most have a story to tell about one particularly strong and resolute slave who resists white authority, and most remark on how avowedly Christian slaveholders are worse than the ones who aren't especially religious. All these elements can be found in Jacobs, as can two others whose significance may easily escape contemporary readers. First, slave narratives were always printed with testimonials and portraits as well as other prefatory material attesting to the author's existence and truthfulness; second, with astonishing consistency, the narratives' opening sentences begin, "I was born . . ." Such features in the published narratives served to combat charges that the books and stories were mere abolitionist propaganda, heavily doctored or in fact authored by white zealots. The testimonials, portraits, and especially the ability to put into writing the words *I was born* were ways for the author to insist upon his or her very existence as a human being, a man or a woman capable of thought, feeling, and speech.

Jacobs's narrative differs significantly from slave narratives written by men in several important ways. First, she makes a specific appeal to a *female* audience, the Northern white sisterhood who might be aroused to outrage by her story. Women could not yet vote in the United States, but Jacobs hoped for action they might take outside of suffrage to persuade men to vote against slavery. Second, she speaks with great frankness of the sexual persecution she endured, of the sexual choices she made within the constraints of slavery, and of how the sexual subjugation of

---

[7] William Wells Brown: (1814–1884) An escaped slave and author of *Narrative of William W. Brown, a Fugitive Slave, Written by Himself* (1847).

[8] Charles W. Chesnutt: (1858–1932) Son of emancipated blacks who wrote about social injustice in such novels as *The Goophered Grapevine* (1887), the first published novel by a black American writer.

[9] W. E. B. DuBois: (1868–1963) Scholar and editor known for *The Souls of Black Folk* (1903), an account of African American history; see Book 6.

[10] Richard Wright: (1908–1960) Black novelist from Mississippi who wrote the autobiographical *Black Boy* (1945) and *Native Son* (1940).

[11] Ralph Ellison: (1914–1994) Author of the semiautobiographical classic novel about a black man's search for identity in New York City, *Invisible Man* (1952).

[12] James Baldwin: (1924–1987) African American novelist and nonfiction writer; see Book 6.

black women by white men poisons black and white families alike. Finally, while many male slave narratives center on an unattached heroic young man who contrives mainly by his own strength and wits to win his way to freedom, Jacobs tells of a resourceful and mutually supportive network of courageous women, in and out of slavery, who are working to liberate one another and to free one another's children.

■ CONNECTIONS

Equiano, *The Interesting Narrative of the Life of Olaudah Equiano* (Book 4). *Incidents* both continues the genre of the slave narrative represented by Equiano's *Life* and transforms it by writing of the degradations peculiar to female slaves. Which generic characteristics do both works share? What does Jacobs add to the genre?

Rassundari Devi, *Amar Jiban*, p. 831; Woolf, *A Room of One's Own* (Book 6); *In the World:* Love, Marriage, and the Education of Women (Book 4). Many texts by women stress the importance of reading and writing in the fight against oppression. What role does education play in the works of Devi, Woolf, and the writers in *In the World:* Love, Marriage, and the Education of Women? How is literacy important to the women in Devi's and Woolf's texts? What differences are there between the notions of literacy that each of these texts promotes?

Pardo Bazán, "The Revolver," p. 696; Gilman, *The Yellow Wallpaper*, p. 941; Higuchi Ichiyo, "The Thirteenth Night," p. 1107. Jacobs reports that apologists for slavery describe it as "a beautiful 'patriarchal institution.'" In what sense can "patriarchal" be understood as a positive term? Can any of these meanings be applied to the patriarchal institution of marriage challenged in the works of Gilman, Pardo Bazán, and Higuchi Ichiyo?

Jefferson, The Declaration of Independence (Book 4); *In the World:* Emancipation, p. 814. The ideal of freedom is pervasive in the literature of the eighteenth and nineteenth centuries, from the liberty proclaimed in The Declaration of Independence and the notion of "free trade" promoted by Adam Smith and other laissez-faire economists to the cause of emancipation itself. What does Harriet Jacobs mean by *freedom* in relation to the texts in the *In the World:* Emancipation section? Make a list of the different definitions of freedom found in the works you have read thus far. Which of these meanings would be most important to Linda Brent?

■ FURTHER RESEARCH

Biography

Yellin, Jean Fagin, ed. *Incidents in the Life of a Slave Girl.* 1987. Includes etchings, photographs, maps, and descriptions of people and places in Jacobs's narrative, along with Yellin's account of Jacobs's life.

Background and Criticism

Baker, Houston A. Jr. *Blues, Ideology, and Afro-American Literature.* 1987.

Davis, Charles T., and Henry Louis Gates Jr. Introduction to *The Slave's Narrative.* 1991.

Garfield, Deborah M., and Rafia Zafar, eds. *Harriet Jacobs and* Incidents in the Life of a Slave Girl: *New Critical Essays.* 1996.

Johnson, Yvonne. *The Voices of African American Women: The Use of Narrative and Authorial Voice in the Works of Harriet Jacobs, Zora Neale Hurston, and Alice Walker.* 1998.

McKay, Nellie, and Frances Smith Foster, eds. Incidents in the Life of a Slave Girl: *Contexts, Criticisms.* 2001.

Olney, James. "'I Was Born': Slave Narratives, Their Status as Autobiography and as Literature," in Davis and Gates, *The Slave's Narrative*, pp. 148–74.

FROM

∾ Incidents in the Life of a Slave Girl

CHAPTER 1. CHILDHOOD

I was born a slave; but I never knew it till six years of happy childhood had passed away. My father was a carpenter, and considered so intelligent and skillful in his trade, that, when buildings out of the common line were to be erected, he was sent for from long distances, to be head workman. On condition of paying his mistress two hundred dollars a year, and supporting himself, he was allowed to work at his trade, and manage his own affairs. His strongest wish was to purchase his children; but, though he several times offered his hard earnings for that purpose, he never succeeded. In complexion my parents were a light shade of brownish yellow, and were termed mulattoes. They lived together in a comfortable home; and, though we were all slaves, I was so fondly shielded that I never dreamed I was a piece of mer- chandise, trusted to them for safe keeping, and liable to be demanded of them at any moment. I had one brother, William, who was two years younger than myself—a bright, affectionate child. I had also a great treasure in my maternal grandmother, who was a remarkable woman in many respects. She was the daughter of a planter in South Carolina, who, at his death, left her mother and his three children free, with money to go to St. Augustine, where they had relatives. It was during the Revolution- ary War; and they were captured on their passage, carried back, and sold to different purchasers. Such was the story my grandmother used to tell me; but I do not re- member all the particulars. She was a little girl when she was captured and sold to the keeper of a large hotel. I have often heard her tell how hard she fared during childhood. But as she grew older she evinced so much intelligence, and was so faith- ful, that her master and mistress could not help seeing it was for their interest to take care of such a valuable piece of property. She became an indispensable personage in the household, officiating in all capacities, from cook and wet nurse to seamstress. She was much praised for her cooking; and her nice crackers became so famous in the neighborhood that many people were desirous of obtaining them. In conse- quence of numerous requests of this kind, she asked permission of her mistress to bake crackers at night, after all the household work was done; and she obtained leave to do it, provided she would clothe herself and her children from the profits. Upon

---

Incidents in the Life of a Slave Girl. As Charles T. Davis and Henry Louis Gates Jr. note in *The Slave's Narrative,* twentieth-century historians continued to be more likely to detect "bias" in the slaves' accounts and "authenticity" in the masters'. Jacobs's story, especially her startling account of seven years spent in a crawl space, was read skeptically by many until 1985, when Jean Fagin Yellin brought to light letters, house blueprints, and other documents that proved Jacobs's authorship and her reliability. Characterizing *Incidents* as one of "the two archetypes of the genre of the slave narrative," (the other is Frederick Douglass's account of his life) Yellin confirms the work's histori- cal accuracy as well as its literary significance.

these terms, after working hard all day for her mistress, she began her midnight bakings, assisted by her two oldest children. The business proved profitable; and each year she laid by a little, which was saved for a fund to purchase her children. Her master died, and the property was divided among his heirs. The widow had her dower in the hotel, which she continued to keep open. My grandmother remained in her service as a slave; but her children were divided among her master's children. As she had five, Benjamin, the youngest one, was sold, in order that each heir might have an equal portion of dollars and cents. There was so little difference in our ages that he seemed more like my brother than my uncle. He was a bright, handsome lad, nearly white; for he inherited the complexion my grandmother had derived from Anglo-Saxon ancestors. Though only ten years old, seven hundred and twenty dollars were paid for him. His sale was a terrible blow to my grandmother; but she was naturally hopeful, and she went to work with renewed energy, trusting in time to be able to purchase some of her children. She had laid up three hundred dollars, which her mistress one day begged as a loan, promising to pay her soon. The reader probably knows that no promise or writing given to a slave is legally binding; for, according to Southern laws, a slave, *being* property, can *hold* no property. When my grandmother lent her hard earnings to her mistress, she trusted solely to her honor. The honor of a slaveholder to a slave!

To this good grandmother I was indebted for many comforts. My brother Willie and I often received portions of the crackers, cakes, and preserves she made to sell; and after we ceased to be children we were indebted to her for many more important services.

Such were the unusually fortunate circumstances of my early childhood. When I was six years old, my mother died; and then, for the first time, I learned, by the talk around me, that I was a slave. My mother's mistress was the daughter of my grandmother's mistress. She was the foster sister of my mother; they were both nourished at my grandmother's breast. In fact, my mother had been weaned at three months old, that the babe of the mistress might obtain sufficient food. They played together as children; and, when they became women, my mother was a most faithful servant to her whiter foster sister. On her death-bed her mistress promised that her children should never suffer for any thing; and during her lifetime she kept her word. They all spoke kindly of my dead mother, who had been a slave merely in name, but in nature was noble and womanly. I grieved for her, and my young mind was troubled with the thought who would now take care of me and my little brother. I was told that my home was now to be with her mistress; and I found it a happy one. No toilsome or disagreeable duties were imposed upon me. My mistress was so kind to me that I was always glad to do her bidding, and proud to labor for her as much as my young years would permit. I would sit by her side for hours, sewing diligently, with a heart as free from care as that of any free-born white child. When she thought I was tired, she would send me out to run and jump; and away I bounded, to gather berries or flowers to decorate her room. Those were happy days — too happy to last. The slave child had no thought for the morrow; but there came that blight, which too surely waits on every human being born to be a chattel.

When I was nearly twelve years old, my kind mistress sickened and died. As I saw the cheek grow paler, and the eye more glassy, how earnestly I prayed in my heart that she might live! I loved her; for she had been almost like a mother to me. My prayers were not answered. She died, and they buried her in the little churchyard, where, day after day, my tears fell upon her grave.

I was sent to spend a week with my grandmother. I was now old enough to begin to think of the future; and again and again I asked myself what they would do with me. I felt sure I should never find another mistress so kind as the one who was gone. She had promised my dying mother that her children should never suffer for any thing; and when I remembered that, and recalled her many proofs of attachment to me, I could not help having some hopes that she had left me free. My friends were almost certain it would be so. They thought she would be sure to do it, on account of my mother's love and faithful service. But, alas! we all know that the memory of a faithful slave does not avail much to save her children from the auction block.

After a brief period of suspense, the will of my mistress was read, and we learned that she had bequeathed me to her sister's daughter, a child of five years old. So vanished our hopes. My mistress had taught me the precepts of God's Word: "Thou shalt love thy neighbor as thyself." "Whatsoever ye would that men should do unto you, do ye even so unto them." But I was her slave, and I suppose she did not recognize me as her neighbor. I would give much to blot out from my memory that one great wrong. As a child, I loved my mistress; and, looking back on the happy days I spent with her, I try to think with less bitterness of this act of injustice. While I was with her, she taught me to read and spell; and for this privilege, which so rarely falls to the lot of a slave, I bless her memory.

She possessed but few slaves; and at her death those were all distributed among her relatives. Five of them were my grandmother's children, and had shared the same milk that nourished her mother's children. Notwithstanding my grand-mother's long and faithful service to her owners, not one of her children escaped the auction block. These God-breathing machines are no more, in the sight of their masters, than the cotton they plant, or the horses they tend.

CHAPTER 2. THE NEW MASTER AND MISTRESS

Dr. Flint, a physician in the neighborhood, had married the sister of my mistress, and I was now the property of their little daughter. It was not without murmuring that I prepared for my new home; and what added to my unhappiness, was the fact that my brother William was purchased by the same family. My father, by his nature, as well as by the habit of transacting business as a skillful mechanic, had more of the feelings of a freeman than is common among slaves. My brother was a spirited boy; and being brought up under such influences, he early detested the name of master and mistress. One day, when his father and his mistress had happened to call him at the same time, he hesitated between the two; being perplexed to know which had the strongest claim upon his obedience. He finally concluded to go to his mistress. When my father reproved him for it, he said, "You both called me, and I didn't know which I ought to go to first."

"You are *my* child," replied our father, "and when I call you, you should come immediately, if you have to pass through fire and water."

Poor Willie! He was now to learn his first lesson of obedience to a master. Grandmother tried to cheer us with hopeful words, and they found an echo in the credulous hearts of youth.

When we entered our new home we encountered cold looks, cold words, and cold treatment. We were glad when the night came. On my narrow bed I moaned and wept, I felt so desolate and alone.

I had been there nearly a year, when a dear little friend of mine was buried. I heard her mother sob, as the clods fell on the coffin of her only child, and I turned away from the grave, feeling thankful that I still had something left to love. I met my grandmother, who said, "Come with me, Linda;" and from her tone I knew that something sad had happened. She led me apart from the people, and then said, "My child, your father is dead." Dead! How could I believe it? He had died so suddenly I had not even heard that he was sick. I went home with my grandmother. My heart rebelled against God, who had taken from me mother, father, mistress, and friend. The good grandmother tried to comfort me. "Who knows the ways of God?" said she. "Perhaps they have been kindly taken from the evil days to come." Years afterwards I often thought of this. She promised to be a mother to her grandchildren, so far as she might be permitted to do so; and strengthened by her love, I returned to my master's. I thought I should be allowed to go to my father's house the next morning; but I was ordered to go for flowers, that my mistress's house might be decorated for an evening party. I spent the day gathering flowers and weaving them into festoons, while the dead body of my father was lying within a mile of me. What cared my owners for that? he was merely a piece of property. Moreover, they thought he had spoiled his children, by teaching them to feel that they were human beings. This was blasphemous doctrine for a slave to teach; presumptuous in him, and dangerous to the masters.

The next day I followed his remains to a humble grave beside that of my dear mother. There were those who knew my father's worth, and respected his memory.

My home now seemed more dreary than ever. The laugh of the little slave-children sounded harsh and cruel. It was selfish to feel so about the joy of others. My brother moved about with a very grave face. I tried to comfort him, by saying, "Take courage, Willie; brighter days will come by and by."

"You don't know any thing about it, Linda," he replied. "We shall have to stay here all our days; we shall never be free."

I argued that we were growing older and stronger, and that perhaps we might, before long, be allowed to hire our own time, and then we could earn money to buy our freedom. William declared this was much easier to say than to do; moreover, he did not intend to *buy* his freedom. We held daily controversies upon this subject.

Little attention was paid to the slaves' meals in Dr. Flint's house. If they could catch a bit of food while it was going, well and good. I gave myself no trouble on that score, for on my various errands I passed my grandmother's house, where there was always something to spare for me. I was frequently threatened with punishment if I stopped there; and my grandmother, to avoid detaining me, often stood at the gate with something for my breakfast or dinner. I was indebted to *her* for all my comforts, spiritual or temporal. It was *her* labor that supplied my scanty wardrobe. I have a vivid recollection of the linsey-woolsey dress given me every winter by Mrs. Flint. How I hated it! It was one of the badges of slavery.

While my grandmother was thus helping to support me from her hard earnings, the three hundred dollars she had lent her mistress were never repaid. When her mistress died, her son-in-law, Dr. Flint, was appointed executor. When grandmother applied to him for payment, he said the estate was insolvent, and the law prohibited payment. It did not, however, prohibit him from retaining the silver candelabra, which had been purchased with that money. I presume they will be handed down in the family, from generation to generation.

My grandmother's mistress had always promised her that, at her death, she should be free; and it was said that in her will she made good the promise. But when the estate was settled, Dr. Flint told the faithful old servant that, under existing circumstances, it was necessary she should be sold.

On the appointed day, the customary advertisement was posted up, proclaiming that there would be a "public sale of negroes, horses, &c." Dr. Flint called to tell my grandmother that he was unwilling to wound her feelings by putting her up at auction, and that he would prefer to dispose of her at private sale. My grandmother saw through his hypocrisy; she understood very well that he was ashamed of the job. She was a very spirited woman, and if he was base enough to sell her, when her mistress intended she should be free, she was determined the public should know it. She had for a long time supplied many families with crackers and preserves; consequently, "Aunt Marthy," as she was called, was generally known, and every body who knew her respected her intelligence and good character. Her long and faithful service in the family was also well known, and the intention of her mistress to leave her free. When the day of sale came, she took her place among the chattels, and at the first call she sprang upon the auction-block. Many voices called out, "Shame! Shame! Who is going to sell *you*, Aunt Marthy? Don't stand there! That is no place for *you*." Without saying a word, she quietly awaited her fate. No one bid for her. At last, a feeble voice said, "Fifty dollars." It came from a maiden lady, seventy years old, the sister of my grandmother's deceased mistress. She had lived forty years under the same roof with my grandmother; she knew how faithfully she had served her owners, and how cruelly she had been defrauded of her rights; and she resolved to protect her. The auctioneer waited for a higher bid; but her wishes were respected; no one bid above her. She could neither read nor write; and when the bill of sale was made out, she signed it with a cross. But what consequence was that, when she had a big heart overflowing with human kindness? She gave the old servant her freedom.

At that time, my grandmother was just fifty years old. Laborious years had passed since then; and now my brother and I were slaves to the man who had defrauded her of her money, and tried to defraud her of her freedom. One of my mother's sisters, called Aunt Nancy, was also a slave in his family. She was a kind, good aunt to me; and supplied the place of both housekeeper and waiting maid to her mistress. She was, in fact, at the beginning and end of every thing.

Mrs. Flint, like many southern women, was totally deficient in energy. She had not strength to superintend her household affairs; but her nerves were so strong, that she could sit in her easy chair and see a woman whipped, till the blood trickled from every stroke of the lash. She was a member of the church; but partaking of the Lord's supper did not seem to put her in a Christian frame of mind. If dinner was not served at the exact time on that particular Sunday, she would station herself in the kitchen, and wait till it was dished, and then spit in all the kettles and pans that had been used for cooking. She did this to prevent the cook and her children from eking out their meager fare with the remains of the gravy and other scrapings. The slaves could get nothing to eat except what she chose to give them. Provisions were weighed out by the pound and ounce, three times a day. I can assure you she gave them no chance to eat wheat bread from her flour barrel. She knew how many biscuits a quart of flour would make, and exactly what size they ought to be.

Dr. Flint was an epicure. The cook never sent a dinner to his table without fear and trembling; for if there happened to be a dish not to his liking, he would either order her to be whipped, or compel her to eat every mouthful of it in his presence. The poor, hungry creature might not have objected to eating it; but she did object to having her master cram it down her throat till she choked.

They had a pet dog that was a nuisance in the house. The cook was ordered to make some Indian mush for him. He refused to eat, and when his head was held over it, the froth flowed from his mouth into the basin. He died a few minutes after. When Dr. Flint came in, he said the mush had not been well cooked, and that was the reason the animal would not eat it. He sent for the cook, and compelled her to eat it. He thought that the woman's stomach was stronger than the dog's; but her sufferings afterwards proved that he was mistaken. This poor woman endured many cruelties from her master and mistress; sometimes she was locked up, away from her nursing baby, for a whole day and night.

When I had been in the family a few weeks, one of the plantation slaves was brought to town, by order of his master. It was near night when he arrived, and Dr. Flint ordered him to be taken to the work house, and tied up to the joist, so that his feet would just escape the ground. In that situation he was to wait till the doctor had taken his tea. I shall never forget that night. Never before, in my life, had I heard hundreds of blows fall, in succession, on a human being. His piteous groans, and his "O, pray don't, massa," rang in my ear for months afterwards. There were many conjectures as to the cause of this terrible punishment. Some said master accused him of stealing corn; others said the slave had quarrelled with his wife, in presence of the overseer, and had accused his master of being the father of her child. They were both black, and the child was very fair.

I went into the work house next morning, and saw the cowhide still wet with blood, and the boards all covered with gore. The poor man lived, and continued to quarrel with his wife. A few months afterwards Dr. Flint handed them both over to a slavetrader. The guilty man put their value into his pocket, and had the satisfaction of knowing that they were out of sight and hearing. When the mother was delivered into the trader's hands, she said, "You *promised* to treat me well." To which he replied, "You have let your tongue run too far; damn you!" She had forgotten that it was a crime for a slave to tell who was the father of her child.

From others than the master persecution also comes in such cases. I once saw a young slave girl dying soon after the birth of a child nearly white. In her agony she cried out, "O Lord, come and take me!" Her mistress stood by, and mocked at her like an incarnate fiend. "You suffer, do you?" she exclaimed. "I am glad of it. You deserve it all, and more too."

The girl's mother said, "The baby is dead, thank God; and I hope my poor child will soon be in heaven, too."

"Heaven!" retorted the mistress. "There is no such place for the like of her and her bastard."

The poor mother turned away, sobbing. Her dying daughter called her, feebly, and as she bent over her, I heard her say, "Don't grieve so, mother; God knows all about it; and HE will have mercy upon me."

Her sufferings, afterwards, became so intense, that her mistress felt unable to stay; but when she left the room, the scornful smile was still on her lips. Seven children called her mother. The poor black woman had but the one child, whose eyes she saw closing in death, while she thanked God for taking her away from the greater bitterness of life.

CHAPTER 5. THE TRIALS OF GIRLHOOD

During the first years of my service in Dr. Flint's family, I was accustomed to share some indulgences with the children of my mistress. Though this seemed to me no more than right, I was grateful for it, and tried to merit the kindness by the faithful discharge of my duties. But I now entered on my fifteenth year—a sad epoch in the life of a slave girl. My master began to whisper foul words in my ear. Young as I was, I could not remain ignorant of their import. I tried to treat them with indifference or contempt. The master's age, my extreme youth, and the fear that his conduct would be reported to my grandmother, made him bear this treatment for many months. He was a crafty man, and resorted to many means to accomplish his purposes. Sometimes he had stormy, terrific ways, that made his victims tremble; sometimes he assumed a gentleness that he thought must surely subdue. Of the two, I preferred his stormy moods, although they left me trembling. He tried his utmost to corrupt the pure principles my grandmother had instilled. He peopled my young mind with unclean images, such as only a vile monster could think of. I turned from him with disgust and hatred. But he was my master. I was compelled to live under the same roof with him—where I saw a man forty years my senior daily violating the most sacred commandments of nature. He told me I was his property; that I must be subject to his will in all things. My soul revolted against the mean tyranny. But where could I turn for protection? No matter whether the slave girl be as black as ebony or as fair as her mistress. In either case, there is no shadow of law to protect her from insult, from violence, or even from death; all these are inflicted by fiends who bear the shape of men. The mistress, who ought to protect the helpless victim, has no other feelings towards her but those of jealousy and rage. The degradation, the wrongs, the vices, that grow out of slavery, are more than I can describe. They are greater than you would willingly believe. Surely, if you credited one half the truths that are told you concerning the helpless millions suffering in this cruel bondage, you at the north would not help to tighten the yoke. You surely would refuse to do for the master, on your own soil, the mean and cruel work which trained blood-hounds and the lowest class of whites do for him at the south.

Every where the years bring to all enough of sin and sorrow; but in slavery the very dawn of life is darkened by these shadows. Even the little child, who is accustomed to wait on her mistress and her children, will learn, before she is twelve years old, why it is that her mistress hates such and such a one among the slaves. Perhaps the child's own mother is among those hated ones. She listens to violent outbreaks of jealous passion, and cannot help understanding what is the cause. She will become prematurely knowing in evil things. Soon she will learn to tremble when she hears her master's footfall. She will be compelled to realize that she is no longer a child. If God has bestowed beauty upon her, it will prove her greatest curse. That which commands admiration in the white woman only hastens the degradation of the female slave. I know that some are too much brutalized by slavery to feel the humiliation of their position; but many slaves feel it most acutely, and shrink from the memory of it. I cannot tell how much I suffered in the presence of these wrongs, nor how I am still pained by the retrospect. My master met me at every turn, reminding me that I belonged to him, and swearing by heaven and earth that he would compel me to submit to him. If I went out for a breath of fresh air, after a day of unwearied toil, his footsteps dogged me. If I knelt by my mother's grave, his dark shadow fell on me even there. The light heart which nature had given me became heavy with sad forebodings. The other slaves in my master's house noticed the change. Many of them pitied me; but none dared to ask the cause. They had no need to inquire. They knew too well the guilty practices under that roof; and they were aware that to speak of them was an offence that never went unpunished.

I longed for some one to confide in. I would have given the world to have laid my head on my grandmother's faithful bosom, and told her all my troubles. But Dr. Flint swore he would kill me, if I was not as silent as the grave. Then, although my grandmother was all in all to me, I feared her as well as loved her. I had been accustomed to look up to her with a respect bordering upon awe. I was very young, and felt shamefaced about telling her such impure things, especially as I knew her to be very strict on such subjects. Moreover, she was a woman of a high spirit. She was usually very quiet in her demeanor; but if her indignation was once roused, it was not very easily quelled. I had been told that she once chased a white gentleman with a loaded pistol, because he insulted one of her daughters. I dreaded the consequences of a violent outbreak; and both pride and fear kept me silent. But though I did not confide in my grandmother, and even evaded her vigilant watchfulness and inquiry, her presence in the neighborhood was some protection to me. Though she had been a slave, Dr. Flint was afraid of her. He dreaded her scorching rebukes. Moreover, she was known and patronized by many people; and he did not wish to have his villainy made public. It was lucky for me that I did not live on a distant plantation, but in a town not so large that the inhabitants were ignorant of each other's affairs. Bad as are the laws and customs in a slaveholding community, the doctor, as a professional man, deemed it prudent to keep up some outward show of decency.

O, what days and nights of fear and sorrow that man caused me! Reader, it is not to awaken sympathy for myself that I am telling you truthfully what I suffered in slavery. I do it to kindle a flame of compassion in your hearts for my sisters who are still in bondage, suffering as I once suffered.

I once saw two beautiful children playing together. One was a fair white child; the other was her slave, and also her sister. When I saw them embracing each other, and heard their joyous laughter, I turned sadly away from the lovely sight. I foresaw the inevitable blight that would fall on the little slave's heart. I knew how soon her laughter would be changed to sighs. The fair child grew up to be a still fairer woman. From childhood to womanhood her pathway was blooming with flowers, and overarched by a sunny sky. Scarcely one day of her life had been clouded when the sun rose on her happy bridal morning.

How had those years dealt with her slave sister, the little playmate of her childhood? She, also, was very beautiful; but the flowers and sunshine of love were not for her. She drank the cup of sin, and shame, and misery, whereof her persecuted race are compelled to drink.

In view of these things, why are ye silent, ye free men and women of the north? Why do your tongues falter in maintenance of the right? Would that I had more ability! But my heart is so full, and my pen is so weak! There are noble men and women who plead for us, striving to help those who cannot help themselves. God bless them! God give them strength and courage to go on! God bless those, every where, who are laboring to advance the cause of humanity!

Chapter 6. The Jealous Mistress

I would ten thousand times rather that my children should be the half-starved paupers of Ireland than to be the most pampered among the slaves of America. I would rather drudge out my life on a cotton plantation, till the grave opened to give me rest, than to live with an unprincipled master and a jealous mistress. The felon's home in a penitentiary is preferable. He may repent, and turn from the error of his ways, and so find peace; but it is not so with a favorite slave. She is not allowed to have any pride of character. It is deemed a crime in her to wish to be virtuous.

Mrs. Flint possessed the key to her husband's character before I was born. She might have used this knowledge to counsel and to screen the young and the innocent among her slaves; but for them she had no sympathy. They were the objects of her constant suspicion and malevolence. She watched her husband with unceasing vigilance; but he was well practised in means to evade it. What he could not find opportunity to say in words he manifested in signs. He invented more than were ever thought of in a deaf and dumb asylum. I let them pass, as if I did not understand what he meant; and many were the curses and threats bestowed on me for my stupidity. One day he caught me teaching myself to write. He frowned, as if he was not well pleased; but I suppose he came to the conclusion that such an accomplishment might help to advance his favorite scheme. Before long, notes were often slipped into my hand. I would return them, saying, "I can't read them, sir." "Can't you?" he replied; "then I must read them to you." He always finished the reading by asking, "Do you understand?" Sometimes he would complain of the heat of the tea room, and order his supper to be placed on a small table in the piazza. He would seat himself there with a well-satisfied smile, and tell me to stand by and brush away the flies. He would eat very slowly, pausing between the mouthfuls. These intervals were employed in describing the happiness I was so foolishly throwing away, and in threatening me with the penalty that finally awaited my stubborn disobedience. He boasted much of the forbearance he had exercised towards me, and reminded me that there was a limit to his patience. When I succeeded in avoiding opportunities for him to talk to me at home, I was ordered to come to his office, to do some errand. When there, I was obliged to stand and listen to such language as he saw fit to address to me. Sometimes I so openly expressed my contempt for him that he would become violently enraged, and I wondered why he did not strike me. Circumstanced as he was, he probably thought it was better policy to be forbearing. But the state of things grew worse and worse daily. In desperation I told him that I must and would apply to my grandmother for protection. He threatened me with death, and worse than death, if I made any complaint to her. Strange to say, I did not despair. I was naturally of a buoyant disposition, and always I had a hope of somehow getting out of his clutches. Like many a poor, simple slave before me, I trusted that some threads of joy would yet be woven into my dark destiny.

I had entered my sixteenth year, and every day it became more apparent that my presence was intolerable to Mrs. Flint. Angry words frequently passed between her and her husband. He had never punished me himself, and he would not allow any body else to punish me. In that respect, she was never satisfied; but, in her angry moods, no terms were too vile for her to bestow upon me. Yet I, whom she detested so bitterly, had far more pity for her than he had, whose duty it was to make her life happy. I never wronged her, or wished to wrong her; and one word of kindness from her would have brought me to her feet.

After repeated quarrels between the doctor and his wife, he announced his intention to take his youngest daughter, then four years old, to sleep in his apartment. It was necessary that a servant should sleep in the same room, to be on hand if the child stirred. I was selected for that office, and informed for what purpose that arrangement had been made. By managing to keep within sight of people, as much as possible, during the day time, I had hitherto succeeded in eluding my master, though a razor was often held to my throat to force me to change this line of policy. At night I slept by the side of my great aunt, where I felt safe. He was too prudent to come into her room. She was an old woman, and had been in the family many years. Moreover, as a married man, and a professional man, he deemed it necessary to save appearances in some degree. But he resolved to remove the obstacle in the way of his scheme; and he thought he had planned it so that he should evade suspicion. He was well aware how much I prized my refuge by the side of my old aunt, and he determined to dispossess me of it. The first night the doctor had the little child in his room alone. The next morning, I was ordered to take my station as nurse the follow-ing night. A kind Providence interposed in my favor. During the day Mrs. Flint heard of this new arrangement, and a storm followed. I rejoiced to hear it rage.

After a while my mistress sent for me to come to her room. Her first question was, "Did you know you were to sleep in the doctor's room?"

"Yes, ma'am."

"Who told you?"

"My master."

"Will you answer truly all the questions I ask?"

"Yes, ma'am."

"Tell me, then, as you hope to be forgiven, are you innocent of what I have accused you?"

"I am."

She handed me a Bible, and said, "Lay your hand on your heart, kiss this holy book, and swear before God that you tell me the truth."

I took the oath she required, and I did it with a clear conscience.

"You have taken God's holy word to testify your innocence," said she. "If you have deceived me, beware! Now take this stool, sit down, look me directly in the face, and tell me all that has passed between your master and you."

I did as she ordered. As I went on with my account her color changed frequently, she wept, and sometimes groaned. She spoke in tones so sad, that I was touched by her grief. The tears came to my eyes; but I was soon convinced that her emotions arose from anger and wounded pride. She felt that her marriage vows were desecrated, her dignity insulted; but she had no compassion for the poor victim of her husband's per-fidy. She pitied herself as a martyr; but she was incapable of feeling for the condition of shame and misery in which her unfortunate, helpless slave was placed.

Yet perhaps she had some touch of feeling for me; for when the conference was ended, she spoke kindly, and promised to protect me. I should have been much com-forted by this assurance if I could have had confidence in it; but my experiences in slavery had filled me with distrust. She was not a very refined woman, and had not much control over her passions. I was an object of her jealousy, and, consequently, of her hatred; and I knew I could not expect kindness or confidence from her under the circumstances in which I was placed. I could not blame her. Slaveholders' wives feel as other women would under similar circumstances. The fire of her temper kindled from small sparks, and now the flame became so intense that the doctor was obliged to give up his intended arrangement.

I knew I had ignited the torch, and I expected to suffer for it afterwards; but I felt too thankful to my mistress for the timely aid she rendered me to care much about that. She now took me to sleep in a room adjoining her own. There I was an object of her especial care, though not of her especial comfort, for she spent many a sleepless night to watch over me. Sometimes I woke up, and found her bending over me. At other times she whispered in my ear, as though it was her husband who was speaking to me, and listened to hear what I would answer. If she startled me, on such occa-sions, she would glide stealthily away; and the next morning she would tell me I had been talking in my sleep, and ask who I was talking to. At last, I began to be fearful for my life. It had been often threatened; and you can imagine, better than I can describe, what an unpleasant sensation it must produce to wake up in the dead of night and find a jealous woman bending over you. Terrible as this experience was, I had fears that it would give place to one more terrible.

My mistress grew weary of her vigils; they did not prove satisfactory. She changed her tactics. She now tried the trick of accusing my master of crime, in my presence, and gave my name as the author of the accusation. To my utter astonishment, he replied, "I don't believe it: but if she did acknowledge it, you tortured her into exposing me." Tortured into exposing him! Truly, Satan had no difficulty in distinguishing the color of his soul! I understood his object in making this false representation. It was to show me that I gained nothing by seeking the protection of my mistress; that the power was still all in his own hands. I pitied Mrs. Flint. She was a second wife, many years the junior of her husband; and the hoary-headed miscreant was enough to try the patience of a wiser and better woman. She was completely foiled, and knew not how to proceed. She would gladly have had me flogged for my supposed false oath; but, as I have already stated, the doctor never allowed any one to whip me. The old sinner was politic. The application of the lash might have led to remarks that would have exposed him in the eyes of his children and grandchildren. How often did I rejoice that I lived in a town where all the inhabitants knew each other! If I had been on a remote plantation, or lost among the multitude of a crowded city, I should not be a living woman at this day.

The secrets of slavery are concealed like those of the Inquisition. My master was, to my knowledge, the father of eleven slaves. But did the mothers dare to tell who was the father of their children? Did the other slaves dare to allude to it, except in whispers among themselves? No, indeed! They knew too well the terrible consequences.

My grandmother could not avoid seeing things which excited her suspicions. She was uneasy about me, and tried various ways to buy me; but the neverchanging answer was always repeated: "Linda does not belong to *me*. She is my daughter's property, and I have no legal right to sell her." The conscientious man! He was too scrupulous to *sell* me; but he had no scruples whatever about committing a much greater wrong against the helpless young girl placed under his guardianship, as his daughter's property. Sometimes my persecutor would ask me whether I would like to be sold. I told him I would rather be sold to any body than to lead such a life as I did. On such occasions he would assume the air of a very injured individual, and reproach me for my ingratitude. "Did I not take you into the house, and make you the companion of my own children?" he would say. "Have I ever treated you like a negro? I have never allowed you to be punished, not even to please your mistress. And this is the recompense I get, you ungrateful girl!" I answered that he had reasons of his own for screening me from punishment, and that the course he pursued made my mistress hate me and persecute me. If I wept, he would say, "Poor child! Don't cry! don't cry! I will make peace for you with your mistress. Only let me arrange matters in my own way. Poor, foolish girl! you don't know what is for your own good. I would cherish you. I would make a lady of you. Now go, and think of all I have promised you."

I did think of it.

Reader, I draw no imaginary pictures of southern homes. I am telling you the plain truth. Yet when victims make their escape from this wild beast of Slavery, northerners consent to act the part of bloodhounds, and hunt the poor fugitive back into his den, "full of dead men's bones, and all uncleanness." Nay, more, they are not only willing, but proud, to give their daughters in marriage to slaveholders. The poor girls have romantic notions of a sunny clime, and of the flowering vines that all the year round shade a happy home. To what disappointments are they destined! The young wife soon learns that the husband in whose hands she has placed her happiness pays no regard to his marriage vows. Children of every shade of complexion play with her own fair babies, and too well she knows that they are born unto him of his own household. Jealousy and hatred enter the flowery home, and it is ravaged of its loveliness.

Southern women often marry a man knowing that he is the father of many little slaves. They do not trouble themselves about it. They regard such children as property, as marketable as the pigs on the plantation, and it is seldom that they do not make them aware of this by passing them into the slavetrader's hands as soon as possible, and thus getting them out of their sight. I am glad to say there are some honorable exceptions.

I have myself known two southern wives who exhorted their husbands to free those slaves towards whom they stood in a "parental relation;" and their request was granted. These husbands blushed before the superior nobleness of their wives' natures. Though they had only counselled them to do that which it was their duty to do, it commanded their respect, and rendered their conduct more exemplary. Concealment was at an end, and confidence took the place of distrust.

Though this bad institution deadens the moral sense, even in white women, to a fearful extent, it is not altogether extinct. I have heard southern ladies say of Mr. Such a one, "He not only thinks it no disgrace to be the father of those little niggers, but he is not ashamed to call himself their master. I declare, such things ought not to be tolerated in any decent society!"

Chapter 7. The Lover

Why does the slave ever love? Why allow the tendrils of the heart to twine around objects which may at any moment be wrenched away by the hand of violence? When separations come by the hand of death, the pious soul can bow in resignation, and say, "Not my will, but thine be done, O Lord!" But when the ruthless hand of man strikes the blow, regardless of the misery he causes, it is hard to be submissive. I did not reason thus when I was a young girl. Youth will be youth. I loved, and I indulged the hope that the dark clouds around me would turn out a bright lining. I forgot that in the land of my birth the shadows are too dense for light to penetrate. A land

"Where laughter is not mirth; nor thought the mind;
Nor words a language; nor e'en men mankind.
Where cries reply to curses, shrieks to blows,
And each is tortured in his separate hell."[1]

There was in the neighborhood a young colored carpenter; a free born man. We had been well acquainted in childhood, and frequently met together afterwards. We became mutually attached, and he proposed to marry me. I loved him with all the ardor of a young girl's first love. But when I reflected that I was a slave, and that the laws gave no sanction to the marriage of such, my heart sank within me. My lover wanted to buy me; but I knew that Dr. Flint was too willful and arbitrary a man to consent to that arrangement. From him, I was sure of experiencing all sorts of opposition, and I had nothing to hope from my mistress. She would have been delighted to have got rid of me, but not in that way. It would have relieved her mind of a burden if she could have seen me sold to some distant state, but if I was married near home I should be just as much in her husband's power as I had previously been,— for the husband of a slave has no power to protect her. Moreover, my mistress, like many others, seemed to think that slaves had no right to any family ties of their own; that they were created merely to wait upon the family of the mistress. I once heard her abuse a young slave girl, who told her that a colored man wanted to make her his wife. "I will have you peeled and pickled,[2] my lady," said she, "if I even hear you mention that subject again. Do you suppose that I will have you tending *my* children with the children of that nigger?" The girl to whom she said this had a mulatto child, of course not acknowledged by its father. The poor black man who loved her would have been proud to acknowledge his helpless offspring.

Many and anxious were the thoughts I revolved in my mind. I was at a loss what to do. Above all things, I was desirous to spare my lover the insults that had cut so deeply into my own soul. I talked with my grandmother about it, and partly told her my fears. I did not dare to tell her the worst. She had long suspected all was not right, and if I confirmed her suspicions I knew a storm would rise that would prove the overthrow of all my hopes.

This love-dream had been my support through many trials; and I could not bear to run the risk of having it suddenly dissipated. There was a lady in the neighborhood, a particular friend of Dr. Flint's, who often visited the house. I had a great respect for her, and she had always manifested a friendly interest in me. Grandmother thought she would have great influence with the doctor. I went to this lady, and told her my story. I told her I was aware that my lover's being a free-born man would prove a great objection; but he wanted to buy me; and if Dr. Flint would consent to that arrangement, I felt sure he would be willing to pay any reasonable price. She knew that Mrs. Flint disliked me; therefore, I ventured to suggest that perhaps my mistress would approve of my being sold, as that would rid her of me. The lady

---

[1] "Where . . . hell": George Gordon, Lord Byron, "The Lament of Tasso," iv, 7–10.

[2] **peeled and pickled:** The practice of whipping a slave and then rinsing the wounds with salt water.

listened with kindly sympathy, and promised to do her utmost to promote my wishes. She had an interview with the doctor, and I believe she pleaded my cause earnestly; but it was all to no purpose.

How I dreaded my master now! Every minute I expected to be summoned to his presence; but the day passed, and I heard nothing from him. The next morning, a message was brought to me: "Master wants you in his study." I found the door ajar, and I stood a moment gazing at the hateful man who claimed a right to rule me, body and soul. I entered, and tried to appear calm. I did not want him to know how my heart was bleeding. He looked fixedly at me, with an expression which seemed to say, "I have half a mind to kill you on the spot." At last he broke the silence, and that was a relief to both of us.

"So you want to be married, do you?" said he, "and to a free nigger."

"Yes, sir."

"Well, I'll soon convince you whether I am your master, or the nigger fellow you honor so highly. If you *must* have a husband, you may take up with one of my slaves."

What a situation I should be in, as the wife of one of *his* slaves, even if my heart had been interested!

I replied, "Don't you suppose, sir, that a slave can have some preference about marrying? Do you suppose that all men are alike to her?"

"Do you love this nigger?" said he, abruptly.

"Yes, sir."

"How dare you tell me so!" he exclaimed, in great wrath. After a slight pause, he added, "I supposed you thought more of yourself; that you felt above the insults of such puppies."

I replied, "If he is a puppy I am a puppy, for we are both of the negro race. It is right and honorable for us to love each other. The man you call a puppy never insulted me, sir; and he would not love me if he did not believe me to be a virtuous woman."

He sprang upon me like a tiger, and gave me a stunning blow. It was the first time he had ever struck me; and fear did not enable me to control my anger. When I had recovered a little from the effects, I exclaimed, "You have struck me for answering you honestly. How I despise you!"

There was silence for some minutes. Perhaps he was deciding what should be my punishment; or, perhaps, he wanted to give me time to reflect on what I had said and to whom I had said it. Finally, he asked, "Do you know what you have said?"

"Yes, sir; but your treatment drove me to it."

"Do you know that I have a right to do as I like with you, — that I can kill you, if I please?"

"You have tried to kill me, and I wish you had; but you have no right to do as you like with me."

"Silence!" he exclaimed, in a thundering voice. "By heavens, girl, you forget yourself too far! Are you mad? If you are, I will soon bring you to your senses. Do you think any other master would bear what I have borne from you this morning? Many masters would have killed you on the spot. How would you like to be sent to jail for your insolence?"

"I know I have been disrespectful, sir," I replied; "but you drove me to it; I couldn't help it. As for the jail, there would be more peace for me there than there is here."

"You deserve to go there," said he, "and to be under such treatment, that you would forget the meaning of the word *peace*. It would do you good. It would take some of your high notions out of you. But I am not ready to send you there yet, notwithstanding your ingratitude for all my kindness and forbearance. You have been the plague of my life. I have wanted to make you happy, and I have been repaid with the basest ingratitude; but though you have proved yourself incapable of appreciating my kindness, I will be lenient towards you, Linda. I will give you one more chance to redeem your character. If you behave yourself and do as I require, I will forgive you and treat you as I always have done; but if you disobey me, I will punish you as I would the meanest slave on my plantation. Never let me hear that fellow's name mentioned again. If I ever know of your speaking to him, I will cowhide you both; and if I catch him lurking about my premises, I will shoot him as soon as I would a dog. Do you hear what I say? I'll teach you a lesson about marriage and free niggers! Now go, and let this be the last time I have occasion to speak to you on this subject."

Reader, did you ever hate? I hope not. I never did but once; and I trust I never shall again. Somebody has called it "the atmosphere of hell;" and I believe it is so.

For a fortnight the doctor did not speak to me. He thought to mortify me; to make me feel that I had disgraced myself by receiving the honorable addresses of a respectable colored man, in preference to the base proposals of a white man. But though his lips disdained to address me, his eyes were very loquacious. No animal ever watched its prey more narrowly than he watched me. He knew that I could write, though he had failed to make me read his letters; and he was now troubled lest I should exchange letters with another man. After a while he became weary of silence; and I was sorry for it. One morning, as he passed through the hall, to leave the house, he contrived to thrust a note into my hand. I thought I had better read it, and spare myself the vexation of having him read it to me. It expressed regret for the blow he had given me, and reminded me that I myself was wholly to blame for it. He hoped I had become convinced of the injury I was doing myself by incurring his displeasure. He wrote that he had made up his mind to go to Louisiana; that he should take several slaves with him, and intended I should be one of the number. My mistress would remain where she was; therefore I should have nothing to fear from that quarter. If I merited kindness from him, he assured me that it would be lavishly bestowed. He begged me to think over the matter, and answer the following day.

The next morning I was called to carry a pair of scissors to his room. I laid them on the table, with the letter beside them. He thought it was my answer, and did not call me back. I went as usual to attend my young mistress to and from school. He met me in the street, and ordered me to stop at his office on my way back. When I entered, he showed me his letter, and asked me why I had not answered it. I replied, "I am your daughter's property, and it is in your power to send me, or take me, wherever you please." He said he was very glad to find me so willing to go, and that we should start early in the autumn. He had a large practice in the town, and I rather thought he had made up the story merely to frighten me. However that might be, I was determined that I would never go to Louisiana with him.

Summer passed away, and early in the autumn Dr. Flint's eldest son was sent to Louisiana to examine the country, with a view to emigrating. That news did not disturb me. I knew very well that I should not be sent with *him*. That I had not been taken to the plantation before this time, was owing to the fact that his son was there. He was jealous of his son; and jealousy of the overseer had kept him from punishing me by sending me into the fields to work. Is it strange that I was not proud of these protectors? As for the overseer, he was a man for whom I had less respect than I had for a bloodhound.

Young Mr. Flint did not bring back a favorable report of Louisiana, and I heard no more of that scheme. Soon after this, my lover met me at the corner of the street, and I stopped to speak to him. Looking up, I saw my master watching us from his window. I hurried home, trembling with fear. I was sent for, immediately, to go to his room. He met me with a blow. "When is mistress to be married?" said he, in a sneering tone. A shower of oaths and imprecations followed. How thankful I was that my lover was a free man, that my tyrant had no power to flog him for speaking to me in the street!

Again and again I revolved in my mind how all this would end. There was no hope that the doctor would consent to sell me on any terms. He had an iron will, and was determined to keep me, and to conquer me. My lover was an intelligent and religious man. Even if he could have obtained permission to marry me while I was a slave, the marriage would give him no power to protect me from my master. It would have made him miserable to witness the insults I should have been subjected to. And then, if we had children, I knew they must "follow the condition of the mother." What a terrible blight that would be on the heart of a free, intelligent father! For *his* sake, I felt that I ought not to link his fate with my own unhappy destiny. He was going to Savannah to see about a little property left him by an uncle; and hard as it was to bring my feelings to it, I earnestly entreated him not to come back. I advised him to go to the Free States, where his tongue would not be tied, and where his intelligence would be of more avail to him. He left me, still hoping the day would come when I could be bought. With me the lamp of hope had gone out. The dream of my girlhood was over. I felt lonely and desolate.

Still I was not stripped of all. I still had my good grandmother, and my affectionate brother. When he put his arms round my neck, and looked into my eyes, as if to read there the troubles I dared not tell, I felt that I still had something to love. But even that pleasant emotion was chilled by the reflection that he might be torn from me at any moment, by some sudden freak of my master. If he had known how we love each other, I think he would have exulted in separating us. We often planned together how we could get to the north. But, as William remarked, such things are easier said than done. My movements were very closely watched, and we had no means of getting any money to defray our expenses. As for grandmother, she was strongly opposed to her children's undertaking any such project. She had not forgotten poor Benjamin's[3] sufferings, and she was afraid that if another child tried to escape, he would have a similar or a worse fate. To me, nothing seemed more dreadful than my present life. I said to myself, "William *must* be free. He shall go to the north, and I will follow him." Many a slave sister has formed the same plans.

Chapter 10. A Perilous Passage in the Slave Girl's Life

After my lover went away, Dr. Flint contrived a new plan. He seemed to have an idea that my fear of my mistress was his greatest obstacle. In the blandest tones, he told me that he was going to build a small house for me, in a secluded place, four miles away from the town. I shuddered; but I was constrained to listen, while he talked of his intention to give me a home of my own, and to make a lady of me. Hitherto, I had escaped my dreaded fate, by being in the midst of people. My grandmother had already had high words with my master about me. She had told him pretty plainly what she thought of his character, and there was considerable gossip in the neighborhood about our affairs, to which the open-mouthed jealousy of Mrs. Flint contributed not a little. When my master said he was going to build a house for me, and that he could do it with little trouble and expense, I was in hopes something would happen to frustrate his scheme; but I soon heard that the house was actually begun. I vowed before my Maker that I would never enter it. I had rather toil on the plantation from dawn till dark; I had rather live and die in jail, than drag on, from day to day, through such a living death. I was determined that the master, whom I so hated and loathed, who had blighted the prospects of my youth, and made my life a desert, should not, after my long struggle with him, succeed at last in trampling his victim under his feet. I would do any thing, every thing, for the sake of defeating him. What *could* I do? I thought and thought, till I became desperate, and made a plunge into the abyss.

And now, reader, I come to a period in my unhappy life, which I would gladly forget if I could. The remembrance fills me with sorrow and shame. It pains me to tell you of it; but I have promised to tell you the truth, and I will do it honestly, let it cost me what it may. I will not try to screen myself behind the plea of compulsion from a master; for it was not so. Neither can I plead ignorance or thoughtlessness. For years, my master had done his utmost to pollute my mind with foul images, and to destroy the pure principles inculcated by my grandmother, and the good mistress of my childhood. The influences of slavery had had the same effect on me that they had on other young girls; they had made me prematurely knowing, concerning the evil ways of the world. I knew what I did, and I did it with deliberate calculation.

But, O, ye happy women, whose purity has been sheltered from childhood, who have been free to choose the objects of your affection, whose homes are protected by

---

[3] **Benjamin:** Jacobs's grandmother's younger son Benjamin had attempted to escape and was recaptured, jailed, and, sick and weak after months of imprisonment, sold to a slave trader. He escaped again and made it safely to New York.

law, do not judge the poor desolate slave girl too severely! If slavery had been abolished, I, also, could have married the man of my choice; I could have had a home shielded by the laws; and I should have been spared the painful task of confessing what I am now about to relate; but all my prospects had been blighted by slavery. I wanted to keep myself pure; and, under the most adverse circumstances, I tried hard to preserve my self-respect; but I was struggling alone in the powerful grasp of the demon Slavery; and the monster proved too strong for me. I felt as if I was forsaken by God and man; as if all my efforts must be frustrated; and I became reckless in my despair.

I have told you that Dr. Flint's persecutions and his wife's jealousy had given rise to some gossip in the neighborhood. Among others, it chanced that a white unmarried gentleman had obtained some knowledge of the circumstances in which I was placed. He knew my grandmother, and often spoke to me in the street. He became interested for me, and asked questions about my master, which I answered in part. He expressed a great deal of sympathy, and a wish to aid me. He constantly sought opportunities to see me, and wrote to me frequently. I was a poor slave girl, only fifteen years old.

So much attention from a superior person was, of course, flattering; for human nature is the same in all. I also felt grateful for his sympathy, and encouraged by his kind words. It seemed to me a great thing to have such a friend. By degrees, a more tender feeling crept into my heart. He was an educated and eloquent gentleman; too eloquent, alas, for the poor slave girl who trusted in him. Of course I saw whither all this was tending. I knew the impassable gulf between us; but to be an object of interest to a man who is not married, and who is not her master, is agreeable to the pride and feelings of a slave, if her miserable situation has left her any pride or sentiment. It seems less degrading to give one's self, than to submit to compulsion. There is something akin to freedom in having a lover who has no control over you, except that which he gains by kindness and attachment. A master may treat you as rudely as he pleases, and you dare not speak; moreover, the wrong does not seem so great with an unmarried man, as with one who has a wife to be made unhappy. There may be sophistry in all this; but the condition of a slave confuses all principles of morality, and, in fact, renders the practice of them impossible.

When I found that my master had actually begun to build the lonely cottage, other feelings mixed with those I have described. Revenge, and calculations of interest, were added to flattered vanity and sincere gratitude for kindness. I knew nothing would enrage Dr. Flint so much as to know that I favored another; and it was something to triumph over my tyrant even in that small way. I thought he would revenge himself by selling me, and I was sure my friend, Mr. Sands, would buy me. He was a man of more generosity and feeling than my master, and I thought my freedom could be easily obtained from him. The crisis of my fate now came so near that I was desperate. I shuddered to think of being the mother of children that should be owned by my old tyrant. I knew that as soon as a new fancy took him, his victims were sold far off to get rid of them; especially if they had children. I had seen several women sold, with his babies at the breast. He never allowed his offspring by slaves to remain long in sight of himself and his wife. Of a man who was not my master I could ask to have my children well supported; and in this case, I felt confident I should obtain the boon. I also felt quite sure that they would be made free. With all these thoughts revolving in my mind, and seeing no other way of escaping the doom I so much dreaded, I made a headlong plunge. Pity me, and pardon me, O virtuous reader! You never knew what it is to be a slave; to be entirely unprotected by law or custom; to have the laws reduce you to the condition of a chattel, entirely subject to the will of another. You never exhausted your ingenuity in avoiding the snares, and eluding the power of a hated tyrant; you never shuddered at the sound of his foot-steps, and trembled within hearing of his voice. I know I did wrong. No one can feel it more sensibly than I do. The painful and humiliating memory will haunt me to my dying day. Still, in looking back, calmly, on the events of my life, I feel that the slave woman ought not to be judged by the same standard as others.

The months passed on. I had many unhappy hours. I secretly mourned over the sorrow I was bringing on my grandmother, who had so tried to shield me from harm. I knew that I was the greatest comfort of her old age, and that it was a source of pride to her that I had not degraded myself, like most of the slaves. I wanted to confess to her that I was no longer worthy of her love; but I could not utter the dreaded words.

As for Dr. Flint, I had a feeling of satisfaction and triumph in the thought of telling *him.* From time to time he told me of his intended arrangements, and I was silent. At last, he came and told me the cottage was completed, and ordered me to go to it. I told him I would never enter it. He said, "I have heard enough of such talk as that. You shall go, if you are carried by force; and you shall remain there."

I replied, "I will never go there. In a few months I shall be a mother."

He stood and looked at me in dumb amazement, and left the house without a word. I thought I should be happy in my triumph over him. But now that the truth was out, and my relatives would hear of it, I felt wretched. Humble as were their cir-cumstances, they had pride in my good character. Now, how could I look them in the face? My self-respect was gone! I had resolved that I would be virtuous, though I was a slave. I had said, "Let the storm beat! I will brave it till I die." And now, how humil-iated I felt!

I went to my grandmother. My lips moved to make confession, but the words stuck in my throat. I sat down in the shade of a tree at her door and began to sew. I think she saw something unusual was the matter with me. The mother of slaves is very watchful. She knows there is no security for her children. After they have entered their teens she lives in daily expectation of trouble. This leads to many ques-tions. If the girl is of a sensitive nature, timidity keeps her from answering truthfully, and this well-meant course has a tendency to drive her from maternal counsels. Presently, in came my mistress, like a mad woman, and accused me concerning her husband. My grandmother, whose suspicions had been previously awakened, believed what she said. She exclaimed, "O Linda! has it come to this? I had rather see you dead than to see you as you now are. You are a disgrace to your dead mother." She tore from my fingers my mother's wedding ring and her silver thimble. "Go away!" she exclaimed, "and never come to my house, again." Her reproaches fell so hot and heavy, that they left me no chance to answer. Bitter tears, such as the eyes never shed but once, were my only answer. I rose from my seat, but fell back again, sobbing. She did not speak to me; but the tears were running down her furrowed cheeks, and they scorched me like fire. She had always been so kind to me! *So* kind! How I longed to throw myself at her feet, and tell her all the truth! But she had ordered me to go, and never to come there again. After a few minutes, I mustered strength, and started to obey her. With what feelings did I now close that little gate, which I used to open with such an eager hand in my childhood! It closed upon me with a sound I never heard before.

Where could I go? I was afraid to return to my master's. I walked on recklessly, not caring where I went, or what would become of me. When I had gone four or five miles, fatigue compelled me to stop. I sat down on the stump of an old tree. The stars were shining through the boughs above me. How they mocked me, with their bright, calm light! The hours passed by, and as I sat there alone a chilliness and deadly sickness came over me. I sank on the ground. My mind was full of horrid thoughts. I prayed to die; but the prayer was not answered. At last, with great effort I roused myself, and walked some distance further, to the house of a woman who had been a friend of my mother. When I told her why I was there, she spoke soothingly to me; but I could not be comforted. I thought I could bear my shame if I could only be reconciled to my grandmother. I longed to open my heart to her. I thought if she could know the real state of the case, and all I had been bearing for years, she would perhaps judge me less harshly. My friend advised me to send for her. I did so; but days of agonizing suspense passed before she came. Had she utterly forsaken me? No. She came at last. I knelt before her, and told her the things that had poisoned my life; how long I had been persecuted; that I saw no way of escape; and in an hour of extremity I had become desperate. She listened in silence. I told her I would bear any thing and do any thing, if in time I had hopes of obtaining her forgiveness. I begged of her to pity me, for my dead mother's sake. And she did pity me. She did not say, "I forgive you;" but she looked at me lovingly, with her eyes full of tears. She laid her old hand gently on my head, and murmured, "Poor child! Poor child!"

CHAPTER 12. FEAR OF INSURRECTION

Not far from this time Nat Turner's[4] insurrection broke out, and the news threw our town into great commotion. Strange that they should be alarmed, when their slaves were so "contented and happy"! But so it was.

It was always the custom to have a muster every year. On that occasion every white man shouldered his musket. The citizens and the so-called country gentlemen wore military uniforms. The poor whites took their places in the ranks in every-day dress, some without shoes, some without hats. This grand occasion had already passed; and when the slaves were told there was to be another muster, they were sur-

---

[4] **Nat Turner:** Led a slave insurrection on August 21 and 22, 1831, in Southhampton County, Virginia, near Jacobs's home in Edenton, North Carolina, in which fifty-five white people were killed. Months of brutal terrorist attacks on both slave and freed African Americans followed in the wake of the rebellion.

prised and rejoiced. Poor creatures! They thought it was going to be a holiday. I was informed of the true state of affairs, and imparted it to the few I could trust. Most gladly would I have proclaimed it to every slave; but I dared not. All could not be relied on. Mighty is the power of the torturing lash.

By sunrise, people were pouring in from every quarter within twenty miles of the town. I knew the houses were to be searched; and I expected it would be done by country bullies and the poor whites. I knew nothing annoyed them so much as to see colored people living in comfort and respectability; so I made arrangements for them with especial care. I arranged every thing in my grandmother's house as neatly as possible. I put white quilts on the beds, and decorated some of the rooms with flowers. When all was arranged, I sat down at the window to watch. Far as my eye could reach, it rested on a motley crowd of soldiers. Drums and fifes were discoursing martial music. The men were divided into companies of sixteen, each headed by a captain. Orders were given, and the wild scouts rushed in every direction, wherever a colored face was to be found.

It was a grand opportunity for the low whites, who had no negroes of their own to scourge. They exulted in such a chance to exercise a little brief authority, and show their subserviency to the slaveholders; not reflecting that the power which trampled on the colored people also kept themselves in poverty, ignorance, and moral degradation. Those who never witnessed such scenes can hardly believe what I know was inflicted at this time on innocent men, women, and children, against whom there was not the slightest ground for suspicion. Colored people and slaves who lived in remote parts of the town suffered in an especial manner. In some cases the searchers scattered powder and shot among their clothes, and then sent other parties to find them, and bring them forward as proof that they were plotting insurrection. Every where men, women, and children were whipped till the blood stood in puddles at their feet. Some received five hundred lashes; others were tied hands and feet, and tortured with a bucking paddle, which blisters the skin terribly. The dwellings of the colored people, unless they happened to be protected by some influential white person, who was nigh at hand, were robbed of clothing and every thing else the marauders thought worth carrying away. All day long these unfeeling wretches went round, like a troop of demons, terrifying and tormenting the helpless. At night, they formed themselves into patrol bands, and went wherever they chose among the colored people, acting out their brutal will. Many women hid themselves in woods and swamps, to keep out of their way. If any of the husbands or fathers told of these outrages, they were tied up to the public whipping post, and cruelly scourged for telling lies about white men. The consternation was universal. No two people that had the slightest tinge of color in their faces dared to be seen talking together.

I entertained no positive fears about our household, because we were in the midst of white families who would protect us. We were ready to receive the soldiers whenever they came. It was not long before we heard the tramp of feet and the sound of voices. The door was rudely pushed open; and in they tumbled, like a pack of hungry wolves. They snatched at every thing within their reach. Every box, trunk, closet, and corner underwent a thorough examination. A box in one of the drawers containing some silver change was eagerly pounced upon. When I stepped forward to take it from them, one of the soldiers turned and said angrily, "What d'ye foller us fur? D'ye s'pose white folks is come to steal?"

I replied, "You have come to search; but you have searched that box, and I will take it, if you please."

At that moment I saw a white gentleman who was friendly to us; and I called to him, and asked him to have the goodness to come in and stay till the search was over. He readily complied. His entrance into the house brought in the captain of the company, whose business it was to guard the outside of the house, and see that none of the inmates left it. This officer was Mr. Litch, the wealthy slaveholder whom I mentioned, in the account of neighboring planters, as being notorious for his cruelty. He felt above soiling his hands with the search. He merely gave orders; and, if a bit of writing was discovered, it was carried to him by his ignorant followers, who were unable to read.

My grandmother had a large trunk of bedding and table cloths. When that was opened, there was a great shout of surprise; and one exclaimed, "Where'd the damned niggers git all dis sheet an' table clarf?"

My grandmother, emboldened by the presence of our white protector, said, "You may be sure we didn't pilfer 'em from *your* houses."

"Look here, mammy," said a grim-looking fellow without any coat, "you seem to feel mighty gran' 'cause you got all them 'ere fixens. White folks oughter have 'em all."

His remarks were interrupted by a chorus of voices shouting, "We's got 'em! We's got 'em! Dis 'ere yaller gal's got letters!"

There was a general rush for the supposed letter, which, upon examination, proved to be some verses written to me by a friend. In packing away my things, I had overlooked them. When their captain informed them of their contents, they seemed much disappointed. He inquired of me who wrote them. I told him it was one of my friends. "Can you read them?" he asked. When I told him I could, he swore, and raved, and tore the paper into bits. "Bring me all your letters!" said he, in a commanding tone. I told him I had none. "Don't be afraid," he continued, in an insinuating way. "Bring them all to me. Nobody shall do you any harm." Seeing I did not move to obey him, his pleasant tone changed to oaths and threats. "Who writes to you? half free niggers?" inquired he. I replied, "O, no; most of my letters are from white people. Some request me to burn them after they are read, and some I destroy without reading."

An exclamation of surprise from some of the company put a stop to our conversation. Some silver spoons which ornamented an old-fashioned buffet had just been discovered. My grandmother was in the habit of preserving fruit for many ladies in the town, and of preparing suppers for parties; consequently she had many jars of preserves. The closet that contained these was next invaded, and the contents tasted. One of them, who was helping himself freely, tapped his neighbor on the shoulder, and said, "Wal done! Don't wonder de niggers want to kill all de white folks, when dey live on 'sarves" [meaning preserves]. I stretched out my hand to take the jar, saying, "You were not sent here to search for sweetmeats."

"And what *were* we sent for?" said the captain, bristling up to me. I evaded the question.

The search of the house was completed, and nothing found to condemn us. They next proceeded to the garden, and knocked about every bush and vine, with no better success. The captain called his men together, and, after a short consultation, the order to march was given. As they passed out of the gate, the captain turned back, and pronounced a malediction on the house. He said it ought to be burned to the ground, and each of its inmates receive thirty-nine lashes. We came out of this affair very fortunately; not losing any thing except some wearing apparel.

Towards evening the turbulence increased. The soldiers, stimulated by drink, committed still greater cruelties. Shrieks and shouts continually rent the air. Not daring to go to the door, I peeped under the window curtain. I saw a mob dragging along a number of colored people, each white man, with his musket upraised, threatening instant death if they did not stop their shrieks. Among the prisoners was a respectable old colored minister. They had found a few parcels of shot in his house, which his wife had for years used to balance her scales. For this they were going to shoot him on Court House Green. What a spectacle was that for a civilized country! A rabble, staggering under intoxication, assuming to be the administrators of justice!

The better class of the community exerted their influence to save the innocent, persecuted people; and in several instances they succeeded, by keeping them shut up in jail till the excitement abated. At last the white citizens found that their own property was not safe from the lawless rabble they had summoned to protect them. They rallied the drunken swarm, drove them back into the country, and set a guard over the town.

The next day, the town patrols were commissioned to search colored people that lived out of the city; and the most shocking outrages were committed with perfect impunity. Every day for a fortnight, if I looked out, I saw horsemen with some poor panting negro tied to their saddles, and compelled by the lash to keep up with their speed, till they arrived at the jail yard. Those who had been whipped too unmercifully to walk were washed with brine, tossed into a cart, and carried to jail. One black man, who had not fortitude to endure scourging, promised to give information about the conspiracy. But it turned out that he knew nothing at all. He had not even heard the name of Nat Turner. The poor fellow had, however, made up a story, which augmented his own sufferings and those of the colored people.

The day patrol continued for some weeks, and at sundown a night guard was substituted. Nothing at all was proved against the colored people, bond or free. The wrath of the slaveholders was somewhat appeased by the capture of Nat Turner. The imprisoned were released. The slaves were sent to their masters, and the free were permitted to return to their ravaged homes. Visiting was strictly forbidden on the plantations. The slaves begged the privilege of again meeting at their little church in the woods, with their burying ground around it. It was built by the colored people, and they had no higher happiness than to meet there and sing hymns together, and pour out their hearts in spontaneous prayer. Their request was denied, and the church was demolished. They were permitted to attend the white churches, a certain portion of the galleries being appropriated to their use. There, when every body else had partaken of the communion, and the benediction had been pronounced, the minister said, "Come down, now, my colored friends." They obeyed the summons, and partook of the bread and wine, in commemoration of the meek and lowly Jesus, who said, "God is your Father, and all ye are brethren."

CHAPTER 13. THE CHURCH AND SLAVERY

After the alarm caused by Nat Turner's insurrection had subsided, the slave-holders came to the conclusion that it would be well to give the slaves enough of religious instruction to keep them from murdering their masters. The Episcopal clergyman offered to hold a separate service on Sundays for their benefit. His colored members were very few, and also very respectable—a fact which I presume had some weight with him. The difficulty was to decide on a suitable place for them to worship. The Methodist and Baptist churches admitted them in the afternoon; but their carpets and cushions were not so costly as those at the Episcopal church. It was at last decided that they should meet at the house of a free colored man, who was a member.

I was invited to attend, because I could read. Sunday evening came, and, trusting to the cover of night, I ventured out. I rarely ventured out by daylight, for I always went with fear, expecting at every turn to encounter Dr. Flint, who was sure to turn me back, or order me to his office to inquire where I got my bonnet, or some other article of dress. When the Rev. Mr. Pike came, there were some twenty persons present. The reverend gentleman knelt in prayer, then seated himself, and requested all present, who could read, to open their books, while he gave out the portions he wished them to repeat or respond to.

His text was, "Servants, be obedient to them that are your masters according to the flesh, with fear and trembling, in singleness of your heart, as unto Christ."

Pious Mr. Pike brushed up his hair till it stood upright, and, in deep, solemn tones, began: "Hearken, ye servants! Give strict heed unto my words. You are rebellious sinners. Your hearts are filled with all manner of evil. 'Tis the devil who tempts you. God is angry with you, and will surely punish you, if you don't forsake your wicked ways. You that live in town are eye-servants behind your master's back. Instead of serving your masters faithfully, which is pleasing in the sight of your heavenly Master, you are idle, and shirk your work. God sees you. You tell lies. God hears you. Instead of being engaged in worshipping him, you are hidden away somewhere, feasting on your master's substance; tossing coffee-grounds with some wicked fortuneteller, or cutting cards with another old hag. Your masters may not find you out, but God sees you, and will punish you. O, the depravity of your hearts! When your master's work is done, are you quietly together, thinking of the goodness of God to such sinful creatures? No; you are quarrelling, and tying up little bags of roots to bury under the door-steps to poison each other with. God sees you. You men steal away to every grog shop to sell your master's corn, that you may buy rum to drink. God sees you. You sneak into the back streets, or among the bushes, to pitch coppers. Although your masters may not find you out, God sees you; and he will punish you. You must forsake your sinful ways, and be faithful servants. Obey your old master and your young master — your old mistress and your young mistress. If you disobey your earthly master, you offend your heavenly Master. You must obey God's commandments. When you go from here, don't stop at the corners of the streets to talk, but go directly home, and let your master and mistress see that you have come."

The benediction was pronounced. We went home, highly amused at brother Pike's gospel teaching, and we determined to hear him again. I went the next Sabbath evening, and heard pretty much a repetition of the last discourse. At the close of the meeting, Mr. Pike informed us that he found it very inconvenient to meet at the friend's house, and he should be glad to see us, every Sunday evening, at his own kitchen.

I went home with the feeling that I had heard the Reverend Mr. Pike for the last time. Some of his members repaired to his house, and found that the kitchen sported two tallow candles; the first time, I am sure, since its present occupant owned it, for the servants never had any thing but pine knots. It was so long before the reverend gentleman descended from his comfortable parlor that the slaves left, and went to enjoy a Methodist shout. They never seem so happy as when shouting and singing at religious meetings. Many of them are sincere, and nearer to the gate of heaven than sanctimonious Mr. Pike, and other longfaced Christians, who see wounded Samaritans, and pass by on the other side.

The slaves generally compose their own songs and hymns; and they do not trouble their heads much about the measure. They often sing the following verses:

> "Old Satan is one busy ole man;
>   He rolls dem blocks all in my way;
> But Jesus is my bosom friend;
>   He rolls dem blocks away.

> "If I had died when I was young,
>   Den how my stam'ring tongue would have sung;
> But I am ole, and now I stand
>   A narrow chance for to tread dat heavenly land."

I well remember one occasion when I attended a Methodist class meeting. I went with a burdened spirit, and happened to sit next a poor, bereaved mother, whose heart was still heavier than mine. The class leader was the town constable — a man who bought and sold slaves, who whipped his brethren and sisters of the church at the public whipping post, in jail or out of jail. He was ready to perform that Christian office any where for fifty cents. This white-faced, black-hearted brother came near us, and said to the stricken woman, "Sister, can't you tell us how the Lord deals with your soul? Do you love him as you did formerly?"

She rose to her feet, and said, in piteous tones, "My Lord and Master, help me! My load is more than I can bear. God has hid himself from me, and I am left in darkness and misery." Then, striking her breast, she continued, "I can't tell you what is in here! They've got all my children. Last week they took the last one. God only knows where they've sold her. They let me have her sixteen years, and then — O! O! Pray for her brothers and sisters! I've got nothing to live for now. God make my time short!"

She sat down, quivering in every limb. I saw that constable class leader become crimson in the face with suppressed laughter, while he held up his handkerchief, that those who were weeping for the poor woman's calamity might not see his merriment. Then, with assumed gravity, he said to the bereaved mother, "Sister, pray to the Lord that every dispensation of his divine will may be sanctified to the good of your poor needy soul!"

The congregation struck up a hymn, and sung as though they were as free as the birds that warbled round us, —

"Ole Satan thought he had a mighty aim;
He missed my soul, and caught my sins.
Cry Amen, cry Amen, cry Amen to God!

"He took my sins upon his back;
Went muttering and grumbling down to hell.
Cry Amen, cry Amen, cry Amen to God!

"Ole Satan's church is here below.
Up to God's free church I hope to go.
Cry Amen, cry Amen, cry Amen to God!"

Precious are such moments to the poor slaves. If you were to hear them at such times, you might think they were happy. But can that hour of singing and shouting sustain them through the dreary week, toiling without wages, under constant dread of the lash?

The Episcopal clergyman, who, ever since my earliest recollection, had been a sort of god among the slaveholders, concluded, as his family was large, that he must go where money was more abundant. A very different clergyman took his place. The change was very agreeable to the colored people, who said, "God has sent us a good man this time." They loved him, and their children followed him for a smile or a kind word. Even the slaveholders felt his influence. He brought to the rectory five slaves. His wife taught them to read and write, and to be useful to her and themselves. As soon as he was settled, he turned his attention to the needy slaves around him. He urged upon his parishioners the duty of having a meeting expressly for them every Sunday, with a sermon adapted to their comprehension. After much argument and importunity, it was finally agreed that they might occupy the gallery of the church on Sunday evenings. Many colored people, hitherto unaccustomed to attend church, now gladly went to hear the gospel preached. The sermons were simple, and they understood them. Moreover, it was the first time they had ever been addressed as human beings. It was not long before his white parishioners began to be dissatisfied. He was accused of preaching better sermons to the negroes than he did to them. He honestly confessed that he bestowed more pains upon those sermons than upon any others; for the slaves were reared in such ignorance that it was a difficult task to adapt himself to their comprehension. Dissensions arose in the parish. Some wanted he should preach to them in the evening, and to the slaves in the afternoon. In the midst of these disputings his wife died, after a very short illness. Her slaves gathered round her dying bed in great sorrow. She said, "I have tried to do you good and promote your happiness; and if I have failed, it has not been for want of interest in your welfare. Do not weep for me; but prepare for the new duties that lie before you. I leave you all free. May we meet in a better world." Her liberated slaves were sent away, with funds to establish them comfortably. The colored people will long bless the memory of that truly Christian woman. Soon after her death her husband preached his farewell sermon, and many tears were shed at his departure.

Several years after, he passed through our town and preached to his former congregation. In his afternoon sermon he addressed the colored people. "My friends," said he, "it affords me great happiness to have an opportunity of speaking to you again. For two years I have been striving to do something for the colored people of my own parish; but nothing is yet accomplished. I have not even preached a sermon to them. Try to live according to the word of God, my friends. Your skin is darker than mine; but God judges men by their hearts, not by the color of their skins." This was strange doctrine from a southern pulpit. It was very offensive to slaveholders. They said he and his wife had made fools of their slaves, and that he preached like a fool to the negroes.

I knew an old black man, whose piety and childlike trust in God were beautiful to witness. At fifty-three years old he joined the Baptist church. He had a most earnest desire to learn to read. He thought he should know how to serve God better if he could only read the Bible. He came to me, and begged me to teach him. He said he could not pay me, for he had no money; but he would bring me nice fruit when the season for it came. I asked him if he didn't know it was contrary to law; and that slaves were whipped and imprisoned for teaching each other to read. This brought the tears into his eyes. "Don't be troubled, uncle Fred," said I. "I have no thoughts of refusing to teach you. I only told you of the law, that you might know the danger, and be on your guard." He thought he could plan to come three times a week without its being suspected. I selected a quiet nook, where no intruder was likely to penetrate, and there I taught him his A, B, C. Considering his age, his progress was astonishing. As soon as he could spell in two syllables he wanted to spell out words in the Bible. The happy smile that illuminated his face put joy into my heart. After spelling out a few words, he paused, and said, "Honey, it 'pears when I can read dis good book I shall be nearer to God. White man is got all de sense. He can larn easy. It ain't easy for ole black man like me. I only wants to read dis book, dat I may know how to live; den I hab no fear 'bout dying."

I tried to encourage him by speaking of the rapid progress he had made. "Hab patience, child," he replied. "I larns slow."

I had no need of patience. His gratitude, and the happiness I imparted, were more than a recompense for all my trouble.

At the end of six months he had read through the New Testament, and could find any text in it. One day, when he had recited unusually well, I said, "Uncle Fred, how do you manage to get your lessons so well?"

"Lord bress you, chile," he replied. "You nebber gibs me a lesson dat I don't pray to God to help me to understan' what I spells and what I reads. And he *does* help me, chile. Bress his holy name!"

There are thousands, who, like good uncle Fred, are thirsting for the water of life; but the law forbids it, and the churches withhold it. They send the Bible to heathen abroad, and neglect the heathen at home. I am glad that missionaries go out to the dark corners of the earth; but I ask them not to overlook the dark corners at home. Talk to American slaveholders as you talk to savages in Africa. Tell *them* it is wrong to traffic in men. Tell them it is sinful to sell their own children, and atrocious to violate their own daughters. Tell them that all men are brethren, and that man has no right to shut out the light of knowledge from his brother. Tell them they are answerable to God for sealing up the Fountain of Life from souls that are thirsting for it.

There are men who would gladly undertake such missionary work as this; but, alas! their number is small. They are hated by the south, and would be driven from its soil, or dragged to prison to die, as others have been before them. The field is ripe for the harvest, and awaits the reapers. Perhaps the great grandchildren of uncle Fred may have freely imparted to them the divine treasures, which he sought by stealth, at the risk of the prison and the scourge.

Are doctors of divinity blind, or are they hypocrites? I suppose some are the one, and some the other; but I think if they felt the interest in the poor and the lowly, that they ought to feel, they would not be so *easily* blinded. A clergyman who goes to the south, for the first time, has usually some feeling, however vague, that slavery is wrong. The slaveholder suspects this, and plays his game accordingly. He makes himself as agreeable as possible; talks on theology, and other kindred topics. The reverend gentleman is asked to invoke a blessing on a table loaded with luxuries. After dinner he walks round the premises, and sees the beautiful groves and flowering vines, and the comfortable huts of favored household slaves. The southerner invites him to talk with these slaves. He asks them if they want to be free, and they say, "O, no, massa." This is sufficient to satisfy him. He comes home to publish a "South-Side View of Slavery," and to complain of the exaggerations of abolitionists. He assures people that he has been to the south, and seen slavery for himself; that it is a beautiful "patriarchal institution;" that the slaves don't want their freedom; that they have hallelujah meetings, and other religious privileges.

What does *he* know of the half-starved wretches toiling from dawn till dark on the plantations? of mothers shrieking for their children, torn from their arms by slave traders? of young girls dragged down into moral filth? of pools of blood around the whipping post? of hounds trained to tear human flesh? of men screwed into cotton gins to die? The slaveholder showed him none of these things, and the slaves dared not tell of them if he had asked them.

There is a great difference between Christianity and religion at the south. If a man goes to the communion table, and pays money into the treasury of the church, no matter if it be the price of blood, he is called religious. If a pastor has offspring by a woman not his wife, the church dismiss him, if she is a white woman; but if she is colored, it does not hinder his continuing to be their good shepherd.

When I was told that Dr. Flint had joined the Episcopal church, I was much surprised. I supposed that religion had a purifying effect on the character of men; but the worst persecutions I endured from him were after he was a communicant. The conversation of the doctor, the day after he had been confirmed, certainly gave *me* no indication that he had "renounced the devil and all his works." In answer to some of his usual talk, I reminded him that he had just joined the church. "Yes, Linda," said he. "It was proper for me to do so. I am getting on in years, and my position in society requires it, and it puts an end to all the damned slang. You would do well to join the church, too, Linda."

"There are sinners enough in it already," rejoined I. "If I could be allowed to live like a Christian, I should be glad."

"You can do what I require; and if you are faithful to me, you will be as virtuous as my wife," he replied.

I answered that the Bible didn't say so.

His voice became hoarse with rage. "How dare you preach to me about your infernal Bible!" he exclaimed. "What right have you, who are my negro, to talk to me about what you would like, and what you wouldn't like? I am your master, and you shall obey me."

No wonder the slaves sing, —

"Ole Satan's church is here below;
Up to God's free church I hope to go."

CHAPTER 21. THE LOOPHOLE OF RETREAT[5]

A small shed had been added to my grandmother's house years ago. Some boards were laid across the joists at the top, and between these boards and the roof was a very small garret, never occupied by any thing but rats and mice. It was a pent roof, covered with nothing but shingles, according to the southern custom for such buildings. The garret was only nine feet long and seven wide. The highest part was three feet high, and sloped down abruptly to the loose board floor. There was no admission for either light or air. My uncle Phillip, who was a carpenter, had very skillfully made a concealed trap-door, which communicated with the storeroom. He had been doing this while I was waiting in the swamp. The storeroom opened upon a piazza. To this hole I was conveyed as soon as I entered the house. The air was stifling; the darkness total. A bed had been spread on the floor. I could sleep quite comfortably on one side; but the slope was so sudden that I could not turn on the other without hitting the roof. The rats and mice ran over my bed; but I was weary, and I slept such sleep as the wretched may, when a tempest has passed over them. Morning

---

[5] In the missing chapters Dr. Flint has continued his persecution of Jacobs. When she resists his overtures, he punishes her by sending her to his plantation, separating her from her two young children. Eventually, Jacobs escapes from the plantation and hides in a storeroom provided by a sympathetic white woman. Flint, frustrated and angry from his unsuccessful search for Jacobs, sells her children and her brother to a slave trader, but by a ruse they are in turn purchased by their white but unacknowledged father, Mr. Sands. When Flint is about to discover Jacobs's hiding place, she escapes, and goes into hiding in her grandmother's house.

came. I knew it only by the noises I heard; for in my small den day and night were all the same. I suffered for air even more than for light. But I was not comfortless. I heard the voices of my children. There was joy and there was sadness in the sound. It made my tears flow. How I longed to speak to them! I was eager to look on their faces; but there was no hole, no crack, through which I could peep. This continued darkness was oppressive. It seemed horrible to sit or lie in a cramped position day after day, without one gleam of light. Yet I would have chosen this, rather than my lot as a slave, though white people considered it an easy one; and it was so compared with the fate of others. I was never cruelly over-worked; I was never lacerated with the whip from head to foot; I was never so beaten and bruised that I could not turn from one side to the other; I never had my heel-strings cut to prevent my running away; I was never chained to a log and forced to drag it about, while I toiled in the fields from morning till night; I was never branded with hot iron, or torn by blood-hounds. On the contrary, I had always been kindly treated, and tenderly cared for, until I came into the hands of Dr. Flint. I had never wished for freedom till then. But though my life in slavery was comparatively devoid of hardships, God pity the woman who is compelled to lead such a life!

My food was passed up to me through the trap-door my uncle had contrived; and my grandmother, my uncle Phillip, and aunt Nancy would seize such opportunities as they could, to mount up there and chat with me at the opening. But of course this was not safe in the daytime. It must all be done in darkness. It was impossible for me to move in an erect position, but I crawled about my den for exercise. One day I hit my head against something, and found it was a gimlet.[6] My uncle had left it sticking there when he made the trap-door. I was as rejoiced as Robinson Crusoe could have been at finding such a treasure. It put a lucky thought into my head. I said to myself, "Now I will have some light. Now I will see my children." I did not dare to begin my work during the daytime, for fear of attracting attention. But I groped round; and having found the side next the street, where I could frequently see my children, I stuck the gimlet in and waited for evening. I bored three rows of holes, one above another; then I bored out the interstices between. I thus succeeded in making one hole about an inch long and an inch broad. I sat by it till late into the night, to enjoy the little whiff of air that floated in. In the morning I watched for my children. The first person I saw in the street was Dr. Flint. I had a shuddering, superstitious feeling that it was a bad omen. Several familiar faces passed by. At last I heard the merry laugh of children, and presently two sweet little faces were looking up at me, as though they knew I was there, and were conscious of the joy they imparted. How I longed to *tell* them I was there!

My condition was now a little improved. But for weeks I was tormented by hundreds of little red insects, fine as a needle's point, that pierced through my skin, and produced an intolerable burning. The good grandmother gave me herb teas and cooling medicines, and finally I got rid of them. The heat of my den was intense, for nothing but thin shingles protected me from the scorching summer's sun. But I had

---

[6] **gimlet:** A small hand tool for boring holes.

my consolations. Through my peeping-hole I could watch the children, and when they were near enough, I could hear their talk. Aunt Nancy brought me all the news she could hear at Dr. Flint's. From her I learned that the doctor had written to New York to a colored woman, who had been born and raised in our neighborhood, and had breathed his contaminating atmosphere. He offered her a reward if she could find out any thing about me. I know not what was the nature of her reply; but he soon after started for New York in haste, saying to his family that he had business of importance to transact. I peeped at him as he passed on his way to the steamboat. It was a satisfaction to have miles of land and water between us, even for a little while; and it was a still greater satisfaction to know that he believed me to be in the Free States. My little den seemed less dreary than it had done. He returned, as he did from his former journey to New York, without obtaining any satisfactory information. When he passed our house next morning, Benny was standing at the gate. He had heard them say that he had gone to find me, and he called out, "Dr. Flint, did you bring my mother home? I want to see her." The doctor stamped his foot at him in a rage, and exclaimed, "Get out of the way, you little damned rascal! If you don't, I'll cut off your head."

Benny ran terrified into the house, saying, "You can't put me in jail again. I don't belong to you now." It was well that the wind carried the words away from the doctor's ear. I told my grandmother of it, when we had our next conference at the trapdoor; and begged of her not to allow the children to be impertinent to the irascible old man.

Autumn came, with a pleasant abatement of heat. My eyes had become accustomed to the dim light, and by holding my book or work in a certain position near the aperture I contrived to read and sew. That was a great relief to the tedious monotony of my life. But when winter came, the cold penetrated through the thin shingle roof, and I was dreadfully chilled. The winters there are not so long, or so severe, as in northern latitudes; but the houses are not built to shelter from cold, and my little den was peculiarly comfortless. The kind grandmother brought me bedclothes and warm drinks. Often I was obliged to lie in bed all day to keep comfortable; but with all my precautions, my shoulders and feet were frostbitten. O, those long, gloomy days, with no object for my eye to rest upon, and no thoughts to occupy my mind, except the dreary past and the uncertain future! I was thankful when there came a day sufficiently mild for me to wrap myself up and sit at the loophole to watch the passers by. Southerners have the habit of stopping and talking in the streets, and I heard many conversations not intended to meet my ears. I heard slave-hunters planning how to catch some poor fugitive. Several times I heard allusions to Dr. Flint, myself, and the history of my children, who, perhaps, were playing near the gate. One would say, "I wouldn't move my little finger to catch her, as old Flint's property." Another would say, "I'll catch *any* nigger for the reward. A man ought to have what belongs to him, if he *is* a damned brute." The opinion was often expressed that I was in the Free States. Very rarely did any one suggest that I might be in the vicinity. Had the least suspicion rested on my grandmother's house, it would have been burned to the ground. But it was the last place they thought of. Yet there was no place, where slavery existed, that could have afforded me so good a place of concealment.

Dr. Flint and his family repeatedly tried to coax and bribe my children to tell something they had heard said about me. One day the doctor took them into a shop, and offered them some bright little silver pieces and gay handkerchiefs if they would tell where their mother was. Ellen shrank away from him, and would not speak; but Benny spoke up, and said, "Dr. Flint, I don't know where my mother is. I guess she's in New York; and when you go there again, I wish you'd ask her to come home, for I want to see her; but if you put her in jail, or tell her you'll cut her head off, I'll tell her to go right back."

CHAPTER 23. STILL IN PRISON

When spring returned, and I took in the little patch of green the aperture commanded, I asked myself how many more summers and winters I must be condemned to spend thus. I longed to draw in a plentiful draught of fresh air, to stretch my cramped limbs, to have room to stand erect, to feel the earth under my feet again. My relatives were constantly on the lookout for a chance of escape; but none offered that seemed practicable, and even tolerably safe. The hot summer came again, and made the turpentine drop from the thin roof over my head.

During the long nights I was restless for want of air, and I had no room to toss and turn. There was but one compensation; the atmosphere was so stifled that even mosquitos would not condescend to buzz in it. With all my detestation of Dr. Flint, I could hardly wish him a worse punishment, either in this world or that which is to come, than to suffer what I suffered in one single summer. Yet the laws allowed *him* to be out in the free air, while I, guiltless of crime, was pent up here, as the only means of avoiding the cruelties the laws allowed him to inflict upon me! I don't know what kept life within me. Again and again, I thought I should die before long; but I saw the leaves of another autumn whirl through the air, and felt the touch of another winter. In summer the most terrible thunder storms were acceptable, for the rain came through the roof, and I rolled up my bed that it might cool the hot boards under it. Later in the season, storms sometimes wet my clothes through and through, and that was not comfortable when the air grew chilly. Moderate storms I could keep out by filling the chinks with oakum.

But uncomfortable as my situation was, I had glimpses of things out of doors, which made me thankful for my wretched hiding-place. One day I saw a slave pass our gate, muttering, "It's his own, and he can kill it if he will." My grandmother told me that woman's history. Her mistress had that day seen her baby for the first time, and in the lineaments of its fair face she saw a likeness to her husband. She turned the bondwoman and her child out of doors, and forbade her ever to return. The slave went to her master, and told him what had happened. He promised to talk with her mistress, and make it all right. The next day she and her baby were sold to a Georgia trader.

Another time I saw a woman rush wildly by, pursued by two men. She was a slave, the wet nurse of her mistress's children. For some trifling offence her mistress ordered her to be stripped and whipped. To escape the degradation and the torture, she rushed to the river, jumped in, and ended her wrongs in death.

Senator Brown, of Mississippi, could not be ignorant of many such facts as these, for they are of frequent occurrence in every Southern State. Yet he stood up in the Congress of the United States, and declared that slavery was "a great moral, social, and political blessing; a blessing to the master, and a blessing to the slave!"[7]

I suffered much more during the second winter than I did during the first. My limbs were benumbed by inaction, and the cold filled them with cramp. I had a very painful sensation of coldness in my head; even my face and tongue stiffened, and I lost the power of speech. Of course it was impossible, under the circumstances, to summon any physician. My brother William came and did all he could for me. Uncle Phillip also watched tenderly over me; and poor grandmother crept up and down to inquire whether there were any signs of returning life. I was restored to consciousness by the dashing of cold water in my face, and found myself leaning against my brother's arm, while he bent over me with streaming eyes. He afterwards told me he thought I was dying, for I had been in an unconscious state sixteen hours. I next became delirious, and was in great danger of betraying myself and my friends. To prevent this, they stupefied me with drugs. I remained in bed six weeks, weary in body and sick at heart. How to get medical advice was the question. William finally went to a Thompsonian[8] doctor, and described himself as having all my pains and aches. He returned with herbs, roots, and ointment. He was especially charged to rub on the ointment by a fire; but how could a fire be made in my little den? Charcoal in a furnace was tried, but there was no outlet for the gas, and it nearly cost me my life. Afterwards coals, already kindled, were brought up in an iron pan, and placed on bricks. I was so weak, and it was so long since I had enjoyed the warmth of a fire, that those few coals actually made me weep. I think the medicines did me some good; but my recovery was very slow. Dark thoughts passed through my mind as I lay there day after day. I tried to be thankful for my little cell, dismal as it was, and even to love it, as part of the price I had paid for the redemption of my children. Sometimes I thought God was a compassionate Father, who would forgive my sins for the sake of my sufferings. At other times, it seemed to me there was no justice or mercy in the divine government. I asked why the curse of slavery was permitted to exist, and why I had been so persecuted and wronged from youth upward. These things took the shape of mystery, which is to this day not so clear to my soul as I trust it will be hereafter.

In the midst of my illness, grandmother broke down under the weight of anxiety and toil. The idea of losing her, who had always been my best friend and a mother to my children, was the sorest trial I had yet had. O, how earnestly I prayed that she might recover! How hard it seemed, that I could not tend upon her, who had so long and so tenderly watched over me!

One day the screams of a child nerved me with strength to crawl to my peeping-hole, and I saw my son covered with blood. A fierce dog, usually kept chained, had

---

[7] **"a great . . . slave!"**: Jacobs refers to a speech made by Albert G. Brown (1813–1880) on February 24, 1854, during congressional debate on the Kansas–Nebraska Bill.

[8] **Thompsonian**: Named after Samuel Thompson (1763–1843), a doctor who attempted to cure disease by raising the internal body temperature.

seized and bitten him. A doctor was sent for, and I heard the groans and screams of my child while the wounds were being sewed up. O, what torture to a mother's heart, to listen to this and be unable to go to him!

But childhood is like a day in spring, alternately shower and sunshine. Before night Benny was bright and lively, threatening the destruction of the dog; and great was his delight when the doctor told him the next day that the dog had bitten another boy and been shot. Benny recovered from his wounds; but it was long before he could walk.

When my grandmother's illness became known, many ladies, who were her customers, called to bring her some little comforts, and to inquire whether she had every thing she wanted. Aunt Nancy one night asked permission to watch with her sick mother, and Mrs. Flint replied, "I don't see any need of your going. I can't spare you." But when she found other ladies in the neighborhood were so attentive, not wishing to be outdone in Christian charity, she also sallied forth, in magnificent condescension, and stood by the bedside of her who had loved her in her infancy, and who had been repaid by such grievous wrongs. She seemed surprised to find her so ill, and scolded uncle Phillip for not sending for Dr. Flint. She herself sent for him immediately, and he came. Secure as I was in my retreat, I should have been terrified if I had known he was so near me. He pronounced my grandmother in a very critical situation, and said if her attending physician wished it, he would visit her. Nobody wished to have him coming to the house at all hours, and we were not disposed to give him a chance to make out a long bill.

As Mrs. Flint went out, Sally told her the reason Benny was lame was, that a dog had bitten him. "I'm glad of it," replied she. "I wish he had killed him. It would be good news to send to his mother. *Her* day will come. The dogs will grab *her* yet." With these Christian words she and her husband departed, and, to my great satisfaction, returned no more.

I heard from Uncle Phillip, with feelings of unspeakable joy and gratitude, that the crisis was passed and grandmother would live. I could now say from my heart, "God is merciful. He has spared me the anguish of feeling that I caused her death."

Chapter 29. Preparations for Escape

I hardly expect that the reader will credit me, when I affirm that I lived in that little dismal hole, almost deprived of light and air, and with no space to move my limbs, for nearly seven years.[9] But it is a fact; and to me a sad one, even now; for my body still suffers from the effects of that long imprisonment, to say nothing of my soul. Members of my family, now living in New York and Boston, can testify to the truth of what I say.

Countless were the nights that I sat late at the little loophole scarcely large enough to give me a glimpse of one twinkling star. There, I heard the patrols and slave-hunters conferring together about the capture of runaways, well knowing how rejoiced they would be to catch me.

---

[9] seven years: Jacobs lived in her grandmother's attic crawl space from August 1835 to June 1842.

Season after season, year after year, I peeped at my children's faces, and heard their sweet voices, with a heart yearning all the while to say, "Your mother is here." Sometimes it appeared to me as if ages had rolled away since I entered upon that gloomy, monotonous existence. At times, I was stupefied and listless; at other times I became very impatient to know when these dark years would end, and I should again be allowed to feel the sunshine, and breathe the pure air.

After Ellen[10] left us, this feeling increased. Mr. Sands had agreed that Benny might go to the north whenever his Uncle Phillip could go with him; and I was anxious to be there also, to watch over my children, and protect them so far as I was able. Moreover, I was likely to be drowned out of my den, if I remained much longer; for the slight roof was getting badly out of repair, and Uncle Phillip was afraid to remove the shingles, lest some one should get a glimpse of me. When storms occurred in the night, they spread mats and bits of carpet, which in the morning appeared to have been laid out to dry; but to cover the roof in the daytime might have attracted attention. Consequently, my clothes and bedding were often drenched; a process by which the pains and aches in my cramped and stiffened limbs were greatly increased. I revolved various plans of escape in my mind, which I sometimes imparted to my grandmother, when she came to whisper with me at the trap-door. The kind-hearted old woman had an intense sympathy for runaways. She had known too much of the cruelties inflicted on those who were captured. Her memory always flew back at once to the sufferings of her bright and handsome son, Benjamin, the youngest and dearest of her flock. So, whenever I alluded to the subject, she would groan out, "O, don't think of it, child. You'll break my heart." I had no good old Aunt Nancy now to encourage me; but my brother William and my children were continually beckoning me to the north.

And now I must go back a few months in my story. I have stated that the first of January was the time for selling slaves, or leasing them out to new masters. If time were counted by heart-throbs, the poor slaves might reckon years of suffering during that festival so joyous to the free. On the New Year's day preceding my aunt's death, one of my friends, named Fanny, was to be sold at auction, to pay her master's debts. My thoughts were with her during all the day, and at night I anxiously inquired what had been her fate. I was told that she had been sold to one master, and her four little girls to another master, far distant; that she had escaped from her purchaser, and was not to be found. Her mother was the old Aggie I have spoken of. She lived in a small tenement belonging to my grandmother, and built on the same lot with her own house. Her dwelling was searched and watched, and that brought the patrols so near me that I was obliged to keep very close in my den. The hunters were somehow eluded; and not long afterwards Benny accidentally caught sight of Fanny in her mother's hut. He told his grandmother, who charged him never to speak of it, explaining to him the frightful consequences; and he never betrayed the trust. Aggie little dreamed that my grandmother knew where her daughter was concealed, and that the stooping form of her old neighbor was bending under a similar burden of

---

[10] Ellen: Jacobs's daughter; she had been sent by Mr. Sands to live in the North to escape the machinations of Flint, who claimed he still owned her.

anxiety and fear; but these dangerous secrets deepened the sympathy between the two old persecuted mothers.

My friend Fanny and I remained many weeks hidden within call of each other; but she was unconscious of the fact. I longed to have her share my den, which seemed a more secure retreat than her own; but I had brought so much trouble on my grandmother, that it seemed wrong to ask her to incur greater risks. My restlessness increased. I had lived too long in bodily pain and anguish of spirit. Always I was in dread that by some accident, or some contrivance, slavery would succeed in snatching my children from me. This thought drove me nearly frantic, and I determined to steer for the North Star[11] at all hazards. At this crisis, Providence opened an unexpected way for me to escape. My friend Peter came one evening, and asked to speak with me. "Your day has come, Linda," said he. "I have found a chance for you to go to the Free States. You have a fortnight to decide." The news seemed too good to be true; but Peter explained his arrangements, and told me all that was necessary was for me to say I would go. I was going to answer him with a joyful yes, when the thought of Benny came to my mind. I told him the temptation was exceedingly strong, but I was terribly afraid of Dr. Flint's alleged power over my child, and that I could not go and leave him behind. Peter remonstrated earnestly. He said such a good chance might never occur again; that Benny was free, and could be sent to me; and that for the sake of my children's welfare I ought not to hesitate a moment. I told him I would consult with Uncle Phillip. My uncle rejoiced in the plan, and bade me go by all means. He promised, if his life was spared, that he would either bring or send my son to me as soon as I reached a place of safety. I resolved to go, but thought nothing had better be said to my grandmother till very near the time of departure. But my uncle thought she would feel it more keenly if I left her so suddenly. "I will reason with her," said he, "and convince her how necessary it is, not only for your sake, but for hers also. You cannot be blind to the fact that she is sinking under her burdens." I was not blind to it. I knew that my concealment was an ever-present source of anxiety, and that the older she grew the more nervously fearful she was of discovery. My uncle talked with her, and finally succeeded in persuading her that it was absolutely necessary for me to seize the chance so unexpectedly offered.

The anticipation of being a free woman proved almost too much for my weak frame. The excitement stimulated me, and at the same time bewildered me. I made busy preparations for my journey, and for my son to follow me. I resolved to have an interview with him before I went, that I might give him cautions and advice, and tell him how anxiously I should be waiting for him at the north. Grandmother stole up to me as often as possible to whisper words of counsel. She insisted upon my writing to Dr. Flint, as soon as I arrived in the Free States, and asking him to sell me to her. She said she would sacrifice her house, and all she had in the world, for the sake of having me safe with my children in any part of the world. If she could only live to know *that* she could die in peace. I promised the dear old faithful friend that I would write to her as soon as I arrived, and put the letter in a safe way to reach her; but in

---

[11] **North Star:** Runaway slaves, who often traveled by night, were guided by this star.

my own mind I resolved that not another cent of her hard earnings should be spent to pay rapacious slaveholders for what they called their property. And even if I had not been unwilling to buy what I had already a right to possess, common humanity would have prevented me from accepting the generous offer, at the expense of turning my aged relative out of house and home, when she was trembling on the brink of the grave.

I was to escape in a vessel; but I forbear to mention any further particulars. I was in readiness, but the vessel was unexpectedly detained several days. Meantime, news came to town of a most horrible murder committed on a fugitive slave, named James. Charity, the mother of this unfortunate young man, had been an old acquaintance of ours. I have told the shocking particulars of his death, in my description of some of the neighboring slaveholders. My grandmother, always nervously sensitive about runaways, was terribly frightened. She felt sure that a similar fate awaited me, if I did not desist from my enterprise. She sobbed, and groaned, and entreated me not to go. Her excessive fear was somewhat contagious, and my heart was not proof against her extreme agony. I was grievously disappointed, but I promised to relinquish my project.

When my friend Peter was apprised of this, he was both disappointed and vexed. He said, that judging from our past experience, it would be a long time before I had such another chance to throw away. I told him it need not be thrown away; that I had a friend concealed near by, who would be glad enough to take the place that had been provided for me. I told him about poor Fanny, and the kind-hearted, noble fellow, who never turned his back upon any body in distress, white or black, expressed his readiness to help her. Aggie was much surprised when she found that we knew her secret. She was rejoiced to hear of such a chance for Fanny, and arrangements were made for her to go on board the vessel the next night. They both supposed that I had long been at the north, therefore my name was not mentioned in the transaction. Fanny was carried on board at the appointed time, and stowed away in a very small cabin. This accommodation had been purchased at a price that would pay for a voyage to England. But when one proposes to go to fine old England, they stop to calculate whether they can afford the cost of the pleasure; while in making a bargain to escape from slavery, the trembling victim is ready to say, "Take all I have, only don't betray me!"

The next morning I peeped through my loophole, and saw that it was dark and cloudy. At night I received news that the wind was ahead, and the vessel had not sailed. I was exceedingly anxious about Fanny, and Peter too, who was running a tremendous risk at my instigation. Next day the wind and weather remained the same. Poor Fanny had been half dead with fright when they carried her on board, and I could readily imagine how she must be suffering now. Grandmother came often to my den, to say how thankful she was I did not go. On the third morning she rapped for me to come down to the storeroom. The poor old sufferer was breaking down under her weight of trouble. She was easily flurried now. I found her in a nervous, excited state, but I was not aware that she had forgotten to lock the door behind her, as usual. She was exceedingly worried about the detention of the vessel. She was afraid all would be discovered, and then Fanny, and Peter, and I, would all be tortured to death, and Phillip would be utterly ruined, and her house would be torn down. Poor Peter! If he should die such a horrible death as the poor slave James had lately done, and all for his kindness in trying to help me, how dreadful it would be for us all! Alas, the thought was familiar to me, and had sent many a sharp pang through my heart. I tried to suppress my own anxiety, and speak soothingly to her. She brought in some allusion to Aunt Nancy, the dear daughter she had recently buried, and then she lost all control of herself As she stood there, trembling and sobbing, a voice from the piazza called out, "Whar is you, Aunt Marthy?" Grandmother was startled, and in her agitation opened the door, without thinking of me. In stepped Jenny, the mischievous housemaid, who had tried to enter my room, when I was concealed in the house of my white benefactress. "I's bin huntin ebery whar for you, Aunt Marthy," said she. "My missis wants you to send her some crackers." I had slunk down behind a barrel, which entirely screened me, but I imagined that Jenny was looking directly at the spot, and my heart beat violently. My grandmother immediately thought what she had done, and went out quickly with Jenny to count the crackers locking the door after her. She returned to me, in a few minutes, the perfect picture of despair. "Poor child!" she exclaimed, "my carelessness has ruined you. The boat ain't gone yet. Get ready immediately, and go with Fanny. I ain't got another word to say against it now; for there's no telling what may happen this day."

Uncle Phillip was sent for, and he agreed with his mother in thinking that Jenny would inform Dr. Flint in less than twenty-four hours. He advised getting me on board the boat, if possible; if not, I had better keep very still in my den, where they could not find me without tearing the house down. He said it would not do for him to move in the matter, because suspicion would be immediately excited; but he promised to communicate with Peter. I felt reluctant to apply to him again, having implicated him too much already; but there seemed to be no alternative. Vexed as Peter had been by my indecision, he was true to his generous nature, and said at once that he would do his best to help me, trusting I should show myself a stronger woman this time.

He immediately proceeded to the wharf, and found that the wind had shifted, and the vessel was slowly beating down stream. On some pretext of urgent necessity, he offered two boatmen a dollar apiece to catch up with her. He was of lighter complexion than the boatmen he hired, and when the captain saw them coming so rapidly, he thought officers were pursuing his vessel in search of the runaway slave he had on board. They hoisted sails, but the boat gained upon them, and the indefatigable Peter sprang on board.

The captain at once recognized him. Peter asked him to go below, to speak about a bad bill he had given him. When he told his errand, the captain replied, "Why, the woman's here already; and I've put her where you or the devil would have a tough job to find her."

"But it is another woman I want to bring," said Peter. "*She* is in great distress, too, and you shall be paid any thing within reason, if you'll stop and take her."

"What's her name?" inquired the captain.

"Linda," he replied.

"That's the name of the woman already here," rejoined the captain. "By George! I believe you mean to betray me."

"O!" exclaimed Peter, "God knows I wouldn't harm a hair of your head. I am too grateful to you. But there really *is* another woman in great danger. Do have the humanity to stop and take her!"

After a while they came to an understanding. Fanny, not dreaming I was any where about in that region, had assumed my name, though she had called herself Johnson. "Linda is a common name," said Peter, "and the woman I want to bring is Linda Brent."

The captain agreed to wait at a certain place till evening, being handsomely paid for his detention.

Of course, the day was an anxious one for us all. But we concluded that if Jenny had seen me, she would be too wise to let her mistress know of it; and that she probably would not get a chance to see Dr. Flint's family till evening, for I knew very well what were the rules in that household. I afterwards believed that she did not see me; for nothing ever came of it, and she was one of those base characters that would have jumped to betray a suffering fellow being for the sake of thirty pieces of silver.

I made all my arrangements to go on board as soon as it was dusk. The intervening time I resolved to spend with my son. I had not spoken to him for seven years, though I had been under the same roof, and seen him every day, when I was well enough to sit at the loophole. I did not dare to venture beyond the storeroom; so they brought him there, and locked us up together, in a place concealed from the piazza door. It was an agitating interview for both of us. After we had talked and wept together for a little while, he said, "Mother, I'm glad you're going away. I wish I could go with you. I knew you was here; and I have been *so* afraid they would come and catch you!"

I was greatly surprised, and asked him how he had found it out.

He replied, "I was standing under the eaves, one day, before Ellen went away, and I heard somebody cough up over the wood shed. I don't know what made me think it was you, but I did think so. I missed Ellen, the night before she went away; and grandmother brought her back into the room in the night; and I thought maybe she'd been to see *you,* before she went, for I heard grandmother whisper to her, 'Now go to sleep; and remember never to tell.'"

I asked him if he ever mentioned his suspicions to his sister. He said he never did; but after he heard the cough, if he saw her playing with other children on that side of the house, he always tried to coax her round to the other side, for fear they would hear me cough, too. He said he had kept a close lookout for Dr. Flint, and if he saw him speak to a constable, or a patrol, he always told grandmother. I now recollected that I had seen him manifest uneasiness, when people were on that side of the house, and I had at the time been puzzled to conjecture a motive for his actions. Such prudence may seem extraordinary in a boy of twelve years, but slaves, being surrounded by mysteries, deceptions, and dangers, early learn to be suspicious and watchful, and prematurely cautious and cunning. He had never asked a question of grandmother, or Uncle Phillip, and I had often heard him chime in with other children, when they spoke of my being at the north.

I told him I was now really going to the Free States, and if he was a good, honest boy, and a loving child to his dear old grandmother, the Lord would bless him, and bring him to me, and we and Ellen would live together. He began to tell me that grandmother had not eaten any thing all day. While he was speaking, the door was unlocked, and she came in with a small bag of money, which she wanted me to take. I begged her to keep a part of it, at least, to pay for Benny's being sent to the north; but she insisted, while her tears were falling fast, that I should take the whole. "You may be sick among strangers," she said, "and they would send you to the poorhouse to die." Ah, that good grandmother!

For the last time I went up to my nook. Its desolate appearance no longer chilled me, for the light of hope had risen in my soul. Yet, even with the blessed prospect of freedom before me, I felt very sad at leaving forever that old homestead, where I had been sheltered so long by the dear old grandmother; where I had dreamed my first young dream of love; and where, after that had faded away, my children came to twine themselves so closely round my desolate heart. As the hour approached for me to leave, I again descended to the storeroom. My grandmother and Benny were there. She took me by the hand, and said, "Linda, let us pray." We knelt down together, with my child pressed to my heart, and my other arm round the faithful, loving old friend I was about to leave forever. On no other occasion has it ever been my lot to listen to so fervent a supplication for mercy and protection. It thrilled through my heart, and inspired me with trust in God.

Peter was waiting for me in the street. I was soon by his side, faint in body, but strong of purpose. I did not look back upon the old place, though I felt that I should never see it again.

Chapter 30. Northward Bound

I never could tell how we reached the wharf. My brain was all of a whirl, and my limbs tottered under me. At an appointed place we met my uncle Phillip, who had started before us on a different route, that he might reach the wharf first, and give us timely warning if there was any danger. A row-boat was in readiness. As I was about to step in, I felt something pull me gently, and turning round I saw Benny, looking pale and anxious. He whispered in my ear, "I've been peeping into the doctor's window, and he's at home. Good by, mother. Don't cry; I'll come." He hastened away. I clasped the hand of my good uncle, to whom I owed so much, and of Peter, the brave, generous friend who had volunteered to run such terrible risks to secure my safety. To this day I remember how his bright face beamed with joy, when he told me he had discovered a safe method for me to escape. Yet that intelligent, enterprising, noble-hearted man was a chattel! Liable, by the laws of a country that calls itself civilized, to be sold with horses and pigs! We parted in silence. Our hearts were all too full for words!

Swiftly the boat glided over the water. After a while, one of the sailors said, "Don't be down-hearted, madam. We will take you safely to your husband, in ———." At first I could not imagine what he meant; but I had presence of mind to think that it probably referred to something the captain had told him; so I thanked him, and said I hoped we should have pleasant weather.

When I entered the vessel the captain came forward to meet me. He was an elderly man, with a pleasant countenance. He showed me to a little box of a cabin, where sat my friend Fanny. She started as if she had seen a spectre. She gazed on me in utter astonishment, and exclaimed, "Linda? can this be *you*? or is it your ghost?" When we were locked in each other's arms, my overwrought feelings could no longer be restrained. My sobs reached the ears of the captain, who came and very kindly reminded us, that for his safety, as well as our own, it would be prudent for us not to attract any attention. He said that when there was a sail in sight he wished us to keep below; but at other times, he had no objection to our being on deck. He assured us that he would keep a good lookout, and if we acted prudently, he thought we should be in no danger. He had represented us as women going to meet our husbands in ———. We thanked him, and promised to observe carefully all the directions he gave us.

Fanny and I now talked by ourselves, low and quietly, in our little cabin. She told me of the sufferings she had gone through in making her escape, and of her terrors while she was concealed in her mother's house. Above all, she dwelt on the agony of separation from all her children on that dreadful auction day. She could scarcely credit me, when I told her of the place where I had passed nearly seven years. "We have the same sorrows," said I. "No," replied she, "you are going to see your children soon, and there is no hope that I shall ever even hear from mine."

The vessel was soon under way, but we made slow progress. The wind was against us. I should not have cared for this, if we had been out of sight of the town; but until there were miles of water between us and our enemies, we were filled with constant apprehensions that the constables would come on board. Neither could I feel quite at ease with the captain and his men. I was an entire stranger to that class of people, and I had heard that sailors were rough, and sometimes cruel. We were so completely in their power, that if they were bad men, our situation would be dreadful. Now that the captain was paid for our passage, might he not be tempted to make more money by giving us up to those who claimed us as property? I was naturally of a confiding disposition, but slavery had made me suspicious of every body. Fanny did not share my distrust of the captain or his men. She said she was afraid at first, but she had been on board three days while the vessel lay in the dock, and nobody had betrayed her, or treated her otherwise than kindly.

The captain soon came to advise us to go on deck for fresh air. His friendly and respectful manner, combined with Fanny's testimony, reassured me, and we went with him. He placed us in a comfortable seat, and occasionally entered into conversation. He told us he was a Southerner by birth, and had spent the greater part of his life in the Slave States, and that he had recently lost a brother who traded in slaves. "But," said he, "it is a pitiable and degrading business, and I always felt ashamed to acknowledge my brother in connection with it." As we passed Snaky Swamp, he pointed to it, and said, "There is a slave territory that defies all the laws." I thought of the terrible days I had spent there,[12] and though it was not called Dismal Swamp, it made me feel very dismal as I looked at it.

---

[12] **terrible days . . . there:** Before hiding in her grandmother's attic, Jacobs hid for a few nights in a snake-infested swamp.

I shall never forget that night. The balmy air of spring was so refreshing! And how shall I describe my sensations when we were fairly sailing on Chesapeake Bay? O, the beautiful sunshine! the exhilarating breeze! and I could enjoy them without fear or restraint. I had never realized what grand things air and sunlight are till I had been deprived of them.

Ten days after we left land we were approaching Philadelphia. The captain said we should arrive there in the night, but he thought we had better wait till morning, and go on shore in broad daylight, as the best way to avoid suspicion.

I replied, "You know best. But will you stay on board and protect us?"

He saw that I was suspicious, and he said he was sorry, now that he had brought us to the end of our voyage, to find I had so little confidence in him. Ah, if he had ever been a slave he would have known how difficult it was to trust a white man. He assured us that we might sleep through the night without fear; that he would take care we were not left unprotected. Be it said to the honor of this captain, Southerner as he was, that if Fanny and I had been white ladies, and our passage lawfully engaged, he could not have treated us more respectfully. My intelligent friend, Peter, had rightly estimated the character of the man to whose honor he had intrusted us.

The next morning I was on deck as soon as the day dawned. I called Fanny to see the sun rise, for the first time in our lives, on free soil; for such I *then* believed it to be. We watched the reddening sky, and saw the great orb come up slowly out of the water, as it seemed. Soon the waves began to sparkle, and every thing caught the beautiful glow. Before us lay the city of strangers. We looked at each other, and the eyes of both were moistened with tears. We had escaped from slavery, and we supposed ourselves to be safe from the hunters. But we were alone in the world, and we had left dear ties behind us; ties cruelly sundered by the demon Slavery.

❧ AFRICAN AMERICAN FOLK SONGS

The themes of SLAVE NARRATIVES—the injustice of slavery, the suffering it brought to those it held captive, and the desire for escape and freedom—appeared also in spirituals, songs of Southern slaves, now recognized as some of America's greatest music. W. E. B. DuBois characterized spirituals in 1903 as "the sole American music, . . . the most beautiful expression of human experience from this side of the seas." Combining African and American elements, most spirituals date from the eighteenth century and the first half of the nineteenth century and were passed down orally from one generation to the next. After the Civil War, the songs were written down and performed by groups such as the Fisk Jubilee Singers, from Nashville, Tennessee, who in 1871 were the first choral group to include spirituals in a concert program. The response they received was so positive that soon they and similar choral groups were performing spirituals throughout the United States and abroad.

The Slave's Christianity.   Most spirituals are based on biblical stories or Christian hymns. The slaves' relationship with Christianity, however, was problematic, for Christianity was the religion of the slave masters. Howard Thurman, an African American theologian, suggests that some of the power of spirituals derives from this paradoxical connection. In *Deep River,* his study of spirituals, he remarks: "When the master gave the slave his (the master's) God, for a long time it meant that it was difficult to disentangle religious experience from slavery sanction. . . . By some amazing but vastly creative spiritual insight the slave undertook the redemption of a religion that the master had profaned in his midst." Spirituals sometimes made a clear distinction between those who professed to be Christians and those who really were; the chorus of "All God's Chillun Got Wings," for example, reminds the listener that everybody that "talks about heaven ain't goin' there."

The Christianity of spirituals is grounded in personal experience, not in theological doctrines. Praying consoles the singer who "feel[s] like a motherless chile" in a spiritual that prefigures the blues. Spirituals often give personal testimony of the ways in which the liberating Bible stories affect the singer. "Were you there when they crucified my Lord?" asks a spiritual that recounts the story of Jesus' death and resurrection; the sung response tells of how the singer is moved: "Sometimes it causes me to tremble, tremble, tremble." When a group of African Americans visiting

> The sole American music, . . . the most beautiful expression of human experience from this side of the seas.
>
> – W. E. B. DuBois on "The Sorrow Songs"

In de Lan' o' Cotton, 1899
Freed slaves in the South had scant employment prospects; many, like those seen in this photograph, continued to work on cotton plantations. (Library of Congress)

Slave Quarters,
Hermitage
Plantation, outside
Savannah, GA, 1900
*Typically, slave houses
lacked windowpanes
and provided only the
most basic shelter.
(Library of Congress)*

India met Mahatma Gandhi,[1] a HINDU, he asked them to sing this spiritual, which for him transcended its Christian origins in its theme and emotional intensity.

Emancipation, The Great Theme.   The great themes of the slaves' Christianity and their spirituals are freedom and deliverance. "Didn't my Lord deliver Daniel?" one spiritual asks, leading to the rhetorical question, "And why not every man?" The stories of Moses leading the Israelites out of bondage and crossing over the river Jordan into the Promised Land and of Jesus' death and resurrection were sung as tales of deliverance from the trials of this life. "Before I'd be a slave," the spiritual "Oh Freedom" laments, "I'd be buried in my grave,/ And go home to my Lord and be free."

The mention of freedom in spirituals was often a coded message about escape. In spirituals such as "Go Down, Moses," Egypt stood for the institution of slavery and the journey to the Promised Land represented the Underground Railroad and freedom in the North. Harriet Tubman,[2] who led many slaves to freedom, was known as "Moses," who led the Israelites out of slavery in Egypt to the Promised Land; she used "Go Down, Moses" as a code to rally those slaves who sought to escape. "Follow the Drinkin' Gourd" even provided a kind of map to slaves who would use the Big Dipper to guide them northward at night.

---

[1] **Mahatma Gandhi:** (1869–1948) Indian independence leader; see Book 6.

[2] **Harriet Tubman:** (c. 1820–1913) After escaping slavery herself in 1849, Tubman was perhaps the hardest working "conductor" on the Underground Railway, leading more than 300 slaves to freedom and earning the nickname "Moses."

African American Work Songs.   The spiritual "Hold On!" links biblical stories of Noah and Mary to an agricultural metaphor—plowing a field, which was work familiar to almost every slave. By the end of the song, the straight furrow has become the straight path to heaven and, by implication, the road to the "promised land" of the North. This spiritual "work song," its rhythms and repetitions attuned to the rhythms of physical work, foreshadows such post-slavery work songs as "John Henry," which describes the superhuman effort of a pile driver on the railroad, who gave his life to prove that he was stronger than the new mechanical steam drill.

■ CONNECTIONS

Hebrew Scriptures, Exodus (Book 1); Rowlandson, *Narrative of the Captivity and Restoration of Mrs. Mary Rowlandson* **(Book 4).** The most important source of imagery in spirituals is the Bible, particularly the account of the Exodus of the Hebrew people from Egypt, where they were slaves, and their journey to the Promised Land. Mary Rowlandson makes similar biblical allusions in the account of her captivity. Would Rowlandson and the creators of the spirituals agree on the allegorical equivalents of the Israelites' bondage in Egypt or the Promised Land?

In the World: **Heroes and Heroines, p. 179; Goethe,** *Faust,* **p. 29; Pushkin,** *The Bronze Horseman,* **p. 339.** The nineteenth century, as *In the World:* Heroes and Heroines suggests, made heroes of empire builders and charismatic leaders such as Napoleon. Heroic qualities are celebrated in Goethe's *Faust* and Pushkin's *Bronze Horseman.* Faust and Peter the Great bring suffering as well as benefit to mankind; their projects entail sacrifice as well as achievement. Consider John Henry in the context of such heroism. What are Henry's heroic qualities? What suffering results from his accomplishments? How does his hero story reflect the context of slavery and its aftermath?

■ FURTHER RESEARCH

Collections
Johnson, James Weldon, and J. Rosamond Johnson. *The Book of American Negro Spirituals.* 1925; *The Second Book of Negro Spirituals.* 1926.

Criticism and Commentary
Dixon, Christa K. *Negro Spirituals: From Bible to Folk Song.* 1976.
DuBois, W. E. B. "The Sorrow Songs," from *The Souls of Black Folk.* 1903.
Johnson, James Weldon. "O Black and Unknown Bards." 1930.
Lovell, John Jr. *Black Song: The Forge and the Flame.* 1972.
Thurman, Howard. *Deep River.* 1945.

∽ Go Down, Moses

Go down, Moses,
Way down in Egypt land,
Tell ol' Pharaoh,
Let my people go!

1.

When Israel was in Egypt's land,
    Let my people go.
Oppressed so hard they could not stand,
    Let my people go.

2.

Thus said the Lord, bold Moses said, . . .
If not I'll smite your firstborn dead. . . .

3.

No more shall they in bondage toil; . . .
Let them come out with Egypt's spoil. . . .

4.

When Israel out of Egypt came . . .
And left the proud oppressive land, . . .

5.

O, 'twas a dark and dismal night . . .
When Moses led the Israelites. . . .

6.

'Twas good ole Moses and Aaron, too, . . .
'Twas they that led the armies through. . . .

"Go Down, Moses." This spiritual is based on the account of Moses leading the Hebrews out of slavery in Egypt in Exodus, chapters 1–15 (Hebrew Scriptures). The veiled message in this spiritual was that freedom could be attained in the North by following Moses—Harriet Tubman—on the Underground Railway.

7.

The Lord told Moses what to do . . .
To lead the children of Israel through. . . .

8.

O come along, Moses, you'll not get lost; . . .
Stretch out your rod and come across. . . .

9.

As Israel stood by the water side, . . .
At the command of God it did divide. . . .

10.

When they had reached the other shore . . .
They sang a song of triumph o'er. . . .

11.

Pharaoh said he would go across, . . .
But Pharaoh and his host were lost. . . .

12.

O, Moses, the cloud shall cleave the way, . . .
A fire by night, a shade by day. . . .

13.

You'll not get lost in the wilderness . . .
With a lighted candle in your breast. . . .

14.

Jordan shall stand up like a wall, . . .
And the walls of Jericho shall fall. . . .

15.

Your foes shall not before you stand, . . .
And you'll possess fair Canaan's land. . . .

16.

'Twas just about at harvest time . . .
When Joshua led his host divine. . . .

17.

O let us all from bondage flee . . .
And let us all in Christ be free. . . .

18.

We need not always weep and moan . . .
And wear these slavery chains forlorn. . . .

19.

This world's a wilderness of woe; . . .
O, let us on to Canaan go. . . .

20.

What a beautiful morning that will be . . .
When time breaks up in eternity. . . .

21.

O brethren, brethren, you'd better be engaged, . . .
For the devil he's out on a big rampage. . . .

22.

The devil he thought he had me fast, . . .
But I thought I'd break his chains at last. . . .

23.

O take yer shoes from off your feet . . .
And walk into the golden street. . . .

24.

I'll tell you what I likes de best: . . .
It is the shouting Methodist. . . .

25.

I do believe without a doubt . . .
That a Christian has the right to shout. . . .

∾ Deep River

Deep river, my home is over Jordan,
Deep river, Lord, I want to cross over into campground.
Lord, I want to cross over into campground,
Lord, I want to cross over into campground.

Oh, chillun, Oh, don't you want to go to that gospel feast,
That promised land, that land where all is peace?
Walk into heaven, and take my seat,
And cast my crown at Jesus' feet,[1]
Lord, I want to cross over into campground.

10   Deep river, my home is over Jordan,
Deep river, Lord, I want to cross over into campground.
Lord, I want to cross over into campground,
Lord, I want to cross over into campground,

"Deep River."   The deep river in this spiritual is on one level the river Jordan, the river of passage for the Israelites in Exodus and later the river in which Jesus is baptized. On a figurative level it is the river that divides this life from the next, and perhaps in a more concrete but masked reference, the Ohio River, which divided the North from the South.

---

[1] **And cast . . . feet:** An allusion to Revelation 4:10–11: "The four and twenty elders fall down before him that sat on the throne, and worship him that liveth for ever and ever, and cast down their crowns before the throne, saying, Thou art worthy, O Lord, to receive glory and honor and power."

✎ Follow the Drinkin' Gourd

Follow the drinkin' gourd! (2x)
For the old man is a-waitin' for to carry you to freedom
If you follow the drinkin' gourd

When the sun comes up & the first quail calls / Follow . . .
For the old man is a-waitin' for to carry you . . . / Follow . . .

The river bank will make a mighty good road
The dead trees will show you the way
Left foot, peg foot, travelin' on . . . / Follow . . .

10   The river ends between two hills / Follow . . .
There's another river on the other side . . . / Follow . . .

"Follow the Drinkin' Gourd." The "gourd" in this song is the Big Dipper, a guide to the North Star that pointed the way to freedom in the North or in Canada for escaping slaves traveling at night.

✎ Sometimes I Feel Like a Motherless Chile

1.

Sometimes I feel like a motherless chile,
Sometimes I feel like a motherless chile,
Sometimes I feel like a motherless chile,
Far, far away from home,
A long, long ways from home.

Then I get down on my knees an' pray.
Get down on my knees an' pray.

2.

Sometimes I feel like I'm almost gone,
Sometimes I feel like I'm almost gone,
Sometimes I feel like I'm almost gone,

"Sometimes I Feel Like a Motherless Chile." In tone and imagery this spiritual foreshadows the blues, especially such songs as "Motherless Children Have a Hard Time When the Mother Is Dead."

Far, far away from home,
A long, long ways from home.

Then I get down on my knees an' pray,
Get down on my knees an' pray.

∾ Hold On!

Keep your hand on-a dat plow!
    Hold on!
Hold on! Hold on!
Keep your hand right on-a dat plow!
    Hold on!

1.

Noah, Noah, lemme come in,
Doors all fastened an de winders pinned.
Keep your hand on-a dat plow!
Noah said, You done lost yo' track,
Can't plow straight an' keep a-lookin' back.

2.

Sister Mary had a gold chain;
Every link was my Jesus' name.
Keep your hand on-a dat plow!
Keep on plowin' an' don't you tire;
Every row goes hi'er an' hi'er.

3.

Ef you wanner git to Heben
I'll tell you how:
Keep your hand right on-a dat plow!
Ef dat plow stays in-a your hand,
Land you straight in de Promise' Land.

"Hold On!" This song combines the work of plowing a field with religious imagery to evoke passage to the Promised Land.

∾ John Henry

John Henry was a little baby
Sittin' on his papa's knee
He picked up a hammer & a little piece of steel
Said "Hammer's gonna be the death of me, Lord, Lord!
Hammer's gonna be the death of me"

The captain said to John Henry
"Gonna bring that steam drill 'round
Gonna bring that steam drill out on the job
Gonna whop that steel on down Lord, Lord / Whop . . ."

10 John Henry told his captain
"A man ain't nothin' but a man
But before I let your steam drill beat me down
I'd die with a hammer in my hand . . ."

John Henry said to his shaker
"Shaker, why don't you sing?
I'm throwin' 30 lbs. from my hips on down
Just listen to that cold steel ring . . ."

John Henry said to his Shaker
"Shaker, you'd better pray
20 'Cause if I miss that little piece of steel
Tomorrow be your buryin' day!"

The Shaker said to John Henry
"I think this mountain's cavin' in!"
John Henry said to his Shaker, "Man
That ain't nothin' but my hammer suckin' wind!"

The man that invented the steam drill
Thought he was mighty fine
But John Henry made 15 ft.
The steam drill only made nine . . .

"John Henry." This familiar folk song, a Negro work song from the post-slavery period, is said to be based on a real event that took place in the Swannanoa Tunnel in West Virginia in the 1870s. In the song, John Henry becomes a mythic figure—like Paul Bunyan or Lincoln—symbolizing human strength that resists the power of the machine.

30 John Henry hammered in the mountain
His hammer was striking fire
But he worked so hard, he broke his poor heart
He laid down his hammer & he died . . .

John Henry had a little woman
Her name was Polly Ann
John Henry took sick & went to his bed
Polly Ann drove steel like a man . . .

John Henry had a little baby
You could hold him in the palm of your hand
40 The last words I heard that poor boy say
"My daddy was a steel-driving man . . ."

They took John Henry to the graveyard
And they buried him in the sand
And every locomotive comes a-roaring by
Says "There lies a steel-driving man . . ."

Well every Monday morning
When the bluebirds begin to sing
You can hear John Henry a mile or more
You can hear John Henry's hammer ring . . .

Emancipation

In classical Rome, *emancipation* was a term used to denote a father setting his son free from his authority; by the nineteenth century, the term had come to mean freeing men, women, and children from slavery, an institution described by its defenders as paternal. The emancipation, or abolition, movement begun in the late eighteenth century at about the same time as the French and American Revolutions, became one of the defining movements of the 1800s, which might be called the century of emancipation. Spirituals, which made freedom their great subject, and SLAVE NARRATIVES, which climaxed with slaves' escape from captivity, were important literary expressions of this theme. Emancipation was also central to much of the philosophical, economic, and political thought of the period.

SLAVERY AND EMANCIPATION

Americans associate the term *emancipation* with the Emancipation Proclamation issued by President Abraham Lincoln, the "Great Emancipator," on January 1, 1863. That edict, which freed slaves in the Southern states, was confirmed by the thirteenth amendment to the Constitution passed at the conclusion of the Civil War. In a prolonged struggle, abolitionists in England and the United States had managed to end the slave trade in 1808 and had achieved incremental victories along the way, but it took the Civil War and a courageous president to end slavery in the States. Even **Frederick Douglass,** the African American activist and abolitionist who thought Lincoln had taken too long to decide on emancipation, nevertheless celebrated the Proclamation in his *Emancipation*

p. 821

Eugène Delacroix, *July 28th 1830, Liberty Leading the People*. Oil on canvas
On July 28, 1830, the revolution in France replaced the reactionary king Charles X with Louis Philippe, the "Citizen King." Although Louis Philippe was thought to bring liberty to France, he, too, ended up abdicating, during the revolution of February 1848. Nevertheless, this painting, celebrating the revolutionary ideals of liberty and freedom as well as the date Louis Philippe took power, stands as a worldwide symbol of emancipation from tyranny. (Art Resource)

Proclaimed as "the most important of any to which the President of the United States has ever signed his name."

SLAVE NARRATIVES

The emancipation movement in Britain and the United States was rooted in Evangelical Protestantism. Quakers, Baptists, and Wesleyan Methodists, believing in the equality of all men before God and in the individual's free will to choose divine grace, were especially tireless in working to end slavery. Lincoln, though not a zealous abolitionist, grounded his belief in emancipation in a concept of spiritual freedom. "This is a world of compensation," he wrote in a letter to H. L. Pierce, "and he who would be no slave must consent to have no

> The most important of any to which the President of the United States has ever signed his name.
> — FREDERICK DOUGLASS on the Emancipation Proclamation

slave. Those who deny freedom to others deserve it not for themselves, and, under a just God, cannot long retain it." One of the ways abolitionists in America and Europe promoted their cause was by collecting and publishing slave narratives, such as those of Olaudah Equiano and Linda Brent. These autobiographical accounts described the rigorous work performed by slaves, the cruel treatment they received, the inhumanity arising from their status as "property," which ignored marital and family relationships, their desire for freedom, attempted escapes, and, usually, the ultimate emancipation of the narrator. Often these stories were oral narratives that had been recorded and "edited" by an abolitionist coauthor. Such was the case with *The History of Mary Prince: A West Indian Slave Related by Herself,* a British slave narrative from the early years of the century.

p. 826

A WORLDWIDE MOVEMENT

After years of agitation, Britain withdrew from the slave trade in 1808 and abolished slavery in its West Indian colonies in 1834. Shortly afterwards, Denmark, Sweden, France, and Holland took similar measures, followed by Spain and Portugal. The last country in the Americas to abolish slavery was Brazil, in 1888. About one century from the time the emancipation movement began, its mission in the Western Hemisphere was complete. To the east, Tsar Alexander II had abolished serfdom in Russia in 1861. There had also been actions taken against slavery in many non-Western countries, such as Turkey, Tunisia, and Egypt.

Even without the efforts of Evangelical reformers, slavery would probably have disappeared in time — made obsolete by industrialization. Slavery in the West Indies and the southern United States and serfdom in Russia were systems largely confined to plantations and feudal estates in agricultural economies. The new capitalist economy called for free trade and free markets, including a free market for labor. Workers had to be free to move from the country to the cities and free to sell their labor to the employer offering the best wage. Unlike the "paternal" slave owner, who was responsible for the well-being of his or her slaves and serfs before and after their working years, the factory owner had only to pay a day's wages for a day's work. Karl Marx argued that the new factory workers were not really free at all. The industrial proletariat, he contended, were really

And by virtue of the power and for the purposes aforesaid, I do order and declare that all persons held as slaves within said designated states and parts of states are, and henceforward shall be, free; and that the executive Government of the United States, including the military and naval authorities thereof, will recognize the freedom of said persons.

– PRESIDENT ABRAHAM LINCOLN, Emancipation Proclamation, January 1, 1863

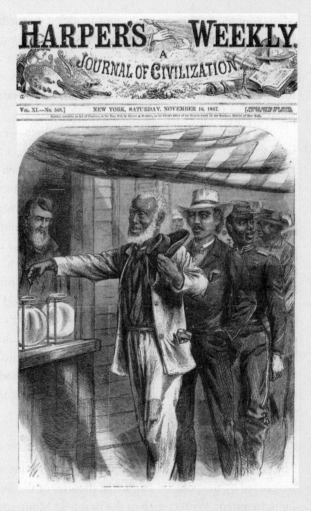

Cover of *Harper's Weekly,* **"The First Vote"**
Soon after slavery was outlawed, a series of constitutional amendments granted African Americans the right to vote. Although many whites in the South used intimidation, even murder, to protest this advancement, African Americans still exercised their newfound right. (Schomburg Center for Research in Black Culture, New York Public Library)

"wage slaves," compelled in order to survive to accept an unfair market wage in a bargain stacked against them.

THE EMANCIPATION OF WOMEN

The concept of emancipation spread from the abolition of slavery to other freedom movements, including the feminist movement, which by the end of the nineteenth century had fostered a generation of "emancipated women" who questioned patriarchal authority and sought equal property rights as well as the right to vote. The watershed year for American feminists was 1848, when a convention held in Seneca Falls, New York, led by Elizabeth Cady Stanton and Lucretia

p. 827

Mott, adopted a series of resolutions modeled on the Declaration of Independence that amounted to a manifesto of the women's rights movement. That same year Marx and Engels published *The Communist Manifesto* and revolution swept through Europe, where battles for democratic rights were waged in the streets in France, Germany, Austria, and Britain.

Several of the literary works in this anthology — especially those by Ibsen, Pardo Bazán, Chopin, and Gilman — reflect the era's growing awareness of the situation of Western women and their desire to be free from oppression. A similar consciousness was emerging in non-Western societies, as indicated in works by Higuchi Ichiyo and Rabindranath Tagore. In her autobiography, **Amar Jiban**, **Rassundari Devi** describes the experience of being a child bride in traditional Indian village culture. Married at twelve to a stranger, Devi is separated from her family and assigned an unfamiliar role in a new household. Though not composed as a political polemic, *Amar Jiban* has many themes in common with other emancipation literature of the nineteenth century: the confining cultural restraints that make her a virtual prisoner in her husband's household, her sense of isolation and abandonment, her desire to read and write. Devi's diary thus became a document in the cause of the emancipation of women.

uh-MAR jee-BAHN

p. 831

ruh-soon-DAH-ree

DAY-vee

THE IDEA OF FREEDOM

The evangelical fervor that prompted the abolitionist movement was supported by the political and social theories of the European Enlightenment. Writers such as the Baron de Montesquieu,[1] who argued that the separation of the three powers of government — executive, legislative, and judicial — protected the citizen from tyranny, and Thomas Paine,[2] who preached the radical philosophy of the rights of man, made *liberté* one of the catchwords of the French Revolution. *Liberté* defined freedom in a new, individualistic manner, as the power to choose one's life without interference from

This is a world of compensation, and he who would be no slave must consent to have no slave. Those who deny freedom to others deserve it not for themselves, and, under a just God, cannot long retain it.

– ABRAHAM LINCOLN, letter to H. L. Pierce

---

[1] **Baron de Montesquieu:** Charles Louis de Secondat, Baron de la Brède et de Montesquieu (1689–1755), French jurist and political philosopher known for *The Spirit of the Laws* (1750), which compared monarchy, republican government, and despotism.

[2] **Thomas Paine:** (1737–1809) American writer and radical political theorist; author of *Common Sense* (1776), *The Rights of Man* (1791–92), and *The Age of Reason* (1794–95).

society as long as one's choices did not adversely affect others. The classic essay articulating freedom in these terms is John Stuart Mill's *On Liberty* (1859). The excerpts that follow present Mill's definition of liberty and his discussion of why a person cannot be free to sell himself into bondage. **Swami Vivekananda**'s notion of freedom, which he sees as the end purpose of life, derives from an inner, spiritual understanding. He is less concerned with external laws that control the tyranny of the majority than he is with the inner journey of the individual toward spiritual freedom, and as such is closer to such Western existentialists as Kierkegaard and Sartre[3] than to such RATIONALIST UTILITARIANS as Mill. **Muhammed Iqbal**, an Indian Muslim, in *Freedom* defines that term by contrasting the characteristics of the freeman with those of the bondman, or slave. This strategy would seem to suggest that Iqbal's idea of freedom is defined by its opposite, but the metaphors he uses to describe freedom suggest their own inherent meaning.

Rabindranath Tagore's parable "Emancipation" resembles the tales in *The Thousand and One Nights*. It tells of Vajarasin's emancipation from prison, effected by the sacrifice of another man's life. The ambivalence of the tale makes its title, at the very least, ironic. One wonders whether Tagore had in mind spiritual freedom of the sort described by Vivekananda or whether he was thinking in more political terms, particularly about the emancipation of India from British colonial rule.

p. 834

p. 840
SWAH-mee
vi-vay-kuh-NAHN-duh

p. 841
moo-HAH-med
ik-BAHL

p. 842
rub-in-druh-NAHTH
tuh-GORE

■ CONNECTIONS

Equiano, *The Interesting Narrative of the Life of Olaudah Equiano* (Book 4); **Jacobs**, *Incidents in the Life of a Slave Girl*, p. 760; **Stowe**, *Uncle Tom's Cabin*, p. 194; *In the World*: Colonialism (Book 6). Slavery is the subject of the narratives, *The Interesting Narrative of the Life of Olaudah Equiano* and Harriet Jacobs's *Incidents in the Life of a Slave Girl*, and a significant topic in *In the World*: Colonialism. The story of the death of Uncle Tom, from the most famous of all antislavery novels, Harriet Beecher Stowe's *Uncle Tom's Cabin*, appears in *In the World*: Heroes and Heroism.

Chekhov, *The Cherry Orchard*, p. 708. In *The Cherry Orchard*, Lopakhin, the son of a serf and an emancipated serf himself, makes much of his personal history; Chekhov uses Lopakhin's change in station as an indicator of the sweeping changes taking place in Russia at the time of the play. Do Chekhov's characters see the emancipation of the serfs as a positive historical development? Does Chekhov?

---

[3] **Sartre:** Jean-Paul Sartre (1905–1980), existentialist whose philosophy stresses the necessity of individual choice.

Goethe, *Faust*, p. 29; Dostoevsky, "The Grand Inquisitor," p. 541. The concept of freedom plays an important role in many works of nineteenth-century literature. It is fundamental, for example, to Goethe's transformation of the Faust legend, for even though Goethe's Faust makes a deal with the devil, he does not sign over his free will, and in the end he is redeemed by the choices he makes and by his continued striving. In Dostoevsky's "The Grand Inquisitor," freedom is the choice offered to mankind by Jesus. How is freedom defined in these two works?

Ibsen, *Hedda Gabler*, p. 561; Pardo Bazán, "The Revolver," p. 696; Chopin, "The Story of an Hour," p. 931; Gilman, *The Yellow Wallpaper*, p. 941; Higuchi Ichiyo, "The Thirteenth Night," p. 1107. Freedom takes on different meanings in the works of many nineteenth-century women authors. The word *free* is used with considerable irony in both Chopin's "Story of an Hour" and Pardo Bazán's "Revolver." In various ways, Ibsen's Hedda Gabler, the woman in the attic in Gilman's *Yellow Wallpaper*, and Oseki in Higuchi Ichiyo's "The Thirteenth Night" are trapped in patriarchal prisons from which they seek to free themselves. How would the women in each of these works define *freedom*?

■ PRONUNCIATION

Amar Jiban: uh-MAR jee-BAHN
Muhammed Iqbal: moo-HAH-med ik-BAHL
Palanquin: puh-LANG-kwin
Potajia: poh-tah-JAH
Ramdia: rahm-DEE-uh
Shyama: SHYAH-muh
Uttiya: OO-tee-yuh
Vajrasen: vuj-ruh-SANE
Rabindranath Tagore: rub-in-druh-NAHTH tuh-GORE
Rassundari Devi: ruh-soon-DAH-ree DAY-vee
Swami Vivekananda: SWAH-mee vi-vay-kuh-NAHN-duh

FREDERICK DOUGLASS
1818–1895

Born a slave in Tuckahoe, Maryland, Frederick Douglass escaped from slavery in 1838 and went on to become a journalist, orator, and one of the abolitionist movement's most effective spokespersons. His first autobiography, *Narrative of the Life of Frederick Douglass, an American Slave* (1845), was a slave narrative that established his credibility as an abolitionist leader. Later in life, after a distinguished career in journalism and government service, he wrote *The Life and Times of Frederick Douglass* (1882), a second autobiography. His remarks on the Emancipation Proclamation and President Lincoln are taken from the October 1862 issue of a magazine he published, *Douglass' Monthly.*

Portrait of Frederick Douglass, 1856

This photograph was taken of the abolitionist and statesman Frederick Douglass about seven years before Lincoln signed the Emancipation Proclamation, which freed all U.S. slaves. (National Portrait Gallery/Art Resource)

[R]ead the proclamation for it is the most important of any to which the President of the United States has ever signed his name.

– FREDERICK DOUGLASS

It [Emancipation Proclamation] recognizes and declares the real nature of the contest [in the Civil War], and places the North on the side of justice and civilization, and the rebels on the side of robbery and barbarism.

– FREDERICK DOUGLASS

Emancipation Proclaimed

Common sense, the necessities of the war, to say nothing of the dictation of justice and humanity have at last prevailed. We shout for joy that we live to record this righteous decree. *Abraham Lincoln,* President of the United States, Commander-in-Chief of the army and navy, in his own peculiar, cautious, forbearing, and hesitating way, slow, but we hope sure, has, while the loyal heart was near breaking with despair, proclaimed and declared: *"That on the First of January, in the Year of Our Lord One Thousand, Eight Hundred and Sixty-three, All Persons Held as Slaves Within Any State or Any Designated Part of a State, The People Whereof Shall Then be in Rebellion Against the United States, Shall be Thenceforward and Forever Free."* "Free forever" oh! long enslaved millions, whose cries have so vexed the air and sky, suffer on a few more days in sorrow, the hour of your deliverance draws nigh! Oh! Ye millions of free and loyal men who have earnestly sought to free your bleeding country from the dreadful ravages of revolution and anarchy, lift up now your voices with joy and thanksgiving for with freedom to the slave will come peace and safety to your country. President Lincoln has embraced in this proclamation the law of Congress passed more than six months ago, prohibiting the employment of any part of the army and naval forces of the United States, to return fugitive slaves to their masters, commanded all officers of the army and navy to respect and obey its provisions. He has still further declared his intention to urge upon the Legislature of all the slave States not in rebellion the immediate or gradual abolishment of slavery. But read the proclamation for it is the most important of any to which the President of the United States has ever signed his name.

Opinions will widely differ as to the practical effect of this measure upon the war. All that class at the North who have not lost their affection for slavery will regard the measure as the very worst that could be devised, and as likely to lead to endless mischief. All their plans for the future have been projected with a view to a reconstruction of the American Government upon the basis of compromise between slaveholding and non-slaveholding States. The thought of a country unified in sentiments, objects, and ideas, has not entered into their political calculations, and hence this newly declared policy of the Government, which contemplates one glorious homogeneous people, doing away at a blow with the whole class of compromisers and corrupters, will meet their stern opposition. Will that opposition prevail? Will it lead the President to reconsider and retract? Not a word of it. Abraham Lincoln may be slow, Abraham Lincoln may desire peace even at the price of leaving our terrible national sore untouched, to fester on for generations, but Abraham Lincoln is not the man to reconsider, retract, and contradict words and purposes solemnly proclaimed over his official signature.

The careful, and we think, the slothful deliberation which he has observed in reaching this obvious policy, is a guarantee against retraction. But even if the temper and spirit of the President himself were other than what they are, events greater than the President, events which have slowly wrung this proclamation from him may be relied on to carry him forward in the same direction. To look back now would only load him with heavier evils, while diminishing his ability, for overcoming those with which he now has to contend. To recall his proclamation would only increase rebel pride, rebel sense of power and would be hailed as a direct admission of weakness on the part of the Federal Government, while it would cause heaviness of heart and depression of national enthusiasm all over the loyal North and West. No, Abraham Lincoln will take no step backward. His word has gone out over the country and the world, giving joy and gladness to the friends of freedom and progress wherever those words are read, and he will stand by them, and carry them out to the letter. If he has taught us to confide in nothing else, he has taught us to confide in his word. The want of Constitutional power, the want of military power, the tendency of the measure to intensify Southern hate, and to exasperate the rebels, the tendency to drive from him all that class of Democrats at the North, whose loyalty has been conditioned on his restoring the union as it was, slavery and all, have all been considered, and he has taken his ground notwithstanding. The President doubtless saw, as we see, that it is not more absurd to talk about restoring the union, without hurting slavery, than restoring the union without hurting the rebels. As to exasperating the

South, there can be no more in the cup than the cup will hold, and that was full already. The whole situation having been carefully scanned, before Mr. Lincoln could be made to budge an inch, he will now stand his ground. Border State influence, and the influence of half-loyal men, have been exerted and have done their worst. The end of these two influences is implied in this proclamation. Hereafter, the inspiration as well as the men and the money for carrying on the war will come from the North, and not from half-loyal border States.

The effect of this paper upon the disposition of Europe will be great and increasing. It changes the character of the war in European eyes and gives it an important principle as an object, instead of national pride and interest. It recognizes and declares the real nature of the contest, and places the North on the side of justice and civilization, and the rebels on the side of robbery and barbarism. It will disarm all purpose on the part of European Government to intervene in favor of the rebels and thus cast off at a blow one source of rebel power. All through the war thus far, the rebel ambassadors in foreign countries have been able to silence all expression of sympathy with the North as to slavery. With much more than a show of truth, they said that the Federal Government, no more than the Confederate Government, contemplated the abolition of slavery.

But will not this measure be frowned upon by our officers and men in the field? We have heard of many thousands who have resolved that they will throw up their commissions and lay down their arms, just so soon as they are required to carry on a war against slavery. Making all allowances for exaggeration there are doubtless far too many of this sort in the loyal army. Putting this kind of loyalty and patriotism to the test, will be one of the best collateral effects of the measure. Any man who leaves the field on such a ground will be an argument in favor of the proclamation, and will prove that his heart has been more with slavery than with his country. Let the army be cleansed from all such proslavery vermin, and its health and strength will be greatly improved. But there can be no reason to fear the loss of many officers or men by resignation or desertion. We have no doubt that the measure was brought to the attention of most of our leading Generals, and blind as some of them have seemed to be in the earlier part of the war, most of them have seen enough to convince them that there can be no end to this war that does not end slavery. At any rate, we may hope that for every pro-slavery man that shall start from the ranks of our loyal army, there will be two anti-slavery men to fill up the vacancy, and in this war one truly devoted to the cause of Emancipation is worth two of the opposite sort.

Whether slavery will be abolished in the manner now proposed by President Lincoln, depends of course upon two conditions, the first specified and the second implied. The first is that the slave States shall be in rebellion on and after the first day of January 1863 and the second is we must have the ability to put down that rebellion. About the first there can be very little doubt. The South is thoroughly in earnest and confident. It has staked everything upon the rebellion. Its experience thus far in the field has rather increased its hopes of final success than diminished them. Its armies now hold us at bay at all points, and the war is confined to the border States slave and free. If Richmond were in our hands and Virginia at our mercy, the vast regions beyond would still remain to be subdued. But the rebels confront us on the Potomac, the Ohio, and the Mississippi. Kentucky, Maryland, Missouri, and Virginia are in debate on the battlefields and their people are divided by the line which separates treason from loyalty. In short we are yet, after eighteen months of war, confined to the outer margin of the rebellion. We have scarcely more than touched the surface of the terrible evil. It has been raising large quantities of food during the past summer. While the masters have been fighting abroad, the slaves have been busy working at home to supply them with the means of continuing the struggle. They will not down at the bidding of this Proclamation, but may be safely relied upon till January and long after January. A month or two will put an end to general fighting for the winter. When the leaves fall we shall hear again of bad roads, winter quarters, and spring campaigns. The South which has thus far withstood our arms will not fall at once before our pens. All fears for the abolition of slavery arising from this apprehension may be dismissed. Whoever, therefore, lives to see the first day of next January, should Abraham Lincoln be then alive and President of the United States, may confidently look in the morning papers for the final proclamation, granting freedom, and freedom forever, to all slaves within the rebel States. On the next point nothing need be said. We have full power to put down the rebellion. Unless one man is more than a match for four, unless the South breeds braver and better men than the North, unless slavery is more precious than liberty, unless a just cause kindles a feebler enthusiasm than a wicked and villainous one, the men of the loyal States will put down this rebellion and slavery, and all the sooner will they put down that rebellion by coupling slavery with that object. Tenderness towards slavery has been the loyal weakness during the war. Fighting the slaveholders with one hand and holding the slaves with the other, has been fairly tried and has failed. We have now inaugurated a wiser and better policy, a policy which is better for the loyal cause than an hundred thousand armed men. The Star Spangled Banner is now the harbinger of Liberty and the millions in bondage, inured to hardships, accustomed to toil, ready to suffer, ready to fight, to dare and to die, will rally under that banner wherever they see it gloriously unfolded to the breeze. Now let the Government go forward in its mission of Liberty as the only condition of peace and union, by weeding out the army and navy of all such officers as the late Col. Miles, whose sympathies are now known to have been with the rebels. Let only the men who assent heartily to the wisdom and the justice of the anti-slavery policy of the Government be lifted into command; let the black man have an arm as well as a heart in this war, and the tide of battle which has thus far only waved backward and forward, will steadily set in our favor. The rebellion suppressed, slavery abolished, and America will, higher than ever, sit as a queen among the nations of the earth.

Now for the work. During the interval between now and next January, let every friend of the long enslaved bondman do his utmost in swelling the tide of anti-slavery sentiment, by writing, speaking, money, and example. Let our aim be to make the North a unit in favor of the President's policy, and see to it that our voices and votes, shall forever extinguish that latent and malignant sentiment at the North, which has from the first cheered on the rebels in their atrocious crimes against the union, and has systematically sought to paralyze the national arm in striking down the slaveholding rebellion. We are ready for this service or any other, in this, we trust the last struggle with the monster slavery.

MARY PRINCE
c. 1788–?

The first black British woman to escape from slavery and publish a book about her experiences, Mary Prince described her life as a West Indian slave in *The History of Mary Prince*, published in London and Edinburgh in 1831. Its description of slavery from a woman's point of view made it particularly alarming and persuasive as literature for the abolition movement, especially at a time when Parliament was debating a bill to end slavery in the British colonies. The book went through three editions in its first year. The passage excerpted here ends the narrative with Prince's adamant assertion that all slaves desire freedom, countering the propaganda of pro-slavery forces who contended that many slaves were content with their situation.

> The man that says slaves be quite happy in slavery — that they don't want to be free — that man is either ignorant or a lying person. I never heard a slave say so.
>
> – MARY PRINCE

Henry L. Stephans, *The Parting, "Buy us too,"* 1863
This illustration, drawn in the year African Americans were freed from slavery, portrays what had been a common occurrence — a family being broken apart. The cold slave owner shows no compassion toward his slave's wife and child. (Library of Congress)

THE PARTING "Buy us too."

The History of Mary Prince
A West Indian Slave Related by Herself

I still live in the hope that God will find a way to give me my liberty, and give me back to my husband. I endeavour to keep down my fretting, and to leave all to Him, for he knows what is good for me better than I know myself. Yet, I must confess, I find it a hard and heavy task to do so.

I am often much vexed, and I feel great sorrow when I hear some people in this country say, that the slaves do not need better usage, and do not want to be free.[1] They believe the foreign people,[2] who deceive them, and say slaves are happy. I say, Not so. How can slaves be happy when they have the halter round their neck and the whip upon their back? and are disgraced and thought no more of than beasts?— and are separated from their mothers, and husbands, and children, and sisters, just as cattle are sold and separated? Is it happiness for a driver in the field to take down his wife or sister or child, and strip them, and whip them in such a disgraceful manner?—women that have had children exposed in the open field to shame! There is no modesty or decency shown by the owner to his slaves; men, women, and children are exposed alike. Since I have been here I have often wondered how English people can go out into the West Indies and act in such a beastly manner. But when they go to the West Indies, they forget God and all feeling of shame, I think, since they can see and do such things. They tie up slaves like hogs—moor[3] them up like cattle, and they lick them, so as hogs, or cattle, or horses never were flogged;—and yet they come home and say, and make some good people believe, that slaves don't want to get out of slavery. But they put a cloak about the truth. It is not so. All slaves want to be free—to be free is very sweet. I will say the truth to English people who may read this history that my good friend, Miss S——, is now writing down for me. I have been a slave myself—I know what slaves feel—I can tell by myself what other slaves feel, and by what they have told me. The man that says slaves be quite happy in slavery—that they don't want to be free—that man is either ignorant or a lying person. I never heard a slave say so. I never heard a Buckra man[4] say so, till I heard tell of it in England. Such people ought to be ashamed of themselves. They can't do without slaves, they say. What's the reason they can't do without slaves as well as in England? No slaves here—no whips—no stocks—no punishment, except for wicked people. They hire servants in England; and if they don't like them, they send them away: they can't lick them. Let them work ever so hard in England, they are far better off than slaves. If they get a bad master, they give warning and go hire to another. They have their liberty. That's just what *we* want. We don't mind hard work,

---

[1] The whole of this paragraph, especially, is given as nearly as was possible in Mary's precise words. [Original editor]

[2] foreign people: Anglo West Indians.

[3] moor: West Indian for "to fasten or tie up."

[4] Buckra man: A white man in the West Indies.

if we had proper treatment, and proper wages like English servants, and proper time given in the week to keep us from breaking the Sabbath. But they won't give it; they will have work—work—work, night and day, sick or well, till we are quite done up; and we must not speak up nor look amiss, however much we be abused. And then when we are quite done up, who cares for us, more than for a lame horse? This is slavery. I tell it to let English people know the truth; and I hope they will never leave off to pray God, and call loud to the great King of England, till all the poor blacks be given free, and slavery done up for evermore.

ᘓ Elizabeth Cady Stanton
1815–1902

ᘓ Lucretia Mott
1793–1880

Two leaders of the American feminist movement in the mid nineteenth century, Elizabeth Cady Stanton and Lucretia Mott, after attending a World Anti-Slavery Convention in London where women delegates were denied the opportunity to speak, convened a meeting on women's rights in Seneca Falls, New York, on July 19, 1848. Their *Declaration of Sentiments and Resolutions* drafted for the meeting began Stanton's lifelong career of writing about women's issues and working for change. The document modeled its language and rhetoric in the *Declaration of Independence* and applies that document's principles to women. Stanton's early collaboration with Mott preceded her more sustained relationship with Susan B. Anthony, begun in 1851, in which Anthony served as organizer and researcher and Stanton as writer and orator.

> The history of mankind is a history of repeated injuries and usurpations on the part of man toward woman, having in direct object the establishment of an absolute tyranny over her.
>
> – Elizabeth Cady Stanton and Lucretia Mott

ᘓ Declaration of Sentiments and Resolutions, Seneca Falls

When, in the course of human events, it becomes necessary for one portion of the family of man to assume among the people of the earth a position different from that which they have hitherto occupied, but one to which the laws of nature and of nature's God entitle them, a decent respect to the opinions of mankind requires that they should declare the causes that impel them to such a course.

We hold these truths to be self-evident: that all men and women are created equal; that they are endowed by their Creator with certain inalienable rights; that among these are life, liberty, and the pursuit of happiness; that to secure these rights governments are instituted, deriving their just power from the consent of the governed. Whenever any form of government becomes destructive of these ends, it is the right of those who suffer from it to refuse allegiance to it, and to insist upon the institution of a new government, laying its foundation on such principles, and organizing its powers in such form, as to them shall seem most likely to effect their safety and happiness. Prudence, indeed, will dictate that governments long established should not be changed for light and transient causes; and accordingly all experience hath shown that mankind are more disposed to suffer, while evils are sufferable, than to right themselves by abolishing the forms to which they were accustomed. But when a long train of abuses and usurpations, pursuing invariably the same object evinces a design to reduce them under absolute despotism, it is their duty to throw off such government, and to provide new guards for their future security. Such has been the patient sufferance of the women under this government, and such is now the necessity which constrains them to demand the equal station to which they are entitled.

The history of mankind is a history of repeated injuries and usurpations on the part of man toward woman, having in direct object the establishment of an absolute tyranny over her. To prove this, let facts be submitted to a candid world.

He has never permitted her to exercise her inalienable right to the elective franchise.

He has compelled her to submit to laws, in the formation of which she had no voice.

He has withheld from her rights which are given to the most ignorant and degraded men — both natives and foreigners.

Having deprived her of this first right of a citizen, the elective franchise, thereby leaving her without representation in the halls of legislation, he has oppressed her on all sides.

He has made her, if married, in the eye of the law, civilly dead.

He has taken from her all right in property, even to the wages she earns.

He has made her, morally, an irresponsible being, as she can commit many crimes with impunity, provided they be done in the presence of her husband. In the covenant of marriage, she is compelled to promise obedience to her husband, he becoming, to all intents and purposes, her master — the law giving him power to deprive her of her liberty, and to administer chastisement.

He has so framed the laws of divorce, as to what shall be the proper causes, and in case of separation, to whom the guardianship of the children shall be given, as to be wholly regardless of the happiness of women — the law, in all cases, going upon a false supposition of the supremacy of man, and giving all power into his hands.

After depriving her of all rights as a married woman, if single, and the owner of property, he has taxed her to support a government which recognizes her only when her property can be made profitable to it.

He has monopolized nearly all the profitable employments, and from those she is permitted to follow, she receives but a scanty remuneration. He closes against her all the avenues to wealth and distinction which he considers most honorable to himself. As a teacher of theology, medicine, or law, she is not known.

He has denied her the facilities for obtaining a thorough education, all colleges being closed against her.

He allows her in Church, as well as State, but a subordinate position, claiming Apostolic authority for her exclusion from the ministry, and, with some exceptions, from any public participation in the affairs of the Church.

He has created a false public sentiment by giving to the world a different code of morals for men and women, by which moral delinquencies which exclude women from society, are not only tolerated, but deemed of little account in man.

He has usurped the prerogative of Jehovah himself, claiming it as his right to assign for her a sphere of action, when that belongs to her conscience and to her God.

He has endeavored, in every way that he could, to destroy her confidence in her own powers, to lessen her self-respect, and to make her willing to lead a dependent and abject life.

Now, in view of this entire disfranchisement of one-half the people of this country, their social and religious degradation—in view of the unjust laws above mentioned, and because women do feel themselves aggrieved, oppressed, and fraudulently deprived of their most sacred rights, we insist that they have immediate admission to all the rights and privileges which belong to them as citizens of the United States.

In entering upon the great work before us, we anticipate no small amount of misconception, misrepresentation, and ridicule; but we shall use every instrumentality within our power to effect our object. We shall employ agents, circulate tracts, petition the State and National legislatures, and endeavor to enlist the pulpit and the press in our behalf. We hope this Convention will be followed by a series of Conventions embracing every part of the country.

RESOLUTIONS

Whereas, The great precept of nature is conceded to be, that "man shall pursue his own true and substantial happiness." Blackstone[1] in his Commentaries remarks, that this law of Nature being coeval with mankind, and dictated by God himself, is of course superior in obligation to any other. It is binding over all the globe, in all countries and at all times; no human laws are of any validity if contrary to this, and such of them as are valid, derive all their force, and all their validity, and all their authority, mediately and immediately, from this original; therefore,

Resolved, That such laws as conflict, in any way, with the true and substantial

---

[1] **Blackstone:** Sir William Blackstone (1723–1780), professor of law at Oxford University; his *Commentaries on the Law of England* (1765–69) codified and organized the body of English law.

happiness of woman, are contrary to the great precept of nature and of no validity, for this is "superior in obligation to any other."

Resolved, That all laws which prevent woman from occupying such a station in society as her conscience shall dictate, or which place her in a position inferior to that of man, are contrary to the great precept of nature, and therefore of no force or authority.

Resolved, That woman is man's equal—was intended to be so by the Creator, and the highest good of the race demands that she should be recognized as such.

Resolved, That the women of this country ought to be enlightened in regard to the laws under which they live, that they may no longer publish their degradation by declaring themselves satisfied with their present position, nor their ignorance, by asserting that they have all the rights they want.

Resolved, That inasmuch as man, while claiming for himself intellectual superiority, does accord to woman moral superiority, it is pre-eminently his duty to encourage her to speak and teach, as she has an opportunity, in all religious assemblies.

Resolved, That the same amount of virtue, delicacy, and refinement of behavior that is required of woman in the social state, should also be required of man, and the same transgressions should be visited with equal severity on both man and woman.

Resolved, That the objection of indelicacy and impropriety, which is so often brought against woman when she addresses a public audience, comes with a very ill-grace from those who encourage, by their attendance, her appearance on stage, in the concert, or in feats of the circus.

Resolved, That woman has too long rested satisfied in the circumscribed limits which corrupt customs and a perverted application of the Scriptures have marked out for her, and that it is time she should move in the enlarged sphere which her great Creator has assigned her.

Resolved, That it is the duty of the women of this country to secure to themselves their sacred right to the elective franchise.

Resolved, That the equality of human rights results necessarily from the fact of the identity of the race in capabilities and responsibilities.

Resolved, therefore, That, being invested by the Creator with the same capabilities, and the same consciousness of responsibility for their exercise, it is demonstrably the right and duty of woman, equally with man, to promote every righteous cause by every righteous means; and especially in regard to the great subjects of morals and religion, it is self-evidently her right to participate with her brother in teaching them, both in private and in public, by writing and by speaking, by any instrumentalities proper to be used, and in any assemblies proper to be held; and this being a self-evident truth growing out of the divinely implanted principles of human nature, any custom or authority adverse to it, whether modern or wearing the hoary sanction of antiquity, is to be regarded as a self-evident falsehood, and at war with mankind.

Resolved, That the speedy success of our cause depends upon the zealous and untiring efforts of both men and women, for the overthrow of the monopoly of the pulpit, and for the securing to woman an equal participation with men in the various trades, professions, and commerce.

RASSUNDARI DEVI
C. 1810–?

Rassundari Devi's *Amar Jiban* (*My Life,* 1876) was the first autobiography to be published in Bengali. Born in the village of Potajia at the beginning of the nineteenth century and raised by her mother after her father's death, Devi, following Indian custom, was married at age twelve and sent to live in her husband's family home. In the following excerpt, she describes this traumatic episode; in later sections, she details the drudgery of her life as a housekeeper and a mother and tells of how she secretly taught herself to read and write, accomplishments that enable her to compose her autobiography as she nears the end of her life. Though Devi wrote without an ideological agenda, her story is an important text in the emancipation literature of the nineteenth century.

Our selections are translated by Tanika Sarkar, lecturer in history at the Jawaharlal Nehru University in Delhi and author of *Words To Win: The Making of Amar Jiban: A Modern Autobiography* (1987).

> If I am asked to describe my state of mind, I would say that it was very much like the sacrificial goat being dragged to the altar, the same hopeless situation, the same agonized screams.
>
> – RASSUNDARI DEVI

FROM

Amar Jiban (My Life)

Translated by Tanika Sarkar

THE THIRD COMPOSITION

. . . The news made me very happy indeed. I would be married. There would be music, I would hear the women ululating. How exciting that would be! Yet I felt scared at the same time. I cannot express the apprehensions that came to my mind. Meanwhile the various things necessary for the ceremony began to arrive. Relatives and guests began pouring in. I was scared to death by all this. I did not talk to anyone and spent most of the time weeping. Everybody did their best to reassure me. They embraced me, but the unspoken agony in my mind did not lift.

Later on I was cheered up by the ornaments, the red wedding sari, and the wedding music. I forgot my earlier worries and went about laughing and watching the elaborate preparations. My happiness knew no bounds. When everything was over the next day, I heard people asking my mother, "Are they leaving today?" I thought they were referring to the guests. Then the music started. There was an air of festivity. The guests must be leaving now, I thought. It made me happy and I went about following my mother. Presently everybody assembled inside the house. Some looked happy, but others were in tears. That made me feel really frightened. Then my brother, aunts, uncles, and my mother all took me in their arms by turn as they burst into tears. Their tears made me so sad that I began to cry too. I knew mother was

831

going to hand me over to the other family. I tightened my hold on her and pleaded, "Don't give me over to them, Mother!" That made everybody present even more upset. They broke down and tried to say nice words to console me. My mother took me in her arms and said, "You are a good girl, you understand everything, don't you? God is with us, you needn't be afraid. You are going to come back to us in a few days' time. Every girl has to go to her in-laws' house. Nobody else cries like this. There is no reason to be so upset. Please calm down and talk to me." But I was trembling all over with fear. I was quite unable to speak. Somehow I managed to say through my tears: "Are you sure that God will go with me?" Mother promptly reassured me that he most certainly would. "He will be with you all the time, so stop crying now." But in spite of her soothing words my apprehensions kept growing and I could not check my tears.

With great effort they took me away from my mother. I still feel sad when I think of the state of mind I was in and the agony I was going through. As a matter of fact it is indeed a sad thing to leave one's parents, settle in some other place, and live under other people. A place where your parents are no longer your own. But such is the will of God, so it is praiseworthy.

I clung to whomever came to pick me up and went on weeping incessantly. Everyone, old and young, was moved to tears. Eventually they managed to put me into a palanquin,[1] which was not the one intended for me. No sooner was I seated inside than the bearers started marching off. With none of my near ones close by I sank into a deep depression. Since there was no way out, I started praying through my tears: "Please be with me, God." If I am asked to describe my state of mind, I would say that it was very much like the sacrificial goat being dragged to the altar, the same hopeless situation, the same agonized screams. I could see none of my relatives near me. I was miserable, and in tears I kept calling for my mother. I also prayed with all my heart as Mother had told me to. If you ever feel afraid, think of God, she had said.

All these thoughts went through my mind as I sat weeping. Very soon I felt too parched to cry.

The Fourth Composition

Unable to cry any more I fell into deep sleep. I had no idea what happened after that and where I was taken.

When I woke up the next morning I found myself on a boat with none of my relations near me. All the people who came and talked were strangers. I thought of my mother and other members of the family, the affectionate neighbors, my playmates. Where were they now and where was I? So I started to weep once again. My heart felt as if it would break. All the people in the boat tried to console me. But that increased my misery because their kind words reminded me of the affection of my own people. Tears streamed down endlessly—I just couldn't stop them. I cried till I

---

[1] palanquin: A litter carried on the shoulders of two or four bearers.

was out of breath. Besides the boat ride was a new experience and it made me feel sick. All I could do in my desperation was to think of God, and I did that, though the predominant emotion I felt was fear. But Mother had said, speak the name of God if you are afraid. So I just kept on repeating my prayers.

Only God will understand the predicament I was in—nobody else can have any idea. Even now I remember those days. The caged bird, the fish caught in the net.

Since it was the will of God, however, it was no use feeling sorry for myself. I am only writing about what I felt at the time. I do not know how other girls feel. Perhaps they do not feel as miserable as I did. Actually there are no obvious reasons for my sadness but the tears came constantly because I had to leave my own people.

People put birds in cages for their own amusement. Well, I was like a caged bird. And I would have to remain in this cage for life. I would never be freed. We spent a few more days on the boat. Then I heard people say that we were about to reach home. For one moment I thought they meant my home. It gave rise to mixed emotions and also to fear. God only knows what went through my mind. All I could do was cry—I spent all my days and nights crying. Strange are the ways of God! Your laws are so wonderful! You have taken me from my dear mother and from others I love so much and have brought me to this distant place. That night we landed. We arrived at their house and saw different people taking part in all sorts of merrymaking. But none of them was from my part of the country. I did not know a single one of them. I began to weep again. I was so upset that the stream of tears did not cease. Everybody tried to assure me that this was my home—that all these people and everything that I saw was mine—and that I had no reason to cry. From now on I would have to live here and look after the house. There was no reason to be upset. But even as they spoke, my longing increased because I knew I wouldn't be able to see my family. Sorrow engulfed me like a raging forest fire. Those who have had such experiences perhaps know how useless words seem in times of sorrow. If somebody loses her son, is it wise to rebuke her? Or ask her not to lament, saying he must have been an enemy in an earlier birth: "He was not your son really. He wouldn't have left you if he had been so. He was a plunderer—don't ever utter his name. . . ."

THE FIFTH COMPOSITION

My day used to begin very early—and there was no respite from housework till long past midnight. I could not rest, even for a moment. But thanks to the grace of God I did everything in a spirit of duty. No work seemed too tiring. Because God wished it, I managed to gradually finish all the household tasks. I was only fourteen then. Around this time, the idea that I should learn how to read books entered my mind. But unfortunately girls were not supposed to read in those days. "What is the world coming to?" they used to say. "To think that women will be doing the work of men! Never heard of it before. In this new age even this has come to be true! These days women are becoming famous and men seem good for nothing. Such strange things never happened before. There was even a woman ruler on the throne. Who knows what other changes are in store for us! The way things are going, a decent man will very soon lose his caste. Pretty soon the womenfolk will get together and study books."

When I overheard these conversations I used to feel really scared. I had never dared to tell anyone about my desires—but now I became afraid that they might come to know what was on my mind. I dared not look at a page with written letters on it, in case they attributed it to my desire for learning. But I prayed constantly to God. I said, "Please, God, help me learn, so that I can read religious books. Dear God, friend of the poor, I invoke your name only for this." I used to say, "God, you have brought me so far from my village Potajia—a journey of three days and three nights to Ramdia. You have made me leave my friends and my relations and have brought me to this faraway place. And now, this village of Ramdia has become my home. How strange that is! When I did not know how to do any housework, even the slightest attempt would please my mother. She used to praise me before the others. Look at me now. I am no longer free. I have learned to work for others. And there is so much I should do. These people have become very dear to me. . . ." All these thoughts raced through my mind and I would shed tears, hiding my face in the sari that was drawn over my head. Nobody knew of my sorrow. How could they know, for my face lay hidden. "Only you knew because you are my father, my God, the heart of my heart, the life of my life, the very cream of kindness. I float in your kindness all the time. You have been with me through good days and bad days. You know all that I have experienced; I cannot keep anything back from you. . . ."

∾ JOHN STUART MILL
1806–1873

> The only part of the conduct of any one, for which he is amenable to society, is that which concerns others. In the part which merely concerns himself, his independence is, of right, absolute. Over himself, over his own body and mind, the individual is sovereign.
>
> – JOHN STUART MILL

Political philosopher and social theorist, John Stuart Mill wrote essays treating many of the central social issues of his own day and beyond. The son of utilitarian philosopher James Mill, he was homeschooled by his father, learning Greek, Latin, mathematics, economics, and philosophy as a young child. He later regretted the lack of literature and art in his curriculum, and in *Principles of Political Economy* (1848), *Autobiography* (1873), and *The Subjection of Women* (1869) he sought to broaden the scope of utilitarian thought. His essay *On Liberty* (1859) is the classic examination of the danger of the tyranny of the majority. Mill calls for institutional measures like the Bill of Rights in the United States Constitution to protect individual liberty and to counter the tendencies toward tyranny and mediocrity inherent in democratic societies.

"Franchise for females," "Pray clear the way for these
A-Persons," *Punch,* March 30, 1867, Engraving
*This satirical drawing criticizes women's voting rights and
John Stuart Mill (center), a highly influential thinker and
writer on the issue of personal freedom. Mill is making way
for women to vote, as angered men look on. (Mary Evans
Picture Library)*

FROM

∾ On Liberty

The object of this Essay is to assert one very simple principle, as entitled to govern absolutely the dealings of society with the individual in the way of compulsion and control, whether the means used be physical force in the form of legal penalties, or the moral coercion of public opinion. That principle is, that the sole end for which mankind are warranted, individually or collectively, in interfering with the liberty of action of any of their number, is self-protection. That the only purpose for which power can be rightfully exercised over any member of a civilised community, against his will, is to prevent harm to others. His own good, either physical or moral, is not a sufficient warrant. He cannot rightfully be compelled to do or forbear because it will be better for him to do so, because it will make him happier, because, in the opinions of others, to do so would be wise, or even right. These are good reasons for remonstrating with him, or reasoning with him, or persuading him, or entreating him, but not for compelling him, or visiting him with any evil in case he do otherwise. To justify that, the conduct from which it is desired to deter him must be calculated to produce evil to some one else. The only part of the conduct of any one, for which he is amenable to society, is that which concerns others. In the part which merely concerns himself, his independence is, of right, absolute. Over himself, over his own body and mind, the individual is sovereign.

It is, perhaps, hardly necessary to say that this doctrine is meant to apply only to human beings in the maturity of their faculties. We are not speaking of children, or of young persons below the age which the law may fix as that of manhood or womanhood. Those who are still in a state to require being taken care of by others, must be protected against their own actions as well as against external injury. For the same reason, we may leave out of consideration those backward states of society in which the race itself may be considered as in its nonage. The early difficulties in the way of spontaneous progress are so great, that there is seldom any choice of means for overcoming them; and a ruler full of the spirit of improvement is warranted in the use of any expedients that will attain an end, perhaps otherwise unattainable. Despotism is a legitimate mode of government in dealing with barbarians, provided the end be their improvement, and the means justified by actually affecting that end. Liberty, as a principle, has no application to any state of things anterior to the time when mankind have become capable of being improved by free and equal discussion. Until then, there is nothing for them but implicit obedience to an Akbar or a Charlemagne,[1] if they are so fortunate as to find one. But as soon as mankind have attained the capacity of being guided to their own improvement by conviction or persuasion (a period long since reached in all nations with whom we need here concern ourselves), compulsion, either in the direct form or in that of pains and penalties for non-compliance, is no longer admissible as a means to their own good, and justifiable only for the security of others.

It is proper to state that I forego any advantage which could be derived to my argument from the idea of abstract right, as a thing independent of utility. I regard utility as the ultimate appeal on all ethical questions; but it must be utility in the largest sense, grounded on the permanent interests of a man as a progressive being. Those interests, I contend, authorise the subjection of individual spontaneity to external control, only in respect to those actions of each, which concern the interest of other people. If any one does an act hurtful to others, there is a *prima facie* case for punishing him, by law, or, where legal penalties are not safely applicable, by general disapprobation. There are also many positive acts for the benefit of others, which he may rightfully be compelled to perform; such as to give evidence in a court of justice; to bear his fair share in the common defence, or in any other joint work necessary to the interest of the society of which he enjoys the protection; and to perform certain acts of individual beneficence, such as saving a fellow creature's life, or interposing to protect the defenceless against ill-usage, things which whenever it is obviously a man's duty to do, he may rightfully be made responsible to society for not doing. A person may cause evil to others not only by his actions but by his inaction, and in either case he is justly accountable to them for the injury. The latter case, it is true, requires a much more cautious exercise of compulsion than the former. To make any one answerable for doing evil to others is the rule; to make him answerable for not preventing evil is, comparatively speaking, the exception. Yet there are many

---

[1] an Akbar or a Charlemagne: Akbar (1542–1605), greatest of the Mughal emperors in India; noted for his administrative reforms and his policy of religious tolerance. Charlemagne, also Charles the Great or Charles I (742–814), king of the Franks and emperor of the Romans.

cases clear enough and grave enough to justify that exception. In all things which regard the external relations of the individual, he is *de jure*[2] amenable to those whose interests are concerned, and, if need be, to society as their protector. There are often good reasons for not holding him to the responsibility; but these reasons must arise from the special expediencies of the case: either because it is a kind of case in which he is on the whole likely to act better, when left to his own discretion, than when controlled in any way in which society have it in their power to control him; or because the attempt to exercise control would produce other evils, greater than those which it would prevent. When such reasons as these preclude the enforcement of responsibility, the conscience of the agent himself should step into the vacant judgment seat, and protect those interests of others which have no external protection; judging himself all the more rigidly, because the case does not admit of his being made accountable to the judgment of his fellow creatures.

But there is a sphere of action in which society, as distinguished from the individual, has, if any, only an indirect interest; comprehending all that portion of a person's life and conduct which affects only himself, or if it also affects others, only with their free, voluntary, and undeceived consent and participation. When I say only himself, I mean directly, and in the first instance; for whatever affects himself, may affect others through himself; and the objection which may be grounded on this contingency, will receive consideration in the sequel. This, then, is the appropriate region of human liberty. It comprises, first, the inward domain of consciousness; demanding liberty of conscience in the most comprehensive sense; liberty of thought and feeling; absolute freedom of opinion and sentiment on all subjects, practical or speculative, scientific, moral, or theological. The liberty of expressing and publishing opinions may seem to fall under a different principle, since it belongs to that part of the conduct of an individual which concerns other people; but, being almost of as much importance as the liberty of thought itself, and resting in great part on the same reasons, is practically inseparable from it. Secondly, the principle requires liberty of tastes and pursuits; of framing the plan of our life to suit our own character; of doing as we like, subject to such consequences as may follow: without impediment from our fellow creatures, so long as what we do does not harm them, even though they should think our conduct foolish, perverse, or wrong. Thirdly, from this liberty of each individual, follows the liberty, within the same limits, of combination among individuals; freedom to unite, for any purpose not involving harm to others: the persons combining being supposed to be of full age, and not forced or deceived.

No society in which these liberties are not, on the whole, respected, is free, whatever may be its form of government; and none is completely free in which they do not exist absolute and unqualified. The only freedom which deserves the name, is that of pursuing our own good in our own way, so long as we do not attempt to deprive others of theirs, or impede their efforts to obtain it. Each is the proper guardian of his own health, whether bodily, *or* mental and spiritual. Mankind are

---

[2] *de jure:* According to the law.

greater gainers by suffering each other to live as seems good to themselves, than by compelling each to live as seems good to the rest.

Though this doctrine is anything but new, and, to some persons, may have the air of a truism, there is no doctrine which stands more directly opposed to the general tendency of existing opinion and practice. Society has expended fully as much effort in the attempt (according to its lights) to compel people to conform to its notions of personal as of social excellence. The ancient commonwealths thought themselves entitled to practise, and the ancient philosophers countenanced, the regulation of every part of private conduct by public authority, on the ground that the State had a deep interest in the whole bodily and mental discipline of every one of its citizens; a mode of thinking which may have been admissible in small republics surrounded by powerful enemies, in constant peril of being subverted by foreign attack or internal commotion, and to which even a short interval of relaxed energy and self-command might so easily be fatal that they could not afford to wait for the salutary permanent effects of freedom. In the modern world, the greater size of political communities, and, above all, the separation between spiritual and temporal authority (which placed the direction of men's consciences in other hands than those which controlled their worldly affairs), prevented so great an interference by law in the details of private life; but the engines of moral repression have been wielded more strenuously against divergence from the reigning opinion in self-regarding, than even in social matters; religion, the most powerful of the elements which have entered into the formation of moral feeling, having almost always been governed either by the ambition of a hierarchy, seeking control over every department of human conduct, or by the spirit of Puritanism. And some of those modern reformers who have placed themselves in strongest opposition to the religions of the past, have been noway behind either churches or sects in their assertion of the right of spiritual domination: M. Comte,[3] in particular, whose social system, as unfolded in his *Système de Politique Positive,* aims at establishing (though by moral more than by legal appliances) a despotism of society over the individual, surpassing anything contemplated in the political ideal of the most rigid disciplinarian among the ancient philosophers.

Apart from the peculiar tenets of individual thinkers, there is also in the world at large an increasing inclination to stretch unduly the powers of society over the individual, both by the force of opinion and even by that of legislation; and as the tendency of all the changes taking place in the world is to strengthen society, and diminish the power of the individual, this encroachment is not one of the evils which tend spontaneously to disappear, but, on the contrary, to grow more and more formidable. The disposition of mankind, whether as rulers or as fellow-citizens, to impose their own opinions and inclinations as a rule of conduct on others, is so energetically supported by some of the best and by some of the worst feelings incident to human nature, that it is hardly ever kept under restraint by anything but want of power; and as the power is not declining, but growing, unless a strong

---

[3] Comte: August Comte (1798–1857), French philosopher and founder of the Positivist school, whose central theory related the stages in the development of science to the stages of social evolution.

barrier of moral conviction can be raised against the mischief, we must expect, in the present circumstances of the world, to see it increase. . . .

It was pointed out in an early part of this Essay, that the liberty of the individual, in things wherein the individual is alone concerned, implies a corresponding liberty in any number of individuals to regulate by mutual agreement such things as regard them jointly, and regard no persons but themselves. This question presents no difficulty, so long as the will of all the persons implicated remains unaltered; but since that will may change, it is often necessary, even in things in which they alone are concerned, that they should enter into engagements with one another; and when they do, it is fit, as a general rule, that those engagements should be kept. Yet, in the laws, probably, of every country, this general rule has some exceptions. Not only persons are not held to engagements which violate the rights of third parties, but it is sometimes considered a sufficient reason for releasing them from an engagement, that it is injurious to themselves. In this and most other civilised countries, for example, an engagement by which a person should sell himself, or allow himself to be sold, as a slave, would be null and void; neither enforced by law nor by opinion. The ground for thus limiting his power of voluntarily disposing of his own lot in life, is apparent, and is very clearly seen in this extreme case. The reason for not interfering, unless for the sake of others, with a person's voluntary acts, is consideration for his liberty. His voluntary choice is evidence that what he so chooses is desirable, or at least endurable, to him, and his good is on the whole best provided for by allowing him to take his own means of pursuing it. But by selling himself for a slave, he abdicates his liberty; he foregoes any future use of it beyond that single act. He therefore defeats, in his own case, the very purpose which is the justification of allowing him to dispose of himself. He is no longer free; but is thenceforth in a position which has no longer the presumption in its favour, that would be afforded by his voluntarily remaining in it. The principle of freedom cannot require that he should be free not to be free. It is not freedom to be allowed to alienate his freedom. These reasons, the force of which is so conspicuous in this peculiar case, are evidently of far wider application; yet a limit is everywhere set to them by the necessities of life, which continually require, not indeed that we should resign our freedom, but that we should consent to this and the other limitation of it. The principle, however, which demands uncontrolled freedom of action in all that concerns only the agents themselves, requires that those who have become bound to one another, in things which concern no third party, should be able to release one another from the engagement: and even without such voluntary release there are perhaps no contracts or engagements, except those that relate to money or money's worth, of which one can venture to say that there ought to be no liberty whatever of retractation.

SWAMI VIVEKANANDA

1863–1902

Swami Vivekananda
meditating

*Portrait of the Hindu
saint and leader of the
Vedanta movement.
(Ramakrishna-
Vivekananda Center
of New York)*

Hindu saint and leader of the Vedanta movement in the late nineteenth century, Swami Vivekananda asserts that freedom is the "goal of all nature." He contends that freedom does not depend on institutional guarantees but rather derives from the individual's inner awareness. The divergent concepts of freedom in Vivekananda and John Stuart Mill are reflected in the conflict in Tagore's "Broken Ties."

The selections from Swami Vivekananda, written in English, were taken from a selection of his writings, *Living at the Source,* edited by Ann Myren and Dorothy Madison (1993). Their selections came from *The Complete Works of Swami Vivekananda,* 8 vols., published in Calcutta (1884–87).

FROM

On Freedom

The soul cries ever, "Freedom, O Freedom!" With the conception of God as a perfectly free Being, man cannot rest eternally in this bondage. Higher he must go, and unless the struggle were for himself, he would think it too severe. Man says to himself, "I am a born slave, I am bound; nevertheless, there is a Being who is not bound by nature. He is free and Master of nature." The conception of God, therefore, is as essential and as fundamental a part of mind as is the idea of bondage. Both are the outcome of the idea of freedom. There cannot be life, even in the plant, without the idea of freedom. (1:335–36) . . .

The awakening of the soul to its bondage and its effort to stand up and assert itself—this is called life. Success in this struggle is called evolution. The eventual triumph, when all the slavery is blown away, is called salvation, nirvana, freedom. Everything in the universe is struggling for liberty. When I am bound by nature, by name and form, by time, space, and causality, I do not know what I truly am. But even in this bondage my real Self is not completely lost. I strain against the bonds; one by one they break, and I become conscious of my innate grandeur. Then comes complete liberation. I attain to the clearest and fullest consciousness of myself—

I know that I am the infinite spirit, the master of nature, not its slave. Beyond all differentiation and combination, beyond space, time, and causation, I am that I am. (8:249)

The goal to be reached is freedom. I disagree with the idea that freedom is obedience to the laws of nature. I do not understand what that means. According to the history of human progress, it is disobedience to nature that has constituted that progress. (8:257) . . .

To advance oneself toward freedom—physical, mental, and spiritual—and help others to do so, is the supreme prize of man. Those social rules which stand in the way of the unfoldment of this freedom are injurious, and steps should be taken to destroy them speedily. Those institutions should be encouraged by which men advance in the path of freedom. (5:147)

Man must have education. They speak of democracy, of the equality of all men, these days. But how will a man know he is equal with all? He must have a strong brain, a clear mind free of nonsensical ideas; he must pierce through the mass of superstitions encrusting his mind to the pure truth that is in his inmost Self. Then he will know that all perfections, all powers are already within himself, that these have not to be given him by others. When he realizes this, he becomes free that moment, he achieves equality. He also realizes that everyone else is equally as perfect as he, and he does not have to exercise any power, physical, mental, or moral, over his brother men. He abandons the idea that there was ever any man who was lower than himself. Then he can talk of equality; not until then. (8:94)

If you think that you are bound, you remain bound; you make your own bondage. If you know that you are free, you are free this moment. This is knowledge, knowledge of freedom. Freedom is the goal of all nature. (2:462)

ॐ MUHAMMAD IQBAL
1877–1938

Poet and philosopher of the Islamic revival in India, Muhammad Iqbal was the greatest Urdu writer of his time. Although he died before India gained independence in 1947, his vision of an Islamic community based on righteousness and equality inspired Muslim intellectuals and earned him the reputation as the spiritual founder of Pakistan. Educated in Europe, Iqbal blended Western ideas with classical Islamic influences, especially the poet Rumi, to construct an activist philosophy that advocated self-development as a way to overcome the injustices of colonialism, capitalist exploitation, and the imbalances between rich and poor, East and West.

The translation is by V. G. Kiernan from his *Poems from Iqbal* (1955).

❧ Freedom

Translated by V. G. Kiernan

The freeman's veins are firm as veins of granite;
The bondman's weak as tendrils of the vine,
And his heart too despairing and repining—
The free heart has life's tingling breath to fan it.
Quick pulse, clear vision, are the freeman's treasure;
The unfree, to kindness and affection dead,
Has no more wealth than tears of his own shedding
And those glib words he has in such good measure.

Bondman and free can never come to accord:
One is the heavens' lackey, one their lord.

❧ RABINDRANATH TAGORE
1861–1941

Much like the tales collected in *The Thousand and One Nights,* Tagore's short story "Emancipation" involves a merchant, a princess, and the cruel agents of a king. It is not a realistic story describing Indian life in Tagore's time, yet the author may have been writing on a metaphorical level about the emancipation of his nation from British colonial rule or from entrenched traditions, such as the Indian caste system. An internationalist who sought to blend the best of East and West in modern India, Tagore was distrustful of the intense nationalism that accompanied the Indian independence movement, an ambivalence that may help to explain this enigmatic parable.

The translator, not identified in the first and only American edition in 1925, was probably a similar group to that Tagore identified in the American edition of *The Hungry Stones and Other Stories,* which included Tagore himself, the Reverend E. J. Thompson, C. F. Andrews, Panna Lal Basu, Prabhat Kumar Mukerji, and the sister Nivedita. Clearly Tagore had an important role in translating his works into English.

❧ Emancipation

"Theft from the king's treasury!" The cry ran through the town. The thief must be found, or there will be trouble for the officer of the guards.

Vajrasen, a stranger from a foreign port, came to sell horses in the town, and, robbed by a band of robbers of all his earnings, was lying in a ruined temple outside the walls. They charged him with the theft, chained him, and led him through the streets to the prison.

Proud Shyama, of a perilous charm, sat in her balcony idly watching the passing crowd. Suddenly she shuddered, and cried to her attendant: "Alas, who is that god-like young man with a noble face, led in chains like a common thief? Ask the officer in my name to bring him in before me."

The chief of the guards came with the prisoner, and said to Shyama: "Your favour is untimely, my lady; I must hasten to do the king's bidding."

Vajrasen quickly raised his head, and broke out: "What caprice is this of yours, woman, to bring me in from the street to mock me with your cruel curiosity?"

"Mock you!" cried Shyama; "I could gladly take your chains upon my limbs in exchange for my jewels."

Then turning to the officer, she said: "Take all the money I have, and set him free."

He bowed, and said: "It cannot be. A victim we must have to stay the king's wrath."

"I ask only two days' respite for the prisoner," urged Shyama. The officer smiled, and consented.

On the end of his second night in prison, Vajrasen said his prayers, and sat waiting for his last moment, when suddenly the door opened, and the woman appeared with a lamp in her hand, and at her signal the guard unchained the prisoner.

"You have come to me with that lamp, merciful woman," said he, "like the dawn with her morning star after a night of delirious fever."

"Merciful indeed," Shyama cried, and broke out in wild laughter, till tears came with a burst, and she sobbed, and said: "There is no stone brick in this prison-tower harder than this woman's heart." And clutching the prisoner's hand she dragged him out of the gates.

On the Varuna's bank the sun rose. A boat was waiting at the landing. "Come to the boat with me, stranger youth," Shyama said. "Only know that I have cut all bonds, and I drift in the same boat with you."

Swiftly the boat glided on. Merrily sang the birds. "Tell me, my love," asked Vajrasen, "what untold wealth did you spend to buy my freedom?"

"Hush, not now," said Shyama.

Morning wore on to noon. Village women had gone back home with their clothes dripping from their bath, and pitchers filled with water. Marketing was over. The village path glared in the sun all lonely.

In the warm gusts of the noontide wind Shyama's veil dropped from her face. Vajrasen murmured in her ears: "You freed me from a bond that was brief to bind me in a bond everlasting. Let me know how it was done." The woman drew her veil over her face, and said: "Not now, my beloved."

The day waned, and it darkened. The breeze died away. The crescent moon glimmered feebly at the edge of the steel-black water.

Shyama sat in the dark, resting her head on the youth's shoulder. Her hair fell loose on his arms.

"What I did for you was hard, beloved," she said in a faint whisper, "but it is harder to tell you. I shall tell it in a few words. It was the love-sick boy Uttiya who took your place, charging himself with the theft, and making me a present of his life. My greatest sin has been committed for the love of you, my best beloved."

While she spoke the crescent moon had set. The stillness of the forest was heavy with the sleep of countless birds.

Slowly the youth's arm slipped from the woman's waist. Silence round them became hard and cold as stone.

Suddenly the woman fell at his feet, and clung to his knee crying: "Forgive me, my love. Leave it to my God to punish me for my sin."

Snatching his feet away, Vajrasen hoarsely cried: "That my life should be bought by the price of a sin! That every breath of mine should be accursed!"

He stood up, and leapt from the boat on the bank, and entered the forest. He walked on and on till the path closed and the dense trees, tangled with creepers, stopped him with fantastic gestures.

Tired, he sat on the ground. But who was it that followed him in silence, the long dark way, and stood at his back like a phantom?

"Will you not leave me?" shouted Vajrasen.

In a moment the woman fell upon him with an impetuous flood of caresses; with her tumbling hair and trailing robes, with her showering kisses and panting breath she covered him all over.

In a voice choked with pent-up tears, she said: "No, no; I shall never leave you. I have sinned for you. Strike me, if you will; kill me with your own hands."

The still blackness of the forest shivered for a moment; a horror ran through the twisting roots of trees underground. A groan and a smothered breath rose through the night, and a body fell down upon the withered leaves.

The morning sun flashed on the far-away spire of the temple when Vajrasen came out of the woods. He wandered in the hot sun the whole day by the river on the sandy waste, and never rested for a moment.

In the evening he went back aimlessly to the boat. There on the bed lay an anklet. He clutched it, and pressed it to his heart till it bruised him. He fell prone upon the blue mantle left lying in a heap in the corner, hid his face in its folds, and from its silken touch and evasive fragrance struggled to absorb into his being the memory of a dear living body.

The night shook with a tense and tingling silence. The moon disappeared behind the trees. Vajrasen stood up, and stretched out his arms towards the woods, and called: "Come, my love, come."

Suddenly a figure came out of the darkness, and stood on the brink of the water. "Come, love, come."

"I have come, my beloved. Your dear hands failed to kill me. It is my doom to live."

Shyama came, and stood before the youth. He looked at her face, he moved a step to take her in his arms—then thrust her away with both hands, and cried: "Why, oh why did you come back?"

He shut his eyes, turning his face, and said: "Go, go; leave me."

For a minute the woman stood silent before she knelt at his feet and bowed low. Then she rose, and went up the river-bank, and vanished in the vague of the woods like a dream merging into sleep; and Vajrasen, with aching heart, sat silent in the boat.

❧ HERMAN MELVILLE
1819–1891

Herman Melville
in Headshoulders
Photo, c. 1870s
to 1880s
*Melville in middle
age. (Bettman/
Corbis)*

In the span of the six years from 1850 to 1855, in a decade characterized by F. O. Matthiewson as the American Renaissance, Emerson published *Representative Men* (1850), Thoreau, *Walden* (1854), Hawthorne, *The Scarlet Letter* (1850) and *The House of Seven Gables* (1851), Harriet Beecher Stowe, *Uncle Tom's Cabin* (1852), and Whitman, *Leaves of Grass* (1855). It's hard to find any six-year period with a richer trove of literary treasures. And that is without counting what may arguably be the most important American literary work of the time, Herman Melville's *Moby Dick,* published in 1851, when Melville was only thirty-two years old. This formidable work, with its encyclopedic treatment of whaling and its philosophic engagement with the big questions of life, seems to be the work of a much older writer. Thoroughly American in its ambitious and brash philosophizing, *Moby Dick* may come closer than any other work of American literature to the elusive status of the "great American novel." It is at the same time one of the monuments of world literature, transcending its origins as an adventure story by an American sailor to become one of the great philosophic novels of the nineteenth century, along with Dostoevsky's *The Brothers Karamazov* (1879–80), Tolstoy's *War and Peace* (1866–69), and Dickens's *Little Dorrit* (1855).

Melville's Childhood.   Although he was descended from prominent colonial American families, Herman Melville was not a child of privilege. His father, a dry goods merchant, died bankrupt when Herman was twelve, and his mother took him, his elder brother, **Gansevoort**, and six younger children to Albany where the family could live more cheaply than in New York City. There Herman began a series of occupations by working six days a week as a clerk in the New York State Bank. In his teens he went on to clerk in his brother's store, take care of his uncle's farm, teach at a district school, and earn a certificate in surveying and engineering. He also attended school for short periods during these years and began writing, submitting short articles to Albany-area newspapers.

Education on a Whaleboat.   In 1839, when he was twenty, Melville began his real education when he signed on as a hired boy on the *St. Lawrence* and sailed to Liverpool, a trip he later wrote about in *Redburn, His First Voyage* (1849). When he returned to the States, he briefly tried teaching again and took an exploratory trip west to look over opportunities there before returning to seafaring. In 1841 he joined the crew of the whaler *Acushnet* bound for the Pacific. During the next four years, on a series of voyages and stopovers in the Pacific, he gathered the experiences that he would later draw on in much of his literary work. He could claim, as Ishmael, the narrator of *Moby Dick,* does, that "a whale-ship was my Yale College and my Harvard." He stayed with the *Acushnet* for eighteen months before jumping ship in the Marquesas Islands, curious to confirm the natives' notoriety for cannibalism and sexual license. His first novel, *Typee: A Peep at Polynesian Life* (1846), was based on the several weeks he spent on those islands. Shipping out on an Australian whaler, he was briefly imprisoned in Tahiti with other members of the crew for failing to carry out shipboard duties. He lingered in Tahiti and spent time in Hawaii between other voyages before enlisting in the American navy, where he was assigned to the frigate *United States* and a fourteen-month voyage to Boston.

Early Work.   From his experiences during these seafaring years, Melville created nearly all his fiction. After *Typee* (1846), Melville wrote **Omoo:** *A Narrative of Adventures in the South Seas* (1847), which tells of his voyage to Tahiti and his imprisonment there. *Redburn* is an account of his first voyage to Liverpool, and *White Jacket* (1850) is about his time aboard the *United States*. These early works earned Melville a reputation as a travel writer and a novelist of the sea, but he had larger ambitions. In 1849 he had written *Mardi,* which turned sea travel into political and religious allegory, an experiment that did not sit well with his readers. Nevertheless, Melville turned again to allegory in 1851 in his masterpiece, *Moby Dick,* a novel that uses the genre of a seagoing adventure story to tell an allegorical and symbolic tale about a young man's search for the meaning of life and community.

oh-MOO

Melville and Hawthorne.   Melville's maturation from a travel writer to a great symbolic novelist owed something to his relationship with Nathaniel Hawthorne. After he married in 1847, Melville moved to a farm outside Pittsfield, Masssachusetts, near the home of Hawthorne. Hawthorne at the time was America's premier novelist, an artist whom Melville described as the "American Shakespeare" and to whom he would dedicate *Moby Dick.* For Melville, his mentor's works were models of philosophical novels that treated serious themes, such as the relation of good and evil, symbolically. Hawthorne found in Melville an honest searcher for whom the great philosophical issues were open and troubling questions. "He can neither believe, nor be comfortable in his unbelief," Hawthorne wrote of Melville in *Notebooks;* "If he were a religious man, he would be one of the most truly religious and reverential; he has a very high and noble nature, and better worth of immortality than most of us."

Moby Dick.   Melville first adopted a symbolic method in his works in the late 1840s. The method reached its peak in *Moby Dick* — a story of the whaling ship *Pequod,* the maniacal Captain Ahab, and the captain's obsessive search for a great white whale. With a crew recruited from all corners of the earth, Ahab searches across the immensity of the Pacific Ocean for the whale that will ultimately destroy him, his ship, and all the members of his crew except for Ishmael, the one survivor who lives to tell the story. The novel is both a compendium of information about whales and whaling and a work of symbolic imagery that reminds the reader

www   For more information about Melville and "Bartelby the Scrivener," see *World Literature Online* at bedfordstmartins .com/worldlit.

that this is much more than an adventure story: Ahab's artificial leg,
made from the ivory of a whale's jawbone; a crew of cannibals and Pacific
Islanders who perform strange pagan rites; a harpoon tempered in the
blood of the pagan harpooners; a coffin that serves as a sea chest. The
overriding central symbol, Moby Dick, the name Ahab gives to the white
whale, comprises the contradictory possibilities of the human search for

meaning and the inevitable frustration of that quest: The white whale embodies both good and evil, God and meaninglessness, creation and destruction.

Moby Dick was not enthusiastically received when it first appeared, and writing it may have taken more out of Melville than even he knew. After 1851 his productivity declined and he was troubled by periods of depression and despair. The best of his later works were *The Confidence Man* (1857), a satire of American attitudes and morals set on a Mississippi riverboat, *The Piazza Tales* (1856), a collection of short stories that included "Bartleby," and the posthumously published novella *Billy Budd* (1924). In the mid-1860s, troubled by the lack of acceptance for his work and in need of money, Melville largely gave up writing and took a job as a customs inspector that he held for nineteen years.

Bartleby. "Bartleby the Scrivener," written after *Moby Dick* in 1853, is often read as an autobiographical story about a writer, a scrivener, who faces a psychological "wall" and "prefers" not to write. Melville's own psychological despair upon completing *Moby Dick* and learning that his readers failed to comprehend or accept the work became the material out of which he fashioned this parable of the enigmatic scrivener and his employer. If "Bartleby" is an autobiographical narrative, it is one told not with self-pity but with a gallows humor that turns the Dead Letter Office into a literary graveyard and the Tombs into Bartleby's Westminster Abbey.[1]

Whatever its sources in Melville's own life, "Bartleby" has a symbolic richness comparable to that of *Moby Dick*. Commentators have found in it a satiric commentary on the superficiality of American life, an attack on lawyers, a story of class struggle, a critique of materialistic capitalism, an affirmation of the civil disobedience and passive resistance advocated by Thoreau and Gandhi, a biography of a saintlike Christ figure, a clinical study of a madman, and a story that prefigures the work of Kafka and Camus[2] in the twentieth century. There is some truth to each of these interpretations and to others too numerous to catalog here.

Melville first published "Bartleby" anonymously, and his technique in the story seems designed to maintain his anonymity. By telling the story through the lawyer, Melville hides his own intentions. Consequently, critics have debated whether Melville was sympathetic with his narrator or intent on satirizing him. Some have found the lawyer charitable and understanding; others consider him conventional and hardhearted. Through point of view, Melville manages to conceal himself and his attitude toward the story and to render the narrator as enigmatic as Bartleby. Clearly "Bartleby," like *Moby Dick,* is a work intended, as Keats says of his mysterious Grecian urn, to "tease us out of thought" by

> It is strange how he persists — and has persisted ever since I knew him, and probably long before — in wondering to-and-fro over these deserts, as dismal and monotonous as the sand hills amid which we were sitting.
>
> – NATHANIEL HAWTHORNE, *Notebooks*

---

[1] **Westminster Abbey:** A cathedral in London where the famous and distinguished are buried.

[2] **Kafka and Camus:** Franz Kafka (1883–1924), German novelist and short story writer of enigmatic parables of the oppressiveness of modern life, such as *The Trial* (1925); Albert Camus (1913–1960), French Algerian existential novelist whose characters face an absurd and meaningless world, as in *The Stranger* (1942).

eluding easy classification or interpretation. In the end Bartleby remains uniquely himself, an unforgettable character whose "I would prefer not to" becomes as lodged in our consciousness as Scrooge's "Bah, humbug" in Dickens's *Christmas Carol*. Bartleby contradicts conventional expectations: His negativity makes him visible and his passivity makes him heroic.

■ CONNECTIONS

In the World: Heroes and Heroines, p. 179; Camus, *The Stranger* (Book 6). Consider Bartleby in light of the discussions of heroism in *In the World:* Heroes and Heroines. Is Bartleby heroic in refusing to act?

In the World: Society and Its Discontents, p. 663; Goethe, *Faust*, p. 29. Bartleby's illness—his forlornness and despair—is seen as lunacy by his coworkers and employer, but could it also be seen as the "sickness unto death" that Kierkegaard defines as the first stage in salvation? Consider Bartleby's end in relation to Faust's. In what ways are their final days triumphant?

Fuentes, *The Prisoner of Las Lomas* (Book 6). Part of our difficulty in understanding Bartleby stems from the fact that the narrator himself doesn't comprehend him. Melville could be said to have chosen the lawyer as his narrator in order to create mystery. Why does the narrator have difficulty understanding and dealing with Bartleby? Is he deluded? Compare him with Fuentes's narrator in *The Prisoner of Las Lomas*. Is that narrator deluded? What about their individual situations does each narrator have difficulty comprehending?

■ FURTHER RESEARCH

Biography
Howard, Leon. *Herman Melville: A Biography.* 1951.
Parker, Hershel. *Herman Melville: A Biography.* 1996.
Robertson-Lorant, Laurie. *Melville: A Biography.* 1996.

Criticism
Bryant, John. *A Companion to Melville Studies.* 1986.
Fredricks, Nancy. *Melville's Art of Democracy.* 1995.
Inge, M. Thomas, ed. *Bartleby the Inscrutable: A Collection of Commentary on Herman Melville's Tale "Bartleby the Scrivener."* 1979.
McCall, Dan. *The Silence of Bartleby.* 1989.
Vincent, Howard P., ed. "Bartleby the Scrivener: *The Melville Annual / A Symposium.*" 1965.

■ PRONUNCIATION

Acushnet: uh-KUSH-net
Gansevoort: GANS-vohrt
Omoo: oh-MOO

⌒ Bartleby the Scrivener

I am a rather elderly man. The nature of my avocations, for the last thirty years, has brought me into more than ordinary contact with what would seem an interesting and somewhat singular set of men, of whom, as yet, nothing, that I know of, has ever been written — I mean, the law-copyists, or scriveners. I have known very many of them, professionally and privately, and, if I pleased, could relate divers histories, at which good-natured gentlemen might smile, and sentimental souls might weep. But I waive the biographies of all other scriveners, for a few passages in the life of Bartleby, who was a scrivener, the strangest I ever saw, or heard of. While, of other law-copyists, I might write the complete life, of Bartleby nothing of that sort can be done. I believe that no materials exist for a full and satisfactory biography of this man. It is an irreparable loss to literature. Bartleby was one of those beings of whom nothing is ascertainable, except from the original sources, and, in his case, those are very small. What my own astonished eyes saw of Bartleby, *that* is all I know of him, except, indeed, one vague report, which will appear in the sequel.

Ere introducing the scrivener, as he first appeared to me, it is fit I make some mention of myself, my *employés,* my business, my chambers, and general surroundings; because some such description is indispensable to an adequate understanding of the chief character about to be presented. Imprimis:[1] I am a man who, from his youth upwards, has been filled with a profound conviction that the easiest way of life is the best. Hence, though I belong to a profession proverbially energetic and nervous, even to turbulence, at times, yet nothing of that sort have I ever suffered to invade my peace. I am one of those unambitious lawyers who never addresses a jury, or in any way draw down public applause; but, in the cool tranquillity of a snug retreat, do a snug business among rich men's bonds, and mortgages, and title-deeds.

"Bartleby the Scrivener."   First appearing anonymously in *Putnam's Magazine* in 1853, "Bartleby" was Melville's first published story. Its title has led many critics to equate the occupation of scrivener with that of writer and to interpret the story's Wall Street setting as indicative of writer's block. Wall Street, located in the world of commerce, is a realm totally outside the otherworldly one that Bartleby inhabits. If the reader enters Melville's story with conventional expectations, he may, like the narrator, find himself baffled by, but at the same time drawn in and sympathetic toward, the strange scrivener. Being told almost nothing about Bartleby's life beyond what the narrator can observe, the reader, like the narrator, is forced to understand Bartleby on his own terms, with no excuses from his past or explanations from his creator to rationalize his troubling presence.

To make sense of the story the reader must evaluate the narrator and the reliability of his account of Bartleby. The narrator's history, his language, and the changes in his attitude toward his clerk may help in defining the terms of the puzzle. But in the end Bartleby may remain enigmatic, both alter ego to the narrator and social outcast, passive and negatively self-assertive, victim and hero.

---

[1] Imprimis: In the first place.

All who know me, consider me an eminently *safe* man. The late John Jacob Astor,[2] a personage little given to poetic enthusiasm, had no hesitation in pronouncing my first grand point to be prudence; my next, method. I do not speak it in vanity, but simply record the fact, that I was not unemployed in my profession by the late John Jacob Astor; a name which, I admit, I love to repeat; for it hath a rounded and orbicular sound to it, and rings like unto bullion. I will freely add, that I was not insensible to the late John Jacob Astor's good opinion.

Some time prior to the period at which this little history begins, my avocations had been largely increased. The good old office, now extinct in the State of New York, of a Master in Chancery, had been conferred upon me. It was not a very arduous office, but very pleasantly remunerative. I seldom lose my temper; much more seldom indulge in dangerous indignation at wrongs and outrages; but I must be permitted to be rash here and declare, that I consider the sudden and violent abrogation of the office of Master in Chancery,[3] by the new Constitution, as a—— premature act; inasmuch as I had counted upon a lifelease of the profits, whereas I only received those of a few short years. But this is by the way.

My chambers were up stairs, at No. — Wall Street. At one end, they looked upon the white wall of the interior of a spacious skylight shaft, penetrating the building from top to bottom.

This view might have been considered rather tame than otherwise, deficient in what landscape painters call "life." But, if so, the view from the other end of my chambers offered, at least, a contrast, if nothing more. In that direction, my windows commanded an unobstructed view of a lofty brick wall, black by age and everlasting shade; which wall required no spyglass to bring out its lurking beauties, but, for the benefit of all near-sighted spectators, was pushed up to within ten feet of my window-panes. Owing to the great height of the surrounding buildings, and my chambers being on the second floor, the interval between this wall and mine not a little resembled a huge square cistern.

At the period just preceding the advent of Bartleby, I had two persons as copyists in my employment, and a promising lad as an office-boy. First, Turkey; second, Nippers; third, Ginger Nut. These may seem names, the like of which are not usually found in the Directory. In truth, they were nicknames, mutually conferred upon each other by my three clerks, and were deemed expressive of their respective persons or characters. Turkey was a short, pursy Englishman, of about my own age — that is, somewhere not far from sixty. In the morning, one might say, his face was of a fine florid hue, but after twelve o'clock, meridian — his dinner hour — it blazed like a grate full of Christmas coals; and continued blazing — but, as it were, with a gradual wane — till six o'clock, P.M., or thereabouts; after which, I saw no more of the proprietor of the face, which, gaining its meridian with the sun, seemed to set with

---

[2] John Jacob Astor: (1768–1848) Businessman who made a fortune in the fur trade and was the wealthiest landlord in New York City in 1848.

[3] Master in Chancery: When the new constitution abolished the position of Master of Chancery, the narrator lost a sinecure — an undemanding salaried job — that had guaranteed him a steady income.

it, to rise, culminate, and decline the following day, with the like regularity and un-diminished glory. There are many singular coincidences I have known in the course of my life, not the least among which was the fact, that, exactly when Turkey dis-played his fullest beams from his red and radiant countenance, just then, too, at that critical moment, began the daily period when I considered his business capacities as seriously disturbed for the remainder of the twenty-four hours. Not that he was absolutely idle, or averse to business then; far from it. The difficulty was, he was apt to be altogether too energetic. There was a strange, inflamed, flurried, flighty reck-lessness of activity about him. He would be incautious in dipping his pen into his inkstand. All his blots upon my documents were dropped there after twelve o'clock, meridian. Indeed, not only would he be reckless, and sadly given to making blots in the afternoon, but, some days, he went further, and was rather noisy. At such times, too, his face flamed with augmented blazonry, as if cannel coal had been heaped on anthracite. He made an unpleasant racket with his chair; spilled his sand-box; in mending his pens, impatiently split them all to pieces, and threw them on the floor in a sudden passion; stood up, and leaned over his table, boxing his papers about in a most indecorous manner, very sad to behold in an elderly man like him. Neverthe-less, as he was in many ways a most valuable person to me, and all the time before twelve o'clock meridian, was the quickest, steadiest creature, too, accomplishing a great deal of work in a style not easily to be matched — for these reasons, I was will-ing to overlook his eccentricities, though, indeed, occasionally, I remonstrated with him. I did this very gently, however, because, though the civilest, nay, the blandest and most reverential of men in the morning, yet, in the afternoon, he was disposed, upon provocation, to be slightly rash with his tongue — in fact, insolent. Now, valu-ing his morning services as I did, and resolved not to lose them — yet, at the same time, made uncomfortable by his inflamed way after twelve o'clock — and being a man of peace, unwilling by my admonitions to call forth unseemly retorts from him, I took upon me, one Saturday noon (he was always worse on Saturdays) to hint to him, very kindly, that, perhaps, now that he was growing old, it might be well to abridge his labors; in short, he need not come to my chambers after twelve o'clock, but, dinner over, had best go home to his lodgings, and rest himself till teatime. But no; he insisted upon his afternoon devotions. His countenance became intolerably fervid, as he oratorically assured me — gesticulating with a long ruler at the other end of the room — that if his services in the morning were useful, how indispensa-ble, then, in the afternoon?

"With submission, sir," said Turkey, on this occasion, "I consider myself your right-hand man. In the morning I but marshal and deploy my columns; but in the afternoon I put myself at their head, and gallantly charge the foe, thus" — and he made a violent thrust with the ruler.

"But the blots, Turkey," intimated I.

"True; but, with submission, sir, behold these hairs! I am getting old. Surely, sir, a blot or two of a warm afternoon is not to be severely urged against gray hairs. Old age — even if it blot the page — is honorable. With submission, sir, we *both* are get-ting old."

This appeal to my fellow feeling was hardly to be resisted. At all events, I saw that go he would not. So, I made up my mind to let him stay, resolving, nevertheless, to see to it that, during the afternoon, he had to do with my less important papers.

Nippers, the second on my list, was a whiskered, sallow, and upon the whole, rather piratical-looking young man, of about five and twenty. I always deemed him the victim of two evil powers—ambition and indigestion. The ambition was evinced by a certain impatience of the duties of a mere copyist, an unwarrantable usurpation of strictly professional affairs, such as the original drawing up of legal documents. The indigestion seemed betokened in an occasional nervous testiness and grinning irritability, causing the teeth to audibly grind together over mistakes committed in copying; unnecessary maledictions, hissed, rather than spoken, in the heat of business; and especially by a continual discontent with the height of the table where he worked. Though of a very ingenious, mechanical turn, Nippers could never get this table to suit him. He put chips under it, blocks of various sorts, bits of pasteboard, and at last went so far as to attempt an exquisite adjustment, by final pieces of folded blotting paper. But no invention would answer. If, for the sake of easing his back, he brought the table lid at a sharp angle well up towards his chin, and wrote there like a man using the steep roof of a Dutch house for his desk, then he declared that it stopped the circulation in his arms. If now he lowered the table to his waistbands, and stooped over it in writing, then there was a sore aching in his back. In short, the truth of the matter was, Nippers knew not what he wanted. Or, if he wanted anything, it was to be rid of a scrivener's table altogether. Among the manifestations of his diseased ambition was a fondness he had for receiving visits from certain ambiguous-looking fellows in seedy coats, whom he called his clients. Indeed, I was aware that not only was he, at times, considerable of a ward politician, but he occasionally did a little business at the Justices' courts, and was not unknown on the steps of the Tombs.[4] I have good reason to believe, however, that one individual who called upon him at my chambers, and who, with a grand air, he insisted was his client, was no other than a dun, and the alleged title deed, a bill. But, with all his failings, and the annoyances he caused me, Nippers, like his compatriot Turkey, was a very useful man to me; wrote a neat, swift hand; and, when he chose, was not deficient in a gentlemanly sort of deportment. Added to this, he always dressed in a gentlemanly sort of way; and so, incidentally, reflected credit upon my chambers. Whereas, with respect to Turkey, I had much ado to keep him from being a reproach to me. His clothes were apt to look oily, and smell of eating houses. He wore his pantaloons very loose and baggy in summer. His coats were execrable; his hat not to be handled. But while the hat was a thing of indifference to me, inasmuch as his natural civility and deference, as a dependent Englishman, always led him to doff it the moment he entered the room, yet his coat was another matter. Concerning his coats, I reasoned with him; but with no effect. The truth was, I suppose, that a man with so small an income could not afford to sport such a lustrous face and a lustrous coat at one and the same time. As Nippers once observed, Turkey's money went chiefly for red ink. One winter day, I presented Turkey with a highly respectable-looking coat of my own—a padded gray coat, of a most comfortable warmth, and which buttoned

---

[4] **the Tombs:** The maximum security prison in New York City.

straight up from the knee to the neck. I thought Turkey would appreciate the favor, and abate his rashness and obstreperousness of afternoons. But no; I verily believe that buttoning himself up in so downy and blanketlike a coat had a pernicious effect upon him—upon the same principle that too much oats are bad for horses. In fact, precisely as a rash, restive horse is said to feel his oats, so Turkey felt his coat. It made him insolent. He was a man whom prosperity harmed.

Though, concerning the self-indulgent habits of Turkey, I had my own private surmises, yet, touching Nippers, I was well persuaded that, whatever might be his faults in other respects, he was, at least, a temperate young man. But, indeed, nature herself seemed to have been his vintner, and, at his birth, charged him so thoroughly with an irritable, brandylike disposition, that all subsequent potations were needless. When I consider how, amid the stillness of my chambers, Nippers would sometimes impatiently rise from his seat, and stooping over his table, spread his arms wide apart, seize the whole desk, and move it, and jerk it, with a grim, grinding motion on the floor, as if the table were a perverse voluntary agent and vexing him, I plainly perceive that, for Nippers, brandy and water were altogether superfluous.

It was fortunate for me that, owing to its peculiar cause—indigestion—the irritability and consequent nervousness of Nippers were mainly observable in the morning, while in the afternoon he was comparatively mild. So that, Turkey's paroxysms only coming on about twelve o'clock, I never had to do with their eccentricities at one time. Their fits relieved each other, like guards. When Nippers's was on, Turkey's was off; and *vice versa*. This was a good natural arrangement, under the circumstances.

Ginger Nut, the third on my list, was a lad some twelve years old. His father was a carman, ambitious of seeing his son on the bench instead of a cart, before he died. So he sent him to my office, as student at law, errand boy, cleaner, and sweeper, at the rate of one dollar a week. He had a little desk to himself; but he did not use it much. Upon inspection, the drawer exhibited a great array of the shells of various sorts of nuts. Indeed, to this quick-witted youth, the whole noble science of the law was contained in a nutshell. Not the least among the employments of Ginger Nut, as well as one which he discharged with the most alacrity, was his duty as cake and apple purveyor for Turkey and Nippers. Copying law-papers being proverbially a dry, husky sort of business, my two scriveners were fain to moisten their mouths very often with Spitzenbergs,[5] to be had at the numerous stalls nigh the Custom House and Post Office. Also, they sent Ginger Nut very frequently for that peculiar cake—small, flat, round, and very spicy—after which he had been named by them. Of a cold morning, when business was but dull, Turkey would gobble up scores of these cakes, as if they were mere wafers—indeed, they sell them at the rate of six or eight for a penny—the scrape of his pen blending with the crunching of the crisp particles in his mouth. Rashest of all the fiery afternoon blunders and flurried rashnesses of Turkey was his once moistening a ginger cake between his lips and clapping it onto a mortgage for a seal. I came within an ace of dismissing him then. But he mollified me by making an oriental bow, and saying—

---

[5] Spitzenbergs: A variety of apple.

"With submission, sir, it was generous of me to find you in stationery on my own account."

Now my original business—that of a conveyancer and title hunter, and drawer-up of recondite documents of all sorts—was considerably increased by receiving the master's office. There was now great work for scriveners. Not only must I push the clerks already with me, but I must have additional help.

In answer to my advertisement, a motionless young man one morning stood upon my office threshold, the door being open, for it was summer. I can see that figure now—pallidly neat, pitiably respectable, incurably forlorn! It was Bartleby.

After a few words touching his qualifications, I engaged him, glad to have among my corps of copyists a man of so singularly sedate an aspect, which I thought might operate beneficially upon the flighty temper of Turkey, and the fiery one of Nippers.

I should have stated before that ground-glass folding doors divided my premises into two parts, one of which was occupied by my scriveners, the other by myself. According to my humor, I threw open these doors, or closed them. I resolved to assign Bartleby a corner by the folding doors, but on my side of them, so as to have this quiet man within easy call, in case any trifling thing was to be done. I placed his desk close up to a small side window in that part of the room, a window which originally had afforded a lateral view of certain grimy backyards and bricks, but which, owing to subsequent erections, commanded at present no view at all, though it gave some light. Within three feet of the panes was a wall, and the light came down from far above, between two lofty buildings, as from a very small opening in a dome. Still further to a satisfactory arrangement, I procured a high green folding screen, which might entirely isolate Bartleby from my sight, though not remove him from my voice. And thus, in a manner, privacy and society were conjoined.

At first, Bartleby did an extraordinary quantity of writing. As if long famishing for something to copy, he seemed to gorge himself on my documents. There was no pause for digestion. He ran a day and night line, copying by sunlight and by candle-light. I should have been quite delighted with his application, had he been cheerfully industrious. But he wrote on silently, palely, mechanically.

It is, of course, an indispensable part of a scrivener's business to verify the accuracy of his copy, word by word. Where there are two or more scriveners in an office, they assist each other in this examination, one reading from the copy, the other holding the original. It is a very dull, wearisome, and lethargic affair. I can readily imagine that, to some sanguine temperaments, it would be altogether intolerable. For example, I cannot credit that the mettlesome poet, Byron, would have contentedly sat down with Bartleby to examine a law document of, say five hundred pages, closely written in a crimpy hand.

Now and then, in the haste of business, it had been my habit to assist in comparing some brief document myself, calling Turkey or Nippers for this purpose. One object I had, in placing Bartleby so handy to me behind the screen, was to avail myself of his services on such trivial occasions. It was on the third day, I think, of his being with me, and before any necessity had arisen for having his own writing examined, that, being much hurried to complete a small affair I had in hand, I abruptly called to

Bartleby. In my haste and natural expectancy of instant compliance, I sat with my head bent over the original on my desk, and my right hand sideways, and somewhat nervously extended with the copy, so that, immediately upon emerging from his retreat, Bartleby might snatch it and proceed to business without the least delay.

In this very attitude did I sit when I called to him, rapidly stating what it was I wanted him to do—namely, to examine a small paper with me. Imagine my surprise, nay, my consternation, when, without moving from his privacy, Bartleby, in a singularly mild, firm voice, replied, "I would prefer not to."

I sat awhile in perfect silence, rallying my stunned faculties. Immediately it occurred to me that my ears had deceived me, or Bartleby had entirely misunderstood my meaning. I repeated my request in the clearest tone I could assume; but in quite as clear a one came the previous reply, "I would prefer not to."

"Prefer not to," echoed I, rising in high excitement, and crossing the room with a stride. "What do you mean? Are you moonstruck? I want you to help me compare this sheet here—take it," and I thrust it towards him.

"I would prefer not to," said he.

I looked at him steadfastly. His face was leanly composed; his gray eye dimly calm. Not a wrinkle of agitation rippled him. Had there been the least uneasiness, anger, impatience, or impertinence in his manner; in other words, had there been anything ordinarily human about him, doubtless I should have violently dismissed him from the premises. But as it was, I should have as soon thought of turning my pale plaster-of-paris bust of Cicero[6] out of doors. I stood gazing at him awhile, as he went on with his own writing, and then reseated myself at my desk. This is very strange, thought I. What had one best do? But my business hurried me. I concluded to forget the matter for the present, reserving it for my future leisure. So calling Nippers from the other room, the paper was speedily examined.

A few days after this, Bartleby concluded four lengthy documents, being quadruplicates of a week's testimony taken before me in my High Court of Chancery. It became necessary to examine them. It was an important suit, and great accuracy was imperative. Having all things arranged, I called Turkey, Nippers, and Ginger Nut from the next room, meaning to place the four copies in the hands of my four clerks, while I should read from the original. Accordingly, Turkey, Nippers, and Ginger Nut had taken their seats in a row, each with his document in his hand, when I called to Bartleby to join this interesting group.

"Bartleby! quick, I am waiting."

I heard a slow scrape of his chair legs on the uncarpeted floor, and soon he appeared standing at the entrance of his hermitage.

"What is wanted?" said he, mildly.

"The copies, the copies," said I, hurriedly. "We are going to examine them. There—" and I held towards him the fourth quadruplicate.

"I would prefer not to," he said, and gently disappeared behind the screen.

---

[6] Cicero: Marcus Tullius Cicero (106–43 B.C.E.), Roman orator and legal philosopher, hence a figure of symbolic importance to a lawyer.

For a few moments I was turned into a pillar of salt,[7] standing at the head of my seated column of clerks. Recovering myself, I advanced towards the screen, and demanded the reason for such extraordinary conduct.

"*Why* do you refuse?"

"I would prefer not to."

With any other man I should have flown outright into a dreadful passion, scorned all further words, and thrust him ignominiously from my presence. But there was something about Bartleby that not only strangely disarmed me, but in a wonderful manner, touched and disconcerted me. I began to reason with him.

"These are your own copies we are about to examine. It is labor saving to you, because one examination will answer for your four papers. It is common usage. Every copyist is bound to help examine his copy. Is it not so? Will you not speak? Answer!"

"I prefer not to," he replied in a flutelike tone. It seemed to me that, while I had been addressing him, he carefully revolved every statement that I made; fully comprehended the meaning; could not gainsay the irresistible conclusion; but, at the same time, some paramount consideration prevailed with him to reply as he did.

"You are decided, then, not to comply with my request—a request made according to common usage and common sense?"

He briefly gave me to understand, that on that point my judgment was sound. Yes: His decision was irreversible.

It is not seldom the case that, when a man is browbeaten in some unprecedented and violently unreasonable way, he begins to stagger in his own plainest faith. He begins, as it were, vaguely to surmise that, wonderful as it may be, all the justice and all the reason is on the other side. Accordingly, if any disinterested persons are present, he turns to them for some reinforcement of his own faltering mind.

"Turkey," said I, "what do you think of this? Am I not right?"

"With submission, sir," said Turkey, in his blandest tone, "I think that you are."

"Nippers," said I, "what do *you* think of it?"

"I think I should kick him out of the office."

(The reader, of nice perceptions, will here perceive that, it being morning, Turkey's answer is couched in polite and tranquil terms, but Nippers's replies in ill-tempered ones. Or, to repeat a previous sentence, Nippers's ugly mood was on duty, and Turkey's off.)

"Ginger Nut," said I, willing to enlist the smallest suffrage in my behalf, "what do *you* think of it?"

"I think, sir, he's a little *loony*," replied Ginger Nut, with a grin.

"You hear what they say," said I, turning towards the screen, "come forth and do your duty."

But he vouchsafed no reply. I pondered a moment in sore perplexity. But once more business hurried me. I determined again to postpone the consideration of this dilemma to my future leisure. With a little trouble we made out to examine the papers without Bartleby, though at every page or two Turkey deferentially dropped

---

[7] turned . . . salt: The punishment meted out to Lot's wife for looking back. (Genesis 19:26).

his opinion, that this proceeding was quite out of the common; while Nippers, twitching in his chair with a dyspeptic nervousness, ground out, between his set teeth, occasional hissing maledictions against the stubborn oaf behind the screen. And for his (Nippers's) part, this was the first and the last time he would do another man's business without pay.

Meanwhile Bartleby sat in his hermitage, oblivious to everything but his own peculiar business there.

Some days passed, the scrivener being employed upon another lengthy work. His late remarkable conduct led me to regard his ways narrowly. I observed that he never went to dinner; indeed, that he never went anywhere. As yet I had never, of my personal knowledge, known him to be outside of my office. He was a perpetual sentry in the corner. At about eleven o'clock though, in the morning, I noticed that Ginger Nut would advance toward the opening in Bartleby's screen, as if silently beckoned thither by a gesture invisible to me where I sat. The boy would then leave the office, jingling a few pence, and reappear with a handful of ginger nuts, which he delivered in the hermitage, receiving two of the cakes for his trouble.

He lives, then, on ginger nuts, thought I; never eats a dinner, properly speaking; he must be a vegetarian, then; but no; he never eats even vegetables; he eats nothing but ginger nuts. My mind then ran on in reveries concerning the probable effects upon the human constitution of living entirely on ginger nuts. Ginger nuts are so called, because they contain ginger as one of their peculiar constituents, and the final flavoring one. Now, what was ginger? A hot, spicy thing. Was Bartleby hot and spicy? Not at all. Ginger, then, had no effect upon Bartleby. Probably he preferred it should have none.

Nothing so aggravates an earnest person as a passive resistance. If the individual so resisted be of a not inhumane temper, and the resisting one perfectly harmless in his passivity, then, in the better mood of the former, he will endeavor charitably to construe to his imagination what proves impossible to be solved by his judgment. Even so, for the most part, I regarded Bartleby and his ways. Poor fellow! thought I, he means no mischief; it is plain he intends no insolence; his aspect sufficiently evinces that his eccentricities are involuntary. He is useful to me. I can get along with him. If I turn him away, the chances are he will fall in with some less indulgent employer, and then he will be rudely treated, and perhaps driven forth miserably to starve. Yes. Here I can cheaply purchase a delicious self-approval. To befriend Bartleby; to humor him in his strange willfulness, will cost me little or nothing, while I lay up in my soul what will eventually prove a sweet morsel for my conscience. But this mood was not invariable with me. The passiveness of Bartleby sometimes irritated me. I felt strangely goaded on to encounter him in new opposition—to elicit some angry spark from him answerable to my own. But, indeed, I might as well have essayed to strike fire with my knuckles against a bit of Windsor soap. But one afternoon the evil impulse in me mastered me, and the following little scene ensued:

"Bartleby," said I, "when those papers are all copied, I will compare them with you."

"I would prefer not to."

"How? Surely you do not mean to persist in that mulish vagary?"

No answer.

I threw open the folding doors nearby, and, turning upon Turkey and Nippers, exclaimed:

"Bartleby a second time says he won't examine his papers. What do you think of it, Turkey?"

It was afternoon, be it remembered. Turkey sat glowing like a brass boiler; his bald head steaming; his hands reeling among his blotted papers.

"Think of it?" roared Turkey; "I think I'll just step behind his screen, and black his eyes for him!"

So saying, Turkey rose to his feet and threw his arms into a pugilistic position. He was hurrying away to make good his promise, when I detained him, alarmed at the effect of incautiously rousing Turkey's combativeness after dinner.

"Sit down, Turkey," said I, "and hear what Nippers has to say. What do you think of it, Nippers? Would I not be justified in immediately dismissing Bartleby?"

"Excuse me, that is for you to decide, sir. I think his conduct quite unusual, and, indeed, unjust, as regards Turkey and myself. But it may only be a passing whim."

"Ah," exclaimed I, "you have strangely changed your mind, then — you speak very gently of him now."

"All beer," cried Turkey; "gentleness is effects of beer — Nippers and I dined together today. You see how gentle *I* am, sir. Shall I go and black his eyes?"

"You refer to Bartleby, I suppose. No, not today, Turkey," I replied; "pray, put up your fists."

I closed the doors, and again advanced towards Bartleby. I felt additional incentives tempting me to my face. I burned to be rebelled against again. I remembered that Bartleby never left the office.

"Bartleby," said I, "Ginger Nut is away; just step around to the Post Office, won't you?" (it was but a three minutes' walk) "and see if there is anything for me."

"I would prefer not to."

"You *will* not?"

"I *prefer* not."

I staggered to my desk, and sat there in a deep study. My blind inveteracy returned. Was there any other thing in which I could procure myself to be ignominiously repulsed by this lean, penniless wight? — my hired clerk? What added thing is there, perfectly reasonable, that he will be sure to refuse to do?

"Bartleby!"

No answer.

"Bartleby," in a louder tone.

No answer.

"Bartleby," I roared.

Like a very ghost, agreeably to the laws of magical invocation, at the third summons, he appeared at the entrance of his hermitage.

"Go to the next room, and tell Nipper to come to me."

"I prefer not to," he respectfully and slowly said, and mildly disappeared.

"Very good, Bartleby," said I, in a quiet sort of serenely-severe, self-possessed tone, intimating the unalterable purpose of some terrible retribution very close at hand. At the moment I half intended something of the kind. But upon the whole, as it was drawing towards my dinner hour, I thought it best to put on my hat and walk home for the day, suffering much from perplexity and distress of mind.

Shall I acknowledge it? The conclusion of this whole business was, that it soon became a fixed fact of my chambers, that a pale young scrivener, by the name of Bartleby, had a desk there; that he copied for me at the usual rate of four cents a folio (one hundred words); but he was permanently exempt from examining the work done by him, that duty being transferred to Turkey and Nippers, out of compliment, doubtless, to their superior acuteness; moreover, said Bartleby was never, on any account, to be dispatched on the most trivial errand of any sort; and that even if entreated to take upon him such a matter, it was generally understood that he would "prefer not to"—in other words, that he would refuse point-blank.

As days passed on, I became considerably reconciled to Bartleby. His steadiness, his freedom from all dissipation, his incessant industry (except when he chose to throw himself into a standing revery behind his screen), his great stillness, his unalterableness of demeanor under all circumstances, made him a valuable acquisition. One prime thing was this—*he was always there*—first in the morning, continually through the day, and the last at night. I had a singular confidence in his honesty. I felt my most precious papers perfectly safe in his hands. Sometimes, to be sure, I could not, for the very soul of me, avoid falling into sudden spasmodic passions with him. For it was exceeding difficult to bear in mind all the time those strange peculiarities, privileges, and unheard-of exemptions, forming the tacit stipulations on Bartleby's part under which he remained in my office. Now and then, in the eagerness of dispatching pressing business, I would inadvertently summon Bartleby, in a short, rapid tone, to put his finger, say, on the incipient tie of a bit of red tape with which I was about compressing some papers. Of course, from behind the screen the usual answer, "I prefer not to," was sure to come; and then, how could a human creature, with the common infirmities of our nature, refrain from bitterly exclaiming upon such perverseness—such unreasonableness. However, every added repulse of this sort which I received only tended to lessen the probability of my repeating the inadvertence.

Here it must be said that according to the custom of most legal gentlemen occupying chambers in densely populated law buildings, there were several keys to my door. One was kept by a woman residing in the attic, which person weekly scrubbed and daily swept and dusted my apartments. Another was kept by Turkey for convenience' sake. The third I sometimes carried in my own pocket. The fourth I knew not who had.

Now, one Sunday morning I happened to go to Trinity Church, to hear a celebrated preacher, and finding myself rather early on the ground I thought I would walk around to my chambers for a while. Luckily I had my key with me; but upon applying it to the lock, I found it resisted by something inserted from the inside. Quite surprised, I called out; when to my consternation a key was turned from within; and thrusting his lean visage at me, and holding the door ajar, the apparition of Bartleby appeared, in his shirt sleeves, and otherwise in a strangely tattered *déshabillé,* saying quietly that he was sorry, but he was deeply engaged just then, and— preferred not admitting me at present. In a brief word or two, he moreover added, that perhaps I had better walk around the block two or three times, and by that time he would probably have concluded his affairs.

Now, the utterly unsurmised appearance of Bartleby, tenanting my law chambers of a Sunday morning, with his cadaverously gentlemanly nonchalance, yet withal firm and self-possessed, had such a strange effect upon me, that incontinently I slunk away from my own door, and did as desired. But not without sundry twinges of impotent rebellion against the mild effrontery of this unaccountable scrivener. Indeed, it was his wonderful mildness chiefly, which not only disarmed me, but unmanned me, as it were. For I consider that one, for the time, is somehow unmanned when he tranquilly permits his hired clerk to dictate to him, and order him away from his own premises. Furthermore, I was full of uneasiness as to what Bartleby could possibly be doing in my office in his shirt sleeves, and in an otherwise dismantled condition of a Sunday morning. Was anything amiss going on? Nay, that was out of the question. It was not to be thought of for a moment that Bartleby was an immoral person. But what could he be doing there? — copying? Nay again, whatever might be his eccentricities, Bartleby was an eminently decorous person. He would be the last man to sit down to his desk in any state approaching to nudity. Besides, it was Sunday; and there was something about Bartleby that forbade the supposition that he would by any secular occupation violate the proprieties of the day.

Nevertheless, my mind was not pacified; and full of a restless curiosity, at last I returned to the door. Without hindrance I inserted my key, opened it, and entered. Bartleby was not to be seen. I looked round anxiously, peeped behind his screen; but it was very plain that he was gone. Upon more closely examining the place, I surmised that for an indefinite period Bartleby must have eaten, dressed, and slept in my office, and that, too, without plate, mirror, or bed. The cushioned seat of a rickety old sofa in one corner bore the faint impress of a lean, reclining form. Rolled away under his desk, I found a blanket; under the empty grate, a blacking box and brush; on a chair, a tin basin, with soap and a ragged towel; in a newspaper a few crumbs of ginger nuts and a morsel of cheese. Yes, thought I, it is evident enough that Bartleby has been making his home here, keeping bachelor's hall all by himself. Immediately then the thought came sweeping across me, what miserable friendlessness and loneliness are here revealed! His poverty is great; but his solitude, how horrible! Think of it. Of a Sunday, Wall Street is deserted as Petra;[8] and every night of every day it is an emptiness. This building, too, which of weekdays hums with industry and life, at nightfall echoes with sheer vacancy, and all through Sunday is forlorn. And here Bartleby makes his home; sole spectator of a solitude which he has seen all populous — a sort of innocent and transformed Marius[9] brooding among the ruins of Carthage!

For the first time in my life a feeling of overpowering stinging melancholy seized me. Before, I had never experienced aught but a not-unpleasing sadness. The bond of a common humanity now drew me irresistibly to gloom. A fraternal melancholy!

---

[8] Petra: An ancient city in Jordan discovered in 1812 after having been deserted for centuries.

[9] Marius: Caius Marius (157–86 B.C.E.), a plebian who fought in Africa and became a general in the Roman army; he later quarreled with the rulers in Rome and was exiled.

For both I and Bartleby were sons of Adam. I remembered the bright silks and sparkling faces I had seen that day, in gala trim, swanlike sailing down the Mississippi of Broadway; and I contrasted them with the pallid copyist, and thought to myself, Ah, happiness courts the light, so we deem the world is gay; but misery hides aloof, so we deem that misery there is none. These sad fancyings—chimeras, doubtless, of a sick and silly brain—led on to other and more special thoughts, concerning the eccentricities of Bartleby. Presentiments of strange discoveries hovered round me. The scrivener's pale form appeared to me laid out, among uncaring strangers, in its shivering winding sheet.

Suddenly I was attracted by Bartleby's closed desk, the key in open sight left in the lock.

I mean no mischief, seek the gratification of no heartless curiosity, thought I; besides, the desk is mine, and it contents, too, so I will make bold to look within. Everything was methodically arranged, the papers smoothly placed. The pigeon holes were deep, and removing the files of documents, I groped into their recesses. Presently I felt something there, and dragged it out. It was an old bandanna handkerchief, heavy and knotted. I opened it, and saw it was a savings bank.

I now recalled all the quiet mysteries which I had noted in the man. I remembered that he never spoke but to answer; that, though at intervals he had considerable time to himself, yet I had never seen him reading—no, not even a newspaper; that for long periods he would stand looking out, at his pale window behind the screen, upon the dead brick wall; I was quite sure he never visited any refectory or eating house; while his pale face clearly indicated that he never drank beer like Turkey, or tea and coffee even, like other men; that he never went anywhere in particular that I could learn; never went out for a walk, unless, indeed, that was the case at present; that he had declined telling who he was, or whence he came, or whether he had any relatives in the world; that though so thin and pale, he never complained of ill health. And more than all, I remembered a certain unconscious air of pallid—how shall I call it?—of pallid haughtiness, say, or rather an austere reserve about him, which had positively awed me into my tame compliance with his eccentricities, when I had feared to ask him to do the slightest incidental thing for me, even though I might know, from his long-continued motionlessness, that behind his screen he must be standing in one of those dead-wall reveries of his.

Recovering all these things, and coupling them with the recently discovered fact that he made my office his constant abiding place and home, and not forgetful of his morbid moodiness; revolving all these things, a prudential feeling began to steal over me. My first emotions had been those of pure melancholy and sincerest pity; but just in proportion as the forlornness of Bartleby grew and grew to my imagination, did that same melancholy merge into fear, that pity into repulsion. So true it is, and so terrible, too, that up to a certain point the thought or sight of misery enlists our best affections; but, in certain special cases, beyond that point it does not. They err who would assert that invariably this is owing to the inherent selfishness of the human heart. It rather proceeds from a certain hopelessness of remedying excessive and organic ill. To a sensitive being, pity is not seldom pain. And when at last it is perceived that such pity cannot lead to effectual succor, common sense bids the soul be rid of it. What I saw that morning persuaded me that the scrivener was the victim of innate and incurable disorder. I might give alms to his body; but his body did not pain him; it was his soul that suffered, and his soul I could not reach.

I did not accomplish the purpose of going to Trinity Church that morning. Somehow, the things I had seen disqualified me for the time from churchgoing. I walked homeward, thinking what I would do with Bartleby. Finally, I resolved upon this—I would put certain calm questions to him the next morning, touching his history, etc., and if he declined to answer them openly and unreservedly (and I supposed he would prefer not), then to give him a twenty dollar bill over and above whatever I might owe him, and tell him his services were no longer required; but that if in any other way I could assist him, I would be happy to do so, especially if he desired to return to his native place, wherever that might be, I would willingly help to defray the expenses. Moreover, if, after reaching home, he found himself at any time in want of aid, a letter from him would be sure of a reply.

The next morning came.

"Bartleby," said I, gently calling to him behind his screen.

No reply.

"Bartleby," said I, in a still gentler tone, "come here; I am not going to ask you to do anything you would prefer not to do—I simply wish to speak to you."

Upon this he noiselessly slid into view.

"Will you tell me, Bartleby, where you were born?"

"I would prefer not to."

"Will you tell me *anything* about yourself?"

"I would prefer not to."

"But what reasonable objection can you have to speak to me? I feel friendly towards you."

He did not look at me while I spoke, but kept his glance fixed upon my bust of Cicero, which, as I then sat, was directly behind me, some six inches above my head.

"What is your answer, Bartleby," said I, after waiting a considerable time for a reply, during which his countenance remained immovable, only there was the faintest conceivable tremor of the white attenuated mouth.

"At present I prefer to give no answer," he said, and retired into his hermitage.

It was rather weak in me I confess, but his manner, on this occasion, nettled me. Not only did there seem to lurk in it a certain calm disdain, but his perverseness seemed ungrateful, considering the undeniable good usage and indulgence he had received from me.

Again I sat ruminating what I should do. Mortified as I was at his behavior, and resolved as I had been to dismiss him when I entered my office, nevertheless I strangely felt something superstitious knocking at my heart, and forbidding me to carry out my purpose, and denouncing me for a villain if I dared to breathe one bitter word against this forlornest of mankind. At last, familiarly drawing my chair behind his screen, I sat down and said: "Bartleby, never mind, then, about revealing your history; but let me entreat you, as a friend, to comply as far as may be with the usages of this office. Say now, you will help to examine papers tomorrow or next day: In short, say now, that in a day or two you will begin to be a little reasonable:—Say so, Bartleby."

"At present I would prefer not to be a little reasonable," was his mildly cadaverous reply.

Just then the folding doors opened, and Nippers approached. He seemed suffering from an unusually bad night's rest, induced by severer indigestion than common. He overheard those final words of Bartleby.

"*Prefer not*, eh?" gritted Nippers—"I'd *prefer* him, if I were you, sir," addressing me—"I'd *prefer* him; I'd give him preferences, the stubborn mule! What is it, sir, pray, that he *prefers* not to do now?"

Bartleby moved not a limb.

"Mr. Nippers," said I, "I'd prefer that you would withdraw for the present."

Somehow, of late, I had got into the way of involuntarily using this word "prefer" upon all sorts of not exactly suitable occasions. And I trembled to think that my contact with the scrivener had already and seriously affected me in a mental way. And what further and deeper aberration might it not yet produce? This apprehension had not been without efficacy in determining me to summary measures.

As Nippers, looking very sour and sulky, was departing, Turkey blandly and deferentially approached.

"With submission, sir," said he, "yesterday I was thinking about Bartleby here, and I think that if he would but prefer to take a quart of good ale every day, it would do much towards mending him, and enabling him to assist in examining his papers."

"So you have got the word, too," said I, slightly excited.

"With submission, what word, sir," asked Turkey, respectfully crowding himself into the contracted space behind the screen, and by so doing, making me jostle the scrivener. "What word, sir?"

"I would prefer to be left alone here," said Bartleby, as if offended at being mobbed in his privacy.

"*That's* the word, Turkey," said I—"*that's* it."

"Oh, *prefer*? oh yes—queer word. I never use it myself. But, sir, as I was saying, if he would but prefer—"

"Turkey," interrupted I, "you will please withdraw."

"Oh certainly, sir, if you prefer that I should."

As he opened the folding door to retire, Nippers at his desk caught a glimpse of me, and asked whether I would prefer to have a certain paper copied on blue paper or white. He did not in the least roguishly accent the word prefer. It was plain that it involuntarily rolled from his tongue. I thought to myself, surely I must get rid of a demented man, who already has in some degree turned the tongues, if not the heads of myself and clerks. But I thought it prudent not to break the dismission at once.

The next day I noticed that Bartleby did nothing but stand at his window in his dead-wall revery. Upon asking him why he did not write, he said that he had decided upon doing no more writing.

"Why, how now? what next?" exclaimed I, "do no more writing?"

"No more."

"And what is the reason?"

"Do you not see the reason for yourself," he indifferently replied.

I looked steadfastly at him, and perceived that his eyes looked dull and glazed. Instantly it occurred to me, that his unexampled diligence in copying by his dim window for the first few weeks of his stay with me might have temporarily impaired his vision.

I was touched. I said something in condolence with him. I hinted that of course he did wisely in abstaining from writing for a while; and urged him to embrace that opportunity of taking wholesome exercise in the open air. This, however, he did not do. A few days after this, my other clerks being absent, and being in a great hurry to dispatch certain letters by the mail, I thought that, having nothing else earthly to do, Bartleby would surely be less inflexible than usual, and carry these letters to the post office. But he blankly declined. So, much to my inconvenience, I went myself.

Still added days went by. Whether Bartleby's eyes improved or not, I could not say. To all appearance I thought they did. But when I asked him if they did, he vouchsafed no answer. At all events, he would do no copying. At last, in reply to my urgings, he informed me that he had permanently given up copying.

"What!" exclaimed I; "suppose your eyes should get entirely well—better than ever before—would you not copy then?"

"I have given up copying," he answered, and slid aside.

He remained as ever, a fixture in my chamber. Nay—if that were possible—he became still more of a fixture than before. What was to be done? He would do nothing in the office; why should he stay there? In plain fact, he had now become a millstone to me, not only useless as a necklace, but afflictive to bear. Yet I was sorry for him. I speak less than truth when I say that, on his own account, he occasioned me uneasiness. If he would but have named a single relative or friend, I would instantly have written, and urged their taking the poor fellow away to some convenient retreat. But he seemed alone, absolutely alone in the universe. A bit of wreck in the mid-Atlantic. At length, necessities connected with my business tyrannized over all other considerations. Decently as I could, I told Bartleby that in six days' time he must unconditionally leave the office. I warned him to take measures, in the interval, for procuring some other abode. I offered to assist him in his endeavor, if he himself would but take the first step towards a removal. "And when you finally quit me, Bartleby," added I, "I shall see that you go not away entirely unprovided. Six days from this hour, remember."

At the expiration of that period, I peeped behind the screen, and lo! Bartleby was there.

I buttoned up my coat, balanced myself; advanced slowly towards him, touched his shoulder, and said, "The time has come; you must quit this place; I am sorry for you; here is money; but you must go."

"I would prefer not," he replied, with his back still towards me.

"You *must*."

He remained silent.

Now I had an unbounded confidence in this man's common honesty. He had frequently restored to me sixpences and shillings carelessly dropped upon the floor, for I am apt to be very reckless in such shirt-button affairs. The proceeding, then, which followed will not be deemed extraordinary.

"Bartleby," said I, "I owe you twelve dollars on account; here are thirty-two; the odd twenty are yours—Will you take it?" and I handed the bills towards him.

But he made no motion.

"I will leave them here, then," putting them under a weight on the table. Then taking my hat and cane and going to the door, I tranquilly turned and added— "After you have removed your things from these offices, Bartleby, you will of course lock the door—since everyone is now gone for the day but you—and if you please, slip your key underneath the mat, so that I may have it in the morning. I shall not see you again; so good-bye to you. If, hereafter, in your new place of abode, I can be of any service to you, do not fail to advise me by letter. Good-bye, Bartleby, and fare you well."

But he answered not a word; like the last column of some ruined temple, he remained standing mute and solitary in the middle of the otherwise deserted room.

As I walked home in a pensive mood, my vanity got the better of my pity. I could not but highly plume myself on my masterly management in getting rid of Bartleby. Masterly I call it, and such it must appear to any dispassionate thinker. The beauty of my procedure seemed to consist in its perfect quietness. There was no vulgar bullying, no bravado of any sort, no choleric hectoring, and striding to and fro across the apartment, jerking out vehement commands for Bartleby to bundle himself off with his beggarly traps. Nothing of the kind. Without loudly bidding Bartleby depart— as an inferior genius might have done—I *assumed* the ground that depart he must; and upon that assumption built all I had to say. The more I thought over my procedure, the more I was charmed with it. Nevertheless, next morning, upon awakening, I had my doubts—I had somehow slept off the fumes of vanity. One of the coolest and wisest hours a man has, is just after he awakes in the morning. My procedure seemed as sagacious as ever—but only in theory. How it would prove in practice— there was the rub. It was truly a beautiful thought to have assumed Bartleby's departure; but, after all, that assumption was simply my own, and none of Bartleby's. The great point was, not whether I had assumed that he would quit me, but whether he would prefer so to do. He was more a man of preferences than assumptions.

After breakfast, I walked downtown, arguing the probabilities *pro* and *con.* One moment I thought it would prove a miserable failure, and Bartleby would be found all alive at my office as usual; the next moment it seemed certain that I should find his chair empty. And so I kept veering about. At the corner of Broadway and Canal Street, I saw quite an excited group of people standing in earnest conversation.

"I'll take odds he doesn't," said a voice as I passed.

"Doesn't go?—done!" said I; "put up your money."

I was instinctively putting my hand in my pocket to produce my own, when I remembered that this was an election day. The words I had overheard bore no reference to Bartleby, but to the success or nonsuccess of some candidate for the mayoralty. In my intent frame of mind, I had, as it were, imagined that all Broadway shared in my excitement, and were debating the same question with me. I passed on, very thankful that the uproar of the street screened my momentary absentmindedness.

As I had intended, I was earlier than usual at my office door. I stood listening for a moment. All was still. He must be gone. I tried the knob. The door was locked.

Yes, my procedure had worked to a charm; he indeed must be vanished. Yet a certain melancholy mixed with this; I was almost sorry for my brilliant success. I was fumbling under the doormat for the key, which Bartleby was to have left there for me, when accidentally my knee knocked against a panel, producing a summoning sound, and in response a voice came to me from within—"Not yet; I am occupied."

It was Bartleby.

I was thunderstruck. For an instant I stood like the man who, pipe in mouth, was killed one cloudless afternoon long ago in Virginia, by summer lightning; at his own warm open window he was killed, and remained leaning out there upon the dreamy afternoon, till some one touched him, when he fell.

"Not gone!" I murmured at last. But again obeying that wondrous ascendancy which the inscrutable scrivener had over me, and from which ascendancy, for all my chafing, I could not completely escape, I slowly went downstairs and out into the street, and while walking round the block, considered what I should next do in this unheard-of perplexity. Turn the man out by an actual thrusting I could not; to drive him away by calling him hard names would not do; calling in the police was an unpleasant idea; and yet, permit him to enjoy his cadaverous triumph over me— this, too, I could not think of. What was to be done? or, if nothing could be done, was there anything further that I could *assume* in the matter? Yes, as before I had prospectively assumed that Bartleby would depart, so now I might retrospectively assume that departed he was. In the legitimate carrying out of this assumption, I might enter my office in a great hurry, and pretending not to see Bartleby at all, walk straight against him as if he were air. Such a proceeding would in a singular degree have the appearance of a home-thrust. It was hardly possible that Bartleby could withstand such an application of the doctrine of assumptions. But upon second thoughts the success of the plan seemed rather dubious. I resolved to argue the matter over with him again.

"Bartleby," said I, entering the office, with a quietly severe expression, "I am seriously displeased. I am pained, Bartleby, I had thought better of you. I had imagined you of such a gentlemanly organization, that in any delicate dilemma a slight hint would suffice—in short, an assumption. But it appears I am deceived. Why," I added, unaffectedly starting, "you have not even touched that money yet," pointing to it, just where I had left it the evening previous.

He answered nothing.

"Will you, or will you not, quit me?" I now demanded in a sudden passion, advancing close to him.

"I would prefer *not* to quit you," he replied, gently emphasizing the *not*.

"What earthly right have you to stay here? Do you pay any rent? Do you pay my taxes? Or is this property yours?"

He answered nothing.

"Are you ready to go on and write now? Are your eyes recovered? Could you copy a small paper for me this morning? or help examine a few lines? or step round to the post office? In a word, will you do anything at all, to give a coloring to your refusal to depart the premises?"

He silently retired into his hermitage.

I was now in such a state of nervous resentment that I thought it but prudent to check myself at present from further demonstration. Bartleby and I were alone. I remembered the tragedy of the unfortunate Adams and the still more unfortunate Colt[10] in the solitary office of the latter; and how poor Colt, being dreadfully incensed by Adams, and imprudently permitting himself to get wildly excited, was at unawares hurried into his fatal act—an act which certainly no man could possibly deplore more than the actor himself. Often it had occurred to me in my ponderings upon the subject, that had that altercation taken place in the public street, or at a private residence, it would not have terminated as it did. It was the circumstance of being alone in a solitary office, upstairs, of a building entirely unhallowed by humanizing domestic associations—an uncarpeted office, doubtless, of a dusty, haggard sort of appearance—this it must have been, which greatly helped to enhance the irritable desperation of the hapless Colt.

But when this old Adam of resentment rose in me and tempted me concerning Bartleby, I grappled him and threw him. How? Why, simply by recalling the divine injunction: "A new commandment give I unto you, that ye love one another."[11] Yes, this it was that saved me. Aside from higher considerations, charity often operates as a vastly wise and prudent principle—a great safeguard to its possessor. Men have committed murder for jealousy's sake, and anger's sake, and hatred's sake, and selfishness' sake, and spiritual pride's sake; but no man, that ever I heard of, ever committed a diabolical murder for sweet charity's sake. Mere self-interest, then, if no better motive can be enlisted, should, especially with high-tempered men, prompt all beings to charity and philanthropy. At any rate, upon the occasion in question, I strove to drown my exasperated feelings towards the scrivener by benevolently construing his conduct. Poor fellow, poor fellow! thought I, he don't mean anything; and besides, he has seen hard times, and ought to be indulged.

I endeavored, also, immediately to occupy myself, and at the same time to comfort my despondency. I tried to fancy, that in the course of the morning, at such time as might prove agreeable to him, Bartleby, of his own free accord, would emerge from his hermitage and take up some decided line of march in the direction of the door. But no. Half-past twelve o'clock came; Turkey began to glow in the face, overturn his inkstand, and become generally obstreperous; Nippers abated down into quietude and courtesy; Ginger Nut munched his noon apple; and Bartleby remained standing at his window in one of his profoundest dead-wall reveries. Will it be credited? Ought I to acknowledge it? That afternoon I left the office without saying one further word to him.

---

[10] **tragedy . . . Colt:** In a notorious crime of 1842 John C. Colt, who was writing a textbook on bookkeeping, murdered his printer, Samuel Adams, when he became enraged about an overcharge in the printer's bill. After killing Adams with an axe in his office, Colt put the body in a trunk and shipped it to New Orleans. It was discovered en route and Colt was arrested and condemned to be hanged. Colt committed suicide a half hour before his scheduled execution.

[11] **"A new . . . one another":** Jesus' injunction to his disciples (John 13:34).

Some days now passed, during which, at leisure intervals, I looked a little into "Edwards on the Will" and "Priestley on Necessity."[12] Under the circumstances, those books induced a salutary feeling. Gradually I slid into the persuasion that these troubles of mine, touching the scrivener, had been all predestinated from eternity, and Bartleby was billeted upon me for some mysterious purpose of an all-wise Providence, which it was not for a mere mortal like me to fathom. Yes, Bartleby, stay there behind your screen, thought I; I shall persecute you no more; you are harmless and noiseless as any of these old chairs; in short, I never feel so private as when I know you are here. At last I see it, I feel it; I penetrate to the predestinated purpose of my life. I am content. Others may have loftier parts to enact; but my mission in this world, Bartleby, is to furnish you with office-room for such period as you may see fit to remain.

I believe that this wise and blessed frame of mind would have continued with me, had it not been for the unsolicited and uncharitable remarks obtruded upon me by my professional friends who visited the rooms. But thus it often is, that the constant friction of illiberal minds wears out at last the best resolves of the more generous. Though to be sure, when I reflected upon it, it was not strange that people entering my office should be struck by the peculiar aspect of the unaccountable Bartleby, and so be tempted to throw out some sinister observations concerning him. Sometimes an attorney, having business with me, and calling at my office, and finding no one but the scrivener there, would undertake to obtain some sort of precise information from him touching my whereabouts; but without heeding his idle talk, Bartleby would remain standing immovable in the middle of the room. So after contemplating him in that position for a time, the attorney would depart, no wiser than he came.

Also, when a reference was going on, and the room full of lawyers and witnesses, and business driving fast, some deeply occupied legal gentleman present, seeing Bartleby wholly unemployed, would request him to run round to his (the legal gentleman's) office and fetch some papers for him. Thereupon, Bartleby would tranquilly decline, and yet remain idle as before. Then the lawyer would give a great stare, and turn to me. And what could I say? At last I was made aware that all through the circle of my professional acquaintance, a whisper of wonder was running round, having reference to the strange creature I kept at my office. This worried me very much. And as the idea came upon me of his possibly turning out a long-lived man, and keep occupying my chambers, and denying my authority; and perplexing my visitors; and scandalizing my professional reputation; and casting a general gloom over the premises; keeping soul and body together to the last upon his savings (for doubtless he spent but half a dime a day), and in the end perhaps outlive me, and claim possession of my office by right of his perpetual occupancy: As all these dark anticipations crowded upon me more and more, and my friends continually

---

[12] "Edwards . . . Necessity": Jonathan Edwards (1703–1758) was a Puritan cleric whose *Freedom of the Will* (1754) reconciled human will with predestination; Joseph Priestley (1733–1804) was an English scientist and Unitarian theologian whose doctrine of necessity was based on natural determinism.

intruded their relentless remarks upon the apparition in my room; a great change was wrought in me. I resolved to gather all my faculties together, and forever rid me of this intolerable incubus.

Ere revolving any complicated project, however, adapted to this end, I first simply suggested to Bartleby the propriety of his permanent departure. In a calm and serious tone, I commended the idea to his careful and mature consideration. But, having taken three days to meditate upon it, he apprised me, that his original determination remained the same; in short, that he still preferred to abide with me.

What shall I do? I now said to myself, buttoning up my coat to the last button. What shall I do? what ought I to do? what does conscience say I *should* do with this man, or, rather, ghost? Rid myself of him, I must; go, he shall. But how? You will not thrust him, the poor, pale, passive mortal—you will not thrust such a helpless creature out of your door? you will not dishonor yourself by such cruelty? No, I will not, I cannot do that. Rather would I let him live and die here, and then mason up his remains in the wall. What, then, will you do? For all your coaxing, he will not budge. Bribes he leaves under your own paperweight on your table; in short, it is quite plain that he prefers to cling to you.

Then something severe, something unusual must be done. What! surely you will not have him collared by a constable, and commit his innocent pallor to the common jail? And upon what ground could you procure such a thing to be done?—a vagrant, is he? What! he a vagrant, a wanderer, who refuses to budge? It is because he will *not* be a vagrant, then, that you seek to count him *as* a vagrant. That is too absurd. No visible means of support: there I have him. Wrong again: for indubitably he *does* support himself, and that is the only unanswerable proof that any man can show of his possessing the means so to do. No more, then. Since he will not quit me, I must quit him. I will change my offices; I will move elsewhere, and give him fair notice, that if I find him on my new premises I will then proceed against him as a common trespasser.

Acting accordingly, next day I thus addressed him: "I find these chambers too far from the City Hall; the air is unwholesome. In a word, I propose to remove my offices next week, and shall no longer require your services. I tell you this now, in order that you may seek another place."

He made no reply; and nothing more was said.

On the appointed day I engaged carts and men, proceeded to my chambers, and, having but little furniture, everything was removed in a few hours. Throughout, the scrivener remained standing behind the screen, which I directed to be removed the last thing. It was withdrawn; and, being folded up like a huge folio, left him the motionless occupant of a naked room. I stood in the entry watching him a moment, while something from within me upbraided me.

I reentered, with my hand in my pocket—and—and my heart in my mouth.

"Good-bye, Bartleby; I am going—good-bye, and God some way bless you; and take that," slipping something in his hand. But it dropped upon the floor, and then—strange to say—I tore myself from him whom I had so longed to be rid of.

Established in my new quarters, for a day or two I kept the door locked, and started at every footfall in the passages. When I returned to my rooms, after any little absence, I would pause at the threshold for an instant, and attentively listen, ere applying my key. But these fears were needless. Bartleby never came nigh me.

I thought all was going well, when a perturbed-looking stranger visited me, inquiring whether I was the person who had recently occupied rooms at No.—— Wall Street.

Full of forebodings, I replied that I was.

"Then, sir," said the stranger, who proved a lawyer, "you are responsible for the man you left there. He refuses to do any copying; he refuses to do anything; he says he prefers not to; and he refuses to quit the premises."

"I am very sorry, sir," said I, with assumed tranquillity, but an inward tremor, "but, really, the man you allude to is nothing to me—he is no relation or apprentice of mine, that you should hold me responsible for him."

"In mercy's name, who is he?"

"I certainly cannot inform you. I know nothing about him. Formerly I employed him as a copyist; but he has done nothing for me now for some time past."

"I shall settle him, then—good morning, sir."

Several days passed, and I heard nothing more and, though I often felt a charitable prompting to call at the place and see poor Bartleby, yet a certain squeamishness, of I know not what, withheld me.

All is over with him, by this time, thought I, at last, when, through another week, no further intelligence reached me. But, coming to my room the day after, I found several persons waiting at my door in a high state of nervous excitement.

"That's the man—here he comes," cried the foremost one, whom I recognized as the lawyer who had previously called upon me alone.

"You must take him away, sir, at once," cried a portly person among them, advancing upon me, and whom I knew to be the landlord of No. —— Wall Street. "These gentlemen, my tenants, cannot stand it any longer; Mr. B——," pointing to the lawyer, "has turned him out of his room, and he now persists in haunting the building generally, sitting upon the banisters of the stairs by day, and sleeping in the entry by night. Everybody is concerned; clients are leaving the offices; some fears are entertained of a mob; something you must do, and that without delay."

Aghast at this torrent, I fell back before it, and would fain have locked myself in my new quarters. In vain I persisted that Bartleby was nothing to me—no more than to anyone else. In vain—I was the last person known to have anything to do with him, and they held me to the terrible account. Fearful, then, of being exposed in the papers (as one person present obscurely threatened), I considered the matter, and, at length, said, that if the lawyer would give me a confidential interview with the scrivener, in his (the lawyer's) own room, I would, that afternoon, strive my best to rid them of the nuisance they complained of.

Going upstairs to my old haunt, there was Bartleby silently sitting upon the banister at the landing.

"What are you doing here, Bartleby?" said I.

"Sitting upon the banister," he mildly replied.

I motioned him into the lawyer's room, who then left us.

"Bartleby," said I, "are you aware that you are the cause of great tribulation to me, by persisting in occupying the entry after being dismissed from the office?"

No answer.

"Now one of two things must take place. Either you must do something, or something must be done to you. Now what sort of business would you like to engage in? Would you like to reengage in copying for someone?"

"No; I would prefer not to make any change."

"Would you like a clerkship in a dry-goods store?"

"There is too much confinement about that. No, I would not like a clerkship; but I am not particular."

"Too much confinement," I cried, "why, you keep yourself confined all the time!"

"I would prefer not to take a clerkship," he rejoined, as if to settle that little item at once.

"How would a bartender's business suit you? There is no trying of the eyesight in that."

"I would not like it at all; though as I said before, I am not particular."

His unwonted wordiness inspirited me. I returned to the charge.

"Well, then, would you like to travel through the country collecting bills for the merchants? That would improve your health."

"No, I would prefer to be doing something else."

"How, then, would going as a companion to Europe, to entertain some young gentleman with your conversation—how would that suit you?"

"Not at all. It does not strike me that there is anything definite about that. I like to be stationary. But I am not particular."

"Stationary you shall be, then," I cried, now losing all patience, and, for the first time in all my exasperating connection with him, fairly flying into a passion. "If you do not go away from these premises before night, I shall feel bound—indeed, I *am* bound—to—to—to quit the premises myself!" I rather absurdly concluded, knowing not with what possible threat to try to frighten his immobility into compliance. Despairing of all further efforts, I was precipitately leaving him, when a final thought occurred to me—one which had not been wholly unindulged before.

"Bartleby," said I, in the kindest tone I could assume under such exciting circumstances, "will you go home with me now—not to my office, but my dwelling—and remain there till we can conclude upon some convenient arrangement for you at our leisure? Come, let us start now, right away."

"No: at present I would prefer not to make any change at all."

I answered nothing; but, effectually dodging everyone by the suddenness and rapidity of my flight, rushed from the building, ran up Wall Street towards Broadway, and, jumping into the first omnibus, was soon removed from pursuit. As soon as tranquillity returned, I distinctly perceived that I had now done all that I possibly could, both in respect to the demands of the landlord and his tenants, and with regard to my own desire and sense of duty, to benefit Bartleby, and shield him from rude persecution. I now strove to be entirely carefree and quiescent; and my conscience justified me in the attempt; though, indeed, it was not so successful as I could have wished. So fearful was I of being again hunted out by the incensed landlord and his exasperated tenants, that, surrendering my business to Nippers, for a few days, I drove about the upper part of the town and through the suburbs, in my rockaway;[13] crossed over to Jersey City and Hoboken, and paid fugitive visits to Manhattanville and Astoria. In fact, I almost lived in my rockaway for the time.

When again I entered my office, lo, a note from the landlord lay upon the desk. I opened it with trembling hands. It informed me that the writer had sent to the police, and had Bartleby removed to the Tombs as a vagrant. Moreover, since I knew more about him than anyone else, he wished me to appear at that place, and make a suitable statement of the facts. These tidings had a conflicting effect upon me. At first I was indignant; but, at last, almost approved. The landlord's energetic, summary disposition, had led him to adopt a procedure which I do not think I would have decided upon myself; and yet, as a last resort, under such peculiar circumstances, it seemed the only plan.

As I afterwards learned, the poor scrivener, when told that he must be conducted to the Tombs, offered not the slightest obstacle, but, in his pale, unmoving way, silently acquiesced.

Some of the compassionate and curious bystanders joined the party; and headed by one of the constables arm in arm with Bartleby, the silent procession filed its way through all the noise, and heat, and joy of the roaring thoroughfares at noon.

The same day I received the note, I went to the Tombs, or, to speak more properly, the Halls of Justice. Seeking the right officer, I stated the purpose of my call, and was informed that the individual I described was, indeed, within. I then assured the functionary that Bartleby was a perfectly honest man, and greatly to be compassionated, however unaccountably eccentric. I narrated all I knew, and closed by suggesting the idea of letting him remain in as indulgent confinement as possible, till something less harsh might be done—though, indeed, I hardly knew what. At all events, if nothing else could be decided upon, the almshouse must receive him. I then begged to have an interview.

Being under no disgraceful charge, and quite serene and harmless in all his ways, they had permitted him freely to wander about the prison, and, especially, in the inclosed grass-platted yards thereof. And so I found him there, standing all alone in the quietest of the yards, his face towards a high wall, while all around, from the narrow slits of the jail windows, I thought I saw peering out upon him the eyes of murderers and thieves.

"Bartleby!"

"I know you," he said, without looking round—"and I want nothing to say to you."

"It was not I that brought you here, Bartleby," said I, keenly pained at his implied suspicion. "And to you, this should not be so vile a place. Nothing reproachful attaches to you by being here. And see, it is not so sad a place as one might think. Look, there is the sky, and here is the grass."

---

[13] rockaway: A four-wheeled carriage.

"I know where I am," he replied, but would say nothing more, and so I left him.

As I entered the corridor again, a broad meatlike man, in an apron, accosted me, and, jerking his thumb over his shoulder, said — "Is that your friend?"

"Yes."

"Does he want to starve? If he does, let him live on the prison fare, that's all."

"Who are you?" asked I, not knowing what to make of such an unofficially speaking person in such a place.

"I am the grub-man. Such gentlemen as have friends here, hire me to provide them with something good to eat."

"Is this so?" said I, turning to the turnkey.

He said it was.

"Well, then," said I, slipping some silver into the grub-man's hands (for so they called him), "I want you to give particular attention to my friend there; let him have the best dinner you can get. And you must be as polite to him as possible."

"Introduce me, will you?" said the grub-man, looking at me with an expression which seemed to say he was all impatience for an opportunity to give a specimen of his breeding.

Thinking it would prove of benefit to the scrivener, I acquiesced; and, asking the grub-man his name, went up with him to Bartleby.

"Bartleby, this is a friend; you will find him very useful to you."

"Your sarvant, sir, your sarvant," said the grub-man, making a low salutation behind his apron. "Hope you find it pleasant here, sir; nice grounds — cool apartments — hope you'll stay with us some time — try to make it agreeable. What will you have for dinner today?"

"I prefer not to dine today," said Bartleby, turning away. "It would disagree with me; I am unused to dinners." So saying, he slowly moved to the other side of the inclosure, and took up a position fronting the dead wall.

"How's this?" said the grub-man, addressing me with a stare of astonishment. "He's odd, ain't he?"

"I think he is a little deranged," said I, sadly.

"Deranged? deranged, is it? Well, now, upon my word, I thought that friend of yourn was a gentleman forger; they are always pale and genteel-like, them forgers. I can't help pity 'em — can't help it, sir. Did you know Monroe Edwards?" he added, touchingly, and paused. Then, laying his hand piteously on my shoulder, sighed, "He died of consumption at Sing-Sing.[14] So you weren't acquainted with Monroe?"

"No, I was never socially acquainted with any forgers. But I cannot stop longer. Look to my friend yonder. You will not lose by it. I will see you again."

Some few days after this, I again obtained admission to the Tombs, and went through the corridors in quest of Bartleby; but without finding him.

"I saw him coming from his cell not long ago," said a turnkey, "maybe he's gone to loiter in the yards."

So I went in that direction.

---

[14] **Sing-Sing:** Site of the New York State penitentiary.

"Are you looking for the silent man?" said another turnkey, passing me. "Yonder he lies—sleeping in the yard there. 'Tis not twenty minutes since I saw him lie down."

The yard was entirely quiet. It was not accessible to the common prisoners. The surrounding walls, of amazing thickness, kept off all sounds behind them. The Egyptian character of the masonry weighed upon me with its gloom. But a soft imprisoned turf grew underfoot. The heart of the eternal pyramids, it seemed, wherein, by some strange magic, through the clefts, grass seed, dropped by birds, had sprung.

Strangely huddled at the base of the wall, his knees drawn up, and lying on his side, his head touching the cold stones, I saw the wasted Bartleby. But nothing stirred. I paused; then went close up to him; stooped over, and saw that his dim eyes were open; otherwise he seemed profoundly sleeping. Something prompted me to touch him. I felt his hand, when a tingling shiver ran up my arm and down my spine to my feet.

The round face of the grub-man peered upon me now. "His dinner is ready. Won't he dine today, either? Or does he live without dining?"

"Lives without dining," said I, and closed the eyes.

"Eh!—He's asleep, ain't he?"

"With kings and counselors," murmured I.

There would seem little need for proceeding further in this history. Imagination will readily supply the meager recital of poor Bartleby's interment. But, ere parting with the reader, let me say, that if this little narrative has sufficiently interested him, to awaken curiosity as to who Bartleby was, and what manner of life he led prior to the present narrator's making his acquaintance, I can only reply, that in such curiosity I fully share, but am wholly unable to gratify it. Yet here I hardly know whether I should divulge one little item of rumor, which came to my ear a few months after the scrivener's decease. Upon what basis it rested, I could never ascertain; and hence, how true it is I cannot now tell. But, inasmuch as this vague report has not been without a certain suggestive interest to me, however sad, it may prove the same with some others; and so I will briefly mention it. The report was this: that Bartleby had been a subordinate clerk in the Dead Letter Office at Washington, from which he had been suddenly removed by a change in the administration. When I think over this rumor, hardly can I express the emotions which seize me. Dead letters! does it not sound like dead men? Conceive a man by nature and misfortune prone to a pallid hopelessness, can any business seem more fitted to heighten it than that of continually handling these dead letters, and assorting them for the flames? For by the cartload they are annually burned. Sometimes from out the folded paper the pale clerk takes a ring—the finger it was meant for, perhaps, molders in the grave; a bank note sent in swiftest charity—he whom it would relieve, nor eats nor hungers any more; pardon for those who died despairing; hope for those who died unhoping; good tidings for those who died stifled by unrelieved calamities. On errands of life, these letters speed to death.

Ah, Bartleby! Ah, humanity!

✍ WALT WHITMAN
1819–1892

Walt Whitman has had a tremendous influence on American poetry, both in form and content. He attempted to create a truly indigenous American poetry, one that would match in rhythm and image the unique and incredible variety and breadth of the American landscape and the American people. He was a poet of the new American democracy, of people who were largely absent from the European tradition of poetry: the working classes, women, slaves, prostitutes, felons, adventurers. He was a poet of great empathy, excluding no one and nothing from his vast range of subjects. The great Chilean poet Pablo Neruda[1] could not remember when he first read Whitman, but thanked him because "you gathered / for me / everything; / everything that came forth / was harvested by you / galloping in the alfalfa, / picking poppies for me, / visiting the rivers, / coming into the kitchens / in the afternoon." As Whitman says himself again and again, he is the poet of both the beautiful and the plain, the body and the soul; and his sexual honesty and refusal to feel ashamed of the body was a slap in the face to VICTORIAN[2] prudishness.

Although Whitman is thought of as an American original, his influences included contemporary literature. He was especially affected by Ralph Waldo Emerson's TRANSCENDENTALISM as well as by an eclectic range of beliefs that located divinity within humans as well as outside of them. He trusted intuition, revered nature, and respected the common man. Whitman celebrated nationalism and was part of the ongoing search for an American identity separate from European culture and classical Greek and Roman influences. As he told one of his disciples, "Everything comes out of the dirt — everything comes out of the people . . . not university people . . . people, people, just people." Whitman worked at projecting a hearty and very public persona in his poetry; by the end of his life, his face was emblazoned on cigar boxes, and a Whitman fan club in England venerated a lock of his hair and a stuffed canary that had once been his pet.

A Born Observer.   Whitman was born at West Hills, on Long Island, on May 31, 1819, the second of eight children of a loving mother and the father for whom he was named. The elder Walt, according to his son, was "mean, angered, unjust," an alcoholic who had trouble making ends meet. Whitman's best legacy from his father was political; Thomas Paine[3]

Gabriel Harnson, Daguerreotype of Walt Whitman, c. 1853
Whitman at middle age had a certain ruggedness about him that suggested a wise and well-traveled man. (Oscar Lion Collection, Rare Book Division, Humanities and Social Sciences Library, New York Public Library)

www   For links to more information about Whitman and a quiz on *Song of Myself,* see World Literature Online at bedfordstmartins .com/worldlit.

---

[1] Pablo Neruda: (1904–1973) A Chilean, Neruda is one of the most important poets of the twentieth century; through his poems he searched for ways of identifying the peoples of the Americas, understanding their violent histories, and unifying them into a common vision.

[2] Victorian: Refers to the reign of Queen Victoria (r. 1837–1901) and the values of respectability, conservatism, and prudery.

[3] Thomas Paine: (1737–1809) American revolutionary patriot and liberal thinker.

was a family friend, and the Whitmans supported liberal and feminist causes. When Whitman was four, his father abandoned farming and turned to building or buying houses and quickly selling them; the family moved almost yearly. Whitman deeply loved his mother and his baby brother, Jeff, but household life on the whole was cramped and harsh, and Walt left school at twelve for a string of jobs as a printer's devil (an apprentice), teacher, house builder, and newspaper editor. Above all, like other great Naturalists and poets, the young Whitman was a born voyeur, loafer, and eavesdropper, a friendly spy taking note of nesting birds, seasonal weeds, and molting snakes, and a hanger-out registering the sights, sounds, and smells of working people's lives. He gave voice to some of his ideas about democracy and America at this time in editorials for the Brooklyn *Eagle*.

Travel America.   A trip in 1848 opened his eyes to the vastness and wonder of the American landscape and the possibilities of the frontier; he went down the Ohio and Mississippi Rivers to New Orleans, back north again to Chicago, then east by way of the Great Lakes and the Hudson River.

Whitman's early writings, such as his sentimental novel *Franklin Evans: Or, The Inebriate,* showed little promise. But the imaginative soil out of which *Leaves of Grass* came to flower in 1855 was, as Whitman said, "plowed and manured" well before he began to write that astonishing work. In 1855, he published the book at his own expense. It contained twelve poems and a preface that made plain that Whitman knew he was doing something important and daring. It would remain his chief work, and throughout his life he continually enlarged, revised, rearranged, and lovingly tended to it, adding to it out of all he experienced.

The Effects of the Civil War.   In 1861, when his brother George suffered a mild wound in the Civil War at Fredericksburg, Virginia, Whitman traveled to Washington to take care of him and there found a second true vocation as a nurse, an unpaid "wound dresser" tending the injured and soothing the dying. Eventually, Whitman found a clerkship in the Indian Bureau in the Department of Interior to support himself. He fetched candy, pickles, and tobacco for the patients, played word games with them, or just listened to them talk of war and home.

The Good Gray Poet.   Sightings of President Lincoln in the streets of the capital moved Whitman profoundly. Although the two never met, tradition has it that Lincoln admired *Leaves of Grass* and on seeing Whitman in a crowd remarked, "He looks like a man." At Lincoln's death, Whitman wrote "When Lilacs Last in the Dooryard Bloomed," one of the great elegiac poems of Western literature. After the war, he was forced out of his job when the Secretary of the Interior came across a copy of *Leaves of Grass* and charged the poet with obscenity; friends rallied, and William D. O'Connor wrote a passionate defense of Whitman in a pamphlet entitled *The Good Gray Poet,* a name Whitman retained. Whitman was even appointed to a clerkship in the Attorney General's office. In 1871 he published the fifth edition of *Leaves of Grass* as well as *Democratic Vistas,* a plea to Americans to beware of materialism and to seek instead a visionary, spiritual, and cultural democracy, a theme echoed in his poem, "Passage to India." But Whitman was not a pure democrat; he fiercely opposed universal suffrage, especially for freed slaves.

The man who boasted "I sound my barbaric yawp over the roofs of the world" was secretive about his inner life, and there are nearly as many mysteries about the private Whitman as there are regarding his greatest American contemporary, Emily Dickinson.[4] Whitman's actual sexual history was one of his most guarded secrets. No sexual relationship of his, heterosexual or gay, has ever been documented. His allusions to past mistresses and illegitimate children seem to be balanced by an expressed attraction to young working-class men. It is difficult to label the historical Whitman by referencing portions of his poems; he tends to adopt a collective persona whose central affection is a love for all creatures. If anything, one might call Whitman omnisexual or omnipassionate, since his eroticism flowed outward in multiple directions.

Since having contracted malaria during his stint as a nurse, Whitman's health had been poor. Then in 1873 he had a stroke and returned north to New Jersey to recuperate at his brother George's house; his mother died soon after. Still, he continued to revise and rearrange *Leaves,* and his fame grew to cult status in the United States and Europe. In 1879, this poet who had imaginatively cataloged the North American continent at last saw for himself the American West, as far as the Rockies: "... wonders, revelations I wouldn't have missed for my life ... the Prairie States, the real America," he reported. Whitman died in Camden, New Jersey on March 26, 1892.

An American Poet & *Leaves of Grass*.   The 1855 edition of *Leaves of Grass* got almost no critical notice except for anonymous reviews by its author. But Ralph Waldo Emerson wrote, "I greet you at the beginning of a great career, which must yet have had a long foreground somewhere, for such a start." Without asking permission, Whitman used Emerson's letter to promote his book; Emerson didn't seem to mind, but the literary establishment thought this self-promotion confirmed Whitman's vulgarity. For the frontispiece to the book Whitman chose an engraving of himself lounging in an open-necked shirt like "one of the roughs," the plain working men he admired and to whom he sought to give voice.

During his years of editing, carpentering, and writing formulaic fiction, Whitman was also tirelessly reading — Shakespeare, the Bible, Greek and Roman literature, the English Romantics,[5] and the Bhagavad Gita[6]

"I greet you at the beginning of a great career, which yet must have had a long foreground somewhere, for such a start. I rubbed my eyes a little, to see if this sunbeam were no illusion; but the solid sense of the book is a sober certainty."

– RALPH WALDO EMERSON, about the first edition of *Leaves of Grass* in a letter to Whitman, 1855

---

[4] Emily Dickinson: (1830–1886) Innovative American poet of wit and depth.

[5] English Romantics: Romantic poets, including William Wordsworth, Samuel Taylor Coleridge, and John Keats. See pp. 236, 255, and 281.

[6] Bhagavad Gita: (first century C.E.) Ancient Hindu wisdom text that deals with the spiritual tools necessary for survival.

and other Asian texts. From his contemporaries he mainly gauged how he did *not* want to write: He would avoid "rippling" cadences, elaborate "poetical images," a "tedious and affected" voice. Music — folk songs and spirituals, grand opera and oratorios — enraptured him. From opera especially he learned the techniques of antiphony (responsive chanting), long, flexible, narrative lines, and setting off powerful lyric sections in the manner of arias, or solos. He was casting aside conventional poetic forms, trying instead to catch the rhythms of "the grand American expression" in what is now called free verse, "brawny enough and limber and fun enough" to match any poetry.

Song of Myself.   *Song of Myself,* a poem of several sections within *Leaves of Grass,* is Whitman's epic. Its hero is not a warrior like Homer's[7] Odysseus nor a wandering soul like Dante's[8] Medieval pilgrim in *The Divine Comedy.* Whitman's "Me Myself" is both spirit and body, "hankering, gross, mystical, nude," a self that contains all creation and has empathetic connections to dinosaurs, runaway slaves, Bowery prostitutes, opera singers, longshoremen, alligators snoozing on riverbanks, and the remotest of stars. Against the advice of Emerson and others, in the third *Leaves* edition in 1860, *Song of Myself* included two sections now titled "Children of Adam" and "Calamus." The poems of the former deal in a frank way with heterosexual love: "It is I, you women, I make my way, / I am stern, acrid, large, undissuadable, but I love you, / I do not hurt you any more than is necessary for you, / I pour the stuff to start sons and daughters fit for these States." In the "Calamus" poems, Whitman celebrates male relationships, "the dear love of comrades." With these new verses, Whitman lost many advocates.

"Passage to India."   In 1871, just two years before his crippling paralytic stroke, Whitman completed "Passage to India," an extended poem that celebrates two major engineering feats: the joining of the Union Pacific and the Central Pacific railroads in Utah on May 10, 1869, and the completion of the Suez Canal in 1869. For Whitman, these events mean more than a physical connection between East and West, a journey begun by Columbus in 1492; they symbolize a spiritual relationship with India and the East and the opportunity to connect with and learn from the wisdom of that part of the world. Like many intellectuals in the nineteenth century, Whitman believed that the ancient scriptures of India — the VEDAS[9] and the Bhagavad Gita — contained profound, illuminating insights about the divine.

Whitman's is a uniquely American, democratic self, one that "mutter[s] the word En Masse." His heroic act is to apprehend and pass on the

---

[7] Homer: (eighth century B.C.E.) Credited with *The Iliad* and *The Odyssey.*

[8] Dante: (1265–1321), Italian poet who wrote *The Divine Comedy,* the journey of a pilgrim through hell, purgatory, and heaven.

[9] Vedas: Four books in Sanskrit that date from 1200 B.C.E. and contain poems, litanies, and songs about deities and the origins and workings of the cosmos.

revelation of the democracy of creation, a vision available to all. And yet he is not special, he is no miracle, except in the way all things, even the ants and the "heap'd stones, elder, mullein, and pokeweed" are miracles. Whitman assures the reader in the haunting last lines of *Song of Myself* that he is hanging out, loafing somewhere, encouraging the reader's own journey to discover universal democracy:

> Failing to fetch me at first keep encouraged,
> Missing me one place search another,
> I stop somewhere waiting for you.

One measure of Walt Whitman is the praise he receives from other writers, past and present, and how he revealed to them their own creativity and self-worth. With his writing's free rhythms and open structure, his sexual directness, his colloquial vocabulary, and his democratic inclusion of all peoples in his poetry, he has empowered generations of readers.

■ CONNECTIONS

Pablo Neruda, *Poems,* **Book 6.** A few of the great poets reach across social class, religion, gender, and nationality to become, indeed, international poets. Pablo Neruda speaks to the hearts and souls of Chileans in his work while also touching various classes and races of people in other parts of the world. What characteristics of Whitman's poetry indicate that his writing, like Neruda's, is directed at a wide spectrum of humanity?

William Blake, *Songs of Innocence and Experience,* **p. 208.** A number of nineteenth-century poets made political statements in their work about the need for radical social change. William Blake's *Songs of Innocence and Experience* reveals the sufferings of the lower classes in London. As the poet of democracy, how does Whitman use his writings to promote social change?

Homer, *The Iliad* **and** *The Odyssey,* **Book 1.** The great epic poets made use of long lists of people and events to provide background and historical context for their stories. In his epics *The Iliad* and *The Odyssey,* Homer devotes numerous passages to lists of warriors, armies, and ships. Does Whitman in *Leaves of Grass,* which is sometimes called an American epic, effectively use catalogs or lists?

■ FURTHER RESEARCH

Biography
Allen, Gay Wilson. *The Solitary Singer: A Critical Biography of Walt Whitman.* 1955.
Kaplan, Justin. *Walt Whitman.* 1980.

History & Culture
Reynolds, David S. *Beneath the American Renaissance: The Subversive Imagination in the Age of Emerson and Melville.* 1988.

Criticism
Miller, E. H. *"Song of Myself": A Mosaic of Interpretations.* 1989.

FROM

☙ Song of Myself

1

I Celebrate myself, and sing myself,
And what I assume you shall assume,
For every atom belonging to me as good belongs to you.

I loafe and invite my soul,
I lean and loafe at my ease observing a spear of summer grass.

My tongue, every atom of my blood, form'd from this soil, this air,
Born here of parents born here from parents the same, and their parents the same,
I, now thirty-seven years old in perfect health begin,
Hoping to cease not till death.

10 Creeds and schools in abeyance,
Retiring back a while sufficed at what they are, but never forgotten,
I harbor for good or bad, I permit to speak at every hazard,
Nature without check with original energy.

2

Houses and rooms are full of perfumes, the shelves are crowded with perfumes,
I breathe the fragrance myself and know it and like it,
The distillation would intoxicate me also, but I shall not let it.

The atmosphere is not a perfume, it has no taste of the distillation, it is odorless,
It is for my mouth forever, I am in love with it,

"**Song of Myself.**" Whitman's epic is a multisectioned poem included in the poet's masterwork, *Leaves of Grass*. At first it seems as if the poem's speaker is interested only in himself, but then he begins to speak for others as well; "I" expands into a "we" of great diversity. The popular section six uses grass as a metaphor to connect with various objects and with human beings. An important theme is struck in section twenty-one when Whitman says, "I am the poet of the Body and I am the poet of the Soul." He breaks through Victorian prudery and celebrates the sacredness and beauty of the physical body. Body and soul merge in section forty-eight. The poet's sympathies extend to animals in section thirty-two. The epic, like Whitman's whole body of poetry, is characterized by small vignettes or sketches as well as by long lists or catalogs. An honesty and calm attitude toward death are found in section forty-nine. Section fifty shows Whitman's prescience about living beyond his mortality through his writing.

I will go to the bank by the wood and become undisguised and naked,
20 I am mad for it to be in contact with me.

The smoke of my own breath,
Echoes, ripples, buzz'd whispers, love-root, silk-thread, crotch and vine,
My respiration and inspiration, the beating of my heart, the passing of blood and
    air through my lungs,
The sniff of green leaves and dry leaves, and of the shore and dark-color'd searocks,
    and of hay in the barn,
The sound of the belch'd words of my voice loos'd to the eddies of the wind,
A few light kisses, a few embraces, a reaching around of arms,
The play of shine and shade on the trees as the supple boughs wag,
The delight alone or in the rush of the streets, or along the fields and hill-sides,
The feeling of health, the full-noon trill, the song of me rising from bed and
    meeting the sun.

30 Have you reckon'd a thousand acres much? have you reckon'd the earth much?
Have you practis'd so long to learn to read?
Have you felt so proud to get at the meaning of poems?

Stop this day and night with me and you shall possess the origin of all poems,
You shall possess the good of the earth and sun, (there are millions of suns left,)
You shall no longer take things at second or third hand, nor look through the eyes
    of the dead, nor feed on the spectres in books,
You shall not look through my eyes either, nor take things from me,
You shall listen to all sides and filter them from your self.

5

I believe in you my soul, the other I am must not abase itself to you,
And you must not be abased to the other.

40 Loafe with me on the grass, loose the stop from your throat,
Not words, not music or rhyme I want, not custom or lecture, not even the best,
Only the lull I like, the hum of your valvèd voice.

I mind how once we lay such a transparent summer morning,
How you settled your head athwart my hips and gently turn'd over upon me,
And parted the shirt from my bosom-bone, and plunged your tongue to my bare-
    stript heart,
And reach'd till you felt my beard, and reach'd till you held my feet.

Swiftly arose and spread around me the peace and knowledge that pass all the
    argument of the earth,

And I know that the hand of God is the promise of my own,
And I know that the spirit of God is the brother of my own,
50 And that all the men ever born are also my brothers, and the women my sisters and
      lovers,
And that a kelson[1] of the creation is love,
And limitless are leaves stiff or drooping in the fields,
And brown ants in the little wells beneath them,
And mossy scabs of the worm fence, heap'd stones, elder, mullein and pokeweed.

6

A child said *What is the grass?* fetching it to me with full hands;
How could I answer the child? I do not know what it is any more than he.
I guess it must be the flag of my disposition, out of hopeful green stuff woven.

Or I guess it is the handkerchief of the Lord,
A scented gift and remembrancer designedly dropt,
60 Bearing the owner's name someway in the corners, that we may see and remark, and
      say *Whose?*

Or I guess the grass is itself a child, the produced babe of the vegetation.

Or I guess it is a uniform hieroglyphic,
And it means, Sprouting alike in broad zones and narrow zones,
Growing among black folks as among white,
Kanuck,[2] Tuckahoe,[3] Congressman, Cuff,[4] I give them the same, I receive them the
      same.

And now it seems to me the beautiful uncut hair of graves.

Tenderly will I use you curling grass,
It may be you transpire from the breasts of young men,
It may be if I had known them I would have loved them,
70 It may be you are from old people, or from offspring taken soon out of their
      mothers' laps,
And here you are the mothers' laps.

This grass is very dark to be from the white heads of old mothers,
Darker than the colorless beards of old men,
Dark to come from under the faint red roofs of mouths.

-----

[1] kelson: The superstructure of a ship's keel.   [2] Kanuck: French Canadian.   [3] Tuckahoe: Resident of tidewater Virginia.   [4] Cuff: African American.

O I perceive after all so many uttering tongues,
And I perceive they do not come from the roofs of mouths for nothing.

I wish I could translate the hints about the dead young men and women,
And the hints about old men and mothers, and the offspring taken soon out of their
　　laps.

What do you think has become of the young and old men?
80 And what do you think has become of the women and children?

They are alive and well somewhere,
The smallest sprout shows there is really no death,
And if ever there was it led forward life, and does not wait at the end to arrest it,
And ceas'd the moment life appear'd.
All goes onward and outward, nothing collapses,
And to die is different from what any one supposed, and luckier.

16

I am of old and young, of the foolish as much as the wise,
Regardless of others, ever regardful of others,
Maternal as well as paternal, a child as well as a man,
90 Stuff'd with the stuff that is coarse and stuff'd with the stuff that is fine,
One of the Nation of many nations, the smallest the same and the largest the same,
A Southerner soon as a Northerner, a planter nonchalant and hospitable down by
　　the Oconee I live,
A Yankee bound my own way ready for trade, my joints the limberest joints on
　　earth and the sternest joints on earth,
A Kentuckian walking the vale of the Elkhorn in my deer-skin leggings, a
　　Louisianian or Georgian,
A boatman over lakes or bays or along coasts, a Hoosier, Badger, Buckeye;[5]

At home on Kanadian snow-shoes or up in the bush, or with fishermen off
　　Newfoundland,
At home in the fleet of ice-boats, sailing with the rest and tacking,
At home on the hills of Vermont or in the woods of Maine, or the Texan ranch,
Comrade of Californians, comrade of free North-Westerners, (loving their big
　　proportions,)
100 Comrade of raftsmen and coalmen, comrade of all who shake hands and welcome
　　to drink and meat,

---

[5] **Hoosier . . . Buckeye:** Nicknames, respectively, for natives of Indiana, Wisconsin, and Ohio.

A learner with the simplest, a teacher of the thoughtfulest,
A novice beginning yet experient of myriads of seasons,
Of every hue and caste am I, of every rank and religion,
A farmer, mechanic, artist, gentleman, sailor, Quaker,
Prisoner, fancy-man, rowdy, lawyer, physician, priest,
I resist any thing better than my own diversity,
Breathe the air but leave plenty after me,
And am not stuck up, and am in my place.

(The moth and the fish-eggs are in their place,
110 The bright suns I see and the dark suns I cannot see are in their place,
The palpable is in its place and the impalpable is in its place.)

17

These are really the thoughts of all men in all ages and lands, they are not original
    with me,
If they are not yours as much as mine they are nothing, or next to nothing,
If they are not the riddle and the untying of the riddle they are nothing,
If they are not just as close as they are distant they are nothing.

This is the grass that grows wherever the land is and the water is,
This the common air that bathes the globe.

20

Who goes there? hankering, gross, mystical, nude;
How is it I extract strength from the beef I eat?

120 What is a man anyhow? what am I? what are you?

All I mark as my own you shall offset it with your own,
Else it were time lost listening to me.

I do not snivel that snivel the world over,
That months are vacuums and the ground but wallow and filth.

Whimpering and truckling fold with powders for invalids, conformity goes to the
    fourth-remov'd,
I wear my hat as I please indoors or out.

Why should I pray? why should I venerate and be ceremonious?

Having pried through the strata, analyzed to a hair, counsel'd with doctors and
    calculated close,
I find no sweeter fat than sticks to my own bones.

130 In all people I see myself, none more and not one a barleycorn less,
And the good or bad I say of myself I say of them.

I know I am solid and sound,
To me the converging objects of the universe perpetually flow,
All are written to me, and I must get what the writing means.

I know I am deathless,
I know this orbit of mine cannot be swept by a carpenter's compass,
I know I shall not pass like a child's carlacue[6] cut with a burnt stick at night.

I know I am august,
I do not trouble my spirit to vindicate itself or be understood,
140 I see that the elementary laws never apologize,
(I reckon I behave no prouder than the level I plant my house by, after all.)
I exist as I am, that is enough,
If no other in the world be aware I sit content,
And if each and all be aware I sit content.

One world is aware and by far the largest to me, and that is myself,
And whether I come to my own to-day or in ten thousand or ten million years,
I can cheerfully take it now, or with equal cheerfulness I can wait.

My foothold is tenon'd and mortis'd in granite,
I laugh at what you call dissolution,
150 And I know the amplitude of time.

21

I am the poet of the Body and I am the poet of the Soul,
The pleasures of heaven are with me and the pains of hell are with me,
The first I graft and increase upon myself, the latter I translate into a new tongue.

I am the poet of the woman the same as the man,
And I say it is as great to be a woman as to be a man,
And I say there is nothing greater than the mother of men.

---

[6] carlacue: A curlicue.

I chant the chant of dilation or pride,
We have had ducking and deprecating about enough,
I show that size is only development.

160   Have you outstript the rest? are you the President?
It is a trifle, they will more than arrive there every one, and still pass on.

I am he that walks with the tender and growing night,
I call to the earth and sea half-held by the night.

Press close bare-bosom'd night — press close magnetic nourishing night!
Night of south winds — night of the large few stars!
Still nodding night — mad naked summer night.

Smile O voluptuous cool-breath'd earth!
Earth of the slumbering and liquid trees!
Earth of departed sunset — earth of the mountains misty-topt!
170   Earth of the vitreous pour of the full moon just tinged with blue!
Earth of shine and dark mottling the tide of the river!
Earth of the limpid gray of clouds brighter and clearer for my sake!
Far-swooping elbow'd earth — rich apple-blossom'd earth!
Smile, for your lover comes.

Prodigal, you have given me love, — therefore I to you give love!
O unspeakable passionate love.

24

Walt Whitman, a kosmos, of Manhattan the son,
Turbulent, fleshy, sensual, eating, drinking and breeding,
No sentimentalist, no stander above men and women or apart from them,
180   No more modest than immodest.

Unscrew the locks from the doors!
Unscrew the doors themselves from their jambs!

Whoever degrades another degrades me,
And whatever is done or said returns at last to me.

Through me the afflatus surging and surging, through me the current and index.

I speak the pass-word primeval, I give the sign of democracy,
By God! I will accept nothing which all cannot have their counterpart of on the
    same terms.

Through me many long dumb voices,
Voices of the interminable generations of prisoners and slaves,
190 Voices of the diseas'd and despairing and of thieves and dwarfs,
Voices of cycles of preparation and accretion,
And of the threads that connect the stars, and of wombs and of the father-stuff,
And of the rights of them the others are down upon,
Of the deform'd, trivial, flat, foolish, despised,
Fog in the air, beetles rolling balls of dung.

Through me forbidden voices,
Voices of sexes and lusts, voices veil'd and I remove the veil,
Voices indecent by me clarified and transfigur'd.

I do not press my fingers across my mouth,
200 I keep as delicate around the bowels as around the head and heart,
Copulation is no more rank to me than death is.

I believe in the flesh and the appetites,
Seeing, hearing, feeling, are miracles, and each part and tag of me is a miracle.

Divine am I inside and out, and I make holy whatever I touch or am touch'd
     from,
The scent of these arm-pits aroma finer than prayer,
This head more than churches, bibles, and all the creeds.

If I worship one thing more than another it shall be the spread of my own body, or
     any part of it,
Translucent mould of me it shall be you!
Shaded ledges and rests it shall be you!
210 Firm masculine colter⁷ it shall be you!
Whatever goes to the tilth of me it shall be you!
You my rich blood! your milky stream pale strippings of my life!
Breast that presses against other breasts it shall be you!
My brain it shall be your occult convolutions!
Root of wash'd sweet-flag! timorous pond-snipe! nest of guarded duplicate eggs! it
     shall be you!
Mix'd tussled hay of head, beard, brawn, it shall be you!
Trickling sap of maple, fibre of manly wheat, it shall be you!
Sun so generous it shall be you!
Vapors lighting and shading my face it shall be you!
220 You sweaty brooks and dews it shall be you!
Winds whose soft-tickling genitals rub against me it shall be you!

---

⁷ **colter:** The cutting edge of a plow; metaphorically, the penis.

Broad muscular fields, branches of live oak, loving lounger in my winding paths, it
    shall be you!
Hands I have taken, face I have kiss'd, mortal I have ever touch'd, it shall be you.

I dote on myself, there is that lot of me and all so luscious,
Each moment and whatever happens thrills me with joy,
I cannot tell how my ankles bend, nor whence the cause of my faintest wish,
Nor the cause of the friendship I emit, nor the cause of the friendship I take
    again.

That I walk up my stoop, I pause to consider if it really be,
A morning-glory at my window satisfies me more than the metaphysics of books.

230 To behold the day-break!
The little light fades the immense and diaphanous shadows,
The air tastes good to my palate.

Hefts of the moving world at innocent gambols silently rising freshly exuding,
Scooting obliquely high and low.

Something I cannot see puts upward libidinous prongs,
Seas of bright juice suffuse heaven.

The earth by the sky staid with, the daily close of their junction,
The heav'd challenge from the east that moment over my head,
The mocking taunt. See then whether you shall be master!

28

240 Is this then a touch? quivering me to a new identity,
Flames and ether making a rush for my veins,
Treacherous tip of me reaching and crowding to help them,
My flesh and blood playing out lightning to strike what is hardly different from
    myself,
On all sides prurient provokers stiffening my limbs,
Straining the udder of my heart for its withheld drip,
Behaving licentious toward me, taking no denial,
Depriving me of my best as for a purpose,
Unbuttoning my clothes, holding me by the bare waist,
Deluding my confusion with the calm of the sunlight and pasture-fields,
250 Immodestly sliding the fellow-senses away,
They bribed to swap off with touch and go and graze at the edges of me,
No consideration, no regard for my draining strength or my anger,

Fetching the rest of the herd around to enjoy them a while,
Then all uniting to stand on a headland and worry me.

The sentries desert every other part of me,
They have left me helpless to a red marauder,
They all come to the headland to witness and assist against me.

I am given up by traitors,
I talk wildly, I have lost my wits, I and nobody else am the greatest traitor,
260 I went myself first to the headland, my own hands carried me there.

You villain touch! what are you doing? my breath is tight in its throat,
Unclench your floodgates, you are too much for me.

29

Blind loving wrestling touch, sheath'd hooded sharp-tooth'd touch!
Did it make you ache so, leaving me?

Parting track'd by arriving, perpetual payment of perpetual loan,
Rich showering rain, and recompense richer afterward.

Sprouts take and accumulate, stand by the curb prolific and vital,
Landscapes projected masculine, full-sized and golden.

31

I believe a leaf of grass is no less than the journey-work of the stars,
270 And the pismire is equally perfect, and a grain of sand, and the egg of the wren,
And the tree-toad is a chef-d'œuvre for the highest,
And the running blackberry would adorn the parlors of heaven,
And the narrowest hinge in my hand puts to scorn all machinery,
And the cow crunching with depress'd head surpasses any statue,
And a mouse is miracle enough to stagger sextillions of infidels.

I find I incorporate gneiss, coal, long-threaded moss, fruits, grains, esculent roots,
And am stucco'd with quadrupeds and birds all over,
And have distanced what is behind me for good reasons,
But call any thing back again when I desire it.

280 In vain the speeding or shyness,
In vain the plutonic rocks send their old heat against my approach,
In vain the mastodon retreats beneath its own powder'd bones,

In vain objects stand leagues off and assume manifold shapes,
In vain the ocean settling in hollows and the great monsters lying low,
In vain the buzzard houses herself with the sky,
In vain the snake slides through the creepers and logs,
In vain the elk takes to the inner passes of the woods,
In vain the razor-bill'd auk sails far north to Labrador,
I follow quickly, I ascend to the nest in the fissure of the cliff.

32

290 I think I could turn and live with animals, they are so placid and self-contain'd,
I stand and look at them long and long.

They do not sweat and whine about their condition,
They do not lie awake in the dark and weep for their sins,
They do not make me sick discussing their duty to God,
Not one is dissatisfied, not one is demented with the mania of owning things,
Not one kneels to another, nor to his kind that lived thousands of years ago,
Not one is respectable or unhappy over the whole earth.

So they show their relations to me and I accept them,
They bring me tokens of myself, they evince them plainly in their possession.

300 I wonder where they get those tokens,
Did I pass that way huge times ago and negligently drop them?

Myself moving forward then and now and forever,
Gathering and showing more always and with velocity,
Infinite and omnigenous, and the like of these among them,
Not too exclusive toward the reachers of my remembrancers,

Picking out here one that I love, and now go with him on brotherly terms.

A gigantic beauty of a stallion, fresh and responsive to my caresses,
Head high in the forehead, wide between the ears,
Limbs glossy and supple, tail dusting the ground,
310 Eyes full of sparkling wickedness, ears finely cut, flexibly moving.

His nostrils dilate as my heels embrace him,
His well-built limbs tremble with pleasure as we race around and return.

I but use you a minute, then I resign you, stallion,
Why do I need your paces when I myself out-gallop them?
Even as I stand or sit passing faster than you.

33

Space and Time! now I see it is true, what I guess'd at,
What I guess'd when I loaf'd on the grass,
What I guess'd while I lay alone in my bed,
And again as I walk'd the beach under the paling stars of the morning.

320 My ties and ballasts leave me, my elbows rest in sea-gaps,
I skirt sierras, my palms cover continents,
I am afoot with my vision.

By the city's quadrangular houses — in log huts, camping with lumbermen,
Along the ruts of the turnpike, along the dry gulch and rivulet bed,
Weeding my onion-patch or hoeing rows of carrots and parsnips, crossing
      savannas, trailing in forests,
Prospecting, gold-digging, girdling the trees of a new purchase,
Scorch'd ankle-deep by the hot sand, hauling my boat down the shallow river,
Where the panther walks to and fro on a limb overhead, where the buck turns
      furiously at the hunter,
Where the rattlesnake suns his flabby length on a rock, where the otter is feeding on
      fish,
330 Where the alligator in his tough pimples sleeps by the bayou,
Where the black bear is searching for roots or honey, where the beaver pats the mud
      with his paddle-shaped tail;
Over the growing sugar, over the yellow-flower'd cotton plant, over the rice in its
      low moist field,
Over the sharp-peak'd farm house, with its scallop'd scum and slender shoots from
      the gutters,
Over the western persimmon, over the long-leav'd corn, over the delicate blue-
      flower flax,
Over the white and brown buckwheat, a hummer and buzzer there with the rest,
Over the dusky green of the rye as it ripples and shades in the breeze;
Scaling mountains, pulling myself cautiously up, holding on by low scragged
      limbs,
Walking the path worn in the grass and beat through the leaves of the brush,
Where the quail is whistling betwixt the woods and the wheat-lot,
340 Where the bat flies in the Seventh-month eve, where the great goldbug drops
      through the dark,
Where the brook puts out of the roots of the old tree and flows to the meadow,
Where cattle stand and shake away flies with the tremulous shuddering of their
      hides,
Where the cheese-cloth hangs in the kitchen, where andirons straddle the hearth-
      slab, where cobwebs fall in festoons from the rafters;
Where trip-hammers crash, where the press is whirling its cylinders,
Wherever the human heart beats with terrible throes under its ribs,

Where the pear-shaped balloon is floating aloft, (floating in it myself and looking
    composedly down,)

Looking in at the shop-windows of Broadway the whole forenoon, flatting the flesh
    of my nose on the thick plate glass,
Wandering the same afternoon with my face turn'd up to the clouds, or down a lane
    or along the beach,
My right and left arms round the sides of two friends, and I in the middle;
350 Coming home with the silent and dark-cheek'd bush-boy, (behind me he rides at
    the drape of the day,)
Far from the settlements studying the print of animals' feet, or the moccasin print,
By the cot in the hospital reaching lemonade to a feverish patient,
Nigh the coffin'd corpse when all is still, examining with a candle;
Voyaging to every port to dicker and adventure,
Hurrying with the modern crowd as eager and fickle as any,
Hot toward one I hate, ready in my madness to knife him,
Solitary at midnight in my back yard, my thoughts gone from me a long while,
Walking the old hills of Judæa with the beautiful gentle God by my side,
Speeding through space, speeding through heaven and the stars,
360 Speeding amid the seven satellites and the broad ring, and the diameter of eighty
    thousand miles,
Speeding with tail'd meteors, throwing fire-balls like the rest,
Carrying the crescent child that carries its own full mother in its belly,
Storming, enjoying, planning, loving, cautioning,
Backing and filling, appearing and disappearing,
I tread day and night such roads.

48

I have said that the soul is not more than the body,
And I have said that the body is not more than the soul,
And nothing, not God, is greater to one than one's self is,
And whoever walks a furlong without sympathy walks to his own funeral drest in
    his shroud,
370 And I or you pocketless of a dime may purchase the pick of the earth,
And to glance with an eye or show a bean in its pod confounds the learning of all
    times,
And there is no trade or employment but the young man following it may become a
    hero,
And there is no object so soft but it makes a hub for the wheel'd universe,
And I say to any man or woman, Let your soul stand cool and composed before a
    million universes.

And I say to mankind, Be not curious about God,
For I who am curious about each am not curious about God,
(No array of terms can say how much I am at peace about God and about death.)

I hear and behold God in every object, yet understand God not in the least,
Nor do I understand who there can be more wonderful than myself.

380 Why should I wish to see God better than this day?
I see something of God each hour of the twenty-four, and each moment then,
In the faces of men and women I see God, and in my own face in the glass,
I find letters from God dropt in the street, and every one is sign'd by God's name,
And I leave them where they are, for I know that wheresoe'er I go,
Others will punctually come for ever and ever.

49

And as to you Death, and you bitter hug of mortality, it is idle to try to
    alarm me.

To his work without flinching the accoucheur[8] comes,
I see the elder-hand pressing receiving supporting,
I recline by the sills of the exquisite flexible doors,
390 And mark the outlet, and mark the relief and escape.

And as to you Corpse I think you are good manure, but that does not offend me,
I smell the white roses sweet-scented and growing,
I reach to the leafy lips, I reach to the polish'd breasts of melons.

And as to you Life I reckon you are the leavings of many deaths,
(No doubt I have died myself ten thousand times before.)

I hear you whispering there O stars of heaven,
O suns—O grass of graves—O perpetual transfers and promotions,
If you do not say any thing how can I say any thing?

Of the turbid pool that lies in the autumn forest,
400 Of the moon that descends the steeps of the soughing twilight,
Toss, sparkles of day and dusk—toss on the black stems that decay in the muck,
Toss to the moaning gibberish of the dry limbs.

---

[8] accoucheur: A midwife or obstetrician.

I ascend from the moon, I ascend from the night,
I perceive that the ghastly glimmer is noonday sunbeams reflected,
And debouch to the steady and central from the offspring great or small.

50

There is that in me — I do not know what it is — but I know it is in me.

Wrench'd and sweaty — calm and cool then my body becomes,
I sleep — I sleep long.

I do not know it — it is without name — it is a word unsaid,
410   It is not in any dictionary, utterance, symbol.

Something it swings on more than the earth I swing on,
To it the creation is the friend whose embracing awakes me.
Perhaps I might tell more. Outlines! I plead for my brothers and sisters.
Do you see O my brothers and sisters?
It is not chaos or death — it is form, union, plan — it is eternal life — it is
    Happiness.

51

The past and present wilt — I have fill'd them, emptied them,
And proceed to fill my next fold of the future.

Listener up there! what have you to confide to me?
Look in my face while I snuff the sidle of evening,
420   (Talk honestly, no one else hears you, and I stay only a minute longer.)

Do I contradict myself?
Very well then I contradict myself,
(I am large, I contain multitudes.)

I concentrate toward them that are nigh, I wait on the door-slab.

Who has done his day's work? who will soonest be through with his supper?
Who wishes to walk with me?

Will you speak before I am gone? will you prove already too late?

52

The spotted hawk swoops by and accuses me, he complains of my gab and my
    loitering.

I too am not a bit tamed, I too am untranslatable,
430 I sound my barbaric yawp over the roofs of the world.

The last scud of day holds back for me,
It flings my likeness after the rest and true as any on the shadow'd wilds,
It coaxes me to the vapor and the dusk.

I depart as air, I shake my white locks at the runaway sun,
I effuse my flesh in eddies, and drift it in lacy jags.

I bequeath myself to the dirt to grow from the grass I love,
If you want me again look for me under your boot-soles.

You will hardly know who I am or what I mean,
But I shall be good health to you nevertheless,
440 And filter and fibre your blood.

Failing to fetch me at first keep encouraged,
Missing me one place search another,
I stop somewhere waiting for you.

✑ Passage to India

1

Singing my days,
Singing the great achievements of the present,
Singing the strong light works of engineers,
Our modern wonders, (the antique ponderous Seven[1] outvied,)
In the Old World the east the Suez canal,[2]

"Passage to India." This poem is carefully structured: The first three sections speak of the physical connections between India and the West; the middle sections look "down the slopes" of history at the various explorers of world routes; the final three sections explore spiritual possibilities for the imagination. Whitman's poetry soars to the soulful union of the New World and the "Elder Brother"—God—that transcends time and space.

---

[1] Seven: The Seven Wonders of the World: the Egyptian pyramids, the Mausoleum at Halicarnassus, the Temple of Artemis at Ephesus, the Hanging Gardens of Babylon, the Colossus of Rhodes, the statue of Zeus at Olympia, and the lighthouse at Alexandria.
[2] Suez canal: Joining the Mediterranean and Red Seas, opened November 17, 1869.

The New by its mighty railroad[3] spann'd,
The seas inlaid with eloquent gentle wires;[4]
Yet first to sound, and ever sound, the cry with thee O soul,
The Past! the Past! the Past!

The Past—the dark unfathom'd retrospect!
The teeming gulf—the sleepers and the shadows!
The past—the infinite greatness of the past!
For what is the present after all but a growth out of the past?
(As a projectile form'd, impell'd, passing a certain line, still keeps on,
So the present, utterly form'd, impell'd by the past.)

2

Passage O soul to India!
Eclaircise[5] the myths Asiatic, the primitive fables.

Not you alone proud truths of the world,
Nor you alone ye facts of modern science,
But myths and fables of eld,° Asia's, Africa's fables,   antiquity
The far-darting beams of the spirit, the unloos'd dreams,
The deep diving bibles and legends,
The daring plots of the poets, the elder religions;
O you temples fairer than lilies pour'd over by the rising sun!
O you fables spurning the known, eluding the hold of the known, mounting to
    heaven!
You lofty and dazzling towers, pinnacled, red as roses, burnish'd with gold!
Towers of fables immortal fashion'd from mortal dreams!
You too I welcome and fully the same as the rest!
You too with joy I sing.

Passage to India!
Lo, soul, seest thou not God's purpose from the first?
The earth to be spann'd, connected by network,
The races, neighbors, to marry and be given in marriage,
The oceans to be cross'd, the distant brought near,
The lands to be welded together.
A worship new I sing,

---

[3] railroad: The Union Pacific and the Central Pacific railroads joined at Promontory, Utah, May 10, 1869.

[4] The seas . . . wires: The laying of the Atlantic cable connecting the United States with Europe was completed in 1866.

[5] Eclaircise: French for "clear up."

You captains, voyagers, explorers, yours,
You engineers, you architects, machinists, yours,
You, not for trade or transportation only,
But in God's name, and for thy sake O soul.

3

Passage to India!
Lo soul for thee of tableaus twain,
I see in one the Suez canal initiated, open'd,
I see the procession of steamships, the Empress Eugenie's[6] leading the van,
I mark from on deck the strange landscape, the pure sky, the level sand in the
    distance,
I pass swiftly the picturesque groups, the workmen gather'd,
The gigantic dredging machines.

In one again, different, (yet thine, all thine, O soul, the same,)
I see over my own continent the Pacific railroad surmounting every barrier,
I see continual trains of cars winding along the Platte carrying freight and passengers,
I hear the locomotives rushing and roaring, and the shrill steam-whistle,
I hear the echoes reverberate through the grandest scenery in the world,
I cross the Laramie plains, I note the rocks on grotesque shapes, the buttes,
I see the plentiful larkspur and wild onions, the barren, colorless, sage-deserts,
I see in glimpses afar or towering immediately above me the great mountains, I see
    the Wind river and the Wahsatch mountains,
I see the Monument mountain and the Eagle's Nest, I pass the Promontory, I ascend
    the Nevadas,
I scan the noble Elk mountain and wind around its base,
I see the Humboldt range, I thread the valley and cross the river,
I see the clear waters of lake Tahoe, I see forests of majestic pines,
Or crossing the great desert, the alkaline plains, I behold enchanting mirages of
    waters and meadows,
Marking through these and after all, in duplicate slender lines,
Bridging the three or four thousand miles of land travel,
Tying the Eastern to the Western sea,
The road between Europe and Asia.

(Ah Genoese[7] thy dream! thy dream!
Centuries after thou art laid in thy grave,
The shore thou foundest verifies thy dream.)

---

[6] **Empress Eugenie:** (1826–1920) Empress of France from 1853 to 1870 and wife of Napoleon III; Eugénie was
aboard the *L'Aigle,* the boat that led the opening ceremonies of the Suez Canal.

[7] **Genoese:** Christopher Columbus.

4

Passage to India!
Struggles of many a captain, tales of many a sailor dead,
Over my mood stealing and spreading they come,
Like clouds and cloudlets in the unreach'd sky.

Along all history, down the slopes,
As a rivulet running, sinking now, and now again to the surface rising,
A ceaseless thought, a varied train—lo, soul, to thee, thy sight, they rise,
The plans, the voyages again, the expeditions,
Again Vasco de Gama[8] sails forth,
Again the knowledge gain'd, the mariner's compass,
Lands found and nations born, thou born America,
For purpose vast, man's long probation fill'd,
Thou rondure° of the world at last accomplish'd.   roundness

5

O vast Rondure, swimming in space,
Cover'd all over with visible power and beauty,
Alternate light and day and the teeming spiritual darkness,
Unspeakable high processions of sun and moon and countless stars above,
Below, the manifold grass and waters, animals, mountains, trees,
With inscrutable purpose, some hidden prophetic intention,
Now first it seems my thought begins to span thee.

Down from the gardens of Asia descending radiating,
Adam and Eve appear, then their myriad progeny after them,
Wandering, yearning, curious, with restless explorations,
With questionings, baffled, formless, feverish, with never-happy hearts,
With that sad incessant refrain, *Wherefore unsatisfied soul?* and *Whither O mocking life?*

Ah who shall soothe these feverish children?
Who justify these restless explorations?
Who speak the secret of impassive earth?
Who bind it to us? what is this separate Nature so unnatural?
What is this earth to our affections? (unloving earth, without a throb to answer ours,
Cold earth, the place of graves.)

---

[8] Vasco de Gama: Portuguese navigator who was the first European to sail around Africa and reach India by sea (1497–98).

Yet soul be sure the first intent remains, and shall be carried out,
Perhaps even now the time has arrived.

After the seas are all cross'd, (as they seem already cross'd,)
After the great captains and engineers have accomplish'd their work,
After the noble inventors, after the scientists, the chemist, the geologist, ethnologist,
Finally shall come the poet worthy that name,
The true son of God shall come singing his songs.

Then not your deeds only O voyagers, O scientists and inventors, shall be justified,
All these hearts as of fretted children shall be sooth'd,
All affection shall be fully responded to, the secret shall be told,
All these separations and gaps shall be taken up and hook'd and link'd together,
The whole earth, this cold, impassive, voiceless earth, shall be completely justified,
Trinitas divine[9] shall be gloriously accomplish'd and compacted by the true son of
    God, the poet,
(He shall indeed pass the straits and conquer the mountains,
He shall double the cape of Good Hope to some purpose,)
Nature and Man shall be disjoin'd and diffused no more,
The true son of God shall absolutely fuse them.

6

Year at whose wide-flung door I sing!
Year of the purpose accomplish'd!
Year of the marriage of continents, climates and oceans!
(No mere doge of Venice[10] now wedding the Adriatic,)
I see O year in you the vast terraqueous globe given and giving all,
Europe to Asia, Africa join'd, and they to the New World,
The lands, geographies, dancing before you, holding a festival garland,
As brides and bridegrooms hand in hand.

Passage to India!
Cooling airs from Caucasus far, soothing cradle of man,
The river Euphrates[11] flowing, the past lit up again.

Lo soul, the retrospect brought forward,
The old, most populous, wealthiest of earth's lands,

---

[9] Trinitas divine: A Christian doctrine that sees God as a trinity: Father, Son, and Holy Ghost.

[10] doge of Venice: The ruler of Venice; during the thirteenth and fourteenth centuries, Venice was a major sea power in the eastern Mediterranean.

[11] soothing . . . Euphrates: Mesopotamia, on the Tigris and Euphrates Rivers, is known traditionally as the birthplace of civilization.

The streams of the Indus and the Ganges and their many affluents,
(I my shores of America walking to-day behold, resuming all,)
The tale of Alexander[12] on his warlike marches suddenly dying,
On one side China and on the other side Persia and Arabia,
To the south the great seas and the bay of Bengal,
The flowing literatures, tremendous epics, religions, castes,
Old occult Brahma[13] interminably far back, the tender and junior Buddha,[14]
Central and southern empires and all their belongings, possessors,
The wars of Tamerlane,[15] the reign of Aurungzebe,[16]
The traders, rulers, explorers, Moslems, Venetians, Byzantium, the Arabs,
    Portuguese,
The first travelers famous yet, Marco Polo, Batouta the Moor,[17]
Doubts to be solv'd, the map incognita, blanks to be fill'd,
The foot of man unstay'd, the hands never at rest,
Thyself O soul that will not brook a challenge.
The mediæval navigators rise before me,
The world of 1492, with its awaken'd enterprise,
Something swelling in humanity now like the sap of the earth in spring,
The sunset splendor of chivalry declining.

And who art thou sad shade?
Gigantic, visionary, thyself a visionary,
With majestic limbs and pious beaming eyes,
Spreading around with every look of thine a golden world,
Enhuing it with gorgeous hues.

As the chief histrion,
Down to the footlights walks in some great scena,
Dominating the rest I see the Admiral[18] himself,
(History's type of courage, action, faith,)
Behold him sail from Palos leading his little fleet,

---

[12] **Alexander:** The Greek Alexander the Great extended his empire into India and then suddenly died on his return journey from a fever in 323 B.C.E.

[13] **Brahma:** In Hinduism, the absolute God (Brahman) is made up of three persons: Brahma, the creator; Vishnu, the preserver; and Shiva, the dissolver.

[14] **Buddha:** Sixth century B.C.E. founder of Buddhism; called "junior" by Whitman because there are older religious traditions in India and the Middle East.

[15] **Tamerlane:** (1336?–1405) Mongol warrior whose empire stretched from the Black Sea to the Ganges.

[16] **Aurungzebe:** Or Aurangzeb (1618–1707), the last Mughal emperor of India.

[17] **Marco . . . Moor:** Marco Polo (1254–1324) was a Venetian traveler to China; Batouta the Moor (1303–1377) was a traveler in Africa and Asia. Both men were traders as well as explorers.

[18] **The Admiral:** Columbus, known as "the Admiral of the Ocean Sea." He sailed from the Spanish seaport of Palos on August 3, 1492.

His voyage behold, his return, his great fame,
His misfortunes, calumniators, behold him a prisoner, chain'd,
Behold his dejection, poverty, death.

(Curious in time I stand, noting the efforts of heroes,
Is the deferment long? bitter the slander, poverty, death?
Lies the seed unreck'd for centuries in the ground? lo, to God's due occasion,
Uprising in the night, it sprouts, blooms,
And fills the earth with use and beauty.)

7

Passage indeed O soul to primal thought,
Not lands and seas alone, thy own clear freshness,
The young maturity of brood and bloom,
To realms of budding bibles.

O soul, repressless, I with thee and thou with me,
Thy circumnavigation of the world begin,
Of man, the voyage of his mind's return,
To reason's early paradise,
Back, back to wisdom's birth, to innocent intuitions,
Again with fair creation.

8

O we can wait no longer,
We too take ship O soul,
Joyous we too launch out on trackless seas,
Fearless for unknown shores on waves of ecstasy to sail,
Amid the wafting winds, (thou pressing me to thee, I thee to me, O soul,)
Caroling free, singing our song of God,
Chanting our chant of pleasant exploration.
With laugh and many a kiss,
(Let others deprecate, let others weep for sin, remorse, humiliation,)
O soul, thou pleasest me, I thee.

Ah more than any priest O soul we too believe in God,
But with the mystery of God we dare not dally.

O soul thou pleasest me, I thee,
Sailing these seas or on the hills, or waking in the night,
Thoughts, silent thoughts, of Time and Space and Death, like waters
    flowing,
Bear me indeed as through the regions infinite,

Whose air I breathe, whose ripples hear, lave me all over,
Bathe me O God in thee, mounting to thee,
I and my soul to range in range of thee.

O Thou transcendent,
Nameless, the fibre and the breath,
Light of the light, shedding forth universes, thou centre of them,
Thou mightier centre of the true, the good, the loving,
Thou moral, spiritual fountain—affection's source—thou reservoir,
(O pensive soul of me—O thirst unsatisfied—waitest not there?
Waitest not haply for us somewhere there the Comrade perfect?)
Thou pulse—thou motive of the stars, suns, systems,
That, circling, move in order, safe, harmonious,
Athwart the shapeless vastnesses of space,
How should I think, how breathe a single breath, how speak, if, out of myself,
I could not launch, to those, superior universes?

Swiftly I shrivel at the thought of God,
At Nature and its wonders, Time and Space and Death
But that I, turning, call to thee O soul, thou actual Me,
And lo, thou gently masterest the orbs,
Thou matest Time, smilest content at Death,
And fillest, swellest full the vastnesses of Space.

Greater than stars or suns,
Bounding O soul thou journeyest forth;
What love than thine and ours could wider amplify?
What aspirations, wishes, outvie thine and ours O soul?
What dreams of the ideal? what plans of purity, perfection, strength,
What cheerful willingness for others' sake to give up all?
For others' sake to suffer all?

Reckoning ahead O soul, when thou, the time achiev'd,
The seas all cross'd, weather'd the capes, the voyage done.
Surrounded, copest, frontest God, yieldest, the aim attain'd,
As fill'd with friendship, love complete, the Elder Brother found,
The Younger melts in fondness in his arms.

9

Passage to more than India!
Are thy wings plumed indeed for such far flights?
O soul, voyagest thou indeed on voyages like those?
Disportest thou on waters such as those?

Soundest below the Sanscrit and the Vedas?[19]
Then have thy bent unleash'd.

Passage to you, your shores, ye aged fierce enigmas!
Passage to you, to mastership of you, ye strangling problems!
You, strew'd with the wrecks of skeletons, that, living, never reach'd you.

Passage to more than India!
O secret of the earth and sky!
Of you O waters of the sea! O winding creeks and rivers!
Of you O woods and fields! of you strong mountains of my land!
Of you O prairies! of you gray rocks!
O morning red! O clouds! O rain and snows!
O day and night, passage to you!

O sun and moon and all you stars! Sirius and Jupiter!
Passage to you!

Passage, immediate passage! the blood burns in my veins!
Away O soul! hoist instantly the anchor!
Cut the hawsers—haul out—shake out every sail!
Have we not stood here like trees in the ground long enough?
Have we not grovel'd here long enough, eating and drinking like mere brutes?
Have we not darken'd and dazed ourselves with books long enough?

Sail forth—steer for the deep waters only,
Reckless O soul, exploring, I with thee, and thou with me,
For we are bound where mariner has not yet dared to go,
And we will risk the ship, ourselves and all.

O my brave soul!
O farther farther sail!
O daring joy, but safe! are they not all the seas of God?
O farther, farther, farther sail!

---

[19] **the Vedas:** Four books written in Sanskrit that date from 1,200 B.C.E. and contain poems, litanies, and songs about deities and the origins and workings of the cosmos.

✑ Facing West from California's Shores

Facing west from California's shores,
Inquiring, tireless, seeking what is yet unfound,
I, a child, very old, over waves, towards the house of maternity, the land of
     migrations, look afar,
Look off the shores of my Western sea, the circle almost circled;
For starting westward from Hindustan, from the vales of Kashmere,
From Asia, from the north, from the God, the sage, and the hero,
From the south, from the flowery peninsulas and the spice islands,
Long having wander'd since, round the earth having wander'd,
Now I face home again, very pleas'd and joyous,
10 (But where is what I started for so long ago?
and why is it yet unfound?)

"Facing West from California's Shores." Unlike "Passage to India," which also provides a connection to the East, "Facing West from California's Shore" extends Whitman's vision westward as he searches for the "house of maternity," the cultural cradle of civilization that gave rise to migrations to the West and became the basis for the great variety of peoples and beliefs in the United States. With a very enlightened perspective for his times, Whitman pays tribute to the religious influence of India as well as other parts of Asia. The questions that conclude the poem suggest that Whitman is uncertain whether he has been able to link the world to his American experience.

✑ EMILY DICKINSON
1830–1886

www For more information about Dickinson and a quiz on her poems, see *World Literature Online* at bedfordstmartins.com/worldlit.

Stylistically, Emily Dickinson's poems may not have had much influence on succeeding generations of writers; it is hard to name a single poet whose poems look or sound like Dickinson's crafted miniatures. Still, her legacy has been vast, especially (but not only) for women, in that she, like her contemporary Walt Whitman, has taught writers audacity. The female voices that speak in Emily Dickinson's poems are daring, subversive, and uncompromising; they weigh old assumptions and find them wanting, speak of desires deemed improper by society, defy convention, and invite cataclysm. Dickinson's work reminds us that the Romantic hero, the person who tests the limits of God's and society's tolerance, who always thirsts for something beyond, who experiences suicidal despair and shattering joy, can be a woman writing in an upstairs bedroom.

A Secluded Life.   In some ways, we know a fair amount about Emily Dickinson. But we know little of her inner life except that it was intense. We do not know the name or even the sex of the person to whom in the early 1860s she wrote a series of anguished and openly erotic love letters, nor do we know whether those letters were ever sent. And we do not know why, after a rather lively childhood and adolescence, she sought a more and more secluded life.

Dickinson was born on December 10, 1830, in Amherst, Massachusetts, a beautiful village in the Berkshire hills whose vigorous intellectual life centered around Amherst College, for which her father and later her brother Austin served as treasurer. The Dickinson children were in awe all their lives of their stern but affectionate father, and Dickinson was exceptionally close to her brother, Austin, and her sister, Lavinia. Dickinson herself had an excellent education at Amherst Academy, and later, a single year at Mount Holyoke Female Seminary. Dickinson's was not the typical watered-down "female curriculum" of her day; her basic knowledge of botany, astronomy, physics, theology, and other subjects is evident throughout her poems. At Mount Holyoke, Dickinson revealed her independent turn of mind. When Mary Lyon, the revered founder, asked the assembled students to rise if they hoped to become Christians, only Dickinson remained seated. As is abundantly evident from her poems, Dickinson balked at conventional pieties and at easy answers to theological questions.

The beginning of Dickinson's gradual withdrawal from society can probably be dated from her leaving Mount Holyoke. As many have pointed out, her isolation may have been strategic. The amount of housework, child care, and social obligation visited upon even an unmarried daughter in a large family allowed little time for poetry. Later in her life, in the upstairs bedroom where she did most of her writing, Dickinson once pantomimed for her niece the act of locking herself in her room, saying "It's just a turn—and freedom, Mattie!"

Worldly Contact.   After Dickinson's departure from Mount Holyoke, she made a few trips with her family. In 1855, she visited Washington and Philadelphia with her father, then serving a term in Congress. In Philadelphia she met the married minister Charles Wadsworth, perhaps the person to whom, in the late 1850s and early 1860s, she addressed the "Master letters," painful expressions of hopeless longing that may never have been mailed.

Dickinson had written poems from adolescence on, but in the early 1860s—the time of the emotional crises hinted at in the Master letters—her creativity burgeoned. In 1862, in response to an essay by Thomas Wentworth Higginson in *The Atlantic Monthly* giving advice to young would-be writers, Dickinson sent him four poems, asking him in an unsigned letter to tell her whether he thought they "breathed"; she penciled her name lightly on a card, which she enclosed in a separate envelope. Higginson was too conventional to appreciate fully Dickinson's work—he often objected to the unorthodoxy of her grammar and vocabulary—but he was a generous lifelong mentor. Her childhood friend Helen Hunt Jackson (1830–1885), author of the popular romance *Ramona*, also respected Dickinson's work and kept urging her to publish, but her pleas were largely in vain. Dickinson cringed at the way her few published poems were altered and regularized by editors, and her reluctance to have her work tampered with may partially explain why she didn't send more of it out into the world. Certainly, even those closest to her did not guess how prolifically she wrote. At times during the 1860s, Dickinson seems to have written one or more poems a day.

Last Years. Death was never far from any nineteenth-century household, but particular deaths were especially painful for Dickinson—several young men she had known died during the Civil War; her father, in 1874; her favorite nephew, Gilbert, in 1883; her beloved friend Judge Otis Lord, the following year. Not only death, but the slow process of dying, was a very present reality for Dickinson. Her mother, no brilliant intellectual but a pleasant and nurturing woman when she was well, became essentially an invalid in 1855, and until her death in 1882 the responsibility of nursing her fell mostly to Emily and Lavinia, the unmarried daughters.

In 1882, Dickinson's adored elder brother Austin embarked on a passionate, adulterous affair with Mabel Loomis Todd, the artistic young wife of an Amherst professor, a relationship that would endure until Austin's death in 1895. The lovers did not seek to divorce their partners, although everyone in both families knew what was going on, and the affair seems to have been an open secret throughout the scandalized community. Emily and Lavinia, at whose house the lovers often trysted, were apparently caught in the crossfire of family loyalties, but neither sister recorded a word about the situation.

In her last years, Dickinson saw no one face-to-face except certain family members and household servants, allowing her rare guests to sit in an adjacent room and speak to her through a door left slightly ajar. She died on May 15, 1886, of Bright's disease. Shortly afterward, Lavinia discovered nearly eighteen hundred poems in various drawers and initially gave them to Austin's wife, Susan, with the thought that Susan might oversee their publication. Two years later, when Susan had made no effort to do so, Lavinia took the poems back and gave them to Dickinson's old mentor, Higginson, and Mabel Loomis Todd, herself something of a poet. The two jointly oversaw two small editions of selected poems in 1890 and 1891; in 1896, Todd brought out a third selection. These editions did exactly what Dickinson had disapproved of previously with their smoothing-out and normalizing of her distinctive voice. Thomas Johnson's edition of 1955, nearly seventy years after Dickinson's death, was the first to attempt to reproduce the poems as Dickinson had recorded them.

The Poet's Voice. Dickinson once claimed to Higginson that her major influences were Keats,[1] the Brownings,[2] and the Bible; elsewhere, she would name Shakespeare and her lexicon as the books she depended on. She disavowed knowing her greatest poetic contemporary, Walt Whitman, whose work she had been told was "disgraceful." But the style of her verse was shaped by very homely influences indeed—principally, the "common meter" of hymn books. Her poems were also influenced by valentines and memorial verses for the dead, both avidly written and collected by genteel Amherst residents.

With these conventional pieces for reading material and music, Emily Dickinson somehow forged her extraordinary poems, the more extraordinary because the revolutionary things they say occur within such everyday structures. In hymn meter, she wonders whether God is not playing a game of hide-and-seek with his children, one that might end, horribly, with the major player having gone away, leaving people staring at their deaths into a nothingness; she takes the supposedly comforting phrase "the Lord giveth, and the Lord taketh away" and pushes it to its logical extreme, envisioning a God who is at once a stingy banker, a sneaky burglar, and overall a father to whose capricious principles of spiritual economy we are subjected as he gives us people to love and then snatches them away. Elsewhere, she envisions ecstatic erotic unions with a figure who may be a mortal lover, a version of Christ, or both; in either case, these are poems that defy and demand more and harder answers than churches or preachers may provide. Dickinson prefers painful truth, however discouraging, to anything less. Her eye for natural subjects is matchless; like Whitman, she is able to see beyond the usual pretty subject. Her poems deal with rats, frogs, snakes, and bats as well as bluebirds, and she looks steadily at nature's darker side.

Perhaps most compelling of all is Dickinson's exploration of female power and powerlessness. She unflinchingly records a dream in which a flaccid worm she'd thoughtlessly let stay in her bedroom turns into a menacing male snake "ringed with power"; she pictures a spirited girl child who inwardly thwarts all adult efforts to repress her; she envisions standing in relation to some master, whether God or a human lover, as a gun to its owner, with its explosive power to kill directed at fellow female creatures. In a poem that for many modern readers seems to evoke experience of repeated sexual abuse, Dickinson asserts that a woman's life amounts to brief moments of feverish freedom bracketed by long periods of helpless oppression.

---

[1] **Keats:** (1795–1821) John Keats, the most symbolic of the English Romantic poets; his work suggested ways of handling symbolism to Dickinson.

[2] **the Brownings:** Robert Browning (1812–1889) and his wife, Elizabeth Barrett Browning (1806–1861), two renowned British Victorian poets who married in 1846 and moved to Florence, Italy. Elizabeth was an invalid most of her life due to a youthful riding accident. Their precarious relationship and passionate poetry made them popular favorites in both England and America.

In addressing such subjects Dickinson defied nineteenth-century theology, patriarchy, and the ideal of the woman as "the angel in the house." Coming from a woman in small-town New England in the nineteenth century, that was heroism indeed.

■ CONNECTIONS

John Donne, "The Canonization," "Holy Sonnet 14," "Good Friday, 1613. Riding Westward," Poems (Book 3). Like many of her contemporaries, Dickinson explored her connection with God in her poetry. In the seventeenth century, Donne had questioned the role of the divine in human existence. What do these two investigations reveal about how each of these authors approaches belief in the divine? How does each portray the relationship between the individual and God?

Mary Rowlandson, *Narrative* (Book 4); Margery Kempe, *The Book of Margery Kempe* (Book 3). Religion and death are controlling forces in Dickinson's poetry. These concerns cross all boundaries and time periods. Note that Rowlandson's consolation in her captivity is that she is serving God's needs, and Kempe's ability to cope with rejection is buffered by her belief that she is serving God's will. What trials and tests does Dickinson record in her poetry? How does Dickinson's approach to her own trials and sufferings compare or contrast with that of Rowlandson and Kempe?

Charlotte Perkins Gilman, *The Yellow Wallpaper* (p. 941); Virginia Woolf, *A Room of One's Own* (Book 6). As a struggling female writer, Dickinson speaks in many ways for women of the nineteenth century. Her unorthodox views and approaches to poetry led to widespread criticism, yet she is recognized as one of the most important American poets of her age. Look at the works of Woolf and Gilman and examine the ways they threaten to revolutionize the view of women for their time periods. In what ways do these texts question or reveal the injustice of the patriarchal system that confines women?

■ FURTHER RESEARCH

Editions
Johnson, Thomas H., ed. *The Poems of Emily Dickinson*. 3 vols. 1951, 1955.
Johnson, Thomas H., and Theodora Ward, eds. *The Letters of Emily Dickinson*. 3 vols. 1958.

Biography
Sewall, Richard. *The Life of Emily Dickinson*. 2 vols. 1974.

Criticism
Dobson, J. *Dickinson and the Strategies of Reticence: The Woman Writer in Nineteenth Century America*. 1989.
Farr, Judith. *The Passion of Emily Dickinson*. 1992.
Ferlazzo, Paul J., ed. *Critical Essays on Emily Dickinson*. 1984.
Howe, Susan. *My Emily Dickinson*. 1985.
Juhasz, Suzanne, ed. *Feminist Critics Read Emily Dickinson*. 1983.
Smith, Martha Nell. *Rowing in Eden: Rereading Emily Dickinson*. 1992.

ᴄᴡ I know that He exists

I know that He exists.
Somewhere—in Silence—
He has hid his rare life
From our gross eyes.

'Tis an instant's play.
'Tis a fond Ambush—
Just to make Bliss
Earn her own surprise!

But—should the play
10   Prove piercing earnest—
Should the glee—glaze—
In Death's—stiff—stare—

Would not the fun
Look too expensive!
Would not the jest—
Have crawled too far!

"I know that He exists"; "I never lost as much but twice". Dickinson, who did not feel that publication was the first business of a poet, saw only ten of her poems published—anonymously and without her permission—during her lifetime. After Dickinson died, her sister Lavinia found some 1,800 poems in Emily's dresser. Though some of the poems had been carefully copied out and hand-sewn into booklets, others had been jotted down on scraps of paper and on the backs of envelopes, making preparation for publication a difficult task.

Like the young woman at Mount Holyoke Female Seminary who alone would not stand when asked to do so if she wished to become a Christian, the mature Dickinson constantly played with the paradoxes of Christian belief and the hope of salvation. These subjects coupled with provocative images of death give much of her poetry a stark, grim quality. Yet there is often wit around the edges of her serious metaphysical musings; Dickinson likes to tease the meaning out of images that appear inappropriate to her subject. Thus God, refusing to show Himself, lays a trap, a "fond Ambush"; yet, Dickinson wonders, in the face of Death might not God carry the "fun" too far? And in "I never lost as much but twice," to take another example, God, who takes away a loved one, is addressed as a "Burglar" and a "Banker" who impoverishes the poet.

I never lost as much but twice

I never lost as much but twice,
And that was in the sod.
Twice have I stood a beggar
Before the door of God!

Angels—twice descending
Reimbursed my store—
Burglar! Banker—Father!
I am poor once more!

A narrow Fellow in the Grass

A narrow Fellow in the Grass
Occasionally rides—
You may have met Him—did you not
His notice sudden is—
The Grass divides as with a Comb—
A spotted shaft is seen—
And then it closes at your feet
And opens further on—

He likes a Boggy Acre
10 A Floor too cool for Corn—
Yet when a Boy, and Barefoot—
I more than once at Noon
Have passed, I thought, a Whip lash
Unbraiding in the Sun
When stooping to secure it
It wrinkled, and was gone—

Several of Nature's People
I know, and they know me—

"A narrow Fellow in the Grass"; "Split the Lark — and you'll find the Music —"; "In Winter in my Room". Dickinson manipulates images of nature, revealing both its improbable beauty and its hidden danger. "A narrow Fellow in the Grass" calls forth extravagant memories of discovery but also excites a shudder of fear: "Zero at the Bone". In "Split the Lark" the Skeptic Thomas thinks he will uncover the source of the lark's music only when he opens its bloody breast, yet the death of the lark stops the music altogether. The "worm" in "In Winter in my Room" metamorphoses into a snake, turning the childish game the poet has played into a nightmare.

I feel for them a transport
20 Of cordiality—

But never met this Fellow
Attended, or alone
Without a tighter breathing
And Zero at the Bone—

∾ Split the Lark—and you'll find the Music—

Split the Lark—and you'll find the Music—
Bulb after Bulb, in Silver rolled—
Scantily dealt to the Summer Morning
Saved for your Ear when Lutes be old.

Loose the Flood—you shall find it patent—
Gush after Gush, reserved for you—
Scarlet Experiment! Sceptic Thomas![1]
Now, do you doubt that your Bird was true?

---

[1] **Sceptic Thomas:** "Doubting Thomas," the disciple who declared he would not believe Jesus had risen unless he could place his fingers in Jesus' wounds; see John 20:24–29.

∾ In Winter in my Room

In Winter in my Room
I came upon a Worm—
Pink, lank and warm—
But as he was a worm
And worms presume
Not quite with him at home—
Secured him by a string
To something neighboring
And went along.

10 A Trifle afterward
A thing occurred
I'd not believe it if I heard
But state with creeping blood—
A snake with mottles rare
Surveyed my chamber floor

In feature as the worm before
But ringed with power—

The very string with which
I tied him—too
20 When he was mean and new
That string was there—

I shrank—"How fair you are"!
Propitiation's claw—
"Afraid," he hissed
"Of me"?
"No cordiality"—
He fathomed me—
Then to a Rhythm *Slim*
Secreted in his Form
30 As Patterns swim
Projected him.

That time I flew
Both eyes his way
Lest he pursue
Nor ever ceased to run
Till in a distant Town
Towns on from mine
I set me down
This was a dream.

∾ They shut me up in Prose—

They shut me up in Prose—
As when a little Girl
They put me in the Closet—
Because they liked me "still"—

"They shut me up in Prose —"; *"Much Madness is divinest Sense"*; *"I like a look of Agony"*; *"Wild Nights — Wild Nights!"*. Even in her seeming isolation Dickinson resists confinement. "They shut me up in Prose—" shows her resisting "Captivity," while "Much Madness is divinest Sense" warns us that although true reason will often discern what public understanding cannot, the original intellect may pay a heavy price for being different. In her search for the authentic, Dickinson praises the beads of sweat as genuine marks of pain: "I like a look of Agony, / Because I know it's true—". But she also upholds excess of feeling in "Wild Nights." Her attraction to excess is part of her rejection of the superficial, the common, and the traditional.

Still! Could themself have peeped—
And seen my Brain—go round—
They might as wise have lodged a Bird
For Treason—in the Pound—
Himself has but to will
10 And easy as a Star
Abolish his Captivity—
And laugh—No more have I—

Much Madness is divinest Sense—

Much Madness is divinest Sense—
To a discerning Eye—
Much Sense—the starkest Madness—
'Tis the Majority
In this, as All, prevail—
Assent—and you are sane—
Demur—you're straightway dangerous—
And handled with a Chain—

I like a look of Agony

I like a look of Agony,
Because I know it's true—
Men do not sham Convulsion,
Nor simulate, a Throe—

The Eyes glaze once—and that is Death—
Impossible to feign
The Beads upon the Forehead
By homely Anguish strung.

Wild Nights—Wild Nights!

Wild Nights—Wild Nights!
Were I with thee
Wild Nights should be
Our luxury!

Futile—the Winds—
To a Heart in port—
Done with the Compass—
Done with the Chart!

Rowing in Eden—
10 Ah, the Sea!
Might I but moor—Tonight—
In Thee!

∾ My Life had stood—a Loaded Gun—

My Life had stood—a Loaded Gun—
In Corners—till a Day
The Owner passed—identified—
And carried Me away—

And now We roam in Sovereign Woods—
And now We hunt the Doe—
And every time I speak for Him—
The Mountains straight reply—

And do I smile, such cordial light
10 Upon the Valley glow—
It is as a Vesuvian[1] face
Had let its pleasure through—

And when at Night—Our good Day done—
I guard My Master's Head—

"My Life had stood — a Loaded Gun —"; "The Soul has Bandaged moments —". Perhaps the most moving of Dickinson's poems are those in which the metaphors go astray, poems whose direction seems to escape the determination of the poet. In "My Life had stood" the image of the gun and its devotion to its master carries most of the poem, but in the last stanza the gun is a lifeless thing, whereas the master contains precious life within him. In "The Soul has Bandaged moments —" the vulnerable soul first confronts terror then enjoys liberty in a variety of metaphorical images, but it is seldom warned, the poet tells us, of the "retaken moments" when it will be recaptured by Horror.

---

[1]Vesuvian: From Mount Vesuvius, in Italy; volcanic.

'Tis better than the Eider-Duck's
Deep Pillow—to have shared—

To foe of His—I'm deadly foe—
None stir the second time—
On whom I lay a Yellow Eye—
20 Or an emphatic Thumb—

Though I than He—may longer live
He longer must—than I—
For I have but the power to kill,
Without—the power to die—

∾ The Soul has Bandaged moments—

The Soul has Bandaged moments—
When too appalled to stir—
She feels some ghastly Fright come up
And stop to look at her—

Salute her—with long fingers—
Caress her freezing hair—
Sip, Goblin, from the very lips
The Lover—hovered—o'er—
Unworthy, that a thought so mean
10 Accost a Theme—so—fair—

The soul has moments of Escape—
When bursting all the doors—
She dances like a Bomb, abroad,
And swings upon the Hours,

As do the Bee—delirious borne—
Long Dungeoned from his Rose—
Touch Liberty—then know no more,
But Noon, and Paradise—

The Soul's retaken moments—
20 When, Felon led along,
With shackles on the plumed feet,
And staples, in the Song,

The Horror welcomes her, again,
These, are not brayed of Tongue—

❧ Success is counted sweetest

Success is counted sweetest
By those who ne'er succeed.
To comprehend a nectar
Requires sorest need.

Not one of all the purple Host
Who took the Flag today
Can tell the definition
So clear of Victory

As he defeated—dying—
10 On whose forbidden ear
The distant strains of triumph
Burst agonized and clear!

"Success is counted sweetest."   The paradox of victory and defeat fascinates Dickinson, as the final poem in this selection suggests. Here, as often is the case, Dickinson confronts a tired old saying, "To the Victor Goes the Spoils," and suggests that only the defeated can truly understand the sweetness of victory. What Whitman often conveys by bombast, Dickinson does by intensifying an image throwing off conventional wisdom to find truth in places least expected.

❧ JOAQUIM MARIA MACHADO DE ASSIS
1839–1908

wah-KEEM
mah-REE-ah
mah-CHAH-*thoh*
thay ah-SEES

With over two hundred short stories and some nine novels to his name, **Joaquim Maria Machado de Assis** is Brazil's greatest writer, but he has only recently become known in the United States. Literature written in Portuguese does not have a solid reputation in the Western world, and Machado de Assis, unfortunately, was not widely translated into English until after World War II. Experts divide his work into two periods: before 1880, when his writings were generally "romantic"—love stories and parlor dramas—and after 1880, when they became critical of the middle class, ironic, and experimental. After 1880, Machado de Assis tends to de-emphasize plot and action and begins to probe beneath the surface of his characters using what could be called psychological **REALISM**, a tendency reminiscent of European writers of that same period, such as Flaubert, Stendahl, and Chekhov. The satiric playfulness of *The Posthumous Mem-*

oirs of Bras Cubas (*Memórias póstumas de Brás Cubas,* 1881) seems to be indebted to Laurence Sterne's *Tristram Shandy.*[1] Machado de Assis's use of literary devices that draw the reader into consciously questioning the boundaries between fiction and reality anticipates the Argentinian writer Jorge Luis Borges.[2] The darkness of the Brazilian's vision seems to reflect the disillusionment of European and American intellectuals with institutions and society around the turn of the century.

Overcoming Obstacles.   Machado de Assis's Portuguese mother, who worked as a washerwoman, died in childbirth, and Joaquim was raised by a woman of mixed race whom his father, himself a mixed-race house painter from Rio de Janeiro, eventually married. After his father died, his stepmother became a cook in a girl's school. Joaquim's formal education was limited to elementary school, but he ultimately overcame poverty and adversity to pursue his dream of becoming a writer. Throughout his life he suffered from physical ailments that undoubtedly curbed his activities: stuttering, eye problems, and epilepsy. In 1856 he became an apprentice printer with the Imprensa Nacional; working first as a typesetter, he later became a proofreader and an editor. His informal education included associating with other writers and translating. Despite Machado de Assis's lack of formal schooling, he was very well read in foreign literature, especially English. In 1869 he married Carolina Augusta, a Portuguese woman, and they settled in Rio where Machado de Assis completed his first collection of short stories, *Stories of Rio de Janeiro* (*Contos fluminenses,* 1869).

From Romance to Realism.   Before 1880, Machado de Assis had published three collections of poetry, the story collections *Stories of Rio de Janeiro* and *Midnight Stories* (*Histórias da meia-noite,* 1873), and four novels; *Resurrection* (*Ressureição,* 1872); *The Hand and the Glove* (*A mão e a luva,* 1874); *Helena* (1876); and *Yayá Garcia* (*Iaiá Garcia,* 1878). These works fall into what is considered Machado de Assis's Romantic phase and are mostly entertaining love stories. During this time he worked as a bureaucrat in various governmental ministries, like Agriculture and Public Roads, and lived a rather quiet life while his energies went into his writing.

In 1878 the Brazilian suffered a physical collapse stemming from stressing his delicate health, and he retreated to a mountain resort for three months. Upon his return to Rio, his writing changed. The publication of *Memórias póstumas de Brás Cubas* in 1881, curiously translated in 1952 as *Epitaph of a Small Winner* (recently translated as *The Posthumous Memoirs of Brás Cubas*), seems to mark a major turning point in Machado de Assis's writing style and attitude towards his subject matter.

> People cannot talk about literary production in Brazil without thinking of Machado de Assis. The perfection of his style and the harmony of all qualities demanded from a great writer make him one of the most (perhaps the most) complete personage of our literature.
>
> – CARLA DIEGUEZ,
> *Joaquim Maria Machado de Assis: A Short Biography*

---

[1] Laurence Sterne: (1713–1768) Wrote *The Life and Opinions of Tristram Shandy* (1767), which is filled with eccentricities, digressions, and incoherencies.

[2] Jorge Luis Borges: (1899–1986), Argentinean short story writer who mixed the elements of fiction and nonfiction while exploring different layers of consciousness and dream realities.

Machado de Assis is arguably the most distinguished writer in Latin America's history. But the rubric "Latin America" runs the risk of misunderstanding his radically hybrid identity. Machado joins wide reading and classical learning in European literature and philosophy with the experience of the social transformations sweeping the Brazil of slavery and empire in the late nineteenth century.

– K. David Jackson,
The New York Times on the Web, 1998

This novel, dedicated to "the first worm that gnawed my flesh," is written from the point of view of someone beyond the grave and addresses the reader with speculations about meaning. In this writer's two other great novels, *Philosopher or Dog?* (*Quincas Borba*, 1892) and *Dom Casmurro* (1900), he continues a theme that links him to such European novelists of the nineteenth century as Honoré de Balzac and Émile Zola—the indifference of the world to the individual life. A far cry from the earlier Romantic who perceived the environment as a reflection of the individual psyche. The work of the last period of Machado de Assis's life is characterized by suggestion and innuendo, the exploration of consciousness.

His last novel, *Counselor Ayres' Memorial* (*Memorial de Ayres*, 1908), represents another change of direction; it celebrates love and fidelity and is an indirect tribute to his wife, Carolina, who died in 1904. When the Brazilian Academy of Letters was founded in 1897, Machado de Assis was elected its president, a position he held until his death in 1908. As an agnostic, he declined to have a priest in attendance at his deathbed.

Recognition Comes Late.   In all, Machado de Assis wrote nine novels, four collections of poetry, more than two hundred short stories, numerous translations, several plays, and hundreds of newspaper columns. Though he experimented with various kinds of writing, from poetry to literary criticism, his reputation in the United States is largely based on his fiction. In style and subject matter, he was far ahead of his Brazilian contemporaries. Nevertheless, he was not recognized in the English-speaking world until after his death. Three short stories were anthologized in *Brazilian Tales* (1921), an edition of Brazilian writers published by Pocket Library in 1921. The publication of the novel *Epitaph of a Small Winner* in 1952, seventy-one years after its publication in Brazil, finally brought Machado de Assis international recognition. The first collection of short stories devoted entirely to him was *The Psychiatrist and Other Stories,* a collection of twelve stories that was published in 1963.

"Adam and Eve."   Originally published in 1885 as "Adão e Eva," the story "Adam and Eve" was published in English in 1977 as part of the collection *The Devil's Church and Other Stories.* The setting for the story is a dinner party at a plantation in the 1700s. During a discussion of the story of Adam and Eve and of whether man or woman is responsible for the Fall, a judge—a symbol of education and thoughtfulness—presents an entirely different version of the story than the one found in Genesis. His tale reflects the ancient **DUALISTIC TRADITION**[3] that the earth was originally the creation and domain of the dark or evil powers—Satan and the fallen angels. In this version, the earth becomes the battleground between good and evil, light and dark. Adam and Eve resist temptation by a female

---

[3] dualistic tradition: Dualism in religion is a belief that there is a god of light and goodness and a deity of evil and darkness, and that these two deities compete for the souls of humans. A final battle is prophesied to take place between them when goodness and light will prevail. The ancient Persian prophet Zoroaster taught the first dualistic doctrines circa 1000 B.C.E. His tenets apparently influenced later Christian teachings about Satan.

Henri Rousseau, *Eve*
This painting shows
the archetypal image
of Eve accepting fruit
from the evil serpent.
(Hamburger
Kunsthalle)

serpent and are welcomed into heaven for their piety; the earth is abandoned to darkness. The guests at the dinner party, including the hostess, have no idea how to interpret the judge's version of the most famous and influential story in the Western world. Adopting a rather ironic attitude, the judge draws a quick conclusion and shifts attention back to the dessert, a subject that his fellow diners can handle.

Machado de Assis wrote this story at about the time in the nineteenth century when science was making claims about geological history and European intellectuals were raising questions concerning the mythical stories in the Book of Genesis, the foundation of Christianity. The story is also a satiric look at the vanities and shallowness of the middle class. In his dissection of character and social class, Machado de Assis tends to emphasize the negative qualities of a class of people that had become self-satisfied, parasitic, and cowardly. His use of irony and ambiguity links him to other modern writers who also take a slanted or fragmented view of reality.

■ CONNECTIONS

Elizabeth Cady Stanton, *Declaration of Sentiments and Resolutions,* **p. 827.** With the rise of science in the nineteenth century, intellectuals began to question the historical truth of religious texts like the Bible. In *The Woman's Bible,* Stanton queries the ways in which gender appears in the Bible and whether women enjoy equality in the Bible or are relegated to second-class status. How does Machado de Assis call the

www For links to more information about Machado de Assis and a quiz on "Adam and Eve," see *World Literature Online* at bedfordstmartins .com/worldlit.

Adam and Eve story into question? Does he think women should be blamed for the world's evil?

Rabindranath Tagore, *Broken Ties,* p. 0000. Intellectual pursuits can lead to critical inquiry and eventually to knowledge, but they can also be superficial, frivolous, and faddish. Tagore portrays both kinds in *The Broken Ties* and shows the dangers of intellectual fads. Machado de Assis appears to approach religious questions more indirectly. How does he expose the shallowness of several characters in his story?

Molière, *Tartuffe* (Book 4). Writers make use of social situations—interactions between characters—to make statements about the relative health of a society. Molière is an expert at setting up situations that unveil the hidden qualities of his characters. How does Machado de Assis make use of the plantation party to give readers insight into his characters?

■ **FURTHER RESEARCH**

Biography

Caldwell, Helen. *Machado de Assis: The Brazilian Master and His Novels.* 1970. Covers Machado de Assis's life, his novels, and a few other writings.

Machado, José Bettencourt. *Machado of Brazil: The Life and Times of Machado de Assis, Brazil's Greatest Novelist.* 1962.

Criticism

Caldwell, Helen. *The Brazilian Othello of Machado de Assis.* 1960. The first extended study of Machado de Assis in English.

Fitz, Earl E. *Machado de Assis.* 1989. Provides an excellent overview of Machado de Assis scholarship.

Nunes, Maria Luisa. *The Craft of an Absolute Winner: Characterization and Narratology in the Novels of Machado de Assis.* 1983.

■ **PRONUNCIATION**

Joaquim Maria Machado de Assis: wah-KEEM mah-REE-ah mah-CHAH-*thoh thay* ah-SEES

ꙮ Adam and Eve

Translated by Jack Schmitt and Lorie Ishimatsu

It was some time during the 1700s that the wife of a Bahian[1] plantation owner, who had invited several intimate friends to dinner, announced a special kind of dessert to one of the guests, who was known to be quite a glutton. He immediately wished to know what it was, and the lady of the house called him a curious fellow. Nothing else was neces-

---

"Adam and Eve." Machado de Assis provided critical distance for his readers by placing this story in the 1700s, and yet the authenticity of the Scriptures was an agonizingly current topic for thinking individuals in the latter half of the nineteenth century. In his story, dinner guests are discussing Adam and Eve and the source of sin. For hundreds of years Western men had blamed women for

---

[1] Bahian: Bahia is a state in the southern half of Brazil.

sary—shortly thereafter, everyone was discussing curiosity, whether it was a mascu-line or a feminine trait and whether Adam or Eve was responsible for the fall from Par-adise. The ladies said it was Adam's fault, and the gentlemen said it was Eve's. The judge didn't say anything and Father Bento, a Carmelite priest, replied with a smile when his hostess, Dona Leonor, asked for his opinion: "I, my dear lady, play the viola." He wasn't lying, for he was no less distinguished as a violist and harpist than as a theologian.

When the judge was called upon, he responded that there was no basis for form-ing an opinion, because the fall from Paradise did not occur in the way it is told in the first book of the Pentateuch,[2] which is apocryphal.[3] Amid the general astonishment, there was laughter from the Carmelite, who knew that the judge was one of the most pious men in the city and also that he was jovial, inventive, and even quite a joker, as long as matters remained priestly and refined. In serious matters, he was very serious.

"Father Bento," said Dona Leonor, "tell Senhor Veloso to be quiet."

"I won't tell him to be quiet," replied the priest, "because I know that everything he says is well intentioned."

"But the Scriptures . . ." said the army commander, João Barbosa.

"Let's leave the Scriptures in peace," interrupted the Carmelite. "Naturally, Sen-hor Veloso is acquainted with other books . . ."

"I know the authentic version of the story," insisted the judge, as he took the plate of sweets Dona Leonor offered him, "and I am ready to tell you what I know, as long as you do not ask me to do otherwise."

"Go on, please tell us!"

"This is how it really happened. In the first place, it wasn't God who created the world, it was Satan . . ."

"Good heavens!" exclaimed the ladies.

"Don't say that name," requested Dona Leonor.

"Yes, it seems that . . ." intervened Father Bento.

"Let's call him the Evil One, then. It was the Evil One who created the world, but God, who could read his thoughts, allowed him to act freely but took care to emend and polish his work, so that salvation or charity would not be left vulnerable to the forces of evil. Divine action soon appeared, because after the Evil One created dark-ness, God created light, and that is how the first day was created. On the second day,

---

the Fall, the event that introduced sin into the world through the temptation of Eve. In Machado de Assis's alternative version of the Genesis story, the serpent is a female, a change that alters the serpent's dynamics with Eve. The final irony, of course, is that with Eve in heaven, there can be no beautiful and powerful women descendants of hers on earth.

The guests appear to be stymied by the judge's challenge to think seriously about the Adam and Eve story. Many readers today are more willing to see the story in mythic or symbolic terms, but Machado de Assis's audience was undoubtedly less experienced in religious debate. Are the judge and the priest the only ones who can entertain a serious discussion about creation? Does the biblical version make any more sense than Machado de Assis's story?

---

[2] **Pentateuch:** The first five books of the Hebrew Scriptures, beginning with the Book of Genesis.

[3] **apocryphal:** Questionable or doubtful with regard to authorship and doctrine.

when the waters were created, storms and hurricanes were born, but the gentle after-noon breezes descended from divine thought. On the third day, the earth was cre-ated, and from it sprang forth the plants, but only those that bear no fruit or flowers: the thorny ones, and the deadly ones, like the hemlock. However, God created the fruit-bearing trees and the plants that nourish or are pleasing to man. Since the Evil One had hollowed out abysses and caverns in the earth, God created the sun, the moon, and the stars—such was the fourth day's work. On the fifth day, the animals of the earth, water, and air were created. We are now approaching the sixth day, and here I ask for your undivided attention."

It wasn't necessary to ask for it, for everyone was staring at him with curiosity.

Veloso continued, saying that on the sixth day Man was created, and Woman soon afterward. Both of them were beautiful, but they possessed only base instincts and lacked souls, which the Evil One could not give them. God infused souls into them with one breath, and noble, pure sentiments with another. Divine grace did not stop there—God caused a garden of delights to sprout forth and led Adam and Eve there, granting them possession of everything. Both fell at the Lord's feet, spilling forth tears of gratitude.

"You will live here," the Lord said to them, "and you may eat all fruits except the ones from this tree, which is the Tree of Knowledge of Good and Evil."

Adam and Eve listened submissively, and when they were left alone, stared at each other in amazement—it seemed that both of them had become different people. Before God granted her noble feelings, Eve had contemplated tying Adam up with a rope, and Adam had desired to beat her. Now, however, they were absorbed in contemplation of one another and the splendid natural scenery. Never before had they known air so pure, water so fresh, or flowers so beautiful and fragrant, nor did the sun spill forth such torrents of light anywhere else. Hand in hand they roamed, laughing heartily at first, because until then they had not known how to laugh. They had no conception of time, and thus their idleness did not give way to tedium—they lived in a state of contemplation. In the evenings they went to see the sun set and the moon rise and counted the stars. It was seldom that they were able to count even a thousand, for they usually fell asleep and slept like two angels.

Naturally, the Evil One became furious when he discovered all this. He couldn't go to Paradise because everything there was averse to him, nor could he bring him-self to confront the Lord. Then, hearing a rustling of dry leaves on the ground, he looked down and saw a serpent. Excited by this discovery, he called to her: "Come here, snake, you creeping bile, venom of venoms, will you be your father's ambassa-dor and reclaim his works?"

With her tail, the serpent made a vague gesture that seemed to be affirmative. The Evil One gave her the power of speech, and she answered that yes, she would go wherever he might send her—to the stars, if he would give her the wings of an eagle; to the sea, if he would reveal to her the secret of breathing under water; to the depths of the earth, if he would teach her the talents of the ant. The malign one rambled on without pause, content and extravagant with her speech, but the Evil One inter-rupted her: "Nothing like that, not to the air, the sea, or the depths of the earth, only to the Garden of Delights, where Adam and Eve live."

"Adam and Eve?"

"Yes, Adam and Eve."

"Two beautiful creatures we saw some time ago, walking as straight and tall as palm trees?"

"The very same ones."

"Oh, I detest them! Adam and Eve? No, no, send me somewhere else. I detest them! The mere sight of them makes me sick. You won't want me to do them any harm . . ."

"But I do!"

"Really? Then I'll go, I'll do whatever you wish, my lord and father. Now hurry and tell me what you want me to do. Bite Eve's heel? I'll bite . . ."

"No," interrupted the Evil One. "I want exactly the opposite. There is a tree in the garden, the Tree of Knowledge of Good and Evil, which they are forbidden to touch and whose fruits they are forbidden to eat. Go, coil yourself up in this tree, and when one of them passes by, call to him gently, pick up one of the fruits, and offer it to him, saying it is the most delicious fruit in the world. If he refuses, you will insist that he take it, saying that he needs only to eat it in order to learn the secret of life itself. Go, go . . ."

"I'll go, but I won't speak to Adam, I'll speak to Eve. I'll go, I'll go. Do you really mean the secret of life itself?"

"Yes, that's right. Go forth, serpent of my flesh, flower of evil, and if you are successful, I swear you'll possess the human part of creation, which is the best part, because you'll have the heels of many Eves to bite and the blood of lots of Adams in which to inject the virus of evil. Go, go, and don't forget . . ."

Forget? She already knew everything by heart. She went and entered the earthly paradise, slithered over to the Tree of Knowledge, coiled herself up, and waited. Eve appeared shortly afterward, walking gracefully and alone, with the confidence of a queen who knows no one will rob of her crown. Torn with envy, the serpent was about to summon poison to her tongue, but she remembered she was there at the Evil One's orders and called Eve with a honeyed voice. Eve was startled.

"Who is calling me?"

"It is I, I'm eating this fruit . . ."

"You wretch! That's the Tree of Knowledge of Good and Evil!"

"That's right. I know everything now, the origin of things and the secret of life. Go on, take a bite, and you'll gain great powers on earth."

"No, you treacherous snake!"

"You fool! How can you refuse the splendor of the ages? Listen to me, do as I say, and you'll be legion, you'll found cities, and your name will be Cleopatra, Dido, Semiramis.[4] Heroes will be born of your womb and you'll be Cornelia.[5] You'll hear a

---

[4] **Cleopatra . . . Semiramis:** Cleopatra (69?–30 B.C.E.) was the enchanting queen of Egypt. Dido was the mythic founder and queen of Carthage, in North Africa. Semiramis was the beautiful, wise legendary queen of Assyria who founded Babylon circa ninth century B.C.E.

[5] **Cornelia:** Roman matron of the second century B.C.E. devoted to her sons, Gaius and Tiberius Gracchus, who became powerful Roman statesmen.

voice from Heaven and you'll be Deborah.[6] You'll sing and you will be Sappho.[7] And one day, should God wish to descend to earth, He will choose your body, and your name will be Mary of Nazareth. What more could you desire? Royalty, poetry, divinity—you're giving up everything because of a foolish obedience. And that's not all. Nature will make you even more beautiful. The brilliant as well as the pale colors of the leaves, the sky, and the night will be reflected in your eyes. The night, in competition with the sun, will revel in your hair. The children of your womb will weave for you the most wonderful garments, create the finest perfumes, and the birds will give you their feathers, the earth its flowers, everything, everything, everything . . ."

Eve listened impassively. Adam arrived, listened to the serpent, and reaffirmed Eve's responses: nothing was worth the risk of losing Paradise, not knowledge, power, or any other earthly illusion. As they said this, they clasped hands and turned away from the serpent, who hurriedly exited to report back to the Evil One . . .

God, who had heard everything, said to Gabriel: "Go, My archangel, descend to the earthly paradise where Adam and Eve live, and take them to eternal bliss, which they deserve for their resistance to the Evil One's temptations."

Then the archangel, placing on his head the helmet which glittered like a thousand suns, traversed the heavens in an instant, reached Adam and Eve, and said to them: "Hail, Adam and Eve. Come with me to Paradise, which you have earned for your resistance to the Evil One's temptations."

Astonished and confused, Adam and Eve bowed their heads in obedience, and Gabriel held out his hands to them. The three ascended to the eternal abode, where hosts of singing angels awaited them.

"Come in, come in. The earth you abandoned is now left to the Evil One's creations, the ferocious and malevolent animals, the harmful and poisonous plants, the unclean air, the swamps. The creeping, vile, biting serpent will reign over the earth, and no creatures like you will ever bring a note of hope and piety to such an abomination."

And that was how Adam and Eve entered Heaven—to the sound of all its zithers, which united their notes in a hymn to the two apostates from Creation . . .

. . . His story finished, the judge handed his plate to Dona Leonor so she could give him more dessert, while the other guests stared at one another in amazement—instead of an explanation, they had heard a puzzling narration, or at least a story without apparent meaning. Dona Leonor was the first to speak: "I was right when I said Senhor Veloso was fooling us. He didn't do what we asked him to do, and it didn't happen the way he said it did. Isn't that right, Father Bento?"

"The honorable judge will know the answer to that," replied the Carmelite, smiling.

And as the judge lifted a spoonful of dessert to his mouth, he said: "On second thought, I don't think any of it actually occurred, but, Dona Leonor, if it had, we wouldn't be here enjoying this dessert, which is in all sincerity perfectly delicious! Is it the work of your old pastry cook from Itapagipe?"[8]

---

[6] **Deborah:** In Hebrew Scriptures, Deborah was a prophetess and one of the judges of Israel (see Judges 4–5).

[7] **Sappho:** A famous Greek poet of the ancient world (c. 600 B.C.E.).

[8] **Itapagipe:** A small town in the state of Minas Gerais, Brazil.

✎ KATE CHOPIN
1851–1904

During the first half of the twentieth century, **Kate Chopin** was thought of as either a minor writer whose stories of Creole life in Louisiana were part of the local-color movement of the late nineteenth century or the author of a scandalous novel. Otherwise, her work was largely ignored until the 1960s, when a new generation of readers discovered the unrelenting Realism and provocative themes beneath the surface of her stories. Her most important work, the novel *The Awakening* (1899), is now recognized as one of the classics of American feminism.

KATE SHOH-pan

Early On. As the daughter of a mother descended from the French Creole aristocracy and an Irish immigrant father who had become a successful merchant in St. Louis, Katherine O'Flaherty, born in 1851, had a privileged childhood. Even though her father died in a railway accident when she was four, she attended Catholic convent schools in St. Louis and made her debut in St. Louis society when she was eighteen. In 1870 she married Oscar Chopin, a Creole cotton trader. After a wedding trip to Europe, the Chopins settled in Louisiana, first in New Orleans and then in **Cloutierville**, in **Natchitoches** Parish, in central Louisiana. They had six children before Oscar died in 1883 of swamp fever. After her husband's death, Chopin, financially independent, moved back to St. Louis with her children, where she began her writing career in earnest, publishing her first poems and stories in 1889.

KLOO-chee-vil
NACK-uh-tish

Local Color and Realism. The most important intellectual influence in her life was probably Frederick Kohlbenheyer, her physician in St. Louis, who became her confidant in the mid-1880s. An agnostic, Kohlbenheyer encouraged her to read Darwin and Thomas Huxley and to give up Catholicism. She also read the work of such American regional writers as Sarah Orne Jewett and Mary E. Wilkins Freeman,[1] local colorists who reproduced the distinctive dialects of their New England characters and described the customs peculiar to their region. Most important, Chopin also read the French Realists Flaubert, Zola, and Maupassant. This reading encouraged the Realist direction of her own writing, as she explored the ways in which her characters were influenced by their environment, as women caught in the social mores of nineteenth-century America, or as members of one of the ethnic and racial groups in Louisiana: Creoles, descendants of the French and Spanish colonists; Cajuns, descendants of eighteenth-century French Canadian immigrants to Louisiana; African Americans; and Native Americans. Maupassant was a particularly

www For links to more information about Chopin and quizzes on "The Story of an Hour" and "Désirée's Baby," see *World Literature Online* at bedfordstmartins .com/worldlit.

---

[1]Jewett . . . Freeman: Sarah Orne Jewett (1849–1909), Maine local colorist, author of many works, including *The Country of the Pointed Firs* (1896); Mary E. Wilkins Freeman (1852–1930), New England local colorist; author of *A Humble Romance* (1887), *Pembroke* (1894), and other works.

A Creole Bovary.

– WILLA CATHER on
The Awakening

ah-kah-DEE

pawn-tuh-LYAY
luh-BRUN
RIGHS

important influence. Chopin translated several of his stories into English, and many of her stories, including "The Story of an Hour" and "Désirée's Baby" use the same kind of irony, tight construction, and surprise turn at the end that typifies Maupassant's work.

Works of the 1890s.   Nearly all of Chopin's literary work was published in the 1890s. She wrote several poems, nearly a hundred stories, and three novels during that decade. Her first novel, *At Fault* (1890), set in the Louisiana backcountry, tells the story of a troubled relationship between a widow and a married man. More of her stories set in the same region began to appear in national magazines, and two collections of stories, *Bayou Folk* (1894) and *A Night in Acadie* (1897), were published. She wrote a second novel, *Young Dr. Gosse,* early in the decade, but later destroyed the manuscript after she could not find a publisher for it.

"A Creole Bovary."   Chopin's reputation, both in her own time and since, has rested largely on *The Awakening* (1899), her third novel. It is the story of Edna **Pontellier**, a young wife and mother, who is awakened to her own desires and feelings through relationships with Robert **Lebrun**, a romantic man she meets while on vacation, and Mademoiselle **Reisz**, an artist. She neglects her social duties and angers her husband, has an affair, leaves her marriage, and finally ends her life by drowning. The novel shocked readers in the 1890s. Reviewers called it a "vulgar story," one that

Edgar Degas, *Interior of the New Orleans Bureau of Cotton Purchasers, 1873. Oil on canvas*
Although Kate Chopin set nearly all her stories in New Orleans—during the first half of the twentieth century she was thought of as a writer of Creole life—there is an unrelenting realism beneath the local color of her stories. (Art Resource)

"should be labeled a poison." Even Willa Cather[2] dismissed it as only "a Creole Bovary," an imitation of Flaubert's novel *Madame Bovary,* about a woman's search for independence, which had similarly scandalized the French. *The Awakening* was banned from libraries, and Chopin was shunned in St. Louis society. Only in the last four decades has Chopin's novel been recognized as much more than a shocking piece of conventional fiction or mock French Realism. In the novel, Chopin adopted the conventions of French Realism to study an American woman coming to an awareness of the confining social conventions that denied her full humanity. Although it is set in Louisiana, as many of Chopin's short stories are, it is much more than a work of regional interest.

The Short Stories.   Their Louisiana settings and the presence of dialect and local customs often led in Chopin's own day to her short stories being relegated to the subgenre of local-color tales.[3] More recently, critics have recognized that Chopin's themes—the search for personal fulfillment, interracial relationships, the conflict between selfhood and sexual desire—transcend localism. These subjects, along with the lyrical conciseness and ironic intensity in her work, place Chopin in the mainstream of late-nineteenth-century Realism, along with Flaubert, Zola, and Maupassant.

"The Story of an Hour" could also have been titled "The Awakening," for it, too, describes a moment of awareness when Mrs. Mallard realizes how she really feels about her life and situation. The news of her husband's death shocks her into an awareness that seems to overtake her against her will. The tight focus of the story and the double surprise in the ending show that Chopin had learned her craft well from Maupassant. Mrs. Mallard's awakening in "The Story of an Hour"—one of the Chopin selections that follow—allies her character with Nora Helmer, the heroine of Ibsen's *Doll's House,* and the woman in Charlotte Perkins Gilman's *Yellow Wallpaper,* as one of the many "new women" in the literature of the period, women who sought to control their own lives rather than be defined by marriage and their relationships to men.

■ CONNECTIONS

E. T. A. Hoffmann, "The Mines of Falun" (p. 298); Higuchi Ichiyo, "The Thirteenth Night," p. 1103. Hoffmann's "Mines of Falun," Ichiyo's "Thirteenth Night," and Chopin's "Story of an Hour" all end ironically. Chopin's story also has a surprise ending, one that's unexpected but that makes sense. Do the other two stories have a surprise ending? What is the nature of the irony with which each of these stories ends?

> Kate Chopin, author of some of the boldest and best stories written in America before 1960.
> – PEGGY SKAGGS, *Kate Chopin,* 1985

---

[2] **Willa Cather:** (1873–1947) Novelist and journalist from Nebraska; in such Realist novels as *O Pioneers!* (1913) and *Death Comes for the Archbishop* (1927), Cather developed themes about life on the American frontier.

[3] **local-color tales:** Stories that seek to portray the people and way of life of a particular region by describing the speech, dress, and customs of its inhabitants.

Henrik Ibsen, *Hedda Gabler,* p. 561; Charlotte Perkins Gilman, *The Yellow Wallpaper,* p. 941. For many women in the nineteenth century, identity and one's place in society was defined by marriage. Mrs. Mallard's sense of liberation on learning of her husband's death is the counterpart to the bondage felt by the woman in Charlotte Perkins Gilman's *Yellow Wallpaper* and by Hedda in Ibsen's *Hedda Gabler.* Do any of these women have control over their lives? What is the nature of the confinement that each experiences? Do any of them escape?

Rabindranath Tagore, *Broken Ties,* p. 986. Understanding a work of literature from another culture often calls for recognizing a given author's cultural assumptions. In "Désirée's Baby," Chopin assumes that readers will understand the ways slavery worked in the American South, the unstated racial attitudes that lead to Désirée's banishment, and the surprise at the end. Look at Tagore's story of Nonibala in chapters four through six of *Broken Ties.* What cultural assumptions are made by Harimohan and Purandar? How does Tagore make these attitudes apparent to a non-Indian reader? Is the ending of Noni's story as surprising as that of "Désirée's Baby"?

■ FURTHER RESEARCH

Biography
Seyersted, Per. *Kate Chopin: A Critical Biography.* 1969.
Toth, Emily. *Kate Chopin: A Solitary Soul.* 1990.

Criticism
Beer, Janet. *Kate Chopin, Edith Wharton, and Charlotte Perkins Gilman: Studies in Short Fiction.* 1997.
Boren, Lynda S., and Sara de Saussure Davis, eds. *Kate Chopin Reconsidered: Beyond the Bayou.* 1999. A collection of critical essays on Chopin and her work.
Ewell, Barbara C. *Kate Chopin.* 1986.
Koloski, Bernard. *Kate Chopin: A Study of the Short Fiction.* 1996.
Petry, Alice Hall. *Critical Essays on Kate Chopin.* 1996. A collection of reviews and contemporary critical essays on Chopin's work.

■ PRONUNCIATION

Kate Chopin: KATE SHOH-pan
Acadie: ah-kah-DEE
Armand Aubigny: ar-MAWND oh-bin-YEE
corbeille: kore-BAY
Coton Maïs: koh-TONE mah-EES
Cloutierville: KLOO-chee-vil
Désirée: deh-zi-RAY
L'Abri: lah-BREE
Lebrun: luh-BRUN, luh-BRENG
Natchitoches: NACK-uh-tish
Négrillon: neh-gree-YAWNG
Pontellier: pawn-tuh-LYAY
Reisz: RIGHS
Valmondé: vahl-mawn-DAY

∾ The Story of an Hour

Knowing that Mrs. Mallard was afflicted with heart trouble, great care was taken to break to her as gently as possible the news of her husband's death.

It was her sister Josephine who told her, in broken sentences; veiled hints that revealed in half concealing. Her husband's friend Richards was there, too, near her. It was he who had been in the newspaper office when intelligence of the railroad disaster was received, with Brently Mallard's name leading the list of "killed." He had only taken the time to assure himself of its truth by a second telegram, and had hastened to forestall any less careful, less tender friend in bearing the sad message.

She did not hear the story as many women have heard the same, with a paralyzed inability to accept its significance. She wept at once, with sudden, wild abandonment, in her sister's arms. When the storm of grief had spent itself she went away to her room alone. She would have no one follow her.

There stood, facing the open window, a comfortable, roomy armchair. Into this she sank, pressed down by a physical exhaustion that haunted her body and seemed to reach into her soul.

She could see in the open square before her house the tops of trees that were all aquiver with the new spring life. The delicious breath of rain was in the air. In the street below a peddler was crying his wares. The notes of a distant song which some one was singing reached her faintly, and countless sparrows were twittering in the eaves.

There were patches of blue sky showing here and there through the clouds that had met and piled one above the other in the west facing her window.

She sat with her head thrown back upon the cushion of the chair, quite motionless, except when a sob came up into her throat and shook her, as a child who has cried itself to sleep continues to sob in its dreams.

She was young, with a fair, calm face, whose lines bespoke repression and even a certain strength. But now there was a dull stare in her eyes, whose gaze was fixed away off yonder on one of those patches of blue sky. It was not a glance of reflection, but rather indicated a suspension of intelligent thought.

There was something coming to her and she was waiting for it, fearfully. What was it? She did not know; it was too subtle and elusive to name. But she felt it, creeping out of the sky, reaching toward her through the sounds, the scents, the color that filled the air.

"The Story of an Hour." First published in *Vogue* magazine in 1894 and included in Chopin's third collection of stories, *A Vocation and a Voice* (1896), this story, like Chopin's major novel, could have been titled "The Awakening." Like that novel, it describes a moment of realization when Mrs. Mallard becomes aware of how she really feels about her situation. The news of her husband's death shocks her into a new consciousness that seems to overtake her against her will. The tight focus of the story and the double surprise of the ending show that Chopin had learned her craft well from Maupassant.

Now her bosom rose and fell tumultuously. She was beginning to recognize this thing that was approaching to possess her, and she was striving to beat it back with her will—as powerless as her two white slender hands would have been.

When she abandoned herself a little whispered word escaped her slightly parted lips. She said it over and over under her breath: "free, free, free!" The vacant stare and the look of terror that had followed it went from her eyes. They stayed keen and bright. Her pulses beat fast, and the coursing blood warmed and relaxed every inch of her body.

She did not stop to ask if it were or were not a monstrous joy that held her. A clear and exalted perception enabled her to dismiss the suggestion as trivial.

She knew that she would weep again when she saw the kind, tender hands folded in death; the face that had never looked save with love upon her, fixed and gray and dead. But she saw beyond that bitter moment a long procession of years to come that would belong to her absolutely. And she opened and spread her arms out to them in welcome.

There would be no one to live for her during those coming years; she would live for herself. There would be no powerful will bending hers in that blind persistence with which men and women believe they have a right to impose a private will upon a fellow-creature. A kind intention or a cruel intention made the act seem no less a crime as she looked upon it in that brief moment of illumination.

And yet she had loved him—sometimes. Often she had not. What did it matter! What could love, the unsolved mystery, count for in face of this possession of self-assertion which she suddenly recognized as the strongest impulse of her being!

"Free! Body and soul free!" she kept whispering.

Josephine was kneeling before the closed door with her lips to the keyhole, imploring for admission. "Louise, open the door! I beg; open the door—you will make yourself ill. What are you doing, Louise? For heaven's sake open the door."

"Go away. I am not making myself ill." No; she was drinking in a very elixir of life through that open window.

Her fancy was running riot along those days ahead of her. Spring days, and summer days, and all sorts of days that would be her own. She breathed a quick prayer that life might be long. It was only yesterday she had thought with a shudder that life might be long.

She arose at length and opened the door to her sister's importunities. There was a feverish triumph in her eyes, and she carried herself unwittingly like a goddess of Victory. She clasped her sister's waist, and together they descended the stairs. Richards stood waiting for them at the bottom.

Some one was opening the front door with a latchkey. It was Brently Mallard who entered, a little travel-stained, composedly carrying his gripsack and umbrella. He had been far from the scene of accident, and did not even know there had been one. He stood amazed at Josephine's piercing cry; at Richards' quick motion to screen him from the view of his wife.

But Richards was too late.

When the doctors came they said she had died of heart disease—of joy that kills.

❧ Désirée's Baby

As the day was pleasant, Madame Valmondé drove over to L'Abri to see Désirée and the baby.

It made her laugh to think of Désirée with a baby. Why, it seemed but yesterday that Désirée was little more than a baby herself; when Monsieur in riding through the gateway of Valmondé had found her lying asleep in the shadow of the big stone pillar.

The little one awoke in his arms and began to cry for "Dada." That was as much as she could do or say. Some people thought she might have strayed there of her own accord, for she was of the toddling age. The prevailing belief was that she had been purposely left by a party of Texans, whose canvas-covered wagon, late in the day, had crossed the ferry that Coton Maïs kept, just below the plantation. In time Madame Valmondé abandoned every speculation but the one that Désirée had been sent to her by a beneficent Providence to be the child of her affection, seeing that she was without child of the flesh. For the girl grew to be beautiful and gentle, affectionate and sincere, — the idol of Valmondé.

It was no wonder, when she stood one day against the stone pillar in whose shadow she had lain asleep, eighteen years before, that Armand Aubigny riding by and seeing her there, had fallen in love with her. That was the way all the Aubignys fell in love, as if struck by a pistol shot. The wonder was that he had not loved her before; for he had known her since his father brought him home from Paris, a boy of eight, after his mother died there. The passion that awoke in him that day, when he saw her at the gate, swept along like an avalanche, or like a prairie fire, or like anything that drives headlong over all obstacles.

Monsieur Valmondé grew practical and wanted things well considered: that is, the girl's obscure origin. Armand looked into her eyes and did not care. He was reminded that she was nameless. What did it matter about a name when he could give her one of the oldest and proudest in Louisiana? He ordered the *corbeille*[1] from Paris, and contained himself with what patience he could until it arrived; then they were married.

Madame Valmondé had not seen Désirée and the baby for four weeks. When she reached L'Abri she shuddered at the first sight of it, as she always did. It was a sad looking place, which for many years had not known the gentle presence of a mistress, old Monsieur Aubigny having married and buried his wife in France, and she

---

"Désirée's Baby." First published in 1892, this story addresses the controversial subject of miscegenation, interracial sexual relationships, the sort of subject European Naturalists such as Emilia Pardo Bazán and Émile Zola treated. The exotic setting, with its suggestions of the Gothic, is given local identity with French place names and customs. The focus of the story on a single issue, the device of the letter, and the ironic reversals at the end again indicate Chopin's debt to Maupassant.

---

[1] *corbeille:* Wedding presents.

having loved her own land too well ever to leave it. The roof came down steep and black like a cowl, reaching out beyond the wide galleries that encircled the yellow stuccoed house. Big, solemn oaks grew close to it, and their thick-leaved, far-reaching branches shadowed it like a pall. Young Aubigny's rule was a strict one, too, and under it his negroes had forgotten how to be gay, as they had been during the old master's easy-going and indulgent lifetime.

The young mother was recovering slowly, and lay full length, in her soft white muslins and laces, upon a couch. The baby was beside her, upon her arm, where he had fallen asleep, at her breast. The yellow nurse woman sat beside a window fanning herself.

Madame Valmondé bent her portly figure over Désirée and kissed her, holding her an instant tenderly in her arms. Then she turned to the child.

"This is not the baby!" she exclaimed, in startled tones. French was the language spoken at Valmondé in those days.

"I knew you would be astonished," laughed Désirée, "at the way he has grown. The little *cochon de lait!*[2] Look at his legs, mamma, and his hands and fingernails,—real finger-nails. Zandrine had to cut them this morning. Isn't it true, Zandrine?"

The woman bowed her turbaned head majestically, "Mais si,[3] Madame."

"And the way he cries," went on Désirée, "is deafening. Armand heard him the other day as far away as La Blanche's cabin."

Madame Valmondé had never removed her eyes from the child. She lifted it and walked with it over to the window that was lightest. She scanned the baby narrowly, then looked as searchingly at Zandrine, whose face was turned to gaze across the fields.

"Yes, the child has grown, has changed," said Madame Valmondé, slowly, as she replaced it beside its mother. "What does Armand say?"

Désirée's face became suffused with a glow that was happiness itself.

"Oh, Armand is the proudest father in the parish, I believe, chiefly because it is a boy, to bear his name; though he says not,—that he would have loved a girl as well. But I know it isn't true. I know he says that to please me. And mamma," she added, drawing Madame Valmondé's head down to her, and speaking in a whisper, "he hasn't punished one of them—not one of them—since baby is born. Even Négrillon, who pretended to have burnt his leg that he might rest from work—he only laughed, and said Négrillon was a great scamp. Oh, mamma, I'm so happy; it frightens me."

What Désirée said was true. Marriage, and later the birth of his son had softened Armand Aubigny's imperious and exacting nature greatly. This was what made the gentle Désirée so happy, for she loved him desperately. When he frowned she trembled, but loved him. When he smiled, she asked no greater blessing of God. But Armand's dark, handsome face had not often been disfigured by frowns since the day he fell in love with her.

When the baby was about three months old, Désirée awoke one day to the conviction that there was something in the air menacing her peace. It was at first too subtle to grasp. It had only been a disquieting suggestion; an air of mystery among

---

[2] *cochon de lait:* A suckling pig.   [3] "Mais si": Yes, indeed.

the blacks; unexpected visits from far-off neighbors who could hardly account for their coming. Then a strange, an awful change in her husband's manner, which she dared not ask him to explain. When he spoke to her, it was with averted eyes, from which the old love-light seemed to have gone out. He absented himself from home; and when there, avoided her presence and that of her child, without excuse. And the very spirit of Satan seemed suddenly to take hold of him in his dealings with the slaves. Désirée was miserable enough to die.

She sat in her room, one hot afternoon, in her *peignoir*,[4] listlessly drawing through her fingers the strands of her long, silky brown hair that hung about her shoulders. The baby, half naked, lay asleep upon her own great mahogany bed, that was like a sumptuous throne, with its satin-lined half-canopy. One of La Blanche's little quadroon[5] boys—half naked too—stood fanning the child slowly with a fan of peacock feathers. Désirée's eyes had been fixed absently and sadly upon the baby, while she was striving to penetrate the threatening mist that she felt closing about her. She looked from her child to the boy who stood beside him, and back again; over and over. "Ah!" It was a cry that she could not help; which she was not conscious of having uttered. The blood turned like ice in her veins, and a clammy moisture gathered upon her face.

She tried to speak to the little quadroon boy; but no sound would come, at first. When he heard his name uttered, he looked up, and his mistress was pointing to the door. He laid aside the great, soft fan, and obediently stole away, over the polished floor, on his bare tiptoes.

She stayed motionless, with gaze riveted upon her child, and her face the picture of fright.

Presently her husband entered the room, and without noticing her, went to a table and began to search among some papers which covered it.

"Armand," she called to him, in a voice which must have stabbed him, if he was human. But he did not notice. "Armand," she said again. Then she rose and tottered towards him. "Armand," she panted once more, clutching his arm, "look at our child. What does it mean? tell me."

He coldly but gently loosened her fingers from about his arm and thrust the hand away from him. "Tell me what it means!" she cried despairingly.

"It means," he answered lightly, "that the child is not white; it means that you are not white."

A quick conception of all that this accusation meant for her nerved her with unwonted courage to deny it. "It is a lie; it is not true, I am white! Look at my hair, it is brown; and my eyes are gray, Armand, you know they are gray. And my skin is fair," seizing his wrist. "Look at my hand; whiter than yours, Armand," she laughed hysterically.

"As white as La Blanche's," he returned cruelly; and went away leaving her alone with their child.

When she could hold a pen in her hand, she sent a despairing letter to Madame Valmondé.

---

[4] *peignoir:* A dressing gown.   [5] quadroon: A person with a quarter part of Negro blood.

"My mother, they tell me I am not white. Armand has told me I am not white. For God's sake tell them it is not true. You must know it is not true. I shall die. I must die. I cannot be so unhappy, and live."

The answer that came was as brief:

"My own Désirée: Come home to Valmondé; back to your mother who loves you. Come with your child."

When the letter reached Désirée she went with it to her husband's study, and laid it open upon the desk before which he sat. She was like a stone image, silent, white, motionless after she placed it there.

In silence he ran his cold eyes over the written words. He said nothing. "Shall I go, Armand?" she asked in tones sharp with agonized suspense.

"Yes, go."

"Do you want me to go."

"Yes, I want you to go."

He thought Almighty God had dealt cruelly and unjustly with him; and felt, somehow, that he was paying Him back in kind when he stabbed thus into his wife's soul. Moreover he no longer loved her, because of the unconscious injury she had brought upon his home and his name.

She turned away like one stunned by a blow, and walked slowly towards the door, hoping he would call her back.

"Good-by, Armand," she moaned.

He did not answer her. That was his last blow at fate.

Désirée went in search of her child. Zandrine was pacing the sombre gallery with it. She took the little one from the nurse's arms with no word of explanation, and descending the steps, walked away, under the live-oak branches.

It was an October afternoon; the sun was just sinking. Out in the still fields the negroes were picking cotton.

Désirée had not changed the thin white garment nor the slippers which she wore. Her hair was uncovered and the sun's rays brought a golden gleam from its brown meshes. She did not take the broad, beaten road which led to the far-off plantation of Valmondé. She walked across a deserted field, where the stubble bruised her tender feet, so delicately shod, and tore her thin gown to shreds.

She disappeared among the reeds and willows that grew thick along the banks of the deep, sluggish bayou; and she did not come back again.

Some weeks later there was a curious scene enacted at L'Abri. In the centre of the smoothly swept back yard was a great bonfire. Armand Aubigny sat in the wide hallway that commanded a view of the spectacle; and it was he who dealt out to a half dozen negroes the material which kept this fire ablaze.

A graceful cradle of willow, with all its dainty furbishings, was laid upon the pyre, which had already been fed with the richness of a priceless *layette*.[6] Then there were silk gowns, and velvet and satin ones added to these; laces, too, and embroideries; bonnets and gloves; for the *corbeille* had been of rare quality.

---

[6] *layette:* An outfit for a new baby.

The last thing to go was a tiny bundle of letters; innocent little scribblings that Désirée had sent to him during the days of their espousal. There was the remnant of one back in the drawer from which he took them. But it was not Désirée's, it was part of an old letter from his mother to his father. He read it. She was thanking God for the blessing of her husband's love: —

"But, above all," she wrote, "night and day, I thank the good God for having so arranged our lives that our dear Armand will never know that his mother, who adores him, belongs to the race that is cursed with the brand of slavery."

ᕓ CHARLOTTE PERKINS GILMAN
1860–1935

Regarded in her own time as the foremost American feminist theorist, Charlotte Perkins Gilman was best known for polemical works such as *Women and Economics* (1898), the bible of the women's movement, which argued that women's dependency on men not only denied women full participation in society but also stunted and distorted the evolution of society itself. "The Yellow Wallpaper" (1892), now recognized as a classic work of American fiction, was largely ignored when it originally appeared. It was rejected for publication by the editor of *The Atlantic Monthly*, who after reading it said, "I could not forgive myself if I made others as miserable as I have made myself." Although American novelist William Dean Howells (1837–1920) included the story in his collection of *Great Modern American Stories* in 1920, "The Yellow Wallpaper" was out of print and forgotten until 1973, when it was reprinted by The Feminist Press. Its publication has helped to establish Gilman as one of many writers who were exploring the situation of women and challenging conventional attitudes and stereotypes at the turn of the century. At the same time that the pioneers of psychoanalysis, Freud and Breuer,[1] were studying female "hysteria" from a male point of view, Gilman was writing about madness from a female perspective. The reappearance of "The Yellow Wallpaper" in the 1970s prompted a revival of interest in Gilman — her troubled personal life, her political activism, and her prolific and varied writing career.

Charlotte Perkins Gilman, c. 1900

Turn-of-the-century portrait of Gilman. (Library of Congress)

Abandoned in Childhood.   Born in Hartford, Connecticut, in 1860, Charlotte Perkins was descended from a number of famous New England writers and advocates of human rights. Her father, Frederic Beecher Perkins, a writer, was the grandson of theologian Lyman Beecher and the

---

[1] **Freud and Breuer:** *Studies in Hysteria,* by Sigmund Freud and Josef Breuer, appeared in 1895. See Book 6.

www   For links to more information about Gilman and a quiz on "The Yellow Wallpaper," see *World Literature Online* at bedfordstmartins .com/worldlit.

nephew of Henry Ward Beecher and Harriet Beecher Stowe,[2] Charlotte's childhood idol. Charlotte's difficulties with patriarchy began early when her father abandoned her mother, herself, and two siblings shortly after she was born, perhaps because doctors had forbidden the couple to have more children. So Charlotte grew up with plenty of reason to question the nineteenth-century's ideal of marriage, which featured a kindly, authoritarian father-provider and a mother who was the flawless "angel in the house," content to accede to the father's wise judgments and to find her fulfillment in comforting, nourishing, and gladdening her family circle. Charlotte's attempts to establish a relationship with her father were rewarded with only occasional letters listing books that she should read and offering no affection.

Charlotte's mother, poor and bitter, decided the best way to protect her children from similar unhappiness was by withholding all physical tenderness from them. "She would not let me caress her," Gilman reported, "and would not caress me unless I was asleep." The young Gilman pretended to be asleep while keeping herself awake, "even using pins to prevent dropping off," so that she could experience the joy of "being gathered into her [mother's] arms, held close and kissed."

Marriage and Madness.   After attending Rhode Island School of Design, Gilman supported herself as an art teacher, governess, and designer of greeting cards. She also began writing poetry. Despite her extreme doubts about marriage, in 1884 she wed Charles Walter Stetson, a pleasant, conventional artist, and immediately grew depressed as household duties infringed on her writing. When her depression deepened with the birth of her daughter ten months after the wedding, Stetson advised her to seek the help of the famous "nerve specialist" S. Weir Mitchell, whose popular "rest cure" for troubled women was a month's regimen of bed rest, heavy meals, baths, and massage, followed by a return to home and full immersion in household duties. He ordered the young mother to keep her baby beside her at all times, to allow herself only two hours of "intellectual life" a day, and above all "never to touch pen, brush, or pencil" for the rest of her life. Gilman followed the prescription, but she grew rapidly worse, bursting into tears at the sight of her child, cuddling a doll she secretly made from rags, and hiding deep in closets to try to escape the fear and despair that stalked her. When she realized that Mitchell's regimen was not working, she returned to writing. In time she was able to describe the pain of her depression in her most famous story, "The Yellow Wallpaper," written a few years later.

A New Beginning.   In 1888 Charlotte Stetson took her daughter and moved to Pasadena, California. After she and Stetson divorced in 1892,

---

[2] Lyman Beecher . . . Stowe: Lyman Beecher (1775–1863), liberal Presbyterian clergyman and author; Henry Ward Beecher (1813–1887), Lyman's son, a Congregational preacher, orator, editor, author, and influential advocate for the abolition of slavery, women's suffrage, and evolution; Harriet Beecher Stowe (1811–1896), Lyman's daughter; abolitionist and novelist who penned *Uncle Tom's Cabin* (1852).

she sent her daughter to live with Stetson, who was now married to her best friend, Grace Ellery Channing. Already notorious as a feminist spokesperson, Gilman was described by a hostile press as a cold and an unnatural mother. But release from marriage and motherhood proved her cure. She went on to a full life as a writer, editor, and lecturer. Eventually, she made a happy second marriage with George Houghton Gilman, and she and her daughter were able to enjoy a close and loving relationship. Far ahead of her time, she advocated both parents sharing in child care, communal households with shared duties, birth control, premarital agreements, and economic and legal rights for women. She also believed in the right to take one's own life; when she learned in 1935 that she had terminal breast cancer, she chose a quiet and dignified suicide.

Gilman's Literary Career.   Gilman's writings cover a wide range of topics and literary genres. In polemical writings such as *Women and Economics: A Study of the Economic Relation between Men and Women as a Factor in Social Evolution* (1898), *Concerning Children* (1900), *The Home* (1903), and *Human Work* (1904), she advocated day-care centers, collective kitchens, and professionalizing household work. *Man-Made World* (1911) and *His Religion and Hers* (1923) argued that violence, war, and a death-obsessed theology were consequences of a too-patriarchal society. In such utopian novels as *Moving a Mountain* (1911), *Herland* (1915), and *With Her in Herland* (1916), Gilman presented the social ills deriving from male competitiveness and imagined a nurturing matriarchal society based on ecological and ethical ideals. Her autobiography, *The Living of Charlotte Perkins Gilman* (1935), is an account of her difficult early years and the achievements of her later life.

"The Yellow Wallpaper."   Gilman's most famous story, "The Yellow Wallpaper," is not strictly autobiographical: Walter Stetson, far from being an overbearing patriarch, helped his wife as best he could and even praised this story, written six years after her crisis. The story first appeared in *The New England Magazine* in 1892. Gilman sent a copy to Dr. Mitchell, who did not reply, but who was said to have later acknowledged to friends that he had altered his methods after reading it. In her autobiography Gilman says that if that was true, she would feel her life had not been in vain.

"The Yellow Wallpaper" is more than an indictment of one particular insensitive doctor or foolish medical treatment, and it is more than just a good psychological horror story; in its brief scope, it takes a devastating look at the oppressive relationships between middle-class husband and wife, doctor and patient, society and artist, and patriarchy and the women in bondage within it. It invokes the **GOTHIC** novel's[3] conventions of the spooky isolated mansion, the mysterious chamber of barred

The Yellow Wallpaper was not intended to drive people crazy, but to save people from being driven crazy, and it worked.

– CHARLOTTE PERKINS GILMAN, 1913

---

[3] **Gothic novel:** A subgenre of the novel, concentrating on mystery, magic, and horror. Especially popular during the late eighteenth and early nineteenth centuries, Gothic novels were often set in castles or mansions with dungeons and secret rooms, which contributed to their atmosphere of mystery.

windows, and the sense of some alien presence in the house. Gilman is partly saying that the true horror story concerns not monsters but nineteenth-century men and women in ordinary marriages and professional relationships. The woman in the story is nameless, even to herself; she is so demoralized she can only whisper the truth of her oppression, can write it only in the most secret of places, and then continues to blame her oppression on her own failure to conform cheerfully to it. Ironically, John—"I am a doctor, dear, and I know"—bases all his "knowledge" on a fantasy of what women are and what they need; the quieter the woman is, the more at peace the doctor believes her to be. The wife's "fancies," on the other hand—that she is growing worse, that John is wrong, that she is in a prison—are real. When she is driven further and further back upon herself, she undertakes her great heroic action against the men and society who are killing her. She does not directly attack them, but by seeing an image of herself in the Rorschach-like wallpaper, she endeavors to free herself. As frightening as the ending is, in a way, the woman has gained some power over her situation; she has found a task in which she can take pride and pleasure, and she can even, by the final lines, express what she truly feels about John. In madness she has found her way to a terrible freedom. The painful power of this story probably accounts for the fact that it remained out of print for nearly fifty years.

■ CONNECTIONS

Goethe, *Faust*, p. 29; Harriet Jacobs, *Incidents in the Life of a Slave Girl*, p. 760; Emily Dickinson, "They shut me up in Prose," p. 914. The depression of the woman in "The Yellow Wallpaper" is a form of captivity or imprisonment, a theme that recurs in several works by women in the nineteenth century, including Jacobs's *Incidents in the Life of a Slave Girl* and Dickinson's "They shut me up in Prose." In varied ways these works depict the restraints placed on women by a patriarchal society in terms of captivity. What restrictions in particular do these works identify? Is Margaret's imprisonment in Goethe's *Faust* an instance of the same theme?

E. T. A. Hoffmann, "The Mines of Falun," p. 298. Gilman employs the conventions of Gothic fiction—the "haunted house," confinement, and the madwoman in the attic, for example—to tell a Realist story. Hoffmann uses Gothic conventions to heighten the Romantic mystery in "The Mines of Falun." What are the Gothic elements in each story and what do they contribute to the stories' overall themes?

Søren Kierkegaard, *The Sickness unto Death*, p. 675; Sigmund Freud, "Case 4: Katharina" (Book 6). Illness is often used metaphorically in literature to reveal an aspect of character or a debilitating social force. Consider "The Yellow Wallpaper" in light of Kierkegaard's discussion of "the sickness unto death." Does the woman's illness in Gilman's story fit the diagnosis offered by Kierkegaard?

■ FURTHER RESEARCH

Biography

Hill, Mary A. *Charlotte Perkins Gilman: The Making of a Radical Feminist, 1860–1896.* 1980.
Lane, Ann J. *To Herland and Beyond: The Life and Work of Charlotte Perkins Gilman.* 1990.
Scharnhorst, Gary. *Charlotte Perkins Gilman.* 1985.

Criticism

Dock, Julie Bates, ed. *Charlotte Perkins Gilman's "The Yellow Wallpaper" and the History of its Publication and Reception: A Critical Edition and Documentary Casebook.* 1998.

Golden, Catherine, ed. *The Yellow Wallpaper.* 1992. A collection of essays on the story and its historical and literary context.

Knight, Denise D. *Charlotte Perkins Gilman: A Study of the Short Fiction.* 1997.

❧ The Yellow Wallpaper

It is very seldom that mere ordinary people like John and myself secure ancestral halls for the summer.

A colonial mansion, a hereditary estate, I would say a haunted house and reach the height of romantic felicity—but that would be asking too much of fate!

Still I will proudly declare that there is something queer about it.

Else, why should it be let so cheaply? And why have stood so long untenanted?

John laughs at me, of course, but one expects that.

John is practical in the extreme. He has no patience with faith, an intense horror of superstition, and he scoffs openly at any talk of things not to be felt and seen and put down in figures.

John is a physician, and *perhaps*—(I would not say it to a living soul, of course, but this is dead paper and a great relief to my mind)—*perhaps* that is one reason I do not get well faster.

You see, he does not believe I am sick! And what can one do?

If a physician of high standing, and one's own husband, assures friends and relatives that there is really nothing the matter with one but temporary nervous depression—a slight hysterical tendency—what is one to do?

My brother is also a physician, and also of high standing, and he says the same thing.

So I take phosphates or phosphites—whichever it is—and tonics, and air and exercise, and journeys, and am absolutely forbidden to "work" until I am well again.

Personally, I disagree with their ideas.

"The Yellow Wallpaper."   In 1892, five years after Charlotte Perkins Gilman underwent a treatment like the one described in this story, "The Yellow Wallpaper" appeared in *The New England Magazine.* Gilman's first husband, George Stetson, reportedly was more enlightened than the husband in the story, and Gilman's illness never reached the depths of madness suffered by its heroine. Gilman declared that she "never had hallucinations or objections to [her] mural decorations" and that after three months on the rest cure she gave it up when she realized it wasn't working. She intended her story as a warning to other women about the dangers of the treatment, and she was gratified when she learned of a woman saved from a similar fate.

Personally, I believe that congenial work, with excitement and change, would do me good.

But what is one to do?

I did write for a while in spite of them; but it *does* exhaust me a good deal—having to be so sly about it, or else meet with heavy opposition.

I sometimes fancy that in my condition, if I had less opposition and more society and stimulus—but John says the very worst thing I can do is to think about my condition, and I confess it always makes me feel bad.

So I will let it alone and talk about the house.

The most beautiful place! It is quite alone, standing well back from the road, quite three miles from the village. It makes me think of English places that you read about, for there are hedges and walls and gates that lock, and lots of separate little houses for the gardeners and people.

There is a *delicious* garden! I never saw such a garden—large and shady, full of box-bordered paths, and lined with long grape-covered arbors with seats under them.

There were greenhouses, but they are all broken now.

There was some legal trouble, I believe, something about the heirs and co-heirs; anyhow, the place has been empty for years.

That spoils my ghostliness, I am afraid, but I don't care—there is something strange about the house—I can feel it.

I even said so to John one moonlight evening, but he said what I felt was a draught, and shut the window.

I get unreasonably angry with John sometimes. I'm sure I never used to be so sensitive. I think it is due to this nervous condition.

But John says if I feel so I shall neglect proper self-control; so I take pains to control myself—before him, at least, and that makes me very tired.

I don't like our room a bit. I wanted one downstairs that opened on the piazza and had roses all over the window, and such pretty old-fashioned chintz hangings! But John would not hear of it.

He said there was only one window and not room for two beds, and no near room for him if he took another.

He is very careful and loving, and hardly lets me stir without special direction.

I have a schedule prescription for each hour in the day; he takes all care from me, and so I feel basely ungrateful not to value it more.

He said he came here solely on my account, that I was to have perfect rest and all the air I could get. "Your exercise depends on your strength, my dear," said he, "and your food somewhat on your appetite; but air you can absorb all the time." So we took the nursery at the top of the house.

It is a big, airy room, the whole floor nearly, with windows that look all ways, and air and sunshine galore. It was nursery first, and then playroom and gymnasium, I should judge, for the windows are barred for little children, and there are rings and things in the walls.

The paint and paper look as if a boys' school had used it. It is stripped off—the paper—in great patches all around the head of my bed, about as far as I can reach, and in a great place on the other side of the room low down. I never saw a worse paper in my life. One of those sprawling, flamboyant patterns committing every artistic sin.

It is dull enough to confuse the eye in following, pronounced enough constantly to irritate and provoke study, and when you follow the lame uncertain curves for a little distance they suddenly commit suicide—plunge off at outrageous angles, destroy themselves in unheard-of contradictions.

The color is repellent, almost revolting; a smouldering unclean yellow, strangely faded by the slow-turning sunlight. It is a dull yet lurid orange in some places, a sickly sulphur tint in others.

No wonder the children hated it! I should hate it myself if I had to live in this room long.

There comes John, and I must put this away—he hates to have me write a word.

We have been here two weeks, and I haven't felt like writing before, since that first day.

I am sitting by the window now, up in this atrocious nursery, and there is nothing to hinder my writing as much as I please, save lack of strength.

John is away all day, and even some nights when his cases are serious.

I am glad my case is not serious!

But these nervous troubles are dreadfully depressing.

John does not know how much I really suffer. He knows there is no reason to suffer, and that satisfies him.

Of course it is only nervousness. It does weigh on me so not to do my duty in any way!

I meant to be such a help to John, such a real rest and comfort, and here I am a comparative burden already!

Nobody would believe what an effort it is to do what little I am able—to dress and entertain, and order things.

It is fortunate Mary is so good with the baby. Such a dear baby!

And yet I *cannot* be with him, it makes me so nervous.

I suppose John never was nervous in his life. He laughs at me so about this wallpaper!

At first he meant to repaper the room, but afterwards he said that I was letting it get the better of me, and that nothing was worse for a nervous patient than to give way to such fancies.

He said that after the wallpaper was changed it would be the heavy bedstead, and then the barred windows, and then that gate at the head of the stairs, and so on.

"You know the place is doing you good," he said, "and really, dear, I don't care to renovate the house just for a three months' rental."

"Then do let us go downstairs," I said. "There are such pretty rooms there."

Then he took me in his arms and called me a blessed little goose, and said he would go down cellar, if I wished, and have it whitewashed into the bargain.

But he is right enough about the beds and windows and things.

It is as airy and comfortable a room as anyone need wish, and, of course, I would not be so silly as to make him uncomfortable just for a whim.

I'm really getting quite fond of the big room, all but that horrid paper.

Out of one window I can see the garden—those mysterious deep-shaded arbors, the riotous old-fashioned flowers, and bushes and gnarly trees.

Out of another I get a lovely view of the bay and a little private wharf belonging to the estate. There is a beautiful shaded lane that runs down there from the house. I always fancy I see people walking in these numerous paths and arbors, but John has cautioned me not to give way to fancy in the least. He says that with my imaginative power and habit of story-making, a nervous weakness like mine is sure to lead to all manner of excited fancies, and that I ought to use my will and good sense to check the tendency. So I try.

I think sometimes that if I were only well enough to write a little it would relieve the press of ideas and rest me.

But I find I get pretty tired when I try.

It is so discouraging not to have any advice and companionship about my work. When I get really well, John says we will ask Cousin Henry and Julia down for a long visit; but he says he would as soon put fireworks in my pillow-case as to let me have those stimulating people about now.

I wish I could get well faster.

But I must not think about that. This paper looks to me as if it *knew* what a vicious influence it had!

There is a recurrent spot where the pattern lolls like a broken neck and two bulbous eyes stare at you upside down.

I get positively angry with the impertinence of it and the everlastingness. Up and down and sideways they crawl, and those absurd unblinking eyes are everywhere. There is one place where two breadths didn't match, and the eyes go all up and down the line, one a little higher than the other.

I never saw so much expression in an inanimate thing before, and we all know how much expression they have! I used to lie awake as a child and get more entertainment and terror out of blank walls and plain furniture than most children could find in a toy-store.

I remember what a kindly wink the knobs of our big old bureau used to have, and there was one chair that always seemed like a strong friend.

I used to feel that if any of the other things looked too fierce I could always hop into that chair and be safe.

The furniture in this room is no worse than inharmonious, however, for we had to bring it all from downstairs. I suppose when this was used as a playroom they had to take the nursery things out, and no wonder! I never saw such ravages as the children have made here.

The wallpaper, as I said before, is torn off in spots, and it sticketh closer than a brother—they must have had perseverance as well as hatred.

Then the floor is scratched and gouged and splintered, the plaster itself is dug out here and there, and this great heavy bed, which is all we found in the room, looks as if it had been through the wars.

But I don't mind it a bit—only the paper.

There comes John's sister. Such a dear girl as she is, and so careful of me! I must not let her find me writing.

She is a perfect and enthusiastic housekeeper, and hopes for no better profession. I verily believe she thinks it is the writing which made me sick!

But I can write when she is out, and see her a long way off from these windows.

There is one that commands the road, a lovely shaded winding road, and one that just looks off over the country. A lovely country, too, full of great elms and velvet meadows.

This wallpaper has a kind of sub-pattern in a different shade, a particularly irritating one, for you can only see it in certain lights, and not clearly then.

But in the places where it isn't faded and where the sun is just so—I can see a strange, provoking, formless sort of figure that seems to skulk about behind that silly and conspicuous front design.

There's sister on the stairs!

Well, the Fourth of July is over! The people are all gone, and I am tired out. John thought it might do me good to see a little company, so we just had Mother and Nellie and the children down for a week.

Of course I didn't do a thing. Jennie sees to everything now.

But it tired me all the same.

John says if I don't pick up faster he shall send me to Weir Mitchell[1] in the fall.

But I don't want to go there at all. I had a friend who was in his hands once, and she says he is just like John and my brother, only more so!

Besides, it is such an undertaking to go so far.

I don't feel as if it was worthwhile to turn my hand over for anything, and I'm getting dreadfully fretful and querulous.

I cry at nothing, and cry most of the time.

Of course I don't when John is here, or anybody else, but when I am alone.

And I am alone a good deal just now. John is kept in town very often by serious cases, and Jennie is good and lets me alone when I want her to.

So I walk a little in the garden or down that lovely lane, sit on the porch under the roses, and lie down up here a good deal.

I'm getting really fond of the room in spite of the wallpaper. Perhaps *because* of the wallpaper.

It dwells in my mind so!

I lie here on this great immovable bed—it is nailed down, I believe—and follow that pattern about by the hour. It is as good as gymnastics, I assure you. I start, we'll say, at the bottom, down in the corner over there where it has not been touched, and I determine for the thousandth time that I *will* follow that pointless pattern to some sort of a conclusion.

---

[1] **Weir Mitchell:** S. Weir Mitchell was the name of the actual doctor who prescribed the "rest cure" for Gilman; see headnote.

I know a little of the principle of design, and I know this thing was not arranged on any laws of radiation, or alternation, or repetition, or symmetry, or anything else that I ever heard of.

It is repeated, of course, by the breadths, but not otherwise.

Looked at in one way each breadth stands alone; the bloated curves and flourishes—a kind of "debased Romanesque" with delirium tremens—go waddling up and down in isolated columns of fatuity.

But, on the other hand, they connect diagonally, and the sprawling outlines run off in great slanting waves of optic horror, like a lot of wallowing sea-weeds in full chase.

The whole thing goes horizontally, too, at least it seems so, and I exhaust myself in trying to distinguish the order of its going in that direction.

They have used a horizontal breadth for a frieze, and that adds wonderfully to the confusion.

There is one end of the room where it is almost intact, and there, when the crosslights fade and the low sun shines directly upon it, I can almost fancy radiation after all—the interminable grotesques seem to form around a common center and rush off in headlong plunges of equal distraction.

It makes me tired to follow it. I will take a nap, I guess.

I don't know why I should write this.

I don't want to.

I don't feel able.

And I know John would think it absurd. But I *must* say what I feel and think in some way—it is such a relief!

But the effort is getting to be greater than the relief.

Half the time now I am awfully lazy, and lie down ever so much. John says I mustn't lose my strength, and has me take cod liver oil and lots of tonics and things, to say nothing of ale and wine and rare meat.

Dear John! He loves me very dearly, and hates to have me sick. I tried to have a real earnest reasonable talk with him the other day, and tell him how I wish he would let me go and make a visit to Cousin Henry and Julia.

But he said I wasn't able to go, nor able to stand it after I got there; and I did not make out a very good case for myself, for I was crying before I had finished.

It is getting to be a great effort for me to think straight. Just this nervous weakness, I suppose.

And dear John gathered me up in his arms, and just carried me upstairs and laid me on the bed, and sat by me and read to me till it tired my head.

He said I was his darling and his comfort and all he had, and that I must take care of myself for his sake, and keep well.

He says no one but myself can help me out of it, that I must use my will and self-control and not let any silly fancies run away with me.

There's one comfort—the baby is well and happy, and does not have to occupy this nursery with the horrid wallpaper.

If we had not used it, that blessed child would have! What a fortunate escape!

Why, I wouldn't have a child of mine, an impressionable little thing, live in such a room for worlds.

I never thought of it before, but it is lucky that John kept me here after all; I can stand it so much easier than a baby, you see.

Of course I never mention it to them any more—I am too wise—but I keep watch of it all the same.

There are things in that paper that nobody knows but me, or ever will.

Behind that outside pattern the dim shapes get clearer every day.

It is always the same shape, only very numerous.

And it is like a woman stooping down and creeping about behind that pattern. I don't like it a bit. I wonder—I begin to think—I wish John would take me away from here!

It is so hard to talk to John about my case, because he is so wise, and because he loves me so.

But I tried it last night.

It was moonlight. The moon shines in all around just as the sun does.

I hate to see it sometimes, it creeps so slowly, and always comes in by one window or another.

John was asleep and I hated to waken him, so I kept still and watched the moonlight on that undulating wallpaper till I felt creepy.

The faint figure behind seemed to shake the pattern, just as if she wanted to get out.

I got up softly and went to feel and see if the paper *did* move, and when I came back John was awake.

"What is it, little girl?" he said. "Don't go walking about like that—you'll get cold."

I thought it was a good time to talk, so I told him that I really was not gaining here, and that I wished he would take me away.

"Why, darling!" said he. "Our lease will be up in three weeks, and I can't see how to leave before.

"The repairs are not done at home, and I cannot possibly leave town just now. Of course, if you were in any danger, I could and would, but you really are better, dear, whether you can see it or not. I am a doctor, dear, and I know. You are gaining flesh and color, your appetite is better, I feel really much easier about you."

"I don't weigh a bit more," said I, "nor as much; and my appetite may be better in the evening when you are here but it is worse in the morning when you are away!"

"Bless her little heart!" said he with a big hug. "She shall be as sick as she pleases! But now let's improve the shining hours by going to sleep, and talk about it in the morning!"

"And you won't go away?" I asked gloomily.

"Why, how can I, dear? It is only three weeks more and then we will take a nice little trip of a few days while Jennie is getting the house ready. Really, dear, you are better!"

"Better in body perhaps—" I began, and stopped short, for he sat up straight and looked at me with such a stern, reproachful look that I could not say another word.

"My darling," said he, "I beg of you, for my sake and for our child's sake, as well as for your own, that you will never for one instant let that idea enter your mind! There is nothing so dangerous, so fascinating, to a temperament like yours. It is a false and foolish fancy. Can you not trust me as a physician when I tell you so?"

So of course I said no more on that score, and we went to sleep before long. He thought I was asleep first, but I wasn't and lay there for hours trying to decide whether that front pattern and the back pattern really did move together or separately.

On a pattern like this, by daylight, there is a lack of sequence, a defiance of law, that is a constant irritant to a normal mind.

The color is hideous enough, and unreliable enough, and infuriating enough, but the pattern is torturing.

You think you have mastered it, but just as you get well under way in following, it turns a back-somersault and there you are. It slaps you in the face, knocks you down, and tramples upon you. It is like a bad dream.

The outside pattern is a florid arabesque, reminding one of a fungus. If you can imagine a toadstool in joints, an interminable string of toadstools, budding and sprouting in endless convolutions—why, that is something like it.

That is, sometimes!

There is one marked peculiarity about this paper, a thing nobody seems to notice but myself, and that is that it changes as the light changes.

When the sun shoots in through the east window—I always watch for that first long, straight ray—it changes so quickly that I never can quite believe it.

That is why I watch it always.

By moonlight—the moon shines in all night when there is a moon—I wouldn't know it was the same paper.

At night in any kind of light, in twilight, candlelight, lamplight, and worst of all by moonlight, it becomes bars! The outside pattern, I mean, and the woman behind it is as plain as can be.

I didn't realize for a long time what the thing was that showed behind, that dim sub-pattern, but now I am quite sure it is a woman.

By daylight she is subdued, quiet. I fancy it is the pattern that keeps her so still. It is so puzzling. It keeps me quiet by the hour.

I lie down ever so much now. John says it is good for me, and to sleep all I can.

Indeed he started the habit by making me lie down for an hour after each meal.

It is a very bad habit, I am convinced, for you see, I don't sleep.

And that cultivates deceit, for I don't tell them I'm awake—oh, no!

The fact is I am getting a little afraid of John.

He seems very queer sometimes, and even Jennie has an inexplicable look.

It strikes me occasionally, just as a scientific hypothesis, that perhaps it is the paper!

I have watched John when he did not know I was looking, and come into the room suddenly on the most innocent excuses, and I've caught him several times *looking at the paper!* And Jennie too. I caught Jennie with her hand on it once.

She didn't know I was in the room, and when I asked her in a quiet, a very quiet voice, with the most restrained manner possible, what she was doing with the paper—she turned around as if she had been caught stealing, and looked quite angry—asked me why I should frighten her so!

Then she said that the paper stained everything it touched, that she had found yellow smooches on all my clothes and John's and she wished we would be more careful!

Did not that sound innocent? But I know she was studying that pattern, and I am determined that nobody shall find it out but myself!

Life is very much more exciting now than it used to be. You see, I have something more to expect, to look forward to, to watch. I really do eat better, and am more quiet than I was.

John is so pleased to see me improve! He laughed a little the other day, and said I seemed to be flourishing in spite of my wallpaper.

I turned it off with a laugh. I had no intention of telling him it was *because* of the wallpaper—he would make fun of me. He might even want to take me away.

I don't want to leave now until I have found it out. There is a week more, and I think that will be enough.

I'm feeling so much better!

I don't sleep much at night, for it is so interesting to watch developments; but I sleep a good deal in the daytime.

In the daytime it is tiresome and perplexing.

There are always new shoots on the fungus, and new shades of yellow all over it. I cannot keep count of them, though I have tried conscientiously.

It is the strangest yellow, that wallpaper! It makes me think of all the yellow things I ever saw—not beautiful ones like buttercups, but old, foul, bad yellow things.

But there is something else about that paper—the smell! I noticed it the moment we came into the room, but with so much air and sun it was not bad. Now we have had a week of fog and rain, and whether the windows are open or not, the smell is here.

It creeps all over the house.

I find it hovering in the dining-room, skulking in the parlor, hiding in the hall, lying in wait for me on the stairs.

It gets into my hair.

Even when I go to ride, if I turn my head suddenly and surprise it—there is that smell!

Such a peculiar odor, too! I have spent hours in trying to analyze it, to find what it smelled like.

It is not bad—at first—and very gentle, but quite the subtlest, most enduring odor I ever met.

In this damp weather it is awful. I wake up in the night and find it hanging over me.

It used to disturb me at first. I thought seriously of burning the house—to reach the smell.

But now I am used to it. The only thing I can think of that it is like is the *color* of the paper! A yellow smell.

There is a very funny mark on this wall, low down, near the mopboard. A streak that runs around the room. It goes behind every piece of furniture, except the bed, a long, straight, even *smooch,* as if it had been rubbed over and over.

I wonder how it was done and who did it, and what they did it for. Round and round and round—round and round and round—it makes me dizzy!

I really have discovered something at last.

Through watching so much at night, when it changes so, I have finally found out.

The front pattern *does* move—and no wonder! The woman behind shakes it!

Sometimes I think there are a great many women behind, and sometimes only one, and she crawls around fast, and her crawling shakes it all over.

Then in the very bright spots she keeps still, and in the very shady spots she just takes hold of the bars and shakes them hard.

And she is all the time trying to climb through. But nobody could climb through that pattern—it strangles so; I think that is why it has so many heads.

They get through, and then the pattern strangles them off and turns them upside down, and makes their eyes white!

If those heads were covered or taken off it would not be half so bad.

I think that woman gets out in the daytime!

And I'll tell you why—privately—I've seen her!

I can see her out of every one of my windows!

It is the same woman, I know, for she is always creeping, and most women do not creep by daylight.

I see her in that long shaded lane, creeping up and down. I see her in those dark grape arbors, creeping all around the garden.

I see her on that long road under the trees, creeping along, and when a carriage comes she hides under the blackberry vines.

I don't blame her a bit. It must be very humiliating to be caught creeping by daylight!

I always lock the door when I creep by daylight. I can't do it at night, for I know John would suspect something at once.

And John is so queer now that I don't want to irritate him. I wish he would take another room! Besides, I don't want anybody to get that woman out at night but myself.

I often wonder if I could see her out of all the windows at once.

But, turn as fast as I can, I can only see out of one at one time.

And though I always see her, she *may* be able to creep faster than I can turn! I have watched her sometimes away off in the open country, creeping as fast as a cloud shadow in a wind.

If only that top pattern could be gotten off from the under one! I mean to try it, little by little.

I have found out another funny thing, but I shan't tell it this time! It does not do to trust people too much.

There are only two more days to get this paper off, and I believe John is beginning to notice. I don't like the look in his eyes.

And I heard him ask Jennie a lot of professional questions about me. She had a very good report to give.

She said I slept a good deal in the daytime.

John knows I don't sleep very well at night, for all I'm so quiet!

He asked me all sorts of questions, too, and pretended to be very loving and kind.

As if I couldn't see through him!

Still, I don't wonder he acts so, sleeping under this paper for three months.

It only interests me, but I feel sure John and Jennie are affected by it.

Hurrah! This is the last day, but it is enough. John is to stay in town over night, and won't be out until this evening.

Jennie wanted to sleep with me—the sly thing; but I told her I should undoubtedly rest better for a night all alone.

That was clever, for really I wasn't alone a bit! As soon as it was moonlight and that poor thing began to crawl and shake the pattern, I got up and ran to help her.

I pulled and she shook. I shook and she pulled, and before morning we had peeled off yards of that paper.

A strip about as high as my head and half around the room.

And then when the sun came and that awful pattern began to laugh at me, I declared I would finish it today!

We go away tomorrow, and they are moving all my furniture down again to leave things as they were before.

Jennie looked at the wall in amazement, but I told her merrily that I did it out of pure spite at the vicious thing.

She laughed and said she wouldn't mind doing it herself, but I must not get tired.

How she betrayed herself that time!

But I am here, and no person touches this paper but Me—not *alive!*

She tried to get me out of the room—it was too patent! But I said it was so quiet and empty and clean now that I believed I would lie down again and sleep all I could, and not to wake me even for dinner—I would call when I woke.

So now she is gone, and the servants are gone, and the things are gone, and there is nothing left but that great bedstead nailed down, with the canvas mattress we found on it.

We shall sleep downstairs tonight, and take the boat home tomorrow.

I quite enjoy the room, now it is bare again.

How those children did tear about here!

This bedstead is fairly gnawed!

But I must get to work.

I have locked the door and thrown the key down into the front path.

I don't want to go out, and I don't want to have anybody come in, till John comes.

I want to astonish him.

I've got a rope up here that even Jennie did not find. If that woman does get out, and tries to get away, I can tie her!

But I forgot I could not reach far without anything to stand on!

This bed will *not* move!

I tried to lift and push it until I was lame, and then I got so angry I bit off a little piece at one corner—but it hurt my teeth.

Then I peeled off all the paper I could reach standing on the floor. It sticks horribly and the pattern just enjoys it! All those strangled heads and bulbous eyes and waddling fungus growths just shriek with derision!

I am getting angry enough to do something desperate. To jump out of the window would be admirable exercise, but the bars are too strong even to try.

Besides I wouldn't do it. Of course not. I know well enough that a step like that is improper and might be misconstrued.

I don't like to *look* out of the windows even—there are so many of those creeping women, and they creep so fast.

I wonder if they all come out of that wallpaper as I did?

But I am securely fastened now by my well-hidden rope—you don't get *me* out in the road there!

I suppose I shall have to get back behind the pattern when it comes night, and that is hard!

It is so pleasant to be out in this great room and creep around as I please!

I don't want to go outside. I won't, even if Jennie asks me to.

For outside you have to creep on the ground, and everything is green instead of yellow.

But here I can creep smoothly on the floor, and my shoulder just fits in that long smooch around the wall, so I cannot lose my way.

Why, there's John at the door!

It is no use, young man, you can't open it!

How he does call and pound!

Now he's crying to Jennie for an axe.

It would be a shame to break down that beautiful door!

"John, dear!" said I in the gentlest voice. "The key is down by the front steps, under a plantain leaf!"

That silenced him for a few moments.

Then he said, very quietly indeed, "Open the door, my darling!"

"I can't," said I. "The key is down by the front door under a plantain leaf!" And then I said it again, several times, very gently and slowly, and said it so often that he had to go and see, and he got it of course, and came in. He stopped short by the door.

"What is the matter?" he cried. "For God's sake, what are you doing!"

I kept on creeping just the same, but I looked at him over my shoulder.

"I've got out at last," said I, "in spite of you and Jane. And I've pulled off most of the paper, so you can't put me back!"

Now why should that man have fainted? But he did, and right across my path by the wall, so that I had to creep over him every time!

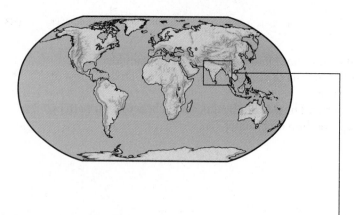

Expansion of the British Empire in India, 1805–58

At the end of the nineteenth century, the British had control of the whole of the Indian subcontinent. To achieve that end, Great Britain had expelled the French from southern India, the Russians from the north, and native Hindu Maratha forces from central and northern India during the first half of the century. In 1858 England's role in India was challenged when the Sepoys, native troops within the British army, rose up against the English in what is sometimes called the first Indian war of independence.

INDIA
Jewel in the Colonial Crown

ᘓ In the nineteenth century the British would consolidate and extend their
power in India, gaining control of the whole Indian subcontinent through a series
of colonial wars and through taking advantage of the divisions in the region after
the collapse of the Mughal empire. During the first half of the century the British
were occupied with expelling the French from southern India, challenging the Russians on the northern borders and in Afghanistan, defeating the Hɪɴᴅᴜ Marathi
forces in central and northern India, and pushing out from their central power
base in Bengal to take over neighboring states and prevent incursions over the
borders. Up until the 1830s, the British took largely an economic and legal interest
in India and made little attempt to impose European culture on the Indian people.
With the growing influence of evangelical Christians in the British government
after passage of the Reform Bill of 1832, however, missionaries were sent to India
and English was declared the medium of instruction in many Indian schools.
Along with the English language a new curriculum including English literature,
philosophy, and political and social theory was adopted for Indian schools. While
many Indians welcomed the opportunity to study and gain access to Western ideas
and science, the imposition of Western culture also sparked resistance. The second
half of the century saw a revival of interest in Hinduism, protests against the
excesses of British colonialism, and the beginnings of an independence movement.

THE SEPOY REBELLION

Symbolically, the Sepoy Rebellion of 1857–58 was the century's defining event in
Indian-British relations. The Sepoys, native troops in the British army, had over
the years protested several times against their treatment by British officers. When
some of their perquisites were cut and they were no longer exempted from foreign
service—an assignment that violated some caste rules—the Sepoys were angered.
Ordered to bite off the ends of cartridges that were lubricated with a mixture of

Calcutta c. 1900

By the nineteenth century the British would consolidate and extend their power across most of India. Along with the English language, a curriculum including English literature, philosophy, and political and social theory was introduced into Indian schools. Although the British held deep economic and legal interests in India, severe poverty still reigned in much of the subcontinent. Scenes such as the one pictured here were common, with large groups of people bathing or performing religious rituals in the dirty waters of the Ganges. (Getty Images)

cow and pig fat—offensive to both Hindus and Muslims—they took up arms. In a series of rebellions at Delhi, Lucknow, Peshawar, and several other sites across northern and central India, the Sepoys challenged the British. The disturbances lasted over a year, from May 1857 until July 1858. Although the military revolt never expanded into a broader national movement, the soldiers had considerable sympathy and covert support from conservative landowners and religious leaders who were distrustful of Westernization.

After a successful military campaign to put down the rebellion, the British pulled back from the liberalizing measures they had instituted before the uprising. They abandoned their attempts to abolish *suttee* (the ritual burning of widows on their husbands' funeral pyres), infanticide of unwanted daughters, and the traditional ban on widows remarrying. Traditional factions of Indian society who resisted Westernization were placated. The British also abolished the British East India Company, which had administered the colony for the British, and placed India under the direct rule of the crown. They reorganized the army, increasing the percentage of European troops and providing some opportunities for Indian troops to be promoted into positions of limited authority. They also opened up positions in the colonial administration to Indians and established a policy of limited consultation with them on political and legislative issues. These measures pleased the Westernized middle class, who had been disappointed by the British decision to abandon reform of the caste system and the marriage laws.

NATIONALISM AND THE BEGINNING OF THE INDEPENDENCE MOVEMENT

Although the Sepoy Rebellion has sometimes been called the first Indian war of independence, it is perhaps better described as an assertion of Indian traditionalism and nationalism. The more progressive forces that formed the Congress Movement in the 1880s — the real beginning of the campaign for independence — came from the Westernized middle class. The inspiration for the Congress Movement came from leaders like the Hindu Ram Mohun Roy (1772–1833), who sought to reform Hindu polytheism and unite Hindu and Christian ideas. This reforming impulse, promoted by several prominent teachers and leaders during the century, reached its quintessential expression in the Tagore family. Debendranath Tagore (1817–1905), a follower of Ram Mohun Roy, took over leadership of the movement after Roy's death; he sought to return Hinduism to monotheism, founded schools, and promoted the cause of national liberation. Among his fourteen children were poets, artists, and intellectuals, most notably Rabindranath (1861–1941) (p. 973) who in 1913 was the first Asian to win the Nobel Prize for literature.

ISLAMIC INDIA

The Tagores were Hindu reformers, and the Congress Movement, even though it included some Muslim members, was predominantly Hindu. The Muslim perspective on Indian nationalism and independence differed somewhat from that of the Hindus. Only a century or so past the dissolution of the Mughal empire, Indian Muslims tended to look back with a certain nostalgia at the nation's former glory. There is in the poetry of Ghalib (1797–1869), for example, a sense of loss and despair, that things always change, and that happiness is fleeting, traditional themes in Islamic poetry that have particular poignancy in the historical context in which Ghalib was working. At the same time there is also a tough-minded realism expressed in such lines as "Spring doesn't last long but at least it *is* spring." Among the Islamic reformers who sought to extend that spring was Syed Ahmad

The Nineteenth Century: The Partition of Bengal, 1905

The jewel in the crown of British India was Bengal, the area in eastern India surrounding Calcutta and constituting what are now the Indian states of West Bengal, Bihar, and Orissa, as well as the nation of Bangladesh. Although Calcutta had long been the administrative center of the British raj (a Hindi word for *rule*), in 1900 it was also the intellectual and cultural capital of the region, the center of the Bengali literary and artistic renaissance. With a population of more than 85 million, the area became increasingly difficult for the British to govern, so in 1905 Lord Curzon, viceroy of India, convinced the British colonial administration in London to partition Bengal into two parts.

The Partition divided Bengal into Western Bengal, population 54 million (42 million Hindus, 9 million Muslims), and Eastern Bengal and Assam, population 31 million (18 million Muslims, 12 million Hindus). Although there was some Muslim support for the plan because it created a separate district in which there would be a Muslim majority, Hindu opinion was adamantly against it. Indian nationalism aroused by the National Congress, founded in 1885, surfaced in opposition. The Congress was committed to a policy of national unity. Not only did it oppose the British encouragement of "communalism"—drawing political divisions along religious lines—but it also supported a "one India" policy as a way of getting beyond the patchwork of the states governed by Hindu princes and provincial rulers, maharajas and nawabs, into which post-Mughal India had fragmented. Indian liberals saw their struggle for national unity as comparable to similar movements in Italy and Germany; they considered the Partition another example of a British policy to divide and rule.

Those against the Partition responded with demonstrations, a boycott of British manufactured goods, and a campaign to buy Indian-made textiles. Some extremists carried out a terror campaign against the British and assassinated some colonial officials. The resistance convinced the British to revoke the Partition in 1909 and to make some political reforms, creating more opportunities for Indian participation in government and recognizing some Muslim majority areas. The British also supported the founding of the All India Muslim League in 1906, an organization comparable to the predominantly Hindu National Congress.

The Partition and the response to it had a lasting impact. The movement to make and buy Indian textiles and the boycott of British goods were techniques later employed by Gandhi's nonviolent movement for independence. And the principle of dividing the subcontinent into separate countries according to a region's religion would guide the partition of India and Pakistan in 1947, a decision that remains controversial more than half a century later.

www For more information about the culture and context of India in the nineteenth century, see *World Literature Online* at bedfordstmartins.com/worldlit.

Khan, (1817–1898) (p. 408), who, like the Tagores, developed educational programs that combined traditional Islamic and Western elements.

THE BENGALI RENAISSANCE

Rabindranath Tagore was the central figure in the BENGALI RENAISSANCE, the movement to create a national literature in the Bengali language that would be both Indian and "modern." Educated in the literature of the British ROMANTICS, the Bengali writers were often linked to British authors; Tagore was sometimes called the Shelley of India. Among his colleagues in the movement, poet Madhusudan Datta (1834–1873) was known as the Milton of India, and novelist Bankim Chandra Chatterjee (1838–1894), the Scott of Bengal. Another important writer of the time, playwright Girish Chandra Ghose (1844–1922), seems to have escaped without a Western epithet. Tagore and his colleagues celebrated Indian values and traditions within Western literary forms, like the novel and short story, incorporating some Western ideas, especially the UTILITARIAN philosophies of Jeremy Bentham and John Stuart Mill.

Tagore's novella *Broken Ties* (1916) deals with the tension between traditional Hinduism, represented by Harimohan and the Swami, and Western PRAGMATISM, espoused by Jagomohan and the narrator, Srivilas. The two brothers, Harimohan and Jagomohan, live in a partitioned house, symbolic of the division between traditionalism and modernism in India. The young men, Satish and Srivilas, are on a pilgrimage to negotiate these conflicting influences in their heritage and to forge an identity for themselves. In "The Hungry Stones" (1895) Tagore treats a similar conflict, representing tradition with the Arabian Nights palace and modernity in the figure of the Indian clerk who works for the British colonial administration.

❧ GHALIB (MIRZA ASADULLAH BEG KHAN)
1797–1869

Mirza Asadullah Beg Khan, known by his pen name of Ghalib, is the foremost poet of the Urdu language, a hybrid tongue derived from a combination of Indian dialects and Persian. In some ways, Urdu reflects the cultural and religious synthesis of the Mughal empire in its heyday, during the sixteenth and seventeenth centuries, when under the emperors Akbar, Shah Jahan, and Aurangzeb[1] the Indo-Muslim culture flourished, producing such poets as Tulsidas (1532–1623) and such monuments as the Taj Mahal (completed in 1653). By Ghalib's time, the Mughal empire was in decline, in part from internal conflicts, but especially from changes stemming from the European, particularly British, presence in India. After the Battle of Plassey in which British forces defeated the army of *nawab*[2] Siraj-ud-daula in 1757, England strengthened its power in Bengal and eventually over greater India. By the time of Ghalib's birth in 1797, the British East India Company—the arm of British political authority in India—exerted considerable influence over the remnants of Mughal power in Delhi, where Ghalib lived. In the course of Ghalib's lifetime, the British extended their political, economic, and cultural control throughout India, claiming ownership rights to lands and titles, and taking charge of the country's administration, economy, and communications. Thus, **Ghalib** witnessed the unraveling of India and the increasing influence, for both better and worse, of the British colonial government. A social and psychological record of India's transformations is registered in Ghalib's finely crafted letters, diaries, and poetry.

Early Life.   Ghalib was born in Agra in December 1797 or January 1798 into a wealthy Muslim family with Turkish roots. His father, an army officer, died before Ghalib was five years old, so Ghalib was raised in the household of his wealthy maternal grand-uncle. Around 1810, at age thirteen, Ghalib was married to the daughter of an aristocratic family, and by 1812 he was settled in Delhi, the capital of the declining Mughal empire. Ghalib continued his education in Delhi and began to refine his poetic style. As in China, young men of the ruling classes were expected to achieve a mastery of poetry; Ghalib studied Persian literature, history, and religion with Mulla Abdussamad Harmuzd, an Iranian tutor and scholar who sometimes appears in Ghalib's poetry as a voice addressing the poet's critics. Though Ghalib indicates that he preferred youthful

---

[1] Akbar . . . Aurangzeb: Mughal emperors of India from 1556 to 1605, 1628 to 1658, and 1658 to 1707, respectively. Akbar, known for his just rule, extended the empire; Shah Jahan oversaw the flourishing of culture, including the building of the Taj Mahal; Aurangzeb, after imprisoning his father, further extended the empire's boundaries, but by implementing persecution of the Hindus and Sikhs ultimately weakened his authority over the Indian population.

[2] *nawab:* A provincial ruler in India under the Moghul empire.

diversions, such as playing chess and flying kites, to his studies, he must have excelled at his literary training, for some scholars suggest that many of his major works in Urdu were completed by 1816, when he would have been nineteen years old; others suggest his productive years of writing in Urdu came when he was in his early twenties. Whatever the case, Ghalib compiled a collection of his Urdu poems when he was twenty-four, after which he wrote primarily in Persian until 1847, when as a member of the court of Bahadur Shah Zafar (Bahadur Shah II; r. 1837–1857), the last Mughal emperor, he again wrote in Urdu.

A Troubled Time.   In his twenties Ghalib encountered financial difficulties when family infighting interrupted his pension. In 1831, in his early thirties, he lost a six-year-long lawsuit over his inheritance from his guardian uncle and began what was to become a lifelong nuisance of intermittently filing petitions to the British government to secure a pension. Not until 1847, when he entered the court of Bahadur Shah II at Delhi, did he regain financial security. Ghalib was appointed to write the official history of the Mughal empire, and he resumed writing poetry — panegyric verse, or eulogy, and **ghazals**[3] — and prose in Urdu, a language he had abandoned in his work for some time except to correct the several editions of his poetry issued between 1821 and 1847. After the 1854 death of Ghalib's archrival Zauk, the emperor's tutor in poetry, Ghalib took over that position and completed the first volume of his history of the Mughals. The planned second volume, never completed, was interrupted by the Indian (Sepoy) Mutiny of 1857. Brought on by widespread resentment against British political and cultural policies — land annexation, conscription of Indian men, and insensitivity to Muslim and Hindu customs — the revolt began in May at Meerut, just thirty miles north of Delhi. As a small liberating army, the Sepoys (Indian police) from Meerut advanced to Delhi to liberate Ghalib's patron, Emperor Bahadur Shah II. In succeeding months, the revolt spread to sites beyond Delhi; it lacked unity and direction, however, and was quickly and ruthlessly suppressed. In September 1857 the British deposed Bahadur Shah II, who went into exile in Burma. With the execution of the former emperor's two sons, the Mughal dynasty came to an end. Disenchanted by the atrocities he had witnessed from both sides during the rebellion, Ghalib left an account of the revolt, critical of both the Indian resistance and the British forces, in his diary of 1857 known as *Bouquet of Flowers (Dast-Ambooh)*.

Although Ghalib had been impressed with the results of British influence during a two-year stay, in 1828 and 1829, at the port town of Calcutta, a center of British power, the British response to the rebellion gave him deep pause. At least two of his friends who had survived the

www For links to more information about Ghalib and a quiz on his work, see *World Literature Online* at bedfordstmartins .com/worldlit.

gah-ZAHL

Ghalib
The great Urdu poet Mirza Asadullah Beg Khan, or Ghalib, wrote his poetry as India came under the influence of Britain, bearing witness to great change in his lifetime. (Diodia Picture Library)

---

[3] *ghazals:* Lyric poetry composed of three to seven couplets (called *sh'ir*) that follows a strict rhyme scheme known as *qafiyah,* of *aa ba ca da,* and so on. Strict adherence to the form requires the use of the *radif,* a word that is repeated in a pattern dictated by the first couplet throughout the poem. Literally meaning "dialogue with the beloved," *ghazals* as practiced in Arabia, Persia, Turkey, and India became the predominant form of love poetry.

interrogations and executions in Delhi had had their libraries destroyed. Ghalib himself was left destitute and had to sell off some of his household goods to get by. Eventually obtaining a small allowance from the nawab of Rampur as well as a pension from the new government, Ghalib remained in Delhi as many other Delhians went into exile in the north. He published a collection of letters, *Ud-i-Hindi,* in 1868; written in Urdu, these letters along with his memoir constitute fine examples of Urdu prose style. Ghalib died on February 15, 1869, leaving a legacy of great love poems, or *ghazals,* in the tradition of Hafiz, Rumi, and Kabir.[4]

The *Ghazal*.   While his prose works and letters are remembered for their elegance, Ghalib is most revered for his mastery of the Urdu *ghazal.* The *ghazal* developed from seventh-century Arabic poetry and became a popular poetic form in Persian, Turkish, and eventually Urdu, in which language poets like Ghalib explored the form's full potential. The *ghazal* is a form of lyric poetry composed of three to seven couplets (Ghalib often used five), rhymed *aa ba ca da,* and so on. This rhyme scheme, known as *qafiyah,* is strictly followed. Many classical *ghazals* introduce what is called the ***radif,*** a word or phrase repeated at the end of each couplet in the series, further challenging the poet's skills. The strength of the *ghazal* lies in the couplet, or ***shi'r.*** Each couplet stands alone as a highly condensed and stylized thematic unit that invokes traditional motifs and figures. Each *shi'r* in a *ghazal* may be a self-contained unit that need not flow logically into the next. The *ghazal* in Urdu poetry was thought of as a string of pearls, each *shi'r* contributing to the mood and general sense of the whole, but not, as in the English or Italian sonnet, following a thematic logic. Given the independent character of each *shi'r* in the series, the ghazal is comparable to the Japanese *renga,* whose links among various haiku are often indirect and tonal rather than linear and logical.

The *ghazal* typically offers a reflection on spiritual and secular love, most often from the point of view of a disappointed lover longing after an unattainable object of desire. In this regard, the *ghazal* is similar to European love poetry, particularly the Renaissance love sonnet and the Romantic lyric. As in those traditions, the *ghazal* expresses the seemingly hopeless but ardent desire of a lover faced with the impossibility of ever grasping the elusive beloved. Moreover, the image of the beloved blurs the boundaries between corporeal and spiritual love; as a metaphor for a spiritual object, the beloved always threatens, or promises, to indicate an embodied worldly one. Drawing on traditional imagery dating back to the *ghazal's* origins in Persian and Arabic poetry, the poet focuses on settings such as the desert, the garden, and the drinking

kah-FEE-yah

RAH-deef

SHEER

---

[4] Hafiz . . . Kabir: Hafiz and Rumi were two of the greatest Persian poets from the fourteenth and thirteenth centuries, respectively; Kabir was a great fourteenth-century poet from India who wrote in Hindi. All three are associated with Sufism, a religious strand woven from Muslim and Hindu forms of mysticism, which stresses the longing for an ecstatic union with God.

party, and calls on conventional symbols such as the candle, the nightingale, and the rose. These latter images symbolize the illuminated or enflamed spirit, the lover, or the beloved. A common motif involves a nightingale away seeking its lover in a garden while its nest is being destroyed by worldly forces—the quest for the ideal leading to the neglect of the everyday.

Ghalib's *Ghazals*.   Written from the heart of a fading empire in the throes of colonial conflict, Ghalib's poetry registers the power of a poet and a poetic tradition to endure and adapt as they respond to the pressures, promises, desires, and disappointments that accompany cultural, social, and economic upheaval. While invoking the conventional motifs and themes associated with the *ghazal*, Ghalib, like other virtuoso poets, transforms them into something more. In his hands, the form becomes a distinctive utterance reflecting his personal response to the unsettled conditions of his private and public life: the stress of financial uncertainty, the loss of social status, the desire to embrace life intensely, and a deep sorrow at the collapse of the Mughal empire. Ghalib's *ghazals* are sometimes intensely private and melancholy; at other times they seem oriented toward public expression and they approach satire. More often, the two realms collapse into each other so that the public becomes private and vice versa.

Although Ghalib found life itself a thing worth cherishing, he was keenly aware of, and deeply experienced in, its myriad disappointments and cruelties. In contrast to Sufi poets like Hafiz, whose poetry aspires toward a mystical effacement of the self, Ghalib's poetry embraces the world with an intensity that insinuates a broad range of experience and a desire for fulfillment in the present. Sunil Dutta puts it simply: "One could say that in thought and intellect, Ghalib resembles Rumi and Hafiz, but the emotion of his poems goes in a different direction from the Sufis. Ghalib has great spiritual intensity, but it comes with a worldliness of the sort we associate with Shakespeare more than with Wordsworth or Herbert."[5] Throughout Ghalib's *ghazals* there is a genuine sense of despair, of powers lost, of the futility of human endeavors, and of his own failures. Simultaneously, however, his poetry registers an equally intense sense of striving that is often figured as a manifestation of divine power, as in "Why didn't I shrink in the blaze of that face?" Ghalib's poetry is about the embodiment of spirituality, and part of that embodiment is the language of the verse itself, its rhythm and music. Although the sound of the original Urdu is lost in translation, the success of Ghalib's language is confirmed by the sustained power of his verse, which even today is widely memorized and recited by Urdu speakers in India.

> Sufi poets, when they use the words "wine" and "the tavern," mean the state of the soul, but when Ghalib uses these words, he means wine and taverns.
>
> – SUNIL DUTTA, "Ghalib and His Work," 1999

---

[5] Herbert: George Herbert (1593–1633), an Anglican priest and English metaphysical poet whose verse emphasizes spiritual devotion and a longing for God.

■ **CONNECTIONS**

Dante, *The Divine Comedy* (Book 3); Alexander Pope, *Essay on Man* (Book 4); Matsuo Bashō (Book 4), *Narrow Road through the Backcountry*. Ghalib is a master of the *ghazal,* a form of lyric poetry composed of three to seven couplets following a strict metrical pattern and a rhyme scheme of *aa ba ca,* and so on; the rhymed lines often repeat the same word or phrase. Each couplet usually continues a new poetic idea only loosely associated with those in the surrounding couplets. As a strictly regulated form that allows for considerable diversity, the *ghazal* offers an interesting contrast to other regulated forms, such as the *terza rima* of Dante, the heroic couplet of Pope, the *haikai* of Bashō, or even the sonnet or sestina used by various European poets. Compare these poetic forms. How do they produce or reflect a distinctive, even culturally distinctive, sensibility or way of thinking about poetry? How does the *ghazal* compare with free verse?

John Keats, *Ode to a Nightingale,* p. 288; Rilke, *Duino Elegies* (Book 6). Ghalib's *ghazals* evoke the contradictions of love, in which longing for the beloved reaches a point of fusion with spiritual desire and the lover is consumed by the intensity of his or her desire. As in Keats's odes and Rilke's *Duino Elegies,* desire in Ghalib's work is tinged with disappointment, and romantic love leads to the brink of unhappiness, even as it promises joy. What elements of these poets' verse — for example, style, symbolism, imagery — draw on culturally specific conventions?

■ **FURTHER RESEARCH**

Biography
Russell, Ralph, and Khurshidul Islam. *Ghalib: Life and Letters.* 1969.

Translations and Editions
Ahmad, Aijaz. *Ghazals of Ghalib.* 1971.
Bly, Robert, and Sunil Dutta. *The Lightning Should Have Fallen on Ghalib: Selected Poems of Ghalib.* 1999.

Criticism
Ali, Ahmed. *The Golden Tradition: An Anthology of Urdu Poetry.* 1973.
Faruqi, Shamsur Rhaman, and Frances W. Pritchett. "Lyric Poetry in Urdue: The Ghazal," *Masterworks of Asian Literature in Comparative Perspective.* 1994.
Jafri, Sardar, and Qurratulain Hyder. *Ghalib and His Poetry.* 1970.
Russell, Ralph, and Khurshidul Islam. *Three Mughal Poets.* 1968.
Sadiq, Muhammad. *A History of Urdu Literature.* 1984.

■ **PRONUNCIATION**

Ghalib (Mirza Asadullah Beg Khan): GAH-leeb (MEER-zah ah-sah-doo-LAH BEG KAHN)
ghazal: gah-ZAHL
qafiyah: kah-FEE-yah
radif: RAH-deef
sh'ir: SHEER
srivilas: sree-VEE-lus, shree-VEE-lus
Vaishnava: VIGH-shnuh-vuh

❧ How murderous is the false faith of the rose!

Translated by Shamshur Rahman Faruqi and Frances W. Pritchett

How murderous is the false faith of the rose!
The nightingale's doings amuse the rose.

Celebrate the breeze's freedom: everywhere lie broken
The meshes of the desire-net of the rose.

Deceived, everyone fell for its wave of color.
Oh, the lament of the bloody-voiced lip of the rose!

How happy is that drunken one who, like the rose's shadow
Rests his head on the foot of the rose.

They make me ashamed before the spring breeze —
10 My cup without wine, my heart without desire for the rose.

Your jealous beauty appears in such supreme glory —
Mere blood in my eyes is the charming color of the rose.

Even now, deceived, thinking it to be you
The rose runs recklessly after the rose.

Ghālib, I long to embrace her.
The thought of whom is the rose on the dress of the rose.

"How murderous is the false faith of the rose!" In this particular *ghazal*, each *sh'ir*, or couplet, offers a shift in perspective on the rose, a conventional symbol of the beloved in Persian and Urdu poetry.

A note on the translation: This translation by Shamshur Rahman Faruqi and Frances W. Pritchett is an excellent example of the ghazal's complexity, illustrating the form's *qafiyah*, or rhyme scheme, and the use of the *radif*, a repeated word or phrase, in this case "the rose." The final couplet of this poem provides a signature of the poet's pen name, or *takhallus*; this signature is called a *maqtac* and is present in most classical ghazals.

∾ The happiness of the drop is to die in the river

Literal translation by Aijaz Ahmad

The happiness of the drop is to die in the river;
When the pain exceeds bearable limits, the pain itself becomes the medicine.

Our weakness is such that tears have turned into mere sighing.
Now we really believe that water can turn into air.

When the spring cloud clears after heavy rain, it seems to me as if it were
Weeping so hard that, at the end it simply dies (from excess of grief).

So that you may begin to understand the miracle of the altering/polishing winds,
You should see how the mirror becomes green in spring,[1]

The appearance of the rose has vouchsafed us the desire to witness (and enjoy),
       Ghālib!
10 Whatever the color and condition of things, the eyes should always be open.

"The happiness of the drop is to die in the river." This poem captures the transcience, the desire for self-annihilation, and the mutability associated with Romantic poetry in the West.
   A note on the translation: Four translations of this text are presented here: a literal translation and three poetic versions from the hands of poets Thomas Fitzsimmons, W. S. Merwin, and Robert Bly with Sunil Dutta. The variation in these renderings demonstrates the difficulty of producing anything but an approximation of the literal translation much less the original Urdu poem. By reading these translations together, the English-speaking reader may experience some of the brilliance of the original, refracted as it is through more than one medium.

---

[1] **how the mirror becomes green in spring:** According to Aijaz Ahmad, the Urdu phrase *havai-saiqal,* translated here as "altering/polishing winds," refers to the old way of making mirrors by applying a green polish to the back surface; thus the back of the mirror is always green, while the face of the mirror turns green with mildew in the dampness of spring. Thus the line elides the powers of nature with human artifice.

～ Waterbead ecstasy: dying in a stream

Translated by Thomas Fitzsimmons

Waterbead ecstasy: dying in a stream;
Too strong a pain brings its own balm.

So weak now we weep sighs only;
Learn surely how water turns to air.

Spring cloud thinning after rain:
Dying into its own weeping.

Would you riddle the miracle of the wind's shaping?
Watch how a mirror greens in spring.[1]

Rose, Ghalib, the rose changes gives us our joy in seeing.
10 All colors and kinds, what is should and be open always.

---

[1] **how a mirror greens in spring:** See note 1 of the literal translation of this poem by Aijaz Ahmad; note that "altering/polishing winds" has now become "the wind's shaping."

～ The drop dies in the river

Translated by W. S. Merwin

The drop dies in the river
of its joy
pain goes so far it cures itself

in the spring after the heavy rain the cloud
disappears
that was nothing but tears

in the spring the mirror turns green
holding a miracle
Change the shining wind[1]

10 the rose led us to our eyes

let whatever is be open

---

[1] **the shining wind:** See note 1 of the Aijaz Ahmad translation of this poem and of the Thomas Fitzsimmons version; note that Merwin's rendering makes the role of the wind in polishing the mirror more ambiguous, hence somewhat obscuring the allusion.

∾ When the Sky Clears

Translated by Robert Bly with Sunil Dutta

The drop grows happy by losing itself in the river.
A pain when beyond human range becomes something else.

One man's heart died when he insisted on treating his own problems.
Sometimes people solve jute-knots by rubbing them on rocks.

Since I am weak, I sigh instead of weeping.
My experience tells me that water can change and become air.

The sky abruptly clears following thick clouds and heavy rain.
The clouds, recognizing separation, cried and vanished into nonexistence.

We make the back of the mirror green in order to see our faces.
10 Sometimes nature makes the front of the mirror green as well.[1]

We love seeing the beauty of poppies and lilies.
When the eyes lose themselves in the colors, they are seeing at last.

---

[1] makes the front of the mirror green as well: See note 1 of the Aijaz Ahmad, Thomas Fitzsimmons, and W. S. Merwin translations; note that Bly and Dutta's version calls attention to and even explains the allusion of the polishing of the mirror, perhaps one lost on readers unfamiliar with Ghalib's culture.

❧ Why didn't I shrink in the blaze of that face?

Translated by Adrienne Rich

Why didn't I shrink in the blaze of that face?[1]
I flare up, apprehending the gaze that returned that vision unblinded.

Out in the world they call me a disciple of fire
because the words of my grief fall like a shower of sparks.

Many have fallen in love with the slim neck of the decanter;
seeing you walk, the wave of the wine trembles with envy.

We and the poems we make get bought and sold together;
but we knew all along for whom they were intended.

The lightning-stroke of the vision was meant for us, not for Sinai;
10 the wine should be poured for him who possesses the goblet.

"Why didn't I shrink in the blaze of that face?" The following *ghazals* are a sample of Ghalib's diverse poetic moods and give a sense of the range of his verse. Keep in mind that *ghazals*, like most European lyric poetry, are meant to be recited, not just read silently. Many Urdu speakers even today readily invoke Ghalib's couplets in their everyday conversation.

 A note on the translations: The translations selected here attempt, as much as possible, to capture some of the lyrical quality of Ghalib's verse. The translators are among the finest contemporary American poets: Adrienne Rich, W. S. Merwin, and Robert Bly with Sunil Dutta.

---

[1] **the blaze of that face:** As becomes apparent in line nine, this poem alludes to the story of Moses, to whom God reveals Himself on Mt. Sinai in the form of a flash of burning light, a story that appears in both the Bible and the Qur'an (Koran).

❧ Is it you, O God

Translated by Adrienne Rich

Is it you, O God, whose coming begins to amaze me?
The mirror has turned to a six-tiered ground of waiting.

Every crowded speck of dust has become a whole mist of longing;
if this world is a net, the entire desert is its prey.

The dew has polished the sheen of the flowering branch.
The nights of spring are finished, nightingale.

Don't go unveiled into that valley of Majnoon:[1]
every grain of sand there is an atom of desire.

Nightingale, give me a bundle of sticks for building:
10 I hear the thunder of the first days of our spring.

_____

[1] Majnoon: Majnoon, whose name means "insane," is a legendary lover of Leyla, both of whom are celebrated
in ancient Arabic and Turkish poetry; their love might be compared with that of the legendary Italian lovers
Paulo and Francesca or to that of the pilgrim Dante and his Beatrice in Dante's *Divine Comedy*.

∾ It is a long time since my love stayed with me here

Translated by W. S. Merwin

It is a long time since my love stayed with me here
And the sparkling goblet lit up our evening together.

Again my complaining breath comes hot, showering sparks.
It is a long time since we saw the night filled with flares.

Again the old enemies, heart and eye, come together
Pining for chances to see her, to brood upon her.

Again I long for her to appear on her balcony,
the wind veiling her face in her black hair.

Again the heart yearns for free days and nights, as before,
10 to think of nothing and no one but her.

∾ There are a thousand desires like this

Translated by W. S. Merwin

There are a thousand desires like this, each needing a lifetime.
Of my wishes, many were gratified, but far from enough.

We have heard of Adam driven from paradise.
My fall from grace was far worse, when I left where you live.

At this time they couple my name with drunkenness.
One more age has dawned that needs Jamshed's cup.[1]

Each time we expected sympathy for our failings
the blade of disaster fell, and we were found near death.

Oh preacher, for God's sake do not raise the Kaa'ba's curtain.[2]

10   It may hide one more idol in which there can be no belief.

---

[1] **Jamshed's cup:** Jamshed was a legendary Persian king who could see the future in a magic cup.
[2] **Kaa'ba's curtain:** Kaa'ba was the most important shrine of Islam, a small building housing the Black Stone at the Great Mosque in Mecca. Before Islam, the Kaa'ba was a site of pagan worship.

∾ Don't Skimp with Me Today

Translated by Robert Bly with Sunil Dutta

For tomorrow's sake, don't skimp with me on wine today.
A stingy portion implies a suspicion of heaven's abundance.

The horse of life is galloping; we'll never know the stopping place.
Our hands are not touching the reins, nor our feet the stirrups.

I keep a certain distance from the reality of things.
It's the same distance between me and utter confusion.

The scene, the one looking, and the ability to see are all the same.
If that is so, why am I confused about what is in front of me?

The greatness of a river depends on its magnificent face.
10   If we break it into bubbles and drops and waves, we are lost.

She is not free from her ways to increase her beauty.
The mirror she sees is on the inside of her veil.

What we think is obvious is so far beyond our comprehension.
We are still dreaming even when we dream we are awake.

From the smell of my friend's friend I get the smell of my friend.
Listen, Ghalib, you are busy worshiping God's friend.

∾ A Lamp in a Strong Wind

Translated by Robert Bly with Sunil Dutta

My wailing—oh inventor of torture—is just a mode of petition.
It's really a request for more torture, and not a complaint.

Even though my house is destroyed, I recognize the value of open space.
In the deliciousness of the desert I forget about home.

To the wise, a storm of difficulty may be a school.
The slaps of waves resemble the slaps of a master.

Things have gone so far that she doesn't even say hello.
If I complain to God, she knows my complaints have no effect.

Why are the roses and the tulips losing their elegant colors?
10 Maybe they recognize they are lamps in the path of a strong wind.

In the street where you live I see the splendor of Paradise.
But Paradise is not as crowded as your street.

Ghalib, which mouth are you using when you complain of your exile?
Have you forgotten the unkindness of people in your own city?

∾ The Sword Wound

Translated by Robert Bly with Sunil Dutta

When I describe my condition, you say, "What's your point?"
When you talk to me that way, what am I to say?

Please don't mention again—even in jest—that you torture people.
My problem is that I agree too much with everything you say.

One of her glances works like a sharp knife.
We consider it an act of friendship because the knife-edge doesn't enter the heart.

To me the wound an arrow makes is insufficient.
Some people call a sword wound the opener of the heart.

When I am dead, give the killer a reward for my death.
10 If my tongue gets cut off, send the gift to the knife.

Your lover may not be faithful, but she is your lover.
We could mention the beautiful rolling way she walks.

Spring doesn't last long but at least it *is* spring.
It would be good to mention the scented winds that move through the garden.

Ghalib, once the boat has arrived at the other shore,
Why go on and on about the wickedness of the boatman?

℘ RABINDRANATH TAGORE
1861–1941

Rabindranath Tagore, the leading figure of the Bengali renaissance of the late nineteenth and early twentieth century, was truly a Renaissance man—a poet, novelist, dramatist, essayist, philosopher, journalist, editor, teacher, painter, and musician. The first Asian writer to win the Nobel Prize, Tagore bridged the gulf between East and West; beginning with traditional forms and moving into modernism, he linked the nineteenth and twentieth centuries. More than any figure other than Gandhi,[1] Tagore has come to represent India. William Rothenstein praised him to George Bernard Shaw[2] as the model of Eastern wisdom. To suggest his important place in Indian literature and culture, Monish R. Chatterjee has described Tagore as "a combination of Shakespeare, Goethe, and Voltaire," a view shared by American poet Ezra Pound (1885–1972), who declared that "Tagore sang Bengal into a nation."

rub-in-druh-NAHTH
tuh-GORE

Rabindranath Tagore, 1917
Tagore's iconic long, white beard helps make his visage one of the most recognized in India. (Library of Congress)

A Migratory Bird Having Two Homes.   Born in 1861, the fourteenth child in a prominent Brahmin family of writers and thinkers, Tagore inherited the divided consciousness of colonial India. He described "Western imperialism" as "the greatest trial in [India's] history." The British had instituted an "impersonal empire, where the rulers were over us but not among us," Tagore wrote, and the colonial experience had "so disintegrated and demoralized . . . our people that many wondered if India could ever rise again by the genius of her own people." Nevertheless, Tagore did not reject all things British. He compared himself to "a migratory bird having two homes," Bengal and Britain. His education,

---

[1] Gandhi: Mahatma Gandhi (1869–1948), leader of the Indian independence movement and advocate of nonviolent resistance to colonial rule, a commitment shared by Tagore. See Book 6.

[2] Rothenstein . . . Shaw: William Rothenstein (1872–1945), English painter and writer who hosted Tagore in England in 1911; George Bernard Shaw (1856–1950), Anglo-Irish playwright, critic, and social commentator.

www For links to more information about Tagore and quizzes on his work, see *World Literature Online* at bedfordstmartins .com/worldlit.

partly in Calcutta and partly in England, introduced him to literatures in SANSKRIT,[3] BENGALI, and English, and all three became part of his personal cultural heritage. So his project to regenerate his people and bring them back to "such a thing as our own mind" was based on a program of synthesizing the best from East and West into a new global culture that he called "the Universal human spirit."

Tagore's universalism, a lifelong commitment that would inform his writing and his social and political activities, was inherited from his father and grandfather, both prominent members of the HINDU reform movement, Brahma Samaj. Founded in 1828 by Ram Mohun Roy (1772–1833), the movement sought to rid Hinduism of polytheism, idol worship, and the caste system and to reground its doctrines in reason and intuition. It also accepted some Christian and Islamic doctrines, encouraging a more tolerant and universal religion.

The Bengali Renaissance. While India was called "the jewel in the crown" of British imperialism at the time of Tagore's birth in 1861, by the 1880s the movement for Indian nationalism and independence, the Congress Movement, had begun to challenge British authority on the subcontinent. The BENGALI LITERARY RENAISSANCE[4] was part of this emerging nationalistic consciousness, for it sought to establish a literature and culture that would represent "our reaction against the culture of Europe and its ideals, [and] a newborn sense of self-respect." The new BENGALI literature was written in Bengali, the everyday language of the people of northeast India, as opposed to Sanskrit, the traditional "literary" language of the region, or English, the language of the oppressor. It also departed from traditional poetic forms and mythological subject matter. Instead, in such modern literary forms as the novel and short story, it realistically described the lives of common people, often drawing on folktales and songs for its models and inspiration.

> A whole people, a whole civilization, immeasurably strange to us, seems to have been taken up into this imagination; and yet we are not moved because of its strangeness but because we have met our own image, . . . or heard, perhaps for the first time in literature, our voice as in a dream.
>
> – WILLIAM BUTLER YEATS, 1912

Rediscovering India. Tagore's literary career was ignited by his contact with rural India upon his return from school in England. His father sent him to oversee some family estates in the Ganges River valley, and there Tagore rediscovered his native land. He heard the language of the peasants, learned their songs, and absorbed the unchanging life of rural India. The stories and poems that he wrote in the 1890s and in the first decade of the twentieth century reveal the influence of his time in the country. The works' language is realistic and vernacular, and their literary models are not traditional SANSKRIT poems but the songs and stories of peasants. In the countryside the cosmopolitan Tagore found the enduring themes of India.

---

[3] Sanskrit: The classical language of Hindu culture in India; by the nineteenth century Sanskrit was only a formal written language. Vernacular languages, such as Bengali, were the spoken tongues.

[4] Bengali literary renaissance: A movement in the second half of the nineteenth century to develop a literature in the Bengali language that would describe the everyday life of contemporary Bengal. Besides Tagore, its major figure, other important writers of the movement were Madhusudan Datta (1824–1873), "the Milton of India," and Bankim Chandra Chatterjee (1838–1894), "the Scott of Bengal."

Tagore's short stories, many written in the 1890s, present the differences between city and country as some of the defining divisions of colonial India. Typically in these stories, a city dweller, anglicized by his Western education and contact with the British, is reminded of his Indian roots by an unsettling experience in the countryside. Such is the experience, for example, of the government clerk in "The Hungry Stones." Tagore's poems, many of them songs based on traditional Indian folk songs, caught the attention of Western poets and writers with the publication of his collection, **Gitanjali** *(Song Offerings)*, in 1912, which Tagore himself translated from Bengali into English. William Butler Yeats,[5] who was similarly exploring his heritage through Irish folktale and myth, found a soul-brother in Tagore: "A whole people, a whole civilisation, immeasurably strange to us," Yeats wrote, "seems to have been taken up into this imagination; and yet we are not moved because of its strangeness, but because we have met our own image, . . . or heard, perhaps for the first time in literature, our voice as in a dream." Yeats was so moved by Tagore's work, he exclaimed, "We have found the new Greece!" Largely on the basis of the English *Gitanjali*, Tagore was awarded the Nobel Prize for literature in 1913.

Tagore and Gandhi.   Tagore's novels—the best-known are *Gora* (1910) and *The Home and the World* (*Ghare-baire*, 1916)—are more political than his stories and poems. They present India as desiring independence but saddled with the mentality of a subject nation. Tagore never viewed independence as an end in itself but as part of a process of regaining national self-respect. He believed India needed to value and integrate the best of its Indian and British heritages, rejecting both superstition and colonial subservience. He proudly accepted a knighthood from the British king in 1915, but in 1919 he rebuked the honor in protest of the Amritsar Massacre, in which British troops killed several hundred Indians at a political demonstration. Although Tagore questioned the economic isolationism in Gandhi's program for Indian independence, he saw Gandhi as a figure who synthesized East and West as he himself was trying to do. Gandhi, Tagore wrote, had taken the message of Christianity—the doctrine "that God became man in order to save humanity by taking the burden of its sin and suffering on himself"—and turned it into a principle of nonviolent struggle. In doing so, Gandhi became an expression of "the genius of India [which] has taken from her aggressors the most spiritually significant principle of their culture and fashioned of it a new message of hope for mankind."

The Universal Educator.   Besides writing, Tagore devoted himself to social causes, to the restoration of rural village life in India, and especially to the school he founded in 1901 at Santiniketan, his family estate north of Calcutta. The progressive school, which taught in the Bengali rather

Tagore sang Bengal into a nation.
– EZRA POUND

gee-TAHN-juh-lee

He represents all that is religious, literary, scholarly, and aristocratic in Bengal, and if there were no other representative we should look upon India as the most perfect country in the world.
– WILLIAM ROTHENSTEIN

[5] **William Butler Yeats:** (1865–1939) Irish poet and playwright; Yeats introduced Western writers to Tagore by holding a reading at which Tagore is said to have captivated the audience. See Book 6.

than the English language and encouraged students to follow their own
interests, was based on the traditional "forest schools" of India in which
nature was made the teacher. By 1921, the school had grown to become
Visva Bharati, Tagore's conception of a world university that sought to
reconcile East and West, country and city, and scientific and spiritual
knowledge. He described the university as an institution "for the study of
the different cultures and religions of the world and to create that mutual
sympathy, understanding, and tolerance on which alone can the unity of
mankind rest." Internationally known, Tagore was a world traveler who
often lectured at universities in Europe and America in his later years. He
died in Calcutta in 1941.

■ CONNECTIONS

Arabian Nights (Book 2); Emilia Pardo Bazán, "The Revolver," p. 696. In "The Hungry Stones," Tagore employs the framed-narrative technique characteristic of *Arabian Nights*. What other elements from *Arabian Nights* does Tagore use in the story?
How does Tagore's framed narrative compare with that of Pardo Bazán in "The
Revolver"?

E. T. A. Hoffmann, "The Mines of Falun," p. 298. A supernatural tale like Hoffmann's "Mines of Falun," "The Hungry Stones" describes the dangerous attractions of the night world of the palace, similar to the allure of the mine that destroys
Elis Froebom in Hoffmann's story. Is the symbolism of the palace and the mine
similar? What is the symbolic meaning of each? Would you call "The Hungry
Stones" a Gothic story?

Goethe, *Faust,* p. 29. The "two souls" that divide Faust, the man of intellect, and
Faust, the man of experience, are akin to the two sides of Satish, an Indian conflicted between Western intellectualism and Eastern spirituality in *Broken Ties*. If
Faust's divided consciousness reflects that of Europe in the early nineteenth century, the division within Satish may mirror that of colonial India. What are the similarities and differences between these two characters, and how do their fragmented
selves represent nineteenth-century European and Asian consciousness?

Joseph Conrad, *Heart of Darkness* (Book 6). Like Kurtz in *Heart of Darkness,* Satish is
an extraordinary man. How do the traits that distinguish Satish differ from Kurtz's
outstanding qualities and achievements? Are the narrators in *Heart of Darkness* and
Broken Ties, Marlow and Srivilas, also extraordinary men? What qualities enable
them to survive while Kurtz and Satish die?

■ FURTHER RESEARCH

Biography
Dutta, Krishna. *Rabindranath Tagore: the Myriad-minded Man.* 2000.
Kripalani, Krishna. *Rabindranath Tagore: A Biography.* 1980.

Criticism
Chatterjee, Bhabatosh. *Rabindranath Tagore and the Modern Sensibility.* 1996.
Lago, Mary. "Modes of Questioning in Tagore's Short Stories," *Studies in Short
       Fiction* 5 (Fall 1967), 24–36.
———. *Rabindranath Tagore.* 1976.
Srinivaslyengar, K. R. *Rabindranath Tagore: A Critical Introduction.* 1985.

■ **PRONUNCIATION**

bulbuls: BOOL-boolz
Cahaprasi: chuh-huh-PRUH-see
Dharma: DAR-muh (DHAR-muh)
ghi: GEE
Gitanjali: gee-TAHN-juh-lee
Harimohan: huh-ree-MOH-hun
Jagamohan: juh-guh-MOH-hun
Junagarh Lilandanda: joo-NAH-gar li-lahn-DAHN-duh
Mahatma Gandhi: muh-HAHT-muh GAHN-dee
Magh: MUG, MAHG
moghlai: MOH-gligh, MOO-gligh
nahabat: NAH-baht
narghileh: nar-GEE-leh
Nonibula: noh-ni-BOO-lah
Purandar: poo-rahn-DAR
Rabindranath Tagore: rub-in-druh-NAHTH tuh-GORE
sahebs: SAH-eebz
Sannyasin: sun-YAH-seen
sareng: SAH-reng
Shivatosh: Shi-vuh-TOHSH
Srijut: sree-JOOT, shree-JOOT

℘ The Hungry Stones

My kinsman and myself were returning to Calcutta from our Puja[1] trip when we met the man in a train. From his dress and bearing we took him at first for an up-country Mahomedan, but we were puzzled as we heard him talk. He discoursed upon all subjects so confidently that you might think the Disposer of All Things consulted him at all times in all that He did. Hitherto we had been perfectly happy, as we did not know that secret and unheard-of forces were at work, that the Russians had advanced close to us, that the English had deep and secret policies, that confusion among the native

---

"The Hungry Stones." First published in 1895, this story translates the psychological divisions within its narrator—between his daytime and nighttime selves, his rational and emotional sides—into the divides within Indian society as a whole—between the town and the country, between English governmental bureaucracy and traditional Indian rural culture, between present and the past. The comic plot shows a mysterious castle in the countryside scaring a boy back to the city while the tale's form imitates the FRAMED TALES of the *Arabian Nights* tradition.

The English translation of "The Hungry Stones" appeared in the volume *The Hungry Stones and Other Stories* (1916), which indicated that the works were "translated from the original Bengali by various writers." In the preface Tagore lists these writers as himself and C. F. Andrews, with assistance from E. J. Thompson, Panna Lal Basu, Prabhat Kumar Mukerji, and the Sister Nivedita.

---

[1] Puja: A Hindu religious holiday.

chiefs had come to a head. But our newly-acquired friend said with a sly smile: "There happen more things in heaven and earth, Horatio, than are reported in your newspapers."[2] As we had never stirred out of our homes before, the demeanour of the man struck us dumb with wonder. Be the topic ever so trivial, he would quote science, or comment on the *Vedas*,[3] or repeat quatrains from some Persian poet; and as we had no pretence to a knowledge of science or the *Vedas* or Persian, our admiration for him went on increasing, and my kinsman, a theosophist, was firmly convinced that our fellow-passenger must have been supernaturally inspired by some strange "magnetism" or "occult power," by an "astral body" or something of that kind. He listened to the tritest saying that fell from the lips of our extraordinary companion with devotional rapture, and secretly took down notes of his conversation. I fancy that the extraordinary man saw this, and was a little pleased with it.

When the train reached the junction, we assembled in the waiting-room for the connection. It was then 10 P.M., and as the train, we heard, was likely to be very late, owing to something wrong in the lines, I spread my bed on the table and was about to lie down for a comfortable doze, when the extraordinary person deliberately set about spinning the following yarn. Of course, I could get no sleep that night.

When, owing to a disagreement about some questions of administrative policy, I threw up my post at Junagarh, and entered the service of the Nizam of Hyderabad, they appointed me at once, as a strong young man, collector of cotton duties at Barich.

Barich is a lovely place. The *Susta* "chatters over stony ways and babbles on the pebbles," tripping, like a skillful dancing girl, in through the woods below the lonely hills. A flight of 150 steps rises from the river, and above that flight, on the river's brim and at the foot of the hills, there stands a solitary marble palace. Around it there is no habitation of man — the village and the cotton mart of Barich being far off.

About 250 years ago the Emperor Mahmud Shah II. had built this lonely palace for his pleasure and luxury. In his days jets of rose-water spurted from its fountains, and on the cold marble floors of its spray-cooled rooms young Persian damsels would sit, their hair dishevelled before bathing, and, splashing their soft naked feet in the clear water of the reservoirs, would sing, to the tune of the guitar, the *ghazals*[4] of their vineyards.

The fountains play no longer; the songs have ceased; no longer do snow-white feet step gracefully on the snowy marble. It is but the vast and solitary quarters of cess-collectors like us, men oppressed with solitude and deprived of the society of women. Now, Karim Khan, the old clerk of my office, warned me repeatedly not to take up my abode there. "Pass the day there, if you like," said he, "but never stay the night." I passed it off with a light laugh. The servants said that they would work till

---

[2] "There . . . newspapers: An allusion to Hamlet's remark to Horatio, "There are more things in heaven and earth, Horatio, / Than are dreamt of in your philosophy" (*Hamlet* I, v). [3] *Vedas:* The primary scriptures of Hinduism. [4] *ghazals:* Popular love poems or songs.

dark, and go away at night. I gave my ready assent. The house had such a bad name that even thieves would not venture near it after dark.

At first the solitude of the deserted palace weighed upon me like a nightmare. I would stay out, and work hard as long as possible, then return home at night jaded and tired, go to bed and fall asleep.

Before a week had passed, the place began to exert a weird fascination upon me. It is difficult to describe or to induce people to believe; but I felt as if the whole house was like a living organism slowly and imperceptibly digesting me by the action of some stupefying gastric juice.

Perhaps the process had begun as soon as I set my foot in the house, but I distinctly remember the day on which I first was conscious of it.

It was the beginning of summer, and the market being dull I had no work to do. A little before sunset I was sitting in an arm-chair near the water's edge below the steps. The *Susta* had shrunk and sunk low; a broad patch of sand on the other side glowed with the hues of evening; on this side the pebbles at the bottom of the clear shallow waters were glistening. There was not a breath of wind anywhere, and the still air was laden with an oppressive scent from the spicy shrubs growing on the hills close by.

As the sun sank behind the hill-tops a long dark curtain fell upon the stage of day, and the intervening hills cut short the time in which light and shade mingle at sunset. I thought of going out for a ride, and was about to get up when I heard a footfall on the steps behind. I looked back, but there was no one.

As I sat down again, thinking it to be an illusion, I heard many footfalls, as if a large number of persons were rushing down the steps. A strange thrill of delight, slightly tinged with fear, passed through my frame, and though there was not a figure before my eyes, methought I saw a bevy of joyous maidens coming down the steps to bathe in the *Susta* in that summer evening. Not a sound was in the valley, in the river, or in the palace, to break the silence, but I distinctly heard the maidens' gay and mirthful laugh, like the gurgle of a spring gushing forth in a hundred cascades, as they ran past me, in quick playful pursuit of each other, towards the river, without noticing me at all. As they were invisible to me, so I was, as it were, invisible to them. The river was perfectly calm, but I felt that its still, shallow, and clear waters were stirred suddenly by the splash of many an arm jingling with bracelets, that the girls laughed and dashed and spattered water at one another, that the feet of the fair swimmers tossed the tiny waves up in showers of pearl.

I felt a thrill at my heart—I cannot say whether the excitement was due to fear or delight or curiosity. I had a strong desire to see them more clearly, but naught was visible before me; I thought I could catch all that they said if I only strained my ears; but however hard I strained them, I heard nothing but the chirping of the cicadas in the woods. It seemed as if a dark curtain of 250 years was hanging before me, and I would fain lift a corner of it tremblingly and peer through, though the assembly on the other side was completely enveloped in darkness.

The oppressive closeness of the evening was broken by a sudden gust of wind, and the still surface of the *Susta* rippled and curled like the hair of a nymph, and from the woods wrapt in the evening gloom there came forth a simultaneous murmur, as though they were awakening from a black dream. Call it reality or dream, the momentary glimpse of that invisible mirage reflected from a far-off world, 250 years old, vanished in a flash. The mystic forms that brushed past me with their quick unbodied steps, and loud, voiceless laughter, and threw themselves into the river, did not go back wringing their dripping robes as they went. Like fragrance wafted away by the wind they were dispersed by a single breath of the spring.

Then I was filled with a lively fear that it was the Muse that had taken advantage of my solitude and possessed me—the witch had evidently come to ruin a poor devil like myself making a living by collecting cotton duties. I decided to have a good dinner—it is the empty stomach that all sorts of incurable diseases find an easy prey. I sent for my cook and gave orders for a rich, sumptuous *moghlai*[5] dinner, redolent of spices and *ghi*.

Next morning the whole affair appeared a queer fantasy. With a light heart I put on a *sola*[6] hat like the *sahebs*,[7] and drove out to my work. I was to have written my quarterly report that day, and expected to return late; but before it was dark I was strangely drawn to my house—by what I could not say—I felt they were all waiting, and that I should delay no longer. Leaving my report unfinished I rose, put on my *sola* hat, and startling the dark, shady, desolate path with the rattle of my carriage, I reached the vast silent palace standing on the gloomy skirts of the hills.

On the first floor the stairs led to a very spacious hall, its roof stretching wide over ornamental arches resting on three rows of massive pillars, and groaning day and night under the weight of its own intense solitude. The day had just closed, and the lamps had not yet been lighted. As I pushed the door open a great bustle seemed to follow within, as if a throng of people had broken up in confusion, and rushed out through the doors and windows and corridors and verandas and rooms, to make its hurried escape.

As I saw no one I stood bewildered, my hair on end in a kind of ecstatic delight, and a faint scent of *attar*[8] and unguents almost effaced by age lingered in my nostrils. Standing in the darkness of that vast desolate hall between the rows of those ancient pillars, I could hear the gurgle of fountains plashing on the marble floor, a strange tune on the guitar, the jingle of ornaments and the tinkle of anklets, the clang of bells tolling the hours, the distant note of *nahabat*,[9] the din of the crystal pendants of chandeliers shaken by the breeze, the song of *bulbuls*[10] from the cages in the corridors, the cackle of storks in the gardens, all creating round me a strange unearthly music.

Then I came under such a spell that this intangible, inaccessible, unearthly vision appeared to be the only reality in the world—and all else a mere dream. That I, that is to say, Srijut So-and-so, the eldest son of So-and-so of blessed memory, should be drawing a monthly salary of Rs. 450 by the discharge of my duties as

---

[5] *moghlai:* Spicy food; *ghi* is butter.   [6] *sola:* Pith helmet.   [7] *sahebs:* A term meaning "sir," often applied derisively to the British.   [8] *attar:* A jasmine-scented perfume.   [9] *nahabat:* A musical instrument.   [10] *bulbuls:* Songbirds like nightingales, often mentioned in Persian poetry.

collector of cotton duties, and driving in my dog-cart to my office every day in a short coat and *sola* hat, appeared to me to be such an astonishingly ludicrous illusion that I burst into a horse-laugh, as I stood in the gloom of that vast silent hall.

At that moment my servant entered with a lighted kerosene lamp in his hand. I do not know whether he thought me mad, but it came back to me at once that I was in very deed Srijut So-and-so, son of So-and-so of blessed memory, and that, while our poets, great and small, alone could say whether inside or outside the earth there was a region where unseen fountains perpetually played and fairy guitars, struck by invisible fingers, sent forth an eternal harmony, this at any rate was certain, that I collected duties at the cotton market at Barich, and earned thereby Rs. 450 per mensem as my salary. I laughed in great glee at my curious illusion, as I sat over the newspaper at my camp-table, lighted by the kerosene lamp.

After I had finished my paper and eaten my *moghlai* dinner, I put out the lamp, and lay down on my bed in a small side-room. Through the open window a radiant star, high above the Avalli hills skirted by the darkness of their woods, was gazing intently from millions and millions of miles away in the sky at Mr. Collector lying on a humble camp-bedstead. I wondered and felt amused at the idea, and do not know when I fell asleep or how long I slept; but I suddenly awoke with a start, though I heard no sound and saw no intruder—only the steady bright star on the hilltop had set, and the dim light of the new moon was stealthily entering the room through the open window, as if ashamed of its intrusion.

I saw nobody, but felt as if some one was gently pushing me. As I awoke she said not a word, but beckoned me with her five fingers bedecked with rings to follow her cautiously. I got up noiselessly, and, though not a soul save myself was there in the countless apartments of that deserted palace with its slumbering sounds and waking echoes, I feared at every step lest any one should wake up. Most of the rooms of the palace were always kept closed, and I had never entered them.

I followed breathless and with silent steps my invisible guide—I cannot now say where. What endless dark and narrow passages, what long corridors, what silent and solemn audience-chambers and close secret cells I crossed!

Though I could not see my fair guide, her form was not invisible to my mind's eye—an Arab girl, her arms, hard and smooth as marble, visible through her loose sleeves, a thin veil falling on her face from the fringe of her cap, and a curved dagger at her waist! Methought that one of the thousand and one Arabian Nights had been wafted to me from the world of romance, and that at the dead of night I was wending my way through the dark narrow alleys of slumbering Baghdad to a trysting-place fraught with peril.

At last my fair guide stopped abruptly before a deep blue screen, and seemed to point to something below. There was nothing there, but a sudden dread froze the blood in my heart—methought I saw there on the floor at the foot of the screen a terrible negro eunuch dressed in rich brocade, sitting and dozing with out-stretched legs, with a naked sword on his lap. My fair guide lightly tripped over his legs and held up a fringe of the screen. I could catch a glimpse of a part of the room spread with a Persian carpet—some one was sitting inside on a bed—I could not see her, but only caught a glimpse of two exquisite feet in gold-embroidered slippers, hanging out from loose saffron-coloured *paijamas* and placed idly on the orange-coloured velvet carpet. On one side there was a bluish crystal tray on which a few apples, pears, oranges, and bunches of grapes in plenty, two small cups and a gold-tinted decanter were evidently awaiting the guest. A fragrant intoxicating vapour, issuing from a strange sort of incense that burned within, almost overpowered my senses.

As with trembling heart I made an attempt to step across the outstretched legs of the eunuch, he woke up suddenly with a start, and the sword fell from his lap with a sharp clang on the marble floor.

A terrific scream made me jump, and I saw I was sitting on that camp-bedstead of mine sweating heavily; and the crescent moon looked pale in the morning light like a weary sleepless patient at dawn; and our crazy Meher Ali was crying out, as is his daily custom, "Stand back! Stand back!!" while he went along the lonely road.

Such was the abrupt close of one of my Arabian Nights; but there were yet a thousand nights left.

Then followed a great discord between my days and nights. During the day I would go to my work worn and tired, cursing the bewitching night and her empty dreams, but as night came my daily life with its bonds and shackles of work would appear a petty, false, ludicrous vanity.

After nightfall I was caught and overwhelmed in the snare of a strange intoxication. I would then be transformed into some unknown personage of a bygone age, playing my part in unwritten history; and my short English coat and tight breeches did not suit me in the least. With a red velvet cap on my head, loose *paijamas,* an embroidered vest, a long flowing silk gown, and coloured handkerchiefs scented with *attar,* I would complete my elaborate toilet, sit on a high-cushioned chair, and replace my cigarette with a many-coiled *narghileh*[11] filled with rose-water, as if in eager expectation of a strange meeting with the beloved one.

I have no power to describe the marvellous incidents that unfolded themselves, as the gloom of the night deepened. I felt as if in the curious apartments of that vast edifice the fragments of a beautiful story, which I could follow for some distance, but of which I could never see the end, flew about in a sudden gust of the vernal breeze. And all the same I would wander from room to room in pursuit of them the whole night long.

Amid the eddy of these dream-fragments, amid the smell of *henna* and the twanging of the guitar, amid the waves of air charged with fragrant spray, I would catch like a flash of lightning the momentary glimpse of a fair damsel. She it was who had saffron-coloured *paijamas,* white ruddy soft feet in gold-embroidered slippers with curved toes, a close-fitting bodice wrought with gold, a red cap, from which a golden frill fell on her snowy brow and cheeks.

She had maddened me. In pursuit of her I wandered from room to room, from path to path among the bewildering maze of alleys in the enchanted dreamland of the nether world of sleep.

---

[11] *narghileh:* A water pipe.

Sometimes in the evening, while arraying myself carefully as a prince of the blood-royal before a large mirror, with a candle burning on either side, I would see a sudden reflection of the Persian beauty by the side of my own. A swift turn of her neck, a quick eager glance of intense passion and pain glowing in her large dark eyes, just a suspicion of speech on her dainty red lips, her figure, fair and slim, crowned with youth like a blossoming creeper, quickly uplifted in her graceful tilting gait, a dazzling flash of pain and craving and ecstasy, a smile and a glance and a blaze of jewels and silk; and she melted away. A wild gust of wind, laden with all the fragrance of hills and woods, would put out my light, and I would fling aside my dress and lie down on my bed, my eyes closed and my body thrilling with delight, and there around me in the breeze, amid all the perfume of the woods and hills, floated through the silent gloom many a caress and many a kiss and many a tender touch of hands, and gentle murmurs in my ears, and fragrant breaths on my brow; or a sweetly-perfumed kerchief was wafted again and again on my cheeks. Then slowly a mysterious serpent would twist her stupefying coils about me; and heaving a heavy sigh, I would lapse into insensibility, and then into a profound slumber.

One evening I decided to go out on my horse—I do not know who implored me to stay—but I would listen to no entreaties that day. My English hat and coat were resting on a rack, and I was about to take them down when a sudden whirl-wind, crested with the sands of the *Susta* and the dead leaves of the Avalli hills, caught them up, and whirled them round and round, while a loud peal of merry laughter rose higher and higher, striking all the chords of mirth till it died away in the land of sunset.

I could not go out for my ride, and the next day I gave up my queer English coat and hat for good.

That day again at dead of night I heard the stifled heart-breaking sobs of some one—as if below the bed, below the floor, below the stony foundation of that gigantic palace, from the depths of a dark damp grave, a voice piteously cried and implored me: "Oh, rescue me! Break through these doors of hard illusion, deathlike slumber and fruitless dreams, place me by your side on the saddle, press me to your heart, and, riding through hills and woods and across the river, take me to the warm radiance of your sunny rooms above!"

Who am I? Oh, how can I rescue thee? What drowning beauty, what incarnate passion shall I drag to the shore from this wild eddy of dreams? O lovely ethereal apparition! Where didst thou flourish and when? By what cool spring, under the shade of what date-groves, wast thou born—in the lap of what homeless wanderer in the desert? What Bedouin snatched thee from thy mother's arms, an opening bud plucked from a wild creeper, placed thee on a horse swift as lightning, crossed the burning sands, and took thee to the slave-market of what royal city? And there, what officer of the Badshah,[12] seeing the glory of thy bashful blossoming youth, paid for thee in gold, placed thee in a golden palanquin, and offered thee as a present for the seraglio of his master? And O, the history of that place! The music of the *sareng*,[13] the

---

[12] Badshah: The emperor.   [13] *sareng:* A sort of violin.

jingle of anklets, the occasional flash of daggers and the glowing wine of Shiraz poison, and the piercing flashing glance! What infinite grandeur, what endless servitude! The slave-girls to thy right and left waved the *chamar*,[14] as diamonds flashed from their bracelets; the Badshah, the king of kings, fell on his knees at thy snowy feet in bejewelled shoes, and outside the terrible Abyssinian eunuch, looking like a messenger of death, but clothed like an angel, stood with a naked sword in his hand! Then, O, thou flower of the desert, swept away by the blood-stained dazzling ocean of grandeur, with its foam of jealousy, its rocks and shoals of intrigue, on what shore of cruel death wast thou cast, or in what other land more splendid and more cruel?

Suddenly at this moment that crazy Meher Ali screamed out: "Stand back! Stand back!! All is false! All is false!!" I opened my eyes and saw that it was already light. My *chaprasi*[15] came and handed me my letters, and the cook waited with a *salam*[16] for my orders.

I said: "No, I can stay here no longer." That very day I packed up, and moved to my office. Old Karim Khan smiled a little as he saw me. I felt nettled, but said nothing, and fell to my work.

As evening approached I grew absent-minded; I felt as if I had an appointment to keep; and the work of examining the cotton accounts seemed wholly useless; even the *Nizamat*[17] of the Nizam did not appear to be of much worth. Whatever belonged to the present, whatever was moving and acting and working for bread seemed trivial, meaningless, and contemptible.

I threw my pen down, closed my ledgers, got into my dog-cart, and drove away. I noticed that it stopped of itself at the gate of the marble palace just at the hour of twilight. With quick steps I climbed the stairs, and entered the room.

A heavy silence was reigning within. The dark rooms were looking sullen as if they had taken offence. My heart was full of contrition, but there was no one to whom I could lay it bare, or of whom I could ask forgiveness. I wandered about the dark rooms with a vacant mind. I wished I had a guitar to which I could sing to the unknown: "O fire, the poor moth that made a vain effort to fly away has come back to thee! Forgive it but this once, burn its wings, and consume it in thy flame!"

Suddenly two tear-drops fell from overhead on my brow. Dark masses of clouds overcast the top of the Avalli hills that day. The gloomy woods and the sooty waters of the *Susta* were waiting in terrible suspense and in an ominous calm. Suddenly land, water, and sky shivered, and a wild tempest-blast rushed howling through the distant pathless woods, showing its lightning-teeth like a raving maniac who had broken his chains. The desolate halls of the palace banged their doors, and moaned in the bitterness of anguish.

The servants were all in the office, and there was no one to light the lamps. The night was cloudy and moonless. In the dense gloom within I could distinctly feel that a woman was lying on her face on the carpet below the bed — clasping and

---

[14] *chamar:* Fly whisks.   [15] *chaprasi:* Clerk.   [16] *salam:* A Muslim greeting, accompanied by bowing the head and touching the brow with the right hand.   [17] *Nizamat:* Royalty.

tearing her long dishevelled hair with desperate fingers. Blood was trickling down her fair brow, and she was now laughing a hard, harsh, mirthless laugh, now bursting into violent wringing sobs, now rending her bodice and striking at her bare bosom, as the wind roared in through the open window, and the rain poured in torrents and soaked her through and through.

All night there was no cessation of the storm or of the passionate cry. I wandered from room to room in the dark, with unavailing sorrow. Whom could I console when no one was by? Whose was this intense agony of sorrow? Whence arose this inconsolable grief?

And the mad man cried out: "Stand back! Stand back!! All is false! All is false!!"

I saw that the day had dawned, and Meher Ali was going round and round the palace with his usual cry in that dreadful weather. Suddenly it came to me that perhaps he also had once lived in that house, and that, though he had gone mad, he came there every day, and went round and round, fascinated by the weird spell cast by the marble demon.

Despite the storm and rain I ran to him and asked: "Ho, Meher Ali, what is false?"

The man answered nothing, but pushing me aside went round and round with his frantic cry, like a bird flying fascinated about the jaws of a snake, and made a desperate effort to warn himself by repeating: "Stand back! Stand back!! All is false! All is false!!"

I ran like a mad man through the pelting rain to my office, and asked Karim Khan: "Tell me the meaning of all this!"

What I gathered from that old man was this: That at one time countless unrequited passions and unsatisfied longings and lurid flames of wild blazing pleasure raged within that palace, and that the curse of all the heart-aches and blasted hopes had made its every stone thirsty and hungry, eager to swallow up like a famished ogress any living man who might chance to approach. Not one of those who lived there for three consecutive nights could escape these cruel jaws, save Meher Ali, who had escaped at the cost of his reason.

I asked: "Is there no means whatever of my release?" The old man said: "There is only one means, and that is very difficult. I will tell you what it is, but first you must hear the history of a young Persian girl who once lived in that pleasure-dome. A stranger or a more bitterly heart-rending tragedy was never enacted on this earth."

Just at this moment the coolies announced that the train was coming. So soon? We hurriedly packed up our luggage, as the train steamed in. An English gentleman, apparently just aroused from slumber, was looking out of a first-class carriage endeavouring to read the name of the station. As soon as he caught sight of our fellow-passenger, he cried, "Hallo," and took him into his own compartment. As we got into a second-class carriage, we had no chance of finding out who the man was nor what was the end of his story.

I said: "The man evidently took us for fools and imposed upon us out of fun. The story is pure fabrication from start to finish." The discussion that followed ended in a lifelong rupture between my theosophist kinsman and myself.

❧ Broken Ties

CHAPTER I
UNCLE

1

When I first met Satish he appeared to me like a constellation of stars, his eyes shining, his tapering fingers like flames of fire, his face glowing with a youthful radiance. I was surprised to find that most of his fellow-students hated him, for no other fault than that he resembled himself more than he resembled others. Because with men, as well as with some insects, taking the colour of the surroundings is often the best means of self-protection.

The students in the hostel where I lived could easily guess my reverence for Satish. This caused them discomfort, and they never missed an opportunity of reviling him in my hearing. If you have a speck of grit in your eye it is best not to rub it. And when words smart it is best to leave them unanswered.

But one day the calumny against Satish was so gross that I could not remain silent.

Yet the trouble was that I hardly knew anything about Satish. We never had even a word between us, while some of the other students were his close neighbours, and some his distant relatives. These affirmed, with assurance, that what they said was true; and I affirmed, with even greater assurance, that it was incredible. Then all the residents of the hostel bared their arms, and cried: "What impertinence!"

That night I was vexed to tears. Next day, in an interval between lectures, when Satish was reading a book lying at full length on the grass in College Square, I went

---

Broken Ties. A short BILDUNGSROMAN, a novel describing a young person's education in life, this work was first published in 1916. It links the self-realization of its narrator, Srivilas, with his growing awareness of his cultural identity. He and Satish, his idolized alter-ego, enact the extremes in a divided India in the first two parts of the novella, as they convert from atheists to followers of a mystical guru. As atheists inhabiting half of a partitioned house in Calcutta, a house suggestive of their conflicted country, Srivilas and Satish celebrate the Western values of empiricism, rationality, and materialism derived from the works of the British UTILITARIANS. Going to the opposite extreme to become disciples of the guru Lilananda Swami, the two travel about rural India chanting prayers, beating drums, and seeking ecstatic fulfillment and emotional release. But neither way of life is finally fulfilling. It is Damini, a rebellious follower of Swami, who teaches Srivilas how to be spiritual and physical at the same time. When Srivilas and Satish return to Calcutta, they are part of a new independent generation that offends both pious traditionalists and liberated urbanites. Srivilas's education is not complete until he learns of suffering—when he must deal with Damini's death. By the end of the story, the disparities between Eastern mysticism and Western empiricism have been transcended and Srivilas has managed to reconcile the opposing impulses within himself. Rabindranath Tagore borrowed the form of the novella from the West, but this work's substance is profoundly Indian.

Like Tagore's other early stories, the English translation which appeared in 1925 did not specify a translator. Tagore himself probably had a significant role in the translation.

up to him without any introduction, and spoke to him in a confused manner, scarcely knowing what I said. Satish shut his book, and looked in my face. Those who have not seen his eyes will not know what that look was like.

Satish said to me: "Those who libel me do so, not because they love to know the truth, but because they love to believe evil of me. Therefore it is useless to try to prove to them that the calumny is untrue."

"But," I said, "the liars must be————"

"They are not liars," interrupted Satish.

"I have a neighbour," he went on, "who has epileptic fits. Last winter I gave him a blanket. My servant came to me in a furious temper, and told me that the boy only feigned the disease. These students who malign me are like that servant of mine. They believe what they say. Possibly my fate has awarded me an extra blanket which they think would have suited them better."

I asked him a question: "Is it true what they say, that you are an atheist?"

He said: "Yes."

I bent my head to the ground. I had been arguing with my fellow-students that Satish could not possibly be an atheist.

I had received two severe blows at the outset of my short acquaintance with Satish. I had imagined that he was a Brahman, but I had come to know that Satish belonged to a Bania[1] family, and I in whose veins flowed a bluer blood was bound duly to despise all Banias. Secondly, I had a rooted belief that atheists were worse than murderers, nay, worse even than beef-eaters.

Nobody could have imagined, even in a dream, that I would ever sit down and take my meals with a Bania student, or that my fanatical zeal in the creed of atheism would surpass even that of my instructor. Yet both these things came to pass.

Wilkins was our professor in the College. His learning was on a level with his contempt for his pupils. He felt that it was a menial occupation to teach literature to Bengali students. Therefore, in our Shakespeare class, he would give us the synonym for "cat" as "a quadruped of the feline species." But Satish was excused from taking notes. The Professor told him: "I will make good to you the hours wasted in this class when you come to my room."

The other less favoured students used to ascribe this indulgent treatment of Satish to his fair complexion and to his profession of atheism. Some of the more worldly-wise among them went to Wilkins's study with a great show of enthusiasm to borrow from him some book on Positivism. But he refused, saying that it would be too hard for them. That they should be held unfit even to cultivate atheism made their minds all the more bitter against Satish.

2

Jagamohan was Satish's uncle. He was a notorious atheist of that time. It would be inadequate to say that he did not believe in God. One ought rather to say that he vehemently believed in no God. As the business of a captain in the navy is rather to

---

[1] **Bania:** The Hindu caste of tradesmen.

sink ships than to steer, so it was Jagamohan's business to sink the creed of theism, wherever it put its head above the water.

The order of his arguments ran like this:

(1) If there be a God, then we must owe our intelligence to Him.

(2) But our intelligence clearly tells us that there is no God.

(3) Therefore God Himself tells us that there is no God.

"Yet you Hindus," he would continue, "have the effrontery to say that God exists. For this sin thirty-three million gods and goddesses exact penalties from you people, pulling your ears hard for your disobedience."

Jagamohan was married when he was a mere boy. Before his wife died he had read Malthus.[2] He never married again.

His younger brother, Harimohan, was the father of Satish. Harimohan's nature was so exactly the opposite of his elder brother's that people might suspect me of fabricating it for the purpose of writing a story. But only stories have to be always on their guard to sustain their reader's confidence. Facts have no such responsibility, and laugh at our incredulity. So, in this world, there are abundant instances of two brothers, the exact opposites of one another, like morning and evening.

Harimohan, in his infancy, had been a weakly child. His parents had tried to keep him safe from the attacks of all maladies by barricading him behind amulets and charms, dust taken from holy shrines, and blessings bought from innumerable Brahmans at enormous expense. When Harimohan grew up, he was physically quite robust, yet the tradition of his poor health lingered on in the family. So nobody claimed from him anything more arduous than that he should continue to live. He fulfilled his part, and did hold on to his life. Yet he never allowed his family to forget for a moment that life in his case was more fragile than in most other mortals. Thus he managed to divert towards himself the undivided attention of all his aunts and his mother, and had specially prepared meals served to him. He had less work and more rest than other members of the family. He was never allowed to forget that he was under the special protection, not only of his aforesaid mother and aunts, but also of the countless gods and goddesses presiding in the three regions of earth, heaven, and air. He thus acquired an attitude of prayerful dependence towards all the powers of the world, both seen and unseen — sub-inspectors, wealthy neighbours, highly placed officials, let alone sacred cows and Brahmans.

Jagamohan's anxieties went altogether in an opposite direction. He would give a wide berth to men of power, lest the slightest suspicion of snobbishness should cling to him. It was this same sentiment which had greatly to do with his defiance of the gods. His knees were too stiff to bend before those from whom favour could be expected.

Harimohan got himself married at the proper time, that is to say, long before the time. After three sisters and three brothers, Satish was born. Everybody was struck by his resemblance to his uncle, and Jagamohan took possession of him, as if he were his own son.

---

[2] Malthus: Thomas Malthus (1766–1834), English economist whose *Essay on Population* (1798) argued that population growth would inevitably outpace the growth of the food supply.

At first Harimohan was glad of this, having regard to the educational advantage of the arrangement; for Jagamohan had the reputation of being the most eminent scholar of that period.

He seemed to live within the shell of his English books. It was easy to find the rooms he occupied in the house by the rows of books about the walls, just as it is easy to find out the bed of a stream by its lines of pebbles.

Harimohan petted and spoilt his eldest son, Purandar, to his heart's content. He had an impression that Purandar was too delicate to survive the shock of being denied anything he wanted. His education was neglected. No time was lost in getting him married, and yet nobody could keep him within the connubial limits. If Harimohan's daughter-in-law expressed any disapprobation of his vagaries in that direction, Harimohan would get angry with her and ascribe his son's conduct to her want of tact and charm.

Jagamohan entirely took charge of Satish to save him from similar paternal solicitude. Satish acquired a mastery of the English language while he was still a child, and the inflammatory doctrines of Mill and Bentham[3] set his brain on fire, till he began to burn like a living torch of atheism.

Jagamohan treated Satish, not as his junior, but as his boon companion. He held the opinion that veneration in human nature was a superstition, specially designed to make men into slaves. Some son-in-law of the family wrote to him a letter, with the usual formal beginning:

"To the gracious feet of———"

Jagamohan wrote an answer, arguing with him as follows:

My DEAR NOREN—Neither you nor I know what special significance it gives to the feet to call them "gracious." Therefore the epithet is worse than useless, and had better be dropped. And then it is apt to give one a nervous shock when you address your letter only to the feet, completely ignoring their owner. But you should understand, that so long as my feet are attached to my body, you should never dissociate them from their context.

Next, you should bear in mind that human feet have not the advantage of prehensibility, and it is sheer madness to offer anything to them, confounding their natural function.

Lastly, your use of the plural inflection to the word "feet," instead of the dual, may denote special reverence on your part (because there are animals with four feet which have your particular veneration) but I consider it my duty to disabuse your mind of all errors concerning my own zoological identity.—Yours,   JAGAMOHAN.

Jagamohan used to discuss with Satish subjects which are usually kept out of sight in conversation. If people objected to this plainness of speech with one so young, he would say that you can only drive away hornets by breaking in their nest. So you can only drive away the shamefulness of certain subjects by piercing through the shame itself.

---

[3] **Mill and Bentham:** James Mill (1773–1836) and Jeremy Bentham (1748–1832), English utilitarian philosophers, economic theorists, and political scientists. Utilitarians argued that the purpose of government was to create the greatest happiness for the greatest number.

When Satish had completed his College course, Harimohan tried his best to extricate him from his uncle's sphere of influence. But when once the noose is fixed round the neck, it only grows tighter by pulling at it. Harimohan became more and more annoyed at his brother, the more Satish proved recalcitrant. If this atheism of his son and elder brother had been merely a matter of private opinion, Harimohan could have tolerated It. He was quite ready to pass off dishes of fowl as "kid curry."[4] But matters had now become so desperate that even lies became powerless to white-wash the culprits. What brought things to a head was this:

The positive side of Jagamohan's atheistic creed consisted in doing good to others. He felt a special pride in it, because doing good, for an atheist, was a matter of unmitigated loss. It had no allurements of merit and no deterrents of punishment in the hereafter. If he was asked what concern he had in bringing about "the greatest happiness of the greatest number," he used to answer that his best incentive was that he could expect nothing in return. He would say to Satish:

"Baba,[5] we are atheists. And therefore the very pride of it should keep us absolutely stainless. Because we have no respect for any being higher than ourselves, therefore we must respect ourselves."

There were some leather shops in the neighbourhood kept by Muhammadans. The uncle and nephew bestirred themselves with great zeal in doing good to these Muhammadans and their untouchable leather workers.[6] This made Harimohan beside himself with indignation. Since he knew that any appeal to Scriptures, or to tradition, would have no effect upon these two renegades, he complained to his brother concerning the wasting of his patrimony.

"When my expenditure," his brother answered, "comes up to the amount you have spent upon your full-fed Brahman priests, we shall be quits."

One day Harimohan's people were surprised to find that a preparation was going on in Jagamohan's quarters for a grand feast. The cooks and waiters were all Mussulmans. Harimohan called for his son, and said to him angrily:

"I hear that you are going to give a feast to all your reverend friends, the leather workers."

Satish replied that he was far too poor to think of it. His uncle had invited them.

Purandar, Satish's elder brother, was equally indignant. He threatened to drive all the unclean guests away. When Harimohan expressed his protest to his brother, he answered:

"I never make any objection to your offering food to your idols. You should make no objection to my offering food to my gods."

"Your gods!" exclaimed Harimohan.

"Yes, my gods," his brother answered.

"Have you become a theist all of a sudden?" sneered Harimohan.

---

[4] "Kid curry": In Bengal kid curry is often eaten without blame. But fowl curry would come within the prohibitions. [Translator]

[5] Baba: A term of endearment, literally "father." [Translator]

[6] untouchable . . . workers: As leather is made from the hides of dead animals, those who work in leather are regarded as unclean by orthodox Hindus. Only the very lowest castes are tanners. [Translator]

"No!" his brother replied. "Theists worship the God who is invisible. You idolaters worship gods who are visible, but dumb and deaf. The gods I worship are both visible and audible, and it is impossible not to believe in them."

"Do you really mean to say," cried Harimohan, "that these leather workers and Mussulmans are your gods?"

"Indeed, they are," said Jagamohan; "you shall see their miraculous power when I put food before them. They will actually swallow it, which I defy your gods to do. It delights my heart to see my gods perform such divine wonders. If you are not morally blind, it will delight your heart also."

Purandar came to his uncle, and told him in a high-pitched voice that he was prepared to take desperate measures to stop the proceedings. Jagamohan laughed at him, and said:

"You monkey! If you ever try to lay hands on my gods, you will instantly discover how powerful they are, and I shall not have to do anything to defend them."

Purandar was even a greater coward than his father. He was a tyrant only where he was sure of receiving submission. In this case he did not dare to pick a quarrel with his Muhammadan neighbours. So he came to Satish, and reviled him. Satish gazed at him with those wonderful eyes of his, and remained silent.

The feast was a great success.

3

Harimohan could not take this insult passively. He declared war. The property on whose income the whole family subsisted was a temple endowment. Harimohan brought a suit in the law court against his brother, accusing him of such grave breaches of propriety as made him unworthy of remaining the trustee of a religious endowment. Harimohan had as many witnesses as ever he wished. The whole Hindu neighbourhood was ready to support him.

Jagamohan professed in open court that he had no faith in gods or idols of any description whatever; that all eatable food was for him food to be eaten; that he never bothered his head to find out the particular limb of Brahma from which the Muhammadans had issued, and therefore he had not the smallest hesitation in taking food in their company.

The judge ruled Jagamohan to be unfit to hold the temple property. Jagamohan's lawyers assured him that the decision could be upset by an appeal to the higher Court. But Jagamohan refused to appeal. He said he could not cheat even the gods whom he did not believe in. Only those who had the intelligence to believe such things had the conscience to cheat them.

His friends asked him: "How are you going to maintain yourself?"

He answered: "If I have nothing else to eat, I shall be content to gulp down my last breath."

After this, a partition was made of the family house. A wall was raised from the ground floor to the upper storey, dividing the house into two parts.

Harimohan had great faith in the selfish sanity of prudence in human nature. He was certain that the savour of good living would tempt Satish into his golden trap, away from the empty nest of Jagamohan. But Satish gave another proof that he had neither inherited his father's conscience nor his sanity. He remained with his uncle.

Jagamohan was so accustomed to look upon Satish as his own that he was not surprised to find him remaining on his side after the partition.

But Harimohan knew his brother's temperament very well. He went about talking to people, explaining that the reason why Jagamohan did not let go his hold on Satish was that he expected to make a good thing out of Satish's presence, keeping him as a kind of hostage.

Harimohan almost shed tears while he said to his neighbour: "Could my brother ever imagine that I was going to starve him? Since he is cunning enough to concoct this diabolical plot against me, I shall wait and see whether he is cleverer than I am."

Harimohan's talk about Satish reached Jagamohan's ears. Jagamohan was surprised at his own stupidity in not anticipating such a turn of events.

He said: "Good-bye, Satish."

Satish was absolutely certain that nothing could make Jagamohan change his mind, so he had to take his leave, after having spent his eighteen years of life in his uncle's company.

When Satish had put his books and bedding on the top of the carriage, and driven away, Jagamohan shut the door of his room, and flung himself on the floor. When evening came, and the old servant knocked at the door with the lighted lamp, he got no answer.

Alas for the greatest happiness of the greatest number! The estimate in number is not the only measure of human affairs. The man who counts "one" may go beyond all arithmetic when the heart does the sum. When Satish took his departure, he at once became infinite to Jagamohan.

Satish went into a students' lodging to share a room with one of his friends. Harimohan shed tears while meditating on the neglect of filial duties in this godforsaken age. Harimohan had a very tender heart.

After the partition, Purandar dedicated a room in their portion of the house to the family god. It gave him a peculiar pleasure to know that his uncle must be execrating him for the noise raised every morning and every evening by the sacred conches and prayer gongs.

In order to maintain himself, Satish secured a post as a private tutor. Jagamohan obtained an appointment as head master of a high school. And it became a religious duty with Harimohan and Purandar to persuade parents and guardians to take away their boys from the malign influence of the atheist Jagamohan.

4

One day, after a very long interval of absence, Satish came to Jagamohan. These two had given up the usual form of greeting[7] which passes between elder and younger.

Jagamohan embraced Satish, led him to a chair, and asked him for the news.

---

[7] **usual . . . greeting:** This greeting in Bengal is for the younger to touch the feet of the elder. [Translator]

There was news indeed!

A girl named Nonibala had taken shelter with her widowed mother in the house of the mother's brother. So long as her mother lived, there was no trouble. But a short time ago her mother had died. Her cousins were rascals. One of their friends had taken away this girl. Then, suspecting her of infidelity, after a while he made her life a constant torture. This had happened in the house next to the one where Satish had his tutorship. Satish wanted to save her from this misery, but he had no money or shelter of his own. Therefore he had come to his uncle. The girl was about to give birth to a child.

Jagamohan, when he heard the story, was filled with indignation. He was not the man to calculate coldly the consequence of his deeds, and he at once said to his nephew: "I have the room in which I keep my books. I can put the girl there."

"But what about your books?" Satish asked in surprise. Very few books, however, were now remaining. During the time when he had been unable to secure an appointment, he had been obliged to eke out a living by selling his books.

Jagamohan said: "Bring the girl at once."

"She is waiting downstairs," said Satish. "I have brought her here." Jagamohan ran downstairs, and found the girl crouching in the corner, wrapped in her *sari,* looking like a bundle of clothes.

Jagamohan, in his deep bass voice, said at once: "Come, little Mother, why do you sit in the dust?"

The girl covered her face, and burst into tears. Jagamohan was not a man to give way to emotion, but his eyes were wet as he turned to Satish and said: "The burden that this girl is bearing is ours."

Then he said to the girl: "Mother, don't be shy on my account. My schoolfellows used to call me 'Mad Jagai,' and I am the same madcap even now."

Then, without hesitation, he took the girl by both her hands, and raised her. The veil dropped from off her face.

The girl's face was fresh and young, and there was no line of hardness or vice in it. The inner purity of her heart had not been stained, just as a speck of dust does not soil a flower. Jagamohan took Nonibala to his upper room, and said to her: "Mother, look what a state my room is in! The floor is all unswept. Everything is upside down; and as for myself, I have no fixed hour for my bath or my meals. Now that you have come to my house, everything will be put right, and even this mad Jagai will be made respectable."

Nonibala had never felt before, even when her mother lived, how much one person could be to another; because her mother had looked upon her, not so much as a daughter, but as a young girl who had to be watched.

Jagamohan employed an elderly woman servant to help Nonibala. At first Noni was afraid lest Jagamohan should refuse to take food from her hand because of her impurity. But it turned out that Jagamohan refused to take his meals unless they were cooked and served by Noni.

Jagamohan was aware that a great wave of calumny was about to break over his head. Noni also felt that it was inevitable, and she had no peace of mind. Within a day or two it began.

The servant who waited on her had at first supposed that Noni was Jagamohan's daughter. But she came one day, saying hard things to Noni, and resigned her service in contempt. Noni became pale with fear, thinking of Jagamohan.

Jagamohan said to her: "My little Mother, the full moon is up in the horizon of my life, so the time is ripe for the flood-tide of revilement. But, however muddy the water may become, it will never stain my moonlight."

An aunt of Jagamohan's came to Harimohan's quarters, and said to him: "Jagai, what a disgrace, what a disgrace! Wipe off this stain of sin from your house."

Jagamohan answered: "You are pious people, and this advice is worthy of you. But if I try to drive away all relics of sin, what will become of the sinner?"

Some old grandmother of a woman came to him, and said: "Send this wench away to the hospital. Harimohan is ready to bear all the cost."

Jagamohan said: "But she is my mother. Because some one is ready to pay expenses, should I send my mother to the hospital?"

The grandmother opened her eyes wide with surprise and said: "Who is this you call your mother?"

Jagamohan replied: "She who nourished life within her womb, and risks her life to give birth to children. I cannot call that scoundrel-father of the child 'Father.' He can only cause trouble, keeping himself safely out of it."

Harimohan's whole body shrank with the utter infamy of the thing. That a fallen woman should be sheltered only on the other side of the wall, and in the midst of a household sacred to the memory of generations of mothers and grandmothers! The disgrace was intolerable.

Harimohan at once surmised that Satish was mixed up in this affair, and that his uncle was encouraging him in his shameful conduct. He was so sure of his facts that he went about spreading the news. Jagamohan did not say a single word to contradict him.

"For us atheists," he said, "the only heaven waiting for good deeds is calumny."

The more the rumour of Jagamohan's doings became distorted, the more he seemed to enjoy it, and his laughter rang loud in the sky. Harimohan and respectable people of his class could never imagine that the uncle could go so far as to jest openly on such a subject, and indulge in loud unseemly buffoonery about it with his own nephew.

Though Purandar had been carefully avoiding that part of the house where his uncle lived, he vowed that he would never rest till he had driven the girl away from her shelter.

At the time when Jagamohan had to go to his school he would shut up all access to his quarters, and he would come back the moment he had any leisure to see how Noni was faring.

One day at noon Purandar, with the help of a bamboo ladder, crossed the boundary wall and jumped down into Jagamohan's part of the house. Nonibala had been resting after the morning meal. The door of her room was open. Purandar, when he saw the sleeping figure of Noni, gave a great start, and shouted out in anger: "So *you* are here, are you?"

Noni woke up and saw Purandar before her. She became pale as death, and her limbs shrank under her. She felt powerless to run away or to utter a single word.

Purandar, trembling with rage, shouted out: "Noni!"

Just then Jagamohan entered the room from behind, and cried: "Get out of this room."

Purandar's whole body began to swell up like an angry cat.

Jagamohan said: "If you don't get out at once, I will call in the police."

Purandar darted a terrible glance at Noni, and went out. Noni fainted.

Jagamohan now understood the whole situation. By questioning, he found out that Satish had been aware that Purandar had seduced Noni; but, fearing an angry brawl, he had not informed Jagamohan of the fact.

For days after this incident Noni trembled like a bamboo leaf. Then she gave birth to a dead child.

One midnight Purandar had driven Noni away from her room, kicking her in anger. Since then he had sought her in vain. When he suddenly found her in his uncle's house, he was seized with an uncontrollable passion of jealousy. He was sure that Satish had enticed her away from him, to keep her for his own pleasure, and had then put her in the very next house to his own in order to insult him. This was more than any mortal man could bear.

Harimohan heard all about it. Indeed, Purandar never took any pains to hide these doings from his father, for his father looked upon his son's moral aberrations with a kindly indulgence. But Harimohan thought it contrary to all notions of decency for Satish to snatch away this girl whom his elder brother, Purandar, had looked upon with favour. He devoutly hoped that Purandar would be successful in recovering his spoil.

It was the time of the Christmas holidays. Jagamohan attended Noni night and day. One evening he was translating a novel of Sir Walter Scott's to her, when Purandar burst into the room with another young man.

When Jagamohan was about to call for the police, the young man said: "I am Noni's cousin. I have come to take her away."

Jagamohan caught hold of Purandar by his neck, and shoved him out of the room and down the stairs. He then turned to the other young man and said: "You are a villain and a scoundrel! You assert this cousin's right of yours to wreck her life, not to protect her."

The young man hurried away. But when he had got to a safe distance, he threatened Jagamohan with legal steps in order to rescue his ward.

Noni said within herself: "O Earth, open and swallow me up!"[8]

Jagamohan called Satish, and said to him: "Let me leave this place and go to some up-country town with Noni. It will kill her if this is repeated."

Satish urged that his brother was certain to follow her when once he had got the clue.

---

[8] "O Earth, . . . up!": The reference is to Sita in the Ramayana, who uttered this cry when in extreme trouble. [Translator]

"Then what do you propose?" said Jagamohan.

"Let me marry Noni," was the answer.

"Marry Noni!"

"Yes, according to the civil marriage rites."

Jagamohan stood up and went to Satish, and pressed him to his heart.

5

Since the partition of the house, Harimohan had not once entered the house to see his elder brother. But that day he came in, dishevelled, and said:

"Dada,[9] what disaster is this you are planning?"

"I am saving everybody from disaster," said Jagamohan.

"Satish is just like a son to you," said Harimohan, "and yet you can have the heart to see him married to that woman of the street!"

"Yes," he replied, "I have brought him up almost as my own son, and I consider that my pains have borne fruit at last."

"Dada," said Harimohan, "I humbly acknowledge my defeat at your hands. I am willing to write away half my property to you, if only you will not take revenge on me like this."

Jagamohan started up from his chair and bellowed out:

"You want to throw me your dirty leavings, as you throw a dog a bone! I am an atheist—remember that! I am not a pious man like you! I neither take revenge, nor beg for favours."

Harimohan hastened round to Satish's lodgings. He cried out to him:

"Satish! What in the world are you going to do? Can you think of no other way of ruining yourself? Are you determined to plunge the whole family into this hideous shame?"

Satish answered: "I have no particular desire to marry. I only do it in order to save my family from hideous shame."

Harimohan shouted: "Have you not got the least spark of conscience left in you? That girl, who is almost like a wife to your brother————"

Satish caught him up sharply: "What? Like a wife. Not that word, sir, if you please!"

After that, Harimohan became wildly abusive in his language, and Satish remained silent.

What troubled Harimohan most was that Purandar openly advertised his intention to commit suicide if Satish married Noni. Purandar's wife told him that this would solve a difficult problem—if only he would have the courage to do it.

Satish sedulously avoided Noni all these days, but, when the proposed marriage was settled, Jagamohan asked Satish that Noni and he should try to know each other better before they were united in wedlock. Satish consented.

Jagamohan fixed a date for their first talk together. He said to Noni:

"My little Mother, you must dress yourself up for this occasion."

Noni bent her eyes to the ground.

---

[9] "Dada": Elder brother. [Translator]

"No, no," said he, "don't be shy, Noni. I have a great longing to see you nicely dressed, and you must satisfy my desire."

He had specially selected some Benares silk and a bodice and veil for Noni. He gave these things to her.

Noni prostrated herself at his feet. This made Jagamohan get up hurriedly. He snatched away his feet from her embrace, and said:

"I see, Noni, I have miserably failed in clearing your mind of all this superstitious reverence. I may be your elder in age, but don't you know you are greater than I am, for you are my mother?"

He kissed her on her forehead and said:

"I have had an invitation to go out, and I shall be late back this evening."

Noni clasped his hand and said:

"Baba, I want your blessing to-night."

Jagamohan replied:

"Mother, I see that you are determined to turn me into a theist in my old age. I wouldn't give a brass farthing for a blessing, myself. Yet I cannot help blessing you when I see your face."

Jagamohan put his hand under her chin, and raised her face, and looked into it silently, while tears ran down her cheeks.

6

In the evening a man ran up to the place where Jagamohan was having his dinner, and brought him back to his house.

He found the dead body of Noni, stretched on the bed, dressed in the things he had given her. In her hand was a letter. Satish was standing by her head. Jagamohan opened the letter, and read:

> Baba, forgive me. I could not do what you wanted. I tried my best, but I could never forget him. My thousand salutations to your gracious feet. —NONIBALA, the Sinner.

CHAPTER II
SATISH

1

The last words of Jagamohan, the atheist, to his nephew, Satish, were: "If you have a fancy for funeral ceremony, don't waste it on your uncle,—reserve it for your father."

This is how he came by his death.

When the plague first broke out in Calcutta, the poor citizens were less afraid of the epidemic than of the preventive staff who wore its badge. Satish's father, Harimohan, was sure that their Mussulman neighbours, the untouchable leather-dealers, would be the first to catch it, and thereupon defile him and his kith and kin by dragging them along into a common end. Before he fled from his house, Harimohan went over to offer refuge to his elder brother, saying: "I have taken a house on the river at Kalna, if you———"

"Nonsense!" interrupted Jagamohan. "How can I desert these people?"

"Which people?"

"These leather-dealers of ours."

Harimohan made a grimace and left his brother without further parley. He next proceeded to his son's lodgings, and to him simply said: "Come along."

Satish's refusal was equally laconic. "I have work to do here," he replied.

"As pall-bearer to the leather-dealers, I suppose?"

"Yes, sir; that is, if my services be needed."

"Yes, sir, indeed! You scamp, you scoundrel, you atheist! If need be you're quite ready to consign fourteen generations of your ancestors to perdition, I have no doubt!"

Convinced that the Kali Yuga[10] had touched its lowest depth, Harimohan returned home, despairing of the salvation of his next of kin. In order to protect himself against contamination he covered sheets of foolscap with the name of Kali, the protecting goddess, in his neatest handwriting.

Harimohan left Calcutta. The plague and the preventive officials duly made their appearance in the locality; and for dread of being dragged off to the plague hospital, the wretched victims dared not call in medical aid. After a visit to one of these hospitals, Jagamohan shook his head and remarked: "What if these people are falling ill, — that does not make them criminals."

Jagamohan schemed and contrived till he obtained permission to use his own house as a private plague hospital. Some of us students offered to assist Satish in nursing: There was a qualified doctor among our number.

The first patient in our hospital was a Mussulman. He died. The next was Jagamohan himself. He did not survive either. He said to Satish: "The religion I have all along followed has given me its last reward. There is nothing to complain of."

Satish had never taken the dust[11] of his uncle's feet while living. After Jagamohan's death he made that obeisance for the first and last time.

"Fit death for an atheist!" scoffed Harimohan when he first came across Satish after the cremation.

"That is so, sir!" agreed Satish, proudly.

2

Just as, when the flame is blown out, the light suddenly and completely disappears, so did Satish after his uncle's death. He went out of our ken altogether.

We had never been able to fathom how deeply Satish loved his uncle. Jagamohan was alike father and friend to him, — and, it may be said, son as well; for the old man had been so regardless of himself, so unmindful of worldly concerns, that it used to be one of the chief cares of Satish to look after him and keep him safe from disaster. Thus had Satish received from and given to his uncle his all.

---

[10] **Kali Yuga:** According to the Hindu Shastras the present age, the Kali Yuga, is the Dark Age when Dharma (civilization) will be at its lowest ebb. [Translator]

[11] **taken the dust:** Touching the feet of a revered elder, and then one's own head, is called taking the dust of the feet. It is the formal way of doing reverence. [Translator]

What the bleakness of his bereavement meant for Satish, it was impossible for us to conceive. He struggled against the agony of negation, refusing to believe that such absolute blankness could be true: that there could be emptiness so desolate as to be void even of Truth. If that which seemed one vast "No" had not also its aspect of "Yes," would not the whole universe leak away through its yawning gap into nothingness?

For two years Satish wandered from place to place, — we had no contact with him. We threw ourselves with all the greater zeal into our self-appointed tasks. We made it a special point to shock those who professed belief in any kind of religion, and the fields of good work we selected were such that not a good soul had a good word left for us. Satish had been our flower; when he dropped off, we, the thorns, cast off our sheaths and gloried in our sharpness.

3

Two years had passed since we lost sight of Satish. My mind revolted against harbouring the least thing evil against him, nevertheless I could not help suspecting that the high pitch at which he used to be kept strung must have been flattened down by this shock.

Uncle Jagamohan had once said of a *Sannyasin:*[12] "As the money-changer tests the ring of each coin, so does the world test each man by the response he gives to shocks of loss and pain, and the resistance he offers to the craze for cheap salvation. Those who fail to ring true are cast aside as worthless. These wandering ascetics have been so rejected, as being unfit to take part in the world's commerce, — yet the vagabonds swagger about, boasting that it is they who have renounced the world! The worthy are permitted no loophole of escape from duty, — only withered leaves are allowed to fall off the tree."

Had it come to this, that Satish, of all people, had joined the ranks of the withered and the worthless? Was he, then, fated to leave on the black touchstone of bereavement his mark of spuriousness?

While assailed with these misgivings, news suddenly reached us that Satish (our Satish, if you please!) was making the heavens resound with his cymbals in some out-of-the-way village, singing frenzied *kirtans*[13] as a follower of Lilananda Swami, the Vaishnava revivalist!

It had passed my comprehension, when I first began to know Satish, how he could ever have come to be an atheist. I was now equally at a loss to understand how Lilananda Swami could have managed to lead him in such a dance with his *kirtans.*

And how on earth were we to show our faces? What laughter there would be in the camp of the enemy, — whose number, thanks to our folly, was legion! Our band waxed mightily wroth with Satish. Many of them said they had known from the very first that there was no rational substance in him, — he was all frothy idealism. And I

---

[12] *Sannyasin:* A Brahman ascetic.

[13] *kirtans:* The *kirtan* is a kind of devotional oratorio sung to the accompaniment of drums and cymbals, the libretto ranging over the whole gamut of human emotions, which are made the vehicle for communion with the Divine Lover. As their feelings get worked up, the singers begin to sway their bodies with, and finally dance to, the rhythm. [Translator]

now discovered how much I really loved Satish. He had dealt his ardent sect of atheists their death-blow, yet I could not be angry with him.

Off I started to hunt up Lilananda Swami. River after river I crossed, and trudged over endless fields. The nights I spent in grocers' shops. At last in one of the villages I came up against Satish's party.

It was then two o'clock in the afternoon. I had been hoping to catch Satish alone. Impossible! The cottage which was honoured with the Swami's presence was packed all round with crowds of his disciples. There had been *kirtans* all the morning; those who had come from a distance were now waiting to have their meal served.

As soon as Satish caught sight of me, he dashed up and embraced me fervidly. I was staggered. Satish had always been extremely reserved. His outward calm had been the only measure of his depth of feeling. He now appeared as though intoxicated.

The Swami was resting in the front room, with the door ajar. He could see us. At once came the call, in a deep voice: "Satish!"

Satish was back inside, all in a flurry.

"Who is that?" inquired the Swami.

"Srivilas, a great friend of mine," Satish reported.

During these years I had managed to make a name for myself in our little world. A learned Englishman had remarked, on hearing one of my English speeches: "The man has a wonderful———." But let that be. Why add to the number of my enemies? Suffice it to say that, from the students up to the students' grandparents, the reputation had travelled round that I was a rampaging atheist who could bestride the English language and race her over the hurdles at breakneck speed in the most marvellous manner.

I somehow felt that the Swami was pleased to have me here. He sent for me. I merely hinted at the usual salutation as I entered his room,—that is to say, my joined hands were uplifted, but my head was not lowered.

This did not escape the Swami. "Here, Satish!" he ordered. "Fill me that pipe of mine."

Satish set to work. But as he lit the tinder, it was I who was set ablaze within. Moreover, I was getting fidgety, not knowing where to sit. The only seat in the room was a wooden bedstead on which was spread the Swami's carpet. Not that I confessed to any qualms about occupying a corner of the same carpet on which the great man was installed, but somehow my sitting down did not come off. I remained standing near the door.

It appeared that the Swami was aware of my having won the Premchand-Roychand[14] scholarship. "My son," he said to me, "it is good for the pearl diver if he succeeds in reaching the bottom, but he would die if he had to stay there. He must come up for the free breath of life. If you would live, you must now come up to the light, out of the depths of your learning. You have enjoyed the fruits of your scholarship, now try a taste of the joys of its renunciation."

---

[14] "The Premchand-Roychand: The highest prize at Calcutta University. [Translator]

Satish handed his Master the lighted pipe and sat down on the bare floor near his feet. The Swami leant back and stretched his legs out towards Satish, who began gently to massage them. This was more than I could stand. I left the room. I could, of course, see that this ordering about of Satish and making him fetch and carry was deliberately directed at me.

The Swami went on resting. All the guests were duly served by the householder with a meal of kedgeree. From five o'clock the *kirtans* started again and went on till ten in the night.

When I got Satish alone at last, I said to him: "Look here, Satish! You have been brought up in the atmosphere of freedom from infancy. How have you managed to get yourself entangled in this kind of bondage today? Is Uncle Jagamohan, then, so utterly dead?"

Partly because the playfulness of affection prompted it, partly, perhaps, because precision of description required it, Satish used to reverse the first two syllables of my name and call me Visri.[15]

"Visri," he replied, "while Uncle was alive he gave me freedom in life's field of work, — the freedom which the child gets in the playground. After his death it is he, again, who has given me freedom on the high seas of emotion, — the freedom which the child gains when it comes back to its mother's arms. I have enjoyed to the full the freedom of life's day-time; why should I now deprive myself of the freedom of its evening? Be sure that both these are the gift of that same uncle of ours."

"Whatever you may say," I persisted, "Uncle could have nothing to do with this kind of pipe-filling, leg-massaging business. Surely this is no picture of freedom."

"That," argued Satish, "was the freedom on shore. There Uncle gave full liberty of action to our limbs. This is freedom on the ocean. Here the confinement of the ship is necessary for our progress. That is why my Master keeps me bound to his service. This massaging is helping me to cross over."

"It does not sound so bad," I admitted, "the way you put it. But, all the same, I have no patience with a man who can thrust out his legs at you like that."

"He can do it," explained Satish, "because he has no need of such service. Had it been for himself, he might have felt ashamed to ask it. The need is mine."

I realised that the world into which Satish had been transported had no place for me, his particular friend. The person, whom Satish has so effusively embraced, was not Srivilas, but a representative of all humanity, — just an idea. Such ideas are like wine. When they get into the head any one can be embraced and wept over — I, only as much as anybody else. But whatever joys may be the portion of the ecstatic one, what can such embrace signify to me, the other party? What satisfaction am I to get, merely to be accounted one of the ripples on a grand, difference-obliterating flood, — I, the individual I?

However, further argument was clearly useless. Nor could I make up my mind to desert Satish. So, as his satellite, I also danced from village to village, carried along the current of *kirtan* singing.

---

[15] Visri: Ungainly, ugly. [Translator]

The intoxication of it gradually took hold of me. I also embraced all and sundry, wept without provocation, and tended the feet of the Master. And one day, in a moment of curious exaltation, Satish was revealed to me in a light for which there can be no other name than divine.

4

With the capture of two such egregious, college-educated atheists as we were, the fame of Lilananda Swami spread far and wide. His Calcutta disciples now pressed him to take up his headquarters at the metropolis.

So Swami Lilananda came on to Calcutta.

Shivatosh had been a devoted follower of Lilananda. Whenever the Swami visited Calcutta he had stayed with Shivatosh. And it was the one delight of Shivatosh's life to serve the Master, together with all his disciples, when they thus honoured his house. When he died he bequeathed all his property to the Swami, leaving only a life-interest in the income to his young childless widow. It was his hope that this house of his would become a pilgrim-centre for the sect.

This was the house where we now went into residence.

During our ecstatic progress through the villages I had been in an elated mood, which I now found it difficult to keep up in Calcutta. In the wonderland of emotion, where we had been revelling, the mystic drama of the courting of the Bride within us and the Bridegroom who is everywhere was being played. And a fitting accompaniment to it had been the symphony of the broad grazing greens, the shaded ferry landing-places, the enraptured expanse of the noonday leisure, the deep evening silences vibrant with the tremolo of cicadas. Ours had been a dream progress to which the open skies of the countryside offered no obstacle. But with our arrival at Calcutta we knocked our heads against its hardness, we got jostled by its crowds, and our dream was at an end.

Yet, was not this the same Calcutta where, within the confines of our students' lodgings, we had once put our whole soul into our studies, by day and by night; where we had pondered over and discussed the problems of our country with our fellow-students in the College Square; where we had served as volunteers at the holding of our National Assemblies; where we had responded to the call of Uncle Jagamohan, and taken the vow to free our minds from all slavery imposed by Society or State? Yes, it was in this self-same Calcutta that, in the flood-tide of our youth, we had pursued our course, regardless of the revilement of stranger and kindred alike, proudly breasting all contrary currents like a boat in full sail. Why, then, should we now fail, in this whirlpool of suffering humanity, ridden with pleasure and pain, driven by hunger and thirst, to keep up the exaltation proper to our tear-drenched cult of emotional Communion?

As I manfully made the attempt, I was beset with doubts at every step. Was I then a mere weakling: unfaithful to my ideal: unworthy of strenuous endeavour? When I turned to Satish, to see how he fared, I found on his countenance no sign to show that Calcutta, for him, represented any geographical reality whatsoever. In the mystic world where he dwelt, all this city life meant no more than a mirage.

5

We two friends took up our quarters, with the Master, in Shivatosh's house. We had come to be his chief disciples, and he would have us constantly near his person.

With our Master and our fellow-disciples we were absorbed day and night in discussing emotions in general and the philosophy of spiritual emotion in particular. Into the very thick of the abstruse complexities which thus engaged our attention, the ripple of a woman's laughter would now and again find its way from the inner apartments.[16] Sometimes there would be heard, in a clear, high-toned voice, the call "Bami!"—evidently a maid-servant of that name.

These were doubtless but trivial interruptions for minds soaring, almost to vanishing point, into the empyrean of idea. But to me they came as a grateful shower of rain upon a parched and thirsty soil. When little touches of life, like shed flower petals, were blown across from the unknown world behind the wall, then all in a moment I could understand that the wonderland of our quest was just there,—where the keys jingled, tied to the corner of Bami's sari; where the sound of the broom rose from the swept floor, and the smell of the cooking from the kitchen,—all trifles, but all true. That world, with its mingling of fine and coarse, bitter and sweet,—that itself was the heaven where Emotion truly held sway.

The name of the widow was Damini. We could catch momentary glimpses of her through opening doors and flapping curtains. But the two of us grew to be so much part and parcel of the Master as to share his privilege,[17] and very soon these doors and curtains were no longer barriers in our case.

Damini[18] was the lightning which gleams within the massed clouds of July. Without, the curves of youth enveloped her in their fulness, within flashed fitful fires. Thus runs an entry in Satish's diary:

> In Nonibala I have seen the Universal Woman in one of her aspects,—the woman who takes on herself the whole burden of sin, who gives up life itself for the sinner's sake, and in dying leaves for the world the balm of immortality. In Damini I see another aspect of Universal Woman. This one has nothing to do with death,—she is the Artist of the Art of Life. She blossoms out, in limitless profusion, in form and scent and movement. She is not for rejection; refuses to entertain the ascetic; and is vowed to resist the least farthing of payment to the tax-gathering Winter Wind.

It is necessary to relate Damini's previous history.

At the time when the coffers of her father, Annada, were overflowing with proceeds of his jute business, Damini was married to Shivatosh. So long, Shivatosh's fortune had consisted only in his pedigree: It could now count a more substantial addition. Annada bestowed on his son-in-law a house in Calcutta and sufficient money to keep him for life. There were also lavish gifts of furniture and ornaments made to his daughter.

---

[16] **inner apartments:** The women's part of the house. [Translator]

[17] Women do not observe *purdah* with religious ascetics. [Translator]

[18] **Damini:** Lightning. [Translator]

Annada, further, made a futile attempt to take Shivatosh into his own business. But the latter had no interest in worldly concerns. An astrologer had once predicted to Shivatosh that, on the happening of a special conjunction of the stars, his soul would gain its emancipation whilst still in the flesh. From that day he lived in this hope alone, and ceased to find charm in riches, or even in objects still more charming. It was while in this frame of mind that he had become a disciple of Lilananda Swami.

In the meantime, with the subsidence of the jute boom, the full force of the adverse wind caught the heavy-laden bark of Annada's fortune and toppled it over. All his property was sold up and he had hardly enough left to make a bare living.

One evening Shivatosh came into the inner apartments and said to his wife: "The Master is here. He has some words of advice for you and bids you attend."

"I cannot go to him now," answered Damini. "I haven't the time."

What? No time! Shivatosh went up nearer and found his wife seated in the gathering dusk, in front of the open safe, with her ornaments spread out before her. "What in the world is keeping you?" inquired he.

"I am arranging my jewels," was the reply.

So that was the reason for her lack of time. Indeed!

The next day, when Damini opened the safe, she found her jewel-box missing. "My jewels?" she exclaimed, turning inquiringly to her husband.

"But you offered them to the Master. Did not his call reach you at the very moment? — for he sees into the minds of men. He has deigned, in his mercy, to save you from the lure of pelf."

Damini's indignation rose to white heat.

"Give me back my ornaments!" she commanded.

"Why, what will you do with them?"

"They were my father's gift to me. I would return them to him."

"They have gone to a better place," said Shivatosh. "Instead of pandering to worldly needs they are dedicated to the service of devotees."

That is how the tyrannical imposition of faith began. And the pious ritual of exorcism, in all its cruelty, continued to be practised in order to rid Damini's mind of its mundane affections and desires.

So, while her father and her little brother were starving by inches, Damini had to prepare daily, with her own hands, meals for the sixty or seventy disciples who thronged the house with the Master. She would sometimes rebelliously leave out the salt, or contrive to get the viands scorched, but that did not avail to gain her any respite from her penance.

At this juncture Shivatosh died: and in departing he awarded his wife the supreme penalty for her want of faith, — he committed his widow, with all her belongings, to the guardianship of the Master.

6

The house was in a constant tumult with rising waves of fervour. Devotees kept streaming in from all quarters to sit at the feet of the Master. And yet Damini, who had gained the Presence without effort of her own, thrust aside her good fortune with contumely.

Did the Master call her for some special mark of his favour she would keep aloof, pleading a headache. If he had occasion to complain of some special omission of personal attention on her part, she would confess to have been away at the theatre. The excuse was lacking in truth, but not in rudeness.

The other women disciples were aghast at Damini's ways. First, her attire was not such as widows[19] should affect. Secondly, she showed no eagerness to drink in the Master's words of wisdom. Lastly, her demeanour had none of the reverential restraint which the Master's presence demanded. "What a shame," exclaimed they. "We have seen many awful women, but not one so outrageous."

The Swami used to smile. "The Lord," said he, "takes a special delight in wrestling with a valiant opponent. When Damini has to own defeat, her surrender will be absolute."

He began to display an exaggerated tolerance for her contumacy. That vexed Damini still more, for she looked on it as a more cunning form of punishment. And one day the Master caught her in a fit of laughter, mimicking to one of her companions the excessive suavity of his manner towards herself. Still he had not a word of rebuke, and repeated simply that the final *dénouement* would be all the more extraordinary, to which end the poor thing was but the instrument of Providence, and so herself not to blame.

This was how we found her when we first came. The *dénouement* was indeed extraordinary. I can hardly bring myself to write on further. Moreover, what happened is so difficult to tell. The network of suffering, which is woven behind the scenes, is not of any pattern set by the Scriptures, nor of our own devising. Hence the frequent discords between the inner and the outer life — discords that hurt, and wail forth in tears.

There came, at length, the dawn when the harsh crust of rebelliousness cracked and fell to pieces, and the flower of self-surrender came through and held up its dew-washed face. Damini's service became so beautiful in its truth that it descended on the devotees like the blessing of the very Divinity of their devotions.

And when Damini's lightning flashes had matured into a steady radiance, Satish looked on her and saw that she was beautiful; but I say this, that Satish gazed only on her beauty, failing to see Damini herself.

In Satish's room there hung a portrait of the Swami sitting in meditation, done on a porcelain medallion. One day he found it on the floor, — in fragments. He put it down to his pet cat. But other little mischiefs began to follow, which were clearly beyond the powers of the cat. There was some kind of disturbance in the air, which now and again broke out in unseen electric shocks.

How others felt, I know not, but a growing pain gnawed at my heart. Sometimes I thought that this constant ecstasy of emotion was proving too much for me. I

---

[19] Hindu widows in Bengal are supposed to dress in simple white (sometimes plain brown silk), without border, or ornamentation. [Translator]

wanted to give it all up and run away. The old work of teaching the leather-dealers' children seemed, in its unalloyed prose, to be now calling me back.

One afternoon when the Master was taking his siesta, and the weary disciples were at rest, Satish for some reason went off into his own room at this unusual hour. His progress was suddenly arrested at the threshold. There was Damini, her thick tresses dishevelled, lying prone on the floor, beating her head on it as she moaned: "Oh, you stone, you stone, have mercy on me, have mercy and kill me outright!"

Satish, trembling from head to foot with a nameless fear, fled from the room.

7

It was a rule with Swami Lilananda to go off once a year to some remote, out-of-the-way place, away from the crowd. With the month of Magh[20] came round the time for his journey. Satish was to attend on him.

I asked to go too. I was worn to the very bone with the incessant emotional excitement of our cult, and felt greatly in need of physical movement as well as of mental quiet.

The Master sent for Damini. "My little mother," he told her, "I am about to leave you for the duration of my travels. Let me arrange for your stay meanwhile with your aunt, as usual."

"I would accompany you," said Damini.

"You could hardly bear it, I am afraid. Our journeying will be troublesome."

"Of course I can bear it," she answered. "Pray have no concern about any trouble of mine."

Lilananda was pleased at this proof of Damini's devotion. In former years, this opportunity had been Damini's holiday time, — the one thing to which she had looked forward through the preceding months. "Miraculous!" thought the Swami. "How wondrously does even stone become as wax in the Lord's melting-pot of emotion."

So Damini had her way, and came along with us.

8

The spot we reached, after hours of tramping in the sun, was a little promontory on the sea-coast, shaded by cocoa-nut palms. Profound was the solitude and the tranquillity which reigned there, as the gentle rustle of the palm tassels merged into the idle plash of the girdling sea. The place looked like a tired hand of the sleepy shore, limply fallen upon the surface of the waters. On this open hand stood a bluish-green hill, and inside the hill was a sculptured cave-temple of bygone days, which, for all its serene beauty, was the cause of much disquiet amongst antiquarians as to the origin, style, and subject-matter of its sculptures.

Our intention had been to return to the village where we had made our halt, after paying a visit to this temple. That was now seen to be impossible. The day was fast declining, and the moon was long past its full. Lilananda Swami at length decided that we should pass the night in the cave.

---

[20] **month of Magh:** January–February. [Translator]

All four of us sat down to rest on the sandy soil beneath the cocoa-nut groves fringing the sea. The sunset glow bent lower and lower over the western horizon, as though Day was making its parting obeisance to approaching Night.

The Master's voice broke forth in song—one of his own composition:

The day has waned, when at last we meet at the turning;
And as I try to see thy face, the last ray of evening fades into the night.

We had heard the song before, but never with such complete *rapport* between singer, audience, and surroundings. Damini was affected to tears. The Swami went on to the second verse:

I shall not grieve that the darkness comes between thee and my sight, —
Only, for a moment, stand before me, that I may kiss thy feet and wipe them
*   with my hair.*

When he had come to the end, the placid even-tide, enveloping sky and waters, was filled, like some ripe, golden fruit, with the bursting sweetness of melody.

Damini rose and went up to the Master. As she prostrated herself at his feet, her loose hair slipped off her shoulders and was scattered over the ground on either side. She remained long thus before she raised her head.

9 *(From Satish's Diary)*

There were several chambers within the temple. In one of these I spread my blanket and laid myself down. The darkness pent up inside the cave seemed alive, like some great black monster, its damp breath bedewing my body. I began to be haunted by the idea that this was the first of all created animals, born in the beginning of time, with no eyes or ears, but just one enormous appetite. Confined within this cavern for endless ages it knew nothing, having no mind; but having sensibility it felt; and wept and wept in silence.

Fatigue overpowered my limbs like a dead weight, but sleep came not. Some bird, or perhaps bat, flitted in from the outside, or out from the inside,—its wings beating the air as it flew from darkness to darkness; when the draught reached my body it sent a shiver through me, making my flesh creep.

I thought I would go and get some sleep outside. But I could not recollect the direction in which the entrance was. As I crawled on my hands and knees along the way which appeared the right one, I knocked against the cave wall. When I tried a different side, I nearly tumbled into a hollow in which the water dripping through the cracks had collected.

I crawled back to my blanket and stretched myself on it again. Again was I possessed with the fancy that I had been taken right into the creature's maw and could not extricate myself; that I was the victim of a blind hunger which was licking me with its slimy saliva, through which I would be sucked and digested noiselessly, little by little.

I felt that only sleep could save me. My living, waking consciousness was evidently unable to bear such close embrace of this horrible, suffocating obscurity—fit only for the dead to suffer. I cannot say how long after it came upon me,—or whether it was really sleep at all,—but a thin veil of oblivion fell at last over my senses. And while in such half-conscious state I actually felt a deep breathing somewhere near my bare feet. Surely it was not that primeval creature of my imagining!

Then something seemed to cling about my feet. Some real wild animal this time,—was my first thought. But there was nothing furry in its touch. What if it was some species of serpent or reptile, of features and body unknown to me, of whose method of absorbing its prey I could form no idea? All the more loathsome seemed the softness of it,—of this terrible, unknown mass of hunger.

What between dread and disgust, I could not even utter a cry. I tried to push it away with ineffectual thrusts with my legs. Its face seemed to be touching my feet, on which its panting breath fell thickly. What kind of a face had it, I wondered. I launched a more vigorous kick as the stupor left me. I had at first supposed there was no fur, but what felt like a mane now brushed across my legs. I struggled up into a sitting posture.

Something stole away in the darkness. There was also a curious kind of sound. Could it have been sobbing?

Chapter III
Damini

1

We are back in our quarters in the village, near a temple, in a two-storeyed house belonging to one of the Swami's disciples, which had been placed at our disposal. Since our return we see but little of Damini, though she is still in charge of our household affairs. She has made friends with the neighbouring women, and spends most of her spare time in going about with them from one house to another.

The Swami is not particularly pleased. Damini's heart, thinks he, does not yet respond to the call of the ethereal heights. All its fondness is still for earthen walls. In her daily work of looking after the devotees,—formerly like an act of worship with her,—a trace of weariness has become noticeable. She makes mistakes. Her service has lost its radiance.

The Master, at heart, begins to be afraid of her again. Between her brows there darkens a gathering frown; her temple is ruffled with fitful breezes; the loosening knot of her hair lowers over her neck; the pressure of her lips, the gleams from the corner of her eye, her sudden wayward gestures presage a rebellious storm.

The Swami turned to his *kirtans* with renewed attention. The wandering bee, he hoped, would be brought to drink deep of the honey, once enticed in by its fragrance. And so the short cool days were filled to the brim with the foaming wine of ecstatic song.

But no, Damini refused to be caught. The exasperated Swami laughed out one day: "The Lord is out hunting: the resolute flight of the deer adds zest to the chase: but succumb she must, in the end."

When we had first come to know Damini, she was not to be found among the band of devotees clustering round the Master. That, however, did not attract our notice then. But now, her empty place had become conspicuous. Her frequent absences smote us tempestuously.

The Swami put this down to her pride, and that hurt his own pride. As for me,—but what does it matter what I thought?

One day the Master mustered up courage to say in his most dulcet tones: "Damini, my little mother, do you think you will have a little time to spare this afternoon? If so————"

"No," said Damini.

"Would you mind telling me why?"

"I have to assist in making sweetmeats at the Nandi's."

"Sweetmeats? What for?"

"They have a wedding on."

"Is your assistance so indispensably————?"

"I promised to be there."

Damini whisked out of the room without waiting for further questioning.

Satish, who was there with us, was dumbfounded. So many men of learning, wealth, and fame had surrendered at the feet of the Master, and this slip of a girl,—what gave her such hardihood of assurance?

Another evening Damini happened to be at home. The Master had addressed himself to some specially important topic. After his discourse had progressed awhile, something in our faces gave him pause. He found our attention wandering. On looking round he discovered that Damini, who had been seated in the room, sewing in hand, was not to be seen. He understood the reason of our distraction. She was not there, not there, not there,—the refrain now kept worrying him too. He began to lose the thread of his discourse, and at last gave it up altogether.

The Swami left the room and went off to Damini's door. "Damini," he called. "Why are you all alone here? Will you not come and join us?"

"I am engaged," said Damini.

The baffled Swami could see, as he passed by the half-open door, a captive kite in a cage. It had somehow struck against the telegraph wires, and had been lying wounded when Damini rescued it from the pestering crows, and she had been tending it since.

The kite was not the only object which engaged Damini's solicitude. There was a mongrel pup, whose looks were on a par with its breeding. It was discord personified. Whenever it heard our cymbals, it would look up to heaven and voice forth a prolonged complaint. The gods, being fortunate, did not feel bound to give it a hearing. The poor mortals whose ears happened to be within reach were woefully agonised.

One afternoon, when Damini was engaged in practising horticulture in sundry cracked pots on the roof-terrace, Satish came up and asked her point-blank: "Why is it you have given up coming over there altogether?"

"Over where?"

"To the Master."

"Why, what need have you people of me?"

"We have no need,—but surely the need is yours."

"No, no!" flung out Damini. "Not at all, not at all!"

Taken aback by her heat, Satish gazed at her in silence. Then he mused aloud: "Your mind lacks peace. If you would gain peace————"

"Peace from you,—you who are consumed day and night with your excitement,—where have *you* the peace to give? Leave me alone, I beg and pray you. I was at peace. I would be at peace."

"You see but the waves on the surface. If you have the patience to dive deep, you will find all calm there."

Damini wrung her hands as she cried: "I beseech you, for the Lord's sake, don't insist on my diving downwards. If only you will give up all hope of my conversion, I may yet live."

2

My experience has never been large enough to enable me to penetrate the mysteries of woman's mind. Judging from what little I have seen of the surface from the outside, I have come to the belief that women are ever ready to bestow their heart where sorrow cannot but be their lot. They will either string their garland of acceptance[21] for some brute of a man who will trample it under foot and defile it in the mire of his passions, or dedicate it to some idealist, on whose neck it will get no hold, attenuated as he is, like the dream-stuff of his imaginings.

When left to do their own choosing, women invariably reject ordinary men like me, made up of gross and fine, who know woman to be just woman,—that is to say, neither a doll of clay made to serve for our pastime, nor a transcendental melody to be evoked at our master touch. They reject us, because we have neither the forceful delusions of the flesh, nor the roseate illusions of fancy: we can neither break them on the wheel of our desire, nor melt them in the glow of our fervour to be cast in the mould of our ideal.

Because we know them only for what they are, they may be friendly, but cannot love us. We are their true refuge, for they can rely on our devotion; but our self-dedication comes so easy that they forget it has a price. So the only reward we get is to be used for their purposes; perchance to win their respect. But I am afraid my excursions into the region of psychology are merely due to personal grievances, which have my own experience behind them. The fact probably is, what we thus lose is really our gain,—anyway, that is how we may console ourselves.

Damini avoids the Master because she cannot bear him. She fights shy of Satish because for him her feelings are of the opposite description. I am the only person, near at hand, with whom there is no question either of love or hate. So whenever I am with her, Damini talks away to me of unimportant matters concerning the old days, the present times, or the daily happenings at the neighbours' houses. These talks usually take place on the shaded part of the roof-terrace, which serves as a passage between our several rooms on the second storey, where Damini sits slicing betel-nuts.

---

[21] garland of acceptance: In the old days, when a girl had to choose between several suitors, she signified her choice by putting a garland round the neck of the accepted one. [Translator]

What I could not understand was, how these trifling talks should have attracted the notice of Satish's emotion-clouded vision. Even suppose the circumstance was not so trifling, had I not often been told that, in the world where Satish dwelt, there were no such disturbing things as circumstances at all? The Mystic Union, in which personified cosmic forces were assisting, was an eternal drama, not an historical episode. Those who are rapt with the undying flute strains, borne along by the ceaseless zephyrs which play on the banks of the ever-flowing Jamuna[22] of that mystic paradise, have no eyes or ears left for the ephemeral doings immediately around them. This much at least is certain, that before our return from the cave, Satish used to be much denser in his perception of worldly events.

For this difference I may have been partly responsible. I also had begun to absent myself from our *kirtans* and discourses, perhaps with a frequency which could not elude even Satish. One day he came round on inquiry, and found me running after Damini's mongoose,—a recent acquisition,—trying to lure it into bondage with a pot of milk, which I had procured from the local milkman. This occupation, viewed as an excuse, was simply hopeless. It could easily have waited till the end of our sitting. For the matter of that, the best thing clearly would have been to leave the mongoose to its own devices, thus at one stroke demonstrating my adherence to the two principal tenets of our cult,—Compassion for all creatures, and Passion for the Lord.

That is why, when Satish came up, I had to feel ashamed. I put down the pot, then and there, and tried to edge away along the path which led back to self-respect.

But Damini's behaviour took me by surprise. She was not in the least abashed as she asked: "Where are you off to, Srivilas Babu?"

I scratched my head, as I mumbled: "I was thinking of joining the———"

"They must have finished by this time. Do sit down."

This coming from Damini, in the presence of Satish, made my ears burn.

Damini turned to Satish. "I am in awful trouble with the mongoose," she said. "Last night it stole a chicken from the Mussulman quarters over there. I dare not leave it loose any longer. Srivilas Babu has promised to look out for a nice big hamper to keep it in."

It seemed to me that it was my devotion to her which Damini was using the mongoose to show off. I was reminded how the Swami had given orders to Satish so as to impress me. The two were the same thing.

Satish made no reply, and his departure was somewhat abrupt. I gazed on Damini and could see her eyes flash out as they followed his disappearing figure; while on her lips there set a hard, enigmatic smile.

What conclusion Damini had come to she herself knew best; the only result apparent to me was that she began to send for me on all kinds of flimsy pretexts. Sometimes she would make sweetmeats, which she pressed on me. One day I could not help suggesting: "Let's offer some to Satish as well."

"That would only annoy him," said Damini.

---

[22]**Jamuna:** A major river in Bengal that flows into the Ganges.

And it happened that Satish, passing that way, caught me in the act of being thus regaled.

In the drama which was being played, the hero and the heroine spoke their parts "aside." I was the one character who, being of no consequence, had to speak out. This sometimes made me curse my lot; none the less, I could not withstand the temptation of the petty cash with which I was paid off, from day to day, for taking up the rôle of middleman.

3

For some days Satish clanged his cymbals and danced his *kirtans* with added vigour. Then one day he came to me and said: "We cannot keep Damini with us any longer."

"Why?" I asked.

"We must free ourselves altogether from the influence of women."

"If that be a necessity," said I, "there must be something radically wrong with our system."

Satish stared at me in amazement.

"Woman is a natural phenomenon," I continued, undaunted, "who will have her place in the world, however much we may try to get rid of her. If your spiritual welfare depends on ignoring her existence, then its pursuit will be like the chasing of a phantom, and will so put you to shame, when the illusion is gone, that you will not know where to hide yourself."

"Oh, stop your philosophising!" exclaimed Satish. "I was talking practical politics. It is only too evident that women are emissaries of Maya,[23] and at Maya's behest ply on us their blandishments,—for they cannot fulfil the design of their Mistress unless they overpower our reason. So we must steer clear of them if we would keep our intellect free."

I was about to make my reply, when Satish stopped me with a gesture, and went on: "Visri, old fellow! let me tell you plainly: if the hand of Maya is not visible to you, that is because you have allowed yourself to be caught in her net. The vision of beauty with which she has ensnared you to-day will vanish, and with the beauty will disappear the spectacles of desire, through which you now see it as greater than all the world. Where the noose of Maya is so glaringly obvious, why be foolhardy enough to take risks?"

"I admit all that," I rejoined. "But, my dear fellow, the all-pervading net of Maya was not cast by my hands, nor do I know the way to escape through it. Since we have not the power to evade Maya, our spiritual striving should help us, while acknowledging her, to rise above her. Because it does not take such a course, we have to flounder about in vain attempts to cut away the half of Truth."

"Well, well, let's have your idea a little more clearly," said Satish.

"We must sail the boat of our life," I proceeded, "along the current of nature, in order to reach beyond it. Our problem is, not how to get rid of this current, but

---

[23] **Maya:** Or Mahamaya, the Hindu goddess who produces illusions of sensory experience.

how to keep the boat afloat in its channel until it is through. For that, a rudder is necessary."

"You people who have ceased to be loyal to the Master,—how can I make you understand that in *him* we have just this rudder? You would regulate your spiritual life according to your own whims. That way death lies!" Satish went to the Master's chamber, and fell to tending his feet with fervour.

The same evening, when Satish lit the Master's pipe, he also put forward his plaint against Maya and her emissaries. The smoking of one pipe, however, did not suffice for its adjudication. Evening after evening, pipe after pipe was exhausted, yet the Master was unable to make up his mind.

From the very beginning Damini had given the Swami no end of trouble. Now the girl had managed to set up this eddy in the midst of the smooth course of the devotees' progress. But Shivatosh had thrown her and her belongings so absolutely on the Master's hands that he knew not how or where to cast her off. What made it more difficult still was that he harboured a secret fear of his ward.

And Satish, in spite of all the doubled and quadrupled enthusiasm which he put into his *kirtans,* in spite of all the pipe-filling and massaging in which he tried to rest his heart, was not allowed to forget for a moment that Maya had taken up her position right across the line of his spiritual advance.

One day some *kirtan* singers of repute had arrived, and were to sing in the evening at the temple next door. The *kirtan* would last far into the night. I managed to slip away after the preliminary overture, having no doubt that, in so thick a crowd, no one would notice my absence.

Damini that evening had completely thrown off her reserve. Things which are difficult to speak of, which refuse to leave one's choking throat, flowed from her lips so simply, so sweetly. It was as if she had suddenly come upon some secret recess in her heart, so long hidden away in darkness,—as if, by some strange chance, she had gained the opportunity to stand before her own self, face to face.

Just at this time Satish came up from behind and stood there hesitating, without our being aware of it at the moment. Not that Damini was saying anything very particular, but there were tears in her eyes,—all her words, in fact, were then welling up from some tear-flooded depth. When Satish arrived, the *kirtan* could not have been anywhere near its end. I divined that he must have been goaded with repeated inward urgings to have left the temple then.

As Satish came round into our view, Damini rose with a start, wiped her eyes, and made off towards her room. Satish, with a tremor in his voice, said: "Damini, will you listen to me? I would have a word with you."

Damini slowly retraced her steps, and came and sat down again. I made as though to take myself off, but an imploring glance from her restrained me from stirring. Satish, who seemed to have made some kind of effort meanwhile, came straight to the point.

"The need," said he to Damini, "which brought the rest of us to the Master, was not yours when you came to him."

"No," avowed Damini expectantly.

"Why, then, do you stay amongst his devotees?"

Damini's eyes flamed up as she cried: "Why do I stay? Because I did not come of my own accord! I was a helpless creature, and everyone knew my lack of faith. Yet I was bound hand and foot by your devotees in this dungeon of devotion. What avenue of escape have you left me?"

"We have now decided," stated Satish, "that if you would go to stay with some relative all your expenses will be found."

"You have decided, have you?"

"Yes."

"Well, then,—I have not!"

"Why, how will that inconvenience you?"

"Am I a pawn in your game, that you devotees should play me, now this way, now the other?"

Satish was struck dumb.

"I did not come," continued Damini, "wanting to please your devotees. And I am not going away at the bidding of the lot of you, merely because I don't happen to please you!"

Damini covered her face with her hands and burst out sobbing as she ran into her room and slammed the door.

Satish did not return to the *kirtan* singing. He sank down in a corner of the adjoining roof-terrace and brooded there in silence.

The sound of the breakers on the distant seashore came, wafted along the south breeze, like despairing sighs, rising up to the watching star clusters, from the very heart of the Earth.

I spent the night wandering round and round along the dark, deserted village lanes.

4

The World of Reality has made a determined onslaught on the Mystic Paradise, within the confines of which the Master sought to keep Satish and myself content by repeatedly filling for us the cup of symbolism with the nectar of idea. Now the clash of the actual with the symbolic bids fair to overturn the latter and spill its emotional contents in the dust. The Master is not blind to this danger.

Satish is no longer himself. Like a paper kite, with its regulating knot gone, he is still high in the skies, but may at any moment begin to gyrate groundwards. There is no falling off as yet in the outward rigour of his devotional and disciplinary exercises, but a closer scrutiny reveals the totter of weakening.

As for my condition, Damini has left nothing so vague in it as to require any guess-work. The more she notices the fear in the Master's face, and the pain in Satish's, the oftener she makes me dance attendance on her.

At last it came to this, that when we were engaged in talk with the Master, Damini would sometimes appear in the doorway and interrupt us with: "Srivilas Babu, would you mind coming over this way?" without even condescending to add what I was wanted for.

The Swami would glance up at me; Satish would glance up at me; I would hesitate for a moment between them and her; then I would glance up at the door,—and in a trice I was off the fence and out of the room. An effort would be made, after my exit, to go on with the talk, but the effort would soon get the better of the talk, whereupon the latter would stop.

Everything seemed to be falling to pieces around us. The old compactness was gone.

We two had come to be the pillars of the sect. The Master could not give up either of us without a struggle. So he ventured once more to make an overture to Damini. "My little mother," said he, "the time is coming for us to proceed to the more arduous part of our journey. You had better return from here."

"Return where?"

"Home, to your aunt."

"That cannot be."

"Why?" asked the Swami.

"First of all," said Damini, "she is not my own aunt at all. Why should she bear my burden?"

"All your expenses shall be borne by us."

"Expenses are not the only burden. It is no part of her duty to be saddled with looking after me."

"But, Damini," urged the Swami in his desperation, "can I keep you with me for ever?"

"Is that a question for me to answer?"

"But where will you go when I am dead?"

"I was never allowed," returned Damini icily, "to have the responsibility of thinking that out. I have been made to realise too well that in this world I have neither home nor property; nothing at all to call my own. That is what makes my burden so heavy to bear. It pleased you to take it up. You shall not now cast it on another!"

Damini went off.

"Lord, have mercy!" sighed the Swami.

Damini had laid on me the command to procure for her some good Bengali books. I need hardly say that by "good" Damini did not mean spiritual, of the quality affected by our sect. Nor need I pause to make it clear that Damini had no compunction in asking anything from me. It has not taken her long to find out that making demands on me was the easiest way of making me amends. Some kinds of trees are all the better for being pruned: that was the kind of person I seemed to be where Damini was concerned.

Well, the books I ordered were unmitigatedly modern. The author was distinctly less influenced by Manu[24] than by Man himself. The packet was delivered by the postman to the Swami. He raised his eyebrows, as he opened it, and asked: "Hullo, Srivilas, what are these for?"

I remained silent.

The Master gingerly turned over some of the pages, as he remarked for my benefit that he had never thought much of the author, having failed to find in his writings the correct spiritual flavour.

---

[24] Manu: The Hindu law-giver. [Translator]

"If you read them carefully, sir," I suddenly blurted out, "you will find his writings not to be lacking in the flavour of Truth." The fact is, rebellion had been long brewing within me. I was feeling done to death with mystic emotion. I was nauseated with shedding tears over abstract human feelings, to the neglect of living human creatures.

The Master blinked at me curiously before he replied: "Very well, my son, carefully read them I will." He tucked the books away under the bolster on which he reclined. I could perceive that his idea was not to surrender them to me.

Damini, from behind the door, must have got wind of this, for at once she stepped in and asked: "Haven't the books you ordered for me arrived yet?"

I remained silent.

"My little mother!" said the Swami. "These books are not fit for you to read."

"How should you know that?"

The Master frowned. "How, at least, could you know better?"

"I have read the author: you, perhaps, have not."

"Why, then, need you read him over again?"

"When *you* have any need," Damini flared up, "nothing is allowed to stand in *your* way. It is only I who am to have no needs!"

"You forget yourself, Damini. I am a *sannyasin*. I have no worldly desires."

"You forget that I am not a *sannyasin*. I have a desire to read these books. Will you kindly let me have them?"

The Swami drew out the books from under his bolster and tossed them across to me. I handed them over to Damini.

In the end, the books that Damini would have read alone by herself, she now began to send for me to read out to her. It was in that same shaded veranda along our rooms that these readings took place. Satish passed and repassed, longing to join in, but could not, unasked.

One day we had come upon a humorous passage, and Damini was rocking with laughter. There was a festival on at the temple and we had supposed that Satish would be there. But we heard a door open behind, through which Satish unexpectedly appeared and came and sat down beside us.

Damini's laughter was at once cut short. I also felt awkward. I wanted badly to say something to Satish, but no words would come, and I went on silently turning over page after page of my book. He rose, and left as abruptly as he had come. Our reading made no further progress that day.

Satish may very likely have understood that while he envied the absence of reserve between Damini and me, its presence was just what I envied in his case. That same day he petitioned the Master to be allowed to go off on a solitary excursion along the sea-coast, promising to be back within a week. "The very thing, my son!" acquiesced the Swami, with enthusiasm.

Satish departed. Damini did not send for me to read to her any more, nor had she anything else to ask of me. Neither did I see her going to her friends, the women of the neighbourhood. She kept her room, with closed doors.

Some days passed thus. One afternoon, when the Master was deep in his siesta, and I was writing a letter seated out on our veranda, Satish suddenly turned up.

Without so much as a glance at me, he walked straight up to Damini's door, knocking as he called: "Damini, Damini."

Damini came out at once. A strangely altered Satish met her inquiring gaze. Like a storm-battered ship, with torn rigging and tattered sails, was his condition, — eyes wild, hair dishevelled, features drawn, garments dusty.

"Damini," said Satish, "I asked you to leave us. That was wrong of me. I beg your forgiveness."

"Oh, don't say that," cried the distressed Damini, clasping her hands.

"You must forgive me," he repeated. "I will never again allow that pride to overcome me, which led me to think I could take you or leave you, according to my own spiritual requirements. Such sin will never cross my mind again, I promise you. Do you also promise me one thing?"

"Command me!" said Damini, making humble obeisance.

"You must join us, and not keep aloof like this."

"I will join you," said Damini. "I will sin no more." Then, as she bowed low again to take the dust of his feet, she repeated, "I will sin no more."

5

The stone was melted again. Damini's bewildering radiance remained undimmed, but it lost its heat. In worship and ritual and service her beauty blossomed out anew. She was never absent from the *kirtan* singing, nor when the Master gave his readings and discourses. There was a change in her raiment also. She reverted to the golden brown of plain tussore,[25] and whenever we saw her she seemed fresh from her toilet.

The severest test came in her intercourse with the Master. When she made her salutation to him, I could catch the glint of severely repressed temper through her half-closed eyelids. I knew very well that she could not bear to take orders from the Master; nevertheless, so complete was her self-suppression, that the Swami was able to screw up the courage to repeat his condemnation of the obnoxious tone of that outrageously modern Bengali writer. The next day there was a heap of flowers near his seat, and under them were the torn pages of the books of the objectionable author.

I had always noticed that the attendance on the Master by Satish was specially intolerable to Damini. Even now, when the Master asked him for some personal service, Damini would try to hustle past Satish and forestall him. This, however, was not possible in every case; and while Satish kept blowing on the tinder to get it into a blaze for the Master's pipe, Damini would have much ado to keep herself in hand by grimly repeating under her breath, "I will sin no more. I will sin no more."

---

[25] **plain tussore:** The tussore silk-worm is a wild variety, and its cocoon has to be used after the moth has cut its way out and flown away, thus not being killed in the process of unwinding the silk. Hence tussore silk is deemed specially suitable for wear on occasions of divine worship. [Translator]

But what Satish had tried for did not come off. On the last occasion of Damini's self-surrender, he had seen the beauty of the surrender only, not of the self behind it. This time Damini herself had become so true for him that she eclipsed all strains of music, and all thoughts of philosophy. Her reality had become so dominant that Satish could no longer lose himself in his visions, nor think of her merely as an aspect of Universal Woman. It was not she who, as before, set off for him the melodies which filled his mind; rather, these melodies had now become part of the halo which encircled her person.

I should not, perhaps, leave out the minor detail that Damini had no longer any use for me. Her demands on me had suddenly ceased altogether. Of my colleagues, who used to assist in beguiling her leisure, the kite was dead, the mongoose had escaped, and as for the mongrel puppy, its manners having offended the Master's susceptibilities, it had been given away. Thus, bereft both of occupation and companionship, I returned to my old place in the assembly surrounding the Master, though the talking and singing and doing that went on there had all alike become horribly distasteful to me.

6

The laboratory of Satish's mind was not amenable to any outside laws. One day, as he was compounding therein, for my special benefit, a weird mixture of ancient philosophy and modern science, with reason as well as emotion promiscuously thrown in, Damini burst in upon us, panting:

"Oh, do come, both of you, come quick!"

"Whatever is the matter?" I cried, as I leapt up.

"Nabin's wife has taken poison, I think," she said.

Nabin was a neighbour, one of our regular *kirtan* singers—an ardent disciple. We hurried after Damini, but when we arrived his wife was dead.

We pieced together her story. Nabin's wife had brought her motherless younger sister to live with them. She was a very pretty girl, and when Nabin's brother had last been home, he was so taken with her that their marriage was speedily arranged. This greatly relieved her elder sister, for, high caste as they were, a suitable bridegroom was not easy to find. The wedding-day had been fixed some months later, when Nabin's brother would have completed his college course. Meanwhile Nabin's wife lit upon the discovery that her husband had seduced her sister. She forthwith insisted on his marrying the unfortunate girl,—for which, as it happened, he did not require much persuasion. The wedding ceremony had just been put through, whereupon the elder sister had made away with herself by taking poison.

There was nothing to be done. The three of us slowly wended our way back, to find the usual throng round the Master. They sang a *kirtan* to him, and he waxed ecstatic in his usual manner, and began to dance with them.

That evening the moon was near its full. One corner of our terrace was overhung by the branch of a *chalta* tree. At the edge of the shadow, under its thick foliage, sat Damini lost in silent thought. Satish was softly pacing up and down our veranda behind her. I had a hobby for diary-writing, in which I was indulging, alone in my room, with the door wide open.

That evening the *koil* [26] could not sleep; stirred by the south breeze the leaves too were speaking out, and the moonlight, shimmering on them, smiled in response. Something must also have stirred within Satish, for he suddenly turned his steps towards the terrace and went and stood near Damini.

Damini looked round with a start, adjusted her *sari* [27] over the back of her head, and rose as if to leave. Satish called, "Damini!"

She stopped at once, and turning to him appealingly with folded hands she said, "My Master, may I ask you a question?"

Satish looked at her inquiringly, but made no reply.

Damini went on: "Tell me truly, of what use to the world is this thing with which your sect is occupied day and night? Whom have you been able to save?"

I came out from my room and stood on the veranda.

Damini continued: "This passion, passion, passion on which you harp,—did you not see it in its true colours to-day? It has neither religion nor duty; it regards neither wife nor brother, nor the sanctuary of home; it knows neither pity nor trust, nor modesty, nor shame. What way have you discovered to save men from the hell of this cruel, shameless, soul-killing passion?"

I could not contain myself, but cried out: "Oh yes, we have hit upon the wonderful device of banishing Woman right away from our territory, so as to make our pursuit of passion quite safe!"

Without paying any heed to my words, Damini spoke on to Satish: "I have learnt nothing at all from your Master. He has never given me one moment's peace of mind. Fire cannot quench fire. The road along which he is taking his devotees leads neither to courage, nor restraint, nor peace. That poor woman who is dead,—her heart's blood was sucked dry by this Fury, Passion, who killed her. Did you not see the hideous countenance of the murderess? For God's sake, my Master, I implore you, do not sacrifice me to that Fury. Oh, save me, for if anybody can save me, it is you!"

For a space all three of us kept silent. So poignant became the silence all around, it seemed to me that the vibrating drone of the *cicadas* was but a swoon-thrill of the pallid sky.

Satish was the first to speak. "Tell me," said he to Damini, "what is it you would have me do for you?"

"Be my *guru*! I would follow none else. Give me some creed—higher than all this—which can save me. Do not let me be destroyed, together with the Divinity which is in me."

Satish drew himself up straight, as he responded: "So be it."

Damini prostrated herself at his feet, her forehead touching the ground, and remained long thus, in reverential adoration, murmuring: "Oh, my Master, my Master, save me, save me, save me from all sin."

---

[26] **koil:** A bird with a hooting call.

[27] **adjusted her *sari*:** A formal recognition of the presence of an elder. [Translator]

7

Once more there was a mighty sensation in our world, and a storm of vitupera-tion in the newspapers—for Satish had again turned renegade.

At first he had defiantly proclaimed active disbelief in all religion and social con-vention. Next, with equal vehemence, he had displayed active belief in gods and god-desses, rites and ceremonies, not excluding the least of them. Now, lastly, he had thrown to the winds all the rubbish-heaps both of religious and irreligious cults, and had retired into such simple peacefulness that no one could even guess what he believed, or what he did not. True, he took up good works as of old; but there was nothing aggressive about it this time.

There was another event over which the newspapers exhausted all their re-sources of sarcasm and virulence. That was the announcement of Damini's marriage with me. The mystery of this marriage none will perhaps fathom,—but why need they?

Chapter IV
Srivilas

1

There was once an indigo factory on this spot. All that now remains of it are some tumble-down rooms belonging to the old house, the rest having crumbled into dust. When returning homewards, after performing Damini's last rites, the place, as we passed by it, somehow appealed to me, and I stayed on alone.

The road leading from the river-side to the factory gate is flanked by an avenue of *sissoo* trees. Two broken pillars still mark the site of the gateway, and portions of the garden wall are standing here and there. The only other memento of the past is the brick-built mound over the grave of some Mussulman servant of the factory. Through its cracks, wild flowering shrubs have sprung up. Covered with blossoms, they sway to the breeze and mock at death, like merry maidens shaking with laugh-ter while they chaff the bridegroom on his wedding-day. The banks of the garden pool have caved in and let the water trickle away, leaving the bottom to serve as a bed for a coriander patch. As I sit out on the roadside, under the shade of the avenue, the scent of the coriander, in flower, goes through and through my brain.

I sit and muse. The factory, of which these remnants are left, like the skeleton of some dead animal by the wayside, was once alive. From it flowed waves of pleasure and pain in a stormy succession, which then seemed to be endless. Its terribly effi-cient English proprietor, who made the very blood of his sweating cultivators run indigo-blue,—how tremendous was he compared to puny me! Nevertheless, Mother Earth girded up her green mantle, undismayed, and set to work so thor-oughly to plaster over the disfigurement wrought by him and his activities, that the few remaining traces require but a touch or two more to vanish for ever.

This scarcely novel reflection, however, was not what my mind ruminated over. "No, no!" it protested. "One dawn does not succeed another merely to smear fresh plaster[28] over the floor. True, the Englishman of the factory, together with the rest of its abominations, are all swept away into oblivion like a handful of dust,—but my Damini!"

Many will not agree with me, I know. Shankaracharya's[29] philosophy spares no one. All the world is *maya,* a trembling dewdrop on the lotus leaf. But Shankaracharya was a *sannyasin.* "Who is your wife, who your son?" were questions he asked, without understanding their meaning. Not being a *sannyasin* myself, I know full well that Damini is not a vanishing dewdrop on the lotus leaf.

But, I am told, there are householders also, who say the same thing. That may be. They are mere householders, who have lost only the mistress of their house. Their home is doubtless *maya,* and so likewise is its mistress. These are their own handiwork, and when done with any broom is good enough for sweeping their fragments clean away.

I did not keep house long enough to settle down as a householder, nor is mine the temperament of a *sannyasin,*—that saved me. So the Damini whom I gained became neither housewife nor *maya.* She ever remained true to herself,—my Damini. Who dares to call her a shadow?

Had I known Damini only as mistress of my house, much of this would never have been written. It is because I knew her in a greater, truer relation, that I have no hesitation in putting down the whole truth, recking nothing of what others may say.

Had it been my lot to live with Damini, as others do in the everyday world, the household routine of toilet and food and repose would have sufficed for me as for them. And after Damini's death, I could have heaved a sigh and exclaimed with Shankaracharya: "Variegated is the world of *maya!*" before hastening to honour the suggestion of some aunt, or other well-meaning elder, by another attempt to sample its variety by marrying again. But I had not adjusted myself to the domestic world, like a foot in a comfortable old shoe. From the very outset I had given up hope of happiness,—no, no, that is saying too much; I was not so non-human as that. Happiness I certainly hoped for, but I did not arrogate to myself the right to claim it.

Why? Because it was I who persuaded Damini to give her consent to our marriage. Not for us was the first auspicious vision[30] in the rosy glow of festive lamps, to the rapturous strains of wedding pipes. We married in the broad light of day, with eyes wide open.

2

When we went away from Lilananda Swami, the time came to think of ways and means, as well as of a sheltering roof. We had all along been more in danger of surfeit

---

[28] **smear fresh plaster:** The wattle-and-daub cottages of a Bengal village are cleaned and renovated every morning by a moist clay mixture being smeared by the housewife over the plinth and floors. [Translator]

[29] **Shankaracharya:** Or Shankara, an eighth-century Hindu theologian, sometimes said to be the founder of the principal sects of Hinduism.

[30] **auspicious vision:** At one stage of the wedding ceremony a red screen is placed round the Bride and Bridegroom, and they are asked to look at each other. This is the Auspicious Vision. [Translator]

than of starvation, with the hospitality which the devotees of the Master pressed on us, wherever we went with him. We had almost come to forget that to be a house-holder involves the acquiring, or building, or at least the renting of a house, so accustomed had we become to cast the burden of its supply upon another, and to look on a house as demanding from us only the duty of making ourselves thoroughly comfortable in it.

At length we recollected that Uncle Jagamohan had bequeathed his share of the house to Satish. Had the will been left in Satish's custody, it would by this time have been wrecked, like a paper boat, on the waves of his emotion. It happened, however, to be with me; for I was the executor. There were three conditions attached to the bequest which I was responsible for carrying out. No religious worship was to be performed in the house. The ground floor was to be used as a school for the leather-dealers' children. And after Satish's death, the whole property was to be applied for the benefit of that community. Piety was the one thing Uncle Jagamohan could not tolerate. He looked on it as more defiling even than worldliness; and probably these provisions, which he facetiously referred to in English as "sanitary precautions," were intended as a safeguard against the excessive piety which prevailed in the adjoining half of the house.

"Come along," I said to Satish. "Let's go to your Calcutta house."

"I am not quite ready for that yet," Satish replied.

I did not understand him.

"There was a day," he explained, "when I relied wholly on reason, only to find at last that reason could not support the whole of life's burden. There was another day, when I placed my reliance on emotion, only to discover it to be a bottomless abyss. The reason and the emotion, you see, were alike mine. Man cannot rely on himself alone. I dare not return to town until I have found my support."

"What then do you suggest?" I asked.

"You two go on to the Calcutta house. I would wander alone for a time. I seem to see glimpses of the shore. If I allow it out of my sight now, I may lose it for ever."

As soon as we were by ourselves, Damini said to me: "That will never do! If he wanders about alone, who is to look after him? Don't you remember in what plight he came back when he last went wandering? The very idea of it fills me with fear."

Shall I tell the truth? This anxiety of Damini's stung me like a hornet, leaving behind the smart of anger. Had not Satish wandered about for two whole years after Uncle Jagamohan's death,—had that killed him? My question did not remain unuttered. Rather, some of the smart of the sting got expressed with it.

"I know, Srivilas Babu," Damini replied. "It takes a great deal to kill a man. But why should he be allowed to suffer at all, so long as the two of us are here to prevent it?"

The two of us! Half of that meant this wretched creature, Srivilas! It is of course a law of the world, that in order to save some people from suffering others shall suffer. All the inhabitants of the earth may be divided into two such classes. Damini had found out to which I belonged. It was compensation, indeed, that she included herself in the same class.

I went and said to Satish: "All right, then, let us postpone our departure to town. We can stay for a time in that dilapidated house on the river-side. They say it is subject to ghostly visitations. This will serve to keep off human visitors."

"And you two?" inquired Satish.

"Like the ghosts, we shall keep in hiding as far as possible."

Satish threw a nervous glance at Damini,—there may have been a suggestion of dread in it.

Damini clasped her hands as she said imploringly: "I have accepted you as my *guru*. Whatever my sins may have been, let them not deprive me of the right to serve you."

3

I must confess that this frenzied pertinacity of Satish's quest is beyond my understanding. There was a time when I would have laughed to scorn the very idea. Now I had ceased to laugh. What Satish was pursuing was fire indeed, no will-o'-the-wisp. When I realised how its heat was consuming him, the old arguments of Uncle Jagamohan's school refused to pass my lips. Of what avail would it be to find, with Herbert Spencer, that the mystic sense might have originated in some ghostly superstition, or that its message could be reduced to some logical absurdity? Did we not see how Satish was burning,—his whole being aglow?

Satish was perhaps better off when his days were passing in one round of excitement,—singing, dancing, serving the Master,—the whole of his spiritual effort exhausting itself in the output of the moment. Since he has lapsed into outward quiet, his spirit refuses to be controlled any longer. There is now no question of seeking emotional satisfaction. The inward struggle for realisation is so tremendous within him, that we are afraid to look on his face.

I could remain silent no longer. "Satish," I suggested, "don't you think it would be better to go to some *guru* who could show you the way and make your spiritual progress easier?"

This only served to annoy him. "Oh, do be quiet, Visri," he broke out irritably. "For goodness' sake keep quiet! What does one want to make it easier for? Delusion alone is easy. Truth is always difficult."

"But would it not be better," I tried again, "if some *guru* were to guide you along the path of Truth?"

Satish was almost beside himself. "Will you never understand," he groaned, "that I am not running after any geographical truth? The Dweller within can only come to me along my own true path. The path of the *guru* can only lead to the *guru's* door."

What a number of opposite principles have I heard enunciated by this same mouth of Satish! I, Srivilas, once the favourite disciple of Uncle Jagamohan,—who would have threatened me with a big stick if I had called him Master,—had actually been made by Satish to massage the legs of Lilananda Swami. And now not even a week has passed but he needs must preach to me in this strain! However, as I dared not smile, I maintained a solemn silence.

"I have now understood," Satish went on, "why our Scriptures say that it is better to die in one's own *dharma*[31] rather than court the terrible fate of taking the *dharma* of another. All else may be accepted as gifts, but if one's *dharma* is not one's own, it does not save, but kills. I cannot gain my God as alms from anybody else. If I get Him at all, it shall be I who win Him. If I do not, even death is better."

I am argumentative by nature, and could not give in so easily. "A poet," said I, "may get a poem from within himself. But he who is not a poet needs must take it from another."

"I am a poet," said Satish, without blenching.

That finished the matter. I came away.

Satish had no regular hours for meals or sleep. There was no knowing where he was to be found next. His body began to take on the unsubstantial keenness of an over-sharpened knife. One felt this could not go on much longer. Yet I could not muster up courage to interfere. Damini, however, was utterly unable to bear it. She was grievously incensed at God's ways. With those who ignored Him, God was powerless, — was it fair thus to take it out of one who was helplessly prostrate at His feet? When Damini used to wax wroth with Lilananda Swami, she knew how to bring it home to him. Alas, she knew not how to bring her feelings home to God!

Anyhow, she spared no pains in trying to get Satish to be regular in satisfying his physical needs. Numberless and ingenious were her contrivances to get this misfit creature to conform to domestic regulations. For a considerable space Satish made no overt objection to her endeavours. But one morning he waded across the shallow river to the broad sand-bed along the opposite bank, and there disappeared from sight.

The sun rose to the meridian; it gradually bent over to the west; but there was no sign of Satish. Damini waited for him, fasting, till she could contain herself no longer. She put some food on a salver, and with it toiled through the knee-deep water, and at last found herself on the sand-bank.

It was a vast expanse on which not a living creature of any kind was to be seen. The sun was cruel. Still more so were the glowing billows of sand, one succeeding the other, like ranks of crouching sentinels guarding the emptiness. As she stood on the edge of this spreading pallor, where all limits seemed to have been lost, where no call could meet with any response, no question with any answer, Damini's heart sank within her. It was as if her world had been wiped away and reduced to the dull blank of original colourlessness. One vast "No" seemed to be stretched at her feet. No sound, no movement, no red of blood, no green of vegetation, no blue of sky, — but only the drab of sand. It looked like the lipless grin of some giant skull, the tongueless cavern of its jaws gaping with an eternal petition of thirst to the unrelenting fiery skies above.

While she was wondering in what direction to proceed, the faint track of footsteps caught Damini's eye. These she pursued, and went on and on, over the undulating surface, till they stopped at a pool on the farther side of a sand-drift. Along the

---

[31] *dharma:* A key concept in Hinduism with many meanings. In this passage, it refers to the essential quality of one's nature.

moist edge of the water could be seen the delicate tracery of the claw-marks of innu-merable water-fowl. Under the shade of the sand-drift sat Satish.

The water was the deepest of deep blue. The fussy snipe were poking about on its margin, bobbing their tails and fluttering their black-and-white wings. At some distance were a flock of wild duck quacking vigorously, and seeming never to get the preening of their feathers done to their own satisfaction. When Damini reached the top of the mound, which formed one bank of the pool, the ducks took themselves off in a body, with a great clamour and beating of wings.

Satish looked round and saw Damini. "Why are you here?" he cried.

"I have brought you something to eat," said Damini.

"I want nothing," said Satish.

"It is very late———" ventured Damini.

"Nothing at all," repeated Satish.

"Let me then wait a little," suggested Damini. "Perhaps later on———?"

"Oh, why will you———" burst out Satish, but as his glance fell on Damini's face he stopped short.

Damini said nothing further. Tray in hand she retraced her steps through the sand, which glared round her like the eye of a tiger in the dark.

Tears had always been rarer in Damini's eyes than lightning flashes. But when I saw her that evening,—seated on the floor, her feet stretched out before her,—she was weeping. When she saw me her tears seemed to burst through some obstruction and showered forth in torrents. I cannot tell what it felt like within my breast. I came near and sat down on one side.

When she had calmed herself a little I inquired: "Why does Satish's health make you so anxious?"

"What else have I to be anxious about?" she asked simply. "All the rest he has to think out for himself. There I can neither understand nor help."

"But consider, Damini," I said. "When man's mind puts forth all its energy into one particular channel, his bodily needs become reduced correspondingly. That is why, in the presence of great joy or great sorrow, man does not hunger or thirst. Satish's state of mind is now such that it will do him no harm even if you do not look after his body."

"I am a woman," replied Damini. "The building up of the body with our own body, with our life itself, is our *dharma*. It is woman's own creation. So when we women see the body suffer, our spirit refuses to be comforted."

"That is why," I retorted, "those who are busy with things of the spirit seem to have no eyes for you, the guardians of mere bodies!"

"Haven't they!" Damini flared up. "So wonderful, rather, is the vision of their eyes, it turns everything topsy-turvy."

"Ah, woman," said I to myself. "That is what fascinates you. Srivilas, my boy, next time you take birth, take good care to be born in the world of topsy-turvydom."

4

The wound which Satish inflicted on Damini that day on the sands had this result, that he could not remove from his mind the agony he had seen in her eyes.

During the succeeding days he had to go through the purgatory of showing her special consideration. It was long since he had freely conversed with us. Now he would send for Damini and talk to her. The experiences and struggles through which he was passing were the subject of these talks.

Damini had never been so exercised by his indifference as she now was by his solicitude. She felt sure this could not last, because the cost was too much to pay. Some day or other Satish's attention would be drawn to the state of the account, and he would discover how high the price was; then would come the crash. The more regular Satish became in his meals and rest, as a good householder should, the more anxious became Damini, the more she felt ashamed of herself. It was almost as if she would be relieved to find Satish becoming rebellious. She seemed to be saying: "You were quite right to hold aloof. Your concern for me is only punishing yourself. That I cannot bear!—I must," she appeared to conclude, "make friends with the neighbours again, and see if I cannot contrive to keep away from the house."

One night we were roused by a sudden shout: "Srivilas! Damini!" It must have been past midnight, but Satish could not have taken count of the hour. How he passed his nights we knew not, but the way he went on seemed to have cowed the very ghosts into flight.

We shook off our slumbers, and came out of our respective rooms to find Satish on the flagged pavement in front of the house, standing alone in the darkness. "I have understood!" he exclaimed as he saw us. "I have no more doubts."

Damini softly went up and sat down on the pavement. Satish absently followed her example and sat down too. I also followed suit.

"If I keep going," said Satish, "in the same direction along which He comes to me, then I shall only be going further and further away from Him. If I proceed in the opposite direction, then only can we meet."

I silently gazed at his flaming eyes. As a geometrical truth what he said was right enough. But what in the world was it all about?

"He loves form," Satish went on, "so He is continually descending towards form. We cannot live by form alone, so we must ascend towards His formlessness. He is free, so His play is within bonds. We are bound, so we find our joy in freedom. All our sorrow is because we cannot understand this."

We kept as silent as the stars.

"Do you not understand, Damini?" pursued Satish. "He who sings proceeds from his joy to the tune; he who hears, from the tune to joy. One comes from freedom into bondage, the other goes from bondage into freedom; only thus can they have their communion. He sings and we hear. He ties the bonds as He sings to us, we untie them as we hear Him."

I cannot say whether Damini understood Satish's words, but she understood Satish. With her hands folded on her lap she kept quite still.

"I was hearing His song through the night," Satish went on, "till in a flash the whole thing became clear to me. Then I could not keep it to myself, and called out to you. All this time I had been trying to fashion Him to suit myself, and so was deprived.—O Desolator! Breaker of ties! Let me be shattered to pieces within you, again and again, for ever and ever. Bonds are not for me, that is why I cannot hold on to bonds for long. Bonds are yours, and so are you kept eternally bound to creation. Play on, then, with our forms and let me take my flight into your formlessness.—O Eternal, you are mine, mine, mine!"—Satish departed into the night towards the river.

After that night, Satish lapsed back into his old ways, forgetful of all claims of rest or nourishment. As to when his mind would rise into the light of ecstasy, or lapse into the depths of gloom, we could make no guess. May God help her who has taken on herself the burden of keeping such a creature within the wholesomeness of worldly habit. . . .

5

It had been stiflingly oppressive the whole day. In the night a great storm burst on us. We had our several rooms along a veranda, in which a light used to be kept burning all night. That was now blown out. The river was lashed into foaming waves, and a flood of rain burst forth from the clouds. The splashing of the waves down below, and the dashing of the torrents from above, played the cymbals in this chaotic revel of the gods. Nothing could be seen of the deafening movements which resounded within the depths of the darkness, and made the sky, like a blind child, break into shivers of fright. Out of the bamboo thickets pierced a scream as of some bereaved giantess. From the mango groves burst the cracking and crashing of breaking timber. The river-side echoed with the deep thuds of falling masses from the crumbling banks. Through the bare ribs of our dilapidated house the keen blasts howled and howled like infuriated beasts.

On such a night the fastenings of the human mind are shaken loose. The storm gains entry and plays havoc within, scattering into disorder its well-arranged furniture of convention, tossing about its curtains of decorous restraint in disturbing revealment. I could not sleep. But what can I write of the thoughts which assailed my sleepless brain? They do not concern this story.

"Who is that?" I heard Satish cry out all of a sudden in the darkness.

"It is I,—Damini," came the reply. "Your windows are open, and the rain is streaming in. I have come to close them."

As she was doing this, she found Satish had got out of his bed. He seemed to stand and hesitate, just for a moment, and then he went out of the room.

Damini went back to her own room and sat long on the threshold. No one returned. The fury of the wind went on increasing in violence.

Damini could sit quiet no longer. She also left the house. It was hardly possible to keep on one's feet in the storm. The sentinels of the revelling gods seemed to be scolding Damini and repeatedly thrusting her back. The rain made desperate attempts to pervade every nook and cranny of the sky.

A flash rent the sky from end to end with terrific tearing thunder. It revealed Satish standing on the river brink. With a supreme effort Damini reached him in one tempestuous rush, outvying the wind. She fell prone at his feet. The shriek of the storm was overcome by her cry: "At your feet, I swear I had no thought of sin against your God! Why punish me thus?"

Satish stood silent.

"Thrust me into the river with your feet, if you would be rid of me. But return you must!"

Satish came back. As he re-entered the house he said: "My need for Him whom I seek is immense, — so absolutely, that I have no need for anything else at all. Damini, have pity on me and leave me to Him."

After a space of silence Damini said: "I will."

6

I knew nothing of this at the time, but heard it all from Damini afterwards. So when I saw through my open door the two returning figures pass along the veranda to their rooms, the desolation of my lot fell heavy on my heart and took me by the throat. I struggled up from my bed. Further sleep was impossible that night.

Next morning, what a changed Damini met my eyes! The demon dance of last night's storm seemed to have left all its ravages on this one forlorn girl. Though I knew nothing of what had happened, I felt bitterly angry with Satish.

"Srivilas Babu," said Damini, "will you take me on to Calcutta?"

I could guess all that these words meant for her; so I asked no question. But, in the midst of the torture within me, I felt the balm of consolation. It was well that Damini should take herself away from here. Repeated buffeting against the rock could only end in the vessel being broken up.

At parting, Damini made her obeisance to Satish, saying: "I have grievously sinned at your feet. May I hope for pardon?"

Satish, with his eyes fixed on the ground, replied: "I also have sinned. Let me first purge my sin away, and then will I claim forgiveness."

It became clear to me, on our way to Calcutta, what a devastating fire had all along been raging within Damini. I was so scorched by its heat that I could not restrain myself from breaking out in revilement of Satish.

Damini stopped me frenziedly. "Don't you dare talk so in my presence!" she exclaimed. "Little do you know what he saved me from! You can only see my sorrow. Had you no eyes for the sorrow he has been through, in order to save me? The hideous tried once to destroy the beautiful, and got well kicked for its pains. — Serve it right! — Serve it right!" — Damini began to beat her breast violently with her clenched hands. I had to hold them back by main force.

When we arrived in the evening, I left Damini at her aunt's and went over to a lodging-house, where I used to be well known. My old acquaintances started at sight of me. "Have you been ill?" they cried.

By next morning's post I got a letter from Damini. "Take me away," she wrote. "There is no room for me here."

It appeared that her aunt would not have her. Scandal about us was all over the town. The Pooja numbers of the weekly newspapers had come out shortly after we had given up Lilananda Swami. All the instruments for our execution had been kept sharpened. The carnage turned out to be worthy of the occasion. In our *shastras*[32] the

---

[32] *shastras:* Hindu scriptures.

sacrifice of she-animals is prohibited. But, in the case of modern human sacrifice, a woman victim seems to add to the zest of the performers. The mention of Damini's name was skilfully avoided. But no less was the skill which did away with all doubt as to the intention. Anyhow, it had resulted in this shrinkage of room in the house of Damini's distant aunt.

Damini had lost her parents. But I had an idea that her brother was living. I asked Damini for his address, but she shook her head, saying they were too poor. The fact was, Damini did not care to place her brother in an awkward position. What if he also came to say there was no room?

"Where will you stay, then?" I had to inquire.

"I will go back to Lilananda Swami."

I could not trust myself to speak for a time, — I was so overcome. Was this, then, the last cruel trick which Fate had held in reserve?

"Will the Swami take you back?" I asked at length.

"Gladly!"

Damini understood men. Sect-mongers rejoice more in capturing adherents than in comprehending truths. Damini was quite right. There would be no dearth of room for her at Lilananda's, but———

"Damini," I said, just at this juncture. "There is another way. If you promise not to be angry, I will mention it."

"Tell me," said Damini.

"If it is at all possible for you to think of marrying a creature, such as I am———"

"What are you saying, Srivilas Babu?" interrupted Damini. "Are you mad?"

"Suppose I am," said I. "One can sometimes solve insoluble problems by becoming mad. Madness is like the wishing carpet of the *Arabian Nights*. It can waft one over the thousand petty considerations which obstruct the everyday world."

"What do you call petty considerations?"

"Such as: What will people think? — What will happen in the future? — and so on, and so forth."

"And what about the vital considerations?"

"What do you call vital?" I asked in my turn.

"Such as, for instance: What will be your fate if you marry a creature like me?" said Damini.

"If that be a vital consideration, I am reassured. For I cannot possibly be in a worse plight than now. Any movement of my prostrate fortune, even though it be a turning over to the other side, cannot but be a sign of improvement."

Of course I could not believe that some telepathic news of my state of mind had never reached Damini. Such news, however, had not, so far, come under the head of "Important" — at least it had not called for any notice to be taken. Now action was definitely demanded of her.

Damini was lost in silent thought.

"Damini," I said, "I am only one of the very ordinary sort of men, — even less, for I am of no account in the world. To marry me, or not to marry me, cannot make enough difference to be worth all this thought."

Tears glistened in Damini's eyes. "Had you been an ordinary man, it would not have cost me a moment's hesitation," she said.

After another long silence, Damini murmured: "You know what I am."

"You also know what I am," I rejoined.

Thus was the proposal mooted, relying more on things unspoken than on what was said.

7

Those who, in the old days, had been under the spell of my English speeches had mostly shaken off their fascination during my absence; except only Naren, who still looked on me as one of the rarest products of the age. A house belonging to him was temporarily vacant. In this we took shelter.

It seemed at first that my proposal would never be rescued from the ditch of silence, into which it had lumbered at the very start; or at all events that it would require any amount of discussion and repair work before it could be hauled back on the high road of "yes" or "no."

But man's mind was evidently created to raise a laugh against mental science, with its sudden practical jokes. In the spring, which now came upon us, the Creator's joyous laughter rang through and through this hired dwelling of ours.

All this while Damini never had the time to notice that I was anybody at all; or it may be that the dazzling light from a different quarter had kept her blinded. Now that her world had shrunk around her, it was reduced to me alone. So she had no help but to look on me with seeing eyes. Perhaps it was the kindness of my fate which contrived that this should be her first sight of me.

By river and hill and seashore have I wandered along with Damini, as one of Lilananda's *kirtan* party, setting the atmosphere on fire with passionate song, to the beat of drum and cymbal. Great sparks of emotion were set free as we rang the changes on the text of the Vaishanava poet: *The noose of love hath bound my heart to thy feet.* Yet the curtain which hid me from Damini was not burnt away.

But what was it that happened in this Calcutta lane? The dingy houses, crowding upon one another, blossomed out like flowers of paradise. Verily God vouchsafed to us a miracle. Out of this brick and mortar He fashioned a harp-string to voice forth His melody. And with His wand He touched me, the least of men, and made me, all in a moment, wonderful.

When the curtain is there, the separation is infinite; when it is lifted, the distance can be crossed in the twinkling of an eye. So it took no time at all. "I was in a dream," said Damini. "It wanted this shock to wake me. Between that 'you' of mine and this 'you' of mine, there was a veil of stupor. I salute my Master again and again, for it is he who dispelled it."

"Damini," I said, "do not keep your gaze on me like that. Before, when you made the discovery that this creation of God is not beautiful, I was able to bear it; but it will be difficult to do so now."

"I am making the discovery," she replied, "that this creation of God has its beauty."

"Your name will go down in history!" I exclaimed. "The planting of the explorer's flag on the South Pole heights was child's play to this discovery of yours. 'Difficult' is not the word for it. You will have achieved the impossible!"

I had never realised before how short our spring month of Phalgun[33] is. It has only thirty days, and each of the days is not a minute more than twenty-four hours. With the infinite time which God has at His disposal, such parsimony I failed to understand!

"This mad freak that you are bent on," said Damini; "what will your people have to say to it?"

"My people are my best friends. So they are sure to turn me out of their house."

"What next?"

"Next it will be for you and me to build up a home, fresh from the very foundations, that will be our own special creation."

"You must also fashion afresh the mistress of your house, from the very beginning. May she also be your creation, with no trace left of her old battered condition!"

We fixed a day in the following month for the wedding. Damini insisted that Satish should be brought over.

"What for?" I asked.

"He must give me away."

Where the madcap was wandering I was not sure. I had written several letters, but with no reply. He could hardly have given up that old haunted house, otherwise my letters would have been returned as undelivered. The chances were that he had not the time to be opening and reading letters.

"Damini," said I, "you must come with me and invite him personally. This is not a case for sending a formal invitation letter. I could have gone by myself, but my courage is not equal to it. For all we know, he may be on the other side of the river, superintending the preening of ducks' feathers. To follow him there is a desperate venture of which you alone are capable!"

Damini smiled. "Did I not swear I would never pursue him there again?"

"You swore you would not go to him with food any more. That does not cover your going over to invite him to a repast!"

8

This time everything passed off smoothly. We each took Satish by one hand and brought him along with us back to Calcutta. He was as pleased as a child receiving a pair of new dolls!

Our idea had been to have a quiet wedding. But Satish would have none of that. Moreover, there were the Mussulman friends of Uncle Jagamohan. When they heard the news, they were so extravagantly jubilant that the neighbours must have thought it was for the Amir of Kabul or the Nizam of Hyderabad, at the very least. But the

---

[33] Phalgun: Spring.

height of revelry was reached by the newspapers in a very orgy of calumny. Our hearts, however, were too full to harbour any resentment. We were quite willing to allow the blood-thirstiness of the readers to be satisfied, and the pockets of the pro-prietors to be filled, — along with our blessings to boot.

"Come and occupy my house, Visri, old fellow," said Satish.

"Come with us, too," I added. "Let us set to work together over again."

"No, thank you," said Satish. "My work is elsewhere."

"You won't be allowed to go till you have assisted at our house-warming," insisted Damini.

This function was not going to be a crowded affair, Satish being the only guest. But it was all very well for him to say: "Come and occupy my house." That had already been done by his father, Harimohan, — not directly, but through a tenant. Harimohan would have entered into possession himself, but his worldly and other-worldly advisers warned him that it was best not to risk it, — a Mussulman having died there of the plague. Of course the tenant to whom it was offered ran the same spiritual and physical risks, but then why need he be told?

How we got the house out of Harimohan's clutches is a long story. The Mussul-man leather-dealers were our chief allies. When they got to know the contents of the will, we found further legal steps to be superfluous.

The allowance which I had all along been getting from home was now stopped. It was all the more of a joy to us to undertake together the toil of setting up house without outside assistance. With the seal of Premchand-Roychand it was not diffi-cult for me to secure a professorship. I was able to supplement my income by pub-lishing notes on the prescribed text-books, which were eagerly availed of as patent nostrums for passing examinations. I need not have done so much, for our own wants were few. But Damini insisted that Satish should not have to worry about his own living while we were here to prevent it.

There was another thing about which Damini did not say a word. I had to attend to it secretly. That was the education of her brother's son and the marriage of his daughter. Both of these matters were beyond the means of her brother himself. His house was barred to us, but pecuniary assistance has no caste to stand in the way of its acceptance. Moreover, acceptance did not necessarily involve acknowledgment. So I had to add the sub-editorship of a newspaper to my other occupations.

Without consulting Damini, I engaged a cook and two servants. Without con-sulting me, Damini sent them packing the very next day. When I objected, she made me conscious how ill-judged was my attempted consideration for her. "If I am not allowed," she said, "to do my share of work while you are slaving away, where am I to hide my shame?"

My work outside and Damini's work at home flowed on together like the con-fluent Ganges and Jumna. Damini also began to teach sewing to the leather-dealers' little girls. She was determined not to take defeat at my hands. I am not enough of a poet to sing how this Calcutta house of ours became Brindaban[34] itself, our labours

---

[34] **Brindaban:** A center for Hindu pilgrimage in north central India.

the flute strains which kept it enraptured. All I can say is that our days did not drag, neither did they merely pass by,—they positively danced along.

One more springtime came and went; but never another.

Ever since her return from the cave-temple Damini had suffered from a pain in her breast, of which, however, she then told no one. This suddenly took a turn for the worse, and when I asked her about it she said: "This is my secret wealth, my touchstone. With it, as dower, I was able to come to you. Otherwise I would not have been worthy."

The doctors, each of them, had a different name for the malady. Neither did they agree in their prescriptions. When my little hoard of gold was blown away between the cross-fire of the doctors' fees and the chemist's bills, the chapter of medicament came to an end, and change of air was advised. As a matter of fact, hardly anything of changeable value was left to us except air.

"Take me to the place from which I brought the pain," said Damini. "It has no dearth of air."

When the month of Magh ended with its full moon and Phalgun began, while the sea heaved and sobbed with the wail of its lonely eternity, Damini, taking the dust of my feet, bade farewell to me with the words:

"I have not had enough of you. May you be mine again in our next birth."

East and West

p. 1040

"Oh, East is East, and West is West, and never the twain shall meet." The opening line of **Rudyard Kipling**'s "The Ballad of East and West" (1889) is often quoted to indicate the impassable gulf between East and West, but the poem actually tells of a meeting between the two cultures and the similarities between them. The poem may be seen as emblematic of the East/West dialogue at the end of the nineteenth and the beginning of the twentieth centuries, in that commentators emphasized the differences between Europe and Asia even as increasing contact and trade were bringing the two worlds closer together. This tension informs *Broken Ties,* in which the characters Satish and Srivilas seek to establish identities in relation to both British "atheism" (an Indian mischaracterization of Western scientific rationalism and UTILITARIANISM) and Indian spiritual traditions. Tagore may exaggerate Jagamohan's "atheism" and the spirituality of Lilananda Swami to suggest the extreme opposites that complicate the search for those who seek some reconciling middle ground.

"ORIENTALISM"

For centuries the West saw the East as mysterious, inscrutable, exotic, and despotic, an attitude described and critiqued in Edward Said's contemporary classic, *Orientalism* (1978). These stereotypes were the products of an imbalance of power that enabled a dominant Europe to characterize Asia as "other" and to ascribe qualities to Asian cultures that were opposite from and even antithetical to those most valued in the West, for example, rationality, empiricism, practicality, and government by representation. The term "oriental," itself Eurocentric—for Asia is "east" only when viewed from

> My contention is that without examining Orientalism as a discourse one cannot possibly understand the enormously systematic discipline by which European culture was able to manage—and even produce—the Orient politically, sociologically, militarily, ideologically, scientifically, and imaginatively during the post-Enlightenment period.
>
> – EDWARD SAID, critic

W. Heine, *Commodore Perry's Visit to Shui Lew Chew, 1856*
Commodore Perry's most well known achievement is breaking Japan's trade barrier after
arriving at Japan in 1853, but he also visited other parts of Asia, including Shui Lew
Chew, in China.

Europe—carried these negative connotations. Although Said's study
concentrates on the Islamic cultures of the Middle East and North
Africa, the dichotomy he describes also applies to the West's treatment of the major cultures of East Asia—India, China, and Japan.

THE ISOLATION OF THE EAST

The West's ability to characterize the East on its own terms was facilitated by the isolation of China and Japan and the colonial status of
India. At the beginning of the nineteenth century, China and Japan

p. 1043

were closed societies that minimized their cultural and economic contact with the rest of the world. This isolation produced a fear of strangers like the Dutch "barbarians" that **Rai Sanyo** describes with "anxious eyes" of suspicion in 1818 in "Dutch Ships." After Perry broke the Japanese trade blockade in 1853, Japan replaced the feudal Tokugawa SHOGUNATE with a constitutional government in the 1860s and opened up to contact, trade, and cultural exchange with the West. By the beginning of the twentieth century in China, a new generation of thinkers influenced by contact with the West challenged traditional CONFUCIANISM and the conservative social structure based on it. Two centuries of British rule had acquainted India with the West. Ironically, Indians who studied the works of John Stuart Mill and other Western political philosophers in British schools were inspired with a desire for freedom from colonial rule. After its first meeting in 1885, the Indian National Congress developed into an independence movement that would, under the leadership of Mahatma Gandhi, eventually free India from Britain in 1947.

CULTURAL EXCHANGE

Along with Western machines, manufactured goods, medicine, and engineering, the East — often reluctantly — also imported Western ideas, especially SCIENTIFIC MATERIALISM, utilitarianism, and PRAGMATISM. In exchange, the East exported arts and crafts — rugs and furniture, Japanese woodblock prints, Chinese porcelain — and religion. Whistler, van Gogh[1] and other Western artists imitated Japanese prints; Western scholars translated the classic spiritual and literary texts of the East; and many Europeans and Americans were

p. 1045

drawn to Eastern literary and spiritual traditions. **Goethe** was influenced by reading Chinese and Persian poetry. The selection from his *Divan of West and East* (1819), prompted by reading the poetry of Muhammad Hafiz, a fourteenth-century Persian poet, is both an imitation of and a tribute to the literature of the East. The American TRANSCENDENTALISTS Thoreau and Emerson[2] also integrated Eastern

---

[1] Whistler, van Gogh: James Whistler (1834–1903), American artist; his "Caprise in Purple and Gold, no. 2 — the Golden Screen" (1871) shows the influence of Japanese prints. Vincent van Gogh (1853–1890), Dutch painter; he imitated Japanese prints in the painting "Japonaiserie: the Bridge in Rain" (1887) as well as others.

[2] Thoreau and Emerson: Ralph Waldo Emerson (1803–1882), American Transcendentalist, poet, and essayist; his interest in Eastern religion and literature is apparent in such poems as "Hamatreya" and "Brahma." Henry

**Empress of India,
1876. Illustration
from "Punch"
magazine**
*Prime Minister
Benjamin Disraeli,
dressed as Aladdin, is
shown here crowning
Queen Victoria as
empress of India in
1876. Victoria
approved of Disraeli's
imperialist views and
his desire to make
Britain the most
powerful nation in
the world. (Getty
Images)*

spiritual beliefs into their work. A series of Indian spiritual
leaders—most notably, Ram Mohun Roy (c. 1778–1833), **Keshub
Chunder Sen** (1838–1884),[3] Swami Vivekananda, and Rabindranath
Tagore—lectured in Europe and America on the spiritual traditions
of the East. **Walt Whitman** reflects this interest in Eastern religions
in the four sides of his "square deific," which bring together religious
traditions from East and West, past and present, and in which "all
the sides [are] needed." If Europe's gift to the world was scientific
materialism, the East, in a characterization accepted by many Asians,
was the source of the world's religions. "And was not Jesus Christ an
Asiatic?" asked Keshub Chunder Sen in an 1866 lecture.

KAY-shoob
CHUN-dur SANE

p. 1049

David Thoreau (1817–1862), American essayist and poet who frequently draws on Eastern classics in *Walden*
and other works.

[3] Roy . . . Sen: Ram Mohun Roy (1772–1833), Hindu philosopher and social and educational reformer who lectured in England in the 1820s and 1830s. Keshub Chunder Sen (1838–1884), Hindu philosopher and social
reformer who attempted to incorporate Christian theology into Hindu thought; a follower of Ram Mohun
Roy, who lectured in England in 1870.

STEREOTYPES AND MISUNDERSTANDINGS

p. 1051

ruh-NAY gay-NONG

Through Eastern eyes, the West was viewed as materialistic, atheistic, aggressive, nationalistic, and too willing to sacrifice the common good for individual gratification. **René Guénon**, a French apologist for the Eastern point of view, spelled out this critique in his 1924 essay *East and West.* Though Asian nations sought to take advantage of Western technology, especially in science and medicine, they hoped to do so without adopting the West's materialism. The challenge was greatest perhaps in India, where two centuries of British colonialism had established British institutions and the rules for association between the two cultures. In the late nineteenth

p. 1055

century, when **Rabindranath Tagore** was writing, these issues were foremost in the minds of a generation that sought to free itself from British domination and engage the West as an equal. Tagore himself hoped that India could transcend chauvinism, or nationalism, and develop a culture that preserved the best of both the British and Indian traditions. In his *Message of India to Japan,* delivered in 1916, Tagore urged Japan, the most advanced of the Asian societies, to temper its Westernization with the spiritual qualities of the East. He particularly hoped to counter the materialism, militarism, and nationalism of the West, but his assumption that India, China, and Japan shared a common spiritual tradition may have been wishful thinking. Many Japanese, fervently nationalistic and obsessed with industrial development, were suspicious

p. 1058

of his proposals. **E. M. Forster**'s novel, *A Passage to India* (1924), describes relations between three major groups in India—Hindus, Muslims, and the British—from a Western perspective. It concerns the misunderstandings produced when Adela Quested, a young British woman traveling in India, believes she has been molested by her Muslim guide while visiting the Marabar Caves. Using the caves as a symbol of India, Forster defines the cultural differences between the characters through their reactions to them. In the chapters excerpted here, Mrs. Moore, Adela's prospective mother-in-law, suffers "culture-shock" when visiting one of the caves. Her confusion and panic foreshadow Adela's hysteria and articulate the difficulties that arise when colonial "masters" and their "subjects" meet as equals.

■ CONNECTIONS

Samuel Taylor Coleridge, "Kubla Khan," p. 260; Walt Whitman, "Passage to India," p. 897; Yeats, "Sailing to Byzantium" (Book 6); T. S. Eliot, *The Waste Land* (Book 6). Allusions to Eastern literature and symbols of the East appear importantly in the works of many Western Romantic poets. Coleridge's "Kubla Khan" is an example of such Romantic orientalism; Whitman's "Passage to India" draws on classic Indian texts; Yeats invokes Byzantium in several poems as a place where East and West meet; and T. S. Eliot concludes *The Waste Land* with a Sanskrit quotation. What Eastern qualities does each poet celebrate?

Rabindranath Tagore, *Broken Ties,* p. 986; Mori Ōgai, "The Dancing Girl," p. 1088. In the East, Western culture has often been seen as threatening. Both Tagore and Ōgai write of young men trying to negotiate an identity that would reconcile Eastern and Western elements. How well do Tagore's Satish and Srivilas and Ōgai's Toyotaro succeed in reconciling these two cultures?

In the World: Crossing Cultures (Book 6). *In the World:* Crossing Cultures includes several works that place Indian writers in today's emerging global culture, a continuation of the East/West dialogue in a contemporary context. How do Salman Rushdie, R. K. Narayan, and Bharati Mukherjee view the differences between East and West?

■ PRONUNCIATION

Abazai: AH-bah-zigh
Aziz: uh-ZEEZ
Bukloh: boo-KLOH, buk-LOH
Jagai: jah-GIGH
Keshub Chunder Sen: KAY-shoob CHUN-dur SANE
Peshawur: peh-SHAH-wur
René Guénon: ruh-NAY gay-NONG
Ressaldar: res-sul-DAR

❧ RUDYARD KIPLING
1865–1936

Born in India, Kipling began his literary career there in 1882 when he returned to Bombay after being educated in England. His stories and poems from the next two decades are nearly all about India and include *Plain Tales from the Hills* (1888), *The Jungle Books* (1894, 1895), and *Kim* (1901). Although popular poems like "The White Man's Burden" (1899; Book 6) and "Gunga Din" (1890) earned Kipling a reputation as an apologist for British imperialism, his work, especially his fiction, often reveals a deep understanding and sympathy for the Indian people. "The Ballad of East and West" (1888) is remembered largely for the opening line of the refrain, "Oh, East is East, and West is West, and never the twain shall meet." The story told in the poem, however, seems to challenge this opening assertion.

But there is neither East nor West, Border, nor Breed, nor Birth, When two strong men stand face to face, though they come from the ends of the earth.

– RUDYARD KIPLING

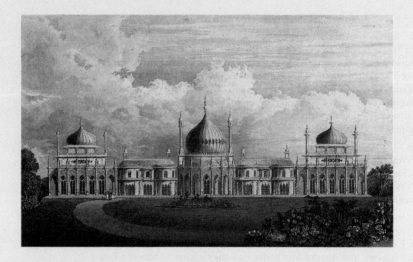

John Nash, *The East Front,* from *Views of the Royal Pavilion,* Brighton, 1826
*The Royal Pavilion in Brighton, England, was built as the seaside residence for King
George IV. Its design is that of an Indian palace and is an example of colonial India's
influence on England. (The Stapleton Collection)*

∾ The Ballad of East and West

Oh, East is East, and West is West, and never the twain shall meet,
Till Earth and Sky stand presently at God's great Judgment Seat;
But there is neither East nor West, Border, nor Breed, nor Birth,
When two strong men stand face to face, though they come from the ends of the earth!

Kamal[1] is out with twenty men to raise the Border side,
And he has lifted[2] the Colonel's mare that is the Colonel's pride.
He has lifted her out of the stable-door between the dawn and the day,
And turned the calkins[3] upon her feet, and ridden her far away.
Then up and spoke the Colonel's son that led a troop of the Guides:[4]
10 "Is there never a man of all my men can say where Kamal hides?"
Then up and spoke Mohammed Khan, the son of the Ressaldar:[5]
"If ye know the track of the morning-mist, ye know where his pickets are.
"At dusk he harries the Abazai — at dawn he is into Bonair,[6]

---

[1]Kamal: Chief of an Afghan tribe.   [2]lifted: stolen   [3]calkins: shoes   [4]Guides: The Queen's Own Corps of
Guides, a unit stationed on the Afghanistan/India border.   [5]Ressaldar: Native captain; the Guides included
both British and colonial soldiers.   [6]Abazai . . . Bonair: Villages on the border, about forty miles apart.

Iranistan, an Oriental
Ville, 1847
*This estate in
Bridgeport, Conn.,
was built for Phineas
Barnum (of the
Barnum & Bailey
Circus) and was
modeled after the
Brighton Pavilion.
(Library of Congress)*

"But he must go by Fort Bukloh to his own place to fare,
"So if ye gallop to Fort Bukloh as fast as a bird can fly,
"By the favour of God ye may cut him off ere he win to the Tongue of Jagai.[7]
"But if he be past the Tongue of Jagai, right swiftly turn ye then,
"For the length and the breadth of that grisly plain is sown with Kamal's men.
"There is rock to the left, and rock to the right, and low lean thorn between,
20 "And ye may hear a breech-bolt snick where never a man is seen."
The Colonel's son has taken a horse, and a raw rough dun was he,
With the mouth of a bell and the heart of Hell, and the head of the gallows-tree.
The Colonel's son to the Fort has won, they bid him stay to eat—
Who rides at the tail of a Border thief, he sits not long at his meat.
He's up and away from Fort Bukloh as fast as he can fly,
Till he was aware of his father's mare in the gut of the Tongue of Jagai,
Till he was aware of his father's mare with Kamal upon her back,
And when he could spy the white of her eye, he made the pistol crack.
He has fired once, he has fired twice, but the whistling ball went wide.
30 "Ye shoot like a soldier," Kamal said. "Show now if ye can ride!"
It's up and over the Tongue of Jagai, as blown dust-devils go,
The dun he fled like a stag of ten,[8] but the mare like a barren doe.
The dun he leaned against the bit and slugged his head above,
But the red mare played with the snafflebars, as a maiden plays with a glove.
There was rock to the left and rock to the right, and low lean thorn between,
And thrice he heard a breech-bolt snick tho' never a man was seen.
They have ridden the low moon out of the sky, their hoofs drum up the dawn,
The dun he went like a wounded bull, but the mare like a new-roused fawn.
The dun he fell at a water-course—in a woeful heap fell he,
40 And Kamal has turned the red mare back, and pulled the rider free.

---

[7] Tongue of Jugai: Mountain ridge in eastern Afghanistan.   [8] stag of ten: A ten-point buck.

He has knocked the pistol out of his hand—small room was there to strive,

"'Twas only by favour of mine," quoth he, "ye rode so long alive:

"There was not a rock for twenty mile, there was not a clump of tree,

"But covered a man of my own men with his rifle cocked on his knee.

"If I had raised my bridle-hand, as I have held it low,

"The little jackals that flee so fast were feasting all in a row.

"If I had bowed my head on my breast, as I have held it high,

"The kite that whistles above us now were gorged till she could not fly."

Lightly answered the Colonel's son: "Do good to bird and beast,

50   "But count who come for the broken meats before thou makest a feast.

"If there should follow a thousand swords to carry my bones away,

"Belike the price of a jackal's meal were more than a thief could pay.

"They will feed their horse on the standing crop; their men on the garnered grain,

"The thatch of the byres[9] will serve their fires when all the cattle are slain.

"But if thou thinkest the price be fair,—thy brethren wait to sup,

"The hound is kin to the jackal-spawn,—howl, dog, and call them up!

"And if thou thinkest the price be high, in steer and gear and stack,

"Give me my father's mare again, and I'll fight my own way back!"

Kamal has gripped him by the hand and set him upon his feet.

60   "No talk shall be of dogs," said he, "when wolf and grey wolf meet.

"May I eat dirt if thou hast hurt of me in deed or breath;

"What dam of lances brought thee forth to jest at the dawn with Death?"

Lightly answered the Colonel's son: "I hold by the blood of my clan:

"Take up the mare for my father's gift—by God, she has carried a man!"

The red mare ran to the Colonel's son, and nuzzled against his breast;

"We be two strong men," said Kamal then, "but she loveth the younger best.

"So she shall go with a lifter's dower, my turquoise-studded rein,

"My 'broidered saddle and saddle-cloth, and silver stirrups twain."

The Colonel's son a pistol drew, and held it muzzle-end,

70   "Ye have taken the one from a foe," said he; "Will ye take the mate from a friend?"

"A gift for a gift," said Kamal straight; "a limb for the risk of a limb.

"Thy father has sent his son to me, I'll send my son to him!"

With that he whistled his only son, that dropped from mountain-crest—

He trod the ling[10] like a buck in spring, and he looked like a lance in rest.

"Now here is thy master," Kamal said, "who leads a troop of the Guides,

"And thou must ride at his left side as shield on shoulder rides.

"Till Death or I cut loose the tie, at camp and board and bed,

"Thy life is his—thy fate it is to guard him with thy head.

"So, thou must eat the White Queen's meat,[11] and all her foes are thine,

80   "And thou must harry thy father's hold for the peace of the Border-line.

"And thou must make a trooper tough and hack thy way to power—

"Belike they will raise thee to Ressaldar when I am hanged in Peshawur."[12]

---

[9] byres: cow stables   [10] ling: heather   [11] the White Queen's meat: The mess for Queen Victoria's troops.
[12] Peshawur: Major city in northwest India, at the foot of the Khyber Pass.

They have looked each other between the eyes, and there they found no fault,
They have taken the Oath of the Brother-in-Blood on leavened bread and salt:
They have taken the Oath of the Brother-in-Blood on fire and fresh-cut sod,
On the hilt and the haft of the Khyber knife, and the Wondrous Names of God.
The Colonel's son he rides the mare and Kamal's boy the dun,
And two have come back to Fort Bukloh where there went forth but one.
And when they drew to the Quarter-Guard, full twenty swords flew clear —
90 There was not a man but carried his feud with the blood of the mountaineer.
"Ha' done! ha' done!" said the Colonel's son. "Put up the steel at your sides!
"Last night ye had struck at a Border thief — to-night 'tis a man of the Guides!"

Oh, East is East, and West is West, and never the twain shall meet,
Till Earth and Sky stand presently at God's great Judgment Seat;
But there is neither East nor West, Border, nor Breed, nor Birth,
When two strong men stand face to face, though they come from the ends of the earth.

~ RAI SANYO
1780–1832

A Japanese historian and poet who wrote in Chinese and is generally regarded as the greatest of such poets in Japanese literature, Rai Sanyo most often treated political and social themes in his work. "Dutch Ships" reflects the distrust of foreigners in Japan in the first half of the nineteenth century.

> Through the streets on all sides the cry breaks forth: "The redhaired Westerners are coming!"
>
> – RAI SANYO

~ Dutch ships (1818)

In Nagasaki Bay, where sky and sea meet to the west,
At heaven's edge a little dot appears.
The cannon of the lookout tower sounds once;
In twenty-five watch stations, bows are bared.
Through the streets on all sides the cry breaks forth:
"The redhaired Westerners are coming!"
Launches set out to meet their ship, we hear the drums echo;
In the distance signal flags are raised to stay alarm.
The ship enters the harbor, a ponderous turtle,
10 So huge that in the shallows it seems sure to ground.

Sadahide Utagawa,
*American Enjoying a
Sunday in Yokohama,*
1861

*After it was opened to
trade in 1853,
Westerners began
traveling to Japan to
experience the
formerly off-limits
land. (Library of
Congress)*

Our little launches, like strung pearls,
Tow it forward amid a clamorous din.
The barbarian hull rises a hundred feet above the sea,
The sighing wind flapping its banners of felt.
Three sails fly amid a thousand lines,
Fixed to engines moving up and down like well-sweeps.
Blackskinned slaves,[1] nimbler than monkeys,
Scale the masts and haul on the lines.
The anchor drops with shouts from the crew;
20   Huge cannon bellow forth again and again their roar.
The barbarian heart is hard to fathom; the Throne ponders
And dares not relax its armed defense.
Alas, wretches, why come they to vex our anxious eyes,

---

[1] **Blackskinned slaves:** Japanese servants of the Dutch. [Translator]

Pursuing countless miles in their greed what gain?
Their ships pitiful leaves upon the monstrous waves,
Crawling like gigantic ants after rancid meat.
Do we not bear ox-knives to kill but a chicken,
Trade our most lovely jewels for thorns?[2]

---

[2] Do we not . . . jewels for thorns?: That is, are not all the alarms and defense measures of the government
unnecessary, and are we not losing by trading with the foreigners? [Translator]

❧ Johann Wolfgang von Goethe
1749–1832

Especially in the latter years of his life, Goethe was passionately committed to the idea of Weltliteratur, literature that would transcend
national identity and speak broadly of the universal human situation,
blending such disparate traditions as those of East and West. He commended the translation of literary works because he thought that it could
promote understanding between different cultures. In two collections of
lyrics, *Chinese-German Hours and Seasons* (1830) and the better-known
Divan of West and East (1819), Goethe sought to close the gap between
Western and Eastern cultures. The poems from *Divan* presented here
were inspired in particular by Goethe's reading of the Persian poet Hafiz
(Muhammad Shams-ud-din, 1320–1389), a master of the *ghazal* who
Goethe said "had no peer." Goethe found in Hafiz a poet who blended
spiritual, mystical love with earthly physical love, and Goethe's lyrics imitate and celebrate Hafiz while they explore Eastern ideas: the circularity
of experience, rebirth, and the melding of the spiritual and the carnal.

The translations which capture the lyric qualities of Goethe's verse
are by Christopher Middleton.

> In my songs do you
> not feel
> That at once I'm one
> and double?
> – Goethe

❧ Unbounded (1814–15)

What makes you great is that you cannot end,
And never to begin you are predestined
Your song revolves as does the starry dome,
Beginning, end for ever more the same;

And what the middle brings will prove to be
What last remains and was initially.

Of poets' joys you are the one true source,
Wave after numberless wave you give to verse.
Lips that of kissing never tire,
10   Song from the breast that sweetly wells,
A throat that's never quenched, on fire,
An honest heart that freely tells.

And though the whole world were to sink,
Hafiz, with you, with you alone
I will compete! Delight, despair,
Let us, the twins, entirely share!
Like you to love, like you to drink
My life and pride I here declare.

Self-fuelled now, my song, ring truer!
20   For you are older, you are newer.

❧ Blessed Longing (1814)

Tell it only to the wise,
For the crowd at once will jeer:
That which is alive I praise,
That which longs for death by fire.

Cooled by passionate love at night,
Procreated, procreating,
You have known the alien feeling
In the calm of candlelight;

Gloom-embraced will lie no more,
10   By the flickering shades obscured,
But are seized by new desire,
To a higher union lured.

Then no distance holds you fast;
Winged, enchanted, on you fly,

Light your longing, and at last,
Moth, you meet the flame and die.

Never prompted to that quest:
Die and dare rebirth!
You remain a dreary guest
20 On our gloomy earth.

❧ Submerged (1815)

Full of crisp curls, a head so round! —
And if in such abundant hair I may
With full hands travel, or return to stay,
Down to my inmost being I feel sound.
If forehead, eyebrow, eye and lips I kiss,
Ever again renewed, I'm sore with bliss.
The five comb-fingers, where should their roaming end?
Already to those curls again they bend.
Nor do the ears refuse their part.
10 They are not flesh, they are not skin,
Such a love-gamut for tenderly-bantering art!
No matter how fondled, here, within
One little head's abundant hair,
For ever forth and back you'll fare.
So, Hafiz, once you used to do,
And we embark on it anew.

❧ Gingo Biloba (1815)

This tree's leaf that from the East
To my garden's been entrusted
Holds a secret sense, and grist
To a man intent on knowledge.

Is it *one*, this thing alive,
By and in itself divided,

Or two beings who connive
That as *one* the world shall see them?

Fitly now I can reveal
10 What the pondered question taught me;
In my songs do you not feel
That at once I'm one and double?

◐ Hatem (1815)[1]

Hold me, curls, securely caught,
To the circle of her face—
Belovèd tawny snakes, with nought
Can I reward your act of grace.

Except this heart, which does persist,
Blooming in youth, as flowers do;
Underneath the snow and mist
An Etna gushes forth to you.

That volcano's earnest brow
10 You put like blush of dawn to shame:
Hatem feels, resurgent now,
The breath of Spring and Summer's flame.

Another bottle, publican!
I drink to her! Happen she'll say,
Finding a heap of ash anon:
"For me he burned his life away."

---

[1] Hatem: A pseudonym adopted by Goethe as a way of identifying himself with poets of the East.

WALT WHITMAN
1819–1892

Largely self-educated, Walt Whitman included Asian texts, especially the Bhagavad Gita, in his voluminous reading of the classics. Whitman's universalism and mysticism have seemed to many Indian readers similar to Hinduism; Rabindranath Tagore declared that "no American had caught the Oriental spirit of mysticism as well as [Whitman]." In "Chanting the Square Deific" (1865–66; 1881), Whitman explores the connections between Eastern and Western religions.

> Jehovah am I
> Old Brahm I, and
> I Saturnius am
>   – WHITMAN,
>   "Chanting the
>   Square Deific"

Chanting the Square Deific

1

Chanting the square deific, out of the One advancing, out of the sides
Out of the old and new, out of the square entirely divine,
Solid, four-sided, (all the sides needed,) from this side Jehovah am I,
Old Brahm I, and I Saturnius am;[1]
Not Time affects me — I am Time, old, modern as any,
Unpersuadable, relentless, executing righteous judgments,
As the Earth, the Father, the brown old Kronos,[2] with laws,
Aged beyond computation, yet ever new, ever with those mighty laws rolling,
Relentless I forgive no man — whoever sins dies — I will have that man's life;
10 Therefore let none expect mercy — have the seasons, gravitation, the appointed
     days, mercy? no more have I,
But as the seasons and gravitation, and as all the appointed days that forgive not,
I dispense from this side judgments inexorable without the least remorse.

2

Consolator most mild, the promis'd one advancing,
With gentle hand extended, the mightier God am I,
Foretold by prophets and poets in their most rapt prophecies and poems,
From this side, lo! the Lord Christ gazes — lo! Hermes I — lo! mine is Hercules'[3]
     face,

---

[1] Jehovah . . . Saturnius am: Jehovah is the nineteenth-century rendering of Yahweh, the god of Judaism; Brahm, or Brahma, the creator god of Hinduism; Saturnius, an important god in the Roman pantheon.

[2] Kronos: In Greek mythology, the father of Zeus. The Romans identified their god Saturnius with Kronos.

[3] Hermes . . . Hercules': Hermes was the messenger and herald of the Greek god; Hercules (Heracles), in Greek mythology, was a mortal hero whose labors were symbolic of the defeat of evil in the world.

All sorrow, labor, suffering, I, tallying it, absorb in myself,
Many times have I been rejected, taunted, put in prison, and crucified, and many
    times shall be again,
All the world have I given up for my dear brothers' and sisters' sake, for the soul's
    sake,
20 Wending my way through the homes of men, rich or poor, with the kiss of affection,
For I am affection, I am the cheer-bringing God, with hope and all-enclosing
    charity,
With indulgent words as to children, with fresh and sane words, mine only,
Young and strong I pass knowing well I am destin'd myself to an early death;
But my charity has no death—my wisdom dies not, neither early nor late,
And my sweet love bequeath'd here and elsewhere never dies.

3

Aloof, dissatisfied, plotting revolt,
Comrade of criminals, brother of slaves,
Crafty, despised, a drudge, ignorant,
With sudra[4] face and worn brow, black, but in the depths of my heart, proud as any,
30 Lifted now and always against whoever scorning assumes to rule me,
Morose, full of guile, full of reminiscences, brooding, with many wiles,
(Though it was thought I was baffled and dispel'd, and my wiles done, but that will
    never be,)
Defiant, I, Satan, still live, still utter words, in new lands duly appearing, (and old
    ones also,)
Permanent here from my side, warlike, equal with any, real as any,
Nor time nor change shall ever change me or my words.

4

Santa Spirita,[5] breather, life,
Beyond the light, lighter than light,
Beyond the flames of hell, joyous, leaping easily above hell,
Beyond Paradise, perfumed solely with mine own perfume,
40 Including all life on earth, touching, including God, including Saviour and Satan,
Ethereal, pervading all, (for without me what were all? what were God?)
Essence of forms, life of the real identities, permanent, positive, (namely the
    unseen,)
Life of the great round world, the sun and stars, and of man, I, the general soul,
Here the square finishing, the solid, I the most solid,
Breathe my breath also through these songs.

---

[4] sudra: The lowest caste in Hinduism.

[5] Santa Spirita: Holy Spirit.

❧ RENÉ GUÉNON
1886–1951

French metaphysician and scholar of world religions, René Guénon began life as a French Catholic, went on to study theosophy, Hinduism, and the other religions of East Asia, and spent twenty years at the end of his life in Cairo as a Muslim. His many books and articles sought to explain the intellectual (or spiritual) traditions of the East to readers in the West. *East and West,* written in 1924 following books on Hinduism and theosophy, critiqued Western scientism as a lower form of knowledge than the metaphysical and truly "intellectual" knowledge of the East.

> Western science means analysis and dispersion; eastern knowledge means synthesis and concentration.
>
> – RÉNE GUÉNON

Kamekichi Tsunajima, *Fashionable Mélange of English Words,* 1887 *The choice of words and the representations on this illustrated page of English terms and their Japanese translations shows the ways in which Japanese culture mixed with the West. (Library of Congress)*

FROM

∿ East and West

Translated by Martin Lings

CIVILIZATION AND PROGRESS

The civilization of the modern West appears in history as a veritable anomaly: among all those which are known to us more or less completely, this civilization is the only one which has developed along purely material lines, and this monstrous development, whose beginning coincides with the so-called Renaissance, has been accompanied, as indeed it was fated to be, by a corresponding intellectual regress; we say corresponding and not equivalent, because here are two orders of things between which there can be no common measure. This regress has reached such a point that the Westerners of to-day no longer know what pure intellect is; in fact they do not even suspect that anything of the kind can exist; hence their disdain, not only for eastern civilization, but also for the Middle Ages of Europe, whose spirit escapes them scarcely less completely. How is the interest of a purely speculative knowledge to be brought home to people for whom intelligence is nothing but a means of acting on matter and turning it to practical ends, and for whom science, in their limited understanding of it, is above all important in so far as it may be applied to industrial purposes? We exaggerate nothing; it only needs a glance at one's surroundings to realize that this is indeed the mentality of the vast majority of our contemporaries; and another glance, this time at philosophy from Francis Bacon and Descartes[1] onwards, could only confirm this impression still further. . . .

But most extraordinary of all is perhaps the claim to set up this abnormal civilization as the very type of all civilization, to regard it as Civilization with a capital letter, and even as the only one which deserves the name. Extraordinary too, and also complementary to this illusion, is the belief in "progress," considered no less absolutely, and naturally identified, at heart, with this material development which absorbs the entire activity of the modern West. It is curious to note how promptly and successfully certain ideas come to spread and impose themselves, provided, of course, that they correspond to the general tendencies of the particular environment and epoch; it is so with these ideas of "civilization" and "progress," which so many people willingly believe universal and necessary, whereas in reality they have been quite recently invented and, even to-day, at least three-quarters of mankind persist either in being ignorant of them or in considering them quite negligible. . . .

There is still another point which is worth noticing: If one examines which branches of the pretended progress most often come up for consideration to-day, which ones are imagined by our contemporaries to be the starting point of all the

---

[1] **Bacon . . . Descartes:** Francis Bacon (1561–1626), English philosopher and essayist who applied the inductive method to science; see Book 3. René Descartes (1596–1650), French philosopher and mathematician; a skeptic who arrived at knowledge of the external world by doubting its existence; see Book 4.

rest, it will be seen that they only amount to two, "material progress" and "moral progress". . . . To be sure, there are some who still talk about "intellectual progress," but for them this phrase is essentially a synonym of "scientific progress," and it applies above all to the development of the experimental sciences and of their applications. Here again there comes to light this degradation of intelligence which ends in identifying it with the most limited and inferior of all its uses, experimenting upon matter for solely practical purposes; the so-called "intellectual progress" is thus no more, to be accurate, than "material progress" itself. . . . Actually it never enters the heads of most Westerners of to-day that intelligence is anything else; for them it no longer amounts even to reason in its Cartesian sense, but to the lowest part of this reason, to its most elementary functions, to what always remains closely connected with this world of the senses which they have made the one exclusive field of their activity. For those who know that there is something else and who persist in giving words their true meaning there can be no question in our time of "intellectual progress," but on the contrary of decadence, or to be still more accurate, of intellectual ruin; and, because there are some lines of development which are incompatible, it is precisely this which is the forfeit paid for "material progress," the only progress whose existence during the last centuries is a real fact: It may be called scientific progress if one insists, but only in an extremely limited acceptance of the word, and a progress which is very much more industrial than scientific. Material development and pure intellectuality go in opposite directions; he who sinks himself in the one becomes necessarily further removed from the other. . . .

The modern world has precisely reversed the natural relations between the different orders of things: once again, it is depreciation of the intellectual order (and even absence of pure intellectuality), and exaggeration of the material and the sentimental orders, which all go together to make the western civilization of to-day an anomaly, not to say a monstrosity.

That is how things look when considered without any prejudice; and that is how they are seen by the most qualified representatives of the eastern civilizations who view them quite without bias, for bias is always something sentimental, not intellectual, and their point of view is purely intellectual. If the people of the West have some difficulty in understanding this attitude, it is because they are incorrigibly prone to judge others according to themselves, and to attribute to them their own concerns, as well as their ways of thinking, and their mental horizon is so narrow that they do not even take into account the possibility of other ones existing; hence their utter failure to understand all the eastern conceptions. This failure is not reciprocated: The Orientals, when they are faced with western science, and when they are willing to give themselves the trouble, have scarcely any difficulty in penetrating and understanding its special branches, because they are used to far wider and deeper speculations, and he that can do the greater can do the less; but in general they feel scarcely any temptation to devote themselves to this work, which, for the sake of things that in their eyes are insignificant, might make them lose sight of, or at least neglect, what is for them the essential. Western science means analysis and dispersion; eastern knowledge means synthesis and concentration; but we shall have occasion to come back to this point. In any case, what the westerners call civilization, the others would call barbarity, because it is precisely lacking in the essential, that is to say a principle of a higher order. By what right do Westerners claim to impose on everyone their own likes and dislikes? Besides, they should not forget that among earthly mankind taken as a whole they form only a minority; of course, this consideration of number proves nothing in our eyes, but it ought to make some impression on people who have invented "universal suffrage," and who believe in its efficacy. If they merely took pleasure in affirming their imagined superiority, the illusion would only do harm to themselves; but their most terrible offence is their proselytizing fury: In them the spirit of conquest goes under the disguise of "moralist" pretexts, and it is in the name of "liberty" that they would force the whole world to imitate them! Most astonishing of all, they genuinely imagine in their infatuation that they enjoy prestige amongst all other peoples; because they are dreaded as a brutal force is dreaded, they believe themselves to be admired; when a man is in danger of being crushed by an avalanche, does it follow that he is smitten with respect and admiration for it? The only impression that, for example, mechanical inventions make on most Orientals is one of deep repulsion; certainly it all seems to them far more harmful than beneficial, and if they find themselves obliged to accept certain things which the present epoch has made necessary, they do so in the hope of future riddance; these things do not interest them, and they will never really interest them. What Westerners call progress is for Orientals nothing but change and instability; and the need for change, so characteristic of modern times, is in their eyes a mark of manifest inferiority: He that has reached a state of equilibrium no longer feels this need, just as he that has found no longer seeks. In these circumstances it is indeed difficult to understand one another, since the same facts give place, on this side and on that, to interpretations which are diametrically opposed. What if the Orientals also sought, after the manner of the West, and by its methods, to impose their own outlook? But one may rest assured: Nothing is more contrary to their nature than propaganda, and such considerations are quite foreign to them; without preaching "liberty," they let others think what they will, and are even indifferent as to what is thought of them. All they ask, in fact, is to be left in peace; but that is just what the people of the West refuse to allow them, and it must be remembered that they went to seek them out in their own home, and have behaved there in a way which might well exasperate the most peaceful of men. We are thus faced with a state of affairs which cannot last indefinitely; there is only one way for the West to make itself bearable: this is, to use the customary language of colonial politics, that it should give up "assimilation" and practice instead "association" in every domain; but that alone would already mean some modification of their mentality, and the understanding of at least one or two of the ideas which form part of our present exposition.

⌘ RABINDRANATH TAGORE

1861–1941

In 1916 Tagore, the leading Indian writer of his day and the first Nobel Prize winner from Asia, went to Japan to urge the Japanese to join in an Asian search for alternatives to the imperialism and nationalism that had propelled the West into World War I. He assumed that Japan, China, and India shared spiritual and aesthetic concerns that could challenge Western materialism. Even though his message was received without much enthusiasm, Tagore continued his efforts to unify Asia with a similar tour of China in 1924. His vision of a world culture that combined the best of Eastern and Western traditions ran counter to the nationalism and industrialism that obsessed Japanese as well as European society.

Tagore's lecture, published in English in Tokyo in 1916, follows British conventions of spelling.

> Japan has imported her food from the West, but not her vital nature. Japan cannot altogether lose and merge herself in the scientific paraphernalia she has acquired from the West and be turned into a mere borrowed machine. She has her own soul which must assert itself over all her requirements.
>
> – RABINDRANATH TAGORE

The Revolt of the Cipayes Is Defeated by the English
The Sepoy, or Indian, Mutiny of 1857–58 was symbolically the defining event in Indian-British relations in the nineteenth century. The Sepoys (Cipayes), Indian troops in the British army, were angered by a series of abuses by the British and took up arms in revolt. The mutiny lasted more than a year, and although it was eventually put down, it is thought of by some as the first Indian war of independence. (The Art Archive/ HarperCollins Publishers)

FROM

◠ The Message of India to Japan

Japan has taught us that we must learn the watchword of the age, in which we live, and answer has to be given to the sentinel of time, if we must escape annihilation. Japan has sent forth her word over Asia, that the old seed has the life germ in it, only it has to be planted in the soil of the new age.

I, for myself, cannot believe that Japan has become what she is by imitating the West. We cannot imitate life, we cannot simulate strength for long, nay, what is more, a mere imitation is a source of weakness. For it hampers our true nature, it is always in our way. It is like dressing our skeleton with another man's skin, giving rise to eternal feuds between the skin and the bones at every movement.

The real truth is that science is not man's nature, it is mere knowledge and training. By knowing the laws of the material universe you do not change your deeper humanity. You can borrow knowledge from others, but you cannot borrow temperament.

But in the first incertitude of new knowledge we not only try to learn, but we try to imitate. That is to say, with the science that we acquire we try the impossible feat of acquiring the teacher of science himself, who is the product of a history not our own. But in that vain attempt we merely copy his manners and mannerisms, those outer forms which are expressions of his historical identity, having their true meaning only with regard to himself. Of course, there are forms which are not merely personal but universal, not historical but scientific, and these can be and have been borrowed by one nation from the other with great advantage. But at the imitative stage of our schooling we cannot distinguish between the essential and the non-essential, between what is transferable and what is not. It is something like the faith of the primitive mind in the magical properties of the accidents of outward forms which accompany some real truth. We are afraid of leaving out something valuable and efficacious by not swallowing the husk with the kernel. But while our greed delights in wholesale appropriation, it is the function of our vital nature to assimilate, which is the only true appropriation for a living organism. Where there is life it is sure to assert itself by its choice of acceptance and refusal according to its constitutional necessity. The living organism does not allow itself to grow into its food, it changes its food into its own body. And only thus can it grow strong and not by mere accumulation, or by giving up its personal identity.

Japan has imported her food from the West, but not her vital nature. Japan cannot altogether lose and merge herself in the scientific paraphernalia she has acquired from the West and be turned into a mere borrowed machine. She has her own soul which must assert itself over all her requirements. That she is capable of doing so, and that the process of assimilation is going on, have been amply proved by the signs of vigorous health that she exhibits. And I earnestly hope that Japan may never lose her faith in her own soul in the mere pride of her foreign acquisition. For that pride itself is a humiliation, ultimately leading to poverty and weakness. It is the pride of the fop who sets more store on his new head-dress than on his head itself.

I have not had the opportunity of coming into intimate touch with Japan and forming my own opinion of what she truly is, where is her strength and where lie her dangers. For a person like myself belonging to the East, her present problems and her methods of solution of those problems are matters of utmost interest. The whole world waits to see what this great Eastern nation is going to do with the opportunities and responsibilities she has accepted from the hands of the modern time. If it be a mere reproduction of the West, then the great expectation she has raised will remain unfulfilled. For there are grave questions that the Western civilisation has presented before the world but not completely answered. The conflict between the individual and the state, labour, and capital, the man and the woman; the conflict between the greed of material gain and the spiritual life of man, the organised selfishness of nations and the higher ideals of humanity; the conflict between all the ugly complexities inseparable from giant organisations of commerce and state and the natural instincts of man crying for simplicity and beauty and fullness of leisure, — all these have to be brought to a harmony in a manner not yet dreamt of.

We have seen this great stream of civilisation choking itself from debris carried by its innumerable channels. We have seen that with all its vaunted love of humanity it has proved itself the greatest menace to Man, far worse than the sudden outbursts of nomadic barbarism from which men suffered in the early ages of history. We have seen that, in spite of its boasted love of freedom, it has produced worse forms of slavery than ever were current in earlier societies, — slavery whose chains are unbreakable, either because they are unseen, or because they assume the names and appearance of freedom. We have seen, under the spell of its gigantic sordidness, man losing faith in all the heroic ideals of life which have made him great. We have seen him pelting those ideals with the mud of sarcasm, which has accumulated in the vast system of sewerage, the product of his separation from the purifying influence of great Nature.

Therefore you cannot with a light heart accept the modern civilisation with all its tendencies, methods, and structures, and dream that they are inevitable. You must apply your Eastern mind, your spiritual strength, your love of simplicity, your recognition of social obligation, in order to cut out a new path for this great unwieldy car of progress, shrieking out its loud discords as it runs. You must minimise the immense sacrifice of man's life and freedom that it claims in its every movement. For generations you have felt and thought and worked, have enjoyed and worshipped in your own special manner; and this cannot be cast off like old clothes. It is in your blood, in the marrow of your bones, in the texture of your flesh, in the tissue of your brains; and it must modify everything you lay your hands upon, without your knowing, even against your wishes. Once you did solve the problems of man to your own satisfaction, you had your philosophy of life and evolved your own art of living. All this you must apply to the present situation and out of it will arise a new creation and not a mere repetition, a creation which the soul of your people will own for itself and proudly offer to the world as its tribute to the welfare of man. Of all countries in Asia, here in Japan you have the freedom to use the materials you have gathered from the West according to your genius and your need. You are fortunately not hampered from the outside, therefore your responsibility is all the greater, for in your voice Asia shall answer the questions that Europe has submitted to the conference of Man. In your land the experiments will be carried on by which the East will change the aspects of the modern civilisation, infusing life in it where it is a machine, substituting human heart for cold expediency, not caring so much for power and success as for harmonious and living growth, for truth and beauty.

E. M. FORSTER
1879–1970

Devils are of the North, and poems can be written about them, but no one could romanticize the Marabar because it robbed infinity and eternity of their vastness, the only quality that accommodates them to mankind.

– E. M. FORSTER, *A Passage to India*

English novelist, short story writer, and critic, Edward Morgan Forster often wrote about cross-cultural situations, especially about English travelers in foreign lands. In *Where Angels Fear to Tread* (1905) and *A Room with a View* (1908), for example, he contrasted repressed middle-class British culture with the freer life in Italy. *A Passage to India* (1924), his last novel, dramatized relations between Hindus, Muslims, and the British in colonial India. Forster drew on two visits to India, in 1912 and 1922, for his story, which explores the misunderstandings brought about by cultural differences. In the novel, Adela Quested, a young Englishwoman, goes to India as the prospective bride of a colonial administrator. In her naive quest to understand Indians and to meet them as equals, she distances herself from the society of the British colonials and disregards established rules of interaction between the two cultures. The crisis point of her journey comes on a visit to the Marabar Caves, used by Forster as a symbol of India, when she believes that her Muslim guide has molested her. Her hysterical response to the caves is foreshadowed in the selection below in which Mrs. Moore, Adela's prospective mother-in-law, is also panicked by the nihilistic confusion she encounters inside of them.

FROM

A Passage to India

CHAPTER 12

The Ganges, though flowing from the foot of Vishnu and through Siva's hair,[1] is not an ancient stream. Geology, looking further than religion, knows of a time when neither the river nor the Himalayas that nourished it existed, and an ocean flowed

---

[1]Ganges . . . Siva's hair: In Hindu mythology, the sacred River Ganges was said to issue from the foot of Vishnu and descend through the locks of Siva, two gods who, with Brahma (the Creator), form the Hindu trinity; Vishnu is the preserver, Siva, the destroyer and restorer.

Colonial Life c. 1890
The British colonizers of India were impressed with its natural resources and wildlife. This colonial-era house is full of trophies, such as a tiger-skin rug and the heads of animals killed in hunts. (Getty Images)

over the holy places of Hindustan.[2] The mountains rose, their debris silted up the ocean, the gods took their seats on them and contrived the river, and the India we call immemorial came into being. But India is really far older. In the days of the pre-historic ocean the southern part of the peninsula already existed, and the high places of Dravidia[3] have been land since land began, and have seen on the one side the sinking of a continent that joined them to Africa, and on the other the upheaval of the Himalayas from a sea. They are older than anything in the world. No water has ever covered them, and the sun who has watched them for countless aeons may still discern in their outlines forms that were his before our globe was torn from his bosom. If flesh of the sun's flesh is to be touched anywhere, it is here, among the incredible antiquity of these hills.

Yet even they are altering. As Himalayan India rose, this India, the primal, has been depressed, and is slowly re-entering the curve of the earth. It may be that in aeons to come an ocean will flow here too, and cover the sun-born rocks with slime. Meanwhile the plain of the Ganges encroaches on them with something of the sea's action. They are sinking beneath the newer lands. Their main mass is untouched, but at the edge their outposts have been cut off and stand knee-deep, throat-deep, in the advancing soil. There is something unspeakable in these outposts. They are like nothing else in the world, and a glimpse of them makes the breath catch. They rise abruptly, insanely, without the proportion that is kept by the wildest hills elsewhere, they bear no relation to anything dreamt or seen. To call them 'uncanny' suggests ghosts, and they are older than all spirit. Hinduism has scratched and plastered a few rocks, but the shrines are unfrequented, as if pilgrims, who generally seek the extraordinary, had here found too much of it. Some saddhus[4] did once settle in a cave, but they were smoked out, and even Buddha, who must have passed this way

---

[2] **Hindustan:** The part of northern India stretching from the Punjab to Assam.   [3] **Dravidia:** Southern India.
[4] **saddhus:** Hindu holy men.

down to the Bo Tree of Gya,[5] shunned a renunciation more complete than his own, and has left no legend of struggle or victory in the Marabar.

The caves are readily described. A tunnel eight feet long, five feet high, three feet wide, leads to a circular chamber about twenty feet in diameter. This arrangement occurs again and again throughout the group of hills, and this is all, this is a Marabar Cave. Having seen one such cave, having seen two, having seen three, four, fourteen, twenty-four, the visitor returns to Chandrapore[6] uncertain whether he has had an interesting experience or a dull one or any experience at all. He finds it difficult to discuss the caves, or to keep them apart in his mind, for the pattern never varies, and no carving, not even a bees'-nest or a bat, distinguishes one from another. Nothing, nothing attaches to them, and their reputation—for they have one—does not depend upon human speech. It is as if the surrounding plain or the passing birds have taken upon themselves to exclaim 'extraordinary,' and the word has taken root in the air, and been inhaled by mankind.

They are dark caves. Even when they open towards the sun, very little light penetrates down the entrance tunnel into the circular chamber. There is little to see, and no eye to see it, until the visitor arrives for his five minutes, and strikes a match. Immediately another flame rises in the depths of the rock and moves towards the surface like an imprisoned spirit: the walls of the circular chamber have been most marvellously polished. The two flames approach and strive to unite, but cannot, because one of them breathes air, the other stone. A mirror inlaid with lovely colours divides the lovers, delicate stars of pink and grey interpose, exquisite nebulae, shadings fainter than the tail of a comet or the midday moon, all the evanescent life of the granite, only here visible. Fists and fingers thrust above the advancing soil—here at last is their skin, finer than any covering acquired by the animals, smoother than windless water, more voluptuous than love. The radiance increases, the flames touch one another, kiss, expire. The cave is dark again, like all the caves.

Only the wall of the circular chamber has been polished thus. The sides of the tunnel are left rough, they impinge as an afterthought upon the internal perfection. An entrance was necessary, so mankind made one. But elsewhere, deeper in the granite, are there certain chambers that have no entrances? Chambers never unsealed since the arrival of the gods. Local report declares that these exceed in number those that can be visited, as the dead exceed the living—four hundred of them, four thousand or million. Nothing is inside them, they were sealed up before the creation of pestilence or treasure; if mankind grew curious and excavated, nothing, nothing would be added to the sum of good or evil. One of them is rumoured within the boulder that swings on the summit of the highest of the hills; a bubble-shaped cave that has neither ceiling nor floor, and mirrors its own darkness in every direction infinitely. If the boulder falls and smashes, the cave will smash too— empty as an Easter egg. The boulder because of its hollowness sways in the wind, and even moves when a crow perches upon it: hence its name and the name of its stupendous pedestal: the Kawa Dol.

---

[5] Bo Tree of Gya: The tree under which Buddha sat when he received enlightenment.

[6] Chandrapore: Fictional town based on Bankipore near Patna in northern India.

Chapter 14

Most of life is so dull that there is nothing to be said about it, and the books and talk that would describe it as interesting are obliged to exaggerate, in the hope of justifying their own existence. Inside its cocoon of work or social obligation, the human spirit slumbers for the most part, registering the distinction between pleasure and pain, but not nearly as alert as we pretend. There are periods in the most thrilling day during which nothing happens, and though we continue to exclaim, 'I do enjoy myself,' or, 'I am horrified,' we are insincere. 'As far as I feel anything, it is enjoyment, horror'—it's no more than that really, and a perfectly adjusted organism would be silent.

It so happened that Mrs Moore and Miss Quested had felt nothing acutely for a fortnight. They had lived more or less inside cocoons, and the difference between them was that the elder lady accepted her own apathy, while the younger resented hers. It was Adela's faith that the whole stream of events is important and interesting, and if she grew bored she blamed herself severely and compelled her lips to utter enthusiasms. This was the only insincerity in a character otherwise sincere, and it was indeed the intellectual protest of her youth. She was particularly vexed now because she was both in India and engaged to be married, which double event should have made every instant sublime.

India was certainly dim this morning, though seen under the auspices of Indians. . . .

The train crossed a nullah.[7] 'Pomper, pomper, pomper,' was the sound that the wheels made as they trundled over the bridge, moving very slowly. A hundred yards on came a second nullah, then a third, suggesting the neighbourhood of higher ground. . . . Her thoughts ever veered to the manageable future, and to the Anglo-Indian life she had decided to endure. And as she appraised it with its adjuncts of Turtons and Burtons, the train accompanied her sentences, 'pomper, pomper,' the train half asleep, going nowhere in particular and with no passenger of importance in any of its carriages, the branch-line train, lost on a low embankment between dull fields. Its message—for it had one—avoided her well-equipped mind. Far away behind her, with a shriek that meant business, rushed the Mail, connecting up important towns such as Calcutta and Lahore, where interesting events occur and personalities are developed. She understood that. Unfortunately, India has few important towns. India is the country, fields, fields, then hills, jungle, hills, and more fields. The branch line stops, the road is only practicable for cars to a point, the bullock-carts lumber down the side tracks, paths fray out into the cultivation, and disappear near a splash of red paint. How can the mind take hold of such a country? Generations of invaders have tried, but they remain in exile. The important towns they build are only retreats, their quarrels the malaise of men who cannot find their way home. India knows of their trouble. She knows of the whole world's trouble, to its uttermost depth. She calls 'Come' through her hundred mouths, through objects ridiculous and august. But come to what? She has never defined. She is not a promise, only an appeal.

'I will fetch you from Simla[8] when it's cool enough. I will unbottle you in fact,'

---

[7] nullah: A ravine or gully.   [8] Simla: Summer resort in the Himalayas of northwestern India; formerly the headquarters for the British army.

continued the reliable girl. 'We then see some of the Mogul[9] stuff—how appalling if we let you miss the Taj![10]—and then I will see you off at Bombay. Your last glimpse of this country really shall be interesting.' But Mrs Moore had fallen asleep, exhausted by the early start. She was in rather low health, and ought not to have attempted the expedition, but had pulled herself together in case the pleasure of the other should suffer. Her dreams were of the same texture, but there it was her other children who were wanting something, Stella and Ralph, and she was explaining to them that she could not be in two families at once. When she awoke, Adela had ceased to plan, and leant out of a window, saying, 'They're rather wonderful.'

Astonishing even from the rise of the civil station, here the Marabar were gods to whom earth is a ghost. Kawa Dol was nearest. It shot up in a single slab, on whose summit one rock was poised;—if a mass so great can be called one rock. Behind it, recumbent, were the hills that contained the other caves, isolated each from his neighbour by broad channels of the plain. The assemblage, ten in all, shifted a little as the train crept past them, as if observing its arrival.

'I'd not have missed this for anything,' said the girl, exaggerating her enthusiasm. 'Look, the sun's rising—this'll be absolutely magnificent—come quickly—look. I wouldn't have missed this for anything.' . . .

As she spoke, the sky to the left turned angry orange. Colour throbbed and mounted behind a pattern of trees, grew in intensity, was yet brighter, incredibly brighter, strained from without against the globe of the air. They awaited the miracle. But at the supreme moment, when night should have died and day lived, nothing occurred. It was as if virtue had failed in the celestial fount. The hues in the east decayed, the hills seemed dimmer though in fact better lit, and a profound disappointment entered with the morning breeze. Why, when the chamber was prepared, did the bridegroom not enter with trumpets and shawms, as humanity expects? The sun rose without splendour. He was presently observed trailing yellowish behind the trees, or against the insipid sky, and touching the bodies already at work in the fields.

'Ah, that must be the false dawn—isn't it caused by dust in the upper layers of the atmosphere that couldn't fall down during the night? I think Mr McBryde said so. Well, I must admit that England has it as regards sunrises. Do you remember Grasmere?'[11]

'Ah, dearest Grasmere!' Its little lakes and mountains were beloved by them all. Romantic yet manageable, it sprang from a kindlier planet. Here an untidy plain stretched to the knees of the Marabar.

'Good morning, good morning, put on your topis,'[12] shouted Aziz from farther down the train. 'Put on your topis at once, the early sun is highly dangerous for heads. I speak as a doctor.'

'Good morning, good morning, put on your own.'

'Not for my thick head,' he laughed, banging it and holding up pads of his hair.

'Nice creature he is,' murmured Adela.

---

[9] **Mogul:** Muslim empire of India from 1526 to 1857.   [10] **The Taj!:** The Taj Mahal in Agra, considered one of the most beautiful buildings in the world.   [11] **Grasmere:** Resort town in the Lake District in northwest England.   [12] **topis:** Caps.

'Listen — Mohammed Latif[13] says "Good morning" next.' Various pointless jests.

'Dr Aziz, what's happened to your hills? The train has forgotten to stop.'

'Perhaps it is a circular train and goes back to Chandrapore without a break. Who knows!'

Having wandered off into the plain for a mile, the train slowed up against an elephant. There was a platform too, but it shrivelled into insignificance. An elephant, waving her painted forehead at the morn! 'Oh, what a surprise!' called the ladies politely. Aziz said nothing, but he nearly burst with pride and relief. The elephant was the one grand feature of the picnic, and God alone knew what he had gone through to obtain her. Semi-official, she was best approached through the Nawab Bahadur, who was best approached through Nureddin, but he never answered letters, but his mother had great influence with him and was a friend of Hamidullah Begum's, who had been excessively kind and had promised to call on her provided the broken shutter of the purdah carriage came back soon enough from Calcutta. That an elephant should descend from so long and so slender a string filled Aziz with content, and with humorous appreciation of the East, where the friends of friends are a reality, where everything gets done sometime, and sooner or later everyone gets his share of happiness. And Mohammed Latif was likewise content, because two of the guests had missed the train, and consequently he could ride on the howdah instead of following in a cart, and the servants were content because an elephant increased their self-esteem, and they tumbled out the luggage into the dust with shouts and bangs, issuing orders to one another, and convulsed with goodwill.

'It takes an hour to get there, an hour to get back, and two hours for the caves, which we will call three,' said Aziz, smiling charmingly. There was suddenly something regal about him. 'The train back is at eleven-thirty, and you will be sitting down to your tiffin[14] in Chandrapore with Mr Heaslop at exactly your usual hour, namely, one-fifteen. I know everything about you. Four hours — quite a small expedition — and an hour extra for misfortunes, which occur somewhat frequently among my people. My idea is to plan everything without consulting you; but you, Mrs Moore, or Miss Quested, you are at any moment to make alterations if you wish, even if it means giving up the caves. Do you agree? Then mount this wild animal.'

The elephant had knelt, grey and isolated, like another hill. They climbed up the ladder, and he mounted shikar[15] fashion, treading first on the sharp edge of the heel and then into the looped-up tail. When Mohammed Latif followed him, the servant who held the end of the tail let go of it according to previous instructions, so that the poor relative slipped and had to cling to the netting over the buttocks. It was a little piece of Court buffoonery, and distressed only the ladies, whom it was intended to divert. Both of them disliked practical jokes. Then the beast rose in two shattering movements, and poised them ten feet above the plain. Immediately below was the scurf of life that an elephant always collects round its feet — villagers, naked babies. The servants flung crockery into tongas.[16] Hassan annexed the stallion intended for Aziz, and defied Mahmoud Ali's man from its altitude. . . . The train . . . wobbled

---

[13] Mohammed Latif: A friend of Dr. Aziz who helps him with the arrangements for the trip to the Marabar caves. [14] tiffin: Lunch. [15] shikar: Hunter. [16] tongas: Two-wheeled, horse-drawn carriages.

away through the fields, turning its head this way and that like a centipede. And the only other movement to be seen was a movement as of antennae, really the counterpoises of the wells which rose and fell on their pivots of mud all over the plain and dispersed a feeble flow of water. The scene was agreeable rather than not in the mild morning air, but there was little colour in it, and no vitality.

As the elephant moved towards the hills (the pale sun had by this time saluted them to the base, and pencilled shadows down their creases) a new quality occurred, a spiritual silence which invaded more senses than the ear. Life went on as usual, but had no consequences, that is to say, sounds did not echo or thoughts develop. Everything seemed cut off at its root, and therefore infected with illusion. For instance, there were some mounds by the edge of the track, low, serrated, and touched with whitewash. What were these mounds — graves, breasts of the goddess Parvati?[17] The villagers beneath gave both replies. Again, there was a confusion about a snake which was never cleared up. Miss Quested saw a thin, dark object reared on end at the farther side of a watercourse, and said, 'A snake!' The villagers agreed, and Aziz explained: yes, a black cobra, very venomous, who had reared himself up to watch the passing of the elephant. But when she looked through Ronny's field-glasses, she found it wasn't a snake, but the withered and twisted stump of a toddy-palm. So she said, 'It isn't a snake.' The villagers contradicted her. She had put the word into their minds, and they refused to abandon it. Aziz admitted that it looked like a tree through the glasses, but insisted that it was a black cobra really, and improvised some rubbish about protective mimicry. Nothing was explained, and yet there was no romance. Films of heat, radiated from the Kawa Dol precipices, increased the confusion. They came at irregular intervals and moved capriciously. A patch of field would jump as if it was being fried, and then lie quiet. As they drew closer the radiation stopped.

The elephant walked straight at the Kawa Dol as if she would knock for admission with her forehead, then swerved, and followed a path round its base. The stones plunged straight into the earth, like cliffs into the sea, and while Miss Quested was remarking on this, and saying that it was striking, the plain quietly disappeared, peeled off, so to speak, and nothing was to be seen on either side but the granite, very dead and quiet. The sky dominated as usual, but seemed unhealthily near, adhering like a ceiling to the summits of the precipices. It was as if the contents of the corridor had never been changed. Occupied by his own munificence, Aziz noticed nothing. His guests noticed a little. They did not feel that it was an attractive place or quite worth visiting, and wished it could have turned into some Mohammedan object, such as a mosque, which their host would have appreciated and explained. His ignorance became evident, and was really rather a drawback. In spite of his gay, confident talk, he had no notion how to treat this particular aspect of India. . . .

The corridor narrowed, then widened into a sort of tray. Here, more or less, was their goal. A ruined tank held a little water which would do for the animals, and close above the mud was punched a black hole — the first of the caves. Three hills encircled the tray. Two of them pumped out heat busily, but the third was in shadow, and here they camped.

---

[17] **Parvati:** The consort, or spouse, of Siva.

'A horrid, stuffy place really,' murmured Mrs Moore to herself.

'How quick your servants are!' Miss Quested exclaimed. For a cloth had already been laid, with a vase of artificial flowers in its centre, and Mahmoud Ali's butler offered them poached eggs and tea for the second time.

'I thought we would eat this before our caves, and breakfast after.'

'Isn't this breakfast?'

'This breakfast? Did you think I should treat you so strangely?' He had been warned that English people never stop eating, and that he had better nourish them every two hours until a solid meal was ready.

'How very well it is all arranged.'

'That you shall tell me when I return to Chandrapore. Whatever disgraces I bring upon myself, you remain my guests.' He spoke gravely now. They were dependent on him for a few hours, and he felt grateful to them for placing themselves in such a position. All was well so far; the elephant held a fresh-cut bough to her lips, the tonga shafts stuck up into the air, the kitchen-boy peeled potatoes, Hassan shouted, and Mohammed Latif stood as he ought, with a peeled switch in his hand. The expedition was a success, and it was Indian; an obscure young man had been allowed to show courtesy to visitors from another country, which is what all Indians long to do — even cynics like Mohammed Ali — but they never have the chance. Hospitality had been achieved, they were 'his' guests; his honour was involved in their happiness, and any discomfort they endured would tear his own soul.

Like most Orientals, Aziz overrated hospitality, mistaking it for intimacy, and not seeing that it is tainted with the sense of possession. It was only when Mrs Moore or Fielding[18] was near him that he saw further, and knew that it is more blessed to receive than to give. These two had strange and beautiful effects on him — they were his friends, his for ever, and he theirs for ever; he loved them so much that giving and receiving became one. He loved them even better than the Hamidullahs, because he had surmounted obstacles to meet them, and this stimulates a generous mind. Their images remained somewhere in his soul up to his dying day, permanent additions. He looked at her now as she sat on a deck-chair, sipping his tea, and had for a moment a joy that held the seeds of its own decay, for it would lead him to think, 'Oh, what more can I do for her?' and so back to the dull round of hospitality. The black bullets of his eyes filled with soft expressive light, and he said, 'Do you ever remember our mosque, Mrs Moore?'

'I do. I do,' she said, suddenly vital and young.

'And how rough and rude I was, and how good you were.'

'And how happy we both were.'

'Friendships last longest that begin like that, I think. Shall I ever entertain your other children?'

'Do you know about the others? She will never talk about them to me,' said Miss Quested, unintentionally breaking a spell.

'Ralph and Stella, yes, I know everything about them. But we must not forget to visit our caves. One of the dreams of my life is accomplished in having you both here

---

[18] Fielding: English friend of Dr. Aziz. He is a teacher and somewhat of an outsider in the community of British colonials.

as my guests. You cannot imagine how you have honoured me. I feel like the Emperor Babur."[19]

'Why like him?' she inquired, rising.

'Because my ancestors came down with him from Afghanistan. They joined him at Herat. He also had often no more elephants than one, none sometimes, but he never ceased showing hospitality. When he fought or hunted or ran away, he would always stop for a time among hills, just like us; he would never let go of hospitality and pleasure, and if there was only a little food, he would have it arranged nicely, and if only one musical instrument, he would compel it to play a beautiful tune. I take him as my ideal. He is the poor gentleman, and he became a great king.'

'I thought another Emperor is your favourite—I forget the name—you mentioned him at Mr Fielding's: what my book calls Aurangzebe.'[20]

'Alamgir? Oh yes, he was of course the more pious. But Babur—never in his whole life did he betray a friend, so I can only think of him this morning. And you know how he died? He laid down his life for his son. A death far more difficult than battle. They were caught in the heat. They should have gone back to Kabul for the bad weather, but could not for reasons of state, and at Agra Humayun fell sick. Babur walked round the bed three times, and said, 'I have borne it away', and he did bear it away; the fever left his son and came to him instead, and he died. That is why I prefer Babur to Alamgir. I ought not to do so, but I do. However, I mustn't delay you. I see you are ready to start.'

'Not at all,' she said, sitting down by Mrs Moore again. 'We enjoy talk like this very much.' For at last he was talking about what he knew and felt, talking as he had in Fielding's garden-house; he was again the Oriental guide whom they appreciated.

'I always enjoy conversing about the Moguls. It is the chief pleasure I know. You see, those first six emperors were all most wonderful men, and as soon as one of them is mentioned, no matter which, I forget everything else in the world except the other five. You could not find six such kings in all the countries of the earth, not, I mean, coming one after the other father, son.'

'Tell us something about Akbar.'[21]

'Ah, you have heard the name of Akbar. Good. Hamidullah—whom you shall meet—will tell you that Akbar is the greatest of all. I say, "Yes, Akbar is very wonderful, but half a Hindu; he was not a true Moslem," which makes Hamidullah cry, "No more was Babur, he drank wine." But Babur always repented afterwards, which makes the entire difference, and Akbar never repented of the new religion he invented instead of the Holy Koran.'

'But wasn't Akbar's new religion very fine? It was to embrace the whole of India.'

'Miss Quested, fine but foolish. You keep your religion, I mine. That is the best. Nothing embraces the whole of India, nothing, nothing, and that was Akbar's mistake.'

'Oh, do you feel that, Dr Aziz?' she said thoughtfully. 'I hope you're not right.

---

[19] Emperor Babur: (1483–1530) First Mughal emperor. According to legend, he rescued his son Humayun, who became the second emperor, from a mortal illness by taking the disease on himself and dying. [20] Aurangzebe: Aurangzebe (1618–1707), Mughal emperor from 1659 to 1707 who took the title Alamgir as ruler. [21] Akbar: (1542–1605) Son of Humayun, greatest of the Mughal emperors, Akbar was noted for his reforms of the government and his religious tolerance. He developed a monotheistic religion, synthesizing Islam, Zoroastrianism, and Christianity.

There will have to be something universal in this country—I don't say religion, for I'm not religious, but something, or how else are barriers to be broken down?'

She was only recommending the universal brotherhood he sometimes dreamed of, but as soon as it was put into prose it became untrue.

'Take my own case,' she continued—it was indeed her own case that had animated her. 'I don't know whether you happen to have heard, but I'm going to marry Mr Heaslop.'

'On which my heartiest congratulations.'

'Mrs Moore, may I put our difficulty to Dr Aziz—I mean our Anglo-Indian one?'

'It is your difficulty, not mine, my dear.'

'Ah, that's true. Well, by marrying Mr Heaslop, I shall become what is known as an Anglo-Indian.'

He held up his hand in protest. 'Impossible. Take back such a terrible remark.'

'But I shall; it's inevitable. I can't avoid the label. What I do hope to avoid is the mentality. Women like—' She stopped, not quite liking to mention names; she would boldly have said 'Mrs Turton and Mrs Callendar' a fortnight ago. 'Some women are so—well, ungenerous and snobby about Indians, and I should feel too ashamed for words if I turned like them, but—and here's my difficulty—there's nothing special about me, nothing specially good or strong, which will help me to resist my environment and avoid becoming like them. I've most lamentable defects. That's why I want Akbar's "universal religion" or the equivalent to keep me decent and sensible. Do you see what I mean?'

Her remarks pleased him, but his mind shut up tight because she had alluded to her marriage. He was not going to be mixed up in that side of things. 'You are certain to be happy with any relative of Mrs Moore's,' he said with a formal bow.

'Oh, my happiness—that's quite another problem. I want to consult you about this Anglo-Indian difficulty. Can you give me any advice?'

'You are absolutely unlike the others, I assure you. You will never be rude to my people.'

'I am told we all get rude after a year.'

'Then you are told a lie,' he flashed, for she had spoken the truth and it touched him on the raw; it was itself an insult in these particular circumstances. He recovered himself at once and laughed, but her error broke up their conversation—their civilization it had almost been—which scattered like the petals of a desert flower, and left them in the middle of the hills. 'Come along,' he said, holding out a hand to each. They got up a little reluctantly, and addressed themselves to sightseeing.

The first cave was tolerably convenient. They skirted the puddle of water, and then climbed up over some unattractive stones, the sun crashing on their backs. Bending their heads, they disappeared one by one into the interior of the hills. The small black hole gaped where their varied forms and colours had momentarily functioned. They were sucked in like water down a drain. Bland and bald rose the precipices; bland and glutinous the sky that connected the precipices; solid and white, a Brahminy kite flapped between the rocks with a clumsiness that seemed intentional. Before man, with his itch for the seemly, had been born, the planet must have looked thus. The kite flapped away . . . Before birds, perhaps . . . And then the hole belched and humanity returned.

A Marabar cave had been horrid as far as Mrs Moore was concerned, for she had nearly fainted in it, and had some difficulty in preventing herself from saying so as soon as she got into the air again. It was natural enough: She had always suffered from faintness, and the cave had become too full, because all their retinue followed them. Crammed with villagers and servants, the circular chamber began to smell. She lost Aziz in the dark, didn't know who touched her, couldn't breathe, and some vile naked thing struck her face and settled on her mouth like a pad. She tried to regain the entrance tunnel, but an influx of villagers swept her back. She hit her head. For an instant she went mad, hitting and gasping like a fanatic. For not only did the crush and stench alarm her; there was also a terrifying echo. . . .

There are some exquisite echoes in India; there is the whisper round the dome at Bijapur;[22] there are the long, solid sentences that voyage through the air at Mandu, and return unbroken to their creator. The echo in a Marabar cave is not like these, it is entirely devoid of distinction. Whatever is said, the same monotonous noise replies, and quivers up and down the walls until it is absorbed into the roof. 'Boum' is the sound as far as the human alphabet can express it, or 'bou-oum', or 'ou-boum',—utterly dull. Hope, politeness, the blowing of a nose, the squeak of a boot, all produce 'boum.' Even the striking of a match starts a little worm coiling, which is too small to complete a circle, but is eternally watchful. And if several people talk at once, an overlapping howling noise begins, echoes generate echoes, and the cave is stuffed with a snake composed of small snakes, which writhe independently.

After Mrs Moore all the others poured out. She had given the signal for the reflux. Aziz and Adela both emerged smiling, and she did not want him to think his treat was a failure, so smiled too. As each person emerged she looked for a villain, but none was there, and she realized that she had been among the mildest individuals, whose only desire was to honour her, and that the naked pad was a poor little baby, astride its mother's hip. Nothing evil had been in the cave, but she had not enjoyed herself; no, she had not enjoyed herself, and she decided not to visit a second one.

'Did you see the reflection of his match—rather pretty?' asked Adela.

'I forget . . .'

'But he says this isn't a good cave, the best are on the Kawa Dol.'

'I don't think I shall go on to there. I dislike climbing.'

'Very well, let's sit down again in the shade until breakfast's ready.'

'Ah, but that'll disappoint him so; he has taken such trouble. You should go on; you don't mind.'

'Perhaps I ought to,' said the girl, indifferent to what she did, but desirous of being amiable.

The servants, etc., were scrambling back to the camp, pursued by grave censures from Mohammed Latif. Aziz came to help the guests over the rocks. He was at the summit of his powers, vigorous and humble, too sure of himself to resent criticism, and he was sincerely pleased when he heard they were altering his plans. 'Certainly, Miss Quested, so you and I will go together, and leave Mrs Moore here, and we will not be long, yet we will not hurry, because we know that will be her wish.'

'Quite right. I'm sorry not to come too, but I'm a poor walker.'

'Dear Mrs Moore, what does anything matter so long as you are my guests? I am

---

[22] Bijapur: An ancient city in southern India; among its monuments is the mausoleum of Mohammed Adil Shah known as the Gol Gumbaz, the Round Dome.

very glad you are *not* coming, which sounds strange, but you are treating me with true frankness, as a friend.'

'Yes, I am your friend,' she said, laying her hand on his sleeve, and thinking, despite her fatigue, how very charming, how very good, he was, and how deeply she desired his happiness. 'So may I make another suggestion? Don't let so many people come with you this time. I think you may find it more convenient.'

'Exactly, exactly,' he cried, and, rushing to the other extreme, forbade all except one guide to accompany Miss Quested and him to the Kawa Dol. 'Is that all right?' he inquired.

'Quite right, now enjoy yourselves, and when you come back tell me all about it.' And she sank into the deck-chair.

If they reached the big pocket of caves, they would be away nearly an hour. She took out her writing-pad, and began, 'Dear Stella, Dear Ralph,' then stopped, and looked at the queer valley and their feeble invasion of it. Even the elephant had become a nobody. Her eye rose from it to the entrance tunnel. No, she did not wish to repeat that experience. The more she thought over it, the more disagreeable and frightening it became. She minded it much more now than at the time. The crush and the smells she could forget, but the echo began in some indescribable way to undermine her hold on life. Coming at a moment when she chanced to be fatigued, it had managed to murmur, 'Pathos, piety, courage—they exist, but are identical, and so is filth. Everything exists, nothing has value.' If one had spoken vileness in that place, or quoted lofty poetry, the comment would have been the same— 'ou-boum'. If one had spoken with the tongues of angels and pleaded for all the unhappiness and misunderstanding in the world, past, present, and to come, for all the misery men must undergo whatever their opinion and position, and however much they dodge or bluff—it would amount to the same, the serpent would descend and return to the ceiling. Devils are of the North, and poems can be written about them, but no one could romanticize the Marabar because it robbed infinity and eternity of their vastness, the only quality that accommodates them to mankind.

She tried to go on with her letter, reminding herself that she was only an elderly woman who had got up too early in the morning and journeyed too far, that the despair creeping over her was merely her despair, her personal weakness, and that even if she got a sunstroke and went mad the rest of the world would go on. But suddenly, at the edge of her mind, Religion appeared, poor little talkative Christianity, and she knew that all its divine words from 'Let there be Light' to 'It is finished'[23] only amounted to 'boum.' Then she was terrified over an area larger than usual; the universe, never comprehensible to her intellect, offered no repose to her soul, the mood of the last two months took definite form at last, and she realized that she didn't want to write to her children, didn't want to communicate with anyone, not even with God. She sat motionless with horror, and, when old Mohammed Latif came up to her, thought he would notice a difference. For a time she thought, 'I am going to be ill,' to comfort herself, then she surrendered to the vision. She lost all interest, even in Aziz, and the affectionate and sincere words that she had spoken to him seemed no longer hers but the air's.

---

[23] **"Let there be Light" to "It is finished":** The first words of the Creator in Genesis, 1:3, and the last words of Jesus on the cross, John 19:30.

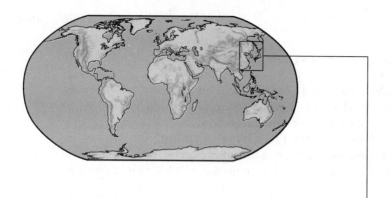

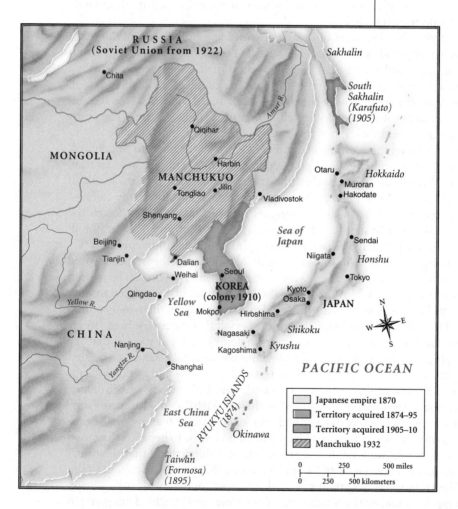

Japanese Acquisitions, 1870–1932

The collapse of the Tokugawa shogunate and the advent of the Meiji Restoration opened Japan to the rest of Asia and the world. By the end of the nineteenth century, the development of industry and modernization of the military gave rise to Japanese imperialism. Japan first fought China, acquiring the Ryukyu Islands in 1874 and the island of Taiwan (Formosa) in 1895. Japan's imperialistic sights soon turned to the mainland, where it colonized Korea in 1910 and defeated the Chinese to win Manchukuo in 1932.

JAPAN
From Isolation to Nationalism

Unlike many European nations that at the beginning of the nineteenth century were disunified collections of competing duchies, Japan entered the century as a nation unified under the Tokugawa shogunate, a military government that had ruled during a period of peace and stability of nearly two hundred years. Tokugawa rulers had consolidated their power in 1603 after a long series of wars between rival feudal lords. Maintaining a divine-right emperor as a mere spectacle of power in Kyoto, the SHOGUNATE made Edo (now Tokyo) the functional center of power. National unity was maintained by rules that curtailed the power of feudal houses — other than that of the Tokugawa — and protected the nation from all foreign influences. In 1639 the shogunate repressed Christianity, forbade travel outside of Japan, and excluded all foreigners except the Dutch, who were granted a small commercial outpost on an island in Nagasaki harbor. Japan would remain isolated from the rest of the world for more than 200 years, until the middle of the nineteenth century.

THE EDO PERIOD

During the Tokugawa, or Edo, period, Japanese education and social practices were grounded in NEO-CONFUCIANIST doctrines that promoted a hierarchically ordered society divided into distinct groups: warriors, or SAMURAI, at the top, followed by farmers, artisans, and merchants. To maintain their position, the Tokugawa shoguns undermined the power and influence of competing feudal families. But beginning in the eighteenth century, the merchant classes, like those in the West, were gaining in wealth and influence. To accommodate the growing stature of this urban bourgeoisie, the shoguns allowed "pleasure quarters" to thrive in the major cities. In these "licensed districts" where merchants could spend their wealth on courtesans, diversions, and entertainment, a new popular culture thrived. Two of its most noteworthy creations were KABUKI theater and the woodblock print.

Rather than drawing on classical drama or classical painting for their models, Kabuki dramatists wrote about the pleasure quarters, and woodblock artists made popular portraits of Kabuki actors in costume for their famous roles.

By the beginning of the nineteenth century, the shogunate was caught in the contradictions of its rule. By undermining other feudal families it had weakened the social structure that supported its conservative class system and Japan's traditional ethical code. Many of the feudal families were so financially strapped they could no longer retain samurai, and many warriors were thus reduced to *ronin,* masterless wanderers. Moreover, by allowing the pleasure quarters and their alternative culture, the Tokugawa rulers had encouraged the social forces that would, in the middle of the century, produce the radical changes that came with the MEIJI RESTORATION.

OPENING TO THE WEST

Like their European contemporaries, Japanese writers of the nineteenth century witnessed rapid social and economic changes: The decline of neo-Confucianism and the rigid social hierarchy it had helped to legitimate, an acceleration of demand to reform government to better accommodate a rising middle class, the gradual opening to trade with the West, a growing dependence on money as a means of exchange, and the commercialization of art and literature. In 1854 the lifespan of the Tokugawa shogunate was shortened when Commodore Perry got the Japanese to sign the Treaty of Kanagawa, which opened Japanese ports to American ships. Four years later the Commercial Treaty of 1858 between the United States and Japan opened more ports and brought Japan into the world of international trade. These treaties were strongly opposed by conservative clans who thought the Tokugawa shogun was selling out their national identity. A number of clan leaders, who called themselves the Satcho Hito group, overthrew the Tokugawa in a brief but bloody rebellion in the 1860s, took control of the government, and led the Japanese into the modern world through the so-called Meiji Restoration.

THE MEIJI RESTORATION

The Meiji leaders appealed to Japanese conservatism by characterizing their revolution as one that sought to restore the emperor, who took the name of Meiji, to a position of honor. Meiji leaders moved the imperial palace from its peripheral location in Kyoto to Edo (now Tokyo), the center of political power. Their policies, however, were not conservative. They encouraged a careful exchange of ideas and technology with the West, announcing in the charter of 1868 that "knowledge shall be sought from all the world and thus shall the foundation of the Imperial polity be strengthened." Entering the world marketplace of ideas and commodities

Kobaysgu Kiyochika, Scene from the Sino-Japanese War in Korea.
Woodblock engraving
This graphic scene from the late nineteenth century shows a very different Japan from
that of a century before. After Commodore Perry's arrival in 1853, Japan opened its doors
to the West and to its Asian neighbors. Its industry and military developed quickly, and
Japan was encouraged to expand its borders, first engaging in the Sino-Japanese War
with China over the Korean peninsula. (The Bridgeman Art Library)

involved major changes in Japanese educational, legal, military, and industrial
systems; one area that remained sacred, however, was religion. Traditional Shintoism was promoted under the Meiji leadership, both as a spiritual practice and as a
source of national identity under the emperor, said to be a descendant of the Sun
Goddess, the central divinity in Shintoism. Even when a parliamentary government
that protected the civil rights of Japanese citizens was established under the constitution of 1889, the emperor's place remained secure; article three of the constitution
stated that the emperor was "sacred and inviolable." The emperor became the symbolic representative of the nationalistic fervor that gripped the modernizing nation.
Loyalty to the emperor, the development of industry, and the modernization of the

military enabled Japan to defeat first China in 1894 and then Russia, which was trying to gain territory to Manchuria and Korea, in 1905. After these victories, Western leaders recognized Japan as a major world power.

LITERATURE OF THE LATE EDO PERIOD

Takizawa Bakin (1767–1848) (p. 1076) is a writer who represents the contradictions of this period. Born into the samurai class, he was reduced to the status of a *ronin*. To support himself he married into the merchant class and became himself a kind of literary merchant, turning out chapbooks for the commercial market. His major works, historical romances that hearken back to the feudal times before the Tokugawa period, are about a way of life that had been displaced. His works are similar to the historical novels of such Western **ROMANTIC** writers as Sir Walter Scott (1771–1832) and Alexandre Dumas (1802–1870), who celebrated the Scottish and French past at a time when European feudalism was being overthrown by the revolutionary changes of the eighteenth century. Bakin's contemporaries, the poets Kagawa Kageki (1768–1843), Uchiyama Mayumi (1784–1852), and *HAIKAI* master Kobayashi Issa (1762–1826), turned away from the imitation of Chinese and Japanese classics and rejected the use of conventional poetic devices and diction in favor of a more personal style. Kobayashi Issa's *A Year in My Life* (1879), for example, a journal of prose and poetry, is about the death of his daughter.

LITERATURE OF THE MEIJI PERIOD

As part of its modernization program, the Meiji government abolished feudal class distinctions. It even provided a subsidy to former samurai to enable them to go into business. For many former warriors the attitude required in the business world was too radical a change, however, and most of their enterprises failed. Many writers of the period dealt with the psychological dislocations that resulted from the nation's sudden move to modernization. Inazo Nitobé (1862–1932) ascribed the samurai's difficulties to the differences between the feudal code and the ethics of the business world. Westernization, or modernization — terms that were nearly synonymous at the time — prompted a nostalgic interest in Japanese feudal traditions. The historical romances of Takizawa Bakin enjoyed a revival late in the century, and there was a reawakened interest in **BUSHIDO**, the ethical code of samurai. Nitobé's best-selling book, *Bushido: The Soul of Japan* (1899), went through numerous editions in the first two decades of the twentieth century.

WWW   For more information about the culture and context of Japan in the nineteenth century, see *World Literature Online* at bedfordstmartins.com/worldlit.

Nineteenth Century: Perry and the Opening of Japan

With westward expansion and the conquest of California, the United States sought to become a power in the Pacific by expanding its whaling industry and its trade with China. The Japanese policy of closing its waters to foreign ships blocked the most direct routes to China and denied American ships the opportunity to secure water and provisions in Japanese ports. In 1853 President Millard Fillmore sent Commodore Matthew C. Perry to Japan with a letter demanding negotiations. On July 8, when Perry entered the fortified harbor at Uraga, at the mouth of Edo Bay, the two-century-old policy of isolation, symbolically at least, came to an end.

Perry anchored his "black ships"—two sailing ships and two steam warships—in Edo Bay and refused orders to leave. When a comet flamed through the night sky on the evening of his arrival, he took it as an omen that "our present attempt to bring a singular and isolated people into the family of civilized nations may succeed without bloodshed." Nevertheless, Perry threatened to go ashore with "a suitable force," determined "to demand as a right, and not to solicit as a favour, those acts of courtesy which are due from one civilized country to another." After realizing that they were too weak to expel Perry, the Japanese accepted his documents. Perry promised to return the following year for an answer.

In February 1854 Perry reentered Edo Bay with twice as many ships and with gifts for the Japanese. To the shogun, Perry gave a miniature railway with 350 feet of eighteen-inch track, a telegraph with three miles of wire, and other industrial products from the West.

Each Japanese official received a clock, a sword, a rifle, a revolver, and five gallons of whisky. In return the Japanese gave the Americans pottery, textiles, bronzes, and laquerware; they agreed to open two ports, Shimoda and Hakodate, to American ships in need of supplies and to allow an American consulate at Shimoda. Although these were very limited concessions, the long-standing policy of isolation had been broken. Soon other Western nations negotiated treaties with the Japanese, and the United States set out to open up trade with Japan and to obtain permission for American missionaries to embark on the island. The decision of the shogun to settle with Perry in 1854 hastened the end of the Tokugawa regime, which came with the Meiji Restoration in 1867.

Commodore Perry Arrives in Japan, August 7, 1853. During the Tokugawa shogunate, Japan strictly enforced its policy prohibiting foreign trade, especially with the West. In the wake of Commodore Perry's trips to Japan in 1853 and 1854, when the American Perry started negotiations that led to the end of the Japanese trade blockade, the Tokugawa regime lost power. It was replaced with a constitutional government in the 1860s that opened up contact, trade, and cultural exchange with the West. (The Art Archive/British Museum)

As one of their strategies for rapid modernization, Meiji leaders sent young intellectuals abroad to gather ideas for rebuilding the Japanese system. Among these emissaries sent to Europe was Mori Ōgai (1862–1922), a physician who combined his scientific training with a grounding in both Asian and European literature. When he returned from Europe he gave up medicine to take up writing. He became one of the major literary figures of the time as he sought in his work to combine an appreciation of Western scientific achievements with traditional Japanese values, balancing Western individualism with a Japanese deference to authority and assumption of public responsibilities.

Although many of Ōgai's contemporaries slavishly imitated the techniques and perspectives of such Western Realists as French novelists Gustave Flaubert and Émile Zola and the Russian Ivan Turgenev, Ōgai sought a balance of Western and Eastern qualities in his work. He used his influence as editor of an important literary magazine to encourage writers with similar goals, such as novelist Soseki Natsume (1867–1916). One of the young writers that Ōgai published was Higuchi Ichiyo (1872–1896), who also sought to create a Japanese Realism. Although she was influenced by the dominant Realism of the period, Ichiyo had been educated in the Chinese and Japanese classics. Her stories about the search for identity in the rapidly changing society of her time, in which she tempers Realist description with a poignant Romanticism, draw on her personal experience as one of the victims of change.

ꙮ Takizawa Bakin
1767–1848

tah-kee-ZAH-wah
bah-KEEN

toh-koo-GAH-wah

The most important novelist of the late Tokugawa period, **Takizawa Bakin** was one of the earliest professional writers in Japan. Later in life he used the money from his writing to reestablish his family's honor and social position in the samurai class, a level of minor nobility. Bakin's tales are historical romances usually set in the fourteenth and fifteenth centuries, when struggles between warring clans were shaping the future course of Japan. He created a mythic version of an aristocratic ancestral Japan. His vision may have been particularly appealing in the final years of **Tokugawa** rule, a time when feudal traditions were disappearing. Bakin's appeal revived again in the late nineteenth century when Japanese nationalism was at its height, leading Japanese writer Mori Ōgai to exclaim that Takizawa Bakin "lives again."

Early Life as a Samurai.   Bakin was born in 1767, the third son of a
SAMURAI. He was trained for service as a samurai, but when he was thirteen he gave up his position with a master and set out on his own as a
ronin (a masterless, wandering warrior), leaving behind his mother and
two elder brothers. During his adolescence, Bakin briefly held several
posts as a samurai, but he also explored many other professions—Confucian scholar, comic poet, calligrapher, fortune teller, dealer in patent
medicines, and physician. Bakin summarized his early life in a letter to
his friend **Suzuki Bokushi:**

> When I was fourteen I studied Confucian scholarship and medi-
> cine, and when I was twenty-four I gave up my samurai status and
> lived in the city, ignoring thoughts of power or profit. Because I had
> no regular job and feared that I might turn into a drifter, I became a
> municipal servant, at least in name. . . . I have worried lest I bring
> shame on my ancestors, and thus I have been very circumspect in
> my actions.

By the time Bakin was in his early twenties, the Takizawa family had been
decimated. His father died in 1775, his mother died ten years later, and his
eldest brother died in 1786. Bakin gave up his last samurai post in 1788,
expecting his remaining elder brother, Rabun, to carry on the family
name and position; when Rabun died in 1798, Bakin was left as the eldest
son. From that point on he devoted himself to reestablishing the family
name, honor, and social position.

Beginning as a Writer.   In the early 1790s Bakin had decided to become
an author and sought the advice and help of **Santo Kyoden** (1761–1816),[1] a
popular writer of the day. Kyoden helped him publish his first story, *A
Night at the Hachiman Shrine* (*Tsukai hatashite nibu kyogen*, 1791), and
employed him briefly as a ghostwriter. Most of Bakin's early works are
KIBYOSHI[2] and GOKAN,[3] two forms of popular writing that featured many
illustrations, often telling their stories "comic book" style, with the dialogue incorporated into illustrations. In 1793 Santo Kyoden arranged for
Bakin to marry a well-to-do widow who owned a shoe business.
Although this unequal marriage placed him well below his birth station,
his wife's business did support him during his years as an apprentice
writer. By the end of the century Bakin was producing an average of ten
kibyoshi a year.

Inventing the Historical Romance.   The family responsibilities that
Bakin took on after his brother's death in 1798 seemed to redirect his
work in a more serious direction. He began the new century by writing

soo-ZOO-kee
boh-KOO-shee

SAHN-toh KYOH-den

For his romantic
fiction that extolled
samurai ideals, he
deserves a place
among the world's
great storytellers. He
stands without peer
as the eminent Edo
author.
– LEON M. ZOLBROD,
Takizawa Bakin, 1967

---

[1] Santo Kyoden: (1761–1816) Popular author of such *kibyoshi* as *A Wanton Edo Born* (1775) and *Confucius a la
mode* (1789) and *yomihon* such as *Water Margin of the Loyal Retainers* (1799–1801).

[2] *kibyoshi*: Literally, "yellow back"; simple illustrated books usually concerned with life in the licensed quarters.

[3] *gokan:* Chapbooks combining pictures and text, often adapting classic Chinese or Japanese stories.

www For links to more information about Bakin and a quiz on *Hakkenden (Eight Dogs)*, see *World Literature Online* at bedfordstmartins .com/worldlit.

mee-nah-MOH-toh
tah-meh-TOH-moh
hahn-SHEE-shee

soh-HAH-koo

MAY-jee

travel diaries in the manner of Bashō, but he discovered his forte when he began writing YOMIHON⁴ (books for reading, rather than picture books) on didactic, historical themes. In his first such work, *Love Is Made in Heaven* (*Geppyokien*, 1803), virtue is rewarded and wickedness inevitably punished; the same is true in all his later historical tales. This first *yomihon* was the first successful historical novel written in Edo (Tokyo) and signaled a cultural shift in nineteenth-century Japan, as Edo replaced Kyoto and Osaka as the cultural center of the nation. In the decade following *Love Is Made in Heaven*, Bakin published another thirteen novels, including *Crescent Moon* (*Chinsetsu yumiharizuki*, 1806), the story of **Minamoto Tametomo** (1139–1170), a legendary bowman who strives to restore his family's fortunes, and *The Complete Story of O'San and Hanshichi* (*Sanshichi zenden nanka no Yume*, 1808), in which **Hanshichi**, son of a former samurai, overcomes the bad karma in his family's past and restores both his family's fortunes and those of his lord.

Hakkenden.   Takizawa Bakin's masterwork is *Nansoo Satomi Hakkenden*, which roughly translates as *The Legend of Nansoo Satomi and the Eight Dogs*. The longest work of Japanese fiction, its 181 chapters were written and published over the twenty-eight years between 1814 and 1842. While he was writing this tale about the restoration of the Satomi clan, Bakin was working to restore his own family. His son **Sohaku**, however, was not the successful samurai that Bakin had wished for; after the young man died in 1835, the despairing author bought a samurai post for his eight-year-old grandson, Taro. By this time Bakin's own health was failing. Almost totally blind, he dictated the last third of *Eight Dogs* to his daughter-in-law. When he died at eighty-two in 1848, Bakin was at work on another long-running *yomihon, Biographies of Chivalrous Men* (*Kaikan kyoki kyokakuden*, 1831–49).

The Theme of Restoration.   Takizawa Bakin's great theme, repeated in nearly all of his epic historical romances, is the restoration of family position and honor. In *Crescent Moon*, for example, Minamoto Tametomo's family is stripped of its hereditary position during the Hogen Insurrection (1156) and the Heiji Rising (1159–60). Tametomo sets out to restore the family's lost privileges and, with the magical aid of some tame wolves and white cranes, he succeeds in doing so. *Eight Dogs,* set in the fifteenth century, recounts the adventures of eight samurai, all of whom are magically related to a mythic dog, as they restore the Satomi clan. Popular in their own day, Bakin's novels had a revival in the late nineteenth century during the MEIJI RESTORATION, when Japan restored the emperor and sought to return to a place of international importance through industrialization.

---

⁴ *yomihon:* Serious, often didactic "reading books" (rather than picture books). This genre, popular in the early nineteenth century, was often made up of historical romances influenced by classic Chinese fiction.

■ CONNECTIONS

Goethe, *Faust,* p. 29. Like Shino who sacrifices his relationship with Hamaji to pursue a higher duty, Goethe's Faust sacrifices Margaret and her family and Baucis and Philemon as he pursues his wider goals. How does Faust justify abandoning Margaret and later dispossessing Baucis and Philemon? What is Shino's justification for leaving Hamaji? How are these characters' reasons representative of their cultures?

Virgil, *The Aeneid* (Book 1); Kalidasa, *Shakuntala* (Book 2). The conflict between public and domestic life is felt today by women who seek to have both a professional career and a family. In classic literature, heroes such as Aeneas in Virgil's *Aeneid* or King Duyshanta in Kalidasa's *Shakuntala* must choose between love and duty as a warrior or a king. Consider the nature of the conflict in *The Aeneid, Shakuntala,* and *Hakkenden.* How is it resolved in each case? How do you explain the reuniting of Shakuntala and Duyshanta? Could Kalidasa's solution work in the cases of Aeneas and Dido or Shino and Hamaji?

■ FURTHER RESEARCH

Biography and Criticism
Zolbrod, Leon M. *Takizawa Bakin.* 1967.

Historical Background
Keene, Donald. *World within Walls: Japanese Literature of the Pre-Modern Era, 1600–1867.* 1976.

■ PRONUNCIATION

Takizawa Bakin: tah-kee-ZAH-wah bah-KEEN
Hamaji: HAH-mah-jee
Hanshichi: hahn-SHEE-chee
Meiji: MAY-jee
Minamoto Tametomo: mee-nah-MOH-toh tah-meh-TOH-moh
Santo Kyoden: SAHN-toh KYOH-den
Shino: SHEE-noh
Sohaku: soh-HAH-koo
Suzuki Bokushi: soo-ZOO-kee boh-KOO-shee
Tokugawa: toh-koo-GAH-wah

ॐ Hakkenden

Translated by Donald Keene

SHINO AND HAMAJI

Shino had gone to bed, but could not sleep in his impatience for the dawn. His head was filled with thoughts about the future. He realized that he was alone, that there was no one to stop him from leaving, but he could not help feeling unhappy that he was now to go far from the graves of his parents and the place where he was born. Hamaji, who regretted his departure no less than he, slipped out of bed and, taking care lest her parents now snoring in the back room should waken, those parents toward whom she felt a resentment she could not voice, she soundlessly stepped over the threshold of the barrier of her maiden reserve, which had hitherto kept her from going to Shino. Her knees trembled, and she could scarcely walk. How dreary, sad, bitter, and hateful the inconstant world now seemed.

When Hamaji came close to Shino's pillow, he saw that someone had entered his room. He drew his sword to him and sprang to his feet. "Who is it?" he cried, but no sound answered him. He wondered uneasily whether some enemy had come to observe whether he was asleep, with the intent of stabbing him to death. He grew more and more tense. He flashed the light of the lamp and peered into the darkness. Then he saw that it was Hamaji. Without warning she had appeared, and now lay motionless on the other side of the mosquito netting, seemingly shaken by grief but unwilling to reveal it by her tears.

Shino was a brave soldier who would not flinch before the fiercest enemy, but now he was disturbed. Controlling his emotions, he left the mosquito netting and, unfastening the cords by which the netting hung, drew his pallet to where she lay. "Hamaji, what has brought you here in the middle of the night, when you should be sleeping? Have you never heard the proverb, 'Don't arouse suspicion by tying your

---

Hakkenden, or *The Legend of Nansoo Satomi and the Eight Dogs.* Set in the fifteenth century, this novel is about the restoration of the Satomi clan. In its recovery and return to prominence, the family is aided by eight miraculous samurai. Linked spiritually to a mythic dog, each of the eight warriors has a name beginning with "dog" and represents one of the Confucian virtues—benevolence, righteousness, courtesy, wisdom, fidelity, loyalty, filial piety, and service to elders. The section excerpted here describes the first of the dog-samurai, Inuzaka Shino, who represents filial piety, as he leaves his fiancée to set out on his mission. Had he not possessed so strong a sense of duty—filial piety—this episode might have ended as a love suicide, a traditional alternative ending that Bakin seems to have in mind in the didactic concluding paragraph of the chapter.

This chapter is the only one of *Hakkenden* to have been translated into English. The novel is a classic in Japan, however, where it has recently been made into a popular series of animated films. The translation is by Donald Keene, the foremost American scholar and translator of Japanese literature of the twentieth century.

shoes in a melon field[1] or by lifting your arms to straighten your hat under a plum tree'?" When he had thus admonished her, Hamaji, brushing away her tears, lifted her head in indignation. "How cruel of you to ask me in that impersonal way why I have come! If we were joined but casually, and husband and wife only in name, you might well speak in that way, but were we not wedded with my parents' consent? Whatever might be the proper behavior under normal circumstances, it is heartless of you tonight, our last night for farewells, to order me out with a careless word. You are pretending not to know what I feel because you are afraid that it might bring discredit to you. How hardhearted of you!"

Shino sighed in spite of himself. "I am not made of wood or stone, and whether I wish it or not, I know what tender emotions are. But it can serve no purpose for me to voice my feelings — it will only arouse the antipathy of your parents. I know that you will be true to me, and you must know what lies within my heart. Koga is a bare forty miles from here — it takes no more than three or four days to make the journey there and back. Please wait till I return."

He tried to persuade her, but Hamaji, wiping her eyes, exclaimed, "What you say is false. Once you leave here, what will ever make you return? The bird in the cage longs for the sky because it misses its friends; when a man leaves his home it must be because he is thinking of his advancement. You cannot depend on the likes and dislikes of my parents.[2] They are sending you off now because you are in the way, and they have no desire for your return. Once you leave here, when will you come back? Tonight is the last we have of parting. . . .

"Ever since the seventh moon of last year the little stream of our love has been dammed and its passage cut, but one thing remains unchanged, like the downward flow of water, the sincerity of my heart. Not a day has passed but that I have prayed morning and night for your safety, success, and prosperity, but you remain extremely hard of heart. Is it because of duty to your aunt that you are deserting your wife? If you had in you one-hundredth of the depth of feeling that I have, you would say to me, 'For one reason or another the day of my return may be doubtful. Let us steal off secretly, together.' We are man and wife — who would slander you as being my paramour? But however cruel I think you are, I cannot, with my woman's heart, bear separation from you. Rather than that I be deserted and left to die of longing for you, kill me with your sword. I shall wait for you in the world to come, a hundred years if need be." To these she added many words of persuasion, relating one after another the painful griefs she bore, and though she kept herself from weeping aloud, a thousand tears coursed down to soak her sleeves.

Shino could not very well say that it would bring embarrassment if her voice were heard outside the room, and since there was no way now to undo the ties that bound them, he could only sigh sadly. He said, with his hands folded on his knees, "Every one of your reproaches is justified, but what can I do, Hamaji? My departure

---

[1] "Don't arouse . . . melon field": That is, the mere fact that Hamaji is in Shino's room will make people think that they have been making love, just as if a man stoops in a melon field, it is assumed that he is stealing a melon. [Translator]

[2] my parents: That is, Hamaji's foster parents.

is by command of my uncle and aunt. I know that they are really sending me to a distant place so as to get a new husband for you. The problem is that I am, and yet I am not, your husband.[3] Your parents probably suspect our true feelings. However, if now I let myself be guided by my emotions and take you off with me, what man will not say that it was a deed of lust? It will be painful for you to remain behind, but it will be for my sake. And if I go, though it is difficult for me to do so, will that not also be for your sake? Even if we are parted for a brief while, as long as our hearts remain constant a time will surely come when we can be fully married. Please go back to bed before your parents awaken. Please go quickly."

His words were in vain; she remained as she was and merely shook her head. "Having gone this far, it doesn't matter any longer.[4] If my parents waken to find me here and reprove me for it, I too shall have something to say. I will not move from here unless I hear you say that you want me to go with you. Otherwise, kill me." Weak as is a woman's will, hers was firmly set and would not alter.

Shino was quite at a loss. A note of irritation came into his voice, although he still kept it low. "You still do not understand. As long as we remain alive a time will surely come when we can meet. How can death be the proper state for man? If you interfere with me, now that I have this rare chance of winning success granted to me by my aunt and uncle, you are not my wife. Perhaps you are an enemy from a previous existence."

Hamaji sank deeper in tears. "There is nothing I can do when you make me feel that if I obtain my heart's desire I shall become your enemy. If my thoughts are really selfish, I shall put them aside and remain here. May your journey be a safe one. Be careful lest, these terribly hot days, you get sunstroke on the way. In the winter months when the wind blows down the northern mountains, send me messages about yourself with the wind. I shall think only of the fact that you are alive and safe. If the weakening thread of my life should break, now will be our parting for this existence, and all I shall have to depend upon is the yet unseen world to come. Our ties are certain to endure through both worlds. Please never change your heart." Thus she spoke of uncertainties; however wise her prayers may have seemed, the heart of this innocent maiden was pitiful.

Shino in spite of himself also felt downcast, and unable to comfort her could only nod. There was nothing else for him to say. Just then the first cock-crow announced the dawn, and Shino, pulling himself together, said, "In a few moments your parents will waken. Hurry! Hurry!"

Hamaji at last got up, and recited the poem,

"*Yo mo akeba*	Now that dawn has come
Kitsu ni hamenan	Perhaps the foxes will eat
Kudakake no	Those cursed roosters,
Madaki ni nakite	Crowing in the early morn,
Sena wo yaritsutsu	Chasing you away from me.[5]

---

[3] "The problem . . . your husband": Shino and Hamaji have been engaged with the consent of her foster parents, but a wedding ceremony has not actually taken place. [Translator]   [4] "Having gone . . . longer": Hamaji thinks that she has already destroyed her reputation. [Translator]   [5] Quoted from *The Tales of Ise*, 13. This tale is of a traveler in the north of Japan who spends one night with a country girl and then leaves her. [Translator]

That poem was inspired by the casual love of a traveler, but now is the moment of separation with a departing husband. If the cocks do not crow the sky will not grow light; if the dawn does not come, no one will waken. Oh, hateful crowing of the cock! For us only are there no nights of meeting—between us stands an unyielding barrier. Even the moon at dawn brings only sorrow."

As she murmured these words, about to leave, there was a cough outside the door and a faint rapping on the door. "The cocks have crowed, are you not awake yet?" It was his servant who called. Shino hastily answered and the man withdrew to the kitchen. "Quickly, before he returns!" Shino said, pushing her out. Hamaji, her eyelids swollen from weeping, looked back from the darkness where she stood, but her eyes were too misted with tears for her to see him. She leant against the wall a moment, and then went to weep in her room.

Sadder even than parting at death is parting in life, than which is nothing sadder. Ah, rare indeed is this maiden! Yet has she to share a bedquilt with her husband, yet to range her pillow by his and sleep with entwined arms. Their love was more admirable than that of a century of ordinary husbands and wives. Shino, though drawn by love, does not waver in his heart, but by being faithful to his love, maintains the proper separation between men and women. Those who wander in the maze of the passions show insufficient wisdom and a lack of discrimination. Few of all the many young people who have once approached the brink have escaped being drowned. But here we have a case of a righteous husband and a chaste wife. Hamaji's love was not one of pleasures and lust. Shino's sighs were of sorrow, and not of weakness. Hamaji's love is still to be sought; men like Shino are rarer than ever.

∿ Mori Ōgai
1862–1922

An army doctor who became the equivalent of the Surgeon General, Mori Ōgai may seem an unlikely candidate to be considered one of the greatest writers of the Meiji period. Steeped in the tradition of the samurai, Japanese and Chinese literature, and European science and literature, Ōgai was one of the first Japanese writers whose birth, education, and career spanned the newly formed bridge between East and West. Although loyal to the values of the Japanese oligarchy (government by the few) and to the traditional rule of *giri*, or obligation to one's public responsibilities, Ōgai also appreciated some of the values of the West, including its emphasis on individual talent, personal freedom, and feeling. Concerned with the conflict between *giri* and *ninjo*, personal feeling, that characterizes the literature of the Tokugawa era, Ōgai 's work negotiates the line between disciplined deference to authority and responsibil-

MOH-ree OH-gigh

www For links to more information about Ōgai and a quiz on "The Dancing Girl," see *World Literature Online* at bedfordstmartins .com/worldlit.

ity to oneself. Many of Ōgai's literary works deal with contact between the Japanese and Europeans, particularly Germans, and in his writing Ōgai tries to integrate the positive aspects of both cultures without compromising his strong sense of national identity.

Education.   Mori Ōgai was born Mori Rintaro in 1862 in the small town of Tsuwano in western Japan. Keeping up a tradition that went back several generations, Ōgai's father Shizuo was a doctor in the service of the *daimyō*, or feudal lord, and Ōgai received the education to follow in his father's footsteps. By age five, he began the study of the Chinese philosophers Confucius (c. 551–479 B.C.E.) and Mencius (372–289 B.C.E.), and at age seven he entered the fief school, where he excelled at his study of Chinese philosophy, mathematics, medicine, and Dutch, winning annual prizes for his scholarship. Shortly after the dissolution of the fiefdoms, Ōgai left Tsuwano for Tokyo, where he took up the study of German— the language of choice for medical professionals—and lived with Nishi Amane, a prominent scholar and bureaucrat in the Department of Military Affairs, whose special interest was Western civilization. By 1874 Ōgai, two years underage, enrolled in the preparatory course for medical school and began his medical training under the direction of German professors in 1877 at the University of Tokyo, from which he graduated in 1881. In that same year he entered the Medical Corps, hoping to travel to Europe.

Travel to Germany.   Within three years, Ōgai received orders to go to Berlin to study hygiene and the administration of medicine in the German army. In Germany, he pursued his medical studies, read widely in German literature and philosophy, including the works of the German writers Goethe (1749–1832), and Heine (1797–1856), and fell in love with a German woman. He left a diary, *Doitsu nikki*, of these years, and some of his impressions of this time show up in his earliest short stories, written shortly after his return to Japan. "The Dancing Girl," ("*Maihime,*" 1890), Ōgai 's first short story, describes the disappointed love affair of Ōta Toyotarō, who, like Ōgai, had been sent to Berlin to study German culture. Other stories that treat the German experience are "A Record of Froth on the Water" ("Utakata no ki") and "The Courier" ("Fumizukai").

Soldier and Scholar.   When he returned to Japan in the fall of 1888, after visiting London and Paris, Ōgai started a literary magazine called *Shiragami zōshi,* in which he published his own and other works of fiction, translations of European and American writers, and literary criticism. Ōgai also published a collection of translations called *Vestiges* (*Omokage*), in which he developed a new form and diction. In addition, he became involved in public health and in urban planning projects, taking up the cause of the working classes who needed housing and health care. After a year-long, unsuccessful marriage that ended in 1890 and a one-year tour of Korea during the Sɪɴᴏ-Jᴀᴘᴀɴᴇꜱᴇ Wᴀʀ[1] in 1894, Ōgai founded an avant-garde journal called *Remarkable Notes* (*Mezamashi-gusa*), which ended in 1900 when he entered what he called his "years of exile" in the remote town of Kokura, banished for his zealous attempt to move Japanese science and art into the modern era too quickly.

In 1902, at the age of forty, Ōgai returned to Tokyo and began another journal, *Eternal Grasses* (*Mannensō*), only to have another war— the Rᴜꜱꜱᴏ-Jᴀᴘᴀɴᴇꜱᴇ[2] Wᴀʀ of 1904–05—interrupt his work as a writer, critic, scholar, and translator. With the end of the war, Ōgai returned to Tokyo and focused his energies on an incredible array of literary tasks. He wrote and produced plays, actively seeking to modernize Japanese drama; translated works of European literature and philosophy; and wrote poetry and fiction. Among the works of this later period are his translations of Henrik Ibsen's *John Gabriel Borkman* (1909) and Goethe's *Faust* (1913); *Shizuka*, a historical drama based on a traditional character from the Nō and Kabuki theater;[3] *Mask* (*Kamen*), a play that speaks out against Naturalism and argues that in the interest of social harmony one should cloak emotions that would disturb others; and the autobiographical quartet of novels *Vita Sexualis* (*Vita sekusuarisu*, 1909, which was banned), *Youth* (*Seinen*, 1911), *Wild Geese* (*Gan*, 1913), and *Destruction* (*Kaijin*), which remained unfinished.

History and Philosophy.   In a key story of 1912, "As If," Ōgai had explored the way history might serve as a means of overcoming the contradictions of modern society. Based in part on the ideas of Hans Vaihinger's[4] *Philosophy of As If* (1911), this story amounts to a philosophical account of the need for a reasoned exploration of the past in order to gain a critical distance on the myths of the present. Critics suggest that this story marks a turning point in Ōgai's thinking, and after its publication he devoted a great deal of his time to historical research and writing. Although he explored a broad range of Japanese history, his primary focus was on the Tokugawa era, a time that represented for him political

---

[1] **Sino-Japanese War:** In 1894, the Qing dynasty in China declared war on the Japanese, who were making advances on the Korean peninsula, to which China laid claims; the Japanese defeated the Chinese, who were forced to give up what is now Taiwan and the Liaotung peninsula in southern Manchuria.

[2] **Russo-Japanese War:** In 1904, war broke out between Japan and Russia, who was contesting Japanese influence in Korea; Japan defeated the Russian fleet off the coast of Korea in 1905, and Russia conceded its loss. Russia's defeat shocked observers around the world and signaled Japan's rise as an imperial power.

[3] *Nō* **and Kabuki theater:** *Nō* is the highly elaborate and ritualistic classical theater of Japan known for its minimalist approach to plot, scenery, and stage effects as well as the Zen-like mastery of its actors. Kabuki is a form of popular Japanese drama using live actors, which developed in the sixteenth and seventeenth centuries alongside the puppet theater; both puppet and live Japanese theater often share the same plots and stories.

[4] **Hans Vaihinger:** (1852–1933) German philosopher whose studies of Kant and Nietzsche led him to conclude that human beings cannot truly know anything but use language to construct philosophical systems that suit their needs and then act "as if" those systems were true. In Vaihinger's view, people live their lives according to useful fictions.

My own study of Ōgai has convinced me (and many generations of Japanese would agree) that Ōgai is not only a commanding figure in his own tradition but a paradigm of modern man in his relentless attempt to look at the emptiness of life objectively and without pious illusion.

– J. THOMAS RIMER,
Preface to *Mori Ōgai*,
1975

and social stability as well as spiritual renewal. Among these stories is "The Last Will and Testament of Okitsu Yagoemon" (1912), a historically displaced meditation on the ritual suicide of General Nogi following the death of Emperor Meiji in 1912. Ōgai also wrote a story set in the Middle Ages, "Sansho the Bailiff" ("*Sanshō dayū*"), and some stories dealing with China, including "*Kanzan Jitoku*" concerning the celebrated Han Shan[5] (c. eighth century), the author of the Cold Mountain poems. Ōgai's interest in historical themes, incidents, and people also led him to write three historical biographies, including *Shibue Chusai* (1916), which tells the story of a doctor from the late Tokugawa period; many Japanese readers regard this piece as Ōgai's masterwork. Shibue's education and career as a doctor in the late Tokugawa period were close enough to Ōgai's to allow him to create a kind of spiritual and intellectual double of himself in the biography. As he fought a kidney ailment and possibly a long-term tuberculosis in the last years of his life, Mori Ōgai tenaciously clung to what he called his "will to write," working and writing almost to the very end of his life on July 9, 1922.

Romantic Fiction.   Known as one of the greatest literary stylists of the Meiji period, Mori Ōgai produced a prodigious body of work in a wide variety of genres, including poetry, drama, the novel, the short story, essays, historical tales, and translations of European writers, particularly Goethe and Ibsen, his favorites. Against the prevailing current of literary NATURALISM, Ōgai adopted a more ROMANTIC aesthetic and criticized Naturalist writers, such as French novelist Émile Zola (1840–1902), for their stark description of unpalatable emotion. Ōgai preferred to remove his reader from the drudgery of the everyday; as he noted in "On the Novel" ("*Shosetsuron*," 1889), the "desire to seek real facts has never hindered dreams of visiting the Infinite."

Early Stories.   In part because of the extensive historical detail Ōgai brings to his writing, many of his works remain untranslated from Japanese. He began his literary career with a burst of activity from 1889 to 1891, when he was in his late twenties, after returning from a four-year tour in Germany as an army medical officer. In those years he published translations of German, French, American, and Russian literature in periodicals, including his own literary magazine founded in 1889, as well as three short stories—"The Dancing Girl," "A Record of Froth on the Water," and "The Courier"—about the love between a Japanese man and a German woman, set in Germany. "The Dancing Girl," Ōgai's first published short story, was written in 1890 and gives a fictionalized account of his own love affair with a young German woman, though the degree to which it matches his exact experience is debatable. "A Record of Froth on the Water," written in the same year, presents a somewhat brighter,

---

[5] Han Shan: "Cold Mountain" was the site of a Buddhist temple in China; the more than three hundred verses known as the "Cold Mountain" poems and attributed to a Buddhist monk named Han Shan were written sometime between 600 and 800 C.E., probably by more than one hand.

though finally tragic, picture of the love between a Japanese artist, Kose, and a German woman, Marie, who visit the Starnbergersee, near Munich, where Marie drowns after the couple witnesses the drowning of "mad" King Ludwig. King Ludwig functions as a key allusion in T. S. Eliot's *Wasteland*, which was not published until 1922. The Ludwig subtext in Ōgai's stories demonstrates, in part, the writer's aim to inform his Japanese readers about European, particularly German, culture.

"The Dancing Girl."   Although the body of Ōgai's work is formidable, "The Dancing Girl" (1890), presented here, has received considerable attention from literary critics and scholars. Partly autobiographical, the story deals with Ōgai's experience in Germany as a medical officer who falls in love with a German woman, only to leave her, pregnant, at the end of his tour. Ōgai himself wrote that "['The Dancing Girl'] is not based on the truth, although there has been a lot of that kind of talk," and he notes, rightly, that stories with similar plots abound. In the story, **Ōta Toyotarō**, the protagonist, arrives in Berlin on an official mission to study. When unfavorable reports lead to his dismissal, he decides to stay on, continue his studies on his own, and live with his German girlfriend, Elise, a ballet dancer. Eventually, Ōta learns that he can return to Japan and restore his name, but only if he leaves Elise, who is now pregnant. Much of the story revolves around his anguished attempt to decide between his homeland and his love. Torn between a traditional sense of obligation to Japan and a newfound individualism, Ōta in many ways personifies the predicament of many Japanese intellectuals in the late nineteenth and early twentieth century who were divided between their indigenous culture and the influences of the West.

OH-tah
toh-yoh-TAH-roh

■ CONNECTIONS

Homer, *The Odyssey* (Book 1); Virgil, *The Aeneid* (Book 1). A recurrent motif in stories from predominantly patriarchal cultures involves a male hero who is distracted from some higher purpose by falling in love with, or being seduced by, a woman. When these stories involve questions of national identity, the woman is often of foreign origin, as in the case of the female figures — Circe and Nausicaa — who threaten to block Odysseus's return to Ithaca in *The Odyssey;* and Dido, whose love detains Aeneas from his mission to found a new homeland in Virgil's *Aeneid.* In "The Dancing Girl," Ota is torn between his duty to Japan and his newly discovered autonomy, symbolized by his relationship with his German lover, Elise. Taking into account the wide cultural and historical divide between the Greek and Roman epics and Ōgai's short story about late-nineteenth-century Japan, why do you think these texts share the structural device of a foreign woman as blocking agent?

Rabindranath Tagore, *Broken Ties*, p. 986; James Joyce, *The Dead* (Book 6). In staging Ōta's internal struggle between returning to Japan and staying with Elise, Ōgai's "Dancing Girl" dramatizes the tension between different value systems through the intimate relationship of two people from different cultures. By way of contrast, in Tagore's *Broken Ties* and Joyce's *The Dead,* women symbolize the homeland (like Penelope in *The Odyssey*) from which the male protagonists are to various degrees alienated: Damini represents traditional India, and Gretta, native Ireland. How are women used to figure or negotiate questions of national identity in these stories?

Tanizaki Junichiro, *Aguri* (Book 6). Written at a time when Japan was deeply self-conscious and ambivalent about the effects of Westernization on its culture, "The Dancing Girl" is a good example of how literature absorbs the key questions of its historical moment and attempts to work through them. Tanizaki's *"Aguri"* also deals with the influence of the West on Japanese society and culture. In it a woman acts as a symbolic agent, this time of Japan's fascination with European fashion, which makes the woman more alluring to Okada. How do these two stories depict the West and Japan's fascination with it? Do the differences between them suggest a shift in Japan's attitude toward the West between the 1890s and 1922?

■ FURTHER RESEARCH

Critical Biography
Bowring, Richard. *Mori Ōgai and the Modernization of Japanese Culture.* 1979.
Johnson, Eric W. "The Historical Fiction and Biography of Mori Ōgai," *The Journal of the Association of Teachers of Japanese.* November 1972.
Rimer, J. Thomas. *Mori Ōgai.* 1975.

Editions
Rimer, J. Thomas. *Youth and Other Stories.* 1994.
———. *Saiki Koi and Other Stories.* 1977.

■ PRONUNCIATION

Mori Ōgai: MOH-ree OH-gigh
Ōta Toyotarō: OH-tah toh-yoh-TAH-roh

❧ The Dancing Girl

Translated by Richard Bowring

They have finished loading the coal, and the tables here in the second-class saloon stand in silence. Even the bright glare from the electric lights seems wasted, for tonight the group of card players who usually gather here of an evening are staying in a hotel and I am left alone on board.

"The Dancing Girl." Mori Ōgai launched his career as a writer of fiction with this story, the first of three written in 1890 and 1891 about tragic love affairs between a Japanese man and a German woman. Based in part on his own experience, "The Dancing Girl" tells the tale of Ōta Toyotarō, a Japanese man sent to study in Berlin, and the dancer Elise. Unfavorable reports from a fellow Japanese lead to Ōta's dismissal from government service, and when he learns that his mother has died back home, he decides to continue his studies on his own. Nonetheless, when Ōta finds he has a chance to be reconciled with his family and country, he decides to return to Japan, leaving his pregnant girlfriend behind. Torn between his sense of obligation to Japan and Western individualism, Ōta personifies in many ways the predicament of many Japanese intellectuals of Ōgai's time and beyond who were divided between traditional Japanese culture and the influences of the West.

The translation and notes are those of Richard Bowring, unless otherwise indicated.

It is now five years since the hopes I cherished for so long were fulfilled and I received orders to go to Europe. When I arrived here in the port of Saigon, I was struck by the strangeness of everything I saw and heard. I wonder how many thousands of words I wrote every day as I jotted down random thoughts in my travel diary. It was published in a newspaper at the time and was highly praised, but now I shudder to think how any sensitive person must have reacted to my childish ideas and my presumptuous rhetoric. I even recorded details of the common flora and fauna, the geology, and the local customs as if they were rarities. Now, on my way home, the notebooks that I bought intending to use for a diary remain untouched. Could it be that while studying in Germany I developed a kind of *nil admirari* attitude? No, there is another reason.

Returning to Japan, I feel a very different person from when I set out. Not only do I still feel dissatisfied with my studies, but I have also learned how sad this transient life can be. I am now aware of the fallibility of human emotions, but in particular I realize what a fickle heart I have myself. To whom could I possibly show a record of fleeting impressions that might well be right one day and wrong the next? Perhaps this is why my diary was never written. No, there is another reason.

Twenty days or more have passed since we left Brindisi.[1] Usually it is the custom at sea to while away the cares of travel even in the company of utter strangers, but I have shut myself up in my cabin under the pretext of feeling somewhat indisposed. I seldom speak to my fellow travelers, for I am tormented by a hidden remorse.

At first this pain was a mere wisp of cloud that brushed against my heart, hiding the mountain scenery of Switzerland and dulling my interest in Italy's ancient ruins. Then gradually I grew weary of life and weary of myself, and suffered the most heart-rending anguish. Now, remorse has settled in the depths of my heart, the merest shadow. And yet, with everything I read and see it causes me renewed pain, evoking feelings of extreme nostalgia, like a form reflected in a mirror or the echo of a voice.

How can I ever rid myself of such remorse? If it were of a different nature I could perhaps soothe my feelings by expressing them in poetry. But it is so deeply engraved upon my heart that I fear this is impossible. And yet, as there is no one here this evening, and it will be some while before the cabin boy comes to turn off the light, I think I will try to record the outline of my story here.

Thanks to a very strict education at home since childhood, my studies lacked nothing, despite the fact that I had lost my father at an early age. When I studied at the school in my former fief, and in the preparatory course for the university in Tokyo, and later in the Faculty of Law, the name Ōta Toyotarō was always at the top of the list. Thus, no doubt, I brought some comfort to my mother who had found in me, her only child, the strength to go through life. At nineteen I received my degree and was praised for having achieved greater honor than had any other student since the founding of the university. I joined a government department and spent three pleasant years in Tokyo with my mother, whom I had called up from the country. Being especially high in the estimation of the head of my department, I was then

---

[1] Brindisi: A port town in southeastern Italy.

given orders to travel to Europe and study matters connected with my particular section. Stirred by the thought that now I had the opportunity to make my name and raise my family fortunes, I was not too sorry to leave even my mother, although she was over fifty. So it was that I left home far behind and arrived in Berlin.

I had the vague hope of accomplishing great feats and was used to working hard under pressure. But suddenly here I was, standing in the middle of this most modern of European capitals. My eyes were dazzled by its brilliance, my mind was dazed by the riot of color. To translate Unter den Linden[2] as 'under the Bodhi tree' would suggest a quiet secluded spot. But just come and see the groups of men and women sauntering along the pavements that line each side of that great thoroughfare as it runs, straight as a die, through the city. It was still in the days when Wilhelm I[3] would come to his window and gaze down upon his capital. The tall, broad-shouldered officers in their colorful dress uniform, and the attractive girls, their hair made up in the Parisian style, were everywhere a delight to the eye. Carriages ran silently on asphalt roads. Just visible in the clear sky between the towering buildings were fountains cascading with the sound of heavy rain. Looking into the distance, one could see the statue of the goddess on the victory column. She seemed to be floating halfway to heaven from the midst of the green trees on the other side of the Brandenburg Gate.[4] All these myriad sights were gathered so close at hand that it was quite bewildering for the newcomer. But I had promised myself that I would not be impressed by such captivating scenes of beauty and I continually closed my mind to these external objects that bore in on me.

The Prussian officials were all happy to welcome me when I pulled on the bell rope, asked for an interview, and handed over my open letter of introduction, explaining to them why I had come. They promised to tell me whatever I wished to know once formal application had been received from the Legation. I was fortunate enough to have learned both French and German at home, and no sooner was I introduced than they asked where and when I had learned to speak so well.

I had already obtained official permission to enter Berlin University and so I enrolled to study politics whenever my duties might permit. After one or two months, when the official preliminaries had been carried out and my investigations were making good progress, I sent off a report on the most urgent matters, and the rest I wrote down in a number of notebooks. As far as the university was concerned, there was no chance of providing special courses for would-be politicians, as I had naively hoped. I was irresolute for a while, but then, deciding to attend two or three law lectures, I paid the fee and went to listen.

---

[2] Unter den Linden: A street lined with lime trees in Berlin. Ōgai may also allude to the classic poem by Walter von der Vogelweide (c. 1170–1230), a medieval German lyric poet. The linden is a lime tree; the Bodhi tree is the sacred fig tree, associated with Gautama Buddha, who attained enlightenment meditating beneath this "tree of wisdom."

[3] Wilhelm I: (1797–1888) King of Prussia from 1861–1888, who appointed Otto von Bismarck as prime minister in 1862; after Bismarck oversaw the unification of German states under Prussia, Wilhelm was emperor of Germany from 1871 until his death in 1888. [Ed.]

[4] Brandenburg Gate: A magnificent gate in Berlin, designed in the Doric style by Karl Langhaus and completed in 1791.

Some three years passed in this way like a dream. But there is always a time when, come what may, one's true nature reveals itself. I had obeyed my father's dying words and had done what my mother had taught me. From the beginning I had studied willingly, proud to hear myself praised as an infant prodigy, and later I had labored unremittingly in the happy knowledge that my department head was pleased with my excellent work. But all that time I had been a mere passive, mechanical being with no real awareness of myself. Now, however, at the age of twenty-five, perhaps because I had been exposed to the liberal ways of the university for some time, there grew within me a kind of uneasiness; it seemed as if my real self, which had been lying dormant deep down, was gradually appearing on the surface and threatening my former assumed self. I realized that I would be happy neither as a high-flying politician nor as a lawyer learning statutes off by heart and pronouncing sentence.

My mother, I thought to myself, had tried to make me into a walking dictionary, and my department head had tried to turn me into an incarnation of the law. The former I might just be able to stand, but the latter was out of the question. Up to then I had answered him with scrupulous care even in quite trifling matters, but from that time on, I often argued in my reports that one should not be bothered with petty legal details. Once a person grasped the spirit of the law, I grandly said, everything would solve itself. In the university I abandoned the law lectures, and became more interested in history and literature; eventually I moved into the world of the arts.

My department head had obviously tried to turn me into a machine that could be manipulated as he desired. He could hardly have been very pleased with someone who entertained such independent ideas and held such unusual views. I was in a precarious situation. If that were all, however, it would not have been enough to undermine my position. But among the students studying at Berlin at the time was an influential group with whom I did not see eye to eye. They were only suspicious of me at first, but then they began to slander me. They may have had good reason.

Attributing the fact that I neither drank nor played billiards with them to apparent stubbornness and self-restraint on my part, they ridiculed and envied me. But this was because they did not know me. How could anyone else know the reason for my behavior when I did not know it myself? I felt like the leaves of the silk-tree which shrink and shy away when they are touched. I felt as unsure of myself as a young girl. Ever since my youth I had followed the advice of my elders and kept to the path of learning and obedience. If I had succeeded, it was not through being courageous. I might have seemed capable of arduous study, but I had deceived not only myself but others too. I had simply followed a path that I was made to follow. The fact that external matters did not disturb me was not because I had the courage to reject them or ignore them, but rather because I was afraid and tied myself hand and foot. Before I left home I was convinced I was a man of talent. I believed deeply in my own powers of endurance. Yes, but even that was short-lived. I felt quite the hero until the ship left Yokohama, but then I found myself weeping uncontrollably. I thought it strange at the time, but it was my true nature showing through. Perhaps it had been with me from my birth; or perhaps it came about because my father died and I was brought up by my mother.

The ridicule of the students was only to be expected, but it was stupid of them to be jealous of such a weak and pitiful mind.

I used to see women sitting in the cafés soliciting for custom; their faces were heavily made up and their clothes were gaudy. But I never had the courage to go and approach them. Nor did I have the nerve to join in with those men about town, with their tall hats, their pince-nez, and that aristocratic nasal accent so peculiar to Prussians. Not having the heart for such things, I found I could not mix with my more lively fellow countrymen, and because of this barrier between us, they bore a grudge against me. Then they started telling tales, and thus I was accused of crimes I had not committed and had to put up with so much hardship in so short a time.

One evening I sauntered through the Tiergarten and then walked down Unter den Linden. On the way back to my lodgings in Monbijoustrasse, I came in front of the old church in Klosterstrasse. How many times, I wonder, had I passed through that sea of lights, entered this gloomy passage, and stood enraptured, gazing at the three-hundred-year-old church that lay set back from the road. Opposite it stood some houses with the washing hanging out to dry on poles on the roofs, and a bar where an old Jew with long whiskers was standing idly by the door; there was also a tenement house with one flight of steps running directly to the upper rooms and another leading down to the home of a blacksmith who lived in the cellar.

Just as I was walking past I noticed a young girl sobbing against the closed door of the church. She must have been about sixteen or seventeen. Her light golden hair flowed down from under the scarf around her head, and her dress was spotlessly clean. Surprised by my footsteps, she turned around. Only a poet could really do her justice. Her eyes were blue and clear, but filled with a wistful sadness. They were shaded by long eyelashes which half hid her tears. Why was it that in one glance over her shoulder she pierced the defenses of my heart?

Perhaps it was because of some profound grief that she was standing there in tears oblivious of all else. The coward in me was overcome by compassion and sympathy, and without thinking I went to her side.

'Why are you crying?' I asked. 'Perhaps because I am a stranger here I may be able to help you all the more.' I was astounded by my audacity.

Startled, she stared into my sallow face, but she must have seen my sincerity from my expression.

'You look a kind sort of person,' she sobbed. 'Not cruel like him or my mother!'

Her tears had stopped for a moment, but now they overflowed again and ran down her lovely cheeks.

'Help me! You must help me from having to lose all sense of shame. My mother beat me because I did not agree to his proposal. My father has just died and we have to bury him tomorrow. But we don't have a penny in the house.'

She dissolved into tears again. I gazed at her as she hung her head and trembled.

'If I am to take you home, you must calm down,' I said. 'Don't let everyone hear you. We're out in the street.'

She had inadvertently lain her head on my shoulder while I was speaking. Suddenly she looked up and, giving me the same startled glance as before, she fled from me in shame.

She walked quickly, as if unwilling for people to see her, and I followed. Through a large door across the road from the church was a flight of old worn stone steps. Up these steps on the third floor was a door so small that one needed to bend down to enter. The girl pulled on the twisted end of a rusty piece of wire.

'Who's there?' came a hoarse voice from inside.

'It's Elise. I'm back.'

She had hardly finished speaking when the door was roughly pulled open by an old woman. Although her hair was graying and her brow clearly showed the traces of poverty and suffering, it was not an evil face. She was wearing an old dress of some wool and cotton material and had on some dirty slippers. When Elise pointed to me and went inside, the old woman slammed the door in my face as if she had been waiting impatiently.

I stood there vacantly for a while. Then, by the light of an oil lamp, I noticed a name painted on the door in lacquer: 'Ernst Weigert,' and below, 'Tailor.' I presumed it was the name of the girl's dead father. Inside I heard voices raised as if in argument, then all was quiet again. The door was reopened, and the old woman, apologizing profusely for such impolite behavior, invited me in.

The door opened into the kitchen. On the right was a low window with spotlessly clean linen curtains. On the left was a roughly-built brick stove. The door of the room facing me was half open and I saw inside a bed covered with a white sheet. The dead man must have been lying there. She opened a door next to the stove and led me to an attic; it faced onto the street and had no real ceiling. The beams sloping down from the corners of the roof to the window were covered with paper, and below that, where there was only room enough to stoop, was a bed. On the table in the middle of the room was spread a beautiful woollen cloth on which were arranged two books, a photograph album, and a vase with a bunch of flowers. They seemed somehow too expensive for the place. Standing shyly beside the table was the girl.

She was exceedingly attractive. In the lamplight her pallid face had a faint blush, and the slender beauty of her hands and feet seemed hardly to belong to the daughter of a poor family. She waited until the old woman had left the room and then spoke. She had a slight accent.

'It was thoughtless of me to lead you here. Please forgive me. But you looked so very kind. You won't despise me, will you. I suppose you don't know Schaumberg, the man we were relying on for my father's funeral tomorrow. He's the manager at the Viktoria Theater. I have been working for him for two years so I thought he was bound to help us; but he took advantage of our misfortune and tried to force me to do what he wished. You must help. I promise to pay you back from the little I earn, even if I have to go hungry. If not, then my mother says. . . .'

She burst into tears and stood there trembling. There was an irresistible appeal in her eyes as she gazed up at me. Did she know the effect her eyes had on me, or was it unintentional?

I had two or three silver marks in my pocket, but that would probably not have been enough. So I took off my watch and laid it on the table.

'This will help you for the time being,' I said. 'Tell the pawnbroker's man if he calls on Ōta at 3 Monbijoustrasse, I'll redeem it.'

The girl looked startled but grateful. As I put out my hand to say goodbye, she raised it to her lips and covered it with tears.

Alas, what evil fate brought her to my lodgings to thank me? She looked so beautiful there standing by the window where I used to sit reading all day long surrounded by the works of Schopenhauer and Schiller.[5] From that time on our relationship gradually deepened. When my countrymen got to know, they immediately assumed that I was seeking my pleasures in the company of dancing girls. But it was as yet nothing more than a foolish trifling affair.

One of my fellow countrymen — I will not give his name, but he was known as a mischief-maker — reported to my department head that I was frequenting theaters and seeking the company of actresses. My superior was in any case resentful that I was neglecting my proper studies, and so he eventually told the Legation to abolish my post and terminate my employment. The Minister at the Legation passed this order on, advising me that they would pay the fare if I returned home immediately, but that I could expect no official help if I decided to stay on. I asked for one week's grace, and it was while I was thus worrying what to do that I received two letters which brought me the most intense pain I think I have ever suffered. They had both been sent at almost the same time, but one was written by my mother and the other by a friend telling me of her death, the death of the mother who was so dear to me. I cannot bear to repeat here what she wrote. Tears prevent my pen from writing more.

The relationship between Elise and myself had in fact been more innocent than had appeared to others. Her father had been poor and her education had been meager. At the age of fifteen she had answered an advertisement by a dancing master and had learned that disreputable trade. When she had finished the course, she went to the Viktoria Theater and was now the second dancer of the group. But the life of a dancer is precarious. As the writer Hackländer[6] has said, they are today's slaves, tied by a poor wage and driven hard with rehearsals in the daytime and performances at night. In the theater dressing room they can make up and dress themselves in beautiful clothes; but outside they often do not have enough clothes or food for themselves and life is very hard for those who have to support their parents or families. It was said that, as a result, it was rare for them not to fall into the lowest of all professions.

Elise had escaped this fate, partly owing to her modest nature and partly because of her father's careful protection. Ever since a child, she had in fact liked reading, but all she could lay her hands on were poor novels of the type lent by the circulating libraries, known by their cry of 'Colportage.' After meeting me, she began to read the books I lent her, and gradually her tastes improved and she lost her accent. Soon the mistakes in her letters to me became fewer. And so there had grown up between us a kind of teacher–pupil relationship. When she heard of my untimely dismissal, she went pale. I concealed the fact that it was connected with her, but she

---

[5] **Schopenhauer and Schiller:** Arthur Schopenhauer (1788–1860), German philosopher influenced by Hindu thought; Friedrich von Schiller (1759–1805), German writer of literary, critical, and historical works.

[6] **Hackländer:** Friedrich Wilhelm von Hackländer (1807–1877), a minor German novelist and playwright.

asked me not to tell her mother. She was afraid that if her mother knew I had lost financial support for my studies she would want nothing more to do with me.

There is no need to describe it in detail here, but it was about this time that my feeling for her suddenly changed to one of love and the bond between us deepened. The most important decision of my life lay before me. It was a time of real crisis. Some perhaps may wonder and criticize my behavior, but my affection for Elise had been strong ever since our first meeting, and now I could read in her expression sympathy for my misfortune and sadness at the prospect of parting. The way she stood there, a picture of loveliness, her hair hanging loose — I was distraught by so much suffering and powerless in the face of such enchantment.

The day I had arranged to meet the Minister approached. Fate was pressing. If I returned home like this, I should have failed in my studies and bear a disgraced name. I would never be able to re-establish myself. But on the other hand, if I stayed, I could not see any way of obtaining funds to support my studies.

At this point, my friend Aizawa Kenkichi, with whom I am now travelling home, came to my aid. He was private secretary to Count Amakata in Tokyo, and he saw the report of my dismissal in the Official Gazette. He persuaded the editor of a certain newspaper to make me their foreign correspondent, so I could stay in Berlin and send back reports on various topics such as politics and the arts.

The salary they offered was a pittance, but by changing my lodgings and eating lunch at a cheaper restaurant, I would just be able to make ends meet. While I was trying to decide, Elise showed her love by throwing me a life line. I don't know how she did it, but she managed to win over her mother, and I was accepted as a lodger in their rooms. It was not long before Elise and I found ourselves pooling our meager resources, and managed, even in the midst of all our troubles, to enjoy life.

After breakfast, Elise either went to rehearsals, or, when she was free, would stay at home. I would go to the coffee shop on Königsstrasse with its narrow frontage and its long deep interior. There, in a room lit by an open skylight, I used to read all the newspapers and jot down the odd note or two in pencil. Here would come young men with no regular job, old men who lived quite happily by lending out the little money that they had, and jobbers stealing time off from their work at the Exchange to put their feet up for a while. I wonder what they made of the strange Japanese who sat among them writing busily on the cold stone table, quite oblivious that the cup of coffee the waitress had brought was getting cold, and who was always going back and forth to the wall where the newspapers were hanging open in long wooden frames. When Elise had rehearsals, she would call in about one o'clock on her way home. Some of the people there must have looked askance when we left together, myself and this girl who seemed as if she could dance in the palm of your hand.

I neglected my studies. When she came home from the theater, Elise would sit in a chair and sew, and I would write my articles on the table by her side, using the faint light of the lamp hanging from the ceiling. These articles were quite unlike my earlier reports when I had raked up onto paper the dead leaves of laws and statutes. Now I wrote about the lively political scene and criticized the latest trends in literature and the arts, carefully composing the articles to the best of my ability, more in the style of Heine than Börne.[7] During this time Wilhelm I and Friedrich III[8] died in quick succession. Writing particularly detailed reports on subjects such as the accession of the new emperor and the fall of Bismarck,[9] I found myself from then on much busier than I had expected, and it was difficult to read the few books I had or return to my studies. I had not cancelled my registration at the university, but I could not afford to pay the fees and so seldom went to any lectures.

Yes, I neglected my studies. But I did become expert in a different sphere—popular education, for this was more advanced in Germany than in any other European country. No sooner had I become a correspondent than I was constantly reading and writing about the variety of excellent discussions appearing in the newspapers and journals, and I brought to this work the perception gained from my studies as a university student. My knowledge of the world, which up to then had been rather limited, thus became much broader, and I reached a stage undreamed of by most of my compatriots studying there. They could barely read the editorials in the German newspapers.

Then came the winter of 1888. They spread grit on the pavements of the main streets and shoveled the snow into piles. Although the ground in the Klosterstrasse area was bumpy and uneven, the surface became smooth with ice. It was sad to see the starved sparrows frozen to death on the ground when you opened the door in the mornings. We lit a fire in the stove to warm the room, but it was still unbearably cold. The north European winter penetrated the stone walls and pierced our cotton clothes. A few evenings before, Elise had fainted on stage and had been helped home by some friends. She felt ill from then on and rested. But she brought up whatever she tried to eat and it was her mother who first suggested that it might be morning sickness. Even without this my future was uncertain. What could I possibly do if it were true?

It was Sunday morning. I was at home, but felt somewhat uneasy. Elise did not feel bad enough to go to bed; she sat on a chair drawn up close to the small fireplace but said little. There was the sound of someone at the door and her mother, who had been in the kitchen, hurried in with a letter for me. I recognized Aizawa's handwriting immediately, but the stamp was Prussian and it was postmarked Berlin. Feeling puzzled, I opened the letter. The news was totally unexpected: 'Arrived yesterday evening as part of Count Amakata's suite. The Count says he wants to see you immediately. If your fortunes are ever to be restored, now is the time. Excuse brevity but sent in great haste.'

---

[7] Heine . . . Börne: **Heinrich Heine** (1797–1856), a leading liberal German writer and poet, who worked in Paris as a foreign correspondent for German newspapers; Karl Ludwig Börne (1786–1837), German republican writer and satirist. Heine, whose style is more subtle and ironic than Börne's, which is overtly satirical and polemical, looked up to Börne as a young man and wrote a tribute to him.

[8] Friedrich III: (1831–1888) King of Prussia and emperor of Germany; successor to Wilhelm I, Friedrich ruled for just three months from March to June 1888, before dying of cancer. He was succeeded by his son, Wilhelm II. [Ed.]

[9] Bismarck: Otto von Bismarck (1815–1898), German statesman who brought Germany under Prussian rule; prime minister of Prussia from 1862 to 1890 and the first chancellor of Germany, from 1871 to 1890. Bismarck was dismissed by Wilhelm II. [Ed.]

I stared at the letter.

'Is it from home?' asked Elise. 'It's not bad news, is it?'

She was probably thinking it was connected with my salary from the newspaper.

'No,' I replied. 'There's no need to worry. You've heard me mention Aizawa. Well, he's just arrived in Berlin with his Minister. He wants to see me. He says it's urgent, so I'd better go along without delay.'

Not even a mother seeing off her beloved only child could have been more solicitous. Thinking I was to have an interview with the Count, Elise fought back her illness. She chose a clean white shirt and got out my *Gehrock,* a coat with two rows of buttons, which she had carefully stored away. She helped me into it, and even tied my cravat for me.

'Now no one will be able to say you look a disgrace. Look in my mirror,' she said. 'Why so miserable? I wish I could come too!'

She straightened my suit a little.

'But when I see you dressed up like this, you somehow don't look like my Toyotarō.'

She thought for a moment.

'If you do become rich and famous, you'll never leave me, will you. Even if my illness does not turn out to be what Mother says it is.'

'What! Rich and famous?' I smiled. 'I lost the desire to enter politics years ago. I don't even want to see the Count. I'm just going to meet an old friend whom I have not seen for a very long time.'

The first-class *Droschke*[10] that her mother had ordered drew up under the window, the wheels creaking in the snow. I put on my gloves, slung my slightly soiled overcoat about my shoulders without putting my arms through the sleeves, and picked up my hat. I kissed Elise goodbye and went downstairs. She opened the ice-covered window to see me off, her hair blowing in the north wind.

I got out at the entrance to the Kaiserhof. Inquiring the room number of Private Secretary Aizawa from the doorman, I climbed the marble staircase. It had been a long time since I had last been there. I came to an antechamber where there was a plush sofa by the central pillar and directly ahead a mirror. Here I took off my coat and, passing along a corridor, arrived at Aizawa's door. I hesitated a little. How would he greet me? When we were at university together, he had been so impressed by my correct behavior. I entered the room and we met face to face. He seemed stouter and sturdier than of old, but he had the same naturally cheerful disposition and did not appear to be concerned about my misconduct. But we were given no time to discuss in detail what had happened since we had last met, for I was called in and interviewed by the Count. He entrusted me with the translation of some urgent documents written in German. I accepted them and took my leave. Aizawa followed me out and invited me to lunch.

During the meal it was he who asked all the questions and I who gave the

---

[10] *Droschke:* A carriage for hire.

answers, because his career had been in the main uneventful, whereas the story of my life was full of troubles and adversity.

He listened as I told him about my unhappy experiences with complete frankness. He was often surprised, but never tried to blame me. On the contrary he ridiculed my boorish countrymen. But when I had finished my tale he became serious and remonstrated with me. Things had reached this pass because I was basically weak-willed, but there was no point in laboring the fact now, he said. Nevertheless, how long could a man of talent and learning like myself remain emotionally involved with a mere chit of a girl and lead such an aimless life? At this stage Count Amakata merely needed me for my German. Since he knew the reason for my dismissal, Aizawa would make no attempt to make him change his preconception of me — it would do neither of us any good if the Count were to think that we were trying to deceive him. But there was no better way to recommend people than by displaying their talents. I should show the Count how good I was and so try to win his confidence. As for the girl, she might be sincerely in love with me and our passions deeply involved, but there was certainly no meeting of minds — I had merely allowed myself to slip into what was an accepted practice. I must decide to give her up, he urged.

When he mapped out my future like this, I felt like a man adrift who spies a mountain in the distance. But the mountain was still covered in cloud. I was not sure whether I would reach it, or even if I did, whether it would bring satisfaction. Life was pleasant even in the midst of poverty and Elise's love was hard to reject. Being so weak-willed I could make no decision there and then, so I merely promised to follow my friend's advice for a while, and try and break off the affair. When it came to losing something close to me, I could resist my enemies, but never could refuse my friends.

We parted about four o'clock. As I came out of the hotel restaurant the wind hit me in the face. A fire had been burning in a big tiled stove inside, so when the double glass doors closed behind me and I stood outside in the open, the cold of the afternoon pierced my thin overcoat and seemed all the more intense. I shivered, and there was a strange chill in my heart too.

I finished the translation in one night. Thereafter I found myself going to the Kaiserhof quite often. At first the Count spoke only of business, but after a while he brought up various things that had happened at home recently and asked my opinion. When the occasion arose, he would tell me about the mistakes people had made on the voyage out, and would burst out laughing.

A month went by. Then one day he suddenly turned to me.

'I'm leaving for Russia tomorrow. Will you come with me?' he asked.

I had not seen Aizawa for several days as he was busy with official business, and the request took me totally by surprise.

'How could I refuse?' I replied.

I must confess that I did not answer as the result of a quick decision. When I am suddenly asked a question by someone whom I trust, I instantly agree without weighing up the consequences. Not only do I agree, but, despite knowing how difficult the matter will be, I often hide my initial thoughtlessness by persevering and carrying it out.

That day I was given not only the translation fee but also my travel money. When I got home I gave the fee to Elise. With this she would be able to support herself and her mother until such time as I returned from Russia. She said she had been to see a doctor, who confirmed that she was pregnant. Being anaemic she hadn't realized her condition for some months. She had also received a message from the theater telling her that she had been dismissed as she had been away for so long. She had only been off work for a month, so there was probably some other reason for such severity. Believing implicitly in my sincerity, she did not seem unduly worried about the impending journey.

The journey was not long by train and so there was little to prepare. I just packed into a small suitcase a hired black suit, a copy of the *Almanach de Gotha,* and two or three dictionaries. In view of recent depressing events, I felt it would be miserable for Elise after my departure. I was also anxious lest she should cry at the station, so I took the step of sending her and her mother out early the next morning to visit friends. I collected up my things and locked the door on my way out, leaving the key with the cobbler who lived at the entrance.

What is there to tell of my travels in Russia? My duties as an interpreter suddenly lifted me from the mundane and dropped me above the clouds into the Russian court. Accompanying the Count's party, I went to St. Petersburg, where I was overwhelmed by the ornate architecture of the palace, which represented for me the greatest splendors of Paris transported into the midst of ice and snow. Above all I remember the countless flickering yellow candles, the light reflected by the multitude of decorations and epaulets, and the fluttering fans of the court ladies, who forgot the cold outside as they sat in the warmth from the exquisitely carved and inlaid fireplaces. As I was the most fluent French speaker in the party, I had to circulate between host and guest and interpret for them.

But I had not forgotten Elise. How could I? She sent me letters every day. On the day I left, she had wanted to avoid the unaccustomed sadness of sitting alone by lamplight, and so had talked late into the night at a friend's house. Then, feeling tired, she returned home and immediately went to bed. Next morning, she wondered if she had not just dreamed she was alone. But when she got up, her depression and sense of loneliness were worse than the time when she had been scratching a living and had not known where the next meal was coming from. This was what she told me in her first letter.

Later letters seemed to be written in great distress, and each of them began in the same way.

'Ah! Only now do I realize the depth of my love for you. As you say you have no close relatives at home, you will stay here if you find you can make a good living, won't you? My love must tie you here to me. Even if that proves impossible and you have to return home, I could easily come with my mother. But where would we get the money for the fare? I had always intended to stay here and wait for the day you became famous, whatever I had to do. But the pain of separation grows stronger every day, even though you are only on a short trip and have only been away about twenty days. It was a mistake to have thought that parting was just a passing sorrow. My pregnancy is at last beginning to be obvious, so you cannot reject me now, whatever happens. I quarrel a lot with Mother. But she has given in, now she sees how much more determined I am than I used to be. When I travel home with you, she's talking of going to stay with some distant relatives who live on a farm near Stettin. If, as you say in your last letter, you are doing important work for the Minister, we can somehow manage the fare. How I long for the day you return to Berlin.'

It was only after reading this letter that I really understood my predicament. How could I have been so insensitive! I had been proud to have made a decision about my own course of action and that of others unrelated to me. But it had been made in entirely favorable rather than adverse conditions. When I tried to clarify my relationship with others, the emotions that I had formerly trusted became confused.

I was already on very good terms with the Count. But in my shortsightedness I only took into consideration the duties that I was then undertaking. The gods might have known how this was connected to my hopes for the future, but I never gave it a thought. Was my passion cooling? When Aizawa had first recommended me, I had felt that the Count's confidence would be hard to gain, but now I had to some extent won his trust. When Aizawa had said things like, 'If we continue to work together after you return to Japan,' I wondered whether he had really been hinting that this was what the Count was saying. It was true that Aizawa was my friend, but he would not have been able to tell me openly since it was an official matter. Now that I thought about it, I wondered whether he had perhaps told the Count what I had rashly promised him — that I was going to sever my connections with Elise.

When I first came to Germany, I thought that I had discovered my true nature, and I swore never to become used as a machine again. But perhaps it was merely the pride of a bird that had been given momentary freedom to flap its wings and yet still had its legs bound. There was no way I could loose the bonds. The rope had first been in the hands of my department head, and now, alas, it was in the hands of the Count.

It happened to be New Year's Day when I returned to Berlin with the Count's party. I left them at the station and took a cab home. In Berlin no one sleeps on New Year's Eve and it is the custom to lie in late the next morning. Every single house was quiet. The snow on the road had frozen hard into ruts in the bitter cold and shone brightly in the sunlight. The cab turned into Klosterstrasse and pulled up at the entrance to the house. I heard a window open but saw nothing from inside the cab. I got the driver to take my bag and was just about to climb the steps when Elise came flying down to meet me. She cried out and flung her arms around my neck. At this the driver was a little startled and mumbled something in his beard that I could not hear.

'Oh! Welcome home! I would have died if you had not returned!' she cried.

Up to now I had prevaricated. At times the thought of Japan and the desire to seek fame seemed to overcome my love, but at this precise moment all my hesitation left me and I hugged her. She laid her head on my shoulder and wept tears of happiness.

'Which floor do I take it to?' growled the driver as he hurried up the stairs with the luggage.

I gave a few silver coins to her mother, who had come to the door to meet me, and asked her to pay the driver. Elise held me by the hand and hurried into the room. I was surprised to see a pile of white cotton and lace lying on the table. She laughed and pointed to the pile.

'What do you think of all the preparations?' she said.

She picked up a piece of material and I saw it was a baby's nappy.

'You cannot imagine how happy I am!' she said. 'I wonder if our child will have your dark eyes. Ah, your eyes that I have only been able to dream about. When it's born, you will do the right thing, won't you? You'll give it your name and no one else's, won't you?'

She hung her head.

'You may laugh at me for being silly, but I will be so happy the day we go to church.'

Her uplifted eyes were full of tears.

I did not call on the Count for two or three days because I thought he might be tired from the journey, and so I stayed at home. Then, one evening, a messenger came bearing an invitation. When I arrived, the Count greeted me warmly and thanked me for my work in Russia. He then asked me whether I felt like returning to Japan with him. I knew so much and my knowledge of languages alone was of great value, he said. He had thought that, seeing I had been so long in Germany, I might have some ties here, but he had asked Aizawa and had been relieved to hear that this was not the case.

I could not possibly deny what appeared to be the situation. I was shaken, but of course found it impossible to contradict what Aizawa had told him. If I did not take this chance, I might lose not only my homeland but also the very means by which I might retrieve my good name. I was suddenly struck by the thought that I might die in this sea of humanity, in this vast European capital. I showed my lack of moral fiber and agreed to go.

It was shameless. What could I say to Elise when I returned? As I left the hotel my mind was in indescribable turmoil. I wandered, deep in thought, not caring where I was going. Time and time again I was cursed at by the drivers of carriages that I bumped into and I jumped back startled. After a while I looked around and found I was in the Tiergarten. I half collapsed onto a bench by the side of the path. My head was on fire and felt as if someone were pounding it with a hammer as I leaned back. How long did I lie there like a corpse? The terrible cold creeping into the marrow of my bones woke me up. It was nighttime and the thickly falling snow had piled up an inch high on my shoulders and the peak of my cap.

It must have been past eleven. Even the tracks of the horse-drawn trams along Mohabit and Karlstrasse were buried under the snow and the gas lamps around the Brandenburg Gate gave out a bleak light. My feet were frozen stiff when I tried to get up, and I had to rub them with my hands before I could move.

I walked slowly and it must have been past midnight when I got to Kloster-strasse. I don't know how I got there. It was early January and the bars and tea shops on Unter den Linden must have been full, but I remember nothing of that. I was completely obsessed by the thought that I had committed an unforgivable crime.

In the fourth-floor attic Elise was evidently not yet asleep, for a bright gleam of light shone out into the night sky. The falling snowflakes were like a flock of small white birds, and the light kept on disappearing and reappearing as if the plaything of the wind. As I went in through the door I realized how weary I was. The pain in my joints was so unbearable that I half crawled up the stairs. I went through the kitchen, opened the door of the room, and stumbled inside. Elise was sewing nappies by the table and turned round.

'What have you been doing?' she gasped. 'Just look at you!'

She had good reason to be shocked. My face was as pale as a corpse. I had lost my cap somewhere on the way and my hair was in a frightful mess. My clothes were torn and dirty from the muddy snow as I had stumbled many times along the road.

I remember trying to reply, but I could say nothing. Unable to stand because my knees were shaking so violently, I tried to grab a chair, but then I fell to the floor.

It was some weeks later that I regained consciousness. I had just babbled in a high fever while Elise tended me. Then one day Aizawa had come to visit me, saw for himself what I had hidden from him, and arranged matters by only telling the Count that I was ill. When I first set eyes on Elise again, tending me at the bedside, I was shocked at her altered appearance. She had become terribly thin and her blood-shot eyes were sunk into her gray cheeks. With Aizawa's help she had not wanted for daily necessities, it was true, but this same benefactor had spiritually killed her.

As he told me later, she had heard from Aizawa about the promise I had given him and how I had agreed to the Count's proposal that evening. She had jumped up from her chair, her face ashen pale, and crying out, 'Toyotarō! How could you deceive me!', she had suddenly collapsed. Aizawa had called her mother and together they had put her to bed. When she awoke some time later, her eyes were fixed in a stare and she could not recognize those around her. She cried out my name, abused me, tore her hair, and bit the coverlet. Then she suddenly seemed to remember something and started to look for it. Everything her mother gave her she threw away, except the nappies that were on the table. These she stared at for a moment, then pressed them to her face and burst into tears.

From that time on, she was never violent, but her mind was almost completely unhinged and she became as simple-minded as a child. The doctor said there was no hope of recovery, for it was an illness called paranoia that had been brought on by sudden excessive emotion. They tried to remove her to the Dalldorf Asylum, but she cried out and refused to go. She would continually clasp a nappy to her breast and bring it out to look at, and this seemed to make her content. Although she did not leave my sickbed, she did not seem to be really aware of what was going on. Just occasionally she would repeat the word 'medicine,' as if remembering it.

I recovered from my illness completely. How often did I hold her living corpse in my arms and shed bitter tears? When I left with the Count for the journey back to Japan, I discussed the matter with Aizawa and gave her mother enough to eke out a bare existence; I also left some money to pay for the birth of the child that I had left in the womb of the poor mad girl.

Friends like Aizawa Kenkichi are rare indeed, and yet to this very day there remains a part of me that curses him.

✍ HIGUCHI ICHIYO (HIGUCHI NITSUKO)
1872–1896

The biography of **Higuchi Ichiyo** has all the elements of the mythic tale of the Romantic writer struggling in abject poverty to survive and to continue writing. The tale often ends with the writer's great work being discovered only after he or she has died. Ichiyo's story has a somewhat happier ending. Her talents were widely recognized in the final year of her life, but she died at the age of 24 from tuberculosis. Although she was writing at a time when many of the younger Japanese writers were excited by the new ideas entering Japan from the West and were imitating European Realists like Flaubert and Zola, Ichiyo, educated in the Japanese and Chinese classics, drew instead on Asian sources. She is one of the important **REALISTS** of the late nineteenth century, and the realism of her stories has a distinctly Japanese character. Mori Ōgai, writing about her novella *Child's Play* (1895), said: "What is extraordinary about *Child's Play* is that the characters are not those beastlike creatures one so often encounters in Ibsen or Zola, whose techniques the so-called [Japanese] naturalists have tried imitating. They are real, human individuals that we laugh and cry with."

Ichiyo's Traditional Education.   Ichiyo was born Higuchi **Nitsuko** in 1872, the fifth child and second daughter of an ambitious peasant farmer, Higuchi Noriyoshi, who had left the country for Edo (Tokyo) in hopes of raising his social station. He worked his way up through menial jobs to bureaucratic positions and managed to buy his way into the SAMURAI class in 1867, just at the time when Japan was Westernizing and doing away with traditional class distinctions. Higuchi was a devoted traditionalist; he sent his bookish daughter to a private school with a classical curriculum where she was known as a voracious reader. One legend has it that at age seven she read all 106 volumes of Takizawa Bakin's *Hakkenden* in three days. She also had a reputation for being snobbish and aloof. Nitsuko's mother did not share her husband's passion for the classics, and she resisted his efforts to "overeducate" their daughter. When Nitsuko was eleven, her mother withdrew the girl from school; for the next three years Nitsuko stayed at home learning domestic skills. Her mother relented when Nitsuko was fourteen, and the teenager was enrolled in the Haginoya, a private finishing school for girls that emphasized poetry writing and the study of literary classics. Even though Nitsuko was intimidated by the wealth and social assurance of her schoolmates, she excelled at writing poetry in the classical manner and won a poetry competition at the school.

Family Disasters.   In 1887, when Nitsuko was fifteen, her father was forcibly retired from his job, an event that initiated a series of disasters. A few months later the eldest son in the family died. Then Noriyoshi invested his retirement savings in a partnership, but like many former

hee-GOO-chee
ee-chee-YOH

NEE-tsoo-koh

www For links to more information about Ichiyo and a quiz on "The Thirteenth Night," see *World Literature Online* at bedfordstmartins .com/worldlit.

samurai he had no head for business and the enterprise failed. When Nitsuko was seventeen, her father died, leaving the family without resources. The three women of the household, Nitsuko, her mother, and her younger sister, worked at menial jobs to support themselves, but they slipped further and further into poverty. In 1893 they gathered their meager resources and moved from their respectable neighborhood to one of the poorest sections of the city, **Ryusenji**, a crowded enclave on the outskirts of town, next to the red-light district. There they opened a small shop selling candy and trinkets. But they too were not suited for business; the shop failed within a few months.

Writing to Survive.   During these years of hardship and struggle, Nitsuko did some teaching, administrative, and custodial work at the Haginoya. She also set out to learn how to write fiction, hoping that she could earn some money as an author. She arranged an informal student/teacher relationship with **Nakarai Tosui**, a writer of serial novels for the newspapers. Her work did not resemble the formulaic potboilers he turned out for the market; nevertheless, he recognized and encouraged her talent. Her first story, "Flowers at Dusk" ("*Yamizakura*"), had been published in 1892 in a literary journal edited by Nakarai Tosui. For this publication, following Japanese custom, Nitsuko took the literary name Higuchi Ichiyo, a common practice among Japanese writers who are often referred to by their pen name alone. In the next two years, Ichiyo published several more stories, relatively plotless mood pieces about unrequited love, loneliness, and isolation.

The major change in her work came with her family's move to the slums. There the streets and alleys were crowded with people on the fringes of society searching for ways to survive. The conventional RoMANTICISM of the early tales gave way to stories about the children of the streets, prostitutes, and the poor grubbing for money. The deaths of family members, financial hardship, and Ichiyo's experience in Ryunsenji inspired a realism that tapped into the pain of her own struggle and melded with her training in classical poetry. The result can be called poetic Realism.

Child's Play.   The fullest expression of her mature vision appeared in the last two years of her life, especially in *Child's Play* (*Takekurabe*, 1895), the novella that brought her recognition and approval from the literary establishment as well as from a wider popular audience. *Child's Play* is Ichiyo's most sustained work, a coming-of-age story centering on three adolescents: Midori, who will grow up to become a prostitute like her older sister; Shota, a gang leader who aspires to become a pawnbroker like his father; and Nobu, an awkward youth who is about to go off to seminary to study for the priesthood. The story takes place during a festival in late August, a holiday marking the end of summer and also their childhood. Told against the sociologically realistic background of teen gangs in the streets of Tokyo, the story individualizes its characters, their hopes and fears. Ichiyo's interior view of her characters enables the reader to understand their ambivalence about growing up and their painful inability to

ryoo-SEN-jee

na-KAH-ree

toh-SOO-ee

tah-keh-koo-RAH-beh

communicate with one another and transcend the inevitable loneliness of their impending adulthood. Their lives are already determined.

Ichiyo's Literary Achievement.

When she died at 24, Ichiyo left behind several thousand poems — mostly from her school days — several literary essays, twenty-one short stories, and a multivolume diary. Her reputation rests on four or five of the stories and on the diary she wrote throughout her life, particularly the last five years. Her training as a poet had honed her skills at evoking mood and place, qualities ever present in her fiction. Her characters, especially the petty tradesmen, rickshawmen, courtesans, and street people in her mature work, were drawn from the people she observed in the streets and alleys of Ryusenji. Ichiyo's use of realistic detail and disparate scenes derived, as Robert Danly has demonstrated, from the influence of **Ihara Saikaku** (1642–1693),[1] the seventeenth-century Realist who was rediscovered by the Meiji writers of the late nineteenth century. Ichiyo's inspiration was wholly Japanese. Had she lived longer, the promise of these early works would surely have flowered, earning her a place beside the other women who so importantly shaped the course of Japanese fiction — **Sei Shonagon** and **Lady Murasaki**.[2]

Ichiyo's Feminism.

"The Thirteenth Night" ("*Jusan'ya,*" 1895), one of Ichiyo's mature works, could be called a feminist story, for its subject is similar to that of Ibsen's *Doll's House* and Gilman's "Yellow Wallpaper." Like Ibsen's Nora Helmer, **Oseki** is leaving her husband and child to live on her own. The story does not dramatize the abusive relationship with her husband that leads to Oseki's decision; rather it begins when she arrives at her parents' house to tell them of her decision. The dialogue with her parents articulates her own doubts and inner conflict. Her sympathetic mother gives voice to Oseki's anger and self-pity; her father expresses Oseki's sense of social obligation, family loyalty, and responsibility to her child. If we cannot imagine Nora Helmer returning to her husband, it is equally hard to picture Oseki living successfully apart from hers. She has no clear vision of an alternative to her marriage. The concluding scene, when she walks in the moonlight with **Roku**, the rickshawman who might have been her husband, is not presented romantically as a glimpse at a lost opportunity but rather as a look at a life that would have been even less fulfilling than her unhappy marriage. The moon on this thirteenth night does not bring tranquility; it makes both Oseki and Roku aware of their lost childhood dreams and of their suffering in adulthood. Oseki returns to her marriage chastened by the knowledge that there are no better alternatives for her.

I do not hesitate to confer on Ichiyo the title of true poet.

– MORI ŌGAI

ee-HAH-rah
sigh-KAH-koo

SAY shoh-NAH-gone
moo-rah-SAH-kee
joo-sahn-YAH

oh-SEH-kee

ROH-koo

---

[1] **Ihara Saikaku:** (1642–1693) Writer of Realist fiction who was "rediscovered" by the Japanese Realists of the late nineteenth century.

[2] **Sei Shonagon:** (c. 966–c. 1017) *The Pillow Book of Sei Shonagon,* a diary of Sei's observations and fascinations, is the earliest example of autobiographical fiction and is one of the great works of Japanese literature; *The Tale of Genji* by Murasaki Shikibu (978–1015), or **Lady Murasaki**, has been called the first great novel in world literature.

■ CONNECTIONS

Gustave Flaubert, "A Simple Heart," p. 439. Realists seek to present an accurate and unbiased picture of the everyday life of their characters. Compare Ichiyo as a Realist with Flaubert. How objective is the narration in "The Thirteenth Night" and in "A Simple Heart"? Is the author's attitude toward his or her characters detectable? What do the endings of these two stories say about the lives of their heroines?

Henrik Ibsen, *Hedda Gabler*, p. 561. In one of the most controversial plays of the nineteenth century, Ibsen's *Doll's House* (1879), Nora Helmer leaves her husband and children to seek independence and fulfillment. Ibsen develops a similar theme in the story of Thea Elvstead in *Hedda Gabler;* Elvstead finds meaning outside her marriage as a creative collaborator with Løvborg and Tesman. Think about Elvstead's reasons for leaving her marriage and Oseki's motives for leaving and then returning to hers. What cultural factors contribute to these two women's decisions?

Elizabeth Cady Stanton and Lucretia Mott, "Declaration of Sentiments and Resolutions," p. 827. Consider Ichiyo's feminism in light of "Declaration of Sentiments" by American feminists Stanton and Mott. Which of their positions could Oseki subscribe to? Which might she reject?

■ FURTHER RESEARCH

Biography and Criticism

Danly, Robert. *In the Shade of Spring Leaves: The Life and Writings of Higuchi Ichiyo, A Woman of Letters in Meiji Japan.* 1981. Includes excellent translations of nine of Ichiyo's stories.

Keene, Donald. *Dawn to the West.* 1984. Places Ichiyo in the context of Japanese literary history.

■ PRONUNCIATION

Higuchi Ichiyo (Higuchi Nitsuko): hee-GOO-chee ee-chee-YOH (NITS-koh, NEE-tsoo-koh)
Asakusa: ah-sah-KOO-sah
Harada Isamu: hah-RAH-dah ee-SAH-moo
Hirokōji: hee-roh-KOH-jee
Hsi Shih: shee-SHUR
Ihara Saikaku: ee-HAH-rah sigh-KAH-koo
Inosuke: ee-noh-SOO-kee
Jusan'ya: joo-sahn-YAH
Kōsaka Roku: koh-SAH-kah ROH-koo
Murasaki: moo-rah-SAH-kee
Nakari Tosui: nah-KAH-ree toh-SOO-ee
Ogawamachi: oh-gah-wah-MOO-chee
Oseki: oh-SEH-kee
Ryusenji: ryoo-SEN-jee
Saitō Kazue: SIGH-toh kah-ZOO-eh
Sarugakuchō: sah-roo-gah-KOO-choh
Sei Shonagon: SAY shoh-NAH-gone
Shinzaka: shin-ZAH-kah
Sotoori: soh-TOH-ree, soh-toh-OH-ree
Surugadai: soo-roo-GAH-digh
Takekurabe: tah-keh-koo-RAH-beh
Tarō: TAH-roh
Ueno: oo-EH-noh

☙ The Thirteenth Night (Jūsan'ya)

Translated by Robert Lyons Danly

Ordinarily, Oseki rode in a handsome black rickshaw, and, when her parents heard the sound of it approaching their gate, they would run out to greet her. Tonight however, she had hired a rickshaw on the street corner. She paid the driver, sent him away, and stood dejectedly at the door to her parents' house.

Inside, she could hear her father talking in the same loud voice as always. "You could say I'm one of the lucky ones. We have good children. Never a speck of trouble when they were growing up. People are always praising them. And we've never wanted for a thing, have we? Don't think I'm not thankful."

He would be talking to her mother, then. It gave Oseki pause. How was she going to broach the question of divorce when they were so happy, so unaware of things? What a sermon there would be! She was a mother herself, and it wasn't easy, God knows, leaving little Tarō behind. It was a bit late now to be bringing her parents such startling news. The last thing she wanted was to destroy their happiness, as if it were so many bubbles on a stream. For a moment, she felt the urge to go back without saying anything. She could go on just as before—mother to Tarō, wife to Isamu—and her parents could go on boasting of a son-in-law with an imperial appointment. So long as she was careful, nothing would have to change. The little gifts of food they liked, the spending money now and then, all the filial courtesies would continue. But if she had her way and went through with the divorce, it would be the end of everything. Tarō would be miserable with a stepmother. In a single instant, her parents would lose the only reason they had to hold their heads high. There was no telling what people would think of her. And her brother's future—any basis for his success in life—would be swept away by her selfishness and her caprice. Perhaps she *should* go back home to her husband. No! She couldn't. He was inhuman, and she trembled at the thought of him and reeled against the lattice at the gate.

Inside they heard the noise. "Who's there?" her father called out. "Some urchin at the wrong house, I suppose."

But the sound outside turned to laughter. "Papa, it's me." It was a lovely voice.

"Who is it?" Her father pushed back the sliding door. "Oseki! What are you doing here? And without a rickshaw, or your maid? Hurry up—come in. What a

---

"The Thirteenth Night" ("Jūsan'ya"). This story, published in 1895, treats its realistic subject matter—the pain of Oseki's abusive marriage and Roku's struggle to survive—in the poetic context of a moon-viewing ceremony. The ironic use of both Realist and Romantic modes evokes the disillusionment that both characters experience as they recall their childhood dreams and return to the struggles of their adult lives.

The contemporary translation by Robert Lyons Danly nicely captures the poetic qualities in the story.

surprise! No, we certainly weren't expecting you. Don't bother about the door, I'll get it. Let's go into the other room. We can see the moon from there. Here, use a cushion. No, no, use a cushion, the mats are dirty. I told the landlord, but he says we have to wait till the matting people can get around to making new ones. Don't be so polite with us—you'll get dirty if you don't take a cushion. Well, well, it's awfully late for you to be visiting. Is everyone all right?"

Her father treated her with the usual courtesy, and it made Oseki feel uncomfortable. She disliked it when they deferred to her as the wife of someone important.

"Yes, everyone's fine, in spite of the weather." There, she had managed to bring her emotions under control. "I'm sorry for not coming sooner. How are you?"

"I've been fine. Not so much as a sneeze. Your mother has one of her fainting spells now and then, but it's nothing to speak of. If she lies down for a few hours, it goes away." From his hearty laugh, she could tell he was in good health.

"I don't see Inosuke. Has he gone out somewhere? Still studying hard?"

"He's just left for night school. He's had a promotion, Oseki, thanks to you," her mother said ebulliently as she served the tea. "His supervisor is quite fond of him. Everything seems to be going well. It's thanks to our having Harada Isamu for a son-in-law, of course. Not a day goes by we don't acknowledge it. Ino isn't very good with words, and I know that when he sees Isamu, he probably doesn't express his gratitude as fully as he might. You know about these things, Oseki. I hope you'll let Isamu know how grateful we are to him, and always do your best to make him happy. See to it that he keeps on taking an interest in Ino. How is Tarō in this weather? This change in the seasons! I could do without it. Is he still up to his old tricks? You should have brought him with you tonight. Grandpa and I would have liked to see him."

"I thought I would, but he goes to bed so early. He was already asleep when I left. He really is full of the dickens, and he never listens to reason. When I go out, he wants to go too. He follows me around the house and keeps a good eye on me. He's a handful, all right! I don't know what makes him that way."

She felt overcome with remorse at the thought of the little son she had abandoned. In her resolve to find a new life, she had left him sleeping in his bed. He would probably be awake by now, and calling for her, giving the maids no end of trouble. No treats would placate him tonight. His nursemaid and the housekeeper would end up threatening to wash their hands of him and feed him to the devil if he didn't behave himself. "The poor thing!" she wanted to cry out. But seeing her parents in such a happy mood, she held her tongue. Instead, she took several puffs on her pipe, coughing into her sleeve to hide her tears.

"By the old calendar, it's the thirteenth night.[1] You may think I'm old-fashioned," her mother said, "but I made some dumplings to offer to the moon, like the old moon-viewing parties. I know you like them. I thought I'd have Inosuke bring you some. But you know how self-conscious he is, he didn't want to have any

---

[1] **thirteenth night:** By the old lunar calendar, it was the thirteenth night of the ninth month. On this night, along with the night of the fifteenth of the eighth month, moon-viewing parties were held, and delicacies, including special dumplings, were offered to friends and to the moon. [Translator]

part of it. So I didn't send you any on the fifteenth, and then I didn't think I ought to start in now.[2] Still, I did want you to have some — it's like a dream, that you've come tonight. It's as if you read my mind! You must have all kinds of good things to eat at home, Oseki, but it's not often you can have your mother's cooking, is it? Let's see you eat some beans and chestnuts — you used to like them so when you were little. Tonight you can forget you're a married woman. Be your old self, don't worry about your manners.

"You know, your father and I are always talking about your success. What an extraordinary match you've made, how wonderful it is, the circles you move in, how impressive you are. But I'm sure it's not easy being the wife of someone as important as Isamu. Why, it's hard just to have people under you — maids to manage, guests to entertain. Not to mention the problem of coming from a poor family like ours. I'll bet you have to be on your toes all the time to make a good impression. Your father and I are well aware of all this. That's why we don't want to make a nuisance of ourselves, much as we would like to see more of you and little Tarō. Sometimes, you know, we pass in front of your gate, in our cotton clothes and carrying our old umbrellas, and we look up at the bamboo blinds on the second floor and wonder to ourselves what you're doing. Then we walk on by. If only your own family were a little better off, you wouldn't have to be so ashamed of us. With all your other problems, if your father and mother were from a higher station, it would be one less thing for you to worry about . . . But what good does it do to talk like this? I can't even send over any dumplings for moon-viewing without being ashamed of the box. I know how you must feel."

Delighted as she was with her daughter's visit, all too quickly the woman had recalled anew how seldom these occasions were, how little freedom she had to see her own daughter.

"I really am an undutiful child," Oseki said, as if to allay her mother's regrets about their humble station. "I may look grand dressed up in soft silks and riding in a private rickshaw, but I can't even help my own parents. I've only helped myself. I'd be much happier doing piecework and living at home with you."

"Don't be a fool!" her father said. "You should never talk that way. What married woman supports her parents? When you were here, you were our daughter. But you're married now, you're the wife of Harada Isamu. Your . . .

. . . of Saitō Kazue, all the laughter and tears in the world could never reinstate her as the mother of Harada Tarō. She might well have no fondness for her husband, but forgetting her child would not be so easy. After they were separated, she would find herself yearning for him more and more. She would come to long for those days when she endured the ordeal for the sake of being with Tarō. It was Oseki's misfortune to have been born so beautiful, and to have married above herself.

When he thought about her hardships, the man's pity for his daughter doubled. "Oseki, you may think I'm heartless, that I don't understand your situation. But I'm not saying any of this to scold you: when people come from different backgrounds,

---

[2] It was considered bad form to offer the dumplings on only one of the two moon-viewing dates. [Translator]

it's only natural their ways of thinking aren't always going to be the same. I'm sure you're doing your best to please Isamu. But that doesn't mean everything is fine and dandy—not in his eyes, anyway. Isamu is a smart man. He knows what's what. I don't think he means to be unreasonable with you. It's often the case, though: men who are hardworking and admired by the world can sometimes be very selfish. Away from home they hide their swollen heads. With their families they let their hair down; they take out all the discontent they bring home from the office. It must be terribly hard on you to be the target of all Isamu's grievances.

"On the other hand, your responsibilities as the wife of a man like Isamu are of another kind altogether. You're not married to someone in the ward office, you know—some fellow who lights the fire underneath the kettle for you and goes off to work every day with lunch box tied to his waist. You can't compare Isamu's place in society with an ordinary office worker's. Even if he is fussy and a little difficult sometimes, it's still a wife's duty to humor her husband. You can never tell, but I'd be surprised if there are many wives who enjoy completely happy relations with their husbands. If you think you're the only one in a bind like this, Oseki, it'll only embitter you. Fact is, it's a burden many people have to bear. What with the difference in your backgrounds, it's natural you'd meet with more suffering than a wife whose husband comes from the same class.

"Your mother talks big, but remember: the fine salary your brother is making is all thanks to Isamu. They say the light a parent sheds on his child is sevenfold.[3] In that case, the benefits we've received from Isamu must be tenfold! His way of helping out is to do things behind the scenes, but we're indebted to him nonetheless. It's trying for you, Oseki, I know. Think what your marriage means to us, though, and to Inosuke, and to Tarō. If you've been able to put up with things this long, surely you can continue. And how do you know a divorce is the answer? Isamu would have custody of Tarō, and you'd be my daughter again. Once the bonds are cut, there's no going back—even for a glimpse of little Tarō. If you're going to cry over spilt milk, you might as well do your crying as the wife of Harada. All right? Wouldn't that be better, Oseki? Get hold of yourself and go home tonight as if nothing had happened. Go on being just as careful as you have been. Even if you don't tell us anything more after this, we'll know now, we'll all understand how you feel. We'll share your tears with you." As he urged his daughter to bow to the inevitable, he too wiped a tear from his eyes.

Sobbing, Oseki gave in to his advice. "It was selfish of me to think of a divorce. You're right. If I couldn't see Tarō, there'd be no point in living. I might flee my present sorrows, but what kind of future would I have? If I could think of myself as already dead, that would solve everything . . . Then Tarō would have both his parents with him. It was a foolish idea I had, and I've troubled you with the whole unpleasant business. From tonight I will consider myself dead—a spirit who watches over Tarō. That way I can bear Isamu's cruelty for a hundred years to come. You've

---

[3] **the light . . . sevenfold:** "Nana hikari dokoro ka tō hikari mo shite" in the original, which alludes to the saying, "Oya no hikari wa nana hikari": The light (i.e., favors and influence) of one's parents is sevenfold. [Translator]

convinced me, Papa. Don't worry. I won't mention any of this again." No sooner had she wiped her eyes than fresh tears came.

"Poor child!" her mother sobbed.

At that moment even the bright moon looked disconsolate. Even the wild grasses in the vase, picked by her brother Inosuke from the thicket along the back bank, swayed as if to offer their sympathy.

Her parents' house was at the foot of Shinzaka in Ueno,[4] on the road toward Surugadai. It was a shady, secluded spot. But tonight the moon shone brilliantly, and on the main street it was as light as midday. Her parents were not patrons of any of the rickshaw stations; from their window they hailed a rickshawman as he went by.

"Well, then, if you agree, Oseki, I think you'd better be off. Going out without permission while your husband's away, you'll have a lot of explaining to do. It's getting late. It won't take long by rickshaw, though. We'll come soon and talk about things. But tonight you'd best get back." Her father led her by the hand as if to drag her out. The pity he felt for Oseki did not preclude his desire to see the matter settled quietly.

Oseki was resigned to her fate. "That's the end of it, this talk. I'm going home. I'm still Harada's wife. Isamu mustn't know about tonight. Inosuke still has the backing of an important man. Don't worry. As long as you are all happy, I won't have any regrets. I won't do anything rash, so please, you mustn't worry. From now on, I'll consider myself Isamu's property. I'll do whatever he says. Well, I'd better go. Say hello to Inosuke when he comes home. Take care of yourselves. The next time, I'll come with happy news." It was apparent in the way she rose to leave that Oseki had no choice in all of this.

Taking her purse, with what little money she had, Oseki's mother went out to the rickshaw driver. "How much is it to Surugadai?"

"No, Mother. I'll pay. Thank you anyway." Her voice was subdued as she touched her sleeve to her face to brush a tear. Quietly, she passed through the front door and stepped into the rickshaw.

Inside the house, her father coughed to clear his voice, and, from the sound of it, he too was crying.

The faint cry of crickets sounded mournful in the moonglow and the autumn wind. No sooner had they reached Ueno than Oseki was given a start.

"I'm sorry," the man said, abruptly putting down the poles of the rickshaw. "I can't take you any farther. I won't charge you anything."

Oseki was astonished. "What? What am I supposed to do? I'm in a hurry. I'll pay you extra, please try. I'm not going to find another rickshaw in a lonely place like this, now, am I? Come on, do stop grumbling and take me home." She trembled slightly as she implored him.

"I'm not asking you to pay double. I'm asking you to let me stop. Please get out. I can't take you any farther. I'm too tired."

---

[4] Ueno: District on the northern edge of Tokyo, a commercial center for the merchant and artisan classes. Surugadai was a shopping area to the south.

"Are you sick? What's the matter?" She began to raise her voice. "You can't just drop me here and say you're tired."

"Forgive me. I'm too tired, really." He held the lantern in his hand and stepped aside from the poles of the rickshaw.

"What a selfish man you are! All right, I won't ask you to take me all the way, just to where I can find another rickshaw. I'll pay you—at least go as far as Hirokōji." She spoke in a soft voice to cajole him.

"Well, you are a young lady. I suppose it wouldn't be very nice of me to leave you here, in this forsaken spot. It was wrong of me. All right, let's go. I'll take you there. I must have scared you."

When he picked up the lantern to be off, he did not seem so rough, and Oseki breathed a sigh of relief. Feeling safe in his charge, she looked into the man's face. He was twenty-five or -six, of dark complexion and a wiry build. He was not very tall. Wait—that face now turned away from her in the moonlight! She knew it! His name was on the tip of her tongue, but she hesitated to utter it.

"Is it you?" she asked before she knew what she was saying.

"Hm?" Surprised, he turned around to look at her.

"Goodness! It *is* you. Surely you haven't forgotten me, have you?" She slipped down from the rickshaw, never taking her eyes from him.

"Saitō Oseki? I'm ashamed for you to see me like this. How could I have known it was you—without eyes in the back of my head? I should have recognized you from your voice. I guess I've gotten pretty stupid," he said, avoiding her look.

Oseki studied him from head to toe. "No, no. If we had met walking in the street, I wouldn't have recognized you. Until just now I thought you were a stranger, only a rickshawman. Why should you have recognized me? Forgive *me*. How long have you been doing this? You're not overworking yourself, are you? You look frail. I heard somewhere that your aunt closed the shop in Ogawamachi and moved to the country-side. I'm not the person I used to be, either. Things get in the way of what we want," she sighed. "I haven't been able to visit you or even write you a letter. Where are you living now? How is your wife? Do you have children? Now and then I go to see the shops[5] in Ogawamachi. The old store looks the same as always. It's the same tobacco shop, only it's called the Notoya now. Whenever I go by, I look at it and think to myself, 'That's where Kōsaka Roku lived when we were children.' Remember how we used to sneak a smoke on the way to school? What little know-it-alls we were! I've always wondered where you'd gone, what you were doing now. Anyone as gentle as you would be having a hard time of it. I worried about you. When I go home to see my parents, I ask if anyone's heard what became of you. It's been five years since I moved away from Sarugakuchō, and all that time I've never heard a thing. How I've missed you!" She seemed to have forgotten that she was a married woman as she deluged him with her questions.

"I'm ashamed how low I've fallen," he said as he took his towel and wiped the sweat from his forehead. "I don't even have a place I can call home any more. I sleep

---

[5] Ogawamachi: An area of small shops south of Ueno.

upstairs in a cheap inn in Asakusa[6] run by a man named Murata. Some days I spend the whole day there, doing nothing. Some days, like tonight, I work until late pulling the rickshaw. Then when I get tired of it, I loaf again: my life's just going up in smoke. I heard that you were still as beautiful as ever, Oseki, and that you were someone's wife now. I always hoped that, by some slim chance, I'd see you again and we'd be able to talk once more. My life isn't worth anything, I didn't think it mattered what happened to me—but if I hadn't gone on living, I couldn't have met you tonight. Gosh, I'm glad you recognized me! Thank you, Oseki." He looked down at the ground.

There were tears in her eyes as Oseki tried to console him. "You're not the only one to suffer in this sad world . . . Tell me something about your wife."

"You probably knew her. She was the daughter of the Sugitas, kitty-corner from us. The one people were always complimenting for her fair skin and her pretty figure. Well, I was leading a bad life—out carousing, never coming home—which one of my pig-headed relatives mistook for proof that I ought to get married. Mother put her glasses on and began looking for candidates and soon settled on the Sugita girl. She kept pestering me, so I finally gave in. We were married just about the time I heard that you were expecting. And then, a year later, people were congratulating us. But you don't think a few baby's toys were enough to make me change my ways, do you? People think that with a pretty wife a man will stop playing around, and with a child he'll become more serious. But it wouldn't have mattered what beauty of a wife I had. Ono no Komachi, Lady Hsi Shih, Princess Sotoori[7] herself dancing before my eyes—my bad habits wouldn't have changed. Why should a little thing that reeks of its mother's milk inspire some sort of religious awakening in a man? I fooled around to my heart's content and drank myself silly. I neglected my family, I had no use for work. It got to the point where I didn't have a chopstick to my name. That was three years ago. My mother went to live with my sister, who had gone to the provinces to marry. My wife took the baby and returned to her folks. We haven't had a thing to do with each other since. The baby was a girl, anyway, so I never missed her much. I heard she died late last year of typhoid. Girls are precocious, though—I bet she didn't die without remembering her papa. If she'd lived, she would have been five this year. I don't know why I'm telling you all this—it's not really very interesting."

A smile played across his somber face. "If I'd known it was you, Oseki, I wouldn't have been so gruff tonight. Come on, get in and I'll take you home. I must have given you a good scare. You know, I'm not much of a rickshawman, even. I don't get any thrill out of clutching these poles, I'll tell you that. What does a fellow like me have to look forward to? Making a living like a horse, like some ox! You think I'm happy when I get a few coins? You think a little wine's going to drive my sorrows away? I'm

---

[6] Asakusa: A district in northeastern Tokyo; formerly the pleasure quarters for the old Edo.

[7] Ono . . . Sotoori: All three women were legendary beauties. Komachi was the great poetess of the early Heian period, who was ranked by Ki no Tsurayuki as one of the Six Poetic Geniuses. Hsi Shih (Sei Shi in Japanese) was the beloved of a Chinese warlord in the Chou dynasty, who offered her to a rival who defeated him in battle. The rival thereupon became so enamoured of Hsi Shih that he neglected his state and let it fall to ruin. Sotoori-hime was a consort to Emperor Ingyō (376–453). [Translator]

really fed up with it. Who cares if I have a passenger? When I'm tired, that's it! I don't go any farther. Pretty selfish and disgusting, aren't I? Well, come on, get in."

"What! Do you think I could ride now that I know who you are? It was different when I didn't know it was you. But I will ask you to walk with me as far as Hirokōji. *Please.* I'm afraid to stay here alone. We can talk along the way." Oseki held up the bottom of her kimono as she walked. The clatter of her lacquered sandals rang despondently against the cobblestones.

Of all her friends, he was the one she had never quite forgotten: Kōsaka's boy at the tobacco stall in Ogawamachi, where everything was always ship-shape. Now his skin was dark and he looked pretty shabby, but in the old days he had cut a different figure, in his fine matched cottons and his snappy apron. What a charmer he was then! So friendly and grown-up. He was just a boy, but the store did better under him than it had when his father was alive. Everyone thought so highly of him, he was so intelligent. He had certainly changed . . . After her engagement was announced, as she remembered it, had become another person, wild and dissipated. The decline was so extraordinary, it seemed as if some evil spirit had taken hold of him. That's what people said. And tonight he looked it. It was pitiful . . . She would never have dreamt that Kōsaka Roku would end up living in a cheap rooming house.

He had been in love with her once, and, from the time she was twelve until she was seventeen, they saw each other every day. She used to imagine it would be like to sit behind the counter of the tobacco shop, reading the paper and waiting on customers. But then a stranger came along and asked her to marry him. Her parents pressed her, how could she defy them? She had always hoped to marry Roku, though he had never made any overtures, it was true. In the end, her parents persuaded her, and she told herself that her dreams of helping Roku run the shop were only that—the dreams of a schoolgirl, puppy love. She put him out of her mind and resigned herself to marrying Harada. It had not been easy; until the last moment, there were tears in Oseki's eyes for Kōsaka Roku. He must have yearned for her, too. Perhaps she was even the cause of his ruin. How repellent he must find it to see her tonight, looking smug and matronly. She was not as happy and contented as she might look, she wanted to tell him. She turned to him, wondering what he was thinking, but his face was blank, and he did not appear to be rejoicing in this rare encounter.

They came out into Hirokōji. Here Oseki would be able to find a rickshaw. She took some money from her purse and gently wrapped it in chrysanthemum paper. "Forgive me, Roku, for being rude," she said, offering it to him. "Please buy yourself some paper handkerchiefs or something. I haven't seen you in so long—there are so many things I'd like to say. It's hard to put them into words . . . Take good care of yourself, Roku, so your mother doesn't worry. I'll pray for you. I want to see the old Roku I used to know, with that fine shop again. Good-by."

He took the paper from her. "I shouldn't accept this. But since it's from you, I will. As a keepsake. I hate to say good-by to you, Oseki. It's been like a dream, seeing you again. Well, I'll be going too, then. It's lonely on the road late at night, isn't it?"

He started off with the empty rickshaw behind him, and when he had gone a little way he turned back to look at her. He was heading east; she would be going south. The branches of the willow trees trailed beside her in the moonlight as she walked, dispirited, along the main road. One living on the second floor of Murata's boardinghouse; the other, the wife of the great Harada: each knew his share of sadness in life.

GLOSSARY OF LITERARY AND CRITICAL TERMS

Absurd Literary movement that evolved in France in the 1950s. The Absurdists saw the universe as irrational and meaningless. They rejected conventional PLOT and DIALOGUE in their work, emphasizing the incoherence of the world.

Accent The emphasis, or stress, given to a syllable or word in pronunciation. Accents can be used to emphasize a particular word in a sentence: *Is* she con*tent* with the *con*tents of the *yel*low *pack*age?

Acmeists A group of twentieth-century Russian poets, most notably Anna Akhmatova (1889–1966), who rejected Symbolism in favor of linguistic clarity.

Acropolis The most fortified part of a Greek city, located on a hill; the most famous acropolis is in Athens and is the site of the Parthenon.

Act A major division in the action of a play. In many full-length plays, acts are further divided into SCENES, which often mark a point in the action when the location changes or when a new character arrives.

Age of Pericles The golden age of Athens in the fifth century B.C.E. when Pericles (c. 495–429 B.C.E.) was the head of the Athenian government. During this period, Athenian democ-

racy reached its height; the Parthenon was constructed and drama and music flourished.

Agnosticism The belief that the existence of God or anything beyond material phenomena can be neither proved nor disproved. The French ENLIGHTENMENT philosopher François Voltaire (1694–1778) is considered by many to be the father of agnosticism. The term *agnostic,* however, was first used by the English biologist Thomas Huxley (1825–1895) in 1869.

Ahasuarus, the Wandering Jew A legendary figure during ancient times who was said to have mocked Jesus en route to the crucifixion and was therefore doomed to wander the earth in penance until Judgment Day.

Allegory A narrative in which the characters, settings, and episodes stand for something else. Traditionally, most allegories come in the form of stories that correlate to spiritual concepts; examples of these can be found in Dante's *Divine Comedy* (1321). Some later allegories allude to political, historical, and sociological ideas.

Alliteration The repetition of the same consonant sound or sounds in a sequence of words, usually at the beginning of a word or stressed syllable: "*d*escen*d*ing *d*ew *d*rops"; "*l*uscious *l*emons." The repetition is based on the sounds of the letters, not the spelling of the words; for example, "*keen*" and "*car*" alliterate, but "*car*" and "*cite*" do not, even though both begin with *c*. Used sparingly, alliteration can intensify ideas by emphasizing key words.

Allusion A brief reference to a person, place, thing, event, or idea in history or literature. These references can be to a scene from one of Shakespeare's plays, a historic figure, a war, a great love story, a biblical authority, or anything else that might enrich an author's work. Allusions imply that the writer and the reader share similar knowledge and function as a kind of shorthand.

Ambiguity Allows for two or more simultaneous interpretations of a word, phrase, action, or situation, all of whose meanings are supported by the work. Deliberate ambiguity can contribute to the effectiveness and richness of a piece of writing; unintentional ambiguity obscures meaning and may confuse readers.

Anagram A word or phrase made up of the same letters as another word or phrase; *heart* is an anagram of *earth*. Often considered merely an exercise of one's ingenuity, anagrams are sometimes used by writers to conceal proper names, veil messages, or suggest important connections between words, such as between *hated* and *death*.

Antagonist The character, force, or collection of forces in fiction or drama that opposes the PROTAGONIST and gives rise to the conflict in the story; an opponent of the protagonist, such as Caliban in Shakespeare's play *The Tempest*.

Antihero A PROTAGONIST who has the opposite of most of the traditional attributes of a hero. He or she may be bewildered, ineffectual, deluded, or merely pathetic. Often what antiheroes learn, if they learn anything at all, is that they are isolated in an existence devoid of God or any absolute value.

Apartheid The South African system of official racial segregation, which was established in 1948 and lasted until the early 1990s. The term *apartheid* means "state of being separate." Apartheid divided people into racial categories — colored, or Indian, as well as black and white — and severely limited the movements and activities of the colored and black groups, giving particular privilege to people of European heritage. After intense international pressure, the resistance movement leader, Nelson Mandela (b. 1918), was released from prison in 1990. One year later he became the country's first black president.

Apostrophe A statement or address made either to an implied interlocutor, sometimes a nonhuman figure or PERSONIFICATION. Apostrophes often provide a speaker with the opportunity to reveal his or her internal thoughts.

Archetype A universal symbol that evokes deep and sometimes unconscious responses in a reader. In literature, characters, images, and themes that symbolize universal meanings and basic human experiences are considered archetypes. Common literary archetypes include quests, initiations, scapegoats, descents to the underworld, and ascents to heaven.

Aryans A people who settled in Iran (Persia) and northern India in prehistoric times. Their language was also called Aryan, and it gave rise to the Indo-European languages of South Asia. Linguists now use the term *Aryan* to refer to Indo-Aryan languages. In the nineteenth and twentieth century the term was appropriated (most infamously by Adolf Hitler and the Nazi government) to define a "pure" race of people responsible for the progress of the modern world and superior to non-Aryans.

Aside In drama, a speech directed to the audience that supposedly is not audible to the other characters onstage.

Associationism A British eighteenth- and nineteenth-century school of philosophy that derived its ideas from, among others, philosophers John Locke (1632–1704) and David Hume (1711–1776). Associationists believed that one's view of reality is formed from bits and pieces of sensations that join together through patterns of association.

Assonance The repetition of vowel sounds in nearby words, as in "as*lee*p under a tr*ee*" or "*each evening*." When the words also share similar endings, as in "as*leep* in the *deep*," rhyme occurs. Assonance is an effective means of emphasizing important words.

Atheism The belief that God does not exist and that the Earth evolved naturally.

Avant-garde Writers, artists, filmmakers, and musicians whose work is innovative, experimental, or unconventional.

Bataan Death March The forced march of 10,000 American and 65,000 Filipino soldiers who were captured in 1942 by the Japanese on the Bataan Peninsula of the Philippines during World War II; the prisoners of war, many of whom were suffering from exhaustion, malaria, and other ailments, were compelled to march 55 miles from Marivales to San Fernando. They were then packed into railroad cars and taken to Capas, where they were made to march another 8 miles to a prison camp. Up to 650 Americans and some 10,000 Filipinos died before reaching the camp, where still many others died.

Ballad An uncomplicated verse originally meant to be sung; it generally tells a dramatic tale or simple story. Ballads are associated with the oral traditions or folklore of common people. The folk ballad stanza usually consists of four lines of alternating tetrameter (four accented syllables) and trimeter (three accented syllables) following a rhyme scheme of *abab* or *abcb*.

Ballad stanza A four-line stanza, known as a QUATRAIN, consisting of alternating eight- and six-syllable lines. Usually, only the second and fourth lines rhyme (an *abcb* pattern). Samuel Taylor Coleridge adapted the ballad stanza in *The Rime of the Ancient Mariner* (1798).

Battle of Dresden A battle in 1813 outside the capital of Saxony, where Napoleon defeated an allied army of 400,000 men. It was Napoleon's last great victory before his final defeat one year later.

Battle of Plassey Plassey was the village in West Bengal, India, where the British defeated the Bengal army in 1757, which led to Britain's domination of northeast India.

Bengali Traditional language of Bengal in eastern India, now the national language of Bangladesh and the official language of the West Bengal region of India; also, someone who comes from Bangladesh or West Bengal.

Bengali literary renaissance A movement in the second half of the nineteenth century to develop literature in the Bengali language that would describe the everyday life of contemporary Bengal. Rabindranath Tagore, Madhusudan Dutta, and Bankim Chandra Chatterjee were important writers of the movement.

Bhagavad Gita An ancient text of Hindu wisdom from the first century B.C.E. or first century C.E. inserted into the epic poem *The Mahabharata.*

Bible-based calendar Calendar based on Scripture that dates the creation of the earth at 4004 B.C.E. Archbishop James Ussher constructed it in the mid seventeenth century.

Bildungsroman A novel that traces the PROTAGONIST's development, generally from birth or childhood into maturity. An early prototype is Goethe's *Wilhelm Meister's Apprenticeship* (1795–96). The form has flourished in the ensuing two centuries and includes such modern masterpieces as James Joyce's *Portrait of the Artist as a Young Man* (1916).

Bill of Rights A document that spells out the rights of a citizen in either England or the United States of America. The American Bill of Rights, the first ten amendments to the Constitution, was ratified in 1791 and guarantees freedom of religion, press, assembly, and petition; the right to bear arms; protection under the law; and the right to a speedy trial. See also ENGLISH BILL OF RIGHTS.

Biographical criticism An approach to literature that maintains that knowledge of an author's life experiences can aid in the understanding of his or her work. Although biographical information can sometimes complicate one's interpretation of a work and some FORMALIST CRITICS, such as the NEW

CRITICS, disparage the use of an author's biography as a tool for textual interpretation, learning about the life of an author can often enrich a reader's appreciation for that author's work.

Blank verse Unrhymed IAMBIC PENTAMETER. Blank verse is the form closest to the natural rhythms of English speech and is therefore the most common pattern found in traditional English narrative and dramatic poetry, from Shakespeare to the writers of the early twentieth century.

Bolshevik Revolution The revolution in Russia in 1917 in which the government of the hereditary tsar was overthrown and replaced by a Communist regime under the leadership of Vladimir Lenin. After the Bolshevik Revolution, the Russian empire became the Union of Soviet Socialist Republics, or USSR.

Bourgeoisie Prosperous urban middle class that emerged in the wake of the INDUSTRIAL REVOLUTION and gained wealth and power in the nineteenth century. In MARXIST theory, the bourgeoisie is identified as the owners and operators of industry, as opposed to the PROLETARIAT, who live by the sale of their labor.

Brahman In the UPANISHADS—sacred Hindu texts—Brahman is the ultimate reality that transcends all names and descriptions and is the single unifying essence of the universe. A brahman, or brahmin, is also a Hindu priest and thus of the highest caste in the traditional Hindu caste system.

Brahmanism A religion that recognizes the creator, Brahma, and the priestly class of brahmans who administer Hindu rituals.

Buddhism A religion founded in India in the sixth century B.C.E. by Siddhartha Gautama, the Buddha. While Buddhism has taken different forms in the many areas of the world to which it has spread, its central tenet is that life is suffering caused by desire. In order to obtain salvation, or nirvana, one must transcend desire through following an eightfold path that includes the practice of right action and right mindfulness.

Bunraku New name for JORURI, traditional Japanese puppet theater.

Bushido The code of honor and conduct of the Japanese SAMURAI class. *Bushido* emphasizes self-discipline and bravery.

Byronic hero A character based on the heroes in the poems of Lord Byron (1788–1824), such as Childe Harold, Manfred, and Cain. The Byronic hero is an outsider, even an outlaw—proud, defiant, and moody—who seems burdened by an undefined sense of guilt or misery.

Cacophony In literature, language that is discordant and difficult to pronounce, such as the line "never my numb plunker fumbles" from John Updike's "Player Piano." Cacophony (from the Greek for "bad sound") may be unintentional, or it may be used for deliberate dramatic effect; also refers to the combination of loud, jarring sounds.

Caesura A pause within a line of poetry that contributes to the line's RHYTHM. A caesura can occur anywhere within a line and need not be indicated by punctuation. In SCANSION, caesuras are indicated by a double vertical line.

Canon The works generally considered by scholars, critics, and teachers to be the most important to read and study and that collectively constitute the masterpieces of literature. Since the 1960s, the traditional English and American literary canons, consisting mostly of works by white male writers, have been expanding to include many female writers and writers of varying ethnic backgrounds.

Captivity narratives Autobiographical accounts detailing American colonists' experiences as prisoners of Native Americans; extremely popular from the late seventeenth century through the nineteenth century. Often written to illustrate spiritual or moral growth through trials, these narratives typically describe a dramatic capture and lengthy travels and ordeals, culminating in escape or release. Much was made of the divide between "savage" and "civilized" society, of fear of assimilation into an alien culture, and of the promise of salvation for the chosen few.

Carpe diem Latin phrase meaning "seize the day." This is a common literary theme, especially in lyric poetry, conveying that life is short, time is fleeting, and one should make the most of present pleasures. Andrew Marvell's poem "To His Coy Mistress" is a good example.

Catharsis Meaning "purgation," or the release of the emotions of pity and fear by the audience at the end of a tragedy. In *Poetics,* Aristotle discusses the importance of catharsis. The audience faces the misfortunes of the PROTAGONIST, which elicit pity and compassion. Simultaneously, the audience confronts the protagonist's failure, thus receiving a frightening reminder of human limitations and frailties.

Character, characterization A character is a person presented in a dramatic or narrative work; characterization is the process by which a writer makes a character seem real to the reader.

Chivalric romances Idealized stories from the medieval period that espoused the values of a sophisticated courtly society. These tales centered around the lives of knights who were faithful to God, king, and country and willing to sacrifice themselves for these causes and for the love and protection of women. Chivalric romances were highly moral and fanciful, often pitting knights against dark or supernatural forces.

Chorus In Greek tragedies, a group of people who serve mainly as commentators on the play's characters and events, adding to the audience's understanding of a play by expressing traditional moral, religious, and social attitudes. The role of the chorus is occasionally used by modern playwrights.

Cliché An idea or expression that has become tired and trite from overuse. Clichés often anesthetize readers and are usually signs of weak writing.

Closet drama A play that is to be read rather than performed onstage. In closet dramas, literary art outweighs all other considerations.

Colloquial Informal diction that reflects casual, conversational language and often includes slang expressions.

Comedy A work intended to interest, involve, and amuse readers or an audience, in which no terrible disaster occurs and which ends happily for the main characters.

Comic epic One of the earliest English novelists, Henry Fielding (1707–1754) characterized the kind of literature he was creating in his novel *Joseph Andrews* (1742) as "a comic epic in prose," thus distinguishing it from serious or tragic epic poems that treated noble characters and elevated subjects. His novel was about common people and everyday events.

Comic relief A humorous scene or incident that alleviates tension in an otherwise serious work. Often these moments enhance the thematic significance of a story in addition to providing humor.

Communist A supporter of the political system in which all property and wealth is owned collectively by and shared equally among all members of society. Communism derived largely from the theories of Karl Marx and Friedrich Engels, as presented in *The Communist Manifesto* (1848).

Conflict In a literary work, the struggle within the PLOT between opposing forces. The PROTAGONIST is engaged in a conflict with the ANTAGONIST.

Confucianism A religion/philosophy that has influenced Chinese and East Asian spirituality and culture for over two thousand years. Based on the writings of Confucius (Kongfuzi; 551–479 B.C.E.), Confucianism asserts that humans can improve and even perfect themselves through education and moral reform. In its various manifestations, Confucianism has affected the social and political evolution of China and East Asia while providing a spiritual and moral template.

Connotation Implications going beyond the literal meaning of a word that derive from how the word has been commonly used and from ideas or things associated with it. For example, the word *eagle* in the United States connotes ideas of liberty and freedom that have little to do with the term's literal meaning.

Consonance A common type of near-rhyme or half rhyme that consists of identical consonant sounds preceded by different vowel sounds: *home, same; worth, breath.*

Continental Congress Assembly of delegates representing the thirteen British colonies in North America. The First Continental Congress convened in 1774 and drafted a petition to King George III; the Second Continental Congress met in 1775, organized an army under the leadership of George Washington, and adopted the Declaration of Independence on July 4, 1776.

Convention A characteristic of a literary GENRE that is understood and accepted by readers and audiences because it has become familiar. For example, the division of a play into acts and scenes is a dramatic convention, as are SOLILOQUIES and ASIDES.

Cosmogony A theory that explains the origins of the universe.

Council of Areopagus Council in Athens—named after the place where it held its meetings—that was the political forum prior to the establishment of the COUNCIL OF FOUR HUNDRED. Areopagus later remained active as a criminal court.

Council of Four Hundred A council established by Solon in Athens in 594 B.C.E. as a rival to the COUNCIL OF AREOPAGUS, which, according to Solon, had become too corrupt. Solon granted each of Athens's social classes equal representation in the senate. Each class was represented by one hundred men.

Couplet A two-line, rhymed stanza. Pope is the master of the HEROIC COUPLET, a two-line, rhymed, iambic-pentameter stanza that completes its thought within the closed two-line form.

Creole The culture and language of some of the Spanish and French settlers of South and North America. Many Creoles speak a mixed form of French, Spanish, and English.

Crimean War (1853–1856) A war fought on the Crimean peninsula in the Black Sea between the Russians and the allied forces of the British, the French, and the Ottoman Turks. The war arose from religious conflicts in the Middle East. When Austria threatened to enter the war, Russia agreed to peace terms resulting in the Treaty of Paris (1856), but the shift in power had long-lasting effects, notably the unification of Germany and Italy.

Crisis The moment in a work of drama or fiction where the elements of the conflict reach the point of maximum tension. The crisis is part of the work's structure but is not necessarily the emotional crescendo, or climax.

Critical realism Politically driven, early-twentieth-century school of Chinese literature pioneered by Lu Xun (1881–1936); examines societal tendencies through the actions of realistic characters.

Cubism An early-twentieth-century movement centered in France, primarily in painting and collage, that attempted to show objects from several perspectives at once; proponents included the artists Pablo Picasso (1881–1973) and Georges Braque (1882–1963).

Cultural criticism An approach to literature that focuses on the historical as well as the social, political, and economic contexts of a work. Popular culture—mass-produced and mass-consumed cultural artifacts ranging from advertising to popular fiction to television to rock music—is seen on equal footing with "high culture." Cultural critics use widely eclectic strategies, such as NEW HISTORICISM, psychology, gender studies, and DECONSTRUCTION, to analyze not only literary texts but everything from radio talk shows to comic strips, calendar art, commercials, travel guides, and baseball cards.

Dadaism An early-twentieth-century AVANT-GARDE movement inaugurated by French poets Tristan Tzara (1896–1963) and Hans Arp (1887–1966) and German poet Hugo Ball (1886–1927), all living in Zurich during World War I. Stressing irrationality and the absurdity of life in an era of mechanized mass-destruction, dadaism is often seen as nihilistic; in its emphasis on free association and instinctive composition, it can be viewed as a precursor to surrealism. The French painter Marcel Duchamp (1887–1968) may be dadaism's most renowned practitioner.

Daoism (Taoism) A religion / philosophy based on the *Dao De Jing* of Laozi (Lao-tzu) that emphasizes individual freedom, spontaneity, mystical experience, and self-transformation, and is the antithesis of CONFUCIANISM. In pursuit of the *dao,* or the Way—the eternal creative reality that is the essence of all things—practitioners embrace simplicity and reject learned wisdom. The Daoist tradition has flourished in China and East Asia for two thousand years.

Decembrist Revolt After the death of Tsar Alexander I (r. 1801–25), a group of liberal officers, many of whom had served in the Napoleonic Wars, attempted in December 1825 to depose his heir, Nicholas I (r. 1825–55), in the hope of bringing to power a ruler who would guarantee them a constitutional monarchy. The officers were crushed by Nicholas, who punished them severely to discourage other reform-minded Russians.

Deconstructionism An approach to literature that suggests that literary works do not yield single fixed meanings because language can never say exactly what one intends it to mean. Deconstructionism seeks to destabilize meaning by examining the gaps in and ambiguities of a text's language. Deconstructionists pay close attention to language in order to discover and describe how a variety of close readings can be generated.

Deism An unorthodox religious philosophy prominent in the seventeenth and eighteenth centuries in northern Europe and America. Deists believe that religious knowledge can be arrived at through reason rather than through revelation or formal religious instruction. Deism constructs God as a rational architect of an orderly world; the deist God creates the world and sets it in motion but does not become directly involved in human affairs.

Denouement French term meaning "unraveling" or "unknotting" used to describe the resolution of a PLOT following the climax.

Dialect A type of informal DICTION. Dialects are spoken by definable groups of people from a particular geographic region, economic group, or social class. Writers use dialect to express and contrast the education, class, and social and regional backgrounds of their characters.

Dialogue Verbal exchange between CHARACTERS. Dialogue reveals firsthand characters' thoughts, responses, and emotional states, and thus makes the characters real to readers or the audience.

Diaspora The wide dispersion of a people or a culture that was formerly located in one place. Two historical diasporas of note are the diaspora of the Jews from Palestine following the Roman destruction of the Second Temple in 70 C.E. and the African diaspora caused by the slave trade. Both the Jews and the Africans were dispersed across many continents.

Diction A writer's choice of words, phrases, sentence structure, and figurative language, which combine to help create meaning.

Didactic poetry Poetry designed to teach an ethical, moral, or religious lesson.

Dionysus The god of wine in Greek mythology, whose cult originated in Thrace and Phrygia—north and east of the Greek peninsula. Dionysus was often blamed for people's irrational behavior and for chaotic situations. However, many Greeks also believed that Dionysus taught them good farming skills, especially those related to wine production. Greek tragedy evolved from a ceremony that honored Dionysus, and the theater in Athens was dedicated to him.

Doggerel A derogatory term for poetry whose subject is trite and whose rhythm and sounds are monotonously heavy-handed.

Drama Derived from the Greek word *dram,* meaning "to do" or "to perform," the term *drama* may refer to a single play, a group of plays, or to plays in general. Drama is designed to be performed in a theater: Actors take on the roles of its characters, perform indicated actions, and deliver the script's DIALOGUE.

Dramatic monologue A type of lyric or narrative poem in which a speaker addresses an imagined and distinct but silent audience in such a way as to reveal a dramatic situation and, often unintentionally, some aspect of the speaker's temperament or personality.

Dualistic tradition Religious and philosophical doctrine dating from ancient times in which the antagonistic forces of good and evil determine the course of events.

Early Modern era Period extending from about 1500 to 1800, marked by the advent of colonialism and capitalism.

Edenic New World Early European immigrants to the New World often described it as a new Eden, a Garden of Paradise.

Edo The ancient name for Tokyo. During the TOKUGAWA period (1600–1868), Edo became the imperial capital of Japan.

Eight-legged essay The *ba-gu wen,* an essay of eight parts written on a Confucian theme and developed during the MING DYNASTY in China (1368–1644) as a requirement for the civil service examinations.

Electra complex The female version of the Oedipus complex as theorized by Sigmund Freud to describe a daughter's unconscious rivalry with her mother for her father's attention. The name comes from the Greek legend of Electra, who avenged the death of her father by plotting the death of her mother.

Elegiac couplets The conventional strophic form of Latin elegiac love poetry, consisting of one dactylic hexameter line followed by one dactylic pentameter line. A dactylic hexameter line is composed of six feet, each foot comprising one long, or accented, and two short, or unaccented, syllables; the sixth foot may be shortened by one or two syllables; the pentameter line consists of five such feet. The elegiac couplet is also known as a "distich."

Elegy A mournful, contemplative lyric poem often ending in consolation, written to commemorate someone who has died. *Elegy* may also refer to a serious, meditative poem that expresses the speaker's melancholy thoughts.

Elysian land In Greek mythology, some fortunate mortals spend their afterlife in the bliss of the Elysian Fields, or Islands of the Blest, rather than in Hades, the underworld.

End-stopped line A line in a poem after which a pause occurs. End-stopped lines reflect normal speech patterns and are often marked by punctuation.

English Bill of Rights Formally known as "An Act declaring the Rights and Liberties of the Subject, and settling the Succession of the Crown," the English Bill of Rights was passed in December 1689. It conferred the crown upon William and Mary, who succeeded the ousted James II; it stated that no Catholic would ever be king or queen of England, extended civil rights and liberties to the people of England, and confirmed Parliament's power in a constitutional government. See also BILL OF RIGHTS.

Enjambment In poetry, a line continuing without a pause into the next line for its meaning; also called a run-on line.

Enlightenment Refers to a period of time in Europe from the late seventeenth through the eighteenth century, also called the Age of Reason, in which reason, human progress, and order were venerated. The Enlightenment intensified the process of secularization that had begun during the Renaissance and favored the use of empirical science to resolve social problems. Enlightenment philosophers questioned the existing forms of education and politics and fought tyranny and social injustice. Enlightenment ideas led to the American and French Revolutions in the late 1700s. Leading philosophers also questioned the Bible and gave rise to a new movement of freethinkers—people who rejected the church's dogma and encouraged rational inquiry and speculation.

Ennui French for boredom or lack of interest; the term is associated with a widespread discontent with the pleasures of the modern world.

Eos The Greek goddess of the dawn who loved the young men Cleitus, Cephalus, and Orion, the hunter.

Epic A long narrative poem told in a formal, elevated style that focuses on a serious subject and chronicles heroic deeds and events important to a culture or nation.

Epigram A brief, pointed, and witty poem that usually makes a satiric or humorous point. Epigrams are most often written in couplets but can be written in any form.

Epiphany In fiction, when a character suddenly experiences a deep realization about himself or herself; a truth which is grasped in an ordinary rather than a melodramatic moment.

Eros The Greek god of love, associated with both passion and fertility. Freud used the term *Eros* in modern times to signify the human life-drive (desire) at war with THANATOS, the death-drive.

Euphony From the Greek for "good sound"; refers to language that is smooth and musically pleasant to the ear.

Existentialism A school of modern philosophy associated with Jean-Paul Sartre (1905–1980) and Albert Camus (1913–1960) that dominated European thought in the years following World War II. Existentialists are interested in the nature of consciousness and emphasize the role of individual will in shaping existence. Existentialism holds that discrete, willful acts of choice create the only meaning that exists in an otherwise meaningless universe.

Exposition A narrative device often used at the beginning of a work that provides necessary background information about characters and their circumstances. Exposition explains such matters as what has gone on before, the relationships between characters, theme, and conflict.

Expressionism An artistic and literary movement that originated in Germany in the early twentieth century. Expressionism departs from the conventions of realism to focus on the inner impressions or moods of a character or of the artist. Influenced by the increased mechanization of the modern world and by MARXISM, expressionism often reveals the alienation of the individual.

Fabliau Although the *fabliau* originated in France as a comic or satiric tale in verse, by the time of Giovanni Boccaccio (1313–1375) and Geoffrey Chaucer (1340–1400) the term also stood for bawdy and ribald prose tales like "The Miller's Tale" in Chaucer's *Canterbury Tales* or Boccaccio's "Rustico and Alibech."

Farce A form of humor based on exaggerated, improbable incongruities. Farce involves rapid shifts in action and emotion as well as slapstick comedy and extravagant dialogue.

Fascism An ideology that combines dictatorial government, militarism, control of the personal freedom of a people, extreme nationalism, and government control of business. Fascism peaked between the 1920s and '40s, when Adolf Hitler, Benito Mussolini, and Francisco Franco gained power in Germany, Italy, and Spain respectively.

Feminism A school of thought that examines the oppression, subjugation, or inequality of women. Feminism has flourished since the middle of the twentieth century and has taken different forms, focusing variously on language, the meaning of power, and the institutions that perpetuate sexism.

Feminist criticism An approach to literature that seeks to correct or supplement a predominantly male-dominated critical perspective with a feminist consciousness. Feminist criticism places literature in a social context and uses a broad range of disciplines, including history, sociology, psychology, and linguistics, to provide interpretations that are sensitive to feminist issues.

Fenian Society A secret organization of Irish nationalists founded in 1858 promoting Irish independence from England by means of violent revolution. The organization was named after the Fenians, professional soldiers who served Irish kings in third-century Ireland. With support from cells among Irish emigrants in America, South Africa, and Australia, the Fenian Society, led by James Stephens, launched a rebellion in 1867 that, although it failed, helped to galvanize political opposition to English rule and call attention to the problems in Ireland.

Feudal aristocracy A system of government that existed in Europe in the Middle Ages. The feudal system refers to a mode of agricultural production in which peasants worked for landowners, or lords, in return for debt forgiveness, food, and governmental responsibilities such as military protection. The lords or landowners constitute the upper class, or aristocracy, but at the top of the hierarchy was the monarch who controlled the government and the granting of fiefs, or tracts of land.

Figures of speech Ways of using language that deviate from the literal, denotative meanings of words in order to suggest additional meanings or effects. Figures of speech say one thing in terms of something else, such as when an eager funeral director is described as a vulture.

Fin de siècle French for "end of the century"; generally refers to the final years of the nineteenth century, a time characterized by decadence and ENNUI. Artists of this era romanticized drug addiction and prostitution; open sexuality, including homosexuality, also marked the period. In Paris and Vienna, the Art Nouveau movement in the fine arts flourished and was informed by the blossoming of radical ideas in the wake of the Paris Commune of 1871. Notable fin-de-siècle figures include artists such as Aubrey Beardsley and writers such as Oscar Wilde.

Fixed form A poem characterized by a fixed pattern of lines, syllables, or meter. A SONNET is a fixed form of poetry because it must have fourteen lines.

Flashback A literary or dramatic device that allows a past occurrence to be inserted into the chronological order of a narrative.

Floating World (*ukiyo-e*) A Japanese artistic movement that flourished in the seventeenth, eighteenth, and nineteenth centuries in Tokyo. Ukiyo-e depicts the floating or sorrowful world; its most frequent media are woodblock prints, books, and drawings. Originally considered a popular rather than a high art, ukiyo-e treated literary, classic, and historical themes within a contemporary context, and it was particularly appealing to the emerging merchant classes.

Flying Dutchman The legend of a ghostly ship doomed to sail for eternity. If a vision of it appears to sailors, it signals imminent disaster. Most versions of the story have the captain of the ship playing dice or gambling with the Devil.

Foil A character in a literary work or drama whose behavior or values contrast with those of another character, typically the PROTAGONIST.

Foot A poetic foot is a poem's unit of measurement and decides the rhythm. In English, the iambic, or ascending, foot is the most common.

Foreshadowing Providing hints of what is to happen next in order to build suspense.

Formalist A type of criticism dominant in the early twentieth century that emphasizes the form of an artwork. Two of its prominent schools are Russian formalism, which favors the form of an artwork over its content and argues for the necessity of literature to defamiliarize the ordinary objects of the world, and American NEW CRITICISM, which treats a work of art as an object and seeks to understand it through close, careful analysis.

Formula literature Literature that fulfills a reader's expectations. In detective novels, for instance, the plot may vary among different works, but in the end the detective solves the case in all of them. Science fiction, romance, and Westerns are other examples of formula literature.

Found poem An ordinary collection of words that can be understood differently when arranged or labeled as a poem. A found poem could be something as banal as a "to do" list or personal advertisement, but the poet who "finds" it argues that it has special, unintentional value when presented as a poem.

Founding myth A story that explains how a particular nation or culture came to be, such as Virgil's *Aeneid*, which describes the founding of Rome. Many epic poems, sometimes called national epics, are founding myths.

Four classes In Hindu tradition, humans are created as one of four classes, or *varna:* in descending order, the BRAHMANS (priests), the *Ksatriya* (warriors), the *Vaisya* (merchants and farmers), and the *Sudra* (laborers and servants).

Framed narration Also called *framed tale.* A story within a story. In Chaucer's *Canterbury Tales,* each pilgrim's story is framed by the story of the pilgrimage itself. This device, used by writers from ancient times to the present, enjoyed particular popularity during the thirteenth, fourteenth, and fifteenth centuries and was most fully developed in *The Arabian Nights,* a work in which the framing is multilayered.

Free association A Freudian exercise wherein a patient relates to an analyst anything that comes to his or her mind, no matter how illogical or apparently trivial, without any attempt to censor, shape, or otherwise organize the material. In literature, the term refers to a free flow of the mind's thoughts; it is an important element of stream-of-consciousness writing.

Free verse Highly irregular poetry; typically, free verse does not rhyme.

French Revolution The first of four major revolutions in France in the late eighteenth and nineteenth centuries; it began with the storming of the Bastille in 1789 and ended in the coup of the Eighteenth Brumaire, on November 9–10, 1799, when Napoleon overthrew the revolutionary government. The original goal of the revolution had been to establish a constitutional monarchy that would transfer power from the nobility, headed by King Louis XVI, and the clergy to the middle classes. That aim was abandoned, however, when the king and queen were beheaded in 1793 and a republic was created.

French Symbolists Symbolism was an AVANT-GARDE movement in France in the late nineteenth century that arose from revolutionary experiments with language, verse form, and the use of symbols in the poetry of Stéphane Mallarmé (1842–1898) and Paul Verlaine (1844–1896); according to the Symbolists,

poetic language should not delineate ideas but rather evoke feeling and moods, insinuate impressions and connections. French Symbolism, which often is extended to include the poetry of Charles Baudelaire (1821–1867) and Arthur Rimbaud (1854–1891), who anticipated some of its principles, exerted a profound influence on modernist poetry in Russia as well as throughout Europe and the United States.

Freudian criticism A method of literary criticism associated with Freud's theories of psychoanalysis. Early Freudian critics sought to illustrate how literature is shaped by the unconscious desires of the author, but the term has developed and become more broadly defined to encompass many schools of thought that link psychoanalysis to the interpretation of literature.

Gay and lesbian criticism School of literary criticism that focuses on the representation of homosexuality in literature; also interested in how homosexuals read literature and to what extent sexuality and gender is culturally constructed.

Gender criticism Literary school that analyzes how an author's or a reader's sex affects the writing and reading experiences.

Genre A category of artistic works or literary compositions that have a distinctive style or content. Poetry, fiction, and drama are genres. Different genres have dominated at various times and places: In eighteenth-century Europe, the dramatic comedy was the preferred form of theater; in the nineteenth century, the novel was the dominant genre.

Genroku period (1688–1703) A Japanese cultural period during the EDO era when a growing number of affluent *chonin,* or townsmen, sought diversion in the FLOATING WORLD, or *ukiyo-e*—city districts where courtesans, along with theater, dance, song, and the arts, flourished.

German Romanticism A German form of nineteenth-century Romanticism. In addition to German Romantic poets like Friedrich Holderlin (1770–1843), Novalis (1772–1801), and Heinrich Heine (1797–1856), Germany produced the Romantic theorists Friedrich Schlegel (1772–1829), F. W. J. Schelling (1775–1854), and August Wilhelm Schlegel (1767–1845), who believed that the Christian myth needed to be replaced with a modern one.

Ghazal A form of lyric poetry composed of three to seven couplets, called *sh'ir*, that follow the strict rhyme scheme of *aa ba ca da*, and so on, known as the *qafiyah*. Strict adherence to the form requires the use of the *radif*, a word that is repeated in a pattern dictated by the first couplet, throughout the poem. Literally meaning "dialogue with the beloved," the *ghazal*, as practiced in Arabia, Persia, Turkey, and India beginning around 1200, became the predominant form for love poetry.

Giri Japanese term for social duty and responsibility.

Glorious Revolution of 1688 The forced abdication of the Catholic king James II of England, whose attempts to exercise royal authority over Parliament galvanized the largely Protestant English nation against him. Although largely a bloodless revolution, some fighting between Catholics and Protestants took place in Ireland and Scotland.

Gnostics Members of an ancient sect in the Middle East who believed that hidden knowledge held the key to the universe. Throughout history there have been Gnostics who have formed secret societies with secret scriptures and who have believed they understood the workings of the cosmos.

Gokan A book combining pictures and text; often adapted from classic Chinese or Japanese stories.

Gothic A style of literature (especially novels) in the late eighteenth and early nineteenth centuries that reacted against the mannered decorum of earlier literature. Gothic novels explore the darker side of human experience; they are often set in the past and in foreign countries, and they employ elements of horror, mystery, and the supernatural.

Gothic novel A subgenre of the novel whose works concentrate on mystery, magic, and horror. Especially popular during the late eighteenth and early nineteenth centuries, gothic novels are often set in castles or mansions whose dungeons or secret rooms contribute to the atmosphere of mystery.

Greater Dionysia In ancient Greece, dramas were performed at festivals that honored the god Dionysus: the Lenaea during January and February and the Greater Dionysia in March and April. The best tragedies and comedies were awarded prizes by an Athenian jury.

Hadith Islamic source of religious law and moral guidance. According to tradition, the Hadith were passed down orally to the prophet Muhammad, and today they are critical to the study of the early development of Islam.

Haikai A form of Japanese linked verse that flourished from the sixteenth through the nineteenth centuries, *haikai* is a sequence of alternating stanzas usually composed by two or more writers. The sequence opens with a *hokku*, a three-line stanza of seventeen syllables that alternate 5, 7, 5; the hokku is followed by alternating three- and two-line stanzas of seventeen and fourteen syllables, respectively. Bashō, the greatest of the haikai masters, preferred a sequence of thirty-six stanzas. Haikai is distinguished from RENGA, an earlier form of Japanese linked verse, primarily by diction and tone; whereas renga, with its origins in court poetry, uses elevated diction and reflects a cultivated seriousness, haikai introduces more colloquial diction, is more lighthearted, and treats common aspects of human experience. The hokku eventually became a separate form, now known as HAIKU.

Haiku Unrhymed Japanese poetic form that consists of seventeen syllables arranged in three lines. Although its origins can be traced to the seventeenth century, it is the most popular poetic form in Japan today. See HAIKAI.

Hamartia Error or flaw. In ancient Greek tragedies, the hero falls through his own *hamartia*.

Hellene Greek.

Heroic couplet A rhymed, iambic-pentameter stanza of two lines that completes its thought within the two-line form. Alexander Pope

(1688–1744), the most accomplished practitioner of the form in English, included this couplet in his *Essay on Criticism:* "True wit is nature to advantage dressed, / What oft was thought, but ne'er so well expressed."

Hexameter couplets The conventional strophic form of Greek and Latin epic poetry consisting of two dactylic hexameter lines; each line is composed of six feet and each foot comprises one long (accented) and two short (unaccented) syllables. The final foot is known as a catalectic foot, for it is generally shortened by one or two syllables.

Hieros gamos Literally, "sacred marriage"; a fertility ritual in which the god-king or priest-king is united with the goddess or priestess-queen in order to provide a model for the kingdom and establish the king's right to rule.

Hinduism The major religion of India, based upon the ancient doctrines found in the SANSKRIT texts known as the VEDAS and the UPANISHADS, dating from 1000 B.C.E.

Historical criticism An approach to literature that uses history as a means of understanding a literary work. Such criticism moves beyond both the facts of an author's life and the text itself to examine the social and intellectual contexts in which the author composed the work.

Homeric Hymns At one time attributed to Homer, the *Homeric Hymns* (seventh–sixth centuries B.C.E.) are now believed to have been created by poets from a Homeric school or simply in the style of Homer. Five of the longer hymns contain important stories about gods such as Demeter, DIONYSUS, Apollo, Aphrodite, and Hermes.

Hubris Exaggerated pride or arrogance; in Greek tragedies, hubris always causes fatal errors.

Huguenots French Protestant members of the Reformed Church established in France by John Calvin in about 1555. Due to religious persecution, many fled to other countries in the sixteenth and seventeenth centuries.

Hyperbole An exaggerated figure of speech; for example, "I nearly died laughing."

Iambic pentameter A poetic line made up of five feet, or iambs, or a ten-syllable line.

Ibsenism After the plays of Norwegian dramatist Henrik Ibsen (1828–1906): a concern in drama with social problems treated realistically rather than romantically.

Idealism Philosophical Idealism in its various forms holds that objects of perception are in reality mental constructs and not the material objects themselves.

Image The two types of images are literal and figurative. Literal images are very detailed, almost photographic; figurative images are more abstract and often use symbols, such as this image of the night in T. S. Eliot's "The Love Song of J. Alfred Prufrock" (1917):

> Let us go then, you and I,
> When the evening is spread out
>   against the sky
> Like a patient etherized upon a table

Industrial Revolution Advancements in mechanization beginning in the mid eighteenth century that transformed manufacturing, transportation, and agriculture over the next century and a half. Most historians regard the Industrial Revolution as the phenomenon that has had the largest impact on the present, changing the Western world from a rural to an urban society and moving the workplace from the fields to the factories. Because of it, the economy changed rapidly, and the production of goods increased exponentially, raising the West's standard of living. The new working class, however, lived in horrible conditions in the cities.

Industrialization The process of building factories and mass producing goods; typically, also part of urbanization.

Inquisition A medieval institution set up by the Roman Catholic pope to judge and convict anyone who might constitute a threat to papal power. The threats took various forms, including heresy, witchcraft, alchemy, and sorcery. The Inquisition held a great amount of power in medieval Europe, especially in southern European countries. The most powerful was the Spanish Inquisition, authorized in 1478, which executed thousands of victims, among them Jews, Muslims, and heretics, through public burning.

Irish Literary Renaissance A movement of the late nineteenth century of Irish writers, including William Butler Yeats (1865–1939), Lady Gregory (1852–1932), and J. M. Synge (1871–1909), who aimed to revitalize Irish literature and to renew interest in and revaluate Irish myth, legend, folklore, history, and literature. The literary renaissance was part of a broader cultural effervescence in Ireland in the late 1890s that included the founding of the Gaelic League, which promoted the use of the Irish language, and the startup of the Gaelic Athletic Association, which restored Irish sports.

Irony A device used in writing and speech to deliberately express ideas so they can be understood in two ways. In drama, irony occurs when a character does not know something that the other characters or the audience knows.

Jainism A religion founded in India in the sixth century B.C.E. by Vardhaman, who is known as Mahavira, or the "great hero." Formed in direct opposition to the rigid ritualism and hierarchical structure of traditional Hinduism, Jainism espoused asceticism, renunciation of the world, nonviolence, and the sanctity of all living beings.

Jewish mysticism Like all forms of mysticism, Jewish mysticism focuses on learning and practices that lead to unity with the creator; its teachings are referred to as the Cabala, or Kabala.

Joruri The form of puppet theater that developed in Japan in the seventeenth and eighteenth centuries in which expert puppeteers manipulate lifelike dolls while a master chanter, accompanied by the SAMISEN, sings and chants the story, speaks for the characters, and describes the scenes. The term derives from *ningyo,* meaning puppet or doll, and *joruri,* which alludes to the often-told story of Lady Joruri, the main character of a popular story dating back to the fifteenth century who was the subject of the first puppet play. Today joruri is known as BUNRAKU,

after the great puppeteer Bunraku-ken Uemura (d. 1810), and Bunraku-ken Uemura II (1813–1873), who established a puppet theater in Osaka in 1842 after interest in joruri declined.

Judgment of Paris In Greek legend, Paris (Alexandros) was selected by the god Zeus to judge which of three goddesses was the most beautiful. He chose Aphrodite, who bribed him by agreeing to help him seduce Helen, the most beautiful woman alive. His stealing of Helen and refusal to return her was the cause of the Trojan War.

Julian calendar Calendar used from the time of Julius Caesar, c. 46 B.C.E., until 1582, when it was generally replaced by the Gregorian calendar, which is still in wide use today.

Kabuki A popular form of Japanese theater primarily about and aimed at the middle classes and that uses only male actors; Kabuki developed in the sixteenth and seventeenth centuries, parallel to JORURI, or puppet theater, which often shares the same plots and stories and even the same plays.

Kibyoshi Literally, "yellow back"; a simple illustrated book usually concerned with life in the licensed quarters.

Laissez-faire A French phrase meaning "let them do"; a doctrine in classical economics that asserts the economy should operate on its own, without interference from the government.

Leatherstocking Tales Novels by James Fenimore Cooper (1789–1851), including *The Pioneers* (1823), *The Last of the Mohicans* (1826), *The Prairie* (1827), *The Pathfinder* (1840), and *The Deerslayer* (1841). All featured a PROTAGONIST nicknamed "Leatherstocking."

Leitmotifs Themes, brief passages, or single words repeated within a work.

Leviathan A dragon or sea monster mentioned in the Hebrew Scriptures, suggesting an ancient combat myth. See Isaiah 51:9–10, Isaiah 27:1, Psalm 74:12–14, Psalm 89:10, and Job 26:12–13. See also RAHAB.

Liberalism An ideology that rejects authoritarian government and defends freedom of speech, association, and religion as well as the right to own property. Liberalism evolved during the ENLIGHTENMENT and became the dominant political idea of the nineteenth century. Both the American and French Revolutions were based on liberal thought.

Limerick A humorous, sometimes nonsensical poem of five lines, with a strict scheme of meter and rhyme.

Line A sequence of words. In poetry, lines are typically measured by the number of feet they contain.

Literary epic A literary epic—as distinguished from folk epics such as the *Mahabharata* or *The Iliad*—that are made up of somewhat loosely linked episodes and closely follow oral conventions—is written with self-conscious artistry, has a tightly knit organic unity, and is stylistically rooted in a written, literate culture. In actuality, great epics often blur the distinction between the oral or folk epic and the literary epic.

Local-color tales Stories that seek to portray the people and way of life of a particular region by describing the speech, dress, and customs of its inhabitants.

Lyric A brief poem that reflects the imagination and emotion of the speaker. With its etymology in the word *lyre,* a lyric poem was originally meant to be sung to the accompaniment of a lyre, a medieval stringed instrument that is associated with poetic inspiration. Although modern lyric poetry is not necessarily meant to be sung, it does retain its melodic quality. Lyric poetry is highly subjective and informed by the speaker's imagination; it has flourished throughout literary history.

Magical realism A movement in fiction in which REALIST technique is used to narrate stories that combine mundane and miraculous events, everyday realities and the supernatural. The term is most often used to describe the work of Colombian novelist Gabriel García Márquez (b. 1928), Mexican author Carlos Fuentes (b. 1928), Peruvian novelist Mario Vargas Llosa (b. 1936), and Argentine author Julio Cortázar (1914–1984).

Manchu Also known as the Jurchen, a people who lived northeast of the Great Wall of China, in the area now known as Manchuria; when civil disturbances weakened the authority of the Ming emperor, the Manchu, with the assistance of some from inside China, took control of Beijing and founded a new empire. Their dynasty, known as the QING or Manchu dynasty, lasted from 1644 to 1911.

Manifest Destiny Term coined in 1845 for the American belief that the United States was not only destined but obligated to expand its territory westward to the Pacific Ocean.

Marxism A school of thought based on the writings of German Socialist thinker Karl Marx. Among its main tenets are the ideas that class struggle is the central element of Western culture, that a capitalist class thrives by exploiting the labor of a working class, and that workers must struggle to overcome their capitalist exploiters through revolution and thereafter establish a socialist society in which private property does not exist and all people have collective control of the means of production and distribution.

Marxist criticism Literary criticism that evolved from Karl Marx's political and economic theories. Marxist critics believe that texts must be understood in terms of the social class and the economic and political positions of their characters and plot.

Masque Developed in the Renaissance, masques are highly stylized and structured performances with an often mythological or allegorical plot, combining drama, music, song, and dance in an elaborate display.

Materialism A worldview that explains the nature of reality in terms of physical matter and material conditions rather than by way of ideas, emotions, or the supernatural.

Mathnavi Persian poetic form used for romantic, epic, didactic, and other types of poems whose subjects demand a lengthy treatment; its verse structure is similar to that of the Western heroic couplet, but with two rhyming halves in a single line.

Meiji Restoration After years of feudal reign in Japan, the emperor was restored to his position in 1868. He adopted *Meiji,* meaning "enlightened rule," as the name of his era. In this period, massive INDUSTRIALIZATION took place in Japan, which became a significant competitor for world power. The military was also strengthened to combat European and American imperialism.

Melodrama A dramatic genre characterized by suspense, romance, and sensation. Melodramas typically have a happy ending.

Mestizos Peoples in the Americas of mixed ethnic or cultural heritage, usually a combination of Spanish and Native American.

Metaphor A comparison of two things that does not use the words *like* or *as.* For example, "love is a rose."

Meter The rhythm of a poem based on the number of syllables in each line and which syllables are accented. See also FOOT.

Michiyuki A conventional form in Japanese drama (and also in fiction) wherein a character's thoughts and feelings are evoked through the places he or she visits on a journey; often, by means of symbolism and allusion, the journey suggests a spiritual transformation.

Middle Passage The transatlantic journey from West Africa to the Caribbean or the Americas of slave ships transporting their human cargo during the time of the slave trade (sixteenth–nineteenth centuries).

Millenarianism A utopian belief that the end of time is imminent, after which there will be a thousand-year era of perfect peace on earth.

Ming dynasty (1368–1644) Founded by Zhu Yuan-zhang, who restored native Chinese rule from the Mongols who had ruled China during the previous Yuan dynasty (1271–1368) established by Kubla Khan. The Ming dynasty saw a flourishing of Chinese culture, the restoration of Confucianism, and the rise of the arts, including porcelain, architecture, drama, and the novel.

Mock epic A form that parodies the EPIC by treating a trivial subject in the elevated style of the epic, employing such conventions as an invocation to the muse, an extended simile, and a heroic epithet that burlesques its subject.

Modernism In its broadest sense, this term refers to European writing and art from approximately 1914, the beginning of World War I, to about 1945, the end of World War II. Although many writers of this time continued to work with the forms of fiction and poetry that had been in place since the nineteenth century, others such as James Joyce (1882–1941), Virginia Woolf (1882–1941), William Faulkner (1897–1962), Rainer Maria Rilke (1875–1926), and Thomas Mann (1875–1955) broke with the past, introducing experimentation and innovation in structure, style, and language. *Modernism* can also refer to a spirit of innovation and experimentation, or the break with nineteenth-century aesthetic and literary thinking and forms, or the exploration of psychological states of mind, alienation, and social rupture that characterized the era between the two world wars.

Monologue A speech of significant length delivered by one person; in drama, a CHARACTER talks to himself or reveals personal secrets without addressing another character.

Mystery religions Mystery cults were very popular in ancient Greece and Rome for at least one thousand years, beginning around 1000 B.C.E. The details of each cult were kept a secret, but all cults shared a rigorous rite of initiation, a concern about death, and a hope for immortality centered on a deity who had personal knowledge of the afterlife. The most popular Greek versions were the Orphic and Eleusinian mysteries. The mysteries of Isis and Mithra were favored in the Roman world.

Mythological criticism A type of literary criticism that focuses on the archetypal stories common to all cultures. Initiated by Carl Jung in the early twentieth century, mythological criticism seeks to reveal how the structures lodged deep in the human consciousness take the form of archetypal stories and are the basis for literature. Jung identified four principal ARCHETYPES that together constitute the Self: Shadow (rejected evil), Anima (feminine side of male self), Animus (masculine

side of female self), and Spirit (wise old man or woman).

Narrative poem A poem with only one basic rule: It must tell a story. Ballads, epics, and romances are typically narrative poems.

Narrator The voice that in fiction describes the PLOT or action of a story. The narrator can speak in the first or the third person and, depending on the effect the author wishes to create, can be very visible or almost invisible (an explicit or an implicit narrator); he or she can be involved in the plot or be more distant. See also POINT OF VIEW and SPEAKER.

Naturalism A late-nineteenth-century literary school that sought to apply scientific objectivity to the novel. Led by Émile Zola (1840–1902) and influenced by Darwinism, Naturalists created characters who were ordinary people, whose lives were shaped by the forces of heredity and the environment.

Nawab The title given to a local Muslim ruler in India during the Mughal empire (1526–1857).

Négritude A literary movement founded in the early 1930s by three Black Francophone writers in Paris: Léopold Sédar Senghor (1906–2001), Aimé Césaire (b. 1913), and Léon Damas (1912–1978). In their work, these Négritude writers protested French colonial rule and the European assumption of superiority. They wanted their writings, which honored the traditions and special qualities of the African and Caribbean peoples, to inspire independence movements in the colonies.

Neoclassicism A style of art and architecture that was characterized by the simple, symmetrical forms of classical Greek and Roman art. It originated as a reaction to the Rococo and Baroque styles and was the result of a revival of classical thought in Europe and America. Neoclassical writing characterized the Augustan Age, a period comprising roughly the first half of the eighteenth century. Its name suggests an analogy to the reign of Emperor Augustus in the Roman Empire (63 B.C.E.–14 C.E.), when many of the great Latin poets, especially Virgil, were writing.

Neo-Confucianism Refers generally to the philosophical tradition in China and Japan based on the thought of Confucius (551–479 B.C.E.) and his commentators, particularly Mencius (370–290 B.C.E.) and Zhu Xi (1130–1200). Neo-Confucianism, which arose during the Sung dynasty (960–1279), asserts that the understanding of things must be based on an understanding of their underlying principles; in moral and political philosophy, it emphasizes the study of history, loyalty to family and nation, and order.

Neo-Sensualism Also known as the New Sensibilities or New Perceptionist school, this approach was founded by Kawabata Yasunari and other AVANT-GARDE writers, including Yokomitsu Riichi (1898–1947), and headquartered at the University of Tokyo in the 1920s. In 1924 these writers founded a magazine called *The Literary Age.* Influenced by European writers as well as by Japanese poetic traditions and *Nō* drama, neo-Sensualists sought to break with the confessional style of REALIST and NATURALIST writers and aimed for a more purely aesthetic, nonlinear style of fiction writing.

Neo-Shintoism *Shinto* is a term given to indigenous Japanese beliefs as distinguished from Buddhism, which was introduced to Japan in the sixth century C.E. In the seventeenth century, Shinto and Confucianist ideals came into contact with one another and produced an ideology that emphasized political philosophy and valued the virtues of wisdom, benevolence, and courage.

New Criticism A type of formalist literary criticism that completely disregards historical and biographical information to focus on the actual text. The New Critics perform a close reading of a work and give special attention to technical devices such as symbols and images and, in poetry, rhythm.

New Historicism A literary school developed as a reaction to NEW CRITICISM in the 1980s; presently, it is one of the leading schools of literary criticism. Like the nineteenth-century historicists, the New Historicists argue that historical and other external contexts must be part of textual analysis.

Nigerian-Biafran War Nigerian civil war that started when the Igbo people declared the eastern region of Nigeria an independent state named the Republic of Biafra. Recognized by only three countries, Biafra was almost immediately attacked by Nigerian troops. After a bloody fight resulting in close to three million casualties, the Biafran government surrendered in January 1970.

Ninjo Japanese term that denotes human feelings or passion, drives that often come into conflict with GIRI, or social duty and responsibility.

Nō The highly elaborate and ritualistic classical theater of Japan, known for its minimalist approach to plot, scenery, and stage effects and the stately performance and Zen-like mastery of its actors; *nō* means "talent" or "accomplishment." The great master and theorist of *Nō* drama is Zeami Motokiyo (1363–1443), who wrote several of the most famous *Nō* plays, including *Atsumori* and *The Lady Aoi.*

Novel An extended work of fictional prose narrative. The novel is a modern outgrowth of earlier genres such as the romance. There is considerable debate as to the origins of the novel; some critics trace it to Cervantes's *Don Quixote* in 1605. In England, the novel came into being in the beginning of the eighteenth century and has since developed far beyond its original realistic and moralistic aims, making it one of the most flexible of literary genres.

Octave A STANZA of eight lines in poetry.

Ode An elevated form of LYRIC generally written on a single theme, using varied metric and rhyme patterns. With the ode, poets working within classical schemes can introduce considerable innovation. There are three major types of odes in English: the Pindaric, or Regular; the Horatian; and the Irregular. The Pindaric ode is structured by three-strophe divisions, modulating between the strophe, antistrophe, and epode, which vary in tone. The Horatian ode uses only one STANZA type with variation introduced within each stanza. The Irregular ode, sometimes called the English ode, allows wide variety among stanza forms, rhyme schemes, and metrical patterns.

Oedipus complex A term from Freudian psychoanalysis that refers to the unconscious male desire to kill one's own father and to sleep with one's own mother. The term derives from the Greek myth of Oedipus, who unknowingly murdered his father and married his mother; his self-inflicted punishment was to blind himself. FREUDIAN CRITICS do not take the complex or the story literally, but frequently use it to examine in literature the guilt associated with sexual desire and competition with or hostility toward one's father.

Onomatopoeia A word that sounds like the thing it refers to: for example, the *buzz* of bees.

Open form Also known as FREE VERSE. A type of poetry that does not follow established conventions of METER, RHYME, and STANZA.

Organic form The concept that the structure of a literary work develops according to an internal logic. The literary work grows and becomes an organic whole that follows the principles of nature, not mechanics. The created work of art is akin to a growing plant that relies on all of its parts working together.

Orientalism The academic study and knowledge of the Middle East and Asia that developed during the imperialism of the nineteenth century. Orientalism is a Western approach to understanding the cultures, languages, and religions of the East. Especially in the early studies, the Orient was seen as exotic and romantic, but its inhabitants were regarded as uncivilized and inferior. Although by now these views have been challenged and changed, they are arguably still prevalent.

Oxymoron A rhetorical figure of speech in which contradictory terms are combined, such as "jumbo shrimp" and "deafening silence."

Parable A short narrative designed to teach a lesson about life in which the moral isn't directly stated; a form popular during biblical times.

Paradox An argument or opinion that is contradictory but true. For instance, "You have to be cruel to be kind."

Paraphrase To rewrite or say the same thing using different words.

Parian White marble from the Greek island of Paros.

Parody A humorous imitation of another, usually serious, work. Parody can be a form of literary criticism that exposes defects in a work, or it can function as an acknowledgement of a work's cultural and literary importance.

Patois A regional dialect of a language.

Peloponnesian War (431–404 B.C.E.) War between the Athenian and Spartan alliance systems that encompassed most of the Greek world. The war set new standards for warfare—Athens used the navy to support the land offensive, for instance—but the new tactics also prolonged the fight; instead of there being one decisive battle, the war dragged on for three decades. Eventually, Athens was defeated, and Sparta took over the defeated power's overseas empire.

Persian Wars A series of wars between a coalition of Greek city-states and the Persian empire fought between 500 and 449 B.C.E.; the Greek victory set the stage for the flourishing of Greek culture.

Persona Literally, a persona is a mask. In literature, a persona is a speaker created by a writer to tell a story or to speak in a poem. A persona is not a character in a story or narrative, nor does a persona necessarily directly reflect the author's personal voice. A persona is a separate self, created by and distinct from the author, through which he or she speaks.

Personification A figure of speech in which abstractions or inanimate objects are given human qualities or form.

Picaresque Term used to describe a novel that is loosely structured around a succession of episodes that focus on a rather thinly drawn *picaro*, or hero. The hero's adventures generally provide a sweeping and detailed view of a society and its customs, which are often satirized by the writer. Examples include Cervantes's *Don Quixote* and Voltaire's *Candide*.

Picture poem A poem whose lines form the image of the object it describes.

Plot The pattern of events or the story told in a narrative or drama.

Point of view The perspective from which the author, SPEAKER, or NARRATOR presents a story. A point of view might be localized within a CHARACTER, in which case the story is told from a first-person point of view. There is a range of possibilities between first-person point of view and omniscience, wherein the story is told from a perspective unlimited by time, place, or character.

Polis Greek term meaning "city"; designates the Greek city-states, such as Athens and Sparta, that arose in the sixth century B.C.E.

Postcolonial criticism Literary analysis of works produced in countries such as India, Africa, and the Caribbean that were once under the control of a colonial power. In some cases the term refers to the analysis of works about the colony written by authors who have been heavily influenced by the colonizing culture.

Postcolonialism The social, political, cultural, and economic practices that arose in response and resistance to colonialism and imperialism. This term also refers to the historical period following the colonial era, corresponding roughly to the second half of the twentieth century.

Postmodernism A literary and artistic movement that flourished in the late twentieth century as both a departure from and a development of MODERNISM. Postmodernism is frequently characterized by self-consciousness and self-reflexiveness: Postmodern literature is aware of the way it operates in a long literary tradition and responds to this awareness by revealing or referring to itself. Postmodern literature differs from modern literature in its emphasis on surface rather than depth, humor rather than psychological anguish, and space rather than time.

Pragmatism A philosophical approach that explains meaning and truth in terms of the application of ideas and beliefs to practical action.

Pre-Raphaelites A group of artists and writers, including John Everett Millais (1829–1896),

Dante Gabriel Rossetti (1828–1882), and William Holman Hunt (1827–1910), who rebelled against convention in poetry and painting by means of a strict adherence to details of nature; they aimed to capture what they perceived to be the truth, simplicity, and clarity of medieval painting—its pure colors, spiritual or mystical ambience, and sensuousness.

Problem play A drama in which the conflict arises from contemporary social problems. Bernard Shaw's *Mrs. Warren's Profession* (1893) and Shakespeare's *All's Well That Ends Well* (1602–04) are problem plays.

Proletariat The modern industrial working class, which, as defined by Karl Marx, lives solely by the sale of its labor. See also BOURGEOISIE.

Prologue Text that typically is placed prior to an introduction or that replaces a traditional introduction; often discusses events of importance for the general understanding of the narrative.

Prose poem A poem printed as prose without attention to line breaks. The prose poem argues for the flexibility of poetry by eschewing strict attention to METER and even RHYTHM, yet the language of a prose poem is frequently figurative and characterized by other poetic conventions such as ALLITERATION or internal rhyme.

Protagonist A leading figure or the main character in a drama or other literary work.

Protestant work ethic German sociologist Max Weber (1864–1920) first linked Protestantism to the habits of diligence and hard work that contributed to the rise of capitalism. The Puritans, whose form of Protestantism influenced early American life, interpreted prosperity resulting from work as a sign of God's favor.

Psychological criticism An approach to literature that draws on psychoanalytic theories, especially those of Sigmund Freud (1856–1939) and Jacques Lacan (1901–1981), to understand more fully the text, the writer, and the reader.

Pun A play on words that relies on a word's having more than one meaning or sounding like another word.

Purdah Practice adopted by some Muslims and Hindus that obscures women from public sight by mandating that they wear concealing clothing, especially veils. The custom originated in the seventh century C.E. and is still common in Islamic countries, though it has largely disappeared in Hinduism.

Qing dynasty (1644–1911) Also known as the Manchu dynasty, named after the MANCHU, a people from the north of China who took over China in 1644 with the help of rebel Chinese; the last dynasty in Chinese history, the Qing saw an increase in the influence of foreign interests and trade.

Quatrain A stanza of four lines in a poem.

Qur'an Or Koran; the sacred scriptures of Islam.

Rahab A term appearing several times in the Hebrew Scriptures; literally means "stormer," an allusion to the ancient monster of chaos in earlier Semitic creation myths. See also LEVIATHAN.

Rastafarianism An African-influenced religion that originated in the Caribbean in the twentieth century; venerates the former emperor of Ethiopia, Haile Selassie, forbids the cutting of hair, and embraces black culture and identity.

Rationalist Utilitarianism Revolutionary way of thinking established by, among others, Leon Trotsky (1879–1940). The Rationalist Utilitarians adopted the ethical theory proposed by John Stuart Mill (1806–1873) that all political actions should be directed toward achieving the greatest good for the greatest number of people. Mill, however, believed that decisions based on direct observation should determine action, while the Rationalist Utilitarians held that logical reasoning should play that role.

Reader-response criticism A critical approach to literature in which the primary focus falls on the reader, or the process of reading, not on the author. Reader-response critics believe that a literary work does not possess a fixed idea or meaning; meaning is a function of the perspective of the reader.

Realism Most broadly defined, realism is the attempt to represent the world accurately in literature. As a literary movement, Realism flourished in Russia, France, England, and America in the latter half of the nineteenth century. It emphasized not only accurate representation but the "truth," usually expressed as the consequence of a moral choice. Realist writers deemphasized the shaping power of the imagination and concerned themselves with the experiences of ordinary, middle-class subjects and the dilemmas they faced.

Recognition Based on the Greek concept of tragedy, recognition, or *anagnorisis,* is the point in a story when the PROTAGONIST discovers the truth about his or her situation. Usually this results in a drastic change in the course of the plot.

Reformation Also known as the Protestant Reformation, this sixteenth-century challenge to the authority of the Catholic Church caused a permanent rift in the Christian world, with those loyal to the pope remaining Catholic and those rejecting papal authority forming new Protestant faiths such as the Anglican, Lutheran, Calvinist, Anabaptist, and Presbyterian. The Reformation originated — and was most successful — in Northern Europe, especially Germany; its notable leaders include Martin Luther and John Calvin.

Renaissance man A term used to describe someone accomplished in many disciplines, especially in both science and the arts, like Leonardo da Vinci and other figures from the European Renaissance who were talented in many fields.

Renaissance sonneteers Poets of the European Renaissance who wrote fourteen-line love poems, often addressed to lovers who resisted or ignored their entreaties. Two types of Renaissance sonnets are commonly identified, the Italian and the English. These are alternatively known as the Petrarchan, after the Italian poet Petrarch who originated the form, and the Shakespearean, after the form's preeminent English practitioner. The major difference between the two types is that the Italian usually has five rhymes and the English seven.

Renga A form of traditional Japanese court poetry that uses elevated diction and links a number of haiku-like poems. Usually written by two or more poets who alternate verses, the traditional *renga* is a succession of three- and two-line compositions that evokes a particular season in each verse.

Resolution The point in the plot of a narrative work or drama that occurs after the climax and generally establishes a new understanding; also known as *falling action.*

Reversal The point in the plot of a story or drama when the fortunes of the PROTAGONIST change unexpectedly; also known as the *peripiteia.*

Revolution of 1830 In July 1830, the opponents of King Charles X (r. 1818–24) took to the streets of Paris to protest his corruption and the undermining of liberal reforms. Charles abdicated the throne, and bankers and industrialists brought in King Louis-Philippe (r. 1830–48), who promised to uphold the reforms Charles had tried to dissolve.

Revolution of 1848 Often called the February Revolution, when French king Louis-Philippe (r. 1830–48) was overthrown and the Second Republic was established. This revolution inspired uprisings in many European countries.

Rhyme The repetition of identical or similar-sounding words or syllables, usually accented, in lines of poetry. Rhymes may be at the end of lines or internal to the lines.

Rhythm The pattern of stressed and unstressed syllables in prose and especially in poetry that can lend emphasis, reinforce a sound association, or suggest regularity or recurrence. The rhythm of a literary work can affect the emotional response of the reader or listener.

Romantic hero The PROTAGONIST of a romance, novel, or poem who is shaped by experiences that frequently take the form of combat, love, or adventure. The romantic hero is judged by his actions more than his thoughts, and he is often on a journey that will affect his moral development.

Romanticism A literary and artistic movement that swept through Europe in the early nineteenth century; its defiance of neoclassical principles and rationalism roughly parallels the political upheaval of the French Revolution, with which it is often associated. Romanticism in its simplest form exalts nature, the innocence of children and rustics, private emotion and experience, and the pursuit of political freedom and spiritual transcendence.

Rosetta stone A slab of basalt inscribed with texts in hieroglyphic, demotic, and Greek. Found by Napoleon's troops in Northern Egypt in 1799, it enabled Egyptologist J.-F. Champollion (1790–1832) to decipher Egyptian hieroglyphics for the first time (1821).

Russo-Japanese War (1904–1905) Russia's aggressive Far-Eastern policy following the SINO-JAPANESE WAR (1894–95) and the Russian construction of a railway across Manchuria resulted in increasing animosity between the two nations. Russia twice violated the treaty with China and lost the year-long war with Japan, destabilizing Russian power in the region.

Salamis Site of an important naval battle where the Greek fleet defeated the Persians in 480 B.C.E.

Samian War The Samian War (441–439 B.C.E.) was fought to bring the island of Samos—which had broken off from the league of Greek states led by Athens—back into the alliance and into compliance with Athenian hegemony.

Samisen A three-stringed instrument with a long fretless neck and a nearly square sound box introduced in Japan in the late sixteenth century; the samisen became the preferred instrument for accompanying the narration of JORURI.

Samsara A HINDU term for the cycle of birth, life, death, and rebirth; many Hindu practices aimed at obtaining release, *moksa*, from the otherwise endless repetition of life and death.

Samurai Japanese feudal aristocrat and member of the hereditary warrior class. Denied recognition in the MEIJI RESTORATION (1867).

Sanskrit The classical language of ancient India, in which many of the major HINDU religious and literary texts were written.

Satire A literary or dramatic genre whose works, such as Jonathan Swift's (1667–1745) *Gulliver's Travels*, attack and ridicule human behavior.

Scansion A system of poetic analysis that involves dividing lines into feet and examining patterns of stressed and unstressed syllables. Scansion is a mechanical way of breaking down verse in order to understand the regularities and irregularities of its METER.

Scene In drama, a subdivision of an ACT.

Script The written version or text of a play or movie that is used by the actors.

Sentimentality Extravagant emotion; T. S. Eliot defined this as "emotion in excess of the facts."

Sepoy The name given to Indians serving in the British army.

Sepoy Mutiny A rebellion in southern India in 1857 started by local Sepoys in reaction to regulations that violated their religion. The rebellion ended in 1858 after the British army intervened.

Sestet A STANZA of six lines; the last stanza of a Petrarchan SONNET is a sestet.

Setting The time, place, and social environment that frame the characters in a story.

Shinju play A play culminating in suicide; one of three major types of JORURI plays. The others are the *jidaimono*, or history play, and the *sewamono*, a play about contemporary domestic life. Some critics see the *shinju* play as a type of *sewamono*.

Shogun A military ruler of feudal Japan between 1192 and 1867. The shogunate was an inherited position in the military that operated under the nominal control of the emperor.

Simile A figure of speech, introduced by *like* or *as*, in which two things are compared as equals.

Sino-Japanese War (1894–1895) A conflict between Japan and China that revealed the weakness of the declining Chinese empire and the emerging strength of Japan. The war, which developed from a conflict over the control of Korea, culminated in Japan's victory: China recognized the independence of Korea, ceded Taiwan, and lifted trade restrictions with Japan.

Slave narrative Autobiographical narrative by a former slave describing his or her life and mistreatment under slavery, attempts to escape, and ultimate liberation. The narratives, which employed many devices from popular fiction, were accompanied by testimonials to their authenticity.

Slavophile Literally, someone who admires Slavs, a people of Eastern Europe. In nineteenth-century Russia, the term referred to someone who believed in the national traditions of Russia, who felt that Russia had the true religion, and who believed he or she was destined to export Russian teachings and establish the kingdom of God on earth.

Social Realism A type of realism that concentrates on the unpleasant realities of the modern world and attempts to expose injustice and to encourage political reaction.

Socialist Realism A standard for art and literature developed in the Soviet Union in the 1930s; it demanded that art depict the life of the people realistically and celebrate the ideals of the revolution. Mao Zedong (1893–1976) enforced similar standards in China after the People's Republic was established in 1949.

Sociological criticism School of literary criticism that seeks to place a work of art in its social context and define the relationship between the two. Like Marxist critics, sociological critics are oriented toward social class, political ideology, gender roles, and economic conditions in their analyses.

Soliloquy A literary or dramatic discourse in which a character speaks without addressing a listener.

Sonnet A fourteen-line LYRIC poem. The first basic sonnet form is the Italian or Petrarchan sonnet, which is divided into an eight-line octet and a six-line SESTET, each with a specific but varied rhyme pattern. The English or Shakespearean sonnet is divided into three four-line QUATRAINS followed by a two-line COUPLET; the quatrains are rhymed *abab cdcd efef* and the couplet is also end rhymed, *gg.*

Sophists Literally, wise men. Greek teachers who provided instruction in logic and rhetoric to pupils who could afford their expensive fees. Rhetoric was a new discipline whose study was observed to provide an advantage in politics and in the courts. Soon *Sophist* came to mean one who used methods of argumentation that undermined traditional beliefs and manipulated reality. When Socrates (c. 470–399 B.C.E.) challenged the authority of the Sophists, he was brought to trial and executed.

Spanish civil war (1936–39) War between the Falange Fascist Party led by General Francisco Franco and liberal republican loyalist forces; often seen as the staging ground for World War II. The war ended with republican defeat and the establishment of a right-wing dictatorship.

Speaker The person or PERSONA who speaks in a poem — often a created identity who cannot be equated with the poet.

Spiritual autobiography An autobiography that gives special importance to self-examination, interpretation of Scripture, and belief in predestination. St. Augustine's *Confessions* (c. 400), detailing a life of sin, conversion, and spiritual rebirth, is generally regarded as the archetypal spiritual autobiography.

St. Augustine (354–430) Influential Catholic theologian from North Africa whose *Confessions* (c. 400) tells the story of his conversion to Christianity.

St. Francis (c. 1181–1226) Founder of the Franciscan religious order; known for his kindness.

Stage directions Written directions explaining how actors are to move onstage. See also SCRIPT.

Stanza A poetic verse of two or more lines, sometimes characterized by a common pattern of RHYME and METER.

Stock responses Predictable responses to language and symbols. See also CLICHÉ.

Stream of consciousness A term first used by the American philosopher and psychologist William James (1842–1910) to denote the often disjointed and even incoherent flow of ideas, sensations, thoughts, and images running through the conscious mind at any given moment. In literature, "stream of consciousness" generally refers to novels or short stories that attempt to achieve psychological realism by depicting the raw, unedited contents of a character's mind. Such depictions may involve "interior monologues" wherein an author presents a character's thoughts either with (indirect) or without (direct) any commentary, ordering, or editing. This device, associated with high modernism, reached its height in the work of James Joyce.

Stress A syllable receiving emphasis in accordance with a metrical pattern.

Sturm und Drang Literally, "storm and stress." Refers to a period of intense literary activity in the late eighteenth century associated with Idealism and the revolt against stale convention. The movement was named after a play about the American Revolution, and its leading participants included Goethe (1749–1832) and Schiller (1759–1805).

Style The distinctive manner in which an author writes and thus makes his or her work unique. A style provides a kind of literary signature for the writer.

Subplot A PLOT subordinate to the main plot of a literary work or drama.

Superman Also called "overman," or *Übermensch* in German. A term introduced by the German philosopher Friedrich Nietzsche (1844–1900) to denote a superior man who would exercise creative power and live at a level of experience beyond the standards of good and evil and thus represent the goal of human evolution.

Surrealism An aesthetic movement centered in twentieth-century France that extolled the direct and free expression of the unconscious as understood by Freudian psychology; proponents of surrealism include the writer André Breton (1896–1966), who wrote *Manifesto of Surrealism* in 1924; the filmmaker Jean Cocteau (1889–1963); and the painters Salvador Dalí (1904–1989) from France and Joan Miró (1893–1983) from Spain. A combination of precise, realistic detail and dreamlike fantasy characterizes surrealism.

Suspense The anxious emotion of the audience or reader anticipating the outcome of a story or drama, typically having to do with the fate of the PROTAGONIST or another character with whom a sympathetic attachment has been formed.

Symbol A representative of something by association. Though a symbol is often confused with a metaphor, a metaphor compares two dissimilar things while a symbol associates two things. For example, the *word* "tree" is a symbol for an *actual* tree. Some symbols have values that are accepted by most people. A flag, for instance, is for many a symbol of national pride, just as a cross is widely seen as a symbol of Christianity. Knowledge of a symbol's cultural context is sometimes necessary to understand its meaning; an apple pie is an American symbol of innocence that a Japanese person, for example, would not necessarily recognize.

Symbolism As the French writer Paul Valéry (1871–1945) notes in *The Existence of Symbolism* (1939), Symbolism "was not a school. On the contrary, it included many schools of the most divergent types." Symbolism generally refers to a movement among poets in France anticipated in the work of Charles Baudelaire (1821–1867) and Arthur Rimbaud (1854–1891) but practiced as a self-conscious movement by Stéphane Mallarmé (1842–1898), Paul Verlaine (1844–1896), and Jules Laforgue (1860–1887). Symbolists sought to convey the fluidity and evocative harmony of music in their work, and to capture tones, fragrances, sensations, and intuitions rather than concrete images or rational ideas.

Syncretism The attempt to combine differing beliefs, such as philosophy and religion, or two religious systems, such as Christianity and a native African tradition.

Syntax The way parts of speech are arranged in a sentence.

Tantrism A minor HINDU tradition written down in scriptures called Tantras. Tantrism holds the supreme deity to be feminine and teaches that spiritual liberation can be won through erotic practices.

Terza rima A verse form composed of iambic three-line STANZAS. The triplets have ten- or eleven-syllable lines. Terza rima is used to perhaps its most brilliant end in Dante's (1265–1321) *Divine Comedy*.

Tetragrammaton The four consonants of the Hebrew alphabet YHWH used to approximate God's secret name; this name and its utterances are believed to contain special powers.

Thanatos "Death" in Greek. According to Sigmund Freud, our two primary drives are EROS (love) and Thanatos (death).

Theater of the absurd A school of modernist, non-realistic drama especially influential from the 1950s to the '70s. Italian playwright Eugene Ionesco described its subject matter as "man . . . lost in the world, [so] all his actions become senseless, absurd, useless."

Theme A topic of discussion or a point of view embodied in a work of art.

Theosophical Society Founded in 1875 in London by Helena Petrovna Blavatsky in order to promote the reconciliation of Eastern religious doctrines with Western mysticism. Blavatsky, who wrote *Isis Unveiled* (1877) and faced charges of charlatanism, believed in the spiritual nature of things, the reincarnation of the soul, and the power of grasping one's spiritual essence, particularly by means of mystical experience.

Thesis The presentation of a purpose or hypothetical proposition, or a dissertation with an original point based on research.

Tokugawa era (1600–1868) Period of Japanese history named after Tokugawa Ieyasu (1542–1616), who was named shogun in 1603; also known as the EDO era because Tokugawa made Edo (now Tokyo) the capital. The early Tokugawa was a period of international isolation, political stability, nation building, and prosperity for the middle classes; it was also a time of great literary and cultural growth, particularly in the popular cultural forms such as KABUKI and JORURI (puppet) theater, the popular novel, and colored woodblock art, all aimed at the flourishing middle classes.

The Tokugawa era ended in 1867 when a group of disaffected SAMURAI restored imperial rule under the teenage emperor Meiji (r. 1867–1912) in the MEIJI RESTORATION and opened Japan's doors to Western trade and cultural exchange.

Tone A manner of expression in writing that indicates a certain attitude toward the subject or the implied audience.

Totalitarianism A system of centralized government in which a single unopposed party exerts total and repressive control over a country's political, social, economic, and cultural life.

Tragedy A dramatic or literary form originating in Greece that deals with serious human actions and issues. The actions must create feelings of fear and compassion in the spectator that are later released (CATHARSIS). Typically, the main character is of a high stature or rank, so his or her fall is substantial. Even though tragedies are sad, they seem both just and believable. The tragedy raises serious moral and philosophical questions about the meaning of life and fate.

Tragicomedy A drama that combines tragedy and comedy and in which moral values are particularly questioned or ridiculed.

Transcendentalism A philosophy derived from ROMANTICISM that flourished in the United States in the early nineteenth century. American writers Ralph Waldo Emerson and Henry David Thoreau championed and articulated the philosophy, which contends that the individual mind has the capability to transcend the human institutions that seek to fetter it. The transcendentalists believed that the most valuable pursuit was to experience, reflect upon, and study nature and its relation to the individual.

Travel narratives A form of narrative that recounts the incidents that occur and the people and things that the narrator meets and sees while visiting a place with which she or he is typically unfamiliar. Prose and poetic accounts about exploration and adventure in unfamiliar lands and places as well as in more or less familiar locations are considered travel narratives. Such narratives typically are told episodically and chronologically, engage in elaborate strategies to validate their authenticity, and raise important and complex questions about the representation of the "other" — that is, the ability of the traveler to depict accurately the people, places, and cultures he or she is describing.

Triplet   In poetry, a group of three lines of verse.

Ukiyo-e   A school of Japanese woodblock printing arising in the EDO period that captured images of everyday life in the FLOATING WORLD (*ukiyo*). The greatest *ukiyo-e* artists include Moronobu (c. 1618–c. 1694), Harunobu (1725–1770), and Hiroshige (1797–1858).

Ukiyo-zoshi   "Stories of the FLOATING WORLD" or "tales of the floating world"; a Japanese style of fiction associated with the hundred-year period from about 1683 to 1783 that took as its subject matter the everyday lives of *chonin*, or townspeople, and was written in colloquial language. Ihara Saikaku is said to be the originator of *ukiyo-zoshi*; many authors in this tradition not only imitated his style but plagiarized his works.

Ultraists   A group of Spanish writers who influenced Jorge Luis Borges. The Ultraists rejected middle-class materialism and sought refuge in the artifice of poetry and in exotic images and metaphors.

Understatement   A figure of speech that says less than what is intended.

Upanishads   A body of sacred texts dating from the seventh century B.C.E. that provide a mystical development of and commentary on earlier Vedic texts.

Urdu   An Indo-European language closely related to Hindi. Urdu is the official language of Pakistan and is also spoken in India and Bangladesh.

Utilitarianism   An ethical tradition dating from the late eighteenth century that assumes an action is right if it promotes happiness of both the agent and those affected by the act. Judgments of right and wrong depend upon the consequence of an action rather than strictly on motives.

Vedas   The earliest Indian sacred texts, written in SANSKRIT, dating from sometime between 1000 and 500 B.C.E.; they contain hymns and ritual lore considered to be revelation, or *sruti*.

Verisimo   Italian school of literary Realism influenced by Gustave Flaubert and Émile Zola.

Vernacular fiction   Fiction that attempts to capture accurately the typical speech, mannerisms, or dialect of region. *The Satyricon* of the Roman author Petronius is often considered the first work of vernacular fiction.

Verse   Poetic writing arranged according to a metrical pattern and composed of a varied number of lines.

Victorian   In English history, *Victorian* refers to the age of Queen Victoria (1837–1901) and the values of respectability, social conservatism, and sexual repression characteristic of that time.

Villanelle   Originally a complicated French verse form that appeared in English in the 1800s. The villanelle is a nineteen-line poem of five tercets (three-line STANZAS) and a final two-rhyme QUATRAIN. The first and third line of the first tercet repeat alternately, closing the succeeding stanzas.

Wampanoag   One of several Algonquin peoples residing in New England in the seventeenth century. Their territory extended from Narragansett Bay to Cape Cod.

Well-made play   The plays of Augustin Eugène Scribe (1791–1861) and those of his followers, whose popular comedies were especially in vogue during the second half of the nineteenth century, established the rules for the "well-made play." The well-made play was carefully constructed around a single situation that built scene by scene to a climactic revelation. The situation usually involved a misunderstanding, a secret, or a suppressed document that, when discovered, prompted a REVERSAL and a DENOUEMENT. The dialogue was colloquial and realistic, and the subject matter commonplace and trivial. The well-made play was intended to amuse, not instruct.

Weltliteratur Term coined by Goethe for works of literature that transcend local and national concerns to treat universal human themes.

Yin and yang A pair of opposites derived from a dualistic system of ancient Chinese philosophy; symbolically representing the sun and the moon, *yang* is positive, active, and strong, while *yin* is negative, passive, and weak. All things in the universe are formed from the dynamic interaction of these forces.

Yomihon A serious, often didactic "reading book," as opposed to a picture book. This GENRE, popular in the early nineteenth century, often presented historical romances influenced by classic Chinese fiction.

Zen A prominent school of Buddhism that seeks to reveal the essence of the enlightened mind. Zen teaches that everyone has the potential to attain enlightenment but that most are unaware of this potential because they are ignorant. The way to attain enlightenment is through transcending the boundaries of common thought, and the method of study is most frequently the intense, personal instruction of a student by a Zen master.

Acknowledgments (continued from p. iv)

Charles Baudelaire, "To the Reader," translated by Stanley Kunitz, from *The Collected Poems.* Copyright © 2000 by Stanley Kunitz. Reprinted with the permission of W. W. Norton & Company, Inc. "The Albatross" and "Correspondences," translated by Richard Wilbur, "Hymn to Beauty," translated by Dorothy Martin, "Her Hair," translated by Doreen Bell, and "Old Pluvius, month of rains, in peevish mood" from "Spleen," translated by Kenneth O. Hansen, from *Flowers of Evil, Revised Edition,* edited by Martheil and Jackson Mathews. Copyright © 1955, 1962, 1989 by New Directions Publishing Corporation. Reprinted with the permission of the publishers. "Carrion," translated by Richard Howard, from *Les Fleurs du Mal.* Copyright © 1982 by Richard Howard. Reprinted with the permission of the translator. "The Swan," translated by Kate Flores and "The Voyage," translated by Barbara Gibbs, from Angel Flores, ed., *An Anthology of French Poetry From Nerval to Valery in English Translation With French Originals* (New York: Anchor Books, 1958). Reprinted with the permission of the Estate of Angel Flores. "Spleen," translated by Sir John Squire, from *Poems and Baudelaire Flowers* (London: The New Age Press, 1909). Reprinted with the permission of Raglan Squire. "To Every Man His Chimera," "Crowds," "Windows," and "Anywhere Out of the World" from *Paris Spleen,* translated by Louis Varèse. Copyright 1947, © 1955, 1962, 1970 by New Directions Publishing Corporation. Reprinted with the permission of the publishers.

Emilia Pardo Bazan, "The Oldest Story" from *Torn Lace and Other Stories,* translated by Maria Cristina Urruela. Reprinted with the permission of the Modern Language Association. "The Revolver," translated by Angel Flores, from *Spanish Stories,* edited by Angel Flores (New York: Bantam, 1960). Reprinted with the permission of the Estate of Angel Flores.

Anton Chekhov, "The Cherry Orchard" from *Four Plays,* translated by David Magarshack. Copyright © 1969 by David Magarshack. Reprinted with the permission of Hill and Wang, a division of Farrar, Straus & Giroux, LLC.

Emily Dickinson, from *The Poems of Emily Dickinson,* edited by Thomas H. Johnson, "The soul has bandaged moments," #512, "They shut me up in prose," 613 and "My life has stood—a loaded gun," #754. Copyright by the President and Fellows of Harvard College. Copyright 1951, © 1955, 1979 by the President and Fellows of Harvard College. Reprinted with the permission of The Belknap Press of Harvard University Press.

Fyodor Dostoevsky, "Notes from Underground," translated by Ralph E. Matlaw, from *Notes from Underground and The Grand Inquisitor.* Copyright © 1960,

1988 by E. P. Dutton. Reprinted with the permission of Dutton, a division of Penguin Putnam Inc.

Gustave Flaubert, "A Simple Heart" from *Three Tales,* translated by A. McDowell. Copyright 1924 by Alfred A. Knopf, Inc. Reprinted with the permission of Alfred A. Knopf, a division of Random House, Inc.

"Follow the Drinkin' Gourd" Words and Music by Ronnie Gilbert, Lee Hays, Fred Hellerman & Pete Seeger. TRO Copyright 1951 and renewed © 1979 Folkways Music Publishers, Inc., New York, NY. Used by permission.

E. M. Forster, excerpt from *A Passage to India* (New York: Harcourt, 1924). Copyright 1924 by Harcourt, renewed 1952 by E. M. Forster. Reprinted with the permission of The Provost and Scholars of King's College, Cambridge and The Society of Authors as Literary Representatives of the E. M. Forster Estate.

Ghalib (Mirza Asadullah Beg Khan), "How murderous is the false faith of the rose!" translated by Shamsur Rahman Faruqi and Frances W. Pritchett. Reprinted by permission of the translators. Ghazal V ["The happiness of the drop is to die in the river"], translated by Aijaz Ahmad, from *Ghazals of Ghalib.* Copyright © 1971 by Columbia University Press. Reprinted with the permission of the publisher. Ghazal V ["Waterbead ecstasy: dying in a stream"], translated by Thomas Fitzsimmons. Reprinted with the permission of the translator. Ghazals XXVI ["It is a long time since my love stayed with me here"] and XXXVII ["There are a thousand desires like this, each needing a lifetime"], translated by W. S. Merwin. Copyright © by W. S. Merwin. Reprinted with the permission of The Wylie Agency, Inc. Ghazal V ["The drop dies in the river"], translated by W. S. Merwin, from *East Window: The Asian Translations.* Copyright © 1998 by W. S. Merwin. Reprinted with the permission of Copper Canyon Press, P.O. Box 271, Port Townsend, WA 98368-0271. "When the Sky Clears," "Don't Skimp with Me Today," "A Lamp in a Strong Wind," and "The Sword Wound" from *The Lightning Should Have Fallen on Ghalib: Selected Poems of Ghalib,* translated by Robert Bly and Sunil Dutta (Hopewell, New Jersey: The Ecco Press, 1999). Reprinted with the permission of Robert Bly. Ghazals X ["Why didn't I shrink in the blaze of that face?"] and XX ["Is it you, O God, whose coming begins to amaze me?"], translated by Adrienne Rich with Aijaz Ahmad, from *Ghazals of Ghalib* (New York: Columbia University Press, 1971). Reprinted with the permission of the author and Frances Goldin Literary Agent.

Johan Wolfgang von Goethe, "Prologue in Heaven" and excerpts from Parts I and II from *Faust,* translated by Charles E. Passage. Copyright © 1965 by Macmillan Publishing Company. Reprinted with the permission of the publishers. "Unbounded," "Blessed Longing," "Submerged," "Gingo Biloba," and "Hatem" from *Selected Poems*, translated by Michael Hamburger et al., edited by Christopher Middleton. Copyright © 1994 by Princeton University Press. Reprinted with the permission of the publishers.

René Guénon, excerpts from *East and West*, translated by Martin Lings (Ghent, New York: Sophia Perennis, 2001). Copyright © 2001 by Martin Lings. Reprinted with permission.

Heinrich Heine, "The Grenadiers" and "The Minnesingers," translated by Louis Untermeyer, "The Silesian Weavers" and "The Slave Ship," translated by Aaron Kramer, from *The Poetry of Heinrich Heine*, edited by Frederic Ewen. Copyright © 1969 by Citadel Press, Inc. Reprinted with the permission of Citadel Press/Kensington Publishing Corporation. "The Asra," "The Migratory Rats," and "Morphine" from *Heinrich Heine: Lyric Poems and Ballads*, translated by Ernst Feise. Copyright © 1961, 1989 by University of Pittsburgh Press. Reprinted with the permission of University of Pittsburgh Press.

Higuchi Ichiyo, "The Thirteenth Night" from *In the Shade of Spring Leaves: The Life and Writings of Higuchi Ichiyo, A Woman of Letters in Meiji Japan*, translated by Robert Lyons Danly. Copyright © 1981 by Robert Lyons Danly. Reprinted with the permission of W. W. Norton & Company, Inc.

Hirata Atsutane, "The Creator God" from *Sources of Japanese Tradition, Volume II*, edited by William Theodore de Bary. Copyright © 1958 by Columbia University Press. Reprinted with the permission of Columbia University Press.

Hu Shih, "Science and Philosophy of Life" from *Sources of Chinese Tradition*, edited by W. Theodore de Bary. Copyright © 1960 by Columbia University Press. Reprinted with the permission of Columbia University Press.

Henrik Ibsen, *Hedda Gabler*, translated by Nicholas Rudall. English translation copyright © 1992 by Nicholas Rudall. Reprinted with the permission of Ivan R. Dee, Inc.

Muhammed Iqbal, "Freedom" from *Poems by Iqbal*, translated by V.G. Kiernan. Reprinted with the permission of John Murray (Publishers), Ltd.

Syed Ahmed Khan, "The Qur'an and Science" from *Sources of Indian Tradition*, compiled by William Theodore de Bary, Stephen N. Hay, Royal Weiler and Andrew Yarrow. Copyright © 1958 by Columbia University Press. Reprinted with the permission of Columbia University Press.

Soren Kierkegaard, "The Universality of the Sickness (Despair)" from *The Sickness Unto Death: A Christian Psychological Exposition for Upbuilding and Awakening*, translated by Howard V. Hong and Edna H. Hong. Copyright © 1980 by Princeton University . Reprinted with the permission of the publishers.

Mori Ogai, "The Dancing Girl" translated by Richard Bowring, *Monumenta Nipponica* 30, no. 2 (1975). Copyright © 1975 by Monumenta Nipponica, Tokyo. Reprinted with the permission of *Monumenta Nipponica* and the translator.

Gérard de Nerval (Gérard Labrunie), "Pardonable Audacity for Faust" from *Observations on Goethe's Faust*, translated by Howard E. Hugo, from *The Romantic Reader*. Copyright © 1957 by The Viking Press. Reprinted with the permission of Viking Penguin, a division of Penguin Putnam Inc.

Friedrich Nietzsche, excerpt from "The Gay Science" and 1,3 from "Thus Spoke Zarathustra" from *The Portable Nietzsche*, translated by Walter Kaufman. Copyright 1954 by The Viking Press, renewed © 1982 by Viking Penguin Inc. Reprinted with the permission of Viking Penguin, a division of Penguin Putnam Inc.

Alexander Pushkin, "The Bronze Horseman" from *Selected Poems of Alexander Pushkin*, translated by D. M. Thomas (New York: Viking, 1982). Copyright © 1982 by D. M. Thomas. Reprinted with the permission of John Johnson, Ltd. Authors' Agent, London.

Rai Sanyo, "Dutch Ships," translated by Donald Keene, from *Anthology of Japanese Literature*, edited by Donald Keene. Copyright © 1955 by Grove Press, Inc. Reprinted with the permission of Grove/Atlantic, Inc.

Swami Vivekananda, excerpts from *Living at the Source*, edited by Ann Myren and Dorothy Madison. Copyright © 1993 by the Vivekananda Foundation. Reprinted with the permission of Shambhala Publications, Inc.

Émile Zola, excerpt from "Preface to the Second Edition" from *Thérèse Raquin*, translated by Leonard Tancock. Copyright © 1962 by Leonard Tancock. Reprinted with the permission of Penguin Books, Ltd.

Image Credits

Page 14: Musée de la Ville de Paris, Musée Carnavalet, Paris, France/Lauro-Giraudon-Bridgeman Art Library

Page 22: The Art Archive/Civiche Raccolte Museo L. Bailo Treviso/Dagli Orti

Page 24: Kavaler/Art Resource, NY

Page 26: Courtesy of the Trustees of the Boston Public Library

Page 180: Kunsthistorichesches Museum, Vienna

Page 185: Scala/Art Resource, NY

Page 189: Copyright: Hamburger Kunsthalle. Photographer: Elke Welford, Hamburg

Page 199: The Art Archive

Page 204: National Trust Photographic Library/John Hommond

Page 209: The Pierpont Morgan Library/Art Resource, NY

Page 211: Image Select/Art Resource, NY

Page 236: © Austrian Archives/CORBIS

Page 239: Library of Congress, LC-USZ62-122525

Page 255: Private Collection/Bridgeman Art Library

Page 256: Central Saint Martins College of Art and Design, London, UK/Bridgeman Art Library

Page 281: Austrian Archives/CORBIS

Page 316: Bibliothèque National, Paris, France/Giraudon/Bridgeman Art Library

Page 335: Giraudon/Art Resource, NY

Page 337: Stapleton Collection, UK/Bridgeman Art Library

Page 349: © Austrian Archives/CORBIS

Page 350: Hulton/Archive

Page 381: Image Select/Art Resource, NY

Page 385: Image Select/Art Resource, NY

Page 388: Hulton/Archive

Page 390: Erich Lessing/Art Resource, NY

Page 394: Private Collection/Bridgeman Art Library

Page 397: Private Collection/Bridgeman Art Library

Page 400: National Portrait Gallery, Smithsonian Institution/Art Resource

Page 406: The Art Archive/Rijksmuseum voor Volkenkunde Leiden (Leyden)/Dagli Orti

Page 408: Private Collection/Bonhams, London, UK/Bridgeman Art Library

Page 412: © CORBIS

Page 414: Giraudon/Art Resource, NY

Page 436: Bibliothèque Nationale, Paris/Bridgeman Art Library

Page 462: Giraudon/Art Resource, NY

Page 557: © Austrian Archives/CORBIS

Page 617: Library of Congress, LC-USZ62-128302

Page 664: The Art Archive

Page 666: © Bettmann/CORBIS

Page 667: © Underwood & Underwood/CORBIS

Page 669: Bibliothèque Nationale, Paris, France/Archives Charmet/Bridgeman Art Library

Page 671: Courtesy of the Trustees of the Boston Public Library

Page 675: © Bettmann/CORBIS

Page 676: Foto Marburg/Art Resource, NY

Page 704: Snark/Art Resource, NY

Page 750: Library of Congress, LC-USZ62-108448

Page 753: Private Collection/Bridgeman Art Library

Page 757: Courtesy of the N.C. Office of Archives and History

Page 803: Library of Congress, LC-USZ62-89498

Page 804: Library of Congress, LC-USZ62-103293

Page 815: Erich Lessing/Art Resource, NY

Page 817: Schomburg Center for Research in Black Culture, New York Public Library

Page 821: National Portrait Gallery, Washington D.C./Art Resource, NY

Page 825: Library of Congress, LC-USZ62-41838

Page 835: Mary Evans Picture Library

Page 840: Ramakrishna-Vivekananda Center of New York

Page 846: © Bettmann/CORBIS

Page 848: © Bettmann/CORBIS

Page 877: Oscar Lion Collection, The Rare Book Division, Humanities and Social Sciences Library, New York Public Library

Page 921: Copyright: Hamburger Kunsthalle. Photographer: Elke Welford, Hamburg

Page 928: Erich Lessing/Art Resource, NY

Page 937: Library of Congress, LC-USZ62-106490

Page 956: Hulton/Archive

Page 961: Dinodia Picture Library

Page 973: Library of Congress, LC-USZ62-095518

Page 1035: Library of Congress, LC-USZ62-099468

Page 1037: Hulton/Archive

Page 1040: Private Collection/The Stapleton Collection/Bridgeman Art Library

Page 1041: Library of Congress, LC-USZ62-16947

Page 1044: Library of Congress, LC-USZ62-089704

Page 1051: Library of Congress, LC-USZ62-089703

Page 1055: The Art Archive/HarperCollins Publishers

Page 1059: Hulton/Archive

Page 1073: Victoria & Albert Museum, London, UK/Bridgeman Art Library

Page 1075: The Art Archive/British Museum

INDEX